Hellenic Studies 47

THE EPIC RHAPSODE AND HIS CRAFT

Recent Titles in the Hellenic Studies Series

The Web of Athenaeus

Eusebius of Caesarea
Tradition and Innovations

Homeric Durability
Telling Time in the Iliad

Paideia and Cult
Christian Initiation in Theodore of Mopsuestia

Imperial Geographies in Byzantine and Ottoman Space

Loving Humanity, Learning, and Being Honored
The Foundations of Leadership in Xenophon's Education of Cyrus

The Theory and Practice of Life
Isocrates and the Philosophers

From Listeners to Viewers
Space in the Iliad

Aspects of History and Epic in Ancient Iran
From Gaumāta to Wahnām

Homer's Versicolored Fabric
The Evocative Power of Ancient Greek Epic Word-Making

Christianity and Hellenism in the Fifth-Century Greek East
Theodoret's Apologetics against the Greeks in Context

The Master of Signs
Signs and the Interpretation of Signs in Herodotus' Histories

Eve of the Festival
Making Myth in Odyssey 19

Kleos in a Minor Key
The Homeric Education of a Little Prince

Plato's Counterfeit Sophists

Multitextuality in Homer's Iliad
The Witness of the Ptolemaic Papyri

Tragedy, Authority, and Trickery
The Poetics of Embedded Letters in Josephus

A Californian Hymn to Homer

http://chs.harvard.edu/chs/publications

THE EPIC RHAPSODE AND HIS CRAFT
Homeric Performance in a Diachronic Perspective

José M. González

CENTER FOR HELLENIC STUDIES
Trustees for Harvard University
Washington, D.C.
Distributed by Harvard University Press
Cambridge, Massachusetts, and London, England
2013

The Epic Rhapsode and His Craft: Homeric Performance in a Diachronic Perspective
    by José M. González
Copyright © 2013 Center for Hellenic Studies, Trustees for Harvard University
All Rights Reserved.
Published by Center for Hellenic Studies, Trustees for Harvard University,
    Washington, D.C.
Distributed by Harvard University Press, Cambridge, Massachusetts, and
    London, England
Production: Kristin Murphy Romano
Cover design: Joni Godlove
Printed by Edwards Brothers, Inc., Ann Arbor, MI and Lillington, NC

On the cover: The centaur Kheiron teaches Akhilleus to sing to the lyre, a skill he
    exhibits in *Iliad* 9.
From the Basilica at Herculaneum, now in the Museo Archeologico Nazionale, Naples.
Photo, Erich Lessing / Art Resource, NY.

ISBN: 9780674055896
Library of Congress Control Number: 2014956282

PARENTIBUS CARISSIMIS
JOSÉ MIGUEL ET MARÍA AGUSTINA

Key to the Books of
the *Iliad* and the *Odyssey*

A	*Iliad* 1		α	*Odyssey* 1
B	*Iliad* 2		β	*Odyssey* 2
Γ	*Iliad* 3		γ	*Odyssey* 3
Δ	*Iliad* 4		δ	*Odyssey* 4
E	*Iliad* 5		ε	*Odyssey* 5
Z	*Iliad* 6		ζ	*Odyssey* 6
H	*Iliad* 7		η	*Odyssey* 7
Θ	*Iliad* 8		θ	*Odyssey* 8
I	*Iliad* 9		ι	*Odyssey* 9
K	*Iliad* 10		κ	*Odyssey* 10
Λ	*Iliad* 11		λ	*Odyssey* 11
M	*Iliad* 12		μ	*Odyssey* 12
N	*Iliad* 13		ν	*Odyssey* 13
Ξ	*Iliad* 14		ξ	*Odyssey* 14
O	*Iliad* 15		ο	*Odyssey* 15
Π	*Iliad* 16		π	*Odyssey* 16
P	*Iliad* 17		ρ	*Odyssey* 17
Σ	*Iliad* 18		σ	*Odyssey* 18
T	*Iliad* 19		τ	*Odyssey* 19
Y	*Iliad* 20		υ	*Odyssey* 20
Φ	*Iliad* 21		φ	*Odyssey* 21
X	*Iliad* 22		χ	*Odyssey* 22
Ψ	*Iliad* 23		ψ	*Odyssey* 23
Ω	*Iliad* 24		ω	*Odyssey* 24

Contents

Acknowledgments xi

Introduction 1

Part I The 'Homeric Question'

1 Dictation Theories and Pre-Hellenic Literacy 15
   1.1 Statement of the Problem 15
   1.2 Albert Lord's Dictation Theory 18
   1.3 Richard Janko's Dictation Theory 24
   1.4 Written Epics from the Near East 29
   1.5 Written Phoenician Literature 33

2 Dictation Theories and Archaic Art 41
   2.1 M. L. West's Dictation Theory 42
   2.2 Artistic Iconography 46
      2.2.1 Alleged illustrations of the *Iliad* 49
      2.2.2 Alleged illustrations of the *Odyssey* 56
      2.2.3 A fluid sixth-century Homer 64
   2.3 Homer, a Writing Poet? 68

3 The Technology of Writing 71

4 The Euboian Connection 81
   4.1 The Cultural Argument 81
   4.2 The Linguistic Argument 85
      4.2.1 The third CL 85
      4.2.2 Dating the second CL 89
      4.2.3 Dipylon *oinokhoē* 97
      4.2.4 Syllabification of -nw- clusters 105

Contents

5 Archaic Inscriptions before 650 BC 111

  5.1 The Inscription from Cumae 116

    5.1.1 *hisa* 118

    5.1.2 Missing iotas? 121

    5.1.3 *tinnuna* 123

    5.1.4 The alleged meaning 127

  5.2 Nestor's Cup (*CEG* no. 454) 129

    5.2.1 δ' ἄν versus δέ κε 133

    5.2.2 κεῖνος versus ἐκεῖνος 134

    5.2.3 καλλιστεφανο Αφροδιτες 137

    5.2.4 An eighth-century bookhand? 141

6 Early Homeric Scholarship and Editions 147

  6.1 Ajax and Salamis 148

  6.2 Theagenes of Rhegion 156

  6.3 The Name 'Homer' 167

Part II Rhapsodic Performance in Pre-Classical Greece

7 Homer the Rhapsode 173

  7.1 Notional Fixity in Oral Poetry 173

  7.2 Invoking the Muses 183

    7.2.1 Efficacious speech 201

    7.2.2 Quoted speech 207

    7.2.3 The singer, instrument of the Muse 208

8 Hesiod the Rhapsode 219

  8.1 Mantic Poetry 219

    8.1.1 Hesiod's *Dichterweihe* 219

    8.1.2 Revealing the song 224

    8.1.3 The divine will 230

  8.2 Of Truth and Lies 235

  8.3 Μάντις and Προφήτης 267

    8.3.1 Ecstasy 267

    8.3.2 The Delphic Oracle 270

8.3.3 Oracular verse... 284

8.4 Plato and Inspired Poetry... 289

Part III Rhapsodic Performance in High-Classical Athens

9 The Rhapsode in Classical Athens 293

9.1 Of Transcripts and Scripts.. 293

9.2 The Rhapsode as Ὑποκριτής....................................... 296

9.3 The Rhapsode as Ἐπαινέτης.. 305

9.4 The Rhapsode and Ὑπόκρισις 308

9.5 Alkidamas' *On the Sophists* 311

9.6 Ῥαψῳδέω in Isokrates and Plato................................. 318

10 The Rhapsode in Performance 331

10.1 Understanding the Rhapsode 331

10.1.1 Etymology 336

10.1.2 Stitching the song: creative work? 338

10.2 Understanding Rhapsodic Performance.................... 341

10.2.1 Non-melodic recitation?................................... 343

10.2.2 Ῥάπτω and Homeric artistry 356

10.2.3 Rhapsodic sequencing and relay poetics 367

10.2.3.1 Kallimakhos and the rhapsodes 367

10.2.3.2 δέγμενος/δεδεγμένος 371

10.2.3.3 Cooperation and contest 377

10.2.3.4 The Panathenaic rule 382

10.2.3.5 οἴμη and οἶμος..................................... 392

10.2.3.6 ὕμνος... 396

10.2.4 Earliest attestations of ῥαψῳδός.................... 399

10.2.5 The *differentia* of the rhapsodic craft............ 416

10.2.6 Stitching or weaving? 419

Part IV Rhapsodic Performance in the Late Classical and
Post-Classical Periods

11 The Performance of Drama and Epic in Late-Classical Athens 435

11.1 The Reforms of Lykourgos 435

11.2 Demetrios of Phaleron and the Rhapsodes 447

Contents

11.2.1 Rhapsodes and *homēristai* 447

11.2.2 The reforms of Demetrios of Phaleron............................ 466

11.3 Actors at the Panathenaia? 476

12 The Performance of Homer after IV BC 479

12.1 The Τεχνῖται of Dionysos 479

12.2 The Τεχνῖται and Specialization 484

12.3 Rhapsodes in the Inscriptional Record 488

12.3.1 Prosopography of rhapsodes 491

Part V Aristotle on Performance

13 Rhapsodic *hypokrisis* and Aristotelian *lexis* 521

13.1 Why Aristotle on Ὑπόκρισις Matters.............................. 521

13.2 Relationship between Λέξις and Ὑπόκρισις........................ 524

13.3 Ὑπόκρισις, Not a Detour 531

13.4 Ὑπόκρισις, Not Just in *Rhetoric* III.1 533

13.5 Semantic Development of Ὑπόκρισις and Λέξις 544

13.5.1 Φαντασία, 'mere fancy'? 551

13.6 Φαντασία in the Rhetoric 561

14 The Aristotelian *tekhnē* of *hypokrisis* 579

14.1 Technical *hypokrisis*.. 579

14.2 *Hypokrisis* and the Use of Writing 593

Conclusion 641

Appendix: The Origin of the Term *hypokritēs* 647

Bibliography.. 667

Index of Ancient Literary Sources.................................... 749

Index of Documentary Sources 775

Index of Rhapsodes.. 779

Index of Greek Terms 783

General Index... 789

Acknowledgments

Like Homeric poetry, this book has benefited from the hands of many masters. It is a pleasure to acknowledge here the debts I have incurred while writing it. I am grateful to the departments of Classical Studies at Harvard University, the University of Oregon, and Duke University, and to the Center for Hellenic Studies in Washington D.C., where various stages of this project were conceived and executed. They are all most supportive and congenial research environments. I thank Albert Henrichs, Carolyn Higbie, and Nino Luraghi for their input at an early stage, when the core of my argument took shape as a doctoral dissertation at Harvard. Their intellectual generosity, wise guidance, sharp eyes, and superb scholarship saved me from many errors. They should not, of course, be held responsible for the final product. My gratitude also to Craig Melchert, historical linguist extraordinaire, who generously advised me on Lycian and Carian. Most of all, a special thank you to Gregory Nagy, whose fertile mind, imaginative scholarship, inexhaustible energy, and sheer pleasure in classical scholarship have been and remain a constant source of inspiration. His support, good sense, and encouragement have been crucial in helping me reach the end of this, at times, very long road. I could not have hoped for a better friend.

Others have contributed in ways less tangible but just as meaningful. I thank my brother Luis and my sister Carmen, who were always near when help was needed. To Daniel, Gabriel, and Sara, thank you for your cheerful patience and understanding on the many occasions when Papá could not play with you because he had to get back to "the book." I hope that some day you too will read it with profit and will conclude that it was worth the effort. I love you all. My gratitude to Lauren, the love of my life, for her unfailing joy and optimism and for making our house a home during these busy times. Above all, for their life-long devotion, commitment, and sacrificial love, I thank my parents, José Miguel and María Agustina, who never tired of repeating "le mieux est l'ennemi du bien." They must have wondered if this book would ever see the light of day. I owe them a debt of love that can never be repaid. To them I dedicate this work.

S.D.G.

"FOR THE LORD IS GOOD;
HIS LOVINGKINDNESS IS EVERLASTING,
AND HIS FAITHFULNESS TO ALL GENERATIONS."
PSALM 100:5

Ῥητέον, ἦν δ᾽ ἐγώ· καίτοι φιλία γέ τίς με καὶ αἰδὼς ἐκ
παιδὸς ἔχουσα περὶ Ὁμήρου ἀποκωλύει λέγειν. ἔοικε μὲν γὰρ
τῶν καλῶν ἀπάντων τούτων τῶν τραγικῶν πρῶτος διδάσκαλός τε καὶ ἡγεμὼν γενέσθαι. ἀλλ᾽ οὐ γὰρ πρό γε τῆς ἀληθείας
τιμητέος ἀνήρ, ἀλλ᾽, ὃ λέγω, ῥητέον.

Plato Republic X, 595b9–c4

Introduction

THIS BOOK STUDIES the performance of Homeric poetry in Greece from the archaic period to Hellenistic and Roman imperial times. I focus on the rhapsode—on the changing nature of his training and recitation. My underlying claim is that a diachronic understanding[1] of this professional and his craft is possible only when he is seen in his archaic cultural connection to the prophet and in his relation—spanning the archaic and classical periods—to orators and actors. There is a sense in which it is legitimate to view the ῥαψῳδός as a sort of προφήτης and ὑποκριτής and as a performer who engages in ὑπόκρισις. Explaining why and how these assertions hold true is central to this book. An equivalent way to frame my subject is to focus on the related triad ὑπόκρισις, ὑποκριτής, and ὑποκρίνεσθαι. Modern scholars will doubtless associate ὑπόκρισις with rhetorical theory, where it designates the speaker's 'delivery'; and ὑποκριτής with the dramatic stage, the common label in classical Athens for a tragic or a comic actor. Therefore it might seem strange at first to select this triad as the fulcrum of an inquiry into the performance of Homeric poetry in ancient Greece. But, in fact, my investigation shows that a proper grasp of the cultural significance of Homeric epic and the changing nature of its performance over time must consider the manner and contexts in which the Greeks themselves used these terms in their cultural discourse. What emerges from such a study is that often our modern terms 'performance', 'performer', and 'to perform' are, in ways that this book makes clear, best rendered by ὑπόκρισις, ὑποκριτής, and ὑποκρίνεσθαι. This is by no means an obvious claim. I do not mean it absolutely and it shall be my concern to justify this assertion. After all, ὑποκριτής and ῥαψῳδός are never used interchangeably; and ὑποκρίνεσθαι is not classed with καταλέγειν or ἀείδειν among the verbs associated with the recitation of Homeric poetry. Moreover, it seems obvious that ὑπόκρισις and ὑποκριτής, whatever their connection with epic poetry, reach beyond its boundaries into the domains of oratory and drama.

---

[1] By 'diachronic understanding' I mean a grasp of the rhapsode's place in the performance culture of ancient Greece that takes into account the full chronological sweep of the systemic evolution of his craft and performance genre, that is, how these changed over time in accordance with their own internal dynamics and the dynamics of the surrounding culture as *systems*.

But the first observation is undercut by Sokrates' repeated juxtaposition of ῥαψῳδός and ὑποκριτής when he refers in Plato's *Iōn* to members of the rhapsodic profession.[2] And the second must be qualified by the occasional yet significant use of ὑποκρίνεσθαι in the Homeric poems when a character answers questions that call for interpretation. Even if this constitutes, as I believe, a semantic borrowing from the domain of oracular interpretation, one should still consider whether this affects in any way the poetics of epic performance. Its characters, after all, are engaging in the interpretation of traditional epic material in contexts that are especially significant to the course of the poems' plots. And if the rhapsode himself, from a certain point of view explored here, may be construed as the *hermēneus* of his tradition, the parallel between interpreting rhapsodes and interpreting epic characters may be thought to have something to contribute to our understanding of the poetics involved. Finally, I note that the third observation above is only to be expected, since neither among us is 'performance' or 'performer' circumscribed to the recitation of poetry. Though our own culture generally reserves 'performance' for the artist on stage before an audience (whether a singer, a musician, or an actor), a broader meaning is in evidence when we talk about the 'performance' of a lawyer at a trial or of a politician campaigning for office at a public event.

Indeed, the notion of 'social performance' has confidently entered our scholarly discourse and our cultural imagination. This is the more basic sense in which ὑπόκρισις appears in the literature of the classical period. In view is the 'delivery' before the audience, an individual's deportment when he is in the spotlight, on the 'public stage,' so to say. The analysis of this concept took place in connection with the discipline of rhetoric, where the public discourse of an emerging democratic society called for rules of engagement between a citizen and the assembled polis, whether on the political or the forensic stage. Its goal was to secure the welfare of the individual and, ideally, at the same time advance the good of his community. But together with the earliest extant reflection on the art of the orator and, particularly, on his delivery, we meet with the explicit realization that rhetorical ὑπόκρισις was intimately tied, historically and conceptually, to the art of the actor on the dramatic stage and the rhapsode before a festival audience. We find clear testimonies to this effect in Alkidamas' *On the Sophists* §14 and Aristotle's *Rhetoric* III.1. Some have thought these statements the consequence of a late convergence between the three domains of epic, dramatic, and rhetorical performance, driven primarily by the Athenians' love for tragedy and comedy and by the importance of self-characterization for the speaker who hoped to convince his audience. The result of this convergence

---

[2] Cf. *Iōn* 532d6–e1 and 535e10–536a1.

would have been a corruption of the political arena by the theater—the wretched theatrocracy of Plato's *Laws* 701a3—and a similar corruption by an exaggerated mimetic impulse of what should have been the 'purer' narrative mode of the rhapsodic performance of Homer—a distortion noted by Aristotle in the *Poetics* 26 and hinted at by Plato in the *Republic* 392e–396.

I do not deny that such cultural pressures existed: they did, and they made their influence felt. Arguably, in the sphere of Homeric performance the result was the natural issue of the poetry's own mimetic potential. But if we focus too narrowly on this dynamic of convergence alone, we shall fail to appreciate that the connections between these three great performance domains of classical Athens—rhapsody, oratory, and drama—are older and more consequential than a growing appreciation of histrionic emphases in performance. Indeed, taking up a suggestion by Koller 1957, I argue that, diachronically speaking, ὑποκρίνεσθαι and ὑποκριτής originally pertained to the prophet as the intermediary between the oracular god and an inquiring seeker. As a middleman, the prophet was said to 'interpret' the divine message: he was the ὑποκριτής, the 'interpreter'. But mediation is a notion that allows for varying constructions, depending on what is thought of as the source and as the final addressee. Insofar as the god himself was not heard apart from his prophet, in practice the word of the latter might also be considered a source in its own right. Then the verb ὑποκρίνεσθαι and its agent noun would not underscore the interpretive act as much as the attendant notion of a speech-act: the authoritative and efficacious divine speech that carried the force and ability of the god to bring to pass what he declared. In time, the notion of performative speech gained semantic priority over the notion of interpretive speech, and the verb was used for festival performances on stage, eventually connoting histrionic delivery since the dramatic stage was the preeminent context for such usage.

Oracles, of course, are not the only form of divine speech. Epic poetry openly declares its status as the speech of the Muse. It is therefore conceptually related to mantic poetry and casts the rhapsode as a mediating agent who conveys the divine song to his audience. Thus, in the cultural context of archaic Greece, he inherited many of the notions associated with the prophet in his mediating role. These conceptual parallels become all the more significant in the light of Koller's suggestion that the dramatic actor was called ὑποκριτής because he was initially viewed from the perspective of his hermeneutic function—as adding his commentary to, and elaborating upon, the song of the chorus. Although ultimately I cannot accept his proposal without significant modifications, I credit Koller with a fundamental insight: epic and drama cannot be fully appreciated as performance genres except in their diachronic and historical interconnections. Koller's contribution must be modified, however, in two important and related directions. The first follows from diachronic analysis: it was the rhapsode at the earliest stages, not the actor at the inception of drama, who was viewed as discharging a hermeneutic function, specifically in his epic mediation between the Muse and the audience. The second follows from combined diachronic and historical analysis: as the preeminent archaic model of the performer, it was to rhapsodic ὑπόκρισις understood as 'performance' or 'delivery' that the emerging actor looked for professional inspiration and guidance. It is insufficient, therefore, to think of the lines of influence between the dramatic stage and rhapsodic recitation as unidirectional, from the former to the latter, exhibited solely by the increasing theatricality of the rhapsode's delivery so clear during the fourth century BC and later. At the earliest stages of its development, the acting trade considered the performing bard as the model to emulate, adopting such techniques as might be transferable to the new occasion, self-consciously developing in the tragic genre the mimetic potential intrinsic to Homeric poetry. In the course of time the influence exerted became mutual, and it is for this reason that a clear picture of the epic rhapsode and his craft in their full diachronic sweep emerges only when they are viewed in a performance milieu where drama gradually gained cultural preeminence. Despised by some among the intellectual elite, generally admired by the common man, actors were envied by many on account of their public prominence, and their influence upon public speakers—'performers' in an extended sense—is well known.[3] Just as momentous, I contend, was their influence upon rhapsodes. Parts III–IV of this book trace this influence from late archaic through Hellenistic and Roman imperial times.

As noted above, drama was not alone in providing the reciter of Homeric poetry with a historical connection to a performance domain other than his own. Just as significant was the relation between rhapsodes and orators. Here, again, the ties were not simply the universals of the performer-audience interaction, significant though these are. For the growth of the art of rhetoric came by the hand of intellectuals that might be loosely classed among the sophists, a group whose boundaries cannot be drawn too tightly.[4] And the rise of the sophists must be seen, I believe, partly in imitation of, partly in competitive reaction to, rhapsodes in their hermeneutic/explanatory role vis-à-vis epic poetry.[5] The universals of the performance situation alone would urge the study of oratorical delivery, ὑπόκρισις, in the context of a diachronic investigation of the epic rhapsode and his craft. But the historical connection between rhapsodes, the rise of the sophists, and the development of oratorical theory commends the view that the cultural factors that shaped the emergence and evolution of rhetorical

---

[3] Cf., for example, Hall 1995.
[4] Cf. Kerferd 1950.
[5] The parallel between rhapsodes and sophists is acknowledged by Pfeiffer 1968:1.16.

delivery were similarly at work, *mutatis mutandis*, among rhapsodes. This is my rationale in Part V for the detailed reading of Aristotle's discussion of ὑπόκρισις in *Rhetoric* III.1–12 and of Alkidamas' *On the Sophists* in Part III.

An outline of my investigation follows here.

Part I concerns what is usually called the 'Homeric Question.' Although I hope to have made meaningful contributions to various aspects of this enduring debate, my purpose here is chiefly polemical. Diachronic and historical analysis convinces me that the basic contours of the so-called 'evolutionary model' for the textual fixation of Homeric epic, championed by Gregory Nagy, is essentially right.[6] Among all the competing models proposed, it alone is historically plausible and diachronically sound. It alone comports with the song culture of ancient Greece in its historical particularities and diachronic tendencies. And yet a growing consensus in the last thirty years has been coalescing around the notion that the Homeric poems where fixed in writing towards the end of the eighth century BC. There is some variety among the proponents of this consensus, some extending the date into the seventh and even the sixth centuries; some regarding the fixation as the outcome of dictation, some proposing that the author (call him 'Homer') wrote them down himself—perhaps even devising the Greek alphabet for this very purpose. The alleged existence of an eighth- or seventh-century 'monumental poet' largely responsible for the text of *our Iliad* and *Odyssey* and for its preservation in writing represents a fundamental challenge to the evolutionary model and calls into question its understanding of the performance culture of ancient Greece. If true, its implications for our grasp and appreciation of the epic rhapsode and his craft would be sweeping. At the very least, it would tend to confirm the tired dichotomy between the 'creative singer/poet' and the 'reproducing rhapsode.' Although reflexively embraced by many, my work shows that this dichotomy is profoundly misleading. To clear the ground for the more constructive Parts II–V, Part I takes a rather selective journey through the Homeric Question, revisiting those issues and publications that seem to me to pose the more formidable and productive objections to what I remain convinced is the soundest and most plausible way to conceptualize the diachronic evolution of epic performance in ancient Greece. In my survey the reader will find familiar topics side by side with perhaps a few surprises. Among the subjects covered are: modern dictation theories; the relation between epic narrative and archaic art; the technology of writing; recent attempts to displace Athens with Euboia as the place where Homeric poetry achieved its definitive shape; the oldest archaic inscriptions, which I survey for clues about literacy and the soundness of the claim that our modern editions of the *Iliad*

---

[6]   See below, p. 17.

and the *Odyssey* can be traced more or less in simple linear fashion back to a late eighth- or early seventh-century manuscript; and early Homeric scholarship and editions, which I probe for what they imply about the diachronic evolution of the epic rhapsode and his craft. Some of this material is rather technical and I invite my reader to sample it at will. This, my review of, and contribution to, the *status quaestionis*, is intended to vindicate the understanding of the song culture of ancient Greece in the context of which I conduct my diachronic study in Parts II–V. These later chapters may be read with profit without Part I. Still, *The Epic Rhapsode and His Craft* will be most compelling and rewarding to those who choose to join me in revisiting the Homeric Question.

Part II of the book regards rhapsodic performance in pre-classical Greece. It comprises two chapters, the first on what I call the 'Homeric model' of rhapsodic performance craft, the second, on the 'Hesiodic model.' Here I take up one of the most puzzling aspects of the performance of Homeric poetry: the 'notional fixity' of the oral tradition.[7] This notion consists in the perception among insiders to the culture (the singer and his audience) that the bard always sang one and the same 'story'—or 'poem,' for there was no self-conscious distinction drawn at this level between the content sung and the composition that embodied it. They all shared this perception, even though, in actual fact, the performer recomposed his song on every new occasion using traditional language, themes, and thematic sequence. Notional fixity is not only part of the archaic performance poetics of Homeric epic: though with a gradual narrowing of the range of textual variation possible, it survived into the classical period. Thus a diachronic study of Homeric rhapsodic performance is only complete when the implications of this notional fixity are understood. In this section of the book I argue that it had its roots in the common ideology that informed archaic views of epic poetry and mantic/oracular poetry. My analysis explores this widely acknowledged kinship and what it entails for a right understanding of the epic rhapsode and his craft. It suggests that this same notional fixity facilitated the rise of the mythic figure of 'Homer' as the culture hero and author of the *Iliad* and the *Odyssey*. The parallel between prophet and rhapsode as mediating communication between the divine and human realms illuminates the argument of Plato's *Iōn*, specifically, the philosopher's irony when on two occasions he has Sokrates pair ῥαψῳδός and ὑποκριτής to describe Ion and those who, like him, make their living by reciting Homer's poems. Indeed, the twinning of these terms simultaneously looks back to the earlier meaning of ὑποκριτής as 'interpreter' (of dreams and oracles) and to the tendency among

---

[7] 'Notional fixity' is my own term for what Nagy (1996b:69) calls the "distinctly nonoccasional and at least *notionally* unchanging" character of the epic poetry of the *Iliad* and the *Odyssey* (his emphasis).

rhapsodes, already evident during the fourth century BC, to exaggerate their stage presence and overemphasize the mimetic cast of their delivery.

Part III focuses on the connections and mutual influence between oratory and rhapsody with respect to their increasing use of writing to aid future performances. The principal textual witness here is Alkidamas' broadside *On the Sophists.* In essence, my argument is that the cultural pressures that brought about the growing dependence of orators on the memorization of written speeches were also at work among rhapsodes. The parallel between these two performance domains—Alkidamas himself makes the connection in a passing mention of rhapsodes in §14—is a happy one for the modern scholar, for there is very little evidence (and only indirect) that bears on rhapsodes, while the development among orators receives explicit attention. What, then, do we learn? So long as public speaking was the province of the exceptionally gifted 'natural' orator, there was comparatively little need for an explicit science that would point the road to successful performance. As soon, however, as greater numbers of men of average skill either were enticed or else found it necessary to become involved in the democratic process, and thus had to address and persuade a public audience—or as soon as the increasingly litigious society made it a matter of personal survival to have the requisite skill to convince a jury of one's innocence or of an opponent's guilt—instruction and training in the art of rhetoric became desirable, if not essential to full and effective citizenship. A deficient natural gift for improvisation was bound to be compensated for not primarily by an attempt, difficult and of limited promise, to develop the corresponding skill but rather by a reliance on the memorization of written drafts carefully composed in advance of the address. The ensuing demand not only produced the logographers, but also led speakers who did not depend on the scripts of professional writers to develop their own to aid their training and rehearsing. A similar dynamic, I believe, can be posited for the performance of Homeric poetry. The life-long apprenticeship from youth up that might eventually produce a bard able to recompose his traditional material in performance must have been exceptional in the Athens of the late fifth century BC. The high appreciation in which Ionian bards were held[8] suggests that their technique was more faithfully traditional and compared positively with the average Athenian's.

---

[8]   One need only remember the prominence of the Homeridai of Khios as arbiters of the Homeric tradition and supreme judges of rhapsodic performance, a reputation to which Plato's *Iōn* 530d7–8, *Phaidros* 252b4–5, and *Republic* 599e5–6 allude. I may also mention the Kreophyleioi of Samos, from whom according to Plutarch the Spartan lawgiver Lykourgos is supposed to have received the Homeric poems (*Lykourgos* 4.4). Although Kreophylos himself may not have enjoyed a good reputation in Athens (cf. Graziosi 2002:217–220, who cites Plato's *Republic* 600b6–c1), the very fact that a rivalry between the Kreophyleioi and the Homeridai might be hinted at testifies to a high estimate of the former's proficiency as rhapsodes. Finally, it is worth noting that even

Athenian education at that time seems to have emphasized memorization and recitation of 'the classics' (with the rise of an increasingly canonical corpus) and featured a growing use of written material.[9] It is from this pedagogic milieu (supplemented, no doubt, with a heavy additional focus on Homer and attention to current rhapsodic recitations) that the Athenian rhapsodes hailed. It was only natural, then, that any effort made towards the mastery of the traditional language and thematic material would have depended to some degree on the memorization of transcripts of performances that had already proved successful before a festival audience. This dependence amounted to a self-reinforcing tendency, a dynamic that grew in strength with the passing of time. Its outcome, gradual but inexorable, was a fixation of the texts of the *Iliad* and the *Odyssey*, not by the historical accident of an act of dictation but by a process driven by the changing performance practices of rhapsodes in their training and public recitations. In the chapter entitled "The Rhapsode in Performance" I build upon the insights gained in Parts I–II and produce a diachronic synthesis of ancient Greek conceptions of the epic rhapsode and his craft. My study in Part III of the cultural forces that encouraged the increasing use of writing in the performance of Homeric poetry is complemented by a general survey in Part IV of the rhapsodic trade and rhapsodic performance practices from late classical down to Hellenistic and Roman imperial times. There I give particular attention to the formative periods of Lykourgos and Demetrios of Phaleron in the late fourth century BC. I also include a prosopography of known rhapsodes.

Part V of the book focuses on the concept of 'delivery' in Aristotle's *Rhetoric* III.1–12, the sole surviving extended analysis from classical Greece where the term is explicitly introduced. The only other significant treatment is the *Phaidros*, where Plato does not, in any way comparable to Aristotle, explicitly mention ὑπόκρισις or its connection with the performance of actors on the stage and rhapsodes in their recitals of epic. This section of the book is concerned with this analysis, setting Aristotle's observations in the context of earlier attempts to deal with oratorical delivery. But scholars have commonly argued that in his *Rhetoric* Aristotle touches on delivery only in a passing, dismissive way: he sets delivery aside, they say, in favor of a concept of 'style', λέξις, that is purged from its connections with the ethically objectionable ὑπόκρισις. I disagree. I believe that Aristotle's concept of style is different in emphasis from the later one

---

Ion himself—conceited, to be sure, but nonetheless portrayed as successful—is said to hail from Ephesos, a choice that is unlikely to be accidental.

9   Plato's *Prōtagoras* 325e4–6, for example, notes that [οἱ διδάσκαλοι] παρατιθέασιν αὐτοῖς [sc. τοῖς παισὶ] ἐπὶ τῶν βάθρων ἀναγιγνώσκειν ποιητῶν ἀγαθῶν ποιήματα καὶ ἐκμανθάνειν ἀναγκάζουσιν. See the recent treatments by Griffith 2001:66–71 (67n144 lists other passages), Ford 2002:194–197 (195n26 has further bibliography), and Morgan 1999.

familiar to us, developed in an age of literacy that had largely abandoned the predominantly oral habits of the earlier song culture. Aristotle's λέξις cannot be understood apart from delivery, and ὑπόκρισις is correspondingly in view throughout the first twelve chapters of *Rhetoric* III. The consensus interpretation I oppose hinges on an understanding of the word φαντασία in *Rhetoric* III.1 that glosses it as 'mere show' or 'ostentation'. An adequate rebuttal of this view requires a survey of Aristotle's use of this and semantically related terms in the *Rhetoric* and other writings. This necessary work yields additional insights into the philosopher's view of rhetoric and of the orator as the agent called to shape the perception of the audience in a democratic society. Aristotle's treatment of delivery is also of great value in improving our understanding of a matter that is of the utmost importance to any study of Homeric performance in classical Athens: how the use of writing came to play a role in the preparation and delivery of speeches. What cultural forces had a hand in bringing about this momentous technical development? A careful reading of Aristotle (complemented by Alkidamas and, to a lesser extent, Isokrates) suggests how we should think of the parallel development among rhapsodes as they too increasingly used transcripts of earlier performances as scripts for future recitals. My detailed exegetical and cultural analysis of *Rhetoric* III.1-12 (especially of chapters 1 and 12) should be of especial interest to students of ancient Greek rhetoric.

I conclude the book with an appendix on the origin of the label ὑποκριτής for the dramatic actor. This appendix constitutes a self-contained diachronic study of this old *zētēma*, which I hope will draw the attention of anyone curious about the origins of the genre of Attic drama.

A few comments to help the reader are in order. I was asked by the editors to abbreviate neither the titles of ancient works nor the names of their authors. Applying this simple rule with stylistic consistency has proved difficult and I have often had to trade off consistency for clarity and ease of reference. For some authors I have used established English titles (Plato *Symposium*, Aristotle *Rhetoric*) but have reverted to Latin when the Latin title enjoyed greater currency (Aristotle *De anima*). I preferred Greek when it was unlikely to compromise clarity (Xenophon *Apomnēmoneumata* for *Memorabilia*); and, if possible, I tried to adhere to a given choice for other works by the same author (hence Xenophon *Symposion* not *Symposium*). I have endeavored to use the Greek style of transliteration throughout: Akhilleus, Thoukydides, etc. In so doing I remain attached to the grapheme 'y' for the upsilon (*hymnos* rather than *humnos*). Authors whose works I usually cite by their English (Plato *Laws*) or their Latin

(Lucian *Bis accusatus*) titles—as the case may be—will nonetheless feature transliterated Greek name-titles (Plato *Menōn*, Lucian *Hēsiodos*). All the same, I have not hesitated to use longstanding English equivalents when the transliteration seemed immoderately unfamiliar (Plato not Platon, Ajax not Aias, *Hymn to Apollo* not *Hymn to Apollōn*). When transliterating titles I use ē for η and ō for ω (Ion the rhapsode but Plato *Iōn*). I refer to the Homeric hymns either by the number (*Homeric Hymn* 19) or by the name (*Hymn to Pan*). If ambiguous, *Hymn to ...* always refers to a so-called 'major' Homeric hymn (*Hymn to Aphrodite* is *Homeric Hymn* 5, not *Homeric Hymn* 6 or 10). To be sure, all such stylistic choices depend on personal preference and perfect consistency is neither desirable nor possible. I beg the reader's indulgence both for the occasional inconsistency and for any spellings he finds disconcerting.

The editors also requested that I write out in full the titles of journals in the bibliography (*Harvard Studies in Classical Philology* rather than *HSCP*) as well as all year and page ranges (1989–1990:1134–1135 rather than 1989–90:1134f.). I trust that clarity will be served by the long arrays of numbers that often follow. For help with any remaining abbreviations, the reader should consult the *Oxford Classical Dictionary*, the LSJ, the *DGE* (=*Diccionario Griego-Español*), and *Brill's New Pauly*. I use double quotes for quotations, single quotes elsewhere, reversing the style for quotes within quotes. If translations and glosses are in view, I have been careful to leave the punctuation outside the single quotes. Finally, I have adopted the time-tested practice of referring to the books of the *Iliad* with Greek capitals and to the books of the *Odyssey* with lower-case Greek letters. This may take at first some adjusting, but in a book like this any other practice would have been unbearably cumbersome. I trust that the reader's initial discomfort will be more than compensated for by enhanced clarity.

Undoubtedly, some will be disappointed to learn that I have not covered a topic of their interest. But I could not reasonably do much more within the bounds of what is already a rather long book. I do not claim that *The Epic Rhapsode and His Craft* is a comprehensive treatise on all things rhapsodic. I never intended it to be such. In particular, I believe that much remains to be done with regard to the pedagogic role played by rhapsodes in the late archaic and classical periods, especially in relation to the sophists. My focus throughout has been on diachrony, on understanding origins and evolving practices. I have not sought to conduct an exhaustive synchronic investigation of the epic rhapsode and his craft for any one period.

As I end this introduction, I take the opportunity to say something about the tone of this study. I doubt not but some will find it unduly polemical at times. The field of Homeric studies is (in)famous for its polemics and I anticipate, with some regret, that this book will make some enemies. If so, may it be for its substance, not its tone. I can only assure my critics that I have written it with respect and admiration for the scholars that honor its pages with their objections and disagreements. The vigor with which I engage them can be safely assumed to be directly proportional to my esteem for their work. Certainly, I intend no personal attack and I hope that no personal offense will be taken. I trust that most will take my criticism for what it is, an expression of my regard for their scholarship and a tribute of gratitude for all I have learned from them. Whatever I have accomplished, I have done by standing on their shoulders. I could not have done it without them. If I have written trenchantly, I have done so not only with the courage of conviction but also with the humbling certainty that many errors have gone undetected despite my best efforts. I make mine the words of a much greater scholar who, anticipating the charge that his research sought to "make nonsense of a great deal of classical scholarship," replied: "I have not thought of my argument in those terms, nor would I make so extravagant a claim for my conclusions. There is, so far as I know, only one way of making nonsense of scholarship: to give habit the status of authority and thus allow it to suffocate radical curiosity."[10] It is in the spirit of this radical curiosity that I give to the world *The Epic Rhapsode and His Craft.* I beg the reader's forbearance of its blemishes and solicit for its argument the favor of his fair and honest criticism. For this, he will earn my thanks.

---

[10] Dover 1968b:195.

PART I

THE 'HOMERIC QUESTION'

1

Dictation Theories and Pre-Hellenic Literacy

1.1 Statement of the Problem

THE ENDURING FASCINATION of the Homeric poems attests to their undeniable artistic integrity. These are not haphazard products, cobbled together unredacted by one or more editors from independently preexisting songs. The architecture of their themes and plot construction evince sophisticated long-distance correspondences that I would not hesitate to label prolepses and analepses. The patent artistic integrity of the *Iliad* and the *Odyssey* must provide a fixed point to any theory of their genesis and eventual writing. On the other hand, we have ample, and in my view, incontrovertible, evidence that anchors them to the oral song culture of ancient Greece. These poems were composed *in performance*, with the aid of traditional themes and a sophisticated traditional diction, and without the use of writing. This inescapable conclusion follows from the internal evidence of the poetry, as it is illuminated by Milman Parry's and Albert B. Lord's studies of living Southslavic oral poetic traditions.[1] The attempts to chart a way between the Scylla of their primary orality and the Charybdis of their artistic integrity constitute the chronicle of twentieth-century Homeric scholarship. There are still those who hold to a substantially written composition. They believe in the historical reality of a poet 'Homer,' who, pen in hand, charted and executed the composition of the poems. But these are lone voices, unwilling to come to terms with the implications of Parry's and Lord's scholarship.

Of greater influence are those who accept the reality of a singer of exceptional skill—let us call him 'Homer'—in complete command of the techniques of oral composition, who either himself wrote down or else dictated to an amanuensis an especially fulsome version of his poems. The differences of

---

[1] Janko 1998a provides a helpful review of the evidence and defends the oral nature of the poems' origin. As I explain below, however, I cannot agree with Janko's dictation theory. Jensen 2011 provides a full-scale comparative review of the 'Homeric Problem' in light of modern fieldwork on oral epic traditions.

detail between versions of this theory are many: some think Homer[2] was illiterate and therefore could only have dictated to another;[3] others, following Lord, go further and assert that a working knowledge of literacy (as seems requisite for the task of committing almost thirty thousand hexameter lines to paper[4]) would have denaturalized the poet's oral technique and must be ruled out;[5] yet others point out that the skill of writing may be inorganically related to the techniques of oral composition, and that Homer's writing down remains a possibility.[6] Common to all versions, however, is the notion that we should consider the resulting written texts as inorganically related to the oral compositional technique: writing will have affected, but not overruled, the singer's traditional compositional *modus operandi*. From the point of view of Homeric poetry *as a system*, the writing down of the poems was not a diachronic development but a historical accident.[7]

This book explores an alternative to such dictation (or autographic) theories, which I consider historically implausible and diachronically impossible. The author, and still the most eloquent exponent, of this alternative is Gregory

---

[2]   I will usually refrain from placing Homer in scare-quotes. The reader should bear in mind that scholars' use of this traditional name does not necessarily imply their acceptance of ancient biographical traditions or even that this was the name of the singer who is often called the "monumental composer."

[3]   Reece 2005 reviews and defends oral-dictation as the most plausible mode for the recording of the Homeric poems. Although useful in various ways, his summary is not reliable when it mischaracterizes the evolutionary model, implying that it advocates unchanged and unabated fluidity in the degree of recomposition in performance during the classical and Hellenistic periods (so at 77 and 84). Reece also caricatures the model when he intimates that, if true, one should expect the Homeric epics to be "simply a collection of loosely related episodes, ... the predictable result of a process of compilation by various hands over a long period, or of a process of gradual accretion within an impersonal oral tradition" (56; cf. 65). As to Atticisms in the Homeric poems, which he surveys in 80–86, much more can be said than he does there, including evidence that he overlooks. But a comprehensive—and necessarily technical—answer to Reece's challenge (84) must wait for another occasion. I maintain, however, that on balance the data, objectively viewed, support the true claims of the evolutionary model and hardly constitute an Attic dialectal "veneer."

[4]   I am using 'paper' generically for any potential substrate.

[5]   Lord 1991:43.

[6]   Janko 1998a:3, with reference to so-called "transitional texts." But see the adjustments suggested by Jensen (1980:90), who prefers "oral autograph" for such hypothetical written texts.

[7]   In keeping with its original linguistic meaning, I label 'diachronic' those aspects that follow from the development of the poetic tradition as a literary and linguistic system. 'Diachronic' encompasses the outworking of systemic tendencies. 'Historical,' on the other hand, denotes all that took place or is assumed to have taken place. When opposed to 'diachronic,' 'historical' refers to what does not flow from, and cannot be predicted on the basis of, the evolving tendencies of the system. Diachrony must be open to the corrective of history, for accidents cannot be excluded *a priori*. But, in the absence of strongly supporting evidence, the scholar who engages in historical reconstruction cannot expect conjectured historical accidents to overrule with plausibility otherwise anticipated diachronic developments.

Nagy, who in a series of books and articles has described what he calls "an evolutionary model" for the making of Homeric poetry.[8] Because I agree with Nagy's proposal and follow it in its basic outlines, I devote this and the chapter that follows to a critique of the main dictation theories in print. I hope to make clear why I find dictation theories implausible in the extreme and Nagy's alternative eminently preferable. Nagy combines the comparative evidence about the composition and performance of Homeric poetry with the evidence for its diffusion during the archaic and classical periods. Just as the dynamics of performance shaped the manner of composition (the creation of, and recourse to, traditional diction and themes), so also the dynamics of diffusion shaped the evolution of this poetic medium. The main *comparanda* are the living epic traditions of India. Fieldwork has shown that the greater their diffusion, the less occasional they become as the performer seeks the acceptance of a growing target audience. Wider diffusion is also correlated with the increasing professionalization of the performer. This fact is of obvious significance to the focus of this book. Choices of subjects and their particular variants, thematic emphases and de-emphases, are carefully tuned to the breadth of audience reception. One may readily appreciate the difficulty in mastering a repertoire of many detailed versions, each possessing the local color appropriate to a narrow audience. Also clear is the corresponding advantage of converging on a common denominator suitable for the most general kinds of audiences. As with all comparative work, the study of Indian epic traditions reveals both significant similarities and dissimilarities with the Greek ones. In particular, a semantic shift from hero to god is perceptible in those epic traditions that have experienced the widest diffusion and become most normative. This stands in contrast with the Greek focus on the hero's mortality. But the insight remains valid that diffusion deeply affects the dynamics of reception that obtain between the performer and his audiences, and has the potential to shape his subject matter and composition.

Nagy also draws attention to the role that festivals may play in elevating local poetry to supralocal status.[9] This too is instructive, for it suggests that we consider the role of the Panathenaia in Athens and other relevant festivals elsewhere as centers of diffusion that may potentially attract supralocal performers and audiences.[10] One may envision the drawing of public and performers to a

---

[8]   First proposed in 1981, it is found most conveniently in Nagy 1996b:26–63, and at greater length in Nagy 1995.

[9]   Nagy 1995:169 and Nagy 1996b:52.

[10]   If wide attendance at first helps to ground the reputation of the festival, once its prestige has solidified it no longer needs a pervasively supralocal audience, or even a majority of supralocal performers, to continue to exert its influence. At that stage, the tastes of a largely local festival audience may be considered normative and cast a long shadow over the performance of the given poetry elsewhere.

central venue as a centripetal force that subjects the reception of epic poetry to the common demands of the progressively integrated and standardized tastes of its festival audience. At the end of the festival, when outside performers leave and visitors return to their locations of origin, they act as centrifugal agents of diffusion, taking with them and advertising as they may those performances that have enjoyed the greatest success. When there are competing centers of diffusion, the process of homogenization to which recurring festivals give place creates over time recognizable local variants of supralocal projection, whose influence at regional and supraregional levels depends on the perceived prestige of the corresponding festival. In the ancient Greek case, I note the so-called 'city editions' of the Homeric poems (κατὰ πόλεις or πολιτικαί), which at first probably represented epic versions independent from the Athenian, but in the long run may have evolved into syntheses of locally received variants and the more canonical (i.e. Panhellenic) Athenian version.[11] The repeated convergence of performers and audience on a dominant venue matches the convergence over time of local variants on a comparatively more canonical, Panhellenic version. This pattern of diffusion is the key to more unified traditions. Because Athens in the sixth and fifth centuries BC (if not before) became *the* dominant center for the performance of Homeric poetry,[12] this book will focus on the performance practice of rhapsodes in Athens.

1.2 Albert Lord's Dictation Theory

I start with Lord's own dictation theory, first published in Lord 1953 and now conveniently reprinted in Lord 1991:38–48.[13] His towering reputation and centrality to the study of oral poetic traditions make his views the necessary point of reference of all later dictation theories. Familiarity with his formulation clarifies the critical ways in which he differs from later exponents of dictation, who have eagerly, but with doubtful legitimacy, used him to support their own theories. The central contention that issues from Lord's work is that the hypothetical text that might emerge from the dictation to an amanuensis by an oral traditional singer remains a historical accident, organically unconnected to the workings of the oral tradition. Diachronically, it would be as trivial and inconsequential as it is historically implausible. This follows from Lord's

---

[11] See Allen 1924:283–296; van der Valk 1949:14–21; Citti 1966; Janko 1992:26n29; Nagy 1996c:147–148; and Cassio 2002:117 and n. 58. For the aesthetics of common reception, see "koine (Homer)" in the index of Nagy 1996c.

[12] This is Nagy's "definitive period" (1996b:42).

[13] Regarding the claim that Parry articulated a dictation theory of his own, see Nagy 2003:66–67.

consideration of possible sources for the impetus to record the song in writing.[14] Even if we assume *arguendo* that it was available to them, accomplished oral poets would not think of turning to writing from their accustomed composition in performance. This is especially so when writing was still rudimentary. What would make them dissatisfied with the long-established mode of composition? Nor could they need writing as a mnemonic aid, since their training and life-long practice would have taught them to perform without the extraneous need to memorize a script. Nor can the impetus to memorialize a song provide a plausible motivation. When the tradition has been orally handed down to an oral poet and he brings it to life in performance, what would suggest to him the need for anything other than oral transmission to the succeeding generations? Why should he be anxious that his songs would be lost without a written record? Nor do oral traditional singers share our notion of 'word' (see below, p. 174), which would make them eager to preserve verbatim a particular performance.

Lord therefore concludes that the impetus must have come from an outside source, but he does not speculate about the historical circumstances of a possible dictation event or the ensuing transmission of the resulting transcript. He only notes that our texts may go back to "an early period of collecting" which is otherwise unknown.[15] Here, Lord writes presumably under the influence of his own field experience as a collector of living oral traditions. It is precisely his commendable refusal to speculate that is responsible for his historically implausible theory. If he had carefully considered the circumstances that must have obtained in archaic Greece, the technical obstacle to the alleged dictation, and the role that the hypothetical transcript would have had to play in the song culture to make its way through the archaic, classical, and Hellenistic periods into the medieval *paradosis* and, finally, into our hands, I am confident that he would have written otherwise. But we must not lose sight of the central implication that flows from his deep grasp of the workings of oral traditional composition in performance: so long as the oral tradition was vigorous and supple, no hypothetical record of one singer's performance, whatever its quality, could have arrested the centuries-old rhapsodic practice and become a controlling canonical text that performers would have to memorize and perform by rote.[16] For Lord, dictation preserved the primacy of oral performance and guaranteed the

---

[14] Lord 1991:44.

[15] Lord 1991:44. To the suggestion of an external impetus by an appreciating audience "who recognized the special merit of the *Iliad*," one may oppose Sealey's comment that "as far as can be discovered, those Greeks had learnt to recognize merit, not in songs, but in singer" (both quotes are from Sealey 1957:330).

[16] So Nagy 1996b:32: "[H]ow exactly was such a dictated text supposed to be used for the process of performance? How could a dictated text automatically become a script, a prompt, for the performer who dictated it, let alone for any other performer?"

culturally *inorganic*, marginal status of the resulting transcript—a transcript, in his view, whose existence was demanded by the surviving texts. Thus, his article on the oral dictated text was an attempt to harmonize the model of composition in performance derived from his fieldwork with the survival of the *Iliad* and the *Odyssey* as written texts.[17] The greatness of the man and his scholarship is not diminished by his failure to answer adequately questions that he never pondered. It is paradoxical that his authority has been borrowed to prop up dictation theories that are incompatible with his model of oral composition. Even if the implausible historical accident of dictation had actually happened, the resulting transcript would have been irrelevant to the diachronic development of the text of the poems and largely marginal to their transmission.[18]

Here it is appropriate to consider the impact of dictation on the practice of a singer accustomed to compose in performance before an audience. Those who do not dismiss Lord's work out of hand, but still think that the *Iliad* and the *Odyssey* cannot owe their monumental dimensions to the ordinary circumstances of oral composition in performance, find an escape in what they think are the unhurried conditions of dictation. Once again, Lord himself seems to lend his aid: "It is impossible to believe that the *Iliad* and the *Odyssey* as we have them represent exactly the songs as actually sung in normal performance by Homer; their length and consequent richness of content, the perfection of their lines, suggest some reliance on writing"; and again: "The very length of the Homeric poems is the best proof that they are the products of the moment of dictation rather than that of singing. The leisureliness of their tempo, the fullness of their telling, are also indication of this method" (Lord 1991:45 and 46). But these comments might give the false impression that dictation comes easy to the bard, a welcome relief from the pressures of composition before an audience, a process that ensures the successful production of a high-quality composition. Nothing is further from the truth: "One might think that dictating gave the singer the leisure to plan the words and their placing in the line ... . First of all, however, dictating is not a leisurely process; neither the singer nor the scribe has patience for long pauses for deliberation ... . But more especially, a mood and a tempo ... are established which produce the balanced utterances of the poet. Not conscious planning but the rhythm of that particular process of composition calls forth the structures" (Lord 1991:12). Lord's corrective makes clear that, if dictation succeeds at all, it is not because it supplants the ordinary

---

[17]   Cf. Lord 1991:45. This is why it is not, in fact, paradoxical at all, *pace* Cassio 2002:107, that one "who had explored the techniques of oral composition in more depth than anybody else" supported a culturally marginal dictation model. Furthermore, it is hardly true of Lord's proposal "that the transcript became an indispensable basis of all subsequent recitations" (107).

[18]   Hence the comments by Sealey 1957:329–330.

psychology of composition in performance by the conscious premeditation of the literate poet. Only the rhythm is changed, and, with the change of rhythm comes a tendency to ornamentation and structural elaboration.[19] But it is the exceptional singer who can successfully adjust to the unaccustomed rhythm, and the exceptional scribe who can move at the requisite speed and provide the stimulation and feedback the singer needs and would otherwise get from his regular audience.

For as long as recording devices were not available, many were the instances of failed attempts to record a dictated performance. As Lord (1991:12) notes in a marked understatement, "not all singers can dictate successfully." To this, he adds the following caution: "It is vastly important that we do not make the unthinking mistake of believing that the process of dictation frees the singer to manipulate words in accordance with an entirely new system of poetics. Clearly he has time to plan his line in advance, but this is more of a hindrance than a help to the singer who is accustomed to rapid-fire association and composition" (Lord 1960:128). Given the ways in which dictation interferes with the regular practice of the singer, how it upsets the usual psychology and rhythm of composition, it is hardly surprising that the literature contains many examples of frustrating attempts to record dictated performances and their inferior products. Thus Radloff (1990:85–86) complains about the deficient compositions that resulted when the Kirgiz singers performed for dictation:

> Unfortunately, I must concede that despite all my efforts I did not succeed in completely reproducing the singers' songs. The repeated singing of the same song, the slow dictations, and my frequent interruptions slackened the singer's excitement, which is often necessary for good singing. He could only dictate in a fatigued and lax manner what he had recited to me with fervor a short time before. Although I was generous with applause and gifts to encourage the singer, these could not make up for natural motivation. Therefore, the recorded verses have lost much of their freshness.

The great Serbian scholar Vuk Stefanović Karadžić met with comparable difficulties when he sought to record the songs of Old Milija:

---

[19] Lord 1960: "One should emphasize, however, that these changes or differences are not caused by the singer's conscious or deliberate choice of an order of words or of words themselves for any other reason than the influence of the surrounding rhythmic structure. ... The singer is struggling with the traditional patterns under unusual circumstances ... ; he is, indeed, striving to maintain, not to depart, from the tradition" (127–128). Cf. Lord 1991:11.

[W]hen I met Milija, instead of happiness I found nothing but toil and trouble. Like nearly all the other 'singers' (who are nothing but singers), he couldn't recite the ballads in the proper order but only sing them. And not only that; without spirits, he'd become so confused and decrepit ... that he couldn't even sing always in the proper order. When I saw this I could think of nothing better than to make sure that he sang each song to me several times until I'd got it well enough by heart to know when he was skipping something; then I'd ask him to sing it slowly to me, drawling out the words, and would write after him, as quickly as I could. When I'd copied down a song like this, he'd have to sing it to me again, and I'd look at my manuscript to see if it was all written down properly.[20]

It is important to quote at length from these field experiences, because the modern armchair scholar is prone to underestimate the difficulty of dictation and its chances of failure. These examples should make us reluctant to assume too readily that an alleged eighth- or seventh-century dictation might plausibly explain the genesis of the written Homeric poems. On this sole basis the historical accident of dictation cannot be positively ruled out, but the need of this scenario for the co-occurrence of a series of exceptional circumstances hardly recommends it as a plausible origin. Not only would we need an exceptional oral singer with incomparable mastery of his traditional practice of composition in performance; he will also have had the assistance of an exceptionally gifted scribe with the intelligence and skill to prompt his successful dictation; and he will have had to prove himself an extraordinary reciter of a prodigious poem under the abnormal and unprecedented circumstances of dictation.

Lord 1954:8 serves to emphasize how unfamiliar these must have felt to an oral traditional singer accustomed to compose in performance. Lacking the rhythm his instrument imparts to his verse and the critical acclaim of an audience to spur his effort, the singer finds dictation the most difficult of all methods of collection:

Without a good audience the singer tends to shorten his song ... . The scribe must know how to induce the singer to form good verses, even if it means putting the gusle into the singer's hands from time to time to restore the proper rhythm to the singer's mind. Moreover, the scribe must also take the place of the audience ... [H]e must assure the singer ... that he is a discerning audience who will tolerate nothing less than the best which the singer can produce. This takes great skill; for the scribe

---

[20] Wilson 1970:169. Cf. Koljević 1980:314–318.

is working against the evil of ennui both of himself and of the singer. Epic songs are long. In normal rapid performance they frequently take many hours. In the slow process of writing and of dictating line after line, hours are not infrequently stretched to days. The singer is unused to such slow composition. His mind frequently runs ahead several lines while the scribe is writing the last one which he dictated, and the scribe must be constantly alert to this propensity. Yet all this guiding of the singer by the scribe, this nursing of the song, must be done without the scribe in any way inserting himself or his ideas into the song. He may suggest that something isn't consistent, but he can never advise what the correct way would be.

The hypothesis of an oral dictation of the Homeric poems in the archaic period requires the co-occurrence in a common setting of an extraordinarily skilled oral singer and an exceptionally sensitive scribe, together with the technology of writing and the means to defray the attendant costs. Extreme skepticism about the reality of such a remarkable historical accident seems justified.[21]

It remains to understand how the evolutionary model can account for the monumentality of the poems. One can understand the tendency towards comprehensiveness as part and parcel of the Panhellenic aesthetics of reception and its normative status. The intense cultural focus on the Homeric poetic tradition over against other poetry, which subjects the Homeric poems to constant elaboration and augmentation, is reflected by Lykourgos' statement in *Against Leōkratēs* §102 that, of all poets', Homer's ἔπη *alone* should be performed at the penteteric Panathenaia. Consider in this light the way Karadžić describes the growth of heroic poems: "The poems have not immediately, in their beginning, become as they are, but one man begins and composes as he can, and then going from mouth to mouth the poem grows and becomes more beautiful, and sometimes shrivels and is spoilt; for as one man can talk more clearly and beautifully than another, so he can sing and speak poems."[22] When shaped by convergent cultural forces of reception, long-lasting traditional recomposition in performance may foster the growth of a notional thematic totality, of which any performance only constitutes a partial view. A good example of one such convergent force would be the 'Panathenaic rule,' which would have required rhapsodes to perform sequential subject matter.[23] The suggestion of legal compulsion in these late *testimonia* need not be taken at face value. Diachronic developments in ancient Greece were often reimagined as the decisive action of

---

[21] The implausibility would hardly be relieved by assuming an autographic text instead.

[22] Cited in Koljević 1980:322.

[23] In [Plato's] *Hipparkhos* 228b and Diogenes Laertios 1.57. More on this below, pp. 382ff.

one individual. It would not surprise us if what the rhapsodes felt as the growing insistence by the Panathenaic audience to perform Homeric subject matter in a particular sequence—the audience knows how to reward and how to punish— would have been attributed to the initiative of Solon or Hipparkhos. The eventual written text of such notional totality, what Nagy (1996b:76) calls "the singular marvel of ultimate [poetic] expansion," would naturally expand to the monumental dimensions familiar to us. Aelian's *Varia Historia* 13.14 makes clear that the ancients could readily conceive of the poems in terms of episodes.[24] What the prevailing taste might consider the highlights, at least, would probably be performed more often and receive a corresponding title. This would not lessen the notional totality which would at length result largely in the poems as we know them today. This diachronic development is the explanation of the poems' monumentality which scholars, including Lord, have found puzzling apart from the historical accident of dictation.[25]

1.3 Richard Janko's Dictation Theory

Richard Janko has elaborated his dictation theory most fully in Janko 1990 and Janko 1998a. He is primarily motivated by two convictions. The first, that in Janko 1982 he proved conclusively through statistical linguistic analysis that the Homeric poems were fixed in writing in the late eighth century BC. In a recent review, he confidently affirms that "this demonstration ... has yet to be refuted,"[26] and this study has been very influential. Haslam 1997:80 serves to make the point. He quiets his misgivings about an early fixation of the Homeric poems with an appeal to the work of Janko.[27] The second conviction is that the Homeric poems exhibit the sorts of mistakes and inconsistencies that may be expected from the crucible of composition in performance. For an autographic text, these mistakes would be *lapsus calami*; for a dictated one, *lapsus linguae*.

---

[24] Cf. Ford 1997.

[25] For an Indian epic *comparandum*, cited by Nagy 1996b:77, cf. Blackburn et al. 1989: "[W]hen an epic story is well-known to the audience, the complete story, from beginning to end, is rarely presented in performance—or even in a series of performances. The full story is sometimes found in written and published texts, but we prefer to speak of an epic tradition that encompasses not only text and performance but also what is unwritten and unperformed" (11).

[26] Janko 1998b:207; cf. Janko 1990:329–330.

[27] "Even the most naively optimistic scholar may feel uneasy when invited to believe that what we have happens to be just what Homer sang ... . But where the former theory [that there were no written texts until the middle of the sixth century] founders ... is in its inability adequately to account for the early textual fixation implied by certain details of the linguistic constitution of the poems. Janko's comparative statistical study ... shows that the Homeric poems' linguistic evolution was arrested at a very early point."

But Janko 1982 is as influential as it is methodologically flawed. The matter is too complex to be reviewed here, and a detailed critique must be relegated to future work. But it is worth noting that he has not convinced West, who in the exposition of his own dictation theory[28] observes that from a demonstration that the language of the *Iliad* and the *Odyssey* is less modern than other hexameter poems one may not readily infer that they were composed earlier. One need not be wedded to a nineteenth-century view of a thoroughly artificial Homeric *Kunstsprache* to embrace the currency of 'productive archaisms' in a singer's oral composition (cf. West 1995:204–205).[29] In his 2008 dissertation and a recent article, Brandtly Jones claims that the approach of Janko 1982 "is fundamentally and pervasively flawed" and that "his methods fail to date [the epic texts] in either a relative or an absolute manner."[30]

Regarding his second conviction, Janko argues that a poem composed with the aid of writing would exhibit a "much smoother surface" (1998a:7) and he presents a few examples that illustrate the dictum *nescit vox missa reverti* (7–9). These he thinks sufficient to refute the performance-driven model of gradual textual fixation advanced by Nagy (cf. 1998a:12n63), who in turn has answered them in Nagy 2003:49–71. But it is worth commenting on an especially well-known case introduced in Janko 1990:328, 331–332 and elaborated in Janko 1992:99–100.[31] This concerns N 410–423, where Deiphobos strikes Hypsenor and 'immediately loosed his knees' (εἶθαρ δ᾽ ὑπὸ γούνατ᾽ ἔλυσε 412). This expression (with or without ὑπό, and with γυῖα or γούνατα) is used often for a fatal blow that dissipates the limbs' vital force, e.g. at Δ 469 Ζ 27 Η 12 Λ 240 579 Ο 435 Π 312 400 Ρ 349 524 Ω 498 ξ 236 ω 381 (and presumably at Ε 176 Λ 260 Ν 360 Ο 291 581 Π 425 465). But sometimes it is clearly not (Π 805 Φ 406 425 Ψ 726), or at least by itself not necessarily, fatal,[32] even though parallel instances of the type of wound involved might point in this direction (Η 16 compared to Ε 43–47). The expression is further used simply to express weakness (θ 233), instability (σ 242), weariness (Η 6 υ 118), or feebleness induced by strong emotion (Ν 85 Σ 31 Φ 114 δ 703 ε 297 406 σ 212 341 χ 68 147 ψ 205 ω 345). Since death coincides with, or often follows, a fall in battle, 'to loose the limbs' becomes an easy metonymy for 'to kill'. But Π 805, where the fall precedes the wound, and Φ 406 425, where death is an impossible outcome (not to mention Ψ 726, while wrestling), make clear

---

[28] On which see below, pp. 42ff.

[29] Related concerns are expressed by Clay 1997:490–492 and Burgess 2001:52–53. For Janko's disapproval of West, see Janko 1998a:1.

[30] Jones 2010:290; cf. Jones 2008.

[31] I single out this particular instance because Janko's recurrence to it hints of its special significance to him.

[32] X 335 is a special case: either proleptically, of Hektor's impending death, or *stricto sensu* of the collapse of his limbs (ἤριπε δ᾽ ἐν κονίης 330).

that the stricter meaning (i.e. provoking the collapse of the limbs) can be evoked even in the context of fighting. Indeed, σ 238 242 explicitly play on the ambiguity of whether death attends the loosening of the limbs.[33] The parallels establish that it is not impossible, if perhaps surprising, to use the expression where a wounded fighter falls to the ground but does not die (at least immediately) from his wounds. That Deiphobos at N 416 and Idomeneus at N 447 should think so is understandable, but we need not take their perception or inference as normative.[34] In fact, Leaf (1900–1902:2.33) *ad* N 420–423 observes that it is unusual for two Greek heroes to leave the fight to carry a dead body back to the ships (they merely draw it within their lines to prevent despoiling); whereas this development is well motivated if they are carrying back a wounded leader. And he adds that while βαρέα στενάχων is otherwise used in the *Iliad* only of wounded warriors (Θ 334 N 538 Ξ 432), the *Odyssey* applies it to those in distress (δ 516 ε 420 κ 76 ψ 317), like the near identical βαρὺ στενάχων in the *Iliad* (Α 364 Δ 153 Ι 16 Π 20 Σ 70 78 323 Ψ 60). There is nothing in the context or diction of Janko's alleged example of an irreversible performance mistake to force the interpretation that Hypsenor *had* to be dead and could not groan; or to suggest that in making Mekisteus and Alastor, his carriers, groan heavily the passage would necessarily be felt as departing from regular epic diction. It is impossible, in other words, to conclude that Aristarkhos' στενάχοντε, his alternative to the vulgate στενάχοντα at N 423, must have been an emendation without textual support.[35] The scholiast's judgment that reading στενάχοντα is laughable (γελοῖον), usually (and perhaps correctly) ascribed to Aristarkhos too, cannot decide the matter. The Alexandrian scholar did not understand that Homeric poetry had had its genesis through traditional recomposition in performance. Presented with the alternative, he (or his disciples) could judge στενάχοντα laughable on the basis of his own proclivity to integrate his disappointed expectation of a dead Hypsenor with the particulars of the context and his feel of Homeric diction. In creating either reading, a singer in performance would clothe his choice of a particular outcome (a wounded but living or a dead Hypsenor) with the language customary to fighting contexts according to his particular feel of the semantic boundaries of this conventional diction. One singer might feel unsuitable the temporary survival and groaning of a wounded hero whose limbs had

---

[33] Note in particular Odysseus' reasoning at σ 90–94. A comparable ambiguity, this time between death or love as the loosening agent, seems in view at ξ 69.

[34] Leaf 1900–1902:2.33 *ad* N 420–423 remarks that "it would be quite unlike the Epic style to represent him [i.e. Deiphobos] as mistaken without explicitly saying so." I do not find the force of this sentiment decisive.

[35] Nagy 2004:114 observes that στενάχοντες occupies the same verse-final slot at ξ 354, to which I add that μεγάλα, which precedes στενάχοντες there, is a variant of βαρέα in βαρέα στενάχοντα at ψ 317. For the notion of the (Byzantine) 'vulgate' text, see Janko 1992:20–22.

been loosened; he might then produce στενάχοντε.[36] Another might not share the scruple and produce στενάχοντα instead. Varying degrees of tolerance for what are perceived as potentially problematic statements, and a corresponding willingness to accept (and harmonize them with the context) or reject them are typical of the reception of especially authoritative texts. One need only think of the charge, often levied by the skeptic, that the Bible is full of contradictions, an objection that many believers readily counter with an array of harmonizing strategies. In the case of Homeric poetry, the singer himself is an instrument of creation, transmission, and reception, and the production of multiforms in performance is subject to the same considerations of acceptable subject matter and diction. I might add that I find implausible the notion that 'Homer nodded off' in the short space of thirteen lines; or that (incredibly) having nodded off, his skilled scribe (for skilled he must have been to produce the alleged dictated texts) would have failed to bring this to his attention, as Nikola would do during his transcriptions of Southslavic songs.[37] Under the circumstances of dictation as envisioned by Janko, the notion of an 'irreversible' mistake (*nescit ... reverti*) is psychologically implausible. It requires that the singer never hear again, or ask to have read back to him, what he has previously dictated. Otherwise, would he not have noticed the 'laughable' incongruity and instructed the scribe to make the necessary changes? How are we to explain his lack of interest in the product of what would have been, under any scenario, both a stunning departure from his regular practice and a prodigious feat of historical innovation?[38]

Janko (1990:330) asserts that the technical obstacles to the writing down of the *Iliad* and the *Odyssey* in the late eighth century have been "much exaggerated." He notes that the alphabet had been derived from the Phoenicians no later than 775 BC (which precedes by about half a century his date for the *Iliad*); he declares that writing materials were available, with the sole support of Herodotos 5.58;[39] and he suggests that contact with the Near East, where written epics (he claims) circulated widely, might have prompted a similar feat among the Greeks. The first two matters are best taken up individually, and I will do

---

[36] And perhaps not have two others leave the battlefield to take him back to the boats.

[37] Cf. Nagy 2004:113–115 for a somewhat different solution. As Nagy observes, how plausible is Janko's view that for half a millennium N 402–423 "happily coexisted with the version of N 423 that featured στενάχοντα—until Aristarkhos in the second century BCE finally offered his 'solution'"?

[38] That Janko does not grapple with this psychological implausibility seems incongruous with his perplexity when he considers Nagy's evolutionary model: "[O]ne is entitled to ask why the resulting texts contain so many minor oddities, which would surely have been tidied up in any process of this kind" (Janko 1998a:12n63).

[39] The historian notes that early Ionians used leather; Janko adds, "as did the Phoenicians and Arameans" (1998a:12n63).

so below. For now, I simply note, first, that the date of the derivation of the alphabet, while an obvious *terminus post quem*, is not the primary concern. Of greater interest is why the alphabet might have been created and to what uses it might have been put at such an early stage.[40] Second, that, even if Herodotos can be made to imply the currency and ready availability of leather for writing, it is very unlikely that the Greeks would have used this expensive substrate for the almost certainly commercial purposes for which the alphabet was invented.[41] This suggests that at the earliest stages of alphabetic adoption, users would have not resorted to the use of leather. But that is the same early stage at which the poems are supposed to have been written down. That hardly recommends leather for transcripts of epic performances, to say nothing of the substantial amounts of substrate required for the thousands of lines in the poems as we

[40] This, again, is the distinction between the diachronic—what one might expect from the natural development of culture as a system—and the historical, which might have room, however implausible, for an anomalous, early application of the alphabet to a novel use for which it had not been created.

[41] Cf. Csapo et al. 2000:103–105. Johnston 1983:67 adds a concern for the "personal marking of property." That proprietorial and commercial interests encouraged the use of writing is not only the most likely, but also the consensus, view. So, for example, Ruijgh 1995:37–38: "[I]l est légitime d'admettre que l'usage de l'alphabet grec, adopté en vue de la comptabilité commerciale, a été limité à l'administration économique pendant plusiers siècles" (38). Cf. Woodard 1997a:252 (and n. 15) regarding the minority view of Powell 1991 that the alphabet was created to record Homeric poetry: "[A] writing system ... expressly engineered for such a high-minded and noble purpose as recording poetry ... seems not altogether probable." This theory is also contradicted by the failure of the early scripts to distinguish long and short vowels, a feature that is of central prosodic significance (cf. Woodard 1997a:243n111 and 253). To the notion that, phonologically, a syllabary was too indeterminate "to have served as a practical vehicle for recording ambitious poetic compositions" (Powell 1991:113), Woodard 1997a:254 replies that "the syllabic script of Cyprus was an effective means for recording the Greek language and, as such, could certainly be used for writing verse compositions. Powell has confused language with script" (cf. Consani 2008:154–155, who underlines the natural agreement of syllabic systems with "speakers' spontaneous analysis of [the] linguistic *continuum*, as it is operated when writing a text"). Robb 1994, like Powell, doubts that the alphabet was designed for commercial purposes. Its initial motive was "to record the hexameters of dedications" (8). His argument is circumstantial and turns on the character of the earliest surviving inscriptions and it is vulnerable to the same objections levied against Powell's. It is true that archeology has not unearthed any alphabetic commercial records. But it is surely for these, not for the monumental Homeric poems, that we expect the use of perishable and easily reusable substrates that would not have survived. If the Linear B tablets had not been preserved by the fires, who would have suspected that the Mycenaean palaces had kept administrative records? A recent opponent of the commercial origin is Schnapp-Gourbeillon 2002:255–314. She allows Iron-Age Euboian aristocrats both the practice of commerce and the use of writing (279). But even though she owns that writing must have remained marginal vis-à-vis performance (296), her treatment is culturally simplistic at key points. One example must suffice: "[O]n est conduit à penser que l'impulsion menant à la rédaction de cette oeuvre ne s'est produite qu'en raison de sa qualité, son originalité extrême, tellement au-delà du reste de la production épique que l'obligation d'écrire s'est pratiquement imposée d'elle-même" (294).

know them. But if we resort to the more reasonable conjecture of the use of papyri, plausibility is on the side of papyri not being available to the Greeks at this early stage.[42]

1.4 Written Epics from the Near East

Janko's third argument, that written epics circulated widely in the Near East, needs further qualification. When the particular nature of this written record and the social circles of its diffusion are understood, this argument loses much of its force.[43] I can best make my point by restricting the argument to one of the NE epics that received the widest diffusion, the epic of *Gilgamesh*.[44] What follows is heavily indebted to George 2003, the most recent authoritative editor of the epic, and all page references are to this work unless otherwise stated. We must bear in mind, however, that the centralized administration typical of NE rulers, with its extensive archives and a professional class of scribes, marks an immediate and important departure from the setting of Dark-Age and archaic Greece. Actions and developments that are readily intelligible in a court setting that values written literacy highly cannot, without justification, be assumed to apply to Greek Dark-Age and early-archaic centers of power. Another factor that makes NE epics a parallel of doubtful applicability is the unlikelihood that the Greeks would have been directly exposed to Mesopotamian culture. NE literary and cultural practices mediated by the civilizations of the Levant would seem of higher relevance. A final fact of stark difference: even so long a poem as the standard version of *Gilgamesh* did not have more than about three thousand lines;[45] compare that to the almost 15,700 of our *Iliad* and over 12,100 of our *Odyssey*! The combination of a significantly smaller poem and a social class dedicated to writing and archiving makes the recording of *Gilgamesh* and its written

[42] Even the assumption that papyri might have been used faces significant obstacles, technical and economic. (Janko 1998a:12 recognizes the need for considerable time and resources.) For the availability and use of leather and papyri, see below, p. 73.

[43] Following the lead of Burkert (1992:25–33), West (1988:170) offers a different reason when he traces the impetus back to the Greeks' contact with the Phoenicians and the Aramaeans from North Syria. (Among the Greeks, the Euboians are principally in view, with a possible role for Cyprus.) Perhaps under the influence of the intervening Burkert 1992 and West 1997, Janko 1998a:12 abandons his 1990 reference to the Near East in favor of "the written epics of the Levant," singling out "the written literature of the Phoenicians" in 12n64 (cf. Burkert 1992:32–33). The existence and character of a written Phoenician literature is an important matter I take up below, see pp. 33ff.

[44] As George 2003:39 notes, of the great narrative poems only the *Enuma elish* exceeds *Gilgamesh* in the number of first-millennium sources.

[45] Excluding Tablet XII, which most scholars agree does not belong in the series: "The eleven tablets of the epic vary in length from 183 to 326 lines of poetry, so that the whole composition would originally have been about 3,000 lines long" (George 1999:xxviii).

transmission a *diachronic* development of NE culture, not (as would be the corresponding writing of Homeric poetry at the alleged time) a *historical* accident, impossible to rule out but of extreme improbability.

There are four primary stages in the composition and transmission of *Gilgamesh*: the Sumerian stage (down to 2300 BC), and the Old-Babylonian (OB) period (2000–1600 BC), the Middle Babylonian (MB) and Assyrian period (1600–1000 BC), and the Neo-Babylonian (NB) and Neo-Assyrian period (1000–400 BC).[46] To these, George adds consideration of *Gilgamesh* outside the cuneiform tradition. The oldest fragment of the epic comes from Nippur and dates to the Ur III Neo-Sumerian period (2100-2000 BC). Much of the extant Sumerian literature at the time was set down in King Shulgi's academies of Nippur and Ur and was adopted as the regular curriculum of OB scribal schools.[47] Most extant manuscripts of *Gilgamesh* go back to eighteenth-century OB scribal apprentices, but George is reasonably certain that the literature represented there goes back to the Ur III period as court entertainment (7). By the OB period it was limited to scribal circles (8). The Babylonian (i.e. the Akkadian, not Sumerian) version of *Gilgamesh* was not part of the scribal curriculum in the eighteenth century. And yet, a few scraps of an Akkadian *Gilgamesh* among the mass of Sumerian school tablets show that it had already joined the written tradition. George conjectures that "people of this time could have been familiar with Gilgameš stories in the vernacular Akkadian from an oral tradition. The Gilgameš motifs found on terracotta plaques of the Old Babylonian period support such a view, for they are more likely to reflect people's knowledge of orally transmitted stories than to witness popular familiarity with a written version" (17). He further believes that the poem was performed in Akkadian in court circles and the marketplace, and that it was widely known by all social classes. Apprentice scribes familiar with it from repeated performances may have written down favorite passages, and occasionally improvised lines for their own amusement or to relieve their study of Sumerian poetry (18). Notice that there is nothing in this scholar's reconstruction of this stage to support Janko's contention of a wide circulation of written NE epic. The role George assigns to performance seems justified by the presence in the OB version of much material that had no place in the Sumerian canon (20). Although he does not defend the alleged role of performance on the ground of stylistic features supposedly diagnostic of oral telling, which an archaizing mannerism might imitate, he avers that "it is to my mind inconceivable that ancient Mesopotamia was without traditions of oral poetry throughout its long history, both because the majority of people in all periods

---

[46] Cf. Tigay 2002:xxii.
[47] Shulgi's dates are 2094-2047 BC in conventional chronology.

could not read or write and in the light of the strong traditions of oral literature in the more recent Near East" (21).[48] George refuses to speculate how the oral material came to be written. He observes the obvious: a literate people who wanted to leave a record for posterity would naturally resort to writing (22). I might add that the deeply rooted cultural practice of archiving and the possession by individual scribes of personal libraries might serve to motivate the act of recording.[49]

In the late Bronze Age (during the MB period), when Akkadian was the *lingua franca*, cuneiform writing was in much demand in the chanceries of Syria, Palestine, and Anatolia, and, for a brief time, even in Egypt's El-Amarna. Babylonian texts, including the OB *Gilgamesh*, were widely copied by scribal schools throughout the West. Tablets have been found at Emar (southeast of Aleppo, on the Euphrates), Ugarit (on the coast of Syria), Megiddo (in Palestine), and Boğazköy (in Anatolia) (24).[50] The borrowing of Mesopotamian literature was gradual, over several centuries (26). Babylonian high culture had an impact wherever cuneiform was used. South Mesopotamian culture had already been exported to the West (Ebla, Mari, and Tell Beydar) in the early Bronze Age, and archaeologists have found an Old Assyrian pseudo-autobiography of Sargon in a merchant's library in Cappadocia dating to the early second millennium. Babylonian literature influenced Anatolian scribes in the Old Hittite period (seventeenth and sixteenth centuries), and thereafter continued to make its way into this area directly or through the Hurrians (27). Once again, diffusion is driven by scribal training and the spread of cuneiform literacy. Some intellectual exchange must have accompanied regular trade (as witnessed by the merchant mentioned above); but the educated man, not a scribe, who could read and wanted to own a literary text in cuneiform, will have been the exception. The last centuries of the MB period saw the organization of Babylonian literature into canonical series. MB tablets from Nippur show the Akkadian *Gilgamesh* as a text the scribe was to face early in his training (35).

We now reach the Neo-Assyrian period, the most immediately relevant because it overlaps with the derivation of the alphabet in Greece and Janko's dates for the dictation of the Homeric poems. Archaeologists have discovered a library that belonged to a family of 'chief singers' (*nargallu*) from seventh-century Aššur. This seems to support the oral performance of traditional narrative poems. The collection of tablets is "a fairly typical example of a first-millennium private library" (34); it contains school tablets, various documents,

---

[48] Cf. Vogelzang and Vanstiphout 1992.
[49] This seems to be the source of the so-called Pennsylvania (CBS 7771) and Yale (YBC 2178) tablets, fine specimens whose quality suggests permanent library copies (cf. George 1999:xx).
[50] They were also composed in Hittite and Hurrian (George 2003:24n66).

and common texts from the scribal tradition with an atypical emphasis on hymns and mythological poems. Which texts these self-styled singers performed, and whether they sang or recited, is not known. Unclear, too, is the connection, if any, these texts have with court performance, and whether Babylonian narrative poetry was still living in the mid-first millennium (35). Not much is known about scribal training in Babylon during that time, although a study suggests an initial phase of exposure to a small selection of *Gilgamesh* and other celebrated poems. It is possible that this pedagogic practice attempted to build upon the early familiarity of Babylonian children with oral versions of this reduced canon (36). Syrian and Anatolian scribal centers, on the other hand, reveal the use of *Gilgamesh* at an advanced stage of the curriculum (35). The Babylonian and Assyrian social circles that possessed written literature during the first millennium (usually in personal library collections built over several generations) included scribes, diviners, exorcists, and cult singers, for whom literacy was necessary. Common are colophons which identify the inscriber of the tablet as the young relative of the owner and explicitly label him as an apprentice or junior professional (37). Literary transmission across generations was restricted to a few professions and it took place within families devoted to the given trade, typically, from father to son. This does not mean that *Gilgamesh* was necessarily unpopular among the educated outside scribal circles. The use of some of its episodes in Mesopotamian art speaks for a wider currency of the legends of Gilgamesh, if not of the poem that bears his name. It seems to me, however, that not much can be advanced with any certainty about its diffusion beyond scribal circles. Writing, collecting, and archiving were immediately, and most intimately, connected with the scribal trade. Apart from these habits of scribal families and the archival and collecting practices of rulers, there is little evidence that, upon hearing the oral performance of *Gilgamesh*, the average literate man would feel the need to acquire a copy for his private use. But one must assume some such scenario as a regular happening, if incidental exposure to NE literary culture (perhaps mediated by Anatolia or the Levant) was to suggest to a wealthy Greek ruler the value of owning a written record of an extensive Homeric performance. The logic and method of such a trans-cultural influence remains as inexplicable to me as the assumed scenario is implausible. George affirms that West's theory of an early seventh-century "hot line" between Assyrian court literature and the *Iliad* (West 1997:627) "supposes that the written epic was put to use as an entertainment in the Neo-Assyrian court. This is an assumption that cannot be proved" (56). Mesopotamian popular literature runs in parallel with scribal high culture but we know nothing about it. Some version of *Gilgamesh* must have been sung even after the written texts reached their several fixed forms. George thinks it unwise to assume that oral performance must have faithfully followed a written version: "Those that could read may have used the written text to refresh their memories, but others that could not probably knew by heart a version of the poem at some remove" (56).

Someone may adduce the alleged presence of NE motifs and narratives (or narrative patterns) in Homeric and Hesiodic poetry as evidence that Greek singers were acquainted with the *written* texts of corresponding NE poems. If so, the choice to write down a Homeric performance might not be, after all, so great a departure from the oral culture of Greece. But George makes two observations that helpfully counter this argument. First, that in the study of trans-cultural influence, one should start with Phoenician and Aramaic literature, which by proximity and contact have a prior claim over NE Babylonian or Assyrian literature (56). This draws attention, once again, to our need to investigate the extent and nature of Phoenician literature.[51] Second, that NE oral as well as written composition often consisted in adapting and stitching together well-known motifs and mythologems, sometimes reusing blocks of existing lines. The intellectual exchange that often accompanied commerce would have made such familiar episodes, standard passages, and staple motifs and narrative patterns the common store of singers and poets composing in the various ancient NE languages (56). Greece, too, would have imported from the eastern Mediterranean such "motifs, episodes, imagery and modes of expression that were always traditional in the narrative poetry of the area or had been adopted into that poetry from Mesopotamia long before" (57). In sum, the theory that the dictation of the Homeric poems followed the trans-cultural model of written circulation characteristic of NE epics fails to persuade: first, because the written circulation alleged is either doubtful or else of a very different character than what is required to support the claim; and, second, because, even if the type of circulation imagined by proponents of this theory had actually existed, there was no tenable cultural vector to bring the requisite influence to bear upon Dark-Age and archaic Greece.

1.5 Written Phoenician Literature

In 1990 Janko had stated that "the impetus to taking down a text like [the *Iliad* or the *Odyssey*] can only have come from the Near East, where written epics were circulating widely" (Janko 1990:330). By 1998, however, the terms of comparison had changed: "One influence on the person responsible for recording must have been knowledge of the existence of written literature, which means the written epics of the Levant" (Janko 1998a:12). At this point, Janko

---

[51] On which see immediately below, section 1.5

cites Burkert (1992:114–120), who does not, however, review any epic from a Levantine culture that might have circulated in writing during the time when we might reasonably expect it to have exerted the alleged influence. Instead, Burkert considers Mesopotamian, Hittite, and Ugaritic literatures. The latter two belonged to civilizations that were defunct by the turn of the first millennium, whereas with the first we are back to the Near East.[52] The reason is clear: there is hardly any Phoenician literature extant, let alone epic. Scholars (especially classical scholars) assume that there was an abundant Aramaic and Phoenician literature, but that it has been lost because it was written on leather and other perishable materials. Even granting that, as a religious text of first importance, the preservation of the Jewish scriptures is *a priori* more likely than the survival of other writings not so intimately tied to religious cult, the complete disappearance of early (i.e. pre-Hellenistic) Phoenician literature is hard to understand if it was so vital and copious as assumed. For Aramaic literature, the only surviving work is the Elephantine *Ahiqar*, cited by Burkert (1992:32) as proof for the transmission of Mesopotamian literature via Syria to Palestine and Egypt. Burkert (like West 1978a:13 before him) assumes the ultimate Mesopotamian origin of *Ahiqar*, but this is far from established, and modern scholars consider more likely that both the narrative and the sayings were composed in Aramaic.[53] The Book of *Ahiqar*, then, does not imply the probable existence of a flourishing book market of Mesopotamian (or Levantine) epics that might have prompted the dictation of the *Iliad*.[54] Scholars since Wendel (1949:93–94) have conjectured a body of Aramaic literature on bookrolls as the link through which features of the cuneiform book format (like the colophon) made their way into Greece.[55] But Wendel supported his theory on the disputed belief that *Ahiqar*'s Assyrian setting betrayed its Assyrian origin. Moreover, the Sultantepe library of clay tablets suggests that Aramaic-speaking communities with interest in Mesopotamian literature enjoyed this literature in its original languages.[56] We must also bear in mind the warning in Rollston 2008:67–71 not to assume that the linear-alphabetic northwest Semitic writing system was attended by a

---

[52] Cf. Burkert 1992: "The establishment of the first Greek library—the *Iliad* written down in twenty-four(?) leather scrolls—and of the great library of Ashurbanipal at Nineveh, who ruled from 668 to 627, may well have taken place at about the same time. Even this may not be totally accidental" (120).

[53] Cf. Vanderkam 1992:120.

[54] Neither does its sapiential cast commend the notion that a written copy of this very work might have provided the impetus for the recording of Greek heroic epic.

[55] Cited with approval by Burkert 1992:32. Cf. West 1997:592–593.

[56] Cf. Gurney 1952.

higher rate of literacy for the Levant of the Iron Age than the far more complex cuneiform script.[57]

But before reviewing our present knowledge of the nature and scope of early Phoenician literature, it is worth pausing for a moment to probe the validity of the 'influence model' espoused by these scholars. Why should we expect a Greek who had come across a Levantine or Near-Eastern epic in written form to think of producing a transcript of the performance of a traditional oral rhapsode? This is an odd notion, rarely examined, which does not withstand scrutiny. The expectation of a cultural borrowing is only reasonable where the borrowed practice meets an existing or incipient need. I do not believe that the scenario in question meets this standard. To put it in terms of a colorful illustration: an inhabitant from a temperate climate who visits the Eskimo would hardly think of borrowing the construction of igloos to meet the need for housing in his own culture. The material, ice, would be scarce or unavailable; the resulting structure would not be durable; and, presumably, his society already has in place adequate building practices to meet the need. So also in the present case. The song culture of archaic Greece was oral. Epic poetry was composed in performance with traditional language and traditional themes; and, crucially, it was preserved and transmitted orally: neither audience nor performer can be plausibly expected to have felt the need to preserve a particular performance, or *a fortiori* a poetic tradition, in writing. The festival calendar, with its seasonally repeated performance venues, gave cultural expression to the enduring character of its songs. Why should acquaintance with a wholly different method of preservation, well suited for a culture built on the foundations of scribal schools and scholars,[58] public and private libraries, extensive administrative archives, and habits of collection[59]—a method, that is, well motivated by, and readily intelligible within the context of, such a culture—prompt a member of the archaic Greek song culture to adopt the alien and culturally inorganic practice? In archaic Greece, the skills and materials needed for the feat of writing the *Iliad* must be assumed as scarce or lacking as ice would be for our hypothetical visitor to the Arctic. And the resulting artifact—a small library of leather or papyrus scrolls, according to some—would be culturally marginal and as unlikely to endure as a structure of ice in the tropical sun. It would neither be used by performers, who would continue to observe their age-long performance practice, nor read by a

---

[57] Cf. Stoddart and Whitley 1988, who highlight the complexities that attend the study of alphabetic literacy. Their study compares the disparate uses and ideological meaning of alphabetic writing in Attica and Crete, and in Greece and Etruria.

[58] Cf. Driver 1976:62–73.

[59] Driver 1976:73–77.

public that, even if it was not largely illiterate, would feel no need to experience in writing what it had hitherto experienced in performance.

Unsuccessful too are the attempts to motivate the borrowing of the alien practice of writing by speculating that it met the emerging need to legitimize monarchic or aristocratic ideology at a time of social turmoil. They flounder in trying to establish that the ideological cast of the *Iliad* or the *Odyssey* is, as the case might be, monarchic (Janko 1998a:13) or aristocratic (Morris 1986:122–126). The attempt to pin down the ideological texture of the poetic tradition relies on the same assumption it is called to support: that the poems were written down substantially as we know them at a point in time in order to advance a particular social agenda. Rather, our analysis must accommodate the fact of recomposition in performance with varying degrees of fluidity during a protracted interval that included the archaic period. This acknowledgment allows the diachronic dynamics of reception to come into focus. The pivotal development and determinative context for this reception is the rise of the polis, with all of its evolving ideological complexities. Proponents of these theories rarely make the effort to explain in detail why the written artifact should actually advance the ends of a monarchy or an aristocracy. Morris (1986:122–126) provides an exception to the rule; I explain below[60] why I find his reasoning unconvincing. Although the argument is not always or necessarily made, it is worth noting that writing *per se* does not favor monarchic, aristocratic, or democratic tendencies, although arguably, depending on the particular social context, it can be used to further any of these political arrangements.

With these preliminary observations in place, I now proceed to survey with Krings 1995 as a guide what is known about Phoenician literature, and to assess whether Burkert, West, and Janko are justified in making it at least partially responsible for the writing of Homeric poetry. It is important to heed her opening warning: the significance of the Phoenician alphabet for Western culture does not *eo ipso* justify the expectation of a commensurately significant Phoenician literature (31). Scholars like Lipiński 1992 have approached the subject largely with generic categories derived from the study of Greco-Roman antiquity. More problematic yet are: the naive inclination to take at face value ancient testimonies about the nature and extent of the Phoenician and Carthaginian literatures; the assumption that what applies to latter-day Carthage must also be applicable to earlier Phoenicia; the failure to consider the possible influence of Greek literature on Carthaginian and later Phoenician works; and the interpretive weight assigned to Pliny's problematic testimony about the existence of a library at

---

[60] See p. 44 n. 16.

Carthage (*Naturalis historia* 18.22–23).[61] Krings (1995:32) pronounces flawed and unfruitful the approach that seeks to argue for the existence of a Carthaginian literature from Greco-Roman sources that make reference to Carthaginian works.

To take the nature and scope of Phoenician literature first, it is the case that many scholars assume that it was rich and considerable. According to Josephus in *Against Apiōn* 1.28, all acknowledged that significant administrative and historical record-keeping distinguished the Phoenicians. We should mark the obvious fact that the writing in view here concerns historical records, not ancient epics that might have prompted the dictation of Homer. But, as it happens, what Josephus declares an uncontested fact is far from certain. The sources he alleges[62] are all suspect in various ways.[63] Although the existence of the alleged Tyrian chronicles cannot be ruled out, it is impossible to ascertain their nature with any confidence.[64]

Philo of Byblos claimed that his *Phoenician History*, which survives in fragments quoted or paraphrased by Porphyry and Eusebius, derived from a Phoenician scholar from before the Trojan War by the name of Sankhouniathon.[65] This erudite Phoenician from the latter half of the second millennium BC is said to have collected and interpreted the cosmogonic writings of Taautos (the Greek Hermes!) stored in the *adyta* of the temples of Ammon.[66] Baumgarten observes that the fragments of Philo's *History* "are virtually the sole testimony to the myths and beliefs of the Phoenicians" (1981:262). Thus, for the last two hundred years, the existence of an early Phoenician literature has hinged primarily upon the historicity of Philo's source and his early date (or, in lieu of this, the early date of his source material).[67] Baumgarten (1981:264–265), Lemaire (1986:217), and Krings (1995:33) all agree in their judgment: in all probability, behind the myth of Sankhouniathon stands a collection of sources of Phoenician cosmogonic lore from the Hellenistic period, redacted in Phoenician or, more likely, Greek. These had been gathered together under the venerable pseudonym, or

---

[61] All of these factors are carefully reviewed with commendable skepticism by Krings 1995. She addresses further the influence of Greek literature in Carthage in Krings 1991.

[62] 'Tyrian chronicles', γράμματα δημοσίᾳ γεγραμμένα (*Against Apiōn* 1.107), mediated by an otherwise unknown Dios (FGH 785); a Phoenician history by Philostratos (FGH 789); and Menander of Ephesos.

[63] These sources are listed, with brief commentary, in Krings 1995:33.

[64] Cf. Lemaire 1986:217–219.

[65] The dating by the Trojan War is Porphyry's. By making him Hesiod's source (Baumgarten 1981:89n89), Philo merely makes Hesiod a *terminus ante quem*.

[66] Baumgarten 1981:10–11, with translation in 63–64.

[67] Krings 1995: "La date et l'historicité de ce Sanchouniathon ont été souvent discutées et sa prétendue oeuvre s'est retrouvée très tôt au coeur d'une bataille d'érudits, révélatrice de la sensibilité persistante des débats sur la 'littérature' phénicienne" (33). For bibliography on the debate, see Lemaire 1986:233n19.

else circulated individually and were later compiled by Philo himself.[68] This raises the question of the antiquity and authenticity of his sources, and—of obvious importance to my argument—of their character, oral or written. For Baumgarten, Philo's mention of Mōt (806:21), the *Zophasēmin* (806:24), and the poetic form of the cosmogony and zoogony establish beyond doubt that their ultimate source was Phoenician.[69] A review of the last argument is instructive. Philo's sources for the cosmogony and zoogony appear to use the poetic device of parallelism familiar from Biblical and Ugaritic literatures. This conclusion, however, is not without its problems, since there are sentences that lack the expected parallelism and others whose alleged parallelism presents alternative explanations.[70] Baumgarten makes two important comments at this point. First, the use of this poetic device does not rule out Greek influence since the Jews employed parallelism in poetry clearly influenced by Greek thought, and even in poems written in Greek.[71] Second, nothing in the syntax or style prevents a date later than the eighth century BC.[72] He also believes that Greek science explains aspects of the cosmogony previously inexplicable, and that its source must therefore date to a time after the sixth century BC and had Greek sources:[73]

> The Hermetic and Gnostic texts cited establish ... that Philo's cosmogony as interpreted here was not *sui generis*. Not only do we have Eudemus' report of a similar Phoenician cosmogony from the fourth century B.C. at the latest, but the neighbors of the Phoenicians were also engaged in reinterpreting their traditional doctrines in the light of Greek philosophy. ... [I]t is tempting to suppose that Philo's source was written in its final form at approximately the same time as *C[orpus] H[ermeticum]* III and the cosmogony of the Nicolaitans. A date at the very end of the first century B.C. or during the first two centuries A.D. seems proper. This would be close to the time when Philo himself was active.

Baumgarten's judgment, then, is that Philo's work contains genuine Phoenician traditions but does not preserve one or more Phoenician texts from hoary

---

[68] Baumgarten (1981:264) favors the notion that there were many sources and that Philo has combined the traditions of at least two cities, Tyre and Byblos. Each source faces the student with dating uncertainties. West (1994a:294n20) remarks that "Sanchuniathon is a genuine Phoenician name (Šakkūnyātōn, 'Shakkun has given'), but of a type not likely to be earlier than 700 B.C."

[69] Baumgarten 1981:96.

[70] Baumgarten 1981:98–99. Note also the very different explanation in West (1994a:296) for what Baumgarten calls parallelism.

[71] Baumgarten 1981:102 and nn. 27–28.

[72] Baumgarten 1981:103.

[73] Baumgarten 1981:122. The passage cited comes from page 128. Cf. West 1994a.

antiquity.[74] One cannot infer from Philo with any confidence the wide circulation during the archaic period of a rich and varied collection of Phoenician myth, heroic or cosmogonic, in *written* form. I do not doubt that, like the civilizations around them, the Phoenicians too had their own myths and corresponding social contexts, private and public, for their telling. But in the absence of compelling evidence the presumption that these myths were composed in, or reduced to, writing and circulated primarily or exclusively as scrolls seems to me unwarranted. I find no convincing rationale to look here for the stimulus to record the Homeric poems in writing.

There is one last piece of evidence from which scholars have sought proof of the existence of epic narratives among the Phoenicians: a silver bowl of Phoenician craftsmanship from ca. 710–675 BC found in a tomb at Praeneste.[75] Another bowl in a poorer condition from Kourion, Cyprus, displays a similar sequence of scenes.[76] West (1997:99) speculates that the story on these bowls "may have been the subject of a Phoenician poem."[77] This is not a safe conclusion. The time is long past when pictorial narratives on Greek vases were commonly assumed to be derivative of particular poetic compositions.[78] Vase artists should not be assumed merely to respond to the initiative of singers. In archaic Greece, the domains of song and of pictorial representation belonged to the same traditional cultural matrix. Both drew on the cultural superset that the French call 'l'imaginaire mythique,' which exists as a symbolic lexicon and a narrative grammar, together with a collection of ever-changing multiform narrative instantiations.[79] Within their respective spheres of work, singers and pictorial artisans both responded to the forces of reception with calibrated

---

[74] Baumgarten 1981:265.

[75] Rome, Museo Archeologico di Villa Giulia, Inv. 61565. Cataloged by Markoe 1985:191 as E2, with photographs in 278–283. A good color photograph can be found in Gehrig and Niemeyer 1990:37, with a description in 186–187.

[76] Metropolitan Museum, Inv. no. 74.51.4556. Cataloged by Markoe 1985:177 as Cy7, with photographs in 254–255.

[77] He is not the first to do so. Called the "Ape Hunt episode" by Markoe 1985:49, he further notes that "the specificity of the theme, the cohesiveness of the story line, and the element of divine intervention ... argue strongly for the supposition that the story itself is not merely the product of a Phoenician artist's vivid imagination but does, in fact, describe a lost fable or epic" (67–68). The reader should ponder these words in the light of my comments immediately below. Note especially Markoe's prejudicial conviction that without the aid of a verbal narrative the artist could not have produced a compelling, cohesive pictorial narrative. Following Clermont-Ganneau 1880:16, Güterbock 1957:69 had characterized it as a "stage play." For the Kourion bowl, see Marquand 1887.

[78] Cf. Goldhill and Osborne 1994:1–11; Hedreen 2001:3–12; and Small 2003.

[79] For Greek pictorial grammar, see Stansbury-O'Donnell 1999; Hedreen 2001:12–18; and Woodford 2003:15–102.

mixtures of tradition and innovation.[80] Just as their works faced similar cultural forces, either domain evolved diachronically under the influence of the other. Although we know little about the corresponding Phoenician domains of poetic song and pictorial representation, it is naive to assume the unidirectional influence long abandoned as fallacious in the case of archaic Greece. The artisan of the silver bowl may have known how to depict a traditional religious motif (let me call it 'divine deliverance of the pious ruler from the attack of a savage') *without* the aid or inspiration of a poetic narrative archetype. But let me agree for the sake of argument that the silver bowl depicts a poem: why should it be an epic and not a brief composition of some other, culturally appropriate, Phoenician genre? And, the more important point for my argument: why should we further assume that this composition circulated primarily, or exclusively, in written form?[81]

To return to Janko, I will close this section by observing that his exposition (in Janko 1998a:13) of the ideological motivation for the dictation of the Homeric poems seems unlikely to survive scrutiny. How precisely are we to imagine that the *written artifact*, as opposed to the *performance* of the poem, buttressed the legitimacy of monarchic rule? Retaining the services of 'Homer' for frequent performance of the poem would seem more effectively to serve such propagandistic ends. The leadership of Agamemnon, moreover, often portrayed as flawed and perplexing, and Akhilleus' brazen challenge to his authority, central to the poem, seem hardly counterbalanced by sentiments such as A 277–279 and I 95–99. If legitimizing 'monarchic' rule (however defined) was the end, many an episode might seem best left out.

---

[80] Cf. Woodford 2003:105–140.

[81] Even if the bowl had been inspired by poetry, it need not have been Phoenician poetry. Produced in Cyprus at the intersection of Greek and oriental cultures, the artist might have used the oriental pictorial motifs to depict a Greek poetic narrative. This is precisely the opinion advanced by Burkert 1992:104. West 1997:100–101 counters that the female sun that rescues the hunter makes clear that the story is of West Semitic origin. The argument is not persuasive: a Phoenician artist might readily translate a Greek narrative into his own artistic conventions. Furthermore, the interpretation of the winged disk is rather fraught, as Clermont-Ganneau 1880:89–92 and Matthäus 2005 show.

2

Dictation Theories and Archaic Art

EVEN AS RECENTLY AS 2001, when he published his *Studies in the Text and Transmission of the Iliad*, M. L. West remained guarded and somewhat vague in his speculations about the circumstances that accompanied the (first) writing of the *Iliad*. On a few matters he had forcefully stated his opinion: "[f]ixity could come only when a text was written down"; "[a]pparently each epic was written down only once"; "the process of writing [the *Iliad*] down was intermittent and extended over many years" (all three in West 2001:3). To be sure, these assertions represented a moderate departure from his earlier brief treatments of the topic, in which he had seemed to embrace a dictation theory of his own.[1] Still, West (2001:4) had left open the possibility that 'Homer' (whom, in a gesture evocative of Wellhausen, he now calls 'P') had used an amanuensis to record his performances. But, unless we are to imagine a long-term association between poet and scribe that spanned the "many years" of the *Iliad*'s writing, the hypothesis that an amanuensis had taken down the oral performances of the great bard could not long survive the conviction that the writing had been intermittent and long-drawn.[2] Accordingly, in his recent monograph on the making of the *Iliad*,[3] West has effectively disposed of the scribe and, with him, of the possibility

---

[1] I review this and his earlier work in the next section.

[2] Less plausible still would have been the alternative of many different scribes, each putting down in writing at various times over many years some one portion of the *Iliad* (presumably, in the same scrolls, which Homer would have kept with him).

[3] West 2011a. Some of his recent speculations are anticipated by West 2000, where he yet remains more open to alternative scenarios. Thus, for example, he allows for one or more poets of the *Odyssey* (485); he regards as "probable enough that the poets responsible for the poems we have were oral poets ... accustomed to perform their works orally and, to some extent, to recompose them in the course of each performance" (486); and, crucially, he concedes that "the texts may have been reduced to written form by dictation, ... not as line-by-line dictation but rather as a process by which the poet recited a whole episode and the scribe (perhaps another poet), or the author-poet himself, then wrote out from memory what he had just heard (or said)" (486). West takes aim at what he calls the "fashionable opinion" that the Homeric poems were "dictated from beginning to end by oral poets and subject to no subsequent editorial redaction" (486). In its remarkable historical and psychological implausibilities, his argument in this article fully

that the poem may be an oral-dictated text.[4] In the process, West disowns his earlier speculations about the setting that made possible the recording of the poem in the context of a performance—a performance that would have been exceptional, because it was allegedly held for the recording of the poetry; but ordinary, because the bard was yet assumed to have composed in the presence of an admiring audience by resorting to his regular oral technique, however disadvantaged by the slow pace of the amanuensis and the interruptions imposed by the mechanics of recording.

Because the West of 2001 and before and the West of 2011a articulate two very different approaches to the same basic question—how the *Iliad* first came to be written down—I will review them in separate sections. First, and for most of this chapter, I will address the dictation theory of the older West, which offers the more serious alternative to the evolutionary model of textual fixation. In the last section of the chapter I will briefly consider his latest formulation on the matter, which in practice depends entirely on a writing poet. West's theory of a writing Homer is more explicit in its details and less guarded in its exposition than his older dictation theory. But it shares with the latter many of its supporting arguments, including his attempt to date the recording of the *Iliad* by an appeal to the artistic record.[5]

2.1 M. L. West's Dictation Theory

West (1990) represents M. L. West's fullest description of his dictation model for the writing down of the *Iliad*.[6] West (1995) seeks in turn to narrow the range of dates for this dictation. Its primary importance lies in the attempt to set a *terminus ante quem* for the currency of the dictated poem by turning to archaic vases that allegedly depict episodes from it (on the assumption that the dictated poem and the *Iliad* known to us are substantially one and the same).[7] As its title "The Date of the *Iliad*" advertises, West (1995) does not focus on the poem's dictation. Nevertheless, he makes several remarks that bear on it. We learn, for example, that the respective authors of the *Iliad* and the *Odyssey* (for him,

---

anticipates the treatment in his monograph, presupposing (among other things) "operations performed on a written text, as it were with scissors and paste."

[4] Although he still leaves open the possibility that Homer "used an amanuensis or a series of amanuenses" (West 2011a:3), the creative process he envisions makes this alternative both impracticable and improbable in the extreme. West elides the intellectual distance that separates his 2001 *Studies* from his 2011 *Making of the* Iliad by repeatedly referring to the former in the latter, as if both were singing from the same hymn sheet.

[5] West 2011a:16, in rather compressed fashion, where he refers to West 1995:207.

[6] Although the *Odyssey* is occasionally mentioned, the *Iliad* is its clear focus.

[7] West 1995:207.

not the same) "were well-known in their own time in the areas in which they were active"; and that their poems "were written texts that other rhapsodes adopted."[8] West 1998b:97 adds that the first written *Iliad* and *Odyssey* to correspond "in form and narrative detail" to our own version of the same "must have existed initially as a bulky collection of leather or papyrus rolls ... in some form of archaic alphabet"; and a "poet-rhapsode [was] responsible for producing this definitive recension of either poem ... ."

Only West 1990 details his preferred model for the writing of the poems.[9] West starts with the assertion that the *Iliad* had already been written down at least by the last quarter of the seventh century.[10] Early literary echoes of, and artistic references to, it dictate its existence "in einer einigermaßen fixierten Form" (33);[11] and fixity is accompanied by literacy.[12] To this fixed text attests the Panathenaic rule, which he credits to Hipparkhos (34).[13] Important to his model is the view that a tradition of oral verse need not be superseded by a written one when a people learns to write. This particular point motivates his cursory review of Lord's work, which dwells on the oralist's concession that there is a possibility, if remote, that the oral poet is literate and himself writes down a poem "at best" comparable in quality to the result of a successful dictation.[14] He then comes to Kirk 1960, who believed that "[t]he Greek tradition passed with

---

8   West1995:206. West 1988:172 suggests that the *Odyssey* was a Euboian poem, whereas the author of the *Iliad* appears to have lived in Asia Minor.

9   In this section, unless otherwise stated, all unattributed quotations come from this article.

10   In West 1995:218 he confines this date to 670–640 BC, with a preference for the decade of 660–650. West 2011a:19 in turn dates to "between 680 and 640" the extended period during which the alleged writing of the *Iliad* took place. "P will have been born around 700, give or take a decade."

11   The once popular search for echoes of the *Iliad* and the *Odyssey* in lyric poetry, and the attempt to prove Homer's priority from such echoes, has now been largely abandoned (cf. Davison 1955). West does not illustrate his claim here with specific examples. To accommodate his contention that Hesiod is older than Homer, he downdates the *Iliad* to a time that makes claims of Iliadic echoes in early lyric impossible or implausible. Thus, it is hardly surprising to find him dismissing alleged parallels in Tyrtaios and Mimnermos, and claiming that only in Alkaios do we at last find a credible literary echo (West 1995:206). His sole concern is to find echoes of Hesiod in the *Iliad* (1995:208–209). Lately, however, West (2011a:16) has changed his mind about Mimnermos, and he now embraces the view that frr. 2.1–4 and 14.1–3 present "reasonably clear echoes of the *Iliad*." To accommodate this revision to his preferred dates he must posit that the *Iliad* became widely known across Greece and "started producing observable effects in art and literature within a generation or so of its creation." However implausible, this assumed explosion of the poem into the awareness of Greek artists everywhere ca. 650 BC is necessary, if a Mimnermos "active sometime in the last third of the seventh century" was to reflect it in his own poetry. Given West's conviction that the writing of the *Iliad* was intermittent and took place over many years, one must wonder what point of time he has in mind when he speaks of "its creation" in the quotation above.

12   The *Odyssey* followed somewhat later.

13   See below, pp. 382ff.

14   Lord 1960:149.

astonishing and probably unique rapidity from its highest point to complete decline" (Kirk 1960:281), and that therefore Homer's poems must have survived in the oral tradition substantially unchanged until they were finally written down some six generations later in sixth-century Athens (Kirk 1960:279). West is right to challenge this idiosyncratic view, although he does not seem principally troubled by the thesis that recomposition in performance was suddenly arrested shortly after it reached its zenith. Lacking a diachronic model of diffusion that could account for textual convergence, he regards oral recomposition strictly as centrifugal.[15] This and his belief in two monumental composers lead West to conclude that we cannot claim to have 'Homer's *Iliad*' unless we have it from the pen of 'Homer': "[S]o gehört dieser Name [Homer] einzig dem Mann, der die *Ilias* zu dem Zeitpunkt komponiert hat, als sie schriftlich festgelegt wurde" (37).

Only on page 43 do we finally learn that West follows Lord's dictation theory. A review of the difficulties faced by an oral bard who dictates privately to a scribe convinces him that the first recording of the *Iliad* must have been a public event, with a self-confident Homer who dictated day after day with the encouragement of an enthusiastic audience, while the scribe or scribes quickly took his verses down (46). The motivation for the undertaking must have come from an aristocratic patron in whose court he performed. Rich merchants may have also played a significant role that he does not specify. The end of the recording would have been to preserve the fine composition for the future (47). By now, these statements should sound familiar to the reader. As noted above, I join Lord in considering this argument anachronistic. And I find unconvincing West's proposal that aristocratic forces lie behind the recording of the *Iliad*.[16]

---

[15] West summarizes Parry 1989 thus: "[D]ie Identität und die Qualität einer *Ilias* [wäre] sehr bald verlorengegangen ... aufgrund der Umformulierungen, die im Lauf einer Zeit der mündlichen Überlieferung unbedingt zustande gekommen wären" (37).

[16] This case has been made, for example, by Morris 1986. The motivation he offers for the aristocrats' need to record the poem in writing reveals a deficient understanding of performance in an oral culture: "Oral poetry is by its nature a two-edged sword; since it is constantly changing, there is no guarantee that the poet will continue to represent the 'right' sort of society among the heroes and gods. Written down, it is a different matter. It is there for everyone to see: the greatest of all the poets, and therefore by definition the man most inspired by the Muses and knowing most about the 'truth,' says it was so. Therefore it was so" (Morris 1986:126). Unexplained is why Homer should adopt an aristocratic viewpoint if, as Morris thinks, he is performing at a *panēgyris* that includes a broad cross-section of society; or why a written transcript should control performance and preclude a change to the alleged aristocratic texture of the poem. I find puzzling his belief that eminently traditional poetry would be open to radical shifts in its portrayal of society (especially, when such a portrayal is the outcome of a rather complex compositional architecture); and that the aristocrats would be so anxious at the prospect of such a change that they would take the unprecedented step of providing themselves with the safeguard of a written version. Implausible, too, is the further notion that the resulting

West concludes with the following scenario for the transmission of the written text (48): the manuscript was kept by the noble who commissioned it; since Homer remained at hand, only rarely would the text have been read or copied. With the passing of time copies, usually partial ones, were produced for two constituents: singers (who must have adopted the text for their own performances) and other aristocrats, who would sooner tender them to hired singers than read them. Once several complete copies are postulated, the fate of the original manuscript becomes largely irrelevant. West does not say so explicitly, but he must believe that one such copy reached Athens in the sixth century in time for the Peisistratean reforms of the Panathenaia.

There are numerous reasons to reject West's scenario as implausible. I have already noted some of them above, to which I add further considerations in the sections that follow. Here I only wish to examine the iconographic evidence with which he buttresses his theory that the *Iliad* was written down towards the middle of the seventh century.[17] The role West assigns to the literature of

---

manuscript would be widely available and frequently consulted ("for all to see"). This involves peculiar assumptions about literacy in the archaic period. Morris does not tell us whether his estimate of Homer as "the greatest of all the poets" is supposed to be local or Panhellenic. If the latter, one may wonder how this surpassing reputation could have been achieved so early and so conclusively; if the former, the need for the written script is questionable where the singer himself could place upon the poem the authoritative stamp of his performance. At all events, the aristocratic ideals of heroic warriors are not easily mapped onto the aristocratic ideology of landed citizens, although a reading of the *Iliad* that emphasizes the hoplite ideals of a middling citizenry is possible (cf. Graziosi 2002:175–177, 240). Assessing the ideological cast of the Homeric poems is an exceedingly difficult matter that I cannot enter upon here. To summarize my view: the reception of Homeric poetry throughout the archaic period was decisively tied with the development of the polis in a Panhellenic context. This commends the assumption that their depiction of 'society'—whatever its disparate strands—is susceptible of an integrated reading that accommodates and appeals broadly to the citizens of the rising polis across space and time (to wit, a reading that is Panhellenic and diachronically valid), even if sometimes it echoes the internal tension that obtained between its social classes. (This integrated reading does not correspond to the "unitary and historical" Homeric society that Whitley 1991:34–37 opposes.) A middle-class member of the demos striving for social advancement might even read aristocratic ideals through the lens of meritocratic achievement, embracing them as his roadmap for upward mobility. Cf. Nicolai 1983; Donlan 1999; and Duplouy 2006.

[17] It is worth noting that many of the valid arguments marshaled in West 1995 for a textual fixation in the seventh century are easily accommodated by the evolutionary model, which allows for the diachronic layering and integration of material from time periods all the way down to the classical era. This includes, for example, alleged references to seventh-century weaponry (209), hints of phalanx formations (209), or the Gorgon on Agamemnon's shield (210). The evolutionary model further accounts for alleged Athenian interpolations as diachronically organic recomposition, albeit within a narrow range characteristic of the last creative phase of the oral tradition. The destruction of Egyptian Thebes by Assurbanipal, which West (following Burkert) offers as a *terminus post quem*, is entirely indifferent to the evolutionary model, for which only a *terminus ante quem*, as the end of the tradition, is of significance. So is the (to my view, fanciful and textually unsupportable) connection with the fall of Babylon that West advocates in pp. 211–216.

Phoenicia is important, because it is designed to add credibility to the averred recording of the *Iliad* in writing, a development that is hard to motivate strictly from within the oral song culture of archaic Greece.[18] Unfortunately for him, as shown above, the argument from the literature of the Levant, when probed, offers little cheer to advocates of dictation. Artistic representations of heroic scenes, on the other hand, if tied with convincing specificity to our[19] *Iliad* and *Odyssey* and if no other motivation can be plausibly suggested, would provide an unquestionable *terminus ante quem* for the fixation of the passages that supplied the subject matter to the artist.[20]

2.2 Artistic Iconography

When seeking to correlate *our* Homeric poems[21] with depictions in vases,[22] the first question to ask is what kind of evidence could prove that, by a particular *terminus*, the Homeric tradition existed substantially in the form familiar to us (as regards thematic scope and plot line).[23] Thus posed, the investigation demands far more than establishing that any one particular depiction matches in the main an episode included in the poems. The qualification "in the main" allows for minor variations of detail but not for salient differences. Inevitably, one scholar will tolerate more or less divergence than another before he is led to conclude that a given vase cannot be harmonized with our poems. He might then ascribe it to another poetic tradition or else to an '*Iliad*' or '*Odyssey*' whose narrative shape was not what we know it to be now.[24] The evolutionary model

---

[18] In other words, a development that cannot be diachronic and can only be an accident of history.

[19] On my emphatic use of 'our,' see immediately below.

[20] Depictions on vases are put to similar use, albeit with less discrimination, by Powell 1991:210–211.

[21] When I refer to *our* Homeric poems I mean the poems as transmitted to us by classical antiquity (i.e. the 'ancient vulgate' text). But for matters of detail and the occasional interpolation, the advocates of dictation equate these with the *ipsissima verba* of the monumental composer.

[22] For important treatments of this topic see Friis Johansen 1967; Fittschen 1969; Kannicht 1982; Cook 1983; Carpenter 1991; Schefold 1991; Ahlberg-Cornell 1992 (not particularly incisive, but a wonderful collection of images); Schefold 1992; Lowenstam 1992; Lowenstam 1993; Schefold 1993; Shapiro 1994; Lowenstam 1997; Snodgrass 1998; Burgess 2001:53–114 (55 for an overview); and Lowenstam 2008. Mackay 1995 studies formulaic elements and traditional composition in vase-painting.

[23] Cf. Lowenstam 1997: "[P]ostulating ignorance of the Homeric poems works conversely too, as Cook asserts: there is no evidence that the painters did not know our *Iliad* and *Odyssey*, nor is it possible to imagine what sort of evidence one might adduce in order to demonstrate that" (54).

[24] Notice that I prefer the fastidious expression 'poetic tradition' to the simpler and more elegant 'poem.' 'Poetic tradition' makes clear that the poetry I have in view is traditional and allows for multiforms within a sufficiently well-defined thematic scope and narrative sequence. A multiform tradition gives the performer a measure of flexibility in the telling. It also precludes the existence of a canonical text that could rule particular versions 'in' or 'out.' But performer and audience can still ascribe a given telling to the 'story of such and such,' even if it diverges

of text fixation readily accounts for such deviations: they are simply multi-forms that reflect the narrative fluidity still existent at the date of the vase. A more radically divergent depiction that is still best assigned to the Iliadic or the Odyssean traditions merely reveals a commensurately more fluid stage. Thus, a serious mismatch between our poems and the ancient pictorial evidence offers strong support for the evolutionary model. To survive, dictation theories must suppose that the written text failed to influence the artists. Unless we adopt the implausible assumption that the respective cultural spheres of singers and pictorial artists were disjoint—i.e. that they neither influenced each other nor drew on a common cultural stock of narratives—we must infer that there was, along with the hypothetical manuscript, a parallel living oral tradition of some vigor that disappeared eventually without a trace. This is a strange and incredible notion. In the face of divergent depictions, the conclusion seems inescapable: there was no written manuscript that can be substantially equated with our poems. Not all rhapsodes performed the stories in the same way, and, if

---

somewhat from previous similar tellings. Such judgments are neither fixed nor incontrovertible (cf. Ford 1997:85–86). In particular, I take the point in Burgess 2001:59 that one must not assume what seems a multiform of an episode of our *Iliad* or *Odyssey eo ipso* to be a multiform of an inferred Iliadic or Odyssean tradition. Instead, it might just be an expansive treatment of a minor part of the broader Trojan-War tradition. The adoption of either alternative depends on what view we take of the entire tradition at the relevant chronological stage: was there a narrower tradition that by reason of performance practice and audience reception was felt to be recognizably distinct from its parent and sibling(s)? Eventually, with the rise of the notion of authorship, literary judgments about poetic traditions could be, and eventually were, phrased as assessments of authorial authenticity. When this rise coincides (as it did in ancient Greece) with a drastic reduction of the range of multiforms (i.e. when it happens at a time when variants are being strongly marginalized), traditions are reduced to, and equated with, the final version attained by their evolving narratives. It is then, and only then, that we can substitute 'poetic tradition' by 'poem.' When that stage is reached, literary judgment first distinguishes authorship and, under author, one or more poems. In the case of 'Homer,' the further we go back in time the more inclusive the ascription of *Homerica* to him. Cf., for example, the statement of Herodotos at 2.116.6–2.117. Some have argued from Herodotos 5.67 and Pausanias 9.9.5 the ascription to Homer of a Theban epic (e.g. Cingano 1985, with the agreement of Nagy 1990c:22n22 and Burkert 1987:45; *contra* Scott 1921 and 1922). The text of Pausanias 9.9.5 has been doubly emended (see the section below on the name 'Homer') and the ascription to Kallinos of Ephesos must be rejected, but on balance Cingano's inference seems sound. What is not in question is that the canon of works attributed to 'Homer' grows more inclusive the earlier the time considered (cf. Scott 1921:20; Nagy 1990c:22n22, 78–79; and Burgess 2001:8, with bibliography at 8n4). At an early enough date, the poetic traditions represented by the entire cycle (including the *Iliad* and the *Odyssey*) might have been thought of as a grand and all-encompassing Homeric tradition. As particular narrative threads of this grand bundle were woven together into more or less discernible independent narratives, their distinctive and respective scopes would mark them as performance traditions in their own right. Rhapsodes might specialize in some, and not in others.

we are not misled by the comparative evidence, no rhapsode ever performed a story twice in quite the same way.[25]

Potentially, then, vase painting is a strong ally of the evolutionary model and can only prove a weak partner of dictation advocates. For no one agreement is ever sufficient to prove their case, not even a detailed agreement—for what would prevent the currency of *that* version of the telling in a living oral tradition of recomposition in performance? This would only tell us that *our* poem's version of an episode was already exampled in performance at that time. And if the depiction appeared in significant numbers, we could surmise that the particular episode in question, not the entire poem as we know it, had already become crystallized.[26] It seems to me that only under two scenarios could the artistic evidence serve the purposes of dictation advocates. If we should find that the surviving depictions, taken together, cover much of *our* poems' plots;[27] and that, in the vast majority of instances, the textual and pictorial records substantially agree with each other—then we might have good reason to suppose that the vases provide a *terminus ante quem* for a cultural stock of heroic myth whose narrative shape might plausibly be that of our *Iliad* and *Odyssey*. It would be unreasonable to deny the parallel existence of a performance tradition largely in agreement with the art. This *per se* would not prove that the stories rhapsodes told and artists depicted had been written down at the dictation of a monumental composer. But at least the artistic record would not stand decisively in the way of the theory. One other scenario might also help dictation advocates. If we should find one or more extraordinarily detailed, early depictions that thoroughly matched our poems' telling, it would be unreasonable to suppose that the oral tradition had either stumbled then upon the precise version of the vulgate, down to the minutest details; or else that it had crystallized the episode in its final form so early. I submit that neither of these two scenarios obtains.

[25] That oral performance involved recomposition, and not simply the oral delivery of a premeditated and memorized text, is made clear by the extension and economy of the formulaic system of Homeric poetry. This is the sense in which I use 'oral' throughout. Finnegan (1977:73–86) has emphasized the existence of poetry that is not orally composed in performance and yet is composed without the aid of writing. Although such poems as a category of 'oral poetry' are not without interest, when compared with poetry not only composed for, but also in, performance, it is 'oral' in a relatively trivial sense. This is what Lord (1995:197–198) is getting at when he calls such poetry, paradoxically, "written composition without writing." Cf. Janko 1998a:5.

[26] Different parts of the poem (language, subject matter, and narrative sequence) will have crystallized at different times. The more often an episode was performed under similar conditions of reception, the sooner we can expect it to have adopted a standard version.

[27] Snodgrass (1998:130) notes that this is certainly not the case with the *Odyssey*, at least down to the middle of the sixth century. Until that time, even assuming the dubious dependence of artists on our *Odyssey*, we only find depictions of the Sirens and of the Polyphemos episode (intoxication, blinding, and escape). This amounts only to a dismal 2% of the poem's verses! Only with the addition of the Kirke episode does the picture begin to change.

There is therefore no probatory value in the 'sudden' appearance in the record at a particular point in time of numerous vases with heroic themes that can be more or less easily connected to the *Iliad* and the *Odyssey*. Unless either of the two scenarios above applies, such evidence would only indicate a correspondingly sudden rise of public interest in these themes. If so, we can fairly assume the currency of storytelling that included the episodes depicted. This would be as easily explained by a memorable performance that caught the imagination of the public and was emulated by many rhapsodes—a diachronic development—as by a dictated text that suddenly became popular and led oral traditional rhapsodes to exchange their performance habit for rote memorization and recitation of the text's version—a historical accident. If such vases were of scattered geographic provenience, at an early stage diffusion by traveling rhapsodes is more likely than by proliferating copies which artists would be unlikely to acquire and read. The convergence of rhapsodes at a given festival, where one of them might sing a memorable episode to great success and public delight, would explain its adoption by the others. These may then travel on to other festivals, where they might reperform it in its basic outlines. This would suffice to motivate a similar depiction with a different provenience, if in fact one wishes to postulate a straightforward dependence of artists on performers. The influence might also be exerted by the artistic object directly: exported by merchants to another location, it might inspire local artists to more or less faithful reproductions in their own artistic language.

There is, on the contrary, probatory value in the persistence of depictions down to a late date that cannot be explained by anything other than by the cultural currency of ways of telling the story that do not match the poems we know. Now that I have discussed the promise and limitations of this kind of evidence, it is time to review the actual vases.

2.2.1 Alleged illustrations of the *Iliad*

We might start where West (1995:207) does, with the statement by Fittschen (1969:177): "Als wirklich gesicherte Darstellungen aus der Ilias können also nur 5 Vasenbilder gelten die alle dem letzten Viertel des 7. Jhs. angehören (SB 75-79)."[28] The first four are single-fighter depictions. Let us take them in turn.

1. **SB 75:** a badly preserved fragment of a spherical aryballos from the Heraion at Perachora in the Corinthian gulf. Dated by Fittschen to ca. 625 BC, it features a hoplite advancing to the right with leveled lance and a Boiotian shield; opposing him, the tip of the spear and a portion of

---

[28] 'SB' stands for '*Sagenbild*,' and the numbers are Fittschen's.

the shield of another warrior labeled]OP (retrograde), which is, reasonably enough, assumed to be Hektor.[29] The additional inference that this is a duel between Ajax and Hektor and, furthermore, that this duel is *the* duel in *our* H 244–272 is groundless. That a pair of fighters should face off in a vase does not *eo ipso* imply a duel. Even when a melee is in view, the singer regularly narrows his focus to pairs of fighters.[30] Given their prominence—a prominence that may safely be presumed true of the earliest stages of the tradition—it is hardly surprising that the vase painter should choose a confrontation between Ajax (if in fact this is the unidentified fighter) and Hektor (if in fact his is the partially preserved name). There is nothing in this fragment that indicates a necessary dependence on the specific language of the vulgate.

2. **SB 76**: a second Corinthian spherical aryballos, now in the Louvre MNC 669.[31] Dated to the end of the seventh century, this aryballos labels the figures as Ajax (ΑΣϜΑΜ = Αἴϝας in the Corinthian script), advancing with his lance and Boiotian shield, and Hektor,[32] with lance and round shield. Once again, there is nothing in this depiction that establishes its dependence on the vulgate text or that requires that we read this as a duel rather than an engagement during battle. The two fighters appear between horse riders whom Friis Johansen (1967:66) calls "squires": the artist has adopted the fighting convention of his day, when a nobleman did not take to battle in a chariot with a companion driver, but with a squire who held his horse in readiness.[33] The small size of the aryballos commends this sort of self-contained depiction. Even if one believed that a particular episode stands behind the illustration, the space on the fabric and the balance of the composition raises the possibility that the artist has selected this particular face-off from a larger battle narrative.

To explore the interpretive limits set by these vases, it is instructive to consider the Corinthian cup from the beginning of the sixth century

---

[29] Payne et al. 1940:146 no. 1555 and pl. 61 fig. 1555. Also, with a convenient line drawing to facilitate the reading of the faint image, see Ahlberg-Cornell 1992:60 and 309 figs. 87a–b.

[30] Cf. van Wees 1997 and Raaflaub 2006:457.

[31] Discussed by Friis Johansen 1967 at 66, and cataloged as A.2.b at 245. Also Ahlberg-Cornell 1992:59–60 and 310 fig. 88.

[32] Fittschen 1969:173 prints the name as]ΚΤΠΟ[, but the label is not fragmentary. Friis Johansen 1967:66 prints it as ΕΤϘΟ. Ahlberg-Cornell 1992:176n4 gives it as ΗΕΤϘΟΡ. The only image of the inscription I know of is in the *CVA* Louvre vi (France fasc. 9) III C a (*Style Corinthien*) pl. 6, fig. 11 (figs. 9–12 are all from this aryballos). The descriptive catalog (pp. 7–8) reports it as ΚΤΡΟ. My own reading from the picture is ΕΤΡΟ (in the Corinthian script ΒΤΡΟ). (Might the first letter be a Κ corrected to a Β?)

[33] Cf. van Wees 1994:147.

cataloged by Friis Johansen 1967:245 as A.4.a and discussed at 70–75.[34] This cup is now at the Bibliothèque royale de Belgique, Brussels. It depicts two pairs of fighters facing off, flanked by their respective squires, and, under one of the handles, a running man. All the figures are labeled. Hektor is paired with Akhilleus; their squires are Sarpedon and Phoinix. Ajax and Aineias make the other pair; an Ajax and a Hippokles escort them. The running figure is called Dolon. This vase presents numerous interpretive difficulties. There is the otherwise unknown Hippokles and the obvious dislocation of Dolon, who cannot have anything to do with either engagement. Sarpedon and Phoinix make unsuitable squires, and that the artist should have used the name of Akhilleus' old tutor for one of the young mounted squires is striking. But the greatest difficulty is the identity of the pairs and their inclusion on the same vase. The choices call into question the attempt to infer a particular version of the Iliadic tradition from archaic vases. When Hektor and Akhilleus face off in *Iliad* 22, Sarpedon is already dead. And Ajax never meets Aineias in battle. It is interesting to note how Friis Johansen (1967:73–74) argues that this cup betrays neither ignorance nor a cavalier disregard of the poem. He suggests that the unaccountable fight between Ajax and Aineias responds to the painter's desire "to depict famous battles near Troy" (73). Here Friis Johansen is using "famous" in a loose sense: not 'well-known,' because it was narrated in a celebrated passage of the *Iliad* (we know this fight never occurred). He must therefore mean that the painter wished to choose famous fighters from the *Iliad* and depict their engagement near Troy, indifferent to whether the *Iliad* narrated them or not. But this rationale would permit the selection of any two famous heroes from either side. Taken seriously, it would block the inference that a paring of Ajax and Hektor in the previous *aryballoi* must refer to the duel in *Iliad* 7: Ajax and Hektor would seem eminently reasonable choices for a "famous battle near Troy" (with 'famous' in the sense elucidated above) even without narrative backing. At first, the reference to P 752–754 seems to help Friis Johansen's case: it mentions the Aiantes fighting together and holding off the Trojans, while Aineias and Hektor press upon them. These verses place Ajax and Aineias together, motivate the name Ajax for the squire, and mention Hektor. The Aiantes, however, often fight together.[35] In this regard, the

---

[34] For the date, see Friis Johansen 1967:75.

[35] That they appear together "time and again" in *our Iliad* hardly justifies Friis Johansen's assertion that "[t]he very fact that they are united on the vase is felt to be a reminiscence of the Iliad" (1967:73). Why must we assume that this was peculiar to *our* version of the poem? It may

passage is hardly exceptional and their joint appearance does not single it out for the attention of the scholar. But note what Friis Johansen has done with the text: an incidental association between the Aiantes and Aineias which *does not* feature a direct engagement of Ajax and Aineias is made into the inspiration for precisely such an engagement; and what was a melee over the body of Patroklos that involved many of the famous heroes from either side is offered as the textual motivation for a scene that Friis Johansen considers a natural counterpart of Akhilleus and Hektor's *duel*. If we did not have the *Iliad*, the logic applied to the *aryballoi* above would lead us to conclude that the painter had illustrated a poem that narrated two duels: one between Hektor and Akhilleus, and another between Aineias and Ajax. This conclusion strongly suggests that the evidence cannot yield the proof that dictation advocates are looking for.

3. **SB 77**: a third spherical aryballos, now in the Allard Pierson Museum, Amsterdam.[36] From the last quarter of the seventh century, it depicts a warrior with leveled spear who pursues another in retreat. Labels identify them as AEFAM (=Αεϝας) and BAOP (=Εαορ), which are interpreted as misspellings of Ajax and Hektor. This second fighter (Hektor) looks over his shoulder and raises his left arm in a gesture that Friis Johansen (and Fittschen after him) interpreted as the hurling of a stone at Ajax. It is hard to resist the impression that this refers specifically to the *Iliad* 7 duel. But Snodgrass (1998:112) deflates the expectation: "[T]he rock is an illusion: a recent close examination of the surface of the *aryballos* has shown that Hektor's hand is empty."[37] His caution is well advised: "As with other depictions of this popular subject, the case for dependence on the *Iliad* account has to be established; it cannot be simply assumed" (112).

4. **SB 78**: the famous Rhodian plate in the British Museum (A 749)[38] that depicts the fight of Menelaos and Hektor over the body of Euphorbos (the figures are all labeled). It is dated to near the end of the seventh

---

be a very old association, valid for early multiforms of the Iliadic tradition, long before it had crystallized in the form of our current poem.

[36] Cataloged by Friis Johansen 1967:245 as A.2.a and discussed at 64.

[37] Snodgrass refers at 176 to Cook (1983:2n11), who puzzled by Friis Johansen's mistake writes, "though the surface is worn, it is quite evident on inspection that the surface between Hector's fingers and thumb was never painted." Ahlberg-Cornell (1992:60n23) perpetuates Friis Johansen's error, resting the false inference *contra* Cook merely on the shape of the hand. This simply will not do.

[38] Cataloged by Friis Johansen 1967:279 as C.10 and discussed at 77–80. Also in Snodgrass 1998:105–109.

century.[39] Friis Johansen (1967:77–78) thinks it incontrovertible that the source of the names is P 1–113. But there is an embarrassing problem: the narrative is emphatic that Menelaos does *not* confront Hektor. After pondering the odds of facing him victoriously, he decides to withdraw (P 97–101). Our *Iliad* makes the plate unintelligible. This artifact would sooner make the case for a multiform in which the engagement comes to pass than for the vulgate text. Snodgrass (1998:106) observes that the artist hints at Menelaos' eventual victory by using the Argive alphabet to write the Doric form of the heroes' names.[40] Might this be a reference to a known Argive multiform? This proposal is supported by Pausanias' report that Euphorbos' shield, which Menelaos had brought from Troy, could be found at the Argive Heraion: "There was, then, an alternative tradition that somehow Menelaos had prevailed at this juncture. ... [L]ocal pride ... could still prevail over the authority of Homer in the time of Pausanias" (Snodgrass 1998:107). After ably disposing of some minor problems for this interpretation in 108, Snodgrass notes that we only have two options: we must consider the plate either of non-Homeric inspiration or an anti-Homeric Argive reaction. The latter alternative hinges on the unproven premise that the vulgate version of the episode was widespread and dominant at this early time and could serve as a foil to an epichoric counter-tradition. Snodgrass is right: in the absence of compelling support for the premise, the more economical (and, I might add, plausible) hypothesis assumes the existence of rival multiforms that are not derivative from the eventual canonical version.[41]

[39] Snodgrass 1998:105. For Friis Johansen (1967:79), whom Fittschen follows, it is from the last quarter of the seventh century.

[40] Cf. Jeffery 1990:154.

[41] After a discussion steered by neoanalysis, Burgess (2001:81) concludes that "the Rhodian plate and Argive tradition are actually 'Iliadic-derived' phenomena." His argument is based on the assumption that Euphorbos appeared for the first time in the *Iliad*'s version of the death of Patroklos, a version that he deems an innovative expansion of the traditional, rather minor narrative of this event (80). The allegation of innovation, in turn, is justified by the premise that Euphorbos never had a mythological role outside his participation in the death of Patroklos (80). In other words: Euphorbos must be strictly Iliadic (as opposed to traditional)—for Burgess, the *Iliad* at many points is an innovative departure from the tradition—because we cannot find him in any other context but the one the *Iliad* presents, viz. Patroklos' death. Hence a variant Argive telling must be a derivative reaction to the Iliadic. Burgess does not consider that his argument can be inverted. If strict priority must be posited, could we not assert just as well that Euphorbos must be an original Argive element (whether innovated upon a traditional version or not) because he had no mythological role outside his participation in the death of Patroklos as told by Argive poetry? And that, therefore, the canonical Iliadic version must be a derivative reaction? Against my inversion Burgess might insist that "[l]ocal traditions do not usually arise unless they serve the interests of a certain place" (Burgess 2001:78). But the same can be said of the version that ultimately attained Panhellenic status. It is naive to suppose that only local, and not Panhellenic,

5. **SB 79**: a spherical aryballos from a private collection in Basel dated to ca. 625 BC.[42] It depicts a warrior in a chariot drawn by two horses next to the chariot driver. According to Friis Johansen (1967:76), the warrior is labeled]ΑΤΡΟϘΛΟΣ. He also observes that the horses appear as yet quite still and infers that this represents Patroklos' setting out to battle in Π 144–154. There is only one problem: the vulgate is emphatic that to the immortal Xanthos and Balios Automedon harnessed the mortal Pedasos. If the artist were following our *Iliad*, *three* horses should be pulling the chariot. No less than ten verses are devoted to this detail (145–154), the last three to the addition of Pedasos as a trace-horse. The detail is significant because Sarpedon kills the horse some three hundred lines later (Π 466–476), endangering the chariot with his collapse and forcing Automedon to cut him loose to save the day. One might argue that the size of the aryballos limited the number to two. But this seems special pleading: the vase would prove familiarity with our *Iliad* insofar as it follows it—except where it does not follow it. Were there no available pictorial conventions, perhaps a smaller depiction or overlapping horses, that would have enabled the artist to include all three horses?

---

versions serve specific interests. The portrayal of Menelaos in either case (confronting or failing to confront Hektor) makes a point of characterization and possibly ideology. My critique points out a general weakness of neoanalysis: its view of sources, if superior to the rigid *Quellenkritik* of the old analysts, is still insufficiently sensitive to the vibrant dynamics of recomposition that mark long-lasting Homeric performance traditions. (This limitation also renders problematic neoanalytic attempts to identify Homeric innovations of traditional myth.) I submit that it is ultimately impossible to ascribe precedence to either the Argive or the Iliadic version. We can only characterize one as epichoric and the other as Panhellenic. These labels speak to their differential diffusion and reception, not to their chronological priority. One should allow for the likelihood of interactive recomposition, namely, that over a period of time rhapsodes in performance recomposed one multiform in more or less deliberate competition with the other. I would only add that a putative Argive tradition need not be thought of as a "shadow of the *Iliad*" (to use Burgess's term at 80; cf. 60). We simply do not know, and cannot guess, the thematic scope of the Argive tradition, its degree of coherence, and the extent of its agreement with our *Iliad*. But, reciprocally, neither can we in the absence of specific evidence assume any particular stage of development (as to thematic scope, plot sequence, etc.) for other divergent local versions and for what eventually became the Panhellenic canonical one. At best we can only oppose an Argive multiform of this particular episode ('Menelaos confronts Hektor over the body of Euphorbos') to another, ultimately Panhellenic multiform ('Menelaos does not confront Hektor over the body of Euphorbos'). Further inferences about the reason for Euphorbos' demise in the Argive tradition and how this episode contributes to the overall plot of a presumed unitary Argive poem remain speculative. That Burgess's review of the artistic record does not so much inform, as it is accommodated to, his neoanalytic premises is clear from his conclusion that the fight over Patroklos' body is traditional, while the funeral games are a Homeric invention, *despite* the lack of correspondence between the Iliadic account and two early-sixth-century representations of the chariot race (Burgess 2001:83–84).

[42] Cataloged by Friis Johansen 1967:247 as A.13 and discussed at 75–76. Cf. Snodgrass 1998:104–105.

These are all the examples adduced by Fittschen. Some are inconclusive; others actually undermine the very point for which proponents of dictation would proffer them. To these, Snodgrass adds a discussion of the Chest of Kypselos (1998:109–116), dated by most to "around or, more likely, after 600 BC" (115). This is a complicated case because the artifact has not survived and we depend on educated guesses and the detailed testimony of Pausanias. The attendant uncertainty is hardly a foundation on which to support the factuality of an early-archaic dictated transcript as the source of our *Iliad*. But even if we allow this evidence, the verdict is decidedly disappointing to dictation advocates: at best we have a generic fight between Hektor and Ajax without any proof of detailed adherence to *Iliad* 7 (so Snodgrass 1998:112); and a vignette that represents Agamemnon fighting Koon (a possible reference to Λ 248–263).[43] Snodgrass views the latter as significant, because he thinks that it is an "obscure episode" (111) unlikely to exist in more than one source. But his judgment depends on the anachronistic notion that the multiform Homeric tradition already existed as more or less well defined poems, and that no more than one at a time is likely to have included episodes deemed "obscure." It seems to me that his logic is self-contradictory: if the Chest, by his own admission "a prestigious work," devoted a panel to this episode, what other independent evidence do we have to argue that the artist made the bizarre selection of an obscure episode for this work? If we must pronounce on the obscurity or fame of a particular episode, it would seem fairer to take its depiction on the Chest as proof of its popularity in the area in which it was produced. Otherwise we run the risk of misjudging the prominence merely on the basis of *our own* likelihood to recall a given passage from our *Iliad*![44] And there is, moreover, the dissonant fact that the two verses that accompanied the panel cannot be found in our *Iliad*:[45] Ἰφιδάμας οὗτός τε Κόων περιμάρναται αὐτοῦ; and οὗτος μὲν Φόβος ἐστὶ βροτῶν, ὁ δ᾽ ἔχων Ἀγαμέμνων. It is not hard to imagine a narrative that would accommodate the first hexameter. The present tense of περιμάρναται and the deictic οὗτος require that it be part of a direct speech. They might be the words of some Trojan, rallying the forces on his side to help Koon as he fights for his

---

[43] It is doubtful whether the verse inscription 'Koon is fighting for Iphidamas' is compatible with the narrative that unfolds there.

[44] Why else does Snodgrass regard it as obscure, except that the *Iliad* involves Koon only once in action? But does not the mention at T 52–53 in fact argue against the perception that this is an obscure episode?

[45] Pausanias 5.19.4. Since what Pausanias describes does not seem to fit the *Iliad*'s version, it is not possible to find a single verse (or even two) from our text that would have served as label. If the chest had depicted Koon's dragging of Iphidamas, the following two (both from our text, with only one slight modification to the second) would serve: ἤτοι ὅ δ᾽ Ἰφιδάμαντα κασίγνητον καὶ ὄπατρον | ἕλκε Κόων μεμαώς, καὶ ἀΰτει πάντας ἀρίστους (cf. Λ 257–258).

brother's corpse: ἔνθ' ὅ γε δειλὸς κεῖται ἐπὶ χθονὶ πουλυβοτείρῃ | Ἰφιδάμας οὗτός τε Κόων περιμάρναται αὐτοῦ.[46] The two names, Iphidamas and Koon, render unlikely the existence in our poems of close parallels for these verses. But we find οὗτος with the same metrical shape in this very *sedes* in Θ 358 Π 30 χ 49 (οὗτός γε). Concerning περιμάρναται, ἐμεῦ πέρι μάρναο is attested at Π 497. περιμάρναται shares with πέρι μάρναο prosodic shape and *sedes*; the scholia *ad loc.* make clear that it could just as well be read with Aristarkhos as περιμάρναο and be construed with the genitive. This shows that the diction of the first verse quoted by Pausanias is arguably traditional, and my purpose in supplying it with a hypothetical setting is only to show that the inscription might be well taken as evidence of a traditional multiform that departs from the version in our *Iliad*.[47]

2.2.2 Alleged illustrations of the *Odyssey*

I turn now to possible depictions of the *Odyssey*. Fittschen (1969:192–193) lists five.[48] We can deal with these rather more summarily than with the alleged

[46] 'There he lies, wretched, on the bounteous earth | Iphidamas, and Koon there is fighting about him!' ἔνθ' ὅ τε δειλὸς appears at N 278; an exchange of τε for γε follows readily from verse-initial ἔνθ' ὅ γε at B 314 724 Δ 293 E 155 etc. That δειλός can be applied to the fallen as an expression of pity in the sense of 'unlucky' is clear, for example, from E 574. κεῖται ἐπὶ χθονὶ πουλυβοτείρῃ is found at Γ 195; Φ 426 shows that the adjective πουλυβότειρα is allowable for the context of a vanquished foe lying on the ground. For οὗτος as deictic for 'there' cf., for example, K 341 477 (the former proves that the proximity denoted by ἔνθα is compatible with οὗτος).

[47] Two other possible representations are dismissed by West 1995:207n21: **SB 74** (Fittschen 1969:172–173), a Cycladic relief amphora from the second quarter of the seventh century, which *may* depict (cf. Snodgrass 1998:127), but almost certainly does not, a procession of women with a *peplos* that could be connected with Z 286–300 (cf. Friis Johansen 1967:272–275). And a Melian neck amphora from the middle of the seventh century, whose neck (only partially preserved) seems to depict a naked man and a robed female, facing each other, with a shield in the middle. Scholars have identified these as Thetis and Akhilleus and suggested that this may be the arming of *Iliad* 19. Friis Johansen (1967:104–122) accepted the identification of the figures but countered that this was not the Iliadic arming; rather, the amphora depicted an earlier arming before the departure for Troy. Lowenstam 1993 subjected Friis Johansen's arguments to searching criticism. He states that "doubts about whether these two vases [the Melian neck amphora and an Attic *lekanis*] represent Achilleus and Thetis" are in fact legitimate (213). At any rate, he rejects the notion that arming scenes with Akhilleus in early vases have their setting in Phthia, but this "does not necessarily indicate that the vases illustrate the scene in the nineteenth book of the *Iliad*" (214). The episode is important and must have existed in some version at early textual stages of greater fluidity. There is simply nothing in this Melian amphora (even granting the doubtful identities) that points us to *our Iliad*. Cf. Lowenstam 1993:216.

[48] Burgess (2001:101–102) cautions us against assuming too readily that these images reflect an Odyssean tradition. If we grant the existence of an independent (perhaps older) folk story (with multiforms), in the absence of labeling or accompanying illustrations that are arguably Homeric, a Homeric interpretation is not the only alternative. I will assume the best case scenario for the advocates of dictation, namely, that the images that have been adduced as illustrations of the *Odyssey* actually have a connection to the Odyssean tradition. Hurwit has recently tried to revive the ascription to the *Odyssey*, now largely abandoned (2011:2n6; cf., for

illustrations of the *Iliad*. Three of them portray the blinding of Polyphemos. Two of them are dated to the second quarter, and one to the middle, of the seventh century. As Snodgrass (1998:90) observes, these are all large, ambitious vases from three different parts of the Greek world (Eleusis, Argos, and Etruria) that appear within some twenty years from each other before 650 BC. There is a fourth depiction, not in Fittschen 1969, on a large Etruscan storage *pithos* that Snodgrass judges not much later in date.[49] Those who consider the *Odyssey* manifestly younger than the *Iliad* may be startled that it should seem to make its appearance in the artistic record "when the impact of the *Iliad* can only be dimly perceived" (Snodgrass 1998:90). To advance my conclusion: not one of these vases suggests by a preponderance of the evidence—let alone demand that we accept—that our *Odyssey* has inspired the depiction. As a self-contained episode in Odysseus' *nostos*, one may readily imagine that some version of the hero's encounter with Polyphemos would have been part of the Odyssean tradition from a very early stage. However, there is not the degree of correspondence between the details of the paintings and of the narrative as we know it to commend the theory that a transcript substantially identical to our *Odyssey* had been dictated by a monumental composer and—having reached Attika, Argos, and Etruria—inspired these illustrations.

1. **SB 111**: the first vase is the celebrated Protoattic Eleusis amphora at the Eleusis Museum, dated to the second quarter of the seventh century.[50] A bearded Polyphemos sits leaning against the right frame of the neck, holding a cup in his right hand, while three figures (the front one in white, with shading, must be Odysseus) drive a spear horizontally into his eye. But the narrative of our *Odyssey* states clearly that Odysseus used a large stake, not a spear, which he carefully fashioned out of a

---

example, Ahlberg-Cornell 1992:27–28), of a shipwreck on a late-geometric Athenian *oinokhoē* (Munich, Staatliche Antikensammlungen und Glyptothek, inv. no. 8696). Whatever one thinks of the merits of his argument—I myself disagree with it often in matters of detail and think that the scene is best interpreted as a metaphorical restatement of elite symposiastic values; cf. Slater 1976, with Arkhilokhos' fr. 13 W—the careful qualifications with which Hurwit accompanies his attribution are surely significant. The severe discrepancies between the image and the story as we know it from μ 415–425 lead him to emphasize that "the *Odyssey* of Homer was not the only telling of the tale"; the vase's background may be a story of Odysseus "that we know nothing about" (2011:4). Had 'our' *Odyssey* been in existence at this early date, one must admit that "[it] was not authoritative or canonical in the seventh century" (5). At any rate, for my own argument surely the crucial point is that the vase's failure to illustrate the putative shipwreck of Odysseus with any degree of faithfulness—rather, its striking divergence from the known text— rob it of any probative value for a poetic text allegedly fixed in the eighth century BC.

[49] All these are discussed in Lowenstam 2008:13–17 and, though less incisively, at greater length in Giuliani 2003:96–112.

[50] Cf. Ahlberg-Cornell 1992:221 no. 74.

section a fathom's length that he cut from a great 'club' or 'staff' (μέγα ῥόπαλον ι 319) used by the Cyclops. It was made smooth, and its tip was sharpened and hardened in the fire (ι 319–328). The fashioning of the weapon receives great attention, and it makes the use of the spear in this vase unaccountable with reference to the vulgate. I do not consider determinative, however, the discrepancy in the number of men who drive the stake into Polyphemos' eye; ι 335 gives a count of five, but the space on the neck would have certainly encouraged the painter to abridge it as necessary, even if he had intended to portray the vulgate version. Another disagreement with our text is that the Cyclops is not lying supine, as ι 371 notes (ὕπτιος). That on the amphora Polyphemos holds a cup can be excused by the principle of synoptic depiction, according to which the temporal axis of the narrative is represented by a collapse of two or more sequential stages into one representation. The cup points to the drunkenness that makes the Cyclops vulnerable; it does not imply an attempt by the artist to paint him drinking even as the spear is being thrust into his eye.[51] Finally, since the Cyclops was lying on the floor in a drunken stupor, the stake was driven *down* into his eye:[52] '[My companions] took and thrust (ἐνέρεισαν) the stake of olive-wood (μοχλὸν ... ἐλάϊνον) ... into his eye; and I, putting my weight upon it (ἐφύπερθεν ἐρεισθείς), whirled it' (ι 382–384).[53] This action is arguably harder to depict on a vase than a near horizontal thrust, but the poem devotes such painstaking attention to it that one cannot compare text to vase and endorse with any confidence the notion that the latter is inspired by the former. The additional difficulty that the vase seems to depict a two-eyed being is not decisive: the Homeric text speaks of one eye whose gouging renders the Cyclops blind. But how could the vase painter depict this anatomical feature in a figure shown in profile?

---

[51] For the synoptic technique, see Snodgrass 1987:135–146, 153–156; Lowenstam 1992:173–174; Snodgrass 1998:57–58, 61–66; and Stansbury-O'Donnell 1999:5–7.

[52] I do not mean a strict vertical, which would preclude five men from simultaneously grasping the stake. But the thrust cannot be a near or strict horizontal. ι 372 fastidiously details that Polyphemos bent his thick neck sideways (i.e. he drooped his head to one side). This exposed his eye to a thrust from above at some angle from the vertical. This realistic detail facilitates his vomiting and the joint thrust of the four companions. It does not, as Snodgrass (1998:93) thinks, imply a horizontal thrust inconsistent with the remaining diction of the passage, allegedly betraying an earlier version that assumed verticality. Odysseus' action and the simile rule this out.

[53] Aristarkhos read ἐρεισθείς, for which the vulgate offers ἀερθείς, 'lifted up' or 'aloft'. Whichever the reading, the language and the simile that follows make clear that the stake is driven from above. Cf. Heubeck in Heubeck and Hoekstra 1989:34 and Snodgrass 1998:94.

2. **SB 112**: a fragment from an Argive *kratēr*, at the Museum of Argos and dated to the second quarter of the seventh century.[54] Its artistic composition is very similar to the one on the neck of the Eleusis amphora, except that the Cyclops does not hold a wine cup. He is (again) apparently depicted as two-eyed and semi-recumbent on what seems a pile of rocks; at least three men drive the stake (no distinction is made between them but for the leading figure's slightly smaller size);[55] the weapon seems a long and rather thin stake; and the thrust is near horizontal. This illustration shares all the difficulties of the former and, like it, fails to prove direct dependence on our *Odyssey*. ι 321–324 point to a stake much thicker than, and not as long as, the one depicted here (cf. Snodgrass 1998:95).

3. **SB 113**: a western Greek *kratēr* dated to ca. 650 BC, in the Musei Capitolini, Rome.[56] Significantly, this vase depicts five identical figures driving the stake into the eye of the Cyclops. The one farthest away from him braces his foot against the left frame of the picture. The weapon is still too thin and long, the thrust strictly horizontal, and Polyphemos sits on the floor to the right, propping himself up with an arm. An object that looks like a box in wickerwork stands on a pole behind the Cyclops. The pole features another, smaller object halfway up. The numerical agreement with our *Odyssey* is undeniable, and the two objects on the pole have been identified with a milk pail and a cheese rack. One may also argue that the elements that are not in agreement (the horizontality of the thrust, a sitting Polyphemos, the dimensions of the stake) all respond to the pictorial limitations imposed by the fabric. These considerations are not easy to dismiss. I do not wish to espouse the prejudicial notion that, on balance, every surviving vase demonstrates that episodes from the Homeric poems *as we know them* did not exist or were not current as early as the seventh century. After all, they must have come into existence at some point; why should a vase not agree occasionally in one or more details with what became the final vulgate version? The number of assailants in this *kratēr* may evince precisely that kind

---

54 Cf. Ahlberg-Cornell 1992:221 no. 75.
55 Of the third figure, only the leg is partially preserved.
56 In Latacz et al. 2008:417 no. 170, Claudia Braun remarks on its stylistic similarity to the Protoattic Eleusis amphora (see above, SB 111). She accordingly revises its date to 680/670. But the Protoattic amphora itself is usually dated only to the second quarter of the seventh century BC. Therefore, placing SB 113 at the upper boundary seems unwarranted. Snodgrass (1998:91) speculates that it was "probably made in Etruria by a Greek exile who signs his name on this very picture, Aristonothos." On the interpretation of this vase, see Dougherty 2003.

of agreement. The narrative, with its strongly marked folk elements, is memorable and seems to have been famous by the end of the seventh century.[57] Although it was probably a self-standing episode, we should reckon its multiforms among the potential constituents of the Odyssean *nostos* poetic tradition. Whether it had been integrated with other such episodes into a larger performance unit is doubtful (see below). If the evolutionary model of Homeric poetry is right in its understanding of textual fixation, we have every reason to assume a differentially early fixation of those episodes that were performed most often. The blinding of Polyphemos provides a good candidate for this early fixation, and this fact *may* lie behind the striking numerical agreement which may be accidental but cannot be gainsaid. There is no need for a dictation theory, with its myriad difficulties, to explain it. On the other hand, I am not so sure about the import of the objects on the pole. Even if they have been correctly identified, a narrative that portrayed Polyphemos as a shepherd, living off his flock, would suggest these details both to the performer and the artist. If there is anything exceptional in their inclusion on the *kratēr*, it is the artist's desire to particularize the setting by the addition of 'stage' props.[58] This vase by itself cannot bear the burden of a dictation theory, especially in the light of its own, and the other vases', divergences of detail.

4. The fourth vase is an Etruscan *pithos* from ca. 625 BC (cf. Snodgrass 1998:96) now in the J. Paul Getty Museum in Malibu, California.[59] It depicts the Cyclops of the same size as his assailants, sitting on a stool. A wine jar (not a skin, as in the poem) stands between him and the three men pushing a stake with a near horizontal, slightly upward thrust. Two men lean on the weapon; a third has only a hand on it (the other is on his waist). The stake is more realistically portrayed as a tooled branch or trunk: from a swelling butt it tapers off as it approaches a (perhaps two-eyed?) Polyphemos in profile. Snodgrass (1998:96) thinks that the figure who only applies one hand to the stake might be trying to twist it (cf. ι 384); this is possible, but far from certain. He also considers the choice of weapon significant. I agree that here, for the first time, there is a more realistic depiction of a stake that might be obtained from a tree.

---

[57] For the folk elements see Hansen 1997, esp. 449–450; and Burgess 2001:95, 97, with bibliography at 227nn170–176.

[58] As Burgess (2001:101) notes, sheep are common in the folk versions of the blinded ogre and items peculiar to shepherds cannot therefore establish direct dependence on the Odyssean tradition, let alone *our Odyssey*. Cf. Cook 1983:4.

[59] Getty 96.AE.135, dated by the Museum staff to 650–625 BC.

But what else should we think the weapons in **SB 112** and **SB 113** to have been?[60] The swelling butt and tapering width of this stake add realistic details that would suggest themselves just as naturally to a singer as to a vase painter. There is no reason to assume the dependence of the vase on a particular poetic version. A thicker staff more in line with the narrative in the *Odyssey* and a more vertical downward thrust would have made for more impressive coincidences.[61]

There are two engraved bronze reliefs, one from Samos dated to ca. 625 BC[62] and another, slightly later, from Olympia, and dated to the sixth century.[63] More important than these additional survivals is a fact of great significance, noted by Snodgrass (1998:98), which suggests that, insofar as these depictions were inspired by poetry, the Cyclops episode was a self-standing performance unit that was not integrated with other episodes and themes that we would recognize as Odyssean. This fact is the startling circumstance that the Olympia bronze relief is followed by fifty years of iconographic silence: "So whatever this phenomenon represents, it is not the dawn of a great age of Odyssean iconography."[64] It is unlikely that we meet here with a short-lived burst of interest in a recently dictated poem, whose written text makes its way across the Aegean and into Etruria, only to disappear shortly thereafter. Why the sole apparent interest in *this* episode? Why should the other memorable passages—the Sirens, Kirke, etc.—fail similarly to capture the imagination of the public? And what could have caused the hiatus? Furthermore, if disinterest is to blame, why the sudden and sustained resurgence later in the sixth century? The likeliest explanation, I believe, is that this story had not been integrated with any other of the memorable episodes from the Odyssean tradition and that it was

---

[60] Burgess (2001:229n198) thinks that the Protoattic amphora might feature not a spear but a spit. This is possible, perhaps probable; ordinarily there would not be any way to tell the difference. I do not think that what looks like a spearhead can be a flame. Also interesting is his response to critics who argue that the long and thin stakes may be fairly taken as the artists' rendering of what the *Odyssey* envisions as a rather thick staff: "if we relax our demands on the artists, why should we not view the weapons as inexact renderings of a spit rather than inexact renderings of the Homeric narrative?" (106).

[61] For a downward thrust against a Polyphemos lying on his back, see Carpenter 1991:238, fig. 341, a red-figure *kalyx kratēr* that may have been inspired by Euripides' *Cyclops* 455–463 (but the Cyclops on the *kratēr* seems to have three eyes, not the one that Euripides mentions in line 21).

[62] **SB 114**, Archaeological Museum in Vathy, Samos, B 1680. In Ahlberg-Cornell 1992:221 no. 77 and 343 fig. 153. It preserves two warriors and part of a third advancing leftward, holding up a horizontal stake above their heads.

[63] Olympia Museum M 108, Ahlberg-Cornell 1992:221 no. 78 and 344 fig. 154. The fragment depicts one warrior advancing towards the left, sword by thigh, holding up high by his head a horizontal stake.

[64] This was already remarked upon by Cook 1983:4.

correspondingly known as an self-standing lay and performed more frequently than competing themes which were not selected by the artists. Admittedly, this still does not explain the hiatus (more on this immediately below), but it lessens the puzzle in that it does not assume an inexplicable neglect during the seventh century and the ensuing hiatus of every other episode from an existing, more or less unitary *Odyssey*. Assuming *arguendo* the artist's dependence on epic poetry for his themes, the temporal hiatus and geographic scatter of the illustrations are easier to understand if the vagaries of where and when traveling rhapsodes performed and of their interaction with artists are responsible for where and when these five objects were manufactured.[65] Plausible explanations are harder to formulate if the leading cause of these depictions was a dramatic irruption into the Greek world of an unprecedented cultural artifact, a dictated text of the *Odyssey*.

Lowenstam (2008:15–16) has suggested, in fact, a historical rationale for what we perceive to be a somewhat sudden appearance of the Cyclops episode in the artistic record in such disparate locations. His proposal also explains why the episode would have been a preferentially performed item of the rhapsodes' repertoire. Society as a whole, and hence artists and rhapsodes, must have been responding to the changed circumstances in the Greek world of the time. A significant development, and itself an important contributor to the dynamic of Panhellenism, was the greater mobility that had accompanied the increase in trade, colonization, and a growing and vigorous cultural contact during the eighth century.[66] Travel, exploration, and contact with non-Greek societies— evidenced by the fact that two of the surviving vases, the *kratēr* and the *pithos*, are Etruscan—must have aroused hopes for profit and anxieties about reception not unlike the ones that frame the story of Odysseus and the Cyclops.[67] It is not hard to see the parallel between Odysseus the wanderer and the traders and colonists who were setting out into new lands.[68] To this, we should add the

---

[65] Cook (1983:4) suggests what he calls a "possible, but rather creaky explanation" that relies solely on the exportation of wares. Noting the report of a Corinthian *skyphos* or *kotylē* that perished in World War II, he argues that the motif might have been popularized by exported Corinthian pottery.

[66] See, for example, Osborne 1996:104–129, esp. 119–127.

[67] Osborne (1996:125) writes that "contact with Etruria did not mean simply access to desirable minerals, but also meant contact with a different people, differently organised and offering a model for emulation."

[68] Cf. α 2–3 in our *Odyssey*. Hurwit (2011:5n14) complains that "the Getty pithos fits the paradigm [of Greeks exploring foreign lands and dealing with non-Greek 'Others'] a little awkwardly (since the Etruscans were some of the 'Others' the Greeks were encountering)." But Dougherty 2003 explores precisely the tension between the *kratēr*'s iconography of cultural conflict and the "cooperative, bicultural circumstances of its production" (36; see esp. 48–49). Even if one does not fully embrace her conjectural argument, she successfully highlights the potential

use of this episode on funerary vases, which reveals its import as a narrative of victory over death.[69] That the knowledge and performance of a story so relevant to central cultural concerns should have accompanied travelers into the new world is only to be expected.[70] The seventh-, rather than eighth-century date must have something to do with developments in pictorial technique. It is probably not an accident, as Lowenstam (2008:13) astutely noted, that these artists were all using relatively new techniques. Only when the impetus from cultural change and these technological innovations converged did the story, already in circulation both as a folk motif and as a part of the rhapsodic repertoire, become a favorite of vase painters. The hiatus that ensued after the end of the seventh century might be tentatively attributed to the more settled circumstances of the sixth century, when the old anxieties were no longer keenly felt.

The picture I have reviewed above is unchanged if we add the only other few objects that could possibly derive from our *Odyssey*:[71] a mid-seventh-century Protoattic *oinokhoē*,[72] a bronze relief from a tripod leg from Olympia,[73] and two ivory *pyxides* in Florence,[74] all dated to the end of the seventh century. All depict the escape from Polyphemos' cave. None seriously departs from the vulgate except in such details as we might fairly think conditioned by the fabric.[75] It is hard to escape the conclusion that we simply do not have the kind of evidence that would suggest that the *Odyssey*, even in oral performance—let alone written form—had suddenly become available in the seventh century. The dictation theory fails to receive any support. It is, rather, seriously contradicted. If all we have is a long-standing oral tradition of composition in performance, we need not assume that the complex of Odyssean myth had reached any particular

---

complexity of the Etruscan elite reappropriation of Greek culture. Despite Dougherty's agreement with scholars who place the production and circulation of the *Odyssey* in the second half of the eighth century, she still emphasizes that our "*Odyssey* is but one historically contingent inflection of ... the 'ur-myth' of Odysseus' return" and "[is] not the only way that the story of Odysseus' return could be told" (49).

[69] See Burgess 1999 and Burgess 2001:110, 112 (bibliography in 232n228). Cf. Smith 2005, who remarks on the use of the blinding of Polyphemos on the funerary amphora of Eleusis and on a Corinthian *alabastron* dated to ca. 560, now at the Metropolitan Museum of Art in New York (76.12.6). The escape from the cave is often depicted on funerary *lēkythoi*.

[70] Lowenstam 2008:17.

[71] A further illustration on a middle Protocorinthian *skyphos* apparently perished during World War II. Cf. Fittschen 1969:193n915. Cook (1983:4n23) calls it a "Corinthian kotyle" (cf. Herbert 1977:14n7).

[72] **SB 115**, in the Museum of Aigina (inv. 10824).

[73] **SB 116** (B 7000).

[74] Museo Archeologico 82193 and 73846.

[75] Snodgrass (1998:99) writes about the Protoattic jug that "here we are not dealing with a unique Homeric version: the correspondence with the *Odyssey* is pleasing, but does not prove dependence on it."

overall textual shape or stage as a performance tradition. Under such circumstances, the artists' thematic selectivity simply need not speak with specificity to the repertoire and practice of the Homeric rhapsode. The dictation advocate who seeks in illustrations evidence for a *terminus ante quem* does not enjoy this freedom to dissociate the vagaries of the artistic record from the availability and diffusion of the written manuscript. As Snodgrass (1998:99–100) concludes: "It might be possible for a literary scholar to mount an argument that a much shorter lay, corresponding to what was later defined as Book 9, began to be recited over a wide area of the Greek world and beyond, towards the middle of the seventh century BC; but that would be an argument in which the artistic evidence could not possibly be decisive."

2.2.3 A fluid sixth-century Homer

I turn now to two examples that illustrate the fluidity of the Homeric tradition in the sixth century.[76] The first is the depiction of the funeral games for Patroklos on the François Vase (cf. Ψ 262–652). The identification of the frieze is ensured by the presence of Akhilleus as umpire. The chariots competing are five, which agrees with the five contestants in the *Iliad*. They are, however, driven by four horses apiece. Although the *Iliad* knows of four-horse chariots (Θ 185 Λ 699), the regular practice, followed at the funeral games, called for two horses. Kleitias' depiction of four appears to be an anachronism driven by the star equestrian event at the Panathenaia[77] (the vase is Attic black-figure). Except for Diomedes, who is shown in third position, the names of the contestants do not match the account in the *Iliad*. Odysseus(?) is shown as the winner (spelled Olyteus), followed by Automedon; the fourth and fifth contestants, Damasippos and Hippothoon, are unknown to the *Iliad* as Akhaian names.[78] It is perhaps not coincidental that the name Ἱππόθοος is borne by a son of Priam (Ω 251) and by a Trojan ally, the leader of the Pelasgians (B 840 etc.); incidentally, this proves that the name fits epic poetry and its meter. The name Δαμάσιππος is not exampled in the Homeric poems, but is attested in Apollodoros *Bibliothēkē* 3.10.6 (§126) as the brother of Penelope, Odysseus' wife. It too suits the epic meter. Diomedes' position and Kleitias' choice for the other contestants seems inescapable evidence that he is following another version of the race.[79] It is unlikely at this late date

---

[76] For other possibilities, see Lowenstam 1992; Lowenstam 1997; and Snodgrass 1998.

[77] Neils 1992:34 and Kyle 2007:160–161.

[78] Besides Diomedes, the other contestants in *Iliad* 23 are Antilokhos, Menelaos, Meriones, and Eumelos.

[79] It would have been perverse of Kleitias to choose somewhat arbitrary horse compound filler names in the face of the (*ex hypothesi*) well-known Iliadic narrative that had inspired his depiction, a narrative that should have readily supplied him with 'Homer's' own different choices.

(ca. 570) that the race existed as a self-standing performance unit which to the mind of performer and audience bore no organic relation to a poetic tradition substantially like our *Iliad* in shape. It is unlikely, too, that it belonged to an independent myth, whether we imagine this myth as poetry or as a prose narrative that was current beyond the circles of professional performance. The race is not easily conceivable as an element of a folktale; what would the subject of that unattested myth be? Furthermore, that the additional names readily lend themselves to epic treatment seems to me significant. Arguably, the additional representation in Shapiro (1994:37 figs. 21–22) follows the familiar version more closely; this further supports the notion that variant representations should be considered in the specific context of Iliadic performance. Lowenstam suggested that, by his choice and order of contestants, Kleitias deliberately sought to articulate the rivalry between Odysseus and Akhilleus.[80] This view depends on an over-subtle interpretation of Akhilleus, who stands as umpire by the finish line, as an implicit contestant and victor in the race. And it appears particularly improbable if the vase was intended for export to Etruria. The vase stands largely as a mute object. It is hard to imagine that it could convey this clever reading to a patron, even one familiar with traditional myth and sensitive to the possibilities of narrative elaboration. A depiction whose theme approaches the topical and makes a simple point lends itself to mythic treatment: the painter need only choose an episode that illustrates the relevant topic. Such illustrations might depart from the more familiar form of the myth, if the disparities are easily grasped in the topical context of the theme. This is what Lowenstam proposes here. That he should call his reading of Kleitias' version "[the painter's] own *interpretation*" (1992:177, my emphasis) shows that it is hardly intelligible apart from (an almost certainly poetic) narrative. The competing explanation that Kleitias was ignorant and lacked informed advice or else simply did not care what names he used seems implausible considering the effort expended in naming numerous figures on the vase and the accuracy of the other names.[81] Another Athenian vase from the first decades of the sixth century, a fragment from a *dinos* by Sophilos, supports the view that we are dealing with Iliadic multiforms. The illustration states the subject, ΠΑΤΡΟϘΛΥΣ ΑΤΛΑ. Only the

---

[80] Lowenstam 1992:176 and 189.

[81] This is Beazley's reaction: "These are all good heroic names, but Kleitias, left to himself, did not remember the field, and could not find anyone who did; his learned friend was not at hand" (Beazley 1986:32). Snodgrass (1998:120) adds: "[T]he 'learned friend' is the person assumed by Beazley to be responsible for the otherwise generally accurate distribution of name-inscriptions on the vase." Like Beazley, Giuliani (2003:143–146) believes that Kleitias remembered the basic outline of 'Homer's' version (available only at the occasional oral performance) but not the detailed names, and he had no recourse but to reach into the "nomenklatorische Vorratskiste" (146).

horses of one chariot are preserved; they race towards bleachers full of viewing public. We cannot be certain that this is the winning chariot, although the assumption seems plausible. Over the chariot are found the remains of a name, which Immerwahr (1990:21 no. 62) reads as]ιος. Neither as the beginning nor as the end of a word does this match our *Iliad*; and if this is the winning chariot driver, neither does it match Kleitias' choice.

Another important example, reviewed at length by Lowenstam (1997:35–39, with figs. 3–5 at 75–76), concerns a fragmentary *hydria* at the Vatican dated to 560/50.[82] It depicts in unusual detail the fight around a fallen Sarpedon (all figures are labeled). A striking departure from our *Iliad*, however, is that Pyraikhmes is shown alive and under attack by a figure whose label is not preserved, and whose identity might be Patroklos.[83] Pyraikhmes, the leader of the Paionians, is Patroklos' first casualty when he joins the fight (Π 284–292). As Eustathios long ago noted[84] and Lowenstam (1997:36) writes, the felling of 'Fire-spear' and the consequent scattering of the Trojans verbally reenacts Patroklos' success in averting the attempt to burn the ships.[85] This gives peculiar significance to his death at the opening of Patroklos' *aristeia* and makes implausible the view that the vase painter was mistakenly attempting to reproduce our *Iliad*.[86] The degree of detail renders the explanation of a "folk transmission" unlikely: such non-professional tellings tend toward simplification.[87] And the suggestion that the painter was trying to develop his own alternative timeline, independently of a competing performed version, assumes a naive estimate of the power of images. In all likelihood, from the point of reception, the painter's deliberate attempt to contradict so blatantly a known poetic version would have met with a "baffled or censorious" response from a potential patron.[88] The best and most economical explanation is that of an Iliadic multiform.[89] With adequate modifications to the plot familiar to us, a rhapsode in performance could motivate the alternative sequence of events. I must emphasize, however, that this hypothetical alternative must not be seen as derivative from our *Iliad*; we can only guess which version was more popular in Athens at any one time. From the point of view of traditional oral recomposition in performance, neither version is primary or derivative, even though, in actual historical fact,

---

[82] Vatican 35617.
[83] "[His] name was probably inscribed in the missing area near his head" (Lowenstam 1997:36).
[84] Van der Valk 1971–1987:3.851.17.
[85] Note Π 293: ἐκ νηῶν δ' ἔλασεν, κατὰ δ' ἔσβεσεν αἰθόμενον πῦρ.
[86] Lowenstam 1997: "This explanation might be more cogent for simple vases, but our painter has shown remarkable knowledge of the myths associated with our *Iliad* and *Odyssey*" (37).
[87] Lowenstam 1997:37.
[88] Lowenstam 1997:38.
[89] So also Burgess 2001:61, cautiously.

a rhapsode might have deliberately composed the one in competition with a previous performance of the other.

I can now summarize the conclusions of Lowenstam's and Snodgrass's probing studies. Lowenstam writes:

> The tentative conclusion here, then, is that some Greek vases furnish evidence of epic stories that, though related to the Iliadic and Odyssean traditions from which the Homeric poems themselves descend, do not depend on our *Iliad* and *Odyssey*.[90]

And:

> [T]he present analysis of poetic lines quoted by the vase-painters and used by other artisans from the eighth to the fifth centuries does suggest an intriguing conclusion: although painters were quoting lines from epic, including one pertaining to Iliadic matter, for some reason or other they never cite or allude to our Homeric poems.[91]

Similarly fatal to dictation theories are Snodgrass's numerical estimates. Surveying the number of epic depictions of the Trojan saga down to the 530s, he observes that, despite the increase in absolute number, the proportion of scenes with 'Homeric' subjects has not risen compared to the seventh-century. The 30% for the period that ends ca. 600 BC drops slightly to 29% for 600–530 BC: "This constitutes another blow against the theory ... that some major expansion of the Homeric epics took place in the earlier sixth century, and resulted in a sudden extension of the range of Homeric subjects in art."[92] With reference to this same period of 600–530 BC, Snodgrass (1998:147) adds: "[O]f those artists who choose a subject from the Homeric epics, perhaps one in twelve or fifteen shows signs of having actually used Homer as his source. Among the much larger group who depict *any* legendary episode, there is apparently a higher ratio than before, but still perhaps only one in 40 or 50." These calculations lie behind this summary:[93]

> First, if a picture has legendary or mythical but otherwise equivocal subject-matter and we are uncertain whether or not it portrays an event

---

[90] Lowenstam 1997:52.

[91] Lowenstam 1997:54. Also: "This study suggests that the *Iliad* and *Odyssey* either were not composed in a form recognizable to us before the end of the sixth century B.C.E. or, if earlier, did not gain authority until that date or slightly later" (1997:66).

[92] Snodgrass 1998:145. He adds that at least until the end of the sixth century there was no artistic wave that favored Homer as a source for the Trojan story.

[93] Snodgrass 1998:150, his emphasis.

narrated in the *Iliad* or the *Odyssey* then, other things being equal, there is perhaps a one-in-ten chance, perhaps slightly better, that it does so.

Secondly and more debatably, when we are sure that the subject-matter *is* taken from the events narrated in the *Iliad* or the *Odyssey* then, other things being equal, there is appreciably less than a one-in-ten chance that they demonstrably reflect a knowledge of the poem.

2.3 Homer, a Writing Poet?

As I noted at the beginning of this chapter, West (2011a) has radically reconceived the process that resulted in the writing of the *Iliad*. In this monograph, he takes principal aim at "the Oralists" and their "dogma that the Homeric epics are 'oral dictated texts'" (West 2011a:4). With "oralist" he seems to refer to scholars like Albert B. Lord and Richard Janko. For reasons best known to him, West refuses to engage with the evolutionary model.[94] I do not know if his silence is one of indifference, contempt, or ignorance, but it is a pity that those of us who believe in the model's essential correctness have not been able to profit from the productive opposition of his learned argument.[95] At any rate, his *Making of the* Iliad labors under the fallacy of the excluded middle, as if the only alternatives were an intermittently writing and revising Homer and a one-time, linear dictation of an oral performance. Whether or not "the Oralists ... are helpless in the face of [the poem's discontinuities]" (2011a:5), this is certainly not the case with the evolutionary model, which features no "sequential dictation" and allows for "second thoughts" (13) on the part of a long array of recomposing bards. I suspect that West deliberately neglects the evolutionary model, because he is unable to accept that a gradual textual fixation might issue from the converging forces of competitive and cooperative performance at the heart of rhapsodic poetics.[96] According to him, one can only account for the many structural problems of

---

[94]   His bibliography in West 2011a:332–334 does not include a single exponent of the evolutionary model. Although, judging from his earlier publications, this seems to be West's long-standing practice, in this case at least one might ascribe his peculiar selection to the rhetorical effort to show, by deliberate reference only to "[scholars] not generally read nowadays" (v), that the work of Milman Parry and Albert B. Lord has now been finally superseded. West seeks to obviate the writings of the "Oralists" with the rediscovery that whichever limited matters they had correctly ascertained were, after all, "what everyone believed in the eighteenth century and many in the nineteenth" (1). One may therefore happily dispense with their comparative studies of oral epic traditions and return to the long overlooked insights of a pre-Parryan scholarship. Note the telling section heading on page 55: "Most of this was seen long ago." Cf. West 2011b.

[95]   Does he have this model in view where he notes that "[t]he assumption of plural authorship cannot solve the difficulty [of the embassy duals]"? (West 2011a:14).

[96]   See below, pp. 377ff.

the *Iliad* by embracing the "essential point" that Homer "made insertions in parts of the poem that were already fixed; and fixed means written, because if they were only fixed in his head they would naturally have moulded themselves round the insertions more pliably than they have done" (West 2011a:3). As an example of such structural problems he offers the famous crux of the duals in the embassy to Akhilleus: Homer originally conceived the episode with only two envoys. Once he decided to add Phoinix to it, "[h]e ought ... to have rewritten the following passage [after I 168] to get rid of the duals, but he neglected to do so" (13). In González 2015, a work on the diachrony of epic performance, I discuss the 'solution' that follows from the evolutionary model—a solution, I believe, not only more respectful than West is of the oral culture of archaic Greece but also more psychologically realistic. For now, I need only draw attention to the intrinsic implausibility that Homer should have cared so much about his poetry as to make a prodigious effort to write it down, and yet, when a revision made grammatical nonsense of his written text, he should have failed to emend it to reflect his (we must assume) grammatically correct oral version.[97] Or are we to imagine that Homer recited his revised poem with the addition of Phoinix *and* the duals, if in fact (as West intimates) he must have held the duals as manifestly out of place in this new version? There is little comfort to be had in the thought that "[p]robably he did not read through his whole text with a view to ensuring that it flowed smoothly, but simply made additions as they occurred to him" (14). The incongruity between the herculean effort to write down the poem and the alleged neglect to read or properly to revise it is remarkable and, I submit, psychologically inconceivable.

But how about the mechanics of West's scenario, what he calls "the practicalities" (14)? The great scholar asserts that "it boggles the mind"—and well it might, for what he suggests is utterly implausible, even in a much later period

---

[97] Here I pass over the untenable and unexamined assumption that a seventh-century performer's appreciation of the unique value of his poetry—itself a problematic notion—should take the form of a desire and concern to write it down. I am reduced to inferring this as the motivation for the writing (cf. West 2011a:69), because West never directly addresses the 'why' as he does the 'who,' 'when,' 'where,' and 'what.' To a possible memorializing impulse one might add the well-worn judgment that a poem of the complexity of the *Iliad* could only have come into existence through the aid of writing (hence proposition 4 on page 10 that Homer composed "with the aid of writing"). But, once again, we are left to guess that this motivation underlies West's model of the written making of the *Iliad*, for he never tells us how writing was combined with (premeditated) oral composition in Homer's performance practice (see West 2011a:10–11). Did he memorize what he wrote down and subsequently only perform the written version? Just as West reproves "the Oralists" for "fail[ing] to engage seriously with the question of how [the *Iliad* and the *Odyssey*] came about [as written texts]," he too must face the reproach that he never explicitly considers why a performer of oral traditional poetry should have thought to write down his verses in the first place.

that enjoyed an abundance of papyri and ample acquaintance with the technology of writing; all the more is it out of place in the Greece of the seventh century BC. No matter. West disposes of this impassable obstacle with a rhetorical question and a summary non-answer: "How did P, or any patrons who assisted in the matter, obtain all the necessary papyri or whatever material was used? We might judge [getting the poem down in writing] scarcely possible, not worth attempting; yet we know for certain that it was done" (14). For West, then, we must set aside our skepticism, for "we know for certain that it was done." Thus he shrugs off the fatal reefs that would run his theory aground. But how are we to think that Homer made his rather substantial insertions into the written text? "[I]f the book was a papyrus or leather roll, the easiest assumption is that it was done by cutting and pasting, not in the figurative sense ... but by literally cutting the roll in two and pasting in extra sheets" (14). With this astonishing proposal, West achieves no small feat: in his hands, Homer becomes a literal 'rhapsode'—especially if the substrate was leather!—laboriously pasting or stitching his new verses onto the old rolls. I imagine that West would rather have Homer use papyrus—think how the weight of bulky leather rolls might encumber his itinerancy! If so, since the new sheets would have been pasted to the old at the intercolumn (cf. Johnson 2004:x), after the interpolation the resulting flow of the text would be awkward at best (all the more awkward, the more numerous and smaller they were). And I wonder how rolls that featured an increasing number of secondary seams might have fared with the passing of time, whether they would not tend to disintegrate under the stress of use. But such pedantic minutiae need not give us pause: "we know for certain that it was done."[98]

---

[98] West (2011a:431) anticipates the reaction of some of his readers when he imagines their dismissal of his analysis "as a self-indulgent bacchanal of the imagination ('West thinks he knows ...')." Although I do not share this judgment, at times I am perplexed by the combination of naiveté and sophistication.

3

The Technology of Writing

FAVORING A VERY EARLY, NINTH-CENTURY BC ORIGIN and writing of Homeric poetry,[1] Ruijgh 1995 defended the view of a commensurately early derivation of the Greek alphabet ca. 1000 BC.[2] Hence, he pronounced the rightly famous *argumentum ex silentio* by Carpenter 1933 of no probatory value, because early writing substrates were perishable (wood, papyrus, and parchment) and could not be reasonably expected in the archaeological record (Ruijgh 1995:36–38). But this argument has been effectively countered by Burkert (1992:28) and Marek (1993a:33), who note that Carpenter's thesis has only been strengthened by the persistent failure to turn up ceramic shards from before the eighth century with Greek alphabetic writing despite the enormous increase in the number of archaeological discoveries.[3] Ruijgh (1995:38) also adduced the case of Cyprus to show that there are undeniable examples of continuity

---

[1]   Cf. Ruijgh 1995:21–26, received favorably by Janko 1998a:1.
[2]   Cf., for example, Ruijgh 1995:30 and 34.
[3]   Marek (1993a:30–31) has convincingly answered Naveh's arguments for a ca. 1100 BC date (see Marek 1993a:30n18 for bibliography). Various recent *corpora* of geometric inscriptions strengthen Carpenter's point. The oldest inscribed find at the site of the temple of Apollo Daphnephoros in Eretria (Pfyffer et al. 2005:75 no. 64; cf. 2005:52) consists of three letters on a shard from a middle-geometric amphora (i.e. no earlier than the first half of the eighth century; cf. Verdan et al. 2008:135). In Kommos, the earliest Greek letter is a doubtful qoppa or phi of the late eighth or early seventh century (Csapo et al. 2000:111 no. 3). In Pithekoussai, the oldest inscriptions are from ca. 740 BC (Bartoněk and Buchner 1995:165–166 no. 23 and 171–172 no. 31; add to these several LG I letters on amphoras in Bartoněk and Buchner 1995:174–176). In Lefkandi, a sherd with two letters that seems to date back to ca. 775–750 has been brought to light (Bartoněk and Buchner 1995:195 no. B.8 with Powell 1991:14–15 and n. 34). Naxos contributes an eighth-century inscribed *kratēr* sherd (Jeffery 1990:466 no. A). Whether the derivation of the alphabet is to be sought in the northern Levant, as Marek 1993a thinks, or in Cyprus, as Woodard 1997a claims, is too complex a matter for me to enter into here (for the bilingual Assyrian-Aramaic inscription of Tell Fakhariyeh or Fekherye, central to Marek, see Woodard 1997a:243n98). But the agreement of both regarding the mid-ninth- to mid-eighth-century derivation of the alphabet should be noted (cf., for example, Marek 1993a:44 and Woodard 1997a:236). The *terminus ante quem* of 750 must now be revised in light of the graffito from Osteria dell'Osa, securely dated to ca. 770 BC (cf. Watkins 1995a:36–39 and Bartoněk and Buchner 1995:204–205; Sherratt 2003:228n6 advises a cautious assessment). For a recent review of literacy in the archaic period, see Wilson 2009. For

in the use of writing throughout the Dark Age.[4] Lastly attested in the eleventh century, it reappears in an evolved form in the second half of the eighth: "Aucun texte datant de la période 1025–725 ne nous est parvenu, mais il est évident que l'écriture est restée en usage pendant les trois siècles en question, sans doute surtout sur des matériaux périssables." But there are alternatives to Ruijgh's theories that do not presuppose extensive writing on perishable material between the eleventh and the eighth centuries. Egetmeyer (1998:233) believes that there was a contraction in the Dark-Age use of writing in Cyprus, and that Paphos, the provenience of the oldest two seventh-century inscriptions (of about twenty-five extant), was responsible for the preservation of writing: "In dieser Stadt, welche das religiöse Zentrum der Insel ist, konnte die Schrift durch die politisch unruhige Zeit hinübergerettet werden, und kam dann von hier aus zu einem neuen Aufschwung" (242).[5] The Mycenaean Greeks who arrived in Cyprus at the time of the great twelfth-century BC disturbances did not bring Linear B with them, but adopted the Cypriot syllabary instead.[6] Egetmeyer (1998:233) cites as a probable reason for this paradoxical development that the majority of the emigrants set out from the mainland after Linear B had already fallen into disuse. Similarities between Arcadian and Cypriot that are not present in Mycenaean Greek suggest a not insignificant period of time spent in this area of the mainland before the migration. Linear B probably disappeared from continental Greece ca. 1200 BC with one last round of destructive fires that struck the administrative centers.[7] Given the duration of the upheavals, it is likely that it had fallen into disuse in various parts of the mainland at an earlier time. Karageorghis (2002:71–113) examines the archaeological record of these unsettled times and concludes that it is consistent with migrations and extensive political upheavals in the Aegean from the fourteenth

---

    a survey more narrowly focused on alphabetic scripts, see Lemaire 2008. Lazzarini 1999 reconsiders the origin of the Greek alphabet with the most important recent scholarship in view.

[4]   But contrast Palaima (2005:37), who takes issue with a statement by Snodgrass about the "continuous existence of this ancient [Cypro-Minoan] writing system": "[I] wonder how far we can speak of a 'continuous existence of [a] writing system,' when the Cypriote Syllabic script is so different from the Cypro-Minoan in sign repertory and applications."

[5]   Cf. Bazemore 2002. See also Sherratt 2003:227–228, although she probably exaggerates the extent of late Bronze-Age literacy on Cyprus and degree to which writing continued in use during the gap that does not archaeologically attest it.

[6]   Cf. Woodard 1997b:46–51, esp. 47.

[7]   Shelmerdine (1997:581–582) dates the destruction of the palaces to the transitional LH IIIB/IIIC. For Pylos see the detailed analysis of Mountjoy 1997. Especially relevant is Shelmerdine's observation that, despite elements of continuity at certain sites, "the significant change from LH IIIB to LH IIIC is the demise of palatial administration. … [T]he end of Mycenaean bureaucracy meant the end of literacy …" (1997:582). Cf. Driessen 2008 and Morris 1986:121.

through the eleventh century (71).[8] The foundation of separate settlements by the refugees, for example, at Pyla-*Kokkinokremos* (Karageorghis 2002:74–78)[9] and Maa-*Palaeokastro* (Karageorghis 2002:78–81), should have given the immigrants from the mainland opportunity to continue their use of Linear B if it were still current among them when they set out,[10] just as they imported foreign cultural elements like bathtubs, burnished ware, fibulae and gold rivets of Aegean type, and central hearths in communal halls (Karageorghis 2002:78). Therefore, the example of Cyprus does not serve, as Ruijgh intended, to buttress the suggestion of a continuous use of writing during the Dark Age which might justify his early date for the recording of Homeric poetry in writing. On the contrary, the abandonment of Linear B in favor of the Cypriot syllabary suggests that literacy had been largely lost in the mainland by the end of the Mycenaean civilization.[11]

As noted above, some scholars have used Herodotos 5.58 to argue for an eighth-century recording of the Homeric poems on leather. I cannot decisively rule out such a scenario, but it is extremely implausible in the face of the technical complexity and cost of manufacturing durable parchment.[12] That a Dark-Age strong man should have had the technical expertise at hand to prepare the hides of dozens of slaughtered animals for extensive writing stretches credulity. It would take a Persian king to assemble an archive on skins of sheep and goats.[13] That the king of Byblos in the eleventh century should have imported large quantities of papyrus from Egypt despite the attested native use of leather

---

[8] The focus of Karageorghis 2002:71–113 is the Late Cypriot (=LC) iiia, for which he gives the span ca. 1200–1100 BC. Another wave of destruction happened at the transition between LC iiia and LC iiib, ca. 1100, on which see Karageorghis 2002:115–117 and Catlin 1994. For the three waves of destruction at Enkomi, Mountjoy and Gowland (2005:165) give tentative dates of 1130, 1110, and sometime after 1070 BC.

[9] In his unpublished paper, "When did the Greeks first come to Cyprus?," presented at the Cypriot Archaeology Day held by the Royal Ontario Museum on 6 December 2009, Dimitri Nakassis casts doubt on the Aegean identification of the settlers of Pyla-*Kokkinokremos*. Further fieldwork and analysis will be required to bring clarity to this question. For updates see www.pkap.org.

[10] It is always possible that Linear B was in fact used in Cyprus on arrival and yet has left no trace in the record. But unless the migrant Greeks soon abandoned it in favor of the Cypriot syllabary—a development that seems implausible—should we not expect sooner or later to discover at least a scrap of Linear B painted or incised on a vase?

[11] Cf. Palaima 1991: "We can imagine that one of the Aegean Greek settlers who ... shifted from the nearby settlement of Maa-*Palaeokastro* to Palaepaphos-*Skales* when Mycenaean III C:1b pottery was in use—a Greek settler whose speech already had developed away from the standard Mycenaean South Greek of the 13th century B.C. toward the characteristic historical Arcado-Cypriote dialect, and who, we must stress, had no need to be familiar with the highly restricted Linear B script which had suddenly vanished 150 years earlier with the destruction of the palaces on the Mycenaean mainland ..." (454).

[12] Gasparri 2001 calls it a "burdensome material" that called for a "long, complex and minute" preparation. Cf. Ruck 1991.

[13] Diodoros of Sicily 2.32.4.

in the countries bordering on Palestine shows how impractical animal hide was felt to be as a writing substrate already at an early time.[14] This sentiment lies behind the rationale in Herodotos that only ἐν σπάνι βύβλων ('for scarcity of papyrus') did the Ionians resort to διφθέραι.[15] Lewis (1974:86) criticizes scholars who, insisting on the need for writing for the composition of the Homeric poems, infer that the material used was papyrus: "Something more substantial will be required before it can be established that papyrus was a writing material used by the Greeks of the Heroic age."[16] Even so stalwart an advocate of the eighth-century recording of Homer as Powell rejects the use of leather for that purpose.[17] Only in the second half of the seventh century, after Greek mercenaries joined the service of Psammetichus I, and once Greek traders were represented in Naukratis, can papyrus have grown common in the Greek world.[18] Much has been made of the name Βύβλος used by the Greeks to refer to the Phoenician city *Gbl* (Akkadian *Gublu* and Hebrew *Gəbāl*). Some scholars think that Βύβλος is the Hellenized form of *Gbl*, and from this they infer that the Greeks must have called papyrus after the city that was their primary source for it. They conclude, further, that papyrus was imported from Phoenicia before the Greek presence at Naukratis.[19] But as Heubeck (1979:154) writes, following Masson (cited in 154n787), this implies the rather unlikely derivation of Βύβλος from *Gbl*; and the similarly dubious associative chain 'toponym → material → plant.'[20]

Considering the question of the substrate on which a monumental *Iliad* might have been written, Robb (1994:256) observes:

> Excluded as materials ... must be stone, painted (whitened) wooden boards, clay whether fired or not, wax, linen, metals, and bone—all used to preserve writing in the ancient Near East, and some of them in Greece as well. Unless papyrus is assumed (as by Barry Powell), only leather or skins specially prepared would be a plausible candidate. Even so, the motive for that effort—no negligible one even for

---

[14] Cf. Heubeck 1979:155 and Lewis 1974:84. For the use of leather in the Levant see Driver 1976:81–83.

[15] Cf. Jeffery 1990:57–58.

[16] His further comment that "it seems likely that papyrus was in use in Greece by the time of the composition of the *Odyssey*" (Lewis 1974:87) is explained by this apparent belief in a mid- or late-sixth-century composition of the poem (see 87n4).

[17] Powell 2002: "[N]o doubt Homer's poems were recorded on papyrus in the eighth century BC (hardly the expensive and impractical leather, as sometimes thought) ..." (90).

[18] Heubeck 1979:155 and Lewis 1974:87.

[19] So Pfeiffer 1968:22, who dated the introduction of papyrus to the early eighth or late ninth century. Not much follows from the reference to the 'rope of papyrus fibre' (ὅπλον ... βύβλινον) at φ 390–391; cf. Lewis 1974:8, 26 and Jeffery 1962:556–557.

[20] Cf., further, Heubeck 1979:155 and Lewis 1974:7n7.

an experienced scribe in a more literate century—as early as 700 BC frankly eludes me.

Having argued for the unavailability of papyrus at the early date assumed by Ruijgh, Janko, and Powell,[21] it is now time to come to grips with the effort—"no negligible one," as Robb remarks—required to achieve the feat of writing down the full length of the *Iliad* and the *Odyssey*. My purpose here is simply to make a few educated guesses, based on extant papyri, about the necessary length of the rolls and the corresponding writing surface. I will restrict my calculations to the *Iliad*, extrapolating the outcome to the *Odyssey* in a fairly simple-minded fashion. I do not claim any degree of accuracy for the numbers that follow. Since my goal is merely to impress the reader with the difficulty of a task so readily assumed as a historical fact by some, it will be enough to demonstrate that any reasonable estimate of the bookroll length and writing surface area calls for what must be considered imposing quantities of papyrus. In the event, I cannot, once again, completely rule out that so significant an effort might have been expended at so early a time, when the alphabet was in its infancy and writing materials, at best, very scarce. But this adds yet another layer of doubt to the notion of a dictating, and dictated, Homer.

I start with the 'Hawara Homer,' a well-known papyrus of Book 2 of the *Iliad*.[22] The column-to-column width is 23.3 cm and the number of lines in a column, 22.[23] Since the *Iliad* has 15,114 lines without Book 10, and 15,693 with Book 10,[24] the total length required would be 160 and 166.5 meters respectively.[25] To give an easy point of reference, the length of a football field is 91.44 m without, and 109.73 m with, end zones. With the Doloneia, our written text would make its way from end zone to end zone and half-way back to the center of the field. The column height of the papyrus is 14.7 cm. Unfortunately, we do not have the upper margin; the lower margin is no less than 4.8 cm. Excluding the margins, without the Doloneia the surface area would be 23.5 m² (24.5 m² with it). Since the *Odyssey* has 12,110 lines, it is 80% of the length of the *Iliad*

---

[21] The date suggested by West (1995:218), between 670–640 BC ("with perhaps a preference for the decade 660–650") does not suffer from the same degree of implausibility, but it is still too early to assume with any confidence the availability of papyrus.

[22] See Petrie 1889:24–37 and Schironi 2010:140–141 no. 28.

[23] For the terminology used to describe a bookroll, see Johnson 2004:x.

[24] The number varies somewhat depending on the inclusion or exclusion of plus-verses, but, proportionally, the outcome is little affected. On such plus-verses, see the bibliography cited below, p. 79 n. 40.

[25] I have rounded to the nearest half-meter. The error in the calculation is less that one meter, i.e. less than 1%. I do not bother to make these numbers precise, since the uncertainties in the manufacturing of this hypothetical, fantastically long bookroll would exceed the computational error.

without Book 10, i.e. it would take a bookroll approximately 128 m long (more than the length of a football field). Of course, as Johnson (2004:144) explains, actual Homeric rolls only rarely contained more than one book of Homer.[26] A copy of Philodemos' *On Piety* executed in one exceptionally long roll was only about 23 m in comparison.[27] Johnson (2004:148) speculates that MP[3] 980 (*P.Berol.* 16985, also a luxury copy) contained Books 19–22 of the *Iliad* (some 2700 lines) and measured 19 m in length;[28] this corresponds to 106 m for the entire *Iliad* without the Doloneia. But since this and the Hawara Homer are exquisitely executed copies, it will be helpful to consider humbler extant bookrolls of Homer from which to estimate hypothetical full-length volumes. These can be found in Johnson's Table 3.7 (2004:217–230). What follows are rough full-volume length estimates (all without the Doloneia) extrapolated from Johnson's calculations and rounded (up or down) to the nearest half-meter:[29] *P.Oxy.* 0445, 40 m;[30] *P.Oxy.* 3155, 32.5 m; *P.Oxy.* 0687, 95 m; *P.Oxy.* 1815, 96.5 m; *P.Oxy.* 3663, 100.5 m; *P.Oxy.* 3323, 53.5 m; *P.Oxy.* 0020, 133 m; *P.Oxy.* 0223, 133 m; MP[3] 917.1 (*olim* 919), 40.5 m; MP[3] 773, 66 m; MP[3] 855.1, 60 m; MP[3] 819, 61.5 m; MP[3] 830, 64 m; MP[3] 604.1, 62 m; MP[3] 821 (*olim* 822), 69.5 m; MP[3] 991, 79 m; MP[3] 632, 98 m; MP[3] 879, 103 m; MP[3] 962, 144.5 m; MP[3] 998, 56 m;[31] MP[3] 699, 50.5 m; and MP[3] 650, 170.5 m.

To summarize: in my unscientific sample there is a clustering of texts at the approximate lengths of 60 m and 100 m, with outliers as low as 32.5 m (one) and 40 m (two) and as high as 133 m (two), and 144.5 m, 160 m, and 170 m (one each). Under the suggested circumstances of almost experimental writing (i.e. with the alphabet in its infancy and, presumably, scarce training for the amanuensis), the script is unlikely to have been clean, regular, and compact. This would commend a length towards the higher end of the distribution. It is interesting to consider the number of animals it would take to come up with an equivalent writing surface. Since the production of parchment and leather for writing is a rare occupation in the Western world, it is hard to come by the relevant statistical data. I will therefore be using Tanasi et al. 1991, who studied

---

[26] See Schironi 2010, esp. 41–53, for a recent study of rolls with more than one book of hexametric poetry.

[27] Johnson 2004:148. Interesting general observations about bookroll length and roll diameter can be found at 148–151. See also Birt 1882:289–307; Skeat 1982; Lameere 1960:127–147, 166–174; and Schironi 2010:46–47.

[28] Schironi 2010:94–95 no. 5.

[29] I arrive at these rough estimates of length by simple-minded extrapolation. I do not include the Doloneia, often contested as a late interpolation by scholars who adhere to dictation, to make the case as favorable as possible to my opponents. Nevertheless, the reader should note that MP[3] 855.1 (*olim* 857) only contains portions of the very book, the Doloneia, that I am *not* including in the supposed dictated *Iliad*.

[30] MP[3] 778 and Schironi 2010:146–147 no. 31.

[31] Schironi 2010:108–109 no. 12.

the properties of sheep and lamb skins. Each skin was divided into three or four pieces 21 cm long (along the spine), with a width of approximately 48 cm. Although they do not state this explicitly, I assume that a total length of three (63 cm) is more common than four (84 cm), since they have drawn their figures with three. At any rate, the addition of a fourth would scale down the following numbers by a factor of 3/4. Johnson 2004 gives us the column length of the papyri above, to which the upper and lower margins are added (with a question mark when they are not known precisely, but estimated with a moderately high probability). All these numbers are estimated *grosso modo*. There are many uncertainties that could affect the outcome. It is, for example, highly unlikely that all the surface of an animal skin (whether as parchment, which is unthinkable without a well developed technique, or simply as leather) would be usable for writing. The complaints of medieval scribes even about the quality of carefully manufactured parchment are common.[32] Areas often had to be skipped because of various imperfections that made writing on them difficult or impossible. There is also the possibility that cows, not goats or lambs, might be used instead. I do not know how the surface area of an ox hide compares to that of a goat or a lamb. But it is safe to surmise that, even as the number of necessary animal skins would be proportionally diminished if oxen were used, so also the expense involved would be significantly magnified, since a cow is likely much more valuable than a goat or a lamb.[33] Whatever animal one assumes, the cost involved would be great. To illustrate this, I offer below a list of papyri followed by the number of goats necessary for the corresponding surface, assuming that the skin in its entirety is adequate for writing. The numbers in parentheses estimate the additional animal skins required if one allows for the upper and lower margins provided by the papyri. These totals should be scaled down by 3/4 for a lower boundary if one assumes that all the animal skins used are of the longer size (i.e. 84 cm long). Thus, for example, *P.Oxy.* 0020 takes 78 goats (+ 45 with the margins); *P.Oxy.* 0223, 80 (+ 35); *P.Oxy.* 3663, 60 (+ 26); *P.Oxy.* 0445, 32 (+ 8); and MP[3] 998, 39 (+ 9). *P.Oxy.* 3663 provides good reference numbers, since its length, about 100 m, is not a high or low outlier in the distribution reviewed above. One would need 86 goats of average size just for the *Iliad* (with margins, not including Book 10), even if one assumes the complete absence of skin defects that would prevent writing. It should be obvious that this entails a significant sacrifice of personal wealth for the hypothetical recording project.

A major, if not insurmountable, obstacle to dictation is that it is hard to devise a plausible scenario for the transmission of the textual artifact to one of

---

[32] Gullick 1991:149.
[33] Of course, only calves, sheep, and goats are used in the manufacture of parchment.

the sites (Athens, Khios, etc.) that arguably played a role in the dissemination of Homeric epic. Rare is the advocate of dictation who confronts this difficulty; and, invariably, the treatment is vague and rather brief. Janko (1998a:13) merely speculates that "[t]he written transcripts were preserved on Chios among the Homeridae ... ." Why the cession of the precious original should have happened (or how a copy for Khios would have come about) is not addressed. One might take the position that the original transcript remained marginal and did not affect Homeric performance anywhere in the Greek world until 'somehow' it made its way to a center of diffusion (the Homeridai for Janko, Peisistratean Athens for others).[34] This would contradict the notion that the performance of the original poems of Homer (and not of traditions of heroic poetry generally) was widespread during the archaic period and responsible: for the geographically scattered vases that appear to depict Homeric epic;[35] for graffiti like the inscription on 'Nestor's Cup' from Ischia; or for the influence of Homer's language on various archaic lyric poets.[36] Since the *paradosis* was decisively channeled through Athens, we would have to assume that Panathenaic performance was controlled by the original or a faithful copy of it. But this would seem to conflict with the myth of the Peisistratean recension, which assumes a collection of once scattered songs.[37] It would also be more than a little curious that a copy of such venerable authority would not have been explicitly mentioned somewhere in the surviving record (literary, documentary, and scholiastic).[38] We might also have expected a report of the Ptolemies' (real or apocryphal) interest in such a manuscript, like Galen's story of their seizure by deceit of the official Athenian texts of the canonical tragedians for their library.[39] If the Athenian state had possessed an official, authoritative manuscript of the *Iliad* of venerable antiquity to regulate Panathenaic performances, we would expect Athenian bookmakers to popularize its readings, and educated residents

[34] Regarding Powell's dictation theory, Woodard (1997a:253) remarks that "there would obviously be no one able to read the epics once they had been penned by Powell's adapter in his novel script." Powell (1991:232) agrees: "At first, only he could read them." Woodard's remark is valid even if the script was not designed specifically for Homer (or by Homer). Since the alphabet was still in its infancy, what would be the reading public for whom the transcriber expended his considerable efforts?

[35] So Powell 1991:210–211; Janko 1982:230; and West 1995:207, with different *termini post quos*.

[36] Once in vogue, the proclivity among scholars to allege instances of this influence and to trace them immediately to the text of our Homeric poems has now fallen out of favor. See Powell 1991:208 (and Appendix II); cf. Janko 1982:225–228 and Signes Codoñer 2004:301–341.

[37] Allen 1924:224–248; Merkelbach 1952; Davison 1955; Sealey 1957:342–349; Jensen 1980:128–158; Böhme 1983; Aloni 1984; S. West in Heubeck et al. 1988:36–40; Catenacci 1993; Boyd 1995; Nagy 1996c:77–80; Frame 2009:318–328; and Jensen 2011:295–327.

[38] For the notion that the Panathenaic rule might be one such reference, see below, pp. 382ff.

[39] *Commentaria in Hippocratis Epidemias* III, 17a.607 Kühn (*CMG* 5.10.2.1). See below, p. 440.

(Isokrates, Plato, Aristotle, etc.) both to give great deference to its text and to own personal copies of it. In such circumstances, the view that the many quotations that do not match the vulgate must be blamed on a failing memory or on indifference towards verbal accuracy grows implausible. But perhaps such quotations represent the Athenian text? Whence the vulgate, then?[40]

If, on the other hand, one believes in the extensive diffusion of an original transcript, this assumes readily available copies of it throughout the archaic Greek world. And it is not enough that private men embrace it. Since no significantly divergent, alternative text survives, the performers too must have adopted it. This conjures up the image of Greek rhapsodes, far and wide, on pilgrimage to the site of Homer's original transcript, pen and paper in hand, with the intention and skill to read and copy for themselves the venerable text. Or else we must envision an archaic publishing house at the site of the manuscript, selling copies to rhapsodes willing to give up their life-long training and practice of recomposition in performance, and eager to memorize and recite as derivative performers only the rival version.[41] In other words, we would have to multiply manifold the first miracle of literacy that produced the original manuscript. West is typical of other scholars in his failure to explore how his dictation model can account for the textual diffusion he alleges. A quaint autobiographical anecdote reveals his conviction that 'Homer'[42] composed the *Iliad* at Ilios.[43] He offers no motivation for the production of what "must have existed initially as a bulky collection of leather or papyrus rolls." Apparently, he believes that this miracle of early literacy was done "only for intermittent reference"[44] and that the collection of rolls stayed in the poet's possession. He does not tell us why, when, where, and how other oral bards would have adopted this performance script against their regular training and practice; only—with a convenient passive voice—that "occasionally would the written text have been copied."[45] Powell is more forthcoming. Assuming a Euboian audience,[46] he states that, at first, only his alphabetic adapter could read the poems. He goes on to affirm, without motivating the development, that (possibly partial) copies of the poems

---

[40] Apart from oral composition, there is no good explanation for the so-called plus-verses. Cf. S. West 1967b; Nagy 1996c:138–147; and Bird 2010, with bibliography. On plus-verses more generally, see Bolling 1925 and Apthorp 1980.

[41] I note in passing that divergent local writing conventions (to which Greek epichoric alphabets witness) make even more problematic the thought that visitors often copied into their own alphabet a text written in an unfamiliar script; or the alternative notion that many acquired for their personal use local copies in the unfamiliar script.

[42] West does not believe in the authenticity of the name, as we learn in West 1999b.

[43] West 1995:217n43.

[44] At the poet's initiative, then?

[45] All the immediately preceding quotations are from West 1998b:97.

[46] On which see immediately below, pp. 81ff.

circulated among the Euboians (Powell 1991:232). How they are supposed to have learned to read, or else, if they could not, why they should have wished to own such copies, he does not say. Even Homer may have possessed his own copy. Had he, then, learned to read? Did he, too, give up his oral technique in favor of rote memorization and recitation? He further pronounces the Homeridai his descendants, and the eventual owners of the first manuscript or a copy of it.[47] At last, Hipparkhos would have obtained from them the Athenian copy that, as noted above, no extant literary or documentary source explicitly mentions.[48]

[47] These, and the next statement, are from 232–233n32. Powell does not suggest the reason why the descendants of Homer should have moved to, and settled in, Khios.

[48] Powell directs us to his chapter 4, n. 156 (at 216), which includes a reference to [Plato] *Hipparkhos* 228b and to the late and unreliable reports of a Peisistratean recension.

4

The Euboian Connection

4.1 The Cultural Argument

T HIS BOOK ARGUES FOR THE CENTRAL ROLE of Athens in the performance-driven fixation of the Homeric text. Because my argument turns on the dominance of Athens, what Nagy 2001 has called the Panathenaic "bottleneck," I must take some time to review a competing alternative to Athens that has grown increasingly popular during the last thirty years. This alternative goes back to Wathelet 1981, who proposed Euboia as the location in Greece where the Homeric poems were composed and possibly recorded in writing. His theory was motivated by the desire to find an alternative explanation to what scholars dismissively called the "Attic coloring" of the Homeric poems. This label comprises all the dialectal forms deemed Attic as a last analytical resort, that is, because they cannot be ascribed to any other of the dialects long recognized as major constituents of the *Kunstsprache*. Since most scholars assume that the *Iliad* and the *Odyssey* had received its final shape, usually with the help of writing, well before Athens became the conduit of their transmission to posterity, it is an embarrassment for them to find the text somehow affected by Athens' dialect. In the past, two main strategies were adopted to explain away these data. Whenever these forms could be readily emended to earlier dialectal layers, scholars assumed that they were trivial (and mostly unintentional) scribal changes that reflected contemporary linguistic practice. This notion was helped by the fact that often the emended, hypothetical older form cured what scholars deemed prosodic blemishes. When an expedient substitute could not be devised, a second strategy was ready at hand: the passage must be a late, inorganic interpolation, either an attempt to doctor the text or an instance of what is contemptuously labeled a "rhapsodic elaboration." In the search for the 'true Homer,' such suppositious insertions could be cleanly excised and the authentic text saved from the bungling experiments of latter-day poetasters.[1]

---

[1]   Cf. Cassio 1998:16–17.

The paramount motivation driving these strategies was the offense caused by what appeared to be evidence of late Homeric composition, however limited in scope (for this coloring was regularly pronounced "trivial" and "superficial").

But what if one could suggest a source other than Athens for all or most of these data, a source that was old enough to remove the taint of embarrassment? Scholars who embrace an early-archaic recording of Homeric poetry in writing could then allow these forms to stand without the urge to emend or excise them. This is precisely what Wathelet 1981 made possible by substituting Euboia for Athens. The Euboian dialect belongs to the West Ionic variety, and it shares with the Attic some of the traits that had until then been interpreted as Athenian coloring. The theory of a Euboian origin of Homeric poetry had several attractive advantages. The excavations at Lefkandi proved that Euboia was a Greek center of power as early as the ninth century. Thus, the chronology was open for as early a written fixation as one could plausibly defend. The testimony in Hesiod's *Works and Days* 650–657 about the funeral games for Amphidamas was further marshaled to make the case for a vigorous tradition of epic performance on the island in the early archaic period. That Janko had dated Hesiod to the early seventh century, a date widely accepted and roughly in agreement with West's own, lent further credence to the scheme.[2] The cultural importance of Euboia was boosted by the converse contention that during the same period (ninth to the end of the seventh century) Athens had been a cultural backwater. I will show below that this is not true, but it was only too readily accepted by most. Another fact that seemed to buttress the Euboian theory was this island's early role in trade and colonization, which made it a likely and convenient instrument for the diffusion of Homeric poetry. Dramatic corroboration was provided by the discovery in Pithekoussai of an inscribed *skyphos* from the late eighth century with two lines of hexameter that, for many, made clear reference to Pylian Nestor's cup.[3] The regular size and spacing of the characters, together with the use of colons as interpunction between words and perhaps even metrical clauses, prompted Immerwahr to suggest that the inscription reflected Euboian bookhand practices. Voilà: late eighth-century evidence of Euboian poetry *books*! Positing Euboian dictated transcripts of the *Iliad* and the *Odyssey* could not be long in coming. To round out the composition, some suggested that the alphabet had been invented by the Euboians, and at least one scholar, that the purpose of this momentous invention was the recording in writing of Homer's performance. In view of these arguments it is hardly surprising that

---

[2]   See Janko 1982:200 for a convenient diagram, with his reasoning at 228–231. For West's dating of Hesiod's *floruit* to ca. 700 BC, see West 1966:45. West thinks Hesiod to be older than Homer (cf. West 1995:208–209).

[3]   But see below, pp. 129ff.

a number of prominent Homerists would soon espouse a version of Wathelet's Euboian theory: West, Powell, the early Cassio, and Ruijgh are only the more prominent; Janko is sympathetic.[4] It is fair to say that the Euboian theory, at least in its more restricted form, has now become the consensus view. Athens, never in favor, has finally been displaced.

But the narrative is all too clean, and the theory faces insuperable difficulties. I must make clear at the outset that I do not wish to deny that epic poetry—even poetry whose subject matter might reasonably be classed Iliadic or Odyssean—was performed on the island of Euboia during the archaic period, perhaps even during the Dark Ages. And to the extent that Euboian itinerant rhapsodes visited Athens during the sixth and fifth centuries to compete at the Panathenaia, one cannot completely rule out *some* influence of the West Ionic Euboian dialect, even as one must reckon with island Ionic and East Ionic. The case for a significant Euboian influence is muted by the absence of any indication in the Homeric *Vita* traditions that Euboia played a role in the diffusion of Homeric epic.[5] Contrast this silence with traditions that tied Homer to Khios, Smyrna, and other places.[6] All the same, it is possible (and I do not deny) *some*, probably marginal role of Euboia in the diffusion of the *Iliad* and the *Odyssey*.[7]

---

[4] See West 1988:165–172; Powell 1991 *passim*; Cassio 1991–1993:200 (but cf. Cassio 1994:66 and n. 78); and Ruijgh 1995:47–50. Cf. Janko 1992:18n33. Cassio 1998 provides a commendable reexamination of this question that broadly supports my argument here.

[5] One must remember that these *Vita* traditions reflect in biographic form the competition for Panhellenic acceptance by local versions of the Homeric and cyclic poems. By attempting to tie Homer's birth or an episode of his life, including his activity as a composer and performer, to a particular individual or location (city, island, etc.), various parts of Greece sought to appropriate for *their* local versions the symbolic capital of Homer as the Panhellenic poet *per excellence*. This involved not only authorizing—as to 'authorship' and 'authority'—epichoric multiforms of the *Iliad* and the *Odyssey*, but also articulating a relationship between cyclic (and other) poetry and the *Iliad* and the *Odyssey*. For lives of poets generally, see Nagy 1999a:279–288, 296–316 and Nagy 1990c:75–76. For the lives of Homer, see Nagy 2010a:31–47 and Graziosi 2002 *passim* (see "General Index" under "Lives of Homer").

[6] Homer's descent from Mousaios (so *Vita* 6.9 and Gorgias *apud* Proklos' *Khrēstomatheia*, p. 100 line 5 in Allen's edition) arguably regards Athens.

[7] Euboia's place in the poems is no more conspicuous than Athens'. In particular, its ten-line section in the *Catalogue of Ships* is comparable to the immediately following eleven lines that regard Athens. Both locations appear in the initial group headed by the Boiotians, and, as far as strength of numbers, Athens' fifty ships compare favorably with Euboia's forty. (On Athens' and Menestheus' place in the *Catalogue*, see Kirk 1985:179–180 and 206–207.) As Cassio (1998:14) remarks, the Euboian's leader Elephenor is killed early in action at Δ 463–471 and is otherwise absent from the poem (cf. Kirk 1985:387). Athens' Menestheus, also a relatively minor figure, appears considerably more often, with interventions at Δ 327 M 331 373 N 195 690 O 331 (with the Ἀθηναῖοι at Δ 328 N 196 689 O 337). Athens' historical (and celebrated) connection with Salamis, the birthplace of the prominent hero Ajax, who immediately follows the city in the *Catalogue*, might well have sufficed to obviate the need to gratify an Athenian audience with a greater role for Menestheus. Instead, Ajax could be embraced as Athens' own preeminent Iliadic

What I think does not withstand scrutiny is the notion that Euboia exerted decisive influence upon their text during the Dark Age and the archaic period. An exaggerated view of the possible Euboian influence is usually attended by a corresponding devaluation of the cultural importance of Athens at the beginning of the archaic period.[8] Cassio (1998:19) cites with approval the comment by Murray (1993:185) that "[t]he city of Athens remained a centre of occupation throughout the Dark Age, and from about 900 was the most prosperous and advanced community in Greece." To this cultural preeminence witness the fine examples of geometric art by the Dipylon Master and his followers; the abundant eastern imports starting in the 850s; the presence of Attic pottery in the lowest levels of Al Mina; and the presence of eastern goldsmiths in the city in the early eighth century.[9] Only after 730 did the urban center decline until the end of the seventh century. But this decline was accompanied by a resurgence of the Attic countryside,[10] and we cannot therefore make definitive pronouncements about the *cultural* decline, unless we assume without proof that the aristocratic gentry responsible for the rich burials on the countryside could not have supported communal festivals, poetic performance, and the arts. Even during the seventh century, "the city itself remained large, and ... economically advanced in its differentiation into specialized trades and activities, and its attitude to wealth" (Murray 1993:186).[11] Not without reason does Cassio (1998:19) pair the Dipylon *oinokhoē* and the Pithekoussan cup as two of the earliest and most important attestations of metrical composition. At any rate, those who believe in Athens' formative influence on the text of Homer during the sixth and fifth centuries do

---

hero (cf. Shapiro 1989:154–157). And whatever may be said for Euboia as a point of reference in the *Odyssey* (in my opinion, far too much has been made of it; cf. Cassio 1998:14), one cannot read Cook 1995:128–170 without feeling the greater potential debt of the poem to Athens.

[8] E.g. Wathelet 1981:831–833 and Ruijgh 1995:47.

[9] All in Murray 1993:185.

[10] Morris (2000:241–242) observes that grave goods began to decline in Athens before 800, but in the Attic countryside the reverse was true.

[11] Thomas and Conant (1999:84) offer a traditional view of Athenian decline: "[B]y the eighth century its preeminence had disappeared." But they too note that Attic graves surpassed the Athenian in their richness and (citing Whitley) that there may have been an affirmation of local interests vis-à-vis those of the urban center. Their inference of decline from the poverty of Athenian burial goods is challenged by Morris (2000:287–306), who sees in Athens' return to cremation for adults during the seventh century a deliberate elite reaction to the "middling" ideology of citizenship that was in the ascendant elsewhere (288–290). Like Athens' seeming lack of involvement in the Panhellenic games, hoplite warfare, and colonization, the poverty of its burials responded to the attempt by the Athenian elite to "cut themselves off from the growth of polis institutions" and look back "to the simpler religious practices and social relationships of the Dark Age" (294, 302). If Morris is right, one must wonder whether this reaction presupposes a cultural climate that would fail to support the performance of epic poetry or, rather, the precise opposite.

not feel an urgency to oppose to Euboia a culturally and economically thriving Athens from the early ninth to the late eighth century.

4.2 The Linguistic Argument

4.2.1 The third CL

Perhaps the best known proponent of Euboian influence in its strongest form is M. L. West. Ruijgh thinks that West has overstated his position, and himself chooses a weaker form of the theory: Homer visited Euboia for a series of performances and, while on the island, acquired for his *Kunstsprache* metrically convenient Euboian forms that are therefore sparsely represented in the text of the poems.[12] But what are these forms? Are they likely to be of Euboian provenience? We have to do here with the consonantal clusters *-rw-*, *-lw-*, *-nw-*, and *-sw-*, which Ionic simplified in the so-called third compensatory lengthening (henceforth CL) with the corresponding lengthening of the preceding vowel, whereas Euboian, like Attic, simplified them without any CL. Thus *xenwos* had the outcome ξεῖνος in Ionic[13] and ξένος in Attic and Euboian. Principally responsible for popularizing the Euboian origin of Homeric poetry was Wathelet 1981.[14] But does his argument withstand scrutiny? We must remember that this theory attempts to substitute an *early-archaic* (late eighth- or early seventh-century) Euboian formative influence for the impact of Athens on the Homeric text during the archaic[15] and classical periods. The assumption, then, is that the linguistic forces responsible for the Euboian short forms (i.e. the forms that did not suffer CL) must have completed their work by the time these entered the (dictated?)

---

[12] Ruijgh 1995:15–16 and 47–48.

[13] The -ει- stands for the lengthened -ε-, which gave rise to a long, closed /e:/ that contrasts with the inherited, more open /ε:/ represented by the grapheme -η- (or the corresponding sign in an archaic Ionic script).

[14] Previously in Wathelet 1966:154–169 and Wathelet 1970:153–157, and ascribed there tentatively to Aiolic (following Schwyzer *GG* I.228, with bibliography) or else to West Ionic or Attic. See now his recent summation in Wathelet 2008. Wathelet's ascription to West Ionic (Euboian) of forms previously considered Attic was well received by West 1988:166 ("epic-Ionic ... is not East Ionic, it is Central or West Ionic"). Wathelet 1970:155n150 realizes the chronological difficulties of making archaic Euboian the source of these traits: "La date du troisième allongement en Ionie (début du second quart du premier millénaire) semble trop récente, si l'on situe Homère vers 800." He also thought desirable to find a common explanation both for these forms without CL and for instances of the so-called *correptio attica* (1970:155n150). Wackernagel 1970:120–122 had already noted the Aiolic and Euboian options. Of the Aiolic he pointedly noted: "was geht das Lesbische der Sappho den Homer an? Das Äolische, das in Homers Sprache steckt, ist viel älter als jenes." He rejected in turn the Euboic source for reasons of economy: since Attic was unquestionably responsible for *some* forms, *ceteris paribus* it also seemed reasonable to him to ascribe these other to Attic. (Both statements are in Wackernagel 1970:121.)

[15] Starting at least as early as the sixth century BC.

text of the poems.[16] In other words, CL had already happened in Euboia, and the attendant pronunciation affected the composition, performance, and transmission of Homeric poetry there.

But this theory meets with two insurmountable objections. The first is that, as I will demonstrate below, at the early time relevant to the theory clusters with post-consonantal -ϝ- will not have been simplified, and neither alternative outcome (with or without CL) will have been in use. Therefore, the word will have been ξένϝος, not ξένος or ξεῖνος. A second chronological obstacle concerns the process responsible for the alternatives. The simplification with CL follows from a syllabification in speech that assigns the first consonant to the earlier, and the *-w- to the later, syllable: *xen.wos. The simplification that does not result in CL follows from the syllabification *xe.nwos. But I will show below that the inherited Indo-European syllabification is the one exemplified by *-n.w-, in relation to which *-.nw- is an innovation. And this innovation cannot safely be assumed to date from so early at time. If these two objections are sound, a late eighth-century or early seventh-century dictated text would have included the full forms ἔρϝιον (for εἴριον), μόνϝος (for μοῦνος), κενϝός (for κεινός), ξένϝος (for ξεῖνος), etc.[17] After the third CL took place, rhapsodes with sufficient mastery of the Attic dialect could compose verses with short forms like ξένος.[18] Alternatively, attested, metrically secure short forms may reflect selective dialectal updating.[19] Wathelet (1981:831) thinks that he has proof in ἄνοιτο (Σ 473) of the non-Attic character of these forms: although it has not suffered CL, if it were an Attic form, he asserts, one would expect *ἅνοιτο, with the *spiritus asper*. But matters are not this straightforward, despite the witness of ancient grammarians for this Attic dialectal practice.[20] While exhibiting a preference for the *spiritus asper*, examples of the *spiritus lenis* in Attic texts are not hard to come by.[21] Among them: Aristophanes *Clouds* 506 (ἀνύσας), *Frogs* 606 (ἀνύετον),[22] and fr. 2 K-A (ἄνυσον); Pherekrates fr. 44 K-A (ἄνυσον); Plato *Sophist* 230a9 (ἀνύτειν),

---

[16] Alternatively, ordinary Euboian speech during Homer's visits to the island must have exhibited the results of this process, and *xenwos* must have been pronounced ξένος.

[17] For these and similar forms, see Chantraine *GH* I.159–162. He admits, for example, that ξένϝος and καλϝός may have stood in old formulas, but thinks metrical considerations the primary cause for the existence of short and long doublets (ξένος vs. ξεῖνος).

[18] For a convenient list of attested short forms, see Wathelet 1970:154.

[19] This is perhaps the case of ἄνοιτο (Σ 473), from ἄνω < *ἄνϝω (a thematic form of ἄνυμι). *LIV*² 532–533 considers ἄνυμι a reformed *hanāmi (root *senh₂-). As Schulze (1967:107–108) observed, however, ἄνοιτο may hide a metrically equivalent, older ἄνῦτο < *ἄνυιτο.

[20] Cf. Dindorf 1870:46 and Schanz 1881:v.

[21] A strong tendency towards uniform spelling among editors is responsible for printing the *asper* for the *lenis* even in the absence of manuscript support.

[22] Cf. *Frogs* 649 (ἀνύσεις). The Budé edition without ms. support silently adds the *spiritus asper* to these forms.

Sophist 261b6 (ἀνύτων), *Republic* 486c5 (ἀνύτων), *Laws* 650a6 (ἀνύσειεν), etc.; Aristotle *Rhetoric* 1409b4 (ἀνύειν); Aiskhylos fr. 161.2 R (ἄνοις), *Agamemnōn* 935 (ἤνυσεν);[23] Euripides *Bakkhai* 1100 (ἤνυτον), *Andromakhē* 1132 (ἤνεν/ἤνυεν),[24] and *Phoinissai* 453 (ἀνύουσι).[25] The number and variety of manuscript attestations of the *spiritus lenis* hardly suggests scribal alterations. In my opinion, they can only be explained if this pronunciation was allowable and current in Athens during the classical period.[26] This deprives Wathelet's argument of strength, and we are left to consider on other grounds the merit of his suggestion of a Euboian origin for the short forms.

As noted above, the third CL cannot have happened early enough for a hypothetical Homer to use the short (or long!) forms in performance. A dictated transcript would have had the unsimplified consonant clusters (e.g. **xenwos*). It is well-known that the loss of post-consonantal -ϝ- that gave rise to the third CL took place after Attic reversion of [æ:] to [a:][27] following rho.[28] This explains Attic κόρη (< **κόρϝη* < **κόρϝᾱ*), which otherwise would have reverted to κόρα. Attic reversion, in turn, must postdate the second CL, which recreated the sound [a:] in phonological opposition to [æ:].[29] The second CL was caused by the simplification of secondary **-ns-* clusters whose **-s-* came from **-ky-*, **-ty-*, apical stop + σ, or tau before iota.[30] It is unlikely that the reversion alone [ræ:] > [ra:] would have sufficed to recreate the phoneme /a:/. Using the principle of economy developed by Martinet 1955, Ruipérez 1989a offered a compelling explanation for the evolution of the Greek long vowels. He pointed out that, after the first CL had created the new phonemes /e:/ and /o:/,[31] the overloading of the back series sought articulatory relief by pushing in the direction of maximum aperture (65–66). This resulted in the fronting of original /a:/ > /æ:/ in all phonic environments. After /r/, the groups /re:/ /rɛ:/ and /ræ:/ will have realized the corresponding vowel sounds with a comparatively greater aperture (68). Thus,

---

[23] West prints ἤνυσεν without ms. support.

[24] Corrected by Diggle to ἤνον, after Borthwick.

[25] Diggle prints ἀνύτουσιν. These *loci* are simply illustrative of the extent of the practice. This is by no means a comprehensive list.

[26] At the very least, its pervasive use in tragic poetry could have influenced rhapsodes, who, cognizant that Ionic psilosis was the Homeric norm, might readily adopt it.

[27] Both, realizations of original /a:/.

[28] See, for example, Schwyzer *GG* I.187–189 and Sihler 1995:50–51. Sihler argues convincingly for reversion (51). For the chronology of reversion after rho vis-à-vis reversion after epsilon and iota, see Brugmann 1898. In his study of Greek words ending in -αιρα, Peters (1980:250–305) reviews Attic reversion and probes alternative relative orders of the relevant sound changes. He does not attempt an absolute chronology nor does he consider the second or third CLs.

[29] That is, it reintroduced the phoneme /a:/.

[30] See Crespo 1999 and Sihler 1995:217.

[31] I.e. half-close long 'e' and 'o' that contrasted with the half-open original long 'e' and 'o', here represented as /ɛ:/ and /ɔ:/.

/æ:/ after /r/ will have been a slightly different, more open sound than [æ:], what using the IPA I denote [æ̞:].[32] This will have been an allophone of /æ:/, i.e. a combinatorial variant of [æ:] after /r/. It must not, however, be represented as [ra:], as if [æ̞:] = [a:]. This equation is false, for otherwise we would predict ˣπαράη < ˣparaǽ: < ˣpara:(w)ǽ: rather than παρέᾱ < *pareǽ: < *parǽ:(w)œ:.[33] That /ræ:/ appears under the combinatorial variant [ræ̞:] does not change the fact that only after the recreation of the phoneme /a:/ by the second CL could /ræ:/ > /ra:/. For if we assume that post-consonantal -ϝ- in -ρϝ- was absorbed *before* the second CL, we would have (in Attic) *korwǽ: > ˣkorǽ:, and this form in turn would have resulted in κόρα after the recreation of /a:/.[34] To avoid reversion, we need the [æ:] in *korwǽ: to collapse with [ε:] *before* the loss of *-w-; and this can only have happened after the second CL.[35]

---

[32] For basic guidance on phonetics and the I(nternational) P(honetic) A(lphabet), I recommend Catford 2001.

[33] See Sihler 1995:51. For bibliography on this word, see *DMic* II.84–85 s.v. "*pa-ra-wa-jo*." See also Peters 1980:295–304.

[34] In other words, the long vowel that after /w/ was pronounced [æ:] would have been realized as a more open allophone [æ̞:] following the loss of /w/. Only after the second CL would [ræ̞:] > [ra:] and the outcome would be reassigned to the recreated phoneme /a:/. Under this scenario, its final form would have been just the same as if we had started with ˣkora: before [a:] was fronted to [æ:].

[35] Confused by the fact that /æ:/ must have existed as a more open combinatorial variant after /r/, some scholars have suggested that this allophone by itself might have recreated the phoneme /a:/ (cf. Bartoněk 1966:103, López Eire 1970:18, and Crespo 1999:182). The confusion is twofold. /æ:/ after /r/ cannot have been pronounced [a:]. Otherwise, there would have been no fronting in this environment nor any need for reversion. But we have seen that only reversion predicts the correct Attic παρέα. And, as Ruipérez (1989a:67) remarks, one can hardly admit that in /ra:/ the vowel was always realized as [a:], since the /ro:/ that arose from the first CL must have exerted the same structural pressure on /ra:/ that displaced [a:] > [æ:] in other phonic environments. Moreover, this combinatorial variant is *not* a development of ˣ/ræ:/, that is, it is not a sound change that followed the hypothetically preexisting pronunciation ˣ[ræ:]. /æ:/ was always realized after /r/ as the allophone [æ̞:]. This more open realization is a Greek phonetic fact that held true at all times for any vowel that followed /r/ (unless the vowel was already maximally open). The dialect of Naxos serves to illustrate this: different graphemes were used for /a:/, /æ:/ < *a:, and /ε:/ < *e:. (See, for example, Schmitt 1977:101, IV.15.M2, and Schwyzer Del³ 758–759 together with Jeffery 1990, pl. 55, nos. 2, 11.) There was never a ˣ[ræ:] (i.e. a /ræ:/ whose long vowel was pronounced just like the long vowel of /rwæ:/) that developed into [ræ̞:] under a sound change that then ceased, with the result that its outcome could be distinguished from a ˣ[ræ:] that arose later from [rwæ:] by the loss of /w/ (which, under the assumed circumstances, would not have experienced a subsequent opening to [ræ̞:]). Only these false premises could produce two groups, [ræ̞:] and [ræ:], that would merge respectively with /ra:/ and /rε:/ after the second CL. Without such a scenario we are left without a sound that can be phonemically opposed to [æ:] *before* the second CL (here, hypothetically—and falsely—/æ̞:/ and /æ:/ after /r/). This lengthening is therefore prerequisite for the recreation of the phoneme /a:/.

4.2.2 Dating the second CL

The conclusion seems inescapable that the second CL must have *preceded* the Attic reversion of /ræː/ to /raː/. And this reversion, in turn, must have preceded the third CL, which included the loss of -ϝ- in -νϝ-. This suggests a rather late dating for the third CL, because it is almost certain that the second had not yet happened when the Persian *Māda* (for Mede) was borrowed into Greek as Μῆδος[36] or when Καρχηδών was adopted for Carthage.[37] It is true, as Gusmani 1976 demonstrates, that these loanwords cannot date the fronting [aː] > [æː], since e.g. *Māda* could have been borrowed as Μῆδος before the change and undergone the fronting later; or it may have been borrowed after the change, with immediate replacement of [aː] by [æː], because no Greek sound matched the original Persian [aː].[38] But if the second CL had already taken place and [aː] was current in the Greek phonic repertory, we must assume that Μῆδος would have been the Greek reflex unless we appeal to the conjectural substratum influence of non-Greek languages spoken in Asia Minor as the source of the shift away from Persian [aː].[39]

Kretschmer 1907 is perhaps the best known advocate of a substratum influence.[40] Prompted by Herodotos 1.146 he proposed "daß das ionische η auf karischer Aussprache des griechischen ā beruhe" (32). Unfortunately, even after pathbreaking work in the last twenty years[41] we still know very little about Carian today, and Kretschmer's theory remains largely conjectural.[42] To give

---

[36] With a *terminus post quem* of the early seventh century BC (Gusmani, 1976:79).

[37] With a *terminus post quem* of the eighth century (Gusmani 1976:79).

[38] The latter is Gusmani's "ökonomische Lautsubstitution" (Gusmani 1976:81); the former, his "Einreihung" (1976:77). Cf. Szemerényi (1968:145), who pronounces valid the argument that takes the second CL as a *terminus ante quem*, but turns to Πέρσης and Ξέρξης to cast doubt "whether the whole problem [of these loanwords] concerns Greek phonological history at all." Lejeune (1972:235 §249n2) voices similar reservations, but Gusmani (1976:80) has convincingly disposed of these difficulties.

[39] In other words, the Greeks who borrowed *Māda* would have articulated Persian /aː/ under the influence of some non-Greek language that fronted [aː] to [æː]. If so, this phenomenon would be independent of the sound change [aː] > [æː] that followed the first CL and affected all Attic-Ionic speakers. Hence, it could not be integrated into a chronological sequence of Greek sound changes. This subgroup of the Ionic linguistic community would have uttered *Mā-* as [mæː-]. As the loanword spread to the rest (presumably, after [æː] had merged with [εː]), other speakers of Attic-Ionic replaced [mæː-] with [mεː] (ökonomische Lautsubstitution). Hence Μῆδος.

[40] In an earlier work, Kretschmer (1892:286) had not advanced a specific view of the circumstances in which the Ionians allegedly borrowed *Māda* as Μῆδος. He only stated that it must have involved the change of ā to η. Cf. Schwyzer *GG* I.187. I gratefully acknowledge the generous help of H. Craig Melchert with various aspects of my analysis below.

[41] For a comprehensive introduction, see Adiego 2007.

[42] Schwyzer *GG* I.187: "Einleuchtend, aber nicht näher erweisbar ist die Annahme, der Wandel von ā zu η sei vom Karischen aus zunächst ins Ostionische gekommen." Schmitt 1982:375 (under 1.c *Mede*) seems to approve.

it some support, Kretschmer resorted to Lycian, of which a good deal more is known, and tried to make his analysis of it applicable to Carian by pointing out the correspondence of Carian *e* to Lycian *e* (on which see immediately below). Kretschmer was not interested in dating the Ionic change [a:] > [æ:], but he discussed the borrowing of Persian *Māda* in the course of his review of Lycian. There is not much that can be said about Kretschmer's Carian theory, but his approach enables those who argue more generally for the indirect borrowing of Μῆδος not immediately from Persian but from one of the languages spoken in Asia Minor.[43] For this reason, I will consider here the possibility that Ionic Μῆδος might be a Lycian loanword in the light of Kretschmer's review of the Lycian evidence.[44]

Kretschmer assumes that Lycian *Mede* was borrowed from Persian *Māda* and not from the Greek Μῆδος (an alternative that cannot be ruled out and, I would argue, is more probable[45]). If so, its first *e* would correspond to the Persian *ā*. To evaluate the plausibility of this assumption, we need to review his argument in full. Kretschmer claims that the sign for Lycian /e/ at times represents Greek ε, a times Greek α (1907:32–33). Bilingual inscriptions seem to support this assertion. From this fact, he surmises that it must have been "ein offenes *e*" (32), i.e. [ɛ] between [e] and [a]. But, as I will presently show, I do not believe that his inference, though right, is relevant to the case of *Mede*. Hajnal (1995:11) agrees with Kretschmer's inference that Lycian /e/ was open (though not with his further assertion that it was variously rendered by Greek ε and α): "Lykische Vokale sind (zumindest im Vergleich zu den entsprechenden griechischen Phonemen) offensichtlich recht hell (d.h. offen) gesprochen. Dies ergibt sich aus dem Umstand, dass lykische Phoneme in griechischer Transkription

---

[43] Gusmani 1976:82.

[44] It bears emphasizing that Kretschmer does not propose this. He merely suggests the influence of Carian vocal articulation (1907:33): "[D]ie Annahme, das ionische η für ā beruhe auf karischer Artikulation, [entbehrt nicht] eines gewissen Anhaltes in den Tatsachen." Lasso de la Vega (1956:287–289) also favors the substratum theory. But he grounds his support on Kretschmer's doubtful analysis and on Sundwall's wrong ascription of the vocalic sound [æ:] to the Carian sign Κοππα (cf. Adiego 2007:169). Concerning Carian vowels, /a/ is used for Greek α, whereas /e/ is used for Greek η (Adiego 2007:236). Thus, e.g. *ada* > Αδα; and, conversely, Λυσικράτης > *lysikrata-*. (The final *a* for η in *lysikrata-* is a Kaunian accommodation to the lack of *e* in their vocalic system. Kaunian was forced to render the close::open opposition of ε::η by ī::a.) For *e*, consider Οὐλιάδης > *uliade*; and, conversely, *mane* > Μανης. Carian regularly syncopates or reduces unaccented vowels (Adiego 2007:240–241), so that *e* virtually always represents an accented vowel which may also have been phonetically long (if not contrastively). This fact helps to explain the consistent rendering of *e* by η and of *o* by ω. Melchert tells me (*per litteras*): "Even if the Carian vowels were relatively open, I know of nothing to suggest that the Carian *e* was as low as the Lycian. That is, I know of no instances of Carian *e* represented by Greek alpha." Thus, I do not find any support in Adiego 2007 for Kretschmer's notion of a Carian articulation.

[45] See below, p. 93.

durch hellere Laute wiedergegeben werden." Kretschmer is unaware of what Melchert (1992:44) describes as a "very important synchronic phonological rule of Lycian which has grave consequences for [its] historical phonology":[46] any low vowel (*e* or *a*) assimilates in terms of backness to the vowel of the following syllable. This means that, ordinarily, two successive syllables with *a* or *e* in the first only exhibit the sequences *e–i*, *a–u*, *a–a*, and *e–e*. This Lycian rule largely explains the vacillating choice between Greek ε and α to represent Lycian /e/.

Thus, Kretschmer's examples fail to prove that Lycian /e/ might correspond to Greek (and also Persian) [a:] (and, therefore, that Lycian *Mede* may be reasonably expected for Persian *Māda*). For example, Greek Σιδάριος > Lycian *Siderija* (*TL* 1.117)[47] cannot prove that Greek α > Lycian /e/, for the *i* in *-ija* would umlaut a hypothetically preceding Lycian *a* to *e*. Hajnal (1995:11) correctly ascribes the sound [ɛ] to Lycian /e/ on the basis of Greek renderings of Lycian vowels (where obviously the umlaut rule does not apply). He cites Πυβιάλ̣ηι for (dat.) *Pubieleje* (*TL* 117); and Πυριμάτιος for (gen.) *Purihimetehe* (*TL* 6.1–2). Examples like Ερμενηννις < *Erm̃meneni*, where Lycian *e* is now rendered by ε, further support the intermediate character of Lycian /e/. And note the mixed outcome in *Esedeplēmi* > Ασ̣εδεπλεμι̣ς.[48] But even if we grant that, as regards its openness, Lycian /e/ stood between Greek /e/ and /a/, why should we assume its sound to be [ɛ] rather than [æ]? In fact, [æ] is preferable because it is implausible that Greek speakers, whose archaic alphabetic scripts often used the same grapheme for [e], [e:], and [ɛ:], but never for [a]/[a:] and any of the previous three ([e], [e:], or [ɛ:]) should have vacillated between ε/[e] and α/[a] to render [ɛ]. (In other words, hearing the sound [ɛ], which had no place in their phonology, they would have readily associated it with [ɛ:], which did. And /ɛ:/ was unquestionably an 'e-sound' phoneme.) On the other hand, faced with a sound [æ] that could not be readily made to correspond to a current phoneme,[49] it is reasonable to assume that Greek speakers would have rendered it by the phoneme that most nearly approximated [æ]. But the choice of this optimal phonemic match was not obvious. Since [æ] was truly intermediate between α and ε, some vacillation between them is intelligible.

Any wavering between ε and α to render Lycian *e* is less conceivable if this Lycian phoneme was realized as [æ] and Greek speakers still had a phoneme whose sound was [æ:]. Thus, under the transitional circumstances of a fronted **œ:* < **a:*, if speakers of Ionic Greek had initially used the same grapheme for

---

46 See Melchert 1992:44–45 for a full exposition of this umlaut rule.
47 *TL* stands for Kalinka 1901. These texts are also in Friedrich 1932. For an introduction to Lycian see Melchert 2004b.
48 Wörrle 1995:410.
49 That is, for Ionic Greek, after transitional [æ:] had merged with [ɛ:].

*/a:/ and /a/ and where still using it for /æ:/ < */a:/, we would expect them to render Lycian *e* reliably as α.[50] All of this, however, is mere speculation, for the language community that eventually became what we today call Ionic speakers cannot have practiced any writing before the first CL.[51] And where the use of a common grapheme for /a/ and */a:/ was not an established practice, one cannot assume that later /æ:/ and /a/ would have been represented by one and the same script sign. A distinction was made at Naxos (with Amorgos and Keos),[52] where the merger of /æ:/ and /ɛ:/ happens rather late: the epsilon-sign was used for /e/ and original /ɛ:/, the eta-sign for /æ:/ < */a:/, and the alpha-sign for /a/ and /a:/.[53] It is possible that, absent the pressure of a recreated /a:/, the same grapheme might have been used for /æ:/ and /a/, but this, too, is speculation. Elsewhere among the speakers of Attic-Ionic, the same grapheme was used from the earliest times both where we can reconstruct original */a:/ and where words exhibit original */ɛ:/. Most assume that this indicates a complete, early merger, although some scholars have dissented. Any consideration of transitional forms that may have evidenced /æ:/ is unnecessary, however, because, as Bryce (1986:45) notes, "[t]he earliest *clearly* attested evidence for the Lycian script dates to c. 500 B.C., the date assigned to the fragment of an Olpe bearing the name *Pinike* in Lycian characters (*N* 313a)" (his emphasis).[54] He further writes that "the period covered by the datable epichoric inscriptions extended from the last decades of the 5th century down to the last decades of the 4th century" (1986:50).[55] This suggests that the Lycians practiced the inscribing on stone only many decades after the first surviving attestation of their script, and that otherwise undatable inscriptions are likely to belong to this later period. Therefore, we must firmly reckon with Ionians whose phonemic repertory had no /æ:/, only /ɛ:/ and /a:/.

I have spent a fair amount of time on Greek renderings of Lycian to establish the open character of Lycian *e* and to elucidate some of the complexities that must be puzzled out before the written form of a loanword can be made to speak

---

[50] Only after the recreation of /a:/ was [æ:] pushed toward [ɛ:] and /æ:/ eventually merged with /ɛ:/. Only then would the grapheme for /ɛ:/ have been used for any merged vowel sounds that had come from */a:/. Without the structural pressure on [æ:] and the shift to [ɛ:] that ensued, as to openness [æ:] must have been felt closer to [a] than to [e].

[51] The Greek alphabet, in all likelihood, was not even in existence.

[52] Schmitt 1977:101.

[53] See Jeffery 1990:304 no. 11.

[54] Neumann assigned two graffiti to an earlier time: *N* 300a to 580–550 BC, and *N* 330b to the second half of the seventh century. But the provenance of these is Rhodian, and their Lycian identification uncertain (cf. Bryce 1986:45). A number of coins bearing the legend KVB and using Greek script could be dated as early as 520 BC.

[55] E.g. *TL* 117, the Σιδάριος inscription where Lycian *Pubieleje* is rendered into Greek by Πυβιάλμι, dates from the end of the fifth century BC.

to the phonological issues of interest. But the argument at hand is the alleged borrowing of Persian *Māda* into Lycian *Mede*, and the further conjecture that this *Mede* may have been borrowed into Ionian Greek as Μῆδος. *Māda* > *Mede* is puzzling in light of the numerous examples of Persian names with long or short *a* that were borrowed into Lycian with Lycian /a/: *Arssāma* for R̥šāma, *Arttum̃para* for **R̥tambara*, *Humrxxa* for **Humarga*, *Kizzaprñna* and *Zisaprñna* for **Čiçafarnā*,[56] *Miθrapata* and *Mizrppata* for **Miθrapāta*, *Wat[aprdd]ata* for **Vātafradāta*, *Widrñna* for *Vidr̥na*, and *Wizttasppa* for *Vištāspa*.[57] Note, moreover, the obviously relevant *Parz(z)a* (='Persian') for *Pārsa*.[58] An alleged *Mede* < *Māda* is baffling on the assumption that Lycian /e/ corresponds to [æ], but it is utterly implausible if /e/ was [ɛ] instead.[59] The puzzle vanishes, however, if the Lycians borrowed *Mede* from the Ionians. Schmitt (1982:375) rejects this theory with the remark, "noch verschiedene Fälle von *e* statt erwartetem *a*!" But the only incontrovertible case seems to be *Ertaxssiraza*,[60] and this otherwise inexplicable exception must be balanced against all the other cases that reliably borrow Persian /a/ and /aː/ as Lycian /a/. The proposal of a Greek-to-Lycian loan also dispenses with the perplexing length of Μη-: why should the Greeks not have borrowed it simply as ˣΜέδοι? A review of the few unquestionable Lycian-to-Greek loans establishes this expectation. The only exceptions are the occasional long suffixes inevitably used by Greek speakers to incorporate Lycian loanwords into their own morphology (e.g. the masc. ending -της in Πυριβάτης); and *Zrppedun-* (in a Milyan context), which, if we accept its equivalence with Σαρπηδών, is arguably a prosodic remodeling of the unmetrical ˣΣαρπεδών.[61]

There is yet another, even greater obstacle to reading in the Lycian inscriptions a word *Mede* equivalent to our Mede (< Pers. *Māda*). Regarding the superficially promising *Mede* in TL 37.3–4, Melchert writes: "[It] is clearly a personal name. It *could* be the ethnicon used as a personal name, but since this text

56 This is the form in Schmitt 1982:380 no. 2.g; Melchert 2004a gives it as **Çiçafarnā*.

57 All these are found in Schmitt 1982 and Melchert 2004a. Schmitt adds four Lycian names that seem to exhibit Lycian /e/ for Persian /a/ (cf. Schmitt 1982:377 and 383). Two depend on doubtful reconstructions of the Persian: *Erbbina* < **Arbina* (?), whose *E-* at any rate could be due to umlaut; and *Wexssere/Waxssere* < **Hvaxšara* (?) (Schmitt 1982:378 no. 2.c and 382 no. 2.l). Melchert tells me *per litteras*, "I see no compelling reason to believe [Schmitt's] derivations." In the other two, *Ñtarijeuse/i* < **Dārayauš* and *Erijamãna* < **Ariyamanā*, the apparent Lycian /e/ for Persian /a/ may be due to the umlaut rule. This leaves only *Ertaxssiraza* < *R̥taxšaça*. (*Ertẽmi* < Ἄρτεμις, cited in Schmitt 1982:383n65, follows readily from the umlaut rule.)

58 Schmitt 1982:376 no. 1.e and Melchert 2004a s.v.

59 *Pace* Hajnal 1995: "So ist lyk. <↑> /e/ eine Variante von griech. <A>, da lyk. /e/ vermutlich als offenes [ę] gesprochen wird und somit griech. [a] sehr nahe steht" (8). Better, Melchert (*per litteras*): "[T]he [Lycian *e*] vowel must have truly been intermediate (something of the sort of an English [æ] in 'man'." Cf. Catford 2001:131 fig. 40 with 148 fig. 43 and the discussion in 151.

60 As noted above, p. 93 n. 57.

61 Cf. Kretschmer 1907:32 and Kamptz 1982:312–313.

doesn't even give a patronymic, there is no particular reason to assume that this person has such a name, and the personal name *Medemudi* (*TL* 110.1) leaves open the possibility that *Mede* is a perfectly good Lycian name (etymology unknown)" (his emphasis).[62] As to the ablative/instrumental *medezedi* in *TL* 44a.37, Anthony Keen suggested that it might be an adjective 'Median' with the usual Lycian suffix *-ze/i-* for *ethnica*.[63] Melchert writes: "Possible, but the context, as usual in the Xanthos Stele, is far from clear"; and, in any case, the umlaut rule is relevant "and the underlying base could easily have been **mada-*."[64] As to *medese* in *TL* 29.7, it is best to quote Melchert again: "We cannot parse this text with any confidence, but the one thing that is clear is that, despite my and others' attempts to segment the *-se* as the Lycian conjunction 'and', this *will not work!* Lycian *se* 'and' is always *proclitic*, never *enclitic*. So [that] even if *medese* is also some kind of ethnicon modifying *Arttum̃para* (though the case of the resulting phrase would remain unclear), here too the umlaut rule means that we cannot determine the Lycian vocalism of the base. This could still be **mada-*" (his emphasis).[65] With Melchert, then, we must conclude that "the true Lycian representation of Mede is unknown and that claims of its serving as an intermediary for the Greek, while possible, have no positive foundation" (*per litteras*).

If I am right that Lycian borrowed *Mede* from Ionian Μῆδος, it does not matter whether they so did before or after the second CL, so long as the Persian *Māda* had entered Ionic *before* that *terminus*.[66] And the *Einreihung* of masc. Greek *-ος* as Lycian *-e* is possible as the example of Λύσανδρος > *Lusñtre* shows.[67] This substratum theory, then, has many problems, and it raises as many questions as it seeks to answer. Fortunately, we can dispose of it, for, as Ruipérez (1989a:71) notes, his explanation renders superfluous "l'hypothèse qui prétendait expliquer ce changement par l'action du substrat, (ce qui revient, en dernière analyse, à substituer une inconnue à une autre inconnue)."

On the other hand, no recourse to a substratum is possible for Καρχηδών, which must have been borrowed from the West into Ionic from a **Καρχᾱδών* current in a Sicilian Doric dialectal milieu.[68] Scherer 1975 has questioned the

---

[62] *Per litteras.*

[63] *Apud* Melchert 2004a:38. Already in Neumann 1969:380 §19.1b.

[64] *Per litteras.*

[65] *Per litteras.* For attempts to read *-se* as an enclitic or else segment *mede-se* (which can hardly be right, considering the interpunction that follows *medese*), cf. Keen 1998:149–150 and Schmitt 1982:375–376.

[66] Otherwise, it would have been borrowed into Ionic as Μᾶδος, and thence into Lycian as *Mad-*. Lycian *Med-* could reflect [mæ:d-] or [mɛ:d-].

[67] Other twists are possible, such as borrowing Μῆδος as **Meda* (cf. *Exeteija* < Ἑκαταῖος or *Milasañtra* < Μελήσανδρος), which would subsequently umlaut to **Mada-!*

[68] Cf. Friedrich 1921:104 and Laroche 1972:88.

validity of appealing to this word, on the grounds that it may reflect a reformation with a productive -ηδων.[69] While this alternative cannot be excluded,
the independent existence of -ηδων as a productive suffix for foreign names
is poorly supported by the data and its alleged application to the Phoenician
loanword lacks motivation. Far from clear is what precisely the Ionians are
supposed to have reformed. To speak to the alleged suffix first, the analysis of
Greek noun formation shows that the productive ending was -δων, not -ηδων
(Chantraine 1933:360–362 §293). If from a morphological standpoint the suffix
-δων appears as -ηδων (and -εδων), this is because "l'η se retrouve généralement
dans le système verbal ... ou dans d'autres formes nominales."[70] The argument
is not transferable to Qart-ḥadaštī, which commends the attested Carthada[71] and
the suggested *Karthādōn[72] or *Karkhādōn.[73] It is also possible that the reformation of -da into -δων reflects the incorporation of Qart-ḥada- into Greek as
a noun derivative with the suffix -ων. Chantraine (1933:160 §119) notes that
words with the suffix -ων/-ονος do not share the common semantic outlines
of a focused group of derivatives. The majority of these nouns are old Indo-
European survivals. This underlines its productive nature at an early stage. It is
therefore not unreasonable to hold to an early reformation of the Phoenician for
Carthage that resorted to this suffix. There is also some evidence of later derivatives.[74] Scherer (1975:143) adds the proposal that Καλχᾱδών (Chalcedon) in its
Ionian form (Καλχηδών) might have served as the model for Καρχηδών.[75] But
the Megarian foundation of Chalcedon is given as 676 or 685 (cf. CAH 3.3² 160).
Carthage must have come into Greek long before Chalcedon could have influenced the form of its adoption. Moreover, it is odd to suggest that Καλχᾱδών
in its Ionic version would have inspired the Umformung (with an alleged suffix
-ηδων) of a Phoenician name mediated by a Doric dialectal milieu, rather than
its Einreihung with the Doric suffix -ᾱδων which more readily fitted its original
form.[76] Even the existence of an Ionic Καλχηδών for the Megarian Καλχᾱδών

---

[69] Cf. Gusmani 1973:45, which explains 'Lepanto' and 'Scarpanto' as modifications of the original
      'Náupaktos' and 'Kárpathos' after toponyms like 'Ofanto,' 'Levanto,' and 'Taranto.'
[70] Chantraine 1933:362.
[71] The Latin Carthāgō results from progressive dissimilation.
[72] Friedrich 1921:103.
[73] Laroche 1972:88.
[74] Chantraine 1933: ἀρηγών, τρυγών, κατηφών (160). Cf. Schwyzer GG I.486–487.
[75] A recourse to ἀνθρηδών, τενθρηδών, and πεμφρηδών is a shot in the dark. That these could have
      motivated the shape of the Greek name for Carthage is a peculiar proposal.
[76] For the history of Kalkhedon, see Merle 1916 (for its Doric dialect see p. 9). That Karkhedon only
      survives in its Ionic form in the literary sources should not surprise us: Kalkhedon provides a
      good parallel. Only inscriptions preserve its original Doric form. But one does not expect the
      name Karkhādōn of a non-Greek settlement to have been common in inscriptions. Cf. IG VII
      2407.6; FD III 1, 497.17; and SEG 30.1117.7, 30.1118.8 (on these two, see further 32.914), and 52.536.

argues for the Ionians' adoption of this name too at a time when /æ:/ had not merged with /ɛ:/.[77] Critics for whom the change from ā to η in Carthage was not driven by an early-date *ökonomische Lautsubstitution* or *Einreihung*, cannot explain why the name would not have been adopted, even by the Ionians, as Καρχᾱδών.[78] The considerations above render the attempts to neutralize the evidence of Καρχηδών unconvincing.

One final attempt to blunt the implications of these loanwords must be mentioned. Gusmani (1976:82) introduces the notion of "analogische Lautsubstitution": foreign /a:/ would have been automatically replaced by /ɛ:/ because borrowing happened in a linguistic milieu that had embraced this correspondence as an established practice.[79] The only example he adduces (from Schwyzer *GG* I.187n1)[80] is Μιθρήνης in Diodoros of Sicily, from *Μιθρᾶνης < *Miþrā*. But Fischer's Teubner edition of Diodoros prints Μιθρήνη at 17.64.6[81] and Μιθρίνους at 17.21.7.[82] Schmitt (1978:401) s.v. MIΘP-INA remarks concerning the variants Μιθρίνης/Μιθρήνης: "Mag [Μιθρήνης] auch 'nur' eine Handschriftenvariante bei Arrian und Diodor sein, so findet sie sich bei Arrian 3, 16, 5 aber in dem Archetypos der erhaltenen Handschriften und bei Diodor in

---

[77] Establishing this equivalence at a later time would require a transparent morphological or etymological motivation that does not seem to exist. For a parallel, consider Μῆδος, which despite its original Pers. *Māda* only exists in its Ionic form, even in Doric contexts. Only in Cyprus, with its own independent traditional contacts, do we meet *ma-to-i* = Μᾶδοι (*Del³* 679.1). Cf. Forssman 1966:141.

[78] Scherer presumably believes that the second CL had happened by the time of its borrowing, when /a:/ was a working phoneme! Under this scenario, the Ionians would have acquired the name of the settlement from speakers of Doric and they would have had no motivation to replace the Doric ā by the Ionic η.

[79] This automatic substitution would have produced what might be considered parallels to later hyper-Ionic forms.

[80] Also in Scherer 1975:143. Gusmani 1976:80 shows that Ξέρξης is not an example of this alleged practice; nor is Πέρσαι, unless we argue that the borrowing happened *after* the second CL. But even Gusmani speaks of "der wohl ungefähr um die gleiche Zeit [als Meder] entlehnte Name der Perser (iran. *Pārsa*)." If so, it too would have undergone the same process as *Māda*, with the additional shortening of η > ε after /æ:/ merged with /ɛ:/, either because of the fanciful tie with Περσεύς or owing to Osthoff's law. (Peters 1980:318, 333 makes additional suggestions that are independent from Osthoff.) Even if we assumed that it had been borrowed into Greek after the second CL, the opposition *Māda*::Μῆδοι might have motivated the corresponding *Pārsa*::*Πηρσαι (before shortening). This seems at first an example of the "analogische Lautsubstitution" I am opposing here. What makes this one motivated and a permissible theory is the close association of Medes and Persians. This would allow speakers of Ionic, who knew that [a:] in the native *Māda* corresponded to /ɛ:/ in their own dialect, productively to apply this mapping to the closely related *Pārsa*. A fanciful relation to Perseus as their eponym could only help: he was thought to have ruled the Argolid, where original /a:/ was preserved (cf. *CAH* 3.3² 31.). This is the kind of motivation that is missing for *Māda*, which would lack an applicable precedent.

[81] This is the reading of RX; F has Μιθρήνη.

[82] The reading of X. R has Μιθρίννους, and F Μιθρήνους.

dem einzig zuverlässigen Überlieferungszweig."[83] Schmitt also directs pointed criticism at Schwyzer and Scherer for accepting Μιθρήνης.[84]

4.2.3 Dipylon *oinokhoē*

Arguments like Bartoněk's, which turn on a written text of Homer as evidence to prove that the second CL had already happened, are without merit because they beg the question.[85] We must conclude that the third CL can hardly have happened as early as the proponents of the Euboian theory assume. Crespo (1999:166) offers a *terminus post quem* of 800 BC (the earliest possible time for the loanword Καρχηδών), but this is not a good signpost since Μῆδοι brings its down to the turn of the seventh century BC. This date would seem, however, to bring me in conflict with the *terminus ante quem* that Crespo (1999:170–171) offers: the Dipylon *oinokhoē*, dated to the second half of the eighth century. Jeffery's date, ca. 725, is a prudent compromise of the various proposals (Jeffery 1990:76 no. 1; cf. *CEG* 1.239 no. 432). Crespo's rationale is that the word already shows the vowel contraction [æ:(h)ɔ:], i.e. ὀρχεστōν < *ὀρχεστεων < *ὀρχεστ𝛂̄ων < *ὀρχεστᾱων; to which he adds, without comment, that vowels that come from [ɛ:ha] > [eæ:] had probably contracted by the same *terminus*. This does not necessarily challenge my chronology, for the contraction [ɛ:ha] > [eæ:] > [æ:] can be placed before the separation of Attic from Ionic, as Peters (1980:303) does, and hence well before the second CL (see no. 7 in Peters's chronology, printed for convenience immediately below). But Peters also makes the contraction [eɔ:] > [ɔ:] contemporaneous with [eǎ] > [æ:]. Since after rho the latter outcome did not revert (cf., for example, Attic πλήρη < *plēre(s)a), its corresponding contraction must postdate Attic reversion, which in turn postdates the second CL. The combined effect of Crespo's and Peters's chronologies—Crespo cites and, to some extent, depends on Peters—commends the view that the second CL must have happened already by the date of the Dipylon *oinokhoē*. In other words, making the contractions /e/ + /ǎ/ and /e/ + /ɔ:/ concurrent would place the second CL before 725 BC.

The assumed concurrence, however, is hardly necessary, and since it conflicts with the dates I established above other existing alternatives must be considered preferable.[86] In fact, as I will now show, contractions like that of ὀρχεστōν must

---

[83] Μιθρίνην is indeed the sole reading for Arrian's *Anabasis* 3.16.5, which Roos emended to Μιθρήνην after 1.17.3–4 (see his *apparatus ad loc.*).

[84] Schmitt 1978:401n24: "Gleichwohl geht Eduard Schwyzer ... von der Form Μιθρήνης bei Diodor aus, um den Lehrsatz zu begründen, dass 'auch in spätern Transkriptionen ion. ρη für fremdes *rā*' stehe! Hierauf beruht auch Anton Scherer ... ." For all the attestations, with textual notes, see Schmitt 1978:429.

[85] Bartoněk 1966:100. Accepted by Szemerényi 1968:146–147.

[86] Note the similar chronological disjunction between the contraction of /ea:/ and /ea/, more striking—if either of them is—than the one between /eɔ:/ and /ea/ owing to the greater likeness of

have been current in ordinary speech even before Attic grew dialectally distinct from Ionic. This inference follows from adding to the testimony of the Dipylon *oinokhoē* the implications of the form γεννῆται and instances of contraction in Homeric poetry, where especially conducive phonic contexts favored ordinary linguistic practice over the notoriously conservative tendency of traditional epic.

In dating the second CL Crespo seems to follow a sequence like the one proposed by Peters (1980:303), which I reproduce here for convenience:

Common to Attic-Ionic[87]

1. $h \rightarrow \emptyset / V_i$___$V_i$

2. $E_i{:}E_i \rightarrow E_i E_i{:}$

3. $/V_i/ + /V_i/ \rightarrow /V_i{:}/$

4. $[a{:}] \rightarrow [æ{:}]$

5. $[æ{:}] \rightarrow [ɛ{:}] /$___$Cæ{:}$

6. QM

7. $/e/ + /æ{:}/ \rightarrow /æ{:}/, /e/ + /ɛ{:}/ \rightarrow /ɛ{:}/$

Attic

8. $[æ{:}] \rightarrow [a{:}] / r$___

9. $/e/ + \begin{bmatrix} /o/, /o{:}/ \\ /ɔ{:}/ \end{bmatrix} \rightarrow \begin{bmatrix} /o{:}/ \\ /ɔ{:}/ \end{bmatrix}, /e/ + \begin{bmatrix} /a/ \\ /a{:}/ \end{bmatrix} \rightarrow /æ{:}/$

10. $w \rightarrow \emptyset / V$___$V$

11. $E_i{:}E_i \rightarrow E_i E_i{:}$ (reordered)[88]

12. $/V_i/ + /V_i/ \rightarrow /V_i{:}/$ (reordered)

13. QM (reordered)

14. $[æ{:}] \rightarrow [a{:}] / \{i, e\}$___

---

the sounds involved. The former (i.e. contraction of /ea:/) corresponds to no. 7 in Peters 1980:303 ([ea:] > [eæ:] > [æ:]), the latter (i.e. contraction of /ea/), to no. 9. As Peters 1980:274 remarks, "a priori hätte man nun jedoch eine Gleichzeitigkeit der Kontraktionen von /e/ + /ā/ und /e/ + /ǎ/ erwartet." Regarding no. 9, note that [ea:] > [a:] in forms like the fem. acc. pl. χαλκᾶς < *-ea:s < *-eans; but [ea:] > [æ:] in the corresponding nom. sg. (so, χαλκῆ < *-ea:).

[87] C = [-syll] except for y. E = a e o. QM (=Quantitative metathesis) involves $E_i{:}E_j \rightarrow E_i E_j{:}$ with $E_i = /æ{:}/$, /ɛ:/, or /e:/ and $E_j = /a/$ or /o/. For an explanation of these restrictions, see Méndez Dosuna 1993:99 and 109–111.

[88] On the notion of reordering, see the bibliography in Miller 1976:140.

15. Contraction of E_iE_j ($E_i \neq e$)

To these, Peters also appends:[89]

16. $h \rightarrow \emptyset/V_i\_\_V_j$ after 1 and before 6;
17. Shortening of long diphthong, $E: \rightarrow E/\_\_yyV:$, after 10 but no longer after 15
18. Osthoff, still after 9 but no longer after 12

The motivation to place the contraction of /e/ with /ɔ:/ in a sequence prompted by a study of Attic reversion was to explain uncontracted forms like βασιλέως. *If* one must account for such forms not through analogical processes but through sound changes, one would have to place contraction of /e/ and /ɔ:/ before the loss of intervocalic -w- (since Attic εο/εω from *εϝο/εϝω did not contract).[90] And *if* we believe that the contractions of all remaining heterovocalic sequences starting with /e/ were roughly contemporaneous, we would have to assign /e/ + /ɔ:/ and /e/ + /a/ to the same stage. This accounts for 9 and for Crespo's choice of the Dipylon jug's ὀρχεστόν as the *terminus ante quem* for the second CL, which must be placed between 7 and 8. The third CL would follow 10. Only 10 is not a helpful *terminus* for absolute chronology,[91] whereas, if the chronological signposts defended above are right, a post 700 BC date for 8 would provide a good upper boundary for the third CL. But notice my emphasis on the tentative nature of both conditions. Neither is necessary. In fact, the masc. gen. pl. ā-stem contraction in evidence in the Dipylon ὀρχεστόν must have started late during the common Attic-Ionic period and must have been accomplished in Attic well in advance of 8 (i.e. of Attic reversion). A full demonstration of this claim requires that we reevaluate the phenomenon of Q[uantitative] M[etathesis].

Méndez Dosuna 1993 has convincingly shown that the traditional understanding of QM as the phonetic exchange of vocalic quantities cannot be sustained by typological parallels. It also fails to explain an array of data in the literary texts and inscriptions. Méndez Dosuna's theory of synizesis with CL is superior to the alternatives and should be adopted. My abbreviated exposition

---

[89] $V = [+syll, -cons]$.

[90] Crespo 1977:193.

[91] We do not know how much time may have transpired between 9 and 10. Besides, even if we knew that 8 had been completed by 725 BC, this fact would not determine how much earlier it might have taken place. Thus, we could not rule out a third CL that had already happened by the time of a late eighth-century 'Homer.' But one need hardly regard Crespo's *terminus post quem* of 800, not because it is false, but because it is not stringent enough. Crespo has conveniently ignored the evidence of Μῆδοι (which is ca. or post 700), perhaps to accommodate his *terminus ante quem* without contradiction.

of it will use without distinction vocalic sequences that developed from the loss of intervocalic -s-, -y-, and -w- (the phonetic process was the same in all cases). But the reader should bear in mind that -s- and -y- > -h- > -∅- much earlier, and they provide the contexts that gave rise to vocalic contraction (or a preliminary stage thereof) before the Ionic migration. Note also that I intend to apply this model to the masc. gen. pl. ā-stems.[92] I will not consider the further question whether and how this particular case might be extended to other cases, such as *ηου in *νηοῦ > νεώ (cf. Méndez Dosuna 1993:98).

From the restricted set of vowels in contact to which QM applies, the Spanish scholar concludes that QM does not reflect a generic phonotactic restriction on vowel sequences /V:V/. Neither are there non-Greek typological parallels for the process /V:V/ > /VV:/ (1993:99). At this point Méndez Dosuna turns to the Homeric text. Although long forms like βασιλῆος predominate there, as one would expect in a very conservative medium, there are numerous instances of QM, the overwhelming majority of which are in synizesis (εω and εᾱ). Monosyllabic scansion is the ordinary outcome of first-declension masculine εω (ἀγκυλομήτεω). For the gen. pl. of first-declension feminine nouns (ἀγορέων),[93] the subjunctive (στέωμεν), and a few other categories, the scansion ◡ – is rare.[94] Such synizesis is also attested in archaic inscriptions, of which the most famous example is the Nikandre inscription (*CEG* 1.221–222 no. 403 or *Del*³ 758). There we meet with Δεινοδίκηο ... ἀλῆ̄ον, where the Naxian sign here transcribed as η stands for /æ:/ < */a:/.[95] At this point, Méndez Dosuna asserts the central thesis that QM is not an independent phonetic process but one that follows from synizesis. In /V:V/ > /VV:/ the lengthening of the second vowel does not result from the transfer of the first vowel's quantity but from the loss of its syllabic quality and its transformation into a glide: ηο > εω. Glide development and CL are coordinate processes. The outcome is monosyllabic, what had long been considered the metrical license of synizesis.[96] Since the prevocalic shortening *ǣω > * æω in the sequence -ōν < *-εων < *-ǣων < *-ᾱων shares its phonotactic dynamics with QM, it is proper to study the contraction ὀρχεστῶν under that heading.

---

[92] On the genitive singular of masculine ā-stems, see Szemerényi 1956.

[93] Where the meter does not enforce -ᾱων. I hope to explore in a future work the origin of these alleged Aiolisms.

[94] Cf. Chantraine *GH* I.64 for ā-stems. Primary sequences like θεῶν are hardly ever subjected to synizesis.

[95] As Schwyzer *GG* I.245 observes, here η must represent not length but the quality (timbre) of the vowel. For a somewhat different interpretation, see Méndez Dosuna 1993:100n10.

[96] This argument explains what has often been thought a violation of regular accentual patterns in worlds like πόλεων. Following Méndez Dosuna (1993:100n9), I will use more or less interchangeably the terms 'synizesis,' 'glide development,' and 'loss of syllabicity.'

Strictly speaking, of course, since the period of time I am considering precedes Attic reversion, I have in view */-aː(h)ɔːn/ > */-æː(h)ɔːn/ > */-æ̯ɔːn/ ~ -ε̯ων (i.e. -ε̯ων) > -ῶν. The -h- corresponds to intervocalic *-s- and *-y-, but *not* to *-w-. That mid vowels like 'e' might lose syllabicity and develop into glides might seem surprising to classical philologists, who only consider -w- and -y- in the phonemic repertory. But this fact has been conclusively documented for Romanian and Spanish. Chitoran 2002 demonstrates that the Romanian glide-vowel sequence [ya] and the diphthong [ea] (i.e. monosyllabic [ea]) are phonologically different (but there is no phonological difference between [wa] and [oa], which seem to be phonetically neutralized) (220–221). [ya] and [ea] are produced differently: in both the first element is a glide, but they differ in height (210).[97] Bowen and Stockwell (1955:237) cite the following Spanish examples when uttered in rapid conversation: [e̯a] /beatitud/ ('beatitude'), [a̯e] /maestrita/ ('little teacher'),[98] [e̯o] /leonés/ ('of the city of León'), [o̯e] /poetisa/ ('poetess'), [a̯o] /ahorita/ ('right away'), [o̯a] /toallita/ ('little towel').[99] Against the common presumption that loss of syllabicity implies the optimal (or prototypical) glides -y- and -w-, Méndez Dosuna remarks: "The implication is excessive. One thing is to observe that the loss of syllabicity of the *e* ([eV] → [e̯V]) may—and, in fact, usually does—lead to the closing of the semivowel ([e̯V] → [i̯V]) .... Another thing entirely is to establish a necessary relation

---

[97] Cf. Chitoran 2002: "The shorter total duration and transition duration of [ea] are consistent with the representation of the diphthong as a simple segment contained in a syllable nucleus. The longer duration of [ja] supports its representation as a sequence of two segments, filling an onset and a nucleus" (214). Restating her conclusion in the terms used at 209–210, one could say that although both represent glide sequences, -e̯a- and -ya-, their disparate phonetic character subjects them to different morpho-phonetic constraints.

[98] For convenience, here and in the other Spanish examples I use the graphemes to denote the glides without implying that their precise phonetic values are those of the corresponding IPA signs. Hence, 'a̯' should not be taken to imply that this glide has the open quality of a central, maximally open 'a'. As Méndez Dosuna (1993:100 and 100n28) observes, by its own nature a glide cannot be maximally open.

[99] As a native speaker of Spanish I disagree that "[e]ach vowel in the cluster makes a separate syllable" (Bowen and Stockwell 1955:237). This claim accounts for their representation [ĕa] rather than [e̯a] and so on. It is true that the faster and more pronounced the gliding (i.e. the greater the loss of syllabicity), the more /e/ becomes /y/, /o/ becomes /w/, and /a/ becomes /ø/. But even at a high degree of gliding the phonetic realization of /toa-/ in /toallita/ is clearly distinguishable from /tua-/ in /Tuareg/. Cf. Real Academia Española 1973:60 §1.4.15, which regards the Spanish sequences /eo/ and /oe/: "con tendencia al hiato en determinadas voces ... y en general al diptongo en la conversación rápida"; and Real Academia Española 2009–2011:3.339 §8.9i, a recent, authoritative restatement of the same view, now generalized to "secuencias vocálicas formadas por vocales que presentan el rasgo [-alto] (/e/, /o/ y /a/)." Ulivi's formulation in reference to Romanian (*apud* Chitoran 2002:209) offers a more adequate description: compared to [e] and [o], based on the larger amount of frication visible on the spectrogram [j] and [w] are "consonantal." All are glides, but the former two are vocalic (semi-vowels), while the latter are consonantal (semi-consonants).

between both processes; or (what amounts to the same thing) to fuse these two successive and independent stages into one process [eV] → [i̯V]."[100]

For a study of the constraints that allow one language to glide both high and mid vowels, and another, high vowels only, see Casali 1995.[101] Languages that are intolerant of heterosyllabicity resort to the following strategies to resolve hiatus: diphthongization, glide formation, vowel contraction, consonantal epenthesis, and elision.[102] In this case we have to do with glide formation in Ionic, followed by coalescence in Attic. Méndez Dosuna's analysis reveals that monosyllabic (synizetic) ͜εω is actually the expected norm, to which disyllabic ε.ω from QM is secondary and typical of cadences with *rallentando* (101n11).[103] At all events, QM has penetrated the conservative medium of Homeric epic only to a rather limited extent. Although current in everyday speech, in Homer both -ηο- (without QM) and primary -εω prevail over ͜εω, whatever its source.[104] Synizesis of /eo/ in Ionic was not attended by CL because /o/, not /e/, was the vowel that suffered the partial loss of syllabicity and diphthongized, [eǫ] > [eu̯]. In the language of moraic phonology, /e/ and /o/ syllabified as a tautosyllabic nucleus and their moras combined into the bimoraic diphthong.[105] For

---

[100] "La implicación es excesiva. Una cosa es comprobar que la pérdida de silabicidad de *e* ([eV] → [e̯V]) puede—y, de hecho, suele—conducir al cierre de la semivocal ([e̯V] → [i̯V]). ... Otra cosa muy distinta es establecer un determinismo absoluto entre ambos procesos o, lo que viene a ser lo mismo, fusionar estas dos etapas, sucesivas e independientes, en un único proceso [eV] → [i̯V]" (Méndez Dosuna 1993:108n25).

[101] Cf. Rosenthall 1994:56–57.

[102] Casali 1997:497 and 1996:1–2. Casali's dissertation focuses on elision and contraction (which the author calls 'coalescence').

[103] That is, dieresis is used *metri gratia*.

[104] Against the notion that QM is an 'artificial' metrical device, see the persuasive arguments of Méndez Dosuna 1993:104.

[105] For moraic phonology applied to CL, see Hayes 1989. For a recent review of moraic phonology that probes its limitations and explores alternatives, see Kavitskaya 2002:17–35. Although moraic phonology as defined by Hayes 1989 fails to explain tautosyllabic CL caused by onset deletion in some languages (Kavitskaya 2002:27–28), it is well suited for the description of Greek and Latin phonological processes because the growth of the theory was driven in part by them. A phonetically-based approach like Kavitskaya's has much to contribute, but its insights can be incorporated into moraic analysis through language-specific rules. Neither traditional moraic CL nor Kavitskaya's phonologization model are designed to account for the left-to-right CL involved in Greek QM and vowel contraction (Kavitskaya 2002:33 and 187). But the moraic phonology can be readily extended by the addition of language specific rules. Since Greek QM and vowel coalescence do not preserve moras when its bimoraic upper limit is transgressed, it may be best not to think of these processes as involving strict CL, for such CL assumes the conservation of moras. This does not controvert that glide formation exhibits a tendency toward moraic conservation, subject to language-specific limitations. Consider the remarks in Kavitskaya 2002:102 regarding phonetic naturalness and phonologization. The phonologization of a hypothetical trimoraic vowel or vowel-coda that resulted from the phonetic process of glide formation would be subject to the contrastive limit of two moras. Note also how Kavitskaya 2002:99 explains the absence of CL with loss of intervocalic /r/ in Samothraki by reference to a morpheme-structure constraint.

contractions like γένους in Attic, /e/ will have developed into a glide and joined the moraless onset (-νε̥-); its stranded mora will have been filled by spreading the -o- leftward, yielding /oː/;[106] finally, the onset will have been simplified by glide-deletion, with no effect on the quality of the -ν- (i.e. without palatalization) because of the mid-height of [e̥].[107] A clear case of Attic synizesis is στερρός < στερε̥ός. Sihler (1995:223 §233) observes that words like γεννῆται ultimately grew from *geneā- via *γενι̯ᾱ- < *γενε̥ᾱ-.[108] This proves that the development in question (loss of syllabicity of ε and closure into ι̯) must have predated not only Attic reversion but also rule 7 in Peters's sequence above. This crucial observation supports the early date of the contraction ὀρχεστῶν. If so, the Dipylon inscription does not contradict my chronology, for in Attic /eo/ and /eɔː/ coalesced *before* Attic reversion.

Homeric instances of -ω- < -αω-/-αο- support the claim that the contraction which ὀρχεστῶν illustrates predated the individuation of Attic. Leumann (1950:223n20) had already complained that "über die Entwicklung von (āo) ηo zu att. ω statt εω findet man keine Auskunft" in Schwyzer, Lejeune, or Chatzidakis. Thumb and Scherer (1959:255 §311.9a) remind us that the Ionic feminine gen. pl. article was τῶν (in Homer, τάων ×21, twenty of these in the first foot, τῶν ×8). The IE pronominal declension of the feminine gen. pl. article (originally a demonstrative pronoun) was *teh₂sŏm. For feminine and masculine ā-stem nouns, the gen. pl. was *-eh₂ŏm. With the early loss of intervocalic sigma, however, the difference between the near identical *-āhōn and *-āon (*-aōn, remodeled) was obliterated, and Mycenaean Greek offers -āων.[109] The contracted pronominal form must have prompted the corresponding nominal contraction in favorable prosodic and phonic contexts.[110] It is easy to understand, for example, why -έης and -ίης would contract the gen. sg. to -έω and

---

An Optimality Theory of CL is of less interest to me because of its inherently non-derivational approach.

[106] No association lines are crossed. Cf. Kavitskaya 2002:33.

[107] Cf. Méndez Dosuna 1993:111.

[108] Schwyzer 1914:195–196 and Chantraine 1999:222 s.v. γίγνομαι. I cannot accept Peters's substitution of *genewā- for the more plausible *genehā- (1980:254n212; cf. Chantraine 1933:91 §70 and Sihler 1995:52 §56a). Cf. Schwyzer *GG* I.315 for the proposal of an expressive gemination, to which contrast Chantraine's comments. Gemination was the original pandialectal form of CL. Some dialects simplified it after the first wave of palatalizations with the ensuing CL of the preceding vowel (García-Ramón 1982:114 and Sihler 1995:195). Gemination was preserved in the palatalizations with this secondary -y- < -e̥-. From the point of view of moraic phonology, one must distinguish the palatalization caused by the height of the newly formed glide from the lengthening of the palatalized consonant. The mora stranded by glide formation was filled by the palatalized consonant through gemination. Then followed glide deletion. See Méndez Dosuna 1993:112 for στερρός.

[109] Sihler 1995:272–274 §265.4 and §267.

[110] Cf. Peters 1980:268n223 on the influence of πυρῶν upon κριθῶν in πυρῶν ἢ κριθῶν (Λ 69).

-ίω.[111] Desyllabized -ε̯- following an accented ε or ι would soon be lost or coalesce with it (as a homorganic or near homorganic glide):[112] e.g. *-éa:yo > *-éœ:ho > *-éœ:o > *-éœɔ: > /-éɔ:/ for masc. ā-stems. Thus we find ἐϋμμελίω to ἐϋμμελίης (Δ 47 165 Z 449); Βορέω to Βορέης (Ξ 395 Ψ 692 ξ 533); Ἑρμείω (O 214; *v.l.* -είαο); Αἰνείω (E 534; *v.l.* -είεω); Ἀσίω (B 461; *v.l.* Ἀσίῳ).[113]

Synizesis naturally displaces the accent away from the desyllabized glide onto an adjacent element.[114] This displacement can be seen in some Homeric Greek futures. Originally desideratives in *-(h₁)se-,[115] the corresponding form *-ese- that was regular after resonants was extended to verbs in -ίζω. After the loss of the intervocalic sigma, the first epsilon was desyllabized and the accent of the first-person singular displaced to the first mora of the omega, *-éσω > *-ε̯ῶ.[116] This made the sequence rife for contraction after iota by the same principle stated above. Hence, *-ιε̯ῶ > -ιῶ rather early, as we see in κτεριῶ (Σ 334), κομιῶ (o 546), and ἀεικιῶ (X 256).[117]

---

[111] Thumb and Scherer 1959:260 §311.12.

[112] The moraic value of desyllabized glides is zero and their coalescence does not add length. The case of -ύης with gen. sg. -ύω is different. Discounting the effects of analogical leveling, before æ(~y) a long ū could split and develop a homorganic glide: -ū- > -ūϝ-. Therefore, -ύϝ̯ω > -ύίω (Lejeune 1972:169). But in the case of a short upsilon the intervocalic glide would be lost: -ύæω > -ύω. Among the names that Thumb and Scherer (1959:260 §311.12) offer *exempli gratia* are Παγτύω (Miletos), Ἐρασύω (Khios), and Παναμύω (Halikarnassos).

[113] Other examples in Meister 1921:184.

[114] Cf. Méndez Dosuna 1993:124 and n. 64. Read also his illuminating comments regarding the absence of QM in the Homeric *simplices* λαός and νηός, which he relates to morpho-phonological considerations of "phonic volume"; and his further thoughts on τέως and ἕως (112–116).

[115] Sihler 1995:508, 557.

[116] Cf. Sihler 1995:190 §195.a.

[117] Meillet and Vendryes 1979:190 §292, 214 §324. For a different explanation that assumes a textually unattested -ίω, see Wackernagel 1893 and Chantraine *GH* I.451. Glide formation can result in CL to the left or to the right of the glide. Traditional CL compensates to the left, whereas vowel coalescence compensates to the right. Where -εω- > -ε̯ω- we cannot assume that ε̯ was raised to -y- and that the resulting glide palatalized the previous consonant. (This is possible but, since Attic eventually depalatalized such consonants, indeterminable, unless the rule proposed immediately below holds true.) The parallel of Romanian warns us that [ε̯a] and [ya] can be phonologically different. Palatograms of Romanian [Cε̯a] and [Cya] show more contact for [Cya] and contact only on the edges of the palate for [Cε̯a] (Chitoran 2002:209); and -y- in [ya] is longer than -ε̯- in [ε̯a], supporting the notion of a two-segmental /-ya-/ (with non-moraic -y-) and a mono-segmental /ε̯a/ (2002:209 and 205, 207). This suggests the following rule for Greek: when the glide is raised to -y-, CL is leftward and issues in a palatalized geminate; otherwise, it is rightward and issues in contraction (subject to a bimoraic syllabic upper limit). If this rule holds true, gemination would prove original palatalization. A Greek example that did not involve leftward compensation was the so-called Attic future, of which there may be an example at P 451, βαλῶ. Otherwise, we would expect an outcome similar to γεννῆται or πολλό-, with (initially palatalized?) gemination (Sihler 1995:223). But we do not find ˣμεννῶ to μένω or ˣβαλλῶ to βάλλω. In this case we also have to reckon with paradigmatic leveling, since -ε̯- in -ε̯ω [ε̯ɔ:] might be raised to, and approach, -y-, but in -ε̯ει [ε̯e:] it would not.

I hope to have established that at a very early time, when Attic-Ionic was still a single linguistic community, the gen. pl. of ā-stems had already experienced synizesis and coalescence. This must have been pervasive in ordinary speech, although it only made limited inroads into the high register of Homeric speech. But its presence there is unmistakable, and early instances of contraction where the phonic context was especially conducive are also incontrovertible. This renders plausible the proposal that ὀρχεστόν reflects a contraction that predates Attic reversion. Attic developed great tolerance to contraction and commensurate intolerance to hiatus. One may reasonably expect Attic to have finished early the process that Attic-Ionic had already significantly advanced by the time of the migrations.

4.2.4 Syllabification of -nw- clusters

Having disposed of the potential objection raised by the Dipylon *oinokhoē*,[118] I can return to the date of the third CL and advance another reason why this must be placed rather late—in all probability later than the time of Euboian cultural efflorescence during which, according to some scholars, the Homeric poems were committed to writing. The outcome of the third CL assumes for a word like ξένϝος the West Ionic syllabification ξέ.νϝος and the East Ionic ξέν.ϝος.[119] Indeed, Wetzels (1986:310) follows Steriade (1982:120) and shows with CV phonology that the CL in ξεῖνος cannot be explained by reconstructing a stage in which -w- was brought into coda-position by metathesis.[120] Deletion of -w- in an onset -.νϝ- would invoke the "empty node convention" of Ingria (1980:471).[121] Because the resulting West Ionic syllabification ξέ.νος is well formed, there would have been no resyllabification, and hence no impact on the first syllable /kse-/ (i.e. no CL). Matters are different for East Ionic syllabification ξέν.ϝος. Here, deletion of onset -.ϝ- would result in ˣξέν.ος, which is not well formed; the corresponding resyllabification would produce what Hayes named the "double flop":[122] the -ν.- would shift into the melodic slot vacated by the -.ϝ-, and the new empty position is filled in turn by spreading the preceding vowel segment /e/ > /e:/.

---

[118] For the loss of intervocalic ϝ in *παϝιζει, see below, p. 114.

[119] For a short summary of the argument, see Cassio 1998:17–18. Unconvincing is the synchronic view in Chantraine *GH* I.161 that sees both syllabifications as equally available to Ionic rhapsodes and chosen merely for metrical convenience. This begs the question that only a diachronic perspective can hope to answer: how these two forms came to be part of the Homeric system in the first place. Steriade 1982:124–125 follows Chantraine.

[120] Steriade (1982:120) notes that Ionic failed to delete preconsonantal -w- in derived and underived environments alike, so that -VwC- cannot be assumed to have developed into -V̄C-.

[121] Cf. Steriade 1982:114–115.

[122] Hayes 1989:265–266.

Steriade (1982:125) argues that Attic has preserved an archaic version of Common Greek syllabification to which the Ionic syllabification is an innovation.[123] It is true that at times Attic is demonstrably more archaic than Ionic (e.g. in retaining the dual).[124] But if Steriade is right, it is puzzling that epic formulas overwhelmingly reflect the supposed innovative syllabification, and that in turn the allegedly archaic one has not left a deeper mark on Homeric prosody.[125] The proposal that the scansion of Vedic Sanskrit and Homeric Greek reflects innovative syllabification is untenable.[126] Poetic prosody, especially at an advanced stage of development, is doubtless conventional and may depart markedly from ordinary speech. Yet the rules of versification are not set by committee;[127] they develop as stylizations of rhythmic patterns of language and music in performance that gain over time the approval of the audience and gradually acquire traditional authority. One must therefore regard the syllabification entailed by the archaic hexameter as a stylization of the prosody of natural language dominant during the time of its forging.[128] A careful reading of Clements 1990 reveals that syllabification according to the sonority hierarchy is not only dependent on a possibly historically contingent scale of relative sonority (cf., for example, the different relative sonority of -w- and -r- in Attic and Ionic),[129] but also on language specific rules that Miller (1994:8–9) calls

---

[123] She prefers this view—which she supports with a questionable interpretation of Mycenaean Greek spelling, on which see immediately below—because it suits her attempt to establish a universally applicable sound law {s,y} → h/$_\sigma$[___. In order to prevent postconsonantal /y/ > h, she needs to syllabify intervocalic sonorant + -y- clusters as complex onsets. Wetzels (1986:303–309) shows that Steriade's explanation cannot be maintained.

[124] Brugmann-Thumb *GG* 423 §434.

[125] The Attic treatment of *muta cum liquida* is usually considered the innovation. Cf. Ruijgh 1985:120n57.

[126] This view is supported by Steriade 1982; Guion 1996; and Consani 2003, esp. 39–50 (following Pulgram 1981). Cf. Miller 1990:173 nos. 4–5, Miller 1994:17n4, and Baechle 2007:73n24.

[127] Pulgram (1981:86) wonders "why Greek metrics needed more metrically long syllables in its versification than the language provided in the shape of phonologically heavy syllables." His solution: "Could the answer be that Greek metrics was borrowed, in a prehistoric, pre-Homeric period, from a language with another phonological system that had a suitable number of long syllables ... ? Or was this the condition of an earlier pre-Greek or proto-Greek phonological system into whose period falls the origin of Greek metrics ... ?" (86). A little later in the same article he considers the *Rig Veda* and conjectures that "an older syllable-counting metrics in a language relatively rich in light syllables was replaced by a quantitative metrics"; and this, in turn, required perhaps an increase in the number of heavy syllables which were readily supplied by the application of specific metrical rules designed to this end (90).

[128] Devine and Stephens (1994:37–38) argue that "[t]he metrical evidence cannot be discounted because it conflicts with an a priori theory of syllabification ... . It is probably easier to motivate the alternative assumption, namely that the orthographic evidence partially fails to reproduce the syllable divisions of normal speech. ... Writing is a slower activity than speaking, and the writer needs to adopt certain specific strategies to slow down his speech to align it with what is being written."

[129] Cf. Woodard 1997a:77 and 246.

"P[articular] G[rammar] stipulations," "PG exceptions," and "PG restrictions."[130] It is well and good to call the archaic Greek syllabification of Homeric epic typologically "marked"[131] so long as one does not thereby suggest that an artificial metrical convention was operative *ab origine* and that the syllabification of the archaic hexameter never matched the natural speech rhythms of proto-Greek.[132]

Pulgram and his followers might argue that the poetic scansion λεπ.τός was conventional and did not reflect the λε.πτός of everyday speech.[133] But the lengthening in prose of the last vowel of σοφός to form σοφώτερος and σοφώτατος, when contrasted with the unchanged κουφότερος/κουφότατος, supports the view (*pace* Guion 1996:76–77) that prose and poetry shared one notion of light and heavy syllables.[134] Similarly, the accent of trisyllabic neuters in -ιον falls on the stem if the syllable is light but on the ending if heavy: θύριον but πυκτίον and χρῡσίον.[135] Original IE syllabification supports λεπ.τός. Even in Attic, the forms κενότερος and στενότερος point to original forms κενϝός and στενϝός and strongly suggest that IE practice was followed by original Attic syllabification too.[136] What, then, are we to make of Horrocks's claim that Mycenaean ke-se-ni-wi-jo points to /kse.nwios/?[137]

The first thing to be said about ke-se-ni-wi-jo is that it has two spelling variants, ke-se-nu-wi-jo and ke-se-ne-wi-ja. To call the last "exceptional" (so Morpurgo Davies 1987:98, followed by Miller 1994:21) is to beg the question whether the small number of surviving attestations may be fairly thought to render very unlikely the Bronze-Age syllabification /ksen.wios/ (for this syllabification we should expect ˣke-se-wi-jo).[138] At any rate, we should note the agreement of Viredaz (1983:133–134) and Morpurgo Davies (1987:92) that Mycenaean

---

[130] With reference to Vennemann 1988, Guion 1996:79 notes that Steriade's view—which she endorses—of the evolution of syllabification from IE to Mycenaean and Attic violates the so-called 'Coda Law,' even as it observes the competing 'Head Law.' To this, she tellingly adds: "It is unclear which type of change is more natural."

[131] So Miller 1994:9 and 16.

[132] Miller (1994:17n4) thinks that "epic meter is more conservative in terms of syllable division (e.g. Hom. *pat.rí* -˘ vs. Attic *pa.trí* ˘˘ 'to father') than Mycenaean." Woodard 1997a makes the Mycenaean and Cypriot spelling independent of syllable structure (cf., for example, 48), and thus implicitly disputes the orthographic basis for the inference that Mycenaean had already adopted the innovative syllabification.

[133] Cf. Morpurgo Davies 1987:93.

[134] So, λεπτότερος and λεπτότατος.

[135] For the rule and its exceptions see Chandler 1881:101 §343 and 104–107 §§347–352. For these and other examples of prosodic considerations common to poetry and prose, see Morpurgo Davies 1987:93 and Ruijgh 1985:120–121.

[136] These forms were noted by Monro 1992:382–383 §405.3 (first published in 1891). Cf. Cassio 1998:17.

[137] Horrocks 1987:276–279.

[138] The same scribe writes ke-se-ne-wi-ja and ke-se-nu-wi-ja (Morpurgo Davies 1972:107–110). Cf. Viredaz 1983:167 §§29–30. On ke-se-ne-wi-ja see also Consani (2003:94 and 114), who writes that it is evidence of "una sillabazione tipologicamente marcata /ksen.wV/" (114). I agree.

reflected original IE syllabification, and that where its spelling seems to show otherwise, an explanation other than an innovative syllabification must be found. Morpurgo Davies's proposal is that Mycenaean scribes exhibit a stance vis-à-vis the graphic representation of consonantal clusters that is strikingly similar to the one espoused by late grammarians. Indeed, she shows that a Linear B scribe could make a compound explicit by separating the words with an internal divider (this is not done with derivational suffixes) or by marking a graphic hiatus; and that he could treat as a unit a sequence of accented and unaccented words (proclitic or enclitic). This implies a working notion of the word as a unit of utterance (97). From this, she goes on to claim a link between the writing practice of Linear B, Cyprian, and alphabetic Greek. The syllabi-fication commended by late grammarians was neither entirely based upon, nor wholly divorced from, the real syllabic division of the spoken language. It reflected both the phonetic reality and the psychological perception of syllabi-fication (101). For Herodian, if a cluster started a word it could also start a word-internal syllable (e.g. κτίζω vs. τέ.κτων). Allowable word-final consonants may also have influenced his analysis. For Morpurgo Davies, perceptions of syllabic division in Mycenaean Greek were also affected by a combination of real syllabic division and the model provided by word beginnings and ends. To return to /ksenwios/: the -nu-wi- of ke-se-nu-wi-jo would naturally follow from the quick utterance of -nwV-, so that we cannot infer solely from it the existence of words that began with nw-. But the attestation of a complex sign 'nwa'[139] gives it some support. Thus, we can hardly infer from ke-se-ni-wi-jo the syllabification /kse.nwios/.[140]

If Mycenaean, then, does not support the claim that Attic preserved the archaic syllabification ξέ.νϝος, and neither do the forms στενότερος and κενότερος, we must accept the fact that the further we go back in time, the more we are unlikely to meet with the innovative syllabification responsible for the lack of CL in West Ionic after the loss of postconsonantal -w-. Cassio (1998:17–18) is right to affirm that at the time of the migration all Attic-Ionic speakers must have syllabified ξέν.ϝος. It is surely out of the question that a tenth-century rhapsode in Lefkandi could have syllabified ξέ.νϝιος, nor can Attic correption be explained by reference to a Euboian phase during the Geometric Period. The cumulative import of the linguistic arguments reviewed here controverts the now popular view that what scholars before Wathelet had interpreted as

---

[139] Morpurgo Davies 1972:110, used for Ἐνυάλιος and περυσινός (with unexplained -w-).

[140] Cf. Wetzels 1986:312 regarding Mycenaean sonorant + -y- clusters. His article convincingly proves against Steriade the heterosyllabicity of these clusters. Note also his statements about the heterosyllabicity of *ekwo- > i-qo = ikkʷos > ἵππος (312).

Atticisms are best explained as Euboian forms preserved by a hypothetical early-archaic written text of Homer.[141]

Although the main thrust of my criticism has been aimed at the theory of ninth- or eighth-century dictated scripts of the *Iliad* and the *Odyssey*, the same arguments challenge the soundness of West's belief in mid seventh-century texts. Indeed, if, as West (1988:166) claims, "Euboea [was] the area in which the epic language acquired its definitive and normative form," starting with possible performances for the "anonymous king ... at Lefkandi" in the tenth century BC,[142] any instance of a word that would not have suffered CL in West Ionic but is in fact lengthened in our texts is *eo ipso* problematic. For, if West is right, much of the formulaic language would have come into being while the syllabification -C.w- was Panionic. In all words with such clusters, the syllable before the -w- would have scanned long. But if the definitive and normative shape of the texts came into being during 300–350 years of Euboian performances, rhapsodes would have had to adapt the formulaic language to the innovative syllabification as it developed. Hence, most (if not all) of the attested compensatorily lengthened words should have been reduced to the short Euboian forms. In other words, we should not expect ἶσος, ξεῖνος, κοῦρος, κᾱλός, etc., but ἴσος, ξένος, κόρος, κᾰλός, and so on. Not the latter West Ionic forms, but the former East Ionic, would be in need of justification. This must be so, unless we assume such a strong conservative tendency in the system and so little linguistic renovation that, after the loss of postconsonantal -w-, CL was artificially applied under prosodic compulsion against the vernacular West Ionic in order to save the existing formulas. Had this in fact been the case, one can hardly call the centuries of the alleged Euboian phase "definitive and normative"; one might better consider the Euboian bards as a minor, unimportant link in the transmission of texts that might as well, so far as the linguistic and formulaic shape goes, have remained in the hands of East Ionian bards.

None of these difficulties would afflict the Athenian transmission: since the definitive Athenian period in the evolutionary model covered the sixth, fifth,

---

[141] I do not understand how Kavitskaya (2002:51) proposes to supersede an analysis grounded on syllabification like the one by Steriade and Wetzels. Her argument seems to be that in the sequence -VCw- the consonant -C- was heard with a labial off-glide that affected the phonetic duration of the vowel -V-. When the consonant was delabialized, the longer vocalic transition that the labialized consonant had called for was reinterpreted as a longer intrinsic duration of the vowel and phonemicized as such. The logic seems reasonable enough. But Kavitskaya fails to address why the -n- in *ksenwos* should have been labialized in Ionic (with the corresponding phonemicization of the longer vocalic transition after it was delabialized), whereas in Attic such vocalic transition was not phonetically relevant. Surely the difference must lie in the different syllabification strategies effective before such loss.

[142] Cf. West 1988:166n93.

and fourth centuries BC, the poetic language would have come under the influence of the Attic audience and dialect as a fully formed, largely Ionic formulaic system, including East Ionic CL. I am not denying, of course, that performances of 'Homeric' traditions of epic took place in geometric and early-archaic Athens (as they probably did in Euboia and elsewhere). Nor do I wish to imply that the ever-changing poetic language failed to be affected at all by eighth- and seventh-century Attic (although the effect, if it became part of the *paradosis*, would probably be undetectable now, covered over by later Attic influence). More will be said below against a definitive archaic Euboian phase of Homeric epic in connection with the famous Ischian *skyphos*.

5

Archaic Inscriptions before 650 BC

A COLLECTION OF THE EARLIEST INSCRIPTIONS down to 650 BC is conveniently found in Powell 1991:119–186.[1] In this chapter I review the linguistic evidence they contribute and confirm that it agrees with the chronology established above. I will only comment on features that are relevant to my inquiry and will largely pass in silence over the ones that are unproblematic.

Of interest, for example, are the Euboian fragments inscribed with the owner's name Τεισον[(125).[2] This is doubtless Τείσον[ος, the genitive of the broadly attested Τείσων.[3] Τεισ- is derived from τεῖσαι, the aorist of τίνω.[4] Johnston does not date these fragments, but they are surely much earlier than the Eretrian law IG XII.9 1273/4 from ca. 525 BC with the reading τίν[υ]σθα(ι) on which Cassio (1991–1993:190) so heavily relies to argue against the view that τει- should be restored to archaic Greek texts that have rather uniformly transmitted τίνυμαι/τίννυμαι and ἔτισα for τείνυμαι and ἔτεισα.[5] These Euboian fragments disprove Cassio's statement that at least in the West Ionic area during the eighth and seventh centuries the form τείνυμι was not in use: quite the contrary, τεῖσαι presupposes it.[6]

---

[1] All page numbers refer to this work unless otherwise noted. See also Powell 1989. Note that some of Powell's depictions are scarcely accurate and mislead the reader (cf. Johnston 1992). For an earlier catalog, see Heubeck 1979:109–126. I have also consulted the recent editions of Pithekoussan inscriptions by Arena 1994:15–23, Dubois 1995, and Bartoněk and Buchner 1995; and the edition of Eretrian inscriptions, primarily from the sanctuary of Apollo Daphnephoros, by Pfyffer et al. 2005.

[2] Cf. also Johnston 1983:67–68.

[3] See, for example, *LGPN* I (×7), IIIA (×7), IIIB (×9). Cf. Dubois 1995:31 no. 6 and Bartoněk and Buchner 1995:157–158 nos. 6–7.

[4] Cf. Ἰάσων < ἰάσασθαι.

[5] See Brugmann-Thumb *GG* 337. Cf. Hackstein 1997–1998:31n16 and Hackstein 2002:88. Inscription 1273/4 appears in pp. viii–ix of the *addenda ultima* to IG XII.9.

[6] Cassio (1991–1993:196) had noticed τείσε(ι) a couple of lines later in the same Eretrian law and refers to "il contrasto" of τίν[υ]σθαι with it. Presumably, he accepts an otherwise unattested paradigmatic relationship between these two forms, the zero- and the e-grade (see further below, p. 123). That in the Homeric text τίνω and τίνυμαι/τίννυμαι are paradigmatically complementary is no object. Note that τεῖσαι cannot be derived synchronically from *τίνϝω: its aorist would be τῖσαι.

At 127–128 we meet with a late geometric *kratēr* fragment that Johnston (1983:64) has dated to ca. 700 (LG II). The dipinto on it reads]ινος μ' εποιεσε[, and it does not print the -ϝ- in *εποιϝεσε. If this were proof that *all* inner -ϝ- had been lost by the end of the eighth century, it might place some strain on my chronology. But this conclusion is hardly necessary. The dating of Euboian LG pottery presents special challenges.[7] Derivative from Athenian and Corinthian styles in its beginning, scholars remain uncertain how the Euboian artists kept pace with their models. The dearth of stratified deposits and other chronological controls contributes to diverging expert judgments,[8] and the boundary of late-geometric and subgeometric cannot be specified narrowly.[9] Buchner (1970–1971:67), the excavator of Mazzola, the site by the Mezzavia hill where the dipinto was found, did not give the fragment an absolute date. He merely noted of its site that "[it could] be assigned to the period between the middle of the eighth and the beginning of the seventh century," and added that it was deserted during the first quarter of the seventh century (64).[10] By about 680 BC the island exhibits a general pattern of depopulation and the oriental elements in evidence during the LG II disappear from the record.[11] Given that archaeological contexts are often dated by their pottery, in the absence of Buchner's detailed excavation report one cannot know what else he based his chronology upon.[12] Klein (1972:38) thought that the site's pottery

---

[7]   For a general up-to-date study, see Verdan et al. 2008.

[8]   Cf. Coldstream 1995:260.

[9]   Coldstream 2003:438. Verdan et al. 2008:110 write: "Il y a une véritable continuité, dans la production eubéene, entre la fin du Géométrique et le début de l'époque archaïque. On aurait aimé pouvoir conclure en abordant plus en détail cette transition entre les deux périodes, mais les ensembles étudiés ne nous le permettent pas. Il est ailleurs difficile de fixer une limite inférieure pour les plus tardifs d'entre eux." On the beginning of LG I and the transition between LG I and LG II in Pithekoussai, see Verdan et al. 2008:109 and n. 741 (with chronological tables at 135).

[10] For reports on the site see Buchner 1970–1971, Buchner 1972, and Klein 1972 (Buchner's articles depend on Klein's work and tentative conclusions). For a nice derivative summary see Ridgway 1992:91–96, with a bibliographic note at 152.

[11] See Nizzo 2007:84. Descoeudres and Kearsley (1983:28) extend the manufacture of Euboian LG II, type VI chevron *skyphoi* into the early seventh century. This is of relevance if the fragments of Ischian *skyphoi* that they list in 23 as nos. 17–18 are correctly identified as type VI. Nizzo (2007:153) includes under B390(AL)B1 *skyphoi* that could be as late as Level 28, a stratum that he dates to ca. 680 (cf. 2007:85, fig. 39). For Nizzo's adjustment to Coldstream's date of 690 (Coldstream 2003:326–327), see Nizzo 2007:83. Nizzo follows Neeft 1987, with whom Buchner disagrees (Bartoněk and Buchner 1995:201–202, with reference to the discussion in Neeft 1987:372–380).

[12] Buchner (1972:367) seems to corroborate that pottery is the primary (if not the sole) basis: "La ceramica più recente contenuta in questo scarico appartiene al primo quarto del VII sec." In this same work, at 369, he mentions middle Protocorinthian *kotylai*. Similarly, Ridgway 1992: "The investigation yielded remains ... that can be dated by its ceramic finds to the period between the middle of the eighth and the beginning of the seventh centuries" (92). Cf. Descoeudres and Kearsley 1983:10.

"might well suggest the output of a small group of artists in perhaps a single workshop during the second half of the eighth century BC," although he too acknowledged that the construction of the excavated structures from which the pottery was retrieved started ca. 750 and lasted 50–75 years, with the last phase of structure IV beginning by about 700 BC.[13] Presumably these are the reasons why both Jeffery (1976:64) and Johnston (1983:64) chose about 700 BC as the date for the fragment.[14] Thus, downdating the dipinto to the first decades of the seventh century is perhaps not impossible,[15] and this is precisely what Johnston (in Jeffery 1990:453.1a) allows for, where his mature judgment is a date of ca. 700–675.[16]

There is another reason why even a date of ca. 700 BC for the dipinto hardly means that all inner -ϝ- had been lost by the end of the eighth century. Scholars have disagreed whether intervocalic and postconsonantal -ϝ- were lost contemporaneously. On the basis of different reconstructions of Attic reversion, Hoffmann (1891–1898:3.344) thought that -ϝ- had been lost earlier between vowels than after rho. Brugmann seemed to disagree, and only asserted the unproblematic contrast between initial ϝ-, which held out longer, and inner -ϝ-, which was lost at an earlier time regardless of context. But he had to accept that the loss of ϝ in Arcadian between vowels and after ν and its preservation after ρ supported Hoffmann's view.[17] Therefore, even assuming that the dipinto

---

[13] The absolute dates for the various structures seem to me no more than educated guesses based on the assumed chronological boundaries for the occupation of the site and the relative order of the structures and their building phases. The *kratḗr* fragment was retrieved from under one of the foundation stones of structure II (Buchner 1970–1971:67). If Strabo's report of earthquakes (5.247) is credible, tremors and falling boulders from the Mezzavia ridge must have forced repairs and reconstruction on more than one occasion. That all structures but I, which was suddenly abandoned, show signs of reconstruction seems to confirm this view. Klein (1972:36) observes that "[f]allen-down walls elsewhere and constant rebuilding are the sad reminders of harsh natural conditions which ... drove away many of the original colonists." One should assume that this "constant rebuilding," which must have happened sporadically right up to the time when the settlement was abandoned, may occasionally have included the foundation of collapsed walls. Hence, the location of the *kratḗr*'s find does not require a *terminus ante quem* for it of 700.

[14] The year 700 marks the end of Athens' geometric style and the beginning of proto-Attic.

[15] Note the caution of Turfa 1994: "*The First Western Greeks* can't solve all our problems, after all: I still approach absolute chronology for the 8th-7th centuries with great trepidation. The dates of Greek pottery styles are keyed to colony foundations and the like, yet these were often dated by the circular route. Thus, P[ithekoussai] is dated by Coldstream's Geometric scheme, which incorporated material from P[ithekoussai]—probably they are perfectly correct, but there are still no guarantees."

[16] In Bartoněk and Buchner 1995:177 no. 43, Buchner writes: "Johnston ... datiert es 'c. 700'. Es ist anzunehmen, daß es etwas älter ist." Without new evidence or analysis I do not believe that we must follow Buchner.

[17] Brugmann-Thumb *GG* 45. From the sixth-century ϝιόλεως, which he thought a genuine Attic orthographic archaism, Thumb (1898:334) argued that even for Attica there was no need to push

accurately reflects the potter's pronunciation, there is no need to assume that the (occasional?) loss of ϝ after a diphthong ending in iota must imply the wholesale loss of intervocalic and postconsonantal ϝ.[18] Indeed, it is surely significant that the dipinto's phonic context, from which -ϝ- is missing, is no ordinary postvocalic or postconsonantal one, and this for two reasons. First, because the initial π- would have encouraged the loss of ϝ by a dissimilation of labials. Szemerényi (1974:29) makes this phonetic development responsible for the early loss of ϝ in παῖς < *παϝις, even in "so conservative a dialect as Cypriote, which tenaciously preserves intervocalic digamma"; and he adds that "by the same type of dissimilation ... the original πολέϝα, πολέϝων, etc., could very early, and that means *before the general loss of intervocalic digamma*, develop into πολέα, πολέων, etc." (my emphasis). This is, by the way, the reason why the form παίζει rather than *παϝιζει on the Dipylon *oinokhoē* does not pose a problem to my chronology. The second reason to consider the environment exceptional is that, since the iota in the diphthong -οy- would prevent vowel contact upon the loss of -ϝ-, the sequence -$V_i$ywV_j- might well have facilitated an occasional, early neglect of -ϝ-.[19] Thus in Eretria we find both ποιϝ[εσας (IG XII.9 257, ca. 550)[20] and the roughly contemporaneous ποιεσα[ι and ποιει (IG XII.9 1273/4, 3.2–3). Note also the inconsistent use of -ϝ- in ποι]ϝέοι and ποιέοι in the *same* line of the Elean inscription *IvO* 16.18. And the co-occurrence of πρόξενϝος and ἐποίει in early sixth-century Corcyra (IG IX.1 867).[21] Therefore, the attested μ' εποιεσε does not suggest, much less commend, the view that the sequences -εϝᾱ-, like -ε(h)α-, had already devolved into -εᾱ-, with the consequent possibility of contraction.

This view is confirmed by Δηϊδαμαν on an inscription from Amorgos (144).[22] The etymology of δηι- is contested, but it seems fairly certain that *daːw- underlies it (cf. Frisk 1973–1979 s.vv. δαΐ, δαίω, and δήϊος; and Chantraine 1999 s.v. δήϊος). Like πόλ-ις, Δηι- could be an i-stem root extension of *δᾱϝ-: *δᾱϝ-ις,

---

the loss of initial ϝ- to a "vorhistorische, d. h. nebelhafte Epoche." But cf. Threatte 1980:23.

[18] For chronological distinctions in the loss of -w- see Peters 1980:300, who considers (but does not ultimately adopt) a possible loss of -w- before iota (a near-converse of what I am proposing here) prior to Attic reversion after rho, while allowing for other intervocalic losses after the contraction of /e/ + /a/ → /æː/. It is interesting to observe that the context of this particular proposal is *paræːwiyæː* → *paræːyyæː*.

[19] A homorganic glide -oy.ye- would develop for earlier -oy.we-. In time, intervocalic -yy- would weaken and we meet with outcomes like the Euboian μ' εποεσεν (IG XII.9 43, ca. 450). Cf. the Eretrian homorganic glide δυϝε in IG XII.9 1273/4, 2.2.

[20] Del Barrio Vega 1987:216, with Jeffery 1990:85, 87 no. 10 and Pfyffer et al. 2005:79C ("daté du début du 6ᵉ siècle"). Others read ποιϝ[(*SGDI* IV.851–852).

[21] Also *SGDI* 3188 and Buck 1998:294 no. 93.

[22] See Jeffery 1990:293 and 304 no. 15. She tentatively dates it to ca. 700–650. The reading is disputed: Δηιδαμανι (dat.) according to Jeffery (received by Powell and by Ruijgh 1997:583); Δηϊδαμαν (voc.) according to *SGDI* 5351 and IG XII.7 442.

gen. *δᾶϝιος. According to Lejeune (1972:172), the outcome of the intervocalic cluster -wy- in *δᾶϝιος can be explained either as a metathesis -wy- > -yw- or as assimilation -wy- > -yy-. I suggest here again *dæ:wy- > *dæ:yw- with early loss of -w- after -y- and homorganic glide development /dæ:yy-/; or simply (and indistinguishably) *dæ:wy- > *dæ:yy- by an assimilation that is to be dated rather early.

Further confirmation comes from the famous Naxian Nikandre inscription found on Delos and dated ca. 650.[23] Besides the synizesis of Δεινομένεος and the loss of -w- in the cluster Δϝεινο-,[24] of interest is the ἰο- of ἰοχεαίρηι. Its etymology is *ἰσϝ-ος. Lejeune (1972:136 §130) classifies it with the "groupe ancien *-sw- entre voyelles" that experienced voicing *-zw- followed by a softening of the -z- to *-hw- and, in Ionic, its loss with CL. Thus, we have in ἰϝο- the same sequence that obtained for ποιϝ-. Correspondingly, we can expect the same early tendency toward neglect and loss of the -ϝ-.

One final item might be added. It is a Protocorinthian *lēkythos* now in the Boston Museum of Fine Arts, dated to no earlier than ca. 700 and no later than ca. 650.[25] Jeffery (1990:83–84) tentatively ascribed it to Eretria (most scholars think it is Chalcidian). All agree that the alphabet is Euboian (Buck 1998:192 no. 9). Jeffery observes that the date of a copy need not be as early as the date of its original, and she adds that the lettering does not suggest so early a date as ca. 700. The inscription includes the (gen.) name Ἀγασιλέϝō[26] and the verb

---

[23] *CEG* 1.221–222 no. 403, *Del³* 758, Jeffery 1990:303 no. 2. Some date it as late as 625 BC. The word ϙορη instances the loss of -w- after rho (not surprising if its date is no earlier than 650 and perhaps as late as 625), although, strictly speaking, the date that matters is not the Naxian but the Attic for the loss of -w- in -rw- clusters (as a *terminus ante quem* for the second CL). The earliest attested examples of κόρη in Attica seem to be: the Phrasikleia inscription IG I³ 1261 from ca. 540 (κόρε); the now lost IG I³ 509bis, tentatively dated in *DAA* 358 to 558 BC (ϙόρει); and IG I³ 618d from 520–510 BC (κόρει).

[24] Unsurprising at this date, especially since it is rarely preserved by any dialect: Δϝεινία at Corinth (IG IV 358) and in Boiotia (IG VII 2742); Χελιδϝόν in Aitolia (IG IX.1² 1.86); and δϝίς in Corinth (*CEG* 1.189–190 no. 355, with *addenda* in *CEG* 2.303; cf. *SEG* 29.337).

[25] MFA 98.900. It is no. 22 in Jeffery 1990:88, where it is placed under the heading "Inscriptions attributed to Eretria." For Tarbell (1902:45), the vase's first publisher, "the chances appear to be strongly in favor of the view that the vase and inscription were made by a native of Chalcis." Friis Johansen (1923:171) accepted Furtwängler's opinion that it was imitation Protocorinthian and Bechtel's proposal in *SGDI* 5292 of a Boiotian author under Chalcidian influence (he recorded no judgment about its date). Hoppin (1924:3) thought that it belonged "to the middle period of the Proto-Corinthian style before the Oriental influence had made itself felt." It was therefore "not later than the beginning of the seventh century." This is the dating accepted by the Museum's curators ("[e]arly Protocorinthian Period, about 700 B.C."), although Jeffery tentatively prefers ca. 650?, the lower bound in Tarbell 1902:42 ("the latest date that is to be thought of").

[26] Bechtel disputes this reading by Buck on the grounds that it cannot be pure Ionic since ἐποίεσεν lacks intervocalic -ϝ- (*SGDI* 5292). But this assumes what I am disputing here, namely, that

ἐποίἐσεν. Here we see, again, an intervocalic -ϝ- in -λεϝο that coexists with an ἐποίἐσεν that has neglected its own. Buck (1902:47) called the -ϝ- in Ἀγασιλεϝο "the first incontestable example of the preservation of an original ϝ in the Attic-Ionic dialects." Hoffman had opined that the ϝ in Naxian ἀϝυτοῦ and Attic ἀϝυτ[άρ (both secondary glide sounds) proved nothing more than an acquaintance with the character and its sound as it was still being used in Doric.[27] Thumb countered that these words pointed to a not too remote time in which the etymological value of ϝ was still preserved in Attic-Ionic.[28] Buck (1902:47) went further: "As Thumb remarks, there is nothing against the assumption that in the Ionic of the Cyclades and the West the ϝ was still preserved in [the] 8th century *at least*; and this statement might be made to include the early 7th century without fear of controversion" (his emphasis).[29]

5.1 The Inscription from Cumae

The previous section reflects an exhaustive review of all the inscriptions included in Powell (1991:119–186) and mentions all that might seem to call my argument into question. I do not believe that I have met there with any insuperable objection. I have only left out one inscription that deserves a more detailed treatment. This is what follows below. It accompanies two partial abecedaria (Corinthian and Euboian) on an early Protocorinthian conical *lēkythos* discovered at a grave in Cumae and dated to ca. 700 BC.[30] Until recently, the prevailing opinion was that the inscription, *hisamenetinnuna*, in careful and elegant Euboian letters, was a later Etruscan addition, possibly the name of the vase's owner. This judgment

---

-ϝ- after iota was lost more or less contemporaneously with all other intervocalic contexts. (To explain the form, Bechtel proposed a Doric masc. ā-stem genitive ending -ŏ with a stem Ἀγασιλη- reminiscent of Boiotian hypocorisms Μνασίλλει etc.) Thumb and Scherer (1959:261–262) read Ἀγασίλεϝō. But QM before the loss of intervocalic -ϝ- is improbable (cf. Peters 1980:300 and Méndez Dosuna 1993:97), while positing a secondary (i.e. non-etymological) -ϝ- glide where there was once an etymological -ϝ- strikes me as special pleading.

[27] For the Attic]ν ἀϝυτ[άρ, which some read and supplement as ναϝυπ[εγός or]ν ἀϝυτ[ός, see Jeffery 1990:76 no. 7; Threatte 1980:23; and IG I³ 589, whose editors accept it as Attic and date it to ca. 650–600 BC.

[28] Both *apud* Buck 1902:47.

[29] Lejeune 1945:103n1 agrees: "Sur le maintien du digamma et la forme du génitif, il faut donner raison à Buck ... ." Cf. Dubois 1995:59–61 no. 22.

[30] See, with further bibliography: Jeffery 1990:116–117, 130 no. 2; Powell 1991:156; Dubois 1995:36–40 no. 11; and Bartoněk and Buchner 1995:201–204 no. C.2. For the date, see Cassio 1991–1993:187n5 and Colonna 1995:333n35. *SEG* 41.848 contains a summary of the arguments. If Neeft 1987 is right to fix 680/675 as the end date for the EPC globular arybballos—late examples of which were found in the tomb—the *lēkythos* would have a *terminus ante quem* of 675 BC. Buchner disagrees with Neeft, but he admits that if we downdate the *lēkythos*, currently assigned to 700–690, by 10–15 years, "[das macht] im übrigen keinen großen Unterschied" (Bartoněk and Buchner 1995:202).

was not uncontested, however, since a persuasive Etruscan reading had not yet been offered.[31] Cassio is not the first scholar who has sought to construe it as Greek,[32] but his is certainly the most formidable attempt to date.[33] But, as I will show below, I do not think that his impressive *tour de force* ultimately succeeds. Perhaps more importantly, it is also unnecessary, for the convincing analysis of the inscription as unexceptional Etruscan by Colonna (1995:332–341) makes this scholar's view preferable to the problematic Greek of Cassio.[34] Nothing needs to be added to Colonna's able interpretation. He translates, "Hisa Tinnuna 'fa (como dono)'," an extraordinary gift inscription that reflects the ordinary practice of Etrustcan elite gift exchange.[35] Here I will only comment on those aspects of Cassio's analysis whose combined weight makes his argument unsupportable. My criticism is twofold. Not only do I consider his linguistic reasoning wanting or unconvincing. Even if I should accept it for the sake of argument, I find implausible the meaning he ascribes to the inscription. I will take each of these points in turn.

[31] Frederiksen 1984:119 notes that "no recent Etruscologist would accept that the language is Etruscan, and it is hard to detect in its letters or morphology any links with the known languages of Italy." And he adds: "The possibilities seem to be that we have either a pre-Italic native tongue of the Cumae area, or else a yet unidentified tongue spoken by a foreign visitor to Pithecusae and Cumae" (120).

[32] See Cassio 1991–1993:189.

[33] His article was deemed "brilliant" by Watkins 1995a:42. See 42–45 for Watkins's own analysis.

[34] Colonna 1995: "[L]'ipotesi etrusca [è] oggi sostenibile senza forzature di sorta" (336). His reading is approved by Ridgway 1997: "[I]t has been authoritatively argued that the well-known Tataie and the notoriously enigmatic *hisamenetinnuna* (c. 700–690) inscriptions at Cumae represent two more early Etruscans there, of which the latter—Hisa Tinnuna—was, *pace* Frederiksen 1984, 119 and Cassio 1993, using the Euboean version of the Greek alphabet to write, or to have something written, *in his own language*" (336, his emphasis; cf. 337–338). See also Colonna 2002:198.

[35] See Cristofani 1975, esp. 145–152 and Stoddart and Whitley 1988:768. Bartoněk and Buchner 1995:202n15 reject Colonna's interpretation with two arguments. First, they observe that the *lēkythos* was designed for an exclusively funerary use. This follows from its decoration—a serpent that winds around the base of the missing neck—and the failure to turn up similar vases in the settlement of Pithekoussai, although such *lēkythoi* are common as *corredi* both at Pithekoussai and Cumae. This observation may well be true, but I do not see why it should preclude an Etruscan gift to a Greek *corredo* (at least, Ridgway 1997:337 does not think it does). We will never know for sure how the alphabetic inscription ended up on the same vase. In view of the Corinthian style of the *lēkythos*, the switch of script from Euboic to Corinthian commends as its source a Corinthian potter working in Cumae. If so, the presence of the scribbling was not deemed an impediment to the solemn gesture of giving. Buchner and Bartoněk's conjecture that a child of the man who wrote what they think is Greek, on seeing his father write, said, "'ich kann auch schon schreiben' und kritzelte die Buchstaben" (Greek and Corinthian!), is as moving as it is implausible.

5.1.1 *hisa*

Cassio (1991–1993:190) wants to read *hisa* as ἴσα < ϝίσϝα. But as Lejeune (1972:177) explains, the syllabification ϝι.σϝος leads to ἴσος whereas ϝισ.ϝος leads to the East-Ionic ἶσος and to the Hellenistic *koinē* ἴσος.[36] Therefore, Euboian

---

[36] On the *spiritus asper* as a reflex of initial ϝ-, see e.g. Solmsen 1901:186–220, Sommer 1905:83–136, Schwyzer *GG* I.227 §C.d.β4–5, and Sihler 1995:183 §188. There is still much that we do not understand, but, as Sihler notes, that nearly all cases of PIE *w- appearing as *spiritus asper* in Greek are followed by -σ- is unlikely to be a coincidence, even if no broadly accepted phonetic mechanism has been advanced (Sihler 1995:184; cf. Méndez Dosuna 1985:112n57). Schwyzer *GG* I.306 believes that the *koinē* form ἴσος is a hyper-Atticism. The view that its *spiritus asper* is somehow analogical is generally shared (e.g. Sommer 1905:105 and Méndez Dosuna 1985:113). If so, an early form *hisa* for Cassio's conjectured *ϝίσϝα would be impossible. But even granting *ex hypothesi* that such a phonetic development could happen, I note that it is at Ephesos (e.g. *Del*³ 708a3.3, *ante* 321 BC; *IEph* 1435, 322 BC) and Samos (e.g. IG XII.6.1 18, ca. 320 BC) where we find the earliest evidence of non-psilotic ἴσος (which becomes rather common during the Hellenistic period, especially in the expression ἐφ' ἴση καὶ ὁμοίη; cf. Sommer 1905:106n1). This suggests that we only consider the East-Ionic syllabification ϝισ.ϝος as possibly developing into ἶσος (perhaps from the devoicing of the initial ϝ-). Cassio's reading is thwarted by this hypothesis too, which accords with Lejeune 1972:176–177 §183. (On the meaning *ad loc.* of Lejeune's "s (appuyant)" and "s appuyé," see Clédat 1917:71 §60.) I consider immediately below the anomalous case of the Heraklean *hísov* in IG XIV 645.175 (=*Del*³ 62, ca. IV/III BC). That ἶσος is the regular East-Ionic outcome is disputed by Horrocks (1987:277) on the basis of ἴσως in Herodas 2.79. He thinks that Homeric ἶσος reflects artificial lengthening after the loss of postconsonantal -w-, which was needed because the meter had treated syllables before the cluster -σϝ- as heavy. In other words, even though ϝι.σϝος would have been the syllabification in East Ionic before simplification, nevertheless the first syllable ϝι- would have scanned long when the corresponding Homeric verses were composed. (The alternative, that there was no CL although -C.w- was the syllabification before simplification, is precluded by linguistic studies of CL. Horrocks 1987:277 seems to invoke this impossible alternative when he writes that "syllable division prior to simplification should not be assumed to be a reliable guide to syllable quantity after.") "[A]ll cases of short vowel before group with /w/ counted as heavy syllables before the loss of /w/, but only short vowels before liquids and nasals were lengthened in the everyday spoken language of the East Ionic region" (Horrocks 1987:277). I find Horrocks's theory hard to accept. It requires differing syllabification schemes for -Cw- clusters within East Ionic that are not supported by the evidence. One may not with any plausibility allow ἴσως in Herodas 2.79 to trump the ample evidence of Homeric poetry for East-Ionic everyday spoken language except under the questionable assumption that the *Iliad* and the *Odyssey* were fossilized early enough to prevent any linguistic updating in performance. Should we not expect at least one of the seventy-three occurrences of *isos* in Homer to scan ἴσος, just as it does occasionally in Hesiod? (E.g. Hesiod *Works and Days* 752; cf. Edwards 1971:107 and *LfgE* s.v.) In support of his implausible theory, Horrocks adduces the Boiotian inscription no. 37.1 in Buck 1998:227, which features a καλϝόν that scans – ᴗ (=*CEG* 1.178–179 no. 334, with *addenda* in *CEG* 2.302–303, which Hansen dates to "ca. 550–25?"; cf. Buck 1909:80 and *SEG* 29.449). Yet Boiotian is generally held to have simplified -ρϝ- and -νϝ- (and, presumably, -λϝ-) without CL (Bechtel 1963:1.230). If so, the syllabification of καλϝόν before simplification must have been κα.λϝόν. Assuming that this was indeed the syllabification uttered by a hypothetical reader of this inscription, the meter could only be observed by the artificial lengthening to κᾱ- of the first vowel. For what could be the meaning of the statement that "the syllabification was κα.λϝόν," if not that the speaker correlated κα- with the long thesis and -λϝό- with first *breve*? (The closing -ν would syllabify with the following word, ἄγαλμα.) If so, the uses Horrocks cites at 278 must all be instances of

syllabification would call for ἴσα, with the *spiritus lenis*. Adducing the Heraklean hίσον as a parallel bears no weight, since the expected form ἴσον appears twice in the same inscription (*Del³* 62.149 and 170 = Schwyzer 1987:19–25), compared to a single hίσον at 175, and this in a clause that also contains hομολόγως. Its abnormal aspiration is doubtless analogical (cf. hοκτώ at 34 and hενενήκοντα at 36).[37] This is only the first of a number of linguistic objections that can be raised against Cassio's argument.

Moreover, Del Barrio Vega, the foremost authority on the Euboian dialect, believes that word-initial ϝ- was in use in Euboia and its colonies during the

---

metrical license. (Alternatively, they would call *metri gratia* for the syllabification καλ.ϝόν.) Of course, Horrocks does not assume for the inscription the syllabification κα.λϝόν. He adduces it precisely to make the opposite point: that the heaviness of the first syllable (which calls for καλ.ϝόν) does *not* correlate with the simplified Boiotian κᾱλόν attested later—implying that καλ.ϝόν devolves directly into κᾱλόν. But, once again, this impossible postulate is contradicted by linguistic studies of CL, which actually do tie syllabification before simplification to the presence or absence of CL in the outcome. If not metrical license, the truth must be otherwise: there was a change of syllabification from καλ.ϝόν to κα.λϝόν, and it is the latter that results in κᾱλόν. The dates of the inscriptions adduced by Horrocks are: ca. 550–525 BC for *CEG* 1.178–179 no. 334; ca. 625–600 BC for IG IX.1 867 (=*CEG* 1.78–79 no. 143); and ca. 575–550 BC for IG IX.1 869 (=*CEG* 1.80–81 no. 146). IG VII 2533 (=*CEG* 2.195–196 no. 786.iv), dated to ca. 335 (see *CEG* 2.104 *ad* no. 630, with bibliography), should be set aside since the correct reading is not Κορϝείδας but Κορβείδας (so Hansen *ad loc.*, accepted by the *LGPN* III.B.243). Even if it were etymologically derived from κορϝ-, the β for ϝ bespeaks in practice a rather different phonetic value that cannot serve to support Horrocks's argument. (Cf. Blümel 1982:85n70.) The chronological range of the adduced evidence is therefore ca. 625–525. We may extend the lower boundary into the early fifth century if, with Nachmanson (1909:144), we accept that Korinna used the form κόρϝα and we reckon her the contemporary of Pindar. Given that her own name appears in *PMG* 657 as Κόριννα (‿‿–×), we may date the change to the innovative syllabification to the beginning of the fifth century BC. Regarding the simplification of -ρϝ-, Bechtel 1963:1.230 writes: "Die jüngren Inschriften bieten nur Formen mit der Kürze" (i.e. without CL). He is followed by Thumb and Scherer 1959:30 and Blümel 1982:85. But, since the Boiotian script regularly used the same grapheme for o and ω until the end of the fifth century BC (cf. Jeffery 1990:94 and Blümel 1982:32–33), without further information one cannot readily infer the quantity of O in an inscribed KOPA, as the hesitation in *SGDI* 908 shows: "Κωρα- (oder Κορα-)." IG VII 587 prints Κόρα after Meister's later judgment in the "Nachträge" to *SGDI* I (p. 404): "Die Inschrift ist Κόρα zu lesen." He bases his judgment on later inscriptions (with Ionic script) like IG VII 710 which Koumanoudēs (1872–1881:298) dated to the Hellenistic period, when Attic influence cannot be precluded. (Cf. Bottin 2000:90 §39, who lists among Boiotian traits "κώρα < κορϝα.") At any rate, I can readily embrace the consensus that -νϝ- and -ρϝ- were simplified without CL, so long as the intervening adoption of the innovative syllabification -.νϝ- and -.ρϝ- is granted. Be that as it may, even if Horrocks is right, his theory does not require us to depart from the expected Euboian syllabification ϝι.σϝος, which leads not to *hisa* but *isa*.

[37] Cf. Meister 1871:397–403 §8, Bechtel 1963:2.384–385, and Uguzzoni 1968:38 §8. Schwyzer *GG* I.305 §2: "ἴσος nach ὅμοιος." On this matter Méndez Dosuna 1985:111–116 should be consulted. Note his statement at 113: "[E]s muy probable que la analogía haya desempeñado un papel de importancia en casos como los que acabamos de mencionar" (these cases include ἴσος). See also Sihler 1995:184 §188.

seventh and the sixth centuries.[38] Thumb and Scherer (1959:261 §14) claimed that West Ionic had lost ϝ- at an early date and that the attested Euboian use of ϝ- was limited to foreign names like Φᾶχυς and Ϝιό (on Chalcidic vases)[39] and to diphthongal or secondary glides like the ones in Ὀϝατίε̄ς (*SGDI* 5295) and δύϝο (*SEG* 4.64.28–29). But Del Barrio Vega (1987:215) notes: "[W]hy not think that the -w- was still pronounced in the seventh and sixth centuries, and even in the fifth, just as the inscriptions show?"[40] As Kretschmer (1894:71) long ago noted in connection with the Chalcidic vases, at the time of their foundation Cumae and Pithekoussai must have had ϝ in current use, since the Etruscans borrowed it from them for /w/, usually transcribed <v> (e.g. *lavtni*); and, in the south (including Volsinii and Vulci) before the second half of the sixth century, they combined it with -h- in <vh> or <hv> to represent their labial voiceless fricative /f/ (e.g. *vhelmus*).[41] Del Barrio Vega (1987:216) cites two examples from Eretria (the former is disputed): ποιϝ[εσας (IG XII.9 257, ca. 550) and δυϝε (IG XII.9 1273/4, 2.2, ca. 525).[42] To these, add Bartoněk and Buchner 1995:174 no. 36, a single ϝ on an LG II amphora (ca. 725–680).[43] No examples from other Euboian cities or from Oropos survive, but this is not surprising considering that their oldest inscriptions date from the first half of the fifth century.[44] Thus, we should expect ϝίσα (if not ϝίσϝα), rather than hίσα.

---

[38] Del Barrio Vega 1987:215–219 §3.11. Also Del Barrio Vega 1991:21 §9.

[39] Dubois 1995:114–125 no. 43 conveniently collects the inscriptions on these vases.

[40] "Pero, ¿por qué no pensar que la -w- era pronunciada todavía en los siglos VII y VI, e incluso en el s. V, tal como indican las inscripciones?" Similarly in Del Barrio Vega 1991: "[P]ensamos que no hay ningún argumento válido en contra de la existencia de la *digamma* en euboico en los s. VII y VI" (21).

[41] Scholars are not agreed whether Etruscan /f/ was labiodental (Rix 1984:209) or bilabial (Bonfante and Bonfante 2002:77–79 and 125n46; also Lejeune 1966:149). For the origin of the Etruscan alphabet, see Cristofani 1972 and Rix 1984:202.

[42] Both cited above. For the latter, see immediately below.

[43] Bartoněk and Buchner (1995:173) note that "ein ebenso unspezifisches ϝοῖνος (Wein) erscheint unwahrscheinlich." Why this should be so is not explained and they have no better suggestion in its place.

[44] Thumb and Scherer 1959:262 §311.14a attribute ϝοικέōν and ϝοι, the two examples from Rhegion (*SGDI* 5276), to the Doric element of its population (cf. Del Barrio Vega 1987:217–218). Two inscriptions on bronze helmets dedicated by the people of Rhegion to Zeus at Olympia do not preserve intervocalic ϝ: τō̄]ι Διὶ Ῥε̄γῖνοι Γελεαίον (*SEG* 24.303; cf. *SEG* 45.407) and Διὶ Ῥε̄γῖνοι Λοϙ[ρōν (*SEG* 24.305), both dated to VI/V BC. Kunze (1967:101–103) suggests the early fifth century for both, in particular, the late 490s on historical grounds for the former, which Landi (1979:326 no. 225) unaccountably dates to the sixth century. (Cf. Dubois 1995:96–97 nos. 33–34.) If ϝοικέōν and ϝοι are not ascribed to Doric influence and one needs an explanation for the neglect of intervocalic ϝ in Διί, I need only point out that it follows iota and that it stands between two identical vowels.

5.1.2 Missing iotas?

Before I deal with the alleged form τίν(ν)υμαι, I must raise two other objections against Cassio's argument. Faced with the wish to construe *tinnuna* as an infinitive, he declares that the failure to write the final iota has parallels in Attica (for which he cites Threatte 1980:269) and in the Eretrian inscription IG XII.9 1273/4, 1.2.[45] But since Threatte (1980:269) pronounces this a "very rare" phenomenon "doubtless due to careless omission," it is doubtful whether we can legitimately extend the suspicion to the inscription from Cumae, whose beautiful letter forms indicate careful execution. The same charge of carelessness must be levied against the Eretrian inscription (see below, p. 125). The second objection regards his construal of *mene* as μένει. He writes: "In un primo tempo avevo pensato a μένε imperativo ... e dubitavo dell'interpretazione μένε̄ = μένει: sono grato a M. Peters di avermi incoraggiato ad adottare quest'ultima soluzione, che ora mi sembra l'unica giusta" (Cassio 1991–1993:192n25). Lejeune 1972:229–230 §240 does not bear out this license, *pace* Cassio. Its sole support is in the Berezan lead letter dated to ca. 550–500 BC (for which see *SEG* 26.845).[46] But this must be judged indicative of monophthongization that is perhaps characteristic of archaic Milesian, as Dubois (1996:184) suggests, for the writer renders with ε *all* instances of ει, whether infinitives, primary third sg. endings -ει, diphthongs (true and spurious), the monosyllable εἰ, etc.[47] This monophthongization was

[45] On which see below, pp. 123ff.

[46] Dubois 1996:50–55 no. 23; Effenterre and Ruzé 1994–1995:2.261–263 no. 72; Jeffery 1990:478 no. 60c. Most scholars date it to ca. 500 (Jeffery *apud* Chadwick 1973:35: "not far from 500 BC").

[47] Dubois (1996:184) cites other examples of this "propensity" towards monophthongization: "Le phénomène qui ne subsiste quasiment plus à Milet que dans le verbe ἔπε = εἶπε ... était donc vraisemblablement un trait phonologique du milésien du VIIe siècle." The Milesian ἔπεν (Bechtel 1963:3.34) occurs on an inscription from the Delphinion published in Kawerau and Rehm 1914:276–277 no. 132a. Rehm writes that the script is "spätarchaisch, schwerlich lange vor 500." Note the dotted theta Θ, the H-shaped eta, the Α with horizontal crossbar, and the nonsloping epsilon with horizontal bars (add to these the isosceles lambda Λ). For Jeffery 1990:343 no. 39, it is "*c.* 500–480?" and it "bears what is apparently our latest example of a *boustrophedon* text from Miletos" (335). There is a second instance of ἔπεν in Rehm 1958:8 no. 11, an inscription now lost, edited from a squeeze by Haussoullier. Only while surveying the development of the archaic script of Didyma and Miletos does Rehm offer an approximate date for it (1958:1–3). His table on page 2 collects letter forms from no. 11, the inscription from the Delphinion cited above, and others. Not only does Rehm state that no. 11 features the "erreichte Endform" of epsilon (2); it also exhibits the final H-shape of eta and the dotted theta that characterize the third and final phase of the script (1) (Concerning the dotted theta, Rehm 1958:8 observes: "[D]er senkrechte Strich im Θ dürfte Steinverletzung sein. Ich habe Θ notiert.") Hence, the letter shapes of no. 11 are late-archaic. Rehm's vague dating follows by inference from a conjectural date of 540 BC for his key *comparandum*, an inscription by Aiakes, the father of the Samian tyrant Polykrates: "[Die Aeakesinschrift] kann man mit unserer n. 11 wie mit Mil. I 3 n. 31 wohl vergleichen. Für alles, was vor n. 11 liegt, haben wir die Möglichkeit, in die erste Hälfte des 6. Jhs. hinaufzugehen" (3). This probably led Bravo (1980:858) and, after him, *SEG* 30.1291

only a tendency, for it coexists with preserved diphthongs—a tendency that was highly localized to the area of Olbia and might well date to the late archaic period (see previous footnote). This cannot be considered proper motivation for an alleged similar treatment 150–200 years earlier in the carefully inscribed Protocorinthian *lēkythos*. Cassio (1991–1993:192) may be taking a slightly different view when he hints at an error, the imperative μένε for the intended (impersonal) indicative μένει. I do not think this alternative makes the reading any more plausible. Note in contrast the regular ending -ει of ηαιρέσει on Nestor's cup (*CEG* 1.252–253 no. 454)[48] or the κλέφσει of the Tataie *lēkythos* (IG XIV 865),[49] both roughly contemporaneous Euboian inscriptions (the former from Pithekoussai, the latter from Cumae). It is true that Nestor's cup shows exceptional attention to arrangement and lettering; but the consistency of its letter sizes,

---

to date no. 11 to the sixth century, although it is clear that only the *second* half of the sixth century would do justice to Rehm's words. Rehm himself makes clear, however, that 540 is too early and no. 11 must actually be ca. 500. For "Mil. I 3 n. 31" is dated to "nicht lange vor 500" (Kawerau and Rehm 1914:162), confirming Jeffery's assignment to "*c*. 500?" and her judgment that "[a]ccording to the squeeze the lettering should not be earlier than the late archaic period" (Jeffery 1990:335 and 343 no. 36). Jeffery adds that this lettering "may perhaps be compared with that of 39" (335), i.e. with the inscription from the Delphinion that is our only other source of ἔπεν. Unwarranted higher dates for no. 11 are common in the literature. Robinson (1981:350 D-2) gives the "6th cent[ury]" without discussion. Fontenrose (1988:180), similarly, the "early sixth century." As further support for a date of ca. 500, I might cite Newton (1862–1863:2.783 no. 70), who observed that its letters are "rather less archaic" than his no. 66, an inscription that he had assigned to the first half of the sixth century (for Newton's drawing of no. 11, see Roehl 1882:132 no. 489d). Newton's no. 66 is Jeffery 1990:342 no. 22, "*c*. 600–575?" (Fontenrose's and Robinson's dates for the Delphinion inscription are also too early.) I submit that these two contemporaneous, late-archaic Didymaean oracular responses have the same source: an official at Didyma or Miletos who instructed the inscribers, whose tendency to monophthongize ει- was exceptional and did not reflect a Milesian linguistic habit (not even a marginal one). I cannot speculate further about his identity, since we know nothing certain about the archaic administration of the Oracle of Apollo at Didyma. Cf. Fontenrose 1988:45 and Greaves 2002:123–124. I cannot agree with Greaves or Jackson 1995 that no. 11 concerns guidance to private individuals—why inscribe the answer? An anxious question about the propriety of piracy does not seem an endorsement of individual piety suitable for display (cf. Robinson 1981:67). Bravo's view (1980:858) is preferable. Note also Parke (1985:28), who allows for "the community of Miletus" as the questioners. Jackson (1995:95n1) mischaracterizes Jeffery's prudent dating as "non-committal." The few remarks in Günther (1971:18, with nn61–62) add nothing of interest. Dubois apparently assumes that ἔπεν exhibits a genuine Milesian linguistic trait; and that, inasmuch as it is common to Miletos and its colonies but exceptional in the metropolis, it must predate the foundation of Berezan. But all his examples from the area of Olbia are also ca. 500 or later. I wonder if the two Milesian ἔπεν might not reflect a colonial linguistic development that traveled back to the metropolis in the person of the official at Didyma charged with overseeing the inscribing. If so, this monophthongization is late-archaic and not a valid parallel to the alleged Cumaean μενε̄. Another oddity in the Berezan lead letter, perhaps not unrelated to its monophthongal ει, is the dative Ματασυ for Ματασυι (also printed as Ματασιν!). Cf. Miller 1975 and Merkelbach 1975.

[48] With *addenda* in *CEG* 2.304.

[49] Schwyzer 1987:373 no. 786 and Jeffery 1990:240 no. 3.

shapes, and other dimensions are comparable to those in *hisamenetinnuna*. Both resemble what Immerwahr (1990:19) calls "band script." I do not believe that Cassio can successfully maintain that Nestor's cup displays the closing -ει of ηαιρέσει because its writing was "più conservatrice" than the one that presently concerns us, as accords with the impression of great accuracy in its inscribed writing (Cassio 1991–1993:192). Not only because the care and accuracy of their writing are comparable, but also because care is not naturally correlated with 'conservative.' What would correspond to carelessness? Innovation?

5.1.3 *tinnuna*

Cassio (1991–1993:194–200) argues that τίν(ν)υμαι, not τείνυμαι, must have been the West Ionic form current in the eighth and the seventh centuries. His principal piece of evidence is the law of Eretria IG XII.9 1273/4 cited above.[50] But as I noted, the name Τείσων and the subjunctive τείσε⟨ι⟩ in the law (1.3–4) suggest otherwise. The e-grade -νυμι verbs (like δείκνυμι) were a Greek innovation. Indo-European used a zero-grade instead.[51] The synchronic paradigmatic relation between τίνω and τείσαι reflected a diachronic fact.[52] The long iota of Homeric τίνυμαι can only be explained in one of four ways: it may reflect τείνυμαι, a Greek innovative e-grade -νυ- verb built on the original IE e-grade sigma aorist;[53] the length may be analogical, after the East Ionic τίνω;[54] its form may have been τίννυμαι, corrected to τίνυμαι upon simplification of -νν-;[55] or it may be a metrically lengthened *τίνυμαι. The first and second alternatives are possible and acceptable; West (1998a:xxxv) rightly disposes of the fourth. The third is unpersuasive, unless one accepts the notion I am questioning here: that the *paradosis* was primarily in written form. If the text was shaped by an oral *paradosis*, such a simplification could not happen by scribal error. An oral mechanism (like sound change or analogy) that plausibly accounts for the data must then be offered.

What, then, about the Eretrian law? The first thing to note is that the upsilon in τίν[υ]σθα(ι) has been supplied. Editors have near unanimously

---

[50] For its dating to 525 BC see Cairns 1984:148.

[51] Schwyzer *GG* I.697 §γ.

[52] τίνω comes from the zero-grade of the root by -νϝω thematic affixation (Schwyzer *GG* I.698 §η). τείσαι is formed directly upon the root's e-grade. Cf. García-Ramón 2007.

[53] So Chantraine *GH* I.303, after Wackernagel 1970:77–81.

[54] Or by confusion with τίω < *k^wi-ye-, derived from the root aorist of *k^wey/k^wi. Cf. *LIV*² 378. τίω and τίνω are differently derived from the same root (*LIV*² 380).

[55] Accounting for an original derivation with -νν- and motivating the subsequent simplification is problematic. See below, p. 126.

agreed on the supplement.[56] Cassio (1991–1993:196n35) makes much of this, but one cannot dismiss Attic τίνεσθαι out of hand, especially in the face of forms that hint at a measure of Attic dialectal influence.[57] If Cairns (1984:152–153) is right, for lexical and syntactic reasons one cannot accept φ]υγία in line 1.3. Instead, he supplies the Attic neut. pl. ὑγιᾶ. An objection to this supplement on the grounds of its Attic form is lessened by the Attic shape of the otherwise unattested φυγία and by hĘṚẠI, the neatly chiseled out word that follows τείσει

---

[56] Even Wackernagel 1970:255, in his addendum to page 80, without observing that this undermines his argument.

[57] Cassio (1991–1993:198n41) seeks to do away with this (to him) inconvenient alternative by asserting that the τίνομαι attested to by Attic drama in the sense of "mi vendico," like the Homeric τίνυμαι, was never current in ordinary speech: "τίνομαι non abbia mai fatto veramente parte del dialetto attico *parlato*" (202, my emphasis). His argument ails on several counts. First, because it is not clear that the relevant sentence of the inscription, which is notoriously difficult to translate, bears out the meaning "esiga il pagamento della penalità (δίκεν)" (198n41)—that is, it is not clear that the alleged τίν[υ]σθα(ι) is a middle and is to be taken with δίκην in the sense of "vendicarsi" ('to inflict punishment' or 'to take vengeance', with χρέματα δόκιμα in apposition). Furthermore, construing with Cassio the opening ΔIKEN as the object of τίν[υ]σθα(ι) comes at a high cost, for we must then accept the strained hyperbaton of the intervening ἐπεὰν κατομόσει. Effenterre and Ruzé (1994–1995:1.330), who with some hesitation read ΔIKEN as δίκην, reject this unnatural word order and instead suspect that the beginning of the sentence is missing. A second weakness in Cassio's argument is strictly semantic. It concerns the marked division he makes in the application of τίν[υ]σθα(ι) to two separate spheres, the moral ('to exact punishment') and the material ('to exact payment of money'). This division underlies his assertion that for the meaning "vindicarsi" Attic substituted τίνομαι by τιμωροῦμαι, and for "riscuotere una somma di denaro" by πράττω; and it underlies, further, the pivotal claim that Attic also eliminated τίνομαι "nel senso 'mi vendico'" (198 §11). However, that the distinction adduced by Cassio led to differential outcomes in the 'elimination' of τίνομαι depending on its sphere of use is not only questionable but of dubious application to our case: Attic often uses ἀποτίνω for 'to repay' (or 'to compensate for harm'; cf. *DGE* s.v. I.b), and in its passive voice (specifically, ἀποτίνεται, 'is repaid') it appears three times in *Athēnaiōn Politeia* 54.2. This is all that the verb need mean in the inscription: 'let good money be repaid by the third day' (cf. Lysias 1.29). Even if Cassio were right that Attic instances of τίνομαι are all of a high register (1991–1993:202–204)—in essence, a thematic literary equivalent of the athematic epic form—why should this register not be appropriate for the solemn language of legal disposition? At any rate, this assertion is tenuous, for it depends: on the notion that tragedy is invariably distant from everyday speech (presumably, Cassio would similarly dispose of Solon fr. 4.16); on dismissing instances in comedy as paratragic (Aristophanes *Birds* 370) or themselves of a lyric high register (Aristophanes *Women at the Thesmophoria* 686); on making the Herodotean instance at 9.120.10 a superficial thematic adaptation of epic diction (cf. 1.73.4, 2.108.1, 3.75.15, 4.205.2, 6.136.11, etc.); and on dismissing Xenophon's language (*Anabasis* 3.2.6.2; *Kyrou paideia* 1.6.11.9 and 5.4.35.5–6) as poetical and having very little to do with actual Attic usage. Should any other instances of the offending verb exist in Attic, is there any doubt that Cassio would similarly indict them? Even on Cassio's own terms, with so many opportunities for exposure to a τίνομαι allegedly not true to Attic idiom— through Attic tragedy, comedy, historiography, and elegy—one might reasonably question the propriety of classifying this form as non-Attic in the first place.

and has been read as the Attic dative of Hera.[58] These arguably Atticizing forms suggest that τίνεσθαι must be seriously considered.[59] If so, Cassio is left without his main support for an ancient τίν(ν)υμαι. To those who accept the upsilon I would like to make an alternative proposal: that the mason chiseled τίνυσθα in error, intending τείνυσθαι instead. My proposal is conjectural, of course, but no more than the ultimately unprovable existence of the upsilon. The four lines that concern us are all by one hand and make an independent section. Its text is marred by various errors: the iota that should end τίν[ ]σθα is missing; instead of ΤΕΙΣΕΙ, the mason inscribed ΤΕΙΣΕΤ;[60] and if Cairns is correct that hΕRΑΙ is ἧραι for ἆραι, the η for the correct Ionic ᾱ might yet be another error, and so would be the lack of interpunction after ὑγιᾶ. It is apparent that the letter cutter was not a careful worker, a fact that lends some credibility to my conjecture that τι- was supposed to be τει-.

There are only two other alleged examples of τίνυμαι, both from Crete. The first, [τ]ινυμε̣[vo, is of greater significance because of its sixth-century date.[61] But it may only be a mirage: "[L]a forme, souvent citée, [τ]ινυμε̣[vo n'est, à vrai dire, pas identifiable ... . Après ατελειας, le découpage des mots n'est pas satisfaisant sémantiquement. Il est préférable de rester circonspect sur la forme en question."[62] The other is a late fourth-century ἀποτινυ[.[63] Whether the -ι- is long or short cannot be determined. Cassio (1991–1993:194n31) looks for support

---

[58] The sentence is difficult. With the objectionable φυγία it has been translated, "and [there is] exile unless he pays [to Hera?]." But why chisel out 'Hera'? This only makes sense if hΕRΑΙ is not 'to Hera' and instead hides a penalty that was later abolished. (For another view, see Vanderpool and Wallace 1964:386.) If so, Cairns's pairing δόκιμα with κα[ ]υγια and his reading hΕRΑΙ as an apodotic imperatival infinitive makes better sense. The interpunction, however, creates difficulties: "[T]he stone-cutter should have punctuated after ὑγιᾶ but did not" (Cairns 1984:153). That there is an error of neglect is not implausible (see immediately below). I do not know whether to accept the alternative supplement in Cairns (1991:304–305), where he argues that hΕRΑΙ is the aorist ἆραι (from ἄρνυμαι/ἀείρω) with eta for long alpha and its *spiritus asper* borrowed from αἱρέω. The case for the aberrant *asper* is defended in Cairns 1983:22. But the eta for alpha is neither generally Ionic (Smyth 1894:272–273 §305.Ib; Thumb and Scherer 1959:257 §311.10b) nor specifically Euboian (Del Barrio Vega 1987:165 §3.7.1), and Cairns offers no justification for it. Whatever the case, this does not lessen the strength of Cairns's argument for ὑγιᾶ and against φυγία.

[59] Already suggested by Ziebarth in IG XII.9.

[60] Vanderpool and Wallace 1964: "[The letter] was clearly tau, presumably by mistake for iota ... . It seems possible that the stonecutter himself recognized his error and tried to erase the crossbar, for the stone above and around it seems to have been rubbed away" (386). No such solution could fix an omitted epsilon between the tau and the iota of τίν[υ]σθαι. The espilon is too large and adding the horizontal bars to the iota (for τέν-) would not do.

[61] IC 2, Axos no. 1.3.

[62] Bile 1988:238.

[63] IC 2, *Tituli locorum incertorum* no. 1.8.

in the Cretan προδίκνυτι,[64] which scans ⌣⌣–⌣.[65] But as Schwyzer (*GG* I.696n8) remarks, even though it is often regarded as the old zero-grade form of δείκνυμι, various aspects of this second-century BC epigram undermine the notion that it preserves a hoary archaism. Of particular interest is the abbreviation (twice) of the long ᾱ in νᾱός (νᾰόν 10, νᾰῷ 11), which must be *metri gratia*.[66] Since προδεικ- could not be similarly shortened, perhaps the author decided to resort to an artificial zero-grade instead.[67] There is not much, then, to be said for the existence of a zero-grade τίνυμαι other than the alleged case of the Cumae inscription.

If Cassio were correct to suppose the Homeric τίνυμαι comes from τίννυμαι, it is hard to understand why the latter is only represented in some manuscripts. We would have expected it to predominate, since it was in agreement with later Hellenistic use and hence not an obvious target of late scribal tampering.[68] That there are no instances of τείνυμαι, however, need not arouse suspicion, for the analogical pressure of τίνω together with the Hellenistic exchange of -ῑ- for -ει- and predilection for -ννυμι sufficiently accounts for its absence. In the end, therefore, as West (1998a:xxxvi) observes, the most plausible interpretation of the Homeric data is to assume a form τείνυμαι that was expelled from the manuscripts in the Hellenistic period,[69] when τιννυ- was common.

Ultimately unproven and, in my view, unconvincing, is Cassio's theory that -ννυμαι in his alleged τίννυμαι was analogical to σβέννυμι and ἕννυμι,[70] even if we believe that he succeeds in showing that these two verbs are authentic Ionic forms. And one cannot forget that the active form τίνυμι is not attested before the end of the fourth century BC, if in fact the Cretan ἀποτινύ[in *IC* 2, *Tituli locorum incertorum* no. 1.8, is correctly supplemented as ἀποτινύ[μεν.[71] Watkins (1995a:44–45) seeks to improve upon Cassio by assuming a long iota in hῖσα, which is at odds with the absence of CL in Euboian but more easily accounts for the *spiritus asper*; and by suggesting that the inscriber was quoting known poetry but (unintentionally?) distorted his model with the geminate *tinnuna*. In Watkins's reconstruction, the line would have been a perfect pentameter hemistich. But even discounting the arguable opaqueness of the sentence and the implausibility of the vase's alleged function (on which see next), if we are willing to jettison the Euboian character of the inscription, to assume an

---

64   *IC* 1.272–273 Phaistos no. 3.1 (=*SGDI* 5112).
65   Guarducci writes: "In προδίκνυτι (⌣⌣⌣⌣) leges metricas laesas esse apparet" (273).
66   Also attested in *IC* 1.138 Lato no. 24.2 (=*SGDI* 5083), *IC* 1.170–171 Lebena no. 21.2 (=*SGDI* 5088), and *IC* 1.254–255 Olus no. 9.1 (=*SGDI* 5105). Cf. Bechtel 1963:2.676.
67   Even the syllabification is peculiar, προ.δι.κνυ.τι.
68   West 1998a: "τιννυ- [traditur] in paucis quibusdam [libris] neque illis optimis" (xxxvi).
69   But there is no need to reconstruct an original *δίκνυμι.
70   Cassio 1991–1993: "in maniere 'impressionistica', non proporzionale" (196).
71   Cassio 1991–1993:194. Cf. Bile 1988:238.

unknown original that has been unaccountably distorted, and to suppose a literary context that helps to clarify its cryptic conciseness, we have largely lost interpretive control and almost any attractive case can be made at will.

5.1.4 The alleged meaning

To turn away from linguistic matters and address the message: I believe that the meaning Cassio (1991–1993:191–192) gives to his reading is implausible. I have no objection to his brief comments regarding the ideology of strict retribution (and the use of τίνειν with ἶσα, ὁμοῖα, *vel sim.*).[72] But to succeed, Cassio needs to convince us that the following facts are credible: i) the owner of the *lēkythos* thought it necessary or advisable to add on the bottom of the vase a gnomic statement on the certainty of repayment for wrong committed whose target was a hypothetical tomb raider; ii) he did so because he anticipated that the potential tomb raider would look at the bottom of the *lēkythos*, read the inscription, and apply it to himself; iii) his expectation was that somehow this imagined act of reading would protect the tomb or its contents, even though the tomb raider (perforce, if incredibly, literate) could only read the sentence *after* he had broken into the tomb;[73] iv) the meaning suggested, "it is fated (lit. 'it remains') to repay the same,"[74] follows intelligibly from the inscription as it stands.

I need not say much about i–iii to underline their implausibility. One thing is to inscribe prominently a curse on Tataie's *lēkythos* 'he who steals me will go blind'. The statement conspicuously spirals around the body of the vase.[75] Drawing attention to itself, it might actually dissuade a potential thief. Its meaning is also clear: the vase owner is named ('I am Tataie's *lēkythos*'); the threat is issued ('he will go blind'); the condition for its fulfillment, spelled out ('whoever steals me').[76] Compare this with an inscription that would only be read if, of all the objects in the tomb, the intruder should focus on a small vase (the *lēkythos*); he should then pick it up and, having discovered the writing on

---

[72] Cf. Loney 2010, esp. 169–218.

[73] Or else the owner of the vase did not expect anyone to read the text but merely consoled himself by incising the sentiment; or the bare fact of inscribing it and depositing it in the tomb (as a magic spell of sorts) was thought to effect what it stated.

[74] "È fatale pagare le stesse cose" (Cassio 1991–1993:190).

[75] A photograph can be found in Friis Johansen 1923, pl. XV no. 5, or at the British Museum website (search its database for 'Tataie').

[76] There is also a clever correspondence between the punishment by blindness and the act of reading, to which sight is instrumental, through which a potential offender is imagined to learn his fate.

the bottom, try to understand it.[77] But, even if he were to do so, it would be too late: he would have broken into the tomb already. Where then is the deterrence? The controversy regarding *CEG* 1.256 no. 459,[78] whether it is a funerary monument or not, is largely irrelevant.[79] Cassio wishes to prove the existence of funerary curses before 400 BC in order to establish a parallel, even if a hundred years later, perhaps because he feels that his argument labors under the weight of excessive exceptionality. To me, of greater significance is that the meaning of what he alleges as a curse is clear: the threat is stated ('may Zeus utterly destroy him'); the condition for its fulfillment is spelled out ('whoever harms this'). All the examples adduced are of similarly lucid logic: *if* A, *then* B; or *whoever* A, *he/to him* B.

In our inscription, this structure is missing. Unless we assume, with Watkins (see above) a missing literary context that would supplement it with otherwise missing material, according to Cassio we only have the 'B' part: 'it remains to repay the same'. Not only is the 'A' part missing that would specify the identity of the target (e.g. 'whoever robs this tomb'); the 'B' part is impersonal! Not even 'there remains *for you* to repay the same,' resorting for concision to an indefinite 'you.' The indeterminate nature of the *hisa* exacerbates the opaqueness. Laboring already under the weight of mystifying compression, why not state at least the crime? 'It remains [for you] to repay the same for your trespass [into this tomb]'; or 'it is fated [for you] to repay the same for your robbery.' Not so. Add to the lack of a specific target ('you,' 'whoever robs,' *vel sim.*) the lack of a specific crime and a specific punishment. The passage from Aiskhylos' *Suppliants*, which Cassio (1991–1993:191) calls upon to support his argument, is actually detrimental to it. For in lines 434–436 the chorus tells Pelasgos: 'For know [well]: whichever [course] you bring to pass is left to your children and your household, to repay [...] a like justice (penalty?) [for it]'.[80] Regardless of

---

[77] Realizing the utter implausibility of this scenario, Bartoněk and Buchner (1995:202–203) refer the inscription to the sorrow of the father of the deceased child probably interred with the *lēkythos*: "'[D]as Schicksal hat es gewollt, daß du [der Schreiber] das Gleiche erleiden mußt' (wie etwa ein Freund von ihm, oder sein Vater, auf den Tod eines Bruders des Schreibers bezogen?)—oder völlig und ganz allgemein: 'man muß dasselbe als Buße leisten" (203). The proposal stands indicted by these elaborate supplements: the alleged meaning must be read into words that, on this hypothesis, are downright cryptic. Why the child's death should be the father's penance is also baffling. Is this a consolatory message? That a child was probably interred with the *lēkythos* follows from the regular practice of cremation for adults (Buchner, *apud* Cassio 1991–1993:187n2).

[78] With *addenda* in *CEG* 2.304.

[79] Cassio 1991–1993:193.

[80] ἴσθι γάρ· παισὶ τάδε καὶ δόμοις, | ὁπότερ' ἂν κτίσηις, μένει †δρεικ†τίνειν | ὁμοίαν θέμιν (434–436). Scholars are divided whether to read τάδε as the subject of μένει and antecedent of ὁπότερα, with τίνειν ὁμοίαν θέμιν epexegetical to τάδε (and an implicit τῶνδε that depends on θέμιν). So Haupt 1829: "scito, filios tuos domumque tuam, utrumcunque decreveris, manet hoc, ut Marti luant similem poenam" (144; cf. Sandin 2005:199 and Friis Johansen and Whittle 1980:2.338–339).

how one construes the grammar, the target of the implicit threat is clear ('to your children and household') and the content of the threat, well defined ('to repay whichever thing you bring to pass'). Even if μένει is taken impersonally, the statement does not suffer from the opacity of Cassio's reading. Aiskhylos *Agamemnōn* 1563–1564 leads to the same result. With Zeus on the throne standing for the permanence of his cosmic order, we read: μίμνει δὲ μίμνοντος ἐν θρόνῳ Διὸς | παθεῖν τὸν ἔρξαντα· θέσμιον γάρ. Here the infinitive clause ('that the doer [must] suffer') is the subject of μίμνει. The parallel between Zeus remaining on the throne and the principle of justice remaining (as law) on the throne ('for it is settled', θέσμιον γάρ) makes the construction with μίμνειν readily intelligible. Not so in the case of the *lēkythos*: 'to repay the same remains'. Can the inconspicuous writing on the bottom of a *lēkythos* deposited in a tomb be plausibly credited with such an oracular pronouncement?

5.2 Nestor's Cup (*CEG* no. 454)

The purpose of this section is to probe further the notion of a definitive Euboian textual phase during the geometric and early archaic periods. In an excellent article,[81] Cassio seeks to answer the most urgent question that the famous Ischian cup poses for the Homerist: what is the relationship between the inscribed verses and the Homeric epic tradition in circulation towards the late eighth century BC? For ease of reference, I print here the text of the inscription after *CEG* 1.252–253 no. 454, with the substitution of ε[μ]ι for Hansen's ε[ἰμ]ι (on which see footnote 84 below):[82]

> Νέστορός : ε[μ]ι : εὔποτ[ον] : ποτέριον. |
> hὸς δ᾽ ἂν τōδε πίεσι : ποτερί[ο] : αὐτίκα κ̄ενον |
> hίμερος hαιρέσει : καλλιστε[φά]νο : Ἀφροδίτες

Naming a 'Nestor' in close connection with a cup invites *us* to think of Λ 632–637, the celebrated description of Gerenian Nestor's δέπας περικαλλές. But did it

---

Others, with Wecklein (1902:65), take τάδε as the object of τίνειν (in the sense of 'to pay for'). I prefer (and have translated) the former, since τίνειν θέμιν seems to stand for τίνειν δίκην and would call for the gen. of what one repays ('whichever you do, it awaits your children and household to pay the penalty for it'). If ὁμοίαν θέμιν were not present, τάδε could indeed be the direct object of τίνειν (τίνειν τάδε = 'to pay for this'). A third alternative, by Paley (1851:39), is to take ὁπότερα adverbially and include τάδε within its clause (the μένει would be impersonal): "whether you do this [or not], it awaits your children and household to repay a like justice."

[81] Cassio 1994. The bibliography on the cup is voluminous. For items up to 1991, see Powell 1991:163n110 and O. Vox's bibliography in Buchner and Ridgway 1993:751–758. To them, add S. West 1994b and the important contribution by Pavese 1996.

[82] For a translation, see the discussion below.

elicit similar associations in the mind of the late eighth-century symposiast who drank from it? S. West (1994b:14) can help us to set the stage of this review. She notes that "ποτήριον and καλλιστέφανος are not to be found in the Iliad and Odyssey; the convenient-looking phrases αὐτίκα κεῖνον and ἵμερος αἱρήσει do not figure in the Homeric stock formulae."[83] She therefore assigns their pedigree to an otherwise unattested Pylian saga, a poetic tradition less sophisticated than the Iliadic that celebrated the exploits of Nestor's youth. Whether the language on the *skyphos* can be shown to reflect the attested Homeric poems is of great potential significance. If on balance it points elsewhere, this fact would make the alleged Euboian phase of Homeric poetry even less plausible than it already appears. For is it likely that, if something like our *Iliad* was in circulation in late eighth-century Euboia—that, if in fact the performance of this poetic tradition on Euboia was flourishing so vibrantly as to place a definitive and normative Euboian stamp on its language—the earliest attested inscription that arguably refers to a well-known Iliadic hero would fail to echo the formulaic language of the *Iliad*? Even if we conclude that the Nestor on the cup cannot refer to Gerenian Nestor, if on balance the diction of the inscription is shown to be independent from the Homeric tradition as we know it, we must also conclude that this tradition did not serve as the model for the cup, or else that it did under a shape rather different from the one ultimately preserved in writing. But, if it did not serve as its model, unless we posit an unlikely symposiast of unique ability who composed the verses *de novo*, with S. West we must assume the existence of another, similarly vigorous poetic tradition that incorporated a figure by the name Nestor and inspired the poet of the *skyphos*. The alternatives are stark for the proponents of the Euboian phase. If the Homeric tradition was not known in Pithekoussai or was known in a substantially different form from the one preserved by the vulgate, this would render the alleged Euboian phase untenable. In particular, one could not argue that dictated scripts of Euboian performances might be responsible for the written texts of the Homeric poems. But if the Homeric tradition *was* known substantially as we know it and simply failed to be the model of the *skyphos* poet, we would have to accept the coexistence of two vigorous, formulaically disjoint hexametric oral traditions that shared a named figure and, incredibly, a possession peculiar to this figure; and we would have to embrace the corollary of the near complete disappearance from the record of the tradition represented by the *skyphos*. If in fact the verses on Nestor's cup point away from the Homeric diction in *our* texts, I submit that it is far more likely that a 'Homeric' tradition was known in Pithekoussai, but one in

---

[83] Cf. Powell 1991:166n120.

diction and themes different from our own, and yet, as the cup attests, one that included elements (the hero and his cup) still familiar to us from the vulgate.

To advance my own conclusions: Nestor's cup stands in a long line of 'I am' inscriptions that are implicitly performative.[84] They betoken a culture whose 'literature' lived in public and semi-public performance, not in written texts disseminated within circles of readers. On balance, the diction of the cup proves independent from the language of our Homeric poems. Because I do not think composition *de novo* plausible, I believe that the traditions of performance underlying the verses prove that Euboian poetry susceptible of inclusion under the label 'Homeric' was substantially different from the one eventually written down and preserved in our vulgate texts. It is ultimately not of much consequence whether we posit the currency of a Pylian strand of which only echoes survive in the grand Panhellenic tradition. The label 'Homeric' applied to late eighth-century epic traditions circulating in Euboia should be capacious enough to draw into its sphere related stories only obliquely reflected by the final canonical form of the poems. Whether we can, or should, use that label at all becomes largely a question of semantics. What matters is the understanding that we are dealing with a formative period, during which the formulaic diction and the narrative repertory must have been in significant flux. Were we today privy to its contents, we might well recognize some elements and be surprised by others. If something like Λ 632–637 stands behind the verses on the *skyphos*, we must read them ironically. The cup is a humble vase, far from the literary description in type and worth. My guess is that the owner was himself named Nestor. This gave place to the irony and accounts for the resumption of τόδε: 'I [too] am Nestor's cup—[but] one that is good to drink from. Whoever drinks from *this* cup, straightway desire instilled by beautifully garlanded Aphrodite will seize him'. The reason for the τόδε is the implicit contrast established by the irony of the first line. It is as if the cup were boasting, 'I too have Nestor as owner!' Adding, 'I am not the massive four-handled cup, but one that is good to drink from. And whoever drinks from *this* cup will not be refreshed for war,

---

[84] Cf. Nagy 1996b:35–36, who cites Svenbro 1993:26–43. See, further, Pavese 1996:4. From close inspection of the letter sizes on a photograph I became convinced that the correct supplement for the first lacuna is simply ε̄[μ]ι. There was no need to assume the dialectally inappropriate ειμι (Pavese 1996:7–8) or the unidiomatic εστι. I was gratified to learn that Pavese (1996:7) had confirmed by autopsy that the spacing suits a lone μ. The 3rd sg. εστι departs from the sole form attested early, the 1st sg. (of which there is, comparatively speaking, what Hansen 1976:30 justifiably calls a "massive array" of instances). Although it fits the lacuna, it should be rejected, *pace* Watkins 1976:38–39. (Cf. Bartoněk and Buchner 1995:150–151.) Once it is epigraphically unnecessary, the only argument in its favor is the supposed difficulty posed by τόδε as a resumption of ε̄μι. But this difficulty is largely specious. More on this below. The phonetic figure noted by Watkins 1976:39n21 adds support for εστι but cannot outweigh the array of first-singular parallels.

but inflamed with desire.' Had the contrast been drawn explicitly, e.g. with 'too' ('I *too* am Nestor's cup'), a personal pronoun (μου or ἐμοῦ) would have sufficed. With the contrast ironically implicit, the deictic τόδε, which (as many have recognized) serves to mark a contrast, becomes necessary. This motivates what is otherwise an exceptional switch from first to third person.[85] If my reading is right, the switch is only apparent, for the cup continues to speak; only, it refers to itself by an act of verbal pointing.[86]

What follows here is a summary of the findings in Cassio 1994. He argues the case well, although he reaches what I think is the wrong conclusion: that there is no proof that Nestor's cup respects an epic tradition other than the Homeric (65). I could embrace this statement if, by Homeric, Cassio meant a very fluid 'Homeric' tradition that could be thought of as rather different from the ultimately received. But item (b) of his conclusion points in another direction. There he notes that the adjective καλλιστέφανος bespeaks the end, not the beginning, of the epic tradition ("the world of the *Odyssey* and the *Hymns*," 65). This suggests a fixed text of poems that are by and large recognizably the same as our own. Item (c), on the other hand, points away from his first one: the verse-end use of κεῖνος is not Homeric. Cassio realizes that items (a) and (c) are at odds: "Se ci troviamo alla fine della tradizione epica l'autore degli esametri della Coppa deve avere già conosciuto ampiamente un Omero in cui ἐκεῖνος si trovava in fine di esametro ed in *enjambment*" (65). But there is no evidence, only the scholar's wish, for such a 'Homer.' On the contrary, as my review of Cassio's article will presently show, the inscribed hexameters diverge markedly from the attested Homeric idiom in ways more than one. What, then, is to be made of the assertion that the *skyphos* respects no poetic tradition other than the Homeric? The implications of Cassio's concluding item (c), hardly inconsequential for a proper estimation of the late eighth-century shape of the 'Homeric' epic tradition generally, are even starker for the theory of a definite geometric and early-archaic Euboian textual phase: "Se la redazione finale o dei poemi omerici, o della sola *Odissea*, si deve ad aedi euboici, perché sulla Coppa non troviamo ἐκεῖνον? Inoltre, come si è visto, l'uso di δ' ἀν nella Coppa ... si allontana in maniera vistosa dall'uso omerico e in particolare de quello dell'*Odissea*" (65).

---

[85] For the few parallels, all much later and none especially close, see Pavese 1996:16.

[86] Pavese's opposition to inferring from the verses a contrast between two cups is aimed at the view that the first line refers to Nestor's Iliadic δέπας, whereas the τόδε of verse 2 points to the Ischian *skyphos*. He believes that this contrast, otherwise improbable, is only tenable if one supplements εστι (Pavese 1996:16). While I share his rejection of this view (and of εστι), I believe that the contrast presented above is textually justified and makes good interpretive sense.

5.2.1 δ' ἄν versus δέ κε

Cassio does not focus on the non-Homeric εὔποτον or ποτήριον.[87] Instead, he addresses himself to three points that are better able to establish dependence on, or divergence from, the attested Homeric diction: the use of ὃς δ' ἄν; the verse-final κἕνον in enjambment; and the noun-epithet καλλιστεφάνō Ἀφροδίτες. Let us take them up in turn. Since it is followed by a word that starts with a consonant, ὃς δ' ἄν scans – –. As Cassio notes, relative clauses that start – δ' ἄν V- (– ⌣ ⌣) can be replaced without consequence by – δέ κ' V- (– ⌣ ⌣); those that start – δ' ἄν C- (– –) can be replaced by – δέ κε C- (– ⌣ ⌣). In principle, proponents of the evolutionary model have no problem accepting any one Homeric instance of δ' ἄν as authentic. But Cassio is right that, as a rhetorical matter, to convince the skeptic that ὃς δ' ἄν on the *skyphos* conforms to late eighth-century Homeric poems substantially like our own, one would have to find in our vulgate parallel instances of this construction that cannot be trivially changed to ὃς δέ κ(εν). Otherwise, a skeptic could always question the antiquity of the adduced parallel and doubt its relevance. An examination of the poems does not support dependence. Constructions resembling the syntax of the inscription are instanced only four times: ὃν δ' ἄν (Θ 10 Ο 348), ὅσσοι δ' ἄν (Τ 230), and ὃς δ' ἄν (τ 332). All except Τ 230 can be trivially rewritten with κε(ν).[88] We simply do not find the equivalent of ὃς δ' ἄν C-. This contrasts with eleven instances of ὃς δέ κε C- or its equivalent.[89] Sharper still is the numerical contrast between δέ κε C- and δ' ἄν C-, irrespective of syntactic construction, wherever δέ κε and δ' ἄν stand in arsis. There are eight instances of the latter if we allow for οὐδ' ἄν, and three if we do not.[90] The *Odyssey* presents a single instance (of οὐδ' ἄν) against twenty-four of δέ κε. As Cassio observes, the Homeric text often offers δέ κε C- where there would be no prosodic impediment to the Ionic δ' ἄν C-. The cup's inscription, however, follows the Euboian dialect and conspicuously diverges from Homeric usage. This severely undercuts the theory that Euboia was the setting in which the Homeric texts attained their definitive and normative shape, and renders extremely implausible the view that the *Odyssey* "might well be a Euboean poem."[91]

---

[87] The closest parallel to εὔποτος is the epithet for wine ἡδύποτος (e.g. β 340; cf. Dubois 1996:71–72 no. 29). If we assume that an *Iliad* substantially like our own circulated at the time in Euboia, by choosing ποτήριον over δέπας the inscriber neglected a ready means of making clear at the level of diction his reference to the poem.

[88] They are of the form – δ' ἄν V- (– ⌣ ⌣), which can be rewritten – δέ κ' V- (– ⌣ ⌣).

[89] ὁππότερος δέ κε (Γ 71 92 σ 46), τῷ δέ κε (Γ 138 255), ὃς δέ κε (Ρ 229 Ψ 322 857 τ 577 φ 75), ᾧ δέ κε (Ω 531).

[90] These are enumerated in Cassio 1994:57n14, which I have independently checked for accuracy.

[91] West 1988:172. Contrast Pavese 1996:15.

5.2.2 κεῖνος versus ἐκεῖνος

An even greater obstacle to this theory is posed by the use of verse-end κεῖνον in enjambment. Homeric usage is clear: ἐκεῖνος appears at the end of the verse; κεῖνος, elsewhere.[92] In the *Iliad*, verse-end ἐκεῖνος occurs at I 63 646 Λ 653 Σ 188; of these, the first and third are irreducible to κεῖνος. The irreducible cases in the *Odyssey* are twelve.[93] Reciprocally, all κεῖνος at verse-end are reducible to ἐκεῖνος except ἤματι κείνῳ (Β 37 482 Δ 543 Σ 324 Φ 517), οὐδέ τι κείνη (ν 111), and εἵματι κείνου (ξ 501).[94] Because irreducible ἐκεῖνος is often found in enjambment (twice in the *Iliad* and five times in the *Odyssey*), Cassio (1994:59–60) speculates that its preferential adoption for verse-end position and the use of enjambment were related phenomena that entered Homeric diction at a relatively recent date. Hence, if Nestor's cup reflected Homeric diction, we would expect αὐτίκ' ἐκεῖνον.[95] As Cassio (1994:60) remarks, "[il redattore del testo della Coppa] ha usato invece κένον, in fine di esametro ed in *enjambment*, allontanandosi quindi in maniera netta dall'*usus* omerico." This distance is all the more conspicuous if, as Peters (1998:596) thinks, the West Ionic deictic was ἐκεῖνος and not κεῖνος.[96]

---

[92] La Roche 1866:247–250. For exceptions and statistics see below.

[93] β 183 γ 103 113 δ 819 ξ 163 352 ο 330 σ 147 τ 322 ω 288 312 437. Add to these the reducible but probative ο 368; and the verse-final ὄφρ' ἂν ἐκεῖθι at ρ 10, reducible to ὄφρα κε κεῖθι (cf. β 124). In a 'probative' instance one form cannot be turned into the other without changing the transmitted text, i.e. merely by moving the word boundary (e.g. ἐκτήσατο κεῖνος is probative because the alternative word division ἐκτήσατ' ˣὀκεῖνος is not possible). In a 'reducible' instance one form can be turned into the other either by moving the word boundary or by combining a new word boundary with an alternative word end (e.g. τεύχε' ἐκεῖνοι is reducible to τεύχεα κεῖνοι).

[94] Reducible verse-end κεῖνος occurs at α 212 ρ 112 (non-probative) υ 265 (probative). The latter two read ἐκεῖνος in the Laurentianus 32.24.

[95] For the elision of αὐτίκα in this *sedes*, see e.g. κ 237.

[96] "[D]as Pronomen mit der 'jener'-Deixis hat im Westion. m.E. gegen den ersten unserer Inschrift verdankten Anschein doch geradeso wie im Att. und in Homers persönlichem Dialekt ἐκεῖνος und nicht κεῖνος gelautet" (596). In 596n35 he cites with approval Bechtel 1963:3.168: "Soweit die Steine beweiskräftig sind, sagen sie aus, daß in den chalkidischen Städten ἐκεῖνος, in Kleinasien κεῖνος die Form der täglichen Rede war." But Bechtel had no evidence for ἐκεῖνος other than a *defixio* from Cumae on a lead plaque, for which see Dubois 1995:54–57 no. 20 and the photograph in Landi 1979 pl. X (also *SGDI* 5270 with the addendum in vol. 4.889–890). Dubois dates it to the beginning of the fifth century; Landi 1979:231 no. 22 to the fifth century without further specification; both Jeffery 1990:240 no. 16 (tentatively) and Arena 1989:18 no. 21 to 450–425, before the Samnite conquest; and Schwyzer 1987:792a to the fourth century. Thus, by common consent this instance is rather late (certainly, much later than the Ischian *skyphos*). It only proves that ἐκεῖνος was in use at Cumae during the classical period (how broadly, one cannot say without further evidence). Del Barrio Vega (1987:407 §3.34b) supposed that the verses on Nestor's cup were colored by Homeric diction and that κεῖνος was probably not Euboic but Ionic. This cannot be sustained in view of the cup's glaring departures from Homeric diction. (Alternatively, she suggested the utterly improbable aphaeresis αυτικα 'κένον.) After noting that the *defixio* from Cumae *might* be proof that Euboic shared ἐκει- forms with Attic, she prudently declined to assert this ("la falta de más datos nos impide afirmarlo"). Given that Nestor's cup conspicuously departs

Peters tries to turn the cup's use of κὲνον, arguably a high hurdle for the Euboian phase, to this theory's advantage. Because he believes in a monumental poet who hailed from Oropos,[97] he thinks that instances of ἐκεῖνος in the poems reflect Homer's own dialect and are not traditional (not formulaic).[98] From this premise, he infers that the cup's verse-end κεῖνος is precisely what we should expect if the inscriber was aiming at the high register of traditional language, and that he is therefore following ur-Homeric usage—i.e. his poetry is dependent on proto-Homeric diction. Hence, the *skyphos* would not militate against the alleged Euboian phase but show engagement with the proto-Homeric tradition at the place and time Peters imagines the monumental poet composing his definitive version of the tradition. Now, aside from the doubtful contention that ἐκεῖνος is the proper Euboic form, this argument depends on the unprovable claim of an 'archaizing' intent that assays for the high register of what passed for

from the diction of our Homeric poems, one should rather infer that κεῖνος was the form current in early Euboic, just as it was in early Ionic. ἐκει- forms must have been innovated in Euboic, Ionic, and Attic at a later time, perhaps independently. Not only is independent innovation conceivable because the beginning ἐ- was an old inherited deictic particle (Frisk 1973–1979 and Beekes 2010 s.v. ἐκεῖ) and the expressive accumulation of the two particles ἐ-κε- was a natural development; it is also commended by the apparently unrelated appearance of ἐκει- forms in such distant locations as Cumae and Olbia (under which I include Berezan). The instances from Olbia are: ἐκεῖ, in Dubois 1996:146–153 no. 93, dated to 550–525 (*SEG* 36.694, to 525–500); and ἐκεῖνοι, in Dana 2004:6, line 7 (*SEG* 54.694, "late 6th century" after Dana 2004:4; Jeffery 1990:479 no. N, "*c.* 500?"). [Santiago Álvarez and Gardeñes Santiago (2006:60) suggest ἀποδ]ώσε̄· κὲνοι; but however attractive its meaning, this assumes that the first O in]ΟΣΕΚΕΝΟΙ stood for ω, which seems unlikely given that in that same line ἀποδώ | [σε̄ν] is spelled correctly with Ω.] For Attica, the first attested uses of ἐκει- are: κἀκένοι in *CEG* 1.43 no. 70, "*ca. vel post* 500?" (=IG I³ 1231; cf. *CEG* 1.142–143 no. 268 and 1.168–169 no. 313, both with *addenda* in *CEG* 2.302); and ἐκεῖ, IG I³ 6B.33–34, "*ante a.* 460." (Cf. Threatte 1996:328 §62.01b.) There is no reason why ἐκει- forms could not have been in use long before. For Thumb and Scherer 1959:276 §312.13c, "die [ionischen] Belege für ἐκεῖνος sind kaum beweiskräftig" (citing specifically the ἐκε̄νο̄ν from Cumae). With help from Dettori 1996:306–308, Peters 1998:596n35 attributes the use of ἐκει- in Olbia to Attic influence. But Dettori's prooftexts (Dubois 1996:154–155 no. 94 and 160–164 no. 99), *pace* Vinogradov (1997:34), are of doubtful significance for the Ionic dialect of Olbia (Dettori 1996:308 and nn. 62, 65; cf. Bravo 2007:79), for all that they prove the growing presence of Attic speakers in the region; whereas the Olbian texts with ἐκει- exhibit many good Ionic forms and no trace of Attic influence other than the offending ἐκει-. (For the Ionic pedigree of forms like ὁπό[σα see Cassio 1998:16 and Ruijgh 1995:15–16.) For a general survey of ἐκει- versus κει- in Ionic, cf. Smyth 1894:207 §224.15 and 447–449 §564. I must emphasize that even if ἐκεῖνος was a genuine Ionic form (though late and secondary to κεῖνος), Homeric diction must have adopted it after the seventh century, during the definitive period of Athenian transmission (cf. Nagy 1996b:42 and Nagy 2001). For that reason, *ceteris paribus*, Homeric ἐκει- forms, which by then were dominant in Athens, must be considered Atticisms.

97 Peters 1986:319n49 and Peters 1987. Trained as an oral poet in East Ionic epic and familiar with the independent tradition of Boiotian epic, he would have introduced into his compositions forms culled from his own Euboic dialect and the diction of Boiotian epic. According to Peters, the poems were drafted in writing.

98 "[E]ine erst von Homer selbst in die ep. Diktion eingeführte Variante" (596n34).

traditional in late eighth-century Euboia. It also makes the author of the cup's verses at best a parallel conduit of the epic tradition that flowed through Homer into the *Iliad* and the *Odyssey*. If defamiliarizing for the sake of literary effect was the aim of the inscriber, why use the (for Peters) lower-register δ' ἄν? Should we not expect δέ κε?[99] Why not, too, the more traditional ἐυστέφανος? Against Peters's clever argument one can also lay the charge that it is ultimately unfalsifiable: the cup does not follow Homer's dialect, but it is alleged to follow pre-Homeric diction; hence it is not un-Homeric but simply non-Homeric! I would find this reasoning more persuasive if the poems exhibited a greater number of reducible and irreducible verse-end κεῖνος. Is it plausible that Homer's personal (and 'untraditional') dialect could have displaced in all but one case (υ 265) every reducible instance of verse-end κεῖνος?[100] Moreover, if formulas predating Homer instanced κεῖνος both at verse-end[101] and elsewhere, why should Homer have shown such a marked preference for injecting his personal dialect at verse-end?[102] Could he not just as well have innovated with ἐκεῖνος in other *sedes*? In

---

99 Cf. Peters 1998:597n38.

100 All probative verse-final ἐκεῖνος are irreducible save: τεύχε' ἐκεῖνοι (Σ 188), where no manuscript supports τεύχεα κεῖνοι; εἵματ' ἐκείνη (ο 368), where only the long-vanished manuscript of Vespasiano Gonzaga, of unknown date (cf. Allen 1910:5–6), supports εἵματα κείνη; and ἐκτήσατο κεῖνος (υ 265), where the *paradosis* favors κεῖνος but the tenth-century Laurent. 32.24 prints ἐκεῖνος. Instances like οππότεκεινων (Ι 646) are of no probative value, since the aural shape of the verse is identical whatever the assignment of the boundary epsilon. Hence the lack of documentary support for verse-final κεῖνος when the preceding word ends in -α (τεύχεα and εἵματα), since elision actually makes an aural difference. Whereas, whenever it does not, word boundary is a largely indifferent graphic choice as far as the *paradosis* is concerned. We therefore expect the witness of manuscripts that actually mark word boundaries to diverge in indifferent cases, since the choice, if motivated, must follow criteria that performance alone cannot establish. Such are: ὁππότ' ἐκείνων (Ι 646), where there is manuscript support for ὁππότε κείνων (West and Allen print κείνων, van Thiel ἐκείνων); and ἐμὲ κεῖνος (α 212 ρ 112). In sum, υ 265 emerges as the *only* line in the two poems in which the manuscripts support a reducible κεῖνος at verse-end that actually makes an aural difference in performance.

101 At least the irreducible occurrences ἤματι κείνῳ are assumed by Cassio (1994:59) to be traditional.

102 The following other-than-verse-final ἐκεῖνος are not probative because the preceding word ends in epsilon: Η 77 Ξ 250 Ο 148 Ω 90 β 124 δ 731 κ 397 414 λ 390 418 615 ο 346 ρ 110 521 ψ 76 ω 90 313. In these *loci* ἐκεῖνος, if attested at all, is utterly marginal save at Ξ 250, where it is weakly supported, and at δ 731 ρ 110, where it has strong support and van Thiel prints it. Thus, there are only two arguable exceptions among them to the rule of verse-end ἐκεῖνος (about these, see the end of this footnote). Probative exceptions divide into two groups. The first consists of eleven instances for which the manuscripts decisively support κει- forms. They are: Ε 604 δ 152 739 ξ 42 70 122 153 283 π 376 ρ 243 φ 201. The second consists of eight instances for which the manuscripts decisively support ἐκει- forms. They may be subdivided into four patterns: | καὶ γὰρ ἐκείνῳ (β 171; but cf. ξ 70); μετ' ἐκεῖνον (π 151); Ἶρος ἐκεῖνος (σ 239); and | οἷος ἐκειν- (Ο 94 Σ 262 β 272 ξ 491 ο 212). The latter five instances deserve special mention. Three correspond to the repeated unit | οἷος ἐκείνου θυμὸς (Ο 94 Σ 262 ο 212); two, to | οἷος ἐκεῖνος ἔην (β 272 ξ 491). I believe that two factors encouraged their emergence: first, the probably preexisting verse-final οἷος ἐκεῖνος | (Λ 653); second, the pattern | οἷος Ὀδυσσεὺς … (β 59 δ 689 ρ 538 τ 315 φ 94), which will have

sum, Peters is open to the same criticism Cassio (1994:62n48) directs against Dihle for claiming that, although καλλιστέφανος is absent from Homer, it is attested "in der archaischen und archaisierenden, an das Epos anknüpfenden Dichtung": "Adottando questo criterio qualsiasi innovazione degli *Inni* rispetto a Omero può ricevere una patente di grande antichità, e possiamo senza problemi costruirci un *altepischer Sprachschatz* di nostro gradimento."

5.2.3 καλλιστεφανο Αφροδιτες

Cassio (1994:60–64) also probes the expression καλλιστεφανο Αφροδιτες from the point of view of Homeric formulaic diction. From his analysis he concludes that it is a development that presupposes the existence of ἐυστέφανος Κυθέρεια (63). Hence, he believes that it points to the chronological endpoint of the development of epic diction which dates the *Iliad* to a time before the inscribing of the cup: "A mio parere quindi ... è del tutto improbabile ipotizzare per καλλιστεφάνō Ἀφροδίτες un antecedente che non sia quello omerico" (63). I cannot embrace

---

fostered (and have been fostered by) the substitution ἐκει- ~ Ὀδυσ- in β 272 ξ 491. This expression will have been modified and extended to the other cases. Peters's hypothesis of a Homer whose composition at verse-end was more inattentive than at verse-opening (1998:598n39) clashes with the well-known fact that the inherited prosody of IE isosyllabic meters—whence the hexameter descends by expansion and substitution—featured greater metrical freedom at the opening of the verse than at its closing (Nagy 1974:34–36; cf. Miller 1990:172 no. 4 and 174 no. 7). Thus, extreme metrical regularity is a sign of relatively late composition. Viewed synchronically, to enhance compositional flexibility in the face of metrical preferences and requirements, performers innovated within carefully calibrated parameters of traditionality. In the present case, a marked preference for a dactylic fifth foot was best accommodated by the innovative ἐκεῖνος. Whereas verse-end κεῖνος allows for a dactyl only when the preceding syllable is short + open, ἐκεῖνος not only accommodates most short + open syllables (unless they feature an iota, which cannot be elided) but also short + closed syllables (long + open, permitted under epic correption, do not occur). Hence the strong tendency to place ἐκει- forms at verse-end vis-à-vis their marginal appearance elsewhere. The numbers are as follows. Of 27 verse-final instances of κει-/ἐκει-, 7 feature irreducible κεῖνος after iota; 17 ἐκεῖνος (1 non-probative, 14 probative and irreducible, 2 probative and reducible); and 3 κεῖνος (2 non-probative, 1 probative and reducible). Of 169 other-than-verse-final occurrences, 10 feature ἐκεῖνος, two non-probative, the rest probative and reducible. Excluding the older, irreducible verse-end κεῖνος after iota, innovative ἐκεῖνος occurs 85% of the time at verse-end (94%, if we only count probative cases). Reciprocally, it occurs 6% of the time when other-than-verse-end. The well-known exchange in phraseology between the Adonic sequence and the metrical space between the end of the first foot and the trochaic caesura (Householder and Nagy 1972:50)—and, secondarily, between the opening of the verse and the second trochee when Meyer's law is not breached—accounts for the ἐκεῖνος that are not verse-final: -δεμεκεινος (ρ 110) ~ -σεμεκεινος | (ρ 112), cf. α 212; δ 731 ~ I 646; and O 94 etc. ~ Λ 653. Even if performer and audience notionally felt the breaks as the vulgate prints them—there is no telling aurally whether ὁππότε was elided or not—δ 731 does not breach Meyer's law because of the heavy counterbalancing effect of the strong third- and fourth-foot caesuras. The same is true of β 272. As to ξ 491, with a masculine caesura and a bucolic diaeresis, it too avoids the offense of a subsequent trochaic caesura. (Cf. Kirk 1985:23–24.)

his conclusion, which is reached through a chain of doubtful links. Cassio is probably right that -στεφαν- in the sense of 'crown' presupposes the orientalizing period, when the use of the crown in real life spread and became established (62). Perhaps it is also true that the application of εὐστέφανος to goddesses hints at a growing familiarity with statues adorned with crowns or *poloi* (63). The alternation ἐυ- and καλλι- is in evidence in our poems.[103] But this does not establish that καλλιστεφανο Αφροδιτες is derived from, and therefore presupposes, the familiar diction of the *Iliad* and the *Odyssey*. The question to answer is whether καλλιστέφανος or εὐστέφανος is older, if in fact one predates the other and this fact can be ascertained; and, if a priority in time is plausibly established, what rationale suggests that the younger form was actually derived from the older. The poems do not exhibit these adjectives in a suppletive paradigm of formulaic economy, though well they would have, had either of them been long enough in use as an epithet, given their complementary metrical shapes (‒ ‒ ⏑ ⏑ ‒ and ⏑ ‒ ⏑ ⏑ ‒ respectively). εὐστέφανος is used once of Artemis (Φ 511), once of Thebes (T 99), once of the heroine Mykene (β 120, with *v.l.* ἐυπλόκαμος), and three times of Aphrodite (θ 267 288 σ 193). When this goddess is in view, the diction is ἐυστεφάνου τ' Ἀφροδίτης (θ 267), ἐϋστεφάνου Κυθερείης (θ 288), and ἐϋστέφανος Κυθέρεια (σ 193). The latter two are the only cases of Κυθέρεια in the Homeric poems. If we include the hymns and Hesiod, there are nine other instances of it (five in the hymns and four in the *Theogony*). Four of the five epithets of Κυθέρεια in the hymns are εὐστέφανος (twice with the *v.l.* ἰοστέφανος).[104] In the *Theogony* it is accompanied by an epithet twice, and both times it is ἐυστέφανος. The outcome of this survey is that Κυθέρεια takes the epithet ἐυστέφανος in eight of its nine surviving instances. Whereas this appellation is rare in the poems (it appears only twice), Ἀφροδίτη is used forty-two times,[105] and its epithets, other than the sole occurrence of ἐυστέφανος, are δῖα, Διὸς θυγάτηρ/κούρη, φιλομμειδής, and χρυσέη/χρυσείη. All are used more than once except for the single instance of κούρη (Υ 105), an uneconomical spondaic equivalent of the more common θυγάτηρ. Hence, ἐυστέφανος as a divine epithet with the meaning 'well-crowned' (*vel sim.*) cannot have entered the diction of the poems long before the time when the Ischian *skyphos* was inscribed. In the case of Aphrodite, it was preferentially paired with the appellation Κυθέρεια.[106] And καλλιστέφανος appears only twice in archaic epic, namely, in the *Hymn*

---

[103] See Risch 1974:183–184 §68b and Risch 1987:9.

[104] The fifth is Κυπρογενῆ (*Homeric Hymn* 10.1).

[105] Every single time but two at verse-end.

[106] The preference of -στέφανος epithets for Κυθέρεια over Ἀφροδίτης, only marginally noticeable in the *Odyssey*, is clear when we take Hesiod and the Homeric hymns into account: of eleven occurrences, eight correspond to ἐϋστέφανος + Κυθέρεια; the remainder comprise one each of Ἀφροδίτης with ἐϋστέφανος, φιλοστέφανος, and χρυσοστέφανος.

to Demeter. It is true that in Nestor's cup ἐυστεφάνō could not have been used instead of καλλιστέφανō. One might therefore argue that the latter represents the necessary formulaic modification of the former. But if the practice attested by our Homeric poems had served as a model, we would never have expected that a verse ending with Ἀφροδίτ- | should call for an epithet with the metrical shape − − ⌣ ⌣ −: all her epithets in the *Iliad* and the *Odyssey* are of the shapes ⌣ − ⌣ ⌣ − or ⌣ − − − (or subsets thereof like − − and −);[107] none are shaped − − ⌣ ⌣ −. Neither is the hiatus -στεφανο Αφρο- necessary,[108] and Homeric usage would have commended the alternative Κυθερείης, which is also a perfectly acceptable Euboic form.[109] To meet with these two departures from the Homeric versification attested by the extant poems at the very time when the corresponding formulaic canons were allegedly being established undermines Cassio's conclusion that the cup is in fact dependent on the predating diction of the poems. *If* we had found at least one or two occurrences in the Homeric poems of καλλιστέφανός τ' Ἀφροδίτη (*vel sim.*), it might be reasonable to conclude i) that it was a formulaic innovation developed to supplement the metrical shape of the more common epithets; and ii) that it postdated, and probably presupposed, the more numerous

---

[107] χρυσείη does not appear with verse-end Ἀφροδίτης or Κυθέρεια (cf. I 389).

[108] Note that there is no epic correption and that the genitive ending -ου, by contraction of -οο < -οιο, was a monophthong (cf. Sihler 1995:259 §259.8). In the *Iliad* and *Odyssey* the only hiatus that I can find is χρυσῆ Ἀφροδίτη | at X 470 (cf. *Homeric Hymn* 5.93). Of course, χρυσῆ Ἀφροδίτη, of which there are seven examples, all but one at verse end, do not involve hiatus (cf. Schwyzer *GG* I.399 §2.a.α). All other examples of a comparable hiatus are in Hesiod or the Homeric hymns: φιλοστεφάνου Ἀφροδίτης in *Homeric Hymn* 2.102; χρυσῆ Ἀφροδίτη in *Homeric Hymn* 5.93; πολυχρύσου Ἀφροδίτης in *Homeric Hymn* 5.1, 9 and Hesiod's *Theogony* 980, *Works and Days* 521, *Shield* 8, 47, and frr. 185.17 MW, 195.8, 47 MW, 253.3 MW; and χρυσο[σ]τεφάνου Ἀφροδίτης in Hesiod fr. 26.13 MW.

[109] There was no reversion of η > ᾱ in Euboic. I am puzzled by the motive Cassio (1994:63) gives for the hiatus: "Variazione sicuramente dovuta al desiderio di usare il nome proprio tradizionale della dea e non un suo epiteto, e probabilmente anche favorita dal fatto che l'epiteto di Citerea, più tardi diventato semplicemente esornativo, era ancora fortemente sentito come legato all'isola di Citera." I for one cannot divine whether the author of the cup's verses preferred 'Aphrodite' to 'Κυθέρεια' because he thought the latter a mere epithet that fell short in the use of the satisfaction provided by the traditional name. Such psychological musings seem unsafe ground on which to build one's argument. As to the second reason put forward by Cassio, are we to suppose that Κυθέρεια was rejected because it was not sufficiently Panhellenic? And yet the Odyssean tradition had no problem embracing it. Once again, how are we to explain these diverging sensibilities if the cup reflects the poetic milieu that gave the Homeric poems their definitive shape? (Cassio's comment *ibidem* apropos θ 362 only has force if: i) one accepts the view articulated earlier in the same page that the formulaic starting point for the poet of this passage was "senz'altro ἐυστέφανος Κυθέρεια"; and ii) from this view one concludes that any departure from said formula calls for an explanation narrowly motivated by the context. To me it seems safer and more economical to assume that, where the traditional name was possible, *ceteris paribus* it was likely to be used. At θ 267 it could, and so it was; at θ 288 it could not because of the hiatus, and so Κυθερείης was; neither was Aphrodite allowed at σ 193 because of the meter.)

ἐυστέφανος. But to infer this from the Ischian cup one must assume what Cassio set out to prove: that in fact the diction of the *skyphos* derives from the Homeric poems. As the case stands, the only safe verdict is that the cup decisively departs from Homeric usage, and this judgment deals another blow to the theory of a Euboian definitive phase.[110] And even if we should grant *arguendo* that the *Iliad* and the *Odyssey*, in versions substantially like our own, were in circulation in Pithekoussai and that their language inspired the verses on the vase, we are still left with an impossible obstacle to the Euboian theory. For, if καλλιστέφανος and ἐκεῖνος belong to the end stage of the epic tradition, and Euboia is the alleged home of the last and definitive formative stage of the Homeric poems, why the cup's conspicuous departures from Homeric diction? Reciprocally, why do the poems largely or absolutely fail to instance the formulaic practice allegedly current at the time when and place where their text was definitively shaped? No wonder Cassio (1994:66) concludes: "Non mi sento di offrire una soluzione netta di queste aporie; ma c'è da chiedersi se la tesi euboica, per quanto affascinante, non debba essere in tutto o in parte riconsiderata."

One might well be puzzled by Cassio's conviction that *despite* the many departures he acknowledges in his paper the verses of Nestor's cup *must* presuppose Homeric epic—a presupposition that for him does not involve a fluid tradition of multiforms, but largely fixed texts near identical with our own.[111] Although

---

[110] Hackstein (2010:419) expresses a similar prejudice. Speaking of the Dipylon *oinokhoē* and Nestor's cup, he observes that "[b]oth inscriptions are neither exclusively dependent on nor solely repetitive of Homeric diction. Instead of copying, they are innovative in coining epithets and phrases not found in the *Iliad* and *Odyssey*. Such non-Homeric words and phrases, however, can be shown to be generated by the same generative mechanisms that lie behind the diction of the large scale epics ... ." To speak without proof of innovation against the background of the poems' diction is to take as one's starting point the assumption that these inscriptions are derivative of, and presuppose acquaintance with, our Homeric texts (or a near final stage thereof). Even if this were true it cannot be simply asserted, and Hackstein soon hedges by adding that the inscriptions are "not strictly dependent on Homer and may reflect para-Homeric traditions" (420). Indeed, nothing can be inferred from the bare fact that epic composition that might well be parallel to and independent of—or at least have the same standing as—that of the extant poems might have at its disposal "mechanisms" that also lie behind the diction of the *Iliad* and the *Odyssey*. The degree to which independent epic traditions might have shared diction (epithets, prosody, grammatical and lexical productive processes, etc.) can only be settled by particular textual and historical study. *A priori* judgments are not possible.

[111] Cassio (1999:81) attempts a *via media* between Janko's late eighth-century dictated text and Nagy's evolutionary model. But it is clear that he believes in an early textual fixation: "[O] gran parte di quello che sarebbe poi diventato l'*Iliade* e l'*Odissea* circolava già, ovvero, come minimo, ... la dizione utilizzata per Omero era già totalmente cristallizzata a quell'epoca" (70). And, discussing Theagenes of Rhegion and his alleged statement about Apollo's reason to help Khryses, Cassio writes: "Teagene si riferiva a *un certo verso* dell'inizio di *un certo poema* in cui si parlava di Apollo amico di Crise; registrava cioè una variante rapsodica di un verso già strutturato in una narrazione immutabile" (81, his emphasis). More on Theagenes below, p. 156.

he owns that *a priori* it is "anything but unlikely" that epic traditions other than the Homeric might have existed,[112] he avers that in the case of Nestor's cup such proof is not forthcoming. All departures can be explained by the influence of the local dialect. I do not dispute that what Hackstein (2010:421) calls "the practice of translating hexametric epic poetry from one Greek dialect into another" did exist, and that it may legitimately explain language that plausibly postdates the textual fixation of the poems and for which there is good reason to suspect dependence upon them.[113] But this cannot be safely assumed for Nestor's cup, which Cassio regards as only one or two generations younger than the alleged composition of the *Iliad* by Homer.[114] What under different circumstances might have been read as signs of dialectal 'translation' must, in this case, be interpreted as evidence of independent epic diction. Ultimately, we cannot assert that a well defined, independent epic tradition lies behind Nestor's cup. But the independent diction does prevent us from embracing the suggestion that the Homeric poems achieved their normative and definitive form in Euboia during the first few hundred years of the first millennium BC.[115]

5.2.4 An eighth-century bookhand?

In closing, I now turn to the execution of the inscription. The careful letter shapes, the arrangement in three lines (two of them hexameters), and the use of interpunction for the cup's inscription have fostered the fanciful view, startlingly well received, that this inscription proves the existence of an eighth-century book script. The best known exponent of this theory is Immerwahr: "Jeffery remarks that elsewhere in inscriptions poetry is never written in individual lines; but surely in manuscripts such separation must have been customary, especially in epic texts. I would suggest that the graffiti on this vase are influenced by eighth-century book script. ... [W]e must recognize the existence of a more regular script for literary and documentary purposes from the later eighth century on" (1990:19). His judgment was embraced by Cassio 1999: "[È] stato sostenuto già da Heubeck ... e più di recente da H. R. Immerwahr,

---

[112] Cassio 1999: "In se stessa la possibilità dell'esistenza a epoca antica di tradizione epiche diverse da quella omerica a noi nota è tutt'altro che improbabile" (70).

[113] Hackstein's examples *ad loc.* are puzzling. Does he really believe that Corinthian ϝοι in CEG 1.251 no. 452.ii depends on a parallel oral transmission of *Ionic* epic? (Not to mention the assumption, broadly shared but unprovable except by circular recourse to *our* Homeric texts, that Attic-Ionic—he writes "epic Ionic"—had lost word-initial ϝ by the beginning of the eighth century.) But if he only means that ϝοι is an archaism that goes back to a stage that is common to, and predates, both this inscription and Ionic epic, in what sense does he speak of the translation of hexametric epic poetry? One must always bear in mind S. West's warning (1994b:14n27).

[114] Cassio 1994:64 and n. 66.

[115] Cf. the conclusion in Pavese 1996:20.

W. Burkert e M. L. West, che il tipo di scrittura e l'intera *mise en page* del testo graffito ... sarebbero influenzati da scrittura *libraria* dell'VIII secolo a.C." (67).[116] This has now been raised to the next level by Bartoněk and Buchner (1995:183), who propose the existence of a Pithekoussan scribal school. To put these views in perspective it is important to mark that, as noticed above, the writing of the Cumae *lēkythos* is of comparable regularity and shows similar care. 'Calligraphy' (if the anachronism is at all adequate) is surely characteristic of the writer and varies greatly from vase to vase and location to location. It is fair to say that an inscription's careful writing proves that it is not the inscriber's first attempt at writing. It is quite another to claim that only the inscriber's familiarity with a different, pre-existing writing practice (in this case, the writing of poetry books on perishable material) can explain the traits (regularity of script, punctuation, etc.) that make this inscription exceptional. Nothing prevents the view that Pithekoussan inscriptions on the whole may even display greater regularity of arrangement and writing than inscriptions from other locations. It is well conceivable that a skilled and careful artisan may set trends and standards in his local community. If scholars can detect artisans and workshops elsewhere on the basis of their workmanship, why should this not be the case in Pithekoussai?[117]

None of this, however, requires a belief in an eighth-century book market unless one starts with the prejudice that a vase inscription *must* be synchronically derivative of other kinds of writing current in its local culture. This prejudice of synchronic secondary status must be distinguished from the hypothesis, diachronically sound, that, insofar as the Greeks may have derived alphabetic writing from Semitic sources (Phoenician or Aramaic or both), it is reasonable to look for Semitic antecedents for the use of punctuation in Nestor's cup. It makes particular sense to posit such lines of influence at a trading post like Pithekoussai,[118] where a Semitic minority lived side by side with the Greeks. Ridgway (1992:111–118) reviews the evidence for oriental residents at Pithekoussai. An imported amphora with several markings used in an *enkhytrismos* burial is of special importance.[119] Two of these markings can be read as the Aramaic for '200' and 'double'.[120] Since the capacity of the amphora is two-hundred times the average capacity of Attic-Ionic *kotylai*, Ridgway speculates that the vessel contained unguent to be repackaged in Pithekoussai and that it was dispatched with an Aramaic description of its contents in the expectation

---

[116] Burkert and West lean on Immerwahr's judgment.

[117] Note the pertinent observations by Klein 1972:38.

[118] I do not intend to join the debate on the nature of Pithekoussai, whether an *emporion* or an *apoikia*. See the insightful and reasonable observations in Ridgway 1992:107–109 and Crielaard 1996:244.

[119] Ridgway 1992:111–114. For the inscriptions, see Amadasi Guzzo 1987:23–25 and Bartoněk and Buchner 1995:187–188 no. A.1.

[120] For the choice between Aramaic and Phoenician, see Ridgway 1992:153.

that the recipient would understand it. He further suggests that Phoenician Ialysos on Rhodes (where the Nestor *skyphos* was made) was the source whence it was dispatched before it started to be bottled in *aryballoi* at this location for distribution (in the LG II period). The overlap of Aramaic and Phoenician elements is justified by the triangular west Phoenician and Punic religious symbol that points to death and afterlife.[121] This sign relates to the funerary use of the amphora and it suggests that a member of the family (Ridgway proposes the father) was of Levantine origin and observed this non-Greek usage at the interment of his child. Further evidence of Levantine residents in Pithekoussai comes from the Lyre-Player Group seals, scarabs, and Levantine *aryballoi* (probably imported from Rhodes).[122] The number of tombs that contain at least one of these items is about one third of the excavated cemetery population of 750–725 BC. This proportion demonstrates the degree to which the settlement was permeated by Levantine influences.

In contrast to Pithekoussai, ordinarily one cannot assume that Euboian metropoleis had sufficient exposure to foreign Semitic cultural practices— e.g. the alleged recording of poetry on perishable materials—to adopt them in turn. Direct contact with the Levant cannot be assumed and must be demonstrated. Lefkandi's archaeological record indeed proves that it had commercial ties with Egypt and the Levant towards the end of the tenth century.[123] Popham (1994:28–30) argues for direct communication between Euboia and the Syro-Palestinian coast, without the intermediacy of Cyprus as a redistribution center, and for Euboian ships as the vehicles of this commercial exchange. But Sherratt (2003:229–230) has vigorously countered on the basis of the chronological and spatial distribution of Greek early Iron-Age pottery in the east Mediterranean that trade was "almost entirely in the hands of eastern (especially Tyrian) carriers," and that "there is no evidence that the inhabitants of Euboea, or for that matter other Greek-speaking inhabitants of the Aegean, frequently if ever found themselves in the position between the eleventh and eighth centuries of seeing full-blown Cypriot literacy in operation in its own context. Since in this period at least it does not seem to have travelled outside the island, it seems very likely that they did not even know of its existence" (230).[124] Clearly, this

---

[121] Bartoněk and Buchner 1995:188 no. A.1.E.

[122] Ridgway 1992:115.

[123] Popham et al. 1988–1989:118–119; Ridgway 1992:24; Walbaum 1994:54; Popham 1994; Bonnet 1995:656–657; and Crielaard 1996:244.

[124] I cannot accept Sherratt's theory of a fundamental link between Homeric epic and the derivation of the alphabet (2003:232), although she carefully distances herself from the untenable views of Powell 1991. Her objection against a predominantly commercial stimulus for its origin— why this should have happened in the late eighth century and not before (230)—applies to her proposal just as well. (The assertion that the surviving inscriptions are largely non-commercial

judgment would apply *a fortiori* to Aramaic and Phoenician literacy. Moreover, in and of itself trade is not a robust enough context for the cultural exchange that the adoption of foreign writing practices presupposes. Only trade in written artifacts (inscriptions, manuscripts, etc.) could conceivably have brought to the attention of the aristocrats in the Euboian metropoleis the technologies of written literacy that, according to some, the Greeks allegedly adopted from the more advanced Semitic cultures in the eighth century BC. Where Greeks and Arameans (or Phoenicians) lived side by side, however, the stimulus for the adoption of foreign customs can be credibly attributed to the stable and culturally embedded context in which the various cultural practices intersected. The excavations at the sanctuary of Apollo Daphnephoros in Eretria have only turned up one sherd from ca. 800–750 BC inscribed with Semitic letters. Pfyffer et al. (2005:76–77) think that the author might have been a Luwian merchant passing through Eretria, a plausible conjecture given the city's relationship with northern Syria at the time.[125] But mark the contrast in distribution and number between the eighth-century inscriptions found on Pithekoussai and those from Eretria: "[L]e geste d'inscrire, et plus encore celui d'inscrire des lettres, est

---

holds true only under a narrow view of 'commerce'—one that excludes, for example, marks of ownership [cf. Csapo et al. 2000:104]. And one may reasonably counter that, by their very nature, ephemeral commercial records must have been kept on cheap, perishable materials.) As the formulaic system demonstrates, poetry that eventually joined the Panhellenic stream of Homeric epic had been performed long before, even if we postulate a late eighth-century resurgence of itinerancy that transcended local concerns. So also there must have been an increase and invigoration of trade links, with the Greeks actually doing the traveling. Besides, if ethnogenesis was the aim of literacy, how does one explain the plethora of epichoric alphabets? Did all Greeks, everywhere and independently, suddenly seek to define themselves through the adoption of literacy? Sherratt's argument at 233 assumes that all epichoric scripts descend by adaptation from a single invention. This is extremely unlikely (cf. Csapo et al. 2000:105–107, with reference to Cook and Woodhead 1959). Sherratt (2003:232n13) views Homeric diction and the Homeric poems only synchronically, as late eighth-century cultural artifacts. But, for the evolutionary model, no historical singularity privileges that particular *point* in time: diachronically, the dialectal mixture of Homeric diction extends from that point into the past and into the future. Time marks a distinction of degree, not kind. One may indeed speak of a formative Panhellenic period for the Homeric tradition that starts roughly at that time, with an increase in communication, a resurgence of travel and trade, the rise of supra-regional sanctuaries as points of convergence, and the formation of the political communities of metropolis and colony (Nagy 1996b:42). The phenomenon thus envisioned is the gradual reorientation of local praise poetry towards an increasingly Panhellenic audience (Nagy 1986). No such gradualism, much less the reorientation of an existing practice, is involved in the derivation of the alphabet. I do agree, however, that the Homeric poems articulate a Panhellenic linguistic consciousness and I do not doubt that the dialectal mixture of their diction contributed to their Panhellenic performance scope. We know that in the historical period dialects (and, to a lesser extent, epichoric alphabets) were preeminent instruments of intra-Hellenic cultural self-definition, and there is no reason to question that specific instances of writing (not the alphabet in the abstract) could have served to define Greekness against foreignness.

[125] For its potential significance for the origin of the Greek alphabet, see Theurillat 2007.

encore rare dans le sanctuaire au 8ᵉ siècle. Il est plus rarement attesté encore ailleurs à Erétrie."[126] It seems that the use of writing was generally limited to the sanctuary, although only one inscription (Pfyffer et al. 2005:61 no. 5) can be classified as 'religious.'

To return to Pithekoussai and Nestor's cup: the exceptional cremation of a minor and the goods deposited in the tomb where the vase was found (a few silver items, unusual in children's graves, and several oriental *arryballoi*) led Ridgway (1992:116) to make the fascinating proposal that the *skyphos* belonged to a family that was partly non-Greek, probably Levantine. If true, this further commends attributing the inscription's interpunction to Semitic practice, not to the fantasy of an eighth-century book hand. Heubeck (1979:115) is likely right that the punctuation must have been intended to aid the oral performance of the verses.[127] This establishes the unsurprising claim that from time immemorial those acquainted with epic poetry apprehended the individual line of verse as a unit of performance. Their intuition of phrasing extended to sublinear units like metrical cola. Marking these subdivisions visually (whether they were uttered as pauses or reflected by the intonation) cannot be assumed to reflect ordinary practice, as the neglect of word division during the historical period proves.[128] It is possible that the non-Greek owners of the cup needed aids to performance that natives could dispense with. Be that as it may, if the cup's use of interpunction to separate words and clauses really derived from practices observed in the writing of poetry books in circulation at the time, it is inexplicable why later attested papyri fail to follow them. Much more plausible is the provision of aids to oral performance that might help non-native speakers of Greek to read aloud the verses—aids, moreover, familiar to them

---

[126] Pfyffer et al. (2005:58), where they also list the six geometric graffiti from the city, five of them from the same area (E, F, G also in Bartoněk and Buchner 1995:190–193). Cf. Theurillat 2007:336.

[127] The same must be true of the doubling of the lambda in καλλιστεφανō, a visual reminder of the need to draw out the consonant and of the corresponding prosodic length of the syllable καλ-.

[128] For the use of *scriptio continua*, see Wingo 1972:14–15; Turner 1987:8–9; Nagy 2000b; Signes Codoñer 2004:124–128; and Nagy 2009b. If interpunction had been in regular use at such an early time, it is hard to explain why it is absent from so many of the earliest inscriptions; or why punctuation was not in regular use during the classical era (cf. Cassio 2002:127–128 and Aristotle *Sophistical Refutations* 177b). Neither the Derveni papyrus nor Timotheos' *Persians* mark word separation. The writing habits of Mycenaean scribes (cf. Hooker 1980:44–45 and Ferrara 2010:21–22) bespeak a concern to make the texts maximally readable. Considering the challenges posed by the often ambiguous syllabic script, one must not wonder at the regular use of vertical strokes to mark word division (cf. Millard 1970:13). Readers of alphabetic scripts do not face such difficulties, and one can hardly assume the transference of the writing habits of the Mycenaean scribal class to the late eighth century BC. (For the restriction of Linear B to a narrow social class of Mycenaean palace administrators, see Sherratt 2003:228.)

from their original cultural milieu.[129] Indeed, as Lipiński (2001:97 §9.11) notes, the use of punctuation by alphabetic scripts (vertical strokes and interpunction) is attested in the Aramaic Tell Fekherye inscription of the ninth century BC.[130] Ugaritic had already resorted to a small vertical wedge. The practice continued in the west-Semitic inscriptions of the eleventh and tenth centuries.[131] The ninth-century Moabite Mesha inscription[132] uses a dot to separate words and small strokes to mark out sentences and contextual units. Three dots occur in the Lachish ewer from the thirteenth or twelfth century (Cross 1954:20) and in two lines of the Tell Fekherye inscription. Pairs of dots and single dots are even more common.[133]

As to the arrangement of the verses, their placement between the handles will have allowed the owner to view and use them as a prompt to performance while holding up the cup. The alignment seeks to keep the text fully between the handles and in view of the drinker. This *mise en page* seems to have followed a false start with a spelling error (NH- for NE-).[134] The natural distinction in kind between the first line, which identifies the owner and the object, and the following two, which describe its properties, helps to explain the line division. Even without positing that the inscriber understood or felt the hexameter as a unit of composition and performance, the second line was bound to be divided from the third if it was to avoid running against the now isolated NH. It is obvious that the space left between the end of κεvον and NH was not large enough for ἡμερος.

---

[129] There is no need, as Heubeck thinks, for hypothetical epic texts on perishable material to serve as models. All that is required is acquaintance with the Semitic use of punctuation and with the proper performance phrasing of epic hexameters (pauses, intonation, etc.).

[130] Millard and Bordreuil 1982 and Lipiński 1975:2.19–82, esp. 50–51.

[131] Cf. Millard 1970. See Sass 2005 (with Misgav 2009) for the downdating of some of these inscriptions.

[132] Cooke 1903:1–14 and Donner and Röllig 1962–1964 no. 181 (text: 1.33; commentary: 2.168–179).

[133] For later examples of punctuation on vases, see Pavese 1996:20. For Greek generally, see Jeffery 1990:50. For Attica, cf. Jeffery 1990:67, Threatte 1980:73–84, and Immerwahr 1990:168.

[134] Cf. Pavese 1996:19. If Ridgway's proposal of a Rhodian connection is right, perhaps the erroneous H was prompted by the Rhodian use of this sign for /e:/ (see, for example, Jeffery 1990:356 nos. 1–2). Before abandoning what would have been a much less adequate arrangement of the text, the inscriber began to correct H to E. Bartoněk and Buchner (1995:152) write: "[E]in solcher unüberlegter Anfang unter dem Henkel dünkt uns bei einer kalligraphisch und räumlich so gut ausgeführten Inschrift etwas unwahrscheinlich." But the logic is circular: a carefully executed final layout cannot preclude *a priori* a former less careful attempt. Elsewhere the layout and execution is far from infallible: note the ποτοριον for ποτεριον; the tight and uneven spacing of hoσδα (the sigma was perhaps added later); and the nu of ἀν, first omitted, added interlineally in a reduced size under the tau of τοδε. It is not surprising that Bartoněk and Buchner have no alternative explanation for the two isolated letters.

6

Early Homeric Scholarship and Editions

IN THIS SECTION I wish to examine two arguments for an early, sixth-century written fixation of the Homeric poems. One has an Athenian emphasis, as we might expect from the evolutionary model. This model posits a definitive textual stage for the *Iliad* and the *Odyssey*, centralized in Athens, from the middle of the sixth century to the middle of the fourth, during which transcripts of growing significance for performance will have been produced. The arguments to be reviewed are: the Homeric scholarship of Theagenes of Rhegion; and the running quarrel about Salamis between Megara and Athens, with the report of Spartan arbitration which in the view of many implies the existence of an authoritative written copy of the *Iliad*. A third line of investigation focuses on problematic Homeric forms that are sometimes alleged to prove the existence of early copies written in the old Athenian alphabet. These forms are explained as mistaken readings of a text that did not use word separation, had a deficient graphemic repertory for vowels, and simplified sequences of repeated letters (e.g. OO to O). Cassio (2002:109–114 §§2–3, with bibliography) disposes well of this alleged evidence for the early written transmission of the poems.[1] I will not delve into the old chestnut of the Peisistratean redaction, which I consider a myth of origins, other than to point out that the account must be read for what it teaches us about Homeric performance and the assumptions of the ancients about it.[2]

---

[1] Cf. Cassio 1999:80.

[2] For the Peisistratean recension as a myth of origins, see Nagy 1996c:77–80. Note in particular, his acute observation at 80: the various versions of the foundation myth do not aim to prove "the hypothetical existence of some unattested textual transmission of Homer but rather [to explain] the institutional reality of ongoing performances of Homeric song at the Feast of the Panathenaia in Athens. That is, the myth is concerned with the performance of Homer." A few convenient bibliographical items from the massive literature about the alleged recension are Merkelbach 1952, Davison 1955, Sealey 1957:342–349, and Jensen 1980:128–158. (Others have been noted above, p. 78 n. 37.)

6.1 Ajax and Salamis

Cassio (2002:115) represents the consensus when he writes: "In my opinion the text of the *Iliad* must have been fixed for some decades by 560 BC, when the lines Αἴας δ' ἐκ Σαλαμῖνος ἄγεν δυοκαίδεκα νῆας, | στῆσε δ' ἄγων ἵν' Ἀθηναίων ἵσταντο φάλαγγες (*Il.* 2.557f.) were used as evidence by the Athenians against the Megarians in an interstate arbitration over Salamis." The case, however, is hardly that simple. In fact, even if we assume *arguendo* its basic historicity (which is beset by serious doubts), the record best supports that the quarrel played out as one between rival performance traditions and did not hinge on a given written text of the poem.[3] Interpreting the various reports and assessing their soundness is not easy and the list of distinguished attempts is long. But before I make what must needs be a rather brief appraisal of my own, it is good to pause and consider what sort of document might have been produced by Solon at the alleged arbitration—if a written document is actually what the texts imply. For the existence of a late eighth-century written *Iliad*, either in the possession of the Athenian state or else, say, at Khios in the hands of the Homeridai, as the acknowledged, authoritative source of all other copies, should have prevented the Megarians from falsely accusing Solon of forgery and from supplying an alternative of their own to B 557–558; or else it should have made clear that Solon had in fact inserted B 558 into the copy, especially if one accepts the notion that an eighth-century calligraphic bookhand had drafted the text in a suitable archaic script (Euboian?) respecting word boundaries and line divisions. The Spartans in turn should have found it all too easy to check their own copy of this alleged ur-text and establish the truth of the competing claims. No further evidence would have been required.

The reports of course suggest no such thing (see below). Neither do the Homeric manuscripts. The textual status of B 558 is dubious. After a careful review of the evidence, Apthorp (1980:165–178) concludes that there is no good reason to suppose that Aristarkhos found B 558 in more than a few of his manuscripts, whereas there are various reasons to suppose that he did not. West in his Teubner edition agrees: "Ar[istarchus] versum omisit, cum sciret eum non in

---

[3] This is also the view of Shear 2000:99. Although there are many things in her fascinating book to disagree with (cf. Burgess 2000), on this matter she is right: "Megara claimed that the Athenians had added a line to the Salamis entry in the Catalogue of Ships in order to bolster their claim to Salamis. The Athenians stoutly denied the Megarian accusation ... . If written texts of the Catalogue had existed, then the presence of an alteration would have been made immediately obvious by a comparison of the Athenian text with other existing texts. ... The Megarian accusation was only possible in an oral society when the discussion eventually resorted to arguments based on what 'our bards' say as opposed to what 'your bards' say."

omnibus ferri libris."[4] He also lists a number of papyri that do not carry it or (in one case) add it later.[5] That the parodist Matron of Pitana knew it (*Supplementum Hellenisticum* 259–266 no. 534.95–97) gives us a *terminus ante quem* of the late fourth century, although, as Apthorp (1980:171) perceptively observes, this does not entitle us to infer that he found the verse in his text of Homer (if he owned one)—nor even, I would add, that it was regularly performed with the passage. For Plutarch in *Solōn* 10,[6] after reporting that the majority say (οἱ μὲν οὖν πολλοὶ ... λέγουσι) that Solon inserted (ἐμβαλόντα) a verse (ἔπος) in the *Catalogue of Ships* and read it at the trial (B 557–558 follows), records that the Athenians themselves think that this is nonsense (φλυαρίαν). They assert that Solon proved (pointed out?) to the jury that the sons of Ajax had become Athenian citizens and made over their island to them. Solon is further said to have argued his case by comparing Athenian and Megarian burial customs to the way in which the Salaminian dead were buried. The further support of Delphian oracles is noted. Taking Plutarch at face value, the Athenians put little stock in the alleged textual evidence, whether we think that the other arguments were added to it[7] or (what seems to me a more natural reading) that they disowned the 'silly story' of Homer's help through Solon's forgery and substituted for it three alternative lines of reasoning. Apthorp (1980:169) points out that the Athenian denial did not "take the form of a claim that the line is genuine" but "that Solon in fact used other, more respectable, arguments." Although I do not agree with the search for Homer's *ipsissima verba* and judgments about the authenticity of lines whose diction is clearly traditional, if Apthorp's reading is right and Plutarch's report factual, we arguably detect a certain Athenian embarrassment at B 558, as if the circumstances surrounding it had made it notorious. Hence, many may have thought it better suppressed from the performance of the passage and, eventually, from the written texts. This notoriety would sufficiently motivate Matron's parodic reference to it without any need for its textual attestation: "He could well have known the line merely from the story surrounding it. A piquant anecdote like this would certainly have lent itself to an indirect allusion" (Apthorp 1980:171). Notoriety further motivates, as suggested, the line's

---

[4]   I do not wish to join here the debate whether Aristarkhos omitted or simply marked the verse as suspect, a debate that involves the meaning of Aristarchean atheteses and a comprehensive grasp of his editorial principles. (See Apthorp 1980:167 on this issue as it applies to the scholia A to Γ 230 and Δ 273.) I merely note that West, too, agrees that the Alexandrian scholar did not find the verse attested in all of his manuscripts.

[5]   Cf. Apthorp 1980:166.

[6]   Piccirilli 1975:67–73 F 3.

[7]   That is to say, that the 'nonsense' was not the story that Solon had cited Homer but that he had forged the key verse.

suppression even from many an Athenian manuscript, assuming that it was not manufactured for the story, as Bolling (1916:29) thought.

No support for it must be necessarily inferred from Aristotle's comment in the *Rhetoric* 1375b29–31 that the Athenians used Homer as witness concerning Salamis. For a text that included the Athenian section and was followed solely by B 557 would suffice to draw the plausible inference that Ajax and Salamis were an appendix to Menestheus and Athens. As Bolling (1916:29) memorably put it, "B 546–57 in which Aias is made but a tail to the Athenian kite, would be an ample foundation for this legendary use of poetry as evidence." I grant that a version that only featured B 557 for Ajax would be most unsatisfying (if only slightly less than the one we possess). But if we take seriously what the scholia tell us about Aristarkhos' evidence, this seems the most likely scenario for the mainstream of the Athenian *paradosis*. Assuming the historicity of his telling, the Athenian attitude that Plutarch hints at might explain this state of affairs. One can only conjecture what other, less Athenocentric versions might have sung instead. Cingano (2005:143–152) is right that the language in fr. 204.44–51 of the Hesiodic *Catalogue of Women* does not support the assertion by Finkelberg 1988 that Ajax's domain is portrayed as embracing the cities mentioned there (Troizen, Epidauros, Aigina, Mases, Hermione, and Asine). But it does perhaps suggest what modifications to our *Iliad* might have given a section to Ajax commensurate with the hero's relevance and comparable in length to other entries in the *Catalogue of Ships*. Strabo 9.1.10 provides another glimpse of an alternative version, this time, Megarian. We are told that either Solon or Peisistratos interpolated immediately after B 557 the offending B 558 and resorted to Homer as a witness that Salamis had been the Athenians' from the beginning. We also learn that the critics (οἱ κριτικοί) do not accept the verse, because it is contradicted by other statements in the poem. Nevertheless, the Athenians appear to have alleged in their own support 'some such testimony from Homer' (οἱ μὲν δὴ Ἀθηναῖοι τοιαύτην τινὰ σκήψασθαι μαρτυρίαν παρ' Ὁμήρου δοκοῦσιν), to which the Megarians responded with a rival version: οἱ δὲ Μεγαρεῖς ἀντιπαρῳδῆσαι οὕτως "Αἴας δ' ἐκ Σαλαμῖνος ἄγεν νέας, ἔκ τε Πολίχνης, | ἔκ τ' Αἰγειρούσσης Νισαίης τε Τριπόδων τε." ἅ ἐστι χωρία Μεγαρικά.[8] The rare word ἀντιπαρῳδῆσαι might imply mockery, as if the Megarians were making the point that they too could compose *ad hoc* forgeries to their benefit. But we would expect a parody to imitate its model, and there is no imitation of syntax or sound such as we find in the parodic Matron. The Megarian verses open with identical diction up to the thesis of the fourth foot and veer subsequently without any resemblance to the Athenian. For this reason, I think it is better to understand ἀντιπαρῳδῆσαι

---

[8] Cf. Piccirilli 1975:133–134 F 21b.

in its etymological sense: they sang their version alongside (παρά) instead or in return (ἀντί). This is the way Higbie (1997:286) understands it: "the Megarians give this version in reply." There is every reason to think that the Megarian version, substantially different from the Athenian and hardly recognizable as a parody in the ordinary sense of the term, was intended as a genuinely valid multiform.[9] For the more common νῆας, the verses use the comparatively rarer, but by no means unexampled, νέας;[10] and although the quotation does not report the number of boats, there is no reason to suppose that the Megarian version of this entry stopped with the second line quoted. What followed may have stated the missing information. The obvious point of quoting two verses only was to join the poem with the received opening (what in our *Iliad* is the beginning of verse 557) and then to supplant the offending 558 with material favorable to Megara's claims.[11] Strabo's equation of Tripodes with Tripodiskion and his comment that the places mentioned are Megarian suggest that these were not verses composed *ad hoc* to counter the Athenian version. Special erudition was required to understand them as making Megara's point. Rigsby (1987b:100) writes that "a Megarian forger motivated by his city's claim upon Salamis in the face of an Athenian threat should not have spoiled his case by failing to name Megara." And Figueira (1985:268) believes that the group of locations mentioned by the Megarian version "portrays the actual situation ... in the late seventh and sixth centuries."

Hence, the report, if it has a factual core, is best understood as a rivalry of traditional versions. Bolling (1925:16) had noted that "[fama affertur B 558] ab oratore Atheniensi interpolatum esse. Ut haec interpolatio per verba sola fieri intelligatur plane necesse est." And again at 73: "The meaning is clearly that they recited as if genuine extra lines of their own composition, not that they forged and put into circulation copies of the lengthened text." Apthorp (1980:168) thought that Bolling's emphasis on verbal performance went too far and cited παρεγράψαντα (Strabo 9.1.10), ἀναγνῶναι (Plutarch *Solōn* 10.2), and ἐγγράψαι (Diogenes Laertios 1.48) as making explicit reference to Solon's writing. But these can be readily understood as anachronistic details and can hardly be given probative value. Our late sources merely retroject to the alleged 'trial' before

---

[9]   *Pace* Wilamowitz-Moellendorff 1884:243. Cf. FGH 485 F6n28 (vol. 3b, Noten, p. 232): "Ich teile die bedenken von Wilamowitz ... nicht; aus Strabons bezw. Apollodors ausdruck ἀντιπαρωιδῆσαι ist garnichts zu schliessen." Although Jacoby does not think the Megarian verses might have stood in a Megarian ἔκδοσις, Piccirilli (1975:134) writes, "ciò non è però del tutto impossibile."

[10] νέας is not used in the attested *Catalogue of Ships*, but it is in A 487 N 96 101 620 Ξ 392 P 612 γ 153 162 299 δ 582 κ 15 91 λ 124 (=ψ 271) ξ 258 (=ρ 427) and Hesiod *Works and Days* 247, fr. 205.6 MW.

[11] One can readily understand why the beginning of B 557, which states the name and domain of the hero who leads the ensuing contingent, should have arrived at a comparatively more advanced degree of textual fixation sooner than the rest of the section it headed.

the Spartan umpires elements of their own book cultures and known practices attested for classical court proceedings, at which a clerk would read aloud when requested documentary evidence given to him by the parties in advance.[12] For Strabo, Peisistratos or Solon subjoined B 558 to the Athenian section after B 557 so that he may use Homer as a witness (μάρτυρι χρήσασθαι τῷ ποιητῇ). In this way Solon was effectively preparing the written copy to be read at the trial. Plutarch's version is similar: Solon inserted the text into the *Catalogue of Ships* and then read it at the trial (ἐπὶ τῆς δίκης ἀναγνῶναι). Diogenes Laertios does not mention a trial before a panel of Spartans. But there may be an echo of it in his account of Solon's desire to make the case that Athens' possession of Salamis was just (δίκη).[13]

It is important to mark the following methodological observation. Jensen (1980:138) writes that "Solon's interpolation presupposes an already fixed Catalogue of Ships." This kind of claim is often found in connection with apparent or alleged ancient references to specific lines in our Homeric texts. The quotation from Cassio that opens this section is another example of the same. But it involves an inadmissible leap of logic, effected under the spell of our regularized modern editions and their unvarying line numbers. Nothing follows for the entire *Catalogue of Ships*—much less for the entire *Iliad*—from the fact that a few ancient authors mentioned two verses identical to our own B 557–558. Even if we conclude that the ultimate source for the quoted text is early, why should

---

[12] Bonner 1905:54 and 58–59. A party who did not merely refer in a general way to a law but had the clerk read its text aloud was responsible for supplying a truthful copy upon the penalty of death. For Bonner (1927:195–196), there was no established procedure other than a challenge and a suit for perjury to guarantee that evidence so presented was true and accurate. It is not clear whether Harrison (1968–1971:2.134–135) makes the clerk himself responsible for the copy of the law or decree whose text he was to read aloud. His statement that the laxity of citation was improved by "the rule that evidence ... was to be in the form of written depositions read out by the clerk at the trial" (135) implies the view that the clerk either copied the law himself upon request or else checked for accuracy the copy supplied by the litigants. To judge from Demosthenes 19.270, sometimes the clerk was tendered the text only when he was called to read it. For written and oral forensic testimony, see Bonner 1905:46–53; Calhoun 1919; Harrison 1968–1971:2.134–135 and 139; Humphreys 1985b:317 and 321; Todd 1990:29n15; and Pébarthe 2006:315–343. Thomas (1992:148–149) observes that growing confidence in documentary evidence is a fourth-century development (cf. Rubinstein 2000:72–75, with added nuance). Harris (1989:71–73) adds that, even then, "legal practice, like the administration of large-scale business, remained to a considerable extent oral and independent of documents" (at 72). For large domains like the law of sale oral testimony still reigned supreme. Sickinger 2004 offers a complementary perspective, which suggests that "despite the persistence of oral practices, participants in legal actions frequently relied on written texts" (94). He does not, however, directly address the question of the accuracy of the clerk's texts or their source.

[13] Right before he reports on Solon's textual insertion, he recounts the argument based on the coincidence of Salaminian and Athenian burial customs. For Plutarch, both were arguments presented to the Spartan arbitrators.

we be surprised if *some* manuscripts embraced lines whose notoriety drew the attention of commentators and placed them in the very sequence reported by them? It would be fallacious to assert that this or that ancient writer quoted B 558 as if he had one of our modern editions at hand. That is of course not what is usually meant by such a statement. But in the face of sweeping, impermissible inferences like Jensen's or Cassio's, it is hard to resist the impression that the modern scholar has embraced unawares a glaring hysteron proteron.

Of somewhat different cloth are Cassio's remarks about what he deems "an awkward interpolation in the *Nekuia* ... [from] the time of the Peisistratids." To him, the alleged interpolation—the statement that not Herakles but his *eidōlon* was in Hades—"shows by implication that the text in which it was inserted was by then fixed and unalterable" (Cassio 2002:116 and n. 52). Once again, there is slippage in the reasoning. Even if the fact that Odysseus had seen Herakles in Hades was traditional by a certain time, say, the rule of Peisistratos, it does not follow that the text of the *Nekuia* was fixed, nor even that necessarily the lines about Herakles were.[14] I cannot pronounce on the alleged awkwardness of the juxtaposition, which remains a matter of subjective taste. In this judgment, Cassio joins an array of distinguished scholars, ancient and modern. But, for all their skill, their consensus is none the less textually arbitrary and based on a subjective feel for the sequence and thematic material that would make for the best poetry. Focke (1943:228–229) offers a few specimens. He quotes Wilamowitz as saying that "von einer Erhöhung (des Herakles) weiß das Epos nichts und kann es nichts wissen wollen." He reports the judgment of Rohde as "Verlegenheitsauskunft ältester Harmonistik." His own is equally damning: "Theologie, nicht Poesie enthalten die eingeschobenen Verse." The charge of tampering with the text in the interest of harmonizing a perceived divergence can be readily turned around. For if, harried by a scheming Hera, Herakles had achieved apotheosis through self-immolation, would his end not fully agree with Σ 117–119?[15] There is no incongruity with λ 616, *pace* Heubeck, since

---

14 Whether one thinks that this encounter was traditional or not since the earliest identifiable stages of the Odyssean tradition, it is arguably the climax of the *Nekuia*. Cf. Heubeck and Hoekstra 1989: "[t]he encounter with Heracles is deliberately placed last" (114 *ad* 601–627); "[it is] clearly intended as the concluding climax to the episode" (116 *ad* 630–631.) To that extent, it is indispensable to the architecture of the episode as we know it.

15 In other words, one might argue that a keen awareness of the gruesome manner in which he had attained his apotheosis would render psychologically plausible Akhilleus' dwelling on Herakles' death, rather than his divine afterlife, as a *paradeigma* for his own fate. The familiar account of Herakles' death (without the detail of the pyre) is at least as old as Hesiod fr. 25.20–33 MW. It is vain to speculate about Akhilleus' knowledge of Herakles' afterlife and how this information might affect the tenor of his words. His emphasis falls squarely on the event of dying. Even the Hesiodic fragment, which dwells at length on Herakles' present divinity (26–33), describes his end in grim familiar terms: δ[εξ]αμένωι δέ ο[ἱ αἶψα τέλος θανάτοι]ο παρέστη· | καὶ] θάνε καί ῥ'

Herakles is bewailing Odysseus' lot in life, not his own in death, as his words show (especially λ 619 and the imperfect εἶχον in 621). From a textual point of view, Bolling (1925:212) demonstrated long ago that, when the scholia are carefully read, they make clear that λ 604 had not been athetized by Aristarkhos or any other ancient scholar.[16] Rather, the addition of this line, identical to Hesiod *Theogony* 952, must be post-Aristarchean, as its absence from a second-century AD papyrus and some manuscripts confirm. According to the somewhat muddled scholia *ad loc.*, some athetized one or both verses in λ 602–603 and fathered them on Onomakritos. But there is little to recommend this attribution if, as I think, the combination of heroic and divine status for Herakles was already old and deeply traditional in the sixth century.

Indeed, Herakles is hardly an ordinary hero. It has been plausibly argued that, like Helen in Sparta, he was originally a god with a chthonic dimension who was subsequently given an exceptional heroic identity.[17] Burkert reminds us that the complex of immolation and apotheosis recalls Near-Eastern tradition. Cult was offered on Mount Oita at the penteteric fire festival. At Tarsos, in Cilicia, a pyre was prepared yearly for an ancient Anatolian god, Sandes or Sandon in the local language, called Herakles in Greek. Hittite kings were divinized by cremation. And the equation of Herakles and the Phoenician god Melqart, recognized in Herodotos 2.44, explains his cremation at Tyre.[18] Usener (1896:255) once affirmed: "Wir dürfen mit überzeugung den satz aufstellen, dass alle heroen, deren geschichtlichkeit nicht nachweisbar oder wahrscheinlich ist, ursprünglich götter waren." In its application to Herakles, this statement eerily recalls Herodotos 2.44: "My investigations plainly show that Herakles is an ancient god."[19] If so, diachronically speaking, his portrayal as a hero and his presence in Hades would be the innovation—certainly very old and likely a part of the Homeric tradition since its earliest stages—not his dwelling on Olympos in the company of the other gods.[20] Hence, the verses often condemned as an intrusive interpolation could actually reflect a very old stratum of Greek religion. The rationale for classifying them as a later addition to an already fixed text would vanish. In principle, it is still possible, if improbable, that a later

---

Ἀΐδ[αο πολύστονον ἵκε]το δῶμα (24–25). (Like λ 602–603, the Hesiodic report of the hero's divine blessedness could not escape the suspicions of ancient athetizers and is obelized in *P.Oxy.* 2075.) One should consider, moreover, that Herakles' apotheosis is not entirely unrelated to the poetic immortality through which Akhilleus manages to transcend his own death (Σ 121).

16 His analysis should be consulted.

17 Burkert 1985: "[He] is the greatest of the Greek heroes and yet thoroughly untypical" (208).

18 For these statements and the corresponding references, see Burkert 1985:210 and West 1997:465.

19 τὰ μέν νυν ἱστορημένα δηλοῖ σαφέως παλαιὸν θεὸν Ἡρακλέα ἐόντα.

20 The narrative of his apotheosis would serve to harmonize his original divine character with his heroic identity.

addition was made to the poem to accommodate older religious material. But this claim would face the burden of proof—why should older material be a late arrival to the poem?—proof that would be hard to come by considering the utter lack of textual support for it. At any rate, the report that Onomakritos added the offending verses to accommodate a recent elevation of Herakles to divine honors would be demonstrably false.[21]

Be that as it may, even if we grant for the sake of argument that, thematically, Herakles' presence in Hades was chronological prior to the qualification, allegedly added later, that Odysseus had only seen his *eidōlon*, it does not follow that the *text* was already fixed when the qualification was made. Cassio is confusing theme and diction. Thematic material felt to be indispensable to a story need not be attended by already established, equally indispensable verbal expression. A performer may not have felt free to suppress the reference to Herakles, even if—to follow Cassio—he thought it theologically objectionable. But this hardly requires us to hold that he had also memorized specific language, sanctioned by tradition, to narrate the encounter. Cassio's whole argument hinges on his subjective feeling of awkwardness. It leads him to believe that the qualification is clumsy precisely because it does not fit with an already existing, traditional sequence of clauses.[22] Sentencing the whole as "patently absurd" (Cassio 2002:116n52) flies in the face of the uniform textual *paradosis*, which only challenges λ 604. The scholiast calls the other offending material not 'absurd' but νεωτερικόν—i.e. in line with Hesiodic material—and he does not think that its author is Homer. But the surviving copies do not support his judgment. We simply cannot, without further evidence, infer from his comment that he knew of ancient manuscripts that did not contain λ 602–603. That the scholia should ascribe the authorship of λ 604 to Onomakritos is hardly probative, since Herodotos 7.6 made him notorious as a forger and associated him firmly with the editing of religious subject matter.

---

[21] On the other hand, that he added them to accommodate old religious thinking might be true, if sheer conjecture without a shred of documentary support.

[22] Nothing in the logic of the case requires that we condemn λ 602–603 as an *inorganic* interpolation into an already fixed text. This is so, even if we were to accept the view that these verses did not belong in older versions of the poem. Why must we preclude the possibility that it was in the normal course of its diachronic development that rhapsodes *organically* wove into the poetry the (*ex hypothesi*) later theme of Herakles' apotheosis? If so, this would be an ordinary instance of the diachronic layering of themes that follows from a live tradition of poetic recomposition in performance. That is of course not what Cassio has in mind: he is convinced that the offending material bears no organic relation either to its context or to the ordinary growth of the poem and that its insertion does violence to the poetic integrity of the original. It bears saying, once again, that his case turns entirely on the subjective feel of the critic for what makes good poetry, and hence for what 'Homer' (or the authentic tradition) might have composed.

6.2 Theagenes of Rhegion

Theagenes of Rhegion was reported to be one of the first scholars of Homeric poetry.[23] Some even think that he may have been a rhapsode, although this is not stated explicitly anywhere. Cassio has returned to him twice in the recent past[24] and claimed that his work proves the fixation of the text of the *Iliad* by the time of his *floruit*. This claim depends on two pieces of evidence: a report in the scholia A to A 381 and a passage of Porphyry, preserved by the scholia B to Y 67, which illustrates Theagenes' allegorical views of the divine apparatus of Homeric poetry.

Cassio (2002:118) seems especially impressed by the report in the scholia A to A 381: ⟨εὐξαμένου ἤκουσεν⟩ Σέλευκός φησιν, ἐν τῇ Κυπρίᾳ καὶ Κρητικῇ "ἐπεί ῥά νύ οἱ φίλος ἦεν"· καὶ Θεαγένης δὲ οὕτως προφέρεται· ἀπίθανον γὰρ τὸ †οδένυ† λίαν φίλος ἦν.[25] Note that the lemma, which I have taken directly from the manuscript, is not ⟨ἐπεὶ μάλα οἱ φίλος ἦεν⟩ as Erbse and Dindorf print it. These editors quote for our convenience the portion from our critical text that the scholiast's comment directly addresses. The scholiast, however, as might be expected for ease of reference on the page, quotes the beginning of the line he is annotating. This detail is informative because much of the force of Cassio's argument hinges on the impression that Theagenes is offering a relatively minor variant reading to a specific section of a line in our modern editions. As Cassio (2002:118) puts it, "Theagenes quoted a Homeric line (*Il.* 1.381) with a variant." And again: "if our source can be trusted, he quoted a rhapsodic variant in a *specific* line of *our* Homer" (118, his emphasis). With Müller (1891:36), I ascribe the reference to Theagenes in the scholion ultimately to Seleukos, the Homeric grammarian from Alexandria. Otherwise, as our sole source we are left with an anonymous scholiast who obviously postdated Seleukos and yet, more than half a millennium after Theagenes' *floruit*, claimed detailed knowledge of his Homeric views. But crediting Seleukos for the entire scholion only mildly alleviates our problem. For one must wonder, too, how reasonable it is to expect that even Seleukos had access to Theagenes' writings, of whom little more than a few *testimonia* have been preserved.[26] The *floruit* of Seleukos Homerikos, active

---

[23] Recent treatments of Theagenes in the context of early allegoresis can be found in Richardson 1975; Svenbro 1976:108–138; Rispoli 1980; Feeney 1991:8–11; Ramos Jurado 1999; Ford 1999; Ford 2002:68–72; Zumbo 2002; Struck 2004:26–29; and Naddaf 2009 esp. 108–114. Among the older treatments, see Wehrli 1928:88–94.

[24] Cassio 1999:81–82 and 2002:118–119.

[25] On this scholion, besides Erbse 1969–1988 *ad loc.* see Ludwich 1884:1.192 and Müller 1891:35–36.

[26] His section in *Die Fragmente der Vorsokratiker* (1.51–52) is merely a page long.

at the court of Tiberius, is a full five hundred years after Theagenes.[27] According to Müller (1891:30–31), other than with Theagenes, *testimonia* and fragments allege his engagement with Aristophanes of Byzantion (ca. 257–180 BC), Athenokles from Kyzikos (III/II BC), Demetrios of Phaleron (b. ca. 350 BC), Timaios (ca. 350–260 BC), Philokhoros (ca. 340–260 BC), Aristotle, Demetrios Ixion (II BC), a certain Kroton, Aristoxenos (b. ca. 370 BC), Plato, Diodoros Aristophaneios (ca. II BC), and Khamaileon (ca. 350–post 281). Disregarding Plato and Aristotle, whose writings we can assume readily available in much later times, we can see from the list that no authority is older than the end of the fourth century *except* for Theagenes himself, who predates every other name by two hundred years. This seems legitimate cause for suspicion.

But let us grant, for the sake of argument, that the quotation is genuine and accurate. Does it justify Cassio's impression that the text of the *Iliad* was fixed down to the level of line and word by the end of the sixth century?[28] I submit that its implications are rather more diffuse than his emphatic "specific" and "our" convey. For the statement is merely that 'Theagenes proffers (προφέρεται) it so'. The meaning of προφέρεται (the verb is used both in the active and the middle) has a wide range that follows from its basic sense 'to bring forth'. Dickey (2007:257) s.v. glosses it as "to utter, pronounce, use, cite (also in the middle)."[29] Here it may mean no more than that Theagenes 'brings forth in this way' the clause in question—to what end and in what way this evidence is proffered remains to be determined, whether in his writings, as reported by another who heard him recite or read his work, or in yet some other manner. From the scholion to be reviewed below, Wilamowitz-Moellendorff (1931–1932:2.215n2) inferred that Theagenes must have been a rhapsode himself: "Theagenes von Rhegion gilt als der erste, der die Götter in physikalische Mächte umgedeutet hat (Porphyrios zu Y 67), und zwar in einem Buche über Homer. Da wird er ein Rhapsode gewesen sein, denn von diesen verlangte man auch Erklärung." With this, Pfeiffer (1968:1.9–11) agrees.[30] That he wrote is stated both in the second scholion to be reviewed below[31] and in the *Suidas* 2.688 Θ no. 81 (Adler).[32]

---

[27] For general information on Seleukos, see the *New Pauly* s.vv. "[13] S[eleucus] Homericus." See also Müller 1891.

[28] Cassio, of course, does not put his case in such strong terms. But his emphasis on the "specificity" of the line in question once again suggests a modern text with its standard line numbers. That the variant is about two syllables only, ῥά νύ versus μάλα, further evokes the image of a late sixth-century van Thiel laboring over manuscript collations.

[29] Cf. Ludwich 1884:1.113n128.

[30] Wehrli 1928:91 disagrees: "Einfach Rhapsode war er darum nicht, denn dann würde er nicht Grammatiker heißen." Cf. Rispoli 1980:249–250.

[31] [Θεαγένης] πρῶτος ἔγραψε περὶ Ὁμήρου.

[32] εἰσὶ δὲ καὶ ἄλλοι δύο Θεαγένεις, εἷς μὲν ὁ περὶ Ὁμήρου γράψας ... .

Modern studies of Aristarkhos' editorial practice show that from a statement like this one cannot infer that Theagenes necessarily discussed the relative merits of the two variant readings ἐπεὶ μάλα οἱ φίλος ἦεν and ἐπεί ῥά νύ οἱ φίλος ἦεν, and that he expressed a reasoned preference for the one allegedly attested by the Cyprian and Cretan versions. It is just as possible that a Homeric text associated with his name was known to contain the reported variant. Or that he is reported to have recited the motive for Apollo's helping Khryses in agreement with the Cyprian and Cretan editions. In other words, this may have been the one and only way he ever knew or sang the line. If he was indeed defending Homeric poetry against the attacks of Xenophanes and other like critics, it is also possible that he knew the two versions and specifically approved of the second. Assuming that Ludwich's emendation of the *crux* is correct, he may have objected to the intensification of φίλος by μάλα as incredible or unlikely (perhaps even inappropriate) in view of the gods' true nature. ῥά νύ, of course, implied no such thing. Seleukos' interest in Homeric studies and theology (he wrote a Περὶ θεῶν) might explain why he cites Theagenes' opinion here.[33]

But all of this is mere conjecture. In the end, what do we have? The fact that a late sixth-century scholar-cum-rhapsode apparently knew the episode that begins our *Iliad*: he knew that Khryses had petitioned Apollo, and that Apollo had answered his request 'because he was (very?) dear to him'. This is indeed a "specific" line of "our" *Iliad*, but what is there to be surprised at? It is a well-known narrative law that the beginning, the climax, and the end of a story are its fixed points. If a story is in thematic flux, these are the first elements to be established. One may, in fact, say that only when these are settled do we really have a recognizable story.[34] Theagenes lived at the time when we first have

---

[33] The elucidation that starts with ἀπίθανον γὰρ need not be Theagenes' own. As scholia tend to be, the flow of logic is compressed and unclear. To construe the clause with what precedes it one must supply the link. For example, 'And Theagenes also proffers it so. For [he says that] the exaggeration "he was very dear" is unconvincing'. Or, 'Seleukos says that in the Cyprian and the Cretan versions [the reading is] "since he was dear to him". And Theagenes also proffers it so. For [Seleukos says that] the exaggeration "he was very dear" is unconvincing' (that is, Seleukos is the one who objects to μάλα and he adduces Theagenes and the Cyprian and Cretan versions to show that there was an old reading that did not involve the exaggeration he deprecated). Or again, 'And Theagenes also proffers it so. [And it is no wonder that there are texts that do not read μάλα] for the exaggeration "he was very dear" is unconvincing'. Or finally, 'And Theagenes also proffers it so. [This must be the correct reading] for the exaggeration "he was very dear" is unconvincing [and unworthy of Homer]'. I offer these alternatives *exempli gratia* simply to make the point that on the assumed and supplied link depends whether the explanatory clause is Theagenes' or Seleukos' (or even the scholiast's).

[34] The only partial exception is the end. Climax and end are often one and the same. Sometimes the climax is sufficient to round up a narrative, and to the end is left only the tying of loose threads. If so, it may take various forms without affecting the perceived integrity of the story. Tolkien's narrative of *The Lord of the Rings* is of that sort. The Hobbits' return to the Shire ("The Scouring

indisputable proof of an interest in a personal author of the *Iliad* and the *Odyssey*. Chronologically, he heads the list of those who first investigated Homer's poetry, family, and time. Although this report may yet be another example of the ubiquitous search for πρῶτοι εὑρεταί, there is in principle no reason to disbelieve it.[35] This implies that the poems had a sufficiently settled thematic shape to be recognizable units of composition that could be ascribed to an individual. It is not surprising that a line from the beginning of the *Iliad* that touches on the motivation of Apollo in answering Khryses would have a shape similar, though by no means identical, to the one in our vulgate. This last detail, namely, that Theagenes allegedly proffered a *variant* to the reading in our vulgate (whether he knew of another or not) must be duly stressed. If anything, this demonstrates a remaining degree of fluidity, even at the point in the poem where we first expect rigidity of theme and diction.[36] How reasonable is it to turn this into an argument *for* the fixity of the text of the *Iliad*? No necessary implication for the rest of the poem may be legitimately drawn, and, at this relatively late date, the rather limited scope of fixity entailed presents no difficulties to proponents of the evolutionary model.

What of the second scholion, from the scholia B to Y 67, attributed by Dindorf to Porphyry?[37] We do well to heed the warning in Pfeiffer 1968:10 that,

---

of the Shire") is strongly overshadowed in the mind of the reader by the climax of Mount Doom and the victory of Gondor. It is not by chance that Peter Jackson's celebrated movie version does not include this return and ends with the Grey Havens.

[35] περὶ γὰρ τῆς Ὁμήρου ποιήσεως γένους τε αὐτοῦ καὶ χρόνου καθ᾽ ὃν ἤκμασεν προηρεύνησαν πρεσβύτατοι μὲν Θεαγένης τε ὁ Ῥηγῖνος κατὰ Καμβύσην γεγονὼς καὶ Στησίμβροτος ὁ Θάσιος καὶ Ἀντίμαχος ὁ Κολοφώνιος Ἡρόδοτός τε ὁ Ἁλικαρνασσεὺς καὶ Διονύσιος ὁ Ὀλύνθιος … . (Tatian *Oratio ad Graecos* §31.2 Goodspeed [p. 31 Schwarz] = DK 8 1).

[36] Even granting *arguendo* the doubtful reliability of the scholion, for Cassio's point to succeed we must further assume: i) that Theagenes was deliberately proffering a preferred variant (i.e. he knew that his version was one of several); ii) that there was a base text from which his reading was conceived as a departure, i.e. an agreed text broadly received by one and all; iii) that the shape of this text had largely crystallized in a final form, not only as regards the disputed 'line' but also elsewhere. *Pace* Cassio, none of this follows from the scholion.

[37] τοῦ ἀσυμφόρου μὲν ὁ περὶ θεῶν ἔχεται καθόλου λόγος, ὁμοίως δὲ καὶ τοῦ ἀπρεποῦς· οὐ γὰρ πρέποντας τοὺς ὑπὲρ τῶν θεῶν μύθους φησίν. πρὸς δὲ τὴν τοιαύτην κατηγορίαν οἱ μὲν ἀπὸ τῆς λέξεως ἐπιλύουσιν, ἀλληγορίαι πάντα εἰρῆσθαι νομίζοντες ὑπὲρ τῆς τῶν στοιχείων φύσεως, οἷον ⟨ἐν⟩ ἐναντιώσεσι τῶν θεῶν. καὶ γάρ φασι τὸ ξηρὸν τῶι ὑγρῶι καὶ τὸ θερμὸν τῶι ψυχρῶι μάχεσθαι καὶ τὸ κοῦφον τῶι βαρεῖ. ἔτι δὲ τὸ μὲν ὕδωρ σβεστικὸν εἶναι τοῦ πυρός, τὸ δὲ πῦρ ξηραντικὸν τοῦ ὕδατος. ὁμοίως δὲ καὶ πᾶσι στοιχείοις, ἐξ ὧν τὸ πᾶν συνέστηκεν, ὑπάρχει ἡ ἐναντίωσις καὶ κατὰ μέρος μὲν ἐπιδέχεσθαι φθορὰν ἅπαξ, τὰ πάντα δὲ μένειν αἰωνίως. μάχας δὲ διατίθεσθαι αὐτόν, διονομάζοντα τὸ μὲν πῦρ Ἀπόλλωνα καὶ Ἥλιον καὶ Ἥφαιστον, τὸ δὲ ὕδωρ Ποσειδῶνα καὶ Σκάμανδρον, τὴν δ᾽ αὖ σελήνην Ἄρτεμιν, τὸν ἀέρα δὲ Ἥραν καὶ τὰ λοιπά. ὁμοίως ἔσθ᾽ ὅτε καὶ ταῖς διαθέσεσι ὀνόματα θεῶν τιθέναι, τῆι μὲν φρονήσει τὴν Ἀθηνᾶν, τῆι δ᾽ ἀφροσύνηι τὸν Ἄρεα, τῆι δ᾽ ἐπιθυμίαι τὴν Ἀφροδίτην, τῶι λόγωι δὲ τὸν Ἑρμῆν, καὶ προσοικειοῦσι τούτοις· οὗτος μὲν οὖν τρόπος ἀπολογίας ἀρχαῖος ὢν πάνυ καὶ ἀπὸ Θεαγένους τοῦ Ῥηγίνου, ὃς πρῶτος ἔγραψε περὶ Ὁμήρου, τοιοῦτός ἐστιν ἀπὸ τῆς λέξεως (Schrader 1880:240–241 = DK 8 2 =

since the scholion "is obviously derived from a Stoic source," it should be used "with the greatest caution." And Feeney (1991:10) is doubtless right that "[i]t is in the highest degree unlikely that Theagenes devised the full panoply of allegorical technique which we see exemplified in [it]." Indeed, after saying that Homer's account of the gods borders on the unprofitable and unseemly, and that he tells inappropriate stories about them, Porphyry (?) observes that some (οἱ μέν) use the poems' language to solve the difficulty presented by this kind of charge (ἀπὸ τῆς λέξεως ἐπιλύουσιν),[38] holding that everything is said allegorically and stands for the nature of the elements, as e.g. in the disagreements of the gods (οἷον ⟨ἐν⟩ ἐναντιώσεσι τῶν θεῶν). What is striking about the scholion is the utter generality of its references. Not only is Theagenes not identified before the examples of allegorical reading are presented (we meet only with the indefinite 'some'); but the label that should allegedly draw our attention to the famous theomachy of *Iliad* 20 is not the distinctive θεομαχία, 'battle of the gods', but the ordinary and generic ἐναντίωσις, 'disagreement'.[39] Only after a list of element-to-god equivalences do we learn that 'this type of defense, then, being very old and from Theagenes of Rhegion, who first wrote about Homer, proceeds in this manner, from the diction'. Porphyry only establishes a tenuous historical link with the man reputed to be the first exponent of this interpretive strategy. There is not a hint in his presentation that Theagenes' actual writings

---

MacPhail Jr. 2011:240–242). Although I depart from it at several points of significance to my argument, I print for convenience the translation by Ford 1999: "In general, [Homer's] account of the gods tends to be worthless and unsuitable, for the myths he tells about the gods are inappropriate. To such charges as this, some reply on the basis of Homer's way of speaking [*lexis*], holding that everything is said by way of allegory [*allēgoria*] and refers to the nature of the elements, as in the passage where the gods square off against one another. For they say that the dry battles with the wet, the hot with the cold, and the light with the heavy. Moreover, water extinguishes fire while fire evaporates water, so that there is an opposition between all the elements composing the universe, which may suffer destruction in part but remains eternal as a whole. In setting out these battles Homer gives fire the name Apollo, Helius, or Hephaestus, he calls water Poseidon or Scamander, the moon Artemis, the air Hera, and so on. In a similar way he sometimes gives names of the gods to human faculties: intelligence is Athena, folly is Ares, desire Aphrodite, speech Hermes, according to what is characteristic of each. Now this kind of defense is very old and goes back to Theagenes of Rhegium, who first wrote about Homer" (35). Cf. also the translations in Struck 2004:27 and MacPhail Jr. 2011:241–243. For Dindorf's ascription, see Dindorf 1875–1888:3.vii.

38 For the meaning of the expression, see Carroll 1895:40–55 and Combellack 1987 ("the solution based on language," at 219).

39 That θεομαχία was used specifically for literary narratives of divine battles, including Homer's at *Iliad* 20, is clear from Plato *Republic* 378d5; *Protagoras* DK 80 A30; [Longinos] *Peri hypsous* 9 §§5, 8; scholia A *ad* O 212a and bT *ad* Y 4a; Herakleitos *Allegoriae* 52.1; and Proklos *In Platonis Rempublicam commentarii* 1.87.12 Kroll. The word 'battle' (μάχη) does appear a few lines later, but here again it is not the distinctive θεομαχία, which might evoke the specific literary *episode*, but the plural and seemingly generic μάχας (μάχας δὲ διατίθεσθαι αὐτόν).

stand with any specificity behind its details, as Feeney once noted.[40] The scribe who added this scholion to the Venetus B[41] doubtless thought that it helped to illuminate the word ἔναντα at Y 67, which it annotates. This fact does not, however, prove that it was drafted by its author (*ex hypothesi*, Porphyry) with the specific language of *our* theomachy in view; nor does it substantiate the still weaker claim that the precise backdrop for its treatment was this partic-ular Iliadic episode as opposed to divine confrontations generally, of which the theomachy—in whatever textual shape it was known to the author—may well have been a signal instance. Both the non-specific label, ἐναντίωσις, and the lack of a detailed correspondence between the scholion's content and the express language of the episode speak against the proposal that this passage distinctly drives the critique. Before we can accept Cassio's assertion that the work of Theagenes proves the existence in the late sixth century BC of a text of the Iliadic theomachy substantially like our own, we must embrace two tenuous and implausible links: first, that the scholion in its details faithfully repre-sents Theagenes' thought; and, second, that the scholion addresses itself to the theomachy that we know from our text. I have already shown that the former premise is unlikely. I will now demonstrate that the latter, too, is dubious at best.

Indeed, if we should let the Iliadic theomachy guide us, we would expect Apollo to fight Poseidon (Y 67–68 Φ 435–469), Ares Athena (Y 69 Φ 391–414), Hera Artemis (Y 70–71 Φ 479–496), Hermes Leto (Y 72 Φ 497–501), and Hephaistos Skamandros (Y 73–74 Φ 331–382). Of these, Porphyry mentions and argu-ably pairs as "fire" against "water" Apollo and Poseidon, and Hephaistos and Skamandros. But for the pairing to work we must excise Helios as a gloss for Apollo, a detail that is certainly *un*-Homeric. And it is perhaps a little embar-rassing for the allegorical reading that, at least in our *Iliad*, Apollo and Poseidon evade their confrontation. There is no attempt to pair Artemis "the moon" and Hera "the air" (?). If σελήνη is in fact a στοιχεῖον, how are these two "elements" supposed to "fight" each other?[42] Still more difficult to relate to the Homeric

---

[40] Feeney 1991: "It is plain that the author of this passage knows nothing at first hand from Theagenes' writings, and is aware only of a tradition that he was the first to use 'this sort of defence'" (9). Naddaf 2009:125n37 strikes me as unfounded and historically naive.

[41] Venetus graecus 821 (*olim* Marcianus graecus 453) *folio 270 recto*.

[42] Unless the moon is supposed to be "heavy" and the air "light." Little help is to be found in Herakleitos the Allegorist, who in *Allegoriae* 57.2–4 resorted to a fanciful etymology of Artemis (ἀερότεμις from τέμνω) to motivate the confrontation. This work (also known as *Homeric Problems*) must be first-century BC or later (probably ca. AD 100; cf. Russell and Konstan 2005:xi–xii). Hence, his statements, like those of the later Porphyry and the much later Eustathios, *pace* Ramos Jurado (1999:54n75), make no more plausible the suggestion that Theagenes may have adopted a similar interpretive strategy in the late sixth-century BC. The same may be said of the asser-tion that the scholiast's failure to pair Hermes and Leto explicitly is not problematic because "entre los alegoristas es tradicional" (Ramos Jurado 1999:54). None of the allegorists cited is

theomachy are Athena, Ares, Aphrodite, and Hermes. They are equated with 'dispositions' (διαθέσεις). One may readily oppose 'sensibleness' (Athena) to 'senselessness' (Ares). But the pair Aphrodite and Hermes is neither Homeric nor does it make much obvious sense to oppose 'desire' (ἐπιθυμία) to 'speech' (λόγος).[43] If instead we pair Athena not only with Ares but also Aphrodite,[44] Hermes is left without a partner. In the Homeric narrative, he was supposed to face Leto, a divinity that is conveniently left out of the narrative.[45] In the end, the only arguable good fit between our Homeric theomachy and the scholion is Hephaistos and Skamandros. What does all of this tell us about the stage of textual fixation this account implies for the *Iliad*? Very little, I submit. We merely learn that gods were involved in the action and that they had disagreements! Absent the poem, we could not guess that Poseidon and Apollo never fight; we would wonder whom Helios (or Hephaistos) had faced; we would assume that Aphrodite had clashed with Hermes; and we would never suspect that Leto was involved at all. Not much to claim, as Cassio (2002:118) does, that Theagenes' alleged "allegorical interpretation of the battles of the gods in the *Iliad* ... automatically means that a fixed Homer, in which those battles were inescapable, was already in existence." His inference that Theagenes' writing on Homer "must surely mean that written copies of his poems existed and circulated by 530–520 BC" (118) is a similar *non sequitur*. As a rhapsode, Theagenes could surely write (if writing he did) without needing to consult a copy of the poems. Even at a later time when the existence of written excerpts from largely fixed texts are not to be doubted, many who did not make their living performing Homer had an acquaintance with Homeric epic intimate enough to be able to comment on it with specificity and perceptiveness without the

---

any earlier than Herakleitos himself. The question is not whether late allegorists, half a millennium or more after Theagenes' allegedly seminal work, could come up with highly abstract equivalences that would explain the Homeric pairs. After all, something *had* to be made of the received text. What we must consider is whether Theagenes himself could have established such correspondences in a cultural—and, if he was a rhapsode, professional—milieu that must have been closely wedded to Homeric myth and language. Once again, Ramos Jurado (1999:56) fails to persuade when he adduces Anaximander to recommend the proposal that Theagenes could have offered such an exegesis in his own time. If Theagenes had been of the same intellectual cast as Anaximander, he could hardly have thought it necessary to allegorize in the first place (cf. Naddaf 2009:113–114). It is not a coincidence that the Ionian philosopher played no recorded part in the development of allegory; or that Naddaf (2009:109) begs the question of his relationship to Theagenes by asserting on the basis of the scholion that "[i]t is as if Theagenes were a disciple of Anaximander."

[43] The polarity would work if we translated 'passion' and 'reason'. But the λόγος that is attributed to Hermes is not likely to be 'reason', but 'speech'.

[44] Although Aphrodite does not appear in the original list of *Iliad* 20, Athena ends up confronting her too (Φ 423–433).

[45] Like Apollo and Poseidon, Hermes and Leto end up not fighting.

need to refer to written copies. There is no reason to question the existence of partial transcripts of performances by Theagenes' *floruit*, but the "sure" inference that Cassio draws does not seem well grounded in the realities of Greek archaic culture.

I close this section with two examples from Cassio (2002:119–120), which, he thinks, make the point that the alleged written copies in existence by the late archaic period did not prevent new significant modifications or "interpolations." This claim, which highlights Cassio's presuppositions, can help us to understand how existing written versions of one or another of the poems' episodes must have functioned in the culture of the time. The first example regards H 334–335, the two-line proposal to convey home the bones of fallen Greek heroes. According to Cassio, "Jacoby established beyond doubt ... [that this] is an Attic interpolation not earlier than the fifth c. BC."[46] Whether one thinks that Jacoby's argument succeeds or not,[47] these lines are a good example of what must have been true of existing written texts at the time. They will have been considered mere transcripts of individual festival performances: ordinarily, representative of the notional poem but without canonical authority. Rhapsodes may have used them as aids to training and performance, not as scripts to be memorized by rote for subsequent recitation. Individual members of the public may have owned partial texts—perhaps favorite episodes from the larger notional whole, perhaps more or less faithful transcripts of a particularly successful and memorable performance—for private enjoyment, for use at symposia, or, in the case of the few fortunate enough to afford an education, for reading and writing school exercises.[48] Against this understanding of the significance of hypothetical transcripts of the *Iliad* and the *Odyssey*, Cassio's speculations strike me as a distortion of what must have been the cultural reality: "Either the new copies were never checked against the old ones, or, if they were, nobody had the courage to do away with interpolations of central importance to Attic culture" (Cassio 2002:119). Note his presumption: i) that new copies must have exercised a good measure of textual control; ii) that those concerned should have felt a corresponding need to check the new against the old, to defend or enforce a *status quo ante*; iii) that, in this case, there was either an inexplicable lapse of zeal and neglect of duty or else a failure of courage to preserve the existing text. There was, of course, no such thing. We can certainly expect at this late date a significant measure of enforced agreement with the poem's central thematic substance and plot sequence, and even with favorite turns of diction

---

[46] Citing Jacoby 1944.
[47] His article has received near universal praise. But there are a few dissenting voices, on which see Shive 1996, himself a critic.
[48] For the functional differences between transcripts, scripts, and scripture, see Nagy 1996c:110–112.

for memorable passages. But, ordinarily, there will have been no sense of obligation to whatever detailed thematic boundaries the story happened to have at
any one time in a particular telling. The verses in question concern a detail that
a rhapsode should have felt free to recompose in performance—no need here to
use the wooden notion that underlies the inorganic and deprecated 'interpolation.' It is only fair to conclude from their uniformly positive attestation in the
manuscript evidence (whatever the suspicions of scholars, ancient and modern)
that this recomposition was done to magnificent effect and the enthusiastic
embrace of the Panathenaic audience.[49]

The second passage cited by Cassio (2002:119–120), B 11–15 pertains to
the lying dream Zeus sends Agamemnon. This is an example entirely fabri-
cated by the sensitive conscience of the scholar. For, having decided that it was
morally objectionable for Zeus to command a dream to deceive Agamemnon—
here Cassio joins similarly troubled, morally sensitive men from antiquity, like
Hippias of Thasos[50] and Sokrates[51]—he deems a perfectly ordinary example of
textual fluidity an innovation that attempted to remove the alleged embarrassment. There was, of course, no such concern in the minds of the rhapsodes
who happily recomposed either variant; nor, in all likelihood, in the mind of
the average member of the public who listened to their performances.[52] That,
after proffering the plausible pretext of Hera's successful entreaty, instead of
saying "and griefs have been fastened on the Trojans" Zeus should assert "and
we are granting him to win his victory boast" hardly seems to me sensibly to
aggravate Zeus' responsibility (or his guilt, if one must condemn his words).
Without any ancient statement to the effect, which might support the notion
of a deliberate change that seeks moral relief, such judgments lie entirely in
the eye of the beholder. If only this were the sole "explicit and undeniable"
divine moral transgression! Quite another is the ancient case that we can reconstruct from Aristotle's statements in the *Poetics* 1461a21–23 and the *Sophistical
Refutations* 166b1–9. It depends on reading what in our text is B 15, from the
masculine caesura to the end of the verse, as West prints it: δίδομεν δέ οἱ εὖχος

---

[49] We cannot dismiss the possibility, perhaps likelihood, that Aristarkhos had non-Athenian
Homeric manuscripts that did not include the verses. But without testimony to this effect we
simply cannot say. Cf. Erbse's references in his scholia *ad loc.*

[50] Aristotle *Poetics* 1461a22.

[51] Plato *Republic* 383a8.

[52] The moral fabric of ancient thought is often more complex than our own categories allow for.
See, for example, 1 Kings 22:19–23. An understanding of divine testing and double determination that confined culpability to the human sphere, however paradoxical to us, was for many
ancients an effective theodicy that obviated the need to excise offending passages. This is not to
deny that there were then, like today, those who had scruples and who for relief adopted diverse
textual and interpretive strategies.

ἀρέσθαι. Our vulgate reads instead: Τρώεσσι δὲ κήδε' ἐφῆπται (which West prints at B 32 69). Aristotle reports in the *Poetics* that Hippias sought relief for his scruples in a change of 'prosody' (κατὰ δὲ προσῳδίαν, i.e. 'accentuation'). Instead of δίδομεν, he must have read διδόμεν, the infinitive for the imperative, displacing the agency ever so slightly from Zeus to the destructive Dream.[53] Note well that Hippias is reinterpreting what for us is a variant reading to the vulgate. His 'solution' does *not* depend on substituting his own reading for the one in the vulgate. But this is precisely what Cassio's argument would lead us to believe. Aristotle does not tell us that he himself was, or even that many in his own time were, troubled by δίδομεν (he was no purist like Sokrates!). His point is simply to illustrate alleged 'solutions' to alleged 'problems.' Nor does he necessarily imply that he was ignorant of the vulgate reading. It has not occurred to modern scholars, for whom every line has one and only one 'right' version—Homer's—that, in a world tolerant of multiforms, Aristotle need only mention the one form that had given rise both to an objection and to a solution that only affected suprasegmentals. His passing in silence over the vulgate reading does not even mean that no one had found it objectionable: it was simply not susceptible of a solution like Hippias'. It is true that Hippias' strategy betrays a desire to respect the received text to the maximum extent possible. But this is not to deny the reality of multiforms, only to affirm the value placed on traditional variants. As we have learned from the Southslavic oral poetic traditions in performance, and as I explore at length below in chapter 7, Homeric epic, whose rhapsodes recomposed their poems in performance, paradoxically combined a strong claim to a notionally faithful telling (cf. θ 487–491) with the freedom in practice to change themes and diction within a culturally acceptable range. For the Homeric poems, this range grew increasingly narrow with the passing of time. Only when two variants were consciously and polemically opposed did the source of their respective authority come into view and become problematic. This very polemical clash—in this case, played at the level of Panhellenic versus local traditions—is in view in the famous words of the Muses to Hesiod in *Theogony* 27–28.[54] In the context of irreconcilable, competing claims to truth, a tradition's pretension to the authority of true inspiration could be reconceived as the authorship of a uniquely inspired author. This is arguably responsible in large measure for the traditional foregrounding of Hesiod's authorship

---

[53] Cf. Lucas 1968:242–243 and West 2001:175. Examples of this infinitival form (not used for the imperative) are found in Pindar *Nemean* 7.97 and *Isthmian* 8.60. Although not exampled in Homer, διδόμεν would be perfectly regular. Note the comparable τιθέμεν, also for imperative, in Hesiod *Works and Days* 744. In the *Sophistical Refutations* Aristotle seems to broaden the authorship of Hippias' proposal to 'some' (ἔνιοι), if λέγοντες, as seems likely, governs the ὅτι-clause.

[54] See below, pp. 239ff.

vis-à-vis the retiring persona of the Homeric narrator. During its formative period, Homeric epic did not overtly face the challenge of competing traditions. Hence, neither the *Iliad* nor the *Odyssey* explicitly acknowledges any rivals as such. If faced directly with the choice of variants, I do not doubt that Aristotle, like Hippias, might have thought desirable, if not possible, to determine on various grounds which one was truly Homer's. And that, once this determination had been made, there would be no recourse, if morally offended by the choice, but to 'solve' with only minimal textual changes the perceived transgression. An acceptable solution would proceed on the grounds that the received text had been misconstrued or slightly altered by mistake. This must have been Hippias' rationale.[55] At any rate, it is obvious to us—and, in all likelihood, to Aristotle—that Hippias' solution is, to use Lucas's colorful criticism, "poverty-stricken casuistry," "even more pathetic" in light of the Dream's announcement Διὸς δέ τοι ἄγγελός εἰμι (B 26);[56] and, I may add, in light of the specification of Zeus' agency (ἐκ Διός) in Τρώεσσι δὲ κήδε' ἐφῆπται | ἐκ Διός (B 32–33 69–70).[57]

Only one whose judgment is shaped by the experience of literacy, who defaults to thinking of such variants in terms of a morally offended writer bowdlerizing his edition of the *Iliad*, would readily embrace Cassio's conjecture about the origin and rationale for the vulgate reading of B 15. We are under no obligation to believe with him that it is "later than Aristotle" (2002:120). In a song culture where multiforms were not rare and recomposition was the mode of epic performance—however reduced its scope for change—there is no reason to assume that Aristotle knew, or cared to quote, every existing variant. And, if he actually knew both, it is possible, if not probable, that, unlike Cassio, he may have thought them morally equivalent. Were it not for the aims of his argument in the cited *loci*, he might well have quoted either one indifferently. That Aristotle's multiform was not acknowledged by the Alexandrians is

---

[55] It bears repeating that we do not know that Aristotle was similarly offended, that he felt the need to choose between known variants, or that he would even have thought it possible to determine which one was truly Homer's. Tolerance for multiforms is best lived in scholarly skepticism, and in the reception of a public that either does not have the means or does not feel the need or the desire to hold one performer to the version of another.

[56] Lucas 1968:243.

[57] West's decision to print Aristotle's line at B 15, despite the lack of manuscript support, but to respect the vulgate at B 32 69 depends not only on his conviction that "[i]t fits perfectly here" (this and the following two citations are taken from West 2001:175), but presumably also on the belief that Aristotle must not have known the latter in the former's *sedes* ("[T]he quoted hemistich ... must have stood in line 15") and that the Dream is unlikely to have repeated verbatim Zeus' δίδομεν—presumably a 'royal we'—making it his own ("δίδομεν could not metrically be converted into the third person"). But epic practice is to repeat the lines verbatim to the extent that syntax and the change of speaker allow. Hippias' proposal, however untenable on other grounds, allows for this repetition, so long as B 15 uses the infinitive and B 32 69 the indicative. ἐκ Διός in B 33 70 makes clear that the authority behind δίδομεν is not the Dream's, but Zeus'.

doubtless an accident of preservation. We cannot presume to have every state-ment Aristarkhos ever made about variant lines known to him.

6.3 The Name 'Homer'

The earliest reliable attestations of the name 'Homer' (as it happens, along with Hesiod) come from Xenophanes, whose *floruit* is in the second half of the sixth century BC (the reference is explicit in DK 21 B10–11; contextual in B12–13). Somewhat later (ca. 500 BC) are Herakleitos' (DK 22 B42, B56, and B105 = frr. 30, 21, and 63a Marcovich).

The famous fr. 6 (West = 10 Gentili) of Kallinos is rightly classified as *dubium* by West[58]—and not surprisingly. For, as Davison (1968:81–82) notes, we depend on a double emendation of Καλαῖνος to Καλλῖνος (twice) and Θηβαίοις to Θηβαΐς. The second is indifferent to the argument of this section, for any mention of Homer (whatever the connection) would suffice. But I can hardly judge the first emendation sufficiently reliable. Gentili's "prob[avit] Davison" does not accu-rately reflect the rather tepid endorsement of the latter, who merely opines that "there is more to be said" for the first emendation than for the second. The state-ment makes sense as it stands, without any need to emend it:[59] 'And epic poetry (ἔπη) about this war was also composed for the Thebans.[60] When he mentioned [lit., 'having come to the mention of'] this poem (τὰ δὲ ἔπη ταῦτα), Kalainos said that Homer was its composer ...'. Pausanias uses the periphrasis 'to come to the mention of', ἀφικνέομαι ἐς μνήμην, for 'to remember' (5.8.7, 7.19.8), 'to bethink oneself' (7.4.10), and 'to mention' (7.7.4–5). In this last instance, Pausanias uses it to anticipate his future treatment of a subject: 'I shall again mention Kleomenes in my Arcadian narrative'.[61] This is the sort of prosaic periphrasis we should expect of an author who comes to a topic in the course of his narra-tive. The metaphor is one of coming upon (arriving at) something in the course of time, while thinking or in the process of recounting. If one must imagine that Kalainos is a poet, Pausanias' words would seem to require a poem that goes from one topic to another and that, upon reaching the subject of Thebes' war, would include an explicit statement of Homeric authorship. This, we might expect of an Alexandrian poet, say, Kallimakhos. And, not surprisingly, Kalainos has been emended to Kallimakhos with much greater plausibility than to a

---

[58] West 1989–1992:2.245, *index verborum* s.v. Ὅμηρος. For this witness, Bernabé's *Poetae epici graeci* I.21 no. 2 (under *Thebais, Testimonia*) should also be consulted.

[59] Davison 1968: "Θηβαίοις is perfectly intelligible as it stands" (81).

[60] For Homer composing poems or passages *for* various individuals (or cities) in return for liveli-hood or hospitality, see e.g. *Vita Herodotea* 196–207 and 346–354.

[61] Κλεομένους μὲν δὴ καὶ αὖθις ἐν λόγοις τοῖς Ἀρκαδικοῖς ἀφιξόμεθα ἐς μνήμην.

seventh-century Kallinos, of whom we hardly expect scholarship in verse and who, as far as we know, did not pen any literary discussions.[62] Once we surrender the notion that Kallinos of Ephesos is implied, as Scott observes, there is little gain in emending an unknown Kalainos to an unknown Kallinos (1922:359). All the same, the inference seems legitimate that epic poetry on the Theban War (whether referred to by the title Θηβαΐς) was current among the Thebans, and that a scholar of some authority (of time and place unknown, but probably in the late archaic or early classical period) had ascribed it to Homer. We may be troubled not to know the precise identity of this early and weighty authority, but this does not give us leave to extract from the text meaning at the cost of three unnecessary emendations and a somewhat forced reading.

One may still argue that an explicit mention of the *name* 'Homer' is not strictly necessary, and that a mere reference to his *persona* would do. Allusions to 'the blind man from Khios' would be the obvious example. The two oldest instances are the *Hymn to Apollo* 171–173 and a fragment (*apud* Stobaios 4.34.28) ascribed to a 'Simonides' that scholars have variously equated with Semonides of Amorgos or with Simonides of Keos. As to the *Hymn to Apollo*, most now place its composition in the second half of the sixth century (cf. Burkert 1979 and West 2003b:9–12), a date that gains us no greater antiquity than explicit instances of the name. As to Stobaios' fragment, *P.Oxy.* 3965 (fr. 20 West = 7 Gentili) would now seem to confirm that it is not Semonides', but Simonides'— bringing us, once again, to the late sixth century BC (cf. Davison 1968:73–77 and Sider 2001). Furthermore, links at the level of theme or diction between an archaic author and Homeric poetry are not enough to establish a *terminus ante quem* for Homeric authorship, for these are satisfactorily explained by the influence of the epic tradition on other competing poetic production (for the case of Stesikhoros see Burkert 1987); my concern here is strictly with the time when the locus of authority for the performance of Homeric epic moves from 'inspiration' (the god presiding over the public occasion) to the 'authorship' of 'Homer.' One final matter that requires attention is the reference to the Meles, the river of Smyrna, in *Homeric Hymn* 9.3 and the connection (made at least as early as the fifth century BC) with 'Melesigenes,' a competing name for 'Homer.' Graziosi (2002:72–76) helpfully reviews the evidence, reaching, in my opinion, the wrong conclusion: that the link between 'Homer,' the individual poet, and the Meles is at least as old as the hymn, i.e. with a *terminus ante quem* of ca. 600 BC. It is not with her dating of the hymn that I disagree: that a goddess probably native to Anatolia (cf. Lebrun 1987:251–253) should be hymned in her connection with Smyrna is hardly surprising; but given the destruction of the city by

---

[62] Cf. Scott 1922:359.

Alyattes ca. 600 BC and its refoundation as an important urban center only three hundred years later, the composition—here I join the consensus—must be at least late seventh-century, if not older (cf. Cassola 1997:303). On the other hand, the connection of 'Homer' with the Meles or Smyrna (apart from the hymn itself, which I believe does not establish it) is not attested earlier than sometime before the Peloponnesian war.[63] The *Homeric Hymn* 9 alone is left: the view that it makes a connection between a 'Homer' and the Meles has force solely on the assumption that Melesigenes can *only* derive from Smyrna's river. If it could have arisen independently and can be shown to be an apposite choice for a poet's sobriquet, then the connection with Smyrna would easily follow from the false etymology 'born from/by the Meles' (cf. West 2003b:310). Graziosi seems to assume without warrant that, since Smyrna was not a flourishing polis in the classical period, no one would have thought of linking a known 'Melesigenes' with an obscure river Meles. But this ignores the role that the hymn itself may have played—why should we assume that it too would have been obscure? its very transmission suggests otherwise—and the keen biographical interest in Homer's place of origin,[64] which must have been accompanied by what I may call, *faute de mieux*, an 'antiquarian' concern even for the relatively obscure, a concern that the curious must surely have brought to their investigations. If Athens was to own Homer, since it could lay claim (at least in the eyes of some) to the foundation of Smyrna (*Vitae* 4.16 and 5.34), it is only natural that it should tie the poet's name and the river. And so we now come to its etymology, about which Marx (1925:406–407) observes that it must derive from the aorist stem of μέλομαι: "Μελησιγένης wurde ein Mann genannt, der für seine Familie, sein γένος zu sorgen weiss." But, of course, γένος (and the alternative γενεή) need not look forward in time to offspring: it may look backwards to genealogy and race—arguably an adequate generic characterization of the subject matter of Homeric poetry (especially, but not exclusively, its catalogs). To Sokrates' question in Plato's *Iōn* whether Homer had not recounted 'the origins [i.e. 'birth' or 'descent'] of gods and heroes' (γενέσεις καὶ θεῶν καὶ ἡρώων 531c8–d1), the rhapsode answers with an unqualified affirmative. Indeed, taking the perspective of a later age M 23 describes the Trojan War as one in which 'the semi-divine race of men fell in the dust' (κάππεσον ἐν κονίῃσι καὶ ἡμιθέων γένος ἀνδρῶν). And μέλομαι, in turn, is readily used to denote the poet's engagement with the

---

[63] The *Certamen* (cf. Graziosi 2002:73n62), at best, will not get us earlier than the classical period. Kritias (DK 88 B50) only mentions a river, not specifically the Meles, as Homer's father, and, like Stesimbrotos', his *floruit* is, at any rate, late fifth-century. The report that Pindar (fr. 264 Sn-M) made Homer hail from Smyrna (as Graziosi 2002:78 shows) is contradictory and unreliable. Thus, we are left with Euagon's reference in the *Certamen* 20 (as Εὐγαίων), whose *floruit* Fowler (2000:102) places "*ante bellum Peloponnesiacum*."

[64] Starting perhaps with Theagenes of Rhegion, DK 8 1. Cf. Heath 1998:26.

subject matter of his song—the *Odyssey*, for example, mentions the Argonautic tradition in an offhanded way simply by noting that the Argo was everyone's concern (Ἀργὼ πᾶσι μέλουσα μ 70). So I conclude that 'Melesigenes' is a sobriquet that describes 'him whose [poetic] concern is the races [of gods and heroes]'. Applicable to any rhapsode of heroic epic, it hardly proves the antiquity of an *individual* conception of Homeric authorship.

PART II

RHAPSODIC PERFORMANCE IN PRE-CLASSICAL GREECE

7

Homer the Rhapsode

7.1 Notional Fixity in Oral Poetry

IN HIS CLASSIC WORK *THE SINGER OF TALES*, A. B. Lord opened a fascinating window into the mindset of the Southslavic oral poet.[1] During an interview between the singer Đemail Zogić and Nikola Vujnović, Parry's assistant, the following exchange took place:[2]

> N[ikola]: [S]ome singers have told us that as soon as they hear a song from another singer, they can sing it immediately, even if they've heard it only once, ... just as it was, word for word. Is that possible, Đemail?

> Đ[email]: It's possible ... . I know from my own experience. When I was together with my brothers and had nothing to worry about, I would hear a singer sing a song to the gusle, and after an hour I would sing his whole song. I can't write. I would give every word and not make a mistake on a single one ... .

> N: So then, last night you sang a song for us. [...] Was it the same song [you once learned from Suljo Makić], word for word and line for line?

> Đ: The same song, word for word and line for line. I didn't add a single line, and I didn't make a single mistake ... . [...]

> N: Does a singer sing a song which he knows well (not with rhymes, but one of these old Border songs), will he sing it twice the same and sing every line?

---

[1]   In the context of traditional oral poetry, I use 'poet' for 'performer' without implying a claim to creativity or to the unique authorship of the poetry delivered. In this sense 'poet', 'bard', 'singer', and the generic 'performer' are used interchangeably.

[2]   Lord 1960:27 (all ellipses are his, other than the two exceptionally denoted here by '[...]'). A fuller transcript can be found in Lord 1954:1.240–241.

Đ: That is possible. If I were to live for twenty years, I would sing the song which I sang for you here today just the same twenty years from now, word for word.

Commenting on this dialog, Lord noted that Zogić had *not*, in fact, learned the song "word for word and line for line," and yet both performances, Makić's and his own, were two recognizable versions of the same story. This did not mean that Zogić was lying, for oral bards do not have the same notion of 'word' that we as literate people are accustomed to. They follow the old practice, attested in many poetic traditions, of using 'word' for units of utterance of varying length,[3] what Homeric Greek calls ἔπος.[4] From our point of view, we might consider Zogić's protestations an emphatic way of saying 'like,' of asserting his role as guardian of the tradition.[5]

We must distinguish here the perception of the outsider, the ethnographer, from the perspective of the insider, the singer. The ethnographer who studies a singer's actual practice is able to note objectively the empirical differences between two recorded tellings of the same song; the singer, while recomposing the story in performance, so long as he keeps within certain traditional parameters of acceptability, clearly feels at freedom without self-conscious thought to modify it in accordance with his personal skill and the particulars of the occasion. To this, however, he does not admit when faced with the outsider's perspective.[6] At most, he may grant it of other singers, worse or less principled than himself. Accordingly, we need further to distinguish this artistic freedom of an entirely traditional nature and the bard's self-conscious consideration of it, especially in the competitive context of a comparison between himself and other singers or between the better and worse practitioners of his profession.

The exchange above shows that the oral poet can both live the freedom of his traditional art and insist on the notion that his every new performance tells the same story unchanged, "word for word and line for line": for the story must 'tell it the way it was' and modifying it would compromise its truthfulness. As Đemail observes at an earlier point in the same exchange: "[P]eople like the ornamenting of a song ... . There are people who add and ornament a song and

---

[3] Martin 1989:10–14. Note, however, that I am not using 'utterance' in Martin's apparently reified sense. For when he writes that "Homeric diction does not pose the poem as an utterance ... [but as] an authoritative speech-act" (237–238), he seems to divorce 'utterance' from 'speech-act' (though perhaps by 'utterance' he means just the words said, i.e. only the propositional content of the message). I use 'utterance' to denote speech-in-action, the act of vocal expression. The essence of a speech-act, then, is a performative utterance (the so-called 'illocutionary act').

[4] Cf. Koller 1972 and Foley 1995:2–3 (incl. 3n4). See also Schmitt 1967 §20 and §546.

[5] Although, strictly speaking, Zogić does not avow a high degree of resemblance with his model, but rather the exact identity that issues from an act of total appropriation.

[6] Cf. Lord 1954:1.338n37. For more examples see below, n. 7.

say, 'This is the way it was,' but it would be better, brother, if he were to sing it as he heard it and as things happen ... . You can find plenty of people in Novi Pazar who know these songs but who don't know how to sing them clearly, just as things happened, just as Bosnian heroes did their deeds ..." (Lord 1954:1.239).[7] In other words, placing a high value on truth results in a strong insistence on the fixed character of the song, its necessarily unchanging nature from telling to retelling—and yet, all the while, the song *is* being recomposed anew at every performance. The fixity, therefore, is not empirical, but notional: this is what I call the 'notional fixity' of a song or a poetic tradition.[8]

In line with Lord's analysis, I propose that the same notional fixity obtained in the epic tradition of archaic Greece (by which I mean Homeric and Hesiodic poetry). I should emphasize that I am not claiming that the Southslavic *comparandum* in and of itself *proves* that the Greek epic tradition was characterized by notional fixity—this is not my reason for adducing it. But the field work of Parry and Lord shows that notional fixity and an artistic freedom of a traditional sort at times *can* and *do* coexist in certain cultures.[9] Since for many of us this is a strange and extraordinary fact, we need an explicit demonstration that it is possible. This is my reason for adducing the Southslavic oral tradition. My argument for the notional fixity of the Homeric tradition is of a different kind, and principally heuristic: I believe that it is consistent with the worldview that informed the poetic production of epic during the earliest stages of archaic Greece, a worldview conveyed by the surviving texts. It is consistent, in particular, with the claim to divine inspiration. Furthermore, allowing for notional fixity helps us to understand why a poetry cultivated since time immemorial by a long line of oral bards was, in the event, so readily assigned to a single author, Homer, the mythical wordsmith *par excellence*. This development would be hard to conceive had the tradition encouraged change and modification rather than fixity of form and content. Notional fixity, moreover, would have encouraged and contributed to the actual text-fixation of the epic poems in a manner consistent with the performance milieu of ancient Greece. For this reason it is preferable to the most common alternative, the dictation theories I examined in chapters 1–2. As I argued there, such theories do violence to the song culture and fail to account for the dissemination of a hypothetical transcript and its

---

7 Cf. Lord 1954:1.239–240, 1.242–243, 1.245 (Đemail Zogić); 1.266 (Sulejman Makić); 1.338n37 (Salih Ugljanin); 3.60, 3.66, 3.71–72 (Avdo Međedović, though Avdo's perspective is more in line with the realities of oral poetics; see below, p. 210 n. 131). For more on 'ornamenting a song,' see my study of κόσμος below, pp. 194ff. Cf. also Boyd 1994:118–120.

8 This notional fixity applies not only to the transmission from one singer's telling to another singer's retelling, but also to successive retellings by a singer.

9 Barnett 1953, Liep 2001, and Bronner 1992 situate 'creativity,' 'innovation,' and 'tradition' in an anthropological context and explore the ways in which they are culturally relative.

immediate and comprehensive sway over the poems' performance throughout Greece.

By itself notional fixity is not enough to bring about a corresponding performance-driven textual fixity. Here, again, the Southslavic epic tradition serves my purposes, now as a counterexample: Lord never observed any overall textual convergence for its songs. Typically, the thematic and formulaic discrepancies between two versions of a song by different singers were more numerous and serious than the differences between two retellings by the same performer. And where a performer's song revealed a tendency towards textual fixity, it was due to his performing it more frequently.[10] But while notional fixity is not sufficient, I believe it is necessary if textual fixation is to happen gradually by way of performance. Where (to us, paradoxically) notional fixity coexists with a measure of textual fluidity, the audience will expect to hear always 'the same song,' will project its expectations on the performer in ever so subtle and unsubtle ways and will reward him to the extent that he meets them. And, in an agonistic context, performers themselves will seek to outdo each other not only in technical virtuosity, dramatic force, and vividness, but also in the 'accuracy' and 'comprehensiveness' of their telling—in other words, in what may be called truthfulness or veracity, in their faithfulness to the notional integrity of the tradition they are singing about.[11] All these factors, to be ultimately productive, must be helped along by socio-cultural dynamics that will reinforce them. For example, to mention, among the many possible, one that was certainly true of the Homeric tradition: a diffusion of the poetry under the dominant control of one preeminent festival, the Panathenaia, whose prestige must have drawn to one venue the more influential Homeric performers of the time, subjecting them all to the same competitive rules and the expectations of the same audience. Other determinants must have been the Panhellenic cultural exchanges between poleis, and the tendency in Athens towards the end of the fifth century and during the fourth century BC to rely increasingly on the use of written transcripts to train and prepare for actual epic performance.[12]

But this chapter is not about these factors, and if I mention them it is only to suggest how one might build on notional fixity to explore the cultural process that brought about a performance-driven textualization of the Homeric poems.

---

[10] Lord 1981:457–459.

[11] I do not mean to imply that oral traditions can generally and without qualification be viewed as monolithic, integral wholes. But where notional fixity is present, there is necessarily an attendant notional integrity of the story (or set of stories) that are conceived of as unchanging. Neither am I suggesting that notional fixity rules out competition between rival alternatives: this often takes the form of one version presented as the absolute truth and a silent snub of the rest. More on the matter of competition below, p. 236.

[12] For the use of written texts, first as transcripts and eventually as scripts, see below, pp. 311ff.

Neither am I concerned here with showing that Homeric epic was actually recomposed in performance. This is a fact of the ancient Greek song culture that is no longer disputed. What scholars debate is the nature and particulars of the process undergone by the song culture that resulted in the written texts of our *Iliad* and *Odyssey*. Having established that notional fixity and recomposition in performance can coexist, my purpose is to argue that ancient Greek epic did, in fact, enjoy such notional fixity, and that this fixity derived from the well-known kinship between poetry and prophecy that has its most immediate expression in the bard's claim to divine inspiration. My methodology is simple: I focus on key Homeric and Hesiodic passages and consider their portrayal of the medium of poetry and the role of the performer. I take these descriptions 'seriously,' that is, not as mere literary conventions, but as earnest expressions of a cultural paradigm largely shared by the professional and his audience. In other words, in performing these passages the bard says what he means and means what he says.[13] This need not imply that a performer's attitude is one of straightforward sustained seriousness. Individual views and cultures are extremely complex systems, and experience teaches that humor can coexist with earnestness and heart-felt religious feeling. But however hard it may be to articulate it, it is not hard to understand the difference between an invocation as a literary convention and one that not only serves to punctuate the performative situation but is also an authentic expression of belief.

I must emphasize again a methodological conviction that underlies this book: that the analysis of Homeric poetry must be simultaneously synchronic *and* diachronic. Particular attention must be paid to the skewing that arises from the rate at which the medium's self-referential language changes,[14] a rate that is comparatively slower than the medium's overall rate of change. One must also consider the diachronic depth intrinsic to the medium, which can invest terms

---

[13] The matter of 'conventionality' is quite complex and it need not negate serious intent. Traditional Christian wedding vows, for example, have remained unchanged for many generations and are thus highly conventional; yet no one doubts their seriousness or their performative status when uttered by bride and groom during an actual wedding ceremony. Similarly, a degree of conventionality in the mode and description of a poetic initiation or a hymnic invocation need not disallow the possibility of a real engagement with the corresponding religious implications: it may still denote a real transaction between the human actor and his gods. It is helpful, in this connection, to quote Griffith's observation about Hesiod's induction as a performer (his *Dichterweihe*) in the *Theogony*: "I do not doubt that an archaic poet might believe that he had experienced something like what Hesiod describes: Empedocles, Aristeas, and others were not adopting *purely* conventional postures (and where do conventions come from, if not from common human experience?)" (Griffith 1983:48n45, his emphasis).

[14] For example, references to performance practices: agents involved, instruments used, performance occasion, etc. On diachronic skewing, see below, p. 349 n. 60.

that are, from a synchronic point of view, ordinary with thickly layered meanings that resonate with metapoetic echoes in the context of performance.[15]

I take Finnegan's concern (1992:205) that we be careful not to assume that the production of poets automatically stands for the society as a whole, or that the views expressed in oral poetry are *ipso facto* a culture's worldview. It seems right to consider a poet's voice, first of all, as his own, and to view him as a spokesman only when there is further justification to regard him as representative of the values and beliefs of his culture. But in the case of the Homeric and Hesiodic traditions, their preeminence from the very first as *the* paradigm for the cultural life of ancient Greece—for its religion, its intellectual production, and its *paideia*—gives us, I believe, precisely the justification needed to extrapolate, albeit carefully, from the record of its poetry to the worldview of its culture. After all, 'Homer' and 'Hesiod' gave Greece its defining cultural charter.[16]

One last preliminary comment is in order: simply to say that, whenever a bard sang an episode, say, from the Iliadic tradition, he claimed and believed that he was performing a divinely inspired song does not, in and of itself, imply its notional fixity. Something more is necessary, for the Muse might conceivably change her song with every telling. But this would imply that the poet and his audience thought of the epic tradition as 'literary fiction' (to use our anachronistic terms), and restricted the involvement of the goddess to the ability, arguably nothing short of divine, to deliver a compelling story in near flawless hexameters composed in performance. But this, I hope to show, is not the view of inspiration that follows from a careful analysis of the evidence. Just as we would expect the Delphic oracle to give a particular individual the same answer, if he should pose the same question under the same circumstances—whether about the past or the future—on two different occasions,[17] so also when the epic

---

[15] Nagy 2003:39–48, esp. 45–46. See also González 2015.

[16] Cf. Herodotos 2.53.

[17] Some might object to the parallel I am drawing here by citing the example of Kroisos in Herodotos 1.46–49. Wishing to make trial of the oracles of Greece and Lybia in order to learn which, if any, spoke truthfully, Kroisos dispatched embassies that, at a previously agreed time, were to pose a question whose answer was known only to the king himself and to the gods. An objector may counter that on this occasion not all oracles gave the same answer to the same question, posed under the same circumstances. But the logic of the trial is that they should have. The story opposes true to false oracles, whereas my illustration assumes *ex hypothesi* the truthfulness of the oracle. Another, arguably more relevant, objection is the so-called oracle of the wooden wall of Herodotos 7.140–141. (Cf. Evans 1982 and Mikalson 2003:52–56.) There the question, posed twice, is ostensibly the same, as are the circumstances, yet two different answers are given. This, however, is not a valid counterargument, since the two answers are in no way contradictory (even if the tone of the second seemed to the *theopropoi* milder than the first); they merely address two aspects of the same future events: the destruction and burning of Athens (especially its temples) in the first; the protection of the wooden wall and the future confrontation with the Persians at Salamis (with a typically ambiguous oracular hint of

rhapsode stood before his audience to sing a given episode from the story of Troy, their expectation and his was that he would tell it just the same today as he had done yesterday or would do tomorrow; or that two different rhapsodes would perform it just the same. This expectation reflected the notional fixity of the tradition, and wrought upon the performance even when it remained implicit and the culture did not call for its articulation and recognition. Where rhapsodes competed for approval, faithfulness to the 'story' would have been rewarded, and this, in a way that did not necessarily make a distinction between form and content. The virtuosity of form that made a given performance compelling may well *ipso facto* have been judged more faithful. Was it not the song of the Muse? And would not the performance of the goddess, unencumbered by the imperfections of her human instrument, meet with resounding success?[18]

Now, appealing to divine inspiration to argue for notional fixity might be thought an obvious strategy. But this is arguably not the case, for Finkelberg 1990 has viewed the involvement of the Muse as a poetic pretext to innovate.[19] Her analysis pits tradition against divine inspiration, seeing the former as constraining and shackling to individual creativity, and the latter, on the contrary, as liberating: "To the Yugoslav singer, the guarantee of the song's truthfulness is the tradition itself ... . To the Greeks, the guarantee of the song's truthfulness lies in the Muses ... . In other words, while the Yugoslav poet sees himself as first and foremost a preserver of the tradition, the ancient Greek poet sees himself as a mouthpiece of the Muse" (295). This formulation substitutes the scholar's outside perspective for that of the cultural insider. It is true, of course, that the Southslavic singer does not set his performance in the context

---

victory) in the second. But whatever the disparity in tone, the two oracles are largely complementary in substance and, where they overlap, they are in exact agreement with each other: e.g. in enjoining flight from the enemy (140.2 and 141.4) and stressing the inevitability of the impending evil (140.3 and 141.3). It is simply not accurate to say that "Delphi delivered two *contradictory* directions" (Macan 1908:189, my emphasis). More correctly, Kirchberg (1965:91) notes: "Die Pythia gibt ihnen ein zweites Orakel ... . Es ... bekräftigt die Aussagen des ersten Orakels." One genuine element of discontinuity between the rhapsode as mediator of the Muse and the Pythia as mouthpiece of Apollo is that exceptionally—and there is no doubt that Timon's encouragement to the Athenians to approach the oracle a second time as suppliants is very unusual—one might request the god not merely to reveal but to affect the future for the better, since this was arguably within his power. This combination of interrogation and entreaty is beyond the traditional purview of the Muse and, at any rate, only makes sense when the object of one's inquiry is not the past, as is largely the case with Homeric epic. (Homeric poetry rarely addresses matters that lie in the audience's future.) It is in this fusion of the ability to disclose and the ability to affect the future that the performative power of divine speech is best seen. See further below, p. 201.

18   Thus Avdo Međedović equates the "better" song with "the true one" (see below, p. 210 n. 131).

19   With the seeming approval of Grandolini 1996:44n37.

of an invocation of the deity, nor does he claim to be divinely inspired. But it is wrong to cleave Muse and tradition on the grounds that for validation the Slav singer need only appeal to the shared knowledge of his audience and the performances of other singers. The Greek Panhellenic tradition, in eliminating all traces of occasionality, does indeed absolutize its authority as the testimony of the Muse. But tradition it is nonetheless, for the rhetoric of the appeal to the Muses is precisely that they, as eyewitnesses, can tell the story fully and accurately. The rationale would utterly fail if there were not a story to begin with that, to hearers and singers alike, is fixed and well defined. For what accuracy would be involved in reporting a notionally moving target? Thus, in pondering the way the Greek poet "sees himself," one must consider what this rhetoric from within implies about the performer-audience interaction. Merely looking at the situation synchronically, as if the singer had never sung his material before and his every word, given by the Muse, were new to his audience, flattens the diachronic dimension of the poetry and fails to see that the invocation of the Muse is not one particular appeal by an individual singer on one historically contingent occasion; rather, it is emblematic of countless actual performances of the tradition by many rhapsodes and, as such, speaks to the accuracy and reliability—and, therefore, the notional fixity—of the eyewitness report.

A comparable misunderstanding of the working of traditional oral poetry is reflected in the following: "In Yugoslav oral tradition the poet's creativity has no niche to be classed in ... . In the Greek tradition, the idea of the poet's inspiration by the Muse offers an excellent alibi for creative intervention."[20] Here the word 'alibi' is revealing: it shows that the analysis takes only the outsider's stance. Followed to its logical conclusion, we shall have to view the Greek bard as dishonestly evading the reality of his non-traditional innovation and, in order to legitimize his creative freedom, drawing upon a cultural convention merely as a pretext to fend off the charge of singing about "things of which he did not hear from his predecessors."[21] But such reasoning merely projects the outsider's perspective upon the insider. As Nagy (1996b:19) reminds us, "the here-and-now of each new performance is an opportunity for innovation, whether or not any such innovation is explicitly acknowledged in the tradition." We must be careful, however, not to equate the innovation proper to traditional poetry with what he calls the "anxious modernist vision of the creative self," with "creation out of self-contained genius" (Nagy 1990c:55n19). Innovation is possible in oral traditions, but it is culturally specific and itself traditional. So, to return one last time to the alleged 'alibi' of the Greek poet: the corresponding synchronic leveling

---

[20] Finkelberg 1990:296.
[21] Finkelberg 1990:296.

and misconstrual of traditional innovation contradicts the notion of the poetic οἴμη that governs the performances of the Homeric Phemios and Demodokos. When Demodokos is said to start his song οἴμης (θ 74), this should be translated 'from that thematic thread',[22] and, as the metaphor makes clear, it conceptualizes the story as an established sequence that, once picked by the poet, he must faithfully follow.[23] This is what the Muses have implanted in the heart of the bard, 'all sorts of threads' (χ 347–348), not a romantic creative genius. It is helpful here to quote Nagy (1996c:22): "[A] tradition may claim unchangeability as a founding principle while at the same time it keeps itself alive through change ... . Participants in a given tradition may of course choose to ignore any change whatsoever. If they do recognize change, however, either it must be negative or, if it is to be positive, it must not really be change after all. In other words, positive change must be a 'movement' that leads back to something that is known ... [a movement] that aims at the traditional, even the archetypal."

The key, then, to a right understanding of the nature of epic poetry, with its notional fixity, is its claim to inspiration. The poet's appeal to the gods, most commonly the Muses, for divine assistance is already present in the oldest strata of the Homeric and Hesiodic traditions, for this old *topos* of Greek poetics has its roots in the common stock of Indo-European cultural practices.[24] Both the *Iliad* and the *Odyssey* open with invocations of the Muse, and the *Theogony* presents

---

[22] Cf. Durante 1976:176–177. See below, p. 395.

[23] The insistence on an established notional sequence, which answers, in turn, to the notional fixity of the song, is a central tenet of rhapsodic poetics that I will explore at length below in chapter 10. It is reflected by the language of performance as it focuses on the precise narrative 'point of entry': μῆνιν ἄειδε θεὰ ... | ἐξ οὗ δὴ τὰ πρῶτα ... (A 1 6); ἄνδρα μοι ἔννεπε, Μοῦσα ... | τῶν ἁμόθεν γε, θεά, θύγατερ Διός, εἰπὲ καὶ ἡμῖν (α 1 10; this should be rendered 'from a point [along the thread] of these events': the Muse is free to choose her starting point, but notionally the narrative thread is always the same); Μοῦσ' ἄρ' ἀοιδὸν ἀνῆκεν ἀειδέμεναι κλέα ἀνδρῶν, | οἴμης, τῆς τότ' ἄρα κλέος οὐρανὸν εὐρὺν ἵκανε (θ 73–74); ὁ δ' ὁρμηθεὶς θεοῦ ἤρχετο, φαῖνε δ' ἀοιδήν, | ἔνθεν ἑλών, ὡς ... (θ 499–500).

[24] Strictly speaking, it is true, as West (2007:94) observes, that "[o]ther Indo-European traditions have nothing corresponding to the Muses." But the figure of the inspired poetic performer is pervasive, even if his privileged access to divine speech and knowledge is variously articulated by each branch of the IE family. Cf. Thieme 1968b:226–229 and Schmitt 1967 §§89, 95. Specifically on the root of *vates*, see Thieme 1968a and Watkins 2000:101 s.v. "*wet-*." Watkins (1995b:73) illustrates well the variable idiom of IE claims to inspiration: the same root that gives us Μοῦσα, the divine inspireress of Greek bards, also gives us the Vedic *mánma* ('knowledge'), used by *Rig Veda* 4.5.6 in the context of inspiration: "You have placed on me this knowledge, o Agni, like a heavy burden" (Watkins's translation). See, further, Chadwick and Chadwick 1932–1940:1.635–660, 2.624–625; Durante 1968a:255–256; and Durante 1968b:263–264. I cannot, however, agree with Durante (1968b:263) that the Muse merely provides the singer with his narrative material. Nor can I, with him (263), endorse Setti's distinction (based on χ 347–348) between 'creative' singers, responsible for their own repertoire, and those who merely sang what they learned from others (Setti 1958:150). For more on Setti's position and my disagreement with him see below, p. 207 n. 121.

us with Hesiod's poetic initiation or *Dichterweihe* by the Helikonian Muses (more on these passages anon). The ἀοιδός is the 'attendant of the Muses', the Μυσάων θεράπων,[25] a term fraught with ritual implications[26] that defines the singer's relation to the goddesses and their leader, Apollo. The many instances of divinely sanctioned poetry furnish obvious points of contact between traditional oral epic and forms of communication (like oracular speech) between the Greeks and their gods.[27] All this is familiar ground.[28] My goal here is to focus on the performative implications of 'inspiration,' in particular, on the notional fixity of the epic tradition. To this end, this chapter redraws the familiar ideological connections between oracular and poetic speech in the milieu of archaic Greece. This helps me to delineate the worldview that informed the activity of epic rhapsodes. I argue that from the notion of epic as 'divine speech' flowed a 'mentality of fixity' as the characteristic insider's view of Homeric epic, a view that conceptualized this traditional poetry as a notionally unchanging whole, to be faithfully reproduced as the same in every new performance.

---

[25] Hesiod *Theogony* 100 and *Homeric Hymn* 32.20 (to Selene).

[26] Cf. Nagy 1999a:289–300, esp. §4 and §6. For the relation in which Apollo stands to the Muses and, by implication, to the poet, see below, p. 208 n. 123.

[27] A convenient comparative study of the relation between literature and prophecy is Chadwick 1942. See also the relevant chapters of Chadwick and Chadwick 1932–1940, esp. III.839–853.

[28] Hainsworth writes *ad* θ 62–103 concerning the ἀοιδός that "the nature of his skill is mysterious and attributable to divine aid and favour, but this does not set him apart from other craftsmen (diviners, doctors, and carpenters are mentioned at xvii 383–5) or give his art a value beyond that of acrobats and wrestlers" (Heubeck et al. 1988:349). This statement, which might seem to threaten the unique status advocated here for singers in archaic Greece, is an oversimplification: ρ 383–385 does list the μάντις, the ἰητήρ, and the τέκτων along with the ἀοιδός as itinerant δημιουργοί (cf. Hesiod *Works and Days* 25–26), but this hardly justifies our judging them all to be equally valuable and respected. (For a hierarchy of *dēmiourgoi* see Nagy 1990c:56n26.) Hainsworth's comment ignores the rhetorical structure of the passage: a tricolon capped by an entire line devoted to the singer, who is introduced by the emphatic ἢ καί. (Russo et al. 1992:38: "Homer reserves an entire verse for describing his own trade in glowing terms.") I do not mean to imply, however, that the other professions are anything but valuable and, in some respects, it is right to consider them the social equals of the ἀοιδός (especially the μάντις, who also makes a trade of ἔπη). The root *tek*- on which τέκτων is built, was used in Indo-European poetics to describe the activity of the singer (see further below, p. 207 n. 121). The mention of the μάντις, moreover, is not without significance for my argument, although the particular nature of its close tie with the ἀοιδός has to be independently established. But surely the unique love of the Muse for the singer (θ 63) and the honor in which the people hold him (θ 472) distinguish him from doctors, carpenters, acrobats, and wrestlers, elevating him above them. θ 479–481 makes clear, moreover, that such reverence is not peculiar to Demodokos (whose very name etymologizes his reception; cf. the scholia *ad* θ 44) but is shown to all singers generally.

7.2 Invoking the Muses

Let us start, then, with a Homeric invocation of the Muse; specifically, with the familiar claim to derived autopsy, with which the narrator of the *Iliad* opens the *Catalog of Ships* (B 484–493):

ἔσπετε νῦν μοι Μοῦσαι Ὀλύμπια δώματ' ἔχουσαι·
485 ὑμεῖς γὰρ θεαί ἐστε <u>πάρεστέ τε ἴστέ τε πάντα</u>,
ἡμεῖς δὲ <u>κλέος οἶον ἀκούομεν</u> οὐδέ τι <u>ἴδμεν·</u>
οἵ τινες ἡγεμόνες Δαναῶν καὶ κοίρανοι ἦσαν·
πληθὺν δ' οὐκ ἂν ἐγὼ μυθήσομαι οὐδ' ὀνομήνω,
οὐδ' εἴ μοι δέκα μὲν γλῶσσαι, δέκα δὲ στόματ' εἶεν,
490 φωνὴ δ' ἄρρηκτος, χάλκεον δέ μοι ἦτορ ἐνείη,
εἰ μὴ Ὀλυμπιάδες Μοῦσαι Διὸς αἰγιόχοιο
θυγατέρες μνησαίαθ' ὅσοι ὑπὸ Ἴλιον ἦλθον·
ἀρχοὺς αὖ νηῶν ἐρέω νῆάς τε προπάσας.

Tell me now, you Muses who have Olympian dwellings
485 —for you are goddesses and *are present and know all things*
but *we only hear the report (kléos) and know nothing*—
who the leaders and chiefs of the Danaans were.
The multitude I could not tell nor name,
not even if I had ten tongues and ten mouths,
490 an unbreakable voice and a brazen heart within,
unless the Olympian Muses, daughters of aegis-bearing Zeus,
recalled all those who came beneath Ilios.
I will tell in turn of all the ships and their leaders.

The interpretive key to this passage is the rhetorical opposition between *hearing* and *seeing*: the poet and, by extension, his audience 'only hear the *kléos*', the sung report of divine and heroic deeds which constitutes the very medium of epic poetry (ἔκλυον is built on the zero-grade root of κλέϝος). The Muses, on the other hand, were present as divine eyewitnesses at all the events narrated.[29] As Benveniste (1969:2.173–174) remarked of a similar case,[30] the verbs ἴστε and ἴδμεν must be given their full etymological force: not merely 'to know', but

---

[29] On a similar statement at θ 491 touching Demodokos, see below, p. 200.
[30] At T 258 the imperative ἴστω is used to summon Zeus and other gods as witnesses to an oath: ἴστω νῦν Ζεὺς πρῶτα θεῶν ὕπατος καὶ ἄριστος. Benveniste (1969:2.173) observes: "Le but n'est pas seulement de faire connaître aux dieux le texte de l'engagement par lequel on se lie. Il faut rendre ici à *ístō* sa pleine force étymologique: non pas seulement 'qu'il sache', mais proprement 'qu'il *voie*'" (emphasis his). Cf. Bartolotta 2002 and Bartolotta 2005.

specifically 'to see'.[31] One might object to giving ἴδμεν its full force here and not elsewhere. But the peculiar nature of Homeric poetry readily meets this criticism: the meaning 'to see' lies in its diachronic layering and was available to composing bards, especially given the prominence of 'sight' in archaic epic poetics.[32] Hence, the context may always 'reactivate' it, bringing it to the hearer's interpretive awareness. This is the case in this highly marked passage, which self-consciously articulates the epistemology that underlies epic performance: note the πάρεστε, which equates the knowledge of the goddesses not merely with abstract omniscience but, specifically, with that of an *eyewitness*.[33] Thus, in κλέος οἶον ἀκούομεν οὐδέ τι ἴδμεν it would be natural for the audience to oppose ἴδμεν not to κλέος (as many do today) but to ἀκούομεν. Hence my contention that ἴδμεν be given its full etymological force.[34] With the language here one might helpfully compare the encounter of Akhilleus with Aineias at Υ 203–205, which lacks a παρεῖναι to activate the meaning 'to see'. Aineias does not oppose 'seeing/knowing' to 'hearing', for there are things that he and Akhilleus *do* know, and this from hearing. He contrasts, rather, 'knowing' with 'knowing by sight' (ἴδες at 205 is explicitly qualified by ὄψει). In Β 484–486 the goddesses are able to relate the events to the poet in song because they have *seen* them; he himself 'knows nothing' because he lacks autopsy—and here, as often, we meet the stereotype of the blind bard who is endowed with second-sight.[35] But the Muses put him in contact with his subject and supernaturally enable a special kind of 'recollection':[36] unerring knowledge of the heroic past; the bard, 'in turn[,] will tell' his audience, αὖ ... ἐρέω. This infallible power of total recall is designated by the verb μνάομαι and its semantic family (μνῆμα, μιμνήσκω, etc.).[37]

---

[31] Lesher 1981:12–13.

[32] Cf. Mette 1961, Bader 1985, Prier 1989:15–117, Bader 1989:20–22, Bader 1990:44–45, Turkeltaub 2003, and Bakker 2005:92–176.

[33] With πάρεστε here compare θ 491. It also hints that the Muses are at hand and ready to assist the bard.

[34] To be sure, since the word κλέος refers to the act of hearing, it readily builds on the contrast between seeing and hearing. But just as the opposition by itself does not necessarily compromise the epistemological reliability of the poet's hearing—it merely denies him immediate eyewitness access to past events—neither does it question the credibility of the κλέος whose source is the Muse. The ideology of sight so dominates Greek archaic poetics that even so late a writer as Aristotle sometimes melds the visual and the auditory unselfconsciously (e.g. in *Politics* 1336b13–14).

[35] Cf., for example, θ 62–64. For the *topos* of blindness (in particular, Homer's blindness) see Graziosi 2002:125–163.

[36] Usually, the Muses' gift is expressed by δίδωμι with an object such as ἀοιδή or αὐδή (e.g. θ 64). At the time of performance the goddesses are said to impel the bard (Μοῦσ᾽ ἄρ᾽ ἀοιδὸν ἀνῆκεν ἀειδέμεναι κλέα ἀνδρῶν θ 73).

[37] For a fuller understanding of the archaic notions associated with μνάομαι and μνήμη, see Benveniste 1954b. His etymological analysis alone, however, is not enough; one must also survey

In disowning *personal* knowledge of events far removed from the time of his telling and sealed in mythical heroic time, the singer paradoxically claims the divine dispensation of perfect 'memory',[38] i.e. the gift of epic poetry, which, as ever-present and ever-knowing deities, only the Muses have. Thus an acknowledgment of personal ignorance turns into an affirmation of professional aptitude and poetic sufficiency. It would be an error to oppose the κλέος of the tradition to the Muses' song and miss the rhetorical point of the passage.[39] This is what Finkelberg (1990:295) does when, following Lattimore's translation (here, uncharacteristically misleading), she makes too much of his word 'rumor' for κλέος:[40] "[T]he tradition, or 'what we hear,' is ... not envisaged as sufficiently reliable. The true guarantors of the catalogue's authenticity are the omnipresent and omniscient Muses, who inspire the poet and are thus responsible for his song."[41] Not so; the gap, if any, between the report of the Muses and the tradition can only be a rhetorical one: the Muses' song *is* the tradition, and the κλέα ἀνδρῶν that the poet hears *and* sings is the quoted utterance of the Muses. From the point of view of traditional poetry, the way the invocation works is to point out that the authority behind the κλέος—what makes it reliable and trustworthy, and its singing, an authoritative sacral speech-act—is that the Muses,

---

the contexts in which we find 'memory', 'remember', the Muses, etc., and ascertain the views that flow from them. This is what Detienne 1996 does. See also Bakker 2002b.

[38] At Θ 181 Hektor wishes that there be 'a remembrance of devouring fire' when the Trojans reach the ships (μνημοσύνη τις ἔπειτα πυρὸς δηΐοιο γενέσθω). Though at the narrative surface level this wish merely stands periphrastically for 'let someone remember [to bring me] fire', as Nagy (1999a:17 §3n2) remarks, on a metapoetic level it surely calls for its inclusion into the permanent record of epic. And this is what happens at the invocation of Π 112: ἔσπετε νῦν μοι Μοῦσαι Ὀλύμπια δώματ' ἔχουσαι, | ὅππως δὴ πρῶτον πῦρ ἔμπεσε νηυσὶν Ἀχαιῶν.

[39] In fact, the text does not require this opposition, which assumes that the two clauses of B 486 state one and the same fact in positive and negative terms: 'we only hear the *kléos*' = 'we know nothing'. Only then might one draw the false inference that, as far as knowing is concerned, κλέος amounts to 'nothing'. I argue instead that, even on the assumption that this passage draws a contrast, its performance pragmatics leads to the conclusion that it is a rhetorical one between 'we know nothing' and 'you know everything'. In other words, 'we only hear the *kléos*' is equivalent to 'we see/know nothing in and of ourselves'. In view is the ultimate *source* of knowledge—the Muses, not the performer. Hence, the first clause of B 486 amounts to a statement of dependence: 'we only *hear*' what you have *seen* and now choose to *tell* us, i.e. 'the *kléos*'. This is precisely what the rhapsode himself goes on to tell. Because B 486 relates the source of the bard's telling to his hearing the Muses' speech, far from an acknowledgment of ignorance because he only has access to the κλέος, it is rather a statement of authoritative inspiration.

[40] On the meaning of κλέος and the related debate whether κλέος ἄφθιτον is a formula, see Finkelberg 1986; Edwards 1988; Olson 1995:2–3 and 224–227; Watkins 1995b:173–178; Volk 2002; Nagy 2003:45–48; and González 2015.

[41] Ford (1992:59–61) offers a more sensitive reading, but he still wants diachronic nuance when he overlays the metapoetic meaning of κλέος with its "etymological sense ... simply as 'what is heard'." The correct sequence of the diachronic layering is the precise opposite. See also Ford 1992:72–77.

the omniscient witnesses, are the notional source of the report. Setting the Muses against the tradition they themselves recount betrays a serious misunderstanding of oral-traditional poetics and its rhetorical pose. More accurate is Nagy (1999a:16): "[T]he word *kléos* itself betrays the pride of the Hellenic poet through the ages. ... [T]he poet hears *kléos* recited to him by the Muses ... [b]ut then it is actually he who recites it to his audience." In other words, the singer views himself as a link in the transmission of the song, both hearing and conveying authoritative speech, the divine song of the Muses.

Another textual instance of divine inspiration is θ 487–498, where Demodokos is praised by Odysseus for his accurate singing about the taking of Troy as if he himself had witnessed it:

> Δημόδοκ', ἔξοχα δή σε βροτῶν αἰνίζομ' ἁπάντων·
> ἢ σέ γε Μοῦσ' ἐδίδαξε, Διὸς πάϊς, ἢ σέ γ' Ἀπόλλων·
> λίην γὰρ κατὰ κόσμον Ἀχαιῶν οἶτον ἀείδεις,
> 490 ὅσσ' ἔρξαν τ' ἔπαθόν τε καὶ ὅσσ' ἐμόγησαν Ἀχαιοί,
> ὥς τέ που ἢ αὐτὸς παρεὼν ἢ ἄλλου ἀκούσας.
> ἀλλ' ἄγε δὴ μετάβηθι καὶ ἵππου κόσμον ἄεισον
> δουρατέου, τὸν Ἐπειὸς ἐποίησεν σὺν Ἀθήνῃ,
> ὅν ποτ' ἐς ἀκρόπολιν δόλον ἤγαγε δῖος Ὀδυσσεὺς
> 495 ἀνδρῶν ἐμπλήσας, οἳ Ἴλιον ἐξαλάπαξαν.
> αἴ κεν δή μοι ταῦτα κατὰ μοῖραν καταλέξῃς,
> αὐτίκα καὶ πᾶσιν μυθήσομαι ἀνθρώποισιν,
> ὡς ἄρα τοι πρόφρων θεὸς ὤπασε θέσπιν ἀοιδήν.

> Demodokos, truly I praise[42] you above all mortals,
> whether *the Muse*, Zeus' child, *taught you* or *Apollo*;
> for very *well and truly*[43] do you sing of the fate of the Akhaians,
> 490 all they did and suffered and all the Akhaians toiled at,
> as if (it seems) *you yourself were present or heard [of it] from another*
>   [who was].
> But come now, *move along* and *sing the lay*[44] of the horse
> of wood that Epeios made with Athena,
> which once noble Odysseus led to the citadel, an object of deceit,

---

[42] Odysseus' praise of Demodokos (αἰνίζομαι) recalls the characterization of the rhapsode as an ἐπαινέτης of Homer. The word family of αἶνος and αἰνέω signals a metapoetics of reception (cf. Nagy 1999a:234–242; and Nagy 1990c:146–150 with its index s.v. "*ainos*"). See further below, pp. 305ff.

[43] For κατὰ κόσμον I adopt Murray's Loeb translation "well and truly," which nicely captures the implications of this expression for the veracity and artistic excellence of Demodokos' performance.

[44] See immediately below for this translation of κόσμος.

495   after he had filled it with warriors who then sacked Ilios.
If you indeed *relate* to me these things *in due measure*
at once I will declare to all men
that surely the god has readily bestowed on you *divine song.*

In this case, as an alternative to the Muse, Apollo, the god most commonly associated with μαντική, is mentioned as a possible source of the bard's song. The
choice is only apparent: in his engagement with poetry Apollo is often known
as the *Mousēgetēs*,[45] and he works in concert with the Muses, presiding over and
authorizing the performance. The difference between them is one of emphasis:
Apollo is the marked, the Muse the unmarked, choice for the invocation, so that,
even when the Muse alone is addressed, one should also think of the poet as
tacitly calling on Apollo.[46] The divine action is denoted by the verb διδάσκω,
which casts the gods as song-masters and the bard as apprentice-in-training.
From such uses διδάσκω acquires demonstrative and revelatory nuances (cf., for
example, *Hymn to Hermes* 556).[47] Some scholars, however, take strong exception
to the view that Homeric epic portrays inspiration and artistry as complementary.
Finkelberg (1998) represents a sustained and particularly energetic attempt to
challenge precisely that compatibilist reading.[48] Although she does not deny the
practical existence of a complementary relation, she claims that this is not the
express view advanced by the Homeric poems. The realization that 'Homer's'
technique (she believes in a monumental poet) transcends his own alleged articulation of the relationship of inspiration to art sufficiently exhibits the weakness
of her case. She appeals to the notion of diachronic skewing to defend her assertion that Homer violates in practice what he articulates in theory. But diachronic
skewing is a heuristic that restates as a characteristic fact of the diachrony of the
epic medium—specifically, it restates in terms of its different internal rates of
change and renewal—an otherwise indisputable phenomenon: the failure of the
epic medium's performative self-references to reflect the performance of epic
as we know it during the archaic and classical periods. For example, Demodokos'

---

[45] See below, p. 208 n. 123.

[46] However, as Nagy (1999a:301–308) observes, there is a latent opposition between Apollo and his
bard not unlike the ritual antagonism between a hero and the divinity whose τιμή the hero's
deeds challenge the most (cf. 1999a:62–64). This opposition does *not* obtain between the singer
and the Muses (except in cases of blatant defiance, such as Thamyris' at B 594–600).

[47] See below, p. 559 n. 128.

[48] One reviewer considers Finkelberg "a superb logician" and, referring in particular to her second
chapter *exempli gratia*, pronounces the task she sets for herself there "misguided" but "brilliantly
argued" (Pratt 1999–2000:302). Another reviewer declares her book "a salutary reminder of the
beauty of rational discourse" (Morgan 2000:94). But it is pervaded by rigid schematisms that
often lead to forced readings and build up to an implausible overarching argument. Besides the
reviews cited above, see Rutherford 2000, Rotstein 2000, and Rösler 2002.

and Phemios' epic performances as prandial or post-prandial courtly entertainment have little to do with the late-archaic and classical festival performance of Homeric poetry. Diachronic skewing is hardly adequate to justify a broad view of Homeric performance that the poems' outer narrative framework itself gainsays. If Finkelberg had succeeded in establishing the underlying dichotomy that drives her analysis, i.e. a disjunction between poetic inspiration as the source of the detailed poetic material—for which the singer is not responsible—and poetic skill—for which the god is not responsible—she might have some reason to invoke a sort of representational skewing. But not only does she fail to make the case successfully. Note also that the 'skew' in the ordinary understanding of diachronic skewing obtains between the poetic mimesis of performance and the contemporaneous cultural practice. It does not obtain, as it does in Finkelberg's peculiar version of it, between an alleged articulation of inspiration, which for Finkelberg is ideally exampled by the narrative linearity of the catalog, and the undeniable artistry of the poem (with forward- and backward-looking cross-references). Finkelberg's skewing is entirely internal to the epic medium and stands or falls with the accuracy of her readings. A detailed review of her book has no place here, where I must limit myself to sketching a critique.

Her very starting point is a misreading of Plato's *Phaidros* 248d, where Sokrates calls the soul that has seen the most of being *philosophos*, *philokalos*, *mousikos*, and *erōtikos*. The dialog makes clear that these four are complementary descriptions of the philosophical project. Because the same passage ranks the soul of a poet and other mimetic artists in the sixth rank, Finkelberg assumes that there is a disjunction in the very notion of *mousikē*, one that allows it to be ranked high, with the philosophical, and low, with the mimetic. But this misconstrues Plato's appropriation of musical *theōria* as properly philosophical,[49] in opposition to mimetic poetry towards which he is on the whole negative. Finkelberg applies her reading of Plato to the Homeric view of inspiration, disassociating what is 'divine' (the inspired material that she implies Plato should approve of) from what is 'artistic' (the mimetic technique Plato frowns upon). If her reading were right, we would expect Sokrates to approve of Homer's 'inspired' portrayal of the gods and heroes. This is not what happens. How Finkelberg might distinguish in this case between the acceptable inspired material and the unacceptable mimesis of plot construction is hardly clear. At any rate, to point out only one instance in which her rigid analysis fails to account for the facts, notice how διδάσκω is used in θ 481 488 to refer to the divine involvement with the singer's *performance* (ἀείδεις θ 489). Finkelberg would have us expect δίδωμι instead (with

---

[49] Cf. *Phaidros* 259d3–7 and 268e2 with Yunis 2011 *ad loc.* See also Plato *Phaidōn* 60e6–61a4, where Sokrates states in no uncertain terms, ὡς φιλοσοφίας μὲν οὔσης μεγίστης μουσικῆς.

an appropriate object). As if deliberately to confute her thesis, the poem tells us that the Muses or Apollo have *taught* Demodokos, and immediately goes on to state that it is as if he had been present to witness the events in person or else had heard about them from another who did. Clearly, whatever else διδάσκω might entail, it entails at least that the goddesses and Apollo have taught him to relate the subject matter of his song fully and with unfailing accuracy. Finkelberg's assertion that gods are never referred to in connection with skills is directly contradicted by the statement that Epeios built the wooden horse 'with Athena' (σὺν Ἀθήνῃ θ 493). This language may not be as explicit as God's in his selection of Bezalel and Oholiab (Exodus 31:2-6), but it is similar in kind. Even more pointed is Eumaios' affirmation that an outstanding singer learns his skill from the gods: 'As when a man gazes at a singer who taught by the gods sings (θεῶν ἐξ | ἀείδῃ δεδαώς) poetry that is lovely to mortals, and whenever he sings they insatiably desire to listen to him, so he enchanted me while he sat by me in the halls' (ρ 518-521).[50] The use of δεδαώς in the context of *verbal* θέλξις (ἔπε' ἱμερόεντα ρ 519) leaves no doubt that performance skill—not just raw subject matter, however detailed—is in view.[51] As at ρ 519, skill, even expressly τέχνη, is readily associated not only with δαῆναι[52] but also with δαήμων.[53] *Theogony* 22 would appear decisively to refute Finkelberg's contention that the Muses do not teach, but only give, the bard song/singing, when it affirms that '[the Muses] once taught Hesiod beautiful song' (αἵ νύ ποθ' Ἡσίοδον καλὴν ἐδίδαξαν ἀοιδήν). But the scholar shields her argument with yet another arguable dichotomy between ἀοιδή and οἴμη. She observes (which is true) that Hesiodic poetry lacks the term οἴμη, a term that she has previously wedged apart from ἀοιδή and restricted conceptually to 'basic knowledge of the principal events constituting the story and of the order of their succession'.[54] And she remarks that Hesiod therefore uses ἀοιδή inclusively of what she has dichotomously opposed in Homer; but—and this is crucial—*only* in that restricted sense of οἴμη (acquaintance with basic plots) which she feels comfortable assigning to the competence of the bard. The inconsistency should be transparent: what is a polarity in Homer turns out, after all, to regard aspects of one and the same conceptual complex in Hesiod: this alone, I believe, fatally subverts the logic of her argument. But to add to the implausibility, she further requires that we unnaturally restrict our understanding of Hesiod's use of ἀοιδή in *Theogony* 22 to her definition of οἴμη!

[50] ὡς δ' ὅτ' ἀοιδὸν ἀνὴρ ποτιδέρκεται, ὅς τε θεῶν ἐξ | ἀείδῃ δεδαὼς ἔπε' ἱμερόεντα βροτοῖσι, | τοῦ δ' ἄμοτον μεμάασιν ἀκουέμεν, ὁππότ' ἀείδῃ· | ὣς ἐμὲ κεῖνος ἔθελγε παρήμενος ἐν μεγάροισι.
[51] Cf. λ 367-368.
[52] β 61 θ 134 146 448 υ 72 ζ 232-234.
[53] Ο 411-412 (note ὑποθημοσύνῃσιν Ἀθήνης) Ψ 671 θ 159 (to be compared with θ 179-181, in a passage that places skill in comfortable contiguity with divine gifting).
[54] She has done so to evade the (to her) detrimental evidence of θ 481 488.

I agree that ἀοιδή comprehends οἴμη,[55] although not just in Hesiod, and not as the unlikely combination of an alleged Homeric polarity. Finkelberg's proposal loses all force once οἴμη is properly understood, including its artistic side,[56] rather than forced into an impossibly anachronistic schema. But her reading is hardly tenable even on its own terms.[57] That ἀοιδή in *Theogony* 22 is not just the content of the song but 'singing' holistically considered (including every resource of craft, e.g. the use of voice in performance) is supported not only by the adjective λιγυρή in *Works and Days* 659 but also by the coordinate description of Hesiod's initiation only a few verses later: 'they breathed into me a divine voice' (ἐνέπνευσαν δέ μοι αὐδὴν | θέσπιν *Theogony* 31–32), where the variant reading ἀοιδήν for αὐδήν, if in fact a corruption,[58] is eminently reasonable. Note that West *ad loc.* expressly agrees that "ἀοιδή is normally an activity"; he even admits that "it can also be a faculty" (West 1966:165). Finkelberg's understanding of the divine impetus in performance[59] not only fails to do justice to the text in the particulars reviewed above; it also fails to account: for the singer's ability to shift at will from one episode to another (θ 492; cf. θ 499–501) or to start and stop at another's request (θ 43–45 97–107 254–255 536–543); for the description of Odysseus as 'skilled in song' (φ 406); and for the Phaiakians' *sui generis* seamanship (θ 246–247 558ff.).

As I noted above, Finkelberg's book is pervaded by interpretive schematisms of dubious validity.[60] Here I will only examine her dichotomy between 'pleasure' (τέρψις) and 'enchantment' (θέλξις), which if true would be of great consequence for the complementarity of divine inspiration and rhapsodic training I espouse.[61] Finkelberg wants to establish that in a traditional society the performance of a song and its (notional?) text have different functions (Finkelberg 1998:89). This seems a problematic stance to adopt, considering her admission that "[an] oral poem ... is knowable only through its performances" (89), an admission that makes me wonder in what setting the text abstracted from performance ("the linguistic content" 89) could possibly realize its allegedly characteristic function. The opening of her analysis hints at her motives: Homeric song is regularly

---

[55] Note how the poetic induction is reprised in *Works and Days* 659 as ἔνθα με τὸ πρῶτον λιγυρῆς ἐπέβησαν ἀοιδῆς.

[56] See below, pp. 392ff.

[57] West 1966:161 *ad Theogony* 22 suggests that "[p]erhaps Hesiod is here thinking not of the single epiphany but of a period of *practice*" (my emphasis).

[58] I rather deem it a traditional multiform.

[59] See, for example, Finkelberg 1998:38–44.

[60] Rösler 2002:297 speaks of her "willful manner" of handling her subject: "F. behandelt das Thema ... auf durchaus eigenwillige Weise."

[61] I discuss below (pp. 213ff.) another of her interpretive schematisms, this one regarding Phemios' claim to be 'self-taught' (αὐτοδίδακτος χ 347).

associated with pleasure, and this suggests that its verbal artistry is of a piece with its content. But this would undermine Finkelberg's underlying argument that artistry—especially artistry that may in any way be ascribed to bardic skill—does *not* belong in the explicit poetics of Homer. How is the argument to be advanced? First, she distinguishes between the performance, which—such is her claim—alone furnishes pleasure, and the text, which in turn instructs. But the categories of 'usefulness' and 'instruction' are not readily found in the poetic terminology deployed and a proxy must be identified. Finkelberg finds it in 'enchantment', which, unintuitively, for her cannot involve verbal artistry lest her logic be undercut. Therefore, she largely reduces skill to instrumental playing, as if the consequent chanting of the bard did not require coordinate ability or were an insignificant and inessential accident of the 'lovely words' (ρ 519, cf. θ 91) of his performance; or (by way of concession) she contends that references to pleasure apply "*as a rule* to both the song and its musical accompaniment which ... is not intrinsically related to 'singing' proper" (88, my emphasis). The qualification "as a rule" alerts the reader to the existence of textual data (listed in 88n56) that refute her forced schematism. If no skill in the telling (i.e. in the ἀοιδή or performance) is to be ascribed to the bard as an inherent and meaningful aspect of his craft, much less is it to be admitted of the Muses, whose inspiration Finkelberg's impoverished 'poetics of truth' conceptually (if not in practice) contracts to the impartation of developed and detailed narratives and eyewitness catalogs.[62] How does she deal with Homer's emphasis on the pleasure of the bard's singing? In a remarkably implausible reading of the paratactic style of epic as reflecting strict chronological sequence, she takes δ 15–18 to mean that the audience's enjoyment does not follow, but precedes, the performance; and that it is therefore "represented here as a self-contained state of mind that makes [the audience] receptive to the singer's performance—not a sensation that derives from that performance" (90). This typically over-fine distinction is explicitly controverted by her footnote 88n56, not to mention the singer's famous description at ρ 385 as a δημιοεργός who characteristically 'delights by singing' (ὅ κεν τέρπῃσιν ἀείδων). This passage not only makes 'delighting' basic to his craft, but also decidedly places him within a series of τεχνῖται (seers, healers, and carpenters) who serve the people with their respective crafts.[63] After attempting to marginalize

---

[62] So Finkelberg 1998:52 and 59. It bears repeating that this is the view she takes of Homer's explicit poetics, not of the actual and undeniable artistry of the poems: "[W]hat the Homeric poet sees himself as competent in is the range of epic subjects at his disposal and their basic plots, and what he sees himself as ignorant of is the way in which he should expand these subjects by elaborating on them within these basic plots, and the point within the epic saga at which his narrative should start" (53).

[63] Cf. Murray 1981:98. Although pleasure is demonstrably basic to the bard's *singing*, Finkelberg denies that it is basic to his *song* (91).

the pleasure the singer gives, Finkelberg divorces pleasure and enchantment by declaring that according to ρ 518–521 the effect of poetry is not the former but the latter (91). But since these two notions seem *prima facie* perfectly compatible, when not cognate, she must find a definition of θέλξις that excludes delight. This would seem a burdensome charge, since (as already noted) Eumaios explicitly attributes his enchantment to 'lovely words' (ἔπε' ἱμερόεντα ρ 519), and ἱμερόεις is expressly tied to pleasure at α 421–422 (=σ 304–305) Σ 603–604 (cf. ξ 387). No matter; Finkelberg seeks to convince us of the psychologically implausible notion that the 'desire' entailed by 'enchantment' has no bearing on pleasure and regards only the song's 'words'—as if ἔπεα were cold, printed words and not the skillfully performed utterances of the singing bard. θέλγειν, we are told, is only "a ceaseless desire to hear directed towards the content of song" (91). But no sooner has this schematism been set up than it must be carefully qualified: "*though* songs are once referred to as 'spells of mortals' and the singer is described as one who 'ever' enchants his audience, *except* for the song of the Sirens, no specific song sung by an individual singer is ever *explicitly* described as having produced enchantment" (92, my emphasis). Even this narrowly qualified assertion is questionable, for Phemios' song in α 325–327 about 'the return of the Akhaians' explicitly evokes the silent hearing that is the hallmark of enchantment (cf. ρ 513).

A study of the Sirens' episode further undermines Finkelberg's case: "the pleasure produced by the Sirens derives from their voices ... , while their song causes enchantment" (96). Another puzzling dichotomy (song without voices?) that presumably assimilates 'voices' to the 'instrumental music' that she is comfortable ascribing to craft. But the imparting of knowledge that the scholar consigns to θέλγειν (97), as an unprejudiced reader might well expect, is tied to the hearing of the Sirens' 'sweet voice' (μελίγηρυν ἀπὸ στομάτων ὄπ' ἀκοῦσαι μ 187). Their singing (λιγυρὴν δ' ἔντυνον ἀοιδήν μ 183) is thus recapitulated: 'so they said sending forth their beautiful voice' (ὣς φάσαν ἱεῖσαι ὄπα κάλλιμον μ 192). I should state that I am happy to translate φθόγγος and φθογγή as 'the sound of a voice'; and I hardly think that the pleonastic 'we no longer heard the sound of the Sirens' voice or their song' (μ 197–198) requires the view that voice and song refer respectively to sound/tone and content. Regardless of its scholarly pedigree,[64] this interpretation is no less implausibly anachronistic than the polarity Finkelberg hangs upon it. The logic of the narrative is clear: it does not say, 'whoever hears the Sirens' voice derives pleasure'; but 'whoever hears the Sirens' voice ... the Sirens enchant him with their clear-toned song' (λιγυρῇ θέλγουσιν ἀοιδῇ μ 44). Not only is the voice instrumental to enchantment, but

---

[64] Cf., for example, Heubeck and Hoekstra 1989 *ad loc.*

the adjective λιγυρή is undeniably one of quality, not content.[65] But this critique is perhaps unnecessary, for Phemios' song in *Odyssey* 1 sufficiently exposes the fallacy of Finkelberg's dichotomy. There, Penelope describes the bard's songs as θελκτήρια.[66] Finkelberg's contention that the particular song that torments Penelope is enchanting because of its novelty, whereas traditional songs, owing to their well-known subjects, cannot claim enchantment as a typical quality (95), founders on two grounds. First, it fails to understand the diachronic rhetoric in which the poem clothes its own performance: its narrative must present as novel the poem's very traditional subject, namely, the Akhaian νόστος that the rhapsode unfolds.[67] But, second, it also neglects the import of the statement with which Penelope effectively glosses θελκτήρια: they are ἔργ' ἀνδρῶν τε θεῶν τε, τά τε κλείουσιν ἀοιδοί (α 338), whose traditional recurrence in performance is proved by the generalizing τε and the present-tense κλείουσιν.[68] Penelope is not saying that Phemios knows many novel, enchanting stories that no one has ever heard before, but many enchanting stories of divine and heroic deeds which singers ever celebrate in song. Her reference is to a traditional epic repertoire. Telemakhos' response makes this clear when he sets the story of the return apart from the many others that Penelope would rather have Phemios sing by calling it νεωτάτη, 'newest'—a quality in the superlative that the alternative θελκτήρια obviously lack.[69]

What accounts for Finkelberg's convolutions? Apparently, her commitment to the notion that only what is new can possibly enchant, since enchanting allegedly comes solely from the novelty of the information, and new subject matter is decidedly not the property of traditional song. The scholar has painted herself into an interpretative corner that readers not committed to her rigid schema need not share. The notion that Demodokos' performance is not enchanting because otherwise Alkinoos would not have interrupted him (92) is psychologically naive. Finkelberg herself realizes that her reading is self-contradictory:

---

[65] Cf. λιγύφθογγος and λιγύφωνος.

[66] Note the opposition between the 'many other enchantments' and 'this [one] song': Φήμιε, πολλὰ γὰρ ἄλλα βροτῶν θελκτήρια οἶδας | ... ταύτης δ' ἀποπαύε' ἀοιδῆς (α 337–340).

[67] Odysseus, of course, is the last Akhaian to come home from Troy. On this passage, see Nagy 1999a:97–98 §6. See also further below, pp. 365ff.

[68] Cf. Chantraine *GH* II.240 and Smyth §§1876–1877.

[69] Unless one should claim, incredibly, that the many other songs Phemios knows are not recent but he has never yet performed them (i.e. they are old but not traditional and, because they are not well-known, still qualify as potentially 'enchanting'). One might then question how Penelope could possibly be informed, and state so resoundingly, that Phemios knows them. But all of this is oversubtle: the verse actually says that the song of the Akhaian νόστος is the newest to come round to the hearers. Hence, strictly speaking, νεωτάτη is a joint quality of the song and its performance. Conversely, the other θελκτήρια are not 'newest' because the audience has already heard them.

"[W]e should not regard enchantment as a *sine qua non* of Homeric song ... [but] enchantment may be an incidental effect of song ... . However, the fact that Homer calls songs 'spells of mortals' and says of the singer that he 'ever' arouses a 'ceaseless desire to hear' indicates that this effect of song does somehow belong to his basic conception of poetry" (95). This conclusion Finkelberg calls a "problem" in need of a solution, a solution that she claims to find after analyzing the episode of the Sirens. What is it? Well-known songs delight, while new ones enchant. The former would be the norm: "[E]nchantment is that effect of song that results directly from this essential function [of imparting knowledge]. That is why ... *ideally*, the singer ever arouses the 'ceaseless desire to hear', and songs *in general* are 'spells of mortals'" (98, my emphasis). Let the reader be the judge whether Finkelberg has solved her problem or simply restated the interpretive precommitments that first led her to formulate it.

To return to divine song-masters and their bardic apprentices-in-training, in θ 487–498, standing in comfortable contiguity with the acknowledgment of supernatural help, we meet several technical terms of rhapsodic professional practice. This underscores the conceptual compatibility and necessary concurrence of divine assistance and rhapsodic skill.[70] Thus, for example, we find μετάβηθι, 'shift [your song]',[71] answered by ἔνθεν ἑλών ὡς, 'taking it from the point when'. The passage also features κατὰ κόσμον, which recalls the κοσμέω of Plato's *Iōn* 530d7 and the κοσμήτωρ of Homer's epitaph in *Certamen* 337–338,[72] with its punning allusion to the chieftains of epic (A 16 375 Γ 236 σ 152).[73] Its semantics is almost certainly to be related to the κόσμος ἐπέων of Solonic fame (fr. 1.2 W).[74] The adverbial expression is quite frequent,[75] and it can be rendered 'aright', 'duly'. But the root sense of κόσμος is 'good order', and it describes the proper arrangement of the parts into a well ordered whole.[76] For this reason it

---

[70] Cf. Murray 1981, who also argues for the interdependence of inspiration and art in early Greek poetics.

[71] Cf. *Homeric Hymns* 5.293, 9.9, 18.11.

[72] ἐνθάδε τὴν ἱερὴν κεφαλὴν κατὰ γαῖα καλύπτει | ἀνδρῶν ἡρώων κοσμήτορα θεῖον Ὅμηρον.

[73] For more on κόσμος, not only as 'order' but also as 'adornment', see below, chapter 9, p. 302.

[74] For the use and meaning of κόσμος before its adoption by philosophers see Diller 1956. See also Kranz 1938, Kranz 1955–1957, Kerschensteiner 1962, Puhvel 1976, Casevitz 1989, García-Ramón 1993, and Neumann 1995. Building on García-Ramón 1992a and 1992b, Elmer 2013 explores how κόσμος relates to ἔπαινος (speech that builds, embodies, and expresses consensus) in an Indo-European context (48–62, with notes at 245–249). My argument below makes clear why I cannot agree with him that "for the most part the notion of an authoritative and efficacious use of the spoken word is bleached from the Greek reflexes of *kens-" (2013:51).

[75] Most commonly as οὐ κατὰ κόσμον or εὖ κατὰ κόσμον.

[76] Finkelberg (1998:124) reduces the κόσμος in κατὰ κόσμον to "the order of the events as they took place." There is nothing, however, that requires this semantic narrowing and, on the contrary, much that commends our adopting a broader perspective. If the underlying notion of order is not one of linear chronology but of a truthful correspondence with reality, κατὰ κόσμον would

naturally inhabits the metaphorical universe of the artisan, particularly, of the ἀοιδός, whose craft can be denoted by such verbs as τεύχειν (ω 197), ἐντύνειν (μ 183), ἁρμόζειν (Pindar *Pythian* 3.114), δαιδάλλειν (Pindar *Nemean* 11.18), etc.[77] κόσμος, therefore, connotes the ideal of harmony that pervades properly ordered relations of every kind, both social—in Herodotos 1.65.4 it designates the 'constitution' of a polis—and natural—the sophists used it to refer to the universe (Xenophon *Apomnēmoneumata* 1.1.11).[78]

The notion of the song as well ordered speech that is faithful to the struc-ture of reality is so strong in archaic Greek poetics, that not only is κατὰ κόσμον frequent in this context (θ 489, *Hymn to Hermes* 433 479; cf. κοσμῆσαι ἀοιδήν *Homeric Hymn* 7.59) but the very word κόσμος is used metonymically for the song itself.[79] The earliest example of this acceptation is θ 492, in the passage that now concerns us, where Demodokos is to sing the ἵππου κόσμον. By and large modern scholars pass over this expression in silence (Lattimore, for example, does not render it at all) or else take it to mean 'preparation', 'contrivance', 'stratagem'.[80] But it cannot mean 'stratagem' or 'contrivance', for nothing in the

---

no doubt comprehend a full enumeration of all the important events and their correct chrono-logical order. But it would also refer more broadly to a comprehensive narrative of great accuracy and detail that is delivered with compelling artistry (vividness, psychological depth, bold char-acterization, etc.). Such a narrative might include verbatim speeches; it might reveal the hidden thoughts and motivation of its agents; it might meticulously unfold their actions; and so on. Accuracy, comprehensiveness, consistency, a compelling narrative structure, etc. are the sorts of things that make for convincing eyewitness testimony. Therefore, that after hearing the bard sing Demodokos seemed to Odysseus 'as if he himself had been present or had heard from one who was' fails to justify contracting the range of possibilities open to Demodokos' truthful storytelling only to "the order of events." Of course, an accurate narrative would have to respect the actual order of the events, but it would not have to recount them in chronological order. It is this last, narrow sense that Finkelberg privileges and reads into κατὰ κόσμον, in accord with her view that the narrative catalog (a linear, point-by-point account of the action) best embodies the explicit poetics of Homer. Note that the meaning of κοσμέω 'to marshal [troops]' does not entail a temporal order; arguably, it does not even necessarily involve a linear spatial ordering (cf. B 476 M 85–87).

77 In regard to λίην γὰρ κατὰ κόσμον (θ 489), Puhvel (1976:156) writes that "[it] surely ... refers to the preceding Musaic-Apollinian aspect of the performance and means 'for by the best stan-dards of aoedic art'. The following καὶ ἵππου κόσμον ἄεισον then signifies 'give us a piece of your art also about the horse'." Finkelberg (1998:126) observes that "'to order the song' was the oral poets' professional designation of their method of arranging the material at their disposal." I fully agree with this statement, although under "arranging the material" I would include, *contra* Finkelberg, every resource of the rhapsodic craft.

78 Cf. Plato's *Gorgias* 507e6–508a4.

79 I say metonymically, and not metaphorically, for the relation between the song and the order it narrates, as we shall see below, can even be described as one of cause and effect: the song is efficacious, it brings its universe into being.

80 Thus, Diller (1956:51) underlines the importance of the horse's design, the arrangement that made it suitable for its intended purpose: "κόσμος ἵππου [ist] die besondere Ordnung, die dem Trojanischen Pferd zu seinem besonderen Zweck gegeben wurde, daß es Versteck für die bewaff-neten Griechen sein konnte. ... κόσμος [ist] die Zusammenordnung zubereiteter Teile, die an

root meaning of κόσμος ('order') or its natural semantic development ('adorn-ment') suggests 'plan'—unless we stretch it to apply to anything that receives forethought—nor is there any other instance of this alleged sense. Scholars who make this choice try to bridge the gap between 'order' and 'contrivance' by emphasizing the design of the horse, the particular arrangement of its parts that made for a successful stratagem. This corresponds to κατασκευή, the first of three glosses in the scholia *ad loc.*[81] But there are two problems with this: there is still a significant conceptual distance between 'order' and 'design' or 'manufacture',[82] and parallels of this exceptional gloss simply do not exist; but, to me, as serious an obstacle is that, when Demodokos picks up the song, he starts with the departure of the Akhaian ships and the horse already (ἤδη θ 502) standing in the Trojan *agora*, with the warriors in its belly. Not only do we fail to find a description of its manufacture or design, but there is not even a passing comment about its hollow inside, except to say that the Trojan assembly consid-ered splitting the 'hollow wood'—presumably to ascertain whether it contained anything harmful to the city.

Some, however, may point to 'form, fashion', the gloss in LSJ s.v. I.3, for the required parallels. But this subsection is only a mirage, at least insofar as the sense of 'form, fashion' that might be applicable to θ 492 is not elucidated by the other examples:[83] the fragment by Parmenides (DK 28 B8.52)—like the Solonic, also an instance of κόσμος ἐπέων[84]—draws, in my opinion, just like Solon's, on rhapsodic terminology, and therefore does not stand in need of a special

---

das Subjekt herangebracht wird, um es zu besonderem Zweck zu qualifizieren. Vom Subjekt aus gesehen ist κόσμος der Zustand der Qualifikation, der durch die Zurüstung herbeigeführt wird. Das Tun, das die erforderlichen Relationen herstellt, heißt κοσμεῖν." Neumann (1995:206) endorses this view.

[81] If we ignore the objections based on the established meaning of κόσμος and consider only the manner in which Odysseus requests the song, especially the clause 'which Epeios fashioned with Athena's help', we might accept a gloss like 'construction', 'building', or 'fashioning'. And so, with nothing but Odysseus' words to go on, we might be excused for expecting next the performer to narrate Epeios' part: his implements, his skill, how the wood was acquired, the cutting, carving, smoothing, and assembling of the parts, etc. But none of this is forthcoming.

[82] Murray (*Loeb Classical Library*) renders it 'the building of the horse'.

[83] 'Form, fashion' is a remarkably poor choice for a lemma, because its semantic range is so broad. I would pose no objection, for example, to rendering κόσμος in Herodotos 1.99 as 'form', so long as this is understood in the sense of 'arrangement', the procedural order of Deiokes' rule. But no such meaning of 'form' is applicable to ἵππου κόσμος. In the case of Parmenides, LSJ might seem to intend 'form' as 'outward appearance' (again, not applicable to θ 492). But one should expect a lexical subdivision only to include passages where the word in question means one and the same thing.

[84] ἐν τῶι σοι παύω πιστὸν λόγον ἠδὲ νόημα | ἀμφὶς ἀληθείης· δόξας δ' ἀπὸ τοῦδε βροτείας | μάνθανε κόσμον ἐμῶν ἐπέων ἀπατηλὸν ἀκούων (B8.50–52).

acceptation of its own.[85] And the two Herodotean passages actually do not call for the suggested 'form, fashion'. Indeed, in Herodotos 1.99.1[86] κόσμος refers to the procedural form of Deiokes' rule, a civic order reproduced by the arrangement of the houses around the circumference of the outer wall of his palace. This 'urban plan' is a replica of the political κόσμος—the noun, used here in a sense not far from 'constitution' or 'political order'.[87] As to Herodotos 3.22.2,[88] the parallel with the preceding ὅ τι εἴη καὶ ὅκως πεποιημένον seems to suggest (falsely, I am convinced) that here κόσμος might mean 'manufacture'; but one should only embrace this anomalous sense if none of the *established* ones will do. ἐξηγεῖσθαι, I agree, indisputably shows that the answer to the king's question was an 'explanation', but nothing here clinches its subject matter, whether 'manufacture' or something else. I believe that in this passage κόσμος means 'ornament'[89]—which ψέλια and στρεπτὸς περιαυχένιος doubtless are—and that αὐτοῦ refers to τὸν χρυσόν.[90] Thus, the *Ikhthyophagoi* 'explain to him the orna-

---

85 Apparently, it is the use of ἀπατηλός that led to the gloss 'form', as if the goddess were saying: 'henceforth learn the opinions of mortals by listening to the deceptive form of my *epea*'. But the deception is not peculiar to the *form*—there is no obvious change in the poem's form at this point: the utterance in its entirety lacks veracity. (If the *epea* now turn deceptive, it is because the song henceforth is formally indistinguishable from what preceded, yet it no longer publishes divine truth.) On the other hand, if I am right in rendering κόσμος as 'song' or 'lay'—well ordered speech that, in the archaic context, carried the stamp of divine authority—Parmenides' use is natural: he is, after all, quoting divine speech (such is the conceit) uttered in hexameter (hence the ἐμῶν ἐπέων), the meter common to oracles and inspired song. 'Of my *epea*' is a genitive of explanation or material (Smyth §§1322–1323): 'the *kosmos* that is my *epea*' or 'the *kosmos* that is made of my *epea*'; in other words, κόσμος is not a quality, component, or facet of the *epea*, but the very *epea*, described in the rhapsodic language of archaic poetics. The real discontinuity here is that the truthfulness connoted by κόσμος is undermined: this is a significant departure from the symbolic system evoked by the term. The reason is polemical, for what follows is a cosmogony that, unlike Hesiod's theogony, has its source in mortal man, not the Muses. The transfer of κόσμος from the context of authoritative true speech to that of deceitful utterance is rhetorically effective and maximizes the polemical impact of Parmenides' teaching. Cf. Diels 1897:66 (κατὰ κόσμον = "in dem Gefüge seines Baues") and 92 (citing Demokritos DK 68 B21); Untersteiner 1958:XCIXn195, CLXVIIIn9; Bormann 1971:85–86 (κατὰ κόσμον = "der Ordnung entsprechend"; cf. 86n2); and Coxon 1986:218.

86 ταῦτα μὲν δὴ ὁ Δηιόκης ἑωυτῷ τε ἐτείχεε καὶ περὶ τὰ ἑωυτοῦ οἰκία, τὸν δὲ ἄλλον δῆμον πέριξ ἐκέλευε τὸ τεῖχος οἰκέειν. οἰκοδομηθέντων δὲ πάντων κόσμον τόνδε Δηιόκης πρῶτός ἐστι ὁ καταστησάμενος (Herodotos 1.99.1–4). In Asheri 1988 *ad loc*. Antelami translates, "Deiokes pose queste norme" (119); Asheri comments: "Deiokes sarebbe anche il 'primo inventore' del cerimoniale e della burocrazia di corte" (328).

87 Powell 1938 glosses it as 'constitution' (s.v. 2). The presence of the participle καταστησάμενος is, perhaps, no coincidence, since κατάστασις in Herodotos can denote 'political constitution' (e.g. at 2.173.1).

88 δεύτερα δὲ τὸν χρυσὸν εἰρώτα, τὸν στρεπτὸν τὸν περιαυχένιον καὶ τὰ ψέλια· ἐξηγεομένων δὲ τῶν Ἰχθυοφάγων τὸν κόσμον αὐτοῦ γελάσας ὁ βασιλεὺς καὶ νομίσας εἶναί σφεα πέδας εἶπε ὡς παρ' ἑωυτοῖσί εἰσι ῥωμαλεώτεραι τουτέων πέδαι (Herodotos 3.22.2).

89 So also Powell 1938 s.v. 1.

90 Another genitive of material (Smyth §1323). Rosen's *Teubner* prints τὸν χρυσοῦν.

ment of gold'.[91] A more idiomatic translation would be 'when the *Ikhthyophagoi* explained the ornamental use of the gold'.[92]

Having disposed of the alternative 'form, fashion', the choice of the LSJ for θ 492, I can return to my main point, namely, that in this passage ἵππου κόσμος | δουρατέου stands for 'the song of the wooden horse', and that the word for song, κόσμος, belongs to the specialized language of the rhapsode's trade.[93] The third gloss in the scholia, ὑπόθεσις, come closest to its true meaning, despite reducing its rich symbolism to the relative conceptual poverty of 'subject matter'. For the argument of this chapter it is significant that the *Odyssey* itself acknowledges this technical meaning of κόσμος and employs it to refer to the medium of epic poetry; in so doing, it draws the closest of possible relationships between archaic epic song and the ideal of well ordered, efficacious utterance that is proper to the gods.[94] The singer shares with them in the same conceptual universe of

---

[91] As the apparatus shows, the manner of expression is somewhat strained and scribes tried to improve on it: αὐτοῦ competes with αὐτῶν and perhaps αὐτῷ (the apparatus of Hude's *OCT* offers "αὐτῷ V (?)"; but Rosen's *Teubner* reads αὐτοῦ for V also). The awkwardness results from the form of the question, τὸν χρυσὸν εἰρώτα, with 'the gold' followed by 'twisted collar' and 'bracelets' in apposition.

[92] So Rawlinson in *Everyman's Library*. Medaglia (with Rosen) prints χρυσοῦν in Asheri and Medaglia 1990 *ad loc.*, where Fraschetti translates: "In secondo luogo chiese degli oggetti d'oro: la collana e i braccialetti. Quando gli Ittiofagi gli ebbero spiegato il modo di adornarsene ..." (39). The *Ikhthyophagoi* must have explained that the bracelets were for the wrists, and from this the Ethiopian king mistakenly inferred that they must be fetters. The answer may have included a short description of their manufacture, to make clear that the gifts were indeed of gold. Just as with the εἷμα, concerning which the king did not know 'what it was' or 'how it had been made', he may have guessed that the bracelets and the collar were of gold and yet have wondered about their purpose; or he may have suspected that the objects merely looked like gold: asking about their manufacture would have addressed his doubts. ('He asked about the gold', of course, need not imply that the king *knew* it was gold. Herodotos did, and the question is narrated from his perspective.)

[93] Finkelberg (1998:124–126) reaches a similar conclusion through formulaic analysis, adding only her usual insistence on the semantically narrow "ordered sequence of events": "[T]he word *kosmos*, as used in the expression 'sing the order of the Wooden Horse' [is] to be taken as standing for the song of the Wooden Horse itself" (126).

[94] The etymology of κόσμος defended most recently by García-Ramón 1992a and 1993 strengthens my point. He argues that its IE root is *ḱens- and relates it to Latin *censēre*. Its alleged meaning is 'to announce authoritatively', "hablar / dar una estimación con autoridad" (García-Ramón 1992a:40); and, from this primordial sense, by extension, 'to arrange [with the power of speech]' ("la buena disposición resultante de seguir una opinión autorizada" 1992a:45): "[E]n IE *ḱens- coexisten tres noemas ... , a saber /autoridad/, /oralidad/, /opinión, estimación/" (1992a:40–41). "To put in order (by speaking)" is the corresponding wording in Beekes 2010:760. This proposal makes the efficacy of marked speech, its decisive effect on reality, central to the notion of order embodied by κόσμος. κόσμος < *ḱons-mos would be an o-grade *nomen actionis* or *nomen rei actae*. Although Neumann 1995 disagrees with this etymology (he observes at 208 that the order in question "geschieht aber nicht primär oder ausschließlich durch Sprechen"), he admits that it is unimpeachable from the point of view of historical linguistics. Authored by Froehde (1877:311), this reconstruction is endorsed with various degrees of conviction, among others, by

articulated speech because of his inspiration, because through him they reenact the order of reality—past, present, and future—bringing it into being by the speech-act of his performance. Therefore, in the context of the bard's performance κατὰ κόσμον (θ 489) takes on a marked character and points beyond 'aright' or 'duly' to 'as the truth requires', 'exactly as it happened'. This includes, to be sure, the order of events, but it is far more comprehensive, notionally embracing all the dimensions of the story: whatever the song relates, it relates infallibly.[95] θ 491 recapitulates, with slight modifications, B 485–486: Demodokos

---

Brugmann 1907:19 ("nach einer bestimmten Maßgabe und Ordnung, autoritativ kundtun"; he changed his mind in Brugmann 1911:358–363); Boisacq 1938:500–501; Chantraine 1999 s.v.; Walde-Pokorny I.403; Dumézil in *BSL* 42 (1942–1945) xvi ("c'est mettre une notion ou un être à sa place par une appréciation"; reported in "Séance du 21 Avril 1945," pp. xiii-xvi); Risch 1974:45 §19b; Schwyzer *GG* I.492 §III.13.3; and Beekes 2010:759–760 (who pronounces it "[t]he most probable reconstruction").

[95] κατὰ μοῖραν (θ 496) can be viewed from a similar perspective: the gods, especially Zeus, are the ones who assign to all their μοῖρα: ἐπὶ γάρ τοι ἑκάστῳ μοῖραν ἔθηκαν | ἀθάνατοι θνητοῖσιν ἐπὶ ζείδωρον ἄρουραν (τ 592–593). Its root meaning 'portion' probably motivates the choice καταλέξῃς, which suggests a narrative enumeration (cf. Luther 1935:69). The divine dispensation, dramatically enacted by the *kerostasiai* of Θ 69–72 and X 209–213, is too well known to require demonstration; here I will only mention δ 475 *exempli gratia*, which the question (δ 469–470) and answer (δ 472–474) clearly link to the divine will. Now, it is true that the gods are not said personally to kill a hero (with the possible exception of Ares at E 842; and at Π 787–804 Apollo all but spears Patroklos); but the explicit description of a god abandoning his ward immediately before his death (e.g. X 213) clearly proves that μοῖρα and an explicit reference to the divine will are mutually complementary ways of conceptualizing the unfolding of a fixed story that *must* happen. One should not dissociate this theological framework from the traditional quality of the poetry (*pace* Edwards 1991 *ad* P 321): at the notional level, both demand that the integrity of the story be preserved without departure (cf. Π 431–443 X 167–181), even as they reflect the audience's expectation of stability in the telling (cf. ὑπὲρ μοῖραν Υ 336 and ὑπὲρ Διὸς αἶσαν P 321). 'Narrative necessity' is but another way of expressing notional fixity from the perspective of the outsider. For more on μοῖρα and the will of Zeus see Nagy 1999a §17 and §25n2. Note also Luther's perceptive comments: "Die Götter haben jedem Ding seinen Anteil zugewiesen. ... Mit Recht betont Leitzke (S. 9), daß κατὰ μοῖραν umfassend auf die ganze Art des Gesanges geht, sowohl die Richtigkeit und Genauigkeit der Schilderung wie auch den kunstgerechten Vortrag" (Luther 1935:69). Finkelberg 1987 makes a semantic distinction between the κατὰ μοῖραν (⏑–––) that immediately precedes forms of καταλέγω at the end of the verse and the κατὰ μοῖραν (⏑–⏑⏑) that most often precedes verse-end ἔειπε(ς/ν). Because only the former retains the metrical shape that reflects the lost onset *sm- of μοῖρα, Finkelberg thinks that its allegedly distinct meaning must be privileged as the original one. Its sense, she claims, is 'in ordered succession'. Since Homeric speakers apply κατὰ μοῖραν ἔειπες to utterances "not subject to further differentiation" which lack a notion of sequence, there κατὰ μοῖραν must be translated 'rightly' (137). But note that κατὰ μοῖραν κατέλεξας (γ 331) is metrically isomorphic with ἀληθείην κατέλεξα (ρ 122). From this, Finkelberg infers that the sense she attributes to the 'original' κατὰ μοῖραν is the one that ἀληθείη bears. Hence, she concludes, the truthfulness of Homeric poetics and a point-by-point narrative succession are interdependent (138). Although she does not expressly say so, it is clear from her later work (Finkelberg 1998:126–129) that when she speaks of 'point-by-point narrative succession' she has in mind a linear narrative catalog that observes *chronological* sequence. It should be clear from my study below (pp. 367ff.) of

must have been taught by the Muse or Apollo, for his singing is as good as the report of an eyewitness, as if he himself had been present (ἢ αὐτὸς παρεὼν) or had heard it from one who was (ἢ ἄλλου ἀκούσας). Within the narrative framework, Odysseus acknowledges the possibility that the bard may have heard a

rhapsodic sequencing that this is too cramped a notion of Homeric poetics. That κατὰ μοῖραν before a verse-end form of καταλέγω metrically reflects the original shape of the onset of μοῖρα is undeniable. But this type of metrical lengthening in thesis was a productive performance device (cf. Chantraine *GH* I.176–177 §70). Therefore, one may not automatically equate every instance of it with an archaism (cf. Jones 2010 and Hackstein 2002:1–34). The notion of 'point-by-point' storytelling, moreover, if at all present, is more precisely to be found in καταλέγειν, not in κατὰ μοῖραν, which, as my review above of the semantics of μοῖρα demonstrates (cf. especially ὑπὲρ μοῖραν at Y 336), has a richer and more complex meaning than the gloss 'in ordered succession'. See also Π 367 (with M 225), where 'order,' not 'succession,' is in view. καταλέγειν too resists a schematic etymological translation: it is not simply 'to list point by point'. Like our own 'to recount' or the German 'erzählen', it evokes not a mere count or simple list but the structuring of a series of events into a detailed narrative neither precluding rhetorical artistry nor requiring their delivery in strict chronological sequence. Were chronological linearity essential to καταλέγειν, there would be no point to Odysseus' rhetorical question τί πρῶτόν τοι ἔπειτα, τί δ' ὑστάτιον καταλέξω; (ι 14). If the sense of καταλέγειν was the less schematic one I argue for, one readily understands why it must be buttressed by ἀριθμήσας at π 235, where for once κατάλεξον actually means a 'to enumerate'. The fact that κατὰ μοῖραν is sometimes used of statements and actions that are not subject to further differentiation in any obvious way should alert the reader to the inherent weakness of Finkelberg's dichotomy. As it turns out, even her claim that statements with εἰπεῖν are unsusceptible to differentiation overreaches in proportion as it suggests that κατὰ μοῖραν ἔειπες is inapplicable to narrative storytelling: note ἕκαστα in ν 385 and πάντα in A 286 Θ 146 K 169 Ψ 626 Ω 379 σ 170 υ 37 (cf. χ 486). In ν 385, for example, Odysseus qualifies as 'duly spoken' what Athena tells him about the doings of the suitors in his halls and her warning to prepare to deal with them; her message is not an extensive narrative of expanded chronology, but all the same it includes a brief description of past events and present circumstances that the hero declares 'duly spoken'. Similarly, in A 286 Agamemnon calls Nestor's advice to him 'proper', advice that is clothed in a narrative of Nestor's youthful exploits (A 260–272). I do not deny that there is a semantic difference between the statements that use καταλέγειν and the ones that resort to εἰπεῖν. Typically, the former refer to a report or narration, while the latter qualify an expression of wish or advice. Insofar as the notion of propriety entailed by the adverbial phrase κατὰ μοῖραν is closely suited to either meaning, we should expect it to vary somewhat: the propriety of a narrative is different from the propriety of a warning, but in both cases it is defined by its correspondence with social and divine standards of apportionment: truth, accuracy, convenience, timeliness, propitiousness, good will, deference, etc. This correspondence includes destiny and, metapoetically, narrative necessity. Putting excessive emphasis on particular semantic features risks creating an oversimplistic schematism. So, for example, in Ω 379 Hermes' words ταῦτά γε πάντα γέρον κατὰ μοῖραν ἔειπες tell Priam that his assessment of the situation and his praise of Hermes' parents are 'duly spoken'. Whereas in Ω 407, ἄγε δή μοι πᾶσαν ἀληθείην κατάλεξον opens Priam's question to Hermes whether his son Hektor is still by the Akhaian ships or Akhilleus has cut his limbs and fed them to the dogs; arguably, this is hardly a request for a point-by-point narrative of linear chronology. The rigidly oversimple explanation of καταλέγω embraced by Finkelberg also renders φ 212 problematic: Odysseus offers no narrative but a promise to the swineherd and cowherd. I find implausible too the proposal in Radif 2004: κατὰ μοῖραν, she claims, would express that "il canto sarebbe realizzato secondo la sezione di conoscenza di chi lo compone ed espone" (401), i.e. according to personal competence ("competenza personale" 402).

true report from some other Akhaian on his way back from Troy. This is, to be sure, only a rhetorical 'as if' (ὥς τέ που) that underscores the conviction of Demodokos' inspiration in the context of the subsequent challenge to prove, by singing κατὰ μοῖραν about the horse, that the god has readily granted him a 'divine song', θέσπις ἀοιδή (θ 498). The adjective θέσπις itself, from the same root as θεσπέσιος, is a composite *θεσ-σπ- of god, *θεσ-, and the zero-grade of *σεπ-, whence we get ἐννέπω: though θεσπέσιος comes to mean 'of a divine source' or simply 'divine', θέσπις retains its close association with speech and is therefore used of song (α 328 θ 498) or the singer (ρ 385). Its basic meaning is 'uttered by a god', and if it is used more broadly for 'inspired', it is because the song of the poet is notionally the utterance of the god. In later poetry the same adjective is closely connected with oracular speech:[96] the kinship of prophecy and epic song, symbolized by Apollo as the source of the Panhellenic Delphic oracle and his leadership of the Muses, lies at the heart of the description of the epic minstrel by its own poetic medium. The corresponding fixity of the resulting message as an expression of the divine will and the order of reality also carries over into the Homeric tradition of epic. Just as true prophecy offers infallible interpretation or prediction and, by its very nature, though it can be misreported, cannot change at all, neither in form nor substance, so also the epic tradition, notionally spoken by the Muse or Apollo, could not possibly change from one divine telling to another.

7.2.1 Efficacious speech

"Sung speech ... was efficacious speech," says Detienne 1996: "Its peculiar power instituted a symbolicoreligious world that was indeed reality itself" (43). In other words, as I have repeatedly noted, Homeric song in performance is a sacral speech-act, an utterance that realizes its own meaning. In celebrating the deeds of gods and heroes the rhapsode preserves them from oblivion, λήθη, and, by his very singing, assigns to them the status of ἀ-λήθεια. The epic song is true, because it is, at its source, a divine speech-act.[97] Just as the words 'I forgive

---

[96] Two further instances of θέσπις are Euripides *Mēdeia* 425 (the 'divine song of the lyre', the gift of Apollo) and Sophokles *Ikhneutaí* 250 (the 'divine voice' of Hermes' tortoise lyre). Other derivatives from the same root are clearly oracular in meaning: θεσπίσματα, θέσπισις, θεσπιῳδός, etc. According to Koller 1965, θέσπις is a backformation from the compound *θεσπιαοιδός, 'the one who proclaims the oracle through verse', which Koller connects with the epic singer, owing to his practice of starting the recitation of Homeric poetry with the 'oracular verse' of the προοίμιον.

[97] The definition of 'speech-act' used here, though deriving from J. L. Austin's (1975) pioneering work, nevertheless goes beyond it. The most obvious divergence is that for Austin performatives are principally not true or false, but happy or unhappy (though a 'felicity condition' such as legitimate authority—under A.2, p. 15—does apply in either case). Yet common to both is the

you' effect the pardon they promise—and if they are not uttered there is no remission of guilt—so also does the bard's singing underlie the reality of his story. Here we are dealing ultimately with a matter of authority, for without the proper authority the speech-act fails to be efficacious:[98] the seer is qualified by his oracular gift to predict the future infallibly, and the authority of the oracular god stands as guarantee of its fulfillment. One may draw a distinction between the god who brings his prediction to pass and the prophet who conveys it to the inquiring *theōrós*; but it is a logical, not practical, distinction, for without the human instrument there is no oracle at all, and the very words and authority of the god inhere in his mortal representative. So also with the rhapsode: his song, whether about the past or future, by the gift of divine voice, carries in the utterance the force of reality and imposes on the hearers the necessity of its truth. The symbolico-religious character of the speech-act bears with it a heightened emphasis on the comprehensive 'accuracy' of the utterance, down to the minutest details of form, even when such accuracy is not self-consciously measured by the modern standard of a faithful reproduction of some ur-text. But, notionally speaking, the sense that the utterance in its entirety reproduces divine speech—that its performance is a re-presentation of the gods' utterance—endows the song with the notion that it must correspond to what the gods narrate, to what really happened. There is therefore a fixity inherent in the Homeric tradition as a speech-act; or, to say it in another way, the fixity derives from the occasion of its performance, which is presided over by the inspiring god, who makes the song comprehensively authoritative. We must, after all, remember that Homeric epic, as a super-genre, contains a series of performative

---

notion that the speech-act, i.e. the utterance of performative speech, is *doing*, as opposed to just *saying*, something (cf., for example, p. 133). But divine speech may carry with it the force of inevitability, the implication of inexorable fulfillment. This is most readily illustrated by oracles and prophecies, a category of divine speech that regards the future; in which case, the performative character of a promise overlaps with what may at first be thought a merely declarative sentence. Thus, 'you shall die' in 'the day you eat of it you shall surely die' is not so much a statement of future fact as a threat that carries with it divine authority and, implicitly, the promise that God will certainly bring it to pass. To illustrate the same on a strictly human level: we call 'self-fulfilling prophecy' a prediction believed with such conviction by the one who utters it that he acts in accordance with it—not, in our judgment, because of any supernatural necessity, but merely on account of his subjective, yet supremely controlling, persuasion that 'it must happen so.' There is real performative force in the utterance of a prediction that elicits full conviction. *A fortiori*, this is the more so with 'genuine' (from the point of view of a cultural insider) divine speech (speech that need not be only about the future). My parenthetical mention of the cultural insider underscores that a speech-act, as used here, is culturally specific. Cf. Nagy 1999b:22–23: "[A] speech act is a speech act *only when it fits the criteria of the community in which it is being used.* To determine the validity or invalidity of a speech act is to observe its dynamics within the community in question" (his emphasis). For an anthropological, rather than philosophical, approach to speech-acts, see, besides Nagy 1999b, Martin 1989:1–42.

[98] This, by the way, is the archaic concept of lie or ψεῦδος; more on this below, pp. 236ff.

sub-genres, among them the interpretation of dreams and portents, prophecies (by seer-prophets *and* heroes), and divine promises, which are themselves speech-acts that have a sure fulfillment.[99] What still lies in the future from the point of view of the narrative, is simultaneously past 'history' and present reenactment for the festival audience. (Other epic poetry, e.g. the Hesiodic song, may even have a future dimension, a prophetic statement about what 'history' holds, or else pertain to the recurrent fulfillment of seasonal phenomena: weather, crops, etc.) To underline the efficacious nature of epic performance in the archaic setting—its status as a sacral speech-act—it is helpful to consider the word κραίνω in the *Hymn to Hermes* 427 and 559.[100] This verb, which should probably be reconstructed as *κρᾱαίνω, is a denominative from κρᾱα-τος < *$\acute{k}\bar{r}s$-η-, 'head' (cf. Sanskrit *śīrṣṇás* < *$\acute{k}\bar{r}snés$), with the meaning 'to fulfill, to accomplish, to realize, to bring to pass'. For similar semantics one can compare the word 'achieve', which derives from 'chief' (='head') and means 'to bring to a head' or 'to bring to an end' (Latin *ad* and Romance *capum* for Latin *caput*). In the *Iliad* and the *Odyssey* it takes as objects 'injunctions, behest' (ἐφετμάς Ε 508), 'wish' (ἐέλδωρ Α 41 504), and 'word, utterance' (ἔπος υ 115). Thus it is at first striking to read the following description of Hermes' lyre playing and singing (425–428):

> τάχα δὲ λιγέως κιθαρίζων
> γηρύετ' ἀμβολάδην, ἐρατὴ δέ οἱ ἔσπετο φωνή,
> κραίνων ἀθανάτους τε θεοὺς καὶ γαῖαν ἐρεμνὴν
> ὡς τὰ πρῶτα γένοντο καὶ ὡς λάχε μοῖραν ἕκαστος.

> and soon, playing the cithara in clear tones[101]
> *he was striking up his song,*[102] and lovely followed his voice
> *as he told authoritatively of the immortal gods and the dark earth,*
> how they first came to be and how each received his allotted portion.

Not surprisingly, Hermann emended κραίνων to κλείων and Stephanus to αἰνῶν; Hesykhios had already glossed κραίνειν as τιμᾶν; others, departing from the established meaning, had suggested 'to celebrate'. Verses 429 and 432[103] offered the convenient equation κραίνω = γεραίρω (so Allen et al. 1936:334 *ad* 427).[104]

---

[99] For epic as a 'super-genre' see Nagy 1999b:22–23 and 28–29.
[100] See further below, p. 376.
[101] λιγέως is perhaps best construed *apo koinou* with κιθαρίζων and γηρύετο.
[102] I.e. singing a prelude.
[103] Μνημοσύνην μὲν πρῶτα θεῶν ἐγέραιρεν ἀοιδῇ (429); ἀθανάτους ἐγέραιρε θεοὺς Διὸς ἀγλαὸς υἱός (432).
[104] Another artificial attempt at a solution is to read it in the sense of 'bringing [the song] to an end', i.e. ἀποτελῶν (cf. Radermacher 1931:149).

But in a magisterial analysis Benveniste (1969:35–42) shows that κραίνω denotes the exercise of authority, and that, when a god is said to bring to pass a wish,[105] he is, *stricto sensu*, not performing it, but merely welcoming and sanctioning it: by authorizing it, i.e. by backing it with his authority, he sets in motion the course of events that brings it to fulfillment. The essential element in κραίνω, therefore, is authority, and its natural consequence, fulfillment. The vulgate text of I 310 (ἥ περ δὴ κρανέω τε καὶ ὡς τετελεσμένον ἔσται) rightly parallels κραίνειν and τελεῖν, 'to sanction' and 'to bring to pass'.[106]

What are we to make, then, of the use in the *Hymn to Hermes* noted above? How are we to understand κραίνω at 427, where it seems to stand for 'to sing' or 'to celebrate'? Benveniste (1969:40) explains: "The god sings about the origin of [all] things and through his song 'brings into existence' the gods. A daring metaphor, but one that agrees with the role of a poet who is himself a god. A poet causes to exist; things are born in his song."[107] I can further refine Benveniste's point, for Hermes is portrayed here as a bard engaging in hymnic worship: the term ἀμβολάδην corresponds to ἀναβάλλεσθαι, the making of a προοίμιον to precede his theogony; his theme is the immortal gods, their origin and how each received his μοῖρα (here used for τιμή), the subject of many a hymn and, more generally, of Hesiod's *Theogony* with its succession myths. Like Hesiod,[108] first among the gods (πρῶτα) Hermes celebrates Mnēmosynē as mother of the Muses; and, not surprisingly, he relates (ἐνέπων) everything κατὰ κόσμον, a term we now know to belong to rhapsodic practice—one that has the potential to resonate deeply with archaic sacral notions of performance. In fact, Hermes' initial recital offers a *mise en abyme*, for in singing about his own begetting he sends us back to the beginning verses 3–16.

Hermes here performs as the ideal rhapsode that all human bards should seek to imitate: the hymn carefully notes that Mnēmosynē 'received the son of Maia as her portion',[109] which speaks to his engagement with μουσική.[110] Not infrequently does Greek culture portray the gods as archetypes, even of activi-

---

[105] Cf. B 419 for a negative example that involves Zeus.

[106] Cf. Plato's *Lesser Hippias* 365a3. Similarly, at τ 565 ἔπε' ἀκράαντα correspond to dreams that pass through the gates of ivory, in contrast to those that, coming forth through gates of horn, 'bring to pass true things' (ἔτυμα κραίνουσι τ 567). Cf. Empedokles DK 31 B111.2 and Euripides *Iōn* 464 (μαντεύματα κραίνει).

[107] "Le dieu chante l'origine des choses et par son chant 'promeut à l'existence' les dieux. Métaphore hardie, mais qui s'accorde au rôle d'un poète qui est lui-même un dieu. Un poète fait exister; les choses prennent naissance dans son chant."

[108] *Theogony* 34; cf. 36, 53–54.

[109] ἥ γὰρ λάχε Μαιάδος υἱόν (430).

[110] "Die Beziehungen des Hermes zu Mnemosyne und den Musen sind in der musikalischen Natur des Gottes begründet" (Radermacher 1931:150). For Hermes' association with the nymphs, often in the context of dance and song, see Larson 1995:349n25.

ties that, by any reckoning, are eminently human—e.g. animal sacrifice, which (to go no further) in this very hymn involves Hermes himself (*ad* 115–137): this is also the case with rhapsodic performance.[111] It is no objection to my reading to note that Hermes is not singing heroic epic, but a theogony instead: the god starts with a hymnic προοίμιον, which, as I point out below (see p. 233), is the ritual framework of the archaic epic performance. And a theogony, too, is but a particularly elaborate and unusually long hymn, but a hymn nonetheless. The Panhellenic nature of the Homeric tradition is so thoroughgoing that, in the final form in which it has come down to us, it lacks a hymnic opening such as must have regularly preceded it—no hymn, however Panhellenic, which might otherwise have provided traces of occasionality, succeeded in acquiring canonical status as *the* fixed opening (though we have reports, even at a late date, of a written copy of the *Iliad* explicitly framed by such a hymnic προοίμιον). But that, ritually speaking, epic performance took place in the context of a hymn that invoked a presiding deity, at least at sufficiently early stages, is, I believe, unquestionable. And, *a fortiori*, we can assume that the sacral character of hymnic speech did apply to the Homeric tradition in performance.

Later in the same hymn Apollo gives Hermes a ῥάβδος (529). This is not *merely* a rhapsode's staff: it has functions that exceed the bard's emblem of authoritative singing, for it promises to keep him safe, ἀκήριος (530),[112] and the attainment of wealth and fortune, ὄλβος and πλοῦτος (529). Doubtless we are supposed to think here of the κηρύκειον, which makes Hermes χρυσόρραπις (ε 87 κ 277; cf. Pindar *Pythian* 4.178). This gift of Apollo represents Hermes' τιμή[113] and signals his attaining the same honor and wealth that are the privilege of the other gods—a key theme in the hymn;[114] but, I think, it is also legitimate to

---

[111] For a study of Hermes as 'god of music' cf. Hübner 1986.

[112] Perhaps a reference to some sort of τελεταί, which feature Hermes as the divine 'pioneer' in whose steps the initiates follow.

[113] That Hermes' τιμή should come by way of an exchange fits his role as worker of ἐπαμοίβιμα ἔργα (516–517). Nagy 1990a analyzes the exchange as the mythical reenactment of the separation into the distinct realms of poetry and prophecy of what was, at first, an undifferentiated poet-prophet *demiourgos*; once *mantis* and *kērux*, the old labels for the poet-prophet, became semantically specialized and ceased to be appropriate, the general term *aoidos*—he argues—took over the general category. But (this is crucial) "the *aoidos* ... remained in the sacral realm of prophecy, as evidenced by [his] institutional dependence ... on the divine inspiration of the Muse" (1990a:57). As regards the *Hymn to Hermes*, by acquiring the lyre Apollo takes over μουσική as Panhellenic, just as the Panhellenic μαντική of Delphi remains strictly his purview, whereas Hermes is allowed only the ὀμφή conveyed by the 'bee maidens'.

[114] αὐτὰρ ἐγὼ τέχνης ἐπιβήσομαι ἥ τις ἀρίστη | βουκολέων ἐμὲ καὶ σὲ διαμπερές· οὐδὲ θεοῖσι | νῶϊ μετ' ἀθανάτοισιν ἀδώρητοι καὶ ἄλιστοι | αὐτοῦ τῇδε μένοντες ἀνεξόμεθ', ὡς σὺ κελεύεις. | βέλτερον ἤματα πάντα μετ' ἀθανάτοις ὀαρίζειν | πλούσιον ἀφνειὸν πολυλήϊον ἢ κατὰ δῶμα | ἄντρῳ ἐν ἠερόεντι θαασσέμεν· ἀμφὶ δὲ τιμῆς | κἀγὼ τῆς ὁσίης ἐπιβήσομαι ἧς περ Ἀπόλλων (166–173; cf. 460–462, 576).

read it in reference to the χάρις of performance, i.e. the economic reciprocity of patronage—the μισθός and τιμή—we know well from Pindar's poetry.[115] The staff, moreover, will fulfill, ἐπικραίνουσα (531), all the dispositions (θεμούς 531) of good words and deeds (ἐπέων τε καὶ ἔργων 531) which Apollo learns from the utterance (ὀμφή 532)[116] of Zeus.[117] The powers of Hermes' staff are unequivocally subservient to Apollo's gift of μαντεία and do not encroach upon Delphic divination, but it is unquestionable that they encompass the ability to bring to pass Zeus' utterance, as declared by Apollo. Hermes, in his role as a rhapsode, declares authoritatively the utterance of Zeus: the sacral character of his utterance is explicit. The ὀμφή of Zeus is denoted by θεμοί (from τίθημι) of good 'words and deeds': the oracular pronouncement is made of words that have the power to bring about the deeds they declare, and it is legitimate, I think, to read the usual dichotomy—here in reference to Zeus' speech—as a hendiadys, namely, 'performative words'.[118] It is true that Hermes is not known elsewhere as an intermediary of oracular speech, though in his capacity as a messenger or herald (ἄγγελον 3), this function would not be entirely without conceptual precedent. But, even so, interpreting the role of the ῥάβδος in harmony with the rhapsodic language doubtless present in the earlier instance of κραίνω is preferable, I believe, to thinking of Hermes as fulfilling the utterance of Zeus by his direct action: where he is 'instrumental' in some way to the fulfillment of Zeus' will, it is most often in his function as divine herald, where the word of authority is first and last (so at ε 87–90[119]). I wonder if perhaps there is a hint here of the division of labor between the Delphic μάντις and her προφήτης; Hermes might then stand for the tradition of oracular hexametric poetry we know from Delphi.[120]

---

[115] Cf. Nagy 1990c:188–190 and Kurke 1991.

[116] ὀμφή < *song^{u}hā is cognate with the word 'song'.

[117] αὐτὰρ ἔπειτα | ὄλβου καὶ πλούτου δώσω περικαλλέα ῥάβδον | χρυσείην τριπέτηλον, ἀκήριον ἥ σε φυλάξει | πάντας ἐπικραίνουσα θεμοὺς ἐπέων τε καὶ ἔργων | τῶν ἀγαθῶν ὅσα φημὶ δαήμεναι ἐκ Διὸς ὀμφῆς (528–532).

[118] That is, words that are deeds, or deeds that come in the form of words. The emendation θεμούς for the transmitted θεούς at 531 seems certain

[119] τίπτε μοι, Ἑρμεία χρυσόρραπι, εἰλήλουθας, | αἰδοῖός τε φίλος τε; πάρος γε μὲν οὔ τι θαμίζεις. | αὖδα ὅ τι φρονέεις· τελέσαι δέ με θυμὸς ἄνωγεν, | εἰ δύναμαι τελέσαι γε καὶ εἰ τετελεσμένον ἐστίν.

[120] Obviously relevant is the latter part of the hymn, with the three μοῖραι (or σεμναί, as one ms. and most modern editors would have it): sister-bees who live under the fold of Parnassos and whom Apollo grants to Hermes as independent 'teachers' of prophecy; when they feed on honey they 'bring each thing to pass', κραίνουσιν ἕκαστα (559). This is not the place to go into the many interesting issues raised by this puzzling passage (for two helpful assessments see Scheinberg 1979 and Larson 1995). For my argument here, the essential point to bear in mind is that their 'accomplishing' each thing takes place in the context of oracular inquiry (most likely, of cleromancy, cf. Larson 1995:350–351; the use of *astragaloi*, common in gaming, explains the pleasure [τέρπε 565] and the luck [αἴ κε τύχῃσι 566] involved in the inquiry). After feeding

7.2.2 Quoted speech

To return to the Homeric poems, the invocation of the Muses at B 484–493 precedes what is, by any account, a mnemonic feat of the first order. But it would be an error to conclude from this that the goddesses are seen as providing the singer merely with the requisite information, without reference to its poetic form.[121] Not so: from the perspective of the oral tradition "the story's the thing," to use Lord's own words (Lord 1985:37); the audience gathers to hear a tale, and so the focus is not on the specific wording. Though the bard does not set out to 'memorize' the story (in the mechanical sense in which we today tend to think of memorizing), it is still true that, in performance, he 'remembers' it. Hence his natural focus on the story's actors and actions, without implying an anachronistic opposition of form to substance.

But, reciprocally, this does not mean that, from the perspective of the insider to the tradition, the particular words sung, with all their formal features—what

---

on honey they 'tell the truth', ἀληθείην ἀγορεύειν (561)—a statement that underlines the association of κραίνω and ἀλήθεια and recalls the Muses' words to Hesiod, ἴδμεν δ' εὖτ' ἐθέλωμεν ἀληθέα γηρύσασθαι (*Theogony* 28); otherwise, they 'lie' (ψεύδονται 563), which, considering the performative nature of oracular revelation, speaks not so much of its disparity with reality as of its failure to come to pass (cf. B 138 β 202).

[121] This is Setti's stance, calculated to dissociate Homeric performance from oracular delivery, which he views strictly as ecstatic (on the semantics of 'ecstasy,' a word that is often misleading, see below, pp. 267ff.): "[La modalità del dono della poesia] non riguarda, o non riguarda soltanto, una forma o qualità, un grado o perfezione di essa forma, ma più veramente investe il contenuto del canto, la sua essenza, che è essenza di storia e di verità" (Setti 1958:151). And yet commenting on χ 347–348 he does not oppose divine inspiration to Phemios' self-description as αὐτοδίδακτος (150), and even questions the propriety of deriving from this passage a self-conscious distinction between form and substance (152n4). According to Lanata (1963:13–14), Phemios claims to be self-taught not in regard to "il contenuto del suo canto," but to "l'arte, la tecnica poetica con cui dar forma a quel contenuto che gli viene dall'alto." Durante 1968b follows Setti, though with comparatively less nuance: "[D]er Dichter [befolgt] die alte Theorie vom göttlichen Eingreifen ... in Beschränkung auf die Übermittlung des Erzählstoffes" (263); "Folglich beschränkt sich die göttliche Beteiligung darauf, dem Sinn des Aoiden die Kenntnis der Fakten einzuflößen" (277). I can readily agree that the primary reference of οἴμη (χ 347; cf. θ 74 481) is to what Lord calls the 'story', i.e. the sequence of themes that make up his singing (see immediately below). Form is not explicitly in view, simply because the oral bard (at least in those stages of the tradition where the poetry is most fluid) is not self-conscious about his formulaic diction. We are still far here from the poet who conceptualizes his trade as the artful assembly of words painstakingly arranged with an eye to the *formal* beauty of the whole. Not even Pindar's ἐξ ἐπέων ... τέκτονες οἷα σοφοί ἅρμοσαν (*Pythian* 3.113–114) should be read thus. Such ἔπη are *not* individual words (we might be tempted to think of his newly coined adjectives), but the archaic units of utterance: the language is thoroughly traditional, as is the corresponding description, one that likely underlies the identity of Homer as the one who assembles ἔπη together (ὁμ- + ἀρ-; cf. Nagy 1999a:297–300). Pindar's poetics, of course, is not that of archaic epic (witness, for example, his very different use of μῦθος); but his adherence to traditional motifs and language results in a sort of diachronic skewing not unlike the one that shapes the self-reflection of Homeric poetics. (On diachronic skewing, see below, p. 349 n. 60.)

we might call their 'poetic diction'—are indifferent. On the contrary, notionally they are an oral quotation of the Muses' own song, and thus they come with their divine performative sanction: the song of the goddesses is the song of the poet. Recalling that the additive style of oral epic tends to respect the limits of the verse-line by making the syntactical and metrical periods coterminous, Nagy (1999a:272) notes that ἔπος refers to the hexameter line and, by extension, to a unit of poetic utterance; and, consequently, such well-known introductions as καί μιν φωνήσας ἔπεα πτερόεντα προσηύδα, which the master narrator uses to punctuate the beginning of quoted dialog, carry with them the notion of accuracy down to the minutest details of diction. Indeed, the medium of Homeric poetry has developed performative conventions of such a high degree of refinement, that formal features like correption may be found to discriminate between the quoted ἔπος of characters and the quoted ἔπος of the Muse in plain narrative.[122] Such a comprehensive accuracy of quoted speech requires the song's full correspondence to an original—only, here the original has a divine source, a matter of the greatest moment, which implies in turn, as I shall demonstrate in what follows, the notional fixity of the story.

7.2.3 The singer, instrument of the Muse

The epic singer, then, is seen here as the vehicle of the god; not a passive one, to be sure, despite Plato's strictures—which I take up below (p. 267)—but a vehicle all the same, one that makes available in the here-and-now events that transpired long ago. He transcends space and time, and the authority of the Muse or Apollo[123] guarantees the faithfulness of his reperformance of the tradition. As Vernant (1983:75–81) and Detienne 1996 have observed, in this particular capacity archaic poetry embodies the 'social memory' of its oral culture. For this reason Mnēmosynē is conceptualized as the mother of the Muses in Hesiod's

---

[122] Cf. Kelly 1990, cited by Nagy 1999a:272 §7n8. For a critical update of Kelly's work, see Garner 2011.

[123] Apollo and the Muses are often joined together in poetry, e.g. in Hesiod's *Theogony* 94–95: ἐκ γάρ τοι Μουσέων καὶ ἑκηβόλου Ἀπόλλωνος | ἄνδρες ἀοιδοὶ ἔασιν ἐπὶ χθόνα καὶ κιθαρισταί. Cf. A 603–604, *Hymn to Hermes* 450–452, *Hymn to Apollo* 189, Hesiod *Shield* 202–206, Pausanias 5.18.4, Strabo X.3 §10, Plato *Laws* 653d, and Himerios *Orations* 62.7 (p. 226 Colonna). For Apollo as the μουσαγέτας (or μουσηγέτης in Ionic) see Pindar fr. 94c M, IG XII.5 no. 893 (Tenos, III/II BC), *Milet* I.3 no. 145 (Kawerau and Rehm 1914:327), and perhaps Sappho fr. 208 LP (*apud* Himerios). There is even a tradition, ascribed to Eumelos (*PEG* I.114 F17 Bernabé), that made the Muses Apollo's daughters. Fr. 23 of the *lyrica adespota* (*PMG*) features Apollo as the μούσαρχος: σπένδωμεν ταῖς Μνάμας παισὶν Μούσαις | καὶ τῶι μουσάρχωι (τῶι) Λατοῦς υἱεῖ; and IG VII.36 (Megara, *aet. Aug.*) gives him the epithet μούσειος. Though the Muses receive cult in their own right, sometimes they are also associated with Apollo (e.g. Pausanias 8.32.2 and Sokolowski *LSCG* 180). See Farnell 1896–1909:5.434–437. For a complex triangulation of Apollo, the Muses, and the poet in the matter of inspiration in the *Argonautika* of Apollonios of Rhodes, see González 2000. For the poet as the θεράπων of the Muses and Apollo, see Nagy 1999a:289–308 (esp. 291–292, 296–297, and 305–306).

Theogony 54, and in Khios the Muses themselves were called Μνεῖαι.[124] Time and identity are here entwined, for identity is constructed by the reenactment, again and again, of what is notionally fixed, and the recurrence of sameness is the peculiar work of Memory. When the Muses supernaturally reenact the heroic past in the moment of performance, they thrust the bard *in medias res*, they grant him derived, but infallible, autopsy, so that the events largely take place in their natural order before him.[125] Hence, narrative time by and large simply reflects the straightforward sequence of events;[126] even similes often fail to interrupt its flow, and when the narrator resumes the action, we discover that its progress has not been suspended by the apparent aside.[127]

It is important to remember that the time transcended by the poet is not 'historical' time, that is, his performance does not recover a chronology of events that stands in continuity with contemporaneous history: he views the story, rather, in terms of genesis, genealogies, and becoming;[128] and though he may incorporate a logic of historical evolution—stages, races, epochs—the events remain in the otherwise inaccessible past. Only a later mind-set that has left the archaic mold can concern itself with fixing chronologically the time of the

---

[124] Plutarch *Quaestiones convivales* IX.14.1 (743d): ἐνιαχοῦ δὲ καὶ πάσας, ὥσπερ ἐν Χίῳ, τὰς Μούσας μνείας καλεῖσθαι λέγουσιν. Cf. Pindar *Nemean* 1.12: Μοῖσα μεμνᾶσθαι φιλεῖ.

[125] The structure of the *Odyssey*, it is true, is more elaborate than the *Iliad*'s, since two independent but related thematic strands, the journey of Telemakhos and the return of Odysseus, are twined together into one. But the manner of braiding still reflects the same simplicity of linear development that characterizes the *Iliad*: not only do the events in each thread unfold in linear fashion, but in their mutual relation they observe a type of archaic non-overlap, the so-called 'Zieliński's law,' according to which actions are "related in sequence, as if the second were suspended while the first was in progress" (Heubeck et al. 1988:252). (The pictorial equivalent is the avoidance of overlap in late geometric vases.)

[126] This 'linearity' does not preclude cross-referencing, by which a singer foreshadows a future episode or offers his audience a flash-back to an earlier one. Such chronologically intricate thematic ties can be forged entirely upon the dynamics of oral performance: viewing diachronically a song culture for which a given poetic tradition constitutes a notional whole, a coherent aggregate, nothing prevents a bard from making reference to previous performances by himself or a competitor. Obviously, this strategy will only succeed if the earlier recitals on which he draws are memorable enough for the audience to make the appropriate connections. Then, if the tradition is such that it gradually drives the song to textual fixity, any surviving reference to other performances will be synchronically perceived as cross-references from one episode to another. For more on the diachronic and synchronic aspects of oral cross-referencing, see Nagy 2003:7–19.

[127] O 623–629 furnishes a convenient illustration: Hektor leaps on the battle throng as a wave falls on a ship. But the comparison does not stop here, for the sailors of the simile shudder in fear, and their mental distress is then picked up by the narrative: 'so were the hearts of the Akhaians rent within their breasts' (629). Cf. Edwards 1991:28 and 32.

[128] Genesis emphasizes the (typically remote) origin of what is; genealogies, the connection of past and present by lines of filiation; and becoming, concrete developments. There is no place here for abstract historical process and forces or for objective chronological sequence.

Trojan War or the date of Homer in relation to some near-contemporaneous milestone.[129] This is not to say that the events are not thought of as 'true': insofar as poetry exorcizes the specter of oblivion, the danger of forgetting, λήθη,[130] it is intrinsically ἀλήθεια, and both the archaic singer and his audience view the characters and the events narrated in the poetry as 'factual' and 'real,'[131] though they may remain mysterious, puzzling, and discontinuous if measured against their own experience. But it is not the story that is judged in the light of experience, but experience in the light of the story (often viewed as para-

---

[129] Cf. Wace and Stubbings 1962:386.

[130] Cf. Nagy 1990c:58–60, 66.

[131] For a comparative perspective, consider the statement by Đemail above, pp. 174f. This was not the only time when Parry noted the Yugoslav singers' insistence on telling the story as they "heard it and as things happen[ed]," i.e. just as the "heroes did their deeds." A little later in that same interview Nikola asks Đemail if a singer may lengthen his song if he finds his audience exceptionally attentive: "Đ: He can [lengthen it] if he adds to it, but I do not like to listen to such a song ... N: In other words, as far as you are concerned the song is the song, is that it? Đ: That's it ... Even if it's short, let him sing it as it is. He shouldn't add to it so that he stays there all night, when the events in the story didn't happen that way" (Lord 1954:1.240, his ellipses). Sulejman Makić was similarly emphatic: "I would sing [the song] just as I heard it, whatever was worthwhile; what's the good of adding things that didn't happen. One must sing what one has heard and exactly as it happened. It isn't good to change or to add. No sir" (Lord 1954:1.266). On the other hand, Avdo Međedović, who was most skillful with thematic expansion, expresses himself in a manner that is more self-consciously receptive to the oral poetics of thematic expansion: "N: Kasum said that if two singers don't sing the same song alike, then it isn't a true story. ... he said that if they don't sing it alike, then it can't possibly be true history. A: Well, maybe one of them isn't right, because one of the two may not know the song exactly, and the other may know it better. Whichever is the better is the true one. N: But how can you tell which is the better? A: If you've got two singers, why, you can tell from the first third of the song which is the better. If a singer is any good, he won't borrow things from one song and put them in another" (Lord 1954:3.60, his ellipsis; for ornamentation, see 3.67 and 74). Southslavic oral poetry is by no means the only tradition on record as insisting on high standards of 'truth.' Stone (1988:12–61, esp. 12–13) explains how in the Wọi epic of the Kpelle people of Liberia there are three performance levels: an epic-framing meta-narrative level that "helps establish and reassert the frame of epic as a style of performance" (12); a narrative level, which takes up the interaction between the characters; and a song level, with proverbial content and invocations to the tutelary spirit that presides over the performance. The concern throughout for high standards of notional veracity is remarkable. Thus the constant invocations at the song level for clarity in the telling: "Ee, Maa-laa [= the spirit] bring my voice. | Go, call the diviner to come" (16). Furthermore, Stone (1988:13n3) observes how the protagonist, Wọi, addresses the narrator at the narrative level to bring him on the scene of the action; his design is to buttress the narrator's claims to autopsy and trustworthiness, claims that are often articulated in response to concrete challenges by a questioner: "Q[uestioner]: Are you telling the truth? N[arrator]: Very close. Her stomach reached to the ocean. Q: Were you near? N: Very close" (17). Or again: "Q: Don't lie to me here. N: Very close. Lying, I lie to you?" (19); "Q: Kulung, don't lie to me here. N: I'm not lying. Q: They say you really lie" (20). Though such an explicit register for performer-audience interaction does not exist in Homeric poetry (the invocation of the Muse is the only element that approaches it), this poetry, too, reflects an interest in veracity (albeit much more implicit by comparison) through its sacral scheme of inspiration and the archaic hymnic ritual framework of its performance (on which see further below, p. 233).

digmatic or archetypal), and only when the mythical mentality gives way to critical distance are these terms reversed and we find the tradition subjected to sceptical analysis. But this belongs to a later era.[132] Archaic poetry does not operate with an ordinary correspondence-theory of truth: singing that is divinely authorized, i.e. 'inspired poetry,' reenacts the past, bestows on it 'undying renown,' perpetuates it, preserves it from oblivion; and so, it is tautologically true, necessarily accurate. Notionally, the story cannot be otherwise, for the gods, themselves eyewitnesses, authorize and guarantee its reperformance; and because the hearers, thinking of it as fixed, demand a faithful delivery, feeling their own connection to the story on terms that are themselves permanent, terms that may be grounded either on unchanging ritual, on an aetiological appropriation of the myth, or on the seasonally recurring performance occasion.

Pausanias 9.29 reports an old tradition from Askra, Hesiod's own hometown, according to which the Muses were three in number.[133] A rival to the nine Muses of Thespiai—the city that since the third century BC organized the Boiotian festival of the Μουσεῖα—this variant had the misfortune of not being adopted into the Hesiodic corpus and, having failed to receive Panhellenic status, it has largely remained a footnote in modern scholarship.[134] And yet this tradition is presented as older than its rival, and in all likelihood it is at least as old. For my purposes, however, of particular interest are the names given to the Muses, Μελέτη, Μνήμη, and Ἀοιδή, which constitute a transparent description of the poetic process. Μνήμη, 'Memory', corresponds to the underlying subject matter in its oral-traditional form, and promises its preservation in song; Μελέτη bespeaks the assiduous training and practice of the bard, what William Race, in the case of Pindar, translates as 'premeditation', the poet's "craft and training ground" (*apud* Nagy 1990c:16); and Ἀοιδή captures the performance occasion, the moment of recomposition, for the song exists only in the singing of the bard.[135] Μελέτη, in particular, confirms that the concept of divine influence and inspiration is compatible with the self-conscious training and exertion of the singer's own abilities.[136] Here we must assume that, as with oral traditional poetries the world over, the bard learned from other singers and his training probably took place in the context of apprenticeship: this is the case in every sphere of professional praxis, with every category of δημιουργός. Greek poetry, however, is too competitive to have the singer openly acknowledge his debt to a

---

[132] Cf. Buxton 1999.

[133] See also below, p. 286.

[134] Cf. van Groningen 1948.

[135] It may be, as van Groningen (1948:290) observes, that this particular mythical tradition primarily (or exclusively) regards epic poetry, for which ἀείδειν is the technical performance term *par excellence*.

[136] Cf. Murray 1981:96–97.

human master, and the only evidence left of what must have been the pervasive educational model is the denial by Phemios that he had been taught by another (χ 344–349):[137]

> γουνοῦμαί σ', Ὀδυσεῦ· σὺ δέ μ' αἴδεο καί μ' ἐλέησον.
> 345 αὐτῷ τοι μετόπισθ' ἄχος ἔσσεται, εἴ κεν ἀοιδὸν
> πέφνῃς, ὅς τε θεοῖσι καὶ ἀνθρώποισιν ἀείδω.
> <u>αὐτοδίδακτος δ' εἰμί, θεὸς δέ μοι ἐν φρεσὶν οἴμας</u>
> <u>παντοίας ἐνέφυσεν·</u> ἔοικα δέ τοι παραείδειν
> ὥς τε θεῷ· τῷ μή με λιλαίεο δειροτομῆσαι.

> I implore you, Odysseus; show me regard and mercy.
> 345 You yourself shall be grieved later if you slay me, a singer
> who [ever] sings for [the benefit] of gods and men.
> *I am self-taught, and the god has implanted in my mind lays*
> *of every sort*; I am well suited to sing in your service
> as [in the service of] a god; therefore do not be eager to cut
> my throat.

Phemios' plea emphasizes the sacred status of the singer: we have good reason to believe that δημιουργοί were sacrosanct, that they enjoyed juridical immunity in their itinerant travels,[138] and it is certain that in Hellenistic times they had the protection of Apollo through his Delphic oracle.[139] Phemios deserves αἰδώς, even from the βασιλεύς, because his solemn singing in cult and festival contexts makes him a sacred servant of gods and men.[140] In my opinion, the

---

[137] Cf. above, p. 207 n. 121.

[138] So Nagy 1989:19 and Nagy 1990c:56–57 (who adduces the parallel of the old Irish *áes cerd*; cf. Durante 1968b:268). Such a status for the ἀοιδός in early Greece is consistent with (and even suggested by) the epithet θεῖος (Σ 604 α 336 δ 17 θ 43 47 87 539 etc.), an appellative, too, of heralds (Δ 192 K 315) and rulers (δ 621 691 π 335), similarly sacrosanct on account of their function.

[139] Cf. Ghiron-Bistagne 1976:169–171. Concerning the itinerant actors she observes that "[i]l leur restait cependant à résoudre une difficulté essentielle, dans la nécessité où ils se trouvaient de se déplacer constamment de ville en ville. … La situation, à cet égard, ne devait pas être très différente dans la Grèce du Vᵢᵉᵐᵉ et IVᵢᵉᵐᵉ siècle." In fact, such must have been the case since the eighth-century BC 'renaissance' and the establishment of the Olympic games and the Delphic oracle, the quintessential Panhellenic institutions. For a fourth-century instance see Demosthenes *On the Peace* 6. For more on juridical immunity, see Aneziri 2003:243–252 and the *New Pauly* s.vv. *asylia* and *asylon*.

[140] Cf. Hesiod *Theogony* 93–95: τοίη Μουσάων ἱερὴ δόσις ἀνθρώποισιν. | ἐκ γάρ τοι Μουσέων καὶ ἑκηβόλου Ἀπόλλωνος | ἄνδρες ἀοιδοὶ ἔασιν ἐπὶ χθόνα καὶ κιθαρισταί. Although the benefit the poet confers on the gods (θεοῖσι … ἀείδω χ 346) must be his celebrating their glory before men, we must not forget that poetry at first was sprung from the gods and was created for their pleasure (cf. Hesiod *Theogony* 40–52 and *Hymn to Apollo* 188–206.).

term αὐτοδίδακτος must refer to the process of training,[141] a social reality that fails to receive the explicit recognition of the poetry, to be sure, but must otherwise have been taken for granted by the audience.[142] What our poems feel free rhetorically to acknowledge is the gods in the explicit position of song-masters:[143] Δημόδοκ', ἔξοχα δή σε βροτῶν αἰνίζομ' ἁπάντων· | ἢ σέ γε Μοῦσ' ἐδίδαξε, Διὸς πάϊς, ἢ σέ γ' Ἀπόλλων (θ 487–488; cf. Hesiod *Theogony* 22–23). By professing to be self-taught, Phemios repudiates any debt to a human master-singer, even as he owns to the god one that exceeds the traditional bounds of divine involvement in the genesis of epic song. Hence the verb ἐμφύω,[144] which puts the emphasis on a process of growth for the poetry,[145] almost certainly not during a given performance, but in the course of the poet's life: in other words, it is the conceptual equivalent of a course of apprenticeship. Phemios would be saying, in effect: 'God, who has implanted within me song-threads of every sort, has so distinguished me with his favor that I have never depended on a human master; instead, I have learned my trade by myself, solely with divine assistance.'

In a reading that Morgan (2000:94) calls "perverse" and Rotstein (2000:286), more diplomatically, "arresting," Finkelberg (1998:54–56) forces Phemios' plea

---

[141] See pp. 215f. below on the semantics of this remarkable adjective.

[142] Though this passage has attracted much commentary, most of it fails to make contextual sense. The question that must be answered by any reading is how being αὐτοδίδακτος may move Odysseus to spare Phemios' life. I understand it as a claim to a heightened degree of 'super-natural' involvement in what is already a sacral context. Dougherty 1991 applies the term to the bard's ability to suit his song to the occasion of his performance. (This is essentially the view of Fernández-Galiano in Russo et al. 1992:279–280.) Surely any process of apprenticeship would seek to develop this skill, and, to that extent, being self-taught would imply that this, too, he does not owe to another singer. But I fail to see why, from the perspective of the cultural *insider*, this facet of the singer's trade would be seen to contrast (as Dougherty 1991:94 claims) with the "traditional element of oral poetry" (adequately meeting the expectations of his audience is a core skill of the traditional performer); nor why it should be read as a reference to "innovat[ing] within the tradition" (95), or even why such a rationale may serve as a plea for sparing Phemios' life. When Odysseus articulates his reason for honoring and revering singers, he mentions that the Muse teaches them their traditional craft (θ 479–481; cf. θ 487–489 496–498; for οἴμη as a rhap-sodic *terme d'art* see below, pp. 392ff.). The verb παραείδειν + dat. must mean 'to sing in someone's service', just as παραγίγνομαι means 'to be in attendance upon' (ρ 173) and παραδράω 'to do work in attendance upon, to serve' (ο 324). The unusual personal construction with ἔοικα must mean 'I am well suited to sing in your service as in the service of a god' (cf. Hesiod *Theogony* 91 and θ 173). For more on this passage, see Bakker 1997:137–138 and Grandolini 1996:159–164.

[143] On the rhetorical tendency in the *Odyssey* to downplay the artistry of the bard, see further below, p. 359.

[144] As Setti (1958:150) claims, the following clause at χ 347–348 must be read as explicating the claim the precedes it (cf. Thalmann 1984:126–127). I cannot, however, agree with his dichotomy of the self-taught singer, who composes his own repertoire, vis-à-vis the apprenticed one, who learns and reproduces with only minor variations that of his masters. Such a view misreads the rhet-oric of Phemios' plea in terms of much later canons of individual originality. (Note, in particular, Dougherty's criticism of the notion of 'another poet's song' in Dougherty 1991:98.)

[145] For the etymology and meaning of οἴμη, see below, pp. 392ff.

into her dichotomy of 'taught' and 'given' by equating αὐτοδίδακτος with 'given' and θεὸς ... ἐνέφυσεν with 'taught.' Thus, she arguably interprets them against their plain meaning and import. I explained above my conviction that the two parts of the bard's entreaty are best regarded as complementary. But, if they are to be opposed in line with Finkelberg's polarity, I grant that only her strained assignment upholds her thesis: having made οἴμη the purview of rhapsodic competence (Finkelberg 1998:52) she could not easily grant the god a substantial role in the teaching process[146] or allow the verb ἐμφύω its more natural kinship with divine endowment (cf. Rotstein 2000:286). Although she admits that the connotations of ἐμφύειν "lie in the sphere of natural growth" and that it is therefore "compatible with Homer's understanding of learning as a gradual process of acquiring a given profession" (54–55), she passes in silence over the fact that its subject is θεός and omits any consideration of what this pointed fact entails for her thesis. If the god's implanting of οἶμαι—his making them grow within the heart of the singer—hints at divine involvement with the gradual process of the bard's acquiring his craft, the reading of οἶμαι as basic knowledge of the principal events of the story and of their order would seem unsuitably narrow. Still more puzzling is Finkelberg's interpretation of αὐτοδίδακτος as a reference to what is divinely given. To be sure, she does not articulate this connection explicitly: we would then be faced with the contradictory equations 'self-taught = god-stirred' and 'god-implanted = self-acquired.' But the inference is left to the reader by summarizing her argument thus: "Phemius' 'I am self-taught' stands for the improvisatory aspect of the poet's activity, that is, the one that we have rendered by *aoidē*, or 'singing' proper" (56).

---

[146] One must remember that Finkelberg does not deny that the bard is divinely taught. There are, after all, explicit statements to the contrary. Among them is θ 481, which expressly makes οἴμας the subject matter in which the Muse instructs the singer. This means that the bard has an acknowledged sphere of competence, a craft, for which he is responsible. But since Finkelberg insists that the actual performance, the ἀοιδή, is not a matter of acquired skill—i.e. it is not taught—but consists instead in an improvised elaboration, divinely prompted and divinely sustained, of his acquired skill—and improvisation for which he is therefore not responsible—the scholar must restrict the reach of divine teaching to the impartation of basic competence. This basic competence, she argues, is the singer's knowledge of the basic plots of a range of epic subjects (the οἶμαι), and perhaps instrumental playing (does the Muse also teach him that?); but nothing about formulaic technique, enjambment, versification, thematic sequencing, etc. In other words, the teaching of the Muse is effectively assimilated to a gift, rather than a gradual process of training by which the bard acquires his professional craft. This does not amount to a substantial teaching role for the Muse or Apollo. I, on the other hand, readily grant διδάσκω a revelatory import but add to it the implication that it is ultimately to the Muse too that the artistic excellence of the singer in performance must be credited, even though it has come about through a combination of sedulous training under a human master and the coordinate development of the bard's personal talent—his divine giftedness.

Her logic does not survive scrutiny. She first directs our attention to two other passages that seem to juxtapose divine and human sources for the singer's creative ability: one features the θυμός as the agent that stirs the bard (θ 44–45); the other, the νόος (α 346–349). Finkelberg is driving towards the conclusion that "*autodidaktos* implies neither a deliberate process of acquiring knowledge nor the subject's active participation in this process" (56). In order to establish this claim, she must effectively collapse these two seemingly complementary sources into a primary one, the divine, and its epiphenomenon, the instinctive human 'self-acting' that can only be explained as the outworking of the former. But this requires that we view the θυμός and the νόος as independent 'psychological' foci, autonomous wellsprings of action, whose arbitrary motivation cannot be integrated with the rational mental processes of the individual and therefore relieve him from any responsibility. On this view, such unaccountable actions could only be ascribed to the mysterious operations of the divine sphere. Notions like this track the theories of Snell and his *epigonoi* about the disintegrated Homeric psychology, which rendered man "a sort of loose confederation of quasi-autonomous limbs and organs" (I am quoting from Pelliccia 1995:17, who helpfully reviews the relevant scholarship at 17–27). But by denying that bodily organs (including the θυμός) lack the power of speech, Pelliccia has dealt a deathblow to this 'homuncular' conception of the Homeric self (1995:30).[147] For Pelliccia, "rather than being a precisely or realistically conceived 'organ' or other such entity, [the θυμός] covers a series of obscurities in theology and psychology, and thus serves, *à la* Searle, to plug a conceptual gap" (259). I believe that by and large Homeric psychology evinces no greater complexity or bizarreness than our own: we too may structure our forms of expression around the apparent awareness of a divided self, and sometimes own that our feelings and motives are opaque to our introspection. And we also have the same capacity for a rhetorically opportunistic, self-exculpatory use of these reflective tropes (cf. Pelliccia 1995:209–211). That in Homer the stimulus for action should be ascribed to an internal organ, and that the same organ should now and then serve as the channel through which the gods affect man's actions seem facts neither unfamiliar to our diction nor foreign to our thinking.

The first step in Finkelberg's reading of αὐτοδίδακτος is to neutralize the self-consciousness inherent in αὐτο- (i.e. the active psychological involvement); I have suggested above the underlying reasons why I think this strategy fails (more to come below). The second step is to argue that -δίδακτος actually does not entail the acquisition of knowledge but refers rather to spontaneous action. In effect, she equates αὐτόματος and αὐτοδίδακτος. But -ματος comes

[147] Cf. his chapter 2 *passim.*

215

from the zero-grade verbal *to*-adjective of **men-*, and hence the externally unprompted-action that Finkelberg counter-intuitively assigns to αὐτοδίδακτος seems perfectly in order for αὐτόματος. Still, it would not be arbitrary, unaccountable action, only *externally* unprompted. Not so with -δίδακτος, which one can only cleave from 'teaching' by an exercise of interpretive violence. To justify it, Finkelberg adduces only the admittedly relevant Aiskhylos *Agamemnōn* 990–993, which she explains thus: "What the *autodidaktos* of Aeschylus does imply is that the *thumos* sings of itself, that is, in an unprompted and spontaneous manner. In this, it resembles *automatos* ... . Consequently, semantic associations of *autodidaktos* should be sought not in the area of 'self-teaching' but in that of 'self-acting'" (56). I submit, however, that there is a more plausible reading which does not unnaturally reduce -δίδακτος to -ματος. It builds on the self-referential chorality explored in Henrichs 1994–1995, rare but not unexampled in Aiskhylos (see pp. 59–60). Indeed, in their reflective ode the chorus use αὐτοδίδακτος ... | θυμός (*Agamemnōn* 992–993) to drive home the strength with which the circumstances and events just witnessed force themselves upon their foreboding consciousness, informing their understanding, shaping their expectations, and affecting their emotions. Effectively, then, it is as if no χοροδιδάσκαλος had helped them train for the performance of this particular *stasimon*. Alleging the absence of external training provides the chorus with a mildly meta-theatrical yet forceful way to make their point. That -δίδακτος is not to be emptied of its obvious meaning is further supported by the use of αὐτόμαρτυς at 989, which Fraenkel translates as "myself the witness" (1950:1.151). The passage does not claim that the mind of the chorus is inactive or that it has not reached its conclusions through deliberation (note φρενὸς φίλον θρόνον 983), but, as verse 979 shows, that no one has *externally* bidden or hired it to render its prophetic judgment in song. The terms τερασκόπου 977, μαντιπολεῖ 979 (for which see Fraenkel 1950:2.444 *ad loc.*), and δυσκρίτων ὀνειράτων 981, if they are at all valid contextual parallels to Phemios' plea, argue precisely in favor of a technical interpretation of αὐτοδίδακτος: the exceptional denial that he has been apprenticed to a human song-master points to the ordinary reality of rhapsodic training. I close this section with three statements by Fraenkel which corroborate my reading that in the *Agamemnōn* αὐτοδίδακτος hardly entails a spontaneous singing devoid of craft and without knowledge taught by deliberate thinking: "αὐτοδίδακτος clearly points to the origin and nature of the knowledge of the moral law which occupies the central position in this chorus" (2.446); "φρένες [in 996] ... means 'mind, cogitation, reflection, thought' etc." (2.447); "[i]n *Ag.* 996 the phrase ἔνδικοι φρένες, then, means the thoughts in which there is δίκη ... . In their φρονεῖν the conviction of δράσαντι παθεῖν is contained" (2.449).[148]

---

[148] On φρονεῖν as 'to be wise, to have understanding' see Fraenkel 1950:2.105–106 *ad Agamemnōn* 176.

8

Hesiod the Rhapsode

8.1 Mantic Poetry

8.1.1 Hesiod's *Dichterweihe*

HESIOD'S *DICHTERWEIHE* (*Theogony* 22–34) offers an alternative to the Homeric invocation of the Muses:

> αἵ νύ ποθ᾽ Ἡσίοδον <u>καλὴν ἐδίδαξαν ἀοιδήν</u>,
> ἄρνας ποιμαίνονθ᾽ Ἑλικῶνος ὕπο ζαθέοιο.
> τόνδε δέ με πρώτιστα θεαὶ πρὸς μῦθον ἔειπον,
> 25   Μοῦσαι Ὀλυμπιάδες, κοῦραι Διὸς αἰγιόχοιο·
> ποιμένες ἄγραυλοι, κάκ᾽ ἐλέγχεα, γαστέρες οἶον,
> ἴδμεν ψεύδεα πολλὰ λέγειν ἐτύμοισιν ὁμοῖα,
> ἴδμεν δ᾽ εὖτ᾽ ἐθέλωμεν ἀληθέα γηρύσασθαι.
> ὣς ἔφασαν κοῦραι μεγάλου Διὸς ἀρτιέπειαι,
> 30   καί <u>μοι σκῆπτρον ἔδον</u> δάφνης ἐριθηλέος ὄζον
> δρέψασαι, θηητόν· <u>ἐνέπνευσαν δέ μοι αὐδὴν</u>
> <u>θέσπιν</u>, ἵνα κλείοιμι <u>τά τ᾽ ἐσσόμενα πρό τ᾽ ἐόντα</u>,
> καί μ᾽ ἐκέλονθ᾽ <u>ὑμνεῖν</u> μακάρων γένος αἰὲν ἐόντων,
> σφᾶς δ᾽ αὐτὰς πρῶτόν τε καὶ ὕστατον αἰὲν ἀείδειν.

> They once *taught* Hesiod *beautiful song*
> while shepherding lambs under holy Helikon.
> This was the utterance the goddesses first addressed to me
> 25   the Olympian Muses, daughter of aegis-holding Zeus:
> "Field-dwelling shepherds, base reproaches, mere bellies!
> We know how to tell many lies resembling true things;
> and we know, when willing, how to proclaim truths."
> Thus spoke the ready-voiced daughters of great Zeus,
> 30   and *to me they gave a rod*, a shoot of lush laurel

they plucked, quite the sight; and *they breathed into me a voice
divine*, so that I may celebrate *what shall be and what was*,
and they bade me *hymn* the race of the ever living blessed ones,
but ever to sing them first and last.

Here the Muses call the shepherd Hesiod to celebrate in song 'past and future
things', endowing him for this purpose with the gift of 'divine voice', a voice
(αὐδή) qualified by the adjective θέσπις I have already examined (see above,
p. 201). Just as with Demodokos (θ 481 488), his initiation can be described as the
Muses 'teaching' him beautiful singing (καλὴν ἀοιδήν for καλῶς ἀείδειν). In the
Works and Days 659 the same event receives the wording με ... λιγυρῆς ἐπέβησαν
ἀοιδῆς, '[the Muses] set me on the path of clear song': ἐπιβαίνω with the genitive of the sphere of expertise recalls the language in the *Hymn to Hermes*, where
Hermes' attaining to his due rights, his μοῖρα or τιμή, is expressed as κἀγὼ τῆς
ὁσίης ἐπιβήσομαι ἧς περ Ἀπόλλων (173). Important to my argument here is the
strong accent on the divine origin of Hesiod's poetic voice and song, and that his
purview, just as a seer's, is the past and the future. I will comment further below
(p. 225) on this all encompassing temporal horizon; for now, I should note that
Hesiod's initiation casts him in the role of a poet-seer, just as Homer's persona
better corresponds to the prophet. The σκῆπτρον Hesiod receives (perhaps to
replace a shepherd's crook that goes unmentioned) places him in regard to
authoritative speaking in the same category as kings (Z 159; cf. A 279 B 86 etc.),
priests (A 15 28), seers (λ 91), and heralds (H 277), and assimilates him to a rhapsode who performs with his staff in hand.

To understand the distinction between the μάντις and the προφήτης, the
locus classicus is Plato's *Timaios* 71d–72b:[1] here μαντική is specifically tied to
'enthusiasm' ἐνθουσιασμός, which the philosopher, with his usual tendentiousness, calls foolishness (ἀφροσύνη) and disease (νόσος). But—and this is the
key distinction—if μάντεις are the vehicles of inspired sight, the προφῆται are

---

[1] μεμνημένοι γὰρ τῆς τοῦ πατρὸς ἐπιστολῆς οἱ συστήσαντες ἡμᾶς, ὅτε τὸ θνητὸν ἐπέστελλεν
γένος ὡς ἄριστον εἰς δύναμιν ποιεῖν, οὕτω δὴ κατορθοῦντες καὶ τὸ φαῦλον ἡμῶν, ἵνα ἀληθείας
πῃ προσάπτοιτο, κατέστησαν ἐν τούτῳ τὸ μαντεῖον. ἱκανὸν δὲ σημεῖον ὡς μαντικὴν ἀφροσύνῃ
θεὸς ἀνθρωπίνῃ δέδωκεν· οὐδεὶς γὰρ ἔννους ἐφάπτεται μαντικῆς ἐνθέου καὶ ἀληθοῦς, ἀλλ' ἢ καθ'
ὕπνον τὴν τῆς φρονήσεως πεδηθεὶς δύναμιν ἢ διὰ νόσον, ἢ διά τινα ἐνθουσιασμὸν παραλλάξας.
ἀλλὰ συννοῆσαι μὲν ἔμφρονος τά τε ῥηθέντα ἀναμνησθέντα ὄναρ ἢ ὕπαρ ὑπὸ τῆς μαντικῆς τε
καὶ ἐνθουσιαστικῆς φύσεως, καὶ ὅσα ἂν φαντάσματα ὀφθῇ, πάντα λογισμῷ διελέσθαι ὅπῃ τι
σημαίνει καὶ ὅτῳ μέλλοντος ἢ παρελθόντος ἢ παρόντος κακοῦ ἢ ἀγαθοῦ· τοῦ δὲ μανέντος ἔτι τε
ἐν τούτῳ μένοντος οὐκ ἔργον τὰ φανέντα καὶ φωνηθέντα ὑφ' ἑαυτοῦ κρίνειν, ἀλλ' εὖ καὶ πάλαι
λέγεται τὸ πράττειν καὶ γνῶναι τά τε αὑτοῦ καὶ ἑαυτὸν σώφρονι μόνῳ προσήκειν. ὅθεν δὴ καὶ τὸ
τῶν προφητῶν γένος ἐπὶ ταῖς ἐνθέοις μαντείαις κριτὰς ἐπικαθιστάναι νόμος· οὓς μάντεις αὐτοὺς
ὀνομάζουσί τινες, τὸ πᾶν ἠγνοηκότες ὅτι τῆς δι' αἰνιγμῶν οὗτοι φήμης καὶ φαντάσεως ὑποκριταί,
καὶ οὔτι μάντεις, προφῆται δὲ μαντευομένων δικαιότατα ὀνομάζοιντ' ἄν (*Timaios* 71d5–72b5).

appointed to 'interpret' them, i.e. to sit as judges, κριταί, over their meaning. 'Some', Plato goes on, 'call them μάντεις, being blind to the fact that they are ὑποκριταί of visions and riddling utterances, not μάντεις, and that the most correct label for them would be προφῆται of the utterances of the μάντεις'.[2] As Nagy (1989:26) remarks, the semantic connection between μάντις and μανία holds at the etymological level, both deriving from the root *men- (μανία < *mn̥-ieh₂); but what in the classical era denoted an altered mental state was, diachronically speaking, only a marked meaning of the same family that gives us the Latin *mēns*; this suggests the possibility that at an early stage μάντις did not connote senseless *furor*, but was rather cognate with the mental state denoted by formations with *mnē-* ('have in mind, remember, mention, remind'), which is but an extended form, *mneh₂-*, of *mne-*.[3] In his survey of Homeric passages Casevitz 1992 demonstrates conclusively that there was nothing of 'madness' (in its ordinary sense) in the person and practice of the epic seer. He defines

---

[2]   These two offices seem to have been complementary at an early stage in Jewish religion. So, 1 Samuel 9:9 records the following parenthetical remark: 'Formerly in Israel, when a man went to inquire of God, he used to say, "Come, and let us go to the seer": for he who is called a prophet now was formerly called a seer'. The word for seer is the participle *rō'eh*, from *rā'â*, 'to see, to perceive, to understand'. And though the verb is often used for the visual nature of theophanies, dreams, and visions, there is no evidence that the 'seer' himself obtained knowledge of divine secrets through visions or dreams. The word for prophet, *nābî'*, has been variously connected to *nāḇā'*, 'to bubble forth' (suggesting ecstatic behavior, see below, pp. 267ff.), to *bô'*, 'to enter' (suggesting possession), to the Arabic root that means 'to announce' (suggesting herald), and to the Akkadian for 'to speak, to proclaim'; still others have taken it as passive for 'one called by God'. (The title *nabû*, perhaps 'diviner', is now attested in the Mari texts.) The great disparity in the etymologies discourages our relying on them and recommends, rather, that we look at the internal evidence of the Hebrew scriptures for a proper understanding of the word. There, though the context may occasionally hint at ecstatic behavior, the great majority of instances denote proclamation, authoritative public speaking. So, Exodus 6:29–7:2: '[T]he Lord spoke to Moses, saying, "I am the Lord; speak to Pharaoh king of Egypt all that I speak to you." But Moses said before the Lord, "Behold, I am unskilled in speech: how then will Pharaoh listen to me?" Then the Lord said to Moses, "See, I make you as God to Pharaoh, and your brother Aaron shall be your prophet. You shall speak all that I command you, and your brother Aaron shall speak to Pharaoh"'. Ultimately, what is of greater interest to my argument is that, just as with μάντις and προφήτης, regardless of the etymological distinction in emphasis between *rō'eh* and *nābî'*, 1 Samuel 9:9 seems to make them interchangeable at an early stage, stating that only later, presumably after the former had become specialized, did the latter take over the generic meaning they had both once shared. The LXX usually preserves the etymological force of *rō'eh*, rendering it by ὁ βλέπων (Regnorum I 1:9, 1:11, 1:18, 9:18; Paralipomenon I 9:22) or ὁ ὁρῶν (Isaias 30:10) [or even ἴδετε, 'behold', at Regnorum II 15:27]; but προφήτης is also used on three occasions (Paralipomenon I 26:28; Paralipomenon II 16:7, 16:10). *nābî'*, on the other hand, is always translated προφήτης. The word μάντις is reserved for *qāsam*, 'to divine', a practice that was despised and outlawed in Israel. (Balaam, for example, is called *mantis* in Josue 13:22.)

[3]   Cf. Meillet 1897, Ziehen 1930, Benveniste 1935:83, Roth 1988, Casevitz 1992, Bader 1997 esp. 5–6, Bartolotta 2002:27–32, and Bartolotta 2003. On divination generally, see the bibliography in Casevitz 1992:1n1 and Johnston 2005.

mantis as a specialist who interprets divine signs, who reveals what to others is obscure and hidden.[4] According to him, the seer's practice is not intrinsically oriented towards the future[5] and divides broadly into two categories: the inductive understanding of the reader of signs and the immediate understanding of the inspired seer. Casevitz makes Plato responsible for breaking this semantic unity in order to elevate immediate inspiration over against the charlatanry of traditional inductive divination. This aim required excising from μάντεις the interpretive function, which was conveniently assigned to προφῆται; and tying μάντις and μανία etymologically (a tie that Casevitz disputes) so as to make the seer one who is able to predict the future when he is seized by divinely sent *furor*.[6] Casevitz infers Plato's high regard for inspired divination from *Phaidros* 244c, where Sokrates avers that the finest τέχνη by which the future is discerned would not have been called μανική if μανία had been disdained as shameful. I find Casevitz's view of Plato's motives implausible, not least because in a matter of such import and with so many ramifications it is doubtful that one can make any one Platonic statement the interpretive key to the rest. Those who have tried to ascertain Plato's personal evaluation of poetry, a question that arguably depends on the philosopher's estimation of inspired *mania*, have found their attempt notoriously difficult: not only does irony complicate the interpretive task, but one must also consider, for example, the specific aims of the relevant dialogs and allow for a measure of intellectual development from one to another. Be that as it may, I agree with Casevitz that Plato provides a watershed in the characterization of μανία that opposes it to τέχνη and equates it to being out of one's mind.

Post Platonic scholarship finds it difficult to conceive μανία and the related verb μαίνομαι as a marked degree of intellectual activity, a heightened measure of cognition, indicating an extraordinary degree of mental awareness. This positive estimation, I believe, is the ordinary meaning of this semantic field, of which the negative (often punitive, and brought about by a divine agency) was the loss of mental (and bodily) self-possession and the inability to think aright. Hence, madness is to the increased cognition of ordinary, positive μανία as lies are to archaic truth or ψόγος to epic κλέος: a subordinate, negative image that can only be understood in light of the primary, positive acceptation. *Mania*

---

4   "Le *mantis* qu'Achille propose d'interroger est un spécialiste de l'interprétation des signes divins, il révèle ce qui, aux autres hommes, reste obscur et caché" (Casevitz 1992:3; cf. 11).

5   On Epimenidēs see below, p. 229.

6   In regard to Plato *Timaios* 71d–72b, Casevitz (1992:13–14) writes: "Ainsi Timée … distingue celui qui est en transe et celui qui interprète ce que celui-ci voit ou profère. … *mantis* désigne seulement 'le personnage en proie à la *mania*' … . L'étymologie qui rapproche *mantis* de *mania* est bien un outil de travail, qui aide à rehausser le prestige du *mantis*, mais du seul *mantis* à révérer, celui qui 'délire'; tous les autres devins 'traditionnels' et populaires ne sont plus que des charlatans … ."

implied not a suspension of one's native mental capacities but their elevation, usually in the context of ritual and religious practice. The resulting heightened state combined natural ability, specific training, and divine influence—none overruling the others—in a coordinate exercise of superior judgment.[7] For this reason, Casevitz's attempt to divorce μάντις etymologically from μανία and μαίνομαι is misconceived. Drawing attention to the divergent testimony of the *Etymologicum Magnum* 574.70–73 (cols. 1630–1631 Gaisford),[8] he proposes to relate μάντις to μηνύω instead. Bader (1997:5–6) validates this proposal but shows that Casevitz's motivation is ill-founded and his rationale specious; for μηνύω comes from *$mn̥h_2$-nu-, which is built on the zero-grade enlarged root *$mn̥$-h_2- with dissimilation *μ(ν)η-νυ-. The unexpected outcome ṇ > -αν- before -τι- is variously explained by scholars: Bonfante 1979 deems it an Indo-European dialectal variant;[9] Bader (1997:6), a regular, if older, reflex of the syllabic resonant before a consonantal laryngeal;[10] Bartolotta (2002:30), a common phonetic treatment by proto-Doric, Armenian, and Hittite peoples that attests to their cultural contact in the second millennium BC.[11] The use of the suffix -τις for the agent noun and its failure to assibilate remain puzzling,[12] but Casevitz's proposal to segregate μάντις from μαίνομαι alleviates none of the difficulties.[13]

Not only is μάντις, then, to be traced to *men-. In fact, though some still contest this, the word Muse itself in all likelihood should be traced to the same root in its o-grade, *mon-: μοῦσα < *mon-tu̯a or *mon-ti̯a.[14] We would expect, then, to find traces in the literature of ancient Greece of that undifferentiated usage which employed μάντις and προφήτης interchangeably and which cast the poet, moreover, in a role such that the primeval unity of oracular speech and

---

[7] Plato acknowledges divine influence frequently and natural ability occasionally (e.g. in *Apology* 22c1). But he is keen to deny inspired δημιουργοί both τέχνη, the methodical skill that training imparts, and ἐπιστήμη, the body of knowledge assembled by philosophic inquiry.

[8] ζητητικὸς γάρ ἐστιν ὁ μάντις τοῦ μέλλοντος, οἱονεὶ ὁ τὰ ἀφανῆ καὶ ἄδηλα ζητῶν. Οὐ γὰρ παρὰ τὴν μανίαν ὥς τινες ὑπέλαβον. Διὸ καὶ Ὅμηρος εὔφρονα λέγει τὸν μάντιν.

[9] Cf. Porzio Gernia 1989:82.

[10] "μάντις (< *$mn̥h_2$-ti- > *$manh_2$-ti-, avec traitement *an* de ṇ devant *H* dû au caractère consonantique de la laryngale, et plus ancien que le traitement par 'sonante-voyelle longue' de p. ex. μέ-μνη-μαι, avec chute de *h_2 et allongement compensatoire)" (Bader 1997:6).

[11] Bartolotta 2004 lays out the argument in detail. After endorsing the proposal of a common origin to Phrygian and Armenian in the Thracian Balkans, she adds: "Queste ultime accomunano l'armeno non soltanto col frigio, ma anche col greco, con cui entrambe le lingue presentano numerosi tratti comuni. In quest'ottica, l'esito -αν- di μάντις potrebbe essere una traccia di possibili contatti linguistici e culturali di età preistorica" (Bartolotta 2004:113).

[12] Casevitz 1992:14. If Bartolotta (2004:110–112) is right to locate the cultural roots of μάντις in a proto-Doric milieu, this would explain the failure of -τι- to assibilate (cf. also Buck 1998:57 §61 on ἀντί). See also Thompson 2008, esp. 754 no. 1.h.

[13] On all this see Bonfante 1979, Bartolotta 2002:29–32, Bartolotta 2003, and Bartolotta 2004.

[14] Cf. Watkins 2000:54 s.v. "men-" and Watkins 1995b:73. See Assaël 2000 for a recent review of proposed etymologies and an up-to-date bibliography.

poetic utterance under the figure of the poet-seer might be discernible. This is, indeed, what happens, as we shall see below (see p. 274).

8.1.2 Revealing the song

For now, it is important to underscore the implications of this unity for the nature of the oral tradition. I have in mind here a function of epic poetry that in another work I have called 'revelatory', in that the singer acts as a vehicle for the divine message, conveyed to his audience by the inspiring divinity.[15] We, as modern readers, tend not to think of epic narrative in this sense: we are more attuned to its literary qualities as fictional poetry and it takes an anthropological perspective to realize that its social function and repercussions are more profound. When the singer is viewed from this particular perspective, his role has been called sacred and his speech religious, magic, or sacral.[16] Underlying this anthropological construction is the bard's access to the divine will—I might even say to the divine mind—and his kerygmatic and explanatory mediating role as κῆρυξ and προφήτης. This traditional reflex is so pronounced that, even at the much later and largely conventional stage of Hellenistic poetry, Apollonios of Rhodes, too, builds on it by explicitly including Apollo with the Muses and the poet in a triangle of mediated inspiration, invoking the goddesses in an openly hermeneutic role as ὑποφήτορες of Apollo.[17]

In Greek thought the 'revelation' effected by oracular speech is not ordinary 'speaking', λέγειν, but, as Herakleitos famously noted, 'the giving of signs', σημαίνειν.[18] But σήματα, especially in the context of divine omens,[19] are strongly associated with vision—even inner vision[20]—and this serves to motivate the official title, θεωρός, for an envoy sent to consult an oracle. Etymology suggests that a θεωρός is one sent to observe a sight or spectacle, *θεᾱ-ϝορός (cf. *DELG* s.v.), and indeed it can mean 'spectator'. Its connection with oracular consultation not only confirms the visual quality of the oracle's σημαίνειν, but it also underlines the fixed character of mantic/prophetic revelation: the oracular answer must not be changed; the θεωρός must scrupulously guard its accuracy

---

[15] González 2000:276. Cf. Grandolini 1996:29 (*ad* A 1): "La poesia, perciò, è presentata quale rivelazione da parte della divinità, qui indicata con il termine θεά."

[16] Cf. Detienne 1996:43.

[17] Cf. González 2000.

[18] ὁ ἄναξ, οὗ τὸ μαντεῖόν ἐστι τὸ ἐν Δελφοῖς, οὔτε λέγει οὔτε κρύπτει ἀλλὰ σημαίνει (DK 22 B93 = fr. 14 Marcovich, *apud* Plutarch *De Pythiae oraculis* 404d). As Fontenrose (1978:238) writes, this is not a reference to oracular ambiguity, at least in the context of Plutarch's argument, but an emphatic assertion of the instrumentality of the Pythia and its consequences.

[19] B 308 353 Δ 381 I 236 φ 413 with φαίνω; Θ 171 with τίθημι; N 244 with δείκνυμι; X 30 with τέτυκται (=ἐστί).

[20] Brugmann suggested that σῆμα was cognate with the Sanskrit *dhyā-man*, 'thought'. Cf. *DELG* s.v.

and deliver it just as he received it. And so, Theognis warns: 'An envoy (ἀνὴρ θεωρός) sent to Delphi, Kyrnos, must take care to be straighter (εὐθύτερος) than square or rule or lathe, that man to whom the priestess of the god, making her oracular response, indicates (σημήνῃ) the sacred utterance (ὀμφή) from out the wealthy shrine. You could neither find a cure if you add [to it], nor could you escape fault in the eyes of the gods if you take away'.[21]

The orientation of the epic poet towards the past is no hindrance to his revelatory office. Hesiod, because of his mantic status,[22] was granted by the Muses the gift of song about things past, present, and future (*Theogony* 32, 38).[23] In practice, however, even he kept his focus generally on the past. To be sure, he did sing predictively in *Works and Days* 176–201, and other passages from this poem are similarly oriented towards the future. Such are the verses that make predictions on the basis of the calendar[24] or on the grounds of practices observed and actions effected. The commonplace that, *Theogony* 32 notwithstanding, Hesiod never sang of the future is a widespread misunderstanding that goes back to antiquity.[25] Verdenius (1972:239) claims that "the prophetic element is absent from the *Theogony*." One might counter that *Theogony* 886–900, with its implication that Zeus' rule will last forever, is "prophetic" in nature and no small thematic point in the overall architecture of the poem. But the multifaceted complementarity between the two major Hesiodic poems, which most scholars acknowledge (and is supported by apparent cross-references like *Works and Days* 658–659), argues against limiting the force and metapoetic significance of programmatic passages only to the composition in which they appear.[26] Surely this logic applies *a fortiori* to the verses that narrate Hesiod's *Dichterweihe*, since there alone the tradition defines itself through the deliberate construction of its privileged performer. Hence, it seems reasonable to look for

---

[21] West's translation (1993:71), modified. τόρνου καὶ στάθμης καὶ γνώμονος ἄνδρα θεωρόν | εὐθύτερον χρὴ ⟨ἔ⟩μεν, Κύρνε, φυλασσόμενον, ‖ ᾧτινί κεν Πυθῶνι θεοῦ χρήσασ᾽ ἱέρεια | ὀμφὴν σημήνῃ πίονος ἐξ ἀδύτου· ‖ οὔτε τι γὰρ προσθεὶς οὐδέν κ᾽ ἔτι φάρμακον εὕροις, | οὐδ᾽ ἀφελὼν πρὸς θεῶν ἀμπλακίην προφύγοις (805–810 West).

[22] The mantic quality of Hesiodic poetry as a matter of emphasis is to be contrasted, as noted above (p. 220), with the prophetic character of Homeric epic.

[23] West 1966: "The phrase expresses the close connection between poetry and prophecy which is widespread in early literature. In the absence of written records, the ability to see into the distant past is no less marvellous than the ability to see into the future, and there is no reason for a sharp distinction between the two. Neither is possible without some form of divine revelation" (166).

[24] This is true even if one thinks of it in cyclical terms.

[25] See, for example, Lucian *Hēsiodos* §1.

[26] The complementarity I have in mind concerns Hesiod's persona and its significance for the Hesiodic epic tradition, and it should be sharply distinguished from the views that undergird modern efforts to harmonize narratives from major and minor Hesiodic poems that, although thematically divergent, seem to regard the same topic. Cf. González 2010a:386.

the fruition of the Muses' charge to Hesiod in the *Theogony* not merely within that poem but in the diptych it forms with the *Works and Days*. If the former is primarily (but not exclusively) oriented towards the past, the latter explores the implications of Zeus' Olympian rule for man's present and future. In this connection, Verdenius's remark (1972:239) that *WD* 176ff. speaks of the future "but in a critical, not in a laudatory, tone" fails to appreciate the ways in which divine judgment affirms, and therefore extols, the justice of Zeus.[27] In fact, the reformulation of *Theogony* 38 (εἴρουσαι τά τ' ἐόντα τά τ' ἐσσόμενα πρό τ' ἐόντα) as ἵνα κλείοιμι τά τ' ἐσσόμενα πρό τ' ἐόντα, | καί μ' ἐκέλονθ' ὑμνεῖν μακάρων γένος αἰὲν ἐόντων (*Theogony* 32–33) suggests that the overarching thematic interest of the Hesiodic poetic tradition as a whole is to help the audience explore the present implications of the eternal rule of the blessed gods in its stasis under Zeus' supremacy. The singer carries out this poetic project by narrating the genesis of the pantheon and its divine economy; and by considering the ways in which this economy shapes and directs his (and his audience's) daily experiences and future expectations.

Writing about the relationship of verses 32–33 to verse 38 of the *Theogony*, Leclerc observes: "Pourtant, Hésiode évoque le présent et la vie quotidienne des hommes, dans la *Théogonie*. ... Mais ... ces composantes du mode de vie humain sont étroitement rapportées à la compétence ou à l'initiative d'un dieu ... . Il ne s'agit pas de dresser le catalogue *de ce qui est*, mais d'enraciner cette réalité dans un monde en ordre qui a une histoire, ordre et histoire qu'il importe de faire connaître, *κλείειν*."[28] Both Neitzel (1980:397) and, after him, Clay (1988:330n31) are wrong to assert that the absence of the article τά before πρό τ' ἐόντα *necessarily* implies that the words τά τ' ἐσσόμενα πρό τ' ἐόντα denote a composite, i.e. something that *both* 'was' *and* 'shall be'. From the parallels adduced by Clay (*ad loc.*) only follows that, if the meter had accommodated the second article, one might well have expected τά τ' ἐσσόμενα τά τε πρὸ ἐόντα. This is hardly to the point. Rather, the question to answer is whether the absence of the second τά—an absence that makes the expression metrical—results from the composer's need for syntactic flexibility (and hence fits the canons of archaic epic diction) or from the composer's wish to refer to his subject matter as things whose existence spans the past and the future without dissolution of continuity. It is not hard to settle the question: υ 310 should suffice to disprove Neitzel's and Clay's

---

[27] Strange is Neitzel's contention that the inspired singer will not glorify and praise the future because it is uncertain and he ignores whether it shall be glorious: "Selbst ein von den Musen inspirierter Dichter wird die Zukunft nicht rühmen und verherrlichen, weil sie ungewiß ist" (1980:397). By assuming that Hesiod's inspiration does not (cannot?) involve revelation and the infallible prediction of future events, the scholar begs the question at issue, namely, what τά τ' ἐσσόμενα πρό τ' ἐόντα denotes and what kind of inspiration it presupposes.

[28] See Leclerc 2000:67–70 (the quotation is from 69). See, further, Neitzel 1980:396–398.

assumption that only a strictly parallel syntactic construction that repeats the article τά could allow for the view that *Theogony* 32 is but an epic compression of the fuller verse 38 (with verse 33 further explicating its meaning).[29] For the Greek text of Telemakhos' assertion in υ 309-310, 'for now I perceive and understand each thing, both the good and the evil', runs as follows: ἤδη γὰρ νοέω καὶ οἶδα ἕκαστα, | ἐσθλά τε καὶ τὰ χέρεια. Note that the article is absent before ἐσθλά but present before χέρεια. Yet no one, I think, would argue that the audience should understand the ἐσθλά as indefinite and contrast them with definite χέρεια. Although in this case the article is missing from the first member of the τε καὶ pair and one cannot press the point Neitzel and Clay make in regard to τά τ' ἐσσόμενα πρό τ' ἐόντα, the verse serves to show that epic diction does not require, and for metrical reasons may suppress, the use of the article with one member of an enumerated series without thereby sanctioning readings that hinge on a fussy demand for strictly parallel diction. Even in English, if someone said of Kalkhas that 'he knew what is what is to come and was,' I think that few (if any) would construe the enumeration as bipartite (on the one hand 'what is,' on the other 'what was and is to come'). The gloss that Clay offers for A 70, "he knew both the divine and the human things," is none the more credible for being reasonable on its face. One wonders what qualifies 'human things' for their ascription to the narrow temporal range of the ever-fleeting present. Are we to think of man as having neither a sense of his past nor an expectation of the future to come? Archaic poetry belies this impoverished notion. Does not Kalkhas' interpretation of the present Akhaian predicament (and his prediction of the future) depend on his knowledge of past human actions and present (and future) divine responses? Unsurprisingly, neither the scholia to the *Iliad* nor to the *Theogony* offers an ancient interpreter to whom the contested over-scrupulous syntactic argument suggested itself.

A different kind of objection is Arrighetti's (1998:316-317) insistence that *Theogony* 32 *prima facie* excludes the present from the Muses' charge to Hesiod. What is this excluded present? For the answer, Arrighetti resorts to *Theogony* 369-370 which, in his view, is consistent with "questa esclusione delle cose del presente dal dominio delle conoscenze del poeta" (317).[30] In this

---

[29] Arrighetti 1998: "καί di [*Teogonia*] 33 potrebbe benissimo avere un valore esplicativo rispetto ai contenuti dei vv. 31-32" (315).

[30] The other example adduced by Arrighetti *ad loc.*, the *Nautilia* of *Works and Days* 618-694, seems to me singularly unsuited to make his point, insofar as it explicitly claims that Hesiod's inspiration (the song that the Muses taught him, cf. *Theogony* 22 and *Works and Days* 660-662) covers what for Arrighetti, *ex hypothesi*, belongs to τὰ ἐόντα. Because he is inspired, the bard can sing infallibly of what he himself has no first-hand experience (cf. B 484-486). A contrast of his own making first drew the scholar's attention to this passage: he infers from *Theogony* 32 that the Muses grant Hesiod an omniscience that he disowns in the *Nautilia* (cf. Arrighetti 1998:xxviii). But claims of

passage, Hesiod closes with the following verses a partial enumeration of the offspring of Okeanos and Tethys (*Theogony* 367–370):

> τόσσοι δ' αὖθ' ἕτεροι ποταμοὶ καναχηδὰ ῥέοντες,
> υἱέες Ὠκεανοῦ, τοὺς γείνατο πότνια Τηθύς·
> τῶν ὄνομ' ἀργαλέον πάντων βροτὸν ἄνδρα ἐνισπεῖν,
> οἱ δὲ ἕκαστοι ἴσασιν, ὅσοι περιναιετάουσι.

And there are in turn as many other loud-flowing rivers,
sons of Okeanos, whom queenly Tethys bore,
all of whose names it is hard for a mortal man to tell;
but they each know them who severally dwell around them.

Arrighetti considers this a confession of ignorance and an admission that a full enumeration is impossible. But the text claims no such thing: Hesiod only avers that they are so numerous that a hypothetically exhaustive listing would severely tax a mortal man. The rhetorical point of the statement is to underline the multitude of offspring. There is no admission here of ignorance; only the claim that those who live around each river know its name and, presumably, other relevant details.[31] To infer ignorance from the statement that the singer need not tax himself with telling *all* the names because the locals know them is to elevate 'hard' (ἀργαλέον) to 'impossible' (ἀδύνατον), to disregard the obvious rhetorical emphasis (the high number, not the alleged ignorance of the poet), and to forget that the singer has just exhibited his inspired knowledge by offering a representative sample in his bravura performance, not to mention his explicit avowal to know the precise number (three thousand) of the offspring whose names he allegedly ignores.[32] The point of these verses is not one of epistemology. It is rather a conspicuous corroboration of the Panhellenic

---

omniscience are as specious in regard to Hesiod as they are in regard to Kalkhas: the goddesses do not bid him sing '*all* that shall be and was' but simply 'what shall be and was'. There is, to be sure, an implicit assertion of comprehensiveness that befits the Panhellenic scope of the performer's authority, but hardly one of exhaustive comprehensiveness that would require commensurate omniscience. A common but loose characterization of the epic narrator as 'omniscient' may have led the scholar astray. An omniscient narrator, conventionally understood, is one who knows things that only a god could have revealed to him; the label does not entail that he knows *everything* exhaustively. One may reasonably question if true omniscience is applicable to anyone, whether man or god, including Zeus (cf. *Theogony* 565 and Solmsen 1949:48–49). At any rate, Arrighetti's acknowledgment that Hesiod elsewhere adopts more traditional forms (he adduces three *loci* from the *Theogony*) should have led him to call into question his conflicting interpretation of the *Nautilia* and *Theogony* 367–370.

[31] Cf. West 1966:269 on ἕκαστοι.
[32] Cf. West 1966:268 *ad* 364.

shape of Hesiod's *Theogony*: local rivers are of local, not Panhellenic, concern.[33] The Panhellenic rhapsode therefore omits to list them all and relegates them to the attention of local populations in what amounts to an elegant *praeteritio*. This observation addresses Arrighetti's perplexity about why the poet does not resort to the Muses and ask them to supply him with the names (names which, for Arrighetti, Hesiod ignores).[34] One should not forget that the rivers whose names Hesiod does not mention are divinities too, and, presumably, both their names and any other relevant information (their genealogy, myths, etc.) would not fall under the purview of ordinary experience. Ascertaining such things would call, too, for an inspired and authoritative performer—only, in this case, a *local* bard who sings local poetry.

At his *Dichterweihe*, then, the Muses charge Hesiod with singing that is temporally comprehensive in its consideration of the gods' impact upon the world of man. His song is not to exclude some hypothetical present in favor of the past and the future. Now, granting that even Hesiod often keeps his focus on the past, reciprocally, although oracular inquiries most often involved future concerns, questions about the past, usually about the identity of someone's parents or the cause of some present affliction, were by no means unexampled.[35] We have, moreover, the well-known and puzzling statement by Epimenidēs (*apud* Aristotle *Rhetoric* III.17.10) that 'the past is known already, even by *manteis*'; 'for [Epimenidēs] used to divine not the future, but only about past and obscure matters', the philosopher adds by way of explanation.[36] However we interpret this quotation (which, if sarcastic, squares poorly with the seer's own practice),[37] it is clear that oracular speech could engage the past just as well as the future. But not only with regard to their temporal orientation (their varying emphases notwithstanding) do epic and oracular poetry show a certain affinity; the oracular valence of Homeric poetry, its unfolding of the divine will, is similarly explicit in the diction of the poet. Thus, when at Odysseus' urging Demodokos strikes up his song, the poet tells us that he 'revealed his song', φαῖνε δ' ἀοιδήν (θ 499). φαίνω and φημί, of course, can be traced to the same root, *b^heh_2- (*DELG* s.vv.), and this suggests the semantic development 'to shine'

---

[33] West 1966:269 *ad* 370 cites Ephoros (FGH 70 F20) "[o]n the merely local importance of most rivers."

[34] See Arrighetti 1998:xxix. For the full discussion see pp. xxvi–xxxi and Arrighetti 1992:59–63.

[35] Cf. Fontenrose 1978:17–18, whose D2 category concerns "extraordinary and obscure statements of past or present fact." The corresponding frequency table for "legendary and historical responses" can be found at 21; for "quasi-historical responses," at 45.

[36] τὸ γεγονός, ὃ ἐπιστητὸν ἤδη καὶ τοῖς μάντεσιν, ὡς ἔφη Ἐπιμενίδης ὁ Κρής (ἐκεῖνος γὰρ περὶ τῶν ἐσομένων οὐκ ἐμαντεύετο, ἀλλὰ περὶ τῶν γεγονότων μὲν ἀδήλων δέ) 1418a23–26.

[37] Cf. Cope 1877:3.203 and DK 3 B4.

→ 'to make bright' → 'to make clear' → 'to say' (*LIV*² 68–70).[38] It is not a coincidence that the word chosen is closely related to the manifestation of signs (σ 67
υ 114) or divine epiphanies (E 866 Y 131). Where used, as here, for a statement,
it underlines the marked character of the utterance, whether emphatic (Ξ 127)
or of great significance to the plot (Σ 295). Hence, in terms of the archaic poetics
of the passage, the song presents itself as the semantic equivalent of an oracular
pronouncement. This suits the rhetoric of Odysseus' challenge: αἴ κεν δή μοι
ταῦτα κατὰ μοῖραν καταλέξῃς, | αὐτίκα καὶ πᾶσιν μυθήσομαι ἀνθρώποισιν, | ὡς
ἄρα τοι πρόφρων θεὸς ὤπασε θέσπιν ἀοιδήν (θ 496–498); it also complements the
explicit hymnic framework in which the bard delivers his song: ὁ δ' ὁρμηθεὶς
θεοῦ ἤρχετο (θ 499).

8.1.3 The divine will

Indeed, we should not be surprised at the emphasis on the revelatory character
of the song, a fact that has obvious implications for the worldview that informs
epic performance and, consequently, for the notional fixity of the poetry. The
poems present themselves as the outworking of the divine will, which without
the bard's song would remain at best opaque. This is most emphatically expressed
in the opening lines of the *Iliad*, where the anger of Akhilleus and the subsequent death of many heroes is summarized by Διὸς δ' ἐτελείετο βουλή (A 5). One
might think this a proleptic reference to Zeus' favorable answer to the request
Thetis makes on behalf of her son. But fragment 1 of the *Kypria*[39] reveals that, at
least in other epic traditions (if not in the Iliadic one itself), Zeus was directly
and personally responsible for the Trojan War, which he devised as a strategy
to lessen the earth's overpopulation;[40] significantly, the *Kypria* expresses the
outcome by the phrase ἥρωες κτείνοντο, Διὸς δ' ἐτελείετο βουλή. The plot of
Zeus' conspiracy thickens with Proklos' summary, which adds that Zeus involved
Themis in his planning. Whatever the possible diachronic developments within,
and disagreements between, the traditions that informed the *Kypria* and our
present-day *Iliad*, three factors lead me to consider it reasonably certain that,

---

[38] Cf. Fournier 1946:12–13. It is traditional for lexica to offer two entries for *bʰehₐ- (or *bhā-), one
for 'to shine' and the other for 'to speak' (cf. Watkins 2000 s.v. "*bhā-*"); this does not necessarily
mean that the primitive identity of the two roots is being denied. Concerning φήμη note that it,
too, is marked speech, viz. 'a word of omen' (β 35 υ 100 105; cf. χ 376 and Plato *Timaios* 72b3). See
also Fournier 1946:8–12.

[39] ἦν ὅτε μυρία φῦλα κατὰ χθόνα πλαζόμεν' αἰεὶ | ⟨ἀνθρώπων ἐπίεζε⟩ βαρυστέρνου πλάτος αἴης, |
Ζεὺς δὲ ἰδὼν ἐλέησε καὶ ἐν πυκιναῖς πραπίδεσσι | κουφίσαι ἀνθρώπων παμβώτορα σύνθετο
γαῖαν, | ῥιπίσσας πολέμου μεγάλην ἔριν Ἰλιακοῖο, | ὄφρα κενώσειεν θανάτωι βάρος. οἱ δ' ἐνὶ
Τροίηι | ἥρωες κτείνοντο, Διὸς δ' ἐτελείετο βουλή. (I follow Bernabé's edition.)

[40] Cf. West 1997:480–482 and Burgess 2001:245n59.

notionally speaking, the poetry of the *Iliad*[41] was viewed by its audience from beginning to end as the explication of Zeus' will: first, the unity conveyed by the metaphor of an epic κύκλος, whose authorship, at an early stage, was ascribed solely to Homer;[42] second, the shared thematic and formulaic echoes just noted; and third, the frequent ascription to Zeus[43] of responsibility for the war.

The same can be said of the *Odyssey*. This claim calls for elaboration since, on its face, Zeus disavows any responsibility in the famous *concilium* of the first book and the words σφῆσιν ἀτασθαλίῃσιν (α 34) manifestly pick up on the σφετέρῃσιν ἀτασθαλίῃσιν ὄλοντο of α 7. Moreover, as Maehler (1963:23) notes, there is a sense in which this stress on the blind folly of Odysseus' companions not only reflects a keen interest in exculpating the hero (and generally a focus on

---

[41] It is interesting that the debate whether A 5 and fr. 1.7 of the *Kypria* referred to the same ἱστορία (to use the ancient term) is already joined by the Homeric scholia. Thus, Aristarkhos reportedly construed verse five with the immediately following ἐξ οὗ δὴ τὰ πρῶτα, so as to rule out a preexisting divine animus against the Akhaians and reject the 'fabrications' of the *neōteroi*. Hellenistic scholars, of course, called *neōteroi* all poets chronologically later than Homer, and would therefore have numbered among them anyone associated with the *Cycle*. Consequently, Aristarkhos is rejecting a thematic connection between the βουλὴ Διός in the *Iliad* and in the *Kypria*. The D scholia (in the Venetus A *ad loc.*) fills in the picture: ἄλλοι δὲ ἀπὸ ἱστορίας τινὸς εἶπον εἰρηκέναι τὸν Ὅμηρον. φασὶ γὰρ τὴν γῆν βαρουμένην ὑπὸ ἀνθρώπων πολυπληθείας, μηδεμιᾶς ἀνθρώπων οὔσης εὐσεβείας, αἰτῆσαι τὸν Δία κουφισθῆναι τοῦ ἄχθους. τὸν δὲ Δία, πρῶτον μὲν εὐθὺς ποιῆσαι τὸν Θηβαϊκὸν πόλεμον, δι' οὗ πολλοὺς πάνυ ἀπώλεσεν. ὕστερον δὲ πάλιν συμβούλῳ τῷ Μώμῳ χρησάμενος, ἣν Διὸς βουλὴν Ὅμηρός φησιν, ἐπειδὴ οἷός τε ἦν κεραυνοῖς ἢ κατακλυσμοῖς πάντας διαφθείρειν, ὅπερ τοῦ Μώμου κωλύσαντος, ὑποθεμένου δὲ αὐτῷ γνώμας δύο, τὴν Θέτιδος θνητογαμίαν, καὶ θυγατρὸς καλὴν γένναν, ἐξ ὧν ἀμφοτέρων πόλεμος Ἕλλησί τε καὶ Βαρβάροις ἐγένετο, ἀφ' οὗ συνέβη κουφισθῆναι τὴν γῆν, πολλῶν ἀναιρεθέντων. ἡ δὲ ἱστορία παρὰ Στασίνῳ τῷ τὰ Κύπρια πεποιηκότι ... . καὶ τὰ μὲν παρὰ τοῖς νεωτέροις ἱστορούμενα περὶ τῆς τοῦ Διὸς βουλῆς, ἐστὶ τάδε. (This text is conveniently included by Bernabé as item I in his first apparatus to fr. 1 of the *Kypria*, pp. 43–44.) We need not assume, however, that the oral tradition faced the hearer with a dichotomy of mutually exclusive options. As Burgess (2001:149–150) observes, "it is best to suppose that the reference to the plan of Zeus at *Iliad* 1.5 can suggest both the Iliadic and Cyclic manifestations of this phrase, not just one or the other" (cf. also his n. 61, p. 246). In other words, we should not assume that the *Kypria* 'copied' a fixed *Iliad* or vice versa: the relationship between them was one of oral traditions interacting through recurrent performances in the minds and repertories of individual singers. One should not rule out the possibility that the audience or their bard may have interpreted A 5 in the light of what we now consider cyclic themes.

[42] As Pfeiffer (1968:1.73) rightly observes, Aristotle *Sophistical Refutations* 171a10–11 implies that the Homeric authorship of the Epic Cycle was still widely received even in his time (his own stance against it notwithstanding). Furthermore, Nagy (1996b:38, 89–90) has convincingly argued that the 'circle of poetry' is a metaphor (natural to Indo-European poetics) of a perfect (notional) whole, of a tradition of poetry viewed as a superb composite artifact, whose individual parts are masterfully fitted together by the wordsmith-poet. The archetypal ἀοιδός (once the cause for the notional fixity of the tradition was transferred from the divine to the human realm of individual authorship) is none other than Ὅμ-ηρος, i.e. 'Mr. Com-poser' (see above, p. 207 n. 121). For the ancient attribution of the Cycle to Homer see Nagy 1990c:78 and Burgess 2001:129–130.

[43] Λ 78 Ρ 321 Τ 86–88 α 348 θ 82; cf. θ 579–580.

personal guilt, cf. ψ 67), but also suggests a contrast in emphasis with the Iliadic tradition's foregrounding of the will of Zeus. But matters are more complicated than they appear at first, for after Odysseus escapes from Polyphemos and offers the ram to Zeus in thanksgiving we learn that 'Zeus was contriving how my well-benched ships and my trusty comrades might perish' (ι 554–555). Scholars have seen in this doublet of the anger of Poseidon signs of a reworking of two independent traditions, each of which featured the wrath of only one god as the 'divine narrative engine' of Odysseus' many adventures. Regardless of how we account for Zeus' refusal to heed the offering and however we conceive of it in relation to Poseidon (and here it is hard to deny there is a *coincidence* of purpose), for Heubeck to write that "there is no question here of Zeus being hostile"[44] and add that "[h]e must let events take their course in accordance with Moira" (Russo et al. 1992:41) seems to me inadequate and to fly in the face of the text. Add to this the words of Teiresias, who promises deliverance to the hero and his comrades *despite* Poseidon's anger, if they do not harm the cattle of Helios; otherwise, only Odysseus shall come home, late and in someone else's ship, and find trouble in his house (λ 114–115). The seer's words[45] are an oral quotation of Polyphemos' own curse,[46] and hence it would seem that it is still in Odysseus' power to escape the wrath of Poseidon if only he and his men avoid harm to the flock of Helios: there is no talk here of Moira, as would be natural—were the necessity of fate really in view—in the mouth of a seer who proceeds, in fact, to prophesy about the manner of Odysseus' death. One could counter with narrative necessity: that the hero *must* arrive late, find his palace overrun by suitors, slay them, etc. I agree. But this answer misses the point of my argument, which is that *from within the logic* of the story (call it the narrative or theological framework), some scholars ascribe responsibility for the unfolding plot to Poseidon alone, whereas, in my view, ι 554–555 and the words of Teiresias suggest that Odysseus is not bound by some *moira* to which Zeus yields, but that it is Zeus himself who secures the fulfillment of the Kyklops' curse (with the obvious concurrence of Poseidon). The events on Thrinakia confirm this reading, for Zeus' unfavorable wind there (μ 313 325–326) is the ultimate cause of the men's sacrilege: they are driven by desperation and even in their transgression they take care to be as inoffensive as possible; and Odysseus is overtaken by a protective sleep sent to prevent his hindering his men or sharing in their deed (μ 338 371–373). Furthermore, Zeus is emphatically instrumental in carrying out

---

[44] "[W]e are simply told that he did not accept the offering" (Russo et al. 1992:41).

[45] ὀψὲ κακῶς νεῖαι, ὀλέσας ἄπο πάντας ἑταίρους, | νηὸς ἐπ' ἀλλοτρίης· δήεις δ' ἐν πήματα οἴκῳ.

[46] ὀψὲ κακῶς ἔλθοι, ὀλέσας ἄπο πάντας ἑταίρους, | νηὸς ἐπ' ἀλλοτρίης, εὕροι δ' ἐν πήματα οἴκῳ (ι 534–535).

Helios' punishment and destroying the ship (μ 387–388). Neither must we forget that Zeus was also responsible for the onset of Odysseus' adventures (ι 67).[47]

Contributing further to the revelatory character of Homeric poetry are its many connections to oracles, prophecies, dreams, and omens.[48] I might mention, for example, the omen at Aulis (B 303–330); Kalkhas' prophecy (A 92–100); the intimation of Philoktetes' return (B 724); the prediction of Akhilleus' death by his horse Xanthos (T 415–417); the famous and puzzling Delphic χρησμός about the future strife between Odysseus and Akhilleus (θ 79–80); the self-interpreting dream-omen of Penelope (τ 535–553); the visionary outburst of Theoklymenos (υ 351–357); and Teiresias' prophecy about Odysseus and the oar (λ 119–130). Here, again, Apollonios of Rhodes proved his refined sense of inherited epic conventions by highlighting Apollo's prophecy (φάτις 1.5) as the trigger to the plot of his *Argonautika*.[49]

Accustomed, as we are, to thinking about the constraints of genres (their observance, violations, and modifications) primarily within a self-referential framework of literary conventions—a sort of ahistorical 'New Criticism'—we must make an effort here to recover all the social dimensions attendant on this poetry, especially the religious ones. The invocation of the divinity is still, in this period, fraught with sacral meaning: the Panhellenic nature of the poetry, its strong tendency to eliminate any details tied to local cult and to stylize any remaining instances of prayers and sacrifices, makes the archaic ritual context of Homeric performance very difficult to recover.[50] But here, the practice of using hymns (e.g. the so-called Homeric hymns) as προοίμια[51] to the larger poems (in whatever stage of compositional development and textual fixity) attests to the religious character of the singing of the bard.[52] A typical προοίμιον

---

[47] For a forceful defense of the priority of Zeus' will in the *Odyssey*, presiding over the opposition of Athena to Poseidon, see Reinhardt 1996: "If the world experience of the *Iliad* is the result of a battle in which Zeus remains victorious despite setbacks, then the fates of the *Odyssey* are decided by a game of opposing and yielding, which leaves Zeus as the one on top, the one to whose will all the other gods submit" (87). Cf. Marks 2008.

[48] Cf. Nagy 2003:27 and 21–38 *passim*.

[49] Cf. González 2000:278–279. The prophecy is otherwise known from Pindar *Pythian* 4.71–78 and Pherekydes (FGH 3 F105).

[50] For a succinct statement and analysis of this phenomenon see Nagy 1990c:143n40. Some critics even deny Homeric poetry and its performance any connection at all to cult or ritual. But cf. Nagy 1990b:10–12.

[51] For a look at the poetics of προοίμια see Koller 1956. Cf. Nagy 1990c:353–360 and Nagy 1996c:62–64.

[52] It is currently fashionable to deny a cultic dimension to the Homeric hymns. A recent survey of Greek 'cult songs' tersely dismisses them "partly because they are not cult hymns in any real sense" (Furley and Bremer 2001:1.43). Strictly speaking, it is not clear that they are also being denied a religious dimension, for the same writers oppose their genre (which they call 'rhapsodic') to "all the *other* genres of religious hymns" (1.42, my emphasis), thereby apparently conceding that the Homeric hymns, too, are in some sense 'religious.' A distinction

takes the form of a dialog of sorts: first, the bard addresses himself to the god, beseeching his aid and favor as he presides over the performance (and often celebrating his τιμαί and deeds *seriatim*); the Muse, in turn, replies with her song, which in the mouth of the bard becomes his own song and message to his audience. The *Odyssey* itself provides illustrations of the use of preludes. Indeed, the verb ἀναβάλλειν, as noted,[53] refers to the bard 'striking up' his song (α 155 θ 266 ρ 262); there is also one explicit instance of a hymnic invocation: ὁ δ' ὁρμηθεὶς θεοῦ ἤρχετο (θ 499). Such preambles are further documented by Pindar (*Nemean* 2.3) and Thoukydides (3.104.4), and though neither the *Iliad* nor the *Odyssey* has come down to us accompanied by any one particular προοίμιον, Krates of Mallos knew of a copy of the former poem that included a prelude to Apollo and the Muses. The *Theogony* and the *Works and Days* do open with respective hymns to the Muses and Zeus, though a copy of the *Works and Days* without its first ten lines was shown to Pausanias on his visit to Mount Helikon (9.31.4).[54] In fact, the entire *Theogony* could be considered a hymn to Zeus, even as it

---

between 'religious' and 'cultic' during the archaic and classical periods, however, is problematic and calls for careful elucidation. But in the section devoted to the Homeric hymns Furley and Bremer wield it without adequate scholarly nuance. If the key difference is the setting and peculiar manner of a hymn's performance, when it comes to the Homeric hymns their treatment fails to address this matter, content with a cursory mention of "rhapsodic competitions at the pan-Hellenic centres" and possibly also "more informal recitations of epic at banquets, for example" (1.43). The reader who wants to understand the distinction between cult and religious songs looks in vain for guidance in the section devoted to 'cult song' (1.14–20): terms that are just as problematic—religious ceremonial, cult images, religious adoration, gifts and offerings, melody and rhythm, epiphanies, congregational singing, etc.—are massed to paint a composite picture that does not fully apply to any one of the hymnic categories selected for treatment. What makes a song a 'cult hymn'? Do we need melody, or is recitation sufficient? Must it be accompanied by dancing? To what degree must its composition, its content, its tone be public? Must it address the divinity directly and must it do so corporately as 'we'? Or is a choral 'I' sufficient? Does the corporate appropriation of an individual hymn (whose original authorial 'I' was not choral) suffice to make it a cult song? Can we tell when this has happened? Must the 'Du-Stil' predominate over the 'Er-Stil'? Why? Must performance take place in the context of a public sacrifice? Questions like these can be multiplied *sine fine*. I do not mean to imply that they should not be posed or that satisfying answers cannot be offered. But it is wrong simply to dismiss the Homeric hymns because they are not 'cult hymns,' without a careful account of the rationale followed. In fact, Furley and Bremer (1.43) themselves list two reasons to resist marginalizing them: cult hymns are not a homogeneous body to begin with, showing significant disparity according to individual cult and genre; and the emphasis on 'objective narrative' (i.e. 'Er-Stil') has to do more with the genre to which they were a prelude than with their character as hymns: the rhapsode, after all, *did* address the god. (Race 1990:103n48 proves that not only is the distinction precarious, but the way in which it is applied to the Homeric hymns, too, is questionable.) Full consideration of the issues involved here, even though obviously relevant, exceeds the limits of the present work. In a future study I intend to carry out a comprehensive analysis of this matter.

53 See above, p. 204.
54 Cf. van Groningen 1948 and West 1978a:137.

contains both a προοίμιον to the Muses (1–115) and, within the same, a micro-hymn to Zeus (71–75).

The religious mindset (I might say piety) that must have pervaded the performance of Homeric epic at its earliest stages need not mean, of course, that there were no other facets to this poetry. Thus, for example, to mention only one that is amply attested, it was also supposed to delight the audience: μῆτερ ἐμή, τί τ' ἄρα φθονέεις ἐρίηρον ἀοιδὸν | τέρπειν ὅππῃ οἱ νόος ὄρνυται; (α 346–347; cf. θ 44–45 and Hesiod *Theogony* 55, 98–103). But even in regard to the pleasure of poetic performance do the gods receive notional priority:[55] τύνη, Μουσάων ἀρχώμεθα, ταὶ Διὶ πατρὶ | ὑμνεῦσαι τέρπουσι μέγαν νόον ἐντὸς Ὀλύμπου (Hesiod *Theogony* 37–38); αὐτίκα δ' ἀθανάτοισι μέλει κίθαρις καὶ ἀοιδή. | Μοῦσαι μέν θ' ἅμα πᾶσαι ἀμειβόμεναι ὀπὶ καλῇ | ὑμνεῦσίν ῥα θεῶν δῶρ' ἄμβροτα ἠδ' ἀνθρώπων | τλημοσύνας, ὅσ' ἔχοντες ὑπ' ἀθανάτοισι θεοῖσι (*Hymn to Apollo* 188–191).

8.2 Of Truth and Lies

If we come down to the classical period, to the late fifth century BC, and consider Plato's *Iōn*, we find that, according to Sokrates' chain of inspiration, Homer, the singer-poet, is possessed by the Muse (*enthousiasmos* works godward) and hence functions as a μάντις before the audience—or, more immediately, before the rhapsode who performs his poetry. There is here an important modification to the archaic picture: starting in the second half of the sixth century BC we find that the epic tradition, heretofore strictly conceptualized as the word of the Muse, is henceforth assigned to a *prōtos heuretēs*,[56] Homer, the archetypal wordsmith *par excellence*.[57] This development, attractive to the Greek mind in its historical simplicity, also took place in other social domains (e.g. lawgiving, animal sacrifice, etc.) and corresponds to that culture's love of aetiologies. But from a sociological perspective, this shift represents a transparent move of the locus of authority for the performance away from the religious—the Muse, who aids the singer and makes his performance authoritative—and towards the secular—a great and inimitable composer, whose original utterance the singer is called to reenact.[58]

[55] See above, p. 212 n. 140. The archetypal nature of divine action is also on display in Hesiod *Theogony* 71–75, where the rule of Zeus and his apportioning τιμαί to the rest of the immortals is celebrated by the Muses at the beginning of Hesiod's song: their theogony is none other than Hesiod's own theogony.

[56] On this concept see Kleingünther 1933.

[57] On the earliest reliable attestations of the name 'Homer,' see above, pp. 167ff.

[58] This move was prerequisite for an openly critical evaluation of the epic tradition.

The issues, however, are the same: authority and veracity remain fungible, and with the evolving nature of authority we find a corresponding redefinition of truthfulness.[59] The living tradition was once tautologically true, for truth was performatively (re)enacted and untruth relegated to oblivion. This did not place all parties beyond the charge of mendacity: it was in the opposition between competing poetic traditions that ψεύδεα may be discovered.[60] Divergences between multiforms of a given myth or song would have been most readily detected at *agōnes* between competing bards or in the rival festival traditions of locales that shared cultural contacts.[61] It is, in fact, primarily in the context of strife (ἔρις), quarrel (νεῖκος), and competing claims that Greek poetry brings matters of truthfulness to the fore. The rhetoric of ψεῦδος and ἀλήθεια reaches out in two complementary directions: there is, on the one hand, a challenge to the audience to embrace or reject the truth claims of the message, dream, or performance;[62] but there is also a direct challenge by the speaker (or performer) to anyone else offering a competing claim (or song) in the context of ἔρις (or an ἀγών, which is but an institutionally regulated form of ἔρις[63]). This conceptual affinity motivates Hesiod's choice in making quarrels, lies, tales, and disputes (Νείκεά τε Ψεύδεά τε Λόγους τ' Ἀμφιλλογίας τε *Theogony* 229) siblings all descended from ἔρις and 'like each other in habits' (συνήθεας ἀλλήλησιν 230).[64] The association between lying and competition resurfaces at Ψ 576, where Menelaos forestalls the charge of lying by calling on Antilokhos to swear that he has not won the horse race with a δόλος; the context is one of arbitration (ἐγὼν αὐτὸς δικάσω … ἰθεῖα γὰρ ἔσται 579–580).[65]

---

[59] The bibliography on the truth claims (or fictive character) of archaic epic is vast. I can only give here a small selection of the relevant literature: Luther 1935, Frisk 1936, Luther 1958, Setti 1958, Accame 1963, Krischer 1965, Detienne 1996 [1967], Adkins 1972, Snell 1975, Levet 1976, Stroh 1976, Pucci 1977, Rösler 1980, Cole 1983, Puelma 1989, Ritoók 1989, Pratt 1993, Gill and Wiseman 1993, Finkelberg 1998, and Levet 2008.

[60] For the concept of ψεῦδος in archaic Greek literature see Luther 1935, Levet 1976:201–235, and Detienne 1996:158n4.

[61] As Nagy (1990c:57) notes, his very itinerancy would have made a singer conscious of local variations.

[62] Cf. ξ 387–389. Odysseus' elaborate lies in the *Odyssey* belong to his program of disguise and recognition, putting his interlocutors to the test. I cannot accept the attempt by Heiden (2007:171–172) to reconceive the articulation of this challenge in Hesiod *Theogony* 26–28 as a "threat to listeners or readers who might find the Muses' songs unbelievable." I find implausible his suggestion that Hesiod adopted a strategy altogether the child of our own postmodern times and disavowed the very distinction between truth and lies to preempt criticism of his poetry. More below, pp. 259ff., on Heiden's semantic argument.

[63] Cf. Hesiod *Works and Days* 24–26.

[64] Theognis 390, too, associates ψεύδεα and οὐλόμεναι ἔριδες.

[65] Other Iliadic occurrences of ψεῦδος pertain to the following contexts: where reputation and family history is involved (Δ 404 E 635); in connection with oath-breaking (Δ 235); with promises (sometimes implicit or assumed), especially divine ones with an oracular or prophetic valence

The conceptual ties between νεῖκος and ψεύδεα illuminate an otherwise puzzling episode in the *Theogony* (775–806), where Styx is presented as the arbiter of divine strife that results in competing truth claims, 'when strife and quarreling arise among the immortals and if any of the gods, who live on Olympos, lies'.[66] A ritual of potential self-incrimination follows, which includes an oath and a libation with the water of Styx. A god who perjures himself lies 'breathless' (νήυτμος 795; ἀνάπνευστος 797) until the end of the year; the image is one of helplessness and ineffectiveness, the conceptual parallel of ἔπε' ἀκράαντα (τ 565),[67] now touching not merely the god's will but his entire person. It is clear, however, that the lack of breath, though in the context of a κῶμα and abstention from food, focuses on the lack of voice, ἄναυδος (797), in what amounts to an inversion of 'authoritative speech': ⟨ἄναυδος⟩ τὸ ἀπαρρησίαστον τῶν ἀσεβῶν χαρακτηρίζει, notes the scholiast.[68] This ordeal, however, is but the start of the appointed punishment, namely, a forced exile of nine years from the company of the gods (εἰνάετες 801; ἐννέα πάντ' ἔτεα 803).[69] Likewise at Ω 222–224, Priam equates ψεῦδος with a ἅλιον ἔπος, an 'idle' or 'fruitless word'. And Hera tricks Zeus into swearing with the following challenge: ψευστήσεις, οὐδ' αὖτε τέλος μύθῳ ἐπιθήσεις (Τ 107); once again, the 'lie' consists in not accomplishing his word, in failing to bring it to pass. Not unrelated are the juxtaposition of μάψ, 'in vain, without result', and οὐ κατὰ κόσμον at Β 214; and the use of μαψιδίως

(Β 349 Μ 164 Φ 276 Ω 222; cf. Luther 1935:87); or where faithful reporting is in view (Ο 159). The case of Β 81 is complex: Zeus intends destruction on the Akhaians and sends an οὖλος ὄνειρος (Β 6), a dream that not only spells ruin but is also false: it is *not* true that Troy may 'now' by taken (cf. Β 37–38). Agamemnon, however, fails to appreciate its deceptive nature—for which he is called νήπιος (Β 38)—and tells the other chieftains. Thus the performer's challenge to his audience devolves on the Akhaian leaders, and it falls to Nestor, standing in for the rest, to fail the test. But, he makes clear, they would have called it a lie (ψεῦδός κεν φαῖμεν Β 81) had any other than Agamemnon told it. Of interest here is that the status of the dream is connected with the speaker's, who tells what amounts to an alternative denouement for the story of Troy: for the city cannot now be taken lest the tradition be falsified (cf. Β 349). This is further brought out by Agamemnon, who turns the dream on its head by telling the army what, from his perspective, is a lie, but arguably, from the point of view of Zeus, is partially true.

[66] ὁππότ' ἔρις καὶ νεῖκος ἐν ἀθανάτοισιν ὄρηται, | καί ῥ' ὅστις ψεύδηται Ὀλύμπια δώματ' ἐχόντων (782–783).

[67] See above, p. 203.

[68] Di Gregorio 1975 *ad loc.* is doubtless right in substituting ἄναυδος for the lemma οὐδέ ποτ' ἀμβροσίης: "οὐδέ – ἀμβροσίης v. 796 ... seclusi et ἄναυδος praeeunte Sittl ut lemma inserui."

[69] The significance of the number nine is not clear (cf. 789–790), but it is noteworthy that it is the same period of time Hephaistos took refuge with Thetis after Hera cast him off Olympos (Σ 400). The Trojan War, of course, lasted nine years, with the city taken only on the tenth (γ 118 ε 107 ξ 240 χ 228); and there is the universal of the nine months of gestation with birth on the tenth, counting inclusively (e.g. *Hymn to Hermes* 11–12; cf. *Theogony* 56, 722–725 and West 1966:341 *ad Theogony* 636); note, moreover, the temporal patterns in Hesiod fr. 304 MW. It is curious, if arguably coincidental, that, Panhellenic festivals being penteteric, the period of impotence covers precisely two such consecutive cycles.

to qualify ψεύδεσθαι at ξ 365. That ψεῦδος can be used to denote a statement's lack of fulfillment shows that, just as ἀλήθεια does not strictly correspond to our notion of 'truth', so does ψεῦδος resist a straightforward mapping onto our notion of 'lie'. Thus, when Nestor, ignorant of recent events, fears that his observations may be found in error, he remarks: ψεύσομαι, ἦ ἔτυμον ἐρέω; κέλεται δέ με θυμός (Κ 534; cf. δ 140). It is not lies, but an erroneous statement he wants to avoid: where we distinguish between misspeaking and lying, Homeric Greek, regardless of culpability, uses ψεῦδος.[70] In sum, then, though ἀληθής and ἀψευδής belong together (*Theogony* 233), in the larger conceptual world of Greek archaic poetics the fundamental opposition is the one between ἀλήθεια and λήθη, not ἀλήθεια and ψεῦδος.[71]

There is an obvious rhetorical point to lying that tries to gain a hearer's favor (ξ 386–389;[72] *Theogony* 78, 709, 789), the coveted goal of the performer: ψεῦδος and θέλγω stand together at Φ 276 and ξ 387; Akhilleus uses ἀπατάω to describe Agamemnon's breach of the heroic code that would have rewarded his service with τιμή and γέρας (Ι 344 371 375); and λ 363–368 contrasts the deceiver who fashions lies (ψεύδεα ἀρτύνειν) to the skillful singer (ἐπιστάμενος) of noble heart (φρένες ἐσθλαί) and shapely words (μορφὴ ἐπέων).[73] But in this last passage the ἀοιδός, as the instrument of the Muse, is still the paragon of

---

[70] *Pace* S. West (in Heubeck et al. 1988 *ad* δ 140), who, dismissing the evidence that ψεύδομαι can denote "unintentionally saying what is not true," is forced to reject the translation, "Shall I be wrong or right in what I say?" But even she admits that Ε 635 could be so taken (and, I would add, *must* be so taken, if we adopt the most natural translation). It is true that the real question, as proved by the rejoinder 'my heart bids me', is whether to speak or to keep silent; but the only reason Helen has a stake in the choice is that she may be wrong if she speaks—here, she is not certain whether in fact the young man before her is Odysseus' son or not. Similarly in error is Adkins (1972:14), who assumes that Helen's statement may revive painful memories of war and cause so acute a feeling of embarrassment that she really does consider lying to disguise her thoughts. This, however, is contradicted by the following κέλεται δέ με θυμός: the choice is between speech and silence, and not between deceitful and truthful speaking, which would call for γάρ, not δέ, as the joining particle ('since I must speak, shall I tell the truth or dissemble?'). Adkins's reading, moreover, would force us to conclude that Helen had openly acknowledged that she might resort to lies: would such an admission be likely to escape opprobrium? If not, why would Helen willingly bring herself under moral condemnation, if, as alleged, she was so eager to escape embarrassment on another account? I find this reading socially and psychologically implausible. Note, further, Levet 1976: "Le ψεῦδος, à l'origine, désigne deux notions différentes, qui sont étroitement associées à la conception ancienne de certains mécanismes psychologiques, le faux par conjecture non conforme à ce qui est et le faux par invention" (234).

[71] In Hesiod's *Theogony*, ψεύδεα (229) corresponds to ἀψευδέα (233) just as ἀληθέα (233) to λήθεται (236). Cf. Detienne 1996:158n4. I cannot accept the view of Simondon (1982:113–114) who considers ἔτυμα and ἀληθέα the basic oppositive pair. More on this below.

[72] For the use of παραπείθω in this connection see Luther 1935:98.

[73] μορφή, with only two occurrences in Homer, is both times used with ἔπεα: μορφὴ ἐπέων (λ 367) and θεὸς μορφὴν ἔπεσι στέφει (θ 170). As *DELG* s.v. notes, μορφή "signifie 'forme' en tant que cette forme dessine un tout en principe harmonieux," and its restriction to speech, however

'truthful' singing, and of him nothing less than unassailable moral probity is conceivable. And yet it is hard to see how a judgment based on the speaker's possession of these qualities would successfully tell the truthful from the lying, especially the artful lying; and this serves well to underline the precarious standing of truth in the context of performance, where competing singers are bent on winning the audience and defeating their opponents. Now, in the face of conflicting performances, only two judgments are open: either the Muse has inspired one singer but *not* another; or else she has filled the mouth of one with 'truth' and of the other with 'lies.' This (perhaps undesirable) state of affairs is but the reflection of the discriminating and variable nature of divine favor: now giving, now taking away, showing or withholding blessing for the gods' own, at times inscrutable, reasons.[74]

In the one recorded instance where archaic poetry grew self-conscious at the boundary of competing traditions, the προοίμιον to Hesiod's *Theogony*, it granted the Muses comprehensive responsibility for traditional poetics and, in good consequence, had to allow for the tantalizing possibility of 'lying inspiration.'[75] In effect, as the Hesiodic theogony makes a bid for Panhellenic

---

accidental, highlights its affinity with the rhapsodic appropriation of κόσμος explored above (p. 194).

[74] Perhaps the most immediately relevant expression of this sentiment is the hymn to Zeus that opens the *Works and Days* (3–8). Cf. also Hesiod *Theogony* 442–443, Y 242–243, and Xenophanes DK 21 B25.

[75] Treatments of Hesiod *Theogony* 26–28 and the surrounding context are legion. Nearly all students of Greek archaic poetry have at some point advanced an interpretation of these famous words. The last fifty years have witnessed a proliferation of philosophical readings of postmodern flavor that make 'lying-as-fiction' fundamental to Hesiodic poetics. I believe that these readings are too clever by half and impossibly anachronistic. They lack cultural motivation and depend on the unlikely notion of an extraordinary individual poetic genius ('Hesiod'), well ahead not only of his own time but, arguably, of most, if not all, of his successors. The words of Detienne (1996:22, quoting in part the opening of Wismann 1996 from an earlier 1993 mimeographed text), although intended as a defense of his structuralist method, seem apposite here: "Is it legitimate to apply to the author of the *Theogony* the modern hermeneutic principle on which the coherence of the work's meaning resides, in the last analysis, on the autonomous decision of a single individual? The constraints of this principle involve accepting the work in its autonomy, the coherence of its meaning, a unitary project, an author at work, and a peerless interpreter responding to the appeal of a peerless author." (For Wismann's answer to Detienne, see Wismann 1996:23–24.) Detienne's objections stand *a fortiori* if instead of poems created by a single, definitive personality we envision a diachronically developing, continental tradition of epic poetry shaped in performance by the hands of many bards. Modern philosophical speculations are oversubtle and ultimately sterile, because one cannot securely embed them in the cultural context of archaic Greece. Thus, for example, with much semantic analysis that is doubtless right and useful Levet 1976 includes sustained psychological speculation about the archaic mind that I, for one, find hard to follow and even harder to ascribe with any plausibility to the time and place of its alleged currency. What is lacking in many studies, Levet's included, is a credible cultural motivation—a motivation that can (I submit) be confidently found only in the dynamics of diffusion and reception central to the performance of traditional epic poetry

status it must at the same time discredit any other local variants.[76] The Muses rebuke the poet with pointed abuse, calling him a 'mere belly', drawing on the *topos* of the man who is willing to do anything to satisfy his hunger; thus, Eumaios tells Odysseus that 'wanderers in need of substance tell idle lies and have no desire to tell the truth (ἀληθέα μυθήσασθαι)' (ξ 124–125; cf. η 215–221 σ 53–54).[77] There is, then, in the Muses' rebuke a stab at the singer who is willing to compromise the veracity of his song by changing it to suit the expectations of local patronage.[78] Katz and Volk (2000:124) object that the 'bellies' of *Theogony* 26 cannot be poets because Hesiod himself (not a group distinct from him) is being addressed. I share their conviction that *Theogony* 27–28 describes two distinct capacities of the Muses and that Hesiod is inspired specifically with the truth (not a mixture of lies and truth, much less an anachronistic category of 'truthful fiction'); and, like them, I think that one may not ignore or give short shrift to verse 26, as often happens with oversubtle philosophical readings. But I do not endorse their refusal, in which they follow Judet de la Combe (1993:26–30), to make poets the target of the Muses' rebuke because this "would entail that Hesiod was already a poet even before encountering the Muses and that the *Dichterweihe* merely transformed him from a poet of lies into a poet of truth" (Katz and Volk 2000:124).[79] This objection only has force if we lose sight of the

---

in the archaic period. (Cf. Nagy 1990b:43.) Such dynamics involve the full mythico-religious context that Detienne emphasizes and readily explain what Levet's treatment unnecessarily convolutes. I cannot in this book thoroughly review the various interpretations offered by modern scholars. I must limit myself to outlining and critiquing a handful of proposals that have proved especially influential in recent times and have in turn encouraged many implausible readings. For a delightful, if ultimately unconvincing, treatment that conveniently reviews modern interpretive approaches to *Theogony* 26–28, see Katz and Volk 2000. Katz and Volk's view that 'mere bellies' refers "to the role that [Hesiod] is about to play, his role as a recipient or, rather, a receptacle of inspiration" (127) is implausible because it would no longer make the term one of opprobrium, thus following awkwardly on κάκ' ἐλέγχεα. I doubt that in the archaic Greek setting allegedly reducing the poet to a passive instrument should have been deemed "a (teasing) insult" (129). I am, however, sympathetic to their intuition that "what the Muses are stressing is the total dependence of a poet on their inspiration, as well as their complete wilfulness in granting it" (127). Two other works that should be singled out for their usefulness are Judet de la Combe 1993 and Leclerc 1993:167–221. See also the convenient collection of articles in Blaise et al. 1996.

[76] So Nagy 1990b:45–47.

[77] Cf. Svenbro 1976:50–59 and Nagy 1999a:229–233, 261 §11n4. To date, the only compelling interpretation of γαστέρες οἶον is Svenbro's proposal as modified by Nagy, according to which the 'mere bellies' indicts poets who, driven by their physical needs, suit their poetry to the demands of a local audience. In contrast to the oversubtle philosophical readings of others, this interpretation alone accommodates concerns that may be plausibly ascribed to a Greek archaic performer of epic; and it alone bespeaks an interest in the poem's obvious Panhellenic stake and scope. On ξ 124–125 see further below, p. 263.

[78] For Odysseus' lies (e.g. τ 203) and his portrayal as a poet's equal, see Nagy 1990b:43–47.

[79] Cf. Verdenius 1972:234.

point of characterizing Hesiod initially as a shepherd: his transformation into a poet of truth is portrayed as utterly comprehensive, as a radical make-over—a rhetorical move necessary to mark him out as falling henceforth under verse 28 of the anaphoric distich, and not under 27. It is true that the Muses admit to inspiring many ψεύδεα also. But this is merely an unavoidable acknowledgment of the traditional character of the local poetry denigrated: the concession serves only to put down its authority in favor of the Panhellenic claims and scope of the Hesiodic *Theogony*. The very performance mode entailed by the pointed choice of λέγειν (27) deflates the clout of Hesiod's rivals.[80] The rebuke to the shepherds is without motivation if they are not somehow involved in a wrong for which they are rightly indicted by the goddesses as κάκ' ἐλέγχεα (26). Their 'moral blemish' is their eager embrace of local poetry under the patronage of local elites, poetry that is now exposed as devoid of truth, a blemish depicted as a character defect that makes them complicit in the perpetuation of the ψεύδεα with which they are punitively inspired and for which they are held morally culpable.[81]

It is the comprehensive and fundamental transformation in the scope and function of Hesiod's poetic activity that accounts for the details of his induction as a Panhellenic singer: he is taught noble song (καλὴν ἐδίδαξαν ἀοιδήν 22), receives the staff of authority (σκῆπτρον 30), and the goddesses breathe into him a voice that carries their divine imprimatur (αὐδὴν | θέσπιν 31–32). These are all conceived as new emblems of authority because they are Panhellenic and, therefore, true in absolute terms.[82] As a willing participant in the local song

[80] This would be so even if, in actual practice, to a cultural outsider the performance of local poetry were formally indistinguishable from the one envisioned for the *Theogony*. The point is not to suggest that the proclamation of truth to which ἀληθέα γηρύσασθαι (28) makes reference is of necessity metrically and melodically different from what local performers might have offered (though, in time, Panhellenic diffusion may affect these too); it is rather to suggest that Hesiod alone enjoys the authority exclusive to *truthful* inspiration. And yet for the cultural insider the song *in its totality*, formally and thematically (to use *our* analytical categories), is reconceived as radically 'other': only now may it be called 'beautiful song', taught by the Muses (22).

[81] The notion that gods may prompt, or somehow be instrumental in bringing about, actions for which they in turn hold their human agents culpable may trouble and perplex us. But it is unquestionably part of the fabric of ancient religious thought. See, for example, my discussion above (p. 231f.) of the will of Zeus in the *Odyssey*. For two Semitic parallels, see 1 Kings 22:19–23 and Ezekiel 14:9. Regarding Zedekiah's statement, 'In what manner did Yaweh's spirit pass from me to speak with you?', De Vries (1985:268) writes: "[W]e interpret his question to mean that since he has prophetic inspiration, how can Micaiah presume to claim the same prophetic inspiration? Micaiah's vision-oracle already offered the answer to this dilemma: a particular prophet can be inspired by Yahweh, even if it is a lying spirit which entices the people to the judgment that Yahweh has prepared for them."

[82] Cf. Nagy 1996a esp. 43. It bears repeating that there is no force to the objection that the rebuke of shepherds as 'mere bellies' cannot have performers in view because Hesiod's initiation—his being taught noble song, his receiving the laurel staff, and his having a wondrous voice breathed

culture, Hesiod enjoyed none of these divine grants and privileges. Given the culture of reception fundamental to traditional poetry, it is also possible to envision him in a double role by turns, both as singer and as member of the audience. To the degree that later pastoral poetry traces its origins to the realities of Greek archaic culture, that is, to the cultural facts that motivated the choice of shepherds as the targets of the Muses' reproach and of the particular shepherd Hesiod as the object of Panhellenic induction, one may well consider shepherds both as source and as promoters of the deprecated local poetry.[83] We shall never know for sure or in full what motivated the Muses' election of a shepherd as addressee and inductee. Doubtless the setting is partly responsible: the Muses set out from Mount Helikon and it is at its foot that Hesiod the shepherd was tending his flock. I am not persuaded by Stoddard's suggestion that the human condition is in view;[84] for, although the need for sustenance (of which 'mere bellies!' is emblematic) marks the distance that separates gods and men, it is hard to see the reason for the pointed choice of shepherds as opposed to any other (menial?) occupation. Only a prejudice against shepherds that the *Works and Days* belies might support this view; but even then, why should an occupation that is *ex hypothesi* denigrated provide a particularly suitable representation of the human condition? If one rejects this rationale, we are left with the

---

into him by the goddesses—shows him not to have been a singer before his encounter with the Muses. His *Dichterweihe in toto*, as well as in its several elements, is not to be read in a rigid and superficial biographic fashion but as embodying and articulating the Panhellenic authority and authorization that he previously lacked and is now invested with. Cf. González (forthcoming).

[83] Note the plural ποιμένες (26), which is entirely natural in the context of a pastoral community of herdsmen-performers, even though admittedly it does not require the view that the Muses are actually speaking to a group of shepherds (cf. Katz and Volk 2000:123n8). Hesiod could readily stand as a representative member through which the larger community is addressed. Cf. Lord 1960:21.

[84] Stoddard 2004:73–79; cf. Clay 2003:57 (with n. 37) and Tsagalis 2006:84. The view of Detienne and Vernant 1989:57–61 is somewhat different and more nuanced. Historically speaking, pastoralism was indeed man's first step towards civilized living. It may therefore function symbolically, as Stoddard suggests (2004:76), as the boundary between the wild and the civilized. This fact, in a sense, is reflected by my argument immediately below, except that I ground it in the economic realities of Greece during the Iron Age and the archaic period. My proposal is therefore rather different from Stoddard's claim that as a social class shepherds symbolize "man's intermediate position between god and beast" (76). I doubt her claim that this more abstract notion may be found as such in the ancient poetry of Greece and the Near East. For example, that a shepherds' hut is where Enkidu is taught the rudiments of civilization (cf. Pritchard 1969:77 Tablet II.ii–iii) seems to me to make precisely the opposite point and to place shepherds decisively on the civilized side of the man-beast divide. (The harshness of their livelihood is acknowledged at ii.22–23, where the ground is called 'the shepherd's bed', and at iii.30–34, where Enkidu watches over herdsmen by chasing and capturing wild animals.) Contrast to Stoddard's claim the arguably civilizing, pervasive Homeric image, readily intelligible to a Greek archaic audience, of the 'shepherd of the hosts' (ποιμὴν λαῶν) who 'orders' (διακοσμέω) his men. For its NE background see West 1997:226–227.

coincidental Helikonian setting as the sole ostensible motivation. Neither does it seem that the Homeric figure of the ruler-shepherd (of Near-Eastern inspiration) stands behind the election. However much *Theogony* 80–103 implicitly elevates the status of the inspired singer to the near-equivalent of the 'heaven-nourished βασιλεύς' (who himself cuts a figure evocative of the singer's) insofar as it weaves them together through kinship of function, the notion that Hesiod's portrayal as a field-dwelling shepherd corresponds in actual fact or proleptically to a ruler seems far-fetched.[85] We are left, I believe, with only one plausible option: field-dwelling shepherds are chosen because they are emblematic of the 'old' economy of the Dark Age, which, even if not strictly pastoral in nature, still gave pastoralism a privileged role that it did not enjoy in the age of the archaic and classical polis.[86] Large-scale pastoralism that would call for the keeping of flocks in the hinterlands of settlements was associated, both in pre-archaic and archaic times, with elites whose place in the social contract of the polis was ever a focus of tension and constant renegotiation.[87] Thus, field-dwelling shepherds would readily stand not only for the rural end of the polarity that opposed countryside to urban settlement,[88] but also for the elites who would wish to

---

[85] The implicit parallel, however, does reinforce the authority of the epic performer, as he confronts and seeks to shape the institutions of power.

[86] For the proposal that pastoralism was of relatively greater importance during the Dark Age, see Snodgrass 1971:379–380, 1980:35–36, 1987:190–209, and 2006:134–135 (first published in 1989). Supportive are Morgan 1990:76, Hanson 1995, and Thomas and Conant 1999:43–45. For criticism, see Cherry 1988, Foxhall 1995, and Howe 2008 (cf. Hall 2007:61). Yet even Howe (2008:25) presents his criticism merely as "an adjustment" to Snodgrass's model of social evolution.

[87] Cf. Hesiod *Works and Days* 120, 308 with Howe 2008:43. Cf. González (forthcoming).

[88] The success of the Greek city as a political project hinged largely on the integration and complementarity of town (ἄστυ or πόλις) and countryside (χώρα or γῆ); in particular, it depended on the ability of its institutions to reconcile the interests of extra-urban landholders (who may have clustered into smaller κῶμαι) and settlers from the ἄστυ (who may also own land outside the urban settlement). Many urban landholders were not from the elite and did not own extensive tracts of land that sustained large-scale grazing. There was, of course, no real urbanization in the archaic period. Before the fifth century, for example, the *astu* of Thespiai was not a major nucleated settlement "but rather a cluster of small village-sized settlements" (cf. Snodgrass 1991:14). For brief statements of the relationship between the polis and its hinterland see Effenterre 1985:203–206; Hansen 2006:101–105; and Hall 2007:67–79, 237–242. For greater detail, cf. Price and Murray 1990 and Rich and Wallace-Hadrill 1991 (especially Snodgrass 1991 and Osborne 1991:120–121). Writing about the tending of herds in classical Athens, Howe 2008 confirms that wealthy Athenians could only graze large herds "in the border areas" (63). After reviewing several *testimonia* (among them, [Demosthenes] 47 and Isaios 6), he observes: "The sheep and goats in the above examples are all treated separately, as herds, usually together with their shepherds, rather than as part of a working farm. Recent archaeological evidence from the Attic countryside seems to support such conclusions about semi-mobile herds of sheep and goats, grazing marginal pastures at some distance from the main agricultural base" (61). Ideologically speaking, when compared to the ideal of the citizen farmer, herding during the classical period remains marginal in the political *imaginaire*. This fact has its roots in ideological developments

retain control of the cultural authority of traditional performers.[89] Theirs is not the small-scale herd-keeping that is associated with the rise and development of the archaic and classical polis.[90] On the contrary, they emphatically live ἄγραυλοι (26), away from the stage on which Panhellenic forces of trade, travel, and professional itinerancy played out.[91] There is no overt reference to the polis in the *Theogony*—although the *Works and Days* has much to say about it—but it can hardly be coincidental that a natural route for the Muses to travel to Mount Olympos from the foot of Mount Helikon near Askra passes through Thespiai.[92]

Some writers, of whom Luther 1935 is representative, approach this passage by placing a false emphasis on the alleged 'individuality' of Hesiod vis-à-vis the anonymous 'Homer.' This is supposed to explain what they view as a radically new, reflective approach to truth and deceit, an approach that now, for the first time, would have problematized the truth-value of poetry, overcoming the identification of the Muses' song with truth.[93] Thus, according to Wismann (1996:17), Hesiod distinguishes "fictive realities" (ψεύδεα, "réalités fictives") that arise

---

that marked the transition from Dark-Age to archaic Greece and that are intimately associated with the rise of the polis and the Panhellenic cultural trends it fostered. Cf. Morris 1991.

[89] However integral to the workings of the polis, large-scale herding remained an elite economic activity in tension with the polity's larger project of equal rights for all citizens (cf. Howe 2008). This means that, not only during the formative period of archaic epic but also for archaic and classical polis audiences, the figure of the field-dwelling shepherd would appear marginal to the current political culture, and his function coded as elite and 'old-world,' standing outside the dominant stream of Panhellenic cultural trends. With regard to the performer's dependence on the patronage of the polis' social elites (and the elites' control of his cultural authority), the view of Svenbro (1976:50–59) dovetails with mine.

[90] Cf. West 1966: "Sheep are conspicuous by their absence in the *Works and Days* (except in the spurious *Days*), appearing only in 516 in a pictorial image illustrating the strength of Boreas. For meat, milk, and skins Hesiod relies consistently on cows and goats" (160).

[91] Hansen 2006:68 writes: "[T]he Greeks distinguished explicitly settlement in a city (*polis*) from settlement in the country (*chora*), and they seem never to have been interested in whether settlement in the country was in villages or on isolated farmsteads. They were much more interested in political structures than in forms of settlement, so they contrasted the people who lived in the *polis* with the people who lived in the *chora* ... and almost all their attention was directed to the *polis*. Living in *komai* (villages) without any real city centre was regarded in the Classical period as an outmoded form of settlement going back to the pre-*polis* age ... ." On ἄγραυλος see Stoddard 2004:74 and n. 35.

[92] This is the context in which one should read the emphatic *inclusio* that frames the Muses' words: Μοῦσαι Ὀλυμπιάδες, κοῦραι Διὸς αἰγιόχοιο (25) and ὥς ἔφασαν κοῦραι μεγάλου Διὸς ἀρτιέπειαι (29) do not primarily serve to emphasize their divine status vis-à-vis the human shepherds, *pace* Stoddard (2004:79) and Tsagalis (2006:84), but the *Olympian*—and hence Panhellenic—status of their inspiration.

[93] Luther 1935: "Im homerischen Epos fallen 'Dichtung' und 'Wahrheit' zusammen. ... Bei Hesiod ist diese Anschauung bereits überwunden" (124); and again: "Der grundsätzliche Unterschied der hesiodischen Einstellung zum ψεῦδος-Phänomen im Vergleich zu der des homerischen Menschen besteht darin, daß Hesiod dasselbe als Problem nimmt. Bei den Dichtern des Epos und den von ihnen gestalteten Helden fehlt jede derartige Reflexion" (138).

from a perfect imitation of "perceptible realities" (ἔτυμα, "réalités sensibles") through the medium of language (λέγειν ἐτύμοισιν ὁμοῖα) from "true realities" (ἀληθέα, "réalités vraies") that seem to depend on a different linguistic register (γηρύσασθαι). Nothing, he adds, suggests that the Muses only reserve for him one half of their powers. Their statement, therefore, reflects no polemic opposition with any other poetry, but hints at the relationship between the speech registers of 'fiction' and 'knowledge.' Wismann is only one of an increasing number of interpreters who refer both 'lies' and 'truth' to Hesiod's own poetic tradition.[94] Clay (2003:58) agrees: "I would draw attention to the hidden, even unconscious, prejudices that have influenced many commentators: Hesiod must be convinced of the absolute truth of his message and therefore his reference to 'lies like the truth' must refer to something outside his own text."[95] The anachronistic frame of mind that underlies such views surfaces fully formed in Heiden's remark: "As quoted by Hesiod in his *Theogony*, the Muses' speech appears to broadcast a threat to listeners or readers who might find the Muses' songs unbelievable and dismiss them as mere lies. A poet about to narrate how Cronus swallowed and regurgitated his children had good reason to worry that his stories would be deemed lies. Hesiod's defense—or his Muses' defense ... [was to disavow] this very distinction [between truth and lies], perhaps hoping in this way to preempt and disable the predictable ... criticism that his stories were lies" (Heiden 2007:171–172).[96]

In truth, commentators like Arrighetti 1992 (against whom Clay takes aim) are not unconsciously prejudiced. They understand that in a traditional song culture performative authority is of fundamental importance to its reception; and that in the culture of archaic Greece this authority was proportional to the perceived validity of its truth claims. The self-reflective epistemological discourse of distinctly postmodern flavor that these scholars ascribe to Hesiod is altogether out of place in his ancient cultural milieu and more at home with the armchair philosophers of the academic halls. The intimate connection between truth and performative authority in the traditional song culture of

---

[94] This is what Katz and Volk (2000:122) call the 'monist' interpretation: "[it] hold[s] that the two verses [*Theogony* 27–28] form a unity and refer to *all* poetry, including Hesiod's own" (their emphasis). Although I call it 'revisionary' below, it is at least as old as Wilamowitz-Moellendorff (1927:49n1): "Ein Dichter, der selbst so viel erfindet, tut gut, es auch den Göttinnen zuzuschreiben, welche ihn begeistern."

[95] She adds: "To refuse to accept the paradoxical character of the text will not make it go away; better to confront it and live with the consequences" (Clay 2003:59n43). Indeed, if it is, and must be, so. But, in fact, what Clay deems a 'paradox' is not inherent to the Hesiodic tradition and is ascribed to it only by choice. To foreclose what are arguably more plausible interpretive choices by denying them legitimacy *a priori* is in fact to beg the question.

[96] For my critique of Heiden's argument see below, pp. 259ff.

ancient Greece has been well documented.[97] It is transparently recognizable, for example, in the Homeric equation between divine inspiration and eyewitness testimony and in the polemical engagement of Xenophanes (fr. B1.22), Solon (fr. 29 W), Pindar (*Nemean* 7.20-27)[98]—and many others—with the truth and authority of poetry; and it underlies the characterization of traditional poetry in performance as the actualization of Memory.[99] Only a substantial discontinuity between the poetics of Homer and the poetics of Hesiod can hope to justify so great and novel a departure. In essence, this would mean that the conceptual cast of Hesiodic poetry was deeply untraditional,[100] a claim that is *prima facie* implausible given its utterly traditional form.[101] If the revisionary scholarship is right, the genealogy of Hesiodic Ψεύδεα is more than a little puzzling (*Theogony* 226-232);[102] and one might well insist that verse 27 should have preceded 26: that the Muses know how to proclaim the truth should have been the foil against which to make the revolutionary claim that they also know how to tell narrative fictions—fictive narratives that the *Theogony* (in part or

---

[97] Almost any treatment of archaic poetics validates this pervasive fact. Convenient starting points are Maehler 1963, Rösler 1980 (whom Bowie 1993 criticizes unpersuasively), Verdenius 1983, and Puelma 1989.

[98] For Pindar's own approach to the poetics of truth, see Verdenius 1983:29n73 and Koning 2010:310-318.

[99] Leclerc's reservations are fully justified: "Il serait ... paradoxal de supposer qu'au moment même de son initiation, le poète prête aux Muses qui le légitiment une intention aussi manifestement contraire aux prétentions véridiques qu'il affiche" (1993:71-72; cf. 206). Unfortunately, Leclerc too ultimately inscribes the 'lies' within the horizon of the 'truth' (at 71); only, she deems them deliberate 'fictions' without the intent to deceive (72) or the distorted product of an imperfect reception (208). The latter alternative, with its subtle displacement of responsibility, does not however survive the clarity with which the Muses own that *they*, not their hearers, are the ones who know how to speak the ψεύδεα. It would be odd indeed to suppose that the Muses actually meant, 'We know how to tell many misunderstandings ... ; and we know, when willing, how to proclaims truths'. With the focus arguably on their will (εὖτ' ἐθέλωμεν 28), it is hard to argue persuasively that the goddesses bear no responsibility for the reception of their words (however we choose to describe them). When willing, they also know, after all, how to proclaim what *ex hypothesi* are truthful, and truthfully apprehended, statements. Leclerc (1993:209) soon substitutes for her suggestion that ψεύδεα are distorted misunderstandings the proposal that they are the accommodations of divine language to the limited cognitive capacities of the audience. Clay (2003:46) is right to complain that "[l]ike many critics, Stroh ignores εὖτ' ἐθέλωμεν in line 28." Cf. Koning 2010:302n17.

[100] Tsagalis 2006: "In this post-Promethean world, divine speech is often an unsolvable riddle, a semantical conundrum whose content humans will always struggle to decypher. ... Keeping its distance from the absolute distinction between truth and falsehood the *Odyssey* is so fond of, the speech of the Muses indicates that the language of the *Theogony* will indeed be a jigsaw puzzle deliberately hard to solve" (85). Tsagalis follows Pratt 1993:110-111.

[101] Cf. Edwards 1971.

[102] Cf. *Theogony* 783-804 and *Works and Days* 708-709.

in full) is said to illustrate. Against all such interpretive subtleties Koning 2010 offers a salutary correction.[103]

I must briefly address two philological arguments often adduced in support of the views criticized above. One concerns the alleged opposition between ἔτυμα and ἀληθέα; the other, the meaning of ὁμοῖα. It has become fashionable to recast *Theogony* 27-28 as an opposition between two types of truth: one, experiential (ἔτυμα), the other, verbal (ἀληθέα). Wismann (1996:18) puts it most succinctly: "Si ἔτυμον désigne, en accord avec l'étymologie (cf. ἐτάζω), une réalité susceptible d'être vérifiée par un critère objectif et quasiment 'expérimental', ἀληθές, au contraire, évoque une réalité qui n'est pas vérifiable par un critère extérieur, mais qui s'impose immédiatement à la conscience." Central to this claim is that these two adjectives articulate an *epistemological* polarity: ἔτυμα may be apprehended by 'experimental observation,' whereas ἀληθέα are unverifiable and propositional. Wismann's added comment that the latter force themselves immediately upon the conscience is his own attempt to reformulate Krischer 1965, the basis of all these readings. I think that this formulation is profoundly misconceived. A full refutation would lead me too far afield and I can only offer a brief critique. But note that all these approaches shift the explicit terms of the opposition from ψεύδεα vs. ἀληθέα to ἔτυμα vs. ἀληθέα.[104] This is only valid, of course, when one identifies ψεύδεα and ἔτυμα, as Heiden 2007, for example, does. Although I can only accept Krischer's article with significant reservations—I believe he oversimplifies the data and, like others, psychologizes them unduly—he is right to emphasize the connection that archaic poetry establishes between speech and ἀληθέα.[105] The proper approach, however, is not to psychologize the etymology,[106] but to take account of the verbal context in

---

[103] Especially at 202–210 and 297–318. I cannot, however, embrace his able defense of the well-known view (if now fallen out of favor) that *Theogony* 27–28 articulates a polemic against Homer, however much his opinion reflects an actual interpretive strand of the ancient reception of Hesiod.

[104] As G. Danek perceptively remarks *apud* Tsagalis 2006:133.

[105] Cf. Porzig 1942:218 and Cole 1983.

[106] So, for example, Krischer 1965: "Die ἀληθείη ist der Bericht, der die Dinge darstellt, wie sie der Sprechende erlebt hat, ohne daß dabei etwas unbemerkt bleibt" (167). After him, in various ways, also Snell 1975:14, Cole 1983:12, Wismann 1996:18, Levet 1976:16, and others. All attempts to motivate the coinage of ἀληθείη and explain its use with reference to the psychology of perception entailed by λανθάνω, λήθω, or a hypothetical *λῆθος (as 'what does not/cannot remain hidden', 'what does not escape notice', or 'what forces itself upon the conscience') seem thin and unconvincing. Why should a marked term newly minted to designate veracity in the telling, which ordinarily depends on the will of the speaker, be correlated with (some version of) the negative of mental neglect? Who in the archaic Greek world could have felt the psychological need, and under what social circumstances, to coin a word whose purported meaning bore so odd a relation to its alleged linguistic forebears? I submit that looking instead to the conceptual universe of archaic Greek traditional performance readily provides a plausible context and motivation for the origin and the desired justification for the usage.

which it is used as a clue to its meaning and origin. I submit that the genesis of ἀληθής and ἀληθείη is not to be found in a general psychological need by the archaic populace for a special term that would mark verbal truthfulness; nor in narrow philosophical circles who made epistemological reflection their business. I submit that their emergence is to be located in the ambit of rhapsodes, i.e. itinerant performers of traditional poetry self-conscious of their social function as repositories and activators of cultural memory. This origin is to be traced to their double (and truly paradoxical) function as agents of Mnēmosynē who both resist the forces of Forgetfulness (Λήθη *Theogony* 227) yet also bring forgetfulness of cares through their singing (λησμοσύνη κακῶν *Theogony* 55). The rhapsode's selection of what was worth preserving out of the sum total of current *mythoi* known to him and his perpetuation of this repertoire in performance can only have sharpened his self-consciousness as a key cultural agent;[107] doubtless the diffusion of this material through his itinerancy must have brought him in contact with potentially conflicting variants that would have sharply problematized the veracity, and hence the authority, of the rival tellings. It is in this polemical context of verbal truthfulness peculiar to the itinerant traditional performer who stakes a claim for the authority of his singing that the semantic contours of ἀληθής and ἀληθείη were delineated.

My account of their origin, if conjectural, enjoys several advantages over the psychological etymologies advanced by previous scholars: first, it provides a plausible cultural motivation—the performance of traditional poetry—and cultural agent—the rhapsode—for their coinage; second, it explains their fundamental verbal orientation—they were coined to characterize the telling of the rhapsode; third, it accounts for their polemical associations—narrative multiforms problematized the truthfulness, and hence authority, that alone secures the favorable audience reception inherent to traditional poetry; fourth, it justifies the curious choice (otherwise inexplicable without implausibly and self-consciously psychologizing the epistemology of perception) of a derivative of **lāth-* ('to escape notice', 'to overlook', and hence 'to forget') for 'truth' and 'truthful'—making the 'memorable' and 'unforgettable' the authoritative repertoire of the rhapsode as the cultural agent of Memory; and, fifth, it is fully consistent with the semantic implications of the earliest contexts in which the word family is used, especially where this use rises plainly from ordinary narrative to the explicitly metapoetic. Such are the *loci* cited above: *Theogony* 227, where Λήθη heads the list of entities born of Strife and Toil that bring about the dissolution of civilized society and is, in retrospect not unsurprisingly

---

[107] Cf. Nagy 1990c: "The latest performance is by necessity a crisis point for the tradition of myth, in that the latest performance determines what continues to be transmitted and what does not" (57–58).

given *Theogony* 27–28, the sibling of Ψεύδεα;[108] and *Theogony* 55, where we are reminded that Mnēmosynē birthed the Olympian Muses to be the forgetfulness of evils, a reminder that the actualization of cultural Memory that takes place in the performance of traditional poetry inexorably entails a corresponding neglect, a turning away of one's mind, from other subjects—here, the evils and cares of ordinary living that pointedly become the theme of the Muses' song in the *Hymn to Apollo* 190–193.[109]

Levet (1976:16) objects to treating the conceptual link between λήθη and ἀληθείη as primary and hence as etymologically productive.[110] As often with this scholar, his meaning is less than perspicuous. Although he accepts a relationship between truth and forgetting, this 'forgetting' is fundamentally a kind of ignorance: "à la différence de la λήθη, cet oubli est intérieur au sujet lui-même et passif: c'est le *λῆθος, sur le nom duquel est bâti l'adjectif ἀληθής" (16). The conjectured *λῆθος is supposed to have disappeared already by Hesiod's time, if not Homer's, from all the Greek dialects.[111] Apparently, the point of his distinction between λήθη and *λῆθος is to expand the semantic field of ἀληθής so as to imply (through its negation) the psychology of λανθάνω, the failure to notice. Thus, he opposes limiting its scope to the middle λανθάνομαι, 'to forget', which he deems too constraining. Luther (1935:11–12) adopted a similar stance and resorted directly to the root *lādh- because it embraced the sense of both the active and the middle. Only, believing that its ground meaning was 'unhiddenness' ("Unverborgenheit")—a property of things—Luther did not endorse Bultmann's etymology ἀ + λῆθος, based on Leo Meyer, who had taken λῆθος as "verheimlichendes Täuschen" and *ἀ-λῆθος as "ohne verheimlichendes Täuschen." Levet, in turn, goes back to a subjective sense and finds the textually attested link with λήθη unhelpful. To be sure, he acknowledges the occasional etymological play the relates memory, forgetfulness, and truth.[112] He grants

---

[108] False, ineffective stories are eventually consigned to oblivion.

[109] Cf. *Theogony* 98–103, especially the antithetical parallelism of αἶψ' ὅ γε δυσφροσυνέων ἐπιλήθεται οὐδέ τι κηδέων | μέμνηται (102–103). For the ways in which archaic Greek Mnēmosynē entails Lēthē see Nagy 1990c:58–59, who builds on the insights of Detienne 1996. (Nagy 1990c:58–68 probes the archaic Greek notion of ἀληθείη.) See also Simondon 1982:128–131, 141–149. West 1966:175 appositely cites *Anthologia Palatina* 10.67.

[110] Cf. Levet 1976:96.

[111] Levet 2008:18n26. Levet seems to endorse a biographic approach to Homeric and Hesiodic poetry that embraces a 'standard' chronology (standard, that is, among scholars of his persuasion).

[112] He denies it to Ψ 359–361, disapprovingly citing Heitsch's words: "ἀλήθεια ist nicht oder nicht nur als Privativbildung zu λανθάνειν zu verstehen und heißt also nicht nur Unverborgenheit, sondern ἀλήθεια ist auch die Negation zu λήθη und ἐπιλανθάνεσθαι und heißt also auch Unvergessenheit" (Heitsch 1968:35, *apud* Levet 1976:96n2). *Pace* Levet, I believe that in this Homeric passage the juxtaposition of μεμνέωτο and ἀληθείην is deliberate and lends itself readily to a metapoetic reading.

it, for example, at *Theogony* 226–232, with qualifications at *Theogony* 233–236, and often elsewhere, but he seems keenly exercised to deny any linguistic reality to the echo between λήθη, ἀληθέα, and λήθεται. For him, this echo is mere rhetorical wordplay.[113] It is not clear to me whether, and in what sense, Levet deems λήθη external or active,[114] unless he takes a view of it similar to the one I am offering here—λήθη as the negative facet of the memorializing poetic tradition—a scenario that seems to me improbable. More nuanced is his recent attempt to revisit this argument. Although he continues to insist that ἀληθής is not to be etymologically related to λήθη but to the conjectured *λῆθος, he correctly observes that the meaning of λήθη is more multifaceted than mere 'forgetfulness' (Levet 2008:19). I agree with this and add that the metapoetic dimension (λήθη as a facet of the poetic tradition in performance) is crucial for a right understanding of it. In this sense, I can embrace Levet's gloss for ἀληθείη as "le non-voilé-dévoilant" (20), a gloss that overlaps with Vernant's study of the Muses of traditional poetry as the daughters of performative Mnēmosynē.[115] If one bears this in mind, it is not hard to understand the conceptual nexus that brings together in *Theogony* 233–236 ἀψευδέα, ἀληθέα, νημερτής, λήθεται, and οἶδεν.[116] As a traditional 'Master of sea animals' figure,[117] Nereus rules the sea in good Hesiodic fashion (cf. *Theogony* 80–92), i.e. by the performance of authoritative speech. Thus, he is called ἀληθής because he embodies and espouses an authoritative poetic tradition. Since this poetic tradition concerns justice, he is said not to forget authoritative ordinances (οὐδὲ θεμίστων | λήθεται) and (in parallel fashion) to know just and propitious counsels (δίκαια καὶ ἤπια δήνεα οἶδεν). In view of his divine knowledge, characteristically comprehensive, his speech carries oracular associations, and therefore, as to its unerring and truthful nature, he is predictably proclaimed ἀψευδής and νημερτής.[118]

---

[113] Levet 2008: "[L]es auteurs anciens ne manquent pas de rapprocher ἀληθής, λήθη et λανθάνω, des origines de la littérature jusqu'au IVᵉ siècle et au-delà encore. Il y a là un fait absolument incontestable. Mais il est impossible de tirer d'une pratique rhétorique des conclusions justes sur la valeur originelle d'ἀληθής et d'ἀληθείη" (19–20).

[114] See immediately above for his words, cited from Levet 1976:16.

[115] Vernant 1985:109–136, at 115: "Le passé ainsi dévoilé est beaucoup plus que l'antécédent du présent: il en est la source. En remontant jusqu'à lui, la remémoration cherche non à situer les événements dans un cadre temporel, mais à atteindre le fond de l'être, à découvrir l'originel, la réalité primordiale dont est issu le cosmos et qui permet de comprendre le devenir dans son ensemble." Although Vernant's monograph is subtitled "Studies in Historical Psychology," his focus on the structures and institutions of culture saves him from the sterile conjectures about individual psychology that often mar Levet's otherwise helpful analysis.

[116] Νηρέα δ' ἀψευδέα καὶ ἀληθέα γείνατο Πόντος | πρεσβύτατον παίδων· αὐτὰρ καλέουσι γέροντα, | οὕνεκα νημερτής τε καὶ ἤπιος, οὐδὲ θεμίστων | λήθεται, ἀλλὰ δίκαια καὶ ἤπια δήνεα οἶδεν. Cf. the convoluted reading in Levet 2008:20–23.

[117] Cf. Burkert 1985:172 with bibliography.

[118] See West 1966:233 on the association of ἀψευδής "with oracles and the like."

To come to Levet's contention that ἀληθής must be derived from the conjectural *λῆθος whose sense is other than the one attested by λήθη, one must point out that his claim is doubly vulnerable. First, because, even if it were true, it does not establish his point that there is a semantic distinction between λήθη and *λῆθος.[119] The latter is conjectured for the archaic period from an *a priori* belief that ἀληθής must reflect a derivation from an s-stem noun. λᾶθος is attested in Hesykhios Λ no. 95 s.v. λάθει, whose gloss ἀκηδίᾳ cannot, without further context, clarify the matter at issue; and in Theokritos 23.24,[120] which, with LSJ s.v., should be deemed the equivalent of λήθη:[121] the lover despairs of quenching his longing—i.e. of forgetting the object of his desire—even if he should drain the potion. Forgetfulness, explicit for him and implicit for the youth, is entailed, with a hint that death will be the ultimate realization of λᾶθος. At any rate, all this focus on a hypothetical archaic *λῆθος is misguided, for there are other more plausible derivations that do not require belief in the complete disappearance from the record of the alleged *λῆθος and its unaccountable replacement by a λήθη *ex hypothesi* of somewhat different sense.[122] Risch (1974:81 §31g)

---

[119] I have no *a priori* objection to Luther's point that, if (as he assumes) ἀληθής were an s-stem derivative of *λῆθος and *if* Theokritos' λᾶθος were its Doric form, it would be a methodological fallacy *eis ipsis* to ascribe Theokritos' sense to the alleged archaic form (Luther 1954:35).

[120] οὐκέτι γάρ σε, | κῶρε, θέλω λυπεῖν ποχ' ὁρώμενος, ἀλλὰ βαδίζω | ἔνθα τύ μευ κατέκρινας, ὅπη λόγος ἥμεν ἀτερπέων | ξυνὸν τοῖσιν ἐρῶσι τὸ φάρμακον, ἔνθα τὸ λᾶθος (Theokritos 23.21–24). The parallel between λᾶθος and φάρμακον is almost certainly intended to recall Helen's celebrated recourse to a φάρμακον in δ 219–226, a remedy that is described as κακῶν ἐπίληθον ἁπάντων (221). The psychology of Helen's drug is complex: it cannot be that it causes a straightforward failure to notice, since the passage avers that one who drinks it would not cry 'even if they should slay before him with the bronze his brother or dear son *and with his eyes he should behold it*' (δ 225–226, my emphasis). Perhaps we are to regard it as causing eventual forgetfulness, if in fact the intended order of events is not its ingestion first, and only then the experience of tragic loss. This is certainly possible with κατατεθναίη, and could be conjectured for δηϊόωεν (then translating: 'even if they should have slain'; note that I do not depend on syntactic arguments for this proposal but merely conjecture a sequence that the syntax does not decisively preclude). But perhaps the most natural reading is that the φάρμακον brings a certain emotional imperviousness that enables the failure to register the (full?) emotional force of subsequent events. This could be regarded as a qualified sense of forgetting just as well as a qualified sense of not noticing or passing over. *Theogony* 53–55 keeps plainly in view its own metapoetic potential. It is worth remarking that even in B 33–34 eventual forgetfulness is only an intensification of actual neglect.

[121] But Gow (1950–1952:2.410) reckons Stephanus's emendation τὸ λάθας worthy of consideration: "sunt, qui pro λᾶθος legendum putent λάθας, ut sit: ἔνθα τὸ φάρμακον τὸ λάθας" (*apud* Reiske 1765–1766:2.38). If Stephanus is right, one could no longer have recourse to Theokritos in this connection.

[122] Kamptz argues that Λῆθος (B 843 P 288), the name of the son of Teutamos and father of Hippothoos, is a backformation from Ληθαῖος or Ληθαῖον πεδίον (Kamptz 1982:111 §36g, 316 §80c; cf. *LfgE* s.v.). It may also be construed as the obvious masculine equivalent of Λήθη and could have been derived directly from it (cf. the *New Pauly* s.v. "Lethus").

derives ἀληθής directly from λήθω, just as ἀσφαλής is from σφάλλω.[123] Chantraine (1933:23 §18) agrees, noting that the feminine suffix -ᾱ was used for deverbatives (here, for λήθη) irrespective of the vocalism of the verbal root. And Schwyzer illustrates well enough the array of deverbative adjectives in -ης, although he (implausibly) maintains that ἀληθής belonged with "verdunkelte Komposita" perceived as a "Simplizia": "Schon für hom. εὐῆρες εὐρρεής ἐυστρεφής φιλομμειδής braucht man keine *ἄρος usw. anzusetzen."[124] Hence, there is no compulsion to accept Levet's insistence upon the conjectural *λῆθος, and a rhapsodic deverbative coinage of ἀληθής, close to λήθη in its metapoetic implications, seems to me the most likely scenario and the hypothesis that best fits the record.

To return to the kind of contrast that is allegedly drawn in *Theogony* 27–28 between ἔτυμα and ἀληθέα, it is important to challenge the supposed epistemological opposition often inferred from it. I admit that there is a semantic difference between these words: ἔτυμος is the unmarked term that applies indifferently to anything that is, to any component of reality insofar as it exists in actual fact or is claimed or assumed to exist. It therefore qualifies things as much as verbal utterances. The latter are reckoned as true in that they reflect reality (or, in a stronger sense, even bring it about). The verbally marked term is ἀληθής, which only in the exceptional case of M 433—considered textually suspect by some—is found as the attribute of something other than speech.[125] Snell's observation that ἀληθής is never applied to divine speech in Homer is only to be expected.[126] For, in drawing attention to the truthfulness of the utterance, it would polemically suggest by implication the possibility that it might not, in fact, reflect the truth. With regard to the Muses, this is beyond the conceptual horizon of Homeric poetry and, as noted above, first appears in the polemical context of the claims to Panhellenic status by Hesiodic theogonic poetry. ἐτεόν and ἔτυμον are used for (the content of) an utterance that corresponds to reality. At B 299–300, for example, Odysseus bids the Akhaians wait and subject to the test of time the truthfulness of Kalkhas' interpretation of the omen of the serpent at Aulis. To the extent that truthful speech has a bearing on reality, one may find in actual experience a measure of confirmation. This is not

---

[123] Cf. Chantraine 1999:1074 s.v. σφάλλω.

[124] *GG* I.513 §III.27a.β. Schwyzer further notes that ἀϊδής has no relation to εἶδος but to ἰδεῖν, nor ἀτυχής το τεῦχος.

[125] Porzig (1942:218) puts it somewhat differently: he calls the usage at M 433 attributive, "sonst substantivisch ἀληθές oder ἀληθέα ebenfalls als Objekt zu Verben des Sagens."

[126] Snell 1975:15. His statement that "[b]ei Homer paßte das ἔτυμον eher für das Wort des Sehers, das ἀληθές eher für das der Musen" follows *a priori* from his tacit (and widely shared) conviction that ἔτυμα are derived from sense perception whereas ἀληθέα are strictly revelatory. This epistemological distinction is misplaced and the contrast is to be differently drawn.

the exclusive property of ἔτυμα but also pertains to ἀληθέα to whatever degree it impacts the here and now of the audience. Scholars who argue otherwise base their logic on the thematic content of the *Theogony*, which is purported to be beyond the ken of mortal man.[127] But this all too easily dismisses the often aetiological import of the poem: for example in its claim that the stone that Kronos swallowed in Zeus' place was the one displayed in Delphi, which could still be seen in Pausanias' day;[128] or in its plain attempt to motivate the Panhellenic outlines of sacrificial practices in the worship of the Olympian gods.[129] This scholarly stance vis-à-vis the contents of the *Theogony* reveals an inadequate understanding of the temporal dimensions and implications of mantic and prophetic speech. Archaic epic concerns itself with the past as the grounds for present realities and the seed of future developments.[130] This is the sense in which Kalkhas' purview embraces the past, present, and future.[131]

The converse of this argument is to assert that in the *Works and Days* Hesiod does not depend on the Muses for his material and performance (or does not depend on them to the same degree as in the *Theogony*). To make this point, Clay (2003:104) draws attention to the use of ἐτήτυμα in *Works and Days* 10, where Hesiod declares, ἐγὼ δέ κε Πέρσῃ ἐτήτυμα μυθησαίμην. She takes the choice of diction as a pointed avoidance of ἀληθέα that is fraught with epistemological implications.[132] Her argument, further developed by Stoddard (2004:80–84),[133] is

---

[127] This is explicitly the stance and contrast in Stoddard 2004.

[128] West 1966:303 on *Theogony* 498–500; cf. Pausanias 10.24.6. It would be irrelevant, of course, whether the stone Pausanias saw was the very one referred to by the *Theogony*. Even if it was not, its existence and availability to Hellenistic *theōroi* would still serve to exhibit the aetiological force of the passage.

[129] Not to mention the implications of its myths for the audience's understanding and conceptualization of the cosmos. On aetiological myths in the *Theogony*, see West 1966:213 (on *Theogony* 154–210), 305 (on *Theogony* 507–616, which West calls "aetiological through and through"), and 401 (on *Theogony* 886–900).

[130] See above, p. 250 n. 115 and pp. 226ff.

[131] Casevitz (1992:4) rightly emphasizes the engagement of the *mantis* with the past. Such engagement occurs with a view to explaining the present and predicting the future. Cf. p. 229 above on Epimenidēs.

[132] Clay 2003: "[I]n the *Works and Days*, where [Hesiod] speaks of human things whose knowledge is granted to men through their own experience, Hesiod can declare to Perses his intention to tell him *etetuma*, 'things as they are'" (78). I do not object to 'things as they are' as a translation of ἐτήτυμα; only I add that to be able to see things as they *really* are one needs the inspired didactic paraenesis of the performer who has been taught by the Muses. On this point Hesiod's authority turns. His is a privileged knowledge that is *not* "granted to men through their own experience." Clay (2003:78n104) is wrong to see in G. Nagy's (1992:50–52) diachronically modulated reading of ἐτήτυμα μυθησαίμην an interpretation that "would blur the important distinction that Hesiod makes between the contents of the two poems." Cf. also Rousseau 1996:110–115.

[133] "[B]y virtue of his mortal status [Hesiod] already has the ability to sing of mortal affairs" (81); "I would argue that this kind of truth [i.e. ἀληθέα] represents for Hesiod the 'eternal truth' of the cosmos, the sort of knowledge that only gods can have" (82); "The adversative force of τύνη·

that the subject matter of the *Works and Days* belongs to the ordinary experience of the audience and does not call for revelatory inspiration.[134] But this argument neglects a fundamental fact: that in the *Works and Days* the goal of the performer is to reveal to his audience the implications of Zeus' eternal rule of justice for the workings of the polis, both in its institutional administration of justice and in the rhythms and practices that inform the lives and activities of its citizens (both brought under the umbrella of cosmic δίκη). Hesiod goes beyond the pose of the wise teacher, whose years of experience lead him to conclude that he has seen it all and there is nothing new under heaven. Rather, he is taught by the Muses to explicate the mind of Zeus to his hearers. His predictive teaching at *Works and Days* 176-201, his riddling αἶνος at 202-212, his privileged knowledge of Zeus' watchers at 252-255, his instruction to the farmer,[135] his disapproval of ignorance at 824[136]—all these are instrumental to his revelatory performance. In essence, Hesiod draws back the curtain that might hinder a clear view of the divine underpinnings of the experience that man has of his own world.[137] By its effect at least, his performance recalls Elisha's prayer to open the eyes of his servant, in order that he might see the horses and chariots of fire protecting them from the king of Syria (2 Kings 6:15-17).[138] The epistemological contrast allegedly entailed by the performer's respective recourse to ἀληθέα in the *Theogony* and ἐτήτυμα in the *Works and Days* is sometimes reformulated as the parallel claim that in the latter poem Hesiod exhibits a degree of autonomy from the Muses at variance with his dependence upon them in the *Theogony*. But this seems untenable in the face of his emphatic reliance upon the goddesses in the *Nautilia* (*Works and Days* 618-694). There, he avers that his didactic authority within the scope of his divine charge is undiminished by the absence of personal

---

ἐγὼ δέ is extremely pronounced ... : 'Zeus, take care of your concerns ... , while I, on the other hand, concern myself with the sorts of truths that mortals know" (83-84). A close reading of her footnote 52 on 82-83 shows how contrived the mapping ἀληθέα → 'divine truths', ἐτήτυμα → 'mortal truths' is.

[134] The scholarly constructed opposition between a revelatory *Theogony* and an empirical *Works and Days* is surprisingly widespread (it is presupposed, for example, by Tsagalis 2006:84). Behind it stands a notion like the one articulated by Wismann (1996:18), which I quoted on p. 247 above.

[135] Nelson 1998: "Hesiod is not teaching us how to farm. He is teaching us what the cycle of the year ... implies about the will of Zeus. ... His intention was rather to show us how the order of Zeus permeates nature and includes ourselves" (57-58).

[136] Cf. *Works and Days* 818. His disapproval should be read against *Works and Days* 765-769.

[137] Cf. Verdenius 1985: "[T]he truths proclaimed by the poet have a much wider scope than that of a personal quarrel: they refer to the good kind of life as contrasted with the wrong kind of life. The *revelation* of these truths was a task imposed on Hes[iod] by the Muses, as appears from *Th.* 27-8" (13, my emphasis).

[138] Or, according to a competing reading, that he might see the assailing Syrian horses and chariots on fire as a sign of their entrapment.

experience and professional skill (σεσοφισμένος)[139] because the Muses have taught him his song (the vehicle for his teaching).[140] The text clearly establishes that, as regards its inspiration or the nature of the performer's authority, the *Nautilia* is not an ostentatious exception to the rule. It is rather an explicit statement of what is elsewhere tacitly the case. For, as he rounds up his introduction to the section, Hesiod grounds his authority in the wondrous hymn the Muses have taught him to sing (*Works and Days* 662), a hymn whose subject matter he calls 'the mind of aegis-bearing Zeus' (*Works and Days* 661). These two assertions are designed to recall the poem's opening hymn to Zeus, in which the Muses celebrate their father Zeus (*Works and Days* 1-2); indeed, verses 3-9 are a hymnic summary of Zeus' mind, whose essential concern is justice and the administration of justice in the world of men.[141] The justice of Zeus underlies the fabric of the cosmos and encompasses the rhythms of farming (*Works and Days* 483-484) as much as the calendar for sailing. This state of affairs is just as one might have expected it, for the poem sets out to explore how Zeus' δίκη informs the workings of the cosmos, seen from the perspective of the archaic (and classical) Greek polis and its citizens. That the *Nautilia* fits within this larger context and does not call for exceptional inspiration or an anomalous source of authority seems further confirmed by its programmatic nature and its centrality to the poem's architecture (at least in its canonical form), a fact generally recognized by scholars.[142]

One other example suffices to dispute Clay's and Stoddard's insistence on drawing from *Works and Days* 10 epistemological implications for the poem's subject matter. In *Works and Days* 814-818 Hesiod observes, 'few know that the thrice-ninth day is the best of the month for starting a wine-jar and putting the yoke on the neck of oxen, mules, and swift-footed horses; and for dragging the swift boat of many benches to the wine-dark sea'. And he closes by asserting that 'few call things truthfully' (παῦροι δέ τ' ἀληθέα κικλήσκουσιν 818).[143] Regarding the use of ἀληθέα, West (1978a:362) writes: "[M]ost people presumably called it τετρὰς φθίνοντος, as Hesiod himself has done in 798. The idea that τρισεινάς is 'truer' implies that the number itself has an intrinsic relation to the day's properties." Note that West's eminently plausible comment is contextually

---

[139] δείξω δή τοι μέτρα πολυφλοίσβοιο θαλάσσης, | οὔτε τι ναυτιλίης σεσοφισμένος οὔτε τι νηῶν (*Works and Days* 648-649).

[140] τόσσον τοι νηῶν γε πεπείρημαι πολυγόμφων· | ἀλλὰ καὶ ὣς ἐρέω Ζηνὸς νόον αἰγιόχοιο· | Μοῦσαι γάρ μ' ἐδίδαξαν ἀθέσφατον ὕμνον ἀείδειν (*Works and Days* 660-662).

[141] Cf. *Works and Days* 105: οὕτως οὔ τί πη ἔστι Διὸς νόον ἐξαλέασθαι; *Works and Days* 483-484: ἄλλοτε δ' ἀλλοῖος Ζηνὸς νόος αἰγιόχοιο, | ἀργαλέος δ' ἄνδρεσσι καταθνητοῖσι νοῆσαι.

[142] Cf. Rosen 1990:99-100.

[143] Or, 'few call it by its true name'. West (1978a:362) notes that "the abnormal adverbial ἀληθέα is developed from ἀληθέα μυθήσασθαι and the like."

grounded and does not hinge on an alleged contrast between ἀληθής and ἔτυμον or ἐτήτυμον;[144] but it serves all the same to deconstruct the harsh epistemological dichotomy between the *Theogony* and the *Works and Days* as regards subject matter, a dichotomy that with the support of Clay, Stoddard, and others has recently gained currency. As if to round the argument against it, West further adds that "in later Greek τὸ ἔτυμον, 'etymology', judged not by historical criteria but by its ability to illuminate the inner nature of the thing" (1978a:362). For traditional epic, this power to illuminate is divinely granted, it transcends man's ordinary ken, however wise with years (note that Hesiod's age is never at issue), and it is precisely the revelatory charge the performer undertakes when he promises to tell Perses 'true things' (ἐτήτυμα μυθησαίμην *Theogony* 10).[145] The choice of ἐτήτυμα over against ἀληθέα is readily explained by the non-polemical focus of the statement: its point is not the veracity of Hesiod's telling but its correspondence with reality. His speech reveals how things really are. The performing seer discloses to his audience the true workings of the world around them and explains how the underlying divine order of the rule of Zeus shapes its present operations and future course. Insofar as ἀληθέα, as the marked term, remained tied to verbal utterances, ἐτήτυμα was the natural choice to apply to their real-world referents. Had the truthfulness of the utterance been at issue, we should have expected ἀληθέα instead. The *Hymn to Demeter* illustrates the distinction well. Verses 44–45 inform us that no one, god or man, was willing to tell Demeter what had happened to her daughter (τῇ δ' οὔ τις ἐτήτυμα μυθήσασθαι | ἤθελεν οὔτε θεῶν οὔτε θνητῶν ἀνθρώπων).[146] Here, the alternative to speaking is silence, not lying. At 121, however, Demeter lies about her identity even as she asserts the truth of her words: ἐγὼ δ' ὑμῖν μυθήσομαι· οὔ τοι ἀεικὲς | ὑμῖν εἰρομένῃσιν ἀληθέα μυθήσασθαι.[147] The choice of ἀληθέα is ironic and pointed.[148] Epic's recourse to ἀληθής is natural either where the veracity of an utterance is at issue, implicitly or explicitly, or where the narrative telling of a character has the metapoetic potential to blend with the authoritative telling of the traditional performer as

---

[144] Even Stoddard (2004:81–82) plays up the significance of Hesiod's diction on the grounds of his "etymologizing tendencies" (81n48). If one accepts her argument, then West's holds true *a fortiori*.

[145] *Works and Days* 768 uses ἀληθείη in regard to the people's (λαοί) true discernment of the days from Zeus through political deliberation (ἀληθείην ... κρίνοντες) that sets the civil calendar. There are actually slightly fewer uses of ἔτυμος (*Theogony* 27) and ἐτήτυμος (*Works and Days* 10) in the major Hesiodic poems than of ἀληθής (*Theogony* 28, 233; *Works and Days* 818) and ἀληθείη (*Works and Days* 768).

[146] An omen that might have conveyed to Demeter what actually happened (ἐτήτυμα) is made concrete as 'a truthful messenger from the birds [of omen]' (οἰωνῶν τις ... ἐτήτυμος ἄγγελος 46).

[147] 'I will tell you; for it is not inappropriate | since you ask, to tell you the truth' (*Hymn to Demeter* 120–121).

[148] Cf. Foley 1994:42.

the agent of cultural memory. The vocabulary of remembrance and forgetfulness is highly specific to each Indo-European language. For example, Latin *obliviscor*, 'to forget', is a metaphor arguably borrowed from the monumentalizing effected by formal (probably epigraphic) writing.[149] And, in contrast to the ancient Greek usage, sometimes it is not remembering but lying that a IE dialect associates with marked mental activity. Such is precisely the case with Latin *mentior*.

I must address now one other point that might be taken to support the specious epistemological argument that wedges ἀληθέα from ἔτυμα. It is the notion that *Theogony* 27 (ἴδμεν ψεύδεα πολλὰ λέγειν ἐτύμοισιν ὁμοῖα) proves ἔτυμα to be non-revelatory, for otherwise their comparison with ψεύδεα presupposed by this verse could not take place. Even when the conclusion is not drawn explicitly in these terms, this view underlies much of the scholarly commentary on the passage. It is implied, for example, by those who claim that the verification of the ἀληθέα of *Theogony* 28 is beyond the power of man, whose purview is 'earthly things' alone (which ἔτυμα are supposed to be). When scholars of this persuasion observe that the register of speech denoted by γηρύσασθαι differs from that of λέγειν, they do not have in mind (as I would) a different authority but altogether a different epistemology.[150] Are their views sound? I submit that the answer is a qualified 'no.' What is the meaning of the statement that the Muses know how to tell 'lies' (to use the customary translation of ψεύδεα) that are 'like *etuma*'?[151] Does it imply that, at least in principle, ἔτυμα are fully under the epistemological control of mortals and that, insofar as the goddesses make known ἔτυμα and like ψεύδεα, mortals can therefore subject that kind of divine inspiration to their own independent judgment, only to find its content plausible because it is consistent with their ordinary experience of the world? Thus posed, these questions tacitly exclude the very relevant fact that the 'ordinary' experience of mortal man also comprehends religious 'facts' and religious teachings, formal and informal, that he has internalized from his youth. Such propositional content shapes his worldview, prompts his ritual action, and gives rise to interpretive frameworks and standards of plausibility

---

[149] Ernout and Meillet 1985:455 s.v. "*obliuiscor.*"

[150] Leclerc 1993: "Contrairement aux ἀληθέα, indéterminés et ainsi absolus, les 'mensonges' s'inscrivent dans l'horizon de la vérité et se définissent par rapport à elle" (71); and: "Le premier terme [sc. ἔτυμος] désigne un type d'exactitude vérifiable dans la réalité sensible" (206). Simondon 1982: "[L]a vérité de l'ἀληθής est de l'ordre de la révélation. La vérité d'ἔτυμος est d'une autre nature, elle est celle 'd'une identité entre une certaine présentation du réel et la réalité elle-même'" (113, quoting from Levet 1976:163).

[151] The Muses do not say ἀληθέσιν ὁμοῖα not only because it is unmetrical but because they are not considering ψεύδεα chiefly as verbal art. Had they used ἀληθέσιν, they would have asserted that the 'many lies' resembled instances of truthful utterance. Their focus is rather on their likeness or correspondence to 'things as they really are'. On Heiden's view of the meaning of ὁμοῖος (Heiden 2007) see p. 259 below.

that structure his understanding of the world around him. Measured against these epistemological filters, plausibility turns out to have a notable 'supernatural' component, taking 'supernatural' in the sense of 'above and beyond what the ordinary worldview would readily account for without the explicit involvement of τὸ δαιμόνιον.' The notion that 'reality' can be immediately apprehended and readily interpreted by an exclusive recourse to ordinary (naturalistic or, as some might call it, practical) experience is simplistic. Aetiologies that explain striking topographic features or important rituals would make for the kind of σήματα that lend plausibility to the epic narrative. By the logic of the argument, local theogonies that made use of them but were otherwise in conflict with Hesiod's Panhellenic version should be ascribed to the Muses' inspiration of ψεύδεα ... ἐτύμοισιν ὁμοῖα. This does not, of course, mean that an appeal to naturalistic facts or ordinary (naturalistic) experience would be able to expose them as lies. By the same token, Hesiod's use of aetiologies in his Panhellenic *Theogony* does not *per se* prove that the contents of *his* poem are or are not ἀληθέα unmixed with ψεύδεα. In Hesiod's polemic with local poetry, his point is that other performers tell lies which hitherto have been inappropriately taken as authoritative only because they were superficially plausible in some way. This lying inspiration is to be traced to the punitive pleasure of the Muses. In the end, the absolute truthfulness on which the traditional authority of the Hesiodic performer depends is secured by Hesiod's *Dichterweihe* alone, and it must rise and fall with the credence the audience gives to it. Overall narrative plausibility, that is, the performer's successful accommodation of foundational elements of the worldview of his audience, is a necessary but not sufficient condition for his authority, and this agreement in essentials gives him the room to challenge the hearers elsewhere. Yet, ultimately, as the marked term for truthful utterance, ἀληθέα must seek to persuade by dint of the speaker's authority.

Standards of plausibility are also in view in the famous Odyssean verse whose phraseology recalls *Theogony* 27: ἴσκε ψεύδεα πολλὰ λέγων ἐτύμοισιν ὁμοῖα (τ 203).[152] During Penelope's lengthy interview with Odysseus, disguised as a beggar (τ 107–307), the hero tells his wife a celebrated Cretan lie that, as Levaniouk (2000:47) writes, "keeps remarkably close to the truth on this occasion." The verse in question prepares the audience for Penelope's tearful reaction (τ 204–209) to news of Aithon's (Odysseus' *nomen loquens*) alleged encounter with her husband. Whereas her interlocutor makes up his Cretan lineage—the specific target of Penelope's question at τ 162–163—he buttresses the plausibility of his answer with details about the island of Crete and her inhabitants.[153]

---

[152] For a translation, see pp. 262–263 below.

[153] Russo (in Russo et al. 1992) observes: "This passage, together with *Il.* ii 645–52, is the earliest description we have of Crete and one of the most important pieces of historical information in Homer."

But as a summary characterization of the hero's tales, τ 203 does not merely regard the immediately preceding exchange but also looks forward to the developments that follow. These focus on Penelope's testing of the beggar's veracity: 'Now indeed I think I will test you, stranger, | whether it is really true that there, with his godlike companions, | you entertained in your halls my husband, as you are declaring'.[154] She then challenges Aithon to describe Odysseus' clothing, his manner, and his comrades. He fulfills her request with an elaborate description that stirs her emotions deeply 'as she recognized the signs (σήματα) which Odysseus accurately exhibited' (τ 250). It is important to mark in passing the visual implications of both σῆμα[155] and φράζω, implications that undermine Heiden's challenge to 'resembling' *vel sim.* as the prevailing translation of ὁμοῖα in *Theogony* 27 (on which see immediately below). The narrative firmly establishes τ 203 in the context of plausible and persuasive deception.

Not so, argues Heiden 2007, who would want to render ψεύδεα ... ἐτύμοισιν ὁμοῖα in *Theogony* 27 as "lies equivalent to truth" with ὁμοῖος as "equivalent with respect to quality" (153). His point is that Hesiod preempts criticism of his *Theogony* by disavowing from the start the very distinction between truth and lie: "The Muses' statement that they told 'lies equivalent to truth' claimed some of truth's authority for the poet's stories whether they were lies or not" (172). According to Heiden, the use of ἔτυμα in verse 27 parallels the use of ἀληθέα in 28: "*Theog.* 27–28 offer little or nothing to discourage a listener from supposing that ἐτύμοισιν and ἀληθέα are synonymous" (171n46). But the text is structured as a contrast between ψεύδεα πολλὰ λέγειν and ἀληθέα γηρύσασθαι, a contrast that would be largely effaced if ψεύδεα are fictions intended by the performer to bear the same cultural authority and epistemological validity as ἀληθέα. Why then the contrast between λέγειν and γηρύσασθαι? Not to mention that the vocabulary of *pseudo-* words, both in Homer and Hesiod, is tinged with moral condemnation.[156] Moreover, *Theogony* 28 would then seem otiose. According to Heiden, the Muses would be saying: "We know how to tell many fictions with the force of truth; and we know, when willing, how to tell truths."

---

[154] νῦν μὲν δή σευ ξεῖνέ γ' ὀίω πειρήσεσθαι, | εἰ ἐτεὸν δὴ κεῖθι σὺν ἀντιθέοισ' ἑτάροισι | ξείνισας ἐν μεγάροισιν ἐμὸν πόσιν, ὡς ἀγορεύεις (τ 215–217).

[155] See above, p. 224. Cf. Nagy 2010b:157.

[156] See, for example, *Theogony* 229, 233, 783; *Works and Days* 78, 709, 789. For Homer, see, for example, Δ 235 Ζ 163 Η 352 Φ 275–276 λ 363–366 ξ 125–127 (with ξ 156–157) ξ 296–297 387–388. Cf. Carlisle 1999 esp. 55–56. Carlisle's conclusion at 91 that "the moral implications" evoked by the notion of 'lie' "are largely missing from Homeric contexts" is not supported by the passages above. But her larger point holds true metapoetically, i.e. from the point of view of inter- and intra-textuality. As she points out, "the speaker of Homeric *pseudea* intends to deceive" insofar as the "*pseudo-*word signals awareness that the promised outcome or reported event is not consistent with events as they will play out, or have played out, in the reality established by the main narrative" (55–56).

But if the fictions are "as good as truth" (Heiden's gloss at 171), why add the statement in verse 28? What would be the significance of their telling truths at all? They might as well tell only fictions as good as truths and be done. On Heiden's hypothesis, rather than the climax of an opposition, *Theogony* 28 seems an afterthought added for the sake of completion with little practical effect. It would be otherwise if a mixture of lies and truths were alleged—lies, ineffectual and without authority; but truths calling for acquiescence and credence. Then, neither verse would be otiose and sifting the wheat from the chaff would face the audience with a real conundrum.

Heiden's argument cannot succeed. He has not understood the meaning of the Muses, as his calling ἐτύμοισιν ὁμοῖα, on the traditional understanding, "merely pleonastic" and "anomalous" shows (Heiden 2007:169). On the same page he also calls the proposition "tautological." But there is nothing otiose about it. Its point is to account for what may well have come as a rude shock to the archaic audience: Hesiod's Olympian Muses disown local poets and demote as lying inspiration what is bound to have hitherto enjoyed authority and prestige with the hearers. How was this possible? It was possible because the 'lies' were irresistible, invincibly compelling in their divinely crafted plausibility.[157] Not all lies are created equal: some are readily spotted. In the face of a Panhellenic challenge, why local poetry should have been so well received begs for an explanation. And what to make of the invocation of Muses by local poets? And of the texture of epichoric narratives, similar in type and form to the subject matter of Hesiod's own *Theogony*, but narratives that, this fact notwithstanding, Hesiod now implies the audience is to cast aside as false? These are the facts that render *Theogony* 26–28 of fundamental consequence for the efficacy of Hesiodic traditional poetry. There is nothing pleonastic, anomalous, or tautological here.

But more narrowly to the philological point Heiden espouses: we may well accept his gloss for ὁμοῖος as "equivalent to X in respect of Y" (or, in a less cumbersome formulation, "like X in Y"), but this hardly decides, as he thinks, the meaning of *Theogony* 27. Once we agree that the identity of 'Y' is to be inferred from the context, why should one grant that this 'Y' is 'didactic value'? The

---

[157] Heiden misses the point when he asserts that the consensus interpretation "would also have us suppose that the Muses used one of their three directly quoted verses merely to announce that they knew how to do what ordinary mortal deceivers could also do" (2007:169). I dispute the notion that ordinary mortal deceivers could lend their 'lies' the degree of authority and favorable cultural reception the Muses' lying inspiration had arguably enjoyed before Hesiod's challenge. But, granting Heiden's contention for the sake of argument, the point would not have been that the Muses could do what ordinary mortal deceivers could also do, but that they had done it at all. Not to mention that, if Heiden is right, there is no *a priori* reason why mortal men could not also successfully resort unaided to the symbolic (fictive) truth-telling he ascribes to Hesiod's Muses.

thrust of Heiden's argument entails that the ψεύδεα are "as good as truth" in that under the proper hermeneutic principles they yield sound truth.[158] But why should we accept this arbitrary choice for 'Y'? This strikes me as an implausibly anachronistic imposition upon the early archaic world by an age accustomed to distinguish the 'higher' truths that narrative imparts from its status as history or fiction. Heiden seems unaware that his 'Y' is neither contextually necessary nor natural, merely an assumption that must itself be judged on its merits. None of the parallels he adduces serve to establish his conclusion. Whether other examples of ὁμοῖος involved or not confusion between the object equated and the corresponding 'X' is only partly to the point, although here too Heiden has overstated his case.[159] What matters is what the context might reasonably lead us to infer as 'Y.' In the context of lying inspiration and the authority of traditional poetry, I submit that the consensus understanding, which makes 'Y' their *prima facie* plausibility, i.e. the persuasiveness on which such authority hinged, is eminently reasonable and much the best contextual choice. Archaic epic poetry makes clear that this persuasiveness was deemed a function of the subject matter's factual veracity. Only with the ascendancy of intellectual elites who challenged the cultural preeminence of Homeric and Hesiodic epic were allegory and other approaches to legitimizing their canonical status developed, approaches that did not rely on an explicit or implicit claim to historical factuality. Heiden is right, then: the ψεύδεα of the Muses are 'equivalent to actually true things', not 'in respect of the validity of their teaching' but 'in respect of their plausibility and persuasiveness.' The Muses delegitimize and deauthorize what the audience has long considered inspired poetry, not by claiming that it is uninspired—its formal kinship with Panhellenic poetry and kindred thematic typology would have effectively blocked this approach—but by qualifying its inspiration as without validity, ineffective—that is, 'false'.

Heiden aims at the wrong target when he criticizes the gloss 'like, resembling' in LSJ s.v. ὁμοῖος: "Cases where ὁμοῖος does denote appearance [in early epic Greek] are not rare. But even in these instances the shared appearance is not usually—if it is ever—a matter of close or deceptive resemblance between two things" (Heiden 2007:158). The scholar overlooks that the potential deceptiveness of the Muses inheres in the terms of comparison, i.e. in the equivalence of ψεύδεα and ἔτυμα, not in the relational ὁμοῖα that links them. To carry conviction, Heiden must independently establish 1) that in the mouth of the Muses

---

[158] Thus, Heiden (2007:171) claims that "the Muses told Hesiod that they spoke only truth"; and that Hesiod's audiences would have to accept his poetry "even when its assertions seemed dubiously believable; for in respect of properties undisclosed but presumably discoverable, the Muses' lies were 'equivalent to truth'" (172).

[159] Heiden 2007:155, 159–160. Cf. Nagy 2010b.

ψεύδεα could intelligibly designate morally indifferent fictions; 2) that such fictions could reasonably be expected to gain the acceptance of archaic Greek audiences for their didactic value; and 3) that these audiences can be plausibly assumed to have extracted the 'true' teaching embedded in these fictive narratives by applying to them highly symbolic hermeneutic principles. Heiden's article does not meet the burden of proof nor will the evidence support it. The language of τ 203, to which I have already drawn attention above, confirms that at issue in the Muses' words is the plausibility of their inspiration, which, justifiably or not, imparts conviction and the sanction of authority to traditional poetry and invests its performer with consequent credibility. The asyndeton of this verse underlines the semantic development within the epic system of diction undergone by ἴσκε, doubtless from ἐίσκω. In this regard, it is analogous to the Latin verb *fingo*, which from 'to shape or mold' develops the acceptations "to modify the expression of (a face), tone of (a voice) ... to assume, take on (a new attitude or sim.)," "to adapt (one's actions, words, situation, etc.)," and "[t]o make (one's expression, language, etc.) false or hypocritical" (so the OLD s.v. 4c, 5b, and 10a). The analogy is even closer if Beekes (2010:1.435) is right to suggest that the underlying IE root *weik-, of uncertain meaning, denotes 'to be fitting'.[160] The newer *ske*-present ἴσκω (from the also new formation ἐίσκω = *ϝε-ϝίκ-σκω, but shedding the reduplication from ἔοικα)[161] would then mean 'to fit or adapt', the acceptation 5b in the OLD for *fingo*. Because the imperfect ἴσκε (=*fingebat*), used absolutely, would serve to round up a speech in the manner of ὣς ἔφατο *vel sim.*—how did he speak? he feigned—it encouraged asyndeta and is in fact only attested asyndetically in Homeric diction.[162] But this should not obscure the fact that in τ 203 the meaning and syntax of ἴσκε is only one step away from those attested for the ordinary factitive ἐίσκω, 'to liken X (acc.) to Y (dat.)' (*LfgE* s.v. ἔοικα I.4).[163] The best translation, then, is 'he was feigning, telling

---

[160] *LIV*² 669-670 suggests the root meaning 'eingehen in, eintreten', whence '"hinzutreten' → 'nahekommen' → 'gleichkommen'." From the point of view of their meaning, the adduced Vedic and Avestan parallels, however, are not entirely convincing.

[161] Chantraine 1999:354 s.v. ἔοικα.

[162] This was noted long ago by Nägelsbach (1834:268-269) and it probably underlies the ancient debate, reflected by the scholia to τ 203 and χ 31, whether to gloss ἴσκε as ἔλεγε or ἤισκε εἴκαζεν ὡμοίου. See also Buttmann 1869:275-279 and Lehrs 1964:97-98.

[163] See the helpful note by Russo in Russo et al. 1992:87 *ad loc.* Of a different persuasion are Wilamowitz-Moellendorff 1927:62 and van der Valk 1949:116 with n. 7. Van der Valk's connection of this ἴσκε to (ἐν)ίσπω is unconvincing (Fernández-Galiano in Russo et al. 1992:225-226 calls it "impossible"; cf. Ameis and Hentze 1889:16 *ad* τ 203). Nägelsbach (after Buttmann) simply suggested emending to ἴσπε. That χ 31 exhibits a further degree of semantic development is undeniable, but it too can be traced to its original meaning. Thus, there is no need for the uneconomical alternative, which finds no further support in the doubtless late epigram ascribed to Simonides (no. 69 in Page 1981:291).

many lies like actual things'. For 'feigning' in the sense of 'inventing [a story]' one might substitute 'simulating'; or the sharper 'dissimulating', which brings out Odysseus' veering from the truth by combining true and false in a plausible mixture.[164] The plausibility that derives from the overall effect (what one might, in the abstract, call the 'appearance' of the lies, i.e. how the ψεύδεα appear to the mind's eye) can be soundly expressed by the translation that Heiden deprecates: "Thus he made the many falsehoods of his tale *seem like* the truth" (so Murray in his *Loeb* translation, my emphasis).[165]

One final argument to be refuted is Levet's insistence (approved by Simondon 1982:113) that ψεύδεα cannot be the opposite of ἀληθέα on the grounds of the coordinate ψεύδονται and οὐδ' ἐθέλουσιν ἀληθέα μυθήσασθαι in ξ 125 (Levet 1976:82–83).[166] This oversubtle reading ignores the possibility of emphasis through antithetical parallelism and seems to assume for the Homeric text the economy of a terse philosophical treatise. What would this view, which is not true to Homeric style, make of Aphrodite's statement, 'I am not a goddess … but a mortal'?[167] If one were to insist on extracting additional information from the second clause of ξ 125, ἐθέλουσιν might provide firmer ground for an argument. Although its meaning can be so weak as to indicate little more than future occurrence, i.e. 'they will not tell the truth', it might also point to the interlocutors' unwillingness to answer truthfully the follow-up questions that Penelope would pose to them in conversation: 'They lie and [when asked by Penelope] are not willing to tell [her] the truth'. One such probing question is precisely in view at τ 215–219. The sequence of tale-telling and questioning is made explicit in the ensuing verses: 'Whoever in his wanderings comes to the land of Ithaca goes to my mistress and tells a deceitful tale (ἀπατήλια βάζει). And after welcoming him, she offers him hospitality and inquires about each particular (ἕκαστα μεταλλᾷ)' (ξ 126–128).

The philosophical musings I have reviewed in this section and their oversubtle hermeneutics all depend on the problematic notion that Hesiod was as an exceptional thinker, well ahead of his times, anomalous in his conviction of the inherently fictive nature of mythic narrative and its capacity to articulate truth. But the individuality that underlies the claims of exceptionality has been overemphasized, and it has to do more with the distinctive character of this poetic tradition than with an individual self-awareness or self-disclosure.[168]

---

[164] Cf. *LfgE* s.v. ἴσκε.

[165] The scholiast *ad loc.* interprets it thus: πολλὰ ψευδῆ λέγων εἴκαζεν, ὥστε ὅμοια εἶναι ἀληθέσιν.

[166] "La présence de οὐδέ et la place de ἀληθέα μυθήσασθαι sont de nature à surprendre. Le refus de la vérité ne devrait-il pas, en effet, constituer le premier temps du mensonge?" (at 83).

[167] *Hymn to Aphrodite* 109–110.

[168] With the frequently quoted ἐγὼ δέ κε Πέρσῃ ἐτήτυμα μυθησαίμην (*Works and Days* 10), commonly construed in opposition to the Muses' song as an innovative affirmation of Hesiod's

Luther (1935:123n1) misreads the Iliadic narrator's dependence on the Muse as insufficiency, and Hesiod's remark as self-sufficiency that reduces the opening hymn to a mere literary convention.[169] Not so; in truth, the real distinction is the slender biographical schema that frames the *Works and Days* as Hesiod's instruction to his brother Perses. This hardly exceeds the bounds of an undeveloped poetic persona, and the real innovation is that it belongs at all in the tradition and serves to articulate its authority in the presentation of its didactic poetry.

---

self-conscious 'I' (e.g. Luther 1935:123), one can readily compare B 488 (πληθὺν δ' οὐκ ἂν ἐγὼ μυθήσομαι οὐδ' ὀνομήνω) and B 490 (ἀρχοὺς αὖ νηῶν ἐρέω νῆάς τε προπάσας). Since Hesiod's 'I' stands at the end of his hymnic προοίμιον, one might also compare the device that regularly closes Homeric hymns (e.g. *Hymn to Demeter* 495, *Hymn to Apollo* 546, *Hymn to Hermes* 580, etc.).

[169] Stoddard (2004:64–65) also finds in the *Theogony* a Hesiod that seizes the initiative from the Muses and refuses to surrender control of his poem to them. But this Hesiod of Hellenistic cast is not to be found in the poem. It is true that the three hymns of the Muses ostensibly differ in their detailed subject matter and structure, a fact to which Clay 1988 has drawn attention; and that Hesiod's song in turn also features its own distinctive shape. I hope to explore the significance of these observations in a future work. Here I need only remark that, as should be expected in traditional poetry, the occasion and audience determine the thematic scope and design of the performance. The various descriptions of the Muses' song in *Theogony* 1–115 have different audiences and occur at various stages in the proem and their journey to Olympos. It is reasonable to suppose that each instance serves a distinct rhetorical end in the argument of the poem and that this sufficiently accounts for its peculiarities. Similarly, Hesiod sings not for the Muses or Zeus but for a human audience. His material and arrangement answer to the needs of his audience. But these are needs that the Muses supply through inspiration as they prompt the rhapsode to sing—it is after all *their* song (22) and voice (31) that the bard utters. There is nothing to the greater specificity of Hesiod's invocation that Stoddard (2004:64) alleges. Her argument survives only through the ellipses of A 2–5 and α 2–9 which give a false impression of unspecificity: each Homeric proem is a *tour de force* of narrative compression, giving in only a few lines the entire scope of each poem's plot. The supposed "detailed list" of divinities which Hesiod allegedly gives the Muses to sing about—what Stoddard (2004:65) thinks as 'exhibit A' of Hesiod's individual initiative—upon inspection dissolves into a predictable and simple enumeration of the entire cosmos: the gods born from earth and heaven, the night, and the briny sea, a thematic scope recapitulated as the genesis of the gods and the earth, the bodies of fresh and salt water, the stars and heaven. This too is a *tour de force* of thematic compression, with predictable Near-Eastern precedents (cf. Genesis 1:1–2), neither more nor less specific than the Homeric parallels and, like them, standing as an outline in a similar relation to the notional narrative totality. And the 'demand' that the narrative start ἐξ ἀρχῆς (115) not only comports with the Muses' charge that Hesiod sing τά τ' ἐσσόμενα πρό τ' ἐόντα (32) and the γένος (33) of the immortals—which as often, and *a fortiori* in a theogonic context, draws attention to their γένεσις—but is no greater a sign of independence from them than the Homeric narrator's 'demand' that the goddess sing about Akhilleus' wrath ἐξ οὗ δὴ τὰ πρῶτα διαστήτην ἐρίσαντε | Ἀτρεΐδης τε ἄναξ ἀνδρῶν καὶ δῖος Ἀχιλλεύς (A 6–7). Stoddard's remark about Hesiod's "intend[ing] to take an active role in shaping the *Theogony*" arises from her flawed presumption of a dichotomy of divine and human involvement in the performance of traditional poetry where, to put it in etic terms, there is in fact creative and artistic cooperation. This is Finkelberg's working hypothesis; only, Stoddard embraces the opposite side of the polarity: "The narrator of the Proem deliberately sets himself up as the guiding force behind the poem and makes clear that ... he is to be considered substantially responsible for the *Theogony*" (Stoddard 2004:67).

This third-person identification of Hesiod, which takes place in line 22 of the hymnic προοίμιον that opens the *Theogony* (1–35), can only be construed as a departure from the greater 'anonymity' of the Homeric poems if we consider the latter strictly without *their* own προοίμια.[170] But it is analogous to the function the *Hymn to Apollo* 157–178 would have performed as a προοίμιον to the *Iliad* or the *Odyssey*, especially if we accept Nagy's suggestion[171] that the Delian Maidens are the local Muses of Delos.[172] It is important that we view the particular use the Homeric and Hesiodic traditions make of their respective archetypal authors not as a biographical curiosity, but as fulfilling a traditional function within their own particular genres, whether a historical core can be recognized or not. Even West, who thinks that the mention of Hesiod's name in the *Theogony* occurs "out of simple pride" (1966:161) and that in the *Works and Days* "Hesiod goes out of his way to be informative about himself and his family" because he is "anxious ... for us to know these things" (1978a:33), must ultimately admit that Perses (his interlocutor brother and complementary 'personality') "is a changeable figure" whose biographical details are sometimes "invented for the purposes of argument" (1978a:40). In the agonistic engagement of the Hesiodic theogony with other local theogonic traditions as it made its bid for Panhellenic status, the opposition between them could not be marked generically (for the polemic was not directed against a different genre, e.g. heroic epic); neither could it be marked by geography, for this would have worked against its Panhellenic drive;[173] it is left, then, to divine election, to the particular favor showed by the Muses to 'Hesiod' the individual, to mark the tradition of poetry he represents as true over against all others. Whereas the truth of Hesiodic poetry is a function of Hesiod's authorization by the Muses (his authority stems from his initiation), in its earliest stages the truth of the Homeric tradition would have been located notionally in the quoted speech of the Muses, without the interposition

---

[170] The actual name 'Hesiod' does not appear again at all, neither in the *Works and Days* nor in the *Theogony*. A pseudo-biographical framework is really operative only in the *Works and Days*, where its terms are a simple opposition between an unnamed ἐγώ (10, 106, 174, 286, 396, 654, 658, 682) and his brother Perses (10, 27, 213, 274, 286, 299, 397, 611, 633, 641).

[171] Nagy 1990c:375–377. Cf. also G. Nagy 1992:127n6.

[172] The 'blind bard from Khios', generally assumed to be 'Homer' (cf. Graziosi 2002:62–66), identifies himself here in the third person through an imagined dialog between a visitor to Delos and the Δηλιάδες. (Their response is conceptualized as the reperformance of the dialog itself.) Just as in the *Works and Days* 10, an emphatic ἐγὼν follows (177).

[173] But even if a geographical label had not been objectionable, still the Hesiodic theogony could not pose as true merely because it was Boiotian, for even Thespiai and nearby Askra, for example, held competing traditions about the Muses (see above, p. 211).

of the individual 'Homer,' whom later generations credited with the authorship of its poems.[174]

The polemical engagement with the tradition remained even after the locus of authority had shifted into the hands of the archetypal Homer; but rival multiforms were now assailed as illegitimate insertions (ἐμποιεῖν) of foreign material into the fixed, notional whole that was his *oeuvre* (just what, according to Herodotos 7.6.3, Onomakritos was accused of doing ἐς τὰ Μουσαίου); or, if the confrontation was with widely received Homeric oral tradition—as, for example, with Pindar's assertion that Odysseus' reputation had been exaggerated at the expense of Ajax' (*Nemean* 7.20–23)—the strategy was to relativize the authority of the tradition by ascribing it not to quoted divine speech but to a manipulative composer or one carried away by his superior skill: here the rhetoric of the indictment would divorce technical skill from the piety that had traced it to the Muse (remember Μελέτη, p. 211 above); with such a break the truthfulness of the song was greatly undercut.

It is important to realize and affirm that the shift from the Muse to Homer was facilitated by the notional fixity of the poetic tradition. The bard's song had once been considered sacral speech, the quoted utterance of the Muse, a veritable speech-act that retold what was, what is, and what is to come—matters that relate to the unchanging order of the cosmos and to events fixed, whether by the record of the past or by the necessity of divine will and prophetic insight. Now, according to the new perspective, Homer—inheriting the conceptual fixity built into the tradition—was said to have sung one thing but not another, and a guild of rhapsodes devoted to the semi-official control and arbitration of the tradition became conceivable, with a corresponding store of 'unpublished' ἔπη (cf. Plato's *Phaidros* 252b4–6). That 'Homer' the individual had no existence independent from the poetic tradition could only be of help: every locale attached such biographical material as reflected its own local appropriation of the poetry, and thus arose a large body of apocryphal anecdotes and competing lives of Homer.[175]

---

[174] As G. Nagy 1992:126 writes: "If there is a historical inference to be made from these differences, it is not that Homer and Hesiod had different attitudes about truth. It is rather that the traditional role of the performer is different in Homeric and Hesiodic poetry." For the conventional nature and function of Hesiod's 'autobiographical' material, cf. Griffith 1983, with an important corrective by G. Nagy 1992. Cf. Nagy 2009a.

[175] See above, p. 83 n. 5.

8.3 Μάντις and Προφήτης

8.3.1 Ecstasy

As remarked above (p. 220) in my study of Hesiod's *Dichterweihe*, the notional fixity of the Homeric tradition has its mirror image in the twin professions of μάντις and προφήτης.[176] Plato—we shall see momentarily—introduces two others: ἑρμηνεύς and ὑποκριτής.[177] The philosopher's testimony, though indispensable, must be carefully weighed. For, having always an axe to grind, his material embraces real facets of his culture while tendentiously recombining the data and redefining their mutual relation. For this reason his dialogs are better characterized as refracting, rather than simply reflecting, Greek culture. Most famously, the *Iōn* puts the strongest possible emphasis on a view of ecstatic possession, during which the subject retains no self-control and is merely the mindless vehicle of the divine presence within him. Before proceeding any further, I must draw attention to the potential confusion that arises from the words 'ecstasy' and 'ecstatic'. Often their use reveals simplistic assumptions about the nature of that divine influence upon the human subject which the Greeks called ἐνθουσιασμός or 'being ἔνθεος'. Scholars ancient and modern, chiefly under Plato's strongly tendentious re-reading of archaic Greek culture, have all too readily assumed that even before Plato the state of mind under such divine influence, regularly glossed by 'ecstasy' and 'ecstatic', was by and large thought to imply a 'being beside oneself', a suppression or annihilation of native cognition. In short, it was thought to render the subject temporarily mad or irrational. But this is not so. As Porzio Gernia (1989:85) observes, Indo-European derivatives of *men-* exhibit well-determined semantic traits that encompass physical and psychic strength, (prophetic) wisdom, poetic inspiration, sacred speaking and singing (including prayers and magic incantations), and madness (sacred and pathological): "Il nucleo semantico che può aver generato questi significati non può essere che la nozione di una conoscenza particolare, non traducibile in termini della nostra cultura attuale e non corrispondente alla nostra conoscenza, di tipo logico-razionale. È un potenziamento della 'mente', intesa come complesso delle facoltà intellettuali e psichiche, come totalità dell'uomo. È uno stato anormale di coscienza nella quale si manifesta

---

[176] Archaic thought ordinarily subsumed under μάντις their respective characteristics, viz. 'revelatory insight' and 'explanation,' even if on occasion it might draw attention to select facets of this semantic complex. This narrowing of semantic focus motivates the Homeric *hapax* ὑποφῆται at Π 235 (on this passage, see González 2000). This and other terms like ὑποφήτωρ are semantically related to προφήτης.

[177] See below, pp. 298f.

un'energia attiva e creativa. Questo particolare stato di coscienza è determinato dall'irruzione del divino, dall'incorporazione e manifestazione di energie di ordine soprannaturale."

A comprehensive review of the misunderstanding induced by Plato must wait for a future work. Here, I limit myself to making only those brief remarks that are needful for the analysis at hand. The *OED* s.v. "ecstasy" furnishes a convenient entry point: "The classical senses of ἔκστασις are 'insanity' and 'bewilderment'; but in late Greek the etymological meaning received another application, namely, 'withdrawal of the soul from the body, mystic or prophetic trance'; hence in later medical writers the word is used for trance, etc., generally. Both the classical and post-classical senses came into the mod[ern] languages, and in the present fig[urative] uses they seem to be blended." Although the *OED* is wrong to declare 'insanity' and 'bewilderment' "the classical senses" without qualification, it helpfully alerts us to the terminological confusion between 'ecstasy' and 'trance'. The mystical tradition understands 'ecstasy' as "the state of rapture in which the body was supposed to become incapable of sensation, while the soul was engaged in the contemplation of divine things" (*OED* s.v. 3.a). Contrast this with *OED* s.v. 3.b: "The state of trance supposed to be a concomitant of prophetic inspiration; hence, Poetic frenzy or rapture." The distinguishing element between them is what *OED* s.v. 4.a in turn defines as "[a]n exalted state of feeling which engrosses the mind to the exclusion of thought; rapture, transport." But since 'trance' is commonly regarded as an "unconscious or insensible condition ... characterized by a more or less prolonged suspension of consciousness and inertness to stimulus" (*OED* s.v. 2), 'ecstasy' defined as a 'state of trance' should appear incompatible with "[p]oetic frenzy or rapture."[178] Rouget (1985:3–12) surveys the divergent use scholars have made of 'trance' and 'ecstasy'. That, unlike 'ecstatic' for 'ecstasy', 'trance' does not have a convenient adjective has contributed not a little to the preferential use of 'ecstasy', which has in time come to incorporate what in some quarters would have been considered peculiar to a 'trance'. Thus, Rouget groups under 'ecstasy' the following concomitants: "immobility, silence, solitude, no crisis, sensory deprivation, recollection, hallucinations"; and under 'trance': "movement, noise, in company, crisis, sensory overstimulation, amnesia, no hallucinations."[179] Some of these are not immediately applicable to Sokrates' and Ion's discussion of inspired performance, and the important *comparandum* of the Pythia's Delphic experience might seem to include, depending on the source, elements of both. But for the purposes of the

---

[178] 'Frenzy' is defined in turn as 'derangement' or 'temporary insanity', chiefly accompanied by 'excitement of paroxysm' (*OED* s.v. A.1). Ordinarily, 'frenzy' is marked by mental and bodily agitation.

[179] Cf., further, Fachner 2006.

discussion at hand, I will use 'ecstatic' in the sense of a mental paroxysm that suspends rationality and renders the subject's cognition passively instrumental to the divinity's aims. I will usually make this meaning clear by adding 'irrational' to it.[180]

Now, as has often been remarked in recent times, wild ecstatic possession that precludes, with any divine influence that might bear upon the subject, a coordinate use of his native cognition—i.e. an altered state of mind indistinguishable from ordinary madness—was not the archaic view of poetic inspiration. Indeed, at no point in the few places where the narrator of the *Iliad* or the *Odyssey* comes to the fore (at invocations of the Muse or when he addresses a character in the story) does he appear as anything other than self-possessed. The same is true of the two bards in the *Odyssey*, Phemios and Demodokos. The latter maintains his self-control at all times, even when he is described as prompted by the god or Muse. Thus, even though θ 73 makes the Muse responsible for the onset of his singing, from θ 87 90–91 we learn that the performance was punctuated by pauses and by the Phaiakian nobles' encouragement to resume the singing: Demodokos' inspiration, then, did not rule out a sensitive singer-audience interaction. Similarly, at θ 492 he is urged by Odysseus to move his song on (μετάβηθι) to the episode of the wooden horse and the sack of Ilion. Demodokos obliges him, starting at the appropriate point (ἔνθεν ἑλὼν ὡς ... θ 500); yet, all the same, he is said to begin his song at the prompting of the god (ὁ δ' ὁρμηθεὶς θεοῦ ἤρχετο θ 499). And this is not all: for Alkinoos, seeing Odysseus cry at the hearing of the story, commands the minstrel to check his singing (θ 537 542), and we have every reason to believe that Demodokos does as he is told. The same can be said of Phemios who, while singing as his νόος moves him[181] and Zeus metes out (α 346–349),[182] is yet assumed by Penelope to have a choice of repertoire, just as he is said at α 154 to sing under the compulsion of the suitors. Furthermore, scholars have noted that even the few μάντεις who appear in the story (e.g. Kalkhas) never show any of the stereotypical traits

---

[180] I do not, however, take this to be the pre-Platonic meaning of the word. For the ancient use and meaning of ἐξίστημι and related words, see Pfister 1939 and 1959, and Des Places 1969:308–320.

[181] This refers to more, I believe, than a personal inclination or preference, for the psychology of the singer, to which νόος here, and θυμός at θ 45, speaks (cf. I 702–703) is not exclusive of divine influence, but rather coordinate with, or instrumental to, it. Thus, according to θ 44, a god has given Demodokos the gift of singing as his θυμός moves him.

[182] In all likelihood, the main thrust of this statement has reference to α 32–33; but I believe it goes beyond it in suggesting that Zeus has not merely made it possible for Phemios to sing of the Danaans' evil doom, but has also given the bard this specific theme as the choice of song for the occasion. Since Penelope's reproach centers on Phemios' selection, merely to argue that the events have happened and are therefore potential songs would not suffice as defense. But to argue that Zeus not only brought the events to pass but also moved the bard to sing about them would be an adequate apology.

of ecstatic oracular delivery.[183] To Setti this has proved so surprising that he has been misled into describing Homeric poetry as the humanistic product of a secular polis culture (Setti 1958:136–138). But this only reveals his narrow view of inspiration, which robs of sacral notions and religious feeling whatever does not correspond to his expectations of an ecstatic oracular milieu. Setti is, in effect, looking for incantatory poetry when he insists on alliteration and rhyme as the *sine qua non* of truly religious poetry (139); but magic is only a narrow domain of a much larger religious landscape.

8.3.2 The Delphic Oracle

To speak only of the most famous of oracular seats, it is hardly a coincidence that the ancients themselves held divergent traditions about Delphi.[184] On these, modern scholars in turn have formulated two radically different reconstructions of the mantic session.[185] Some insist that the Pythia herself, in her right mind, delivered the oracles in prose or hexameters; that she could even be bribed to lie is adduced in support of this view (cf. Herodotos 6.66 and 6.75[186]). Others emphasize the mediation of the προφήτης, who, they suppose, conveyed the suppliant's question to the Pythia and reported back her answer. A few writers go even further, asserting that, in the case of the more important inquiries, he would also 'recompose' her message into hexameters.[187] Most of the literary evidence supports the former reconstruction; owing to his office as priest at Delphi and his writings on the oracle, Plutarch represents a late but distinguished exponent

---

[183] Cf. Nilsson 1967:166 and Tigerstedt 1970:169 with n. 30.

[184] Focusing only on Delphi is justified, I believe, on the grounds that this sanctuary was one of a handful of institutions that in the eighth century BC transcended the local interests of particular Greek city-states. Together with Homeric poetry, the rise of the polis, the proliferation of the alphabet, organized colonizations, and the establishment of the Olympic games, Delphi shaped and was shaped by the dynamic of supra-political communication that we call Panhellenism. Cf. Nagy 1990b:10 and 37. Note the mention of Pytho at I 404–405 and θ 79–81. For Claros, often cited as a close parallel, see Picard 1922:197–220, Parke 1940:86, and Haussoullier 1898.

[185] Cf. Compton 1994.

[186] Cf. Pausanias 3.4.3 and Thoukydides 5.16.2. But one might conceivably imagine some sort of collusion between the Pythia and her προφήτης, in which case the alleged bribery of the prophetess would not bear decisively on the particular division of labor that obtained between them. In fact, collusion is in evidence at Herodotos 6.66, though the historian makes clear that Kobōn was not a προφήτης.

[187] Cf. Parke 1940. That prose was the dominant mode of delivery is stated at Plutarch *De Pythiae oraculis* 403e. (On the choice of form, verse or prose, in relation to the Pythia see Amandry 1980.) Dempsey 1918, a rather extreme supporter of a raving *mantis*, opines that the Pythia's utterances would have been unintelligible apart from the mediation of the προφήτης, whose work it was to put her babblings into articulate speech. Farnell (1896–1909:4.189), more moderate, notes that her "wild utterance" was "probably some kind of articulate speech," which the Ὅσιοι and the προφήτης knew how to interpret.

of it.[188] Indeed, much of *De Pythiae oraculis* is explicitly built on the assumption that the Pythia herself is directly (and primarily, if not solely) responsible not only for the content but also the form of the oracles. The question at issue, after all, is why Delphic oracles are no longer rendered in verse. The reasons offered are several and various; among them is Theon's, who argues that Apollo merely places within the *mantis* the ἀρχὴ τῆς κινήσεως, and she in turn is moved according to her natural endowments: 'For the voice is not the god's, nor the utterance or diction or meter, but the woman's'.[189] This agrees with Herodotos, whose narrative conveys the distinct impression that the Pythia herself delivered her oracles to the inquirers,[190] at times even anticipating their questions and speaking unbidden upon their crossing the threshold of the temple.[191] Thus, Crahay (1956:83) states definitively that "Delphes n'a qu'un seul prophète, dont le rôle exact nous échappe, mais auquel, en tout cas, Hérodote n'attribue jamais de réponse."[192] Now, one might argue that, given Plutarch's late date and his admission that in his own time oracles were no longer in verse, he may simply have been ignorant of the workings of classical and pre-classical Delphi. But he knows of a report that, in the past, 'some men with the gift of poetry' (ποιητικοί τινες ἄνδρες), overhearing the Pythia's words, would 'twine them round extempore with *epē*, meters, and rhythms as containers' (*De Pythiae oraculis* 407b). This is certainly not quite the same as an officially appointed mediating προφήτης, but there is enough overlap that it is hard to believe that Plutarch would have failed to mention the prophet's participation in the recomposition of oracles into verse, had he known about it. After all, he is often well informed about classical Greece, even about subjects of which he had no personal experience; whereas regarding Delphi, his many years at the oracle as priest make his writings on the matter uniquely authoritative. One may retort that it is precisely such first-hand experience that made him incapable of viewing Delphi's early history objectively. At any rate, that he draws on sources at least as old as the fourth century BC is clear from his reference to Theopompos (*De Pythiae oraculis* 403e).[193] We shall never know for sure, but the fact remains that Plutarch never mentions the cooperation of the prophet in composing the oracle, and

---

[188] See, however, Flacelière 1950, who is responding to Amandry 1950. For a general overview of this old *zētēma* see also Nilsson 1958, Fauth 1963, and Fontenrose 1978:196–228.

[189] οὐ γὰρ ἔστι θεοῦ ⟨γ'⟩ ἡ γῆρυς οὐδ' ὁ φθόγγος οὐδ' ἡ λέξις οὐδὲ τὸ μέτρον ἀλλὰ τῆς γυναικός (*De Pythiae oraculis* 397c; cf. also 405c–e).

[190] Typical introductions are ἡ Πυθίη λέγει τάδε (Herodotos 1.65), ἡ Πυθίη χρᾷ τάδε (Herodotos 1.66), or ἡ Πυθίη εἶπε τάδε (Herodotos 1.85).

[191] E.g. Herodotos 1.47, 1.65, 5.92, etc.

[192] Cf. Fontenrose 1978:197 and 212–224.

[193] The same mention also proves that by the fourth century BC some believed that the Pythia herself prophesied in verse, while others rejected this tenet.

the specific duties of this official remain elusive and conjectural.[194] While he is not epigraphically attested, Herodotos 8.37 (cf. 7.111) and Plutarch *De defectu oraculorum* 438b explicitly mention him,[195] but the only text that unequivocally tells of resident poets whose role it was to put the oracles to verse is Strabo 9.3.5: φασὶ ... τὴν Πυθίαν ... ἀποθεσπίζειν ἔμμετρά τε καὶ ἄμετρα· ἐντείνειν δὲ καὶ ταῦτα εἰς μέτρον ποιητάς τινας ὑπουργοῦντας τῷ ἱερῷ. Note, however, that he does not identify these ποιηταί τινες with the προφῆται.

Now, concerning mental states that point to an impaired ability to reason, there are scattered indications of behavior that could be called irrational, but their historicity is dubious. Thus, Strabo (9.3.5) draws attention to the πνεῦμα ἐνθουσιαστικόν that allegedly ascended from the chasm in the *adyton*, inducing the Pythia's prophecies; and Diodoros' legend (16.26) famously records the bizarre behavior of goats that accidentally breathed the vapors, adding that, after many people had leaped into the chasm under their influence, the locals restricted access to a single woman, the prophetess, furnishing her with the tripod as a device to prevent her falling into the chasm too. Lucian, in turn, mentions the chewing of laurel leaves, which was also thought to induce an altered state of mind (*Bis accusatus* §1). Despite the weakness of the evidence, modern scholars have found it hard to shake their attachment to the story of irrational Delphic ecstasy (certainly attested in classical Athens, e.g. in Plato's *Phaidros* 244b). Since the existence of trance-inducing vapors has found no geological support,[196] some have had recourse to self-induced trances

---

[194] If 'prophets' and 'priests' were the same officials, at least in the time of Plutarch—as appears from Nikander being called προφήτης in *De defectu oraculorum* 438b and ἱερεύς in *De E apud Delphos* 386b—it is easier to imagine what functions they may have discharged. In particular, the priest would have presided over the oracular session. Cf. Amandry 1950:119n2.

[195] For other references see Amandry 1950:118–122 and Fontenrose 1978:218n30. If the identity between Delphic priests and prophets is as old as the *Hymn to Apollo* 393–396, some may see support there for a mediating προφήτης; similarly with Euripides *Iōn* 369–372, 413–416, though I personally do not consider the evidential value of these passages high.

[196] The last decade has witnessed new attempts to ground the mantic experience in gaseous emanations of geological origin. Piccardi 2000 tied ancient reports of an oracular chasm to an east-west fault below the Phaedriades, although he did not put forward a gaseous release theory in connection with the Pythia's μαντεία. In fact, he located the original chasm—a coseismic surface rupture—in the temple of Athena. His article was soon followed by De Boer and Hale 2000, De Boer et al. 2001, Spiller et al. 2002, and De Boer and Hale 2002. These scholars claimed to have identified a new fault that ran roughly in a north-south direction, apparently right under the temple of Apollo. They named it the "Kerna fault." Although they could not determine its intersection with the Delphi fault, they inferred from "projections of fault trends" that it lay below this temple (De Boer et al. 2001:708). Furthermore, they held that the combination of faults, bituminous limestone, and rising groundwater caused the emission of volatile hydrocarbon gases (ethane, methane, and ethylene). Of these, ethylene in particular was made responsible for the intoxicating effect of the prophetic vapors allegedly attested by the ancient sources. These proposals were eagerly received by the news media and popular survey articles

(e.g. Burkert 1985:116), while others rightly draw attention to the psychological complexity of trance-like behavior, not all of which can be simply mapped onto "hysterical excitement."[197] Like Strabo, ancient writers who took for granted an irrational, ecstatic Pythia must have assumed that she was nevertheless sufficiently coherent to speak in hexameters, or else that Apollo put the ἔπη in her mouth to deliver while out of her mind—apparently, this latter is the model Sokrates wields in his dialog with Ion—though under this harmonizing

(cf. Krajick 2005:763–764). Soon, however, its central elements were seriously undermined or soundly refuted: the reality of the Kerna fault could not be confirmed by Etiope et al. 2006, who proposed instead two independent fault segments that did not continue under the temple of Apollo (821); they also demonstrated that the site is not prone to the production of ethylene in the amounts necessary to induce neurotoxic effects. As an alternative, they proposed oxygen depletion by the inhalation of CO_2-CH_4, which they associated rather tentatively with the western end of a conjectural subsidiary fault that would run under the temple of Athena and is supposedly disclosed by a linear sequence of springs. The authors, however, freely admitted that "it is difficult to interpret a linear sequence of springs as a fault" (821). They also added into the mix the possible emission of benzene dissolved in the water of the springs as the source of Plutarch's 'sweet smell' (*De defectu oraculorum* 437c). Foster and Lehoux 2007 and Lehoux 2007 strongly rejected the conjectures of De Boer et al. and their positivist leanings. Foster and Lehoux (2007:86), apparently unaware of Etiope et al. 2006, independently concluded that the alleged ethylene intoxication of the Pythia was untenable on geological, toxicological, and historical grounds. Lehoux 2007, slightly later in date and now apprised of the article by Etiope et al., considered their suggestion of oxygen depletion unlikely, given that neither sealed chambers nor long-term incubation were involved. He also noted that these scholars did not offer any actual evidence for benzene. But it was Lehoux's reexamination of the very ancient sources that geological theories seek to explain that proved these theories' most effective refutation. In the face of his devastating critique, Ustinova's (2009:281) dismissal of Lehoux on *a priori* grounds is inadequate and unconvincing. She assumes all too readily that what the Pythia did in the *adyton* was fully visible to inquirers (276; cf., *contra*, Flacelière 1938:98–99 and Roux 1976:136, 149); and that we know in detail from eyewitness testimony what took place during consultations (note the warning to the contrary in Fontenrose 1978:197; cf. 225–228). She also returns to a simplistic reading of the ancient sources that ignores most of the relevant classical scholarship of the twentieth century (e.g. as concerns the πνεῦμα, on which see Roux 1976:154–157 and Fontenrose 1978:197–203). But her greatest weakness is her reliance on the work of De Boer et al. (278), whose defects and limitations are now clear. Although aware of Etiope et al. 2006, she does not seem to realize the extent to which this study undermines the geological intoxication theory. The current state of the art on the controversy is Piccardi et al. 2008, which Ustinova ignores. This exhaustive reconsideration of the geological claims puts another nail in the coffin of the geological intoxication theory. Etiope at al. 2006 conclude that "there is no evidence of a Kerna fault" (6); that "[h]igh concentrations of ethylene ... are thermodynamically impossible and are unrealistic in non-volcanic areas" (15); and that " both 'gas exhalation' and 'chasm' had not physical geological reality during the time of the main functioning of the sanctuary (7th century BC–4th century AD)" (15).

[197] Thus Dodds 1951:87n41. See his stimulating treatment at 71–75 and 295–299, though Plutarch's emphasis in *De defectu oraculorum* 438b on the abnormal nature of the incident fails to bear out Dodds's views about the character of the Pythia's trance.

scenario the specific role of the prophet is hard to determine.[198] Regardless of one's view about the access an ordinary inquirer might have had to the Pythia, as Amandry (1950:168) observes, it is hard to believe that, in the marked occasions of politically momentous institutional inquiries, she would have spoken directly to the θεωρός or θεοπρόπος without prior screening and consideration by the men who ran Delphi. If indeed the prophet got involved especially at such times, we can understand why one can trace back to these instances the greater fraction of the extant oracular verse. Poetry's latitude of form and capacity for ambiguity would have been welcome where powerful clients or delicate 'international' politics were implicated.[199] The confluence of irrational, ecstatic *mantis* and self-possessed prophet was even historicized by Rohde as the arrival in Delphi of Dionysiac elements and their influence on what, until then, would have been communication through incubation and Apollinean oracles of sortilege.[200] Or, at the suggestion of Parke and Wormell (1956a:12–13), the terms might be inverted, with Apollo taking over a primeval oracular seat of Γῆ, which already exhibited elements cognate with the ecstasy of maenadism (an 'ecstasy' that, even more than the Pythia's, was assumed to suspend rational thought and be identical or akin to madness).[201]

Where poets chose to draw on the original sacral dimensions of their profession, they described themselves as prophets (Pindar *Paian* 6.6, Bakkhylides *Epinician* 8.3). A striking, celebrated instance is Pindar fr. 150: μαντεύεο, Μοῖσα, προφατεύσω δ' ἐγώ. On first thought we might be inclined to focus on the apparent dichotomy between the Muse-as-*mantis* and the poet-as-prophet; but once we remember that the voice of the Muse is the song of the poet, this fragment turns out to reflect instead an early stage in which *mantis* and prophet were one and the same. Thus we are not surprised that Teiresias, the Homeric μάντις *par excellence*, is called by Pindar in the same breath 'Zeus' prophet' and

---

[198] It should be emphasized that, except for Lucan (*Pharsalia* 5.169–174, 190–193, 211–218) and the Christian polemicists, the Pythia was never portrayed as raving deliriously, emitting sounds that called for translation into intelligible speech by a mediating interpreter. In the context in which it is introduced, not even Herakleitos' famous fragment about the Sibyl's 'frenzied mouth' (DK 22 B92 = fr. 75 Marcovich, *apud De Pythiae oraculis* 397a) hints at any measure of unintelligibility. Thus Amandry (1950:120) calls "entièrement gratuite" the notion "des sons inarticulés ou des cris sauvages proférés par la Pythie et interprétés par le prophète" (cf. further 19–24).

[199] Cf. Plutarch *De Pythiae oraculis* 407c–d.

[200] Rohde 1925:287–291. Rohde recognized that, according to the Homeric poems, Apollo instructed his seers in an *art*—the art of explaining signs of the gods' will (1925:289; the original German refers to "die 'kunstmässige' Weissagung"). For the relationship between Apollo and Dionysos at Delphi, see Latte 1940.

[201] Dodds (1951:69–70), leaning heavily on Apollo's alleged Anatolian provenance (a theory now largely displaced or abandoned; cf. Burkert 1985:144–145), insisted that ecstasy in some form had always been part of the worship of this god.

'straight *mantis*'.[202] Therefore, Pindar sees himself as intermediary and herald of otherwise hidden divine utterances. The same shifting valance of terminology was in evidence at Delphi. In Aiskhylos' *Eumenides* 18–19, the Pythia calls Apollo both μάντις and Διὸς προφήτης: insofar as he speaks for Zeus, he is his 'prophet'; vis-à-vis the mortals who inquire of him, he is the *mantis*. But taking this logic a step further, the communication of Apollo's prophecy, too, can be similarly re-analyzed: viewed in relation to Apollo, the Pythia is commonly designated προφῆτις,[203] while from the point of view of the mediation of her own προφῆται, though most often simply called ἡ Πυθία, she could also be named μάντις[204] or πρόμαντις.[205] A further echo of this conceptual and terminological state of affairs is furnished by Plato's *Iōn*, where Homer, himself the first link in the chain of inspiration, is described as the ἑρμηνεύς of the Muse. Strictly speaking, as poetic 'composer' (to use our terms) he does not *interpret* a prior message (as the prophet would do with the Pythia's). He can only be said to 'interpret' the utterance of the goddess in the extended sense of the 'original composition' that wells up in his mind and constitutes the very substance of his song. In other words, there is, strictly speaking, no need for explanation and commentary in the ordinary sense, as if his poetry were to be something short of a 'primary text.' But insofar as he has access to and reveals the divine mind in song—i.e. insofar as we view him within the archaic framework—his poetry can be called revelatory, unfolding before our eyes divine truths that would otherwise remain obscure, unintelligible. In that restricted sense he can rightly be called the *hermēneus* of the Muse: he 'reveals the song' (see above, p. 229) and his ἔπη carry the full performative force of a divine utterance.[206]

---

[202] Διὸς ὑψίστου προφάταν ἔξοχον, | ὀρθόμαντιν Τειρεσίαν (*Nemean* 1.60–61).

[203] Cf., for example, Euripides *Iōn* 42, 321, 1322; Plato *Phaidros* 244a8; Plutarch *De Pythiae oraculis* 397c1, 397d1; Plutarch *De defectu oraculorum* 414b6–7.

[204] Aiskhylos *Eumenides* 29.

[205] Herodotos 6.66, 7.111, 7.141; Thoukydides 5.16.2; Pausanias 3.4.3–5, 10.5–6, and 10.13.8; Lucian *Bis accusatus* §1 and *Hermotimos* §60. Cf. Herodotos 8.135, where the 'prophet' of Apollo's temple at Ptŏion is called both πρόμαντις and προφήτης.

[206] This view is strongly supported by Most's survey of the fifth-century usage of ἑρμηνεύς and related words (Most 1986:308–311). He writes that "all the extant passages can be organised into a small number of rationally related groups once the basic meaning of the word has been grasped: it designates the agent that performs any act of translation of signification from one kind of language in which it is invisible or entirely unintelligible into another kind in which it is visible and intelligible" (1986:308). This remark brings into sharp focus my contention that, as ἑρμηνεύς of the Muse, the rhapsode in performance discharged a revelatory function. Cf. Leumann 1942:36–38 no. 73. Capuccino (2005:128–131) embraces Most's conclusions but, misled by Plato, untenably reduces the rhapsode's ἑρμηνεία to his mediating the poet's voice and thought: the voice, by making accessible to the festival public poetry that would otherwise remain beyond their "direct" reach (whatever 'direct' means); and the thought, by performing an exegesis which she defines not as understanding the sense and explaining it but as judging the mind of the poet and acting as his spokesman (131). On her latter point, see my observations

The role of the prophet might seem slightly different in that, notionally, his poetry derives—interprets—the Pythia's utterance. But we must remember that without him the inquirer receives no oracular response, and for this reason only conceptually does his prophecy enjoy a secondary textual status. And thus we are not surprised to find that there was at Delphi a tradition of oral composition, with its own particular formulaic emphases—emphases that were nonetheless traditional to the extent that the necessarily occasional nature of oracular consultation allowed for it.[207] Each inquirer posed his own peculiar question, but their number was high enough and the nature of many must have been repetitive enough that the answers can be safely assumed to have largely followed established patterns. Where such replies were in hexameter, this would have fostered a formulaic tradition of oral poetry responsible for rendering, on short notice, the appropriate answer to each questioner's concerns.

Even from the late, fourth-century perspective of Plato's *Iōn*, the role of the rhapsode vis-à-vis the epic poet remains analogous to the prophet's relationship to the Pythia. Sokrates, it is true, collapses the centuries-long chain of rhapsodic transmission into a privileged beginning, the inspired Homer, who in turn, in the here-and-now, derivatively 'inspires' the Ephesian rhapsode. This constitutes a synchronic recreation of the true diachronic process. Ion is merely a representative caricature of the best in rhapsodic craft that the late fifth-century Greece could offer. We have no reason to assume that the dialog's portrayal of Ion's professional practice is anything but typical of high-classical rhapsodic performance. Precisely because Ion, the Platonic character, is illustrative of the rhapsodic link in the chain that brings the experience of divine inspiration to bear on the festival audience, he represents the characteristic outcome of the traditional process of apprenticeship by which

---

below, p. 300 n. 29; on the former, it is enough to draw attention to the implausibility that the fourth-century Athenian public only had access to the Homeric poems that may qualify as "direct" at rhapsodic performances. *Pace* Capuccino (2005:127n98), quite apart from the fact that the average educated citizen must have committed to memory (in whichever textual form was available to him) many of the poems' celebrated passages, their very centrality to Greek *paideia* (Plato *Prōtagoras* 325e1–326a1 with Xenophon *Symposion* 3.5; cf. Isokrates 2.43) and their increasing availability in writing from the burgeoning book market suggest otherwise. To these facts testifies the well-known anecdote of Alkibiades' punching a teacher who failed to own a copy of Homer (Plutarch *Alkibiadēs* 7.1). On the Athenian book trade see Turner 1977:20–23 and Harris 1989:84–85. On vase depictions of scrolls see Immerwahr 1964 and 1973.

[207] Cf. McLeod 1961 and Andersen 1987. That writing was not used in delivering the answer is clear from Plutarch *De Pythiae oraculis* 397c (καὶ γὰρ εἰ γράφειν ἔδει μὴ λέγειν τοὺς χρησμούς …). Parke and Wormell (1956b:xxix) wisely underline the 'improvisatory' character of most responses (an 'improvisation' that I take here in the sense of oral traditional poetry). For a *formal* study of oracular verse, see Fontenrose 1978:166–195. Helpful analyses can also be found in Parke and Wormell 1956b and Crahay 1956 *passim*, which should be read with McLeod's caveat against source criticism in mind (1961:324–325).

aspiring rhapsodes were professionally trained. Some modern critics dispute the claim that the *Iōn* has anything to say about rhapsodic transmission *stricto sensu*. After all, Sokrates says nothing explicit about Ion's training and the role that other rhapsodes played in it. So, for example, Pelliccia (2003:106) writes that "the *Ion* says nothing about successive rhapsodic performers. The magnetized rings of Socrates' image represent 1) the god, from whom hangs 2) the poet, from whom hangs 3) the performer, from whom hangs 4) the audience. So the concept of rhapsodic succession is not available here for extrapolation." But once Greece had embraced the notion of a *prōtos heuretēs* of Homeric epic,[208] it is not unreasonable to consider a schematic outline that involves precisely the four elements enumerated by Pelliccia a faithful description of the full compass of the process of inspiration—a description that, if anything, elides as a matter of course, rather than precludes, the reality of rhapsodic succession. A superficially synchronic, hypothetical alternative without the notion of an authoritative poet that focused on the godward relationship would have featured three elements: god, rhapsode, and audience; had it sought instead to bring out the manward dimension, it would have included at least two rhapsodes so as to elucidate the *paradosis*, synchronic and diachronic, at the level of training. If Plato's interests and focus reflect neither alternative, one can hardly reproach the philosopher for evincing concerns typical of his age.

Pelliccia's criticism overlooks what is most significant in Plato's ostensibly synchronic account. Diachronic analysis should pay attention not to what agrees with our expectations of a fourth-century critique of the role of inspiration in composition and performance. Rather, it must attend to seemingly dissonant elements that confute our expectations by blending the categories of 'poet' and 'performer' and, in so doing, reveal the underlying diachronic process that the schematic outline abridges. For 'poet' and 'performer' I should rather write 'epic poet' and 'rhapsode,' since by and large Sokrates is strikingly and, I believe, deliberately silent about performers of other genres of poetry. In Sokrates' celebrated description of the magnetic chain (*Iōn* 533c9–535a2), only epic is attributed an explicit intervening link between poet and audience.[209] This is not to

---

[208] See above, p. 235.

[209] At 534d5 Sokrates mentions the paean by Tynnikhos of Khalkis 'which all sing' (ὃν πάντες ᾄδουσι, presumably in a sympotic context). But he never suggests that Tynnikhos inspires those who sing the paean and any inference to this effect is necessarily *ex silentio*. His focus then is solely on the author, who himself owns that his composition was 'an invention of the Muses' (εὕρημά τι Μοισᾶν). I submit that Sokrates owes his near complete failure to mention inspired performers *qua* performers in connection with non-epic genres not simply to what might be thought an accident, namely, that his interlocutor happens to be a rhapsode. Rather, Plato included him alone in the middle of the chain because traditional epic was the *only* genre that featured its performer, the rhapsode, as an indispensable link in its own *paradosis*. During the archaic period

say that other genres of poetry do not call for non-authorial performers; but in their cases Sokrates shows no interest in the second link and does not claim that the non-epic poet 'inspires' his performers.[210] This silence is significant and

this was also true of other genres to a greater or lesser extent, but in the high-classical period rhapsody remained the sole thoroughly traditional performance craft and, for this reason, rhapsodes were still the essential agents responsible for the diffusion, transmission, and preservation of epic poetry. This fact corresponds to the culturally paramount educational role that they and their repertoire played during the archaic and classical periods. Although not explicitly in view, one could argue that the (almost certainly amateur) singers of Tynnikhos' paean also experience a measure of the original divine influence that led to its creation. But if one insists on forcing them into the Platonic scheme, I believe that they would occupy the fourth slot of Pelliccia's list as audience more readily than the third as performers instrumental to the further enthusiasm of a wider audience.

[210] There is only one exception to this silence: Sokrates includes chorus dancers and their trainers and assistant trainers as potential links in the chain: καὶ ὥσπερ ἐκ τῆς λίθου ἐκείνης ὁρμαθὸς πάμπολυς ἐξήρτηται χορευτῶν τε καὶ διδασκάλων καὶ ὑποδιδασκάλων, ἐκ πλαγίου ἐξηρτημένων τῶν τῆς Μούσης ἐκκρεμαμένων δακτυλίων (536a4–7). But there are good reasons not to place rhapsodes in the same category with these dancers and their trainers. Plato has repeatedly drawn attention to dancing as an outward sign of inspiration. Hence the parallel of corybantic and Bacchic dancing at 534a, at which ἐμβῶσιν (534a3) and the winged poets (534b3–4) hint; and hence also the picture at 536b9 of Ion's soul as dancing (ὀρχεῖταί σου ἡ ψυχὴ) once he has heard a 'strain of Homer' (μέλος). This choral recasting of the Ephesian rhapsode immediately precedes Sokrates' observation that Corybantes are well supplied with dance figures and words when they hear the song (μέλος) peculiar to their inspiring deity. The realization that dancing serves Sokrates as leitmotif in his analysis of inspiration cautions us to consider carefully whether in fact the χορευταί of 536a5 are comparable to rhapsodes as derivative mediators of inspiration. I submit that they are not. Indeed, dancers and their trainers are introduced in the flow of the argument precisely where the audience belongs: the viewer is the last link (οὗτός ἐστιν ὁ θεατὴς τῶν δακτυλίων ὁ ἔσχατος 535e7–8); the rhapsode, the middle (ὁ δὲ μέσος σὺ ὁ ῥαψῳδὸς καὶ ὑποκριτής 535e9–536a1); the poet himself, the first (ὁ δὲ πρῶτος αὐτὸς ὁ ποιητής 536a1): 'Through all these the god draws the soul of men wherever he desires, hanging the power from one another; and just as from that stone, a very long chain hangs down, of dancers, trainers, and assistant trainers, suspended *sideways* (ἐκ πλαγίου) from the *links* that hang from the Muse' (536a1–7). Both implicitly, by their place in the argument, and explicitly, by Sokrates' express words, these choreuts are not portrayed as mediating agents of inspiration; for the philosopher himself says that they are suspended '*sideways* from the *links* that hang from the Muse' (my emphasis), a peculiarity that distinguishes them from poets and rhapsodes and that subordinates their 'oblique' experience to the vertical inspiration of the latter. The plural 'links' that hang from the singular 'Muse' further evince that Plato does not envision these dancers, like the rhapsode, as hanging immediately from a given poet (a single link) and at second remove from the Muse. When Sokrates focuses on poets generally as the 'first links' (536b1–2, *nota bene* the plural) he is careful to add that 'one poet is suspended from one Muse, another from another' (535a7–8). There is also the obvious fact that chorus trainers and undertrainers, although professionals of performance, do not 'perform' in the ordinary sense of the word. Only if we picture their trainees as their audience can we press them into the Platonic scheme: but, on balance, the relative order in which Sokrates lists them (χορευτῶν τε καὶ διδασκάλων καὶ ὑποδιδασκάλων 536a5) militates against this reading (one would expect 'dancers, undertrainers, and trainers' or else 'trainers, undertrainers, and dancers'). Given Sokrates' desire to emphasize poetry's impact on the hearer and, in particular, to elevate bodily motion to the level of a characteristic response, it is likely that the choreuts in question are not dithyrambic performers

provides the first remarkable clue that in its full compass the metaphor of the chain only fits the scenario of rhapsodic succession.

This contention finds further support in Plato's deliberate recourse, singularly meaningful for being unexpected, to language that softens the potential divide between Homer and Ion. His diction all but merges their circumstances, aims, and practices. The heart of Sokrates' rhetorical strategy lies in its peculiar movement back and forth between Homer and his rhapsode. This has often puzzled Plato's readers. Murray (1996:112) observes: "[W]ith the image of the magnet P[lato] shifts the focus of the dialogue away from the specific question of Ion's skill (or lack of it) as a rhapsode and moves on to the larger subject of poetic inspiration in general." Murray would have us believe that Ion serves as the narrative pretext for Plato's alleged focus on the poet. The text refutes her. At the opening of his speech Sokrates professes to be seeking an answer to the question not why some poets compose well but why Ion the rhapsode 'speaks well about Homer' (περὶ Ὁμήρου εὖ λέγειν 533d2). At its end, it is true, Ion agrees that 'it is by divine lot that the good poets express to us these things [that come] from the gods' (μοι δοκοῦσι θείᾳ μοίρᾳ ἡμῖν παρὰ τῶν θεῶν ταῦτα οἱ ἀγαθοὶ ποιηταὶ ἑρμηνεύειν 535a4–5); but Sokrates retorts: 'And do you then not, the rhapsodes, in turn express the [work] of the poets? ... Are you then not interpreters of interpreters?' (οὐκοῦν ὑμεῖς αὖ οἱ ῥαψῳδοὶ τὰ τῶν ποιητῶν ἑρμηνεύετε; ... οὐκοῦν ἑρμηνέων ἑρμηνῆς γίγνεσθε; 535a6–9). The chief rhetorical thrust is to merge epic poet and rhapsode and, in effect, to make them near-identical successive links in the *paradosis* that joins inspiring god to audience. It is no accident that epic poets are said to 'speak' (λέγουσι 533e7) 'all these beautiful poems' while 'full of the god and possessed'.[211] The language of composition

---

(who may well have sung and danced, as Pelliccia 2003:100n6 insists) but merely accompanied a *hyporkhēma* (534c4) with their dancing. Hyporchematic dancers did not sing, but mimicked with their σχήματα the words of the song (cf. Di Marco 1973–1974, esp. 330–331 and 332n16; Seaford 1977–1978:87–88; and D'Alessio 2007); and because of their strongly imitative performance, they would have furnished an excellent illustration of the ideal impact of derivative inspiration upon the audience. These considerations support the view that Sokrates' singling out the rhapsode as his sole example of 'the middle link' is hardly accidental; and discourage the notion that the choreuts of 536a5 provide yet another illustration of performers who mediate inspiration. Had Plato wanted to provide a clear parallel to rhapsodes as Pelliccia views them, he could easily have resorted to dramatic actors. In them we would indisputably have what Pelliccia seeks to affirm of the rhapsodes: performers whose inspiration is derivative and who by and large merely memorize the original script of a creative poet. Yet this ready alternative is precisely what is missing from the dialog. See below, p. 299 n. 22.

[211] Murray 1996: "The fact that P[lato] uses this verb of both composition and recitation suggests that he is not interested in distinguishing between the poet as composer and the rhapsode as reciter" (114–115).

is not entirely avoided,[212] but all the same the calibrated diction preponderantly equates to the fullest extent possible the classical rhapsode with his archetypal poetic source. This motivates the addition at 534b9 of λέγοντες to ποιοῦντες, in order that Sokrates may apply his explanation to Ion: 'Seeing, then, that it is not by art that they make and *say* many fine things about these matters, *just as you do about Homer*, but by divine lot, each one is able to do (compose?) well this thing alone to which the Muse has impelled him—one dithyrambs, another encomia, another dance-songs, another epic, another iambic verse' (my emphasis). It is a 'divine power' (θεία ... δύναμις) that moves Ion to speak well (εὖ λέγειν) about Homer (533d3); and 'by divine power' (θείᾳ δυνάμει) that 'they (the composers of dithyrambs, encomia, etc.) speak these things (ταῦτα λέγουσιν), since, if by art they knew how to speak well about one thing (καλῶς ἠπίσταντο λέγειν), then they would too about everything else' (534c5–7). The facts are so arranged that 'we may know that they themselves are not the ones speaking these things (οἱ ταῦτα λέγοντες) ... but the god himself is the one speaking (ὁ λέγων) and through these speaks to us (φθέγγεται)' (534d2–4). Plato's aims are clear: he demotes the artistic accomplishments of poets to make them mere mouthpieces of the god, like chanters of oracles and passively instrumental seers. It is precisely this demotion that levels poets and rhapsodes and equates them both as speakers of another's words, revealing their diachronic continuity. Even though the language of poetic making is not absent, the overriding impression upon the hearer is that poets are speakers of fine things, not much different from Ion the rhapsode who takes supreme pride in his ability to speak well about Homer.

If we seek to excavate the diachronic layers of Plato's description of epic performance in the classical period, we must attend to the rhetorical thrust of the text as it equates Homer, the archetypal poet, and Ion, the representative rhapsode. This realization demonstrates the legitimacy of reading the metaphor of the magnet as a picture of rhapsodic succession: the primary element of discontinuity between these two links is their respective proximity to the ultimate source, the inspiring divinity. But a difference of degree is precisely what one would expect for *successive* links. And Sokrates passes up the opportunity to play up Ion's greater remove from the Muse and to emphasize his derivative status vis-à-vis Homer.[213] In sum, I am not struck by the predictable elements of discontinuity between them; I am struck by how hard Plato works at equal-

---

[212] ποιοῦσιν, for example, appears at 534a2 soon after, picking up on the explicit subject, οἱ μελοποιοί. Cf. ποιεῖν at 534b5.

[213] One might counter, with Graziosi (2002:37–40), that ultimately it is the poet that the philosopher is after, and this explains why Sokrates demotes him to the level of the rhapsode and deliberately merges their respective profiles. But this is hardly an objection to my argument: such a rhetorical strategy can only succeed where its synchronic leveling has a *prima facie* claim to diachronic faithfulness.

izing and merging their profiles. One should not be surprised to find two additional elements that drive home this continuity. Plato has Ion acknowledge the
psychagogic impact of Sokrates' speech: Ion hints that Sokrates' performance
itself illustrates the 'inspiring' effect not of composing, but of speaking well
by divine lot. In so doing, he draws Sokrates' rhetoric within the productive
ambit of epic poets and their rhapsodes as accomplished speakers. Finally, when
Sokrates readies himself to explain why Ion speaks so well about Homer but
shows neither skill nor inclination with regard to Hesiod and Arkhilokhos, the
philosopher remarks: 'Yet further, I think … you have never seen a man who is
terrific at expounding Olympos or Thamyras or Orpheus or Phemios, the rhapsode from Ithaka, but concerning Ion the Ephesian [rhapsode] is at a loss and
cannot contribute what he rhapsodizes well or not' (533b5-c3). Once again, two
rhapsodes—the indisputably creative Phemios and even Ion himself!—are put
on a par with archetypal poets (Olympos, Thamyras, and Orpheus). The significance of this fact is the converse of the Homeridai's claim either to descend from
Homer or to perform his poetry by right of (rhapsodic) succession.[214] Continuity
is the key to Plato's argument, and rhapsodic succession its legitimate corollary.

   Pelliccia (2003:106n20) realizes that Sokrates' mention of Phemios the
rhapsode 'as also a composer of poetry' undermines his argument. His reply
is that the terminological distinction he alleges between the 'creative *aoidos*'
and the 'reduplicating rhapsode' "was not inflexible." To prove that despite
this flexibility a stark divide between them did exist, he holds counterfactually
that, if it had not, when Ion was pressed to say what he *qua* rhapsode was an
expert on, he should have replied with "the Odyssean discussions of Phemius
and Demodocus." It is not clear to me what he means by this: is he suggesting
that, if the notion of rhapsodic succession underlay the picture of the magnet,
we should have expected Ion to reply that he was good at 'singing κατὰ κόσμον'
what the Muse has taught him (θ 488–489)? What, then, about his claim that it
was worthwhile indeed to hear how well 'I have adorned Homer' (κεκόσμηκα τὸν
Ὅμηρον 530d6–7)? This will doubtless not satisfy those who, without proof or
warrant, assert with Pelliccia that "[Homer] is quoted as text" (Pelliccia 2003:107)
or assume that referring to Homeric poetry by the person 'Homer' *eo ipso* is
tantamount to "referring to the *text* of Homer" (109, Pelliccia's emphasis). I
submit instead that Ion's 'adorning' Homer does entail a compositional facet (at
this late stage, of relatively limited range); and that only if this facet is acknowledged can one make sense of the manner in which Plato apparently mixes activities that (to use our terms) seem to correspond, on the one hand, to poetic
composition (Homer's speaking well about various subjects) and, on the other,

---

[214] See below, p. 383.

to literary criticism (Ion's speaking well about Homer). This is the key to a right understanding of the dialog.[215] Ion indeed is called a ἑρμηνεύς of Homer; but it is misleading to affirm that, in this regard, Homer and other kinds of poets are contrasted "with their performers and interpreters" (Pelliccia 2003:107). Poets themselves are called the ἑρμηνῆς of the gods (534e4–5, 535a5). The scholar's main interpretive burden lies in establishing how poets in the exercise of their hermeneutic function differ, if at all, from rhapsodes in their 'interpretation' (530c3–4, 535a7–9). Merely assuming that there is a stark contrast begs the question. Note that *only* rhapsodes are said to 'interpret' their poets. This claim is made extensive to performers of no other genres.[216] I emphasized above that this is deliberate and not the accidental consequence of the dialog's contextual framework. Among performers, 'interpretation' was exclusively the purview of rhapsodes because they were the only traditional performers: their repertoire embraced a well-defined corpus of traditional poetry, and the practice of their trade involved more than the delivery of an unchanging script memorized by rote. Sokrates' observation that the rhapsode must interpret the poet's thought to his audience (τὸν γὰρ ῥαψῳδὸν ἑρμηνέα δεῖ τοῦ ποιητοῦ τῆς διανοίας γίγνεσθαι τοῖς ἀκούουσι 530c3–4) has a close parallel in Phaidros' statement, adduced by Pelliccia at 109, that he has not learned the words of Lysias' speech but will instead go through the general thought of his arguments.[217] The specificity of Phaidros' reference to τὰ ῥήματα is lacking in the case of Ion, the traditional rhapsode. Unlike the young admirer of Lysias, Ion does not seek to memorize his Homer word for word.

Pelliccia puts forward an unwarranted view, self-evident only to those who assume, rather than prove, that Plato's standpoint is *in toto* our own, when he writes that, according to the *Iōn*, "the poet creates something historically, as

---

[215] It is easy to illustrate this (to us, confusing) mixture. As a visible token of 'possession', Sokrates draws attention at 535b to the emotional impact of Homer's poetry on Ion. This comes about by his fine poetic declamation (ὅταν εὖ εἴπῃς ἔπη 535b2), not by a rhapsodic showpiece of literary criticism. And Ion's performance does not fail to pass on to the audience the inspiration he himself has derived from Homer (535d8–e3). The performance of epic verse is Sokrates' illustration of the magnetic chain, a metaphor ostensibly introduced to explain not Ion's inspired poetic declamation but his inspired 'criticism' of Homer, i.e. his inspired 'speaking about' Homer (533c5–8). And yet the metaphor seems at odds not only with its motivation but also with its application, for Sokrates goes on to apply it to Ion's Homeric commentary: οὐ γὰρ τέχνῃ οὐδ' ἐπιστήμῃ περὶ Ὁμήρου λέγεις ἃ λέγεις, ἀλλὰ θείᾳ μοίρᾳ καὶ κατοκωχῇ (536c1–2). Murray (1996:125) *ad loc.* observes: "[H]aving concentrated exclusively on the nature of Ion's performances of Homer, S[ocrates] now slips back into talking about Ion's ability to comment on the poetry."

[216] On the use of ὑποκριτής in the *Iōn*, see below, p. 299 n. 22.

[217] τῷ ὄντι γάρ, ὦ Σώκρατες, παντὸς μᾶλλον τά γε ῥήματα οὐκ ἐξέμαθον· τὴν μέντοι διάνοιαν σχεδὸν ἁπάντων, οἷς ἔφη διαφέρειν τὰ τοῦ ἐρῶντος ἢ τὰ τοῦ μή, ἐν κεφαλαίοις ἕκαστον ἐφεξῆς δίειμι (*Phaidros* 228d1–4).

a one time event, and the thing he creates survives permanently as an entity succeeding generations can come into contact with, take inspiration from, and, above all, perform. This created entity has of course usually been thought of as a text" (2003:107–108). Apart from the all-important fact that rhapsodes alone are explicitly singled out as susceptible *qua* performers of derivative inspiration by their archetypal poet,[218] the chief thrust of the dialog is to portray good poets themselves as mouthpieces of the god ('the god sang' through Tynnikhos 'the most beautiful song' 534e6–7), not as the agents of a defining one-time creation event. In effect, the making (ποιεῖν) is made notionally subservient to the poets' performing (ᾄδειν).[219]

[218] As already noted, one should expect derivative inspiration of performers *qua* performers only where *traditional* poetry is in view, an expectation the text meets.

[219] This is the point of view commonly taken by the Homeric lives. Pelliccia's attempt to preclude this standpoint by a recourse to the aorist aspect is misconceived. Surely γενέσθ[αι] in Pindar's *Nemean* 7.21 does not entail the reading "Odysseus' story became at a historical, one-time event greater than his suffering." Hesitant to press the notion that here Pindar is immediately ascribing the alleged instantaneous change "to the act of creation," Pelliccia writes that the remark refers instead "to a historical event (a change) quite explicitly tied to that act by the prepositional phrase διὰ τὸν ἀδυεπῆ γενέσθ' Ὅμηρον. Once this (allegedly) reputation-changing thing has been brought into being, it remains ever available for characterization in the present tense (ἔπεστι)" (Pelliccia 2003:108). But Pindar does not have any such discontinuous and instantaneous change in view. Race correctly translates the aorist as an English perfect, "Odysseus' story has become greater … ." It is rather what Smyth calls "aorist for perfect" (§1940), which "simply states a past occurrence" and is even "sometimes regarded as a primary tense." The past occurrence often appears under a complexive aspect (§1927), stated nakedly without reference to process, with the speaker's focus on the present condition that results from the verbal action. (Cf. the perfect of ποιέω at 531d2, 531d6, and 533b3. See, further, below, pp. 422ff.) This is the case here, where γενέσθ[αι] *per se* entails nothing at all about the process, gradual or instantaneous, behind it. What matters is that the speaker looking back realizes that today's circumstances constitute a changed state: at some point in the past the story of Odysseus had not exceeded what he had experienced; now it has. The aorist makes no necessary reference to an instantaneous, once-for-all happening. With Pelliccia, one could read it as a simple historical aorist—'the very day Homer wrote/sang the *Odyssey* the hero's reputation exceeded his life's experience'—but this is not the only available grammatical analysis and the notion that Pindar is alleging a discontinuous, all-at-one-time change stretches credulity: if not the act of creation, what is immediately in view? Pelliccia does not say. More superficially plausible is his claim that the ᾖσεν in Plato *Iōn* 535a1 portrays "the original interaction between the muse and the poet … as a one-time historical event" (2003:107). Perhaps so, although the verb 'to sing' draws attention to the (celebrated?) performance of the paean, not to Tynnikhos' composition, which Pelliccia assumes not to occur in performance but to precede it. Here too, however, the aorist may simply be complexive, conveying the bare verbal notion without regard to process (the aorist *per se* does not rule out, for example, repeated performances of the paean, whether or not such reperformances are historically plausible). A good example in English of a complexive preterite would be 'grew up' in 'when he grew up he left his home.' 'To grow' is intrinsically processual. A simple past naturally regards the verbal action complexively without denying the underlying process. A fussier speaker might prefer 'after he had grown up.' To return to Pelliccia's point, only he who has already committed himself to a particular view of the historical process envisioned can read in the aorist a necessary reference to a one-time historical event.

8.3.3 Oracular verse

It is true that oracular poetry was of comparatively low quality and that it was for this reason subjected to mockery and satire.[220] But it is remarkable that, even then, the belief in its divine origin was not surrendered and Apollo was made the butt of jokes by those who could not understand how the *Mousēgetēs* demonstrated less poetic skill than the very Muses he led and poets he inspired.[221] For my purposes, however, the important fact is that the unchanging divine answer, a fixed oracular utterance that could be neither modified nor retracted, was rendered into hexameter by practitioners of a peculiar kind of oral-traditional poetry, even when, conceptually, their mediation was elided in the interest of tracing the utterance immediately to the Pythia—as if the interposing of other human agents might compromise its infallibility.[222] It is notable that, even though iambic was occasionally used in contexts of abuse, when the oracle was not rendered in prose, hexameter was the meter of choice. To explain this fact some adduce the influence of Homeric epic and its cultural ascendancy. But I rather think it must have been the notion of a divine speech-act—a notion shared by epic and oracular poetry—that led both to use ἔπη for the notionally quoted utterance of the gods. This perspective views the system of Homeric poetry on its own archaic cultural terms—with its full sacral dimensions—rather than in the anachronistic terms of a cultural icon, Homer, who imposes his genre by dint of stylistic brilliance. Parke 1981 undertakes a distinguished, but ultimately flawed, attempt to explain the origin of oracular verse at Delphi in terms of the dominant prestige of epic poetry, viewed here strictly as a 'literary' phenomenon used or imitated for its register (elegance, solemnity, etc.).[223] Observing

---

[220] Cf. Todd 1939 and Henrichs 2003:216–222 (with bibliography).

[221] Thus, when Zeus asks Hermes to use greater solemnity in summoning the gods to a meeting, Lucian the satirist has Hermes answer him thus: ἀλλ' ἐποποιῶν, ὦ Ζεῦ, καὶ ῥαψῳδῶν τὰ τοιαῦτα, ἐγὼ δὲ ἥκιστα ποιητικός εἰμι· ὥστε διαφθερῶ τὸ κήρυγμα ἢ ὑπέρμετρα ἢ ἐνδεᾶ συνείρων, καὶ γέλως ἔσται παρ' αὐτοῖς ἐπὶ τῇ ἀμουσίᾳ τῶν ἐπῶν· ὁρῶ γοῦν καὶ τὸν Ἀπόλλω γελώμενον ἐπ' ἐνίοις τῶν χρησμῶν, καίτοι ἐπικρυπτούσης τὰ πολλὰ τῆς ἀσαφείας, ὡς μὴ πάνυ σχολὴν ἄγειν τοὺς ἀκούοντας ἐξετάζειν τὰ μέτρα (*Iuppiter tragoedus* §6). And in Plutarch *De Pythiae oraculis* 396c–d, amazed at the mean and cheap quality of oracular verse, Diogenianos complains: καίτοι μουσηγέτης ὁ θεὸς καὶ τῆς λεγομένης λογιότητος οὐχ ἧττον αὐτῷ [τὸ] καλὸν ἢ τῆς περὶ μέλη καὶ ᾠδὰς [καὶ] εὐφωνίας μετεῖναι καὶ πολὺ τὸν Ἡσίοδον εὐεπείᾳ καὶ τὸν Ὅμηρον ὑπερφθέγγεσθαι· τοὺς δὲ πολλοὺς τῶν χρησμῶν ὁρῶμεν καὶ τοῖς μέτροις καὶ τοῖς ὀνόμασι πλημμελείας καὶ φαυλότητος ἀναπεπλησμένους.

[222] Cf. Iokasta's speech in Sophokles' *Oidipous tyrannos* 707–725.

[223] This is not to deny that these associations existed at a later date. Aristotle, at any rate, considered the heroic meter 'solemn' (*Rhetoric* 1408b32–33). And though at first its use for dedicatory epigrams may have reflected the status of *epos* as the preeminent form of marked utterance—remember that archaic inscriptions speak in their own voice—doubtless in time it must have been fostered by the cultural prestige of epic poetry. Such epigrams, to be sure, are ideologically distant from the divine speech of oracles, but they still furnish a 'performance' of sorts,

that most of the oracles at Delphi down to the time of Alexander were in prose, he argues that the earlier poetic utterances owed their form to a cult of the Muses alleged by Plutarch to have existed of old at the oracular seat, a cult that was only a distant memory in his own time (cf. *De Pythiae oraculis* 402c–d).

Now, it is obvious that, even if we agree that there were fictitious hexameter oracles, versifying prophetic utterances must have been a genuine (if not uniform) practice: why else trouble yourself with meter if all knew that the Pythia only rendered the god's answers in prose? The question, then, is why the poetic form, and specifically the hexameter, should have been used at all. It will not do, I suggest, merely to argue that, during Delphi's earliest stages (no later than the eighth century BC), only the epic hexameter was available to mark speech as solemn against ordinary prose. For even if we grant *ex hypothesi* the priority of hexameter over lyric meters (a view many scholars no longer hold), we must still explain why and in what sense epic poetry was perceived as 'solemn'—i.e. what sort of marked speech it was—and why oracular utterance should have called for the kind of solemnity the epic style could lend. This reasoning, then, brings us back to the argument of this chapter, namely, that the archaic traditions of hexameter poetry were imbued with notions of quoted divine speech. If true, this view makes the use of hexameter poetry at Delphi entirely natural, and there is no longer any reason to make the versification of oracles immediately dependent on antecedent Homeric or Hesiodic traditions. In fact, the association of Apollo and the Muses is Panhellenic and, as far as I can tell, was already fully developed at the earliest stages of the extant oral traditions of epic. Therefore, to argue, as Parke does, that they owe their ties to Delphi, seems to me implausible on chronological and other grounds. Plutarch's passage is the sole witness to an alleged archaic cult of the Muses at Delphi; by itself, it falls far short of establishing this fact: in his own time there was no shrine left, only the story that once there had been one. On what grounds are we to believe it? Only two Simonidean fragments[224] that mention χέρνιβα are marshaled in support, and neither names Delphi explicitly. The proem of Hesiod's *Theogony* (vv. 3, 6) already shows the association of the Muses with fountains and streams of water,[225] and the debate whether the second fragment referred not to Kleiō but to Styx, as Eudoxos claimed, shows how precarious the

---

borrowing the voice of the viewer to utter statements marked by deixis (whether personal pronouns like με or ἐγώ or demonstrative adjectives like τόδε). See Baumbach et al. 2010 for a convenient entry point into the burgeoning field of the archaic and classical Greek epigram.

[224] *PMG* 577a and 577b (Simonides 72a and 72b).

[225] This association should not be confused with the notion, which I believe erroneous, that originally the Muses were nymphs of the mountains and the streams (cf. Farnell 1896–1909:5.434–435), a view embraced by Parke (1981:104) that would require Wackernagel's etymology μοῦσα < *μοντ-ια, with *μοντ- cognate with Latin *mōns* (see *DELG* s.v. μοῦσα).

link is between the first passage and the water that flowed from the oracle of Γῆ. I do not see how these fragments are supposed to prove the existence of a shrine to the Muses predating the 'arrival' of Apollo in Delphi. Even if such a shrine existed (which is far from certain), and even if it was placed in so central a location of the sanctuary (where else should we expect the worship of goddesses subordinate to Apollo but in the shadow of his temple?), what could prove its temporal priority over the worship of the god? It seems to me much more probable that a Panhellenic association of Apollo with the Muses that was both independent from the cult at Delphi and reinforced by the use of the hexameter for the composition of oracles should have found cultic expression, if anywhere at all, at the Panhellenic oracle of Delphi.[226] Besides Plutarch's doubtful testimony, only Pausanias' description (10.19.4) of the pediments of the fourth-century BC temple of Apollo offers further evidence of the ties at Delphi between the Muses and their *Mousēgetēs*: it featured Apollo with Artemis and Leto, the Muses, the setting Sun, and Dionysos with the Thyiades. But this falls short of proving the existence of an archaic shrine to the Muses, or else we should expect, for example, pedimental depictions of Γῆ and Athena, and shrines to Leto and the Sun. It is clear, instead, that the choice of sculptures draws on traditional artistic devices (the setting Sun), Panhellenic myth (the god's mother and sister), and a certain representational symmetry (Apollo and Dionysos, each with his own cortège).

Neither is there support to be found in Plutarch's *Quaestiones convivales* 744c, where his brother observes that the Delphians held the Muses to be three,[227] making them correspond to the notes that define musical intervals (οἱ τὰ διαστήματα παρέχοντες ὅροι). Parke (1981:105) relates this to the "names of the three strings of the primitive lyre," presumably because of 745b, which seems to present φθόγγοι and χορδαί as alternatives. But I believe that these are not contrasted as two *different* options, but are near synonyms naturally juxtaposed for redundancy.[228] That this numeric correlation is said to associate the Muses with τὸ ἁρμονικόν (744c) shows that strings are not in view. In any case, as Parke admits, this equation betrays late schematism and cannot be original. Though a three-string archaic lyre probably did exist, there is reason to

---

[226] Since Delphi was the only truly Panhellenic oracle of Apollo in archaic Greece, it was there alone that the Panhellenic association between Apollo and the Muses was likely to find cultic expression at so early a stage. This explains the absence of a similar cult at other oracles of Apollo (assuming now, for the sake of argument, that the Muses had a shrine at Delphi).

[227] Cf. above, p. 211.

[228] Cf. LSJ s.vv. φθόγγος II.2.b and χορδή II.1.b. Trypho's use of φθόγγοι and χορδαί to parse Lamprias' ὅροι is natural and cannot be pressed for information on the historical development of the lyre.

question that it was widely used or ever held a central position.[229] And if so, why would the number of the Muses be related to the strings of a marginal instrument?[230] Furthermore, the three-string lyre was still in (limited) use in late antiquity (Stella 1978:278), and, at any rate, in music theory the three tones were of abiding significance: thus a schema 'three Muses ⇔ three strings' need not have drawn at all on old lore. But one might argue that, all by itself, the claim that the Delphians, in defiance of Hesiod's canonical number, had taught that the Muses were three (even though the report passes along admittedly late speculation as genuine) might be reason enough to believe that such indeed was the archaic Delphic doctrine.[231] But I wonder, rather, if the triad of Muses might not reflect the indisputably archaic veneration accorded to the Θριαί, a triad of Delphic goddesses, probably the Corycian Nymphs, which, Larson 1995 argues, lie behind the famous 'bee maidens' of the *Hymn to Hermes*.[232] It would not be surprising if the veneration rendered at the Corycian cave had also once been represented at the oracular site itself (though no longer so by the date of

---

[229] I am using 'lyre' in a non-technical sense to stand for φόρμιγξ and κίθαρις. Cf. Guillemin and Duchesne 1935:118.

[230] In her survey of the evolution of the lyre from late Bronze-Age down to geometric times, Stella (1978:277–292) writes that the number of its strings ranged from three to eight. But whereas the hepta- and octachord (with 'chord' designating the 'number of strings', not 'interval') were predominant during the late Mycenaean and Minoan palatial cultures, geometric depictions almost always feature four strings (see pp. 280 and 288). Stella dates the dominance of three strings to remote Cycladic times, but cites in support only the famous Keros harpist (now at the Athens' National Archaeological Museum, no. 3908) and other cycladic fragmentary statues (280, with 280n9). As far as I can see, there is no firm basis on which to infer the number of strings the *trigōnon* might have featured (cf. Zervos 1957 figs. 316, 317, 333–334). Stella's view, then, is only a conjecture, and, with Evans (see immediately below), one might just as well assume that the strings were four (or more!). Now, though there are occasional instances of late Bronze-Age trichord lyres, they are mostly in seals, where limitations of size and their practical nature might have encouraged an artificial simplification of detail (though a gifted artist working on an item of significance may succeed in representing even an octachord; cf. Evans 1928:834, fig. 551). Thus, Evans 1928 accords clear priority to the seven strings (834), calling the three-string "cursive versions" on clay documents (see his fig. 550 c,d) "secondary forms," adding that "too much importance must not be attached to these secondary forms" (cf. 834n3). [Minoan representations of eight strings are common; Evans thinks this is but the doubling of a cycladic tetrachord *trigōnon* (1928:835; cf. Strabo 13.2.4 and other ancient *loci* in Barker 1984–1989:1.49) and he observes that the octa- and heptachords are one and the same, since consecutive tetrachords would have had one tone in common.] As to the geometric lyre, most vases depict it with four strings (cf. Deubner 1929; see also Wegner 1968:2–16, esp. 5 with fig. 5; Stella 1978 pl. LI, figs. 82 and 83; and Guillemin and Duchesne 1935, figs. 26, 29, 30, 32, and 35). Wegner (1968:12) sums up the data well by concluding the the Iron-Age lyre had four strings, and adds that examples of apparent two- and three-string instances "bieten keine Veranlassung, damit zu rechnen, daß es im wirklichen Gebrauch Saitenspiele mit geringerer Saitenbespannung als diejenige der kanonischen Phorminx gegeben habe" (14).

[231] So Teodorsson 1989–1996:3.354.

[232] See above, p. 206 n. 120.

the hymn, cf. line 556). In this connection it is curious that the hymn calls the maidens μοῖραι or σεμναί (depending on the ms.), and that in the dialog that concerns us Plutarch should also link the Muses with the three Fates (*Quaestiones convivales* 745b). To sum up: the veneration of a triad of female goddesses, variously identified by competing traditions, is too entrenched at Delphi to argue with any degree of certainty that the cult of the Muses was archaic and original to the locale, older than the 'arrival' of Apollo (a chronological priority that might lend plausibility to the view that oracular poetry took up the hexametric form in strict dependence on the antecedent poetic tradition of epic).[233] Thus, I conclude that use at Delphi of hexameters to compose its poetic oracles was not derivative of the Homeric or Hesiodic oral traditions of epic, but a related consequence of the notional association of epic diction with divine speech.[234]

---

[233] Note, moreover, that the association of Apollo and the Muses is already attested by A 603–604 and θ 488.

[234] This conclusion would be weakened if one could show that the use of verse at Delphi was exceptional and without parallel at other oracular seats. This is Parke's contention: that versification at Delphi was due to a historical accident found nowhere else, namely, the geographical coincidence of an ancient cult of the Muses with the later prophetic seat of Apollo (Parke 1981). Reports of oracular verse at other locations would involve either be late fabrications or, if true, instances of the influence exerted by Delphi on lesser oracles. Certainty here, as often, is not possible, but Parke's case is not as persuasive as he would make it. After all, there are only two contemporaneous *comparanda*: Dodona and Didyma in Miletos (Parke 1981:102). But from Dodona we have no preserved archaic answers, only a few questions on lead tables which, unsurprisingly, are in prose (cf. Amandry 1950:171–172 and Parke 1967:110–111; more generally, Guarducci 1967–1978:4.74–122, De Gennaro and Santoriello 1994:391–394, and Lhôte 2006). Nothing can be concluded from this: was there ever a *verse* question posed at Delphi? (Cf. Dieterle 1999.) As to Didyma, we have the added complexity of the possible interference of pre-Hellenic Anatolian practices. There are also fourth-century BC reports of one response in hexameters and an iambic line. One might, with Parke (1981:103), dismiss these as late fabrications: this is entirely possible, but we cannot be certain. As to the three extant fragmentary oracular responses, Parke (1981:102) affirms with great confidence that "of two it can safely be said that they are not in verse." And "the third ... can at least be identified as not in hexameters." But matters are not that simple: I note with interest that one of them is in fact analyzed as elegiac by Roehl (1882:132 no. 489). The fragment is now lost, but the surviving squeeze can be found in Harder 1958 no. 11). Harder assumes the integrity of the inscription along its left edge: it would then have to be prose. But after inspecting the squeeze I am not convinced that his view must be accepted, and Roehl's solution cannot be discounted. Now, it is true that an oracle in elegiac would be exceptional (cf. Apuleius *Metamorphoses* 4.33!), but given its transition from non-Hellenic to Hellenic control, I would not think it impossible that, in adopting a Greek meter, Didyma would have experimented with one cognate with hexameter, which had been recently developed in Ionia and was surely current in the compositional practice of local poets. (Fontenrose 1988:180 no. 2 follows Harder. On the meter of oracles cf. Pomtow 1881. I have not been able to locate his obviously relevant *Ad oraculorum quae exstant graecorum editionem prolegomena*, published by Weidmann.) The second of Parke's fragmentary oracular responses, Kawerau and Rehm 1914 no. 132, is inscribed on both sides: side A alone indisputably contains the god's answer, ΘΕΟΣΕΠΕΝ (*sic*, see above, p. 121 n. 47), and, as the editor notes, it fits the iambic trimeter; side B does not, but it is by a later scribe and merely contains sacrificial regulations that, though surely sanctioned by the god, are not part

8.4 Plato and Inspired Poetry

I would like to close this chapter by returning to Plato for a last but very important insight into the ways in which the notional fixity of the Homeric tradition had an impact on its performance. The *Iliad* and the *Odyssey* make clear that ὑποκρίνεσθαι was used in the context of oracular hermeneutics.[235] Though we do not have any pre-classical surviving instances of ὑποκριτής (its *nomen agentis*), the verb is regularly used by Homeric poetry for the interpretation of signs and dreams (M 228 ο 170 τ 535 555; cf. H 407 β 111). In view of the strong association of ὑποκρίνομαι with the interpretation of omens and oracles, and given the notional fixity that attached to divine utterances—to the ἔπη of the Muse and Apollo—the verb also acquired the same connotation of conceptual fixity and, where used, it conveyed that things must necessarily be as they are, or will surely come to pass exactly as predicted. An important example is Penelope's dream-omen. This instance is significant, because the plot's notional fixity is emphatically asserted by the self-interpreting omen. Penelope challenges Odysseus to interpret the dream, requiring him, in effect, to agree or disagree with the tradition of poetry of which he is the protagonist. The narrator quotes Penelope, who quotes the speaking eagle; Odysseus welcomes the challenge and aligns himself with the tradition: 'Lady, in no way is it possible to bend this dream aside and give it another meaning' (ὦ γύναι, οὔ πως ἔστιν ὑποκρίνασθαι ὄνειρον | ἄλλῃ ἀποκλίναντ[α] τ 555–556). The meaning is fixed, and, hence, interpretation can only reperform the quotation.[236]

But consider now Plato's use of ὑποκριτής as a label for the rhapsode[237] in the light of the tension, expounded above (p. 275), between one who is a primary, revelatory *hermēneus* of the god, unfolding the divine will before his audience, and one who is a *hermēneus* of the poet in a derivative, exegetical sense—who, notionally speaking, not only quotes the ἔπη of the poet but also unfolds their meaning. (The distinction turns on whether the *hermēneus* mediates between god and man or between man and man.) Diachronically speaking, the import of this tension is that Plato's rhapsode straddles the shift between the divine Muse as fountain of inspiration and the human poet as the source of the songs

---

of the oracular utterance. (Cf. Fontenrose 1988:180–181 no. 3.) We are left, then, with Kawerau and Rehm 1914 no. 178, which, I agree, must be prose (cf. Fontenrose 1988:179–180 no. 1). I conclude, therefore, that the 'exceptionality' of Delphi (in Parke's sense; see 1981:102) cannot be established.

[235] See below, pp. 297f.

[236] For more on this dream and the mentality of fixity associated with ὑποκρίνεσθαι, see Nagy 2003:21–38, esp. 24–25.

[237] See below, pp. 298f.

he reperforms for his audience.[238] Belonging as he does to a stage when Homeric poetry is relatively less fluid and, insofar as notionally fixed, ascribed to the authorship of Homer, there is a sense, then, in which the Platonic rhapsode finds in his designation as ὑποκριτής a label that comprehends not only the reception and more or less stable reproduction of relatively fixed material, but also his recomposition of what is relatively more fluid. This latter material can be seen under a dual perspective: not only as a ἑρμηνεία of the Muse, in that it is a creative reappropriation of the tradition (a true recomposition in performance), but also as a ἑρμηνεία of the poet, for the rhapsode elaborates upon the relatively more fixed traditional material (notionally ascribed now to the archetypal poet), developing the story through thematic expansion and contraction, 'ornamenting' the plot (with additional, non-essential themes), and providing transitional passages that join episodes whose text is relatively less fluid.

It is in this sense that the rhapsode can truly be called a ὑποκριτής of Homer. In time, as the preponderance of the poetic material grew increasingly fixed, the explanatory function of the rhapsode might have adapted correspondingly, and his personal contribution might have taken to prose comments, not unlike in kind, if perhaps in quality, to the sophistic lectures that came to dominate the cultural scene in late fifth-century Athens. This would spell a direct line between the rhapsodic ὑπόκρισις and the sophistic ἐπιδείξεις to which the former were often unfavorably compared.[239]

Plato's slant in the *Iōn* is now clear: by collapsing poetic and rhapsodic ἑρμηνεῖαι, and exclusively choosing as his model of oracular delivery a wild and ecstatic Pythia, rather than the self-possessed prophet, he upsets the dominant archaic paradigm of poetic inspiration, opting instead for a comparatively late minority one that made irrational *mania* the performer's *modus operandi*. No wonder Ion objected!

---

[238] In actual performance practice the distinction is a matter of degree, for in either case there is some measure of recomposition in accordance with canons of traditional oral poetic production.
[239] See below, pp. 299ff.

PART III

RHAPSODIC PERFORMANCE IN HIGH-CLASSICAL ATHENS

9

The Rhapsode in Classical Athens

9.1 Of Transcripts and Scripts

"[T]HE DRUIDS HAD THEIR OWN COURSE OF TRAINING, in which some pupils remained for up to twenty years, 'so that they could learn by heart a vast number of verses which had not been committed to writing'."[1] So wrote Friedrich August Wolf in his 1795 epoch-making *Prolegomena to Homer*, to which he added plaintively: "How I wish that the Greeks had transmitted to us even that much about their own bards and rhapsodes!"[2] The stark truth is that we have no direct testimony about the life, training, or practice of rhapsodes in Greece; no handbook of ῥαψῳδική, no reliable biographical information about famous rhapsodes, and little that goes beyond anecdotal evidence regarding their methods, the rules under which they competed, and society's estimation of their profession. Therefore, any attempt to construct a view of their trade and its evolving practices must of necessity be conjectural. This does not mean, however, that such an endeavor is pointless; rather, it is irresistible, for any view of the Homeric Problem and the respective roles of orality and writing in classical Athens must be partially based on, and tested against, our conception of these, the preeminent Homeric performers of the time.

This chapter and the ones that follow study the figure of the rhapsode and his performance from the late archaic period down to Hellenistic and Roman imperial times.[3] Our sources are literary, documentary (i.e. papyri), and epigraphical. Some bear direct witness to various aspects of this trade; others

---

[1] The English translation is taken from Wolf 1985:109–110, chap. xxiv. Wolf is quoting from (and slightly modifying) Caesar's *Bellum Gallicum* 6.14. His Latin (from the second edition) runs as follows: "De his quidem postremis [sc. Druidibus] Caesar et Mela referunt, propriam eorum fuisse disciplinam, in qua nonnulli ad vicenos annos permanserint, *ut magnum numerum versuum ediscerent, litteris non mandatorum*" (Wolf 1876:62, his emphasis).

[2] "Quam vellem tantillum nobis Graeci tradidissent de vatibus et rhapsodis suis!" (Wolf 1876:62).

[3] Important works on the rhapsode and rhapsody include Aly 1914; Patzer 1952; Sealey 1957; Ritoók 1962; Ford 1988; Boyd 1994; Collins 2001a and 2001b. See also the bibliography cited in chapter 10 below, pp. 331ff.

do no more than hint at one or another relevant datum. My goal is to fit them all into a larger picture using plausible conjectures and reconstructions. But my treatment aims not just at the descriptive; for the rhapsode is the protagonist of a momentous cultural drama: the evolution of ancient Greece away from primal habits of orality towards cultural modes that depended increasingly on the written word. Thus, I am especially interested in probing the consistency of what we know (or can reasonably reconstruct) about the culture of classical Greece with a theory that makes *performance* largely responsible for the fixation of the text of the Homeric poems.

My point of departure is Gregory Nagy's proposal of a textual fixation[4] of the *Iliad* and the *Odyssey* in five stages spanning a continuum in which, at one end, writing plays no role at all, while, at the other, a largely uniform written text of the poems is slavishly memorized and adhered to in performance.[5] My particular focus here is in the transition from what Nagy calls 'transcripts' to 'scripts.' These are his definitions: "A transcript can be a record of performance, even an aid for performance, but not the equivalent of performance";[6] a script, in turn, is "a narrower category, where the written text is a prerequisite of performance."[7] If we assume that rhapsodes down to the fifth century BC trained and performed without the aid of writing—transcripts may have been in limited circulation, but the professional himself did not rely on them—what intellectual trends and cultural developments might have encouraged their increasing reliance on written records (whether self-produced or acquired through the burgeoning book trade), so that in time (towards the late fourth century and beyond) their performance largely depended on scripts memorized and rehearsed for delivery? Strictly speaking, training and performance that do not use writing might still depend on the slavish memorization of a fixed, but orally transmitted, uniform text, possibly written down and archived where it may be consulted and appealed to by disagreeing schools of performers.[8]

---

4 By 'textual fixation' I mean the gradual process of fixation, not necessarily in writing, of the text of the poems as to their themes, sequence, and form. This objective process is not to be confused with the emic 'notional fixity' considered in section 7.1 (pp. 173ff. above). Notional fixity contributes nonetheless to textual fixation in various ways, for example, by facilitating the rise of 'Homer,' the individual author. By 'objective process' I mean a measurable, actual fixation from the perspective of a cultural outsider.

5 First articulated in Nagy 1981, it is developed further in Nagy 1996b:41–42 and 1996c:107–113.

6 Nagy 1996c:112.

7 Nagy 1996c:112

8 I am neither conceding the intrinsic likelihood nor the historical plausibility of such a scenario. Nor is it material to it, logically speaking, whether one can conceive that the declamation of so long a poem as, for example, the *Iliad* could have accurately reflected, down to its phraseology, a written text that for many generations was only—or primarily—transmitted by word of mouth.

For reasons of historical plausibility,[9] however, and in agreement with Nagy's evolutionary model of textual fixation, I assume instead that at the transcript stage Homeric bards composed their poems in performance using traditional language, themes, and sequence, and that their technique produced a measure of variation consistent with long-standing traditions of composition and delivery. In other words: there was no controlling written ur-text, and memory, always of capital importance, was primarily not an instrument of slavish reproduction, but an aid to a traditional sort of creativity that we may call, not without paradox, 'traditional improvisation.'

In this and the following chapters I explore the transition from transcripts to scripts as follows: first, by situating rhapsodes (ῥαψῳδική) against actors (τραγική) and orators (ῥητορική), highlighting the connections that existed between these three performance trades and their professions, connections recognized already in antiquity; second, by focusing on orators and rhetorical theory in the late fifth- and fourth-century BC Athens and on the cultural forces responsible for the, at the time, polemical introduction of writing into their practice: I consider the ancient terms of this debate and the causes that brought about this disputed development; third, by arguing that, after making the necessary generic adjustments, one can recognize how similar social trends and expectations impinged on rhapsodes and their art, and to this we owe, at least in part, the move from transcripts to scripts in the performance of the Homeric epics. In Part IV (pp. 435ff.) I also examine the late fourth-century age of Lykourgos, the Athenian statesman, and of Demetrios of Phaleron, the

---

A scheme for the textual fixation of the *Iliad* and the *Odyssey* on such terms is very different from the one espoused in these pages.

9   Part I of this book offers a critique of several theories variously adduced to support a conjectural early-archaic recording of the Homeric poems in writing. Proponents of an early fixation of the text resort to speculations that depend on cultural discontinuities and exceptional circumstances. For example, the existence of a ruler of great power and means who realizes the outstanding quality of 'Homer's' performance and insists on owning a written transcript of it. As we have seen, sometimes even the invention of alphabetic writing is tied to the recording of Homeric poetry. The ruler's literacy is tacitly assumed, as is his interest in the written artifact as a natural and culturally obvious aid to memory. Furthermore, advocates of such views must grant the availability of a sufficiently abundant substrate (papyrus? wood? stone?) and the existence of a scribe capable of writing down thousands upon thousands of lines. The poet, never before engaged in such an ambitious recording session, must have been able to adapt to a much slower performance rate than the one he was accustomed to; and yet, somehow, he excelled, without the encouragement of an ordinary audience, and without losing his train of thought while the scribe made haste to inscribe every word he heard. And if this chain of hypotheses is not sufficiently tenuous, one must explain how the diffusion of this extraordinary cultural artifact over so large a geographical extension could have been so effective as to arrest, soon thereafter, a centuries-old habit of composition in performance and impose the uniform, now fixed, text on dozens of itinerant rhapsodes who roamed the Mediterranean basin and almost certainly must have been illiterate. I find reconstructions of this sort difficult to believe.

autocratic pro-Macedonian ἐπιμελητής, both historical figures who, I believe, reinforced the cultural dynamics already at work, hastening the transition from the transcript to the script stage of rhapsodic performance. I end with a survey of the classical, Hellenistic, and Roman imperial records, documentary and epigraphical, on epic performers, many of whom will have declaimed the Homeric poems in a largely fixed, canonical form, with very little, if any, exercise of compositional creativity; and, to that extent, they will have limited their personal artistry largely to the manner of delivery before the audience—voice, dress, gestures—at times, but for the absence of a mask, nearly indistinguishable from the stage presence of tragic and comic actors.

9.2 The Rhapsode as Ὑποκριτής

It was a commonplace of classical antiquity that tragedy had its roots in epic;[10] it is therefore only natural that the acting profession would have looked back

---

[10] Plato makes frequent reference to this: τῶν ποιητῶν οἱ ἄκροι τῆς ποιήσεως ἑκατέρας, κωμῳδίας μὲν Ἐπίχαρμος, τραγῳδίας δὲ Ὅμηρος (Theaitētos 152e4–5), where ἄκροι may refer to Homer's chronological priority (note his pairing with Epikharmos, who some ancient traditions of scholarship, e.g. Aristotle Poetics 1448a33–34, placed at the source of comedy; cf. Pickard-Cambridge 1927:353–363, esp. 355n3); or else it may denote his superior skill (so LSJ s.v. III.1), as other passages suggest (pace Gudeman 1934:109). Passages from the Republic further underline the point: ἔοικε μὲν γὰρ [sc. Ὅμηρος] τῶν καλῶν ἁπάντων τούτων τῶν τραγικῶν πρῶτος διδάσκαλός τε καὶ ἡγεμὼν γενέσθαι (595b10–c2); μετὰ τοῦτο ἐπισκεπτέον τήν τε τραγῳδίαν καὶ τὸν ἡγεμόνα αὐτῆς Ὅμηρον (598d7–8); οἱ γάρ που βέλτιστοι ἡμῶν ἀκροώμενοι Ὁμήρου ἢ ἄλλου τινὸς τῶν τραγῳδοποιῶν (605c10–11); συγχωρεῖν [χρὴ] Ὅμηρον ποιητικώτατον εἶναι καὶ πρῶτον τῶν τραγῳδοποιῶν (607a2–3). It may well be, as Naddaff (2002:40–41) remarks, that Sokrates emphasizes (even exaggerates) the similarities between epic and tragedy to open the way for his own 'atragic' reading of the Iliad (cf. esp. Naddaff 2002:144n10). But this rhetorical strategy can only succeed if Homer as the father of tragedy is already a cultural commonplace. We remember, of course, Aiskhylos' celebrated comment (apud Athenaios 7.347e) that his tragedies were 'slices from Homer's great dinners' ([Αἴσχυλος] τὰς αὑτοῦ τραγῳδίας τεμάχη εἶναι ἔλεγεν τῶν Ὁμήρου μεγάλων δείπνων); this statement probably amounts to more than an acknowledgment that his μῦθοι were cognate with Homer's. A broader reading indeed is supported by Aristotle's parallel between Homer and tragedy (Poetics 1448b31–1449a2), which makes clear that their point of contact is a proportionality (ἀνάλογον) of form (σχῆμα): ὥσπερ δὲ καὶ τὰ σπουδαῖα μάλιστα ποιητὴς Ὅμηρος ἦν (μόνος γὰρ οὐχ ὅτι εὖ ἀλλὰ καὶ μιμήσεις δραματικὰς ἐποίησεν), οὕτως καὶ τὸ τῆς κωμῳδίας σχῆμα πρῶτος ὑπέδειξεν, οὐ ψόγον ἀλλὰ τὸ γελοῖον δραματοποιήσας· ὁ γὰρ Μαργίτης ἀνάλογον ἔχει, ὥσπερ Ἰλιὰς καὶ ἡ Ὀδύσσεια πρὸς τὰς τραγῳδίας, οὕτω καὶ οὗτος πρὸς τὰς κωμῳδίας. (Cf. Lucas 1968:77 ad 1448b35–36.) This cultural topos recurs so frequently among later writers that it can hardly be assumed to go back to the distortion and conflation by Plato of two genres generally perceived as independent. Thus, for example, the Homeric scholia to A 332: πρῶτος δὲ Ὅμηρος πρόσωπα κωφὰ παρήγαγεν εἰς τὴν τραγῳδίαν; and to Z 466: πρῶτος παῖδας εἰσάγει τῇ τραγῳδίᾳ; so also [Plutarch] De Homero 213: ἡ τραγῳδία τὴν ἀρχὴν ἔλαβεν ἐξ Ὁμήρου. Cf. Gudeman 1934:109 for further witnesses (but note that Philostratos Vita Apollonii 6.11 does not refer to Homer, as he claims, but to Aiskhylos). See also Schmid 1908 on the scholia to the Iliad and dramatic μίμησις.

to the rhapsode as a model. Even the term for 'actor', ὑποκριτής, reflects this relationship. Homeric usage connects the cognate verb with the interpretation of signs and dreams.[11] One can therefore affirm that originally ὑποκριτής and ὑποκρίνεσθαι must have had their home among μάντεις, προφῆται, and others responsible for interpreting divine oracles to inquiring seekers. As Else (1959:101–102) notes, the activity denoted by ὑποκρίνεσθαι often took place in the context of rendering an interpretive judgment in reply to a questioner's concern.[12] Koller (1957:102) agrees in substance, glossing the verb as 'to decide for, explain, or clarify to someone else'. The derivatives ὑπόκρισις and ὑποκριτής are only attested much later. The former, first in Pindar's fr. 140b Sn-M,[13] sometimes paraphrased 'in the manner of', already shows role-playing as an established meaning.[14] The latter first appears in the inscriptional *Fasti* (IG II/III² 2318) in connection with the actors' contest instituted in 449 BC at the Dionysia;[15] and a few years later in Aristophanes' *Wasps* 1279, dated to 422 BC, where its meaning cannot be settled by an appeal to either its context or the scholia.[16] ὑποκρίνεσθαι is arguably not a natural choice for stage acting: neither

11 See below, pp. 647ff. The later acceptation 'to answer'—or something that approaches it—does not lack representation in the diachronic layering of the poems (e.g. at Η 407, though cf. Nagy 2003:21–22). Koller (1957:101) believes that this was a semantic development largely restricted to the Ionic dialect and only rarely present in Athenian authors as a literary affectation (e.g. Thoukydides 7.44.5). I take a somewhat different view of this matter.

12 See below, pp. 647ff., for a critique of Else's formulation.

13 The relevant lines are as follows: ἐγὼ μ[‖ παῦρα μελ[ι]ζομεν[‖ [γλώ]σσαργον ἀμφέπω[ν ˪ἐρε- ‖ θίζ˩ομαι πρὸς ἀϋτᾴ[ν ‖ ˪ἁλίο˩υ δελφῖνος ὑπ˪όκρισιν˩, ‖ ˪τὸν μὲν ἀκύμονος ἐν πόντου πελάγει ‖ αὐλῶν ἐκίνησ' ἐρατὸν μέλος˩ (fr. 140b.11–17). I quote the translation in Henderson 1992: "I (however indeed, while hearing him) playing his brief (songs), and fostering (...) with a loud-sounding tongue, am provoked in response to it, acting like a dolphin of the sea, whom the lovely tune of flutes has excited in the expanse of a waveless sea" (148).

14 The construction is best understood as an accusative in apposition to a sentence; cf. Schwyzer *GG* II.86, under 'Akkusativ der Satzapposition.' For the interpretation of this fragment, see Wilamowitz-Moellendorff 1922:500–502, Fileni 1987, and Henderson 1992. As to Lesky's contention that this text once and for all banishes the possibility that originally ὑποκριτής might have meant 'answerer' (Lesky 1956:475), I must confess with Page 1956 that I do not understand the logic of his argument. Perhaps his point is that in Pindar's time the use of ὑπόκρισις must have been intelligible to the audience in terms of its original meaning; and that one should therefore be able to make good sense of the passage if we use the alleged meaning to translate it. But if so, is 'I am provoked ... replying like a dolphin' to be discarded in favor of 'I am provoked ... interpreting like a dolphin'? Clearly neither is admissible except as a metaphor, and this does not gain us any advantage in the argument.

15 It can hardly be doubted that the word is correctly supplied at IG II/III² 2318.70 (=Mette 1977:15 I col. 6.3; cf. Capps 1943:1–3) and its beginning ὑπο̣- is extant at 82 (=Mette 1977:16 I col. 6.15). Cf. Pickard-Cambridge 1988:71–72 and 101–107. I assume that ὑποκριτής is original and not a scribal anachronism. The year when the contest was instituted is variously given as 450/49, 449/48, or 448/47 BC, depending on the details of the reconstruction (see Capps 1903:16–17, 22n62).

16 Cf. Zucchelli 1962:52n98. ὑποκρινόμενον in *Wasps* 53, however, does mean 'to interpret'.

etymology nor the earliest attested meaning commends its use in this setting. Therefore, as Koller (1957:103) pointed out, we must surely assume—the absence of direct evidence to this effect notwithstanding—that ὑποκριτής was *already* in use as the *nomen agentis* applied to the one who rendered the answer of the deity by oracular pronouncement or clarified its meaning or both.[17] Homeric usage makes clear that this can be the only natural setting for the term.

But how, then, does the actor come to be named ὑποκριτής? On the basis of Plato's *Iōn*, Koller concluded that rhapsodes had long been called ὑποκριταί of Homer, not in the sense of 'dramatic actors' but of 'expounders' of his poetry, and that this 'explanation' is the alleged original burden of tragic actors.[18] Although I agree with the general outlines of Koller's argument as it regards the rhapsode, my own detailed examination of this question below (pp. 647ff.) yields a somewhat different rationale for the application of the label ὑποκριτής to the actor. For now, I will only adduce two well-known passages that support Koller: *Iōn* 532d7, where Sokrates refers to Ion and his ilk as ὑμεῖς οἱ ῥαψῳδοὶ καὶ ὑποκριταί;[19] and *Iōn* 535e9–536a1, where Ion, 'the middle ring' in the chain of inspiration, is once again described as ὁ ῥαψῳδὸς καὶ ὑποκριτής.[20] One may counter that there is something of a stage quality to Ion's performance—this is

---

[17] Plato's *Timaios* 72a6–b5, though much later, would lend support to this view: ὅθεν δὴ καὶ τὸ τῶν προφητῶν γένος ἐπὶ ταῖς ἐνθέοις μαντείαις κριτὰς ἐπικαθιστάναι νόμος· οὓς μάντεις αὐτοὺς ὀνομάζουσίν τινες, τὸ πᾶν ἠγνοηκότες ὅτι τῆς δι' αἰνιγμῶν οὗτοι φήμης καὶ φαντάσεως ὑποκριταί, καὶ οὔτι μάντεις, προφῆται δὲ μαντευομένων δικαιότατα ὀνομάζοιντ' ἄν ('whence also it is customary to appoint the class of prophets as judges over inspired oracles; these same ones some call seers in utter ignorance that they are interpreters of utterances and visions [that come] through riddles, and they would most accurately be called not seers but prophets of things divined'). For more on this passage see above, pp. 220f.

[18] See Koller 1957:106. The debate whether ὑποκριτής in drama originally meant 'answerer' or 'expounder' can be most readily joined by reading Lesky 1956, Else 1959, and Zucchelli 1962. See also, more recently, Ley 1983. Nagy (2003:21–38) offers an important modification that complements Koller's insight. He argues that the traditional nature of Homeric poetry—that audiences over the years thought of the rhapsode in performance as 'quoting' the notionally unchanging speeches by the characters in the poems—gives to the instances of ὑποκρίνεσθαι in epic the connotation of "responding by way of performing" (21). This would readily lead to its use in the context of drama.

[19] *Iōn* 532d6–e1: βουλοίμην ἄν σε ἀληθῆ λέγειν, ὦ Ἴων· ἀλλὰ σοφοὶ μέν πού ἐστε ὑμεῖς οἱ ῥαψῳδοὶ καὶ ὑποκριταὶ καὶ ὧν ὑμεῖς ᾄδετε τὰ ποιήματα, ἐγὼ δὲ οὐδὲν ἄλλο ἢ τἀληθῆ λέγω, οἷον εἰκὸς ἰδιώτην ἄνθρωπον ('I wish you were right in saying that, Ion. But surely you yourselves, the rhapsodes-*hypokritai*, are the wise ones, and those whose compositions you sing; while I myself speak the simple truth, as one would expect from an ordinary man [without expertise]').

[20] *Iōn* 535e7–536a1: οἶσθα οὖν ὅτι οὗτός ἐστιν ὁ θεατὴς τῶν δακτυλίων ὁ ἔσχατος, ὧν ἐγὼ ἔλεγον ὑπὸ τῆς Ἡρακλειώτιδος λίθου ἀπ' ἀλλήλων τὴν δύναμιν λαμβάνειν; ὁ δὲ μέσος σὺ ὁ ῥαψῳδὸς καὶ ὑποκριτής, ὁ δὲ πρῶτος αὐτὸς ὁ ποιητής ('Do you realize then that this one, the spectator, is the last of the links which I said receive their force one from another under the influence of the magnet? And you, the rhapsode-*hypokritēs*, are the middle one, while the first is the poet himself').

true, and more on this below.[21] But he is surely not an actor in the traditional sense, however dramatic his delivery. By Plato's time, ὑποκριτής in the sense of tragic or comic actor was well established. And after painting the portrait of an epic performer who disavowed interest in *any* poet other than Homer, we must surely expect that, to remain in character, Plato would have had Ion protest as demeaning the epexegetic καὶ ὑποκριτής that Sokrates repeatedly appends to ὁ ῥαψῳδός if it could only suggest a generic association with poetry other than Homer's.[22] Not so: ὑποκριτής *was* a traditional description of the rhapsode, and this agrees with Ion's unequivocal insistence that an essential part of his profession, on which he expended the greatest effort, was speaking well about Homer (περὶ Ὁμήρου λέγειν):[23] he must not only know the poet's ἔπη but his διάνοια (530b10–c1); he must both declaim the former and be a ἑρμηνεύς of the latter (530c3–4, 535b2).[24]

We do not know what this rhapsodic exposition of Homer was like, and sadly Sokrates prevents Ion from making a demonstration, so we are left to conjecture. It is an error, however, to argue (as some have) that Ion being our only evidence for such an exegetical rhapsodic practitioner, he must be an idiosyncratic creation of Plato, peculiar to this dialog and without a real-life parallel. Surely the force (and point) of Plato's dialog would be lost if Ion were so unrepresentative of the rhapsodes of his day. And one could only judge the focus

---

[21] Bölte 1907 offers a helpful exploration of the dramatic potential of Homeric epic and the ways in which a rhapsode might take advantage of it. Cf. also Throop 1917 and Hornung 1869:9–13.

[22] The use at 532d7 of one article οἱ with two coordinate nouns, οἱ ῥαψῳδοὶ καὶ ὑποκριταί, should suffice to prove that ὑποκριταί is epexegetic and that Sokrates does not have in view two different types of performers (rhapsodes and actors). But, should there be any doubt, when he calls Ion at 535e9–536a1 ὁ ῥαψῳδὸς καὶ ὑποκριτής, he renders the point incontestable. Dramatic actors are never under discussion in the *Iōn*, however much their trade has arguably influenced the rhapsode's practice. From the beginning Sokrates addresses himself solely to performers of epic (τοὺς ῥαψῳδούς 530b5), and ὑποκριτής (or its plural ὑποκριταί) merely draws out to ironic effect an important diachronic facet of their craft. Incidentally, Sokrates takes for granted in *Republic* 395a7 that one and the same individual cannot be a good rhapsode and an accomplished actor, even in real life this was not always necessarily the case.

[23] E.g. 530c9; cf. 533c5–7 and d2.

[24] For more on the rhapsode and the poet as ἑρμηνῆς see above, pp. 275f. and 289f. It is clear that ὑποκριτής passed from the rhapsode to the actor (and not vice versa), since only for the former can one compellingly motivate a term derived from the ambit of μάντεις, προφῆται, and ὑποφῆται. Indeed, those who refuse to embrace the dichotomy between ἀοιδός and ῥαψῳδός disputed in this book have no reason to withhold from the rhapsode the description 'ἑρμηνεύς of the inspiring deity' that Plato applies to the poet in the *Iōn* (534e4–5 and 535a5). When, in the evolution of his profession, an aspect of rhapsodic performance was conceptualized as explanatory of the poetic tradition—when it was thought of and referred to as 'expounding the poet'— it was natural that, to designate the rhapsode in this capacity, the same term would be used that had previously designated his hermeneutic function vis-à-vis the deity (hence *Iōn* 535a6–7 and a9).

of his argument misconceived, with its unrelenting insistence on his superb ability to 'expound Homer',[25] 'speak about Homer',[26] and 'adorn Homer'[27] (not, *nota bene*, 'sing Homer' or 'declaim Homer'). For 'to sing' and 'to declaim' the verbs ᾄδειν, καταλέγειν, or even λέγειν—but λέγειν τὰ Ὁμήρου [ἔπη], not περὶ Ὁμήρου—would have been quite adequate and obvious. But only on two occasions is ᾄδειν used of rhapsodes (at 532d8 and 535b4) and we find λέγειν with ἔπη just once (at 535b2).[28] The emphasis on exposition and critical commentary is everywhere evident: rhapsodes learn not only Homer's ἔπη but also his διάνοια (530b10–c1); a good rhapsode must understand (συνείη) what is said by the poet (530c2–3); Ion classes himself with Metrodoros and Stesimbrotos (530c9–d1); the verb ἐξηγέομαι is applied to his interpreting what Homer and Hesiod say 'regarding divination' (531b5–6); Ion's being 'terrific at Homer' (περὶ Ὁμήρου δεινός) involves competent judgment (κριτὴς ἱκανὸς 532b5; cf. 538d4–5, 539d3); Sokrates compares Ion to one who gives his opinion (ἀποφήνασθαι γνώμην) about a painter (533a4); and he accuses Ion of not making a demonstration (ἐπιδείξειν) of all he knows about Homer (541e3–4; cf. 542a2–3).[29] Even the

---

25 *Iōn* 530d2–3, 535a6–10.

26 *Iōn* 530c8–9, 532c6, 533c5–6, 533d2, 534c1, 536c1, 536d7, 542a5.

27 *Iōn* 530d6–7, 536d3, 536d5–6, 541e2.

28 Cf. 533e7–8 with epic poets, and 537c1–2 with Homer, as the subject.

29 See Capuccino 2005:275 for a helpful "diagram of the exegetic activity of the rhapsode." I cannot, however, accept her understanding of this exegesis, which reduces it to ἑρμηνεύειν and excludes 'explanation' in favor of '[vocal] expression' (194–195). Lacking diachronic depth, her treatment espouses a reductive view of rhapsodic mediation: the rhapsode as mere mouthpiece of the poet (131). There is, to be sure, some truth to her argument: in advocating Homer's διάνοια, rhapsodic exegesis will have offered a positive appraisal of it. But it may none the more thereupon be reduced to mere ἔπαινος: how are we to imagine that the performer gave voice to his approbation? Surely not just by declaiming Homer's verse with verve (as Capuccino herself acknowledges at 166n217). Whatever the subject in which the poet was purported to instruct his public, at the very least the rhapsode would have had to describe in sufficient detail the content of Homer's teaching. Even if this did not call for glossing archaic formulas or illuminating difficult epic syntax, only a cramped definition of 'exegesis' could fail to embrace such activity. This is Pepin's weakness, whom Capuccino follows, when he reduces "exégèse" to "un mouvement d'entrée dans l'intention d'un texte ou d'un message" (Pépin 1975:291), forgetting the reciprocal outward motion entailed by the preverb ἐξ- (cf. Latin 'explico'). Capuccino's analysis is pulled in opposite directions at once. On the one hand, she wants to preserve the rhapsode's active critical engagement; on the other, to the extent that it detracts from his function as 'mere spokesman', she wishes to marginalize this engagement as 'mental' and 'unofficial'. Regarding such 'mental exegesis' she writes: "Insomma, quello che Ione dovrebbe poter fare per essere un *buon* mediatore di Omero, è conoscerne a fondo la mente … ; vale a dire ripercorrere quel dialogo silenzioso dell'anima con se stessa che è il pensiero (*scil.* l'attività del pensare) di qualcuno. … Ma tutto questo non riguarda alcuna attività esegetica o interpretativa; riguarda piuttosto l'importanza che Socrate attribuisce al dialogo …" (192–193, her emphasis; cf. 196). And she elaborates as follows her claim that rhapsodic laudatory exegesis was 'unofficial': "Questo potrebbe far credere che la locuzione Ὁμήρου ἐπαινέτης designi una precisa figura professionale … . Se il rapsodo (soprattutto il rapsodo omerico) era famoso per le sue declamazioni pubbliche, non

topos of the rhapsodes' stupidity,[30] because they knew Homer's ἔπη by heart but were ignorant of their meaning,[31] must be regarded as proof that they regularly *did* attempt an exposition: for how else would their ignorance be so obviously exposed? This, to me, does not seem a case of revealing their deficiency in private conversation only; the accusation has an official ring to it, as if their excellence at performing and poverty in expounding were of a piece with their trade. The contempt in which, according to Xenophon, the milieu of Sokrates held rhapsodes must surely be set in the context of the challenge that rhetors, sophists, and philosophers variously mounted to their cultural authority as custodians of the traditional educational curriculum. Far from standing alone

---

è necessario che lo fosse per frequenti discussioni ... con altri 'esperti' di Omero di fronte a un uditorio meno numeroso" (163–164n211; the limitation to 'discussions with other experts' is a red herring). In her exposition, Capuccino credits Pépin 1975, who refers to Philo's distinction between two λόγοι: the 'mental' one of discursive thought (ὁ ἐν διανοίᾳ) and the audible one of discursive speech (διὰ στόματος καὶ γλώττης); this latter he names the ἑρμηνεύς of the former (*De migratione Abrahami* §§71–73). Rightly understood, however, Philo's distinction hardly justifies Capuccino's collapse of 'interpretation' onto mere '[vocal] expression'. The Alexandrian regards speech as a complex faculty which God has given man to articulate and communicate his thought (*Quis rerum divinarum heres sit* §§105–111). Should one choose to call this faculty 'expression', then it is certainly not just '*vocal* expression', as though some mechanical conveyance of thought into words. If 'expression' in all of its manifold aspects is reconceptualized as mediating communication that issues from a separate source—i.e. as 'putting it into words' (τῇ λέξει σημαίνειν Aristotle *Sophistical Refutations* 166b15–16)—then it is rightly called 'interpretation', for it expounds its content and makes it explicit (cf. Pépin 1975:293). In this sense, ἑρμηνεύειν complements ἐξηγεῖσθαι. This 'interpretation', moreover, is perfectly consonant with the function I have ascribed to the rhapsode as interpreter of the will of Zeus. Divine thought-λόγος and speech-λόγος concur in the figure of the mediating rhapsode whom the Muses inspire.

30 So Xenophon *Apomnēmoneumata* 4.2.10: τί δὲ δὴ βουλόμενος ἀγαθὸς γενέσθαι, ἔφη, ὦ Εὐθύδημε, συλλέγεις τὰ γράμματα; ... ἀλλὰ μὴ ῥαψῳδός; ἔφη· καὶ γὰρ τὰ Ὁμήρου σέ φασιν ἔπη πάντα κεκτῆσθαι. μὰ Δί' οὐκ ἔγωγ', ἔφη· τοὺς γάρ τοι ῥαψῳδοὺς οἶδα τὰ μὲν ἔπη ἀκριβοῦντας, αὐτοὺς δὲ πάνυ ἠλιθίους ὄντας ('"Euthydemos," said Sokrates, "you collect bookrolls in order to become good at what?" ... "Perhaps [you want to be] a rhapsode then?" he said. "For they say that you also own all of Homer's poetry." "By Zeus, not I!" he said. "For I know that rhapsodes hone their verses, but they themselves are very silly"'). And Xenophon *Symposion* 3.5–6: ὁ πατὴρ ὁ ἐπιμελούμενος ὅπως ἀνὴρ ἀγαθὸς γενοίμην ἠνάγκασέ με πάντα τὰ Ὁμήρου ἔπη μαθεῖν· καὶ νῦν δυναίμην ἂν Ἰλιάδα ὅλην καὶ Ὀδύσσειαν ἀπὸ στόματος εἰπεῖν. ἐκεῖνο δ', ἔφη ὁ Ἀντισθένης, λέληθέ σε, ὅτι καὶ οἱ ῥαψῳδοὶ πάντες ἐπίστανται ταῦτα τὰ ἔπη; καὶ πῶς ἄν, ἔφη, λελήθοι ἀκροωμένῳ γε αὐτῶν ὀλίγου ἂν' ἑκάστην ἡμέραν; οἶσθά τι οὖν ἔθνος, ἔφη, ἠλιθιώτερον ῥαψῳδῶν; οὐ μὰ τὸν Δί', ἔφη ὁ Νικήρατος, οὔκουν ἔμοιγε δοκῶ. δῆλον γάρ, ἔφη ὁ Σωκράτης, ὅτι τὰς ὑπονοίας οὐκ ἐπίστανται ('"My father, taking care that I would become a good man, forced me to learn all the poetry of Homer; even now I could recite by heart the entire *Iliad* and *Odyssey*." "But has this escaped your notice," said Antisthenes, "that all rhapsodes know these verses too?" "How could it," said he, "when I used to listen to them almost daily?" "Do you know then any tribe," he said, "sillier than rhapsodes?" "No, by Zeus!" said Nikeratos, "I think certainly not." "For it is clear," said Sokrates, "that they do not know the underlying meaning"'). Cf. Graziosi 2002:22.

31 Xenophon's Sokrates uses the word ὑπόνοιαι (*Symposion* 3.6.7). Cf. the section on Theagenes above, pp. 156ff.

as an exceptional distortion of a tendentious Plato, the *Iōn* corroborates this state of affairs.[32]

Now, how are we to think of this hermeneutic function? Koller (1957:105) suggested that it consisted of "prose speech, mixed with verses, portions of verses, *kola*, *kommata*, with all the characteristics of poetic speech," in sum, "a mixture of poetic speech and everyday prose."[33] This, he proposed, represented the origin of 'literary' prose—though a very poetic one at first[34]—and hence there was a direct line extending from rhapsodic to sophistic ἐπίδειξις. I believe that the outlines of this proposal are essentially correct, and I would only modify it by conjecturing that initially the explanatory function of the rhapsode would have largely consisted of hexameters composed in performance, joining well-known episodes or speeches, effecting transitions between them, elaborating the twists and turns of the poems' plots, as well as the thoughts, feelings, and motivations of participating gods and heroes.[35] On one level, τὸν Ὅμηρον κοσμεῖν, 'to adorn Homer',[36] must have denoted such an elaboration: not the work of an autonomous creativity expressing a rhapsode's individuality, but the traditional recomposition controlled since time immemorial by the notion of 'order', i.e. the κατὰ κόσμον explored in chapter 7.[37] But with the passing of time and the increasing theatricality of rhapsodic performance, the practice of ornamenting Homer would have been gradually reinterpreted, partly as elaborate ὑπόκρισις,[38] partly as the metaphorical adornment of 'praise'. Ion's gorgeous

---

[32] Cf. Graziosi 2002:45 and Capuccino 2005:271–272 with 272n22.

[33] "Sie konnte nur Prosarede sein, untermischt mit Versen, Versteilen, Kolen, Kommata, mit allen Eigenheiten poetischer Sprache, d. h. die Form der Hypokrisis ist eine Mischung von Dichtersprache und Alltagsprosa."

[34] Cf. Aristotle *Rhetoric* 1404a24–28.

[35] The work of Kelly 1990 on the differing rates of correption in Homeric speeches and narrative would seem to support this conjecture. I quote here from his conclusion: "[T]he formulas for the speeches were composed at an earlier date than the formulas for the narrative. The supposition of a proto-epic composed of speeches and a connecting prose narrative is strengthened by the existence of such poems in ... the Indo-European community, and by the dominance of speeches in the Homeric text as it now stands. The transition from speeches to [versified] narrative was effected by means of quoted narrative. ... Narrative, then, not the speeches, remains the locus for innovation" (80–81). By "quoted narrative" Kelly means narrative in the mouth of a Homeric character. Garner 2011 takes issue with Kelly's theory and views correption in Homer not "as an accidental or residual archaism," but "as a dynamic enabler of poetic flexibility" that remained an active, "essential and integral tool" to composition (50).

[36] *Iōn* 530d6–8: καὶ μὴν ἄξιόν γε ἀκοῦσαι, ὦ Σώκρατες, ὡς εὖ κεκόσμηκα τὸν Ὅμηρον· ὥστε οἶμαι ὑπὸ Ὁμηριδῶν ἄξιος εἶναι χρυσῷ στεφάνῳ στεφανωθῆναι ('Really, Sokrates, it is worth hearing how well I have adorned Homer, [so well] that I think I deserve to be crowned with a golden wreath by the Homeridai').

[37] See above, pp. 194ff.

[38] That is, a stage presence marked by a characteristically histrionic use of voice, gestures, and dress.

attire answers to the former;[39] rhapsodic ἔπαινος, which I shall consider presently, to the latter.[40]

The scenario I have outlined here would readily explain Plato's apparent blurring together of the inspired poet (notionally the source of the tradition) and the rhapsodes (notionally the performers and expounders). Indeed, were we to reduce the bard's performance merely to reproducing (as a mechanical feat of memory) what purported to be Homer's *ipsissima verba*, how could this action even begin to suggest the sort of manic inspiration Plato foists on rhapsodes? There would hardly be anything mysterious and godlike in a feat of memory, for Xenophon makes clear that the layman, too, could boast in his ability to recall the entire poems.[41] To Ion's puzzled question, 'How can it be that when someone talks about another poet, I pay no attention, cannot contribute anything worthwhile, and just doze off, but when Homer is mentioned I am immediately awake, pay attention, and have much to say?', Sokrates' answer must be, 'Is it not obvious? Because you have only memorized Homer!' Memorizing thousands of lines of poetry, however impressive an accomplishment to the modern, is quite different from the notion of 'social memory' embodied by the poetic tradition. The latter alone is shrouded in mystery, for it reenacts the past as only autopsy or divine omniscience can (Apollo's or the Muses'; cf. B 484–486 θ 487–491).[42] On the lips of the poet a claim to *that* memory fully justifies some notion of divine influence. One can hardly say the same when access to the tradition is gained by the hard but ordinary labor of a capacious memory exercised in retaining a widely accessible text. It would be hard to tell in that case who looks more foolish: Ion, for asking the question, or Sokrates, for failing to give the obvious answer. On the other hand, an exposition of Homer strictly as a prose lecture would not suffice: without the creative contribution of the rhapsode's own poetry[43] it is again hard to see how the matter of inspiration would be apposite and, if it is, why it should not be made extensive to the likes of Metrodoros of Lampsakos and Stesimbrotos of Thasos (*Iōn* 530c9–d1). An understanding of rhapsodic practice along the lines I have just described accords a unity to the *Iōn* that has been denied to it by many a scholar. Whether poetic inspiration

---

[39] Cf. *Iōn* 530b6 and 535d2.

[40] See below, section 9.3, pp. 305ff. For more on rhapsodic κόσμησις, see Boyd 1994:118–120.

[41] See above, p. 301 n. 30. This does not hold for the archaic appeal to 'memory', which at that time was not conceived as rote learning and *did* connote mystery and divine influence. But in the environment of late fifth- and fourth-century BC Athens, as just remarked, laymen might commit to memory large portions of Homer in an ordinary, mechanical way.

[42] For more on poetry and 'social memory' see above, p. 208. For the poet and divine omniscience see pp. 183ff.

[43] Or without a prose exposition that was fused with his creative poetic elaboration and viewed in immediate continuity with it.

or rhapsodic exposition was its theme has been debated by many, and various strategies devised to subordinate the one to the logic of the other.[44] Yet the troubling dichotomy largely dissipates if rhapsodic exposition shares to some extent the character of poetic composition. This explains why the composing poet and the performing (declaiming and expounding) rhapsode can be handled under a single scheme and assigned the same kind of manic inspiration. At the same time, it preserves the notional priority of the poet as source (author and authority) of the bard's performance, for only through 'Homer' does Ion have access to the Muse. The *afflatus* is mediated, and passes from poet to rhapsode; but, by the same token, the rhapsode is not without his creative inspiration.

Over time, the verse component must have given way to an increasingly large proportion of explanatory prose, a development that would readily account for the implicit comparison of rhapsodes with sophistic orators, who made a living of epideictic displays and educational lessons for a fee and for whom Homeric material often furnished a point of departure.[45] These sophists may have proceeded at first in conscious imitation of, and competition with, rhapsodes. As O'Sullivan (1996:117) writes (displacing the focus from rhapsodes onto poets): "Although rejecting the mode of communication the poets had adopted, and although subjecting them to searching and hostile criticism, the Sophists also seem to have imagined themselves as their successors." I believe that O'Sullivan's emphasis on "mode of communication" (prose versus poetry) is misplaced and that the real fight was about cultural capital and authority, especially in education, broadly conceived.[46] Hence the contempt in which rhapsodes were held by the Greek intelligentsia of the time. As immediate exponents and (at least implicit) claimants of performative authority, rhapsodes made readier and more vulnerable targets than their poetry or—once their traditional repertoire had been ascribed to a distinct author—than the poets whose work they alleged to perform. O'Sullivan is doubtless right to infer from the following facts a live rivalry between sophists and rhapsodes:[47] Protagoras *apud* Plato identified Homer and Hesiod as sophists (*Prōtagoras* 316d6–7; cf. Kratinos fr. 2 K-A); like rhapsodes, sophists dressed in purple robes (Aelian *Varia historia* 12.32); both appeared at the same festivals (Philostratos *Vitae sophistarum* 1.9.493 on Gorgias;

---

[44] For various approaches to the interpretation of the *Iōn*, a sample of the relevant bibliography might include Verdenius 1943, Ladrière 1951, Diller 1955, Wyller 1958, Flashar 1958, Tigerstedt 1969:13–29, Partee 1971, Dorter 1973, Schousen 1986, Velardi 1989, Ott 1992, Janaway 1995:14–35, Harris 1997, and Capuccino 2005.

[45] As the beginning of Plato's *Lesser Hippias* shows. Cf. Culverhouse 2010.

[46] To this fight, prose and the new technology of writing became instrumental. See below, pp. 311ff.

[47] O'Sullivan 1992:67.

Plato *Lesser Hippias* 363c7–d4 on Hippias); and sophists composed speeches and dialogs featuring Homeric characters.[48]

9.3 The Rhapsode as Ἐπαινέτης

One aspect of the *Iōn* where the connection between the rhapsodic and sophistic performance traditions comes clearly to the fore is Plato's use, characteristically pointed, of the terms ἐπαινέω and ἐπαινέτης.[49] On four different occasions do the interlocutors employ them. The first comes after the celebrated metaphor of the magnetic chain, which Sokrates closes with the following words: 'Of this, the cause you are asking me about, why you are at a loss in regard to the rest but not in regard to Homer, is that you are a terrific *epainetēs* of Homer by divine dispensation, not *tekhnē*';[50] to which Ion replies: 'Well said, Sokrates; but I would be surprised if you spoke well enough to convince me that it is raving and possessed that I praise (ἐπαινῶ) Homer'.[51] The other two instances are in the closing exchange between the philosopher and the rhapsode: 'But if you are telling the truth, Ion, that by art and science you are able to praise (ἐπαινεῖν) Homer, you are wronging me'.[52] Faced with this verbal challenge, Ion at last yields his point to Sokrates, who condescendingly ends the dialog with a declaration of victory: 'This nobler title, then, you have in my eyes, Ion, to be an *epainetēs* of Homer not by dint of art, but divine'.[53] One should mark the technical nature claimed by Ion and contested by Sokrates for his 'commendation' of Homer. In 536d6, 'I praise Homer' (Ὅμηρον ἐπαινῶ) is paralleled by 'my speaking *about* Homer' (μου ... λέγοντος περὶ Ὁμήρου 536d7). The mere fact that the agent noun ἐπαινέτης is used acknowledges that 'praising Homer' is an integral part of the rhapsode's profession. Discharging this function well corresponds in 536d3 to being 'well supplied about Homer' (περὶ μὲν Ὁμήρου εὐπορεῖς 536d1–2). Sokrates makes clear at 536b8–c2 that this ample supply goes beyond recalling large amounts of epic verse; for, when Ion has plenty to say (εὐπορεῖς ὅτι λέγῃς), he speaks not Homeric verse but *about* Homer (περὶ Ὁμήρου λέγεις). It is plain, then, that the

---

[48] O'Sullivan 1992:67n32.

[49] See Capuccino 2005:159–167 and Elmer 2013.

[50] *Iōn* 536d1–3: τούτου δ' ἐστὶ τὸ αἴτιον, ὅ μ' ἐρωτᾷς, δι' ὅτι σὺ περὶ μὲν Ὁμήρου εὐπορεῖς, περὶ δὲ τῶν ἄλλων οὔ, ὅτι οὐ τέχνῃ ἀλλὰ θείᾳ μοίρᾳ Ὁμήρου δεινὸς εἶ ἐπαινέτης.

[51] *Iōn* 536d4–6: σὺ μὲν εὖ λέγεις, ὦ Σώκρατες· θαυμάζοιμι μεντἂν εἰ οὕτως εὖ εἴποις, ὥστε με ἀναπεῖσαι ὡς ἐγὼ κατεχόμενος καὶ μαινόμενος Ὅμηρον ἐπαινῶ.

[52] *Iōn* 541e1–3: ἀλλὰ γὰρ σύ, ὦ Ἴων, εἰ μὲν ἀληθῆ λέγεις ὡς τέχνῃ καὶ ἐπιστήμῃ οἷός τε εἶ Ὅμηρον ἐπαινεῖν, ἀδικεῖς.

[53] *Iōn* 542b2–3: τοῦτο τοίνυν τὸ κάλλιον ὑπάρχει σοι παρ' ἡμῖν, ὦ Ἴων, θεῖον εἶναι καὶ μὴ τεχνικὸν περὶ Ὁμήρου ἐπαινέτην.

artistic and scientific quality that Sokrates denies to the rhapsodic profession cannot be reduced to mnemonics.

To these four passages from the *Iōn* we may add three others. In the *Prōtagoras* Sokrates gently chides a *hetairos* for his unwitting departure from Homer's view of a youth's charm when he first shows facial hair: 'But are you not an *epainetēs* of Homer, who said that youth is at its most charming with its first beard, just the age of Alkibiades now?'[54] And in the *Republic* Homer's theology is censured for its questionable morality: 'Though we praise much of Homer, yet this we shall not praise: Zeus' sending of the dream to Agamemnon'.[55] But it is the next passage that makes clear the ultimate implications of 'praising Homer', the claim purveyors of culture—educators, rhapsodes, sophists—staked out in connection with the alleged social benefits of his poetry: 'Surely then, Glaukos, said I, when you meet *epainetai* of Homer who say that this poet has educated Greece and that, with a view to the management of human affairs and our instruction therein, he is worth taking up, learning, and living one's entire life arranged according to him; you must welcome and salute them for being as virtuous as they can, and agree that Homer is *the* Poet of poets and first among tragedians, but you must know that of poetry, only hymns to gods and encomia of virtuous men should be admitted into the city'.[56] The point made here by Homer's 'supporters' (the *epainetai*) is clearly one of pedagogical preeminence, comprehensiveness, and absolute sufficiency. It is hard for us fully to grasp the foundational significance of such a totalizing cultural narrative, whose impact descends into the triviality of a bearded youth's charm as easily as it ascends to statesmanship, military leadership,[57] and the most serious matters of state.[58] But it is precisely against this background that the word ἐπαινέτης acquires the connotation of the Homer enthusiast who makes his poetry the sum total of all necessary learning. This type is best represented by the rhapsode, who makes his living not only declaiming but also exploring and expounding to his audience the significance of his epic repertoire. Several scholars have

---

[54] *Prōtagoras* 309a6–b1: οὐ σὺ μέντοι Ὁμήρου ἐπαινέτης εἶ, ὃς ἔφη χαριεστάτην ἥβην εἶναι τοῦ ⟨πρῶτον⟩ ὑπηνήτου, ἣν νῦν Ἀλκιβιάδης ἔχει;

[55] *Republic* 383a7–8: πολλὰ ἄρα Ὁμήρου ἐπαινοῦντες, ἀλλὰ τοῦτο οὐκ ἐπαινεσόμεθα, τὴν τοῦ ἐνυπνίου πομπὴν ὑπὸ Διὸς τῷ Ἀγαμέμνονι.

[56] *Republic* 606e1–607a5: οὐκοῦν, εἶπον, ὦ Γλαύκων, ὅταν Ὁμήρου ἐπαινέταις ἐντύχῃς λέγουσιν ὡς τὴν Ἑλλάδα πεπαίδευκεν οὗτος ὁ ποιητὴς καὶ πρὸς διοίκησίν τε καὶ παιδείαν τῶν ἀνθρωπίνων πραγμάτων ἄξιος ἀναλαβόντι μανθάνειν τε καὶ κατὰ τοῦτον τὸν ποιητὴν πάντα τὸν αὐτοῦ βίον κατασκευασάμενον ζῆν, φιλεῖν μὲν χρὴ καὶ ἀσπάζεσθαι ὡς ὄντας βελτίστους εἰς ὅσον δύνανται, καὶ συγχωρεῖν Ὅμηρον ποιητικώτατον εἶναι καὶ πρῶτον τῶν τραγῳδοποιῶν, εἰδέναι δὲ ὅτι ὅσον μόνον ὕμνους θεοῖς καὶ ἐγκώμια τοῖς ἀγαθοῖς ποιήσεως παραδεκτέον εἰς πόλιν.

[57] E.g. *Iōn* 541b3–5.

[58] Perhaps the closest parallel in recent history might be the place the Bible held among the early Puritan settlers of Massachusetts.

sensed and commented on the marked character of the term in this context. So Stallbaum 1857a: "Nempe videntur Homeri ἐπαινέται non tam ii dicti esse, qui Homerum laudabant, quam potius illi, qui unice eius sapientiam probabant eamque ita commendabant, ut inde etiam vitae recte sapienterque regendae ac moderandae praecepta haurienda esse arbitrarentur. In quorum numero certe imprimis etiam Homeridae habendi sunt ... . His igitur viris sapientiae Homericae consultis sese adiunxerunt sine dubio etiam rhapsodi ..." (331–332).[59]

A good fourth-century BC illustration, not by a rhapsode but by a statesman who nevertheless adopts the epideictic pose of one, is Lykourgos' *Against Leōkratēs*, dated to 330 BC, where Lykourgos the son of Lykophron (of the deme Boutadai) indicts a certain Leokrates for his flight to Megara right after the defeat of the Athenians and Thebans by Philip II of Makedon at Khaironeia.[60] In §102 he commends to the jury the example of Hektor as follows: βούλομαι δ' ὑμῖν καὶ τὸν Ὅμηρον παρασχέσθαι ἐπαινῶν.[61] As an ἐπαινέτης of Homer, Lykourgos extols patriotism and courage in fighting for one's country. Velardi (1989:34–35) sees in the outline of §§102–104 the pattern that the more professional rhapsodic *epainetai* might have followed in praising Homer: "1) un breve discorso di carattere generale finalizzato ad introdurre i versi, una sorta di prologo contenente anche informazioni storiche sull'istituzione dell'agone rapsodico delle Panatenee e probabilmente, nel caso di una recitazione rapsodica vera e propria, notizie biografiche su Omero (par. 102); 2) la declamazione dei versi (par. 103); 3) un commento del brano recitato (par. 104)" (35). Though perhaps a little too schematic, if one allows for *ad hoc* adjustments to the particulars of each performance his proposal seems, in the main, sound for the late-classical rhapsode.[62] Indeed, the section that precedes Lykourgos' commendation of

---

[59] Cf. Wilamowitz-Moellendorff 1920: "Ὁμήρου ἐπαινέτης, das hier 536d und als letztes Wort des Dialoges steht, von Ion an der ersten Stelle mit Ὅμηρον ἐπαινῶ aufgenommen wird, bezeichnet den, der zu Ehren Homers redet, seine Sache führt, auf ihn schwört. ... Noch der Kreter der Gesetze ist Διὸς ἐπαινέτης 633a" (41n2); and Albini 1954:35 *ad* 536d: "ἐπαινέτης significa 'panegirista', 'encomiatore'. La parola, con cui il dialogo si chiude, ha un valore pregnante." Thus, Velardi (1989:32) concludes: "In realtà ci sono elementi sufficienti per affermare che i due termini [*epainein* ed *epainétes*], almeno in riferimento ad Omero, hanno un preciso valore tecnico."

[60] For a cultural analysis of the speech and, more generally, the times of Lykourgos, see Mikalson 1998:11–45.

[61] I have restored τὸν Ὅμηρον ... ἐπαινῶν, the reading of the manuscripts that Reiske and Koraēs had unnecessarily emended to τῶν Ὁμήρου ... ἐπῶν (which Conomis prints). Not only is ἐπαινέω here paralleled at *Against Leōkratēs* §100, where it is used in connection with Euripides, but it also reflects the conventional diction of *epideixis*, one that, I am arguing, goes back to long-standing rhapsodic practice. Cf. Velardi 1989:33–35.

[62] See above (p. 302) for my own suggestions about the way in which the practice of rhapsodes in performance may have changed with time, and the corresponding evolution in the character of the 'stitching' and exposition (ἐπίδειξις or ἑρμηνεία, depending on the point of view) they would have engaged in.

Homer, with its focus on Euripides' *Erekhtheus*, is explicit about the politician's intent to make poetry serve pedagogical ends (ταῦτα ὦ ἄνδρες τοὺς πατέρας ὑμῶν ἐπαίδευε §101); further emphasis flows from the ensuing contrast between laws that, owing to their brevity, cannot educate (διὰ τὴν συντομίαν οὐ διδάσκουσιν §102) and poets who, by mimesis of choice deeds, persuade men with *logos* and *apodeixis* (equivalent, respectively, to drama's speech and argument on the one hand, and stage production or *opsis* on the other).[63] The goal is the public demonstration, both ἐπίδειξις and the related ἀπόδειξις, which, as Koller (1957:105) argued (see above, p. 302), made the sophists the intellectual heirs (and competitors) of the earlier rhapsodes.[64]

9.4 The Rhapsode and Ὑπόκρισις

So far we have considered how the rhapsodic trade shaped not only the emerging actor, but also the sophist (who was, in effect, the first professional orator and teacher of oratory). But this is not the only direction in which influence was

---

[63] Cf. Humphreys 1985a:216–217. On this passage see further below, pp. 436ff.

[64] ἐπίδειξιν ποιούμενοι πρὸς τοὺς Ἕλληνας (§102); οἱ δὲ ποιηταὶ ... μετὰ λόγου καὶ ἀποδείξεως τοὺς ἀνθρώπους συμπείθουσιν (§102). While the traditional term for the display of oratory and of performance generally is ἐπίδειξις, ἀπόδειξις is closely related to it. And though the latter can be employed in the specialized sense of rhetorical or logical proof, it still retains the flexibility to evoke the demonstrative 'show' of ἐπίδειξις. So, for example, of three instances of ἀποδείκνυμι in Aristotle's *Poetics*, only one (1456a38) more narrowly relates to proving one's point (complementing the refutation of contrary arguments); the other two (1450a7 and 1450b11) pertain more generally to communicating the thoughts of the characters on stage and associate the word with ἀποφαίνεσθαι, the term used by Sokrates in *Iōn* 532e8 and 533a4 for the exegetical function of the specialist (specifically, in painting, but, by implication, also in the rhapsodic art). In other words, ἀπόδειξις is part and parcel of the ἐπιδείξεις of the σοφοί: ἐπίδειξις especially regards the public display before the audience, ἀπόδειξις the public display of the subject matter. Hence the use of ἀποδείξεις to designate the rhetorical speeches by Themistokles of Ilion (Θεμιστοκλῆς ... ἀποδείξεις πεποίηται τῶν ῥητορικῶν λόγων) given in Xanthos in 196 BC (see Robert and Robert 1983:154–156; cf. Pernot 1993:1.50). Robert and Robert (1983:162n27) write: "Il a donné des 'démonstrations', ἀποδείξεις, de son art, à savoir dans des ἐπιδείξεις." And in his *Progymnasmata* 106 (Spengel), Theon of Alexandria explained that *topoi* differ from encomia and invective and are "concerned simply with their subjects and involve no demonstration (χωρὶς ἀποδείξεως)," whereas the other two "are concerned with specific persons and include demonstration (μετὰ ἀποδείξεως)" (the translation is taken from Kennedy 2003 *ad loc.*; cf. Pernot 1993:2.679). This connection is very old indeed: it is attested in [Plato] *Hipparkhos* 228b6–7 (["Ἵππαρχος] ἄλλα τε πολλὰ καὶ καλὰ ἔργα σοφίας ἀπεδείξατο), in Herodotos' proem (Ἡροδότου Θουρίου ἱστορίης ἀπόδεξις ἥδε), and, significantly, in Alkidamas' *On the Sophists* §§29–32, where a failure to understand it has led scholars to emend the ἀποδείξεις of §29 to ἐπιδείξεις, so as to harmonize it with the τῶν ἐπιδείξεων of §31 (see, for example, Mariß 2002:281–282). Cf. Nagy (1990c:217–222), who insists on ἀπόδειξις as 'performance' (rather than 'public presentation') because of its implicit reference to the artistic medium which effects the display. I am in essential agreement with him on this point, but would accept 'public display', either as a direct reference to performance (in the case of rhapsodes, orators, etc.) or else as a metaphor from the world of the performer and his audience. Cf. Bakker 2002a.

exerted. In Athens tragedy soon rivaled and even surpassed epic poetry in popular appeal as the queen of all cultural productions, and in time it also exerted a profound reciprocal influence upon the performance of Homer. Evidence for this can be found in many places, including the *Iōn* itself, for, as I already observed, Ion's performance was powerfully dramatic, with an exaggerated evocation of πάθη,[65] especially ἔλεος and φόβος (535c5–8), the very emotions Aristotle singles out in connection with the κάθαρσις of tragedy (*Poetics* 1449b27–28).[66] Plato, who is never straightforward, must have been playing with the double referent of ὑποκριτής: not only the traditional one, 'expounder [of Homer]'—which is surely the way we are to think Ion heard it—but the far less flattering 'stage actor', with all the negative mimetic nuances the philosopher assigned to it. This, Plato's demeaning ὑπόνοια, would tend to reduce poetry to an instrument for arousing disorderly emotions, primarily through a markedly mimetic delivery. The same unfavorable implication is found in Aristotle's *Poetics* (chapter 26), where, while criticizing exaggerated acting, the philosopher observes that even an epic rhapsode may overdo his gestures.

This pairing of rhapsode and stage actor resurfaces in Aristotle's *Rhetoric* III.1, where we learn that the matter of ὑπόκρισις, 'oral delivery', had only lately come to τραγική and ῥαψῳδική.[67] Happily, the philosopher does not leave us in doubt as to his meaning, but explains that ὑπόκρισις lies in the voice, how its loudness, melodic line, and rhythm should be used to convey πάθος in every circumstance.[68] It is clear, however, that for him delivery was inextricably linked with writing.[69] For in defining the scope of his investigation of λέξις he specifies that it comprehends such principles as can be assembled into a scientific study of

[65] The metaphor of the ring embodies the lines of transmission along which the emotions flow: though we know nothing of the poet, his allegedly manic possession (which portrays him as a bacchant) is a safe index of his own emotional ecstasy; as to the other links, there is no doubt that the magnetic influence takes the form of a rhapsode overcome by his feelings, who in turn overwhelms his audience emotionally. (If we attend to the details, however, the picture is not so tidy; for, contemplating the prize as all but won, Ion combines inner laughter with his and his audience's outward wailing, 535e4–6.) The inclusion of the audience as the terminal link should caution us not to push the metaphor too far, since the audience neither composes nor performs under the influence of such 'possession'—it merely *feels* a powerful emotional influence. The presence of strong πάθη confirms the divine activity, mediated by poet and rhapsode, whose source is the Muse, but its particular effect on each link is peculiar to the link itself: whether it be a poet, a rhapsode, χορευταί, διδάσκαλοι, etc.

[66] Note also the mention of ἐκπλήττειν at *Iōn* 535b2–3, to be compared with ἔκπληξις at *Poetics* 1455a17–18. Cf. Flashar 1958:67–69.

[67] See below, chapter 13 pp. 521ff.

[68] ἔστιν δὲ αὕτη [sc. ὑπόκρισις] μὲν ἐν τῇ φωνῇ, πῶς αὐτῇ δεῖ χρῆσθαι πρὸς ἕκαστον πάθος, οἷον πότε μεγάλῃ καὶ πότε μικρᾷ καὶ μέσῃ, καὶ πῶς τοῖς τόνοις, οἷον ὀξείᾳ καὶ βαρείᾳ καὶ μέσῃ, καὶ ῥυθμοῖς τίσι πρὸς ἕκαστα. τρία γάρ ἐστι περὶ ἃ σκοποῦσιν· ταῦτα δ' ἐστὶ μέγεθος ἁρμονία ῥυθμός (1403b26–31). See below, p. 526.

[69] See below, section 14.2 pp. 593ff.

'delivery';[70] and to illustrate this distinction he remarks that 'written speeches are more effective on account of their *lexis* than their thought'.[71] This comment is most naturally construed to involve writing in the successful deployment of all the expressive resources of 'style', resources that Aristotle views strictly as instruments in the service of effective delivery. Chapter 12 of *Rhetoric* III shows that writing is not a passing concern, even if it seems superficially paradoxical in the context of ὑπόκρισις; for here a distinction is drawn between the *graphic* and *agonistic* styles, the former lending itself best to *precision*, the latter to *delivery*.[72] It soon becomes clear, however, that he assumes that *both* will be written, and that the distinction between them is only how successful a reader will judge the written text, now deprived of its performative setting and voice, as compared to the hearer who sits in the audience when it is delivered.[73] Despite Aristotle's strong emphasis on oral delivery, it is telling that he should state that 'one thing is to know how to speak correct Greek; another, not to be forced to keep silent, should one wish to share with the others—which is precisely what happens to those who do not know how to write'.[74] The connection the philosopher establishes between rhapsodic, dramatic, and oratorical ὑπόκρισις in *Rhetoric* III.1 is all the more significant in that it belongs to a technical discussion with careful definitions and analysis, one that explicitly considers the service that writing can offer to what is a preeminently performative task: the oral delivery of rhetorical speeches. This parallel, I believe, suggested itself to Aristotle because in his own time these professionals of public performance shared the broad outlines of a common methodology, and this as much in their preparation and rehearsal as in their delivery before an audience. We readily understand that, however different in the particulars, the delivery of actor, rhapsode, and orator were but three species of one genus: they all had recourse to the same resources—voice, gestures, and outward appearance—through which they were to express

---

[70] See below, section 14.1 pp. 579ff.

[71] καὶ ἔστιν φύσεως τὸ ὑποκριτικὸν εἶναι, καὶ ἀτεχνότερον, περὶ δὲ τὴν λέξιν ἔντεχνον. διὸ καὶ τοῖς τοῦτο δυναμένοις γίνεται πάλιν ἆθλα, καθάπερ καὶ τοῖς κατὰ τὴν ὑπόκρισιν ῥήτορσιν· οἱ γὰρ γραφόμενοι λόγοι μεῖζον ἰσχύουσι διὰ τὴν λέξιν ἢ διὰ τὴν διάνοιαν (1404a15–19).

[72] ἔστι δὲ λέξις γραφικὴ μὲν ἡ ἀκριβεστάτη, ἀγωνιστικὴ δὲ ἡ ὑποκριτικωτάτη (1413b8–9).

[73] καὶ παραβαλλόμενοι οἱ μὲν τῶν γραφικῶν ἐν τοῖς ἀγῶσι στενοὶ φαίνονται, οἱ δὲ τῶν ῥητόρων, εὖ λεχθέντες, ἰδιωτικοὶ ἐν ταῖς χερσίν. αἴτιον δ' ὅτι ἐν τῷ ἀγῶνι ἁρμόττει τὰ ὑποκριτικά· διὸ καὶ ἀφῃρημένης τῆς ὑποκρίσεως οὐ ποιοῦντα τὸ αὑτῶν ἔργον φαίνεται εὐήθη, οἷον τά τε ἀσύνδετα καὶ τὸ πολλάκις τὸ αὐτὸ εἰπεῖν ἐν τῇ γραφικῇ ὀρθῶς ἀποδοκιμάζεται, ἐν δὲ ἀγωνιστικῇ οὔ, καὶ οἱ ῥήτορες χρῶνται (1413b14–21 from Ross's *OCT*, quoted for convenience; cf. below, p. 623).

[74] τὸ μὲν γάρ ἐστιν ἑλληνίζειν ἐπίστασθαι, τὸ δὲ μὴ ἀναγκάζεσθαι κατασιωπᾶν ἄν τι βούληται μεταδοῦναι τοῖς ἄλλοις, ὅπερ πάσχουσιν οἱ μὴ ἐπιστάμενοι γράφειν (1413b5–8). This statement has confounded many (e.g. Rapp 2002:1.932), and a 'suitable' meaning is extracted by interpolating much that is allegedly tacit (so, for example, Kennedy 1991 *ad loc.*)—material that, in my view, is extraneous to the context. See below, pp. 601ff., for my discussion of this passage and an alternative translation for τὸ μὲν ... τὸ δέ that does not affect the material point here.

ēthos and *pathos*. But the recurrent late-classical association of rhapsodes with ὑποκριταί and ὑπόκρισις, and the contexts in which this happens, also confirm that, by this time, they shared with actors and orators an important aspect of their training: the use of written texts (first in the character of transcripts, then of scripts) to prepare for and secure a successful performance. This was an innovation gradual in coming, for since time immemorial the Homeric rhapsode had relied on recomposing epic poetry in performance; but, as we shall see, it was also a departure from the original practice of orators, which some of the more seasoned among them hotly decried as enervating and harmful to the speaker and his art.

9.5 Alkidamas' *On the Sophists*

On the Sophists is one such broadside that has survived to our time, where Alkidamas expostulates with sophists about their reliance on written drafts for their speeches to court and assembly.[75] His polemic is primarily against the professional[76] who has neglected the 'expertise' (ἱστορία) and 'training' (παιδεία) that would equip him for the intellectually demanding *autoskhediasmos*, i.e. 'extempore speaking',[77] relying instead on writing, a skill open to all regardless of natural ability.[78] Alkidamas' stance is elitist: he prides himself on grounds

---

[75] He does not consider epideictic as a *genus dicendi* (though ἀποδείξεις makes an appearance in §29; see above, p. 308 n. 64). Alkidamas' life and *oeuvre* have recently been the focus of much work. In the past, the interest of scholars has been the alleged rivalry between him and Isokrates. More recently, he has been studied on his own terms for his contribution to the development of rhetoric and the origin of literary criticism. See, for example, Brown 1914:27–42, Milne 1924, Walberer 1938, Gastaldi 1981, Eucken 1983:121–132, Friemann 1990, Ritoók 1991, O'Sullivan 1992, Bons 1998, Liebersohn 1999, Graff 2000 and 2001, Muir 2001, Schloemann 2002, Mariß 2002, and McCoy 2009.

[76] The distinction between the λογογράφος and his client is only once acknowledged: λογογραφήσουσι in §6 does not demand (though it may hint at) the technical meaning familiar to the modern scholar (cf. Mariß 2002:129); in §13, however, the professional speech writer seems in view. On the client/*logographos* relationship see Worthington 1993; on the *logographos* generally see Lavency 1964, Wolff 2007 [1967], Dover 1968b, Usher 1971, Todd 1990b:163–167, Todd 1993:94–96, Iannucci 2001, and Grethlein 2004.

[77] See the still essential study by Brown 1914. See also Hudson-Williams 1951, Hammerstaedt and Terbuyken 1994–1996, Klawitter 1998, and Schloemann 2000.

[78] ἐπειδή τινες τῶν καλουμένων σοφιστῶν ἱστορίας μὲν καὶ παιδείας ἠμελήκασι καὶ τοῦ δύνασθαι λέγειν ὁμοίως τοῖς ἰδιώταις ἀπείρως ἔχουσι, γράφειν δὲ μεμελετηκότες λόγους ... ('since some of the so-called sophists neglect learning and training and, like the layman, do not know how to speak, but being practiced in writing speeches ...' §1); πρῶτον μὲν οὖν ἐντεῦθεν ἄν τις καταφρονήσειε τοῦ γράφειν, ἐξ ὧν ἐστιν εὐεπίθετον καὶ ῥάδιον καὶ τῇ τυχούσῃ φύσει πρόχειρον. εἰπεῖν μὲν γὰρ ἐκ τοῦ παραυτίκα περὶ τοῦ παρατυχόντος ἐπιεικῶς ... οὔτε φύσεως ἁπάσης οὔτε παιδείας τῆς τυχούσης ἐστίν ('first, then, one might deprecate writing for this reason, that it is easily acquired, facile, and readily available to just any natural disposition. For to speak fittingly

other than well-crafted written speeches (an ability that he is nevertheless quick to own),[79] for writing must remain strictly a 'byproduct' (ἐν παρέργῳ), presumably, of speaking.[80] He allows writing even to those who make improvisation the heart of rhetorical practice, but only so long as it is properly subservient to speaking.[81] By opposing ποιηταί to σοφισταί[82] he acknowledges that writing was current among sophists[83] and asserts that too pervasive an influence of writing would assimilate them to craft artisans.[84]

Given the relation between sophists and rhapsodes I have argued for and the role of the latter as performers of poetry, we might anticipate that Alkidamas may mention ῥαψῳδική as a *comparandum* to the orators' use of writing. And indeed we are not disappointed, as we shall see below. But consider first how different the talents are that improvisation and scripted delivery call for.[85] The former requires speaking fittingly about the happenstance (περὶ τοῦ παρατυχόντος), a swift articulation of thoughts and arguments, a felicitous abundance of vocabulary (the resources of language at the level of expression), aiming accurately at the 'opportunity' of the matter at hand (καιρός), and a sensitive speaker-audience interaction that takes adequate account of the desires of the hearers and their shifting moods: in view is τὸ προσῆκον, a goal open indiscriminately neither to every nature nor to whatever training the orator may chance upon. Writing, on the contrary, enjoys leisure of composition (κατὰ σχολήν) and

---

on the spot on whatever matter presents itself ... is neither within the reach of every natural disposition nor attainable by just any training' §3).

[79] οὐχ ὡς ἀλλοτρίαν ἐμαυτοῦ τὴν δύναμιν αὐτῶν ἡγούμενος, ἀλλ᾽ ὡς ἐφ᾽ ἑτέροις μεῖζον φρονῶν ('not considering their ability alien to me, but priding myself more on other grounds' §2).

[80] So Radermacher 1951, who emends the text to τὸ γράφειν ἐν παρέργῳ τοῦ ⟨λέγειν⟩ μελετᾶν οἰόμενος χρῆναι (§2).

[81] Even where writing plays a role, it is ultimately for the hearing (not reading) of the people: ἐπὶ τὴν ἀκρόασιν (§11).

[82] τοὺς ἐπ᾽ αὐτὸ τοῦτο τὸν βίον καταναλίσκοντας ἀπολελεῖφθαι πολὺ καὶ ῥητορικῆς καὶ φιλοσοφίας ὑπειληφώς, καὶ πολὺ δικαιότερον ἂν ποιητὰς ἢ σοφιστὰς προσαγορεύεσθαι νομίζων ('being of the opinion that those who spend their life on this very thing are greatly deficient in their oratorical skill and in philosophy, and considering that one would much more justly call them makers than sophists' §2).

[83] From various sources we know that they kept and used books when the Athenian book trade was still in its infancy and owning scrolls was still considered extraordinary. Cf. Dover 1993:34–35, Pöhlmann 1994:19n19, and O'Sullivan 1996:115–116.

[84] Later on he mentions ποιήματα: οἱ τοῖς ὀνόμασιν ἐξειργασμένοι [sc. λόγοι] καὶ μᾶλλον ποιήμασιν ἢ λόγοις ἐοικότες ('speeches of contrived diction and more like artifacts than speeches' §12). Mariß 2002:180 writes: "Im Hinblick auf die Metapher in dem vorhergehenden ἐξειργασμένοι schwingt bei ποιήματα auch hier die Bedeutung, 'künstl(er)i(s)ch gefertigte Gebilde', mit; den ursprünglichen Sinn von ποιητάς hatte Alkidamas, in einer sprachlich ähnlichen Wendung in §2, polemisch genutzt ... . Der abwertende Unterton klingt auch in ποιήματα an." For the early history of the word 'poet' in its literary sense see Ford 2002:131–157.

[85] All the references in this paragraph are to *On the Sophists* §§3–4.

length of time (ἐν πολλῷ χρόνῳ), and benefits from comparing and collating other sophists' συγγράμματα, culled for compelling thoughts (ἐνθυμήματα) and felicitous expressions (τὰς τῶν εὖ λεγομένων ἐπιτυχίας). Add to these correction, revision, and rewriting (this last, ἀνακαθῆραι, literally, 'cleaning up' the text), and we have the full apparatus of a developed editorial practice.

We can easily transfer this to the rhapsode. He would have been schooled from youth up in traditional composition in performance: his παιδεία was demanding and called for rare natural talent.[86] He would declaim a sort of improvisation that remained within the parameters of traditional themes, diction, and sequence. The unexpected would arise from interaction with his audience—whose desires he would seek to respond to and gratify—and from competing with other rhapsodes under time constraints and the rules that regulated transitions between one bard and the next (e.g. as to thematic continuity). Depending on the format, interruptions from the audience or amoibaic rhapsodic exchanges may not be out of the question. Speed of thought and expressive resourcefulness would be crucial to his success. Conversely, the leisurely drafting and memorizing of a script for oral delivery, away from the competitive pressures of actual performance and assisted by previous transcripts, in search of apposite ἐνθυμήματα and the felicitous verses of others—all the while correcting, revising, and rewriting, both on the advice of others and his own—would have been to the advantage of any who aspired to be a rhapsode but had not enjoyed the life-long apprenticeship that was the *sine qua non* of recomposition-in-performance. The same elitist criticism may be levied in this case: we would have, on the one hand, what called for rigorous, life-long παιδεία and was only open to singularly gifted talent; and, on the other, what was readily acquired, derivative, and easy even for the uninstructed (ἀπαίδευτοι).

Strictly speaking, these two strategies were not mutually exclusive. Surely, the ability to improvise must have spanned a range. Some performers may have employed texts only as transcripts, to be used in rehearsal not for strict memorization but to hone improvisatory delivery. Memory, after all, remained always an essential tool even of the most creative extempore traditional performance, for which Homeric diction functioned as a language, albeit a special one—just as memory is essential for any natural-language ability.[87] Those orators who did not depend primarily (or even regularly) on writing could, by a change in what Alkidamas calls a 'frame of mind' (τὴν τῆς ψυχῆς ἕξιν μεταρρυθμίσαντες §6), draft fitting scripts for their speeches. The same, I think, might be said about the

---

[86] Here, too, there would be an opposition between the ἰδιῶται and the δημιουργός (§§1, 4), and true traditional skill would hardly be εὐεπίθετον (§3).

[87] So, for example, in Plato's *Iōn* memory is mentioned at 537a2–4, and again humorously at 539e7–540a3. Cf. *Lesser Hippias* 368d6–7 and 369a4–8.

production of poetic transcripts by classical rhapsodes who exhibited a limited and occasional dependence on writing. Ultimately, the opposition between αὐτοσχηδιασμός and scripted delivery was one of opportunity versus time and leisure (i.e. καιρός versus χρόνος and σχολή), and it marks a shift away from the creative primacy of the performative setting. Improvisation possessed flexibility, but also uncertainty; scripts, in turn, could only thrive where competitive rules minimized the unexpected and put the emphasis on the stylistic finish of the delivery, with the corresponding depreciation of the skills that must have been the guarantee of victory at the ἀγῶνες among the more traditionally schooled singers: responding to audience feedback and interruptions, thematic contraction and expansion to adjust to the available time and the interests of the hearers, mastery of relay poetics,[88] and so on. It must be the case, therefore, that the transition from transcripts to scripts was facilitated by competitive rules at the Panathenaia that enforced an increasingly fixed thematic sequence. This sequence must have been predictable enough before the actual performance to give a competitive advantage to rhapsodes who chose to draft their recital in advance and commit it to memory.

Unfortunately, we are too poorly informed to know even the outlines of what must be a crucial piece of this cultural puzzle: the change in the extraction—and, hence, the training—of the rhapsodes that competed at the Athenian Panathenaia.[89] The fame of Ionian bards was well established, and we must assume that among them the traditional skill of extempore recomposition still flourished during the classical age. According to a dominant tradition, Homer himself hailed from the region, specifically from Khios, and thus it is only to be expected that, for his dialog with Sokrates, Plato would choose a bard from a city like Ephesos. But the love of Homer, the distinguished place his poetry held in Athens (emphasized by Lykourgos in *Against Leōkratēs* §102), and the social and material benefits to successful prize winners must have tempted the more ambitious Athenians to try their hand at the competition.[90] Since the *Iliad* and

---

[88] That is, a follow-up of one performer by the next that is not only smooth and polished at the thematic level, but also respectful of the generic constraints observed in transitions between poetic sections.

[89] Athens played the central role because of its dominance over the recitation and diffusion of Homeric epic during its defining stage. Cf. Nagy 2001.

[90] There was a comparable shift in the pool of competitors participating in athletic events all throughout Greece. To be sure, this shift did not consist, as must have been the case with Panathenaic rhapsodes, in a gradual displacement of a largely Ionian (i.e. non-Athenian) professionalism by a growing Athenian 'semi-professional amateurism' (to use an oxymoron). Athletic events witnessed instead an increasing involvement of upper middle- and lower-class athletes. While the elite (in Athens, those who belonged to the liturgical class) never withdrew from festival competitions, citizens from the lower rungs of the leisure class, from the hoplite 'middle class,' and even a small number of lower-class individuals gained access, a development that

the *Odyssey* were the pedagogical mainstay (Isokrates *Panēgyrikos* 159), attaining a level of proficiency adequate for a festival appearance might have seemed to aspiring performers not to go much further than committing to memory large portions of the poems. A book-trade copy might serve as a handy script; to be sure, concentration and recall would have to be honed, but the creative center of gravity would be in the delivery (i.e. in the use of voice, gesture, and dress). Extraordinary facility and a quick mind might enable one thus trained to save the day by supplying a suitable line of his own making here and there, should his memory suffer a minor lapse in performance. But this would no longer qualify as true traditional oral composition. There may be a hint of this state of affairs in Xenophon *Apomnēmoneumata* 4.2.10, where Euthydemos' imposing collection of Homeric writings (τὰ Ὁμήρου ἔπη πάντα) gives rise to Sokrates' gibe that perhaps he wishes to become a rhapsode. And from *Symposion* 3.5–6 we learn that Nikeratos' father, wishing to raise his son to be an ἀνὴρ ἀγαθός, had forced him to learn all of Homer's *epē* (πάντα τὰ Ὁμήρου ἔπη μαθεῖν); apparently, this called for daily exposure to rhapsodic recitation (πῶς ἄν ... λελήθοι ἀκροώμενόν γε αὐτῶν ὀλίγου ἂν' ἑκάστην ἡμέραν;),[91] an apprenticeship of such a sort as an ambitious Athenian of means might have been able to procure for himself. In fact, some have even suggested that this may be the same Nikeratos who according to Aristotle (*Rhetoric* 1413a6–9) was bested by Pratys at a rhapsodic competition.[92] If Xenophon's report in the *Symposion* is accurate and his and Aristotle's Nikeratos are one and the same, Nikeratos must have competed

---

led a few disgruntled καλοὶ κἀγαθοί to withdraw into equestrian events, which were beyond the means of all but the wealthiest. Pleket (1975:74) argues that in Athens the *ephēbeia* "functioned as a bridge for members of the urban elite between gymnasium sport and the world of the public contests." I am not, of course, claiming for rhapsodic performance in Athens that a particular social class of citizens had thitherto monopolized the competition. My suggestion is that just as a world of expanding social opportunities for the Athenian upper classes through the *ephēbeia* and the athletic training of the gymnasium enabled their participation in public athletic contests, so also the expanding educational resources and opportunities for the lower rungs of the leisure class (i.e. the upper middle class) and even the growing popular orientation of the Athenian upper-class engagement with the democratic process (an orientation to which their interest in rhetorical training witnesses) must have helped and encouraged some of them to train for, and participate in, the rhapsodic events at the Panathenaia. On wealth, social status, education, and the Athenian democratic process see Ober 1989. For a recent survey of Greek education see Griffith 2001. On social status and Greek sports, see Pleket 2001 [1974, lightly updated]; Pleket 1975:71–74, Young 1984, Pleket 1992, and Golden 2008:23–26. On the *ephēbeia* (whether it already existed in the fifth century and included the *thētes*) see Pleket 2001:183; Rhodes 1993:503; and Raaflaub 1996:157, with 172–173nn148–149. For the Athenian 'middle class' see Hansen 1991:115–116 and Hanson 1996 (with qualifications from van Wees 2001 and 2002; and Gabrielsen 2002).

[91] Cf. Pelliccia 2003:111.

[92] Cf. Ford 2002:196n31. See further below, p. 494 item 2.

as an amateur or else, despite his earlier criticism of rhapsodes, he must have decided to become one himself.[93]

I believe that the parallel sketched above between orators and rhapsodes is not merely conjectural, for, just as Plato and Aristotle do, Alkidamas also couples ὑπόκρισις and the rhapsode's trade:[94] since it is impossible to memorize written speeches on any and every topic, he notes, it necessarily follows that the orator who depends on scripts will improvise some things and mold others; the outcome will look uneven, some of the material approaching ὑπόκρισις and ῥαψῳδία, while the rest looks common and trivial next to the precision of the former. We could read ὑποκρίσει καὶ ῥαψῳδίᾳ (§14) as a hendiadys: 'dramatic rhapsody' (proper to a rhapsode whose declamation is strongly under the influence of stage acting),[95] 'rhapsodic interpretation' (the rhapsode viewed as expounder of Homer),[96] or, quite simply, 'rhapsodic performance'; alternatively, as referring both to stage acting and rhapsodic declamation.[97] Any of these is sufficient for my purposes and shows that for Alkidamas the practice of the rhapsode epitomizes the finish and precision of delivery that corresponds to the use of scripts, drafted in advance of the performance, memorized, and carefully rehearsed with a view to attaining the maximum impact on delivery.

It is curious that scripted material is likened here to ὑπόκρισις for its precision, whereas in Aristotle's *Rhetoric* III.12 it is the *agonistic* style—the one contrasted with the *graphic* as comparatively less precise—that is considered

---

93 Alternatively, he might have found it preferable to acquiesce in the criticism of his dinner companions, feigning to share it rather than mount a defense of rhapsodes in the face of peer pressure. That he reportedly sought the ὑπόνοιαι of the likes of Stesimbrotos and Anaximander shows that he intended to overcome the commonly perceived limitations of the average rhapsodic training.

94 περὶ πάντων μὲν γὰρ τῶν πραγμάτων γεγραμμένους ἐπίστασθαι λόγους ἕν τι τῶν ἀδυνάτων πέφυκεν· ἀνάγκη δ' ἐστίν, ὅταν τις τὰ μὲν αὐτοσχεδιάζῃ, τὰ δὲ τυποῖ, τὸν λόγον ἀνόμοιον ὄντα ψόγον τῷ λέγοντι παρασκευάζειν, καὶ τὰ μὲν ὑποκρίσει καὶ ῥαψῳδίᾳ παραπλήσια δοκεῖν εἶναι, τὰ δὲ ταπεινὰ καὶ φαῦλα φαίνεσθαι παρὰ τὴν ἐκείνων ἀκρίβειαν ('For knowing written speeches about every subject matter is naturally one of life's impossibilities. And, when one improvises some things and [carefully] molds others, it is inevitable that the speech, being uneven, furnish grounds for censuring the speaker; and that the molded portions appear closely to resemble rhapsodic performance while the improvised, next to the precision of the former, seem mean and careless' §14).

95 Schloemann (2000:215n53) suggests "dichterische Deklamation."

96 Whose style would be that of the "gebundene Rede der Kunstprosa" (Koller 1957:104). Koller connects the ὑπόκρισις of §14 to sections 16–17, which regard those who are accustomed to work out speeches in detail and compose them (doubtless, in writing) with precise diction and rhythms. Alkidamas implies that, unable for lack of talent or training to take advantage of the freedom offered by improvisation, sophists are brought back to the figures and rhythms (εἰς ἐκεῖνα τὰ σχήματα καὶ τοὺς ῥυθμοὺς ἀποφέρονται §17) constrained by writing.

97 So Mariß 2002: "Vielmehr steht ὑπόκρισις als Begriff für den Vortrag von dramatischer Dichtung eigenständig neben dem Rezitieren von—in erster Linie—epischen Texten" (195).

the most appropriate for delivery. This is primarily a matter of emphasis, for *Rhetoric* III.1, as we shall see below,[98] also associates ὑπόκρισις with the precision and technical competence that follow from reducing delivery to an art (in particular, to an art that makes use of writing).[99] Nevertheless, the varying emphasis shows that, conceptually, Alkidamas stops short of the more developed notion of a style enabled by writing to which Aristotle takes us, namely, the '*graphic* style', best represented by epideictic speeches. For Alkidamas, just as the orator as writer of speeches resembles a *poiētēs*, a 'speech maker' or 'poet', and his speech recalls a *poiēma* sooner than a *logos*, so also in delivery he smacks more of a rhapsode than a rhetor. Though my argument here does not turn on the precise meaning of ὑποκρίσει καὶ ῥαψῳδίᾳ, I rather incline to 'rhapsodic *hypokrisis*' in the sense of 'performance'.[100] Indeed, one need not read into Alkidamas the terminological distinction between tragic and rhapsodic delivery Aristotle observes in *Poetics* 26 and *Rhetoric* III.1; and though 'poet' may well lurk behind the word ποιητής (§34) and Isokrates shows us that ποιητὴς τῶν λόγων need not mean more than 'maker' or 'composer of speeches',[101] the emphasis

---

[98]   See section 14.1, pp. 579ff.

[99]   Although I do not agree with Schloemann (2000:214) that Aristotle contradicts himself in his use of ὑπόκρισις in *Rhetoric* III.1 vis-à-vis *Rhetoric* III.12, I join him in his conviction, convincingly substantiated by his excellent article, that 'delivery', as a *tekhnē* and not a natural talent, is throughout connected with writing and hence susceptible of displaying a range of stylistic devices and a varying degree of precision.

[100]   Pace Mariß 2002:195.

[101]   Isokrates *Against the Sophists* 15: ἡ δὲ παίδευσις τοὺς μὲν τοιούτους τεχνικωτέρους καὶ πρὸς τὸ ζητεῖν εὐπορωτέρους ἐποίησεν· οἷς γὰρ νῦν ἐντυγχάνουσι πλανώμενοι, ταῦτ' ἐξ ἑτοιμοτέρου λαμβάνειν αὐτοὺς ἐδίδαξεν, τοὺς δὲ καταδεεστέραν τὴν φύσιν ἔχοντας ἀγωνιστὰς μὲν ἀγαθοὺς ἢ λόγων ποιητὰς οὐκ ἂν ἀποτελέσειεν, αὐτοὺς δ' ἂν αὐτῶν προαγάγοι καὶ πρὸς πολλὰ φρονιμωτέρως διακεῖσθαι ποιήσειεν ('Instruction makes such men more technically skillful and more resourceful in their discovery; for it teaches them to take from a readier source the things which they now randomly hit upon. And while it could not make good competitors or speech makers out of those who have an inferior nature, it could lead them on beyond themselves and render them more discerning in many respects'); Isokrates *Antidosis* 192: περὶ μὲν οὖν τῆς φύσεως καὶ τῆς ἐμπειρίας ταῦτα γιγνώσκω· περὶ δὲ τῆς παιδείας οὐκ ἔχω τοιοῦτον λόγον εἰπεῖν· οὔτε γὰρ ὁμοίαν οὔτε παραπλησίαν ἔχει τούτοις τὴν δύναμιν. εἰ γάρ τις διακούσειεν ἅπαντα τὰ περὶ τοὺς λόγους καὶ διακριβωθείη μᾶλλον τῶν ἄλλων, λόγων μὲν ποιητὴς τυχὸν ἂν χαριέστερος γένοιτο τῶν πολλῶν, εἰς ὄχλον δὲ καταστάς, τούτου μόνον ἀποστερηθείς, τοῦ τολμᾶν, οὐδ' ἂν φθέγξασθαι δυνηθείη ('This, then, is what I know about natural talent and experience. But I cannot make a similar point about instruction, for it is neither similar nor about equal to these in power. For if one should exhaustively hear all that concerns oratory and should grow more accomplished than others, he might perhaps become a more pleasing speech maker than the rest. But were he to stand before the crowd lacking this alone, courage, he would not even be able to utter a word').

clearly falls on careful crafting that almost certainly involves writing, yet all the while is oriented towards delivery.[102]

9.6 Ῥαψῳδέω in Isokrates and Plato

Isokrates and Plato both use ῥαψῳδέω in a sense broader than the declamation of verses learned by rote.[103] Indeed, at *Panathēnaikos* 18[104] Isokrates lampoons some in the Lyceum—whom he calls sophists—who claimed to know everything and were quick to show themselves everywhere; in discussing (διαλέγοιντο) the poets, especially the poetry of Hesiod and Homer, they contributed nothing of their own but merely rhapsodized the poets' material (τὰ δ' ἐκείνων

---

[102] Mariß (2002:99–100) essentially agrees with this view, noting that in *On the Sophists*, as in Plato's *Phaidros*, the boundary between 'poet' and 'speech maker' is fluid. With ποιητής Alkidamas may well intend, as Mariß remarks, a disparagement of the orator who places too great a value on precise drafts, suggesting that he rather resembles a manual artisan. In §34, however, it is clear that ποιητὴς λόγων is the rhetorical wordsmith (not the poet) who, excessively dependent on writing, never rises to the level of the true orator. I agree with Mariß (2002:307) that δεινὸς ῥήτωρ and ποιητὴς λόγων are mutually exclusive at the rhetorical level of Alkidamas' diatribe; but I do not think she is correct in denying Isokrates *Against the Sophists* 15 and *Antidosis* 192 a connection with delivery. In *Against the Sophists* 15, ἀγωνιστὰς μὲν ἀγαθοὺς ἢ λόγων ποιητὰς does not establish an opposition ("Gegenbegriff") between ἀγωνισταί and ποιηταί: Isokrates does not specify the relationship between them. But since both are possible outcomes of the sophistic παίδευσις in the case of gifted men, both must *a fortiori* be included in the promise that πολιτικοὶ λόγοι hold for the formation of successful ῥήτορες (*Against the Sophists* 9). Thus, one should also see *both* as connected with delivery, for this is the end of such *logoi*. A man like Isokrates, who mostly writes but does not deliver them, is still at that time an anomaly. Isokrates *Antidosis* 192 confirms this view (*pace* Mariß 2002:306: "[Der Redenschreiber] hat bei ihnen [sc. Isokrates und Platon] jedoch, anders als bei Alkidamas, mit dem Vortrag nichts zu tun"); for here, Isokrates notes, however refined a ποιητὴς λόγων one might be in attaining mastery of all that pertains to speech-making, only let him lack courage and he will not be able to utter a word before a crowd. The obvious implication of this statement is that the ποιητὴς λόγων is not merely a writer, but also a speaker (as Norlin's *Loeb Classical Library* translation renders it; Mathieu's Budé, in turn, offers "un inventeur de discours").

[103] The sense offered by LSJ s.v. for *Phaidros* 277e, 'to repeat by heart or rote', is much too narrow; and restricting it to 'reciting poems' in Isokrates *Panathēnaikos* 18 and 33, though true, is misleading if we do not observe its contextual tie to 'exposition'.

[104] Isokrates *Panathēnaikos* 18: ἀπαντήσαντες γάρ τινές μοι τῶν ἐπιτηδείων ἔλεγον ὡς ἐν τῷ Λυκείῳ συγκαθεζόμενοι τρεῖς ἢ τέτταρες τῶν ἀγελαίων σοφιστῶν καὶ πάντα φασκόντων εἰδέναι καὶ ταχέως πανταχοῦ γιγνομένων διαλέγοιντο περί τε τῶν ἄλλων ποιητῶν καὶ τῆς Ἡσιόδου καὶ τῆς Ὁμήρου ποιήσεως, οὐδὲν μὲν παρ' αὑτῶν λέγοντες, τὰ δ' ἐκείνων ῥαψῳδοῦντες καὶ τῶν πρότερον ἄλλοις τισὶν εἰρημένων τὰ χαριέστατα μνημονεύοντες ('some of my friends met me and told me that three or four of those herdlike, know-it-all sophists, prompt to be everywhere, were sitting together in the Lyceum and discussing the poets, especially the poetry of Hesiod and Homer, saying nothing of their own vintage but rhapsodizing the poets' material and mentioning the finest things uttered before by certain others').

ῥαψῳδοῦντες) and called to mind (μνημονεύοντες)[105] the most sophisticated things that others before them had said.[106] Though satirical in tone, we recognize the basic description of rhapsodes presented by Koller 1957 and defended above: itinerant, they not only declaim what are notionally the verses of Homer (or another poet) but also expound them as modern scholars would expect a sophist to do. This suggests, once again, that the boundary between rhapsode and sophist was more permeable then than it seems to us now. Note also that they were performing before an audience (perhaps small, but a real audience all the same),[107] and that the sophists' ensuing criticism of Isokrates (§19) pertained to his view of poetry and its precise role in education.[108] Some believe that Isokrates reserves ῥαψῳδέω strictly for the verse (the ἔπη) and uses another verb for the exposition (here μνημονεύω, for what is alleged to be rote learning). But without an immediate specific referent for the τά of τὰ ἐκείνων,[109] its indefinite character encourages us to think of the expository part as of a piece with their rhapsodizing.

I am not, of course, denying that the sophists also declaimed poetry. My point is only that ῥαψῳδέω *by itself* (without the aid of μνημονεύω) would have sufficed to denote the interspersing of declamation and commentary that was characteristic of the rhapsode. The clause with μνημονεύω tells us about the caliber and authorship of the comments, but, as the structure of the passage makes clear, the presence of interpretation does not hinge on it. Indeed, the main verb, διαλέγοιντο, is qualified by a participial μὲν ... δὲ opposition: on the μέν hangs 'saying nothing of their own'; the δέ, in turn, subdivides into 'rhapsodizing' and 'mentioning'. If 'rhapsodize' referred strictly to the declamation of ἔπη, it would be an unnecessary intrusion into the logic of the passage; for it would have been sufficient to say that 'they were talking about the poetry of Homer and Hesiod, saying nothing they could claim as their own, but merely mentioning the finest thoughts others before had said about them'. On this assumption, 'rhapsodizing their poetry' would clearly go beyond 'they were talking about their poetry' and would hang limp as a curious addition to the polarity 'not their own thoughts but what others had said'. Moreover, how could

---

[105] 'Repeating by rote' or 'from memory' (so Norlin in the *Loeb Classical Library*) is too tendentious a translation for a verb that simply means 'to call to mind, mention, say' (cf. Lykourgos' *Against Leōkratēs* §110.1). Such a marked gloss (for which there is no support in the LSJ) reads into the text a preconceived view of the activity that these sophists are engaging in.

[106] Cf. Nagy 1996c:122–124.

[107] ἀποδεξαμένων δὲ τῶν περιεστώτων τὴν διατριβὴν αὐτῶν ... (§19).

[108] Cf. §§26 and 33. This may have been *en nuce* the bone of contention between rhapsodes and those whom we today call sophists.

[109] ἔπη is not found in the context and, although ποίησις is, it appears as the object of διαλέγεσθαι περί; i.e. as a subject of discussion, not of declamation.

'reciting their verses' be fairly held against the sophists as indicative of their lack of originality? If, however, 'to rhapsodize' means 'to treat in the manner of a rhapsode', and rhapsodes, as a rule, *both* declaimed poetry *and* commented on it; and if, among sophists, rhapsodes were infamous for their intellectual mediocrity and lack of original thinking (and they arguably were)—then it would have made sense to note, in a show of contempt, that they were 'saying nothing they could claim to be their own original thinking, but merely treating the poets' material with the same mediocrity rhapsodes are wont to, compensating for this deficiency with the most sophisticated commentary of earlier thinkers.' Then ῥαψῳδέω does not hang limp as a superfluous detail, but becomes central to the criticism Isokrates levels against the sophists.

At any rate, whatever else we may say, the entire episode is summarized by διαλέγοιντο, which unites under one conceptual label of verbal exchange both the poetry itself and its exposition. This episode is anomalous only to this extent: the performance dynamics were such that the outcome was a conversation of sorts (rather than a declaimed monologue or a series of them);[110] and yet, though the interlocutors are clearly in basic agreement, the dialog may well have had a competitive dimension (each trying to outdo the others).[111] In a more formal agonistic setting, a sequence of rhapsodes taking in turn to the βῆμα would answer to such emulous repartee. In *Panathēnaikos* 33,[112] looking back on the same event, Isokrates reiterates his characterization of the sophists; only, he now substitutes μνημονεύοντες by ληροῦντας περὶ αὐτῶν, disparaging as sheer prate the exposition of these sophists (just as was done so often to rhapsodes).[113] Once again, when Isokrates in this passage writes of silencing them, he does not merely say 'I think I could silence those who prattle about them', but 'those who rhapsodize their things (τἀκείνων) and prattle about them'. Thus, in effect, he witnesses once more to the unity of declamation and commentary

---

[110] From Plato's *Phaidros* 277e8–9 and Alkidamas' *On the Sophists* §14, one may infer that in the fourth century BC the average rhapsodic showpiece was largely, if not exclusively, monologic, a discourse that made little allowance for substantial input from the audience. With this in view, Hippias' boast in the *Lesser Hippias* 363d that he is ready to answer any question posed to him by his audience can be seen, by comparison, as a pretentious claim for the superiority of his skill as a sophist.

[111] Dialectic, of course, may prove competitive in actual practice.

[112] Isokrates *Panathēnaikos* 33: περὶ μὲν οὖν τῶν πεπαιδευμένων τυγχάνω ταῦτα γιγνώσκων. περὶ δὲ τῆς Ὁμήρου καὶ τῆς Ἡσιόδου καὶ τῆς τῶν ἄλλων ποιήσεως ἐπιθυμῶ μὲν εἰπεῖν, οἶμαι γὰρ ἂν παῦσαι τοὺς ἐν τῷ Λυκείῳ ῥαψῳδοῦντας τἀκείνων καὶ ληροῦντας περὶ αὐτῶν ('These then happen to be my opinions about the educated. Now, I am eager to speak about the poetry of Homer, Hesiod, and the rest, for I think that I could stop those in the Lyceum from rhapsodizing their things and prattling about them').

[113] Cf. the *Suidas* s.v. ῥαψῳδοί: ῥαψῳδῆσαι δέ ἐστι τὸ φλυαρῆσαι (4.287 P no. 71.2–3 Adler); s.v. καταρραψῳδήσει: φλυαρήσει (3.52 K no. 748 Adler); and s.vv. εἰκῇ ῥαψῳδεῖ: ἀντὶ τοῦ φλυαρεῖ (2.524 EI no. 78 Adler).

that underlies Sokrates' conversation with Ion the rhapsode. Isokrates' insistent use of ῥαψῳδέω in connection with the sophists supports the view that he is drawing attention to their manner of commentary, not just their (otherwise unobjectionable) declamation of poetry. Since sophists arguably despised rhapsodic commentary, this description amounted to an effective put-down. It is not clear whether the αὐτῶν is neuter or masculine plural, i.e. whether it refers to the τά of τἀκείνων or the ἐκεῖνοι. If to the former, ληροῦντας περὶ αὐτῶν would overlap in sense with ῥαψῳδοῦντας τἀκείνων for added emphasis; if to the latter (Norlin's choice in the *Loeb Classical Library*), it would stand for 'these poets' and refer more specifically to the biographic accounts that ancient scholars, including rhapsodes, were so fond of.[114]

Plato's *Phaidros* 277e5–278a1 is another passage that connects ῥαψῳδέω not narrowly with some notion of stage acting but with delivery broadly defined:[115]

ὁ δέ γε ἐν μὲν τῷ γεγραμμένῳ λόγῳ περὶ ἑκάστου παιδιάν τε ἡγούμενος πολλὴν ἀναγκαῖον εἶναι, καὶ οὐδένα πώποτε λόγον ἐν μέτρῳ οὐδ' ἄνευ μέτρου μεγάλης ἄξιον σπουδῆς γραφῆναι οὐδὲ λεχθῆναι,[116] ὡς οἱ ῥαψῳδούμενοι ἄνευ ἀνακρίσεως καὶ διδαχῆς πειθοῦς ἕνεκα ἐλέχθησαν, ἀλλὰ τῷ ὄντι αὐτῶν τοὺς βελτίστους εἰδότων ὑπόμνησιν γεγονέναι ...

One who thinks that in a written speech, irrespective of subject, there is bound to be much childish play, and that no speech in verse or prose worthy of much serious attention has ever yet been written and delivered, as the ones rhapsodized without examination and instruction are delivered for the sake of persuasion, but that in reality the best of them are [merely] a reminder to those who [already] know ...

Here Sokrates denies serious consideration to written speeches (ἐν μὲν τῷ γεγραμμένῳ λόγῳ): hence γραφῆναι οὐδὲ λεχθῆναι cannot represent *two* independent alternatives. At issue is the fixity of writing, its inflexibility, which makes it unsuitable to dialog: hence we need *both* γραφῆναι *and* λεχθῆναι. To illustrate the point, Sokrates mentions 'rhapsodized speeches' (οἱ ῥαψῳδούμενοι [sc. λόγοι]), which are spoken (ἐλέχθησαν)[117] without questioning (ἀνάκρισις)

---

[114] Cf. DK 8 1 on Theagenes of Rhegion, on whom see pp. 156ff. above.

[115] Hence, it supports my preferred understanding of Alkidamas' ὑποκρίσει καὶ ῥαψῳδίᾳ as 'rhapsodic *hypokrisis*' and, by implication, the reading of the *Iōn* offered above.

[116] I am following the punctuation of Moreschini's Budé text, placing with Stallbaum 1857b after λεχθῆναι the comma that Burnet (in the *OCT*) had put after γραφῆναι. Read on for my rationale.

[117] An empiric aorist (Smyth §1930) or an aorist of description (Smyth §1932). Yunis (2011:238) calls it "gnomic." The three types are closely related.

or instruction (διδαχή).[118] The words οὐδὲ λεχθῆναι ὡς οἱ ῥαψῳδούμενοι ἄνευ ἀνακρίσεως καὶ διδαχῆς πειθοῦς ἕνεκα ἐλέχθησαν, which Burnet's OCT isolates with commas as a separate clause, are read by some as an afterthought. Yunis (2011:238) illustrates this reading, which I believe neither the context nor the overarching argument of the dialog commends: "no speech in verse or prose that is worth much serious attention has ever yet been written or even spoken as the [speeches] performed by rhapsodes are spoken for the sake of persuasion without [oral] examination and teaching."[119] According to Yunis, Sokrates here "*extends* the category of non-serious discourse beyond written discourse to include oral discourse that eschews individual engagement and the dialectical pursuit of knowledge" (2011:238, my emphasis). I submit that Sokrates does not have an 'extension' of his argument in view, but rather illustrates the deprecated mode of communication—oral delivery that is seen as either subservient or else inferior to the written word—with its foremost exponent in the culture of his time: rhapsodic delivery of epic poetry and commentary that, by this late time in the chronology of textual fixation, was largely (perhaps often decisively) dependent on scripted performance. Yunis has no warrant for introducing "even" in "written or even spoken," an insertion that serves to sever 'written' from 'spoken'. οὐδέ cannot be *both* conjunctive *and* adverbial.[120] His translation

---

[118] Heitsch (1993:64–65) translates, correctly, "ohne die Möglichkeit von Einrede und Erläuterung." Some take ἀνάκρισις as 'preliminary investigation' *vel sim*. But this misses Plato's point that the give-and-take of true conversation cannot happen when the text is already fixed. (Fixity, of course, is relative, allowing for multiple gradations. But, for Plato, shades of gray would only spoil his black and white analysis, and for this reason γραφῆναι should be read as an accurate description of the dominant tendency.) In this case the semantic component 'preliminary' is beside the point (LSJ correctly, *contra* the DGE s.v. ἀνάκρισις), for what matters is the probing of divergent points of view by careful questioning (the basic meaning of ἀνακρίνω). In other words, ἀνάκρισις amounts to the Sokratic ἔλεγχος by another name, and διδαχή is the learning netted by the investigation. Cf. Heitsch 1993:210n481. There is nothing to object, of course, to taking ἀνάκρισις for the question-and-answer format of the preliminary judicial procedure, so long as in the context of *Phaidros* 277e8–9 one limits its import strictly to this format and strips it of the notion 'preliminary'. For more on the Athenian ἀνάκρισις see Harrison 1968–1971:2.94–105 and Todd 1993:126–127.

[119] A similar criticism applies to Hackforth's translation in Hamilton and Cairns 1961.

[120] A quick survey of the adverbial instances adduced by various grammars shows that, in such cases, οὐδέ is never simultaneously conjunctive. As one would expect, δέ can only perform one or the other function. Thus, for example, Smyth §2931 illustrates the adverbial use with ἀλλ' οὐδέ, ὅτ' οὐδέ, οὐδ' εἰ—all three of which exhibit accompanying conjunctions—and οὐδέ with a participle (ὅπου γὰρ ἐγὼ μὲν οὐδὲ πεπονθώς from Demosthenes 21.205). One must not confuse the structure of our *Phaidros* passage with the intensifying progression τὲ ... δέ (Smyth §2981 and K-G II.2.244 §520 Anm. 3). In *Phaidros* 277e we have an outer coordination τὲ ... καὶ depending on ἡγούμενος (τε ἡγούμενος ... , καὶ ...), whose second clause (the καὶ-clause) includes the subordinate coordination γραφῆναι οὐδὲ λεχθῆναι. In actual τὲ ... δέ constructions, what begins as if the speaker expects to add a second member is rounded instead by a contrast. This has the effect of placing emphasis on the second (contrasting) member. Of course, Yunis and those of

has made it into both by glossing it as the conjunctive "or" and adjoining the adverbial "even."[121] Since standing between two infinitives it is surely a conjunction, the only question here is whether, following as it does 'not one' (οὐδένα), its meaning is that of a disjunctive 'or' or a conjunctive 'and'. If the former, we have the negation of both terms of an alternative; if the latter, we have the negation of both members of a combination.[122] The clause is negated by the οὐ- of οὐδένα, while the οὐ- of οὐδέ merely confirms the first negative (Smyth §2761). That οὐ … οὐδέ can have a conjunctive sense, i.e. 'not (A and [then] B)', is clear e.g. from Demosthenes 1.8: 'You should not (οὐ δεῖ), men of Athens, dismiss such

---

his persuasion allege no contrast (or even intensification) between γραφῆναι and λεχθῆναι—only that the latter further illustrates the criticism levied against the former. The related οὔτε … οὐδέ construction, also by way of a contrastive δέ, implies an emphatic second member: '(both) not this but not that'. This can be freely rendered 'neither this nor yet/even that'. Quite apart from the fact that this is not the construction of *Phaidros* 277e, for my claim that δέ cannot be simultaneously conjunctive and adverbial it is important to realize that the 'yet/even' is added to bring out the contrast in translation, and not because δέ performs both functions at once (again, the literal translation is 'neither A but not B'). The intensifying effect—strictly speaking, the outcome of what Smyth considers a "harsh" "combination of copulative and adversative particles" (§2981)—is often brought out further by the addition of emphasizing particles like αὖ, γέ, or μήν (Smyth §2949 and K-G II.2.290 §535g). It bears repeating that Sokrates intends no contrast between 'written' and 'spoken'; the only interpretive point at issue is whether these are two successive facets of a singly conceived delivery or else the second is added as a further independent illustration of the deficiency imputed to writing.

[121] Note that he does not treat thus the immediately preceding ἐν μέτρῳ οὐδ' ἄνευ μέτρου.

[122] To speak about the logical structure of Sokrates' statement, *stricto sensu* '(not A) and (not B)' (i.e. ¬A ∧ ¬B) does not in itself necessarily imply anything about the relationship of A to B; whether these two are conceived as independent alternatives or as somehow connected to each other is a judgment that must be made contextually. Naturally construed, however, Yunis's 'not A or even B' precludes the notion that A and B may be two stages of one larger action. To illustrate with an example: the statement 'I did not swindle the investors or spend other people's money on my pleasures' does not necessarily presuppose (though it may suggest) the charge that the 'money' spent came from the 'investors'; but, naturally construed, 'I did not swindle the investors and spend other people's money on my pleasures' would precisely deny a charge that involves a two-stage process: first, swindling the investors; then, spending the swindled money. The latter corresponds to what I have called the conjunctive, the former to the disjunctive, οὐδέ. I believe that conjunction, not disjunction, is the point of Sokrates' words: 'no speech has ever yet been written and (then) delivered that is worth much serious attention, as the ones rhapsodized are spoken for the sake of persuasion, without examination or instruction'. On my view, 'rhapsodized', as applied to the manner of delivery, by Sokrates' (and, *a fortiori*, Plato's) time would have implied the use of written scripts. To be clear about the nature of my objection to Yunis's translation: perhaps his 'or even' is merely a free rendering intended to convey his judgment that Sokrates' inclusion of λεχθῆναι is an afterthought to γραφῆναι. If so, I believe that he does not do full justice to the local context of *Phaidros* 277e and the overarching argument of the dialog. But by writing '(n)or even', a common (and proper) gloss for οὐδέ in 'οὔτε … οὐδέ' statements, Yunis gives the impression that this choice, and hence the interpretation built on it, is recommended by an objective appeal to semantics and syntax. Footnote 120 immediately above is intended to foreclose this *textual* (as opposed to contextual) justification. Read on, in turn, for my contextual objection.

an opportunity as has befallen you and [in consequence] have that happen (οὐδὲ παθεῖν) to you which you have already experienced many a time before'.[123] From the examples Demosthenes goes on to adduce, it is clear that what he thinks the Athenians will 'suffer' if they waste the opportunity is the loss of power and prosperity consequent on inaction.[124]

Several textual and contextual indices strongly suggest that, throughout the conversation in the *Phaidros*, Sokrates views writing and speaking as complementary aspects that are integral to the process of public delivery. On several occasions we find τε καὶ joining forms of λέγειν and γράφειν. Thus, at 258d Sokrates remarks that writing speeches is not in itself shameful; what is shameful is 'not to speak and write them well' (τὸ μὴ καλῶς λέγειν τε καὶ γράφειν 258d4–5). In its context, the use of a single article τό with two infinitives joined by τε καί suggests (although admittedly it does not require the view) that these verbs articulate two stages of a single process in which 'writing' is held to be of greater relative significance.[125] This is what one would expect if in fact the focus is on the shortcomings of writing as a mode of communication. Sokrates could have pointed in the direction of two independent alternatives by saying λέγειν ἢ γράφειν (cf. 277b6). It would have been, in fact, more natural to counter the charge that writing speeches is inherently shameful with the reply that what is shameful is writing speeches poorly. Why say instead that 'what is shameful is both speaking and writing speeches poorly'? Why introduce the distracting and (*ex hypothesi*) not intrinsically germane *oral* delivery, which is otiose if it has no connection to the matter at issue, namely, the propriety of writing of speeches? The situation is otherwise and hardly puzzling if Sokrates is addressing oral delivery built upon, or seen as second best to, written scripts. This very subject already appears at the beginning of the dialog, where the scroll of Lysias' speech takes center stage. Even the order of the infinitives, first λέγειν and then

---

123 οὐ δεῖ δὴ τοιοῦτον, ὦ ἄνδρες Ἀθηναῖοι, παραπεπτωκότα καιρὸν ἀφεῖναι οὐδὲ παθεῖν ταὐτὸν ὅπερ ἤδη πολλάκις πρότερον πεπόνθατε.

124 The *Loeb Classical Library* translation by Vince reads: "Men of Athens, you must not let slip the opportunity that offers, nor make the blunder you have so often made before." Contextually, it is clear that 'making the blunder' is one and the same with 'letting the opportunity slip'. Hence, 'nor' is not equivalent to 'or not' ('you must not let slip the opportunity or [you must] not make the blunder') but to 'and not': 'you must not let slip the opportunity and [you must] not make the blunder'. The same logic applies to Trevett's translation: "You must not pass up such an opportunity, men of Athens, when it has fallen into your lap, nor suffer the same fate as you have suffered many times already" (2011:33–34).

125 Note how the statement that makes mention of both speaking and writing (258d4–5) is bracketed on either side by a sole reference to 'writing': τοῦτο μὲν ἄρα παντὶ δῆλον, ὅτι οὐκ αἰσχρὸν αὐτό γε τὸ γράφειν λόγους (258d1–2); τίς οὖν ὁ τρόπος τοῦ καλῶς τε καὶ μὴ γράφειν; (258d7). The latter (258d9–11) is of special significance because, by having 277d6–e8 echo its detailed formulation (including the oppositions 'private vs. public' and 'poetry vs. prose'), Sokrates signals the unity of focus of the intervening discussion which he is then bringing to a close.

γράφειν, is commended by Sokrates' argument. In 257d Phaidros observes that men of influence in their polities are ashamed to write speeches and bequeath their writings to posterity because they fear being branded as sophists. The focus here is arguably on deliberative speeches, a view confirmed by Sokrates' witty and tendentious use of the subsequent inscribing of successful motions (the presumed core of a deliberative address) as a counter argument to his interlocutor's observation (257e–258a). Although some deliberative speeches may have been partially written in advance,[126] ordinarily the public would not have thought of them as having preexisted the actual assembly address so much as, if at all, postdating it, their written text offering a possibly edited and polished version of what had transpired.[127] Not so with forensic speeches by *logographoi*, which, whatever the editorial modifications predating their 'publication,' were clearly understood as scripts to serve the litigant's delivery at the trial. In other words, deliberative speeches would commend the order 'both speak and write'; forensic, the order 'both write and speak'.[128] Concerning the former, in 277d7–9, Sokrates also criticizes those who privilege writing as being superior to the spoken word in its capacity for 'permanence' (or 'certainty', βεβαιότητα) and 'clarity' (σαφήνειαν). The text (as punctuated, I think correctly, by the *OCT contra* Yunis 2011 *ad loc.*) suggests that, spurred by the supposed advantages of writing, the individual in question authors a document in the context of passing laws (νόμους τιθείς). It is possible that Sokrates is resorting again tongue-in-cheek to the inscribing of the assembly's resolutions as the target of his criticism; but since he pairs this public dimension of writing with writing in a private capacity (cf. 258d9–10), it is more natural to take his statement to apply more broadly to publishing an edited version of a previously delivered demegoric speech. This motivates the order, first 'speaking' and then 'writing', in the formulation with which Sokrates retakes at 277d1–4 the investigation of whether speaking and writing speeches is honorable or base (περὶ τοῦ καλὸν ἢ αἰσχρὸν εἶναι τὸ λόγους λέγειν τε καὶ γράφειν 277d1–2).

---

[126] Cf. Plutarch's interesting remarks apropos Demosthenes in *Dēmosthenēs* 8.4 and Yunis 1996:175n4, 241–247.

[127] Cf. Hudson-Williams 1951 and Trevett 1996, with 425n2.

[128] This forensic order is not invariably observed where expected. At 261b4, λέγεται precedes γράφεται (περὶ τὰς δίκας λέγεταί τε καὶ γράφεται τέχνη). This may well be because at that point Sokrates' focus for a while has been off the use of writing and on the truth of the orator's subject matter. In redirecting attention, at least in part, to the technology of writing, it is natural for Phaidros to mention Sokrates' focus first (λέγειν) and then add to it what has meanwhile been left out of sight in their conversation. In fact, Sokrates has just defined rhetoric without reference to writing as ψυχαγωγία τις διὰ λόγων, οὐ μόνον ἐν δικαστηρίοις καὶ ὅσοι ἄλλοι δημόσιοι σύλλογοι, ἀλλὰ καὶ ἐν ἰδίοις (261a8–9).

It is true that in the latter part of the *Phaidros*, starting at 257d, Sokrates (for good Platonic reasons) is also preoccupied with the question whether the subject matter of rhetoric is true and not merely persuasive, irrespective of the intervention of writing at any stage in the delivery and of any supposed advantage of writing as a mode of composition and communication. This is not to say that he necessarily denies the possible involvement of writing so much as that his focus is elsewhere and he sidesteps the polemic altogether. Therefore, *Phaidros* 259e1-2, which summarizes the scope of the investigation thus, τὸν λόγον ὅπῃ καλῶς ἔχει λέγειν τε καὶ γράφειν καὶ ὅπῃ μή, σκεπτέον, precedes Sokrates' insistence that one who would speak well and nobly must know 'the truth about what he intends to speak' (τὸ ἀληθὲς ὧν ἂν ἐρεῖν πέρι μέλλῃ 259e5-6). In good consequence, when the *tekhnē* of rhetoric personified upbraids the orator who is ignorant of his subject, she uses λέγειν and neglects to mention γράφειν.[129] But Phaidros soon brings the conversation back to the realities of Athenian life when he draws attention to the courts as the preeminent context for rhetoric; and he does so by reintroducing writing in tandem with speaking. When Sokrates in effect asks, 'Is that what you have been told about the art of rhetoric?', Phaidros replies: 'No by Zeus, not at all so, but that it is chiefly in connection with lawsuits that there is speaking and writing by [oratorical] art, and speaking [by oratorical art] in connection with assembly speaking'.[130] Note the explicit involvement of 'writing' in the forensic setting and its corresponding neglect in the deliberative, which agrees with my suggestion above that the average Athenian would have considered ordinary the involvement of *logographoi* in lawsuits, while writing would not have been immediately associated with preparing and training for demegoric addresses, only with the exceptional publication in writing of assembly speeches after their delivery.[131]

---

[129] The focus on truth also motivates the disjunction λέγει ἢ γράφει at 277b6, where true knowledge of one's subject is again at issue. A comprehensive formulation while making a point that is indifferent to technology—the need to suit with a view to persuasiveness the particular variety of speech to each type of soul—accounts for the disjunctions ἐνδεικνύμενον ἢ λεγόμενον τέχνῃ ποτὲ λεχθήσεται ἢ γραφήσεται (271b7-8). A slightly different rationale explains λέγων ἢ διδάσκων ἢ γράφων (272b1): although their ostensible subject is 'the intending orator' (τὸν μέλλοντα ῥητορικὸν ἔσεσθαι 271d1), in actual fact, as the inclusion of διδάσκων intimates, the teacher of rhetoric is ultimately in view (i.e. a συγγραφεύς like Lysias 272b2-3; cf. 258c8). Hence, the three verbs may well refer respectively to the practice of rhetoric, its instruction, and its codification in a manual. To the extent that such manuals offered illustrative examples and models to imitate, as (partial) instantiations of written oratory they were not dissimilar from written speeches. For this reason, it is not inappropriate to apply γράφων more broadly to them also.

[130] οὐ μὰ τὸν Δί' οὐ παντάπασιν οὕτως, ἀλλὰ μάλιστα μέν πως περὶ τὰς δίκας λέγεταί τε καὶ γράφεται τέχνῃ, λέγεται δὲ καὶ περὶ δημηγορίας (261b3-5).

[131] Yunis 2011: "Athenian politicians did not normally engage in forensic speech-writing or publish texts ... until Demosthenes changed the practice in the mid fourth century" (171).

Sokrates, however, does not restrict his analysis to courtroom speeches, and when consideration of the role of writing in rhetoric is retaken as the focus of the dialog, its scope embraces private and public speeches (277d7), whether prose or poetry (277e7), with the explicit inclusion of passing laws and writing 'political compositions' (νόμους τιθείς, σύγγραμμα πολιτικόν 277d7).[132] In one of the few places where a possible advantage of writing is even envisaged (only to suggest that it does not exist), Sokrates gently mocks Lysias by hinting that perhaps there is a technical 'logographic' reason, inaccessible to the layman, for the arrangement of his written speech (264b7-8).[133] Once he finally addresses the limitations and impact of writing, the focus is on teaching through *listening* to written treatises or manuals. Attention to teaching is only to be expected, for it answers to Sokrates' characteristic interest in deprecating sophistic rhetorical education in favor of dialectic.

Whatever insight we may derive from all this about the role of writing in rhapsodic performance in the fourth century BC follows inferentially or tangentially from the main thrust of the argument. At the same time, one must not fail to notice that the spoken word remains the vehicle for instruction—only, it is no longer the word of dialectic exchange but the reading aloud of written manuals. Faced with Theuth's invention of γράμματα, Thamos observes: 'You provide your students with apparent, not true, wisdom; for, once they become [mere] assiduous hearers of you (πολυήκοοι ... σοι) without instruction, they will think that they are broadly learned, while for the most part ignorant and

---

[132] In fact, as Thompson 1868:142 *ad* 277d observes, "[t]he original question which has been so long delayed, is now shown by Socr[ates] to have been virtually disposed of in the course of the foregone discussions." It is somewhat incongruous that criticism levied against Lysias by τὶς ... τῶν πολιτικῶν (257c4-5) might prompt broad consideration of the role of writing in rhetoric. Lysias, after all, was not an Athenian citizen and could not participate in the city's politics (cf. Yunis 1996:175-176). The speech by Lysias that opens the dialog is best classified as epideictic, a type that according to Aristotle *Rhetoric* 1414a17 did especially invite the written style. The status of Lysias as a resident alien explains Sokrates' expressly widening the scope to ... ἤ τις ἄλλος (277d6). At any rate, the political domains of assembly and courtroom were notoriously porous, and even the profile of the alleged critic is unclear: described as 'one of the *politikoi*', was he "one of our politicians" (with Hackforth in Hamilton and Cairns 1961:503), which suggests a public figure, a professional of politics, or simply "a man [involved] in political life" (with Thompson 1868:83), which suggests an engaged but private citizen?

[133] See Phaidros' reply at 264b9-c1. Seemingly missing Sokrates' ironic use of λογογράφος and its derivatives at 257e3, 258b4, 258c2, and 264b7, Yunis holds that he is referring broadly to "composing speeches": "With regard to λογογραφία S[ocrates] shifts from the conventional sense 'forensic speechwriting,' as used by Ph[aedrus] (257c5), to a literal sense 'composing speeches,' i.e. of any kind" (Yunis 2011:172; cf. 193). Though doubtless right to observe that the term is not restricted to forensic writing, this fact does not imply that it designates anything other than professional wordsmiths who depend on writing for their trade. Only ironically, by a tendentious abuse of its denotation, is it made extensive generally to those who move legislation in the assembly and specifically to Lykourgos, Solon, and Dareios.

hard to be with because they have grown wise only in appearance'.[134] Thamos' objection pertains to the manner of 'instruction': Theuth has discovered various branches of knowledge—number, calculation, geometry, and astronomy—but instead of teaching his disciples face-to-face, exchanging questions and answers, he commits these sciences to writing and expects the students to learn them by reading them aloud or hearing others read them. That this is the sense in which we are to take πολυήκοοι ... σοι is confirmed by Plato's *Laws* 7.810e11. Here the Athenian probes the claim that youths are to be educated by making them assiduous listeners of the poets as they are *read aloud* and by making them acquire through such exposure a broad knowledge of them (πολυηκόους τ' ἐν ταῖς ἀναγνώσεσιν ποιοῦντας καὶ πολυμαθεῖς), even to the point of learning entire poets by heart. Not so; true 'instruction' calls for dynamic oral exchange between teacher and pupil. Therefore, Thamos asserts that the students' listening to Theuth's writings is 'without instruction' (ἄνευ διδαχῆς).[135] Once again, the focus is squarely on denatured discourse that, wedded to writing, has lost its dialectical dynamism.

If the preceding considerations are valid, ῥαψῳδούμενοι at *Phaidros* 277e8 is best construed not as the declamation of poetry, but as a particular style of lecturing, largely based—and this is crucial—on the oral delivery of scripted material, which does not submit to the interrogation of the ἔλεγχος.[136] Even if a speaker so trained did entertain a question, he would probably lack the intellectual nimbleness to meet the καιρός; he may hold the promise of teaching, but it is a vacuous pledge that goes unfulfilled. Note that the addresses Sokrates has in view may be verse or prose: though we may be inclined to take these as alternatives, we might also ponder that the rhapsodic exposition of Homer may well have combined verses of notionally Homeric authorship with verse and prose embellishment and exposition. In short, under my proposal, 'rhapsodized speeches' understood as 'speeches by rhapsodes' will have fully fitted the scenario presented by Sokrates.[137] Although one might construe 'for the sake

---

[134] σοφίας δὲ τοῖς μαθηταῖς δόξαν, οὐκ ἀλήθειαν πορίζεις· πολυήκοοι γάρ σοι γενόμενοι ἄνευ διδαχῆς πολυγνώμονες εἶναι δόξουσιν, ἀγνώμονες ὡς ἐπὶ τὸ πλῆθος ὄντες, καὶ χαλεποὶ συνεῖναι, δοξόσοφοι γεγονότες ἀντὶ σοφῶν (*Phaidros* 275a7–b2).

[135] Cf. *Phaidros* 275c5–d1.

[136] A similar criticism can be found in Plato's *Gorgias* 448d1–10, now directed against sophistic rhetoric, which falls short of the give-and-take that the much more interactive and responsive Sokratic method is capable of. This is perhaps why Gorgias' willingness to take questions as part of his display is noted as remarkable (447c5–8).

[137] Stallbaum 1857b:216 *ad loc.* translates the passage thus: "Qui vero in scripto de quacunque re sermone necessario multum lusum inesse arbitratur, nec unquam ullum sermonem versibus vel sine versibus multo dignum studio scriptum putat aut dictum esse, sicuti ῥαψῳδούμενοι illi sermones nulla adhibita disquisitione et explicatione persuadendi causa recitari consueverunt ... ." And he adds the following note: "In his verba: ὡς οἱ ῥαψῳδούμενοι

of conviction' (πειθοῦς ἕνεκα) under this proposal in reference to the powerful emotions rhapsodes were able to instigate in their audience, the sentiment is most at home where a speech makes an argument and endeavors to sustain it, as rhapsodic interpretation—however deficient in Sokrates' eyes—surely did.

In the final analysis, Alkidamas' criticism of writing strikes us as the swan song of a fast vanishing practice, a swimming against the current whose flow, though the volume be small at first, has shifted its direction irreversibly. Noting the paradox of his writing against writing (§29), he is forced to offer a justification of the written speech. And it is particularly telling that, faced with proving his excellence to those who are not acquainted with his work, he prefers offering a sample of his writing over making a demonstration of his improvisatory prowess, lest his audience, accustomed to the finish of the written piece, should judge him inferior to others who have made scripted delivery the centerpiece of their art (§31). The same competitive pressure, one can only assume, must have been felt by the Athenian rhapsodes: an uneven field that pitted the finish and flourish of a rehearsed script against the older skill of improvisatory recomposition in the hands of lesser practitioners. Truly gifted traditional bards must have dazzled audiences with their singing and would have had little to fear from those who tried to make up with memory and script what they lacked in recompositional mastery. This must have been a matter of gradation, with performers falling at various points along a continuum, not the often cited, but simplistic opposition between "creative singers" and "reproducing rhapsodes." But as soon as the festival rules, whether intentionally or not, accommodated scripted performances, writing conferred a clear competitive advantage to the majority of rhapsodes whose talent, as is always true in any profession, did not approach either extreme. This shift in practice is of a sort that tends to build on itself and is hard to reverse. Once it began, it must have taken over and displaced most of the rhapsodes unwilling to commit themselves fully to it.

— ἐλέχθησαν, nescio cur interpretibus tam multum negotii creaverint. Continent enim explicationem praecedentis οὐδὲ λεχθῆναι. Nam quum Socrates negavisset ullam unquam orationem magno dignam studio scriptam aut dictam esse, alterum hoc accuratius erat explicandum. Monet igitur hoc de iis tantum valere orationibus, quae sine accurata rerum pervestigatione recitarentur eo tantum consilio, ut efficeretur aliqua persuasio. Quod nemo est quin videat de orationibus sophisticis et forensibus esse accipiendum" (216). I would only take issue with the *aut* between *scriptam* and *dictam*: Sokrates does not worry so much about written speeches as about *orally delivered* speeches that, by adhering to a script, speciously supplant the true orality of dialog.

10

The Rhapsode in Performance

I N THE PREVIOUS CHAPTERS I examined the evolution of epic performance from the point of view of inspiration, authority and authorship, and
the increasing adoption of scripted delivery. In this chapter I reconsider the
diachrony of rhapsodic performance more narrowly through the meaning of
ῥαψῳδός and the distinctive recompositional poetics of traditional rhapsodic
delivery.

10.1 Understanding the Rhapsode

The greatest hindrance to a proper understanding of the Homeric rhapsode
and his craft is perhaps the entrenched, and diachronically invalid, opposition
between a 'creative ἀοιδός' and a 'reproducing (uncreative) ῥαψῳδός.' Scholars
who resort to this polarity often seek to preserve compositional creativity up
until the time of the alleged 'monumental composer'—Homer—who, with his
dictated texts, arrested the traditional practice of recomposition in performance. The treatment in Pelliccia (2003:97–98) is typical. Because he explores
this opposition explicitly and at length, I will review his argument below
(pp. 334ff.). A few brief comments will suffice for now to set the background
for my own treatment. On page 97 he offers in two opposing columns a "crude"
outline of the "ends of the spectrum of synchronic possibilities" for the concept
of the rhapsode. The left (a)-column posits: (1a) an oral culture;[1] (2a) a creative
rhapsode who (re-)composes in performance; (3a) a fluid, evolving Homeric
tradition. The right (b)-column espouses: (1b) uncertainty regarding the question of an oral vs. a literate culture; (2b) an uncreative rhapsode performing
memorized texts verbatim; (3b) a fixed text of the *Iliad* and the *Odyssey*. On
page 98 he notes that many proponents of the right-hand (b)-column "are
happy to posit the entire left-hand (a)-column as the pre-historic antecedent
for the historical (b)-column situation; the divide between them is the living

---

[1]   He places "oral" in scare-quotes.

space of Homer himself, and the key event of this interstitial moment is the dictation of the two poems."

But the dichotomy of creative singer versus uncreative rhapsode flies in the face of ancient descriptions of Homer and Hesiod as rhapsodes.[2] To the Greeks, Homer was a rhapsode who traveled the Greek world composing and performing before audiences for a living.[3] Graziosi (2002:47) objects that "[Homer] is never said to be a *rhapsodos*." But since his mode of performance is rhapsodic (ῥαψῳδεῖν, ἐπιδεικνύναι ... ῥαψῳδίαν)[4] and he travels from place to place (περιιόντας, περιέρχεσθαι) like an ordinary rhapsode, her objection is without force.[5] More apropos is her observation that the sources present Homer as composing his poetry first, and only then performing it rhapsodically.[6] This would depart radically from the model of recomposition in performance only if one assumed that by ποιέω the exhaustive word-for-word formulation of the text was meant, and that the ensuing performance was understood as Homer's verbatim delivery of the memorized verses. This assumption arguably paints an odd picture of the great poet/performer sedulously memorizing his own words. Even when writing intervenes, I dispute that this is what the sources require us to believe of Homer. It is more plausible that they take for granted a measure of improvisatory elaboration in performance.[7] After all, even late-classical and

---

[2] Plato *Laws* 658b: εἰκός που τὸν μέν τινα ἐπιδεικνύναι, καθάπερ Ὅμηρος, ῥαψῳδίαν, ἄλλον δὲ κιθαρῳδίαν, κτλ. Plato *Republic* 600d: Ὅμηρον δ' ἄρα οἱ ἐπ' ἐκείνου ... ἢ Ἡσίοδον ῥαψῳδεῖν ἂν περιιόντας εἴων ... ; *Certamen* 55–56: ποιήσαντα γὰρ τὸν Μαργίτην Ὅμηρον περιέρχεσθαι κατὰ πόλιν ῥαψῳδοῦντα. Plato calls Phemios a rhapsode (*Iōn* 533c).

[3] Cf. Wilamowitz-Moellendorff 1916:396–439, esp. 398; and Meyer 1918:335.

[4] See footnote 2 immediately above for the references.

[5] She notes that "[Homer and Hesiod] are assimilated to rhapsodes only when they are said to perform activities which are typical ... of the rhapsodes proper" (Graziosi 2002:33). But the relevant point is surely that they *are* portrayed and said to perform as rhapsodes. The heart of Graziosi's objection is that Homer is not only said to 'rhapsodize' (ῥαψῳδεῖν) but also to 'compose' (ποιεῖν) his poems. This, she believes, sets him apart from 'true' rhapsodes who are never said to compose (even if they arguably do). Graziosi does not consider that if the diachronic development of epic performance is as I argue here, precisely because Homer embodies the authority of Homeric epic one should expect biographical reports to separate his composing from his performing only to bring them together as the two stages of his professional activity. See my discussion immediately below.

[6] E.g. *Certamen* 55–56, quoted in footnote 2 immediately above. For a discussion of the passages in the *Vita* traditions that ascribe composition to Homer, see Nagy 2010a:33–47.

[7] Note, for example, the phrasing of *Vita Herodotea* §15. After leaving Kyme, Homer arrived in Phokaia, where he 'earned his living in the same manner [as before], performing *epē* (ἔπεα ἐνδεικνύμενος 193) sitting in the public lounges'. At this point Thestorides, a teacher and would-be rival performer, 'having learned of Homer's verse-making' (τοῦ Ὁμήρου τὴν ποίησιν 196), made him a proposal. Cf. Nagy 2010a:37–39, in particular his remark at 39 that the unscripted Homer is contrasted with the scripted Thestorides. Homer's transcript becomes Thestorides' script. That the performing of Homer is glossed by 'verse-making' is telling. For ποίησις as *carminum factio* see the *TGL* 6.1305: this is arguably its meaning at *Vita Herodotea* 68, 94, 218, 346, 372, and 375 (372 is

Hellenistic rhapsodic performances arguably featured a degree of recomposition, however limited. Witness the circulation of Ptolemaic papyri with plus-
verses and the variant readings preserved by the indirect *paradosis*. It would be
odd to deny the great Homer at least that much freedom in his own delivery.
Furthermore, one should consider how the Homeric *Vita* traditions would have
likely depicted Homer's activity if in fact they had believed him, as I claim, to
be a rhapsode. By their time, the construction of an authorial source for the
poetry we call Homeric had already taken place—a diachronic process explored
at length earlier in this book.[8] If Homer was to be the archetypal rhapsode
with unequaled mastery of the tradition—i.e. able to shape it definitively into
recognizable 'poems' ascribable to him and to perform it with unsurpassed
authority—the natural way to convey this would have been to posit a prior stage
of composition followed by serial performance. Such a representation need not
even rule out the delivery of 'Homer's poems' by rival performers, as was said of
Thestorides in the *Vita Herodotea* §16: having acquired from Homer the *Phōkais*
and other *epē* in written form, he moved to Khios where he performed them
as his own (τὰ ἔπεα ἐπιδεικνύμενος ὡς ἑωυτοῦ ἐόντα 215–216)[9] and won much
praise. Identifying the real source of the poetry—Homer, not Thestorides—is
clearly the focus of the anecdote, but this should not obscure the fact that the
poem could be performed by anyone with access to it and the requisite skill.

---

of special significance because it summarizes Homer's professional activity); it may also be similarly understood at 112 and 118. The instances at 145 and especially 209 perhaps regard the
product, although verse-making remains in view: Thestorides does not merely want to appropriate the verses of Homer but to supplant him with his own activity as a rival performer. At 336,
349, and 521 we meet other marginal occurrences that straddle the making and the product.
Notice ποιήσας at 350, which West (2003b:383) translates 'writing', perhaps because 'composing
that Odysseus entrusted his household to Mentor' struck him as odd and unfamiliar. But prefer-
ring ποιέω to γράφω, the text emphasizes plot-construction over word-for-word composition, as
one should expect of oral traditional poetry. The only instances of ποίησις for *oeuvre* are at 352,
380, 399, and 513. On occasion, Ps.-Herodotos writes that Homer performed τὰ ἔπεα—once τὰ
ἔπεα τὰ πεποιημένα 143—as if he had in fact recited preexisting verses verbatim. This semantic
slippage is motivated by the archaic meaning of ἔπεα, 'utterances', which does not concern
detailed wording. Hence, 'he performed the *epē* he had composed' could, but need not, mean
that Homer's recitation slavishly followed a mental script. Cf., for example, Υ 204 θ 91 ρ 519. This
brief survey confirms that ποίησις may indeed stand metonymically for its product, i.e. ποίημα
and ποιήματα, but that even then the verbal notion—the 'making' in 'verse-making'—often
remains in view. An intuition of this fact underlies Aphthonios' calling the *Iliad* a ποίησις while
applying ποίημα to 'the fashioning of Akhilleus' armor' (*Progymnasmata* 2.1 in Patillon 2008:113;
cf. *TGL* 6.1305). As the verse-making of a poet, ποίησις readily stands for his *ouvre*, his life's work,
or for a representative collection of his ποιήματα. Cf. Chantraine 1933:287, Lledó Íñigo 1961, and
Durante 1968b:267. For the use of ποίημα and ποίησις in Hellenistic (and later) criticism, see
Ardizzoni 1953, Greenberg 1961, Ardizzoni 1962, and Häussler 1970.

8   See above, chapters 7–8.

9   A similar expression is used of Homer's own performance at 112 and 143 (cf. 193).

My point, in short, is that what Graziosi sees as an objection to Homer's rhapsodic identity is precisely what we would expect if late sources had wanted to describe Homer as a rhapsode (however exceptional in skill). If "*poietai ...* are often contrasted to those who perform their compositions" (Graziosi 2002:47), then surely we must judge significant that the *Vitae* should make Homer the subject *both* of ποιεῖν *and* ῥαψῳδεῖν.[10] Pindar confirms that the rhapsode may be subsumed under the ἀοιδός in *Nemean* 2 (dated tentatively to 485 by Snell and Maehler), which opens with a picture of the Homeridai:[11]

> Ὅθεν περ καὶ Ὁμηρίδαι
> ῥαπτῶν ἐπέων τὰ πόλλ' ἀοιδοί
> ἄρχονται, Διὸς ἐκ προοιμίου ...

Here the nexus between ἀοιδοί and ῥαπτὰ ἔπεα seems entirely unproblematic, and Pindar even compares his own compositional technique to the frequent recourse the Homeridai have to proemial hymns to Zeus (Kurke 1991:42–43). No attention is drawn to a contrast between the creative poet Pindar and, insofar as rhapsodes, allegedly uncreative Homeridai. Nor is there a hint in this lofty opening of the contempt for rhapsodes we find in Xenophon's writings.

Three things must be done to remove Pelliccia's objections to the notion of a creative rhapsode. First, the words "creative" and "verbatim" must be set in a diachronic perspective; this is effectively the overarching goal of this book, and in this connection I have already addressed the heart of Pelliccia's argument in an earlier chapter.[12] Second, the implications of Pelliccia's evidence for verbatim performance in classical Athens must be clarified; this, I do in brief

---

[10] Plato's choice of Phemios, the celebrated Odyssean ἀοιδός, as the archetypal rhapsode (*Iōn* 533c1) further undermines the alleged incompatibility of 'singer' with 'rhapsode'. There is no compelling reason to dismiss this portrayal of Phemios as tendentious or anomalous. The survey in chapter 1 of Graziosi 2002, which leads her to infer "substantial differences" (32) between rhapsodes and singers, lacks sufficient diachronic nuance. It neglects the use of ῥάπτω in the Homeric epics as "dangerous" evidence (23), inconclusive and possibly misleading; it infers too much *ex silentio* from the failure of Homeric poetry to mention rhapsodic composition (24); and it opposes the competitive setting of early instances of ῥαψῳδός to the *Odyssey*'s portrayal of Phemios' and Demodokos' performances (31–32). Her conviction that "the meaning of the term rhapsode must, in the first place, be sought in the fifth-century texts where it first appears" (22) precludes an adequate diachronic analysis and determines from the start the outcome of her survey. One is therefore not surprised to read that "it is attractive to suppose that these terms [*rhaptō* and *rhapsōidos*] indicated a new activity, to be contrasted, perhaps, with that of singers" (24). This is what she calls her "commonsense assumption" (32). But her discussion includes its own corrective, for she acknowledges that, in contesting the claims of the sophists, Plato "is relying on a current view of Homer" as a rhapsodic performer. Had this not been an ordinary and broadly accepted view of him, Sokrates' remark at *Republic* 600d5–e2 would have lacked all force.

[11] *Nemean* 2.1–3.

[12] See above, pp. 277ff.

immediately below. Finally, as I do above (p. 301), the quotations from Xenophon regarding Athenian rhapsodes must be contextualized.[13] Regarding the matter of verbatim performance to which this scholar helpfully draws our attention, it is important to bear in mind that memory is a rather complex faculty, variously deployed in all sorts of intellectual activities. Therefore, a reference to the use of memory does not *eo ipso* entail 'rote memorization' with no tolerance for *mouvance*.[14] Whether such exists and, if so, in what degree, is the question that cannot be begged. One of the more interesting findings of the evidence Pelliccia assembles in 2003:111n30 is precisely the primacy that aurality (and hence orality) still held during the classical period, even where bookrolls were in view.[15] *Phaidros* 228a6–b1 illustrates this well.[16] After all, this dialog is at least in part an examination of the propriety of scripts and the extent to which they may adequately stand for the corresponding performance. Towards its end, the scope of the discussion broadens to consider the role of writing in the preservation and transmission of knowledge,[17] a concern that also informs the conversation in Xenophon's *Apomnēmoneumata* 4.2. Pelliccia makes much of the extensive training of citizen amateurs to deliver previously memorized poetic scripts. But, whatever its import for the availability to the average classical Athenian of a "concept of fixed, absolutely verbatim accuracy" (102), this training entails very little for the classical rhapsodic delivery of Homeric poetry. For what matters is

---

[13] Pelliccia (2003:112) acknowledges, as I do, that we glimpse here "a contemporary debate about education." But, unlike him, I do not think that the passages from Xenophon serve in any significant way to emphasize, even implicitly, the different status of rhapsode and poet. What one might imagine Plato hypothetically doing with Euripides is not to the point. What matters is the traditional authority, cultural and educational, of the rhapsode, an authority that Euripides lacks. Furthermore, the claim that in the Platonic dialog that bears his name Phaidros performs "rhapsode-style" whereas Sokrates performs "as an *aoidos*" (113) is arguable. Since the text does not portray the action in those express terms, it can be obviously so only to those who have already decided how the alleged contrast of rhapsode with poet must be understood, articulated, and applied. The actual opposition in view in the *Phaidros* is the one between scripted and unscripted performance, a matter of vigorous debate in classical Athens. As I show in this book, this debate transcends the craft of the rhapsode. Where it overlaps with the dichotomy between creation and reproduction, it does so partially, not absolutely but in relative terms, as a matter of diachronic development. Scripted delivery by sophists and professional orators, not "professional memorizers" (whatever that may be), is what ἀπομνημονεύσειν in *Phaidros* 228a2 refers to (cf. Plato *Greater Hippias* 285e8).

[14] For the meaning of *mouvance*, see Nagy 1996c:7–38.

[15] Note also that κεκτῆσθαι is used not only of commercial purchases but also of acquiring mastery of a subject. This is the case, for example, in Plato *Laws* 829c8.

[16] εὖ οἶδα ὅτι Λυσίου λόγον ἀκούων ἐκεῖνος οὐ μόνον ἅπαξ ἤκουσεν, ἀλλὰ πολλάκις ἐπαναλαμβάνων ἐκέλευέν οἱ λέγειν, ὁ δὲ ἐπείθετο προθύμως ('Well I know that, hearing Lysias' speech, he [=Phaidros] not only heard it once but, taking it up again often, told him [=Lysias] to deliver it, and [Lysias] eagerly complied').

[17] Cf. Yunis 2011:225–226.

the conscious expectation of performer and audience whether such accuracy was possible, desirable, and requisite *in the delivery of Homeric epic* and not in the amateur performance of the citizen chorus. One must surely weight the fact that ordinarily these citizens were amateurs of rather limited poetic skill, not professionals who could readily recompose in the manner of traditional rhapsodes; that they performed in groups, not solo, and had to coordinate carefully their dancing and singing, both melody and lyrics; and that they did not—and this is crucial—reperform the same pieces time after time. Thus, the poetry in view is not traditional and cannot illuminate the manner of composition and performance of *traditional* poetry. Neither the amateur performers nor their citizen audience would have had the same expectation of, or tolerance for, *mouvance* in these performances that they had for the rhapsodic performance of Homer. And insofar as the audience did not have any independent access to the scripts delivered by choruses other than their actual performance, there is no obvious sense in which these choral performances could have met an alleged expectation of verbatim reproduction. This is not to deny, of course, that an individual interested in acquiring a particular composition, perhaps for its private performance in the setting of the symposium, would not exert every effort to memorize it.[18] Pelliccia's observations about amateur choric performance are interesting but largely pointless for their ostensible focus, the rhapsode, since they are specific to a different genre and emphatically regard performers of poetry that—all agree—are to be sharply distinguished from the authors of their poetic scripts. If one is not to beg the question, the same cannot be said of the rhapsode without further study.[19]

10.1.1 Etymology

Having briefly considered Pelliccia's arguments, I will now seek to advance our understanding of the word ῥαψῳδός by approaching it from the point of view of etymology and usage in the extant texts. Scholars have long agreed that ῥαψῳδός is a composite noun of the τερψίμβροτος type.[20] The first element is verbal (perhaps in origin an abstract verbal noun in -τι-); the second, a noun. Because abstract verbal nouns often echo the aorist, the *terpsimbrotos* compound was closely tied to it in form: τερψι- to τέρψαι, and ῥαψ- to ῥάψαι.[21] Words of this

---

[18] To this speak Theophrastos *Kharaktēres* 27.7, cited by Pelliccia 2003:111n31, and the ᾄδουσι of Plato *Iōn* 534d7.

[19] Pelliccia (2003:102) recognizes this difficulty, and the rest of his article seeks to justify extending his analytical schema to the rhapsode's relationship to Homer.

[20] E.g. Debrunner 1917:39 §79; Knecht 1946; and Patzer 1952:317, 320–321.

[21] From *ῥαπτι- (Schmitt 1967:300–301 §609). Two further examples are: Στησίχορος and στῆσαι; φθεισίμβροτος and φθεῖσαι.

type receive the accent on the first element, but ῥαψῳδός analogically follows the more numerous compounds whose second element conveys a verbal action: χρησμῳδός, ὑμνῳδός, θεσπιῳδός, κιθαρῳδός, etc.[22] The ancients were divided about its etymology, tracing it both to ῥάπτειν and ῥάβδος.[23] As the more transparent, the latter alternative was especially popular: the classical and Hellenistic rhapsode recited without an instrument, clad in gorgeous attire, and leaning on a staff (ῥάβδος).[24] The ῥάβδος was thought the equivalent of Hesiod's σκῆπτρον (*Theogony* 30), itself an emblem of performative authority and the functional equivalent of the singer's instrument. But there is no linguistic path from ῥάβδος to ῥαψῳδός, and although this erroneous etymology may inform the meaning of late instances of the term, it cannot explain its origin or early use.

Pindar is usually thought to vacillate and support both etymologies. I have already quoted *Nemean* 2.1–3, which speaks to ῥάπτειν. *Isthmian* 3/4.55–57 points to ῥάβδος:

> ἀλλ᾽ Ὅμηρός τοι τετίμακεν δι᾽ ἀνθρώπων, ὃς αὐτοῦ
> πᾶσαν ὀρθώσαις ἀρετὰν κατὰ ῥάβδον ἔφρασεν
> θεσπεσίων ἐπέων λοιποῖς ἀθύρειν.

Patzer (1952:316n2), however, remarks that ῥάβδος θεσπεσίων ἐπέων in the first instance cannot be the staff of the rhapsode. It is far more likely that these words point to the preeminent acceptation of ῥάβδος in the Homeric poems, the 'wand' with divine or magic powers that Hermes, Kirke, and Athena wield.[25] Metaphorically, the expression would amount to 'according to/by the enchanting power of his divine poetry'.[26] As Patzer further notes, "[e]ine Anspielung auf den 'stabhaltenden' Rhapsoden liegt freilich vor, aber pindarische Anspielungen zeugen noch nicht für ein gangbares und auch für den Dichter geltendes etymologisches Bewußtsein." Whether or not Patzer is right, the popular connection between the rhapsode and the ῥάβδος, the emblem of

---

[22] Cf. Patzer 1952:317, Schwyzer *GG* I.437–438, Bader 1972:205–206, and Probert 2003:108 §212.

[23] ῥάβ-δος < ῥαπ- (cf. ῥαπίς). Among the witnesses to ῥάβδος, see Dionysios Thrax *Tekhnē grammatikē* §5 (*Grammatici graeci* I.1.8 Uhlig): εἴρηται δὲ ῥαψῳδία †οἱονεὶ ῥαβδῳδία τις οὖσα, ἀπὸ τοῦ δαφνίνῃ ῥάβδῳ περιερχομένους ᾄδειν τὰ Ὁμήρου ποιήματα; and the *scholia vetera* to Pindar *Nemean* 2.1d: τοὺς ῥαψῳδοὺς οἱ μὲν ῥαβδῳδοὺς ἐτυμολογοῦσι διὰ τὸ μετὰ ῥάβδου δηλονότι τὰ Ὁμήρου ἔπη διεξιέναι. Cf. scholia to Plato *Iōn* 530a5 and the near identical Photios *Lexicon* 3.317 no. 68 Theodoridis (=*Suidas* 4.287 P no. 71 Adler). The scholia to Sophokles *Oidipous tyrannos* 391 supports ῥάπτειν: ἡ Σφὶγξ ἡ ῥάπτουσα τὰς ᾠδάς; so also the *Etymologicum Gudianum* s.v. ῥαψῳδία: λόγων συναφή. Cf., further, Ritoók 1962:225n1 and Ford 1988:300n4.

[24] See Shapiro 1998:96 fig. 21 for a depiction on a red-figure neck amphora from ca. 490 BC, now in the British Museum (Vase E270).

[25] Ω 343 ε 47 κ 238 293 319 389 ν 429 π 172 456 ω 2.

[26] So also Wilamowitz-Moellendorff 1922:339n3.

performative authority, is undeniable, even if, as alleged, for Pindar the tie was not etymological.

ῥάπτω, then, is the only valid etymological explanation for the first element of ῥαψῳδός; ᾠδ-, with the appropriate masculine ending -ος, can be traced to ἀοιδή. The etymology of ῥάπτω is disputed. In the past, it was often assigned the root *wṛp-, 'to bend', 'to turn'.[27] But two arguments preclude this analysis. Mycenaean Greek, with its ra-pi-ti-ra₂ (ῥάπτρια) and ra-pte (*ῥαπτήρ; cf. ῥάπτης), "ruine l'étymologie traditionnelle" (Chantraine 1999 s.v.).[28] There is also, as many have recognized, no clear semantic path from 'to turn' to 'to sew/stitch'.[29] Unfortunately, the alternative *serp- is not semantically illuminating because it lacks parallels in other IE languages.[30] For ῥάβδος Patzer (1952:316) offers the gloss "die 'biegsame' Gerte." But why should pliancy in a staff be desirable, much less its defining quality? The contrary can be easily argued. This gloss seems superficially plausible at M 297—the one Homeric use of the word that is clearly related to sewing—if ῥάβδοισι there means 'wires'.[31] One might imagine the golden thread for sewing as a 'pliant rod' of sorts. But the manufacture of the shield is being described from the point of view of its final appearance. It is not easy to imagine a member of the audience visualizing the wires stretched like 'pliant rods' *before* the stitching. It is far more likely that 'stitches' were meant.[32] The scholiast's ῥαβδοειδέσι ῥαφαῖς perhaps hints at the appearance of the stitches: if the artisan sewed the golden thread in and out of the hides along their perimeter, the dashed circle of exposed thread would have looked like a series of small rods.

10.1.2 Stitching the song: creative work?

If ῥάπτω is 'to sew/stitch', how are we to visualize the action of sewing? This question entails two related queries: does the metaphoric use of 'sewing/ stitching' connote creative or uncreative work? What precisely in the practice of

---

[27] Patzer 1952:316n1 ("'krümmen', 'drehen', 'wenden'"); *LIV*² 690, doubtfully ("?[gr. ῥάπτω"; "[s]emantisch und formal unklar, könnte auch Anlaut *sr° haben"); Frisk 1973–79 s.v.; Watkins 2000:99 s.v. "wer-" viii.

[28] Cf. Lejeune 1972:119 §112 and n. 4, and Durante 1968b:278 and n. 43. Full bibliographical references are given in the *DMic* II.221–223 s.vv.

[29] Chantraine 1999: "l'étymologie traditionnelle ... ne convenait guère pour le sens" (967); Lejeune 1972: "Les données mycéniennes ... amènent à écarter la (médiocre) étymologie traditionnelle" (119); *LIV*² 690: "Semantisch und formal unklar." Other words like ῥαμφή, ῥέμβομαι, or ῥάμφος can be related to *wṛp- with greater plausibility.

[30] For the possibility that it is a loanword, see below, p. 428.

[31] Borchhardt *apud* Hainsworth 1993 *ad loc.*; also *LfgE* s.v. ῥάβδος B.2.

[32] So Murray in his *Loeb* translation and Willcock *apud* Hainsworth 1993 *ad loc.* Lattimore translates 'staples'.

the rhapsode might have led him or his audience when the term was first coined to associate his performance with 'sewing/stitching a song'? Related issues are where and when the term was first coined and used, how it gained currency, and why it became the preferred term for the rhapsode. Additionally, one should address the instances of ῥάπτω in the *Iliad* and the *Odyssey* and explain why its metaphoric use regularly refers to contriving evil or devising plots.

It is not hard to establish that early uses of ῥάπτω consistently point to creative work. This is doubtless the case in its metaphoric acceptation 'to contrive', 'to plot', where it takes the objects κακά (Σ 367 γ 118 π 423), φόνον (π 379), and θάνατόν τε μόρον τε (π 421–422). Creativity is explicitly asserted in the celebrated Hesiodic fragment that states, 'I [Hesiod] and Homer sang Phoibos Apollo, stitching [our] song with new hymns' (μέλπομεν ἐν νεαροῖς ὕμνοις ῥάψαντες ἀοιδὴν | Φοῖβον Ἀπόλλωνα, fr. 357 MW). However one construes the grammar and the relationship between ὕμνοι and ἀοιδή,[33] it is impossible to gainsay the adjective νεαροῖς. It is easy to find modern scholars who believe that the label 'rhapsode' was not coined for the reciter of memorized scripts at the twilight of the oral tradition of Homeric epic. If they are right, the rationale for the term must be sought in something other than its alleged contrast with the creative ἀοιδός, in whose hands (by common consent) traditional diction and thematic structure were still malleable. So, for example, Wilamowitz-Moellendorff (1927:175) wrote: "Der Rhapsode will Dichter sein; nichts anderes besagt der Name, aber niemand fragt, wieviel die Muse ihm von dem eingegeben hat, was er vorträgt, zumal der Stoff allmählich den Hörern kaum etwas ganz Neues war." Fränkel (1925:4) translates ῥάπτω ἀοιδήν as "ich erfinde kunstreich ein Lied" and relates ῥάπτω to ἀρτύ(ν)ω. Schwartz (1940:9), a believer in the historicity of Homer, remarked: "[E]in Rhapsode des Namens muß tatsächlich gelebt haben und in einem Kreis ... berühmt geworden sein zu einer Zeit, wo ein Teil der Epen schon bleibende Gestalt gewann, aber die

---

[33] I analyze this fragment at length below, pp. 420ff. Graziosi (2002:33) remarks that "ἐν νεαροῖς ὕμνοις ... may have been a necessary qualification: Homer and Hesiod did not perform in the manner of ordinary rhapsodes, their songs were new." This special pleading reflects her conviction that rhapsodes did not explicitly admit to innovation and that, consequently, no one could have ascribed it to them (34). Rather than an illustration of rhapsodic poetics, for her this fragment espouses an untrue (and idealized) revision of it. But given Telemakhos' celebrated recognition of the novelty of Phemios' song at α 351–352, only a precommitment to wedge apart singer and rhapsode could turn the Hesiodic fragment on its head and make it an example of what rhapsodes did *not* do. I find implausible the notion that it is an aetiology, fashioned by rhapsodes about the origins of their craft, which *does not* however feature rhapsodic recitation, but a manner of performance that diverges from it at the crucial point of innovation. On Graziosi's assumption, it is hard to see how the alleged aetiology could be rhetorically effective and useful to rhapsodes. Her reading moreover implies that neither Homer nor Hesiod had ever performed rhapsodically until they met in Delos to sing Apollo! (34).

Rhapsoden zu dem Vergangenen, das sie rezitierten, noch Neues hinzufügten."
Pagliaro (1951:44) comments that "la qualifica di ῥαψῳδός ... nel senso di chi
'cuce canti altrui' diventa in sè poco qualificante e non necessaria: a chi sarebbe
venuto in mente di darla al cantore, quando nessuno si sentiva impegnato a
distinguere se i canti che costui recitava erano cuciti di epi propri od altrui?"
Durante (1968b:279) so strongly insists on the originality of the rhapsode, that he
even wrongly rejects the notion that the corresponding 'stitching' had anything
to do with preexisting epic songs: "[D]ie Definition dreht sich um einen Punkt
der epischen Dichtung, der—aus der Sicht der Späteren—wichtig erscheinen
kann, der aber sicher eine ganz am Rande liegende Bedeutung einnehmen muß,
wenn wir von Ort und Zeit ausgehen, als der Ausdruck geprägt worden ist."
With a more nuanced view, Patzer (1952:318) writes that "[die] Verwendung
fester vorgegebener 'Werkstücke' nichts mit dichterischer Originalität oder gar
Güte zu tun hat ... sie [ist] so alt wie die epische Dichtung selbst und [war] mit
deren ursprünglichem Stegreifvortrag gegeben ... [E]ine atomistisch verstan-
dene Originalität in der epischen Gattung [konnte] für ein frühgriechisches
Publikum kein Maßstab für Güte sein." Finally, Ford (1988:300) observes that "in
a number of relatively early sources we find ῥαψῳδός, ῥαψῳδία, and ῥαψῳδεῖν
used of performers who do not merely recite the poetry of others but also create
their own"; and he adds that "[i]t is ... unwarranted to attribute to the archaic
age a clear and significant distinction between creative singers and mechani-
cally imitative rhapsodes." This is only a representative sample of those who
variously trace their way to Wolf (1876:60): "Quamvis vero artis huius nomen
videatur posterius esse Homero, ipsa ars et professio iam antiquissimis tempo-
ribus viguit ... nullumque prope fuisse rhapsodum, quin idem probabilis poeta
esset, manifesta historiae vestigia arguunt."

The competing view that 'rhapsode' *stricto sensu* precludes or severely
limits compositional creativity, although broadly represented, is characteristic of modern British scholarship and its American adherents. Even though
Kirk (1962:312) allowed that the stitching metaphor probably referred "not to
the joining of different poems but to the interlocking of phrase with phrase,
verse with verse and theme with theme," he nevertheless made a clear divide
between "the ἀοιδός or true oral singer" (312) and the rhapsode or "reciter, the
performer, the reproducer by rote" (313) who "polluted" the "unadulterated
oral period" (318).[34] If the two Companions to Homer are at all representative
of the consensus where they address themselves to the transmission of the
Homeric text, we must note their agreement on this one point: "[R]hapsodes

---

[34] For Kirk's views on the rhapsodic "expansion or pollution" of Homer, see his index under 'rhapsode' (Kirk 1962:421).

were primarily executants, performing works composed by others, rather than original composers" (Wace and Stubbings 1962:218); "I see no alternative to dictation ... . The Homerids of Chios will have performed hereditary functions, and perhaps the poems ... . A change in mode of performance is signalled by the switch from the Homeric lyre to the Homeric staff: Homer sang (at least, his bards do), rhapsodes recited" (Haslam 1997:81–82). These views mislead for their lack diachronic depth. They retroject classical and late-classical attitudes about rhapsodes that cry for historical contextualization and diachronic nuance. Sometimes we even meet with the claim that 'rhapsode' is a late coinage actually devised to draw a stark contrast between the scripted reciter of epic and the 'true poet.' Advocates of an essential difference between 'rhapsode' and 'singer' or 'poet' often espouse a flat synchronic reading of the Panathenaic rule.[35] Although their interpretation is therefore ahistorical, its fundamental features are in turn judged inherent to rhapsodic performance: epic performers *qua* rhapsodes recited a written script in sequence, each picking up the thread of the story precisely where the previous one left off. Rote memorization and verbatim reproduction are held to be the rhapsode's defining traits. Proper diachronic analysis clarifies where these readings go astray and puts us on the right path to an understanding of rhapsodic performance. Armed with this understanding, we shall be in a position to grasp the essential nature of Homeric poetry and the role of performance in its genesis, diffusion, textualization, and preservation.

10.2 Understanding Rhapsodic Performance

Seeking to determine what precisely about his performance qualified the rhapsode for the label 'song-stitcher', Ford 1988 has put the accent where it belongs: the correct answer must concern something peculiar to him that was intelligible and readily perceptible to the audience. Otherwise, it is hard to see why the new coinage should have been widely received and adopted as apropos. Ford thinks that rhapsody was understood "irrespective of originality" as the "solo presentation, in public, of a poetic text without musical accompaniment" (303). I will deal with his argument presently. For now, mark his emphasis that this sense of the word "is based on an obvious aspect of the performance rather than a literary conception of genre" (305).[36] Since the earliest instances of metaphoric ῥάπτειν do not support the suggestion that ῥαψῳδός is an ironic or

---

[35] See below, pp. 382ff.
[36] "'[S]titching' could signify a clearly audible difference between poetry that is sung and poetry that is not" (Ford 1988:306).

derisive designation (*pace* Schmid and Stählin 1929:1.157[37] and Else 1957b:33), we must look for distinctive thematic or formal characteristics that would distinguish the rhapsode from the more generic ἀοιδός.[38] For Meyer (1918:332) it is his style of performance, the artful stitching together of individual recitations delivered piecemeal over several consecutive days.[39] For Fränkel (1925:4) the emphasis falls on "artful invention," which evil scheming and outstanding oratory share.[40] For Pagliaro (1951:44), rhapsody refers to the technique peculiar to epic recitation, specifically, to individual performers reciting cooperatively their song ('the rhapsody'). For Patzer (1952:323), it is the "'monostichische' Prinzip," that is, the epic singer who composes "[eine] Reihung unzähliger aneinander schließender gleicher Glieder." For Else (1957b:32–33), rhapsodes competed by reciting individual contributions not of their own making, which, "taken together, produced some kind of whole." For Durante (1968b:281), they composed by advancing, intertwining, or plaiting the thread (οἴμη) of their narrative.[41] For Ritoók (1962:228), rhapsodes engaged in sequential delivery, joining their songs one to another before an audience not merely by following an established script but also by composing extemporaneously. All of these proposals have one or more elements of truth; some are even insightful. But, because they were not formulated with the diachronic development of epic performance in view, they often set in opposition mere matters of emphasis that shifted with time or else they set at odds what are in fact distinct stages of the history of Homeric performance. My aim below will be to take what is true, or plausibly true, in the opinions surveyed above, and place it in a diachronic framework that offers an authentic picture of the origins and development of the Homeric rhapsode and his craft.

---

[37] "Der Name, von den Alten verschieden abgeleitet, ist wohl von Haus aus als Spottname gemeint und nach Analogie von κιθαρῳδός, αὐλῳδός ironisch gebildet, da die Rhapsoden mit dem ᾄδειν überhaupt nichts zu tun hatten."

[38] I am not restricting 'formal' (in 'formal characteristics') to a literary conception of genre. In an oral performance culture, 'genre' conceptualized in terms of 'performance occasion' also exhibits 'formal' traits.

[39] Meyer (1918:333) saw a clear example of the corresponding 'seams' in the ending to the *Iliad* that joined it to the *Aithiopis*.

[40] Schmitt (1967:301 §609) is satisfied with the equation ῥαψῳδός = "Gesänge nähend" that he finds in Fränkel. He calls Patzer's requirement for greater specificity "self-imposed" and conflates 'stitching' (ῥάπτω), 'plaiting' (πλέκω), and 'weaving' (ὑφαίνω). He translates ἐν νεαροῖς ὕμνοις ῥάψαντες ἀοιδήν as "in neuen Hymnen ein Lied webend"; ῥαπτῶν ἐπέων … ἀοιδοί as "die Sänger geflochtener Worte." For him apparently 'weben', 'flechten', and 'nähen' are equivalent. Durante (1968b:280–281) makes a similar attempt to explain ῥάπτω not as 'stitching' or 'sewing' but as 'weaving' or 'plaiting' (see below, p. 428).

[41] "Der Rhapsode ist der, der sein dichterisches Werk hervorbringt, indem er den Faden der Erzählung weiterführt, verwickelt oder verflicht."

10.2.1 Non-melodic recitation?

To start with Ford 1988, as I observed above, he argues that the defining qualities of 'rhapsody' were solo delivery and the absence of musical accompaniment—a mode of performance characteristic of stichic and elegiac verse in the classical period[42]—not its degree of originality or its specific association with the meter of epic. In support of his conclusion, he adduces that fourth-century instances of ῥαψῳδός and its derivatives (some of them referring to the fifth century) concerned the performance of poetry other than epic—in particular, poetry by Arkhilokhos. Ford claims that a study of the relevant Aristotelian *loci* confirms that the non-melodic recitation of stichic and elegiac verse is in view.

If there is an overriding objection to Ford's argument, it is that he cannot, and does not even attempt to, explain why the metaphor of sewing or stitching should have been thought apposite to the mode of performance and poetic material peculiar to the rhapsode. What associative semantic path leads from a solo, non-melodic public recitation to 'stitching' a song? Unless he is willing to re-embrace Patzer's view (which he seemingly rejects as insufficient at 301–302),[43] what might possibly suggest the metaphor of stitching to portray performance without instrumental (and vocal) *melos*? Since Ford does not tender any explanation for the coinage of the term ῥαψῳδός, his article only proves what is hardly in dispute: that by the mid fourth century ῥαψῳδέω was applied to the solo, non-melodic public performance of stichic and elegiac verse. But this state of affairs could just as easily be explained as the outcome of a diachronic evolution from 'song' (melic meters with musical accompaniment) to 'poetry' (stichic and elegiac meters, first with reduced melody, then in recitative[44] with or without an instrument, finally simply recited as ordinary, if

---

[42] This assertion must be nuanced. The ordinary context for elegiac poetry was the symposium, where it was "sung with a piper (male or female) providing the accompaniment" (West 1992:25). Ford (1988:303 and n. 25) recognizes this fact, and it is therefore best to understand his restriction in negative terms, as denoting non-melic poetry or "poetry that can be spoken" (even if at times it was not). It is of course impossible to play and to sing to the *auloi* all at once, so that elegy sung to the pipe could not be a strict "solo" performance. One must also qualify the application of Ford's statement to early *iambos*, at least to the *iambos* of Arkhilokhos (cf. Dale 1963:48, West 1992:40, and Rotstein 2010:230–232). For archaic *iambos* as a melic genre, delivered in melic, semi-melic, or non-melic performance, see Bartol 1992:70–71. In drama, aulodic recitative was the mode of performance for certain anapaests, iambic trimeters, dactylic hexameters, and iambic and trochaic tetrameters (West 1992:40 and Pickard-Cambridge 1988:156–167). For epic, see below.

[43] Ford 1988:301–302 reviews previously suggested etymologies. Although he does not explicitly own his rejection of Patzer 1952—he uses the passive "Patzer's view has ... been criticized"—the logic of his argument is that Patzer's treatment fails and the need remains for a new approach.

[44] There is a degree of imprecision in the application of 'recitative' to ancient Greek music and poetry. The *OED* s.v. defines it as "a style of musical declamation intermediate between singing

emphatic, speech, and without instrumental accompaniment).[45] This diachronic scenario allows for the view that *rhapsodic* performance—i.e. the mode of performance peculiar to the professional for whom ῥαψῳδός was originally coined—was at first tied specifically to epic and made use of a κίθαρις or φόρμιγξ (as was true of the Homeric ἀοιδός).

I believe that 'singer' (ἀοιδός) and 'rhapsode' (ῥαψῳδός) were concurrent designations for the performer of epic. Homeric poetry, in a characteristic display of conservatism, does not depict its own performance as it actually was for most of Greek history. It even excludes features already typical of the formative archaic period. Instead, it offers a suitably refracted portrayal of what it must have been in origin or at least imaginatively recreates its melic roots with authentic diachronic insight. As many have noted, neither the *Iliad* nor the *Odyssey* makes explicit reference to the rhapsode or to the stitching of poetry.

---

and ordinary speech." 'Declamation', in turn, is the "uttering of a speech, etc. with studied intonation and gesture." But "intermediate" lacks specificity, and it is sometimes hard to tell the "intonation" of ordinary speech, especially when emphatic, from the "intonation" associated with 'to intone' (="to utter in musical tones; to sing"). Add to this semantic muddle: that 'to chant' and 'to recite in monotone' may be synonyms of 'to intone'; that, among other acceptations, 'to recite', which recalls 'recitative', may denote 'to intone'; and that any of these forms of delivery intermediate between singing and ordinary speech may have instrumental accompaniment. It is obvious, then, that by itself 'recitative' cannot situate a performance in relation to music and ordinary speech. It is easy to illustrate the confusion that ensues. As far as I can tell, West 1992 uses 'recitative' without defining it, as if its meaning were transparent. So, for example, he explains παρακαταλογή as "a technique of reciting verse with instrumental accompaniment" (40). This suggests 'ordinary speech' with an instrument in the background. But a few sentences later, West specifies that "the verses were recited in a more stylized manner" and that "[p]erhaps 'chanted' would be an appropriate term" (40). It is not clear what "stylized" or "chant" imply (monotone?), and we are little helped by the footnote on the same page that informs us that this is a "type of delivery ... intermediate between ordinary speech and song." The problem here is that παρακαταλογή arguably represents an intermediate stage between music and the rather cramped melody that some associate with recitative. At any rate, it is certainly not ordinary speech with an instrumental background. Hence, Nagy (1990c:46n140) is right to warn us that "[i]t may be misleading to some that West 1982.77 [West 1982] uses *recitative* to translate *parakatalogē*." Nagy describes this mode of delivery as intermediate "between sung and spoken," and, by writing thus, he makes clear that for him 'recitative' is stylized speech that *cannot* be considered between "sung and spoken." Nagy's own adjective for such intermediate forms is "reduced melodic" (1990c:46). For him, ordinarily, dactylic hexameter, elegiac distich, and iambic trimeter were recitative: although they still possessed prescribed pitch patterns, we would not recognize these as melody, not even as reduced melody (1990c:19–20). To West's triad of melody, recitative, and ordinary speech, Nagy opposes the graded scale of (full) melody, reduced melody, recitative, monotone, and ordinary speech (but, *nota bene*, his 'recitation' may involve anything between reduced melody and ordinary speech). The limitations of West's terminology are evident in his survey of the music of tragedy. Point (d) in West 1992:351 speaks of passages "recited ... with instrumental accompaniment." From the adjoined footnote, which mentions παρακαταλογή, we learn that what Nagy calls "reduced melody" is in view. The imprecision of 'recitative' is a reflection of its history. See, for example, the *Oxford Companion to Music* s.v.

45 Cf. Nagy 1990c:17–51.

There are good reasons for this silence which I shall detail below.[46] But this no more rules out the application of the name 'rhapsode' to the early-archaic performer of the poems than the failure to mention festivals precludes the eighth- and seventh-century performance of Homeric poetry at various archaic poleis and Panhellenic festivals. As regards the particular mode of performance, ἀοιδός was the unmarked, ῥαψῳδός the marked, term. ἀοιδός was applicable (at least originally) to (professional) performers of all sung poetry, including lyric meters with choral dancing[47]—i.e. to all performers of 'song,' the broader field of marked speech out of which hexameter epic evolved.[48] ῥαψῳδός referred specifically to the performer of traditional epic. It reflected the audience's perception of what was formally and thematically characteristic of this oral traditional medium of recomposition in performance. The formal criterion did not in origin rule out instrumental accompaniment, although I do believe that it regarded a particular type of music and choice of instrument. This is not to say that the rhapsode *qua* rhapsode at any one time necessarily performed with instrumental accompaniment any more than the Homeric singer *qua* singer. Both were, after all, alternative labels for one and the same performer. The point of my argument is that the profile of the rhapsode is no more and no less 'melic' than that of the Homeric singer. The title 'rhapsode' focuses attention on features of his craft that are largely indifferent to the use of an instrument and the presence of melody. The Homeric performer owes to his presence in the poems *qua* ἀοιδός his association to instrument and *melos* in the epic medium. His absence *qua* ῥαψῳδός means that references tying rhapsode, *melos*, and instrumental playing must be sought elsewhere. Whether as 'singer' or 'rhapsode,' with the passing of time the Homeric performer shed the instrument. Since his was the preeminent public performance during the classical period without any instrumental accompaniment, this *differentia* was readily seized then as the defining characteristic of the rhapsodic mode of performance. This explains the easy naivete with which the performance practices of the classical rhapsode were sometimes retrojected without warrant to the archaic period, when a uniform non-melodic practice cannot be assumed. Whether epic poetry was then sung or delivered with reduced melody or as recitative, with or without an instrument, or else merely declaimed as spoken verse, cannot be finally determined for any particular occasion and performer (e.g. Xenophanes, on whom see below, p. 354). It is likely that all modes of performance were used at one time or another, as the medium evolved first towards reduced melody, then to recitative, and, finally, to spoken declamation. If the practice, then, of the fourth-century epic

[46] See pp. 364ff.
[47] Cf. p. 648 n. 5 below.
[48] Cf. Nagy 1990c:33.

performer—and hence the fourth-century use of ῥαψῳδός—does not necessitate a static view of the rhapsode as one who *ab origine* never accompanied his delivery with an instrument, to assume that the rhapsode *qua* rhapsode always declaimed without musical accompaniment is simply to beg the question that must be answered.

But even as Ford fails to explain the coinage of 'rhapsode' and its *differentiae*, he faces three further obstacles. Out of all early stichic and elegiac composers, why should Arkhilokhos alone have formed part of the repertory of rhapsodes? The prologue and ῥῆσις of tragedy, allegedly Thespis' innovations, must have been solo, non-melodic, stichic set speeches. Why then was ῥαψῳδέω never used in connection with them or, for that matter, applied to the performance of the longer spoken passages of Attic drama? (To messenger speeches, for example.) Finally, Ford fails to explain the ready association of ἀείδω and its semantic family with ῥαψῳδός and its derivatives.

To start with this last point first: the usual reply is that ἀείδω often seems interchangeable with verbs of speaking, or that at least it is not always clear that it must mean 'to sing [poetry to melody]'. Therefore, that ῥαψῳδός points to ἀείδω does not necessarily support the claim that rhapsodic performance ever involved a melic component.[49] But the very fact that we are not always able to draw a clear synchronic contrast between verbs of speaking and singing is itself diachronically significant. Just as the marked ῥαψῳδός stands in contrast to the unmarked ἀοιδός, so also ἀείδω and various verbs of speaking (εἰπεῖν, (κατα)λέγειν, ἐννέπειν, etc.) may see their underlying diachronic contrast activated by a given context, even though ordinarily they overlap as synchronically interchangeable within the system of Homeric diction. Whether 'speaking' is the marked, and 'singing' the unmarked, term when the contrast obtains or vice versa depends on the context. The reason for this superficially puzzling semantic structure is that, synchronically, Homeric diction puts on a par older and newer modes of performance (melodic, reduced melodic, and recitative).[50] Diachronic analysis in turn reveals them as successive stages. As Nagy (1990c:21) writes, "[s]elf-references in Archaic Greek poetry may be diachronically valid without being synchronically true."[51] But, to return to ῥαψῳδός, if by the time of its coinage the rhapsode's craft precluded even a reduced melodic delivery, why should the coinage not have resorted to an alternative like λόγος or ῥῆσις,

---

[49] Ford 1988:305 and n. 35. The statement is common: e.g. Wilamowitz-Moellendorff 1916:341. Renehan (1976:91–92) and West (1981:113–114) cite numerous instances in which it is not always clear what synchronic contrast obtains between a verb of 'speaking' and a verb of 'singing.' Cf. Prauscello (2006:97–103), who takes issue with Renehan.

[50] Just to cite one such synchronic leveling: the *Iliad* opens with an address to the Muse to 'sing' (ἄειδε); the *Odyssey* asks her to 'tell' (ἔννεπε).

[51] See Nagy 1990c:21 for his comments about ἀείδω and ἐννέπω.

rather than the potentially melodic ἀοιδή? And if ἀείδω had, in fact, *already* shed its necessary association with melodic singing when ῥαψῳδός was coined, what need was there for a new term, different from ἀοιδός, to designate a performer whose delivery was non-melodic? On the other hand, if ἀοιδός had not lost its intimate association with *melos*, why coin a potentially confusing term whose second element might connote melody (-ῳδός), only to purge its melic connotation with the choice of ῥάπτω for its first? There is something paradoxical, if not incoherent, about the logic. Furthermore, if Ford is right, μέλπω, with its strong semantic association with instrumental song and dance (some might even say, with choral performance),[52] seems an especially perverse choice for the Hesiodic fragment quoted above. Why not resort instead to the traditional and more neutral φαίνομεν or ἐντύομεν, governing ἀοιδήν *apo koinou* with ῥάψαντες?[53]

As is often the case, a learned Hellenistic poet helps to illuminate the diachronic evolution of the rhapsodic craft.[54] Kallimakhos' *Hymn to Zeus* 78–79

[ὑδείομεν] … Φοίβου δὲ λύρης εὖ εἰδότας οἴμους·
'ἐκ δὲ Διὸς βασιλῆες'

[we say that] those who know well the tracks of the lyre belong
     to Phoibos
'but *basileis* are from Zeus'

reprises Hesiod's *Theogony* 94–96:

ἐκ γάρ τοι Μουσέων καὶ ἑκηβόλου Ἀπόλλωνος
ἄνδρες ἀοιδοὶ ἔασιν ἐπὶ χθόνα καὶ κιθαρισταί,
ἐκ δὲ Διὸς βασιλῆες·

For from the Muses and far-shooting Apollo
there are men on the earth who sing and play the cithara,
but *basileis* are from Zeus.

At first, Kallimakhos' reprise seems straightforward: cithara corresponds to lyre, and ἀοιδοί is glossed by εὖ εἰδότες οἴμους. But, as I make clear below (pp. 392ff.), the word οἶμος, intimately related to οἴμη, is peculiar not to the

---

[52] Cf. *LfgE* s.v. This choice is diachronically illuminating, as I hope to show in a future work.

[53] Instead of μέλπομεν ἐν νεαροῖς ὕμνοις ῥάψαντες ἀοιδήν, it might have been, for example, ἀοιδὴν | φαίνομεν ἐν νεαροῖς ὕμνοις ῥάψαντες ἀοιδοί (cf. θ 499) or ἐντύομεν νεαροὺς ὕμνους ῥάψαντες ἀοιδὴν (cf. μ 183 with E 720). I doubt that one must conclude from the distribution of ἐντύνω and ἐντύω in epic that only the former could govern ὕμνους. See *LfgE* s.v. ἐντύ(ν)ω.

[54] For other examples of diachronic insight gained from Hellenistic poetry see González 2000 and 2010b.

unmarked ἀοιδός but to the marked rhapsode. In effect, Kallimakhos has applied to the rhapsode and his craft the Hesiodic reference to the epic 'singer' and his instrument[55]—a refraction of the melic origins of the epic genre. By implicitly substituting the marked, narrower term for the unmarked, broader one while keeping the reference to melic delivery, Kallimakhos confirms that 'rhapsode' is not a late term coined for a reproducing reciter of textually fixed Homeric poems, but a label that focuses attention upon the rhapsodic craft of recomposition of traditional epic themes and diction in performance.

A similar point may be made on the basis of Pindar's *Isthmian* 3/4.55–57, which was already cited above (p. 337) and I shall have a further occasion to revisit below (p. 349). Note the verb ἀθύρειν at 57. As Wilamowitz-Moellendorff (1922:339n3) observed, it is an epexegetic infinitive. As to meaning, after asserting that "[f]erner ist ἀθύρειν immer nur 'spielen'," he glossed it thus: "Homer made the deeds of Ajax conspicuous to future men, to make it easy now to mention them occasionally." But there is more to ἀθύρειν than the bland 'to mention with ease'. Race (1997:167), like Slater (1969:15) before him ("sport with, take delight in"), enlarges the verb's semantic field to embrace the meaning 'to enjoy' ("for future men to enjoy"). Thummer is nearer the truth with "spielend besingen" (1968–1969:74), although he misses the performative implications of ἀθύρειν, which are more pointed that a generic 'playing' or 'playfully', and in the end he reverts to Wilamowitz's "spielerisch leicht." Willcock (1995:80) is right to particularize λοιποῖς to the professional of poetry ("for later poets to make their entertainment from"), although he seems to have in view composition apart from performance and only non-epic poets.[56] I submit that Pindar is

---

[55] I have no doubt that in its contrast of *basileis* to ἄνδρες ἀοιδοὶ … καὶ κιθαρισταί, the *Theogony* included its own performers among the latter. Just as βασιλῆες denotes the class of rulers comprehensively and generically, so also does 'singers … and citharists' potentially embrace all singers of archaic poetry (chiefly, the epic singer). ἀοιδοί and κιθαρισταί coordinately qualify the noun ἄνδρες. They are not two distinct classes of performers but a twofold description of the generic mortal performer. ἔασιν ἐπὶ χθόνα articulates the contrast between the divine and earthly spheres (the Muses and Apollo vs. mortal performers; Zeus vs. the *basileis*). It would be odd to think that to an utterly generic ἄνδρες ἀοιδοί a narrow class of instrumentalists, the κιθαρισταί, had been appended (καὶ κιθαρισταί might also be read epexegetically); or to conclude that 'singer-citharists' comprised a narrow class of performers that excluded the newly inducted 'Hesiod.' Despite its numerous ancient and modern proponents—e.g. Pausanias 9.30.3, who even thought that Hesiod had been barred from competing at Delphi because he had not learned to play the *kitharis* (10.7.3)—the σκῆπτρον of *Theogony* 30 was not a rhapsodic ῥάβδος that precluded a *kitharis* or *phorminx* (cf. *Hymn to Hermes* 210, 425–426, and 529), but an emblem of performative authority. My interpretation makes 'Hesiod' neither less of a rhapsode at *Theogony* 30 (cf. ἀείδειν 34) nor more of a singer at *Theogony* 95. The view that *Theogony* 94–96 includes epic singers even *qua* rhapsodes is supported by *Homeric Hymn* 25.

[56] Cf. Farnell 1930–1932:1.254: "[Homer] hath told the story in the measured roll of his immortal verse, for other poets to disport themselves therewith." Farnell (1930–1932:2.352) approves Wilamowitz's reading of κατὰ ῥάβδον as a metaphor from weaving. But the fragment of

drawing on the language of epic performance, specifically, the performance of the Homeric hymns, which makes ἀθύρω and ἄθυρμα preferred terms for the joyful playing of the lyre and the singing and dancing that regularly accompany it. In the *Hymn to Hermes* 52 the lyre is called a 'lovely plaything' (ἐρατεινὸν ἄθυρμα) and the tortoise is called ἄθυρμα proleptically at 32 and 40. At 484–485 we further learn that, in the context of the 'plentiful banquet, the lovely dance, and the glorious revel',[57] the utterance of the lyre teaches every manner of thing delightful to the mind when she is played (ἀθυρομένη 485) with ease and tender intimacy. *Homeric Hymn* 19.15 portrays Pan 'playing his song (μοῦσαν ἀθύρων) sweetly to the reed pipes'. His is not, as one might think, a solo instrumental performance. To his melodious playing, compared to a lament (θρῆνον 18) and a honey-voiced song (μελίγηρυν ἀοιδήν 18), the mountain nymphs dance and sing (μέλπονται 21), hymning the gods (ὑμνεῦσιν δὲ θεούς 27) and telling of Hermes alone above all,[58] of his love for Dryops' daughter and of Pan, their child. Thus, in circular fashion, what started with the rhapsode's invocation of the Muse to tell of Hermes' child, Pan, becomes in performance one and the same with the hymnic performance of the nymphs, who sing and dance to the piping of Pan himself. This self-referentiality endows the rhapsodic performance of the epic hymn with the representational character of melic *khoreia*. In Pindar, the melic character of the epic performance entailed by ἀθύρειν is clear, and even the scholiast marked it: τὸ δὲ ἀθύρειν ἀντὶ τοῦ μέλπειν καὶ ὑμνεῖν.[59] It is not that in *Isthmian* 3/4.57 Pindar has only rhapsodic performance in view, but that with the language of rhapsodic hymnody he encompasses the performance of all future poets who might make Ajax their theme. That the epic medium should portray the performance of Homeric hymns as melic may be attributed to the conservative impulse that animates diachronic skewing.[60] That Pindar's

---

Kallimakhos (fr. 26 Pfeiffer) on which it is based (see further below, pp. 367ff.) uses the preposition ἐπί, τὸν ἐπὶ ῥάβδῳ μῦθον ὑφαινόμενον. The acceptation of ῥάβδος instanced by Pollux 7.53 ('streak' or 'stripe') does not readily lend itself to construal with ἐπί (one would expect a simple dative or ἐν + dat.). Neither does ἐπὶ ῥάβδῳ seem an instrumental metaphor (one would expect ἐν + dat., cf. Pindar *Olympian* 5.19; ὑπό + gen., cf. Herodotos 1.17; or ἐπί + gen., cf. Bachmann 1928:1.425.9–10). We are simply left with the expression ἡ ἐπὶ ῥάβδῳ ᾠδή as a gloss for ῥαψῳδία or ῥαβδῳδία (Hilgard 1965:28.26 and 315.31). Pausanias 9.30.3 says of Hesiod that he ἐπὶ ῥάβδου δάφνης ᾖδε. Editors up to Bekker printed ἐπὶ ῥάβδῳ with codex Vindobonensis b, but this is a minority reading (Hitzig and Bluemner 1896–1910:3.1.361).

[57] εἰς δαῖτα θάλειαν | καὶ χορὸν ἱμερόεντα καὶ ἐς φιλοκυδέα κῶμον (480–481). The connection between the lyre as an ἄθυρμα and the κῶμος resurfaces in *Pythian* 5.22–23. Cf. Bakkhylides *Epigrammata* 1.3.

[58] With West (2003b:200), I read οἷον for οἶον at 28: Hermes is not just one thematic choice among many *exempli gratia*. He is the preeminent theme of Pan's cortège.

[59] *Scholia vetera* to *Isthmian* 4.63e Drachmann.

[60] On the notion of 'diachronic skewing' see Nagy 2003:39–48. He defines it as the perspective displayed by "the [poetic] medium [where it] refers to itself in terms of earlier stages of its

intertextual echo should embrace this traditional melic representation (note his reference to hymnody at 61, πυρσὸν ὕμνων) betrays a keen sensitivity to the diachronic development of rhapsodic performance.

I believe that Else (1965:59–60) is right to look to the rhapsode and his craft in his search for a model that might have inspired the dramatic prologue, which Themistios, on the authority of Aristotle, ascribed to Thespis.[61] Else's proposal that the rhapsode and his performance help to motivate and explain significant features in the origin and growth of Attic drama agrees with my own convictions, independently arrived at and explored at length in this book.[62] Although I often differ with him in matters of detail, this essential insight is sound and productive. If so, it is all the more surprising that ῥαψῳδέω was never used in connection with the performance of the prologue. The retort that this verb was too closely tied to epic performance to suggest itself in the context of a new genre—however much epic and its professional performer might have inspired various aspects of it—undermines Ford's argument that *stricto sensu* this verb must not be understood as the delivery of epic but as the solo, public performance of non-melodic verse.[63] Neither is the dramatic ῥῆσις the object of ῥαψῳδέω,[64] although, as Else (1965:54) observes, "Wilamowitz pointed out, and Aurelio Peretti later showed in detail, that the structure of the tragic *rhēsis* in the earliest plays of Aeschylus has nothing in common with choral lyric but goes back to Ionian models: epic, elegiac, and iambic poetry."[65]

A third significant objection to Ford's argument is that of non-epic poets Arkhilokhos alone was associated with rhapsodic performance during the

---

own existence" (39). This skewing concerns "self-references in Archaic Greek poetry [that are] diachronically valid without being synchronically true" (Nagy 1990c:21). For example, whereas in the *Odyssey* the setting for the performance of epic is the evening's feast, the earliest historical evidence points to festivals as the performance occasion.

[61] *Oration* 26.316d: καὶ οὐ προσέχομεν Ἀριστοτέλει ὅτι τὸ μὲν πρῶτον ὁ χορὸς εἰσιὼν ᾖδεν εἰς τοὺς θεούς, Θέσπις δὲ πρόλογόν τε καὶ ῥῆσιν ἐξεῦρεν … ;

[62] A clear statement is found in Else 1957b. He credits J. W. Donaldson for the idea (39n6) but notes that his article "did not spring from D[onaldson]'s suggestion." See, for example, Donaldson 1860:61.

[63] "Surely it is no accident that the nome, a *solo performance* and itself ultimately derived from epic song, is the one lyric genre with a formally marked *prooimion*. ... [W]e cannot exclude the possibility that [in the prologue Thespis] appeared in character as the hero of the piece, introducing himself and reminding the audience of the background of his story" (Else 1965:60, my emphasis). Note that I do not endorse the view that the nome "derives from epic song." The undeniable relationship between 'nome' and 'epic' is far more complex.

[64] Cf. Philo *De migratione Abrahami* §111 CW; and Lucian *Symposium* §17.

[65] With regard to the use of ἀείδω + ῥῆσιν at Aristophanes *Clouds* 1371, Herington (1985:225n15) writes that "a tragic rhesis may well on occasion have been intoned in the rhapsodic manner rather than delivered as ordinary speech." The emendation of ᾖσ' to ᾖγ' by Dover 1968a *ad loc.* prompted Renehan 1976:88–92. See, in particular, 90–91 and the treatment by Prauscello 2006:86–104.

classical period (i.e. before the reforms of Demetrios of Phaleron). This suggests that there was something unique about him or his poetry that led to his inclusion in the rhapsodic repertoire. With him alone does Homer share Herakleitos' censure (DK 22 B42), and his is the only name added by Sokrates to Homer and Hesiod as potentially within the expert purview Ion the rhapsode.[66] Had the rhapsodes' engagement with Arkhilokhos merely concerned their public, non-melodic recitation of his iambic, trochaic, or elegiac poetry, why should he alone have been singled out for this honor? The implications of Sokrates' question to Ion are arguably confirmed by Klearkhos, who in the first of his two books *On Riddles* wrote that Simonides of Zakynthos used to rhapsodize the poetry of Arkhilokhos in the theaters, sitting on a stool.[67] Given the date of Klearkhos and the context of Athenaios' passage, it is just possible—but hardly certain—that Simonides' Arkhilokhean performances followed the innovations of Demetrios.[68] Lysanias' assertion (in the first book of his *On Iambic Poets*) that Mnasion the rhapsode in his public performances used to deliver (ὑποκρίνεσθαι)[69] some of the iambs of Semonides[70] only proves that after the reforms of Demetrios and the theatricalization of the rhapsodes, their repertoire embraced material that in the archaic and high-classical periods would never have been thought within their traditional purview.[71] None of this helps to advance Ford's argument, whose interest is not the broadening of the repertoire of rhapsodes but the claim that 'to rhapsodize' *ab origine* concerned a particular type of performance. The paradoxical entailment of his views is that we need not even think of 'rhapsodizing' as the purview of the 'rhapsode'. Any solo performer of non-melodic iambic,

---

[66] Plato *Iōn* 531a1–2 (cf. 532a4–6).

[67] Athenaios 14.620c–d.

[68] Cf. Murray 1996:105 and Bartol 1992:67. Athenaios does not state unequivocally that Simonides performed Arkhilokhos in Athens, but the assumption seems reasonable (Burckhardt 1963:187).

[69] With Bartol (1992:69–70), I do not believe that ὑποκρίνεσθαι here implies an out-and-out histrionic performance (so also Lennartz 2010:295; but cf. Bartol 1992:67–68 and nn17–19; Rotstein 2010:266 is neither incisive nor illuminating). Its use for 'to perform' stands in continuity with what I argue below must have been the original meaning of ὑποκριτής as a label for the actor: neither 'expounder' nor 'answerer', as the long debate thus far has had it, but simply 'performer'. See pp. 647ff.

[70] The text prints Σιμωνίδου, but West (1981:125) is surely right to correct it to Σημωνίδου. See further below, p. 437 n. 6.

[71] The *Suidas* 2.403 E no. 2898 (Adler) makes Lysanias a teacher of Eratosthenes. Hence, he was roughly contemporaneous with Klearkhos. I deal further with Demetrios' reforms below, pp. 466ff. Modifications to the repertory and practices of the rhapsodes, with a growing emphasis on the histrionic potential of their subject matter, were already afoot. These changes must have been prompted by Homer's rivalry with Attic drama for first place in the affections of the Athenians. Faced with the growing popularity of actors, rhapsodes must have been tempted to adopt stage manners that seemed to have gained their rivals the estimation of the people. The many speeches of the *Iliad* and the *Odyssey* gave ample occasion for character acting. Demetrios of Phaleron did not create these changes; he merely formalized and hastened them.

elegiac, or trochaic poems could be said to 'rhapsodize' his material, even if he was not a 'rhapsode' in any traditional sense of the term.[72] The singing of Solon's poetry at the Apatouria (Plato *Timaios* 21b, cited by Ford 1988:302), falls under the category of rhapsodic performance understood as 'relay poetics' (on which more below, pp. 367ff.), that is, the cooperative-competitive stitching of a song by two or more rhapsodes in turn, each taking the thread of the poem precisely where the previous one had left off. The boys' 'rhapsodic competition' (ἆθλα … ῥαψῳδίας *Timaios* 21b3–4) transparently reproduces the arrangements and dynamics operative at the Panathenaia, attributed to festival reforms instigated either by Solon or by Peisistratos (see below, pp. 382ff.).[73]

To return to Arkhilokhos, critics of Notopoulos 1966 may be right that Arkhilokhos did not compose epic poetry now lost to us, although, in light of his versatility,[74] we should not be surprised to learn that epic poetry too had been attributed to him.[75] The most compelling alternative to the existence of Arkhilokhean epic relies on the typological opposition between epic as praise, and iambic as blame, poetry.[76] This proposal views either genre as the Panhellenic endpoint of the centuries-long evolution of Greek musical traditions. The corresponding diachronic development would have resulted in thematic specializations of opposite sign—epic κλέος versus iambic ψόγος—and a musical stylization that crystallized respectively into the dactylic hexameter and the iambic

[72] Apparent support for this claim dissipates on inspection. The statement about Stesikhoros in Athenaios 14.620c adds nothing to the argument since he was not a rhapsode. It is best to regard it as refracting a historical fact: the diachronic trajectory from song to poetry for the genres of epic (including gnomic), iambo-trochaic, and elegiac poetry. That Khamaileon must have thought Stesikhoros an exponent of the practice (adopted by some Hellenistic rhapsodes) of setting epic poetry to music follows not only from the comment Athenaios reports out of his work *On Stēsikhoros*, but is also consistent with [Plutarch] *De musica* 1132b8–c1 and 1133e7–f6. Cf. Nagy 1990c:27 and Russo 1999. A rhapsode's recitation of Empedokles' *Purifications*, even if not traditional in the sense of Homer and Hesiod—it certainly could not have involved oral recomposition—cannot be considered a radical departure from regular practice, since it was, after all, a hexameter poem (cf. Aristotle *Poetics* 1447b18). Little can be extracted from vague references to 'other poets' when Homer and Hesiod are mentioned (e.g. Plato *Iōn* 530b8–9 and 532a5; or Isokrates *Panathēnaikos* 18 and 33): they could well be hexameter poets such as Phokylides, the various putative authors of cyclic epic, etc. (cf. Notopoulos 1966:314).

[73] Mark the use of ᾔσαμεν at *Timaios* 21b7. The movement from 'many poems of many poets' to 'the poetry of Solon'—i.e. from the general to the specific—suggests that ἐλέχθη was the unmarked, ᾔσαμεν the marked description of the mode of performance. In other words, the text tells us that at least Solon's poems were not delivered as ordinary speech.

[74] Scholars admit as 'securely Arkhilokhean' iambic, trochaic, elegiac, and various lyric meters; for subjects, we have invective, consolatory poetry, epigrams, military themes, and many others. It is not unreasonable to imagine an over-zealous attempt to make him a master of all genres and meters—an attempt, therefore, that would also tie him to hexametric poetry.

[75] Ford (1988:302n19) calls Notopoulos's explanation "not convincing." But other scholars are not so quick to dismiss it (cf., for example, Bartol 1992:65n3). Cf. also below, p. 489 n. 44.

[76] Cf. Nagy 1976.

trimeter, both stichic meters performed to reduced melody and recitative speech cadences. The contrasting thematic emphases served broadly complementary cultural functions: public approval and public censure. The complementary uses of epic praise and iambic invective and their shared Panhellenic scope might well account for their joint adoption into the repertoire of the preeminent Panhellenic performers, the rhapsodes.[77] The Homeric *Margites* may itself instance a tradition that, as to form, blended epic and iambic meters precisely to effect a humorous abuse poem of Panhellenic projection.[78] At any rate, granting *ex hypothesi* that it took place, one would have to consider the incorporation of *iambos* into the rhapsodic repertoire a subordinate outcome of the essential character of rhapsodic performance at an already advanced stage of Panhellenic development. Panhellenic iambic invective would have remained a secondary growth that must be understood against the backdrop of the defining rhapsodic mainstream, Panhellenic praise poetry.[79] As perhaps the oldest of all named iambic poets,[80] whatever his biographical reality,[81] Arkhilokhos doubtless embodied the broadest range of traditional iambic poetry. Therefore, his poems would have had the greatest potential for, and claim to, Panhellenic status.[82] This fact would explain why he alone should have been grouped with Homer and Hesiod as the canonical trio of the rhapsodic repertoire. Note that this alternative explanation for the engagement of rhapsodes with Arkhilokhos differs crucially from Ford's proposal. It relies primarily not on formal arguments but on the complementary cultural uses of *iambos* and epic. The fact that both featured non-melodic, stichic verse types perhaps facilitated their joint adoption by one and the same professional. But these thematic considerations are rather more significant than the formal ones that Ford alleges as the *differentia* of ancient 'rhapsody'.

---

[77] Cf. Lavigne 2005:12–57. Strictly speaking, epichoric traditions of praise poetry concern αἶνος/ ἔπαινος rather than epic κλέος. Some of the ways in which this αἶνος converges on, and diverges from, epic κλέος are explored in Nagy 1976:194–199, Nagy 1986, and Nagy 1990c:146–198. Arkhilokhean *iambos*, its local origins notwithstanding, arguably had a Panhellenic projection. Cf. Nagy 1999a:250 §11.

[78] Cf. Nagy 1999a:259 §9 and Lavigne 2005:48–57, both of whom draw attention to Aristotle *Poetics* 1448b24ff. On the *Margites* see Langerbeck 1958, Forderer 1960, Bossi 1986, Lennartz 2010:462–472, and Gostoli 2007.

[79] Cf. Nagy 1999a:253–254 §2.

[80] Only Semonides' *floruit* was thought to rival Arkhilokhos'. Compare Hubbard 1994 and Lennartz 2010:473–474.

[81] Cf. West 1974:27, Nagy 1999a:243–252, and Carey 1986.

[82] This potential itself would have spurred the adoption of Arkhilokhean *iambos* by rhapsodes. Rhapsodic performance, in turn, would have been instrumental to actualizing its Panhellenic promise.

Ultimately, we will never know for sure what singled Arkhilokhos out as a likely companion of Homer and Hesiod in the repertoire of rhapsodes, but given that there are plausible alternatives to Ford's argument, it is not safe to make this assemblage a cornerstone of our interpretation of ῥαψῳδός and ῥαψῳδέω. Finally, even if we can trust Diogenes Laertios' report that Xenophanes 'rhapsodized his own poetry' (αὐτὸς ἐρραψῴδει τὰ ἑαυτοῦ 9.18), we can only guess what form his performance took (reduced melody for his hexameters? speech for elegy and *iambos*?) and whether Diogenes' choice of ἐρραψῴδει is anachronistic or not. By the third century AD, the meaning of ῥαψῳδέω had unquestionably devolved into the looser one that Ford wishes to retroject into the archaic period: solo, non-melodic public recitation of non-lyric meters. But would Xenophanes (or a contemporary of his) have used this verb for his performance? And, if so, for poetry in all the three meters attributed to him? Even if we grant, *arguendo*, the non-melodic character of Xenophanes' recitation of iambic and elegiac poetry, must we assume the same of his performance of hexameter poetry?[83] Perhaps Ford's conjectures are right, but since the alternatives are not implausible we simply cannot know.[84] Even the support sought in Solon's recitation of the *Salamis* is dubious. Plutarch writes that Solon ἐν ᾠδῇ διεξῆλθε τὴν ἐλεγείαν,[85] while both Demosthenes and Polyainos resort to ᾗδε.[86] The poem itself features the celebrated juxtaposition κόσμον ἐπέων ᾠδὴν ἀντ' ἀγορῆς θέμενος, 'having composed a song for my public address, a lay of *epē*'.[87] Here Solon explicitly disowns ordinary public speaking. It is possible that his performance was 'song' and not 'speech' not only because of its meter but also

---

[83] One cannot put much stock in Athenaios 14.632d, which numbers Xenophanes (with Solon, Theognis, and Phokylides) among those who did not bring singing (μελῳδία) to their poems. The passage blames Homer's thoughtless metrical imperfections on his having composed his entire poetry for singing (μεμελοποιηκέναι). If Xenophanes did not exhibit comparable flaws, the logic of the argument would necessarily lead to the conclusion that *melos* played no role in the composition of his verses. Furthermore, if we embrace Athenaios' testimony about Xenophanes, why should we not also accept that Homeric poetry was composed for singing?

[84] It is also possible that by τὰ ἑαυτοῦ Diogenes only meant Xenophanes' hexameter poetry. Before ἀλλὰ καὶ αὐτὸς ἐρραψῴδει τὰ ἑαυτοῦ he wrote: γέγραφε δὲ ἐν ἔπεσι καὶ ἐλεγείας καὶ ἰάμβους καθ' Ἡσιόδου καὶ Ὁμήρου, ἐπικόπτων αὐτῶν τὰ περὶ θεῶν εἰρημένα. Since τὰ περὶ θεῶν εἰρημένα undeniably refers to ἔπη, it is not unreasonable to take τὰ ἑαυτοῦ as τὰ ἑαυτοῦ [ἔπη]. In other words, τὰ ἑαυτοῦ is not to be understood exhaustively as πάντα τὰ ἑαυτοῦ: 'he rhapsodized his own' means that he rhapsodized some of his poetry. Diogenes would then be drawing attention to a glaring inconsistency: however much Xenophanes criticized Homer and Hesiod, yet he himself too (ἀλλὰ καὶ αὐτός) embraced the composition and public delivery of epic verse as an itinerant rhapsode.

[85] Plutarch *Solōn* 8.2. A few lines later we read, τότε δ' ἀσθέντος αὐτοῦ (8.3).

[86] Demosthenes 19.252: ἐλεγεῖα ποιήσας ᾗδε. Polyainos *Stratēgēmata* 1.20.1: ἐλεγεῖα ᾗδε.

[87] Or: 'having composed a song instead of a speech, a lay of *epē*'. For κόσμος in the sense of '(epic) lay' see above, p. 195.

because Solon sang it with the reduced melodic contours typical of rhapsodic delivery without a *kitharis*.

The case of Khairemon's *Centaur* most likely proves the Aristotle could resort to ῥαψῳδία for its etymological sense of 'stitched song'—here a 'mixed song consisting of all meters stitched together' (*Poetics* 1447b22). Ford must be right that, in its context, the *Centaur* is marshaled as an example of a mimesis of non-lyric "mixed meters."[88] But it hardly follows from this that Athenaios was in error when he called it a 'polymetric drama' (δρᾶμα πολύμετρον Athenaios 13.608e). It could still serve as Aristotle's illustration if the non-lyric portions of this alleged 'drama' were of the mixed metrical type.[89] That the *Centaur*, although a drama, should serve to demonstrate the lack of a proper name (cf. ἀνώνυμος at 1447b9) when a mimesis 'only uses meters, and these ... mixing them one with another' might seem problematic, since ordinarily drama calls for *melos* and dancing rhythms. There are two possible explanations for the philosopher's choice. Examples of metrical mixtures of the sort he had in mind were probably rare and hard to find, and only Khairemon, his contemporary, came readily to mind; his work must have contravened Aristotle's feeling for proper dramatic form and, consequently—here at least, though not in the *Rhetoric*—he refused it the corresponding generic label.[90] And, as we learn from *Rhetoric* 1413b12–13 (see further below, pp. 623f.), the λέξις of Khairemon's

---

[88] The text, as often with Aristotle, is difficult to establish, and its meaning dense. I read it thus: ἡ δὲ [τέχνη] μόνον τοῖς λόγοις ψιλοῖς ἢ τοῖς μέτροις καὶ τούτοις εἴτε μιγνῦσα μετ' ἀλλήλων εἴθ' ἑνί τινι γένει χρωμένη τῶν μέτρων ἀνώνυμος τυγχάνει οὖσα μέχρι τοῦ νῦν (*Poetics* 1447a28–b2). The lines that follow illustrate this statement. The larger context shows that τέχνη stands for μίμησις: in 1447a13–16 ἐποποιία and ἡ τῆς τραγῳδίας ποίησις appeared not as products but as activities (i.e. as *the making* of epos and of tragic drama); with them were listed ἡ διθυραμβοποιητικὴ [τέχνη] and other arts, which were all said to be *mimēseis*.

[89] Since trochaics, iambics, and anapaests were regularly mixed in drama, we must assume that Khairemon's mixture went well beyond the ordinary canons.

[90] Since Athenaios called the *Centaur* a 'drama', it must have included some mimesis of action. According to *Rhetoric* III.12, Khairemon's plays also featured speeches. Because these were comparable to those of a λογογράφος in their stylistic precision, in the setting of public debate they struck a 'meager' pose. The further qualification 'polymetric' shows that the *Centaur* did not readily fit the canons of dramatic composition. Cf. Else 1957a:59 and Collard 1970:25–27. As noted above, Aristotle's μικτὴ ῥαψῳδία is not intended as a generic classification, but it is used in its etymological sense of 'a song stitched out of many meters'. Strictly speaking, Aristotle's reluctance to classify the *Centaur* as a drama is not shown by his calling it a μικτὴ ῥαψῳδία— which, insofar as used in its etymological sense, is compatible with an overall dramatic form— but by his claim that no existing label captured its peculiar mimetic character. If naming it a drama had been unproblematic, the *Centaur* could not have served to illustrate the deficiency of existing mimetic nomenclature. *Poetics* 1460a1–2 states that Khairemon mixed iambic trimeters, trochaic tetrameters, and hexameters. I cannot agree with Ford (1988:304) that "[t]he implication [of this passage] is that he combined *only* these" (my emphasis). The text does not necessitate this restriction: its sole entailment is that Khairemon combined *at least* these.

oeuvre was γραφική and, therefore, he, as a poet, ἀναγνωστικός: this hints at Khairemon's emphasis as a composer on the non-choral passages of the *Centaur* and at a comparatively thin mimesis of action. This would have led Aristotle in turn to focus on the mixture of non-lyric meters. The argument of the *Rhetoric ad loc.* actually suggests that Khairemon is brought forward as an 'anagnostic' dramatist, just as Likymnios was as an 'anagnostic' dithyrambist.[91] Someone may object that if as Athenaios reports the *Centaur* had really been a drama, the label 'drama' (or the narrower 'comedy,' 'tragedy,' or 'satyr play,' as the case might be) should have sufficed Aristotle. But this need not follow. Aristotle wants to illustrate the statement that a mimesis that only uses 'meters' has no proper name 'until now'. His point is that poems may have (or poets may use) the same meter and yet be of a very different mimetic character. Labels that merely specify their meter misrepresent their character and cannot be considered adequate nomenclature (the *mimēseis* remain 'anonymous'). The same is true of metrical mixtures: a name that identified the meters used would still fail to capture the nature of the mimesis. As regards nomenclature, the best that one could do with Khairemon on the basis of his *Centaur* would be to call him a poet ('one would have to call him "poet"'). In view of its exceptional mixture of meters, it would be a misrepresentation to call it a drama and thereby suggest its similarity to ordinary tragedies, comedies, or satyr plays.

10.2.2 Ῥάπτω and Homeric artistry

It is time to look at the instances of ῥάπτω and its cognates in the Homeric poems. As I do, I wish to probe the following claims made by scholars in this connection: first, that the poems do not apply ῥάπτω to verbal artistry and therefore the name 'rhapsode' for the epic performer must be post-Homeric;[92] second, that ῥάπτω does not belong among the traditional Indo-European metaphors for poetic composition; and third, that, given its consistent application to plotting

---

[91] Cf. Cope 1877:3.146–147 and Else 1957a:58. The text of *Rhetoric* 1413b8–14 is as follows: ἔστι δὲ λέξις γραφικὴ μὲν ἡ ἀκριβεστάτη, ἀγωνιστικὴ δὲ ἡ ὑποκριτικωτάτη. ταύτης δὲ δύο εἴδη· ἡ μὲν γὰρ ἠθικὴ ἡ δὲ παθητική. διὸ καὶ οἱ ὑποκριταὶ τὰ τοιαῦτα τῶν δραμάτων διώκουσι, καὶ οἱ ποιηταὶ τοὺς τοιούτους. βαστάζονται δὲ οἱ ἀναγνωστικοί, οἷον Χαιρήμων (ἀκριβὴς γὰρ ὥσπερ λογογράφος), καὶ Λικύμνιος τῶν διθυραμβοποιῶν. τὰ τοιαῦτα [δράματα] must be the ἠθικὰ καὶ παθητικὰ δράματα, both subspecies of ἀγωνιστικὰ δράματα. What remains is to illustrate the other side of the classification, γραφικὰ δράματα, which should be ἀκριβῆ (1413b9). This expectation is met when Khairemon is mentioned (ἀκριβὴς γὰρ ὥσπερ λογογράφος 1413b13). But instead of calling him γραφικός, Aristotle focuses on the character of the γραφικὴ λέξις—that its natural outworking is reading (τὸ γὰρ ἔργον αὐτῆς ἀνάγνωσις 1414a17–18; see below, pp. 621ff.). Hence, he labels him ἀναγνωστικός. Nothing in the context suggests, much less requires, that we think of Khairemon as an exponent of a genre other than drama. Cf. Sifakis 2002:157n23 and Innes 2007:159–160.

[92] For the evolutionary model, 'post-Homeric' is an ill-defined *terminus*. We might think of it roughly as 'the time when the text had largely achieved a substantial degree of fixation.'

and scheming, this verb does not designate performance, only composition, and calls into question the alleged practice of recomposition in performance.

Starting with the last point first, my contention is that the Homeric use of ῥάπτω is in every way parallel to that of ὑφαίνω. Insofar as the latter is accepted as a well-established metaphor for composition, so also must the former. The poems (especially the *Odyssey*) use both metaphorically for the fabricating of plots and evil schemes. We may read signal instances of either verb metapoetically with reference to the poem in progress, and, hence, to the performance of its narrative. There are good reasons for the bard's choice of the comparatively more traditional ἀοιδός and ἀείδω in depictions of performance within the poems. Not only because ῥαψῳδός, with its contraction -αοιδ- > -ῳδ- belongs to later stages of the tradition (and correspondingly appears in the Homeric hymns only),[93] but also because the rhetoric of inspiration would be poorly served by a professional label that focuses so squarely on the singer's compositional technique, performance practice, and role in the construction and delivery of the poems.[94] There is no contradiction in archaic thought between divine inspiration and fully conscious human instrumentality. But where artistry is concerned—precisely the aspect emphasized by manufacturing metaphors (carpenter, stitcher, etc.)—the performer is careful to attribute his skill to the goddesses. B 488–493 provides a classic example:[95]

> ἔσπετε νῦν μοι Μοῦσαι 'Ολύμπια δώματ' ἔχουσαι·
> 485 ὑμεῖς γὰρ θεαί ἐστε πάρεστέ τε ἴστέ τε πάντα,
> ἡμεῖς δὲ κλέος οἶον ἀκούομεν οὐδέ τι ἴδμεν·
> οἵ τινες ἡγεμόνες Δαναῶν καὶ κοίρανοι ἦσαν·
> πληθὺν δ' οὐκ ἂν ἐγὼ μυθήσομαι οὐδ' ὀνομήνω,
> οὐδ' εἴ μοι δέκα μὲν γλῶσσαι, δέκα δὲ στόματ' εἶεν,
> 490 φωνὴ δ' ἄρρηκτος, χάλκεον δέ μοι ἦτορ ἐνείη,
> εἰ μὴ 'Ολυμπιάδες Μοῦσαι Διὸς αἰγιόχοιο
> θυγατέρες μνησαίαθ' ὅσοι ὑπὸ "Ιλιον ἦλθον·
> ἀρχοὺς αὖ νηῶν ἐρέω νῆάς τε προπάσας.

B 484–493

Tell me now, you Muses who have Olympian dwellings
485 —for you are goddesses and are present and know all things

---

[93] *Homeric Hymns* 1.18, 2.494, 3.20, 6.2, 30.18, 32.2, and 32.19. (Also Hesiod *Theogony* 48?)

[94] Cf. Ford 1992:35–39.

[95] I have already considered this passage above, pp. 183ff., where it is quoted (and provided with a slightly different translation) in connection with the view of inspiration it entails and its implications for our understanding of the epic medium.

but we only hear the report and know nothing—
who the leaders and chiefs of the Danaans were.
But the host I could neither narrate nor name,
not even if I had ten mouths and tongues,
490   an unbreakable voice and a heart of bronze,
unless the Olympian Muses, daughters of aegis-bearing Zeus,
should mention all those who came beneath Ilios.
I will tell in turn of all the ships and their leaders.

Some scholars, like West (1999a:189-190), have condemned verses 491–492 (or 491–493) without any textual support on the presumption that a later interpolator must have misunderstood the meaning of πληθύς as the number of the ἡγεμόνες Δαναῶν καὶ κοίρανοι (B 487); since the bard *does* go on to enumerate and name them—so goes their conjecture—the interpolator would have felt the need for the exception 'unless the Olympian Muses' etc. I find this hypothesis unnecessary. The αὖ of B 493 marks a contrast between the (allegedly misunderstood) πληθύς and the ἀρχοί. It seems clear to me that the logic of the thought is as follows: 1) tell me, Muses, who the leaders of the Danaans were (B 484 487); 2) I could not list them without you (implied), for you alone were eyewitnesses and can convey the verbal report (κλέος) that we, in turn, hear (as I declare it) (B 485–486); 3) the host I could not tell, regardless of personal vigor and skill—so many were they (B 488–490); 4) *unless* the Muses chose to mention them too (B 491–492); 5) but I will tell the catalog of leaders, for the Muses, whose speech I relay, are enumerating them to me as I speak (B 493). In other words, in 485–486 the singer acknowledges the necessary mediation of the Muses for the catalog of the leaders; ἐρέω at 493 implies that the Muses are answering his request in 484–487 for this catalog. The intervening 488–490 serve rhetorically to underline the immensity of the Greek contingent that sailed to Troy: the singer's abilities—the strength of his voice, his courage—would be insufficient to enumerate them all. Hence, he shies away from the task (which is mentioned solely for rhetorical purposes) and only asks for the leaders. But an allowance must be made for the overriding will of the inspiring goddesses. Who is the singer to limit what a god can or cannot do? Or to limit what the god can or cannot require him to do? Whether we accept the text as uniformly transmitted or as emended by West and others, there remains a rhetorical contrast between the skill and abilities of the poet—which cannot surmount the barrier of time, compensate for his lack of autopsy, and is physically unable to detail in full the massive undertaking of the Trojan expedition—and the capacities of the Muses, who can supply his need and make him equal to the task if so they choose. Individual skill and inspiration must ultimately cooperate in public delivery. They are distinct and complementary, in mutual tension to a degree, although priority is piously assigned to the divine element.

Anther signal instance that makes the same point is Phemios' remarkable plea: αὐτοδίδακτος δ᾽ εἰμί, θεὸς δέ μοι ἐν φρεσὶν οἴμας | παντοίας ἐνέφυσεν (χ 347–348). To underline his divine commission, the singer speaks in the same breath of being 'self-taught' and of the god having caused narratives of every sort to grow in his mind.[96] αὐτο- in αὐτοδίδακτος does not oppose self to god, but emphasizes the divine source of Phemios' song at the expense of his apprenticeship to another master: 'I did not learn my songs from another man, but from god'.[97] The statement implicitly acknowledges that, ordinarily, exceptional skill was coordinately attributed to divine favor and to training under a superior master of the trade. What is commonly complementary can be set in tension or even opposition in order to serve extraordinary rhetorical ends.

Given that the authority of his performance was rhetorically premised on a totalizing view of divine inspiration, it would have been counterproductive for the ἀοιδός to highlight his artistry through the image of sewing or stitching. It is hardly a coincidence that, although the ἀοιδός is famously listed as a δημιοεργός (ρ 383–385), no manufacturing metaphors are applied to the singer of epic by the medium of epic poetry—not just stitching, but also weaving, carpentry, and others are excluded. Diachronic skewing, which by itself would have privileged the relatively more traditional 'singer' and 'singing,' is further reinforced by the underlying rhetorical emphasis on the divine source and the divine authority of the song. It is telling that in two exceptional passages that apply verbs of manual labor and manufacturing to the composition and performance of song the gods and the Sirens are the respective subjects.[98] Where gods and *daimones* are involved, the singer feels free to highlight artistic accomplishment.[99] Otherwise, in the Homeric poems we meet with a discreetly succinct ἐπισταμένως (λ 368); with a δεδαώς to which θεῶν ἒξ is explicitly appended

---

[96] More on this passage above at pp. 213ff.

[97] Cf. Ford 1992:34.

[98] λιγυρὴν δ᾽ ἔντυνον ἀοιδήν [sc. Σειρῆνες] (μ 183; cf. *Homeric Hymn* 20); τεύξουσι δ᾽ ἐπιχθονίοισιν ἀοιδὴν | ἀθάνατοι (ω 197–198).

[99] E.g. *Hymn to Hermes* 483, addressed to Apollo. Because the playing of the lyre is immediately in view, the focus on τέχνη and σοφίη is not problematic. This section of the hymn centers precisely on imparting art and knowledge (cf. 25). See also the simile at ψ 159–162. Without a context it is hard to judge the implications of Hesiod fr. 306 MW. Cf. Ξ 53–54.

(ρ 518–519); or with oblique rhapsodic terminology like κόσμος[100] (but not κοσμέω).[101]

Nevertheless, that the metaphoric use of ῥάπτειν embraced both composition and performance is clear from the later use of ῥάβδος for poetic delivery, a noun (as we have seen) commonly linked to the verb ῥάπτειν by popular etymology. This is arguably the point of Pindar's *Isthmian* 3/4 56–57, [Ὅμηρος] κατὰ ῥάβδον ἔφρασεν | θεσπεσίων ἐπέων, where φράζω refers to a telling that bears the authority of the ῥάβδος.[102] The same point is made by the fragment in the scholia 1d to *Nemean* 2 ascribed to Kallimakhos (cf. fr. 26 Pfeiffer): καὶ τὸν ἐπὶ ῥάβδῳ μῦθον ὑφαινόμενον | ἠνεκὲς ἀείδω δεδεγμένος.[103] It seems clear that in the Hellenistic period ῥάβδος was primarily connected with the rhapsode in performance—what role could the staff play in his private ruminations, away from the public limelight? Kallimakhos portrays his own composition under the guise of rhapsodic performance as 'singing what is being woven with the authority of the ῥάβδος'.

The converse of the rhetorical emphasis on the divine origin of the epic song is a focus on the deceptiveness of self-interested telling. To this, Homeric diction readily applies craft metaphors. Eumaios provides a good example at ξ 131–132, when he asserts that even Odysseus would 'fashion a false story' (ἔπος παρατεκτήναιο) in exchange for a cloak or tunic to wear.[104] This accounts for the negative metaphoric use of ῥάπτειν for plotting and scheming.[105] Following Scheid and Svenbro (1996:111–130), Nagy (1996c:64n23) concedes that of metaphors of weaving and sewing for songmaking only traces survive—with focus on content rather than form—and that the attested Homeric diction is in the process of phasing out the application of such metaphors to performance. This concession may be premature, for there is an alternative interpretation of the evidence that is preferable and does not entail the view that in Homer artisanal metaphors for song-making are vestigial.[106] The rhetorical emphasis on the

---

[100] θ 492 and the ubiquitous κατὰ κόσμον. For more on κόσμος as a rhapsodic term, see above, pp. 194ff.

[101] Used for 'to marshal [troops]', not for 'to arrange [the song]' (cf. *Homeric Hymn* 7.59).

[102] Rumpel 1883:475 s.v. φράζω: "Act. *indico, dico, eloquor*, c. acc." Also Slater 1969:535 s.v. a: "declare, expound." Wilamowitz-Moellendorff (1922:339n3) translates, "Homer hat die Taten des Aias den Späteren deutlich gemacht" and "Homer … [hat] von Aias erzählt." Thummer (1968–1969:2.74) wonders whether to construe κατὰ ῥάβδον with ὀρθώσαις or ἔφρασεν. Its significance as an emblem of authority commends that we take it *apo koinou* with both. See above, p. 337.

[103] See above, p. 349 n. 56. More on this fragment below, pp. 367ff., in connection with relay poetics.

[104] παρα- conveys the contrast of the hypothetically false story with a notional standard of truthfulness.

[105] Planning is at times presented in a positive light, e.g. at Κ 19–20.

[106] Nagy (1996c:64n22) is right to reject Scheid and Svenbro's claim that there were no such metaphors in existence until the later era for which archaic choral lyric is extant. He is also right to

divine source and authority of the song, with the corresponding de-emphasis of the performer's individual artistry, sufficiently accounts for the failure of the medium to recognize *explicitly* the currency of stitching or weaving as metaphors for the performance of epic. Fränkel (1925:3-4) had already anticipated Scheid and Svenbro's argument. β 236, which he took as proof that ῥάπτω signifies invention, not performance, actually shows how design and execution—in metapoetic terms, composition and performance—can be viewed as two sides of one and the same happening: 'But truly I do not at all grudge the proud suitors their *doing* violent deeds in the evil-sewing of their mind'.[107] The example from Herodotos 6.1 only proves that these are distinguishable elements that can, but need not, be chronologically coextensive or have one and the same subject. π 379 in turn does not preclude the performance of a scheme: it only acknowledges that schemes often fail in their execution. The sheer destruction that the suitors were sewing involved the careful keeping of watches, detailed at π 365-370, which were sedulously carried out 'day by day' (ἤματα π 365). Once again, ἐράπτομεν does not denote mere planning but the execution of the suitors' machinations. In γ 118-119 Nestor summarizes the Greek campaign against Troy with the words, εἰνάετες γάρ σφιν κακὰ ῥάπτομεν ἀμφιέποντες | παντοίοισι δόλοισι, μόγις δ' ἐτέλεσσε Κρονίων. The fulfillment of their war effort was long in coming, but this does not relegate the activity of κακὰ ῥάπτειν to arm-chair scheming. If there was any doubt, ἀμφιέποντες, 'assailing them on every side', makes clear that their fighting πόνος was comprehended in the statement, 'for nine years we kept stitching evil against them with all manner of [martial] stratagems'.[108]

---

draw attention to the Homeric use of ὕμνος and οἴμη as counter arguments (66n23).

[107] ἀλλ' ἦ τοι μνηστῆρας ἀγήνορας οὔ τι μεγαίρω | ἔρδειν ἔργα βίαια κακορραφίῃσι νόοιο· (β 235-236). The same observation applies to O 16. After Hera's celebrated deception, Zeus wakes up from his sleep on mount Ida and sees Hektor lying on the plain. Realizing what has happened, he addresses Hera: 'Hera, impossible woman! Forsooth, the trick you contrived with evil intent (κακότεχνος ... σὸς δόλος) has stayed (ἔπαυσε) goodly Hektor from the fight and has routed (ἐφόβησε) his host. I know not but that you may in turn be first to reap the fruits of your grievous evil-stitching' (O 14-17). Hera's κακορραφίη, which stands for her κακότεχνος δόλος, is so far from mere inactive devising that it is personalized and said to have stopped Hektor and routed the Trojan armies.

[108] κακὰ ῥάπτομεν ἀμφιέποντες is not merely "we kept busy plotting" (so Ameis and Hentze 1920:73). ἔπω means "to direct one's energies at someone or something" (so *LfgE* s.v. B), and 'to be busy at' would not be an inadequate rendering if it did not suggest, as I think it does, planning apart from action. A survey of its Homeric use establishes that energetic action with bodily motion is the norm. As the *LfgE* notes: "it is noteworthy that many instances imply manu[facturing] act[ivity] (cf. deriv. ὅπλον) and that the subj. is always a pers[on] w[ith] the exc[eption] of χεῖρες ... and πῦρ/ἀυτμή ... , of animals 1× indir[ectly] in sim[ile]." With the preverb ἀμφι- (a simplex is instanced only at Z 321) it means "attend to, beset, iter[ative] and insistent." One class of instances (*LfgE* s.v. 1a) refers to butchering and preparing meat; the second (1b) is the one that concerns us, "beset an enemy" (i.e. surround and harass, assail on all sides), which Λ 474 γ 118 and Hesiod *Theogony* 696 illustrate; and a third (1c), like the second in meaning, with πῦρ as

The dative παντοίοισι δόλοισι makes explicit the 'material' out of which the final product, κακά, is stitched together. 'Stitching' does not fail to bear fruit at the planning stage but in execution. This hardly prevents its metaphoric application to songmaking that is composed in performance, for it is possible for a rhapsode to perform an utterance that, notionally, does not possess the performative authority to be effective (cf. the epic notion of ψεῦδος explored above, p. 236).[109]

Like ὑφαίνω,[110] ῥάπτω and its derivatives are also used in their literal sense in regard to: the manufacture of Sarpedon's shield;[111] Laertes' 'patched tunic' and 'stitched greaves';[112] a well-sewn (ἐϋρραφής) leather bag (β 354 = β 380); the seams (ῥαφαί) of the straps of Laertes' old shield (χ 186); and winter clothing made of goat skins.[113] Penelope's stratagem (δόλος β 93) to keep the suitors at bay—her promise to marry one of them only after she had completed a shroud (φᾶρος β 97) for Laertes' burial, a web she would weave by day and unravel by night—provides a transitional instance of ὑφαίνω, both literal and metaphorical in that by weaving she was acting out her guileful scheming. Although the bard is never said to 'weave' his song, Penelope's weaving here, like Helen's

---

subject (Π 124 Σ 348 θ 437). It should be clear that ἀμφιέποντες at γ 118 means 'assailing them on all sides', and that κακὰ ῥάπτομεν refers to the execution of their military campaign and stratagems on the battlefield. (S. West's "probably 'carefully, intently', rather than 'pressing them hard'" apud Heubeck et al. 1988:167 seems an unwarranted accommodation to the prejudice that ῥάπτειν must mean plotting apart from action.)

[109] The four Homeric instances of ἄπτερος belong here, if ἀ- is privative (not copulative) and the implication of the statement ὣς ἄρ' ἐφώνησεν, τῇ δ' ἄπτερος ἔπλετο μῦθος is that the corresponding female failed fully to understand the implications of the utterance spoken. If not with certainty, this may be readily argued for ρ 57 τ 29 φ 386; χ 398 can be similarly interpreted if one gives emphasis to the manner in which Telemakhos addresses Eurykleia (ἥ τε γυναικῶν | δμωάων σκοπός ἐσσι κατὰ μέγαρ' ἡμετεράων χ 395–396)—little could she anticipate how Odysseus presently intended to apply her oversight of the servant girls! I cannot go into this famous crux here (for a good review see Russo et al. 1992:22–24), except to remark: 1) that the word was understood in both its privative and copulative senses (see LSJ ad loc.); 2) that ἀπτερέως in Hesiod fr. 204.84 cannot be determinative, for although it may be best understood as copulative ('with wings', i.e. 'swiftly') if the supplied ἐπίθον[το is right, 'silently' (=without demurring) is also possible (as is 'without realizing the implications of what they were doing'!—although, admittedly, such a meaning here can only follow indirectly from the more common application of ἄπτερος to μῦθος). There is, at any rate, no guarantee that the Hesiodic fragment and Homeric epic agree in their use of the opening ἀ-. I find Russo's defense of the equation ἄπτερος = πτερόεις attractive, but it is not without difficulties.

[110] Γ 125–128 Ζ 456 Χ 440 etc.

[111] ἔντοσθεν δὲ βοείας ῥάψε θαμειὰς | χρυσείης ῥάβδοισι διηνεκέσιν περὶ κύκλον (Μ 296–297).

[112] ῥυπόωντα δὲ ἔστο χιτῶνα, | ῥαπτὸν ἀεικέλιον, περὶ δὲ κνήμῃσι βοείας | κνημῖδας ῥαπτὰς δέδετο (ω 227–229).

[113] πρωτογόνων δ' ἐρίφων, ὁπότ' ἂν κρύος ὥριον ἔλθῃ, | δέρματα συρράπτειν νεύρῳ βοός (Hesiod Works and Days 544).

at Γ 125–128,[114] may be read metapoetically to refer to the narrative in action. This accounts for the otherwise unexpected statement that she would not have her weaving perish in vain (β 98). Metapoetically, it restates in concrete narrative terms that Penelope's epic κλέος will never perish.[115] The metaphoric uses of ῥάπτω are of a similar kind.[116] I have already dealt with γ 118 and π 379.[117] There are two other instances, of which one features an exchange between Zeus and Hera after Akhilleus has been roused to fight the Trojans: 'You did it again, after all (ἔπρηξας καὶ ἔπειτα Σ 357) ... you roused fast-footed Akhilleus', he says; to which Hera replies, 'How should I, who claim to be the best of goddesses ... not have stitched evil for the Trojans in my anger?'[118] The emphasis here is on accomplishment in deed (ἔπρηξας 357, τελέσσαι 362), and it is the perspective of a successful performance that must inform our reading of κακὰ ῥάψαι as combining inextricably both devising and doing. The last instance is π 421–423. Having learned from the herald Medon of 'the destruction of her son

---

[114] On Helen's weaving see Nagy 1996c:64n23.

[115] μή μοι μεταμώνια νήματ' ὄληται (=τ 143 ω 133), to be compared with κλέος οὔ ποτ' ὀλεῖται (Β 325 Η 91 ω 196). For Penelope's κλέος, see ω 196–198. It is striking that scholars should expend their energies on the meaning and etymology of μεταμώνια (β 98), which simply adds emphasis to ὄληται, and fail to consider how Penelope's rationale makes sense. The very few exceptions are superficial and generally unilluminating. Translating "so that the threads are not wasted uselessly," Dawe (1993:99) observes that this must be her reply to "why not finish your weaving after your marriage?" Censuring her words as "vague," he poses the follow-up question, "'Why should laying your weaving aside for a little while mean that all your work to day ... is wasted?' We are given no answer, because we are given no question, and Homer hurries us on." The truth is that Penelope's words only make sense metapoetically. There is no compelling reason why she could not weave on after remarrying, unless we assume without evidence that her incorporation into a new household would preclude her continuing to care for her previous father-in-law (in which case, her having finished the shroud would hardly be of help). Even if this had been so, why express anxiety about the spoiling of the 'threads' (νήματα, standing for the ὕφασμα and her labor at the loom) rather than about her failure to provide for Laertes' burial? Why the suitors should think Penelope's rationale valid is another question. Presumably as an expression of piety they considered it right that it should take precedence over her remarriage. At any rate, the point of her weaving, of course, is to stave off her marrying one of the suitors. Were they not to wait for the completion of the φᾶρος, then her weaving—the ruse—would certainly be in vain, and the κλέος of her cunning and marital fidelity would indeed perish. Although harmonizing the three tellings of the ruse (in Books 2, 19, and 24) presents some difficulties, the threefold repetition itself, the prominence the ruse is given at τ 137–158, and the fact that at ω 128–150 the completion of the φᾶρος marks the arrival of Odysseus leave us in no doubt that Penelope's guileful weaving defines her heroic identity and functions as a narrative metaphor of first importance (for the timing, see Heubeck et al. 1988:137). Cf. N. Austin 1975:127, Slatkin 1996:234–236, and Clayton 2004:21–52.

[116] Besides ὑφαίνω, *LfgE* s.v. gives the related terms ἀρτύ(ν)ω, μήδομαι, μηχανάω/-ομαι, μενοινάω, μερμηρίζω, τεκταίνομαι, φράζομαι, φυτεύω, and (later) κασσύω.

[117] See above, pp. 361f.

[118] πῶς δὴ ἔγωγ' ... | οὐκ ὄφελον Τρώεσσι κοτεσσαμένη κακὰ ῥάψαι; (Σ 364–367).

in the halls',[119] Penelope confronts Antinoos: 'Why are you stitching death and doom for Telemakhos ... ? It is impious to stitch evil against each other'.[120] The expression 'destruction in the halls' refers to the exchanges that took place during the assembly of suitors before the gates of Odysseus' house (π 343–344).[121] These included the narrative of what they had unsuccessfully attempted (what Antinoos referred to at π 379 as φόνον αἰπὺν ἐράπτομεν οὐδ' ἐκίχημεν), as well as what they were now intending to do (π 383–384). Hence, ὄλεθρος embraces the performance of past, and the planning of future, actions. That it cannot be strictly limited to *inventio* without *actio* is clear from the startling use of the present ἀποκτείνεις (π 432): 'You are now devouring his household without repayment, you are wooing his wife, and you are murdering his son' (π 431–432). As Hoekstra rightly notes, "ἀποκτείνεις [is] not so much conative as emphatic" (Heubeck and Hoekstra 1989:284). Penelope takes a comprehensive view of Antinoos' doings and encompasses his deeds and counsels as one emphatic imperfective action: 'you are killing Odysseus' son!'[122]

In sum, there is no great difference in the treatment Homeric diction gives to ῥάπτω and ὑφαίνω as metaphors of composition and performance. Both are used in their literal and metaphoric senses. Both are strongly associated with the construction and execution of plans and plots. Whether the corresponding guile is seen in a positive or a negative light only depends on the particular agent and on the narrative's focalization. Since ὑφαίνω is unquestionably a metaphor for composition of Indo-European pedigree, whether ῥάπτω is a south-Aegean loanword or not, one must assume on the basis of this parity of treatment a comparable antiquity to its own metaphors for verbal (and, specifically, poetic) composition. An important finding from my survey above is that there are good rhetorical reasons why neither the *Iliad* nor the *Odyssey* applies artisanal metaphors to the bard's singing, reasons that do not entail a disjunction between composition and performance. Very much to the contrary, my analysis demonstrates that, even in the limited sense in which 'stitching' is applied to individual authorship, one cannot and should not disjoin evil-scheming (composition) and evil-doing (performance). The application of ὑφαίνω to verbal artistry is

---

[119] πεύθετο γὰρ οὗ παιδὸς ἐνὶ μεγάροισιν ὄλεθρον (π 411).

[120] τίη δὲ σὺ Τηλεμάχῳ θάνατόν τε μόρον τε | ῥάπτεις ... | ... οὐδ' ὁσίη κακὰ ῥάπτειν ἀλλή- λοισιν (π 421–423).

[121] Cf. δ 675–678.

[122] Porzig (1942:119–120) observes that τεύχειν ("das eigentliche und allgemeine Verbum für 'hand- werklich verfertigen'" in epic) may be used with an abstract noun as a periphrasis for the verbal action that corresponds to it. This is the case, for example, at υ 11, whose context precludes 'to plan' as the meaning of τεύξειεν: θάνατον ... τεύξειεν is not 'should prepare death' but 'should kill'. Instances like υ 11 unequivocally collapse onto *actio* the *inventio* that τεύχειν connotes at α 277 β 196 κ 18 etc.

explicit in Γ 212 (μύθους καὶ μήδεα πᾶσιν ὕφαινον); as it is to μῆτις in the sense of spoken counsels at Η 324 δ 678 739 etc., and to δόλος at Ζ 187 ε 356 etc. Weaving suggestively accompanied by singing takes place at ε 61–62 and κ 221 227 254. Although there are no instances of ῥάπτειν governing μῦθον *vel sim.*, my analysis suggests that this is merely accidental and not the consequence of some inherent semantic property of the verb. Indeed, in δ 675–676 Penelope is said to have learned the μῦθοι that the suitors were 'building deep in their hearts' (βυσσοδόμευον δ 676, referring to their counsels against Telemakhos before Odysseus' palace). But for the meter, nothing suggests that ἔρραπτον could not have stood for this word from the building trade. Such are indeed the counsels that Penelope will later describe as κακὰ ῥάπτειν.

There is another reason why Homeric poetry was likely to avoid the explicit application of ῥάπτειν to composition and performance. I observed above that the metaphor of stitching is specifically tied to the recomposition of traditional subjects in a traditional epic medium. And yet, from the internal point of view of the epic narrative, the recounted events are recent and their account is news to the hearers and the object of inquiry (e.g. κ 14–16). The best known expression of this perspective is α 351–352. Phemios sings of the woeful return of the Akhaians (α 325–327):

> τοῖσι δ' ἀοιδὸς ἄειδε περικλυτός, οἱ δὲ σιωπῇ
> εἴατ' ἀκούοντες· ὁ δ' Ἀχαιῶν νόστον ἄειδε
> λυγρόν, ὃν ἐκ Τροίης ἐπετείλατο Παλλὰς Ἀθήνη.

> For them sang the famous singer, and they in silence
> sat and listened; he sang of the return of the Akhaians,
> the woeful return from Troy which Pallas Athena laid upon them.

Penelope hears the song and bursts into tears (α 337–341):

> Φήμιε, πολλὰ γὰρ ἄλλα βροτῶν θελκτήρια οἶδας
> ἔργ' ἀνδρῶν τε θεῶν τε, τά τε κλείουσιν ἀοιδοί·
> τῶν ἕν γέ σφιν ἄειδε παρήμενος, οἱ δὲ σιωπῇ
> 340 οἶνον πινόντων· ταύτης δ' ἀποπαύε' ἀοιδῆς
> λυγρῆς ...

> Phemios, since you know many other subjects spellbinding
>   to mortals,
> deeds of men and gods that singers celebrate in song,
> sing for them one of these as you sit here, and let them in silence
> 340 drink their wine; but cease from this woeful song ...

To this Telemakhos replies (α 346–352):

> μῆτερ ἐμή, τί τ᾽ ἄρα φθονέεις ἐρίηρον ἀοιδὸν
> τέρπειν ὅππῃ οἱ νόος ὄρνυται; οὔ νύ τ᾽ ἀοιδοὶ
> αἴτιοι, ἀλλά ποθι Ζεὺς αἴτιος, ὅς τε δίδωσιν
> ἀνδράσιν ἀλφηστῇσιν ὅπως ἐθέλῃσιν ἑκάστῳ.
> 350 τούτῳ δ᾽ οὐ νέμεσις Δαναῶν κακὸν οἶτον ἀείδειν·
> τὴν γὰρ ἀοιδὴν μᾶλλον ἐπικλείουσ᾽ ἄνθρωποι,
> ἥ τις ἀκουόντεσσι νεωτάτη ἀμφιπέληται.

> My mother, why do you begrudge the trusty singer
> to delight as his mind is stirred? It is not the singers
> that are to blame but Zeus, perhaps, who gives
> to men who eat grain, to each one as he will.
> 350 There is no cause for anger that this man here sings the evil
>   doom of the Danaans;
> for men applaud more whichever song
> comes the newest to their ears.

The search for news is the motivation for Telemakhos' journey, first to Nestor and then to Menelaos (α 281–286). It would have been rhetorically ill-advised for the bard to portray Phemios as song-stitching in performance a well-known and well-loved story.[123] Homeric poetry, then, adopts the rhetorical conceit, made effectual by the authoritative mimesis of performance, that it narrates history in progress. Not only are Odysseus' woes the type of novel song that people love; Helen, too, in Ζ 357–358 adopts the perspective of present actors who, in a moment of quiet reflection, ponder how they will be regarded by future generations.[124] This conceit rules out an explicit self-reference to the performance of Homeric poetry as traditional in theme and diction. There are hints here and there that, in point of fact, it was traditional: Demodokos in the far-flung court of Alkinoos (ζ 8 204–205) has heard of the Trojan War (θ 489–491), and so have the Sirens (μ 189–190).[125] The metapoetic appreciation that marks the reception

---

[123] Ford (1988:301) should not insist on novelty as a metaphoric connotation of ῥάπτειν. His glosses "ingenious machination" and "contrivance" are acceptable, and one may add that the schemes recounted advance the plot. But there is nothing inherently novel in them (i.e. new or unusual). ῥάπτειν and other semantically related terms neither imply new thematic material nor unprecedented or anomalous narrative developments.

[124] Cf. Β 119 θ 579–580 ω 199–201.

[125] It is true that the Sirens claim to know 'all that happens on the fruitful earth' (μ 191), but it seems likely from their addressing Odysseus as πολύαινε (μ 184) that they are not claiming omniscience but a comprehensive awareness of all that is 'news' and worthy of song. As has often been remarked, they are like the Muses in this regard (Β 485).

of traditional poetry allows us to take even Helen's words in Z 357–358, and many a reference to κλέος, as affirmations of traditionality (González 2015). But the performance rhetoric of the profoundly traditional Homeric stories is that they are ever new in the telling.

10.2.3 Rhapsodic sequencing and relay poetics

10.2.3.1 Kallimakhos and the rhapsodes

The fragment in the scholia 1d to Pindar *Nemean* 2, ascribed to Kallimakhos, opens a window into fundamental features of the rhapsode's craft. It nicely combines weaving (ὑφαίνω), rhapsody (ῥάβδος), singing (ἀείδειν), and the sequencing of 'relay poetics' (δεδεγμένος; cf. I 191): καὶ τὸν ἐπὶ ῥάβδῳ μῦθον ὑφαινόμενον | ἠνεκὲς ἀείδω δεδεγμένος.[126] These lines were long ago recognized by Wilamowitz-Moellendorff 1911 as verses 5 and 8 of *P.Ryl.* 1.13 (MP³ 203; cf. fr. 26 Pfeiffer = fr. 30 Massimilla). Before attempting a translation, one must decide how the scholiast's suppression of the two intervening lines affected their meaning. Although certainty is impossible, one may reasonably assume that the excerpt preserves the substance of Kallimakhos' point. Indeed, apparently taking πλαγκτύν closely with μῦθον, Wilamowitz offered the following translation: "[D]ie Geschichte, welche zum Stabe gedichtet die Leute der Vorzeit einzeln überliefert haben, erzähle ich im Zusammenhang ihnen nach" (Wilamowitz-Moellendorff 1911:472). But πλαγκτύς, 'wandering', perhaps referred not to 'scattered' transmission but to a transmitted meaning that had wandered away from the authoritative tradition, from the telling sanctioned by the rhapsodic staff. By receiving the story and singing it in continuity with the authentic tradition, Kallimakhos laid claim to its authority. Thus, on the whole I am in agreement with D'Alessio (1996:409n92): "Callimaco rielabora il canto che ha ricevuto dalla tradizione precedente (v.5), che doveva presentarsi discorde (v.7, secondo l'interpretazione di Wilamowitz). Con il termine ἠνεκές il poeta sottolinea in modo esplicito la specifica tecnica di connessione del materiale narrativo ... , che reinterpreta il criterio di continuità contenutistica implicito nel διηνεκές di fr. 1.3." Only, I understand ἠνεκές, 'without a break', not primarily as referring to a continuity of narrative technique but to the unbroken *paradosis* of the authentic tradition.[127] Hence, I offer the following translation of the

---

[126] To fit the hexameter, Bentley corrected δεδεγμένος to δειδεγμένος with no change of sense.

[127] The review of διηνεκές and its usage in van Tress 2004:31–38 is helpful, although I cannot fully endorse it.

excerpt: 'And taking up the story upon the staff woven in uninterrupted sequence I sing' (construing ἠνεκές *apo koinou*).[128]

Together, ἠνεκές and δεδεγμένος express the notion of performative sequence that is at the heart of rhapsodic poetics. As a performer of traditional poetry, there are three complementary ways in which the rhapsode might be said to sing in uninterrupted sequence. First, he situates his song with studied precision along the οἴμη, i.e. the traditional thematic sequence of the narrative plot. Pointers like τῶν ἁμόθεν (α 10) or ἔνθεν (θ 500) serve to locate the starting point of his performance. Second, he stands in a long succession of traditional singers from whom he has received the song and to whom he, in turn, bequeaths it. This succession embodies the authority of the *paradosis* and gives his performance a diachronic depth which the chain of inspiration in Plato's *Iōn*, with the Muse as the fountainhead, celebrates.[129] And third, in the competitive setting rhapsodes take turns singing their song. Such performance in relays became central to the competitive poetics of the Panathenaia, one rhapsode taking up the song right where the preceding one had left off. I call this competitive mode *relay* or *hypoleptic* singing. In Kallimakhos' fragment, the participles δεδεγμένος and ὑφαινόμενον suggest that the last acceptation of sequence is primarily in view and serves as a dramatic synchronic reenactment of the second: the singer himself is the one who stands in continuity with previous performers as he takes up a song in progress. (δι)ηνεκές portrays his performance as an authentic actualization of the rhapsodic tradition.[130] Its point is not that the song never ceases but to validate the performer as a legitimate link in the long

---

[128] Translating more freely: 'Taking up the narrative that carries the authority of the rhapsodic tradition woven in unbroken continuity with it I sing'. Or, assuming μῦθον τὸν ἐπὶ ῥάβδῳ ὑφαινόμενον as the corresponding prose word order: 'I take up and sing in unbroken continuity the story that is/was woven upon [=with?] the staff. This seems the order assumed by Cameron (1995:363), who construes μῦθον with "heard" (for δειδεγμένος?): "I ⟨heard⟩ the story woven with the aid of a staff and tell it from beginning to end." Asper (2004:89–90 fr. 29) implausibly assumes that ὑφαινόμενον is a middle: "und ihn, der am Stab Märchen webt … in steter Folge singe ich, wie ich empfangen habe." The rendering of Ernesti (1761:497) is "Et carmen super virgam contextum perpetuo canto, comiter accipiens."

[129] What one can learn from the *Iōn* about the rhapsode and his craft is explored above, chapter 8 *passim*. Pelliccia (2003:106–108) disputes the legitimacy of placing 'poet' and 'rhapsode' in diachronic continuity and, *a fortiori*, my claim that diachronic analysis reveals the two as overlapping categories. But he fails to take the measure of Plato's late and tendentious perspective, even though at 113 he dismissively anticipates and attempts to forestall this very objection to his analysis. In an author as late as Plato, what is significant is not what separates Homer the poet from Ion the rhapsode, but the ways in which a continuity of function is hinted at. See further above, p. 277.

[130] Given the focus of ῥάπτω on the recomposition of traditional material, Kallimakhos' self-conscious reappropriation of the authentic rhapsodic tradition is better designated by ὑφαίνω. For a somewhat different reading of this fragment that also stresses the programmatic importance of rhapsodic poetics for the *Aitia*, see Durbec 2003.

chain that ties together past and present through the imperishable memory of κλέος. The sequence remains unbroken so long as the narrative is reperformed yearly within the cycle of the festival calendar. This is the continuity of repetition, re-actualization, and reperformance, a continuity of like elements (here, discrete performances) arranged sequentially to make a whole.[131] Taking his place within the authentic *paradosis*, Kallimakhos lays claim to its authority.

The semantics of (δι)ηνεκές can also capture the thematic continuity and original comprehensiveness of the epic cycle.[132] It is in this light that we must read the famous opening to Kallimakhos' *Aitia*, with its ἓν ἄεισμα διηνεκές (fr. 1.3). Whatever its immediate application to his own poetry, these words make rhapsodic poetics the indispensable reference for the Alexandrian's poetic program (ἄεισμα denoting the product of the song as readily as the manner of its singing).[133]

---

[131] διηνεκές has this meaning in Strabo 3.1.3, where ὄρος ... διηνεκές refers to an uninterrupted mountain range; in M 297, where ῥάβδοισι διηνεκέσιν denotes the continuous sequence of gold stitches along the circular perimeter of Sarpedon's shield (on the meaning of ῥάβδος here, see further above, p. 338); and in IG II/III² 1666.b60, where ἐπε]ργάζεσθαι δὲ κατὰ τὸν στοῖχον ἕκαστον (λίθον) διανεκῆ refers to placing stones in a continuous line, one after the other. Cf. *DGE* s.v. A.I.3.

[132] Here I am using 'epic cycle' broadly to refer, in the case of the Trojan-War myth, to all thematically related poems, including the Homeric. Cf. the statement of Proklos *apud* Photios concerning the ancients' appreciation of the ἀκολουθία τῶν ἐν αὐτῷ [sc. τῷ ἐπικῷ κύκλῳ] πραγμάτων (*PEG* I.6 T22 Bernabé = *EGF* 1 T1 Davies).

[133] For an informative and assertive reading of this fragment, see Cameron 1995:339–361. He rightly emphasizes that Aristotle's views of dramatic unity lie behind Kallimakhos' words (343–344). From the perspective of rhapsodic poetics, however, Cameron's attempt to separate temporal from thematic continuity is fallacious (344–345), whatever the understanding of the neoteric Roman poets who glossed ἄεισμα διηνεκές as *perpetuum carmen* (cf. Horace *Carmina* 1.7.6 and Ovid *Metamorphoses* 1.4). This is not the place to compare at length the poems of the cycle with the *Iliad* and the *Odyssey* in regard to their poetics and aesthetics. I will only say that rhapsodic poetics embraced all manifestations of traditional oral epic, including the Homeric poems. But the differential manner in which Athenian festival regulations and audience expectations focused upon the *Iliad* and the *Odyssey*—in particular, the eventual thematic restriction of Panathenaic performance to these two, to the exclusion of cyclic epic, and, consequently, their comparatively more thoroughgoing Panhellenic shaping (cf. Nagy 2001 and Burgess 2001:14)—in their case led the rhapsodic tendency towards comprehensiveness to develop in a correspondingly differential manner. In contrast to the relatively less Panhellenic Trojan-War cyclic poetry, which preserved a longer temporal scope for its plot sequence, the *Iliad* and the *Odyssey* developed their own characteristic comprehensive monumentality by way of forward- and backward-looking references (cf. Burgess 2001:199n34). Aristotle (and the Alexandrians) viewed poems as self-contained products, as unitary collections of verses of specific authorship and with established texts, not as reflecting the potential for thematic expansion and contraction open to traditional performers according to the needs of the moment. The exclusion of the two Homeric poems from the cycle—like the contrast between cyclic poets and Homer—betrays a point of view characteristic of the late classical and Hellenistic periods. One must remember that Aristotle *Sophistical Refutations* 171a7–11 (*PEG* I.2 T8 Bernabé = *EGF* 13–14 T2 Davies) mentions κύκλος in connection with ἡ Ὁμήρου ποίησις. Insofar as a web of traditional myths connected

Rhapsodic poetics regards each new performance as a segment of the notional thematic whole, whatever its particular beginning or end. Its Panhellenic tendency exhibits a marked propensity to embrace within its scope all that there is to say about its subjects.[134] This tendency toward expansion is signaled by the use Homeric poetry makes of διηνεκές and διηνεκέως to qualify the manner of telling. In η 241 Odysseus tells Arete that it would be grievous to narrate his woes fully (διηνεκέως ἀγορεῦσαι), i.e. one after another, continuously, without leaving anything out. It is well known that Odysseus is later compared to an ἀοιδός who possesses 'shapeliness of utterance' (μορφὴ ἐπέων λ 367),[135] a judgment that encourages us to consider his narrative representative of good rhapsodic practice. The length of Odysseus' tale,[136] which doubtless serves to emphasize his long-suffering, also reflects the tendency towards comprehensiveness characteristic of rhapsodic poetics. By way of contrast, the negative use of διηνεκέως at μ 56 and δ 836 shows that, irrespective of the specific point from which the rhapsode takes up his telling, he always keeps the end notionally in view.[137]

---

with the Trojan War existed with a recognizable thematic coherence, this nexus of oral tradition could have been described as a 'Trojan-War cycle' (itself perhaps part of an even larger mythological cycle). This would have been true irrespective of the particular instantiations of such a thematic κύκλος. If Burgess (2001:143–146) is right to infer that the *Kypria* and the *Little Iliad* narrated the complete story of the Trojan War (doubtless with different emphases), the contrast between the comprehensiveness peculiar to such cyclic poems and the comprehensiveness characteristic of the *Iliad* and the *Odyssey* would have been pronounced. (Burgess's central insights about the epic cycle do not depend on his assumption that particular instantiations of the Trojan-War cycle recognizable to the ancients as Proklos' *Kypria*, *Sack of Troy*, *Little Iliad*, etc. were textually fixed at a time earlier than the textual fixation of the Homeric poems. For this view see, for example, Burgess 2001:12 and 198n28.) On all these matters, see Nagy 1990c:72–73, Scaife 1995, Holmberg 1998, and Burgess 2001:12–33.

[134] The well-known strategy of verbal ornamentation characteristic of Akhilleus and the Homeric narrator is a feature of this tendency. Martin (1989:196) has called this phenomenon the "expansion aesthetic" (cf. 205–230). This aesthetic markedly shapes pairs of consecutive Homeric speeches: "He who talks bigger talks better" (Martin 2000:410).

[135] μῦθον δ' ὡς ὅτ' ἀοιδὸς ἐπισταμένως κατέλεξας (λ 368). Eumaios praises him too as a skillful singer with a long tale (ρ 514–521).

[136] λ 328–330, cf. B 488; ρ 515–517.

[137] S. West *ad* δ 836 observes that the "normal meaning [of διηνεκέως] is 'continuously, from beginning to end', but here it must be something like 'positively, explicitly'; a familiar formula ... has been carelessly used" (Heubeck et al. 1988:244). Not so: whether Odysseus is living or dead makes for a notional narrative end-point. One need only remember that, in the judgment of many, both ancient and modern, Penelope's recognition that her husband had ideed returned was (or should have been) the proper τέλος of the *Odyssey* (see Russo et al. 1992:342–345 *ad* ψ 296).

10.2.3.2 δέγμενος/δεδεγμένος

As I mentioned above, a second characteristic element of rhapsodic relay poetics underlined by Kallimakhos' fragment is that of succession: one performer would take up his singing right where a previous one had left off.[138] From the point of view of the *paradosis*, one might restate this sequential singing as one performance taking up the song where a previous one had left off. The verb for 'taking up the baton' is δέχομαι. It involves waiting for the previous rhapsode to finish his singing and taking up the thread of the song at the very thematic juncture that marks the transfer. Such joints, syntactic and thematic, are also in play during solo epic performance as the singer strives to join one verse to another, especially in the technically more taxing cases of enjambment. This passing of the baton, expressive of the inherently agonistic nature of Greek performance, could be gesturally enacted by handing on a staff to the next singer. Each symposiast was handed the myrtle-branch when it was his turn to perform the *skolia*.[139] Rhapsodic serial performance fostered, and was in turn fostered by, a 'poetics of seam-stitching' already inherent in the genre of hexameter epic, with its long arrays of hexameter στίχοι. This mode of delivery is the focus of the various accounts of the so-called Panathenaic rule, which I review below (pp. 382ff.). First, I wish to illustrate the use of δέχομαι to denote relay performance. A clear example in the context of the symposium is the passage in Aristophanes' *Wasps* that starts with verse 1216. After listing the names of his fellow symposiasts, Bdelykleon tells Philokleon: 'In the company of these men see to it that you take up (δέξει) the *skolia* well' (1222).[140] Bdelykleon adds: 'Suppose I am Kleon and I start singing the Harmodios song, and you are to take it up' (δέξει δὲ σύ 1225). And at 1243–1244: 'After him, Aiskhines, the son of Sellos, a learned man skilled in the art of the Muses, will take it up (δέξεται) and he will sing'. Eupolis' fr. 395 K-A provides another instance from a symposiastic context:

---

[138] In various publications, Nagy has championed the study of relay performance and relay poetics, which he has variously called "the esthetics of rhapsodic sequencing" (Nagy 1996c:71) or, more simply, "relay mnemonics" (Nagy 2002:123). Nagy (2002:36–69) provides an incisive exploration of this matter through Plato's writings in the context of the classical Panathenaic festival.

[139] Hesykhios T no. 796: τὴν ἐπιδεξιάν (-δέξια Reitz.)· περιέφερον ἐν τοῖς συμποσίοις ἐπὶ δεξιὰ τὸ πάλαι κιθάραν, εἶτα μυρρίνην, πρὸς ἣν ᾖδον. Cf. the scholia to Aristophanes *Wasps* 1222a (p. 192–193 Koster); the scholia to Plato *Gorgias* 451e; Athenaios 15.693f–694c (vol. 3, p. 535–536 §49 Kaibel); and Plutarch *Quaestiones convivales* 1.1.5 (615a–c). Most of these can be found in Campbell 1993:270–279.

[140] Campbell 1993:271n2 writes: "Lit. 'receiving'; he was expected to continue or to cap the line." Cf. the *DGE* s.v. δέχομαι A.III.4: "recibir y seguir, recoger, continuar cantos conviviales."

'Having taken it up (δεξάμενος) to the right, Sokrates stole the ladling-cup while he sang something of Stesikhoros to the lyre'.[141]

To move on to epic, one should mark the role of the σκῆπτρον in public assembly as a functional parallel to the rhapsodic staff in relay singing.[142] The σκῆπτρον identified the speaker that had the floor, attesting not only to his right to speak but also to the authority of his utterance.[143] Hence the remarkable use Akhilleus makes of it during his oath (A 233–239 245–246).[144] Three passages illustrate the use of δέχομαι to denote relay singing.[145] The first is the fragment by Kallimakhos that introduced us to this notion. According to regular Homeric use, the perfect participle δεδεγμένος, besides the semantically predictable 'having received', and therefore 'taking up', somewhat surprisingly, simply means 'awaiting' or 'expecting'.[146] Therefore, to ears attuned to the Homeric usage, besides positioning Kallimakhos rhetorically as the true heir of the authentic, i.e. the rhapsodic, tradition, there is in δεδεγμένος a distinct echo of our second passage, I 191, where Patroklos waits for the end of Akhilleus' performance. In effect, there is a hint of Kallimakhos' waiting to take up the song of the authentic tradition, a participant in hypoleptic delivery, as if that tradition had never vanished from the sphere of performance which is the life-blood of traditional poetry. The Alexandrian's reception of earlier poetry is not presented as the fruit of library research. It is as tight and immediate as the passing of the baton from rhapsode to rhapsode in relay singing.[147]

I 191, my second illustration, depicts Akhilleus whiling away his time in epic performance.[148] This by itself is remarkable enough, but even more extraordinary is the manner of his performance. Here the hero engages in what amounts,

---

[141] δεξάμενος δὲ Σωκράτης τὴν ἐπιδέξι' ⟨ἄιδων⟩ | Στησιχόρου πρὸς τὴν λύραν οἰνοχόην ἔκλεψεν. Τὸ δεξάμενος, the editors note: "δέχεσθαι cantu excipere."

[142] We do not know that a staff was passed on from bard to bard to signal whose turn it was to take up the song. But it is indisputable that the ῥάβδος was thought a badge of authoritative singing (cf. Hesiod *Theogony* 30 and Pindar's κατὰ ῥάβδον at *Isthmian* 3/4 56–57) and that it was closely associated with performance (see above, p. 360).

[143] B 278–279 Γ 216–219 Σ 503–505 β 37–38 (cf. B 185–186).

[144] Cf. K 321 328 β 80.

[145] For the acceptation 'to take up', what the *LfgE* s.v. I.2 glosses as "jem.m etw. abnehmen, etw. (von jem. in Funktion, Auftrag) übernehmen, um es zu bearbeiten, aufzuwahren, weiterzugeben usw.," see B 186 E 227 (=P 480) P 208 391 α 121 (~ο 282 π 40) ν 72 ο 132 φ 82.

[146] So Leaf 1900–1902: "*expecting*, not 'having received'" (1.477, his emphasis); and Ameis and Hentze 1906: "erwartend" (50), both commenting on Λ 124. The Homeric *loci* are Δ 107 Θ 296 K 62 O 745 Ψ 273 (cf. β 186 and *LfgE* s.v. B.I.5–6 and B.II.5). See Debrunner 1956–1957, esp. 79–80, who resorts to the notion of "intensive Perfekta" (on which cf. K-G II.1.148–150 §384.4).

[147] A corresponding translation might be: 'Waiting [for my turn to take up the song] I sing the story upon the staff woven in unbroken sequence'.

[148] See Nagy 1996c:71–73.

on the lips of the performing rhapsode, to a magnificently self-referential meta-poetic representation of hypoleptic rhapsodizing (I 186–191):

> τὸν δ' εὗρον φρένα τερπόμενον φόρμιγγι λιγείῃ
> καλῇ δαιδαλέῃ, ἐπὶ δ' ἀργύρεον ζυγὸν ἦεν,
> τὴν ἄρετ' ἐξ ἐνάρων πόλιν Ἠετίωνος ὀλέσσας·
> τῇ ὅ γε θυμὸν ἔτερπεν, ἄειδε δ' ἄρα κλέα ἀνδρῶν.
> 190 Πάτροκλος δέ οἱ οἶος ἐναντίος ἦστο σιωπῇ,
> δέγμενος[149] Αἰακίδην ὁπότε λήξειεν ἀείδων.

> Him they found, delighting his mind with the clear-sounding
>   phorminx,
> beautiful, ornamented, and upon it was a silver bridge;
> this he won from the spoils after he destroyed the city of Eëtion.
> He was delighting his heart with it and was singing the glorious
>   deeds of warriors,
> 190 and Patroklos alone sat facing him, in silence,
> waiting for when the son of Aiakos would leave off singing.

This description, which inspired the choice of cover for this book, raises the question of what Patroklos was waiting for. Was he simply waiting for Akhilleus to end his song so that, leaving the phorminx behind, both should move on to other things? Or is he singled out as 'alone opposite him' (οἱ οἶος ἐναντίος), waiting in silence, because he intended next to take the phorminx and continue the singing? The latter, I believe, is the point of the passage. The κιθαρῳδός (and κιθαριστής—it is usually impossible to distinguish them in the artistic record) could perform while sitting.[150] Patroklos is forcefully marked out as alone on a level with his leader, his attention fully engaged in his performance while he waits for him to end. As the scholia *ad loc.* long ago noted, '[Patroklos] is not alone in the hut, but he alone sat waiting for the son of Aiakos opposite him;

---

[149] Scholars are divided whether this is a perfect (Leaf 1900–1902:1.109 *ad* B 794), a present (Hainsworth 1993:88, Schwyzer *GG* I.678 §V.1a.α6), or an aorist participle (Frisk 1973–1979 and Beekes 2010 s.v. δέχομαι). Cf. Chantraine 1999:256 (with further bibliography).

[150] Images of performers seemingly processing or even standing while playing a string instrument of the family of the lyre (cf. West 1992:50) are not rare. But it is not difficult to find some that depict them in the sitting position. Cf. Paquette (1984:84–185, especially 99): "On joue de la cithare debout, plus rarement assis" (C22, C45, C47, and C49 are offered as examples of the latter). In the concert hall one might expect the performer to mount a platform and stand while playing; in the more intimate setting of Akhilleus' tent, the sitting position is more suitable and relaxed (I 193–194). Cf. West 1992:64 and Zschätzsch 2002:29–44, 182–184.

for also Automedon was in the hut' (190a Erbse).[151] It is no coincidence that this pair, the thematic heart of the poem in course, should have been selected to enact an inset of hypoleptic performance. The word ἐναντίος, which can be read as a simple marker of position, inevitably retains a measure of the antagonistic connotations that make it common in the context of hostile engagement. Its deliberate choice lends Patroklos' waiting the competitive undertone that is the hallmark of even the most cooperative kind of relay performance.[152] An audience sensitive to Patroklos' role in the poem and attuned to the hypoleptic performance practiced by competing rhapsodes would have no trouble understanding why he alone is singled out and why he is said to wait specifically for when Akhilleus would leave off singing. The audience would readily detect the metapoetic meaning. Without this motivation, the narrative's focus on the waiting remains puzzling.[153] It is doubtless true, as some have suggested, that we may see

---

[151] Cf. 190b Erbse: "He means either that he alone was sitting or that he alone was opposite him as compared with the rest of the Myrmidons."

[152] Metapoetically speaking, as Akhilleus' *alter ego* Patroklos almost steals the show at the expense of his leader when he dons Akhilleus' armor and joins the fray. Akhilleus in turn proves jealous for his own honor when he considers the consequences of Patroklos' involvement: 'If the loud-thundering husband of Hera grants you to win glory, do not yourself apart from me be eager to fight against the war-loving Trojans—you will make me more dishonored' (Π 87–90; cf. Π 269–274). Patroklos' central role in the plot as Akhilleus' stand-in represents a narrative hypolepsis of sorts. What Patroklos is ready to do at the end of Akhilleus' performance but does not do because the arrival of the embassy interrupts the singing, he actually performs later at the level of the narrative. Then he takes not his master's phorminx but his armor, and re-activates the κλέα ἀνδρῶν not in narrated song but in narrated deeds.

[153] Perceau (2005:71) fails to grapple with the otherwise puzzling character of this important detail. Her citing of θ 87 is not apropos, for the Phaiakians are not portrayed as waiting for the end of the song. The text simply tells us that 'whenever the divine singer would stop singing' Odysseus would dry his tears and draw the cloak off his head. The optative here is iterative, and the ὅτε clause equivalent to a past general condition ('as often as he would' ~ 'if ever he would'). Not so at I 191, where the waiting focuses on an anticipated one-time event; that is, λήξειεν is not iterative, but merely denotes time subsequent to that of the principal verb in secondary sequence (this is what Chantraine GH II.260 §382 calls "valeur éventuelle," to compare with "optatifs de répétition"). Perceau does not appreciate the puzzle because she has convinced herself that I 191 merely underlines the attentive manner of the singing entailed by σιωπῆ—only, we learn now that the respectful hearing does not extend beyond the end of the song. If she is right, the verse conveys a trite and predictable fact, and we are left without a rationale for the focus on Patroklos or for the curious manner of his singling out. Elsewhere, when waiting for a given happening is mentioned (δέχεσθαι + ὁπ(π)ότε), the context makes clear what specific actions were expected to follow right upon the happening. For example, in order to warn the Trojans of the marching of the Akhaians, Iris impersonates Polites, the Trojan sentinel who sat on the tomb of Aisyetes 'waiting for when the Akhaians would sally forth from their ships' (B 794); it is clear that he was then to rush back and report the fact, which Iris does for him (cf. H 415 Σ 524 υ 385–386). Not so here, unless we assume that Patroklos relieves Akhilleus in his singing, an inference commended both by the context and by the nature of epic performance in the culture of archaic and classical Greece.

in Patroklos the narrative equivalent of the rhapsodic audience.[154] This much can be derived from I 190. But there is no reason why the text could not have made clear that he was merely listening to the singing: why the otherwise odd focus on 'waiting for when Akhilleus would leave off singing'?[155] This suggests that, the very moment Akhilleus should leave off singing, Patroklos was going to do something specific, the identity of which would have been readily inferable by the audience. This, I submit, is to take up the lyre and continue the song right where Akhilleus had left off. It never comes to pass, of course, since the embassy arrives to interrupt the relay performance.[156] Perceau (2005:71) objects that "in epic only solos are mentioned, never relay singing by several singers."[157] She is right, of course, if she means singing by characters identified as professional ἀοιδοί. But this is too simplistic an approach to the intricate metapoetic texture and mimetic pragmatics of Homeric epic. I need only cite here the remarks by Tarditi (1968:140) concerning Andromakhe's, Hekabe's, and Helen's laments for Hektor at Ω 720–776: "Ciascuna delle tre donne esprime il suo dolore e rievoca un aspetto dell'umanità o dell'eroismo di Ettore, ciascuna 'cuce' il suo canto in quella, potremmo chiamarla, rapsodia trenodica che viene cosí composta."[158]

---

[154] For the interchangeability of audience and epic characters as a characteristic Homeric device, cf. Nagy 1996c:72n37 with bibliography.

[155] Syntactically, Αἰακίδην has been extracted from the ὁπότε clause, where it would ordinarily sit, and placed into the main clause. Semantically, the object of δέγμενος is not 'the son of Aiakos', but 'when the son of Aiakos would leave off singing'. Leaf 1900–1902:1.385 *ad loc.* writes: "Αἰακίδην is taken proleptically from the rel. clause."

[156] This is generally recognized by scholars. So, for example, Monro 1958: "δέγμενος, 'waiting,' apparently to take up the song: so the Muses sang ἀμειβόμεναι (1.603)" (344); Ameis and Hentze 1930:94 note: "δέγμενος Αἰακίδην gewärtig des Aiakiden, wohl um ihn im Gesange abzulösen: vgl. A 604"; and Hainsworth 1993: "Patroklos is simply listening to Akhilleus, perhaps with the implication that he would take up the song at the point where Akhilleus left off" (88).

[157] She refers here to Hainsworth 1993: "There are many ways of performing heroic song, including the employment of two singers, but the only one described in Homer is that of the solo singer" (88).

[158] I cannot, however, agree with Tarditi's rejection of the inherently competitive character of rhapsodic singing, or with his notion that the close sequencing entailed by οἴμη was incompatible with the festival ἀγών (1968, 141–142). Tarditi bases his views on an excessively rigid notion of rhapsodic sequence that would not survive the addition of a hymnic proem to the epic performance. Whether hymns always preceded an individual rhapsode's performance, even when he followed another in relay singing, cannot be assumed without argument, as Tarditi does. But even if this were so, I dispute the notion that the hymn would necessarily be felt by performer and audience as an interruption that spoiled the narrative and performative sequence. One must also reckon here with the techniques of expansion and contraction, which would allow the rhapsode to create a seam that met the pragmatic demands of his epic delivery. The peculiar genre and function of the hymn should also be taken into account in judging what sort of 'break,' if any, it might have effected in hypoleptic singing. One must also remember that the so-called Homeric hymns were preserved as their own distinct *corpus*, and not as openings to manuscripts of the Homeric poems. In a future work I hope to explore the implications of this fact for our understanding of these hymns in the context of the Panathenaia.

The last example comes from the *Hymn to Hermes* 476–477 and complements I 186–191, for it presents Hermes and Apollo as archetypes for hypoleptic performers. Hermes had struck up his song (γηρύετ' ἀμβολάδην 426, in the manner of a hymnic prelude) and 'ratified the gods' (κραίνων 427),[159] starting with Gaia (427) and detailing their individual shares (μοῖραν 428): 'First among the gods he honored Mnēmosynē in song, the mother of the Muses, for she received the son of Maia as her lot; and the immortal gods the splendid son of Zeus honored according to their seniority and how each was born, relating everything in good order, playing the lyre under his arm' (429–433). As often in the Homeric hymns, this amounts to a transparent self-referential performance that overlaps thematically with the *Hymn to Hermes* and fuses with the rhapsodic delivery of this hymn currently in progress before the audience. At the marvelous sound, Apollo desires to learn the τέχνη of rhapsodic hymnic performance (song and instrumental playing, possibly dancing too).[160] Then comes the enactment of hypolepsis (475–477):

> ἀλλ' ἐπεὶ οὖν τοι θυμὸς ἐπιθύει κιθαρίζειν,
> μέλπεο καὶ κιθάριζε καὶ ἀγλαΐας ἀλέγυνε
> δέγμενος ἐξ ἐμέθεν· ...

> But since your heart is crazy about playing the lyre,
> sing and play it and heed splendid festivity
> taking it[161] up from me; ...

---

[159] Lit., 'to render true by an authoritative speech-act'. On the meaning of this verb in this passage, see further above, p. 203.

[160] Amazed at the θέσπιν ἀοιδήν (442) and θαυμασίην ... νεήφατον ὄσσαν (443)—presumably the combination of Hermes' singing and the 'voice' of the lyre—Apollo asks: τίς τέχνη, τίς μοῦσα ἀμηχανέων μελεδώνων, | τίς τρίβος; (447–448). At first, dancing does not seem to be in view. Hermes 'stands' by Apollo when he performs (στῆ 424). But Apollo identifies himself as a follower of the Olympian Muses, who care about 'dancing and the splendid path of song, and lively *molpē* and the lovely bray of *auloi*' (τῇσι χοροί τε μέλουσι καὶ ἀγλαὸς οἶμος ἀοιδῆς | καὶ μολπὴ τεθαλυῖα καὶ ἱμερόεις βρόμος αὐλῶν 451–452). Not only does μολπή ordinarily involve a combination of singing, instrumental playing, and dancing, but χοροί explicitly refers to dancing (whether by the performer himself or by others to his music or both). On οἶμος, for which I have used here the traditional rendering 'path', see further below, pp. 392ff.

[161] It is an error narrowly to supply κίθαριν as the sole direct object of δέγμενος. The verb does not have an explicit object, and the context commends the verbal notion κιθαρίζειν or the abstract τέχνη as that which Apollo so earnestly desires. To be sure, there is wonder at the instrument Hermes has devised (443), but the focus of Apollo's words are the entire art of κιθαρῳδία—playing the instrument and singing to it. He mentions Hermes' θέσπις ἀοιδή (442); the lyre's ὄσσα (443), described in 444 as something learned; the τέχνη (447), μοῦσα (447), and τρίβος (448) of Hermes' performance; his κιθαρίζειν (455) and μήδεα (456). Some of these may readily include the lyre as a cunning artifact, but they are deliberately broader in scope and embrace playing and singing. Hermes in turn mentions his τέχνη (465) and κιθαρίζειν (475). (The ἔργα at 440 are probably

The key word is δέγμενος, and in context its object must be all that Hermes' τέχνη encompasses—preeminently the lyre, the focus of Apollo's wonder, but also the 'divine song' (442) that the lyre accompanies and perhaps even dancing. Apollo is portrayed as permanently entering upon the art of Hermes (464-465), whose succession is enacted by an archetypal hypoleptic transfer in the course of a rhapsodic hymnic performance. Adopting the manner of a commercial exchange of divine τιμαί, the ceded privileges become the permanent property of the god who receives them.[162]

10.2.3.3 Cooperation and contest

The relay poetics of hypoleptic performance comes in two flavors: one is predominantly cooperative, the other oppositive. But even the cooperative kind retains the antagonistic quality of competitive rivalry. This distinction is easily illustrated with reference to the singing of *skolia* at the symposium. Mure (1854-1859:3.101) writes that each guest whose turn to perform had come was "expected at once to carry on the strain, whether in the way of continuation or repartee." When the connection between one *skolion* and the next was "supplied by innuendos or ambiguous allusions ... to the character or circumstances of the individual performers ... the principle of contrast would often be preferable, in point of effect, to that of conformity" (3.102-103). The cooperative character of relay poetics is at the heart of the Panhellenic process that drove the textual fixation of the Homeric poems. This cooperation was both diachronic—effective between successive rhapsodic performances, the later ones responding to the earlier—and synchronic—one rhapsode at a competitive event artistically stitching his performance in deliberate sequence to that of the previous rhapsode. Traditional diction, including formulaic language, is

---

Hermes' 'accomplishments', not just the lyre, and δῶρον at 442 could be the lyre or, just as well, the skill necessary to devise it and play it well.) This is the context from which a direct object would have to be supplied to δέγμενος, if we must. If so, only the broader τέχνη of κιθαρῳδία will do. But I believe that the reason δέγμενος does not take an explicit direct object and the context does not readily supply one is because relay performance is in view, an acceptation that deploys δέχομαι absolutely (i.e. without an object). What Apollo is to receive and take up is the performance, the singing of the song. This entails, but is not limited to, receiving the lyre, a gesture that is otherwise commended by the archetypal setting. The case of 496 is different. There ὤρεξε and ἐδέξατο have no explicit direct object either, but the preceding context readily supplies the ἑταίρη (478) (cf. μιν 480, if one accepts Ilgen's emendation [Ilgen 1796:41 and 461]; αὐτήν 482 and 486; and ταύτην 490) as the object held out by Hermes and received by Apollo (the κίθαρις of 499).

[162] This hypoleptic transfer, central to the meaning of the hymn, would be contextually reinforced by the reference in 454 to "the passing to the right at young men's feasts" (so West 2003b:149)— i.e. by the reference to the hypoleptic performance practice at the symposium—if in fact this is the correct translation of this line.

doubtless the instrument and product of this cooperation, but not the sole one. The traditional thematic sequence too guided the singing as a path[163] marked out by earlier singers and worn further by the ongoing performance.[164] This cooperative poetics is also in view in the scholion 1d to Pindar's *Nemean 2*:

οἱ δέ φασι τῆς Ὁμήρου ποιήσεως μὴ ὑφ᾽ ἓν συνηγμένης, σποράδην δὲ ἄλλως καὶ κατὰ μέρη διῃρημένης, ὁπότε ῥαψῳδοῖεν αὐτήν, εἱρμῷ τινι καὶ ῥαφῇ παραπλήσιον ποιεῖν, εἰς ἓν αὐτὴν ἄγοντας. οὕτω καὶ ὁ Πίνδαρος ἐκδέδεκται. οἱ δέ, ὅτι κατὰ μέρος πρότερον τῆς ποιήσεως διαδεδομένης τῶν ἀγωνιστῶν ἕκαστος ὅ τι βούλοιτο μέρος ᾖδε, τοῦ δὲ ἄθλου τοῖς νικῶσιν ἀρνὸς ἀποδεδειγμένου προσαγορευθῆναι τότε μὲν ἀρνῳδούς, αὖθις δὲ ἑκατέρας τῆς ποιήσεως εἰσενεχθείσης τοὺς ἀγωνιστὰς οἷον ἀκουμένους πρὸς ἄλληλα τὰ μέρη καὶ τὴν σύμπασαν ποίησιν ἐπιόντας, ῥαψῳδοὺς προσαγορευθῆναι.

Some say that, when the poetry of Homer had not been collected as a single whole and was otherwise scattered and divided into sections, whenever they performed it rhapsodically, they would make something approaching a [coherent plot] sequence[165] or [narrative] stitch-work by bringing this poetry together into one.[166] This is also Pindar's understanding. Others say that, since in former times [Homer's] poetry had been handed down by sections and each of the contestants would sing whichever section he wanted to, a lamb being the designated prize for the victors, the contestants were then called *arnōidoi*; but in turn [they say that], after both poems were introduced, the contestants, 'mending,' so to speak, the parts one to another and going through[167] the entire poetry, were in turn called rhapsodes.[168]

---

[163] Cf. οἶμος ἀοιδῆς in the *Hymn to Hermes* 451.

[164] Cf. τρίβος in the *Hymn to Hermes* 448.

[165] Cf. *DGE* s.v. εἱρμός 3.

[166] Cf. *DGE* s.v. εἷς I.2g.

[167] For ἔπειμι in the sense of 'to traverse', see *TGL* 3.1460–1461 and LSJ s.v. III. Relevant *loci* are: Lucian *Hermotimos* §1.10 MacLeod (ἐπιὼν τῇ μνήμῃ ἕκαστα); Aristophanes *Frogs* 897 (ἔπιτε δαίαν ὁδόν); Plutarch *Periklēs* 17.2 (τοὺς ἐν Ἑλλησπόντῳ καὶ Θράκῃ μέχρι Βυζαντίου τόπους ἐπῇεσαν); Heliodoros *Aithiopika* 2.6.2 (ἐπειρᾶτό τι τῶν ἐγγεγραμμένων ἐπιέναι); Strabo 1.3.7.27–28 ([οἱ ποταμοὶ] οἱ πολλήν τε καὶ μαλακόγειον χώραν ἐπιόντες); δ 411; and perhaps Herodotos 5.74. Cf. LSJ s.v. ἐπέρχομαι III.1–2 and Herodotos 1.30.2.

[168] For a somewhat different translation, see Nagy 1996c:67–68. Eustathios in *Ad Iliadem* offers a helpful reading of this scholion (van der Valk 1971–1987:1.10). By ἑκατέρας τῆς ποιήσεως, he understands the complete poems: ποίησις μὲν γὰρ ἡ ὅλη βίβλος (1.10–11). The scholion's second interpretation assumes the rhapsodes' dependence on notionally integral poems. Eustathios writes: ἢ καὶ ἄλλως, διότι κατὰ μέρος, φασί, τῆς ποιήσεως διαδεδομένης τὴν σύμπασαν ποίησιν ἐπιόντες οἱ ᾄδοντες καὶ τὰ ἐξ ἑκατέρας Ὁμηρικῆς βίβλου συρράπτοντες, ὡς ἐβούλοντο, ῥαψῳδοὶ

Of especial significance here is the claim that, by singing Homeric poetry rhap-sodically, performers refashioned it into a certain thematic sequence (εἱρμός τις) or stitch-work (ῥαφή). This reshaping is imagined as a cooperative endeavor that results in the artistic unity exhibited by the poems. The scholiast further under-lines in the alternative account the collaborative nature of hypoleptic perfor-mance by his use of ἀκεῖσθαι, 'to heal' or 'cure', as a metaphor for 'mending' and 'repairing'. Whereas formerly the poetry had been transmitted, and was corre-spondingly performed, piecemeal, with an overriding competitive focus on indi-vidual prize-winning and a consequent 'willful' injury to the notional integrity of the poems, once the outward circumstances of performance—the introduc-tion of the poems—enforced the 'correct' sequence, the stitching of the contes-tants was reconceived as reparative, i.e. as the integrative recomposition of the erstwhile scattered members. Hence, the performers were no longer called *arnōidoi*, after the prize that was emblematic of their rivalry, but ῥαψῳδοί, after the corrective stitching enforced by the mandatory adherence to the notional canonical sequence. However anachronistic, this elucidation of the terms ἀρνῳδός and ῥαψῳδός (on which see Durbec 2003) illuminates the competitive and cooperative dimensions of rhapsodic performance. In particular, it tellingly acknowledges that, even when such performance was unconstrained and the rhapsode sang whichever parts he wanted, still the practice of his craft effected a narrative whole that exhibited a particular thematic sequence and resembled a kind of stitch-work. In other words, the aesthetics of rhapsodic performance

---

ἐντεῦθεν προσηγορεύθησαν. The scholiast obviously believes that a notional sequence was established with the introduction of the poems, a sequence that stitching rhapsodes were to observe. Unless Eustathios has badly misunderstood the scholion at this one point, in writing ὡς ἐβούλοντο he cannot have had complete freedom of choice in view; only what was consistent with the poems as introduced, namely, the rhapsode's choice of a starting point for his perfor-mance. Going through Homer's poetry in performance, rhapsodes would move from one section to the next as if 'mending' the poetic fabric by respecting and reenacting in song the established connections (or 'seams') between sections. The metaphor of 'mending' served to contrast this performance practice with the one that relied on a notionally rent (κατὰ μέρος) poetic fabric. καὶ τὴν σύμπασαν ποίησιν ἐπιόντας need not imply comprehensive performances of the entire poems. The scholion describes the general practice of rhapsodes, not the specific practice at a given festival (even if one accepts its connection to Argive traditions). To clarify the distinction I am drawing here, it is helpful to consider a parallel: reading through virtually all the Bible over time as practiced in the liturgy of the Roman Catholic Church. This practice aims not at reading the entire biblical text at once but substantially to cover the canonical scriptures within a five-year cycle. The tendency towards comprehensiveness of scope characteristic of Homeric rhapsodic sequencing, the rhapsodic techniques of thematic expansion and contraction, and the traditional referentiality that marks the epic medium—all these rendered any one rhap-sodic performance notionally homologous with performing the entire tradition. Because the rhapsode evoked the entire sequence by his adherence to whichever part of the traditional plot concerned his performance, there was as little need as there was little opportunity to perform the entire *Iliad* and *Odyssey* at any one festival.

may have moved its emphasis from competition to cooperation, but thematic stitching was, and remained, at the heart of the rhapsode's craft.

Competitive performance in the context of the Greek ἀγών is dramatically illustrated by the *Certamen* of Homer and Hesiod.[169] The primary source for the contest has been persuasively identified as the *Mouseion* of Alkidamas,[170] the fourth-century sophist who was featured above (pp. 311ff.) as a signal witness to the increasing dependence of rhapsodes on scripts for their public delivery. Here, I need only recall that Alkidamas made the rhapsode and his craft a chief focus of analysis as he sought to illustrate the importance of improvisation (αὐτοσχεδιασμός) to accomplished oratorical delivery.[171] This suggests that he patterned his imagined ἀγών between Homer and Hesiod after actual rhapsodic dynamics at the Athenian Panathenaia. The *Certamen* features three kinds of competitive challenges:[172] first, as befits two renowned sages, a test of wisdom (75–101, 140–175);[173] second, what interests me now, a series of 'capping' challenges in which Hesiod's deliberately perverse openings try to hinder Homer from successfully taking up the song from his adversary (107–137);[174] third, a solo reperformance by each contestant of a favorite passage from his own poems (180–204). In the second test, the artistry of stitching is dramatically on display as Hesiod does his best to prevent Homer from sewing a sensible seam. Here enjambment, the most challenging technique of hexameter stitching, takes center stage. This is not to suggest that rhapsodes at the Panathenaia must have exchanged one-liners in the manner of the *Certamen*, but

---

[169] Cf. Collins (2004:185–191). Else (1957b:30) had insisted that the label ῥαψῳδός should come from "a concrete occasion on which the 'sewing' would be overt, unmistakable. Such an occasion might be provided by the rhapsodes' contests." Else was anticipated by Pagliaro (1951:43–45), whose own important treatment exhibited greater diachronic insight. Taking up Else's suggestion, Ritoók (1962:228–229) drew attention to the *Certamen*. He also conjectured on the basis of Pindar *Nemean* 2 that hypoleptic performance was only characteristic of the Homeridai (230). There is truth in Else's and Ritoók's proposals, but they are wrong to narrow the characteristic craft of the rhapsode to competitive hypolepsis.

[170] For the initial suggestion, see Nietzsche 1870 and 1873. Relevant scholarship, not all in support of Nietzsche's hypothesis: Abramowicz 1938, Vogt 1959, Hess 1960 with Vogt 1961, Vogt 1962, West 1967a, Richardson 1981, Heldmann 1982, Avezzù 1982:84–87, Kawasaki 1985, O'Sullivan 1992:63–105, and Mariß 2002:21–24. For the controversy about the relevant papyrological finds, see the bibliography cited by O'Sullivan 1992:63–64.

[171] See, for example, Alkidamas *On the Sophists* §14. More on Alkidamas above, pp. 311ff. Richardson (1981:5) writes: "It has often been noted that the theme of improvisation in the *Certamen* forms a strong link with Alcidamas' *On Sophists* ... . Alcidamas seems to have been interested in the story of the contest ... because it gave prominence to the value of improvisation ... ."

[172] Cf. Collins 2004:184.

[173] I cite the line numbers of Allen's *OCT* edition. Wilamowitz-Moellendorff 1929:34–47 and Avezzù 1982:38–51 should also be consulted for the text. West 2003b:318–353 provides a convenient translation.

[174] Collins 2004:177 calls this "the 'epic' part of the *Certamen*."

that Alkidamas extracted the essence of their craft and displayed the overriding technical point at stake when they competed before the public. In all probability, not only would a competing rhapsode have to prove his skill at recomposing Homeric epic, thus demonstrating the ordinary stitching competence entailed by long stretches of solo performance; but the antagonistic challenge to pick up the delivery right where the previous rhapsode had left off would have provided a dramatic opportunity for the first rhapsode to devise a finish that would test to the utmost the ability of the succeeding one to stitch a felicitous seam.

Let us see how Hesiod in the *Certamen* stages the hypoleptic test of Homer's skill. Before he turns to the heart of the challenge, Hesiod provides what is, in effect, an anti-invocation of the Muse (97–101):[175]

Μοῦσ᾽ ἄγε μοι τά τ᾽ ἐόντα τά τ᾽ ἐσσόμενα πρό τ᾽ ἐόντα
τῶν μὲν μηδὲν ἄειδε, σὺ δ᾽ ἄλλης μνῆσαι ἀοιδῆς.
ὁ δὲ Ὅμηρος βουλόμενος ἀκολούθως τὸ ἄπορον λῦσαι φησίν·
οὐδέ ποτ᾽ ἀμφὶ Διὸς τύμβῳ καναχήποδες ἵπποι
ἅρματα συντρίψουσιν ἐρίζοντες περὶ νίκης.

Come now, Muse, to me what is, shall be, and was before—
of these, sing nothing; but *you* [Homer?] give heed to the rest of
    the song.
Homer, wishing to solve the conundrum in a manner that was consistent
    [with Hesiod's invocation], said:
Never shall horses with sounding hoofs around the tomb of Zeus
shatter chariots as they vie for victory.

Note the explicit focus on sequence: Homer wishes his solution to 'follow' (ἀκολούθως 99) Hesiod's challenge.[176] Note also, incidentally, conclusive proof that ἄλλης in the common hymnic transition καὶ ἄλλης μνήσομ᾽ ἀοιδῆς (e.g. *Hymn to Demeter* 495) does not mean 'another song' but 'the rest of the

---

[175] '[Hesiod] turned to asking conumdrums' (ἐπὶ τὴν τῶν ἀπόρων ὥρμησεν ἐπερώτησιν 95) suggests that what follows deliberately frames the 'ambivalent propositions' (τὰς ἀμφιβόλους γνώμας 102–103). But whereas the preceding challenges had involved Hesiod's querying Homer, the anti-invocation cannot be considered a 'question' in the ordinary sense of the word, even if arguably it seeks to put in question Homer's skill. Instead, it is in character very much like the ambivalent one-liners, except that it does not call for enjambment—only for a sequence of thought that validates and builds upon what seems unmanageable nonsense.

[176] The Flinders Petrie papyrus no. 25 (see Allen's edition, p. 225, lines 41–44) merely picks up the language of 95 and is less illuminating.

song':[177] Hesiod is not challenging Homer to think of another song, but to take up the song where he left off and build the following lines upon his anti-invocation.

Seeing that Homer has met the challenge well, Hesiod turns to the ambivalent propositions. I will only quote the first as a representative illustration of the nature of Hesiod's challenges:[178]

⟨Ἡ.⟩ δεῖπνον ἔπειθ' εἵλοντο βοῶν κρέα καὐχένας ἵππων
⟨Ὀ.⟩ ἔκλυον ἱδρώοντας, ἐπεὶ πολέμοιο κορέσθην.

Hesiod: Then they dined on beef and the horses' necks
Homer: sweating, they unyoked after they had their fill of fighting.

We are told that 'speaking many lines Hesiod required Homer to answer each one in turn congruously' (καθ' ἕνα ἕκαστον συμφώνως ἀποκρίνασθαι 104). The verb ἀποκρίνασθαι makes clear that Homer's line is a continuation of Hesiod's; the adverb συμφώνως, that the sequence should be meaningful. Hesiod's challenge hinges on the apparent syntactic parallelism between 'horses' necks' and 'beef'. But Homer uses enjambment to carry the day: 'necks' is now taken by 'they unyoked', and the added participle 'sweating', which qualifies 'necks', serves to strengthen the sequence he has forged.

10.2.3.4 The Panathenaic rule

The drama of competitive hypoleptic performance must have thrilled the audience with its successes and failures. This explains the so-called Panathenaic succession rules, variously reported, among others, by [Plato's] *Hipparkhos* and Diogenes Laertios.[179] First, the report in the *Hipparkhos* 228b5–c1:

Ἱππάρχῳ ... , ὃς ἄλλα τε πολλὰ καὶ καλὰ ἔργα σοφίας ἀπεδείξατο, καὶ τὰ Ὁμήρου ἔπη πρῶτος ἐκόμισεν εἰς τὴν γῆν ταυτηνί, καὶ ἠνάγκασε τοὺς ῥαψῳδοὺς Παναθηναίοις ἐξ ὑπολήψεως ἐφεξῆς αὐτὰ διιέναι, ὥσπερ νῦν ἔτι οἵδε ποιοῦσιν.

[I mean] Hipparkhos ... who displayed many fine accomplishments of learning, above all, he was first to bring the poetry of Homer to this

---

[177] Long ago argued by Koller 1956:177. Mirroring the hymnic use of ἄλλος, ὁ δ' ἄλλος λόγος in [Demosthenes] 61 §2 also means 'the rest of the speech'.

[178] For further analysis, cf. Collins 2004:186–191.

[179] For these and other *testimonia*, see Davison 1955a. Shapiro 1998 offers a fairly traditional reconstruction of the historical context for the Panathenaic rule and its impact on sixth-century BC rhapsodic performance. He pays particular attention to the iconographic evidence from vases.

land here and forced the rhapsodes at the Panathenaia to go through it in sequence by relay, just as they still do now.

The corresponding account in Diogenes Laertios 1.57 runs as follows:

τά τε Ὁμήρου ἐξ ὑποβολῆς γέγραφε ῥαψῳδεῖσθαι, οἷον ὅπου ὁ πρῶτος ἔληξεν, ἐκεῖθεν ἄρχεσθαι τὸν ἐχόμενον.

He has also enacted a law that rhapsodes are to perform the poetry of Homer reactively, that is to say, that the following is to start from that point where the first left off.

In the *Hipparkhos*, the key terms are 'by relay' (ἐξ ὑπολήψεως) and 'in sequence' (ἐφεξῆς). The former is unproblematic: each rhapsode takes up (ὑπολαμβάνω) where the former left off.[180] This expression corresponds closely to ἐκ διαδοχῆς, which the scholia D to A 604 uses to gloss ἀμειβόμεναι· ἐξ ἀμοιβῆς καὶ διαδοχῆς ᾄδουσαι. Like ἐξ ὑπολήψεως, ἐκ διαδοχῆς could be understood not only synchronically but also diachronically: 'Of old they called Homeridai those in the line of Homer who also sang his poetry in [genealogical] succession' (i.e. as his successors).[181] What 'in sequence' (ἐφεξῆς) refers to is not so clear: either to the rhapsodes (one rhapsode after another) or to the subject matter (one episode after another). Collins (2004:193n4) thinks that it refers to "the sequence of performance by rhapsodes, i.e. one after another, rather than to the sequence of poetic material."[182] But unless one can plausibly suggest alternative modes of singing that the specification 'in sequence' is supposed to rule out, what could out-of-sequence rhapsodes be? Is the point simply to rule out the unpredictable sequence that obtains for the singing of *skolia* at a symposium? Collins's view depends on the notion that rhapsodes were enrolled to compete in a particular order agreed to in advance, from which they were not to depart once before the public. That performers participated in some pre-arranged order seems beyond question, but that there was a felt need to rule out a departure from this order seems improbable.[183] Far more likely, especially in view of the scholia to *Nemean 2* reviewed

---

[180] Cf. LSJ s.v. I.3.

[181] Ὁμηρίδας ἔλεγον τὸ μὲν ἀρχαῖον τοὺς ἀπὸ τοῦ Ὁμήρου γένους, οἳ καὶ τὴν ποίησιν αὐτοῦ ἐκ διαδοχῆς ᾖδον (scholion 1c to *Nemean 2*). Although one cannot be dogmatic, on balance the diachronic *paradosis* seems in view here, *pace* Collins 2004:183n9.

[182] So also Boyd 1994:115. Nagy (2002:10) seemingly applies ἐφεξῆς to what he translates as the "poetic utterances of Homer," for he quotes as parallels Plato *Timaios* 23d3–4 and 24a1–2, which involve only one narrator (cf. 15n23).

[183] If the point was to prevent something like the unpredictable passing of the baton at a symposium, ἐφεξῆς was hardly the word to use. Only against an established pattern can the otherwise ambiguous 'in sequence' suffice. To the demand, 'in sequence', the obvious question is, 'in *what*

above (pp. 378ff.), both ἐφεξῆς and ἐξ ὑπολήψεως regard the sequencing of the subject matter: the former requires that episodes follow one another in agreement with an established traditional order;[184] the latter, that there be no thematic gap between two consecutive performances. The Panathenaic rule ascribes what must have been the late-classical and Hellenistic practice to an archaic πρῶτος εὑρετής, either Hipparkhos or Solon. Whether such a rule ever existed and was enforced is beside the point. What matters is that the thematic sequencing fundamental to rhapsodic practice and responsible for the artistic unity of the Homeric poems is re-imagined as the outcome of performance standards that force rhapsodes to recompose (in the sense of 'ordering as an organic whole') an otherwise scattered and disorderly body of Homeric material.

The expression in Diogenes Laertios that I have translated 'reactively', ἐξ ὑποβολῆς, raises difficult interpretive problems.[185] Nevertheless, there is general agreement that it is interchangeable in meaning with ἐξ ὑπολήψεως, however one justifies this conclusion.[186] Diogenes' text is clear on this point, for it appends an explication preceded by the word 'namely' (οἷον).[187] The best analysis of the expression is in Pagliaro (1951:33–37), with whom Nagy (2002:19–21) overlaps. ὑποβάλλω in T 80 is given the Homeric acceptation 'to interrupt', and the derivative ὑποβλήδην in A 292 is accordingly translated 'interruptingly'. But, as Pagliaro (1951:35–36) astutely observes, strictly speaking, Akhilleus does not interrupt Agamemnon at A 292 "perchè, difatti, Agamennone ha potuto terminare di parlare, dicendo tutto quello che aveva da dire." Only if one extends the ordinary meaning of 'to interrupt' so as to embrace a heated follow-up to an otherwise semantically complete statement can one call Akhilleus' reply 'an interruption.' Such a stylized 'interruption' would fit just as well under the interpretation championed by Pagliaro, which I will now develop with minor modifications.[188]

---

sequence'? At a symposium, the arrangement of couches produced a natural sequence against which ἑξῆς would make sense.

[184] As Boyd (1994:115) observes, neither account of the rule requires a *written* text to attest to the traditional sequence. An oral telling of sufficient stability, at least in regard to the order of its episodes, would suffice. The degree to which the prevailing sequence of a received plot might descend to narrative minutiae would have heightened with time.

[185] Cf. Nitzsch 1828:28–40; Boeckh 1858–1874:4.385–396; Hermann 1827–1877:5.300–311; Boeckh's commentary to *CIG* 3088 (vol. 2.675–678); and Hermann 1827–1877:7.65–87. The footnote in Boeckh 1858–1874:4.385 offers a short history of the controversy up to 1874. See also Wilamowitz-Moellendorff 1884:265–266, who assumes that Diogenes Laertios (or his source) used ὑποβολή in error.

[186] Cf., for example, Davison 1955a:11.

[187] *TGL* 5.1830 s.v. οἷον: "Quinetiam redditur 'id est' ... . Sic saepe grammatici." Cf. LSJ s.v. οἷος 5.2.e. This obvious point is not usually observed by modern translations. Davison (1955a:11) correctly renders the clause, "viz. that the succeeding (reciter) should begin where the first left off."

[188] It begs the question to speculate that Agamemnon had more to say but Akhilleus prevents him from speaking on. Nothing in the context demands this view. Its sole basis would be the alleged

Pagliaro emphasizes that one cannot understand ὑποβάλλω at T 80 and ὑποβλήδην at A 292 apart from the use of ἀμβλήδην at X 476, ἀμβολάδην in the *Hymn to Hermes* 426, and ἀναβάλλομαι at α 155 θ 266 ρ 262. In all probability, ἀναβάλλομαι with the infinitive ἀείδειν (and *a fortiori* its absolute use) derives from its use with direct objects like 'tune', 'voice', 'song' *vel sim.* (cf. μέλος ἀμβάλευ in Theokritos 10.22). Instances of it suggest that it was a technical expression from the domain of performance with currency among instrumentalists and singers, including rhapsodes.[189] Because 'striking up the song' was a *terme d'art* for the prelude, in time (how soon we cannot guess) it came to be used absolutely for 'to start a performance'; and, from this, it was only a small distance to the complementary infinitive ἀναβάλλομαι ἀείδειν, 'to start singing'.[190] Because

---

meaning of ὑποβλήδην one is seeking to establish!

[189] I do not restrict 'prelude' to 'instrumental prelude'. Both singing and instrumental playing are wedded in the epic ἀναβολή. Because Pagliaro (1951:31) accepts the narrow sense of prelude, i.e. an instrumental opening that precedes the song, he must reject the connection of ἀναβολή with ἀναβάλλομαι ἀείδειν. No such rejection is necessary, once we consider the diachronic implications of the use of κιθαρῳδία to portray epic performance in the *Odyssey*. For instances beyond Homer of ἀναβάλλομαι as a technical word for performance, see Theokritos 6.20: ἀνεβάλλετο καὶ τάδ' ἄειδεν (abs.); Pindar *Nemean* 7.77: εἴρειν στεφάνους ἐλαφρόν, ἀναβάλεο· (abs.); Aristophanes *Peace* 1269: αὐτοῦ παρ' ἐμὲ στὰν πρότερον ἀναβαλοῦ 'νθαδί (sc. ἄδειν). See further Nonnos *Dionysiaka* 24.242 (with ἀείδειν) and 19.102 (with ἁρμονίην); and Philostratos *Imagines* 1.29. For the corresponding noun ἀναβολή, see Pindar *Pythian* 1.4–5 and the other *loci* in the *DGE* s.v. A.IV.

[190] Egan 2007 claims that, in poetic contexts, "ἀμβολάδην means 'by way of resumption or sequel, after an interval, subsequently' and ἀναβάλλομαι '[to] resume, [to] begin again after an interval'" (55). Since the function of epic proems was to furnish epic performance with a ritually sanctioned beginning, it would hardly be surprising if Homeric (and other epic) narrative should sometimes explicitly feature proems and proemial language. In fact, this book amply demonstrates that in their epic poetry rhapsodes often drew attention to their own performance medium. This chapter surveys many striking signs of this metapoetic tendency. Not the least of them are instances in which technical rhapsodic terms shaped epic diction. I submit that these include uses of ἀμβολάδην and ἀναβάλλομαι in performance contexts, terms that I believe to be proemial in origin (i.e. they regard proems in musical performance, with 'music' broadly understood). Egan, however, does not think their primordial poetic usage proemial: for him they denote, on the one hand, 'resumption'; on the other, 'proem' as a specialized application of the common meaning 'delay', viz. 'proem [that postpones the subsequent phase]'. Although the relationship between these two senses is unclear at first, eventually Egan also subsumes the acceptation 'to resume' under the notion of "delayed or postponed performance" (61). It is plain, then, that for him 'delay' is the *fons et origo* whence the various acceptations issue. Not so. The semantics of ἀναβάλλομαι is to be elucidated otherwise. Both meanings, 'to perform a proem' and 'to delay', derive from the local one 'to cast up' by semantic extension: the former, from 'to cast up [the voice in song]' *vel sim.*; the latter, from 'to cast [further] along' (or 'up', with 'up' notionally associated with 'later' for reasons we can only conjecture; cf. ὅτι, the o-grade of ἔτι, in ὄπισθεν and ὀψέ, on which see Morpurgo Davies 1983). In my view, then, ἀναβάλλομαι 'to delay' and ἀναβάλλομαι 'to strike up' (='to begin to sing/play') are *independent* polysemes, and neither can be reduced to the other. Egan's explanation of the proemial use of this word family—namely, that it comes from viewing the proem as the postponement of the rest of the performance—is unconvincing. Nothing in the ancient Greek song culture would encourage us to accept that a word that meant *ex hypothesi*

performers often employed the verb as the semantic equivalent of 'to begin' when the action that was beginning concerned singing or playing an instrument, the adverbial derivatives ἀμβολάδην and ἀμβλήδην were also taken with a verb of performance (e.g. sing or play) to mean 'to start singing or playing'. It

---

'to postpone' was embraced as characteristically proemial diction. It is implausible that either rhapsodes or their audiences should have likened the marked performative beginning of rhapsodic performance to a delaying utterance, much less characteristically *identified* it as such; nor, by extension, to view the ensuing performance as a "delayed utterance" (56; I do not quarrel with Egan's "fresh start," even though 'fresh' remains too vague to help his argument). This contention alone is so far-fetched that it makes Egan's revisionary thesis inadmissible. Furthermore, to prove the alternative 'to resume after an interval', Egan needs to do more than showcase (what I claim is) proemial language featuring at the beginning (and as the beginning) of a performance that follows *some other* performance; he must also establish that the notion of 'resumption' or 'sequel', which requires an underlying continuity, obtains. Otherwise, his claim is unfalsifiably trivial: for, if *any* performance will do, identifying *some* earlier one that the present allegedly resumes is a trivial task. Such a light burden can hardly be considered probative. The onset of his argument is not reassuring. Egan cites a Pindaric scholion that resorts to the polyseme 'to delay' as one of several alternative interpretations (hardly the most compelling) of ἀμβολάδαν in *Nemean* 10.33: 'he won the Panathenaia twice, not in succession but *anaboladēn*, i.e. with some delay intervening'. His other opening move amounts to a misreading of the scholion to X 476, which makes a *thematic*, not a performative, point—a point, moreover, entirely compatible with the performative sense of ἀμβλήδην ('in proemial fashion' or 'with an overture', see below). This term, the scholiast suggests, points to the fact that Andromakhe starts her mourning not with the current circumstances (Hektor's death and the dragging of his body) but with her own birth in the house of Eëtion (προοίμια was sometimes used generally for 'beginnings'; cf. LSJ s.v. I.2). I do not believe that the scholiast is right, apropos, or compelling. Like Egan, he has failed to take the measure of the performative setting and to see at play the metapoetic tendency that is the signature of just such Homeric contexts. All the same, on its own terms the scholiast's point is clear and intelligible. Egan might argue that ἀμβλήδην picks up on the sequence 'first Hekabe and then Andromakhe' (57), but he will not find any support for this in the language of the scholion (the required performance sequence can hardly be extracted from 'not from the present circumstances'). But if Egan's opening examples fail to make his case, the notion that ἀναβάλλεσθαι means 'to resume [singing] after an interval' (strictly speaking still possible for X 476) cannot be sustained for θ 266. For even if one could prove that Demodokos' Song of Ares and Aphrodite and his earlier performances share an overall notional unity that justifies rendering ἀνεβάλλετο … ἀείδειν at θ 266 as "he ma[de] a *new* start to his singing" (57, with emphasis on 'new', for I do not quarrel with 'he started singing'), the argument stumbles on the language of θ 90: ὅτ' ἂψ ἄρχοιτο καὶ ὀτρύνειαν ἀείδειν refers to an extended series of performances that led the rhapsode repeatedly to cease his singing, and his audience repeatedly to urge him to continue—with Odysseus having the time and opportunity during each break to dry his tears, to pull off the cloak, and to pour libations to the gods. It is clear that, but for the first time, this earlier sequence of performances offered ample occasion for Egan's notion of resuming one's singing after an interval, but ἀναβάλλεσθαι or its equivalent fails to materialize to make the point—unless Egan intends 'new' in "new start" to mark Demodokos' singing about Aphrodite's adultery not as a 'sequel' but as a thematically unconnected song. If so, Egan should exclude 'sequel' and 'to resume' from his definition or else must water it down to a bare 'do again what has been done before in *some* form' (whether the subject is one and the same and the actions stand in continuity or discontinuity). I doubt that such a weak sense is true or even useful. (Comparable refuting arguments can be made about the other *loci* discussed by Egan, including his bizarre interpretation of Arkhimedes' *Problema bovinum* 37–38.)

is often possible to read a given instance with both the broader and the stricter senses in view.[191] This is the case at X 476: 'But when Andromakhe revived and her spirit gathered into her breast, she started wailing (ἀμβλήδην γοόωσα) and spoke among the Trojan women'. I have translated the verse as if ἀμβλήδην γοόωσα stood for ἀνεβάλλετο γοήμεναι; but it is also possible to read it as 'lifting up [her voice] in wailing', and even as a not-so-subtle metapoetic reference to the overture of a song of lamentation. Similarly, one could render κιθαρίζων | γηρύετ' ἀμβολάδην in the *Hymn to Hermes* 425–426 simply as 'he started playing the lyre and singing [to it]';[192] or, in this case, given the emphasis on technical virtuosity, more likely, 'playing the lyre he sang (in the manner of) a prelude'.[193]

To come now to Diogenes Laertios 1.57: here the sense of ὑποβολή can only be understood against the corresponding ἀναβολή, ἀναβάλλομαι, and ἀμβλήδην. It is very hard to stumble upon the correct meaning from an etymological analysis that equates ὑποβάλλω with βάλλειν τι ὑπό τινα or βάλλειν ἑαυτὸν ὑπό τι, i.e. 'to throw down [before someone]' or 'to throw oneself down under'. The former gloss metaphorically amounts to an interruption if one envisions disrupting a speaker by throwing words in his path; but, as I have argued following Pagliaro, no interruption is in view either at A 292 or at T 80.[194] The latter gloss follows Della Seta (1910:335), who contended that, etymologically, the operative notion is "un movimento da farsi da una seconda persona per andare a prendere il peso del canto abbandonato dalla prima." But this rationale seems far-fetched. The meaning becomes clear, however, if we assume that the coinage of the idiom was technical in origin and took place among professional performers. Indeed, one need only suppose that it took the form of a semantic proportion: just as ἀναβάλλομαι is 'to cast up one's melody or voice as one commences the song', so ὑποβάλλομαι would mean 'to cast one's voice in reaction to' words just uttered.[195] Or, reducing the former to its looser acceptation, 'to start singing',

---

[191] The stricter sense would be '[to sing or play] in the manner of a prelude' (='to sing or play a prelude').

[192] Or 'playing the lyre he started singing'.

[193] Or 'he sang and played a prelude on the lyre'.

[194] Here Agamemnon does not interrupt Akhilleus at all. Nor do the Akhaians, whose expressions of joy (T 74) follow what is obviously the end of Akhilleus' address.

[195] That in T 80 we find not the middle but the active ὑββάλλειν is no object, for the potential interchangeability of middle and intransitive active verbal forms is well documented in Homeric diction and specifically exampled for συμβάλλ-ω/-ομαι (cf. Π 565 Φ 578 φ 15 and Μ 377 Υ 335 etc.; see, further, *LfgE* s.v. βάλλω III.1e and 2e). Chantraine writes: "Il arrive parfois, comme nous venons de le supposer pour οὐτάμεναι que les formes actives soient constituées parallèlement à un thème généralement moyen. De la racine de βάλλω il existe un aoriste βλῆτο 'il a été blessé' qui est très bien attesté ... , βλήμενος ... . Mais il existe deux formes à désinences actives qui présentent aussi un sens intransitif 'se rencontrer, attaquer': ξυμβλήμεναι ... et ξυμβλήτην ἀλλήλοιιν ... l'emploi absolu de formes actives au sens intransitif peut être ancien" (*GH* I.380). If ever le verbe ὑποβάλλ- (not the noun ὑποβολή or the adverb ὑποβλήδην) was later borrowed in

one might render the latter as 'to resume singing', with a strong emphasis on the fact that the continuing 'song' (i.e. what is performed next) picks up on, and reacts to, the words just uttered.[196] This is the reason for my translation of ἐξ ὑποβολῆς ... ῥαψῳδεῖσθαι as 'rhapsodes are to perform reactively'. That ὑπό may, and often does, carry this sense was conclusively demonstrated by Else (1959:85–100): "It appears, then, that one important function of ὑπό in early Greek ... was to express psychological nearness or exposure, the experience of being within immediate range of a person or object ... that was felt as having power to menace or protect. It would follow that a verb 'compounded with ὑπό' ... will tend to denote a *reaction or response* to such a situation, if the meaning of the simple verb lends itself to such an idea" (his emphasis).[197] On my theory, archaic and classical audiences should not have found the meaning of ὑββάλλειν or ὑποβλήδην any less transparent than that of ἀναβάλλομαι or ἀμβλήδην. All were similarly technical in origin, all from the ambit of the rhapsode and his craft.

The tight consequence of thought entailed by reactive performance readily shades into immediacy of thematic or temporal sequence.[198] This explains why ἐξ ὑποβολῆς could be used as a synonym of ἐξ ὑπολήψεως and grasped unproblematically as a reference to hypoleptic performance.[199] It is not difficult to understand how the original rhapsodic meaning of ὑποβάλλω could give rise later to the dramatic ὑποβολεύς, 'prompter'. This represents a technical development that, as I chronicle in this book, happened repeatedly: the adoption into the sphere of dramatic performance of an element of the rhapsodic craft, in this case, a modification of the all-important practice of hypoleptic delivery.[200] When the primarily reactive character of hypoboletic performance turns proactive, then ὑποβάλλω can refer to cuing and ἐξ ὑποβολῆς can be understood as 'by cue'. Collins (2004:195) shows that the dynamics of hypolepsis point backward

---

the Homeric sense, we should expect that its sole surviving occurrence at T 80 in (what I argue is merely by accident and indifferently) an intransitive active form (i.e. but for the meter, it *might* have been a middle) would commend its reappearing in the active. Cf. τ 584 with B 436.

[196] Cf. Monro 1897: "ἀνεβάλλετο καλὸν ἀείδειν = 'began the song'; so also ὑποβλήδην 'taking up,' 'interrupting'" (395).

[197] Although I do not agree with his conclusion on ὑποκρίνομαι or embrace all of his analysis (see below, pp. 654ff.), the general point is sound and incontrovertible.

[198] This immediacy is key to Curtius's attempt to motivate the label ὑποκριτής for the tragic actor (Curtius 1866). Although I do not think that his particular application of sequential immediacy to drama is tenable (see below, pp. 658f.) or that the sense of ὑπό was the same in ὑποβάλλω and ὑποκρίνομαι, I do believe that the implication of sequence in the ὑπό of ὑποβολή, projected onto ὑποκριτής, would have encouraged the survival of this agent noun in connection with rhapsodic performance.

[199] With these considerations in view, it is clear that Nagy (2002:21) is right to focus on "picking up the train of thought" as essential to its meaning, *pace* Schmidt in the *LfgE* s.v. ὑποβλήδην B.1.

[200] Cf. Nagy 2002:19.

and forward, i.e. they are inherently reactive and proactive. Song sequencing and seam-stitching necessarily regard how the performer who leaves off sets up the thread that his successor must pick up. This form of cuing is wholly internal to the performance. I do not think, however, that we can dismiss out of hand the possibility raised by Boyd 1994 that at the Panathenaia the transition from one rhapsode to the next was at some point supervised by an official enforcer.[201] There is simply too much we do not know to be dogmatic about this, and it seems reasonable to imagine that there was a need for the external enforcement of competitive fairness.[202] But, whatever the truth of Boyd's proposals, we must bear in mind that external rules would only have reflected (and perhaps enhanced) the intrinsic character and potential of rhapsodic hypoleptic performance and relay poetics.[203] That ὑποβολή in the sense examined here had its cradle among performers is supported by two epigraphical items.[204] The first is a second-century BC inscription from Khios, *CIG* 2214 (=*SIG*³ 959). The second, *CIG* 3088 (=*SIG*³ 960 n. 1), comes from Teos and is similarly dated. Comparing their competitive categories led Boeckh *ad CIG* 3088 to propose that the term ὑποβολή in *CIG* 3088.a1 and a4 stood for what the Khian text calls ῥαψῳδία. This would be strong evidence that ὑποβολή was still understood and used as a rhapsodic *terme d'art*.

The technical origin of the acceptations 'reactive performance' for ὑποβολή, 'to perform reactively' for ὑποβάλλω (i.e. 'to perform in reaction to an earlier performance'), and 'reactively' for ὑποβλήδην (in a performance context) explains why rhapsodes used these words to project the dynamics of their own performance on the delivery of back-to-back speeches by Homeric

---

[201] Collins (2004:195) and Nagy (2002:15n23) both disagree. Such supervision may have been more flexible than Boyd would allow for and need not have involved clocked performances (cf. Boyd 1994:115n16).

[202] Just to mention one thing that is yet to receive significant thought: how did the Panathenaic officials make sure that the first rhapsode did not have an advantage over the succeeding ones, who unlike him were forced to take up the plot at a particular point and had to face the consequent challenge of forming a suitable narrative seam? To my knowledge, only A. Boeckh has mentioned this difficulty, touching upon it in passing during his discussion of ὑποβολή in *CIG* II.676 *ad* no. 3088.

[203] Collins (2004:195) points to living oral traditions, which show how one singer can offer oral cues to another with ease and virtuosity. Thus are links created—of subject matter, diction, etc.— which contribute to tighter dynamics of sequencing. Collins has in mind primarily a combination of proactive and reactive performance practices. In the case of rhapsodic delivery, 'reaction' is chiefly in view, although given the inherently competitive character of such delivery—and the competitive character of the speeches by epic speakers (see immediately below)—we should not discount that, at least in part, one rhapsode may have shaped his performance with a view to constraining the reaction of his successor. By extension, that too would fall under the scope of ἐξ ὑποβολῆς.

[204] Cf. Pagliaro 1951:34 and Collins 2004:196.

characters. Martin 1989 has convincingly demonstrated that the speeches of Homeric characters are more than first-person thematic content to be quoted by the rhapsode in performance. From the viewpoint of pragmatics, as a matter of archaic and classical mimesis, they coalesce so decisively with the rhapsodic delivery in progress that the epic speakers in turn become performers in their own right.[205] This facilitated the application of specialized rhapsodic vocabulary to characterize them. As Martin (2000:410) observes: "The Glaukos and Diomedes exchange, and especially the speeches of Achilles (to Agamemnon, to the embassy, to Lykaon, to Aeneas, and to Hector) all show this consistent use by a second speaker of the first speaker's phrases and topics, but with the added feature that the person who speaks second outdoes the first. ... Furthermore, the paired speeches are carefully matched in structure." I can illustrate the truth of this statement with reference to the first of two relevant Homeric passages, the confrontation between Akhilleus and Agamemnon in the first book of the *Iliad*. Indeed, the point of ὑποβλήδην at A 292 is to mark the ensuing retort by Akhilleus as a supremely pointed answer to Agamemnon's immediately preceding reproaches. The technical adverb underlines the thematic connection as singularly tight. As Kirk (1985:82) writes, Agamemnon "harps obsessively on Akhilleus' domineering behavior." Note his fourfold repetition at A 287–289:

> ἀλλ' ὅδ' ἀνὴρ ἐθέλει περὶ πάντων ἔμμεναι ἄλλων,
> πάντων μὲν κρατέειν ἐθέλει, πάντεσσι δ' ἀνάσσειν,
> πᾶσι δὲ σημαίνειν, ἅ τιν' οὐ πείσεσθαι ὀΐω.

> But this fellow here wants to be above all others,
> wants to rule all, lord it over all,
> to boss all around—wherein I think someone will not obey him.

Akhilleus' retort reacts closely to the formulation of Agamemnon's contemptuous charges (A 293–296):

> ἦ γάρ κεν δειλός τε καὶ οὐτιδανὸς καλεοίμην
> εἰ δὴ σοὶ πᾶν ἔργον ὑπείξομαι ὅττί κεν εἴπῃς·
> 295 ἄλλοισιν δὴ ταῦτ' ἐπιτέλλεο, μὴ γὰρ ἔμοιγε
> σήμαιν'· οὐ γὰρ ἔγωγ' ἔτι σοὶ πείσεσθαι ὀΐω.

> Well might I be called a coward and a nobody
> if I yield to you in everything you say.

---

[205] See especially his chapter "Heroes as Performers" (Martin 1989:89–145).

295 Enjoin these things on others, but do not boss *me* around;
     for *I*, at least, am minded no longer to obey you.

Agamemnon has said, in effect: 'who does *he* think he is, bossing everybody around?' With his rhetorical question at A 290–291, he further implies that, because Akhilleus owes to the gods his stature as a fighter, his greatness gives him no leave to insult others.[206] To paraphrase Akhilleus' retort: 'You will be right that I am a nobody if I yield to you and you still get to boss me around. *I* am the one who will not obey *you!*' As Monro (1958:255) observes, "Achilles echoes l. 289, mockingly." Akhilleus' 'reactive' performance contains strong thematic and verbal echoes that closely mirror the words of the performer (Agamemnon) who has just left off speaking. This amply justifies the narrator's recourse to ὑποβλήδην to qualify the manner of Akhilleus' answer.

A similar analysis explains ὑββάλλειν at T 80. Agamemnon is not indirectly referring to himself, as is often assumed, but rather, as Pagliaro (1951:36–37) argued, to the approval of the Akhaians that immediately followed the end of Akhilleus' address (T 74–75). Irritated by their obvious (and, to Agamemnon, disruptive) approbation of Akhilleus and their implicit reproach of him (cf. T 85–86), Agamemnon admonishes them for their breach of protocol. He remarks that one should 'listen well' (καλὸν ἀκούειν T 79) to him who stands up to address the assembly, and adds that it is not proper to answer him reactively, i.e. to offer his speech what amounts to tactlessly consequent criticism or praise.[207] This is irksome even to one who is skilled. If you react to a speaker with an uproar—he adds—how could anyone hear or speak?[208] The speaker is then hampered, clear-voiced though he be.[209] In this case, the Akhaians' vehement

---

[206] This sentiment is ironic, because Athena has, in fact, commanded Akhilleus not to strike Agamemnon with the sword and only to revile him (A 211).

[207] In this case it is Agamemnon, not Akhilleus, who finds the Akhaians' response tactless. The complementary 'hearing well' and 'not reacting' in the manner deprecated stand in continuity as elements of proper etiquette. An improper reaction might involve, but is hardly limited to, interrupting the speaker. It is doubtful that heroic assemblies live up to the standard articulated here by Agamemnon. But this, of course, is not the point of his self-serving reprimand.

[208] As noted above, Akhilleus' speech reaches an obvious endpoint at T 73 and, *stricto sensu*, the Akhaians' rejoicing does not interrupt it. Agamemnon's rebuke addresses in general terms proper behavior at an assembly (εἰς ἀγορήν T 45), where participants are to speak and to listen by turns. The rowdy reaction of the audience (ἐν πολλῷ ὁμάδῳ T 81) might disrupt the carefully calibrated pragmatics on which rhetorical persuasion often depends, and hence threaten its social objectives. Such unfavorable circumstances might inhibit proper hearing and speaking and strain even a knowledgeable (ἐπισταμένῳ περ ἐόντι T 80) and clear-voiced (λιγύς περ ἐὼν T 82) speaker. One should recall that λιγύς and λιγέως are regularly used to qualify metonymically the eloquent and rhetorically effective speaker (e.g. at Γ 214). Hence, λιγύς is not merely a matter of tone or volume (so, correctly, *LfgE* s.v. B.1b). Cf. Martin 1989:117 and λιγύφθογγος, the epithet of heralds.

[209] For an alternative interpretation, cf. Nagy 2002:21.

approval is the 'reaction' that ὑποβάλλω refers to. The close connection is not wrought, as before, by a detailed response with verbal echoes, but by the audience's immediate, unequivocal, and definitive embrace of Akhilleus' address. What might well have been given verbal expression through one speaker who voiced his approval and the ensuing assent of the rest—see H 399–404 and I 31–51—is here contracted to a two-line, third-person remark by the narrator.

It is important to emphasize that the Panathenaic rule—whatever its status as an actual stipulation—only formalizes what was already at the heart of rhapsodic poetics: the formal and thematic sequencing of which traditional diction and traditional plot were the outcome. Precisely because relay poetics is of the very essence of rhapsodic performance, one would not expect the various accounts of the rule to agree on its author or the time of its introduction. If traditional sequencing is fundamental to the rhapsode's craft, the gradual fixation of the language and plot of epic narrative is the natural outcome of the rhapsodes' cooperative performances, both in their diachronic and synchronic dimensions. That relay performance could be responsible for poems of recognized artistry is strongly suggested by the Hesiodic fragment 357 MW, analyzed at length below (pp. 420ff.). One plausible reading of it would be that Hesiod and Homer cooperated in stitching their respective hymns, the Delian and Pythian sections, as one song, namely, the extant *Hymn to Apollo*.[210]

10.2.3.5 οἴμη and οἶμος

The rhapsodic emphasis on traditional thematic sequencing had another *terme d'art*: οἴμη, which seems to appear in a complementary distribution with the apparently related οἶμος. Bader 1990 offers a thorough and meticulous study of their etymology. She traces their origin, and that of ὑμήν and ὕμνος, to the IE root *sh_2-* 'to link', 'to tie', 'to bind'. Osthoff (1898:161) had related οἴμη to Sanskrit *sā́man-* 'song' and old Norse *seiðr* 'sorcery'. To these, Benveniste (1954a:39–40) had added Hittite *ishamai-* 'song'.[211] Bader (1990:36) reconstructs *$séh_2$-mn̥-* > *sā́man-*, *sh_2-°mi-* > *ishamai-*, one from the e-grade, the other from the zero-grade of the root 'to tie'. For *seiðr* and οἴμη, she posits e- and o-grade extensions to the zero-grade of the root: *sh_2-ei-* > *sai-* > *sei-* and *sh_2-oi-* + *-mā* > οἴμη (1990:36–38). These elegant and persuasive etymologies allow her to relate these terms to the clearly relevant *$ἱμά$ < *sh_2-i-mā$ (from the zero-grade of the root enlargement)[212] and Αἰσίοδος < *sh_2-ei-ti-*—the latter, according to

---

[210] This old idea is explored at length by Martin 2000. See further below, p. 424 n. 345.

[211] Cf. Lazzeroni 1967:53–55.

[212] From *$ἱμά$ derives the secondary formation in -ντ- ἱμάς 'leather strap' (Schwyzer *GG* I.526n5; cf. Beekes 2010:1.590 for the quantity of the anlauting iota). Durante (1976:176 §76) had already connected οἴμη and ἱμάς.

the *Etymologicum Magnum* 452.37 (col. 1293 Gaisford), an Aiolic name for Hesiod (cf. Bader 1990:37 and n. 64).

οἶμος presents an added complication. There is evidence for both a psilotic οἶμος and an aspirated οἷμος.[213] Its single occurrence at Λ 24 apparently refers to the 'stripes' or 'bands' of a breastplate,[214] an acceptation for which there may be further evidence in the Mycenaean *e-re-pa-te-jo-pi o-mo-pi* (KN Se 891), if in fact *o-mo-pi* is οἴμοφι.[215] In Hesiod *Works and Days* 290 it clearly stands for 'way' or 'road' and it parallels ὁδός at 288. This justifies the persistent gloss 'way' *vel sim.*, even in contexts where 'song' is in view and its relation to οἴμη is most immediate. So, for example, in the *Hymn to Hermes* 451, where Apollo says of the Muses that, among other things, they care about 'the splendid path of song', ἀγλαὸς οἶμος ἀοιδῆς.[216] Although I have printed the conventional translation 'path', it is in fact more likely that it should be translated as would οἴμη, 'band', 'cord', or 'thread of song'. The variant ὕμνος ἀοιδῆς (cf. θ 429)[217]—about which Allen and Sikes (1904:336) observed, "it is doubtful if [it] should not be preferred"— puts οἶμος back in the context of the ancient technology of sewing and weaving. A review of ancient usage convinced Osthoff (1898:163) that the οἶμος of song and the οἶμος of path should be ascribed to different roots. Sommer (1905:29) made a proposal that has been well received by those who share Osthoff's conviction: *oi-s-mo-s = *οἶημος, a form attested by Lithuanian *eismė* 'motion'.[218] Bader (1990:36) restates Sommer's form as *h_1oi-(s)mo- (*h_1ei- > εἶμι), and it is to be preferred to Osthoff's *ϝοῖ-μο-ς (related to ἴεμαι 'to desire', 'to pursue'),[219] against which Pagliaro (1951:26) raised valid objections on semantic grounds.

The two outcomes of *sh_2-oi-m-, a first-declension οἴμη and a second-declension οἶμος, illustrate a lexical variation well attested in other cases. Compare: αὐχμός and αὐχμή, δεσμός and δέσμη, θάλαμος and θαλάμη, κάλαμος

---

[213] So Lentz 1867–1870:1.546.16–17 (τὸ οἶμος οἴμῷ δασύνεται). Cf. φροίμιον (LSJ s.v. προοίμιον) and ἄοιμος· ἄπορος (Hesykhios A no. 5665).

[214] See Hainsworth 1993:218–219.

[215] Cf. *DMic* II.24 s.v. "*o-mo-pi*."

[216] For a novel exploration of this motif, see Giannisi 2006. Conceptualizing the performance of song as walking along a path explains the ready use of μεταβαίνω for 'to move along' in the performance (θ 492; *Homeric Hymns* 5.293, 9.9, 18.11). Similar spatial notions may underlie the transitive use of ἐπιβαίνω in Hesiod *Works and Days* 659 for 'to initiate' as a performer ('where [the Muses] first caused me to step [mount? embark?] on clear-sounding song'; cf. *Hymn to Hermes* 464–465). But the parallel (intransitive) use with abstract nouns like ὁσίη (*Hymn to Hermes* 173) and ἀναιδείη (χ 424) makes the precise nature of the metaphor elusive. See Ford 1992:41–43.

[217] On ὕμνος, see further below, pp. 396ff.

[218] For the transposition of the -h- see Lejeune 1972:138 §133.

[219] Osthoff 1898:171. Beekes (2010:2.1058 s.v. οἶμος) suggests that the hiatus δέκα οἶμοι in Λ 24 (τοῦ δ᾿ ἤτοι δέκα οἶμοι ...) "requires [οἶμος with] initial ϝ-." But this is no more necessary here than in B 87 (ἠΰτε ἔθνεα εἶσι ...), where the hiatus ἔθνεα εἶσι hardly justifies positing initial ϝ- for εἶσι.

and καλάμη, γόνος and γονή, etc.[220] Pagliaro (1951:28) speculates that "il tema in -o rappresenta una funzione individuante nei confronti del tema in -ā più generico e collettivo."[221] Hence, οἴμη would be "legame, traccia" whereas οἶμος would be "striscia" (28). This suggestion is helpful, although I am not convinced that the distinction is attested where οἶμος is specifically used in connection with song, and the alternation -o/-ā, where it entails a semantic difference, can be motivated by a range of reasons.[222] That οἶμος had a longer afterlife than οἴμη may well be related to the influence of οἶμος ~ ὁδός (note its occasional feminine construal). After οἶμος had fallen together with οἶμος and by and large become its homophone, the semantic restriction of οἴμη to the technical sphere of rhapsodic performance would have been keenly felt.[223] Unless their intention was to draw narrowly on a background of traditional epic singing, authors would resort to the now unmarked οἶμος more readily than to the marked οἴμη. Later poets who use οἴμη are borrowing language from the rhapsode and his craft and making reference to traditional epic song. This is the case, for example, of *Anakreontea* 34 West, which speaks of cicadas as singers, an image straight out of the metaphoric world of epic.[224] Other late instances of οἴμη as 'song' are: Kallimakhos' *Hymn to Delos* 9; Apollonios Rhodios *Argonautika* 4.150; Manetho *Apotelesmatika* 6.5 and 6.509;[225] [Lykophron] *Alexandra* 11;[226] Oppian *Halieutika* 3.3 and 28; and *Anthologia Graeca* 4.1.17 (οἴνης emended to οἴμης).[227]

---

[220] All these and a few more in Osthoff 1898:163. Whether such forms differ at all one from another in meaning and to what degree is not *a priori* predictable.

[221] Cf. Gagnepain 1959:57–104, with the pair οἶμος/οἴμη at 85–86.

[222] Cf. Wackernagel 1920–1924:2.12–15.

[223] The confusion is well chronicled by Osthoff 1898:163–164.

[224] Γ 151–152; Hesiod *Works and Days* 582–584, *Shield* 393–396.

[225] Ameis et al. 1862:59 and 69 (the pagination noted starts anew with Aratos' *Phainomena*).

[226] οἶμαι of αἰνίγματα, 'lays of dark oracular statements' that were delivered of old in epic verse, following conventions of recomposition in performance. With mantic and oracular poetry, epic shares its cultural beginnings (a matter explored at length above in chapter 8). Like the scholiast, Osthoff 1898:162 (and, with him, many others in recent times) thought that οἶμαι here referred to "'gänge, pfade, weisen' der dunklen reden," adducing τρίβος (11) and κελεύθῳ (12) in the same sentence. I do not deny that οἴμας plays on οἴμους; hence διοίχνει ... οἴμας (10–11). But these are δυσφάτους ... οἴμας, i.e. 'hard to utter' (cf. 713). And τυλίσσων, which more immediately governs οἴμας, evokes the notion of unraveling a thread: "déroule les énigmes" (Hurst 2008:2). One must also recall that the manufacturing of thread—an obvious metaphor for epic composition—involved twisting between one's fingers fibers from the mass of carded wool. For a cognate use of τυλίσσω as 'to roll up', see the scholia to ζ 53 and Eustathios *Ad Odysseam ad* v 107 (Stallbaum 1825–1826:2.42.30–31). There might also be a hint in this verse of Theseus' escaping from the labyrinth by winding up the thread of Ariadne (so Müller 1811:1.6 and Mooney 1921:2n11; *contra*, Holzinger 1895:166). τυλίσσω stands for *convolvo* more often than for *evolvo*.

[227] But οἴμη is used for 'way' in Cougny 1890:486 epigr. 120.16 (on Plotinos) and Quintus of Smyrna 7.320, 9.508.

The *Iliad* instances οἴμη three times, the first two in *Odyssey* 8. In the former, Demodokos sings about a quarrel (νεῖκος θ 75) between Akhilleus and Odysseus: Μοῦσ' ἄρ' ἀοιδὸν ἀνῆκεν ἀειδέμεναι κλέα ἀνδρῶν, | οἴμης, τῆς τότ' ἄρα κλέος οὐρανὸν εὐρὺν ἵκανε (θ 73–74). Here οἴμης is an ablatival genitive of origin, '[starting] from that point in the song-thread whose *kléos* had then reached broad heaven'.[228] This passage sets οἴμη in close connection with the singing of κλέα ἀνδρῶν, as if the song were a cord tying the relevant subject matter along a traditional narrative sequence. In the second, Odysseus speaks in high praise of Demodokos and ἀοιδοί generally, who τιμῆς ἔμμοροί εἰσι καὶ αἰδοῦς, οὕνεκ' ἄρα σφέας | οἴμας Μοῦσ' ἐδίδαξε (θ 479–480). In the third, Phemios pleads for his life with the argument that he is 'self-taught': θεὸς δέ μοι ἐν φρεσὶν οἴμας | παντοίας ἐνέφυσεν (φ 347–348). These last two make the plural οἶμαι the sum total of traditional epic poetry and rhapsodic singing. Pagliaro (1951:29) aptly calls the οἴμη "[il] nesso di eventi che egli vuole sviluppare nella sua narrazione." Because of its traditional character, once the rhapsode has chosen the epic οἴμη and his specific starting point along this song-thread, the sequence it entails constitutes "un dato obiettivo nella esibizione del cantore" (29). The synchronic limitation imposed by what Pagliaro calls "[la] congruenza dell'argomento" is the diachronic outcome of rhapsodic sequencing. The performative continuity is especially obvious in the relation between προοίμιον and οἴμη or οἶμος, the former being the 'starting end' of the rhapsodic performance.[229]

We see, then, that οἴμη and οἶμος, which must be understood etymologically as metaphoric connecting devices (i.e. 'cord' or 'band of song'), were widely used in ancient Greece as metaphors for songmaking and the singing of traditional song. I suggest that these metaphors were so readily applied to Greek epic song because they underlined the tight performance sequencing and narrative connection that is at the heart of rhapsodic singing. They were also the notional ground for the rhapsode's freedom to shift his performance forward and backward along the thematic thread. This freedom was gradually constrained to the point of eventual elimination, as the dynamic of accretion characteristic of Homeric poetry forced the explicit inclusion within the performance of the very stretches of narrative erstwhile bracketed (and only notionally incorporated) by these performative shifts.[230] The binding of verse to verse, speech to speech,

---

[228] The genitive is certainly not one of inverse attraction. Although it is possible to classify it as partitive, with Pagliaro (1951:28 and n. 2), I believe that the rhapsodic usage attested by the syntax of I 97 α 10 θ 500 (cf. Φ 142) decisively points to a genitive of origin. Cf. Schwyzer *GG* II.92 §4e.I.1c and Nagy 1996c:63n19.

[229] Cf. Pagliaro 1951:29 and Nagy 1996c:63. Cf. Nagy 2009b:241 2§109, 330–335 2§§311–323; and Nagy 2010a:79–102.

[230] See p. 23 above on the characteristic tendency of Homeric epic towards 'monumentality,' that is, towards an explicit, no longer merely notional, comprehensiveness in performance that

episode to episode, and performance to performance (or rhapsode to rhapsode) is precisely captured by the image of a 'cord' or '[leather] band of song'. We find across the family of IE languages a similar metaphoric recourse to the technology of sewing in order to describe characteristic qualities of songmaking or singing or both. The old Norse *seiðr* was used for both 'cord' and 'sorcery', a trope that focused attention on the power of song to draw desired objects to the sorcerer (e.g. fish or a person);[231] or, as Heide (2006:164) has recently argued, it signaled that the mental images the sorcerer sent as his emissaries through *seiðr* ritual "could be regarded as something spun: a thread or rope." In Hittite, *ishima(n)-* meant 'string, line, cord, strap'; whereas the cognate *ishamai-* designated 'song, melody'. Commenting on this fact, Puhvel (1984–:2.395) writes that "the semantic tie-in would be 'rhapsodic' in the literal sense," and for his meaning he directs us to Hesiod fr. 357 MW ὕμνοις ῥάψαντες ἀοιδήν. In Greek traditional poetry, the semantic rationale for οἴμη and οἶμος is the sequencing, performative and thematic, that was the defining *differentia* of rhapsodic delivery: "l'οἴμη, in quanto è legame di contenuto nella recitazione di ciascuno e di tutti i cantori partecipanti, costituisce l'argomento e quindi il componimento ispirato a un motivo" (Pagliaro 1951:29).[232]

10.2.3.6 ὕμνος

The conceptual correlative of οἴμη is ὕμνος.[233] Bader (1990:34–35) has shown that it too may be derived etymologically from the root 'to tie, bind'. Furthermore, it is closely related to ὑμήν, which is attested both with a short and with a long υ: ὑμήν, with the sense 'thin skin, membrane' (Apollonios Rhodios *Argonautika* 4.1648), and ὑμήν, with the meaning 'god of wedding' (Theokritos 18.58). ὑμήν follows readily from $*sh_2$- with the affix -u-: ὑμήν < $*sh_2$-u-; ὑμήν, on the other hand,

---

progressively limited the ability of rhapsodes to shift their focus from one episode to another not immediately contiguous along the plot line.

[231] Heide 2006: "In Icelandic *seiðr* tradition, from recent times, attraction dominates and most of the sources have the fixed expression *seiða til sín* 'attract by *seiðr*' ... . In some of the sources, it is as if the victim is pulled by an invisible rope" (164).

[232] Compare Pagliaro's attempt (1951:29) to put this notion in a diachronic perspective by taking into account that it must have referred to creative composition: "L'uso del termine οἴμη nell'Odissea ... fanno pensare che l'innovazione, cioè l'applicazione di questa nozione di 'legame, traccia' alla composizione, sia probabilmente dovuta al fatto che la novità del poetare epico è costituita dal 'legame' contenutistico che informa l'esibizione del cantore, del 'racconto', nei confronti della poesia lirica divisa in membri ... ."

[233] The bibliography on the Greek hymn is voluminous and this is not the place for a review. I will only mention, among recent surveys, Cassio and Cerri 1991, Lattke 1991, Burkert 1994, Devlin 1995, and Furley and Bremer 2001; and the important treatments in Koller 1956, Durante 1976:155–166, Nagy 2000a and 2002:70–98, Vamvouri Ruffy 2004, and Nagy 2009b:189–248 2§§8–122.

resulted from the metathesis of the laryngeal and the affix -u-: *sh_2-u-* > *suh_2-*.[234] Before the suffix *-$mn̥$-* in its long e-grade,[235] the loss of the laryngeal resulted in the compensatory lengthening of the -u-: *suh_2-$mn̥$-* > *$sūmn̥$-*. -μην was used not only for agent nouns like ποιμήν but also for instruments like ὑμήν.[236] Like ὑμήν 'membrane', ὕμνος, with its short -ὔ-, followed from *sh_2-u-* by simple laryngeal loss without metathesis. Bader (1990:26) argues that this was in fact the older treatment (cf. 35 §10.3), and that metathesis arose as a 'reaction' against this loss.[237] Hence, besides the alternation of preconsonantal *sū-* (e.g. *sūtor*) with prevocalic *sŭw-* > *sŭ-* (κασσύω, *suō*)[238] we also find preconsonantal *sŭ-* and, for *sh_2-i-*, preconsonantal *sĭ-*: to the contrastive pair ὑμήν and ὕμνος, add ἱμάω and ἱμάσθλη (and other derivatives of ἱμάς). ὕμνος is a thematic form built on the zero grade of the suffix < *$sŭmn̥$-os*. Durante (1976:155–166) related ὕμνος to the Sanskrit *sŭmná-*, 'benevolence, favor, song offered in tribute'.[239]

Etymologically, then, the notion of 'hymn' is built on a metaphor taken from the art of sewing, one that reifies the performance of epic song as a 'membrane' or, alternatively, as a product manufactured by tying or sewing. The etymology makes the formal and thematic sequence of traditional epic poetry metaphorically emphatic. The original generic meaning of 'hymn' is the unitary product of a rhapsodic performance, i.e. an integral whole of song and singing, the material delivered at a given performance and the performance itself viewed in its totality.[240] Nagy (2002:71) is therefore right to stress that ἀοιδῆς ὕμνον at θ 429 (cf. the variant at *Hymn to Hermes* 451) "conveys the idea of the *totality* of a given performance of song" (his emphasis).[241] Only the generic acceptation in evidence at θ 429 makes sense of the inscription with which Hesiod dedicated his tripod to the Muses after his victory over Homer in the *Certamen*: Ἡσίοδος Μούσαις

---

[234] Bader (1990:34) deals with Sanskrit *syŭman-* 'band, thong, bridle', which is regularly mentioned in connection with ὑμήν.

[235] *-$mn̥$-* is known in long e- and o-grades, -μην and -μων, as well as in the zero grade -μα. Cf. Chantraine 1933:170–174.

[236] Chantraine 1933:174 §133.

[237] Cf. Bader 1990:11 §3.5 and 16 §4.4.

[238] Cf. Bader 1990:25.

[239] Frisk 1973–1979 s.v. ὕμνος was skeptical. Cf. Mayrhofer 1953–1980:3.485 (with references). Beekes 2010:2.1531–1532 surveys the proposed etymologies for ὕμνος without committing himself to any of them.

[240] This totality is notional insofar as hymnic poetics allows the rhapsode the freedom to shift to another point along the narrative thread. Such shifts include the possible transition from a 'hymn' understood in the narrower sense of *prooimion* (e.g. a shorter Homeric hymn) to a subsequent performance of epic. Thus, in practice, to speak from the perspective of a cultural outsider, by shifting the rhapsode may 'bracket' an intervening narrative stretch.

[241] *Pace* Collins (2004:181n4), ἀοιδῆς ὕμνος need not imply "that *humnos* is a subdivision of song." There is no compelling reason to read the genitive thus. One would hardly construe in this manner the English 'a song's performance.'

Ἑλικωνίσι τόνδ' ἀνέθηκεν | ὕμνῳ νικήσας ἐν Χαλκίδι θεῖον Ὅμηρον (213–214). As Martin (2000:414) remarks, "[these] lines may seem odd, because nothing in the narrated contest between the two poets resembles a 'hymn' in the narrower sense; the word [ὕμνῳ] seems to be used in this event as synonymous with *epic verse*" (his emphasis). I would slightly emend this observation to say that ὕμνος is synonymous with a *performance of epic song*. Evelyn-White (1914:587) translates ὕμνῳ νικήσας, "after he had conquered ... in a contest of song"; West (2003b:341) writes, "having defeated in song"—they are doubtless right to avoid the (for us semantically much narrower) 'with a hymn' (*vel sim*.).[242]

Glossed as a 'membrane-song', the Hesiodic fragment that portrays Hesiod and Homer as rhapsodes stitching a song to Apollo 'with new *hymnoi*' gains the technical precision of professional suturing (see below, pp. 420ff.). On the relationship of 'sewing' to 'tying', Bader (1990:33) writes that "'coudre' n'est qu'un emploi spécialisé de 'lier'," and for this reason verbs derived from *sh_2- with the former meaning are based on relatively late forms.[243] It is worth underlining here a fact recognized by many: irrespective of its original etymology, the combination of ὑφαίνω and ὕμνος in Bakkhylides 5.9–10 SM (ὑφάνας ὕμνον)[244] attests to a popular etymology that derived 'hymn' from 'weaving'. Although popular etymologies are irrelevant to the meaning of a word at the time of its coining, they can greatly inform its later uses. I believe this was indeed the case with the word 'hymn.' It might be well to close this section with Bader's own remarks on the use of technical terms to describe the art of singing and song:

L'emploi de formes d'une racine "lier" pour un art poétique qui comprend un chant est conforme à la conception générale de la poésie ... comme comportant des techniques; celles-ci supposent un "agencement" (cf. *h_2er-, §12.1), que peuvent préciser des métaphores de techniques mettant en oeuvre des agencements particuliers ... . [La couture] est une forme particulière du "liage" ... . Pour l'art poétique, c'est probablement un faux problème que d'hésiter ... entre les sens "lier" et "coudre" de la racine [*seh_2-], puisque la couture fut d'abord un liage, et qu'en outre les formes en *seh_2-(i)- du vocabulaire de l'art poétique s'appliquent essentiellement au chant.[245]

---

[242] Cf. the remarks in Vine 1999:575–576. It is not clear whether of old *Certamen* 213–214 was thought compatible with Hesiod *Works and Days* 656–658. The *Works and Days* does not mention Homer, and modern scholars have often identified the ὕμνῳ of *Works and Days* 657 as the *Theogony*—a work whose formal and thematic canons more readily fall under the narrower notion of 'hymn.'

[243] Cf. Bader 1989:23.

[244] See Bakkhylides 19.6–9 SM and Pindar fr. 179 M. Cf. Nünlist 1998:112–116.

[245] "The use of forms of a root 'to bind' for an art of poetry that includes singing is in line with the general concept of poetry ... as entailing technical skills; these assume an 'arrangement'

10.2.4 Earliest attestations of ῥαψῳδός

The earliest attestations of the word ῥαψῳδός all come from the late fifth century BC. They are: Herodotos 5.67, *SGDI* 5786, and Sophokles' *Oidipous tyrannos* 391.[246] From the former two there is very little that can be inferred about the essential character of rhapsodic performance. Herodotos 5.67 relates the intervention of Kleisthenes, the tyrant of Sikyon, against the rhapsodes' performance of 'Homeric poetry' (τῶν Ὁμηρείων ἐπέων εἵνεκα) because it exalted Argos and the Argives, against whom he had then gone to war.[247] Herodotos' report confirms the rhapsodes' association with Homeric poetry. Ὁμήρεια ἔπεα perhaps designates the Homeric poems; or conceivably, as Cingano 1985 argued,[248] epic from the Theban cycle which at that time many still considered of Homeric authorship.[249] From the passage we also learn that rhapsodes took part in festival contests (ἀγωνίζεσθαι).[250] We cannot be certain that ῥαψῳδοί was the label applied to these performers during the rule of Kleisthenes in the late seventh and early sixth centuries. But I see no reason to prefer the view that the coinage of the term postdated these events and that the historian has resorted to an anachronism deliberately or in ignorance. The fourth-century BC (?) tripod inscription from Dodona tells us nothing about the manner of performance.[251] We only learn the name of the rhapsode, Terpsikles, and (presumably) the pride he takes in his trade—a fact, incidentally, that refutes those who believe that 'rhapsode' was coined as a term of shame (unless one accepts the convoluted conjecture that by Terpsikles' time, 'rhapsode' had shed its negative connotations).[252]

(cf. *h_2er-, §12.1), which metaphors of crafts effecting particular arrangements can specify ... . [Sewing] is a particular form of 'bonding' ... . For the art of poetry, to hesitate ... between the senses 'to bind' and 'to sew' of the root [*seh_2-] is probably only a false problem, since sewing was from the start a [type of] bonding, and, furthermore, the forms in *seh_2-(i)- of the vocabulary of the art of poetry apply mainly to singing" (Bader 1990:38–39).

[246] To these, one may add Herakleitos' censure of Homer (DK 22 B42), if the attractive suggestion that ῥαπίζεσθαι puns on ῥάβδος is true. Cf. Nagy 1989:38 and Graziosi 2002:29.

[247] Κλεισθένης γὰρ Ἀργείοισι πολεμήσας τοῦτο μὲν ῥαψῳδοὺς ἔπαυσε ἐν Σικυῶνι ἀγωνίζεσθαι τῶν Ὁμηρείων ἐπέων εἵνεκα, ὅτι Ἀργεῖοί τε καὶ Ἄργος τὰ πολλὰ πάντα ὑμνέαται.

[248] See above, p. 47 n. 24.

[249] See, for example, *PEG* I.22 F1 Bernabé = *EGF* 22 F1 Davies. On the authorship, cf. *PEG* I.21 T5 Bernabé and *EGF* 21 *de Homero auctore* Davies.

[250] Cf. Nagy 1990c:22.

[251] Τερψικλῆς τῶι Δὶ Ναίωι ῥαψωιδὸς ἀνέθηκε (in the Ionic alphabet). Usually dated after Kirchhoff to the mid fifth-century BC, this is only possible if the inscription is by an Ionian artisan. If of local manufacture, I believe rather that it ought to be downdated to sometime in the first half of the fourth century BC. See below, p. 497 item 9.

[252] Cf. Tarditi 1968:144 and Graziosi 2002:25–27.

We are left with Sophokles' *Oidipous tyrannos* 391, which calls the Sphinx ἡ ῥαψῳδὸς ... κύων. Why characterize the Sphinx as a 'rhapsode'? For an answer, Jebb (1893:29) is typical: "ῥαψῳδὸς, chanting her riddle (in hexameter verse), as the public reciters chanted epic poems."[253] It is worth considering that passages which mention the riddle also speak of the Sphinx in ways suitable to the unmarked 'singer'. Euripides *Phoinissai* 48 calls her a 'wise maiden', a pun on the σοφία of the performer and the devious cunning of the female. She is said to perform μοῦσαι (50) whose meaning had to be learned by him who would rid Thebes of her; at 807 in the same play she is said to have 'most discordant songs' (ἀμουσοτάταισι ὠιδαῖς);[254] and in 1028, to have snatched youth away with her 'lyreless Muse' (ἄλυρον ἀμφὶ μοῦσαν), a manner of performance that well suits the classical rhapsode; finally, 1506–1507 speak of her μέλος and call her an ἀοιδός. Euripides *Ēlektra* 471 adds that her catch 'involved song' (ἀοίδιμον ἄγραν).[255] Sophokles *Oidipous tyrannos* 36 also calls her a 'hard singer' (σκληρᾶς ἀοιδοῦ); at 130 she is the Sphinx 'of intricate song' (ποικιλῳδός); and at 1199–1200 she is the 'oracle-chanting maiden' (παρθένον χρησμῳδόν).

What then are we to make of her characterization as a rhapsode? We can safely dismiss some proposals, for example, that she is so called because she engaged Oidipous in an oracular contest.[256] Hesiod fr. 278 MW attests to a contest of seers (specifically, Kalkhas and Mopsos in the *Melampodia*), but nothing in the transmitted multiforms suggests that Oidipous filled the place of a rival chanter of oracles who dared the Sphinx to unravel the meaning of a countering puzzle.[257] Ritoók (1962:229) suggests that the stitching of song by succeeding parties "wäre geeignet, um die Anwendung des Wortes auf die Sphinx zu erklären; die Sphinx hatte ja Rätsel gestellt, an die man die Antwort anzuknüpfen hatte, genau so wie in dem Agon." But competitive song-stitching by consecutive rhapsodes, although important, is but one aspect of the notion of performative sequence at the heart of the rhapsode's craft. It is neither a *sine qua non*—for solo performance of the proper kind may still be characteristically rhapsodic—nor is it plausible to argue that the Sphinx and Oidipous engage in

---

[253] Cf. Bollack (1990:245), who after noting this fact remarks that the mobility associated with the rhapsodic profession may also have suggested the label.

[254] As we shall see, the point of the adjective is not to ascribe their inspiration to a source other than the Muses, but to draw attention to the absence of merriment that ordinarily accompanies all that the Muses oversee.

[255] Another semantic pun.

[256] Cf. Ritoók 1962:229n17. For contests of riddles, see Schultz 1909–1912:2.73–81 and the article by the same in *RE* 1 A (zweite Reihe), coll. 62–125 s.v. "Rätsel," esp. 70–72.

[257] An elegiac version of a possible answer has been transmitted by the scholia to Euripides *Phoinissai* 50 (Schwartz 1887–1891:1.257), but it is clearly of late composition and cannot rival the antiquity of the hexametric account of the riddle, even if the latter is judged post-archaic.

sequential 'verbal tying' (Ritoók uses "anknüpfen" and "verknüpfen") as rhapsodes would do at a festival contest (note Ritoók's words, "genau so wie in dem Agon").[258]

Can the notion of 'rhapsode' propounded in this chapter explain Sophokles' designation of the Sphinx as a 'rhapsode'?[259] I believe the answer is yes. In short, the Sphinx is readily called 'rhapsode' because: 1) her repertoire, formally and thematically, fits comfortably under the umbrella of traditional epic; 2) her manner of performance is characteristically that of the solo rhapsode; and 3) the source of her poetry and the terminology applied to her performance are peculiarly rhapsodic.

The riddle's five hexameter verses are variously transmitted by Athenaios 10.456b (vol. 2, p. 491 §83 Kaibel); by the hypothesis to Sophokles *Oidipous tyrannos* (Dain and Mazon 1955–1960:2.70–71); twice by the scholia to Euripides *Phoinissai*, first in the hypothesis, then (with some changes and Asklepiades as the source)[260] in connection with verse 50 (Schwartz 1887–1891:1.243–244 and 256); the *Anthologia Palatina* 14.64; the scholia to Lykophron 7 Kinkel; and Tzetzes to Lykophron 7 (Scheer 1881–1908:2.11). Lloyd-Jones (1978:60) and Mastronarde (1988:6–7) offer convenient texts with apparatus. All of these are arguably formulaic multiforms of one another that bear the hallmarks of their oral composition and transmission. That Euripides

---

[258] Tarditi's interesting but ultimately unconvincing article is at least right on this point: bearing in mind that, when he uses 'to sew, stitch', he means 'to perform sequentially after another', he is surely right to aver that "la Sfinge non cuciva il suo canto in nessun contesto" (1968:142). Of course, as my argument in this chapter shows, if taken absolutely, the words "in nessun contesto" are wrong.

[259] According to Graziosi (2002:24), the scholiast to *Oidipous tyrannos* 391 complains that calling the Sphinx a 'rhapsode' is anachronistic. But the scholion, whose authority at any rate is limited by its chronological horizon, is not so definitive. In Papageorgius's edition its text reads: τὸ δὲ ὄνομα τοῦ ῥαψῳδοῦ καθ' Ὅμηρον ἢ μεθ' Ὅμηρον ἦν· ⟨ἀνεχρόνισεν οὖν ὁ Σοφοκλῆς⟩. The bracketed sentence (with ἀνεχρόνησεν corrected by Dindorf to ἀνεχρόνισεν) appears only in G (Laurentianus 2725), which also omits ἢ μεθ' Ὅμηρον. Other than in G, the meaning seems to be: 'The word "rhapsode" [='calling her a rhapsode'] was according to (dated to the time of) Homer or postdated Homer'. This observation agrees with the *Suidas* 4.287 P no. 70: 'The word "rhapsode" [*v.l.* "to rhapsodize"] is Homeric, or it may have been post-Homeric'. This is hardly a ringing indictment for anachronism. It is not clear whether the statement is meant absolutely ('the word rhapsode') or is to be limited to the Sphinx ('calling the Sphinx a rhapsode'). In other words, the scholiast may be (tentatively) ascribing to Homer an archaic epic that called the Sphinx a 'rhapsode' and whose usage Sophokles is deemed to follow. The reading of G is puzzling: 'The word "rhapsode" was according to Homer [i.e. "followed Homer"]. Therefore Sophokles was anachronistic'. Does this condemn as anachronistic Sophokles' (alleged) resort to Homeric usage? Hence Schneidewin's plausible conjecture οὐ καθ' Ὅμηρον (*apud* Papageorgius).

[260] This is Asklepiades of Tragilos, whose fragments are in FGH 12 (for the Sphinx, see F7, vol. 1a p. 169).

included a different version in his own *Oidipous* (fr. 540a Kannicht)[261] sharply raised the question of his own source and the source of the more widely reported version. Lloyd-Jones (1963:447) had approved Robert's conjecture that the better-known version (let us call it the 'vulgate')[262] probably came from the *Thēbais* or the *Oidipodeia*:[263] "[T]his version would not have been likely to be quoted by so many writers unless it had even better authority than that of Euripides" (Lloyd-Jones 1978:60). By 1978, his conviction had been undermined by Lesky 1966 [1928], unknown to him in 1963. Lesky's argument combines a hypothetical reconstruction of the *Oidipodeia* that condemns the riddle as a later addition with the observation that, in at least two matters of diction, the vulgate proves to be post-archaic and cannot therefore be ascribed to the epic cycle.

Lesky's further asseveration (1966:319) that, as a seven-thousand-line poem, the *Thebaid* had no room for the riddle displays his overconfidence. No matter. If the riddle belonged in the traditional Theban cycle at all, it merely needs a home there: if not the *Thebaid*, the *Oidipodeia* will do. Another question is whether it is an 'original' or 'secondary' element. Here we need not follow Lesky. Indeed, how much certainty one may have about the specific shape of archaic Theban epic can be judged from Mastronarde's comment:

> Most previous attempts to deal with the poorly documented back-ground to the Thebaid myth ... have been bedevilled by the desire to reconstruct specific literary artifacts of the archaic period ... . Even if such reconstructions inspired more confidence than they do, they would give a misleading impression of the 'sources' of Thebaid myth. For ... the literary distillations which survived in written form repre-sented only a part of a larger oral tradition, a tradition that varied according to time, locale, and artistic temperament of the bards. ... We have the scantiest possible fragments of the epic *Oedipodeia*, while those of the *Thebaid* are so few and uninformative that it can be debated whether they represent one or two poems. ... Equally, our scant knowl-edge of local cults and of the stories attached to them ... must create caution if not despair.[264]

---

[261] Snell et al. 1971–2004:5.1.571–574 nos. 540, 540a, and 540b. For a translation, see Collard and Cropp 2008:13.

[262] I do not call it yet the 'traditional' version, since this is the matter at stake I am seeking to establish: may this vulgate form of the riddle be considered 'traditional' in the same sense that (other?) poetry from the epic cycle is considered 'traditional'?

[263] Robert 1915:1.56–57: "Da ist nun in der Tat doch das weitaus wahrscheinlichste, daß die fünf Hexameter aus einem Epos stammen, mag dies nun die Oidipodie, die Thebais oder eins der anderen epischen Lieder vom Oidipus gewesen sein, deren es gewiß noch viele gegeben hat."

[264] Mastronarde 1994:17–18.

In the face of such uncertainty, Lesky asserts that, although the Sphinx was doubtless featured in the *Oidipodeia*, it was no riddling monster defeated by Oidipous' cleverness, rather, one he vanquished by sheer force (1966:320).[265] But what is the proof that such was the Sphinx of Theban cyclical epic? Lesky refers to the "certain impression" that the Sphinx in the much debated scholion of Peisandros[266] "did not pose riddles, but like other mythic pests merely picked its victims arbitrarily" (320). This comment seems at first incompatible with the scholion's explicit language that "[Oidipous] then married his mother after he solved the riddle."[267] Evidently, Lesky deems this statement one of those small interpolations that can be readily removed from the coherent subject matter of the scholion.[268]

But there is no narrative inconcinnity, much less contradiction, between the Sphinx's use of the riddle and the scholion's statement that she 'seized up small and great and devoured them'. Even her arbitrarily picking out young victims[269] of high and low estate is compatible with her performing the riddle.[270] It was to an audience of male Thebans—which we have no compelling reason to believe excluded the young[271]—that she repeatedly tendered the riddle. Upon

---

[265] A different kind of challenge is raised by Edmunds 1984 in a folklore study of the Sphinx's role in the Oidipous myth. He argues that her presence is an over-determining addition to conventional folklore patterns of patricide and mother-incest. Why this is of little moment for the *Greek* Oidipous myth is best stated by Mastronarde 1994: "We know of no Greek version in which [the Sphinx] was absent." Edmunds's approach is open to arbitrary discretion (cf. Bremmer 1988:46–47). He notes, for example, that, of the two main categories of folktales cognate with the Oidipous legend, one does not feature a parricide: the hero returns to his native land, defeats an invading army, and then marries his widowed mother (1984:158). Why then should we not consider parricide a secondary element? And yet Edmunds assigns the Oidipous legend to the "divine kingship succession narrative" story-pattern, an illustration of which (from the Near-Eastern city of Dunnu) features "parricide and incest ... in successive generations." There is confusion, moreover, in Edmunds's use of the terms 'primary,' 'secondary,' etc. Sometimes a 'primary' motif is one that is 'integral' to the plot; sometimes, it is its 'high point.' But what about a motif that no known version lacks? Does this fact make it 'primary'? If so, *eo ipso* the riddling Sphinx would be 'primary.' That the identity of the divine sponsor of the Sphinx depends on the version or does not exist or goes unmentioned hardly entails the secondary status of the Sphinx. As Mastronarde (1994:19) writes, "[i]n myth some monsters appear as punishment for misdeeds, others are simply present in a locale as a chaotic, destructive force which must be conquered by a god or hero so that human civilization can be founded or maintained" (cf. Gantz 1993:495).

[266] See *PEG* I.17–19 *Argumentum*? Bernabé = FGH 16 F10, vol. 1a pp. 181–182, with commentary in 495–496.

[267] εἶτα ἔγημε τὴν μητέρα λύσας τὸ αἴνιγμα.

[268] Here he follows Bethe. On this, cf. Moret 1984:80–81 with bibliography.

[269] It is clear from the iconographic and literary records that she had a distinct preference for youthful quarry. Cf. Gantz 1993:497.

[270] Cf. Moret 1984:10n6.

[271] It is not difficult to find vases that feature audiences of beardless *and* bearded figures. See, for example, Moret 1984:1.34 fig. 4 (Cat. 33), ca. 470/60 BC, or vol. 2 pl. 18 (Cat. 31), ca. 480.

their failure to solve it, she might well proceed to snatch whomever within her reach she fancied. This is precisely what the scholion to Euripides *Phoinissai* 45 tells us. Difficulties arise only if we presume that all encounters with the Sphinx were one-on-one affairs—a presumption positively refuted by the vases. As Gantz (1993:496) observes, "youths rather than grown men will scarcely have been sent out to try to solve [the riddle]." But if we assume the concurrence of the riddle and youth-snatching, what Gantz pronounces scarcely probable would seem to follow from the literary references to young victims and the graphic emphasis on naked and unbearded preys (although Gantz 1993:496 admits that occasionally there are beards).[272] The consideration of a broader and inclusive male audience disposes of this specious difficulty.

Many have thought that the account by Asklepiades preserved by the Euripidean scholiast was an attempt to bridge a bifurcated mythic tradition that featured, on the one hand, a youth-snatcher and, on the other, a riddle-posing Sphinx. Vase depictions were marshaled to support this view: some showed the Sphinx pursuing or attacking youths; others, assemblies of men (seated and standing) around a Sphinx on a base (usually a column), in all probability listening to her performance and debating the meaning of her riddle and its answer. But the literary sources as transmitted—scholars' suspicions of interpolations notwithstanding—fail to support any such bifurcation, and I believe that the iconographic evidence can readily be interpreted in harmony with the complex of Theban myth as we know it from our written sources. It is true that the earliest surviving items show males in flight, not figures seated or standing around the Sphinx. This seems to be a well-beloved decorative motif for drinking cups. One should not, however, infer *ex silentio* the non-existence of the riddle, for some vases that postdate the time when the riddle is attested still *only* show aggression and flight. A good example is the red-figure cup from ca. 510/500 listed as Cat. 23 by Moret 1984:168 (vol. 2 pl. 14).[273] Vase painting follows its own narrative conventions and one must be wary of making a simplistic correspondence between its iconography and the shape of mythic narrative. Consider, for example, Moret's observation that, although our written sources portray a predatory Sphinx who kills and devours her quarry (see Moret 1984:10n2 for *testimonia*), "les images ne mettent pas en évidence ses instincts carnassiers. Tout au plus s'apprête-t-elle à bondir sur le dernier des fuyards (Cat. 4 et 5).

Moret 1984:33 writes: "Sur plusieurs documents (Cat. 28–30 et 32), les interlocuteurs de la Sphinx sont des adolescents." But "[e]n général, les classes d'âge sont mêlées" (34).

[272] The two oldest items in Moret's catalog (1984:165 nos. 1 and 2), a pair of Siana cups by the C Painter from ca. 570/60, feature divergent choices: on the first, eight beardless youths flee the Sphinx; on the second, five bearded men. Cf. Moret 1984:10.

[273] Beazley Archive Vase no. 200716.

Le plus souvent, elle est immobile (Cat. 2 et 3). La passivité de la Sphinx est le trait dominant, et le plus déroutant, de cette imagerie" (10). Neither does black-figure painting ever show the winged beast flying. But we are hardly to conclude from this evidence either that she could not fly or that in early myth she merely scared and did not attack her victims.[274]

A similar bifurcation on an evolutionary scheme is the proposal that in earlier versions of the myth Oidipous did not defeat the Sphinx by answering her riddle but by sheer force. Mastronarde (1994:20) notes the possibility merely on the grounds of the scholia to Euripides *Phoinissai* 26, which reports that the hero killed the Sphinx and the Teumessian fox, the latter clearly a feat of strength. The reasoning seems hardly safe or necessary.[275] Better the cautious statement that follows: "Yet it is unnecessary and unsafe to assume a subtle (or careless) reference to physical slaying in the phrase σῶμα φονεύσας at *Phoen.* 1507 ... , and the illustrations on vases which have been thought to document the version without the riddle are both later in date than the illustrations of the riddle and open to other interpretations" (20). As it happens, two non-Attic vases attest to the riddle motif only some thirty years after our earliest vases pictured the fleeing victims (the C Painter Siana cups). Moret (1984:64–65) lists them as Cat. 100 and Cat. 101. They are an amphora in the British Museum (B 122) dated to ca. 540 BC and an amphora in Stuttgart (65/15) from ca. 530. The chronological gap between a hypothetical early form of the myth without the riddle and one that featured it is so small as to make the notion implausible and prejudiced.[276]

---

[274] Moret (1984:11) speaks of the "Sphinx's lack of aggressiveness" as a "fundamental particularity of the figurative tradition." See his discussion at 12 about the subordination of the narrative to the need for compositional symmetry and regularity.

[275] See the apposite remarks by Moret (1984:79–80), who is surely right to question on icono-graphic and literary grounds the broadly received dogma that the physical combat between Oidipous and the Sphinx was more primitive and must have preceded the invention of the riddle (cf. Bethe 1891:19–20).

[276] Kock 1961 is no better guide for this matter than Lesky. Early in his article he commits himself to the notion that, in contrast with the cunning figure of later myth, "Oidipus in the *Iliad* [is] a figure of physical strength" (11); and that "the Sphinx *did* enter the Oidipus saga as a creature of brute force and *only later* became the poser of riddles" (10–11, his emphasis). But what does he have as evidence for this? Other than the weight of recognized authorities (Robert, Bethe, Lesky, and Wehrli, all cited at 10n23), he only notes that "we find proof of [the secondary nature of the riddles] in the appearance of the Sphinx" (10). Apparently, "a monster with the body of a lion is a figure of strength and force and hardly compatible with intellectual prowess" (10). No thought is given to the possibility that, whatever its earlier Phoenician background, this "monster" might have been adopted by Theban epic from the start as a figure of force *and* cunning. Or that, even if *ex hypothesi* cunning was not hers in the very early stages of Theban traditions of epic, by the sixth century it was a well established trait and played a role in the *Oidipodeia*. Kock's preju-dice seems to be that *archaic epic* could not have told the story so and that we must wait until the very late archaic period for a bard to come up with the notion. But why? Kock thought Pindar the *terminus ante quem* for the riddle and owned that "about the Sphinx's riddle I follow

Katz 2006 is a *tour de force* that brilliantly demolishes such preconceptions. Devoted to the argument that "the story of the Sphinx and her riddle, if not also her name, goes back to Proto-Indo-European" (176), he offers compelling reasons to believe that 'riddling' (on whose definition see his 165n27) is of the Greek Sphinx's essence. About Edmunds's view that riddling is a secondary accretion in the story of Oidipous, Katz observes that there are plenty of Hellenists skeptical of Edmunds "and I expect that most Indo-Europeanists would be as well" (166n28).[277] To my mind conclusive is his reading of Hesiod *Theogony* 326–332, which follows Gotō 1995 in explaining ἐλεφαίρετο at 330 as "bamboozle (*vel sim.*)":[278] "That it is, according to Hesiod, the Nemean Lion who does the bamboozling, rather than his sister the half-lioness Sphinx herself, is obviously a matter that needs further discussion (see, briefly, Gotō 1995: 366 and 368 n. 10). Still, it is surely not difficult to imagine either that both siblings have a share in riddling or that a trait of the sister has here been applied to the brother."[279]

To move to Lesky's linguistic arguments, they can be reduced to two: that ἀλλάσσω in the vulgate version of the riddle betrays late diction, for its first attested occurrence is as recent as Theognis; and that the use of ἀφαυρός with τάχος (the choice of some manuscripts over the more common μένος) deviates from epic usage. The force of Lesky's arguments may be judged from his own ascription of the riddle to Antimakhos' *Thebaid*. If its alleged source is an author steeped in the archaic epic tradition, any perceived divergence from it must be small indeed.[280] But, in point of fact, this is an idle ascription, devoid of probative value: for, if the late diction Lesky alleges finds thus its convenient 'motivation' in Antimakhos' innovative use of epic diction, so also the riddle's traditional language will follow readily from Antimakhos' conventional

---

Lesky" (1961:21). But we have seen above that one vase depiction dates the motif of the riddle to no later than ca. 540 BC; and we now know of one vase from ca. 520 with fragments of the riddle's text in agreement with the vulgate version, which probably comes from the *Oidipodeia* (see below, p. 413). Given his views, Kock seems oddly unfazed by his admission that "the riddle as motif is as old as the hills" (21).

[277] Of course the pairing of Sphinx and Oidipous might postdate the inherently riddling character of the monster, although Katz offers further reasons for its age in the same footnote.

[278] Katz 2006:177–178, esp. 178n52, with the quotation at 177.

[279] The scholiast *ad loc.* had already written οf ἐλεφαίρετο· ἀντὶ τοῦ ἔβλαπτεν. Ὅμηρος δέ ποτε καὶ ⟨ἀντὶ τοῦ⟩ παρελογίζετο. Translators, however, often prefer the stronger and fatal 'to destroy' *vel sim.* But cf. scholia to Ψ 388 and Maehler 1982–1997:151–152 *ad* Bakkhylides 9.6–9. Modern scholars have hardly improved on the Hesiodic scholiast. West 1966 passes over the verb in silence. The *LfgE* s.v. ἐλεφαίρω offers the sole gloss "heimtückisch, durch Täuschung Schaden zufügen." But, faced with *Theogony* 330, it notes "spez. Nuance unklar" and suggests δήλημα at *Hymn to Apollo* 364 as if it were a parallel.

[280] Lesky himself admits that "Homerische Diktion ist wohl künstlich erstrebt—besonders auffällig der Einsatz eines homerischen Flickens in v. 2–3 = δ 417f.—, nicht aber erreicht" (1966:322).

reuse of Homeric poetry.[281] While this scenario is *a priori* possible, without any specific instances—which are not forthcoming—of ἀφαυρός or ἀλλάσσω in the fragments of the Colophonian that will vindicate his connection to the discontinuous usage charged by Lesky against the vulgate language of the riddle, Antimakhos amounts to little more than a rhetorical filler in Lesky's argument. But what to say about these two points of epic diction? It is true that ἀφαυρός, whose etymology remains unsolved,[282] is almost always used in the Homeric poems to qualify diminished corporal strength. The *LfgE* s.v. glosses it as 'schwach': "[W]ohl das eigentliche (u[nd] nicht weiter spezifizierte) Adj. für körperliche Schwäche; außer M 458 (von der Wirkung eines geschleuderten Felsbrockens) stets unmittelbar von körperlicher Leistungsfähigkeit." The five epic instances bear this out.[283] But it is not against these five, but against the 'exception' of M 458 that we must judge the riddle's use of ἀφαυρότερον with τάχος. There, Hektor lifts up a heavy stone and hurls it against the gate of the Argive wall: 'so Hektor lifted a stone and carried it straight to the boards ... . He came and stood very close by, and leaning his weight into the cast he struck the gate in the middle, having planted his feet well apart so that his projectile may not be too weak'.[284] For my purposes, what matters in Hektor's action is that he is hurling an object[285] and that the force of its impact is directly proportional to the speed imparted. This semantic development is not to be wondered at, since speed is a natural correlate of strength of limb. One would hardly be wrong to translate the last sentence of the passage, 'so that his projectile may not be too slow'. Indeed, the text goes on to note that 'the boards were severed [one from another] this way and that under the onrush (ὑπὸ ῥιπῆς) of the stone' (M 461–462). ῥιπή is always used of fast and impetuous motion. With this in mind, we might re-read υ 110: twelve women worked at the mills grinding barley and wheat; the rest already slept, because they had finished their work,

---

[281] For the combination of tradition and innovation peculiar to Antimakhos' poetry, see Lombardi 1993 and Matthews 1996.

[282] Cf. Beekes 2010:1.176 s.v. His references to "Fur." are to Furnée 1972.

[283] H 237, said of a 'feeble child' (παιδὸς ἀφαυροῦ) who is paired with a woman without fighting experience; H 457, of a god who, compared to Poseidon, is 'much weaker in hand and strength' (πολλὸν ἀφαυρότερος χεῖράς τε μένος τε); O 11, of Ajax, 'not the weakest (ἀφαυρότατος) of the Akhaians'; υ 110, of a woman at a mill who was 'feeblest of all [grinders]' (ἀφαυροτάτη δὲ τέτυκτο); Hesiod *Works and Days* 586, of men during the heat of summer, when they are 'weakest (ἀφαυρότατοι) because Sirius parches their head and knees'.

[284] ὡς Ἕκτωρ ἰθὺς σανίδων φέρε λᾶαν ἀείρας | ... στῆ δὲ μάλ' ἐγγὺς ἰών, καὶ ἐρεισάμενος βάλε μέσσας | εὖ διαβάς, ἵνα μή οἱ ἀφαυρότερον βέλος εἴη (M 453 457–458).

[285] *LfgE* s.v. βέλος B: "missile, projectile ... a generic term for anything cast or propelled with intent to damage: of arrows, spears or stones ... . The epith[ets]: ὠκύ [qualifies βέλεα in the sense] of spears (Ξ 407+) as well as arrows but would not be inappropriate with stones, especially sling-stones (see N 599f. 716)."

'but she alone was not yet ceasing [her work], but was slowest (ἀφαυροτάτη) [of them all]'. We may, of course, translate 'feeblest' rather than 'slowest', but it is clear that the focus is not on her bodily strength but on her slowness: she is taking much longer than her peers to finish her work. They have already gone to bed while she keeps on working. Once again, physical capacity is secondary to what it immediately translates into, i.e. speed. It bears emphasizing that these two make up one third of all the archaic epic instances of the adjective. Hence, for one in every three attested Homeric and Hesiodic occurrences, the gloss 'slow' for ἀφαυρός is at least as natural as, if not more pertinent than, 'weak'. One may therefore question Lesky's opinion that "man [kann] τάχος ἀφαυρόν nach dem sonstigen epischen Gebrauch des Wortes nicht ganz leicht sagen" (1966:319). Homeric usage may well have motivated Aratos' choice of ἀφαυρός in *Phainomena* 227 to express speed (οὐδὲν ἀφαυρότερον τροχάει). The truth is that the degree of discomfort involved in applying ἀφαυρός to inanimate nouns (speed, strength of a bridge, intensity of light, etc.) remains substantially the same from the archaic through the Hellenistic period and beyond.

What about Lesky's other objection, his assertion that ἀλλάσσω in the sense of 'to change' betrays post-archaic epic diction? Once again, my reply is that he is only partially right. It is true that ἀλλάσσω does not appear in the Homeric poems, and that, *ceteris paribus*, ἀμείβω might be considered a 'more traditional' choice (although it would be unmetrical in the same *sedes* and would call for a significant rewording of the riddle). All the same, Lesky has overstated his case, for ἀλλάσσω with the preverb ἐπί *does* occur in Homeric poetry once, at N 359, in a simile of hotly debated meaning:

> τοὶ δ' ἔριδος κρατερῆς καὶ ὁμοιΐου πτολέμοιο
> πεῖραρ ἐπαλλάξαντες ἐπ' ἀμφοτέροισι τάνυσσαν
> ἄρρηκτόν τ' ἄλυτόν τε, τὸ πολλῶν γούνατ' ἔλυσεν.

> N 358–360

> The end of strong strife and leveling war
> alternating it over both [camps] they tensed,
> unbreakable, impossible to undo, which undid the knees of many.

This passage was already a crux in ancient times and the attempts to solve it are numerous.[286] Space prevents me from entering into a detailed exegesis here. I will only make the interpretive choices necessary for my present argument, which focuses on the word ἐπαλλάσσω. Homeric parallels and context show that

---

[286] See Onians 1951:310–342; Michel 1971; Heubeck 1972 with older bibliography at 139n14; and Nothdurft 1978.

the subject τοί must be Zeus and Poseidon (the plural can stand for the expected dual τώ).[287] This identification is confirmed by ἀμφοτέροισι; had τοί stood for the warring camps (Krates' reading), this would privilege the alternative ἀλλήλοισι, apparently reported as a variant by Aristarkhos.[288] πεῖραρ is used metaphorically for the instrument that applies 'strife' and 'war' to both camps[289] and it is effectively a synonym of τέλος (Υ 101; cf. Β 121–122 Γ 291 Π 630). That it is conceived as a rope that effects conflict is clear from the adjectives ἄρρηκτον and ἄλυτον at Ν 360. The main verb τάνυσσαν conveys the tension of war and strife as it is wielded by the rival gods. It suggests the tensing of a bowstring (Δ 124) and is eminently suitable for a rope pulled in opposite directions. τείνω and τανύω are even used directly with ἔρις (Ξ 389 Π 662), πτόλεμος (Μ 436 Ο 413), μάχη (Μ 436 Λ 336 Ο 413), and πόνος (Ρ 400–401).

To come to the verb ἐπαλλάσσω, it arguably presupposes the availability of ἀλλάσσω. Thus, Lesky's contention necessarily contracts to a single point: that ἀλλάσσω *in the meaning used by the riddle* is foreign to epic.[290] But the ἀλλάσσω that underlies the Homeric participle invalidates Lesky's point and refutes his judgment that the riddle cannot therefore have an archaic-epic pedigree. This conclusion would seem to follow, unless of course ἐπαλλάξαντες in Ν 359 so differs in meaning from the riddle's ἀλλάσσει that the latter breaks radically new semantic ground. I do not believe that the evidence supports the requisite degree of semantic discontinuity. The easiest way for me to make this point is to draw attention to the following semantic proportion. Heyne (1802–1822:6.438) translates ἐπαλλάξαντες as "alternando, alternis" and draws attention to Pindar's use of ἐπαμείβεσθαι in *Pythian* 4.226. Heyne obviously construes ἐπαλλάξαντες intransitively. I do not believe that this is necessary. But neither voice is semantically determinative (see below), and my argument applies to the transitive and intransitive constructions just as well. Assuming, with Heyne, an intransitive construction, the semantic proportion is: ἐπαμείβομαι is to ἐπαλλάσσω as ἀμείβομαι is to X. The solution X is the intransitive ἀλλάσσω. For a transitive construction, the corresponding proportion is: ἐπαμείβω::ἐπαλλάσσω ~ ἀμείβω::X. X is now the transitive ἀλλάσσω. This proportion is significant because: 1) no one questions the archaic-epic pedigree of ἐπαλλάσσω in Ν 359;

---

[287] Cf. Janko 1992:92.

[288] Scholia AT to Ν 359a–b Erbse. Cf. Michel 1971:55.

[289] As Michel (1971:55) observes, there is only one πεῖραρ. Hence, the notion that two ropes or the two ends of a rope are being woven or tied together cannot be in play. According to the scholiast *ad loc.*, the latter was Aristarkhos' interpretation, on which see van der Valk 1963:97–99.

[290] Of course, Lesky does not put it so. By pronouncing the use "foreign to epic" ("der Gebrauch ... ist dem Epos fremd") and adding that one would instead expect ἀμείβειν, he makes clear that he objects to the word itself, not just its meaning (Lesky 1966:322).

and 2) Lesky admits that, in contrast to ἀλλάσσει, there would have been no reason to impugn a hypothetical ἀμείβει as post-archaic.[291]

Now follow a few observations in support of the semantic proportion. The context decisively bears Heyne's interpretation.[292] In view is the shifting battle fortune, as Zeus and Poseidon engage in a metaphorical tug of war.[293] This understanding is embraced, among others, by Köppen 1804–1823:4.48–50,[294] Bothe 1832–1834:2.178, Doederlein 1863–1864:2.16,[295] Ameis and Hentze 1905:25,[296] van der Valk 1963:99,[297] Michel 1971:52,[298] Heubeck 1972:142,[299] and Janko 1992:92.[300] The attentive reader of the preceding footnotes will have realized that scholars sometimes take the verb as transitive, sometimes as intransitive. This is not to be wondered at: the English 'to alternate' illustrates the reason well. Like ἐπαλλάσσω, it is as readily transitive ('they stretched the rope of war over both camps, alternating it') as it is intransitive ('alternating, they stretched the rope

---

[291] I have set up two proportions—one for the transitive, another for the intransitive, construction—because Greek usually opposes the transitive ἀμείβω to the intransitive ἀμείβομαι (cf. *DGE* s.v. ἀμείβω), whereas it regularly deploys the active ἀλλάσσω for both. There are exceptions, however, and ἀμείβω is used intransitively at Ψ 712.

[292] Leaf (1900–1902:2.29) remarks that "[t]he general sense of the passage would be better given if we could translate ἐπαλλάξαντες *alternately*. The use of ἀλλάσσειν makes this possible, but we should require the pres. part. in place of the aor." Bergren (1975:48–49) agrees: "[T]he (metrically equivalent) present rather than the aorist participle would be required. The action of ἐπαλλάξαντες, whatever it means, is not continuous." But van der Valk (1963:2.99) long ago corrected this syntactic misunderstanding: "Leaf (ad loc.) says that the participle of the aorist cannot be used in this meaning. However, this participle may convey the idea of concomitant circumstances, cf. Schwyzer, GG II, 388." I address this important syntactic point at length below, pp. 422ff., in connection with Hesiod fr. 357 MW.

[293] Heyne 1802–1822:6.438: "At h. l. Iupiter et Neptunus ἐτάνυσσαν πεῖραρ, utrinque extendunt, arreptis funis oris, nec coeunt et iunguntur, sed recedunt et disiungunt se; ut intento fune alter deficientibus viribus cedat alteri et est ἐπαλλάξαντες, alternando, alternis, dum modo hic funem intendit, modo validius ille." Cf. scholia A to N 359a Erbse; for the game (under σκαπέρδα), see Pollux *Onomastikon* 9 §116 (vol. 2, p. 179 Bethe) and Hesykhios Σ no. 854.

[294] "Ich fasse es so: wechselnd mit dem Ausgang des Kampfs, theilten sie beiden Völkern den Sieg zu, impenderunt utrisque, d. i. ἐπαλλάξαντες ἔδωκαν νίκην ἀμφοτέροις. ... Also ist ἐπαλλάττειν πεῖραρ πολέμου nichts mehr als permutare victoriam; und τανύειν πείρατα πολέμου ἐπί τινι, gleichbedeutend mit διδόναι νίκην τινί" (48–49).

[295] Interpreting τοὶ δὲ as the Akhaians and the Trojans, he translates: "Utrique alternantes vincebant ... victoria in utramque partem varie inclinabat."

[296] "[D]as Leitseil des Kampfes ... spannten sie wechselnd über beide Parteien, ... in verderblicher Wirkung bald für die eine, bald für die andere Partei."

[297] "Now ἐπαλλάττω also has the meaning of 'to alternate'. This meaning especially suits a situation in which a battle remains undecided. Therefore, we must render 'Both gods stretched the rope of war alternating it', i.e. both parties were alternately victorious."

[298] He translates: "Des heftigen Streites und allen gemeinsamen Krieges | Seil spannten sie wechselweise über beide Heere."

[299] Tentatively: "mit wechselndem Erfolg (ἐπαλλάξαντες)?"

[300] "Alternately, they pulled taut the rope of violent strife and equal war over both sides ... , i.e. the two gods made the armies fight a fierce and indecisive battle."

of war over both camps', i.e. 'they stretched by turns'). The transitive meaning is clearly presupposed by those who think that the metaphor describes the tying or knotting of a rope. LSJ s.v. ἐπαλλάσσω I documents the transitive use; II, the intransitive. Aristotle nicely illustrates the ready shift from transitive to intransitive: referring to animals who have interlocking teeth, he features the transitive construction in *Historia animalium* 501a18–19 (καρχαρόδοντα γάρ ἐστιν ὅσα ἐπαλλάττει τοὺς ὀδόντας τοὺς ὀξεῖς) and the intransitive in *De partibus anima-lium* 661b18–19 (τὰ δ᾽ ὀξεῖς καὶ ἐπαλλάττοντας [ὀδόντας ἔχει]). ἀλλάσσω allows for similar transitive and intransitive syntax.[301] The ἐπί of ἐπαλλάσσω, if intransitive, is best understood as referring to the succession of divine turn-taking.[302] If transitive, to the alternating target of the gods' tug of war, now the Akhaians, now the Trojans; or else it should be taken closely with the ἐπ᾽ ἀμφοτέροισι that follows: the πεῖραρ (or τέλος) of war and strife devolves *upon* both camps, now the Akhaians, now the Trojans.[303] I think that word order commends the transitive reading: πεῖραρ immediately precedes ἐπαλλάξαντες and should be taken *apo koinou* with this participle and τάνυσσαν. πεῖραρ lends itself to a triple verbal pun. In the metaphoric tug of war, either god gains the upper hand and is over-come by turns—now Zeus prevailing over Poseidon, now Poseidon over Zeus—according as one or the other succeeds in pulling the 'end' (πεῖραρ) of the rope towards himself. The oppositive pulling explains the tensing (τάνυσσαν) of the rope (πεῖραρ in the sense of σειρή). As the 'end' of the rope moves, now in the direction of Zeus, now of Poseidon, the gods 'repeatedly change' (ἐπαλλάξαντες) the 'end' or 'outcome' (πεῖραρ as τέλος) of the strife and battle (ἔριδος κρατερῆς καὶ ὁμοίου πτολέμοιο), a change that can be readily envisioned as an exchange or alternation: victory is recurrently exchanged for (or alternates with) defeat and vice versa. The (ex)change affects 'both camps' (ἐπ᾽ ἀμφοτέροισι), that is, the divine rivals play out their tug of war 'over', and hence 'upon' or 'against', both

---

[301] *DGE* s.v., which presents under I the transitive 'change, modify, alter, vary'; under II the transitive 'exchange' and 'repay'; under III the intransitive 'alternate, take turns'; and under IV the intransitive 'change, alter'.

[302] LSJ s.v. ἐπί G.4 speaks of "[a]ccumulation of one thing *over* or *besides* another."

[303] This 'sympathetic' construction, in which the preverb and the preposition motivate each other, must be responsible for the variant to Z 230 δ᾽ ἐπ᾽ ἀλλήλοις ἐπαμ. *apud* cod. E⁴ of Porphyry *Quaestiones Homericae* 1.96.24 (Schrader), which Erbse reports in his entry of the *LfgE* s.v. ἀμείβω III.2.a. Schrader himself does not report it, although, following Erbse, I have given the corresponding *locus* in Schrader's edition for ease of reference. On cod. E⁴ see Erbse 1969–1988:1.xx–xxi. Since I have not inspected the manuscript, I cannot tell whether the reading is reported as an unmetrical variant to the Iliadic text or whether the δ᾽ should be suppressed and one should print the resulting asyndetic reading τεύχε᾽ ἐπ᾽ ἀλλήλοις. For the elision, cf. τεύχε᾽ ἐπ᾽ αὐτῷ (Δ 504 etc.). For asyndeton in Homeric poetry, see Hermann 1806:98–100 *ad Hymn to Aphrodite* 177; Thiersch 1826:579–580 §312.33; Nägelsbach 1834:266–280 ("XIV. Beitrag zur Lehre vom homerischen Asyndeton"); Seymour 1895:18–19 §§l–n; and Chantraine *GH* II.351.

military contingents, and hence ἐπί, with Cunliffe (1963:143 s.v. II.1.a), should be understood as 'on, upon' "[i]n pregnant sense" (cf. Δ 178 E 384).[304] Insofar as πεῖραρ stands for a 'rope', it is natural to find the inescapable effect of the divine struggle upon the human agents restated metaphorically as an 'unbreakable' (ἄρρηκτον) rope, whose ends have been tied on either camp with knots that cannot be loosed (cf. θ 274–275).[305] The passage offers one final pun: the πεῖραρ that could not be loosed in turn 'loosed the knees of many'. For my present argument, the main point in all of this is that ἐπαλλάξαντες construed with πεῖραρ as 'outcome' (a sense that Cunliffe 1963 s.v. 2.c renders '[t]he coming to pass') readily translates as 'changing the outcome' (or 'exchanging the outcome [of victory for defeat and vice versa]'). In the riddle of the Sphinx, ἀλλάσσω conveys the (ex)change of one external appearance (φυή) for another,[306] and it is therefore in semantic continuity with the Homeric ἐπαλλάξαντες.

Lesky's linguistic arguments merely prove that, in the form preserved by the vulgate version, the riddle exhibits some features that, relatively speaking, are more recent than the corresponding Homeric ones. But just as the riddle displays formulaic language whose antiquity is neither the subject of skepticism nor without parallels in the Homeric poems, so also are there features in the *Iliad* and the *Odyssey* that some have claimed as interpolations precisely because they seem more recent than the scholar's preferred *termini ante quos* for the poems' composition. The truth is that the riddle's formulaic multiformity proves its oral transmission, just as its traditional diction strongly suggests its oral-traditional composition. Traditional epic poetry, the Theban cycle included, continued to be recomposed in performance with some measure of variability into the classical period. Even if, *arguendo*, we accept Lesky's view that ἀλλάσσω had not entered the poetic language with the meaning and in the construction exampled by the riddle until the time of Theognis—thus dismissing the implications of ἐπαλλάσσω at N 359—this hardly means that the riddle cannot derive from the Theban epic cycle. The *Theognidea* as a poetic corpus spanned the archaic and early classical periods. It too was traditional poetry, not epic but sympotic, whose growth must have had significant chronological overlap with the development of the Theban epic cycle, which rhapsodes continued to recompose in performance during much of the same period. Therefore, one cannot ascribe any one linguistic or lexical use by 'Theognis' to a particular period—certainly not to a period that is *ex hypothesi* later than a supposed dating of the *Oidipodeia*.

---

[304] I believe that the choice of ἐπί with ἀμφοτέροισι is further motivated by the preverb of ἐπαλλάσσω. See n. 303 immediately above.

[305] Either contingent suffers loss as it is pulled together with its divine patron in the direction of his prevailing opponent.

[306] The Homeric meaning is 'form' or 'figure' (see A 115, with Leaf's note *ad loc.*; cf. B 58 Γ 208 etc.).

One need only remember that attempts to fix in time a historical 'Theognis' resulted in seventh- and sixth-century dates as far apart from each other as a hundred years. Lesky's objections only have force under the premises 1) that Theognis marks a *terminus post quem* for the use of ἀλλάσσω that the riddle exhibits; 2) that the text of the *Oidipodeia* was definitively fixed (composed in writing?) sometime in the archaic period and was not subject to recomposition that might have resorted to late-archaic or early-classical diction; and 3) that Theognis 21 can be securely ascribed to a time that postdates the conjectural archaic date by which the *Oidipodeia* had been textually fixed. These premises are at worst fallacious, at best hardly necessary, and in any case not in harmony with the diachronic perspective of epic composition and performance advanced in this book. They do not comport with the culture of performance, epic and sympotic, of archaic and early classical Greece.

As it happens, there is conclusive pictorial evidence for the text of the riddle that dates to ca. 520/10. The Vatican red-figure *kylix* (16541) from about 470 BC had long been the oldest extant (fragmentary) textual witness to the riddle;[307] on it, between the Sphinx and a seated Oidipous, we read a retrograde AITPI. This is presumably κ]αὶ τρί[πον … , i.e. the beginning of the second verse of the riddle.[308] Moret (1984:40) reported the existence of a new witness some fifty years older than the Vatican *kylix*, which has since been published by Kreuzer (1992:86–88).[309] It is a fragmentary Attic black-figure *hydria* from Basel (coll. Cahn 855) dated to 520/10 (Moret:1984 vol. 2 pl. 23). Moret (1984:40) is surely right to underline that "à cette date (520/510 avant J.-C.), la version courante n'a pu être que celle de l'épopée." The photographs in pl. 23 are not easy to read. There is some disagreement whether the letters make sense. Immerwahr in his *Corpus of Attic Vase Inscriptions* no. 2072 writes that "they seem to be nonsense, but see below"—with a reference to Vollkommer (1991:60):

---

[307] Moret 1984:40 and 175 no. 87 (vol. 2 pl. 51.1) = *ARV*² 451.1.

[308] Or κ]αὶ τρί[πουν if we assume the Attic form. This cup is often thought to reflect Aiskhylos' satyr-play *Sphinx*. Cf. Simon 1981:28–31. To weaken its alleged connection with the epic version of the riddle, Lesky 1966:322 suggested that AITPI might stand for καὶ τρία. He added that the space after the second iota supported this reading over against καὶ τρίπον, because it could only accommodate one more letter. (So also Hoffmann 1997:80–82, apparently following Hartwig 1893:664 without argument.) But Lesky's rationale is invalid: whereas the missing kappa of καὶ falls on a line of fracture and we may legitimately assume it was lost, there was never anything after the iota of TPI. The inscription reads]AITPI, not]AITPI[. It might seem odd to us that vase painters should depict speech fragments, but this is a well-established fact which Beazley (1927:348–349) noted in connection with this very cup: "Such snatches of song, it is well known, are not uncommon on archaic red-figured vases. … [S]ometimes the snatch ceases in the middle of the word. … So in the Vatican cup with Oedipus and the Sphinx, all that Douris writes of the riddle is [κ]αὶ τρι … ."

[309] Beazley Archive Vase No. 43112. See also Vollkommer 1991:60 and n. 92.

"Auf dem genannten Fragment ist das Raten [der Bürger] besonders eindringlich wiedergegeben durch die Worte und Sätze, die über das ganze Bild hinweg verstreut sind." Moret prints the readings τετράπουν οὗ and καὶ τρ[,[310] which are in broad agreement with the vulgate version of the riddle.

Perhaps the late sources that quote the vulgate version took it from a tragedy no longer extant that incorporated this excerpt from Theban cyclic hexameter poetry. The scholiast to Euripides *Phoinissai* 50 explicitly cites Asklepiades' *Tragōidoumena* as his source for it. Lloyd-Jones (1978:60) writes that "this does not prove that the riddle was taken from tragedy, but it creates the presumption that it was." If so, Aiskhylos' *Oidipous* seems an obvious candidate.[311] Unlike the strongly innovative Euripides, the more conservative Aiskhylos is likely to have included a version substantially faithful to the rhapsodic recitation of the *Oidipodeia* in his own time.[312] If he is responsible for minor touches of linguistic updating, these cannot have been of any great significance: the failure of the later sources to ascribe the riddle to an author argues in favor of its ultimate traditional origin. In all probability, the original source was regarded as too obvious to call for specification. At the same time, given the tragedians' numerous treatments of Theban myth, one cannot rule out that Asklepiades

---

[310] Without autopsy, a definitive confirmation of Moret is impossible. But judging from a careful inspection of the photographs, he seems to be right. On pl. 23.1 I tentatively read a retrograde and horizontal ΕΠΕΙΔΑΝ ΓΕΡΑΣ. This, Moret reports there as ἐπειδὰν γῆρας. The epsilon graphemes (for ε and η), of admittedly odd shape and defectively drawn like digammas, correspond to Immerwahr 1990:xxii S6. Remarking on this shape in connection with nonsense inscriptions, Immerwahr notes that "although these forms [S6–7] may sometimes represent faulty epsilons, they are often used with consistency and in company with well-written epsilons, and I think it likely that they are to be read as digammas" (1990:140–141). Pl. 23.2 does, in fact, seem to offer regularly shaped epsilons. Nevertheless, I am satisfied that the odd S6's are epsilons too and that the readings reported by Moret are at least substantially right and make good sense. (I cannot say to what degree what appear as odd shapes might be due to faint traces invisible on the photographs.) Also on pl. 23.1 I tentatively read a retrograde, horizontal ΕΤΡΑΠ which shifts direction at the Π and continues downward with ΟΥΝ. If this is Τ]ΕΤΡΑΠΟΥΝ, it agrees with Moret's report of τετράπουν οὗ. But I cannot confirm his οὗ. Two letters follow ΠΟΥΝ; they seem an eta and a upsilon (ὑ?). The vase painter might have intended ΗΟΥ = οὗ. There is, in fact, a precedent for ὑ- ~ οὖ- in the Neandros black-figure cup, Boston 61.1073 dated to ca. 540, which spells ΗΥΤΟΣ for οὗτος (see Threatte 1980:260 and Immerwahr 1990:49 no. 229, 162, and pl. 14.64). At any rate, these readings seem substantially in harmony with the vulgate version of the riddle. The Attic form τετράπουν appears as an (unmetrical) variant in some of the multiforms, e.g. in Athenaios' version (corrected by Kaibel to τετράπον). As is well known, the source of the Attic -ου- remains a puzzle; it should have been -ο-, like the Homeric, or -ω- if from a lengthened grade (cf. Sihler 1995:117–118 §116.1 and Rix 1976:95 §105, 126 §137).

[311] Snell et al. 1971–2004:3.287–288. Cf. Nauck² no. 173.

[312] Tragedy can occasionally incorporate hexameter poetry as necessary (cf. West 1982:98, 128–132). This is precisely what happens, for example, in Euripides' *Oidipous* fr. 540a.7–10 Kannicht (Snell et al. 1971–2004:5.1.573).

may have excerpted from Theban epic the eminently relevant language of the riddle, even if no tragedy actually incorporated the verses.

In light of these considerations, I am not impressed by Lesky's arguments against the ascription of the vulgate version of the riddle to the Theban cycle. Neither seems West (2003a:41)—hardly a proponent of a performance-driven textual fixation of Greek archaic epic—who says of the vulgate version that "[it] is quoted by various sources which go back to Asclepiades of Tragilus .... There is a good chance that he took it from the *Oedipodea*."[313] For my argument it is inconsequential whether the various details associated with the Sphinx and relevant to her characterization as a rhapsode belonged as one coherent narrative in any particular poem. What matters is that they are all traditional features of the Theban myth complex that formed the subject matter of the Theban epic cycle. These features need not even be entirely consistent with each other, much less need they harmonize with later tellings of the Oidipous saga. Discordant details are in the nature of traditional multiforms. Hence, for example, it is not important whether the people of Thebes met 'daily' to discuss the riddle's meaning, as Asklepiades wrote, or just 'often', as we read in Apollodoros. More important is the agreement of these two sources—in all likelihood part of the traditional telling—that the Sphinx performed her riddle to an audience of Theban citizens often, like a rhapsode of rather limited repertory frequently reperforming the traditional poetry of his specialty (and exacting suitable 'compensation' for it).

There is, therefore, good reason to think that the riddle in its vulgate version goes back to well-known Theban cyclic epic. In my analysis of the *Homeric Hymn* 19 to Pan, I remarked on an important mimetic principle characteristic of archaic epic: it exhibits a poetics of performative self-referentiality that blends in complex ways the performance of a character within the narrative with the rhapsodic performance in progress. I also drew attention to Martin 1989, who has shown in detail how this mimetic principle, fundamental to rhapsodic poetics, decisively shapes the delivery of consecutive speeches in the Homeric poems. I suggest that a related kind of pragmatic blending accounts for Sophokles' designation of the Sphinx as a rhapsode. After all, as a singer she is marked by the performance a popular 'excerpt' of a celebrated body of epic. She is to her internal audience what the rhapsode is to the real-world audience. In short, she *is* the narrative's rhapsode. The traditional epic nature of her poetry, which bore the discernible hallmarks of an oral multiform, and the stability of her repertoire add to this portrayal. The riddle's form was the rhapsode's epic hexameter; its riddling subject matter, a recognized subclass

---

[313] A change of mind since West 1978a:293.

of archaic epic, closely allied to oracular and gnomic poetry.[314] As Bollack also noted, her itinerancy is typically rhapsodic: the very line that designates her as the 'she-rhapsode' also alludes to her coming ('when the she-rhapsode was here, the hound', Sophokles *Oidipous tyrannos* 391). Euripides fr. 540a.12 features the word ὕμνον just two lines after Euripides' version of the Sphinx's riddle. In all probability, the dramatist has adopted rhapsodic terminology to typify her performance. Apollodoros *Bibliothēkē* 3.5.8 §52 tells us that, like any other rhapsode, she had learned her riddle from the Muses (μαθοῦσα δὲ αἴνιγμα παρὰ Μουσῶν). And, finally, her recurring performance before an assembled audience of Theban citizens marked her out as an infamous representative of the preeminent archaic performer, the rhapsode. Apollodoros writes: 'after learning her riddle from the Muses, she would sit on Mount Phikion and would tender it to the Thebans ... [who] coming together often (πολλάκις) would search what it was that was being told [by the Sphinx]; and when they would not find it out, after snatching one [of them] she would devour him' (*Bibliothēkē* 3.5.8 §§52–53). The chronological extent of her recurring performances was dilated. Although Apollodoros notes that the citizens assembled to inquire into the meaning of the riddle, we are to imagine this meeting as an audience to the Sphinx's performance, discussing its meaning in her presence. The vases fully bear this out, regularly representing the Thebans gathered around a Sphinx who typically sits on a column. Asklepiades confirms Apollodoros: the Thebans would gather daily in assembly on account of the woeful riddle of the Sphinx. And when they would not understand it, she would seize whomever of the citizens she wanted.[315]

10.2.5 The *differentia* of the rhapsodic craft

Having examined the essential character of rhapsodic performance, studied the relevant Homeric passages, and surveyed the earliest attested instances of ῥαψῳδός, it is time to answer those who seek to divorce the rhapsodes' manner of performance from their poetic technique. These critics will accept relay singing as the defining *differentia* of rhapsodic delivery because the procedure was plain for everyone to see. But they reject the proposal that the solo stitching of traditional epic themes with traditional epic diction was also of the essence of the rhapsodic craft and set its practitioner *qua* 'rhapsode' apart from other kinds of ἀοιδοί. Yet this severance of composition from performance does violence to the fundamental insight that must guide a diachronic understanding of Homeric

---

[314] The scholion to Euripides *Phoinissai* 50 calls her a χρησμολόγος, and her riddle, χρησμοί. Cf. Nagy 1990c:147–150, 328–329 on αἶνος.

[315] Ἀσκληπιάδης δὲ λέγει τοὺς Θηβαίους εἰς ἐκκλησίαν καθ' ἑκάστην ἀθροίζεσθαι διὰ τὸ δυσαίνιγμα τῆς Σφιγγός .... ὁπότε δὲ μὴ συνίοιεν, ἁρπάζειν αὐτὴν ὅντινα ἂν βούλοιτο τῶν πολιτῶν (scholion to Euripides *Phoinissai* 45).

poetry: that the oral bard recomposed his song in performance. This implies that the manner of performance reflects the internal dynamics of composition and vice versa.

It should be clear from my analysis thus far that I view hypoleptic performance as entirely compatible with the poetics entailed by epic song-stitching in solo performance. In fact, I believe that the former was preceded by, and founded upon, the latter, for the principle of sequencing inheres in the composition of epic hexameter poetry and does not depend for its realization on a succession of performers at a festival. It is important, however, to add that rhapsodic compositional sequencing comes to fruition in the practice of relay performance. These two are complementary and intimately related facets of the classical rhapsode and his craft, and as such must be allowed to coexist as defining features. But the compositional sequencing practiced by a single rhapsode in performance holds diachronic priority over relays of several rhapsodes. And unless we are prepared to follow Else (1957b:33) in his judgment that ῥαψῳδός was a late label that issued from the practice of uncreative relay performance at the Panathenaia, we must accept the view that the performer himself or his audience could have coined, and in actual fact did coin, the professional label to make explicit reference to verse- and theme-stitching as was practiced by a solo epic performer.

Why should scholars prejudicially assume that audiences were not conscious of the traditional character of the diction and subject matter of Homeric poetry, and that they could not have tied this quality specifically to the performance of epic and its occasion?[316] Even children intuitively understand the traditional quality of bed-side story telling, as their insistence on a fastidious repetition of well-beloved story lines shows. The claim that the traditional character of the themes and the diction of epic was readily perceptible in their contrast with the themes and formal features of iambic, trochaic, elegiac, and lyric poetry does not entail an anachronistic focus of the epic performer and his audience on what was innovative over against traditional material in his composition. These other types of poetry adopted characteristic dictions peculiar to each and struck their own distinctive balance between tradition and innovation.[317] We should

---

[316] So, for example, Ritoók 1962: "Es fragt sich auch, ob das Publikum im 7. Jahrhundert einen so grossen Unterschied in Hinsicht des Stiles und besonders der stichischen Art fühlte, und ob es gerade diesen Unterschied für etwas so wesentliches hielt, wie Patzer es glaubt" (226).

[317] I am anxious to disown an unproblematic view of 'lyric' as poetry that stands in more or less straightforward synchronic contrast to 'epic.' I believe that epic (formally and thematically) derived diachronically, by a narrowing and stylization of its generic and performance conventions, from the larger whole of geometric and early-archaic Greek song traditions. This hypothesis, which I believe has comparative, anthropological, historical, and methodological support superior to its alternatives, means that archaic lyric in all of its manifold variety, though often thought to follow epic and to reflect epic themes and diction to various degrees, actually

not marvel if this consciously realized perception received a precise articulation via artisanal metaphors. As soon as there were recognizable Iliadic and Odyssean traditions, with determinable thematic outlines and characteristic formulaic diction, there would have been identifiable episodes that a rhapsode in performance would string together in a sequence that in time would develop into the fixed plot lines (οἶμαι) attested by our written versions. 'Stitching' would focus attention on the industry and artistry of the resulting song, made of traditional episodes (the material stitched). All at once, the partial episodes as well as the whole song would have been traditional and also borne the stamp of the performer's recomposition. There would have been no anachronistic focus on his 'creativity,' only on the artistry of the stitching—the felicity of the transitions, the compelling narrative of the stitched sequence, the skill of the diction used to render the individual episodes, the characterization of gods and heroes, the effect of their speeches, the adequacy and impact of the similes, etc.

It would not have been impossible to descend to the level of individual verse stitching. The traditional quality of Homeric epic must have been obvious to anyone who heard the rhapsode give expression to its long-established formal conventions. Scholars who dismiss the predictable formal quality of the hexameter as too abstract for an audience to realize in performance betray a surprising failure of imagination. I find no reason to doubt that listeners could and did perceive as recurring features its reduced pitch accentual melody, its rhythms, caesuras, cadences, and the overall effect of its bridges, cola, and the consistent arrangement of words by their metrical shapes.[318] This quality, cumulatively reinforced by each new line, would create the impression of a long array of near identical units of utterance, each perceptible as an individual whole, yet cleverly stitched by the rhapsode to the preceding and following verse with various

---

represents a parallel development to archaic traditions of epic performance. I do not, of course, *a priori* rule out the possibility of synchronic interactions between them at various points of the diachronic continuum.

[318] Cf. Kirk 1985:17–30 and 1966a, with bibliography. The Latin grammarian Diomedes reflects the ancients' controlling awareness of sequence in epic (and, incidentally, of epic's connection to oracular language) when he writes in his *Ars grammatica* (*GL* 1.484 Keil): "epos autem appellatur, ut Graecis placet, παρὰ τὸ ἕπεσθαι ἐν αὐτῷ τὰ ἑξῆς μέρη τοῖς πρώτοις. praecipue vero hexameter versus epos dicitur, quoniam quidem hoc versu verba responsi in mutuam, ut sic dixerim, consequentiam primus deus vates conprehendit, unde postea abusive verbum et solutae orationis ipsa scriptura consequens ab aliis epos dictum" ('*epos* moreover receives its name, as the Greeks think, "from the succeeding parts in it following the former." It is particularly the hexameter verse, however, that is called *epos*, since indeed the god first as oracle-giver expressed in this verse the words of his response in mutual (con)sequence (so to say), whence later by an abuse of terminology a word even of prose was called *epos* by others because it "follows" by the very writing'). The popular etymology ἔπος < ἕπεσθαι attested by this statement speaks forcefully for the view that notions of sequence are intrinsic to epic poetry.

semantic and morpho-syntactic strategies of periodicity and enjambment.[319] Even verses that are not self-standing semantic units enjoy the completeness of their formal structures. It is arguably the interplay between this prosodic wholeness and the rather common syntactic and semantic overruns[320] that would have impressed the audience the most, with an overall effect that the metaphor of stitching parts into a whole compellingly captures. This is the very effect Kirk (1985:34) notes: "The progressive form of enjambment, in particular, encourages the building up of longer sentences in a linear mode. Sometimes one can almost hear the components of a sentence[321] being cumulated one upon another in an accretive technique that can be prolonged or curtailed by the singer at will." There is no need of the written page to feel the impact of the stitching technique. At first, Homeric epic was sung to the four-string *kitharis* or phorminx.[322] Even if we believe, with West (1981:121–122), that the notes traced the rise and fall of pitch accentual patterns and potentially each verse had its own melodic line, the reduced range of the melodic possibilities vis-à-vis those of lyric (which used the seven string lyre)[323] together with the overriding effect of the hexameter's recurring rhythms, punctuated by the verse-end pause before picking up again, will have conveyed in clear perceptible outlines the traditional architecture of Homeric performance: the rhapsode performed his song by stitching smaller units one onto another—prosodic, formulaic, thematic, etc.—artfully expanding and abridging his material according to the need of the moment. These considerations should meet Ford's desideratum that rhapsody refer to "concrete aspects of the performance or occasion" (1988:302).[324]

10.2.6 Stitching or weaving?

We have seen that etymology supports the view that the rhapsode is an ἀοιδός who 'stitches' or 'sews together' his song. But here I must deal with a final objection: some scholars have used 'stitch' and 'weave' as if they were interchangeable

---

[319] Cf. Kirk 1985:30–37 and 1966b.

[320] Kirk 1985: "[W]hole-sentence verses are now in a minority of one in six or more" (31).

[321] For Kirk, sentence is the supra-linear unit of meaning. His previous section is titled "From verse to sentence."

[322] Or at least it is the Panhellenic stylization of local poetries that were so sung. Cf. West 1981:125–126 and West 1992:52–53.

[323] West 1986:43–44 notes that the hexameter hymn to Asklepios from Epidauros (West 1992:279 no. 11), although written for seven strings (the fashion since the seventh century BC), featured the same melody for every line. After proposing that it may be a traditional one, if slightly modernized, inherited from the archaic period, West adds: "[T]he eighth-century aoidos sang epic poetry on four notes, the four notes to which his phorminx-strings were tuned, and ... he followed the contours given by the word accents. That would mean a different melodic configuration for each verse, though it would be compatible with a broad pattern repeating from line to line" (45).

[324] Cf. Notopoulos 1964:58–59.

terms in practice. The equation, however, distorts the essential character of rhapsodic delivery, which should not be likened to the composition and performance of genres that do not share a comparable traditionality of form and subject matter. This misleading equivalence can only be put to rest once we acquaint ourselves with the technique of sewing in the Greek context. For as Durante (1968b:281n51) has shown, the verb ῥάπτω takes as direct object its product, not its means.[325] Therefore, the metaphor of song-stitching *per se* does not spell out in full the process by which the genesis of the song is envisioned. Our interpretation of the Hesiodic fragment 357 MW, that most important witness to the craft of the rhapsode, will depend crucially on the process entailed by ancient sewing and stitch-work. The scholiast informs us that, according to the late-classical Atthidographer Philokhoros, rhapsodes received their name from their practice of 'composing[326] and stitching the song' (ἀπὸ τοῦ συντιθέναι καὶ ῥάπτειν τὴν ᾠδὴν). In support, the following is allegedly quoted from Hesiod:[327]

> ἐν Δήλῳ τότε πρῶτον ἐγὼ καὶ Ὅμηρος ἀοιδοὶ
> μέλπομεν, ἐν νεαροῖς ὕμνοις ῥάψαντες ἀοιδὴν,
> Φοῖβον Ἀπόλλωνα χρυσάορον, ὃν τέκε Λητώ.[328]

Marx (1925:399) construed the syntax as μέλπομεν ἐν νεαροῖς ὕμνοις ... | Φοῖβον Ἀπόλλωνα and rendered it, "[i]n Delos haben damals zuerst ich und Homeros, die Dichter, besungen in neuen Hymnen, nachdem wir das Lied ersonnen hatten, den Phoibos Apollon." But this translation depends on Fränkel's unincisive "ersinnen" and entails the implausible view that 'Hesiod' is drawing attention to a compositional phase *before* the performance, at which the song(s) would have been stitched. There is a much better explanation for the aorist participle (see below). Clearly the focus of the fragment is on the *performance* in Delos, not on any preliminaries.

A further weakness of Marx's reading is that his punctuation—"μέλπομεν ἐν νεαροῖς ὕμνοις, ῥάψαντες ἀοιδὴν, | ..."—about which he is rather emphatic,[329] is not true to archaic epic diction: whenever archaic epic specifies the manner of performance designated by μέλπειν, μέλπεσθαι, or εὐμολπέω, it invariably resorts either to a simple adverb or, more often, to an accompanying participial

---

[325] "Als Objekt von ῥάπτειν ist ... das Ergebnis der Arbeit und nicht der bearbeitete Stoff anzusehen."

[326] In its etymological sense 'com + ponere' = 'to put together', 'to construct'.

[327] It is not clear whether the quotation too is taken from Philokhoros. The fragment is classified among the "dubia" by Merkelbach and West (fr. 357). The reference to 'Homer' dates it to the late sixth or early fifth century BC.

[328] Because the correct translation of this fragment depends crucially on the analysis below, I forgo a translation here which would seem to beg the question.

[329] "Wie durch die Interpunktion deutlich gemacht ist, gehört μέλπομεν ἐν νεαροῖς ὕμνοις zusammen" (Marx 1925:399).

phrase. To prove the point, I list here all the passages included by the *LfgE* s.vv.: ἐρατὴν δὲ διὰ στόμα ὄσσαν ἱεῖσαι | μέλπονται (Hesiod *Theogony* 65–66); θεαὶ δ᾽ ἐξῆρχον ἀοιδῆς | Μοῦσαι Πιερίδες, λιγὺ μελπομένης εἰκυῖαι (Hesiod *Shield* 205–206); εὐμόλπει μετὰ χερσὶν ἔχων λιγύφωνον ἑταίρην (*Hymn to Hermes* 478); νύμφαι ὀρεστιάδες λιγύμολποι | φοιτῶσαι πυκνὰ ποσσὶν ἐπὶ κρήνῃ μελανύδρῳ | μέλπονται (*Hymn to Pan* 19–21); μετὰ δέ σφιν ἐμέλπετο θεῖος ἀοιδὸς | φορμίζων (δ 17–18). So strong is this compositional habit, that μέλπεσθαι attracts the near-obligatory participle even when it only describes the performance in a rather indirect way; in the following example, its authority and excellence, as well as the corresponding social standing of the performer, are implied by the high regard in which he is held: μετὰ δέ σφιν ἐμέλπετο θεῖος ἀοιδός, | Δημόδοκος, λαοῖσι τετιμένος (ν 27–28). Α 472–474 exhibits a cognate construction: the unqualified participial form μέλποντες is coordinate with another participle, ἀείδοντες, which specifies it: οἳ δὲ πανημέριοι μολπῇ θεὸν ἱλάσκοντο | καλὸν ἀείδοντες παιήονα κοῦροι Ἀχαιῶν | μέλποντες ἑκάεργον.[330] μέλπεσθαι is used without qualification in Π 182 and *Hymn to Hermes* 476. The adjectives in *Hymn to Apollo* 197–198[331] pertain to Artemis' physique; if at all, only οὔτ᾽ αἰσχρή might hint at the quality of her performance. And in Η 241[332] δηΐῳ ... Ἄρηϊ cannot denote instrument or manner[333] but must be a locatival dative ('I know how to sing-and-dance standing my ground [lit. 'in stationary combat'] in destructive battle')[334] or a dative of interest ('I know how to sing-and-dance for hostile Ares in stationary combat').[335]

In light of these parallels, it is perhaps unsurprising that the text is punctuated μέλπομεν, ἐν νεαροῖς ὕμνοις ῥάψαντες ἀοιδήν, | ... by Drachmann in his

---

[330] Because μέλποντες ἑκάεργον reprises the main clause μολπῇ θεὸν ἱλάσκοντο, it functions effectively as μέλποντο ἑκάεργον. This happens to be the reading of *Etymologicum Magnum* 657.4–5, col. 1858 Gaisford (cf. scholia A *ad* A 474a), which is only marginally metrical (cf. West 1982:38 under 'd'; the verse-initial sequence '-οντο CV-', here μέλποντο *ϝε-, is not exampled in Homer or Hesiod). The sixth Pindaric paean, fr. 52(f).15–18, cited as a parallel by the *LfgE* s.v. μέλπω Β.1, exhibits similar syntax. It assigns to the main verb κροτέο[ντι the description of the performance and adds to it the participle μελπ[ό]μεναι qualified simply by θαμινά: τόθι Λατοίδαν | θαμινὰ Δελφῶν κόραι | χθονὸς ὀμφαλὸν παρὰ σκιάεντα μελπ[ό]μεναι | ποδὶ κροτέο[ντι γᾶν θο]ῷ.

[331] τῇσι μὲν οὔτ᾽ αἰσχρὴ μεταμέλπεται οὔτ᾽ ἐλάχεια, | ἀλλὰ μάλα μεγάλη τε ἰδεῖν καὶ εἶδος ἀγητὴ | Ἄρτεμις ἰοχέαιρα (*Hymn to Apollo* 197–199).

[332] οἶδα δ᾽ ἐνὶ σταδίῃ δηΐῳ μέλπεσθαι Ἄρηϊ.

[333] As might be the case with Α 521 Ν 684 Π 79 (so Chantraine *GH* II.78 §106 under "Remarques I").

[334] Perhaps an ironic oxymoron, as Mader suggests in the *LfgE* s.v. Ἄρης Β.2εβ.dd (col. 1261, lines 48–52), where the reference to Π 610 should read Π 617. See generally the *LfgE* s.v. Ἄρης Β.2ε for the god as a metonymy of 'fight, battle'. This locative would parallel the use of ὑσμῖνι in μέμασαν δ᾽ ὑσμῖνι μάχεσθαι (Β 863), for which see Ameis and Hentze 1877:158 and Chantraine *GH* II.78 §106 (under "Remarques I"). Cf. Θ 56.

[335] So Leaf 1900–1902:1.316 ("to dance the war-dance to Ares"; "Hector means, 'I can dance the war-dance not only in mimicry at a feast of Ares, but in grim reality on the battle-field'") and Kirk 1990:268 ("dance for Ares"). Cf. Chantraine *GH* II.73 §95.

Pindaric scholia and by all the editors of Hesiod's fragments without exception: Marckscheffel, Goettling, Kinkel, Sittl, Rzach, Evelyn-White, Merkelbach and West, and Most.[336] Indeed, the Hesiodic fragment follows the uniform usage reviewed above, that is, the verb μέλπομεν (here, in the rarer active voice) is qualified by the participial clause ἐν νεαροῖς ὕμνοις ῥάψαντες ἀοιδήν. Although mistaken in his attempt to construe ἐν νεαροῖς ὕμνοις immediately with μέλπομεν, Marx cited helpful parallels for use of ἐν in adverbial clauses of manner or instrument. For example, Pindar *Olympian* 5.19 refers to 'calling' to the sound of ('accompanied by') Lydian pipes (Λυδίοις ἀπύων ἐν αὐλοῖς); in *Isthmian* 5.27 brave warriors are celebrated with lyres and the many-toned sounds of pipes (κλέονται δ' ἔν τε φορμίγγεσσιν ἐν αὐλῶν τε παμφώνοις ὁμοκλαῖς); in *Nemean* 3.79 Pindar sends a drink to be sung to the accompaniment of the Aiolian breaths of pipes (πόμ' ἀοίδιμον Αἰολίσσιν ἐν πνοαῖσιν αὐλῶν); and Sophokles *Philoktētēs* 1393–1394 envisions arguments that are instrumental to persuasion (τί δῆτ' ἂν ἡμεῖς δρῷμεν, εἰ σέ γ' ἐν λόγοις | πείσειν δυνησόμεσθα μηδὲν ὧν λέγω;).[337] We must now ask ourselves how 'we sang Phoibos Apollo' relates to the participial clause 'stitching the song with/in new hymns'.[338]

A few comments about the aorist participle ῥάψαντες are in order. We know that participles detail aspect, not time.[339] As Kühner-Gerth II.1.197 §389.E notes: "Während [das Partizip des Präsens] die Handlung in ihrer Entwickelung darstellt, bezeichnet [das Partizip des Aorists] dem Momentanbegriffe des Aorists entsprechend dieselbe bloss als Handlung gleichsam begebenheitlich." "Momentan" need not be restricted to duration of time ('instantaneous'). It may also refer to the verbal action seen complexively: "The complexive aorist is used to survey at a glance the course of a past action from beginning to end … . This is often called the 'concentrative' aorist, because it concentrates the entire course of an action to a single point" (Smyth §1927; cf. §1872.c.4). Given the imperfect μέλπομεν, nothing in the syntax would prevent Marx's view that ῥάψαντες had preceded the action of the main verb.[340] But it is well known that, when the participle merely restates the main action under a particular aspect, it can be

---

[336] Marckscheffel 1840:376 fr. 221; Goettling 1878:343 fr. 227; Kinkel 1877:174 fr. 233; Sittl 1889:625 fr. 180; Rzach 1908:221 fr. 265; Evelyn-White 1914:280 *fragmenta dubia* no. 3; Merkelbach and West 1967:176 fr. 357; Most 2007:354 fr. 297. It is so received by the *LfgE* s.v. μέλπω B.2.

[337] All these in Marx 1925:399.

[338] In accordance with my aspectual analysis immediately below, I have translated the aorist with an English present participle and forgo the conventional past participle 'having stitched'.

[339] K-G II.1.182 §389.3: "[sie] bezeichnen ebenfalls nicht die Zeitstufe, sondern nur die Beschaffenheit des durch sie ausgedrückten Verbalbegriffes." Cf. Smyth §1872.

[340] Cf. K-G II.1.199 §389.E, Anm. 8.

coincident with it.[341] I submit that this is precisely the case here: 'we sang by stitching' ('in that we stitched'). In such cases, both the main verb and the participle are usually in the aorist. Although less common, an aorist participle with a future, present, or imperfect main verb are also sometimes found.[342]

But we still need a rationale for the choice of the aorist, since the present participle ῥάπτοντες would have suited the meter just as well. I submit that there are two equally valid alternatives. The first looks to the pragmatic contrast between imperfect and aorist as regards 'focus function':[343] by using the aorist, the fragment draws attention to the act of stitching, viewed complexively, and to its product, the song. The syntax effectively underlines the 'stitching,' i.e. the manner in which the action in progress, 'singing,' comes to pass. It is the concentrative aspect of the aorist that makes possible the pragmatic focus on the stitching.[344] ῥάπτοντες would have placed 'stitching' pragmatically on a level

---

[341] Stahl 1907: "In besonderen Fällen jedoch kann das Partizipium des Aoristes auch bei Gleichzeitigkeit eintreten, und zwar zunächst ... wenn die durch das Partizipium und das übergeordnete Verbum bezeichneten Erscheinungen in der Weise als Tatsachen an sich hingestellt werden, daß sie vollständig zusammenfallen, die eine in der anderen oder durch die andere besteht, in welchem Falle das Partizipium im Deutschen durch 'dadurch daß, damit daß, darin daß' wiedergegeben werden kann" (212–213).

[342] See Stahl 1907:213–214.

[343] Sicking and Stork 1996:103. 'Focus function' concerns the pragmatics of discourse organization: "'[F]ocus function' [is] the part of the unit involved that, from a viewpoint of information, is the most prominent in the sense of being its 'nucleus', or the part 'to which the speaker especially draws the hearer's attention'" (Sicking and Stork 1996:75n121). Sicking surveys "postposed aorist participles" in Herodotean narrative at 51–52. They describe further the action of the main verb or give additional details connected with it. From the viewpoint of Herodotean discourse pragmatics, Sicking shows that this information is not presented as an element of the main sequence of events. These participles are akin to narrative 'footnotes,' although the information they convey is hardly nugatory. In the Hesiodic fragment, ῥάψαντες could be similarly read as an 'aside': "It was then that Homer and I first sang on Delos—we stitched our song with new hymns—[we sang] Phoibos Apollo ... ." This 'aside' is of great interest, for it adds the specific manner of the singing, viewed complexively. Sicking summarizes his investigation thus: "Aorist indicative verb forms and participles 1) are to be assigned focus function (or: are the 'nucleus') in the clause they are part of, and 2) are the predicate of a self-contained statement" (103). Although I believe that Sicking has correctly identified the pragmatic implications of the aorist stem, I also share Wakker's concerns about excessive oversimplification (Wakker 1998). In particular, I too believe that the pragmatic value of the aorist vis-à-vis the present stem can be understood as a consequence of the semantic opposition of the 'complexive' to the 'non-complexive' aspect. Wakker prefers 'completed' and 'not completed' (361–362 and n. 9), where completion may be understood in temporal or discursive terms. I would rather steer clear of labels that seem to privilege time.

[344] As noted, the aorist, as the unmarked verbal stem, does not *per se* imply anything about the temporal extent of the action. It only contemplates it in its 'bare form.' It is sometimes called 'punctual,' and although the 'point' in question is often considered 'a point in time' the aorist does not inherently refer to time at all. In this case, inasmuch as the participle is the unmarked aorist, the syntax does not pronounce on whether the 'stitching' goes on while the song is in progress or else happens before, or at a given point during, the singing. Had it been a present

with 'singing.' The syntax that corresponds to this first alternative parallels that of ἐπαλλάξαντες in N 359, which I studied above. A second explanation is that the fragment portrays Hesiod and Homer as rhapsodes engaged in competitive relay poetics, with Hesiod taking up his singing right where Homer left off his.[345] Since *ex hypothesi* there would have been only one 'seam' at which the performances of Homer and Hesiod were joined—each discrete performance being one of the 'new hymns' stitched together—the stitching would have taken place only once in the course of singing. Hence the aorist.

Whichever our preference, I do not agree with Marx's interpretation, which makes the stitching precede the singing. Neither do the many scholars who, whether instinctively or deliberately, have rendered the aorist as coincident with the imperfect, i.e. 'stitching' (not 'after stitching' or 'having stitched').[346] Rather, the νεαροὶ ὕμνοι are the raw material stitched in performance. This follows from the fact, noted above, that ῥάπτω takes as direct object the product of the sewing/stitching. If 'new hymns' had stood for the song stitched, it should have been in the accusative, in apposition to ἀοιδήν; or 'song' should have been in the genitive and construed with 'new hymns' in the accusative:

---

participle, we would know that the stitching had some overlap with the μέλπομεν; but only the context could settle whether it was a parallel, unconnected action or one upon which the main verb depended. The aorist allows the participial action to receive pragmatic emphasis without prejudging whether it is actually durative or non-durative. This is what Ruipérez (1991:81 §132) calls "aoristo neutro," indifferent to duration. Note his examples *ad loc.* of "neutral aorists" that belong to non-transformative durative semantemes.

[345] See Martin 2000 for the suggestion that fr. 357 MW has the *Hymn to Apollo* in view, stitched together by Homer and Hesiod in competitive performance (the Delian section being Homer's and the Pythian, Hesiod's). Martin's proposal is not new, as his review of previous scholarship shows. Among earlier contributors is Else (1957b:30–31), who taking up Crusius (1895:717–719) had written the following: "Here ἀοιδήν denotes the common content of the whole, viz. Apollo (Ἀπόλλωνα in apposition with ἀοιδήν), which is the joint product of the two bards' efforts while the ὕμνοι are their individual contributions: 'We sang, "stitching" the song [namely Apollo, etc.] in (the medium of, out of) new hymns.'"

[346] Most 2007: "In Delos then for the first time Homer and I, bards, sang, stitching together our song with new hymns" (355); Evelyn-White 1914: "Then first in Delos did I and Homer, singers both, raise our strain—stitching song in new hymns" (281); Nagy 1996c: "Then it was, in Delos, that Homer and I, singers [*aoidoi*], for the first time sang, in new hymns, sewing together [*rháptō*] the song [*aoidē*]" (73); Powell 1997: "In Delos, Homer and I, singers of oral song, sang of Phoebus Apollo ... stitching together oral song in fresh hymns" (31–32); Taplin 1992: "Then first in Delos Homer and I, the singers, stitching together our song in novel hymns" (41n57). On the hypothesis of respective solo performances, the point of the fragment's πρῶτον would not be that Hesiod and Homer had never sung or stitched before. Rather, that they performed together "then for the first time" (never before had they sung for the same audience); or that they performed (together) in Delos "then for the first time" (never before had they sung, or sung together, at the Delian festival). If, on the other hand, we prefer the hypothesis of hypolepsis, πρῶτον would make clear that never before had Hesiod and Homer engaged each other in competitive relay poetics (so Crusius 1895:717).

νεαροὺς ὕμνους ῥάψαντες ἀοιδῆς *vel sim.*, with a properly metrical complement (cf. θ 429). Most (2007:355 fr. 297) is surely right to translate "stitching together our song with new hymns."[347]

The alternative construction that still keeps to the manufacturing metaphor but takes ἐν νεαροῖς ὕμνοις closely with ἀοιδήν is not readily intelligible. Stitching a part into a larger whole is possible, but what kind of 'song' could be stitched in/into new hymns? The resulting construction, moreover, effectively contravenes the usage rule that the product of the stitching should be the direct object of ῥάπτω. At any rate, this unattractive translation would still make the case that ῥάπτω denotes the combining of smaller units of performance into larger ones (in this case, the 'song' into 'new hymns'). Evelyn-White (1914:281 "Doubtful Fragments" no. 3) adopts this alternative and makes it marginally acceptable to the English ear by translating ἀοιδήν, the concrete song of performance ('our song'), merely as 'song' in the abstract (i.e. 'the activity of singing' and, by implication, its product in the abstract). 'Stitching song in new hymns' would be equivalent to 'stitch-singing new hymns', where the awkward 'stitch-singing' stands for 'singing in a stitching mode' (however understood).[348] There is yet another way to take ἐν νεαροῖς ὕμνοις, namely, as the performative context of the activity of stitching. Anakreon illustrates this alternative when he opposes Scythian drinking 'with clatter and shouting over wine (παρ' οἴνῳ)' to drinking moderately 'in [=accompanied by] beautiful hymns (καλοῖς | ... ἐν ὕμνοις)'.[349] The parallel is not perfect, because Anakreon's 'drinking' is only concomitant with the singing of hymns; in the Hesiodic fragment, 'stitching our song' is integral to 'in new hymns'. This reading of the adverbial ἐν-clause does not construe it closely with the manufacturing metaphor of stitching. For this reason, although possible, I think it is less likely and compelling (note that the governing verb is ῥάπτω, not ῥαψῳδέω). It leaves undefined the particulars of

---

[347] Cf. Lucian *Toxaris* §10: πολλοὺς καὶ ἀξιοπίστους μάρτυρας τοὺς ποιητὰς παρεχόμενοι τὴν Ἀχιλλέως καὶ Πατρόκλου φιλίαν ... ἐν καλλίστοις ἔπεσι καὶ μέτροις ῥαψῳδοῦντας. Here, the classification of ἐν καλλίστοις ἔπεσι καὶ μέτροις as an adverbial clause of 'means' shades readily into one of 'manner.' The choice of one over the other depends on how closely the writer is adhering to the manufacturing metaphor. With ῥαψῳδέω, 'manner' might be thought preferable; with ῥάπτω, 'means.'

[348] Evelyn-White's translation sounds acceptable to the English ear because of expressions like 'blowing glass into bottles', where 'into' is not understood locally ('putting glass into existing bottles by blowing') but as capturing the manufacturing process through which the glass is turned into bottles (cf. *OED* s.v. "into" A.I.6a). His "stitching song in new hymns," even as it evokes manner (cf. *OED* s.v. "in" I.12c)—and in so doing impermissibly disregards epic diction— effectively amounts to 'stitching song into new hymns'. This inverts the intended terms of the manufacture, making 'song' the raw material and 'hymns' the product.

[349] ἄγε δηὖτε μηκέτ' οὕτω | πατάγῳ τε κἀλαλητῷ | Σκυθικὴν πόσιν παρ' οἴνῳ | μελετῶμεν, ἀλλὰ καλοῖς | ὑποπίνοντες ἐν ὕμνοις (*PMG* 356b).

song-stitching as a τέχνη: one merely learns that Hesiod and Homer stitched their (joint or respective) songs—with no further specification of manner—in the course of their new (individual or joint) performances.[350]

Now, if one adopts the view that the aorist regards 'focus function' and that ἐν ... ὕμνοις does not specify the performative context of the rhapsodes' singing,[351] how is their stitching with 'new hymns' to be envisioned? Given that the archaic 'hymn' was a unit of performance, one must imagine 'Hesiod' and 'Homer' to have joined smaller discrete performances into individual larger wholes in the course of their respective solo singing. By implication, the circumstances of their delivery would have had to provide notional 'intermissions' as occasions for seams. Something of the kind was true of Demodokos' song in θ 87–92.[352] Alternatively, the point of the fragment may be to represent the larger song as stitched from smaller sections distinguished in turn by metabatic performance shifts—each section being an individual ὕμνος.[353] Or else the 'hymns' must refer to (the subject matter of) previous performances, and applying the adjective 'new' (νεαροί) to them proleptically—*stricto sensu* only true of the resulting song—would be a rhetorical figure not unlike a transferred epithet.[354]

---

[350] Besides Anakreon's fragment and Herodotos 4.35 (where the adverbial clause qualifies ἐπονομάζω), I have not found any other early examples of ἐν ὕμοις or ἐν ὕμνῳ (with or without the interposition of the article and/or an adjective). Cf. Aristophanes *Birds* 906. The plural ἐν ὕμοις is very common with Christian writers but, other than the three cases above, wholly absent until the second century BC. From Philodemos' reference to Ἐμπε⟨δοκλῆς ἐν τ⟩οῖς ὕμνοις in *De pietate* (DK 31 A33) one cannot infer that the expression ἐν τοῖς ὕμνοις goes back to Empedokles' time. The fact that early instances of the adverbial expression should be so rare even with verbs of speech, performance, and the like, commends the interpretation that construes it more closely with the manufacturing metaphor entailed by ῥάπτω.

[351] That is, assuming that 'Hesiod' and 'Homer' are not making just one seam to a joint hypoleptic performance and that the ὕμνοι are instrumental to the stitching.

[352] It would be idle to speculate beyond the little that can be inferred from the fragment itself about the corresponding circumstances of performance.

[353] For 'metabasis' as 'performance shift', see above, p. 194 and p. 397 n. 240. The *Hymn to Apollo* is precisely one such 'larger song' with a thematic bipartition and performative markers—openings (1, 179), closings (165–176, 545–546), and a transition (177–178)—that suggest its analysis into two smaller ὕμνοι. Just as one may speculate that the Hesiodic fragment portrays Homer and Hesiod as stitching together these two 'hymns' into the one resulting song, we may also consider this Homeric hymn a model of the kind of larger 'new composition' a solo performer might claim to have stitched together from smaller ὕμνοι. I do not think the singular number of the noun ἀοιδήν in the fragment an obstacle to this view: it could indeed mean 'we sang (to) Apollo, stitching new hymns together into one joint song'; but the singular may stand, as often, for the (naturally singular) abstract verbal activity of 'singing' (cf. *LfgE* s.v. B.2: "Gesang als Tätigkeit, auch Resultat der Tätigkeit"); or it may adopt the familiar use of singular for plural hardly unique to ancient Greek. Cf., for example, the sentence 'soldiers fought with a brave heart,' which hardly implies the numerical restriction of 'heart' to one.

[354] 'A song of new sewn hymns' ~ 'a new song of sewn hymns.'

In sum, the direct object of ῥάπτω, i.e. the product of the stitching, is the 'song' (ἀοιδήν). The material used, 'new hymns' (ἐν νεαροῖς ὕμνοις). To this Hesiodic fragment we should add the oblique testimony of Pindar about ῥαπτὰ ἔπη (*Nemean* 2.2), which commends equating ἀοιδή with ἔπη. The rhapsode, then, stitches the song of his epic performance out of smaller compositional and performance units, the ὕμνοι. There is no support here for Durante's claim that what the rhapsode stitches into a song is the οἴμη (1968b:281), although οἴμη is arguably a rhapsodic term of great importance for our understanding of the rhapsode and his craft. In his analysis of ῥάπτω, Durante departs from the notion of 'stitching' and favors a meaning largely indistinguishable from 'weaving': "[D]ie antike ἱματιουργική unterscheidet sich nicht deutlich von der ὑφαντική" (1968b:280). His point is that in the ancient world, where rolls of fabric were not readily available for tailoring, sewing and stitching would have been marginal compared to weaving. But Cleland et al. 2007 s.v. "sewing" show that Durante overstates his case. While sewing was only one option for joining fabric, it was hardly rare: "The open side of Greek folded inner garments often seems to have been sewn ... . Other garments (*kandys, chitōn, cheiridōtos*) were completely sewn, including the sleeves, but this manner of construction never became characteristic" (167).[355] Greek dress de-emphasized stitching and embroidery in favor of draping and folds; pins and brooches would have been more desirable than seams. But this does not mean that a metaphor based on stitching units one to another would have been hard for the average individual to grasp.[356]

At any rate, it is broadly acknowledged that skin and leather were materials commonly in use that *did* call for the stitching together of existing pieces.[357] The Linear B *ra-pte*, 'sewer' or 'stitcher',[358] perhaps in connection with armor, and *ra-pi-ti-ra*$_2$, "sewing women,"[359] show that the practice of stitching was old enough to suggest the metaphor 'song-stitcher' as early as the late Bronze Age. Hesiod *Works and Days* 544 provides a well-known example of the manufacturing of winter clothing by stitching together skins of firstborn kids. Durante betrays a strange prejudice when he argues that the rhapsode's craft should be connected with weaving and not stitching because the material most commonly stitched was leather and not fabric. Even if weaving became the dominant metaphor for

---

[355] The sleeves could be buttoned rather than sewn. Cf. Cleland et al. 2007 s.v. "*cheiridōtos*." And s.v. "seams": "Essential to modern dress ... seams were not similarly important in Greek and Roman dress, although many garments were sewn in some way."

[356] Cleland et al. 2007 s.v. "stitching."

[357] Cf. Durante 1968b:280–281, Cleland et al. 2007 s.v. "stitching," and Marcar 2005:37, only to mention three examples.

[358] *DMic* II.221–223 s.v.: "con el significado de 'talabartero' o 'guarnicionero'." Cf. Lindgren 1973:132–133.

[359] Lindgren 1973:134. Cf. "costurera" in *DMic* II.221 s.v.

poetic composition, this does not require us to reduce all craft metaphors to it.[360] Barber (1991:275) remarks with some plausibility that ῥάπτειν must be an old Protogreek loanword from a non PIE language parallel to the IE κασσύω.[361] Her analysis demonstrates that the existence of doublets in the Greek textile vocabulary is common, one of IE descent and the other borrowed from south Aegean substrate languages.[362]

To support his equating ῥάπτειν with 'weaving' Durante resorts to the rare words φορμορραφέω[363] and σχοινορραφέω. The former is a celebrated coinage by Demosthenes which Aiskhines ridicules as 'incredible' (ἀπίθανα). Demosthenes is alleged to have said: ἀμπελουργοῦσί τινες τὴν πόλιν, ἀνατετεμνήκασί τινες τὰ κλήματα τὰ τοῦ δήμου, [ὑποτέτμηται τὰ νεῦρα τῶν πραγμάτων,] φορμορραφούμεθα, ἐπὶ τὰ στενά τινες ὥσπερ τὰς βελόνας διείρουσι (Against Ktēsiphōn 166).[364] The Greek text is uncertain at points, but the reading φορμορραφούμεθα is not. Its meaning, however, is not obvious. It is possible that here the action implied by ῥάπτειν is the plaiting of rush mats. Hesykhios glossed it thus: ὡς φόρμοι κατα(ρ)ραπτόμεθα.[365] But how are we to understand the metaphor of plaiting the Athenian people as rush mats (or their state, if τὰ πράγματα is preferred)? Right after Demosthenes' denunciation that the sinews had been cut, which evokes a body politic held together by ligaments and tendons, we might expect φορμορραφέω to depict an inferior way of political association that hampers the democratic state. Are we to think of each citizen as a plaited rush fiber? It is not clear why the resulting mat should be a natural metaphor for a defective organization (perhaps this adds to the ridicule). But in so close a proximity to needles, might this ῥάπτειν not refer rather to ordinary stitching? The metaphor of 'patchwork' seems immediately intelligible as inferior to 'body politic' and motivates the natural transition to needles. The patches might be individual plaited mats which, once stitched together, would make a rather weak overall structure. Stitching, in fact, may accompany plaiting in the making of rush mats. For example, in Tudor England rushes were plaited together into

---

[360] Cf. Barber 1975:294.

[361] Frisk (1973–1979 s.v.) is skeptical about the derivation *κατ-sju- (cf. Latin suere), but I do not find Lagercrantz's and Kretschmer's objections persuasive (references apud Frisk). Cf. Schwyzer GG I.321, Bader 1990:33, and Chantraine 2009:1313 s.v. κασσύω. LIV² 545 states the IE root as *syewH-.

[362] Barber 1991:277–278.

[363] Cf. φορμορραφίς.

[364] 'Some are pruning the city like a vine, some have cut off the twigs of the demos, [the sinews of the state have been severed,] we are being stitched together like a mat, some are drawing us through narrow straits like needles'.

[365] Hesykhios Φ no. 782.

neat coils which were then sewn into mats.[366] The common acceptations of φορμός are 'basket' and 'mat', both of plaited reed, rush, or another suitable plant.[367] The scholiast to Aristophanes *Wealth* 542 shows that the suitable verb for plaiting is πλέκω, not ῥάπτω:[368] φορμὸς πᾶν πλεκτόν. ἐνταῦθα δὲ τὸ ψιάθιον; and: φορμὸς πᾶν πλέγμα, εἴτε ψιάθιον εἴτε ἄλλο τι.[369] These two activities and the corresponding stages in the manufacturing process should not be conflated. The only instances that bring together ῥάπτω and φορμός are those related to Demosthenes' 'incredible' words. The *TGL* 8.1015 s.v. φορμορραφέω suggests the meaning "In tegete insuo. Vel potius, Ut tegetem trajicio acu." If so, ῥάπτειν here would involve the usual needle work of stitching and not weaving or plaiting— only, not ordinary fabric but mats are involved.[370] For φορμός, the *TGL* 8.1016 collects statements from Hesykhios, Eustathios, the *Suidas*, Theophrastos, the *Etymologicum Magnum*, etc. All of them use πλέκω or derivatives like πλέγμα.[371]

The other example adduced by Durante (1968b:280) is σχοινορραφέω, from the scholia D to K 262, which to 'ῥινοῦ ποιητήν' notes: ἐκ δέρματος γεγονυῖαν, ἐσκυτορραφημένην. This, according to van Thiel's edition,[372] is the reading in ZYQX (his *sigla*). QX also offer ἐσκηνορραφημένην, while Laskaris prints

[366] "The plaiting itself is carried out with the aid of [a] wall beam. A bundle of rushes is tied to the beam and the plaiter works and walks backwards as the plait grows. As the coil increases and will not keep taut it is wound round the beam and the plaiting continues. ... The coils for the body of a mat or carpet are mainly of 9 ply, while the borders are worked of a wider plait. The finished coils are handed over to other women for sewing up. This is done on a special table with a toothed edge to prevent slipping. The sewing must be done with great care. There must be even stitches and no puckering or the mat will not lie flat." This passage, reportedly taken from Doris Stephens's *Memories of Sherington*, is currently found at http://www.mkheritage.co.uk/shhs/rush.htm.

[367] In Herodotos 3.98, Theophrastos *Peri phytōn historia* 2.6.11, and Aristophanes *Wealth* 542 they are made of plaited plant fibers. This seems to be the case also in Theokritos 21.13. In Pausanias 10.29.8 it must refer to coarsely woven fabric, a meaning that is marginally possible in Theokritos too.

[368] Cf. Nünlist 1998:110–112, 114 §3.84.

[369] Cf. the scholia to Aiskhines *Against Ktēsiphon* 379 Dilts. The scholiast struggled to make sense of the expression and read it as 'some are plotting against us': ἀντὶ τοῦ συρράπτουσί τινες καθ' ἡμῶν πράγματα, ἀπὸ τοῦ φορμοῦ. φορμὸς γὰρ λέγεται τὸ ψιαθῶδες πλέγμα, ὡς καὶ ὁ Θουκυδίδης (4, 48) φορμηδὸν λέγει. Note the word πλέγμα; in view of the manufacturing process for plaited rush mats (see above), its relation to συρράπτουσι is unproblematic and does not bear out Durante's claim.

[370] Construing the 'stitching' of φορμορραφέω with εἰς τὰ στενά, the *TGL* s.v. also offers "[i]n tegetem storeamve conjectum insuere. ... Potest enim aliquis in tegete vel storea insui ut calescat, vel sudet."

[371] Hesykhios Φ no. 781: ἀγγεῖόν τι πλεκτὸν ψιάθοις ὡς κόφινος; *Suidas* 4.752 Φ no. 608.3: φορμὸς οὖν πλέγμα, ὡς κόφινος; Theophrastos *Peri phytōn historia* 2.6.11: καὶ πλέκουσιν ἐξ αὐτοῦ τάς τε σπυρίδας καὶ τοὺς φορμούς; *Etymologicum Magnum* 798.57–59 (col. 2233 Gaisford): φορμός ἐστι πλέγμα τινὸς μεγάλου εἴδους, ἐν ᾧ ἐκοιμῶντο οἱ πένητες, ἢ κατετίθεντο τὰ ὄσπρια; etc.

[372] Available at http://kups.ub.uni-koeln.de/1810.

ἐσχοινορραφημένην, the *hapax legomenon* that concerns us.[373] The passage describes a boar's-tusk helmet whose inner structure is leather; the teeth were sewn to it and one to another.[374] The text itself does not mention sewing. For my purposes, the relevant lines are K 261–263: ... ἀμφὶ δέ οἱ κυνέην κεφαλῆφιν | ἔθηκε | ῥινοῦ ποιητήν· πολέσιν δ' ἔντοσθεν ἱμᾶσιν | ἐντέτατο στερεῶς.[375] The scholiast's gloss ἐσκυτορραφημένην is reasonable: one must assume that the manufacturing involved the sewing of leather;[376] neither is 'sewn like a tent' wide of the mark, for the conical leather structure that supported the teeth was not unlike a small tent. But what could Laskaris's *hapax* mean? If it means "stitched with cords," as the LSJ s.v. notes, it is an odd attempt to explain the contested meaning of πολέσιν δ' ἔντοσθεν ἱμᾶσιν | ἐντέτατο στερεῶς. A connection with weaving is marginally possible if σχοῖνος is used of anything twisted or plaited (cf. LSJ s.v. II.1), in this case, twisted or plaited thongs.[377] This seems to be Lorimer's view. She translates, "inside, it was made of thongs tightly strained," and claims that the sense of ἐντέτατο is borne out by E 727–728, which she renders: "[Hera's chariot] was made of ... plaited strips."[378] Cunliffe 1963 s.v. ἐντείνω seems to agree: "to strain tight (with interplaited straps)."

But I wonder whence these scholars have derived the notion that the making of the helmet involves plaiting at all. How plaited thongs should stiffen a leather helmet is a mystery, and as a substrate it would constitute a singularly poor structure onto which to sew the teeth. No wonder Reichel (1901:102) had already refuted these mistaken notions: "Wir nehmen demnach an, dass die Riemen dazu dienten, die Zähne mit der Haube als Nähte dicht zu verbinden."[379] Borchhardt (1972:79) suggests that the helmet might consist of layers of broad leather strips sewn together and protected at the seams by the thongs. He does not, however, discount Lorimer's "plaited" (at 80) on the basis of Hera's char-

---

[373] Laskaris 1517, three pages after the obverse of sheet viiii (the last explicitly numbered before the relevant page).

[374] Somewhat varying descriptions of its manufacture are found at Reichel 1901:101–105; Lorimer 1950:212–213; and Borchhardt 1972:18–28, 79–80. For bibliography, see Buchholz and Wiesner 1977 E 224–225.

[375] 'About [Odysseus'] head [Meriones] placed a helmet made of hide; it was stretched firm within with many thongs'.

[376] From archaeology we know that the boar teeth were sewn to the hide and to each other, but since the text neglects these details one does not expect the scholiast to address them.

[377] Presumably, the scholiast's gloss would mean 'woven with plaited thongs'; i.e. σχοῖνος would stand for the twisted thongs and ῥάπτω, as Durante contends, for 'to weave' or 'to plait'.

[378] Lorimer 1950:213; cf. 326. Borchhardt (1972:79n352) adds three other secondary sources who believe that the helmet itself was made "aus geflochtenen Lederriemen."

[379] "Abgesehen davon, dass es methodischer ist, wenn der Dichter erst die Hauptsache, die Lederhaube, darauf deren Zuthaten, Zähne, Nähte derselben und Filzfutter erwähnt, sind die bildlichen Beispiele, welche die Genannten zur Stütze ihrer Ansicht heranziehen, theilweise missverstanden" (Reichel 1901:102n1).

iot.[380] But ἐντείνω only means 'to stretch tight' and does not prejudge the structure of what is strained. Whereas an intransitive δίφρος ... ἐντέταται[381] is readily
intelligible as 'the chariot floor stretches tight'[382] (the floor stretches within a
frame), 'the helmet stretched tight within with many thongs' is not: there is no
frame to support a hypothetical substrate of tautly strained thongs.[383] In sum,
this is a very uncertain foundation on which to build one's understanding of
ῥάπτω. Other professional terms ending in -ρράφος unproblematically entail
ordinary sewing and stitching: σκηνορράφος ('tentmaker'), κοσκινορράφος
('sewer of leather sieves'),[384] ἡνιορράφος ('saddler'), ἱστιορράφος ('sailpatcher'),
etc. As Durante observes, the preeminent classical professional of sewing and
stitching was the shoemaker.[385] Among other names, he was called νευρορράφος
by classical authors; post-classically, the rarer labels ὑποδηματορράφος and
σκυτορράφος were also used.[386]

[380] Although a majority of scholars believes that the platform of Hera's chariot consisted of plaited
strips, there are exceptions: "[D]oes this mean that the floor is made out of straps under tension,
or that the front and sides are so constituted? Critics differ ... ; the former is surely impracticable, since the leather would stretch and a foot find its way through somehow" (Kirk 1990:132).

[381] For the intransitive value of the perfect and its affinity with the middle voice, see e.g. Sicking and
Stork 1996:130–137. For intransitive middles generally see Schwyzer *GG* II.230. Examples of the
middle intransitive (plu)perfect of τείνω are Sophokles *Antigonē* 600 (τέτατο, 'for the light just
now spread over the last roots in the house of Oidipous'), *Philoktētēs* 857 (ἐκτέταται, 'the man lies
stretched out'), and *Aias* 1402 (ἐκτέταται, 'already much time has elapsed').

[382] The 'gold and silver thongs' would be a dative of material (i.e. 'the body made of gold and silver
thongs stretched out tight'), semantically very close to means and manner. Cf. K-G II.1.438
§425.10 and Smyth §1508c. An English example would be, 'the tapestry stretches out with beautiful embroidery,' where sense makes clear that the 'embroidery' is not strictly instrumental to
the stretching out.

[383] The point is that 'thongs' cannot easily be the (woven or plaited) substrate that 'stretches out'
(in the intransitive sense). They are more plausibly the means by which the helmet is somehow
stretched tight. I suggest that it was by the very process of sewing the boar tusks onto the
hide that the tight stretching was effected. That 'thongs' (ἱμάντες) are used for sewing is clear
from χ 186, where ῥαφαὶ ... ἱμάντων are not, as correctly observed by Fernández-Galiano in
Russo et al. (1992:253, with the concurrence of the *LfgE* s.v. ἱμάς 2d), 'the seams of the straps'
(*vel sim.*) but 'the seams/stitches [made with] thongs' (i.e. ἱμάντων is a genitive of material;
cf. Smyth §1323).

[384] Cf. Harrison 1904:253–254.

[385] ἀφωρισάμεθα καὶ τὴν τρήσει καὶ ῥαφῇ χρωμένην σύνθεσιν, ἧς ἡ πλείστη σκυτοτομική (Plato
Statesman 280c3–5).

[386] Ordinarily, besides the occasional νευρορράφος, classical authors used σκυτοτόμος and σκυτεύς.

PART IV

RHAPSODIC PERFORMANCE
IN THE LATE CLASSICAL
AND POST-CLASSICAL PERIODS

11

The Performance of Drama and Epic in Late-Classical Athens

11.1 The Reforms of Lykourgos

THE CONVERGENCE BETWEEN RHAPSODES AND ACTORS was in evidence toward the end of the fourth century BC. Just as rhapsodes were relying increasingly on scripted rehearsal and memorized performance—with a drastically reduced extemporaneous creativity and textual variation between successive performances and competing performers—so also at the revival of the old plays actors often felt free to modify their scripts so as to give greater scope to a show of histrionic ability. It is possible that now and then a line spoken on the stage to great dramatic effect occurred to the actor on the spot and was then added to the script for future reuse. Other changes must have been planned and rehearsed in advance. This source of textual instability (if I may call it thus) was of a different order than the extempore recomposition of the traditional rhapsode. But, to the degree that the latter used transcripts, the parallel between the bard and the actor was a similar attitude towards the written word as guiding, but ultimately not constraining, the future performance. Scripted recitals must have left behind numerous written copies of portions of the Homeric poems that would in turn resurface in various social settings (schools, symposia, public speeches, and so on) and may have seen their impact augmented by copies for private use and Athens' book trade. At the same time, the expectation of textual fixity and the desirability of a comprehensive canonical version that reflected the most successful recitals (in sum, 'Homer's original') must have encouraged a regulation of festival performances that would be all the easier to conform to and enforce, insofar as one could readily control the standard selected for rehearsal and memorization and judge the delivery against an authoritative script.

Between the battle of Khaironeia and the Lamian war Athenian public life was dominated by Lykourgos, a statesman whose cultural policy not only reflected the convergence between the dramatic and rhapsodic professions but may even be said to have hastened it. This period, so aptly called "Lykourgan Athens" by Mitchel 1973, was characterized by Lykourgos' drive to recover the splendor of Periklean Athens in what must have been the self-conscious emulation of that golden era of imperial glory. An ambitious public building program, the reinvigoration of local cults, the spirited public defense of old-time Marathonian morality,[1] the establishment of new festivals, the reorganization of old ones—all these classisizing endeavors with a view to crowning as normative the accomplishments of the past brought in a silver age of peace and prosperity that left its mark on the Athens of Hellenistic times. To all this Lykourgos added a keen interest in drama and epic poetry on account of their didactic potential,[2] especially the models of virtue they held out for imitation and their power to shape for the better the character and behavior of his fellow citizens. It is no coincidence, then, that his famous statement about Homeric performance in *Against Leōkratēs* §102 follows a long citation from Euripides' *Erekhtheus* that casts Praxithea as a paragon of sacrificial love for the city.[3] Then comes the one and only explicit testimony to the exclusivity of Homeric performance at the greater Panathenaia:

βούλομαι δ' ὑμῖν καὶ τὸν Ὅμηρον παρασχέσθαι ἐπαινῶν.[4] οὕτω γὰρ ὑπέλαβον ὑμῶν οἱ πατέρες σπουδαῖον εἶναι ποιητήν, ὥστε νόμον ἔθεντο καθ' ἑκάστην πεντετηρίδα τῶν Παναθηναίων μόνου τῶν ἄλλων ποιητῶν ῥαψῳδεῖσθαι τὰ ἔπη, ἐπίδειξιν ποιούμενοι πρὸς τοὺς Ἕλληνας, ὅτι τὰ κάλλιστα τῶν ἔργων προῃροῦντο. εἰκότως· οἱ μὲν γὰρ νόμοι διὰ τὴν συντομίαν οὐ διδάσκουσιν, ἀλλ' ἐπιτάττουσιν ἃ δεῖ ποιεῖν, οἱ δὲ ποιηταὶ μιμούμενοι τὸν ἀνθρώπινον βίον, τὰ κάλλιστα τῶν ἔργων ἐκλεξάμενοι, μετὰ λόγου καὶ ἀποδείξεως τοὺς ἀνθρώπους συμπείθουσιν.

I also wish to bring Homer to your attention in praise. For your ancestors considered him a poet of such worth that they passed a law calling for rhapsodic performances at every penteteric Panathenaia of his poetry alone, of all the poets, demonstrating to the Greeks that they preferred the noblest accomplishments. [They did so] fittingly; for laws, being terse, do not instruct but enjoin what one must do; whereas poets, when reenacting man's life, single out the highest accomplishments and with argument and demonstration win men over by persuasion.

---

[1] *Against Leōkratēs* §104 illustrates this commonplace of Athenian public discourse.

[2] See above, p. 308.

[3] In the light of Aristophanes *Frogs*, it is ironic indeed that Euripides would here be extolled as inculcator of civic virtue.

[4] For my restoration of the ms. reading over against Conomis's text, see above, p. 307 n. 61.

Unfortunately, this famous passage does not make clear whether the lesser Panathenaia featured no μουσικοὶ ἀγῶνες—or at least no rhapsodic competition[5]—or else rhapsodes did compete but they were free to declaim other poetry (Hesiod, Arkhilokhos, etc.).[6] It is hard for me to imagine that the lesser Panathenaia could have been devoid of poetic declamation, but one cannot entirely rule out that at one time or another in its long history there may not have been *official* contests. We face here the additional difficulty that the point of view is that of the 330s BC, and although Lykourgos emphasizes that it was the forefathers (οἱ πατέρες) who had passed a law (νόμον ἔθεντο) to the effect that Homer alone be declaimed at the greater Panathenaia—laws that ever since the great period of codification at the turn of the previous century must have provided reliable archival testimony about the past[7]—some degree of uncertainty always remains as to how far back we can project that state of affairs. And we cannot even be sure that this restriction was still in force at the time of Lykourgos (he might be speaking only of past history for its exemplary value, regardless of the situation current at the time of the speech).[8] But if it is true indeed that the great statesman established a canonical version of the great tragedians and made the performances of their plays conform to that canonical text, we can safely guess that, had the practice of exclusive declamation of Homer at the greater Panathenaia lapsed before his ascendancy to power, he would have moved its readoption. Although I have called *Against Leōkratēs* §102 the only remaining explicit statement of the exclusive declamation of Homer at the greater Panathenaia, I should add that the so-called succession rule of Diogenes Laertios 1.57 and [Plato] *Hipparkhos* 228b8–c1[9] also attest indirectly to

[5] For a discussion of this point, see below, p. 472ff. That rhapsodes could be singled out from among the other competitors of μουσικοὶ ἀγῶνες is implicit at *Iōn* 530a5–7, where, to Sokrates' incredulous question whether the locals have established a competition for rhapsodes at the Asklepieia of Epidauros, Ion responds, 'Yes indeed, and of the rest of μουσική too'.

[6] See also below, p. 475. *Iōn* 531a1 shows that Hesiod and Arkhilokhos belonged in the rhapsode's repertoire at least by the time of Sokrates (cf. also 530b8–9). Athenaios 14.620c, citing Khamaileon's *On Stesikhoros*, seems to confirm Sokrates' statement. In all probability, he does not mean to add Mimnermos and Phokylides to the rhapsodic repertoire, as some think. I discuss below (p. 450 n. 58) Athenaios' reason for mentioning them here. In the same passage Athenaios also reports that a certain rhapsode by the name of Mnasion used to act (ὑποκρίνεσθαι) some of Simonides' iambs, and a Kleomenes would rhapsodize (ἐραψῴδησεν) the *Purifications* of Empedokles at Olympia. [The 'Simonides' of the iambs may be Semonides of Amorgos (West 1981:125 with Nagy 1990c:26n46 approving). On the confusion between Simonides of Keos and Semonides of Amorgos see, for example, Hubbard 2001:227.] I will have occasion to return to this text below.

[7] On the reorganization of the Athenian law code between 410–399 BC and the founding of the Metroon, see Sickinger 1999:93–113 and the other studies cited there.

[8] Cf. Frei 1900:63.

[9] Note the ὥσπερ νῦν ἔτι οἵδε ποιοῦσιν (228b9–c1), which brings the practice down at least to the dramatic date of the dialog if not to the times of the pseudonymous author.

it; for if a succeeding rhapsode was to take up wherever the previous had left off, should any of them declaim the poetry of Homer it is hard to imagine under what conditions the rest could fail to perform more of the same. Thus, if there were other authors included in the repertoire, clearly they must have had their own particular competitive events.

Lykourgos was not only concerned with the exaltation of Homeric poetry as ennobling. He was also instrumental in the construction of the Panathenaic stadium and its θέατρον,[10] and responsible for a financial re-organization of the lesser Panathenaia that secured an adequate level of public display[11] and a proper

[10] See [Plutarch] *Lives of the Ten Orators* 841d and the decree at 852c, to which the fragmentary IG II/III² 457 is a witness. Deinias of Erkhia (*APF* 3163) donated the land for the construction (*Lives of the Ten Orators* 841d) and Eudemos of Plataia the teams of oxen for the leveling of the ground (cf. IG II/III² 351 with Schwenk 1985:232–238 no. 48). On the basis of IG II/III² 351.16–18, which states that Eudemos' oxen were 'for the construction of the Panathenaic stadium and theater' (εἰς τὴν ποίησιν τοῦ σταδ[ί]ου ‖ καὶ τοῦ θεάτρου τοῦ Παναθη[ναϊ]- ‖ κοῦ), Romano (1985:451) contends that "if one accepts that the stadium on the Pnyx hill is the Panathenaic Stadium, it follows that the assembly area can be identified as the Panathenaic Theater." But this, in fact, does not follow. No one questions the need for a 'viewing area'—i.e. a θέατρον—from which to follow the athletic events in the stadium. As Pickard-Cambridge (1946:137) long ago asserted, that provision was made for it is all that the expression τοῦ θεάτρου τοῦ Παναθη[ναϊ]- ‖ κοῦ requires us to believe. Whether or no this 'viewing area' was the assembly on the *Pnyx* is of little relevance to me. For alternatives, see Schwenk 1985:238 and Heisserer and Moysey 1986:182. Romano (1985:446–447) himself alleges the existence of embankments for viewing. There is criticism of his proposal in Stanton and Bicknell 1987:88–89, Hintzen-Bohlen 1997:36–37, and Shear 2001:838–840; and a reply in Romano 1996. My particular objection is to Romano's further suggestion that in the late fifth century "the athletic and probably the musical contests" of the Panathenaia were relocated "as part of the logical trend to move to the Pnyx certain civic and religious activities which originally took place in the Agora" (Romano 1985:451). One looks in vain for evidence to validate this claim in Thompson and Wycherley 1972:48–52, which he cites in support of it: nothing other than the assembly itself was ever relocated to the *Pnyx*. At any rate, extant sources are silent about the conjectured late fifth-century transfer to it of the "musical contests." (Romano 1996:80 softens the claim to "at least from the time of Lykourgos and possibly earlier.") Later reports that point to a transfer of rhapsodic performances to the 'theater' never so much as hint that this theater was any other than the well-known one of Dionysos, magnificently refurbished by Lykourgos (see Heisserer and Moysey 1986:181n23). Romano (1996:78–80) does not deny, of course, that the Athenian statesman rebuilt the theater of Dionysos, and he fully recognizes that this and the Panathenaic *theatron* of the inscription are two distinct structures. But his proposal is uneconomical. The fact that the *Pnyx* itself was abandoned in favor of Dionysos' theater not too long after Lykourgos' time as the preferred place of assembly commends the view that the construction that occurred during its third phase was a final and short-lived burst of life that responded to the conservative turn of the Lykourgan era. (Rotroff 1996 and Rotroff and Camp 1996 strongly suggest that Pnyx III should be dated to the time of Lykourgos; cf. Hansen 1996:23–24.) In the absence of incontrovertible counterarguments, one should therefore presume that it is the theater of Dionysos, not the assembly area of *Pnyx* hill, that sources refer to when they mention a Lykourgan-era θέατρον without qualification.

[11] αἱρεθεὶς ὑπὸ τοῦ δήμου χρήματα πολλὰ συνήγαγεν εἰς τὴν ἀκρόπολιν, καὶ παρασκευάσας τῇ θεῷ κόσμον, Νίκας τε ὁλοχρύσους πομπεῖά τε χρυσᾶ καὶ ἀργυρᾶ καὶ κόσμον χρυσοῦν εἰς ἑκατὸν κανηφόρους (*Lives of the Ten Orators* 852b).

supply of oxen for the sacrifice.[12] When we add to this his comprehensive concern for Athenian festivals (including the Dionysia and the new Amphiaraia),[13] one cannot rule out, even if lacking explicit testimony to this effect, that he may have undertaken the regulation of rhapsodic performances at the Panathenaia. Perhaps, as noted above, if the exclusive rhapsodizing of Homer had lapsed before his time, he might have brought it back and enforced it. And if we can trust the tradition that he had standard editions of the three canonical tragedians compiled and that he made sure that stage performance did not diverge from the official text, we might well assume a similar tendency to standardize in some way the text of the *Iliad* and the *Odyssey*, at least by depositing into the archives of Athens written copies of them, if this had not already been done before.[14]

As just noted, Lykourgos' concern was not limited to the excellence of Homer, but also embraced the Dionysia and its dramatic performances (both tragedy and comedy). Once again, the scope of his reforms was comprehensive: he finished the Theater of Dionysos, only half-done when he took up the project,[15] building in stone what until then most likely had been simple earthen embankments and wooden bleachers;[16] he revived the contest for comic actors, to be held in the theater at the Χύτροι, making the victor eligible to participate at the City Dionysia (which was not allowed before),[17] thus taking up an *agōn* that had fallen out of use (*Lives of the Ten Orators* 841f); he honored the three great tragedians with bronze statues (841f); and, most significantly for our present study, he had state officials write down a standard edition of their tragedies, which were publicly kept and enforced on the acting cast at the time of performance:

---

[12] See IG II/III² 334, conveniently discussed by Schwenk 1985:81–94 no. 17 and Rosivach 1991. For further (and more recent) bibliography on this inscription, see below, p. 474 n. 139. On the interpretation of the disputed νέα see also Langdon 1987:55–57.

[13] For this new quadrennial festival which, as one of ten *epimelētai*, he established in 329/28 BC, see Schachter 1981:1.19–26, Schwenk 1985:241–248 no. 50 (=EO 203–205 no. 298 = Manieri 2009:222–224 Oro. 4), Knoepfler 1993, Tracy 1995:92, and Manieri 2009:211–218. EO = Petrakos 1997.

[14] As seems likely from court proceedings in the Attic orators, who often had the clerk read various passages of Homer. The procedure, however, remains elusive, and it is possible that plaintiff or defendant may have given the clerk, in advance of the proceedings, written copies of what he was to read. This might have been the case even with laws and decrees. The record that survives in forensic speeches shows consultation of public *stēlai* and visits to the Metroon (cf. Sickinger 1999:160–170 and the texts cited there). But regardless of the specific procedures, one must assume that effort would be expended by court officials to make sure that what the *grammateus* read to the jury accurately reflected the alleged sources.

[15] ἡμίεργα παραλαβὼν ... τὸ θέατρον τὸ Διονυσιακὸν ἐξειργάσατο (*Lives of the Ten Orators* 852c).

[16] Cf. Pickard-Cambridge 1946:134–174.

[17] καὶ τὸν νικήσαντα εἰς ἄστυ καταλέγεσθαι, πρότερον οὐκ ἐξόν, where εἰς ἄστυ refers to the Διονύσια τὰ ἐν ἄστει—also Διονύσια τὰ ἀστικά, Διονύσια τὰ μεγάλα, or simply Διονύσια, as opposed to τὰ κατ' ἀγροὺς Διονύσια—an expression that gives rise to others such as ἐν ἄστει διδάσκειν or εἰς ἄστυ καθιέναι (cf. Pickard-Cambridge 1988:57n1). For the interpretation of this clause see O'Connor 1908:54–55 and Pickard-Cambridge 1988:15–16.

τὰς τραγῳδίας αὐτῶν ἐν κοινῷ γραψαμένους φυλάττειν καὶ τὸν τῆς πόλεως γραμματέα παραναγινώσκειν τοῖς ὑποκρινομένοις· οὐκ ἐξεῖναι γὰρ ⟨παρ'⟩ αὐτὰς ὑποκρίνεσθαι (841f). As Sickinger (1999:134–135) writes, ἐν κοινῷ is unlikely to denote the place of storage (as, for example, ἐν τῷ δημοσίῳ sometimes referred to the Metroon), for we would then expect the use of the article. But even ἐν τῷ δημοσίῳ could denote at times more broadly 'in the public domain',[18] and glossing ἐν κοινῷ along these lines as 'publicly' would adequately express the contrast between the textual transmission, until then largely in private hands, and the state tutelage and patronage that would now apply. Some seize on this insight to suggest that Lykourgos was not concerned with actors so much as with the deterioration of the *paradosis* if left to private hands.[19] But, if we are to believe this conjecture, how should we imagine that the citizens of Athens became collectively aware of this alleged deleterious transmission and were persuaded to support remedial legislation, unless in fact such privately held texts had been used for public performance? We are thus cast back on the inescapable fact that it was to actors that the law bore primary relation. The secretary of the city was to 'read [the tragedies] along to the actors' (παραναγινώσκειν)[20] to secure a performance faithful to the script.[21]

This testimony by [Plutarch] derives support from Galen, who reports that Ptolemy III Euergetes had used a ruse to acquire the official Athenian scripts of the three tragedians.[22] We do well to be somewhat sceptical of the anecdote's

---

[18] With the generic article; cf. Sickinger 1999:100.

[19] Cf. Garzya 1980:5.

[20] The παρα- conveys the idea of juxtaposition for the purpose of comparison. In the case of written sources it would apply to collation (cf. LSJ s.v.). Here, in turn, the idea is that the speaking actors are compared to the reading secretary, though the specific procedure remains elusive.

[21] For the interpretation of this passage see Nagy 1996c:174–175, who observes that the conjectured ⟨παρ'⟩ is unnecessary, for γάρ, by itself, can mean 'for otherwise' (175n80, with a reference to Denniston 1954:62–63). But we cannot entirely dismiss Bergk's emendation (1872–1887:3.71n247), which makes very good sense and is easy to defend on paleographic grounds: τοῖς δ' ὑποκρινομένοις οὐκ ἐξεῖναι παρ' αὐτὰ ὑποκρίνεσθαι, where παρ' αὐτά means extempore (cf. Hesykhios A no. 8467 s.v. αὐτοσχεδιάζει). The more conservative, sole insertion of παρ' allows the clause to draw directly on the text of the law and to reflect an explicit prohibition by the assembly (see below).

[22] Galen *Commentaria in Hippocratis Epidemias* III, 17a.607 Kühn (*CMG* 5.10.2.1): ὅτι δ' οὕτως ἐσπούδαζε περὶ τὴν ⟨ἁπάντων⟩ τῶν παλαιῶν βιβλίων κτῆσιν ὁ ⟨Πτολεμαῖος⟩ ἐκεῖνος, οὐ μικρὸν εἶναι μαρτύριόν φασιν ὃ πρὸς ⟨Ἀθηναίους⟩ ἔπραξεν. δοὺς γὰρ αὐτοῖς ἐνέχυρα πεντεκαίδεκα τάλαντ' ἀργυρίου καὶ λαβὼν τὰ ⟨Σοφοκλέους⟩ καὶ ⟨Εὐριπίδου⟩ καὶ ⟨Αἰσχύλου⟩ βιβλία χάριν τοῦ γράψαι μόνον ἐξ αὐτῶν, εἶτ' εὐθέως ἀποδοῦναι σῶα, κατασκευάσας πολυτελῶς ἐν χάρταις καλλίστοις, ἃ μὲν ἔλαβε παρ' ⟨Ἀθηναίων⟩ κατέσχεν, ἃ δ' αὐτὸς κατεσκεύασεν ἔπεμψεν αὐτοῖς παρακαλῶν ⟨κατα-⟩ σχεῖν τε τὰ πεντεκαίδεκα τάλαντα καὶ λαβεῖν ἀνθ' ὧν ἔδοσαν βιβλίων παλαιῶν τὰ καινά. τοῖς μὲν οὖν ⟨Ἀθηναίοις⟩, εἰ καὶ μὴ καινὰς ἐπεπόμφει βίβλους, ἀλλὰ κατεσχήκει τὰς παλαιάς, οὐδὲν ἐνῆν ἄλλο ποιεῖν, εἰληφόσι γε τὸ ἀργύριον ἐπὶ συνθήκαις τοιαύταις, ὡς αὐτοὺς ⟨αὐτὸ⟩ κατασχεῖν, εἰ κἀκεῖνος κατάσχοι τὰ βιβλία, καὶ διὰ τοῦτ' ἔλαβόν τε τὰ καινὰ καὶ κατέσχον καὶ τὸ ἀργύριον.

veracity. After all, as far as Hellenic cultural history was concerned, Alexandria portrayed itself as the natural heir to the city of Athens. This meant not only attracting and retaining a distinguished immigrant intelligentsia from the Ptolemaic possessions and beyond,[23] and designing a robust festival calendar of competitive events that would give expression to the royal patronage of the arts and sciences;[24] it also called for a vigorous reappropriation of the past in the tradition of peripatetic scholarship, i.e. based on the study of sources and public lectures, activities that centered around the Library and the Mouseion.[25] Against this intellectual background, it is only natural that the Ptolemies, in open competition with Attalid Pergamum, would emphasize the acquisition of texts, the preeminent cultural artifacts, as a key to cultural supremacy. Ownership of the iconic state scripts would have been a powerful index of the unique authority of Alexandria's dramatic performances as Athens' heir, of the prestige of the royal patron, his Library, and the scholars resident at the Mouseion. Thus, we cannot be entirely sure that a story so obviously favorable to the Ptolemies might not be self-interested, false propaganda. But the singling out of Aiskhylos', Sophokles', and Euripides' works would be hard to understand unless there was some reason to expect that of their works alone did Athens have an official, uniquely authoritative script: no similar story survives about Homeric or Hesiodic epic, Aristophanic comedy, etc.[26] This leads me to conclude that, whether the anecdote actually happened or not, there must have been a widely circulating report of the existence of a standard edition of the three tragedians, precisely what *Lives of the Ten Orators* 841f tells us Lykourgos did with the most important works of fifth-century BC drama.

Recently Bollack 1994 has subjected this passage to a probing analysis. Reviewing the history of interpretation, he concludes that the variously emended οὐκ ἐξεῖναι γὰρ αὐτὰς ὑποκρίνεσθαι points not to a prohibition of performance that might deviate from the officially commissioned text—which casts actors as destabilizing textual forces—but rather to an open recognition of the importance of public performance: without the activity described by the previous clause as

---

[23] Cf. Fraser 1972:1.305–312, esp. 1.306–308.

[24] Unfortunately, we are not as well informed about the Alexandrian festivals as we might wish, but enough remains to point to increasing opportunities for competitive display, including poetry, both in Alexandria and in other Egyptian centers. See Fraser 1972:1.230–233 for the isolympic Ptolemaieia, the Arsinoeia, and the Soteria. See also Fraser 1972:3.37 s.v. "festivals."

[25] For the Mouseion as an institution founded on the peripatetic model of the Athenian Lyceum see Fraser 1972:1.315–318; for the library, Fraser 1972:1.320 (with n. 100 on Aristotle's own collection). See also Weber 1993:74–82.

[26] This implies that, if Metroon copies of the *Iliad* and the *Odyssey* existed, as we suggested above, they must not have been as emblematic and influential for the regulation of Homeric performance as the tragic scripts were for the Athenian stage.

τὸν τῆς πόλεως γραμματέα παραναγινώσκειν τοῖς ὑποκρινομένοις, the texts drawn up might have lacked information essential to performance (musical notation, marks apportioning the lines to the various characters, etc.). In other words, the *grammateus* would have contrasted his text with the ones used by actors with a view to including theatrical cues and textual aids to performance. This is an interesting suggestion, but in the final analysis I find it unconvincing. It does not improve upon previously offered translations of the emended clause, for he too must read it as "for *otherwise* (sinon) they could not perform them" (my emphasis).[27] The question remains why it was not *otherwise* possible to perform them. Ultimately, one cannot be dogmatic about the meaning, but several details, I believe, support the modern consensus. One is the verb παραναγιγνώσκειν, whose usage points to reading something aloud with the aim of comparing it to something else.[28] In forensic contexts, the *grammateus* simply reads aloud, without making corrections or modifications to the substance of his text. In later usage, it may denote an editor who reads carefully against other sources and when he finds discrepancies enters corrections;[29] but if there is truth to the account, in its fourth-century BC setting one must conceive of the procedure along the established lines of forensic practice.[30] And for this, examples such as Demosthenes' *On the Crown* 267, or Aiskhines' *Against Ktēsiphōn* 201 and *On the Embassy* 135 must be of primary significance.[31] This tells against Bollack's inter-

---

[27] Bollack 1994: "... et que le scribe de la cité compare le texte avec les acteurs: il ne serait pas possible, sinon, de les jouer sur scène" (13).

[28] The comparison is sometimes tacit, as in Plato's *Theaitetos* 172e4: the opponent at law reads aloud the ὑπογραφή, which is implicitly compared to the wider scope the speaker may wish to give to his presentation, thus effectively limiting what is admissible.

[29] Such are the late examples in Cameron 1990, which he glosses as 'check' or 'revise', "so long as a caveat is added. There does not seem to be a single text [surveyed] that suggests revision in the sense of addition or expansion ... [I]t would be a perfectly satisfactory word to characterize the careful reading and checking that went to produce the sort of editions here under discussion. It corresponds to the primary meaning of the Latin *recognoscere*, 'to examine, check (a document), in order to establish authenticity, accuracy, etc.'" (125). It must be emphasized, however, that in the earlier (classical) usage, the grammatical subject of παραναγιγνώσκω does not modify the text he is reading, although the goal of the exercise is a contrast often with a view to correcting some excess or transgression. In other words, though many times establishing the comparison or proving the discrepancy is the sole goal, if a correction takes place, it is not the text read as *comparandum* that is changed, but whatever else it is contrasted with.

[30] I am assuming that παραναγιγνώσκειν is the diction of the source used by the *Lives of the Ten Orators*, and that it is therefore to be read according to late-classical usage.

[31] Demosthenes *On the Crown* 267: φέρε δὴ καὶ τὰς τῶν λῃτουργιῶν μαρτυρίας ὧν λελῃτούργηκα ὑμῖν ἀναγνῶ. παρ' ἃς παραναγνῶθι καὶ σύ μοι τὰς ῥήσεις ἃς ἐλυμαίνου. Aiskhines *On the Embassy* 135: ἀκούετε, ὦ Ἀθηναῖοι, τῶν χρόνων παραναγιγνωσκομένων ἐκ τῶν δημοσίων γραμμάτων κτλ. And *Against Ktēsiphōn* 201: ὑπομνήσατ' αὐτὸν [sc. Κτησιφῶντα] ἀθορύβως τὸ σανίδιον λαβεῖν καὶ τοὺς νόμους τῷ ψηφίσματι παραναγνῶναι. The examples in LSJ s.v. show that παραναγιγνώσκω can take the dative of the *comparandum*, and hence means 'to read (aloud) and compare with' (Isokrates 12.17 [cf. 4.120]; Galen *CMG* 5.4.1.2, p. 132 De Lacy; Polybios 2.12.4 proves that

pretation that the *grammateus* would have annotated the state script with histrionic cues. Depending on whether we follow early or late usage, the dative τοῖς ὑποκρινομένοις might mean 'to read aloud and compare with [the lines spoken by] those acting the plays' or simply 'to read aloud in the presence of those acting the plays'.[32] Though we cannot put much weight on this, the use of the participle (as opposed to τοῖς ὑποκριταῖς) might indicate that the action of the secretary takes place as rehearsal is in progress. One could envision a sort of dialog between him and the acting staff at particular points in the performance, whenever the *grammateus* might detect a divergence or the actors might need prompting from the official script. Those who prefer a less directive process may follow Cameron (1990:124), who writes that the secretary might have read out the text in advance to allow actors to correct their own copies against it.[33]

To me, the most persuasive reconstruction takes into account Arnott's suggestive study on the use of prompting in classical drama.[34] Arnott built on an "excursus on the prompter" by Page (1934:98–100), who noted the astonishing absence in sources earlier than the first century AD of any figure that might suggest a prompter. The first occurrence is the word ὑποβολεύς in Philo of Alexandria.[35] But, as Arnott (1967:45) correctly observes, the *loci* adduced by Page do not so much suggest one who reminds of what has been forgotten as one who teaches what to say: "it is an instructor, not a remembrancer." Aiskhines' *On the Embassy* 35 and the acoustics and design of the classical theater all but prove that there was, in fact, no prompter at the time of the performance. And the meaning of ὑποβολεύς, 'instructor', who, Plutarch teaches us,[36] was indeed involved in dramatic production, suggests his equivalence with the διδάσκαλος

---

in later Greek (if not before) it might simply mean 'to read aloud in the presence of others', i.e. publicly, so as to inform an audience about the text of a document. For other instances, see Cameron (1990:124), who observes that "[i]n many of these passages there is a clear implication that the text is being read publicly so that everyone can check what it says."

[32] Bollack (1994:21) suggests the translation "'*face au* texte joué par les acteurs' si τοῖς ὑποκρινομένοις était pris pour un neutre." Though this might not seem at first impossible, LSJ s.v. does not include any examples of the passive and I cannot turn up any either. One should at least say that, on the point of usage, the odds that ὑποκρινομένοις is a middle are overwhelming. (Even the aor. pass. and pf. pass. came to be used as middles.) But in the event, as Bollack (1994:21) notes, the meaning amounts to the same if one takes it, as most do, as a masc. pl. for 'those acting'.

[33] Anticipated by Garzya 1980: "[S]i tratta di un'operazione di collazionamento orale (il canceliere legge, gli attori confrontano con il proprio il testo letto)" (4n6).

[34] Arnott 1967.

[35] E.g. Philo *De migratione Abrahami* 80: "καὶ ἐρεῖς πρὸς αὐτὸν καὶ δώσεις τὰ ῥήματά μου εἰς τὸ στόμα αὐτοῦ", ἴσον τῷ ὑπηχήσεις αὐτῷ τὰ ἐνθυμήματα, ἃ ῥημάτων καὶ λόγων ἀδιαφορεῖ θείων· ἄνευ γὰρ τοῦ ὑποβολέως οὐ φθέγξεται ὁ λόγος, ὑποβολεὺς δὲ λόγου νοῦς, ὡς νοῦ θεός. And Philo *De vita Mosis* II §37: καθάπερ ἐνθουσιῶντες προεφήτευον οὐκ ἄλλα ἄλλοι, τὰ δ' αὐτὰ πάντες ὀνόματα καὶ ῥήματα, ὥσπερ ὑποβολέως ἑκάστοις ἀοράτως ἐνηχοῦντος.

[36] Plutarch *Praecepta gerendae reipublicae* 813e10–f5.

of classical times. This means that he would be responsible for training the acting staff by cuing them during rehearsal, reading out loud their lines for them to repeat after him and memorize in the process. Arnott's description makes this scenario persuasive: "In the modern Greek and Italian theatres the prompter ... is a vital factor in the rehearsal. Actors do not attempt to learn their parts beforehand. At the rehearsal the prompter sits in front of the cast with script in hand. A scene is then rehearsed by the prompter speaking several lines and indicating the actor who is to say them; the actor repeats after him, and so on through the scene. This method may sound incredibly slow and clumsy, but in fact it is remarkably efficient for actors who are trained to it" (Arnott 1967:44). If this was the ancient practice, it explains the absence in our classical sources of any reference to the ὑποβολεύς: he was no other than the poet/producer of the play (who of course would have done more than simply cue his troupe); it also dispenses with the difficulty of supplying the cast (actors and chorus) each with his own copy of the play or at least the lines to memorize; and it readily explains the role of the Lykourgan city secretary: he was to act, in effect, as the textual *didaskalos* at the time of rehearsal, with the producer presumably taking care of all other aspects of acting and production.[37] It is ultimately hard to imagine the mechanics of the procedure, but what the law envisions is clearly state control over the performance of the three great tragedians and the public elevation of their plays to the status of exemplary documents of foundational significance to Lykourgos' policies of cultural revival.[38]

---

[37] This explanation agrees with Rhodes's notion about the 'secretary of the city' (Rhodes 1993:604 *ad Athēnaiōn Politeia* 54.5; cf. Thoukydides 7.10).

[38] Bollack's interesting proposal is also doubtful because it is not easy to see what might move a statesman like Lykourgos to be so self-conscious about the minutiae of performance that he would call for its inclusion in the state script. What we know from ancient papyri (cf. Turner 1977:7) suggests that the book trade annotated scrolls sparsely, mostly with παράγραφοι, if at all, especially in classical times (it is unknown what histrionic scripts might have looked like in comparison), and one can only envision Bollack's scenario after the ascendancy of philological studies in Hellenistic times (see Turner 1968:112–118 and Thompson 1912:60). At all events, for late classical times, Aristotle (*Rhetoric* 1407b13–18) mentions punctuating (διαστίζω) Herakleitos' works, though it is not clear whether he is thinking of the scribe's writing or the reader's utterance. The εὐανάγνωστον of 1407b11 points to the latter (as Wilamowitz-Moellendorff 1910:128n9 and Kennedy 1991:233n73 think), but it is still possible that Aristotle is using the scribe's hardship as an index of the difficulty the reader faces. The use of διαστίζω for a 'punctuation' that consists in *verbal* phrasing must derive from epigraphical practice, though (as Wilamowitz-Moellendorff 1910:128 notes) the epigraphic *interpunctiones* of the sixth century BC had all but disappeared by the philosopher's time (cf. Woodhead 1992:28). *Rhetoric* 1409a20–21 also mentions the παραγραφή, which could be used to mark the end of a period (or, in dramatic texts, to indicate a change of speaker). Also witnessing to the use of signs at the beginning of paragraphs is Isokrates *Antidosis* 59. Wilamowitz-Moellendorff 1910:128 seems justified in saying that "in [büchern] ist dem leser fast nichts gegeben als die 'elemente', die buchstaben."

Whichever reconstruction one finds plausible, attention must be paid to the syntactic structure of the report about Lykourgos' law, for it further illuminates the nature of its impact on actors. Bollack would have us believe that the clause οὐκ ἐξεῖναι is merely an editorial explanation of the charge to the secretary. An earlier comment (about the Χύτροι) is clearly demarcated as such by its form, an accusative absolute (πρότερον οὐκ ἐξόν). The ἐξεῖναι, however, depends on τὸν δὲ [νόμον], and it reports the law's content where its force would be imperatival:[39] the author of the *Lives*, it is true, has partially turned the text of the law into a comment, inserting γάρ (with the subsequent loss of παρ') and substituting οὐκ for what must have been an original μή.[40] In other words, the οὐκ ἐξεῖναι κτλ. reports an explicit prohibition in the Lykourgan law, not merely an explanatory aside to the effect that, without the *grammateus* reading the text and providing histrionic cues to those acting, performances based on the Lykourgan state script would not have been possible.[41]

The intervention of the Athenian state in the performance of drama is made plausible by testimonies about histrionic interpolations in the texts of the plays.[42] Thus, the epitome of Phrynikhos' *Praeparatio sophistica* (p. 69 de Borries) preserves the following comment on the comic line ἐπικαττύειν καὶ πτερνίζειν:[43] τὰ παλαιὰ ἐπισκευάζειν. ἡ μεταφορὰ ἀπὸ τῶν τοῖς παλαιοῖς ὑποδήμασιν ἕτερα καττύματα καὶ πτέρνας προσραπτόντων. λέγουσι δ' ἐπὶ τῶν τὰ παλαιὰ τῶν δραμάτων μεταποιούντων καὶ μεταρραπτούντων. To this Vürtheim (1928:232) writes: "Die alten Dramen wurden wie Schuhe den modernen Füssen passend gemacht." That this was the case with comedies is generally accepted (so Kock and Bergk 1872–1887:3.70n242). But I find no grounds to dismiss it, with Hamilton (1974:400), as "the common practice of Roman *contaminatio*."[44] Note in particular the use of μεταρράπτω, which, at home with the cobbler, also draws on the metaphorical world of rhapsodic recomposition. Already in antiquity there were times when the scholar, on stylistic grounds, would condemn a verse or passage as not genuine. Thus, for example, the second *hypothesis* to the *Rhesos* contains the following remark: καὶ ἐν ἐνίοις δὲ τῶν ἀντιγράφων ἕτερός τις φέρεται

---

[39] The ὡς at 841f8 would be a result clause: 'another [law], to effect that ...'.

[40] Just as the following clause in *Lives of the Ten Orators*: μηδενὶ ἐξεῖναι κτλ.

[41] Instances of ἐξεῖναι in Attic decrees are common.

[42] The best modern introduction is Hamilton 1974. Also read with profit is Page 1934, though frequently criticized as insufficiently mature and unfavorably compared with Jachmann 1982. See also Malzan 1908, Wilamowitz-Moellendorff 1910, Vürtheim 1928:231–248, Cantarella 1930, Reeve 1972 and 1973, Haslam 1979, and Garzya 1980. Falkner (2002, esp. 352–353) offers an interesting reevaluation of scholia that disparage actors and views histrionic interpolations as a struggle between the performer and the scholar for the control of the text.

[43] PCG VIII fr. 599 = *Comica adespota* fr. 46 Kock.

[44] Quintilian's words at *Institutio oratoria* 10.1.66, I agree, are confusing and offer little guidance. Cf. Cantarella 1930:57–58.

πρόλογος, πεζὸς πάνυ καὶ οὐ πρέπων Εὐριπίδῃ· καὶ τάχα ἄν τινες τῶν ὑποκριτῶν διεσκευακότες εἶεν αὐτόν. Such stylistically based comments offer no certain proof that any one particular passage is a histrionic interpolation, but the implication that actors *did* at times modify the authorial text is hard to dismiss, and this lends credence to [Plutarch's] report about Lykourgos and the consensus interpretation above. This is precisely what one would expect from the scattered comments in the literature about the social standing of actors. Two tendencies can be distinguished: the contempt of the learned man, to some degree shared as a stereotype by the populace, and the adulation lavished on the individual star. It is not hard to see how both contradictory impulses might coexist, if we only think of our own culture and the scorn and admiration heaped by turns on modern actors. Plato's strictures against dramatic mimesis for its corrupting potential are well known, but it might be thought exceptional and unrepresentative. Thus, more interesting are the comments by Aristotle and his circle, which likely reflect popular sentiment. The philosopher decries, for example, that 'in the contests actors are now more important than poets',[45] a comment that can be read against the criticism of *Poetics* 26; contemptuous also is the popular designation Διονυσοκόλακες of the τεχνῖται of Dionysos, who include actors among its performers;[46] and the pseudonymous *Problems* poses the question why the artists of Dionysos are for the most part bad characters (πονηροί).[47] We also remember Demosthenes maligning Aiskhines on the grounds of his early stint as an actor (Demosthenes 18.262). The rise of the professional of the stage is a fifth- and fourth-century BC phenomenon (cf. *Rhetoric* 1403b22–24 and Plato's *Laws* 817a–d), for which the institution of a competition for actors at the City Dionysia in 449 BC provides a convenient *terminus ante quem*. So, if there is truth to an anecdote told by Plutarch, it is significant that already in the times of the Spartan king Agesilaos II the actor Kallippides was famous and respected by all the Greeks.[48] That Aristophanes lampooned actors as readily as other well-known citizens (*Frogs* 303, *Peace* 781–786) proves that, from very early on, some at least received much public recognition. We also note the involvement

---

[45] *Rhetoric* 1403b32–34: τὰ μὲν οὖν ἆθλα σχεδὸν ἐκ τῶν ἀγώνων οὗτοι λαμβάνουσιν, καὶ καθάπερ ἐκεῖ μεῖζον δύνανται νῦν τῶν ποιητῶν οἱ ὑποκριταί.

[46] *Rhetoric* 1405a23–25: καὶ ὁ μὲν διονυσοκόλακας, αὐτοὶ δ' αὑτοὺς τεχνίτας καλοῦσιν· ταῦτα δ' ἄμφω μεταφορά, ἡ μὲν ῥυπαινόντων ἡ δὲ τοὐναντίον.

[47] *Problems* 956b11–15: διὰ τί οἱ Διονυσιακοὶ τεχνῖται ὡς ἐπὶ τὸ πολὺ πονηροί εἰσιν; ἢ ὅτι ἥκιστα λόγου σοφίας κοινωνοῦσι διὰ τὸ περὶ τὰς ἀναγκαίας τέχνας τὸ πολὺ μέρος τοῦ βίου εἶναι, καὶ ὅτι ἐν ἀκρασίαις τὸ πολὺ τοῦ βίου εἰσίν, τὰ δὲ καὶ ἐν ἀπορίαις; ἀμφότερα δὲ φαυλότητος παρασκευαστικά.

[48] Plutarch *Agēsílaos* 21.4: καί ποτε Καλλιππίδης ὁ τῶν τραγῳδιῶν ὑποκριτής, ὄνομα καὶ δόξαν ἔχων ἐν τοῖς Ἕλλησι καὶ σπουδαζόμενος ὑπὸ πάντων, κτλ. Cf. Polyainos 6.10.1.

of actors in high-stakes international politics,[49] largely motivated by the delight of the Makedonian ruling dynasty in the performing arts.[50] It is understandable that performers might develop an exaggerated sense of their own importance and, in consequence, seek to modify plays to give greater salience to their roles on stage. This was possible because, starting in the fourth century BC, old plays were revived at the Dionysia,[51] well after the author's passing, a fact that precluded authorial control. Thus, we should not be surprised to read in Aristotle's *Politics* that Theodoros would not allow 'cheap' actors to be brought on stage before him, 'because the audience endears itself to what it hears first'.[52] As Hamilton (1974:401) says, the wording suggests that accommodating Theodoros forced modifications of the plays that went beyond "scenic effects."

11.2 Demetrios of Phaleron and the Rhapsodes

11.2.1 Rhapsodes and *homēristai*

The next defining stage in the cultural history of Athens arrived in 317/16 BC with Kassander's installation of the pro-Makedonian Demetrios of Phaleron as governor of Athens, a position he held until the liberation of the city in 308/307 BC by Demetrios Poliorketes.[53] His most important reform for our purposes is mentioned in passing by Athenaios 14.620b on the authority of the historian Aristokles (*FHG* IV, p. 331),[54] a passage that examines the contribution of rhapsodes to symposia. I quote it in full:[55]

---

[49] See, for example, the second hypothesis to Demosthenes 19 (§2), Demosthenes 19.315, or Demosthenes 5.6.

[50] E.g. Demosthenes 19.192; Plutarch *Alexandros* 10, 29, 72.1; and FGH 125 F4 (Khares *apud* Athenaios 12.538b–539a). Ghiron-Bistagne (1976:154–163) surveys the growing prominence of actors during the fourth century BC and their involvement with the Makedonians.

[51] IG II/III² 2318 records 386 and 339 BC as the respective dates for the first old tragedy and comedy.

[52] *Politics* 1336b27–31: ἴσως γὰρ οὐ κακῶς ἔλεγε τὸ τοιοῦτον Θεόδωρος ὁ τῆς τραγῳδίας ὑποκριτής· οὐθενὶ γὰρ πώποτε παρῆκεν ἑαυτοῦ προεισάγειν, οὐδὲ τῶν εὐτελῶν ὑποκριτῶν, ὡς οἰκειουμένων τῶν θεατῶν ταῖς πρώταις ἀκοαῖς.

[53] For a comprehensive account of Demetrios' life see Ostermann 1847 and 1857, Bayer 1969, and O'Sullivan 2009. Briefer treatments are Wehrli 1968a, Ferguson 1974:38–94, Habicht 1997:53–66, and Mikalson 1998:46–74. For editions of his fragments see Wehrli 1968b and Fortenbaugh and Schütrumpf 2000. (Pages 311–447 of the last item contain important essays on various aspects of his life and works.) For the impact of his philosophical ideas on his policies see Dow and Travis 1943, Gehrke 1978, and Williams 1987. Further bibliography can also be found in Williams 1987:87n2.

[54] Not in Jacoby's FGH. Of Aristokles, Müller writes: "Hoc tantum liquet, Aristoclem qui scripsit de musica chorisque, vixisse Alexandriae post regnum Ptol. Euergetae II (146–117). Id enim colligitur ex Athenaeo (IV, p. 174, B)."

[55] Aristokles' remark, highlighted here, corresponds to fr. 33 Wehrli and fr. 55a SOD (=Fortenbaugh and Schütrumpf 2000) of Demetrios of Phaleron.

οὐκ ἀπελείποντο δὲ ἡμῶν τῶν συμποσίων οὐδὲ ῥαψῳδοί. ἔχαιρε γὰρ τοῖς Ὁμήρου ὁ Λαρήνσιος ὡς ἄλλος οὐδὲ εἷς, ὡς λῆρον ἀποφαίνειν Κάσανδρον τὸν Μακεδονίας βασιλεύσαντα, περὶ οὗ φησι Καρύστιος ἐν Ἱστορικοῖς Ὑπομνήμασιν ὅτι οὕτως ἦν φιλόμηρος ὡς διὰ στόματος ἔχειν τῶν ἐπῶν τὰ πολλά· καὶ Ἰλιὰς ἦν αὐτῷ καὶ Ὀδυσσεία ἰδίως γεγραμμέναι. ὅτι δ᾽ ἐκαλοῦντο οἱ ῥαψῳδοὶ καὶ Ὁμηρισταὶ Ἀριστοκλῆς εἴρηκεν ἐν τῷ περὶ Χορῶν. τοὺς δὲ νῦν Ὁμηριστὰς ὀνομαζομένους πρῶτος εἰς τὰ θέατρα παρήγαγε Δημήτριος ὁ Φαληρεύς. Χαμαιλέων δὲ ἐν τῷ περὶ Στησιχόρου καὶ μελῳδηθῆναί φησιν οὐ μόνον τὰ Ὁμήρου, ἀλλὰ καὶ τὰ Ἡσιόδου καὶ Ἀρχιλόχου, ἔτι δὲ Μιμνέρμου καὶ Φωκυλίδου. Κλέαρχος δ᾽ ἐν τῷ προτέρῳ περὶ Γρίφων "τὰ Ἀρχιλόχου, φησίν, [ὁ] Σιμωνίδης ὁ Ζακύνθιος ἐν τοῖς θεάτροις ἐπὶ δίφρου καθήμενος ἐραψῴδει." Λυσανίας δ᾽ ἐν τῷ πρώτῳ περὶ Ἰαμβοποιῶν Μνασίωνα τὸν ῥαψῳδὸν λέγει ἐν ταῖς δείξεσι τῶν Σιμωνίδου τινὰς ἰάμβων ὑποκρίνεσθαι. τοὺς δ᾽ Ἐμπεδοκλέους Καθαρμοὺς ἐραψῴδησεν Ὀλυμπίασι Κλεομένης ὁ ῥαψῳδός, ὥς φησιν Δικαίαρχος ἐν τῷ Ὀλυμπικῷ. Ἰάσων δ᾽ ἐν τρίτῳ περὶ τῶν Ἀλεξάνδρου Ἱερῶν ἐν Ἀλεξανδρείᾳ φησὶν ἐν τῷ μεγάλῳ θεάτρῳ ὑποκρίνασθαι Ἡγησίαν τὸν κωμῳδὸν τὰ Ἡσιόδου, Ἑρμόφαντον δὲ τὰ Ὁμήρου.

(Athenaios 14.620b–d)

Neither were rhapsodes missing from our symposia. For Larensios took pleasure in the poetry of Homer as no other did, [so much in fact] as to show up Cassander the ruler of Makedon as a trifle [in comparison], about whom Karystios in his *Historical Commentaries* says that he was such a lover of Homer that he had the greater part of his poetry constantly in his mouth; and that the *Iliad* and the *Odyssey* had been written down by him personally. *That rhapsodes used to be called* homēristai *too is reported by Aristokles in his book* On Choruses. *But those called nowadays* homēristai *Demetrios of Phaleron first brought into the theaters.* Khamaileon in his book *On Stesikhoros* says that Homer's poetry was also set to music, and not only Homer's but also Hesiod's and Arkhilokhos', and even Mimnermos' and Phokylides'. Klearkhos in the former book of his work *On Riddles* says that Simonides of Zakynthos used to perform as a rhapsode the poetry of Arkhilokhos in the theaters, sitting on a stool. Lysanias in the first book of his work *On Iambic Composers* says that in his performances Mnasion the rhapsode used to deliver some of the iambs of Simonides. And Kleomenes the rhapsode rhapsodized the *Purifications* of Empedokles at Olympia, as Dikaiarkhos says in his *Olympic Discourse*. Jason in the third book of his work *On Alexander's Offerings* says that

Hegesias the comic actor delivered the poetry of Hesiod in the large theater in Alexandria, and Hermophantos that of Homer.

This passage, with its mention of rhapsodes and *homēristai*, raises the question of the relationship between the two. To approach this matter aright it is vital to notice that Athenaios avows his intention to speak about rhapsodes: 'Nor were rhapsodes (ῥαψῳδοί) missing from our symposia'. Should there be any doubt about the kind of professional he has in mind or the nature of his contribution to the symposium, he adds that Larensios delighted in Homer as no other, reducing Kassander to a trifle by comparison, who so loved the poet that it was reported he knew by heart most of his verse and owned manuscripts of the *Iliad* and the *Odyssey* written in his own hand.[56] It is clear from the contrast drawn that Athenaios' focus is on the text of the poems, and thus, whatever else may be said about the rhapsodes that attended his symposia, at the heart of their performance must have been the epic *verse* of Homer. This is so, whether they declaimed, employed recitative, or sung his lays; whether they used the accompaniment of an instrument; whether they also acted, and, if they did, acted alone (adopting the persona of the character speaking at each point in the narrative) or with others (in semi-dramatic set pieces). Otherwise the comment about Larensios and his comparing favorably with Kassander would be out of place. The sentence that follows makes clear that in Athenaios' mind there is a difference between rhapsodes and *homēristai*. There are, on the one hand, 'the present-day *homēristai*', οἱ νῦν Ὁμηρισταί, and, by implication, on the other, an older kind of *homēristai*, no longer called by this name. Who are these old-time *homēristai*? The answer is: the rhapsodes who are the focus of the section, for Aristokles in his work *On Choruses* had stated 'that rhapsodes were also called *homēristai*'.[57] Doubtless some of these old-style '*homēristai*'—or Hellenistic rhap-

---

[56] Or, less likely, Cassander had the poems "privately copied for him" (so Olson in his *Loeb* translation). O'Sullivan (2009:184–185) traces Athenaios' source to Demokhares' negative assessment of Demetrios. His mention of Demetrios' role in bringing the *homēristai* into the theater "could conceivably have served ... to underscore Demetrius' relationship with Cassander, a relationship through which the city had been subjugated by a Macedonian overlord."

[57] The label *homēristēs* must have been coined during the Hellenistic period, when ῥαψῳδεῖν was readily used for the solo performance of any non-melic poetry, not just epic, and certainly not just *Homeric* epic. Faced with the increasingly specialized professionalism characteristic of the times, some—probably in professional circles—must have felt the need for a narrower term that would distinctly identify the one who focused his repertoire exclusively (or almost exclusively) on the *Iliad* and the *Odyssey*. If Petronius' account is faithful, however, the *homēristai* of later times may well have adopted a somewhat broader repertoire (cf. Hillgruber 2000:65). For a different view on the origin of the word *homēristēs*, see O'Sullivan 2009:184n54. Nagy (1996c:178–179) shows that the agent noun formation in -*istēs*, which correlates with verbs in -*izō*, is already attested in the fourth century BC. This does not mean, of course, that the motivation specific to

sodes—adopted new performance practices that suited the preferences of their time. Such was their 'setting to music' the epic verse of Homer and Hesiod,[58] a late realization of the old melodic potential that inhered diachronically in epic poetry.[59] The late fourth-century BC Peripatetic Khamaileon draws attention to this potential when he ascribes the practice to Stesikhoros.[60] Underlying this performance modality is the notion of 'singing melodically', a mode of delivery that only expresses the potential diachronically intrinsic to the poetic medium. *Stricto sensu*, understood as an extrinsic imposition on the poetic medium, the alternative translation of μελῳδεῖν used above, 'to set to music', is anachronistic.

Why does Athenaios introduce the *homēristai* at all, if the (for him) present-day type does not correspond to the rhapsode? This must be because he goes on to describe the public performances of rhapsodes, presumably as illustrations of the kind of entertainment that, with the proper adjustments to the setting, they enjoyed at their symposia.[61] But the public performances he adduces had

---

the coinage of *homēristēs* was also available then. It is unlikely that this technical designation, faced with the competition of the more popular 'rhapsode', ever gained much currency. But as the *homēristēs*, with roots in the reforms of Demetrios of Phaleron, grew clearly apart from the rhapsode by his emphatically histrionic delivery and the elective abandonment of solo performance for combined acting, the rarer label *homēristēs* was at hand to tell him apart from the conventional rhapsode. See further below, p. 465.

58 This fact motivates the citation of Khamaileon, who makes reference to the established trio (Homer, Hesiod, and Arkhilokhos) and for the sake of completion adds Phokylides and Mimnermos. Phokylides was best known as an epic gnomologist; whether he also wrote elegy is disputed by West 1978b:164n2. Perhaps he is paired with Mimnermos in the ἔτι δέ clause at Athenaios 14.620c4 as a representative of elegy, although other reasons for the pairing are possible. Arkhilokhos' place in the rhapsodic repertoire was already secure in the classical period, but this does not mean, even if it is likely, that *rhapsodes* were specifically the ones who set and performed his poetry to music. That some of them did so with Homer and Hesiod is certain, for only this fact explains why Khamaileon's observation is introduced at this point in the book.

59 Cf. Nagy 1990c:26–27 and Nagy 1996c:160n25.

60 Although Athenaios' report is in the passive voice (μελῳδηθῆναι 620c2) and lacks an explicit agent, only if Khamaileon had believed Stesikhoros to have set ἔπη to μέλος would he have made the reported comment in his book *On Stēsikhoros*, and only then could Athenaios in turn have thought his citation appropriate to the similar practice of some Hellenistic rhapsodes. Cf. Burkert 1987 and Russo 1999, who variously cast Stesikhoros as a competitor or heir to rhapsodic performance traditions. See further above, p. 352 n. 72. μελῳδέω is found at Aristophanes *Birds* 1382 (1381 in some editions) in connection with Kinesias', in *Women at the Thesmophoria* 99 with Agathon's, lyrics. Dunbar (1995:208) *ad Birds* 226 suggests that "a wider meaning of 'sing/recite to instrumental accompaniment', not limited to lyric metre, seems possible here, as in the statement of Aristotle's pupil Chamaileon cited by Athenaios (620c), were μελῳδηθῆναι is used of performing ... presumably with lyre accompaniment." Other occurrences of the verb at Plato *Laws* 655d8; Plutarch *Moralia* 389e9, 430a7, 623b3, 744c5, 1019a3; Lucian *Phalaris* I §13, *De domo* §19, *Adversus indoctum* §12, *De saltatione* §27, *Dialogi marini* I §4, *Dialogi deorum* XI §4; and Apollodoros *Bibliothēkē* 1.9.25 §135.2.

61 That the οὐκ ἀπελείποντο means that the performers themselves attended the symposia, as opposed to their being present as a topic of conversation, follows from the word used at 616e, ἀκροάματα, which LSJ s.v. glosses as 'lectures, singers, or players, esp. during meals'. Cf. Robert 1936:236–237 and Jones 1991:191.

taken place in the theaters and, thus, they invited comparison with the most theatrical of all performers of Homer, the *homēristai*, who at their showiest joined in small acting troupes to mime scenes from the poems, usually bloody fights from the *Iliad*.[62] Athenaios wants to keep rhapsodes and *homēristai* apart and to prevent confusion feels the need to mention the older kind in passing, since the old were once called by the same name as the new. And so we learn the crucial detail that it was Demetrios of Phaleron who 'first introduced the present-day *homēristai* into the theater'.[63]

Now, on the face of it, this statement must be wrong. For there is nothing in the testimonies from the late fourth century BC to suggest the existence then of anything like the *homēristai* of late Hellenistic and Roman imperial times, as will become clear below when we examine what the *homēristai* did for a living. And I find it implausible to think that Demetrios might have devised *de novo* such a colorful profession, without precedent at the time. But, as I noted above, Homeric poetry had great dramatic potential, acknowledged for centuries; and the rhapsode, sensitive to his material, had made increasing use of it, exploiting it for good effect before adoring audiences. So we should not be surprised if he eventually developed a 'subspecialty' that made the acting of well-known episodes the main fare. Thus, the rich robe was exchanged for a proper costume, and the staff for a fitting prop—perhaps a shield and a sword or a spear. In all likelihood, work as a *homēristēs* called for a less prodigious memory, and certainly for little powers of extempore composition. For this loss he compensated with a greater flair for the dramatic in his deportment and a full use of the all the available resources of stagecraft. And in the earliest stages of his development, as he gradually came to be distinguished from the rhapsode by his peculiar emphasis on acting, a clear point of contrast must have been his altogether more slavish dependence on a script for his performance. Thus, to the degree that the rhapsode still recomposed any of his material in performance, it is right to see him at one end, and the average *homēristēs* at the other, in a spectrum that spans the variable degree to which slavish memorization and reproduction—and hence strict adherence to a performance script—and a measure of extempore recomposition were combined in each individual professional declaimer of Homer.

---

[62] As my analysis below will show, I am of the opinion that the current consensus puts too much weight on the miming of battle scenes. The best current overviews of the *homēristai* are Husson 1993 and Hillgruber 2000. See, further, Calderini 1911, Kroll 1918, Heraeus 1930, Robert 1936:237 (esp. n. 4), Robert 1983:183–184, Roueché 1993:15–25, Perpillou-Thomas 1995:229–230, Nagy 1996c:158–182, Garelli-François 2000:504–506, Cucchiarelli 2006, O'Sullivan 2009:182–184, and Gangloff 2010:54–56.

[63] Athenaios 14.620b: τοὺς δὲ νῦν Ὁμηριστὰς ὀνομαζομένους πρῶτος εἰς τὰ θέατρα παρήγαγε Δημήτριος ὁ Φαληρεύς.

So, how should we envision the *homēristai*? What do we learn about them from extant sources? Three are the main literary ones, to which a few papyri and two inscriptions add a small but significant contribution. All of these witnesses date to Roman imperial times. LSJ s.v. ὁμηριστής cites Artemidoros *Oneirokritika* 4.2 and Akhilleus Tatios 3.20, for which the gloss correctly says 'actor of Homeric scenes'. In the first passage Artemidoros draws a parallel between the surgeon, whose cutting draws blood but is not fatal by design, and the *homēristai*, who wound and draw blood but do not intend to kill.[64] As Jones (1991:189) notes, we are surely dealing here with the theatrical antics and stage devices of actors who specialize in Homeric combat, poking each other with their make-believe swords and drawing false blood. Their exaggerated battle miming (πολλοὺς τιτρώσκειν) corresponds to the surgeon's many operations (πολλοὺς ἐχείρισε). As to Akhilleus Tatios, he mentions *homēristai* at 3.20, when Satyros tells the story of a ship attacked by pirates that held among the passengers 'one of those who performs orally (τῷ στόματι δεικνύντων) Homer's poetry in the theaters'.[65] It is important to note the phrase τῷ στόματι δεικνύντων, which makes clear that, from the author's perspective, at the heart of this performer's trade was the recitation of Homer, even though it took place in the theaters and—it soon becomes clear—involved acting out battle scenes.[66]

---

[64] *Oneirokritika* 4.2 Pack: καὶ τῶν τεχνῶν δὲ αἱ δυνάμεις ὅμοιαι, καὶ εἰ τῇ ἐνεργείᾳ εἶεν ἀνόμοιοι, εἰς ταὐτὸν ἀποβαίνουσιν. ὡς Ἀπολλωνίδης ὁ χειρουργὸς ὁμηρίζειν νομίσας καὶ πολλοὺς τιτρώσκειν πολλοὺς ἐχείρισε. καὶ γὰρ οἱ ὁμηρισταὶ τιτρώσκουσι μὲν καὶ αἱμάσσουσιν, ἀλλ' οὐκ ἀποκτεῖναί γε βούλονται· οὕτω δὲ καὶ ὁ χειρουργός (lines 74–79).

[65] καὶ γάρ τις ἐν αὐτοῖς ἦν τῶν τὰ Ὁμήρου τῷ στόματι δεικνύντων ἐν τοῖς θεάτροις· τὴν Ὁμηρικὴν σκευὴν ὁπλισάμενός τε αὐτὸς καὶ τοὺς ἀμφ' αὐτὸν οὕτω σκευάσας ἐπεχείρουν μάχεσθαι (3.20.4).

[66] This fact has not been readily accepted by all. Rightly viewing him as a *homēristēs*, an undue emphasis on his acting was placed by Mitscherlich, who removed τῷ στόματι from his edition, and Berger (*apud* Boden), who emended it to τῷ σχήματι. But Jacobs (1821:670) rightly comments: "τῷ στόματι delendum censet Bipont. [sc. Mitscherlich] aut cum σχήματι permutandum. Hoc *Bergero* in mentem venerat. Sed bene habet vulgata. Rhapsodus describitur, qui Homerica recitabat carmina, idque in scena, non, ut pantomimi, loquacibus digitis usus aut σχήματι, sed τῷ στόματι, *versus recitando*. De quibus recitationibus, quae non multum abhorrebant ab histrionum in comoediis tragoediisque arte, verbum ὑποκρίνεσθαι usurpatur" (his emphasis). Rouché (1993:15) clarifies the difference between mimes and pantomimes thus: "The pantomime, a solo performer, performed a dance, accompanied by music, but without words; the subject matter was drawn from mythology, but was essentially serious, and the pantomime's art is regularly described as τραγικός. Mimes performed in groups, both of men and women, and used words and music to present scenes which were often comic, but also encompassed tragic subjects." For bibliography see Rouché 1993:15nn1–2, esp. Reich 1903 and Wiemken 1972. For a related mention of ὁμηρίζειν in close proximity with ὑποκρίνεσθαι and ὑπόκρισις, see Akhilleus Tatios 8.9 with LSJ s.v. ὁμηρίζω III and Nagy 1996c:164–165. Hillgruber (2000:67n19) has recently approved of Lurje's emendation τῷ σώματι and its alleged support, Plato's *Laws* 814c6–8. But this is hardly a valid parallel, since the passage regards wrestling (πάλη) and proper bodily movement (κίνησις τοῦ σώματος), for which argumentative clarity will indeed require, as the Athenian points out, that speech be joined by physical illustration. A comparable motivation

Therefore, still at this late date *homēristai* need not have been seen primarily in their capacity as stage actors, and a focus may still remain on the poetry itself. A third and earlier instance of the term, this time the Latin *homerista*, occurs in Petronius' *Satyricon* 59, when Trimalchio brings in a band of *homeristae* to entertain his guests.[67] In the Roman setting of Petronius' satire, the boisterous acting is exaggerated for comic effect: the clashing of spear and shield, the shouting, Ajax' raving attack of the boiled calf with unsheathed sword. But, significantly, even here the declamation remains an emphatic component, and the retention of the original Greek verse is striking: '[W]hile the *homeristae* talked to each other in Greek verse, in their usual excessive way, [Trimalchio] intoned the libretto in Latin'.[68] Starr 1987 remarks that *homeristae* were not normal party entertainment among the Roman rich, and that Trimalchio substitutes these low-class performers for the more normal *comoedi*, an improper social disloca-

---

is lacking in the proposed characterization of the *homēristai* as those who 'exhibit with the body the verses of Homer in the theaters'. 'With the body' is simply too crude a description of a performer's technique. On that count, τῷ σχήματι is a far superior alternative. Unfortunately, *P.Duk.* inv. 772 (formerly *P.Rob.* inv. 35), for which Willis (1990:82 in line 19) prints σ[τ]όματι, has a *lacuna* at that very point. Laplace 1993 accepts Willis's reading. Although the papyrus may perhaps accommodate σώματι, it is hard to gainsay a unanimous medieval *paradosis* that, as I will now show, makes good sense. Hillgruber is doubtless right that the characteristic showmanship of *homēristai* motivates the use of δεικνύντων; mention of their professional setting, ἐν τοῖς θεάτροις, prepares the reader for the existence of the σκευή. But why τῷ στόματι? Doubtless because, ordinarily, vocal delivery was central to their success, and Akhilleus Tatios must have felt the need to clarify that with δεικνύντων he was not marginalizing the role of recitation. Incidentally, *pace* Hillgruber and others, I do not believe that there was more than one *homēristēs* on board the ship (he armed those who happened to be around him, τοὺς ἀμφ' αὐτόν). Why else should the author have written τις ... ἦν rather than τινες ... ἦσαν? That *homēristai* often performed solo is an important clue to the nature of their performance. A solo performer cannot effectively play several parts in close succession (perhaps alternating them) without significant recourse to vocal delivery. In support of this observation I cite the epitaph of the mime Vitalis: "Fingebam vultus, habitus ac verba loquentum, | ut plures uno crederes ore loqui" (*Anthologia Latina* I.2.38 no. 487a.15–16; cf. Hillgruber 2000:68n27).

67 *Satyricon* 59.3–7: "'simus ergo, quod melius est, a primitiis hilares et Homeristas spectemus'. intravit factio statim hastisque scuta concrepuit. ipse Trimalchio in pulvino consedit, et cum Homeristae Graecis versibus colloquerentur, ut insolenter solent, ille canora voce Latine legebat librum. mox silentio facto 'scitis' inquit 'quam fabulam agant? Diomedes et Ganymedes duo fratres fuerunt. horum soror erat Helena. Agamemnon illam rapuit et Dianae cervam subiecit. ita nunc Homeros dicit quemadmodum inter se pugnent Troiani et Tarentini. vicit scilicet et Iphigeniam, filiam suam, Achilli dedit uxorem. ob eam rem Aiax insanit et statim argumentum explicabit.' haec ut dixit Trimalchio, clamorem Homeristae sustulerunt, interque familiam discurrentem vitulus in lance du⟨ce⟩naria elixus allatus est, et quidem galeatus. secutus est Aiax strictoque gladio, tamquam insaniret, ⟨vitulum⟩ concidit, ac modo versa modo supina gesticulatus mucrone frust[r]a collegit mirantibusque [vitulum] partitus est."

68 Hillgruber (2000:64.5) disputes the notion that Trimalchio's *liber* was really a "libretto" of the performance. Whether or no the book closely followed the Greek of the *homēristai*, Trimalchio must have expected his guests to consider his words as their Latin equivalent. On the words "ut insolenter solent" see Cucchiarelli 2006.

tion that parallels his use of *comoedi* for Atellan farces (53.13). This transposition is significant in light of the gloss *omeristai* for *atellani* in the *Corpus Glossariorum Latinorum* (=*CGL*; see below, p. 462).

Besides the passages reviewed above, we possess other documentary evidence: four papyri from Oxyrhynkhos and two from the Faiyūm, one inscription from Aphrodisias in Caria, and one other from Noricum.[69] I print them here for the ease of the reader before I discuss them.

Oxyrhynkhos

1. II AD: *P.Oxy.* III 519 (see line 4) = Wilcken *Chrest.* no. 492 = *Feste* 36[70]

> (ὧν) ἀπεδόθη
> Μεχ(εὶρ) κγ
> μίμῳ (δραχμαὶ) υϛ,
> ὁμηριστῇ (δραχμαὶ) ῳμη,
> 5 καὶ ὑπὲρ μου[σ]ι[κῶνᵃ (δραχμαὶ) . . .]
> [ὀ]ρχηστῇ [(δραχμαὶ)] ρ[.]δ

ᵃμου[σ]ι[κῆς] G[renfell]-H[unt].

2. II–III AD: *P.Oxy.* VII 1050 (see line 26) = *Feste* 39[71]

> λόγ(ος) (δραχμῶν) υ.
> ἱερεῦσιᵃ (δραχμαὶ) ξ,
> Νείλῳ (δραχμαὶ) κ,
> θρόνῳ (δραχμαὶ) κ,
> 5 ἱπποκόμ(οις)ᵇ (δραχμαὶ) . ,
> κήρυκιᶜ [
> ξυστάρχ(η) [
> Ὠρείωνι [
> Σεουήρῳ [

---

69 Marek 1993b:144 no. 28 prints a funerary epigram for a Kyros from Lampsakos (date not specified). He suggests that Kyros was a *homēristēs*. I quote the relevant lines (7–12): εἰ δὲ θέλις γενεήν τε καὶ οὔνομα τοῦ- | μὸν ἀκοῦσαι, οὔνομά μοι Κῦρος, | πατρὶς δέ μοι Λάμψακός ἐστιν, | κεῖμαι δ' ἐν γαίῃ Πομπηίου, φῶς τόδε | λείψας, πολλὰ κοσμήσας θυμέ- | λαις τὸν θεῖον Ὅμηρον. Vacat. Cf. *SEG* 43.920.

70 Wilcken *Chrest.* = Mitteis and Wilcken 1912:I.2; *Feste* = Vandoni 1964. See also Hunt and Edgar 1932–1934:2.522–525 no. 402 and Tedeschi 2002:176–177 no. 25. For editions of Greek papyri and other papyrological references see Oates et al. 2001. I print Wilcken's text, except for the erroneously dotted σ of ὁμηριστῇ. Vandoni follows Wilcken but fails to dot several letters.

71 Schmidt = Schmidt 1911; Poliakoff = Poliakoff 1982:91. See also Tedeschi 2002:177–178 no. 26. I print Hunt's text, emended as noted.

10 Βελλαρείνῳ [
    βραβευταῖς [
    πανκρατ(ιαστῶν) ζε[ύγ(ει)
    σφαιρομαχ(ούντων) [ζεύγ(ει)ᵈ
    ἄλ(λῳ) ζεύγ(ει) παν[κρατ(ιαστῶν)
15 Κώφῳ πύκ(τη) [
    φύλ(αξι) θεάτ[ρου
    ῥάντα[ις
    παν . [
    μανγανα[ρίῳᵉ
20 αὐλητ[ῆ
    ἱεροδ[ούλοιςᶠ
    ερ[
    τ[

ᵃἱερευσι Pap. ‖ ᵇἱπποκομ Pap. ‖ ᶜFirst κ of κηρυκι corr. from ἰε ‖ ᵈσφαιρομαχ(ούντων) [ζεύγ(ει) *vel* σφαιρομαχ(οῦσι) [Poliakoff, σφαιρομάχ(οις) [H. ‖ ᵉμανγανα[ρίῳ] or μανγανα[ρίοις Schmidt, μανγάνα[ις Vandoni, μανγανᾳ.[H. ‖ ᶠἱεροδ[Pap.

Col. II
    κ.[
25 μίμῳᵍ [
    ὁμηρισ[τῆ

ᵍμειμῳ Pap.

3. III AD: *P.Osl.* III 189 *verso*, lines 11–13 (see line 12) = *Feste* 13[72]

Παχὼν ῑδ ἐπι . [	May 9
ῑς ἀπόδιξις Ὁμηρι[στῶνᵃ	May 11
ῑθ ἀγὼν ποιητῶν	May 14

ᵃor Ὁμηρι[στοῦ E.-A.]

---

[72] *P.Osl.* = Eitrem and Amundsen 1936. See also Tedeschi 2002:179 no. 28. I print the text as it appears in *P.Osl.* The provenience of this papyrus is unknown. I have followed Husson's plausible suggestion and placed it under Oxyrhynkhos (Husson 1993:96).

455

4. Late III AD: *SB* IV 7336 (see lines 26, 29) = *Feste* 44 (cf. Wormald 1929)[73]

[ὐ(πὲρ) λη]μμάτων ἐνεχ(θέντων) καὶ ὑ(πὲρ) ι[ᵃ
[Ἀμε]ϲυϲίωνᵇ τῶν κυρ[ω]θ[έντων
[. . .]κλαρίῳ [ἐ]λθόντι ἐκ [
ὑ[(πὲρ) ὑ]πολόγουᶜ [
5 κ[ήρ]υκι ὁμοίως [
σαλπικτῇ ὁμοίως [
αἵματος μόσχου [
Ἥρωνι ὁμοίως [
Σφόγ'γῳᵈ ὁμοίως [
10 κωμῳδῷ ὁμοί(ως) [
/ε) — ⟨ τπ Lνε ——[ᵉ
[τ]οῖς Σαραπείοις ὁμοί(ως) νομ[ᶠ
[σ]υνηθείας ὁμοίως [
ἀναλόγουᵍ ὀρχηστοῦ [
15 [.]ηραρίῳ ὁμοίως [
[Ἀ]μοιτᾷ εἰς ϲυλ[. .]ιμου [
[Ἥ]ρωνι τιμή[ματο]ϲʰ [
πανκλυστῇ [
[θυρ]ωρῷ Σαραπείου [
20 [Σαραπ]ίωνι καὶ Ἀμοιτᾷ πανκ[ρατιασταῖς
[ἀλεί]πταιςⁱ γ̄ τιμήματος [
[κ]ωμῳδῷ ὁμοί(ως) [
κήρυκι ὁμοίως [
ξένια κυνώπουʲ [
25 ἀνδρεοκαταμάκτῃ [
ὁμηριστῇ τιμή(ματος) [
τῷ τοῦ ὀρχηστοῦ δραματοθ[έτηιᵏ
ἀναγνώστῃ Σαραπᾷ [
[ἄλλ]ῳ ὁμηριστῇ [
30 [. . .]γύλλῳˡ τιμή(ματος) [

ᵃⁱ[δίου λόγου Tedeschi ‖ ᵇ[Διο?]νυϲίων Wormald, [Ἀμε]ϲυϲίων Bonneau ‖ ᶜυ]πολογω Pap. ‖
ᵈ*sic* ‖ ᵉ(γίνεται) ἐπ(ὶ τὸ αυτὸ) (δραχμαὶ) τπ (ὀβολοὶ) νε–[Vandoni, (γίνονται) ἐπ( ) (δραχμαὶ) τπ
(ῶν) νε–[Tedeschi, ἐ (=αἱ) π(ᾶσαι) Bilabel; L=ῶν ‖ ᶠνομ[ίϲματα? Bilabel ‖ ᵍἀναλόγου Bilabel,
αναλογω Pap. ‖ ʰτειμη[ματο]ϲ Pap. ‖ ⁱ[ἀλεί]πταις Wormald, [αλι]πταις Pap. ‖ ʲκυνώπου Wormald,
κυνοπου Pap. ‖ ᵏδραματοθ[έτηι? Bilabel, prob. Lewis ‖ ˡγ(ρ)ύλλῳ? Tedeschi

---

73 *SB* = *Sammelbuch griechischer Urkunden aus Ägypten* (vol. IV is edited by F. Bilabel). See also
Tedeschi 2002:179–181 no. 29. For the reading [Ἀμε]ϲυϲίων in line 2 see Bonneau 1981:55 and

Faiyūm

    5. Late III AD: *P.Oxy.* VII 1025 (see line 8) = Wilcken *Chrest.* no. 493 = *Feste* 26[74]

        Αὐρήλιοι Ἄγαθος γυ(μνασιάρχης)
        ἔναρχος πρύτανις καὶ
        Ἑρμανοβάμμων ἐξηγ(ητὴς)
        καὶ Δίδυμος ἀρχιερεὺς
5   καὶ Κοπρίας κοσμητὴς
        πόλεως Εὐεργέτιδος
        Αὐρηλίοις Εὐριπᾷ βιολό-
        γῳ καὶ Σαραπᾷ ὁμηριστῇ
        χαίρειν.
10   ἐξαυτῆς ἥκετε, καθὼ̣[ς
        ἔθος ὑμῖν ἐστιν συνπα-
        νηγυρίζειν, συνεορτάσον-
        τες ἐν τῇ πατρῴᾳ ἡ[μῶν
        ἑορτῇ γενεθλίῳ το̣ῦ̣ Κρ̣ό̣ν̣ο̣υ̣
15   θεοῦ μεγίστου ἀναγ . . . . [.ᵃ
        τῶν θεωριῶν ἅμ' αὔ̣[ρ]ιον
        ἥτις ἐστὶν ι ἀγομ̣[έν]ων
        ἐπὶ τὰς ἐξ ἔθους ἡμ[έρ]ας,
        λαμβάνοντες το[ὺς] μισ-
20   θοὺς καὶ τὰ τίμια.ᵇ
        σεσημ(είωμαι).ᶜ
m²   Ἑρμανοβάμμων ἐξηγ(ητὴς)
        ἐρρῶσθαι ὑμᾶς εὔχομ(αι).
m³   Δίδυμος ἀρχιερ(εὺς) ἐρρῶσθ(αι) ὑμᾶς εὔχομ(αι).
m⁴   Κοπρίας ἐρρῶσθαι ὑμᾶς
        εὔχομαι.

ᵃἀναγομέν[ων] Tedeschi, cf. Schuman 1980:15n *ad* no. 5, l. 24 ‖ ᵇτειμια Pap. ‖ ᶜσεσημ(είωμαι)
Wilcken, σεσημ(ειώμεθα) H.

Perpillou-Thomas 1993:81n72; for δραματοθ[έτηι in 27 see Lewis 1981:80. I print the text in SB IV 7336, amended as noted.
[74] See also Hunt and Edgar 1932–1934:2.438–439 no. 359, Collart 1944:142–143, Perpillou-Thomas 1993:107–109, and Tedeschi 2002:168–169. I print Wilcken's text, amended as noted (m² = 2nd hand, etc.).

6. IV.1–2 AD: *P.Bodl.* I 143 (see line 3)[75]

>]ηψ . . .
> . . . .] . ν . . ος νομ(ισμάτια) ς
> ἀννωνῶν ὁμηρικῶν δι(ὰ)
>   Σουχιδοῦ ἐπὶ λ(όγου)   νομ(ισμάτια) ς
> 5 ταμιακῶν α (ἔτους) Ψενύρεως δι(ὰ)
>   Κυρίλλου τρ(απεζίτου) *vacat* (τάλαντα) τκα
> Ἀκυσιλάῳ τρ(απεζίτῃ) [τι]μῆς κριθ(ῆς)
>   ὑπὲρ (ἀρταβῶν) κε *vacat* (τάλαντα) τ
> καὶ ὑπὲρ ναύλου κριθῆς   (τάλαντα) σξς (δηνάρια) Γ
> 10   ὑπὲρ ἄνθρακος κεν(τηναρίων) ιβ (τάλαντα) φ
> . . .] . ι Ναμεσί(ωνος) λ(ιτρῶν) ς καὶ ἐρί[ων]
> λ(ιτρῶν)] ιδ   *vacat 4.6 cm*   (τάλαντα) σν
> ὑπὲ]ρ χρυσίου . ιηπων (τάλαντα) τ
> γί(νεται)] ὁμοῦ νομ(ισμάτια) κ καὶ (τάλαντα) [.]ψλη
> 15 . . . .]αεως γ (ἔτους) εξ( )   (τάλαντα) η
> . . . .] α (ἔτους) Νεμεσᾶς   β (ἔτους) Νεώτερος
> . . . .] γ (ἔτους) Φίλιππος *vacat*

Inscriptions

1. Late III AD, theater at Aphrodisias in Caria, room 6 behind the stage
   front (Roueché 1993:18)

   a.   Δημητρίου ὁμηριστοῦ
        διασκευή
        Α[. . . ca. 9 . . .]Σ

   b.   Ἐγενήσθη Ἀλέξανδρος

2. II AD, from Virunum, Noricum (Heger 1980 and Leppin 1992:194)

   T(itus) Flavius
   Aelianus
   homerista

Papyrus 1, a fragment from an account of expenditures for theatrical performances at Oxyrhynkhos on Mekheir 23 (February), shows the payment of high
sums to a mime (496 drachmas) and a *homēristēs* (448 drachmas), as well as an
allowance for μουσικοί. Papyrus 2 does not preserve the amount paid to the

---

[75] *P.Bodl.* = Salomons 1996. See also Tedeschi 2002:135n226. For the meaning of "1–2" in the dating
see below, p. 492.

homēristēs (or *homēristai*), but here too this specialty follows the mime in the list of expenditures. It records, however, that the priests received 60 drachmas, far less than the mime and *homēristēs* of Papyrus 1. In fact, the υ in line 1 suggests an account total of 400–500 drachmas.[76] From the same papyrus we also learn about the various kinds of entertainers who participated in the public festivities. It is important to note that Papyrus 1 reflects the engagement of a single *homēristēs*. The same may be true of Papyrus 2, if the identity in the relative order between him and the mime can be extended to the number of artists. It is hard to imagine how a specialist in the dramatic reenactment of fighting scenes from the *Iliad* would have been able to perform alone, unless the theatrical element had been subservient to declaiming the poetry. But if Homeric verse was the focus—complemented, to be sure, by costuming, gestures, and whatever else might contribute to a strong stage presence—his performing alone presents hardly any difficulty of execution and is unlikely to have disappointed the expectations of his audience. Husson (1993:97) well realizes this and defends, for example, the restoration of a plural in Papyrus 3. The editors, however, offered in the notes the alternative Ὁμηρι[στοῦ (Eitrem and Amundsen 1936:269), and there is no compelling reason for the printed plural other than the prejudice, disputed here, that a plurality of performers is *a priori* more likely. Husson cannot account, however, for the inescapable singular of Papyrus 1 and the likely one of Papyrus 2. Furthermore, by pairing the ὁμηριστής and the ἄλλος ὁμηριστής of Papyrus 4 (lines 26 and 29), she elides the independence of their respective performances implicit in their separate listing, with two other items intervening.[77] Husson attempts to tie them more closely together by arguing that 'to the reader Sarapas' designates a reader of the text mimed by the actors. But, as Petronius illustrates, we are dealing with mimes who themselves recited their lines, not with pantomimes: Trimalchio's Latin reading does not support Husson since it was designed to render intelligible in real time to a non-Greek dinner audience the boisterous Greek declamation of the *homēristai* themselves. Nothing of the sort would be feasible in a festival context. Nor do I think plausible, despite Nagy's approval, her later suggestion that the ἀναγνώστης may have been a *souffleur* for the *homēristai* (see Nagy 1996c:177). A performance by *homēristai* was doubtless too humble an affair to call for such elaborate help. Moreover, if one insists on relating the ἀναγνώστης to the *homēristai*, one would also have to assign the δραματοθέτης to the same production. We should therefore expect 'of the dance', not 'of the dancer'.[78] A show that involved the hiring

---

[76] The editor translates, "Account of 400 drachmae."

[77] See below, p. 462.

[78] But a choreographer, if that is what the word means (cf. Lewis 1981:80), would sooner belong in a pantomime than in a mime.

of a choreographer and a 'reader' seems too grand an event to account for the anticlimactic 'for another *homēristēs*', which reads like an afterthought. Why not just use a plural to start with? Or at least make the second *homēristēs* immediately follow the first? Hence, we must simply own that we do not know what Sarapas' role as 'reader' was.

The services of a βιολόγος and a lone *homēristēs*—also by the name Sarapas—are engaged in Papyrus 5 for the festival of Kronos' birthday at Ptolemais Euergetis (i.e. Arsinoe) in the Faiyūm. Singular, too, is the occurrence in Inscription 1. As I emphasized above (see p. 452 n. 66), the text of Akhilleus Tatios explicitly states that there was only one *homēristēs* on board the ship. Since he traveled alone, we must presume that he was a solo performer. That he is able to arm 'those about him' (the precise number is not given) only means that his equipment included an array of weapons. This is hardly surprising if his repertoire was broad or his practice was to alternate or act out in succession more than one part in performance. At all events, that he should possess a plurality of weapons adds realistic color to his characterization: over the course of a life-long professional practice any man is likely to build redundancy into the tools and accessories of his trade. One need not conjecture against the text that the *homēristēs* was accompanied by a troupe that is never mentioned; or that, although alone in his journey, his equipment actually belonged to a troupe that had not joined him.[79] Such convolutions, which flow from a discomfort with the evidence for the solo performance of the *homēristēs*, are simply unnecessary. Similarly unwarranted is the supposition that, even though Papyrus 1 mentions only one *homēristēs*, the magnitude of the payment proves that he stands in the account for his troupe as *pars pro toto*.[80] If this were true, why write ὁμηριστῆ instead of ὁμηρισταῖς? If an explicit singular stands unaccountably for the plural with such ease, why should we prefer the plural ὁμηρι[στῶν over the singular ὁμηρι[στοῦ in Papyrus 3? And why should the author of Papyrus 4 have taken the trouble to list the second *homēristēs* and not rather subsume him under the first? There are, moreover, more plausible explanations for the high sums in Papyrus 1 that do not require us to assume the silent existence of a troupe. As Collart (1944:143) remarked, since we do not know the duration of the festival neither do we know what the daily pay was.[81] Note that the same document stipulates a payment of 100 to 200 drachmas (specifically, '1[.]4') for the dancer. In the event, only Petronius' *Satyricon* provides explicit support for the view that *homēristai* acted together as

---

[79] Cf. Hillgruber 2000:67n20.
[80] Hillgruber 2000:68n27 after Heraeus 1930:401.
[81] So also Perpillou-Thomas 1993:231.

a troupe.[82] I do not doubt that this elective mode of performance was occasionally realized. But there is no warrant for the common scholarly prejudice that downplays or rejects solo performance. The record arguably makes this mode of delivery the more common alternative, and in so doing plainly exhibits the centrality of recitation to this most histrionic of Homeric performers.

Having demonstrated that *homēristai* often (if not ordinarily) performed alone, it is time to return to a descriptive survey of the evidence. Papyrus 3 is a calendar, though too fragmentary to discern whether it included accounting details or merely a list of competitive events. Each of the three lines 11–13 takes place on a different day: May 9, 11, and 14. May 14 featured a competition for which poets presumably contributed their own original compositions. As the editors note, the ἀγὼν ποιητῶν apparently belonged to the same festival as the ἀπόδειξις three days earlier. As I emphasized above, despite the plural restored by the editors we simply do not know that said 'display' involved more than one *homēristēs*. Robert (1983:184) underlines the distinction between an ἀγών and an ἀπόδειξις.[83] He points out that in Hellenistic times there were cases in which even the verb ἀγωνίζεσθαι need not have implied a competition against other participants. So, for example, in *SIG*³ 738a (whose text should be compared with Robert's own in Robert 1929:34–36) a χοροψάλτρια by the name of Polygnota is said to have 'competed for three days' (ἀγωνίξατο ἐ[πὶ ἁ]μέρας τρεῖς 7–8) at a time when the Pythian games could not be held because of war (Robert 1929:34; cf. lines 5–6 of the inscription).[84] All the same, such 'displays'—the use of ἀγωνίζεσθαι shows—were never entirely non-competitive, as might be expected from the close ties between entertainment and competition in the ancient festival setting. The crowning, the recourse to ἀγωνίζεσθαι, and the frequent mention in honorary inscriptions of the approval of the audience[85] all point to the ideology of competition underlying the honorary decree. True,

---

[82] The joint acting of *homēristai* may be reasonably inferred from Artemidoros, although the further notion that this was their only mode of performance does not follow. On the doubtful case of Papyrus 6 see below.

[83] "D'autre part, le vocabulaire en ce qui concerne ces deux lignes du papyrus d'Oslo est, pour chacune d'elles, radicalement différent: l'ἀγὼν ποιητῶν est un concours traditionnel, à la fin duquel on proclame le vainqueur; pour les homéristes, il y a une ἀπόδειξις, c'est-à-dire qu'ils sont 'produits'." But there is no established technical use of ἀποδείκνυμι in the sense of 'to produce (a play)', and it is better to view ἀπόδειξις here in terms of its connection with ἐπίδειξις (see above, p. 308 n. 64).

[84] Robert 1929: "Polygnota n'a pas concouru. C'est un usage qui se répand à l'époque hellénistique que les musiciens et les poètes ne se fassent pas entendre seulement dans les concours, mais donnent aussi des auditions (ἐπιδείξεις, ἀκροάσεις) soit en dehors de l'époque des concours, soit à l'occasion des concours" (38–39). Even a crown need not imply a previous competition (so *SIG*³ 450). Cf. Aneziri 2003:222n106.

[85] εὐδοκιμέω, for example, in *SIG*³ 659.5, 737.6, or 738a.7.

the performer at times may not have competed against other rivals, but, even when there was no tangible prize, he would have certainly striven to gain the favor of his audience.[86] The stakes would have been the bestowal of honors at the pleasure of the officials who acted on behalf of the city. If we bear this in mind and accept *ex hypothesi* that the ἀπόδειξις of Papyrus 3 did not involve several rival *homēristai* in competition (or groups of them), it remains the case that only an artist whose performance had won the loudest acclaim would have his honors recorded for a permanent witness. At any rate, Robert's distinction[87] will not decide whether one *homēristēs* or more might have taken part in the 'display'. My study has made clear, however, that ἀπόδειξις cannot be reduced to dramatic production, but encompasses a wide range of public performances, including the declamations of rhapsodes and public lectures by sophists. Still Robert is right that there is a distinction of emphasis between the poets' ἀγών and the ἀπόδειξις of the *homēristēs* (or *homēristai*): the latter put more weight on the *opsis* of the stage.

As I already observed, although Papyrus 4 mentions two *homēristai*, they appear individually as *two different* line items. This strongly suggests that they gave two independent performances, which undercuts the notion of the *homēristēs* as a mime specializing strictly in Homeric fights. Indeed, commenting on Papyrus 4, the editors of Papyrus 3 noted: "ἄλλ]ῳ ὁμηριστῆ—the recital from Homer to be continued after a pause?"[88] Individual performances signal an enduring emphasis on the declamation of poetry. In Papyrus 5 officials from Euergetis engage the services of a *biologos*[89] and a *homēristēs* from Oxyrhynkhos, both regulars, to participate at a local festival (the birthday of Kronos). As I anticipated above, the pairing of these two professionals recurs in the *CGL* II p. 22, 40–42: "Atellani: σκηνικοι· αρχαιολογοι· ‖ βιολογοι· ωσδεοβοι· ‖ διος ομηριστην· δη ‖ τοι· νυχοροι." Despite the textual corruption,[90] we can tell that the *homēristēs* is clearly on a level with the *biologos* and the *atellanus*. Papyrus 6, a list of expenditures from the Faiyūm dated to the first half of the fourth century AD, records 'Homeric *annonae*', which the editor has glossed as "allowances for Homeric actors." By Homeric actors he means *homēristai*, whom he describes after Husson as "actors ... who mimed Homeric battle scenes on the

---

[86] Wörrle 1988:8, lines 44–46 records three days devoted to "mimes and performers and shows for which there are no prizes" when any of the other performers that pleased the city (τῶν ἀρεσκόντων τῇ πόλει) would also be admitted.

[87] See n. 83 immediately above.

[88] Eitrem and Amundsen 1936:269.

[89] A type of mime. Cf. Robert 1936:239–241 and Hillgruber 2000:65n12.

[90] h (=*margo* ed. Steph. Leid. 764.B.8, i.e. the annotations of Franciscus Junius the Younger, on which see *CGL* II pp. xix–xx) offers "ὁμηρισταὶ δετοὶ σὺν χοροῖς." Cf. Heraeus 1930:397 and Hillgruber 2000:65.

stage."[91] Granting *ex hypothesi* that ὁμηρικῶν refers to *homēristai*, the fact that their expenses are lumped together does not prove that they acted together as a troupe. Although possible, this view remains conjectural. The payment of six *solidi* amounts *grosso modo* to three hundredfold the average daily salary of a worker at that time.[92]

As to Inscriptions 1 (a and b), Roueché (1993:19–20) suggests that it was cut on the wall of the doorway to room 6 at the back of the theater stage to mark it as reserved for a Demetrios. The word *homēristēs* is in a different hand (cursive, not square) and apparently was added to identify him further by his trade. (Traces of other inscriptions, surely of previous users, are still visible.) Inscription 1.b is harder to interpret: if it meant '*né* Alexander', why the wish to give his birth name? And if it means 'he acted Alexander' (the Paris of the *Iliad*), why the prominence of that one role? (hardly a martial paragon befitting the stereotype of a bloody *homēristēs*).[93] Inscription 2 witnesses to the vitality of the profession, spanning several centuries, and, in the case of Virunum, extending the declamation of Greek Homeric verse even to provincial cities where—if Petronius' text can serve as a reliable guide—few would have been able to understand it.

To summarize the results of my survey: Husson (1993:93) was right to follow Robert (1936:237n4) in criticizing those who made no distinction between the rhapsode and the *homēristēs*. But my analysis reveals as overdone the emphasis placed since then on their stage acting to the detriment of their recitation. The *homēristēs*, to be sure, may have dressed to impersonate a Homeric character, and his stage delivery, as to voice and gesture, must have exceeded anything

---

[91] Both quotations are at Salomons 1996:265.

[92] For the currency of fourth-century Egypt see Bagnall 1985:9–18, with his equation of νομισμάτιον and *solidus* at 16. Pankiewicz (1989:105) calculates the average daily base salary as 1/56 of a *solidus*. He arrives at this number by averaging amounts attested by several papyri and the Diocletian price edict (see Lauffer 1971). He uses not the Diocletian standard, which struck *solidi* at 60 to the pound of gold, but one that started in AD 309 at the mint in Trier, where 72 were struck. The devalued *solidus* was finally embraced as standard in 324 (cf. Crawford 1975:588–590, Bagnall 1985:15, and Pankiewicz 1989:81–82). The edict specifies 25 *denarii* as the daily pay for an *operarius rusticus* (7.1a Lauffer). The Edict of Maximum Prices (on which see Bagnall 1985:20 and Crawford and Reynolds 1979:197) states the price of a pound of gold at 72,000 *denarii*. This means that 25 *denarii* are 1/40 of the Constantine *solidus*. The other amounts are: 1/60 in P.Oxy. 1499 (three attendants of a public bath in AD 309 are paid monthly wages of one talent in all, i.e. 1,500 *denarii*, which must be divided by three and thirty); per diem payments to workers in AD 314 of 400, 500, and 650 drachmas (four to a *denarius*), i.e. of 1/65, 1/52, and 1/40, since by AD 314 (the date of the document) inflation had increased the price of gold by a factor of 6–7 from the original 40 or 48 talents/pound to 288 (see Sijpesteijn and Worp 1983:52–63 no. 22 at 55–56 for the papyrus; cf. Bagnall and Sijpesteijn 1977:116). The fraction of *solidus* for the daily salary during the first half of the fourth century AD remains within 1/40 and 1/65, with the lower range being more common.

[93] Roueché (1993:19–20) also notes his likely association with a *biologos* attested in a stray find that probably belongs with the texts from the theater.

a classical Athenian audience ever witnessed. But even the most satiric of all literary sources firmly attests to an on-going declamation of the poetic Greek text, and this, even where comprehension was far from guaranteed.[94] The papyri also show us, in all likelihood, *individual* performers who, thus unable to place a heavy emphasis on the choreography of fighting scenes, must have made the spoken word a vital ingredient of their successful demonstrations.[95] The word ἀπόδειξις, which has survived in one of the documents, further ties their performances to the long-standing rhapsodic and rhetorical traditions of public displays. This makes it likely that the statement by the late fourth-century AD grammarian Diomedes,[96] which casts rhapsodes as reciters in the theaters under the name 'Homeristae', is not a misinformed inference from early sources, but a true reflection of the central role that the declamation of the poems (in their original Greek) held even among performers who in time became notorious for their exaggerated stage antics, especially their choreography of battle scenes.[97]

[94] I cite as further, indirect support what Hillgruber (2000:72) writes of the *Ennianista* in Gellius *Noctes Atticae* 18.5, a performer whose trade name must have been formed after the pattern of 'homerista'. That he was an ἀναγνώστης, an educated man experienced in declaiming the *Annales* ("non indoctum hominem, uoce admodum scita et canora Enii annales legere"), undermines Hillgruber's argument that *homēristai* were nothing more than mimes largely unmoored from the original Greek texts who specialized in Homeric motifs.

[95] Someone might object that single mimes too are sometimes mentioned in our documents. But this is a valid objection only on the (false) assumption that mimes always acted in groups. Csapo and Slater (1994:370) state that "mimes acted, sang, and danced without masks, either individually or in a troupe." It is very unlikely that a city would supply with a supporting band of local actors a single out-of-town mime whose services it had engaged (as in Papyrus 5): Roueché (1993:52) is clear that, so far as we can ascertain their status, mimes were associate-performers. Prevented from competing at sacred festivals, their participation in synods of τεχνῖται was barred also (Aneziri 2003:331–332). Although some did form associations in the second and third centuries AD, they remained separate from the artists of Dionysos (332n77). Wiemken's considered judgment is that "[ü]berhaupt ... von stehenden Mimentruppen in der Überlieferung niemals die Rede [ist]; vielmehr waren die Mimen Solisten in ihrem jeweiligen Fach, die auf Tagesgage spielten und von Fall zu Fall herangezogen und zu einem Ensemble vereinigt werden konnten" (1972:182). *Ad hoc* associations, then, seem to have been the norm among them. This is quite different from views of *homēristai*, here disputed, that assume without hesitation that they must have always acted in troupes, a *modus operandi* seemingly required by the further assumption that their sole specialty was the staging of bloody fights.

[96] *GL* 1.484 Keil: "rapsodia dicitur Graece ποιήσεως μέρος ... vel quod olim partes Homerici carminis in theatralibus circulis cum baculo, id est virga, pronuntiabant qui ab eodem Homero dicti Homeristae."

[97] For the opposite view, cf. Garelli-François (2000:504n15), who thinks Diomedes to be wholly derivative of Athenaios 14.620b: he would have neither known what Garelli-François calls "the *homēristai* from the time of Athenaios" (whom she assumes to be very different from the rhapsodes of old) nor the ones attested during the first and second centuries AD (who, she thinks, may have disappeared by the time of Diomedes). I suggest instead that, from his fourth-century perspective, Diomedes incorporated in his synchronic description of rhapsodes elements that came from different stages in the diachronic evolution of epic performance. Ultimately, his words emerge from scrutiny innocent of serious distortion. He is obviously familiar with the

Now, the very name *homēristēs* must have had its origin in the context of the increasing specialization of performers in Hellenistic times.[98] It is then that we find among the αὐληταί the ἀσκαύλης, καλαμαύλης, θρηναύλης, and χοραύλης; among string instrumentalists the πανδουριστής and σαμβυκιστής; among ὀρχησταί the κορδακιστής and παντόμιμος, sometimes referred to as τραγικῆς καὶ ἐνρύθμου κινήσεως ὑποκριτής or μύθων ὀρχηστής; among acrobats the κοντοπέκτης, σκανδαλιστής, and καλοβάτης; among the μῖμοι the κίναιδος, μαλακός, μαγῳδός, ἀρχαιολόγος, and βιολόγος.[99] Such terms could be multiplied. In this cultural and professional context, it is only natural that the ὁμηριστής too would find his place.[100]

---

theatrical setting for rhapsodic performance, relevant both to the post-Phaleronian rhapsodes and to the *homēristai* of later Roman imperial times; hence his "in theatralibus circulis." The relative clause "qui ab eodem Homero dicti Homeristae" is similarly applicable to Hellenistic and Roman imperial performers of Homeric poetry (see above, pp. 449f. with n. 57). Given that he knew the term "homerista," still in use about a century before his own time in connection with the histrionic *homēristai*, it seems to me improbable that he would nevertheless—*ex hypothesi*, if we follow Garelli-François—apply it without historical warrant to the older rhapsodes of Hellenistic times. It is more plausible that he understood the diachronic continuity between classical and Hellenistic rhapsodes and the Roman imperial *homēristai*; and that, therefore, after drawing a rather traditional picture of the rhapsode in performance, he did not think inconsequent to supply the word 'homerista' as his Latin equivalent. Perhaps unexpectedly, the resulting synchronic description is in fact rather accurate.

[98] See above, p. 449 n. 57.

[99] Perpillou-Thomas 1995:226–230. Cf. Bélis 1988 and Chaniotis 1990:90–92 (also table 1, pp. 99–102).

[100] Nagy 1996c:178–180 argues for the late fourth-century BC origin of the term, for which Demetrios of Phaleron himself may be responsible. I agree with the connection between this label and "a decreasing flexibility in the inherited repertoire, ... correlated with an increasing professionalism" (1996c:180). But, as argued above, I do not believe that Demetrios' impact extended beyond a formal control of the performers by the state, i.e. beyond establishing official procedures for the supply, employment, and payment of performers (which might have encouraged further self-regulation and self-organization) and fostering the inherent tendency towards greater theatricality in the practice of Homeric rhapsodes (owing to the new performance venue and perhaps even a desire to indulge Demetrios' delight in a 'good show'). Assuming that Demetrios was responsible for the sobriquet would imply too radical a discontinuity in the performance tradition at the time, rather than the more likely gradual change encouraged by the implicit promotion of already existing cultural tendencies (cf. O'Sullivan 2009:185).

11.2.2 The reforms of Demetrios of Phaleron

My survey, then, puts the rhapsodes of the classical era in continuity with the *homēristai* of Hellenistic and Roman imperial times. There are points of continuity and discontinuity, but it is possible to establish lines of gradual development that lead from one to the other by an increasing emphasis on the dramatic potential of the Homeric poems and a corresponding exploitation of voice, gesture, and dress in their performances before an audience (cf. Nagy 1996c:171). This serves to return us to the text of Athenaios 14.620b and its report about Demetrios of Phaleron as the one responsible for the introduction of the *homēristai* into the theater. It is undeniable that the governor of Athens had a live interest in Homeric poetry: Diogenes Laertios 5.81 includes a Περὶ Ἰλιάδος α′ β′, a Περὶ Ὀδυσσείας α′ β′ γ′ δ′, and a Ὁμηρικὸς α′.[101] The first two must have been *hypomnēmata*; about the latter we can only guess.[102] Thus, he continued the time-honored philological interests of the founder of the Lyceum. Building on Lykourgos' broad restoration of Athens' cultural life, Demetrios was instrumental in bringing about a reorganization of the social mechanisms of dramatic production.[103] In particular, he abolished the χορηγία, which Aristotle in the *Politics* 1309a14–20 had criticized as exacerbating useless spending, harming the fortunes of the rich, and doing little to prevent the unequal prospering of the polis by sections.[104] Lykourgos, too, expressed particular resentment at liturgies that purported to be for the public good (*khorēgia* among them), but benefited only the reputation of the sponsor (*Against Leōkratēs* §139). To these, he opposed truly useful services such as trierarchies. Demetrios adopted this policy in an effort to curtail conspicuous consumption, also legislating limits to funerary spending.[105] One of the few preserved fragments in his own voice expresses his criticism of the *khorēgia*:[106] καὶ τούτων [sc. τῶν χορηγῶν] τοῖς μὲν ἡττηθεῖσι περιῆν προσυβρίσθαι καὶ γεγονέναι καταγελάστους· τοῖς δὲ νικήσασιν ὁ τρίπους ὑπῆρχεν, οὐκ ἀνάθημα τῆς νίκης, ὡς Δημήτριός φησιν, ἀλλ᾽ ἐπίσπεισμα τῶν ἐκκεχυμένων βίων καὶ τῶν ἐκλελοιπότων κενοτάφιον οἴκων. τοιαῦτα γὰρ τὰ ποιητικῆς τέλη

---

[101] Fragments assigned to his *homerica* are 190–193 Wehrli or 143–146 SOD.

[102] Wehrli (1968b:85) suggests a rhetorical declamation, such as he imagines Plato's Ion boasted about when he compared himself with Metrodoros of Lampsakos, Stesimbrotos of Thasos, and Glaukon (530c9–d1). Cf. Bayer 1969:146–147. On Demetrios' philological writings see, further, Montanari 2000.

[103] See O'Sullivan 2009:165–195.

[104] δεῖ δ᾽ ἐν μὲν ταῖς δημοκρατίαις τῶν εὐπόρων φείδεσθαι, μὴ μόνον τῷ τὰς κτήσεις μὴ ποιεῖν ἀναδάστους, ἀλλὰ μηδὲ τοὺς καρπούς, ὃ ἐν ἐνίαις τῶν πολιτειῶν λανθάνει γιγνόμενον, βέλτιον δὲ καὶ βουλομένους κωλύειν λειτουργεῖν τὰς δαπανηρὰς μὲν μὴ χρησίμους δὲ λειτουργίας, οἷον χορηγίας καὶ λαμπαδαρχίας καὶ ὅσαι ἄλλαι τοιαῦται. Cf. *Politics* 1305a3–7 and 1320b2–4.

[105] Cicero *De legibus* 2.63–66 (fr. 135 Wehrli = fr. 53 SOD).

[106] Fr. 136 Wehrli = fr. 115 SOD.

καὶ λαμπρότερον οὐδὲν ἐξ αὐτῶν (Plutarch *De gloria Atheniensium* 349b1-6).[107] Instead of the *khorēgoi*, a state official, the ἀγωνοθέτης, was henceforth in charge of the festival, not only of the Dionysia but also the Lenaia and the Thargelia,[108] but *not* the Panathenaia;[109] and the people were to be the notional *khorēgos*.[110] The effect of these reforms, which probably took place towards the beginning of his tenure,[111] was that from then on actors were the employees of the state. And so we should expect that, with the abolition of the *khorēgia*, Demetrios must have also pursued a more formal arrangement between the polis and the professionals of tragedy and comedy, paying the cast directly in return for making their service at festivals predictable and stable. This would have gone a step beyond the Lykourgan control of the text of the plays through the *grammateus*.[112]

It is ultimately in such a management model—one in which the city formally contracts with her actors and other dramatic staff as a whole—that an important impetus must lie towards the founding of the synod of Dionysian artists some-time later during the third century BC. Doubtless we must credit other factors: economies of scale; the synergism of, and the flexibility offered by, complementary specialties; the ability to negotiate better terms of employment or to secure immunity; a more effective match of supply and demand; etc. But I believe that it must have been the management model first established by Demetrios what proved so convenient to the professionals of drama and others that it was soon to be made permanent in the autonomously organized and self-ruled synods of τεχνῖται. The *terminus ante quem* for Athens' own is the amphictyonic decree IG II/III² 1132 (cf. Aneziri 2003:347-350), dated 279/78 or 278/77 BC. That the

---

[107] With the modern editors, I follow Reiske's emendation ἐπίσπεισμα τῶν ἐκκεχυμένων βίων, which doubtless stands behind the awkward ms. reading ἐπὶ πεισμάτων ἐκκεχυμένον βίον.

[108] Cf. Wilson 2000:272n33.

[109] *Pace* Ferguson 1974:57 and n. 2. Cf. B. Nagy 1978 and 1992:62-65, esp. 64. Although a *temporary* suspension of the *athlothetai*'s responsibility for the Panathenaia in favor of a single *agōnothetēs* cannot be dismissed, it remains entirely speculative.

[110] IG II/III² 3073: ὁ δῆμος ἐ[χορήγει … . Cf. IG II/III² 3074, 3076-3077, 3079, 3081, 3083, and 3086-3088. For more on the *agōnothetēs* see Pickard-Cambridge 1988:91-92, Mikalson 1998:54-59, and Wilson 2000:270-276.

[111] An obvious date would be 317/16 BC, when he was *nomothetēs*. Cf. Wilson 2000:272 and 307-308 (appendix 4).

[112] O'Sullivan (2009:181) suggests that Demetrios did not abolish the *khorēgia* but only "prohibited victorious *khorēgoi* from displaying their prize tripods in lavish shrines." If so, he would only have helped indirectly the decline of the liturgy. O'Sullivan places its actual restructuring under the restored democracy in 307/306 BC. Whether during Demetrios' rule or shortly thereafter, the socio-economic impact of the change would have been the same. Nonetheless, I prefer the traditional ascription to Demetrios. In the light of his far-reaching social concerns and indisput-able policy reforms (on which see Wilson 2000:270-272 and the references above, p. 447 n. 53), O'Sullivan's proposal that the introduction of the *agōnothesia* in 307/306 sought to enhance the prestige of the Antigonids as liberators, although possible, is less compelling a motivation than the Phaleronian's own political project.

Athenian synod was probably the first in existence is admitted by many authorities. This chronological priority both explains its superiority and legitimizes its claims to preeminence vis-à-vis the Isthmian *koinon*, a claim famously upheld by the amphictyonic decree *FD* III 2, 69 (=*SIG*³ 704e) of which IG II/III² 1134 is a copy (cf. Aneziri 2003:368–372). To be sure, its mention of Athens' priority is couched in anachronistic language that projects the situation that obtained ca. 117/16 BC back to archaic and classical times.[113] But all the same, the language would hardly be defensible in the polemical setting of inter-synodical rivalries unless the cultural preeminence of classical Athens had been further buttressed by her pioneering establishment of a *koinon* of Dionysian artists. It is not likely, however, that the Athenian model would have succeeded in the long run and enjoyed as witness to its success the establishment of rival associations in the Corinthian Isthmus, Ionia, and Egypt, had not many of the Hellenistic rulers offered them protection and robust patronage (a practice continued with distinction by late republican and imperial notables and potentates).[114] No longer did 'Dionysiac' contests take place only at a festival to Dionysos; they could also be organized for the festivals of other gods, and even in honor of rulers. Artistic specialties and their representative performers became unmoored from their original settings and transportable to new ones. The dominant factor henceforth was to be the artist himself, his professional persona. This was not, however, an entirely new development. That performers already during the fifth and fourth centuries BC might have enjoyed a loose association of sorts to defend their common interests, and that they had at least the consciousness of a shared professional identity, might be inferred from the (otherwise clearly anachronistic) language of Athenaios 9.407b about Hegemon of Thasos and the

---

[113] Surely the language—ἐπει[δὴ] γεγονέ[ναι κ]αὶ [συνειλέ]χθαι τεχνιτῶν σύνοδον παρ' Ἀθηναίος συμβέβηκε πρῶτον ... (11) and πρῶτός τε πάντων, συναγα⟨γ⟩ὼν τεχνιτῶν σύνοδον [καὶ ἀγωνιστῶν, θ]υμελικ[οὺς καὶ σκ]ηνικ[οὺ]ς ἀγῶνας ἐποίησεν (16–17)—is not intended as a description merely of the founding of third-century BC competitions, but, as the panegyric that follows makes clear, of the invention of all the arts by the Athenians (tragedy, comedy, and others).

[114] See above, p. 447 n. 50. In places like Alexandria, which had not enjoyed, as Athens, centuries of rich cultural traditions and which, for this reason, was subjected by its rulers to a vigorous official policy of Hellenization, the establishment of a guild of artists had obvious advantages for recruiting performers and supplying newly established festivals. Here it was not merely a matter of regulating preexisting religious and cultural forms, but of founding entirely new festivals to give expression to the ideologies of power. There would also be the added benefit of evoking Alexander the Great as Dionysos in his patronage of the arts (cf. Diogenes Laertios 6.63 and Athenaios 12.538f). The respective *termini ante quos* for the non-Athenian κοινά are ca. 270 BC for the Egyptian, ca. 240 BC for the Ionian, and ca. 260 BC for the Isthmian. Following in Alexander's footsteps, influential Romans, too, portrayed themselves under the guise of Bakkhos: so Mark Antony (Athenaios 4.148c) and Caligula (Athenaios 4.148d). By the time of Hadrian and Antoninus Pius, it was no longer a personal claim, but an established honorific address: Ἀδριανὸν Καίσαρα Σεβαστὸν νέον Διόνυσον (Rouché 1993:226 no. 88 iii.3; cf. IG II/III² 1350).

passing comment in Aristotle's *Rhetoric* 1405a23–24. Demetrios' alleged reorganization of the performers cannot be proved, but the environment was certainly ripe for it, and all the circumstantial evidence suggests that it must have taken place.

Although very likely, then, given the abolition of the *khorēgia* and the assumption by the state of the exclusive sponsorship and financing of city festivals, we do not have any explicit mention of a corresponding reorganization of the actors themselves. But we do steal from Athenaios' remark about Demetrios and the rhapsodes a passing glance at his comprehensive concern for the performing arts of the city he ruled. That this cannot have meant a radical change in the fourth-century BC character of Homeric rhapsodic performance, I have argued above in my discussion of the *homēristai*: to be sure, the rhapsode's flair for the dramatic can only have been encouraged by the move, but this would have been merely another step in the gradual march towards the ever increasing influence of scripted acting on what had once been the extempore recomposition of Homeric poetry in performance without mimetic costuming, voice, and gesture.[115] Granting then that there was a change in setting, what did it consist in? One possibility is that it was into the Dionysia itself that Demetrios brought the reciting rhapsodes (with Athenaios' τὰ θέατρα standing not only for the place, but metonymically for the preeminent festival celebrated there). But I believe that this is not very likely: no known inscription so much as hints at the performance of rhapsodes during the feast of Dionysos. And only on the assumption that the performance of the rhapsodes in their new setting was very close to the much later acting of the *homēristai*—an anachronism I cannot accept—is it plausible to imagine them as furnishing ἐμβόλιμα between acts or plays. On the other hand, if they kept their character primarily as reciters of Homeric epic and still did take part in the Dionysia, we would have, in effect, a θυμελικὸς ἀγών.[116] But as Pickard-Cambridge (1946:168) once said, the term θυμελικός was never used for an Athenian competition; perhaps unsurprisingly, for we might expect a city with such long-standing festival traditions, especially after the conservative turn of the Lykourgan era, to have usually respected the broad characteristic outlines of each of her feasts and their peculiar customs. The other alternative, then, is to assume that Demetrios moved the rhapsodic competitions from the

---

[115] This evolution of the performance practice is reflected by late sources, e.g. the *Suidas* s.v. ῥαψῳδοί: οἱ τὰ Ὁμήρου ἔπη ἐν τοῖς θεάτροις ἀπαγγέλλοντες (4.287 P no. 71.1 Adler).

[116] Strictly speaking, θυμελικός referred to the μουσικοὶ ἀγῶνες in the setting of the theater. A mixed competition, with drama and *mousikē* (*rhapsōidia*, *kitharōidia*, *aulōidia*, etc.) would go by the fuller name θυμελικοὶ καὶ σκηνικοὶ ἀγῶνες (or, in the words of Vitruvius V 7.2.6, it would involve *scaenici et thymelici artifices*). Cf. Frei 1900:5–15. As Wörrle (1988:227) observes, later usage under Rome was less precise and sometimes applied to both the shorthand θυμελικοί in contrast to γυμνικοί.

odeion of Perikles to the theater of Dionysos.[117] The reasons for this move are not hard to understand: after Lykourgos rebuilt the theater, the site must have been used with increasing frequency for all sorts of assemblies. It was now a convenient, solid, and safe structure, situated in the heart of the city (as opposed to the slightly more peripheral *Pnyx*).[118] Capacious, it had the convenience of its unimpeded view and its semi-circular shape. The odeion, on the contrary, in all likelihood neither intended nor designed originally as a music hall,[119]

---

[117] So Shear 2001:368. For the odeion of Perikles see Robkin 1976 and 1979, Kotsidu 1991:141–149, Hose 1993, Miller 1997:218–242, Papathanasopoulos 1999 (*non vidi*), Mosconi 2000, Musti 2002, Papathanasopoulos 2003 (*non vidi*), Di Napoli 2004, and Lippolis et al. 2007:561–562. Kotsidu (1991:154) rejects the conjecture of a late fourth-century transfer of the rhapsodes from the odeion to the theater on the basis of IG II/III² 784, which is dated to the middle of the third century BC and mentions a Panathenaic ἀγὼν μουσικός. In her view, if the change of setting had already taken place, one should rather expect to read about a Panathenaic ἀγὼν θυμελικός. But this objection is naive and unpersuasive. At this early date a preference for the adjective θυμελικός over against μουσικός would entail the corresponding contrast, at least implicit, with σκηνικός—a contrast that did not obtain for the Panathenaia, but would have existed if rhapsodic performances had been included in the Dionysia. One must also reckon with the doubtless conservative epigraphic nomenclature, which if at all possible would have likely adhered to the traditional adjective μουσικός in preference to the innovative θυμελικός.

[118] Thompson and Wycherley (1972:50) call the *Pnyx* "a *tour de force* and a freak" and note that "[i]n the end common sense prevailed" when "in the course of the 3rd century, the theater, already used for occasional meetings, became the regular place of assembly."

[119] See, for example, Robkin 1979:10 and Miller 1997:232–235 (esp. 234). Miller notes that the odeion was "singularly poorly designed for such a function" (233). Mosconi 2000:243, which, atypically among recent studies, defends the—at least predominant—use of the building for musical performances, places natural but perhaps misleading emphasis on its peculiar name. Whether or not one agrees with Robkin, her hypothesis that after Perikles' failure to convene the Panhellenic congress he made the staging of μουσικοὶ ἀγῶνες the structure's first prominent use (Robkin 1976:95) would sufficiently account for the conventional name Ὠιδεῖον in contemporary sources. Given the purpose for which the congress was called (cf. Plutarch *Periklēs* 17), Robkin convincingly motivates the symbolism evoked by imitating the pavilion of the Persian king (an imitation that Mosconi 2000:244 declares illusory). On the historicity of the so-called 'congress decree,' see MacDonald 1982 and Stadter 1989:202–203. Miller notes that there are chronological stumbling-blocks to positing the construction (or completion) of the odeion in the early 440s BC, but she does not spell out what these are. The Panhellenic assembly must have been convened after the peace of Kallias (449?) and before beginning work on the Parthenon (447/46 BC). But so long as archaeology fails to illuminate the dating, Robkin's review (1976:36–41) shows that a building project with a foreseeable completion date for the odeion soon enough to house the Periklean congress shortly after 449 BC—and in time for the Panathenaic year of 446/45—is not unfeasible. A doxographic survey of modern scholars confirms this impression: built "shortly after 450 BC" according to Boersma 1970:72, following Shear 1966:118 ("early 440s"); mid-440s in the opinion Camp 2001:101 (who ties it to the ostracism ca. 443 BC of Perikles' opponent Thoukydides, which can only provide a *terminus ante quem*); before the removal of the *mousikoi agōnes* to it "in the 440s" according to Hurwit 2004:279n39 (a date apparently in conflict with the chronology of his table at 254); and, summarizing the consensus, Di Napoli 2004:593 writes "nel decennio 450–440."

was proverbial for its many interior columns (πολύστυλον)[120] and 'many seats' (πολύεδρον).[121] It was a square-shaped building whose 'many seats' must have been wooden bleachers (ἴκρια) built between the columns. Performers must have stood on a wooden platform built for the occasion.[122] Its views and perhaps acoustics were less than ideal,[123] a state of affairs that might well be justified for the similarly constructed Eleusinian Telesterion, for which secrecy recommended roofing and illumination by torches and the columns supporting the roof might be a necessary nuisance. But only a departure from its original purpose would explain why Perikles made the odeion the seat of rhapsodic and perhaps other 'musical' competitions.[124] With the newly refurbished theater of Dionysos available, where already in times past occasional meetings of the *ekklēsia* had been held,[125] at last the Periklean tradition might be relaxed and all competitions other than athletic and equestrian might be held there.[126] With this, Hesykhios Ω no. 39 s.v. ᾠδεῖον agrees: τόπος, ἐν ᾧ

---

[120] Cf. Robkin 1976:23–26.

[121] Robkin 1976:26–28. Cf. Plutarch *Periklēs* 13.9–11. See also Theophrastos *Kharaktēres* 3.3.6–7. Mosconi (2000:234n49) is probably right to reject Miller's novel interpretation of πολύεδρος as 'polyhedral' (Miller 1997:227).

[122] Plato's *Iōn* 535e1–2: καθορῶ γὰρ ἑκάστοτε αὐτοὺς ἄνωθεν ἀπὸ τοῦ βήματος.

[123] We do not know what the acoustics of the building were. Miller (1997:235n207) hedges by calling them "unusual." It certainly lacked the design that has made Greek theaters the world over famous for their ability to convey sound. The roofed enclosure must have helped to palliate its dissipation; but the return to a traditional shape for the auditorium in the construction of the odeia of Agrippa and Herodes suggests that the semi-circular stone theater surpassed what the Periklean odeion could offer. For an interesting exploration of the acoustics of the *Pnyx* and the corresponding limitations on the political process see Johnstone 1996a:116–126.

[124] Whether the transfer applied only to rhapsodes or embraced all other performers of *mousikē* is open to question. Since odeion and theater were immediately adjacent, a division of competitive events between them would have been entirely feasible. It is possible that rhapsodic performances drew more avid audiences and that their solo delivery without melody and instrumental accompaniment commended the more acoustically effective setting of the theater. A measure of variability in the arrangements of venues from one Panathenaic festival to the next is also conceivable. IG II/III² 968 honors Miltiades, son of Zoilos, for his *agōnothesia* of the Panathenaia in a section (ll. 37–55) that refers to events that took place after the archonship of Theaitetos. The inscription notes that 'what needed work on the Acropolis, in the Odeion, and in the *Anakeion* he got ready in a manner that was fitting' (τά τε ἐν ἀκροπόλει προσδεόμε[να ἐργασία]ς καὶ τὰ ἐν τῶι ὠιδείωι | [καὶ τῶι Ἀν]ακεί[ω]ι ἐπεσκεύασεν προσηκ[όντως 47–48). We do not know what precisely took place in the odeion on that occasion, but it is clear that it must have served as one of the venues for the events on the program. The festival is assumed to be the penteteric one of 142/41 BC on the questionable grounds that: i) mention of the odeion entails *mousikoi agōnes*; ii) and 'musical' performances were not held during the lesser Panathenaia (see Shear 2001:101, with the inscription at 1026–1027). See for further consideration p. 472 immediately below.

[125] Cf. McDonald 1943:47–51 and Pickard-Cambridge 1988:68–70.

[126] We learn from Hyperides' *In Defense of the Children of Lykourgos* (fr. 118 Jensen) that the great Athenian statesman also subjected the odeion to construction. The word used, ᾠκοδόμησε, is applied also to the theater (among others). Thus it must mean not 'build' but 'rebuild' or 'refurbish', and the degree of construction and modification implied must be allowed to vary.

πρὶν τὸ θέατρον κατασκευασθῆναι οἱ ῥαψῳδοὶ καὶ οἱ κιθαρῳδοὶ ἠγωνίζοντο.[127] Davison (1958:35) assumes that Hesykhios' theater corresponds to the structure that stood in Perikles' lifetime (built ca. 470 BC, he says). The odeion (whose roofing he assigns to Themistokles) was not in use then, either because the 'musical' contests, if ever housed there, had been transferred to the theater, or simply because they had been discontinued at some earlier point and were not held until Perikles refounded the μουσικῆς ἀγῶνες and returned them to the odeion.[128] But I think that Robkin's analysis[129] makes the hypothesis of a Themistoklean construction of the odeion (based on Vitrivius V 9.1) very unlikely,[130] and that it is therefore better to take Hesykhios' note as the transference of the 'musical' contests, or at least the rhapsodic ones, from the odeion to the theater after Lykourgos' reforms,[131] a move at least began (if not entirely carried out) by Demetrios of Phaleron. It is clear, at any rate, that during Hellenistic times the theater of Dionysos increasingly became the preferred meeting place.[132]

The translation of 'music' contests to the theater need not have been complete. It is possible that the meetings at the odeion continued during the greater Panathenaia, but may have been transferred to the theater for the lesser Panathenaia.[133] This is on the assumption that μουσικοὶ ἀγῶνες were held at the yearly festivals too, a matter that is contested by some scholars. Unfortunately, it is hard to settle this question with certainty, since the celebration of the greater Panathenaia is, to a large degree, involved in resolving calendrical

---

(Cf. Lykourgos' *Against Kēphisodotos* fr. 2 Conomis, which credits Perikles with the construction, οἰκοδομήσας, of the odeion). Robkin (1976:65) suggests that the work for the theater necessitated some modifications to the odeion: the crosswall that connects the west end of the north wall of the odeion to the *analēmma* of the theater, as opposed to the buttresses at the center and east end, may be one such modification. At any rate, no work on the odeion can have compensated for a design unsuited to 'musical' performances.

[127] For a discussion, see Hiller 1873.

[128] The survey of the relevant iconographic record in Kotsidu 1991:104–129 refutes the notion of a hiatus in the celebration of the ἀγῶνες (see her lists in 293–317).

[129] Robkin 1979:8.

[130] *Pace* Papathanasopoulos 2003. Cf. Mosconi 2000:250–270 and Musti 2002.

[131] Davison (1958:34n17) observes: "It should be noted that Hesychius does not say to which theatre he refers; he might be speaking of the 'Periclean' (or even of the Lycurgean) one."

[132] Pollux 8.132.8–133.2 makes reference to this change: ἐνεκλησίαζον δὲ πάλαι μὲν ἐν τῇ Πυκνί· ... αὖθις δὲ τὰ μὲν ἄλλα ἐν τῷ Διονυσιακῷ θεάτρῳ, μόνας δὲ τὰς ἀρχαιρεσίας ἐν τῇ Πυκνί (cf. Wachsmuth 1874:647n2). McDonald (1943:47–51 and 56–61), after examining the epigraphical and literary sources, concludes that starting in the times of Lykourgos' reforms, after which the "[t]heater must have been much the best equipped meeting place in Athens for any large group" (58), regular assemblies there (flagged by the expression ἐκκλησία ἐν τῷ θεάτρῳ) slowly increased in number during the third century BC until the new venue entirely supplanted the *Pnyx* after the first third of the second century BC (cf. 57n74).

[133] For other alternatives, see above, p. 471 n. 124.

matters, with the result that, starting with the Eusebian date of 566 BC, the date of any epigraphical or literary instance of the festival that is associated with 'musical' performances is *eo ipso* adjusted to a year away by some appropriate multiple of four from 566. A case in point is IG II/III² 784, a decree from the archonship of Athenodoros, whom Meritt had once dated to 240/39 BC[134] and more recently redated to 256/55 BC.[135] In either case, the significance of the year is that it corresponds to a lesser Panathenaia (566-240 is not divisible by 4); and since the inscription deals with a μουσικὸς ἀγών,[136] this would seem to prove conclusively that Davison (1958:26) was in fact wrong when he wrote that "it is reasonably certain that the individual competitions [i.e. 'music', athletics, and horse-racing] were instituted in the sixth century and confined to the 'great' Panathenaea." Meritt (1981:82), however, noted that Habicht (1979:137), whose arguments prompted the higher redating, had suggested a "Panathenaic year" (i.e. a year when the greater Panathenaia was held) because the decree mentions *athlothetai*, who many believe were not involved in the lesser festival.[137] Thus, Habicht only considered the Panathenaic years 258/57, 254/53, and 250/49

---

[134] Meritt 1961:234, revalidated in Meritt 1977:176. In agreement is Samuel (1972:215), who places Athenodoros on his second column for "those archons whose placement depends solely upon the reconstruction of the secretary cycle" (211). This was already the dating offered by the editor of IG II/III² 784.

[135] Meritt 1981:79 and 82–83 (cf. p. 94).

[136] IG II/III² 784.7–10: ἐπειδὴ ᵛ οἱ ἀθλοθέται ἐπεμελήθησαν [τῆς διοικήσεως τῶ]- ‖ ν Παναθηναίων ᵛ Ἀγαθαίου Προσπ[αλ]τ[ίου συντελοῦντος κα]- ‖ ὶ τοῦ ἀγῶνος τοῦ τε μουσικοῦ καὶ [τοῦ γυμνικοῦ καὶ τῆς ἱππ]- ‖ οδρομίας ᵛ καὶ τὰ ἄλλα ἅ[παντα κτλ. Cf. Shear 2001:1020–1021, who dates it to 239/38 BC. (She dots several alphas that Kirchner left undotted; otherwise, the text is unchanged and hardly in doubt.)

[137] This matter is complex, since IG I³ 370, with its ἀθλοθέταις ἐς Παναθέναια (line 67) in the section that regards 415/14 BC, the evidence alleged (e.g. by Meritt 1981:82n19 and B. Nagy 1992:63) to prove the involvement of *athlothetai* in the lesser festivals, was long ago argued vigorously by Davison (1958:32) to apply not to the festival that year but to the greater one that followed it (in 414/13). Davison's view has found little favor and is rejected by Meiggs and Lewis (1969:236) among others. And for a good reason: we simply do not know enough about the financial arrangements—who was owed what, which expenses might be incurred on short-term credit, when payment was expected, etc.—categorically to declare the date of the disbursement "administrative nonsense" if intended for the Panathenaia of 415/14 (Davison 1958:32). If *athlothetai* were in charge of the lesser Panathenaia (not of the sacrifices and the procession, for which the *hieropoioi* continued to be responsible, cf. IG I³ 375.6–7 and II/III² 334), this surely implies that this festival too must have included contests with prizes. We might then understand the extravagant sum of nine talents as perhaps "a specially luxurious celebration [of the lesser Panathenaia] after the troubles of the summer" (so Meiggs and Lewis 1969 *ad loc.*). As Rhodes (1993:670) writes, "the title of the athlothetae suggests that their original duty was to organise the contests." This purview harmonizes with the testimony of Plutarch *Periklēs* 13.11, who reports that, after being elected *athlothetēs*, Perikles himself arranged the 'musical' contests. (The force of this observation does not depend on whether *athlothetēs* here has a technical or general sense.)

for Athenodoros' date.[138] The same rationale was accepted by Osborne 1989: "Athenodoros ... needs one of the Great Panathenaic years" (227).[139] I note with

---

[138] "[D]ie traditionelle Datierung auf 240/39 ist nicht nur zu spät, sondern auch deshalb falsch, weil Athenodoros aller Wahrscheinlichkeit nach in ein Jahr der Großen Panathenäen gehört" (Habicht 1979:137). "Es muß sich hier um die Großen Panathenäen handeln, denn die Athlotheten sind 'eine Behörde der penteterisch begangenen Panathenäen', während die Hieropoioi das kleine, jährliche Fest vollständig verwalten" (137).

[139] Osborne (1989:213n14) rejects the ascription of IG II/III² 784 to a lesser Panathenaia on the grounds that the *athlothetai* were responsible for the penteteric, the *hieropoioi* for the yearly, festival. Faced with IG I³ 370, he observes that "there is nothing to indicate that the athlothetai took over the organization of the lesser Panathenaia (as opposed to having a role in its celebration)." But what division of labor, if any, existed between these two sets of officers is precisely the point that should not be begged. Once we grant coordinate roles to athlothetai and hieropoioi, we must also ascertain—and not just gloss over—their respective spheres of responsibility. IG II/III² 334 cannot be adduced to settle the case for an exclusion of the *athlothetai* from the lesser festival. Its date falls between 336 and 330 BC, with preference for 336/35 or 335/34 (Lewis 1959:240). With this, contrast the fact that Rhodes (1993:56) dates Aristotle's *Athēnaiōn Politeia* "towards the end of the 330's" (with possible updates in the first half of the 320s). And yet the Aristotelian text (at 60.1) assigns the administration of the Panathenaic πομπή to the *athlothetai* in apparent contradiction with IG II/III² 334.B18 and B31–32. It seems perverse to hold that Aristotle would have failed to take into account a recent, significant festival reorganization when he heeds other near contemporaneous ones (cf. Rhodes 1993:52 and 610 regarding the Hephaistia). This suggests that the absence of the *athlothetai* from the inscription is to be attributed to its narrow focus on the sacrificial arrangements, naturally subsuming the procession of the cows under them; and that, where we read τοὺς δὲ ἱεροποιοὺς τοὺς διοι[κ]- ‖ [οῦντας τ]ὰ Παναθήναια τὰ κατ' ἐνιαυτὸν (B31–32), we should understand a contextual restriction to sacrifices and the like. I wonder if the syntax of B5–6 does not hint at this restriction. It does not say τἆ]λα ... διοικῆται τὰ περὶ τὴν ἑορτὴν ('so that all the other matters that concern the festival be well administered'), but τἆ]λα ... διοικῆται περὶ τὴν ἑορτὴν ('so that all the other matters [that are the responsibility of *hieropoioi*] be well administered in connection with the festival'). If the *pannychis* was celebrated after the sacrifice on Hekatombaion 28, we may understand the *hieropoioi*'s supervision of it (at B32–33) as concerning the distribution of meat and the regulation of the ensuing feasting (cf. Pritchett 1986:186). The *pannychis* must have included a veritable spectacle of song and dance; cf. Plato *Republic* 328a and Euripides *Hēraklēs* 777–783 (in Euripides note the sequence of sacrifice first and then celebration, and the expression μηνῶν φθινὰς ἁμέρα, on whose meaning see Pritchett 1986:183 and the note *ad loc.* in Garzya 1958:117–118). Parker (2005:257) observes that it is hard to resist the implication that the sequence in B32–34 is chronological; if so, the meat would not have been available for the *pannychis*. But resist it we must. All-night merry-making as a vigil before the climactic procession constitutes distinctly poor timing and suggests weary rather than eager crowds for an audience. The Bendideia in Plato *Republic* 327a–328a sensibly featured a *pannychis* with a torch-race *after* the procession (cf. Clinton 1994:27–28 on the Epidauria). This must have been the Panathenaic order too (so Boegehold 1996:97 and Shear 2001:83 following Pritchett 1986). At any rate, if we hold firmly in view *ex hypothesi* that πομπή and sacrifice preceded the *pannychis*, the sequence in B32–34 would seem associative and unproblematic. Only to us, who are ignorant, would it seem chronological. (Boutsikas 2011:303 assumes without discussion a date of 27 Hekatombaion.) That the *athlothetai* are not mentioned among the officials to whom special portions of meat are distributed seems to me the more significant objection to their involvement in the lesser Panathenaia, at least as reflected by the inscription (cf. Rosivach 1991:440n32; that their office still existed then follows from the late second-century BC IG II/III² 1060, on which see B. Nagy 1978:311).

interest that Tracy (2003:84) now gives the date of Athenodoros as 238/37 BC,[140] and, for a rationale, the terse statement, "Steinhauer, *Νεότερα στοιχεῖα* 47, places him without discussion in 238/37 and indicates the date as certain" (Tracy 2003:2n6). He is referring to Steinhauer 1993:47. That there is no strong consensus emerges from the latter's table on page 36, but I suspect that, in the end, he assigns Athenodoros' archonship to 238/37 on the grounds that, if 'music' was included in the Panathenaia that year, it must have been a greater Panathenaia: the closest fine-tuning of Meritt's original date (240/39) would adjust him up to 242/41 or down to 238/37. Perhaps a more reliable indicator is Lykourgos' *Against Leōkratēs* §102, where the Athenian fathers are said to require Homeric rhapsodic performances καθ' ἑκάστην πεντετηρίδα τῶν Παναθηναίων.[141] Admittedly, it would be odd to speak thus if in fact such contests were held yearly. But other interpretations are possible: perhaps the yearly Panathenaia did include contests of 'music' but did not enforce on rhapsodes the exclusivity of the Homeric repertoire; or else the point may be that in

---

Athēnaiōn Politeia 60.1 is explicit that *athlothetai* hold office for four years, so that their existence during the lesser Panathenaia (whether they received meat or not) should arguably be accepted. Rhodes (1993:606) reads *Athēnaiōn Politeia* 54.7 as precluding *hieropoioi* from involvement in any Panathenaia, and hence in conflict with our inscription; but one might read the exclusion πλὴν Παναθηναίων as 'except the [penteteric] Panathenaia'. This compatible reading posits that *hieropoioi* took the initiative in, and carried the burden of, the administration of the lesser festival; whereas the *athlothetai* did so for the penteteric. All that this view requires is the relatively greater salience of the competitions during the latter and of the procession and sacrifices during the former. This still allows for a complementary and subordinate role at each festival for the other set of officers. It is perhaps the unusual prominence of the contests at the lesser Panathenaia of 415/14 BC that accounts for an involvement of the *athlothetai* more prominent than was customary (and hence their mention to the apparent exclusion of the *hieropoioi*). If this logic is right, the question may be badly posed from the start. One must not assume the absence of contests wherever only *hieropoioi* are mentioned. From *Athēnaiōn Politeia* 54.7 we learn that these yearly officials (ἱεροποιοὶ κατ' ἐνιαυτόν) are to administer all penteteric festivals other than the Panathenaia. Among the enumerated are the Hephastia, the Eleusinia, and perhaps the Herakleia. For the sake of brevity and simply to make the point, I note that IG I³ 82, a decree from 421/20 BC agreed to be about the Hephaistia, explicitly places under the responsibility of *hieropoioi* not only the procession (τὲς δὲ πονπὲς hόπος [ἂν hος κάλλιστα] ‖ πενφθῆι ho[ι hι]εροπ[οι]οὶ ἐπιμελόσθον 24–25) but also the torch-race and the rest of the competition (ποιόντο[ν δ]ὲ [h]οι hιεροπ[οιοὶ hούτος hόστε] ‖ [τὲ]ν λανπαδ[εδρομίαν καὶ] τὸν ἄλλον ἀγόνα γίγνεσθαι καθά[περ τοῖς Προμεθίο]- ‖ [ις τὲ]ν θέαν [hοι λανπάδαρχ]οι ποιõσι 31–33). On this and the related IG I³ 472 and the Hephaistia generally, see Thompson 1969, Parke 1977:171–172, Harrison 1977 (esp. 414), Simon 1983:51–54, and Saito 1999. If *hieropoioi* may and do run contests, there is no reason to conclude that the lesser Panathenaia did not have competitions on a more modest scale simply because we do not find *athlothetai* involved in their administration. On IG II/III² 334, besides the authorities cited above, see Parke 1977:47–49; Schwenk 1985:81–94 (with earlier bibliography); Brulé 1996; and Shear 2001:73–87, 91–94, 1054–1055, 1119–1122 (with discussion of the related IG II/III² 1496; she lists IG II/III² 334 as "Agora XVI 75").

[140] See Tracy 2003:165–168.

[141] See above, pp. 436ff.

the time of the fathers rhapsodic performances during the greater Panathenaia were exclusively of Homeric poetry but this was no longer the case. If so, the comment would have no bearing at all on the lesser Panathenaia. Even if we take the position that in Lykourgos' time no contests of 'music' were held at the lesser festival, nothing hinders the notion that during his tenure as governor of Athens Demetrios of Phaleron might have added them, or at least performances by rhapsodes, as part of his populist policies, which Walbank (1967:358, *ad* Polybios 12.13.10) has characterized as "cheap food and ... entertainments, *panis et circenses*." This might have been the norm henceforth, a norm still observed in 256/55 according to IG II/III² 784 (if this is its correct date!).

Whatever the view adopted, we can agree that the new theater setting must have encouraged the tendency to dramatize the delivery of Homeric poetry, and encouraged even further the dependence of rhapsodes on a carefully rehearsed script such as would maximize the dramatic impact of the performance. The kinship of Homeric epic and tragedy was at last given free course and wide scope, enhanced by the identity of setting—certainly of location if not of time. In what was to be a prelude to the joint participation of actors and rhapsodes in the synods of the artists of Dionysos, both performers were brought into a much closer contact than they had ever enjoyed before, and it is likely that their performances were regulated with similar care by Demetrios, the *epimelētēs* of the city. Nothing would have pleased him better than a heavy dose of theatricality. During his archonship of 309/308 BC he was responsible for the πομπή of the Dionysia,[142] which he gave in great style: a self-moving snail that spewed saliva led the way, and donkeys were marched through the theater (fr. 132.10–11).[143] Demokhares derided him for these (ἐπὶ τούτοις αὐτὸν οὐκ αἰσχύνεσθαι), but Walbank (1967:359) is surely right to conclude that "they were presumably a part of the grandiose show put on by Demetrius and not of any other significance."[144]

11.3 Actors at the Panathenaia?

Answering to the introduction of rhapsodic declamation into the theater, there was a reciprocal inauguration of a dramatic event at the Panathenaia. Relatively speaking, this development was much later in coming, a fact that speaks perhaps of the more traditional character of this old feast and the

---

[142] Cf. Bayer 1969:70–71.

[143] Fr. 132 Wehrli = fr. 89 SOD. Cf. O'Sullivan 2009:182 and 193n83. For the emendation ὄνοι for the ms. ἀνοῖ see Walbank 1967 *ad loc.* The expansion ἄνθρωποι seems much too weak without elaboration and cannot be accepted unless we assume in the text a *lacuna* that supplies further details.

[144] See Athenaios 12.542e (fr. 34 Wehrli = fr. 43a SOD) for another report of the same occasion, according to which the chorus sang to Dionysos in verses that flattered Demetrios.

correspondingly greater reluctance to adopt in it the cultural eclecticism of the more recently founded festivals. The one literary testimony to the innovation comes from Diogenes Laertios 3.56, where we learn that, according to Thrasyllos (the astrologer friend of Tiberius) Plato published his dialogs as tetralogies after the manner of the tragedians, who competed with four plays 'at the Dionysia, Lenaia, Panathenaia, and Χύτροι'.[145] To this we can now add two inscriptions. One is the first-century AD IG II/III² 3157:

[ca. 8]αν ἀ[γωνι]σάμενος κ[υ]-
[κ]λίοις χορο[ῖς] ἀνδρῶν Κεκροπίδι
[φ]υ[λ]ῇ αὐτὸς χορηγῶν καὶ διδάσ-
[κων, κα]ὶ τραγῳδίαν Παναθήναια τ[ὰ]
[μεγά]λα καινὴν διδ[ά]ξας κα[ὶ ca. 5]
[.]αστα τρία ᵛ Ἀθηναίο[ις].

The other, the much earlier *SEG* 41.115, contains an entry at the end of the Panathenaic victor lists for the year 162/61 BC, which records that Zeuxis staged dramatic contests (Tracy and Habicht 1991:189, col. III lines 39–43):

τοὺς δὲ σκηνικοὺς ἀγῶνας π[ca. 10]
40 ⟨Ζ⟩εῦξις ἐποίησε καὶ τοὺς ἐν τα[ca. 10]
σαις τοῖς εὐεργέταις ἡμέραν [ca. 10]
ἀγωνισαμένους εἰσήγαγεν [ca. 11]
τῆς πανηγυρέως ἐπέθηκε [ca. 12]

For line 39 the editors suggest a supplement π[ρῶτος πάντων] or π[άντας καλῶς]: the fragmentary nature of the text does not allow us to determine if this might have been the first time the contests were held (although they cannot have been introduced much earlier).[146] Since Zeuxis' name is inscribed without patronymic or demotic, he must have been mentioned in the preamble to the inscription, now lost. The editors are surely right in suggesting that he must have been the *agōnothetēs* and a man of great influence who either added drama to the festival or staged it with great extravagance. With the restorations καὶ τὰς θυσίας for line 42 and ἐκ τῶν ἰδίων for 43, the following tentative translation is offered: "Zeuxis staged the dramatic contests [admirably?], sponsored? those who contested (on) the day [added?] in th[e _____] in honor of the benefactors

---

[145] Θράσυλλος δέ φησι καὶ κατὰ τὴν τραγικὴν τετραλογίαν ἐκδοῦναι αὐτὸν τοὺς διαλόγους, οἷον ἐκεῖνοι τέτρασι δράμασιν ἠγωνίζοντο—Διονυσίοις, Ληναίοις, Παναθηναίοις, Χύτροις.
[146] Cf. Balabanēs 2007.

of the city, [and] provided [the sacrifices] of the festival [at his own expense]"
(Tracy and Habicht 1991:204).[147]

---

[147] These two inscriptions (with epigraphical commentary, bibliography, and an English translation) can be found in Shear 2001:1080 and 1110–1116.

12

The Performance of Homer after IV BC

A LTHOUGH THE *HOMĒRISTĒS* whom I have already considered[1] takes us decisively into Roman imperial times, I now return more broadly to the performance of Homer during and after the Hellenistic period by professionals who did not concern themselves more narrowly with the acting of Homeric scenes.

12.1 The Τεχνῖται of Dionysos

The last chapter in the performance of epic during Hellenistic and Roman imperial times prominently features the σύνοδοι or κοινά of the so-called οἱ περὶ τὸν Διόνυσον τεχνῖται or simply Διονυσιακοὶ τεχνῖται, to which I have made reference several times already.[2] The rise of these professional associations (in parallel with lower-status artists, such as mimes, who did not enjoy the privileges of membership)[3] meant a privatization in the supply of performers that one would not be wrong to describe, to use a modern term, as the subcontracting of local festivities to professional caterers who could provide everything necessary to stage elaborate festivals. The officials of a given polis would deal directly with representatives of the σύνοδοι for all their hiring needs rather than individually with each performer.[4] The multiplication of theaters all throughout the Greek world (cf. Pausanias 10.4.1), even in smaller cities that could not hope to

---

[1]   See above, section 11.2 pp. 447ff.
[2]   For an older in-depth summary of the Διονυσιακοὶ τεχνῖται see Poland 1934. Shorter surveys are Ghiron-Bistagne 1976:163–171; Pickard-Cambridge 1988:279–321, 365; and Aneziri 2009. Le Guen 2001 and Aneziri 2003 provide excellent comprehensive updates. One should also consult Sifakis 1967 *passim* (esp. Appendix II on the organization of festivals and the Dionysiac guilds).
[3]   See above, p. 464 n. 95.
[4]   See Aneziri 2009:223–224, who underlines the role of Hellenistic kings, political confederations, and religious associations in the organization of many festivals. "Precisely because of the increase in the number of contests and of their geographical expansion, it became increasingly difficult to organize them successfully. This required frequent movements of artists and careful coordination in order to meet the minimum needs of contests, which frequently coincided in date" (Aneziri 2009:224).

fill all the scheduled events with local artists, greatly increased the demand for capable performers and encouraged the internationalization of the cultural life of Greece. Even the more prestigious sacred festivals[5] cultivated ties of friendship with the guilds, acknowledging their services with honorary decrees and grants of rights and privileges. Their aim was to encourage the participation of (and rivalry among) the various synods and, if at all possible, the supply of performances at their own expense as a favor to the city and a pious service to the gods, to be dutifully repaid with such honors as might foster similar benefactions in the future.

We have already seen one important development in the performance of Homeric epic during Hellenistic times, the *homēristai*. These did not, however, belong to the synods of τεχνῖται, at least under this particularly label—i.e. in their narrow character as histrionic reciters of Homeric poetry—perhaps because, like the mimes with whom they were often associated later, they were unable to compete at sacred festivals.[6] But their earliest contemporary attestation, Petronius, dates to the first century AD. And though we must reckon with the accidents of preservation, the over three-hundred-year interval between the end of the classical era and the first instance of the overt declaimer-actor should itself convince us that Homeric poetry must have survived in the hands of other artists who kept its performance alive and a part of the festival setting. And indeed, such is the case with the synods, from which we have epigraphical confirmation that epic generally (and, we must assume, Homeric epic in particular) did not lose its vitality, sustained not by the comparatively rarefied literary reaches of the Alexandrian court and its institutions of high-culture, the library and Mouseion, but by the circle of popular festivals where rhapsodes

---

[5]   In classical times, only the Olympic, Pythian, Isthmian, and Nemean contests, all Panhellenic, enjoyed the status of 'sacred', i.e. they were ἱεροὶ καὶ στεφανῖται because they did not offer money but crowns as prizes. Victors were called ἱερονῖκαι and στεφανῖται (Aneziri 2003:329), and ultimately their reward came from the official recognition of their triumph by their own cities. In exchange for their share of glory their native poleis would grant prerogatives that often entailed material compensation, e.g. the right to ἀτέλεια (exemption from some public burden) or to dine at public expense (Golden 1998:76). One such privilege was the right to drive into the city (εἰσελαύνειν) to public acclaim—the corresponding contest, in imperial times, being labeled εἰσελαστικός (Frisch 1986:38). Competitions that offered money prizes were called θεματικοὶ/ θεματῖται or ταλαντιαῖοι ἀγῶνες (Golden 1998:33 and Aneziri 2003:329). Becoming a sacred victor would increase the likelihood of making even more money in the lesser games or in private engagements for the wealthy, who often rewarded participation with handsome sums. On all these matters see Robert 1989. Golden 1998 offers a concise introduction to ancient Greek sport. For the different categories of games, see Pleket 1975:56–71, Spawforth 1989, and Parker 2004.

[6]   Rhapsodes *qua* rhapsodes did feature as members of the synods and are epigraphically attested among them (Aneziri 2003:208n30 and 428 s.v. ῥαψῳδοί). One cannot rule out that the label *homēristēs* was ever applied to any of them during the Hellenistic period, when the term was first coined and did not yet refer to the out-and-out histrionic performer of Homer.

were still prized performers. Attested as members of the associations are the following professions:[7] σαλπιγκταί; κήρυκες; for poets, τραγικοὶ ποιηταί, κωμικοὶ ποιηταί, ποιηταὶ σατύρων, ποιηταὶ ἐπῶν, ποιηταὶ διθυράμβων, ποιηταὶ προσῳδίου; connected with drama, τραγῳδοί, κωμῳδοί, τραγικοὶ συναγωνισταί, κωμικοὶ συναγωνισταί, διδάσκαλοι (χοροῦ or αὐλητῶν), and τραγικοὶ ὑποδιδάσκαλοι;[8] for dancers (some involved in drama), κωμικοὶ χορευταί, παῖδες χορευταί, ἄνδρες χορευταί, and ὀρχησταί; for instrumentalists, κιθαρισταί or οἱ προσκιθαρίζοντες and αὐληταί or οἱ προσαυλίζοντες; for singers κιθαρῳδοί, αὐλῳδοί, and ᾠδοί; perhaps at times with reduced melody, else merely as declaimers, ῥαψῳδοί; for auxiliary staff, ἱματιομίσθαι and σκευοποιοί. Of course not all are attested for any given synod or inscription, and the role and precise sphere of expertise involved is not always clear to the modern scholar. With the distinction between mere ὑποκριταί and τραγῳδοί or κωμῳδοί, for example, we are familiar from fourth-century BC Athens, when old dramas first (in 386) and then comedies (in 339) were admitted into festivals.[9] The need for new labels must have become necessary at least in part to be able to tell them apart in the *Fasti*. The occasional titles ὑποκριτὴς παλαιᾶς τραγῳδίας[10] and ὑποκριτὴς παλαιᾶς κωμῳδίας[11] gave way decisively to the near exclusive use of τραγῳδός and κωμῳδός (if nothing else, a significant saving of labor for the letter cutter).[12]

I have already considered the circumstances that may have spurred the coining of ὁμηριστής over against the more traditional ῥαψῳδός;[13] even though the former did not belong to the Dionysiac synods (or perhaps because of it), once their respective performance practices had diverged enough to mark them as two different kinds of artists, it may have been a matter of pride and prestige for the latter to set themselves clearly apart from the former.[14] The *homēristēs* not

---

[7] Cf. Aneziri 2003:425–428 table 3. These and other specialties may also be traced through the index in Stephanēs 1988:556–593.

[8] For the meaning of διδάσκαλος, χοροδιδάσκαλος, and ὑποδιδάσκαλος see Sifakis 1967:80–81 and 119–120.

[9] Cf. Pickard-Cambridge 1988:99–100 and IG II/III² 2318.202–203, 317–318 (=Mette 1977:27 col. 10.11–12 and 35 col. 15.14–15). See also Aneziri 2003:212–213.

[10] IG XII.6.1 173. 3 (=Mette 1977:49–50 II.C1a.α; *ante med.* II BC); SEG 36.473? (=Roesch *IThesp* 168, who conjectures καινῆς instead of παλαιᾶς, but see the reservations voiced by Schachter 1981:2.171 no. VII and Manieri 2009:394–395 Thes. 28; II.3–4/I BC); IG VII 420.25 (=Mette 1977:58 II.C4d; ca. 80–50 BC), 1760.29 (=Mette 1977:58–59 II.C5a = Roesch *IThesp* 172; early I BC). Cf. 1773.21 (=Mette 1977:59–60 II.C5c=Roesch *IThesp* 178; II.3–4 AD); and SEG 3.334.37 (=Mette 1977:60–61 II.C5d = Roesch *IThesp* 177; ca. AD 150–160 or after AD 169). *IThesp* = Roesch 2007. Cf. Aneziri 2003:212n52.

[11] SEG 36.473.3; IG VII 420.27, 1760.31, 1773.20; cf. SEG 3.334.35. For their dates and the corresponding numbers in Mette's and Roesch's editions, see the previous footnote.

[12] Aneziri 2003:212–213.

[13] See above, p. 449 n. 57 and p. 465.

[14] Gangloff (2010:70) concludes that during Roman imperial times the more traditional rhapsodic performance was characteristic of mainland Greece (particularly, Boiotia): "L'art des rhapsodes

only declaimed Homeric poetry but was also responsible for the *mise en scène*[15] (especially when several of them worked together to stage fighting duels). The rhapsode, in turn, need not have limited himself strictly to Homeric poetry, though we must assume, if only for reasons of continuity with the classical age, that the *Iliad* and the *Odyssey* remained the mainstay of his repertoire. But the mere presence of ποιηταὶ ἐπῶν shows that the composition of *epos*—here surely in the Aristotelian sense of hexametric poetry[16]—was common and popular.[17] And this, in turn, suggests an expanded repertoire that could draw on relatively recent compositions. Athenaios 14.620c–d witnesses to the performance by rhapsodes not only of Homer, but also of Hesiod, Arkhilokhos, Semonides, and Empedokles.[18] Thus, Klearkhos tells of a Simonides of Zakynthos who sitting on a stool performed Arkhilokhean poetry in the theater as a rhapsode.[19] And from Lysanias we learn that Mnasion the rhapsode delivered the iambs of Semonides in his shows.[20] Note the verb ὑποκρίνεσθαι—here, 'to deliver'[21]—in the context

---

semble donc avoir constitué à l'époque impériale une spécialisation artistique propre à la Grèce continentale, et en particulier à la Béotie, peut-être en relation avec le culte des Muses béotiennes et celui d'Apollon, le Musagète" (61). It is easy to understand why the innovations associated with the more emphatic stage presence of Roman imperial *homēristai* should have been more readily embraced in Asia Minor and Egypt, where epic performance practices were less long-standing. Gangloff (2010:59 with n. 29) helpfully lists the festivals at which rhapsodes are attested during the classical, Hellenistic, and Roman imperial periods (for "*Mouseia* de Delphes" in 59n29 read "*Mouseia* de Thespies").

[15] Just as the τραγῳδός and κωμῳδός, for whom no authoring poet played the role of διδάσκαλος. So Aneziri 2003:213n54, following Ghiron-Bistagne 1976: "Bref, dans les reprises les acteurs retrouvaient les responsabilités des anciens *didascaloi*" (123). This does not mean that *didaskaloi* (or *hypodidaskaloi*, in the case of the Athenian κοινόν) never assisted in the production, as the remarks in Sifakis 1967:80–81, 90, and 119–120 show. For inscriptional instances of διδάσκαλοι and ὑποδιδάσκαλοι, see Aneziri 2003:426–427.

[16] *Sophistical Refutations* 180a20–21 and *Metaphysics* 1023a32–33, 1093a30. Cf. Herodotos 4.29 and 7.220.

[17] Gangloff (2010:70) observes that in the epideictic and competitive settings the popularity of 'poets of epics' in Roman imperial times seems to have declined markedly from its peak during the Hellenistic period. She speculates that their functions in these contexts were responsible for the decline and that perhaps the better epic poets did not compete but appeared instead at πανηγύρεις or other public occasions (as was the case with sophists).

[18] See above, pp. 352 and 448.

[19] Κλέαρχος δ' ἐν τῷ προτέρῳ περὶ Γρίφων τὰ Ἀρχιλόχου, φησίν, [ὁ] Σιμωνίδης ὁ Ζακύνθιος ἐν τοῖς θεάτροις ἐπὶ δίφρου καθήμενος ἐραψῴδει (620c4–7).

[20] Λυσανίας δ' ἐν τῷ πρώτῳ περὶ Ἰαμβοποιῶν Μνασίωνα τὸν ῥαψῳδὸν λέγει ἐν ταῖς δείξεσι τῶν Σιμωνίδου τινὰς ἰάμβων ὑποκρίνεσθαι (620c7–10). For the emendation of the transmitted 'Simonides' to 'Semonides' see above, p. 437 n. 6. Nothing further is known about Mnasion (Steph[anēs] no. 1721) or Simonides of Zakynthos (Steph. 2281). For Stephanēs's numbers see below, p. 486 n. 35.

[21] For my translation of ὑποκρίνεσθαι as 'to deliver' see above, p. 351 with n. 69. Schweighäuser 1801–1807:7.372 writes: "Quod vero ὑποκρίνεσθαι carmina dicuntur rhapsodi, id sonat *recitare cum gestu et actione*. 'Erat enim' (ut perspecte idem Vir summus ibid. pag. 795 ait) 'simillima recitatio

of 'shows' (δείξεις) before a theater audience.[22] Other reported instances of an expanded repertoire are: Kleomenes the rhapsode reciting Empedokles' *Purifications* at Olympia;[23] Hegesias the κωμῳδός (Steph. 1055) and Hermophantos (Steph. 908),[24] perhaps also a comic actor, respectively 'delivering' (ὑποκρίνασθαι) Hesiod[25] and Homer in the great theater in Alexandria.[26] There is no doubt that these are far from the stereotype of a *homēristēs*: they almost certainly performed alone, one even sitting on a stool; and their subject matter (e.g. Hesiod or the

---

actioni scenicae: et rhapsodi voce, vultu, gestu, ipsam rem reddebant, affectus movendo, lacrymis rem miserandam, terrore horrendam, redhibendo etc.' Confer Wolfii *Proleg. ad Hom.* pag. 96."

[22] Cf. p. 453 n. 66 above.

[23] Cf. p. 352 n. 72 above.

[24] For the abbreviation "Steph." see below, p. 492.

[25] The transmitted reading, τὰ Ἡροδότου, was corrected by Meineke to τὰ Ἡσιόδου: "parum mihi credibile videtur Herodoti historias in theatro actas esse, quae res tam mihi mira visa est, ut Herodoto Hesiodi nomen substituere non dubitaverim" (Meineke 1867:297). The *Etymologicum Magnum* 411.43 s.v. ζήτρειον (col. 1175 Gaisford) ascribes a choliambic (ms. 'choriambic') fragment to a Ἡροδότῳ. Gaisford followed Ruhnken (1828:372n) in correcting the name to 'Herodas'. Regarding the unrelated emendation of τὰ Ἡροδότου in Athenaios 14.620d, Bergk (1872–1887:1.1022) preferred Herodas to Hesiod. Crusius (1914:3–4 §2, with 4n) brought together these two unrelated suggestions approvingly (cf. 44n32). But while Ruhnken was doubtless right, the same cannot be said of Bergk and Crusius (or Citelli et al. 2001:4.1601n1). Kaibel's text is properly sectioned: section 12 opens with οὐκ ἀπελείποντο δὲ ἡμῶν τῶν συμποσίων οὐδὲ ῥαψῳδοί, only to delve into nomenclature ('rhapsodes' vs. '*homēristai*'); section 13 opens with nomenclature, καὶ οἱ καλούμενοι δὲ ἱλαρῳδοί, only to assert that these performers συνεχῶς ἡμῖν ἐπεφαίνοντο. This chiastic parallel proves that section 12 is thematically self-contained. Since 'rhapsodes' are its ostensible topic, all the performers mentioned there should be considered ῥαψῳδοί unless the context demands otherwise. Athenaios must have regarded these individuals as rhapsodes because they were known to have performed passages from the standard rhapsodic repertoire (or, at least, dactylic hexameter verse—i.e. 'epic' poetry broadly conceived—that could be readily added to it). This repertoire included not only Homer, Hesiod, and Arkhilokhos, the acknowledged classics (on Arkhilokhos see above, pp. 350ff.), but also the epic poetry of Empedokles' *Purifications*. The inclusion of Semonides' iambs must have been a Hellenistic development that followed the precedent of Arkhilokhos. It was a natural extension insofar as they were considered contemporaries or near contemporaries and the two oldest canonical iambic poets. Whichever genre of Arkhilokhean poetry archaic and classical rhapsodes recited—whether it was epic or not (see above, pp. 352f.)—this development proves that in the Hellenistic period their repertoire included his iambs. The text neither states nor implies that rhapsodes performed the elegies of Mimnermos too. Only for the sake of completion (ἔτι δέ 620c4) is he mentioned by Athenaios among those whose poetry was set to music (or 'performed melodically', μελῳδηθῆναι 620c2). The list of names is not original with Athenaios, but with Khamaileon from whom he takes it in full. That Homer, Hesiod, and Arkhilokhos make this list—not that Phokylides or Mimnermos also do—motivates Athenaios' recourse to Khamaileon in the first place. The thematic focus on rhapsodes both justifies correcting τὰ Ἡροδότου and makes the emendation Herodas distinctly out of place. (For more on setting epic poetry to μέλος, see above, p. 450.)

[26] τοὺς δ' Ἐμπεδοκλέους Καθαρμοὺς ἐραψῴδησεν Ὀλυμπίασι Κλεομένης ὁ ῥαψῳδός, ὥς φησιν Δικαίαρχος ἐν τῷ Ὀλυμπικῷ. Ἰάσων δ' ἐν τρίτῳ περὶ τῶν Ἀλεξάνδρου Ἱερῶν ἐν Ἀλεξανδρείᾳ φησὶν ἐν τῷ μεγάλῳ θεάτρῳ ὑποκρίνασθαι Ἡγησίαν τὸν κωμῳδὸν τὰ Ἡσιόδου, Ἑρμόφαντον δὲ τὰ Ὁμήρου (620d1-7).

Purifications) was far from the bloody fights that scholars regularly associate with *homēristai*. Nor is Hegesias' label as a 'comic actor' in any obvious way related to his theatrical delivery of Hesiodic poetry.

12.2 The Τεχνῖται and Specialization

One aspect of the practice of artists during Hellenistic times that has obvious implications for the partial convergence between rhapsodic and dramatic performance is the matter of specialization. With the passing of time there were two simultaneous movements, in some ways mutually complementary, in some ways the result of opposing tendencies: the one led to finer distinctions between artists and is reflected by the proliferation of titles that described increasingly narrow areas of expertise; the other was embodied by individual artists who crossed the newly defined boundaries, proving that their proficiency extended beyond the confines of a single field and gaining for their accomplishments the right to use more than one professional label. Many years before, Plato's Sokrates had already taken for granted that neither dramatic poets nor actors could successfully cross the generic boundary between tragedy and comedy. Whoever distinguished himself in one could not, by the very nature of mimesis, prove proficient in both.[27] His argument is not fully developed. It appears to depend on the assumption that excellence requires the single-minded pursuit of a goal; and that mimesis, by taking one away from his true self, breaks the requisite unity of being. A similar point of view, but with quite different arguments, is put forth at *Iōn* 534c3–4: now the boundaries between the several compositional genres are set not by personal ability but by the Muse's gift of inspiration. The opposite case is defended at the end of the *Symposium*.[28] There is, however, a crucial distinction here. Sokrates speaks of ὁ τέχνῃ τραγῳδοποιὸς ὤν: if it be granted that the composition of tragic plays is a matter of τέχνη, it follows that one and the same composer can be both a tragedian and a comedian. With this agrees Cicero's sentiment in the *Orator*.[29]

---

[27] *Republic* 395a1–b1: —Σχολῇ ἄρα ἐπιτηδεύσει γέ τι ἅμα τῶν ἀξίων λόγου ἐπιτηδευμάτων καὶ πολλὰ μιμήσεται καὶ ἔσται μιμητικός, ἐπεί που οὐδὲ τὰ δοκοῦντα ἐγγὺς ἀλλήλων εἶναι δύο μιμήματα δύνανται οἱ αὐτοὶ ἅμα εὖ μιμεῖσθαι, οἷον κωμῳδίαν καὶ τραγῳδίαν ποιοῦντες. ἢ οὐ μιμήματε ἄρτι τούτω ἐκάλεις; —Ἔγωγε· καὶ ἀληθῆ γε λέγεις, ὅτι οὐ δύνανται οἱ αὐτοί. οὐδὲ μὴν ῥαψῳδοί γε καὶ ὑποκριταὶ ἅμα. —Ἀληθῆ. —Ἀλλ' οὐδέ τοι ὑποκριταὶ κωμῳδοῖς τε καὶ τραγῳδοῖς οἱ αὐτοί· πάντα δὲ ταῦτα μιμήματα. ἢ οὔ; Note that the objection is extended to rhapsodes and actors.

[28] *Symposium* 223d1–6: τὸ μέντοι κεφάλαιον, ἔφη, προσαναγκάζειν τὸν Σωκράτη ὁμολογεῖν αὐτοὺς τοῦ αὐτοῦ ἀνδρὸς εἶναι κωμῳδίαν καὶ τραγῳδίαν ἐπίστασθαι ποιεῖν, καὶ τὸν τέχνῃ τραγῳδοποιὸν ὄντα ⟨καὶ⟩ κωμῳδοποιὸν εἶναι. For a philosophical analysis of this contrast between the *Iōn* and the *Symposium* see Harris 2001.

[29] Cicero *Orator* 109: "histriones eos vidimus quibus nihil posset in suo genere esse praestantius, qui non solum in dissimillimis personis satis faciebant, cum tamen in suis versarentur, sed et

Thus, we have an acknowledgment, however fortuitous, of the dynamic of specialization that gave rise both to further refined specialties and to the drive by the more ambitious performers to master several of them. But this phenomenon cannot be merely reduced to a matter of bearing labels. We have epigraphical evidence that boundaries were crossed even when the individual in question did not publicly own the corresponding titles.[30] A study of the degree to which professionals exceeded the limits of one specialty is partially hindered by the incompleteness of the inscribed record. It is hazardous, for example, to equate various instances of the same name if the identity of patronymic and place of origin (ethnic or demotic *vel sim.*) cannot be established. As far as the data in our possession allow us to determine it, the general trend is towards an increasing versatility or willingness to exceed in practice one's putative area of expertise. Just to offer an illustration: Sifakis (1967:119) observes that the same persons are sometimes called χοροδιδάσκαλοι, sometimes ὑποδιδάσκαλοι. The old canonical distinction (reflected, for example, by Photios s.v. ὑποδιδάσκαλος) lay between the poet, the διδάσκαλος, and his aid, the ὑποδιδάσκαλος, who was more narrowly concerned with the chorus (ὁ τῶι χορῶι καταλέγων).[31] As the artists traveled around and put on the same performance in the absence of the poet, presumably the ὑποδιδάσκαλος would act as producer. The old opposition was no longer applicable, and the more specific term χοροδιδάσκαλος may now be used to express the added responsibility, while still maintaining the focus on the training of the chorus. A certain Elpinikos, for example, who visited Delphi in 130/29 BC as representative of his guild was described as a tragic ὑποδιδάσκαλος (IG II/III² 1132.46, 72). Two years later, as participant in the second Pythaïs, he was called χοροδιδάσκαλος (*SIG*³ 698.28) and was also numbered among those who sang the paean (*SIG*³ 698.15).[32] But at the first Pythaïs he conducted the choir of boys with Kleon the χοροδιδάσκαλος (*FD* III 2, 11.20–22).[33] Sifakis (1967:120) concludes: "Evidently therefore the *hypodidaskaloi* were qualified musicians, competent to conduct a purely musical performance." We need not, however, press to the corollary that in the second and first centuries BC there was no difference between χοροδιδάσκαλοι and ὑποδιδάσκαλοι.

---

comoedum in tragoediis et tragoedum in comoediis admodum placere vidimus." See also the statement in Aristotle *Politics* 1276b4–6.

[30] Fundamental here is the study by Chaniotis 1990. See also the comments in O'Connor 1908:39–44 and Sifakis 1967:81, 119–120.

[31] Theodoridis 1982–:3.535 no. 195. For the classical use of χοροδιδάσκαλος in connection with drama and lyric see E. Reisch in *RE* V 1, coll. 401–406 s.v. διδάσκαλος and in *RE* III 2, col. 2441 s.v. χοροδιδάσκαλος.

[32] For the Pythaïs see Colin 1905, Boëthius 1918, Daux 1936:521–583 (with an appendix at 708–729), Karila-Cohen 2005a, Karila-Cohen 2005b, and the other references cited in *SEG* 55.28.

[33] Cf. *SIG*³ 696b.

There might have been flexibility in labeling professionals not because the terms were entirely interchangeable, but because the ethos of the professional association allowed for exploration and the acquisition of ever greater expertise in activities related to one's original training. Crossing terminological boundaries was coextensive with a real broadening of technical purview.

This same dynamic was at work at the interface between the dramatic and the rhapsodic trades, and the proliferation of such cross-over in Hellenistic and Roman imperial times was only the logical consequence of the increased professionalism and the mutual influence to which the practices peculiar to the several performers were subjected as they interacted one with another in the context of tightly articulated artistic associations.[34] Using the ground-breaking study by Stephanēs 1988, which includes the fullest prosopography of artists to date, Chaniotis 1990 has collected the following cases in which rhapsodic performance is combined with some other specialty:[35]

1. *(χορευτής), [αὐλῳ]δός, [ῥαψῳ]δός*[36] (2174)

2. (ᾠδός), (τραγικὸς συναγωνιστής), ῥαψῳδός[37] (1146, 1368, 1913)

---

[34] Chaniotis (1990:92–93) seems to work with too strict a definition of specialization when (to use our previous example) he questions whether we can truly consider Elpinikos a master of three specialties: singer, χοροδιδάσκαλος, and ὑποδιδάσκαλος (see his three presuppositions in 89). He is right, of course, that strictly speaking we only have parallel descriptions of a given individual's activities, and these do not reveal what his training or apprenticeship might have been, or which of these activities (if any) was the primary one. But surely it is more important to realize that, moving at the highest professional levels, Elpinikos both had occasion and felt free to participate in the various capacities recorded, and that he was recognized and honored for it. As regards our focus on the degree to which such cross-over occurred, it is only a matter of relative interest whether he achieved the same level of proficiency and success in all of them. More significant is that the cross-over occurred at all.

[35] The numbers refer to Stephanēs's study in Stephanēs 1988, and the identifications and dates (as he gives them) are as follows. **2174:** Πυθοκλῆς Ἀριστάρχου Ἑρμιονεύς, III.2 (=second quarter of the third century BC). **1146:** Θεόδοτος Πυθίωνος Ἀθηναῖος, I.1. **1368:** Κάλλων Κάλλωνος (Ἀθηναῖος), I.1. **1913:** Ξενόφαντος Εὐμάχου (Ἀθηναῖος), I.1. **908:** Ἑρμόφαντος, III.3. **1055:** Ἡγησίας, III.2/3. **1979:** Πόπλιος Αἴλιος Πομπηϊανὸς Παίων Σιδήτης καὶ Ταρσεὺς καὶ Ῥόδιος, II.2 AD. **822:** Εὔρανος (or Ἴρανος) Φρυνίδου Ταναγραῖος, I.1–2 (on whom see Gossage 1975:126n21). **54:** Ἀείμναστος Εὐφραίου Θηβαῖος, II/I. **955:** Μᾶρ. Αὐρ. Εὔκαιρος Ταναγραῖος, III.4 AD. **956:** Κορνήλιος Εὔκαρπος Ἀργεῖος, II/III AD. (For "X/Y" read 'boundary between X and Y'; for "X–Y," 'period from X to Y.')

[36] Also in Le Guen 2001:2.128. The parentheses flag an inference from the context; the italic font, the uncertainty of the label (i.e. the context cannot ensure the inference or the supplement).

[37] Once again, the parentheses indicate that the labels are inferred from the context; the straight font, that the inference is certain. Indeed, ᾠδός and τραγικὸς συναγωνιστής follow unambiguously from the inscribed periphrases τοὺς ἀσομένους τούς [τε παιᾶνας] καὶ τὸν χορόν and τοὺς τούτοις συναγωνιξαμένους (Tracy 1975:61.21 and 62.50). Cf. Le Guen 2001:2.128, who adds a fourth instance, no. 732, a certain Δ]ιονύσιος [Διονυσο]δώρου (Ἀθηναῖος) from the first century BC whom Stephanēs only labels as a singer (ᾠδός). Since I cannot confirm from her own sources Le Guen's additional τραγικὸς συναγωνιστής and ῥαψῳδός, I omit no. 732 from the

3. (κωμικὸς ὑποκριτής), (ῥαψῳδός)   (908)

4. κωμῳδός, *(ῥαψῳδός)*   (1055)

5. [ποιη]τής, μελοποιός, ῥαψ[ῳδός], θεολόγος   (1979)

6. κῆρυξ, [τραγ]ῳδός, κωμικός, ῥαψῳδός   (822)

7. κῆρυξ, ῥαψῳδός   (54, 955, 956)

For my purposes, it is significant that 2–4 and 6 provide six cases in which professional performers are explicitly known to have practiced both as a rhapsode and as an actor. The numbers are small, surely owing to the unlikelihood that the versatility and accomplishments of a given artist in more than one area of expertise would be recorded and the record would survive. The evidence, therefore, is significant well beyond its numbers, and it is doubtless in agreement with the kinship between rhapsody and acting this book explores.[38] Taking all the disciplines into account, we find that most of the combinations show activities that are closely related in their practices. This is predictable, for the training in one made the performer, if not proficient, at least able to try his hand at the others. So, for example, the trained voice of the singer would stand him in good stead as an actor; or the tragic actor, who often sang arias on stage, could with relative ease compete as a singer, especially if (as Chaniotis 1990:93 suggests) he did so with memorable excerpts from plays in which he had acted. This can also be said of those who combined acting and rhapsody: voice, stage presence, and scripted delivery all contributed to the cross-over; the artist need only add the corresponding works to his repertoire. Thus, Chaniotis (1990:93) seems justified in concluding that, "Trotz der häufigen Kombination mehrerer Tätigkeiten, dürfen wir also tatsächlich von einer Spezialisierung reden; es handelt sich zwar nicht immer um eine Spezialisierung in einer bestimmten Tätigkeit, aber doch einer Spezialisierung im Bereich der Kunst."

---

references here. I infer from the corresponding entry in the table of the Athenian τεχνῖται in Le Guen (2001:2.52) that she has assumed the supplement ⟨Διονύσιον⟩ Διονυσοδώρου in her TE 13.32 at 1.114 (=*FD* III 2, 49.32) for one of the τραγικοὶ συναγωνισταί (the inscription omits the accusative in error). Stephanēs lists him by himself as no. 2823. This explains the joint attribution of this profession and of the label ᾠδός (cf. her TE 14.25 at 1.118) to a single individual so named, allegedly, Steph. 732. Her choice is especially confusing, because she prints and translates the usual supplement ⟨Διονυσόδωρον⟩ Διονυσοδώρου (cf. *SIG*³ 728k and Sifakis 1967:169 no. 19) and, apparently, only in her index under Διονυσόδωρος Διονυσοδώρου (at 2.194) calls into question his identity with the individual in TE 13.18. At any rate, I have not been able to guess what other identification allows her also to ascribe the label 'rhapsode' to this same artist.

[38] Commenting on the entire record, not just the instances that include rhapsodes, Chaniotis (1990:93) writes: "Diese 126 Personen sind vielleicht prozentual gesehen eine sehr kleine Minderheit (weniger als 4%); angesichts jedoch der Lücken unserer Überlieferung ist diese Zahl eigentlich sehr hoch."

12.3 Rhapsodes in the Inscriptional Record

An important development in the performance of epic poetry during the Hellenistic period is the rise of the so-called 'poet of epics', ἐπῶν ποιητής, often featured in honorific and festival inscriptions.[39] To be distinguished from the ῥαψῳδός, with whom he frequently appears, he probably composed and performed new epic poetry, whereas the rhapsode must have concerned himself predominantly, if not solely, with the traditional repertoire.[40] Although nothing survives to confirm explicitly that such was the difference between them, it is clear that both he and the rhapsode concerned themselves with epic (the rhapsode, largely so, if not exclusively).[41] We may confidently credit an increasing professionalism among performers with the creation of ever more precise subdisciplines, together with the labels used to tell them apart. Once the specialization of a competitive event had take place—demanding, for example, not only a rhapsodic declamation but, specifically, the declamation of a *new* epic poem, perhaps even composed for the very festival in question—giving proper recognition to the performer made it necessary to distinguish his particular area of accomplishment from others closely related. This need was especially acute for inscribed catalogs of victors, which had to state with the utmost economy of expression the competitive categories that accompanied the name of the winning performer.

I argued above (p. 284) that the association of the epic meter with elevation of style and solemnity of purpose goes back to its religious roots in prophetic and mantic poetry. Indeed, what I have called 'revelatory' poetry[42] made dactylic hexameter the meter of choice. The Homeric poems had acquired the status of cultural icons by the time Aristotle classified the heroic meter as σεμνός (*Rhetoric* 1408b32). Therefore, its selection by the poetic tradition of Greek praise—to which, as we shall see presently,[43] the production of the 'poet of epics' bears a close relation—was natural: it would serve well to celebrate individuals, peoples, cities, islands, countries, or any other subject connected with the circumstances of performance (its location, the performer, his audience,

---

[39] Important studies on the 'poet of epics' are Frei 1900:57–59; Guarducci 1926–1929:631–640; Powell 1929; Pallone 1984; Fantuzzi *apud* Ziegler 1988:XXXIV–LXXXVIII; and Gangloff 2010:63–70.

[40] So, for example, Fantuzzi *apud* Ziegler 1988: "Il *rhapsodós* recitava opere di autori precedenti (più spesso di Omero, si può immaginar dal gradimento testimoniato per questo autore dai papiri ... ; il *poietès epôn* recitava epica propria di tipo tradizionale, cioè mitologica oppure storico-locale" (XXXVI).

[41] See above, p. 482.

[42] See above, section 8.1.2, pp. 224ff.

[43] See below, p. 490.

a patron or an influential citizen, etc.).[44] As Weil (1900b:243) observed, the Greeks did not speak of the ἐπικὸς ποιητής (nor τραγικός or κωμικός, for that matter), because at first ποιητής meant not 'poet', but 'maker': thus, not 'epic maker' but 'maker of epics' (whereas 'epic poet' would have been quite natural). Inscriptional nomenclature was conservative and, even when equating ποιητής with poet became common, it held to the old label. This does not rule out the conjecture that ordinarily the poet of epics would have declaimed his own works. Therefore, the opposition 'rhapsode vs. poet of epics' could be formulated either as 'performer of *traditional* epic vs. performer of *new* epic' or as '*performer* of epic vs. *composer* of epic'. Clearly, one cannot definitely rule out the possibility that, on occasion, the rhapsode might have declaimed what the poet of epics had composed. If so, the competition would have recognized the victorious performer as performer, and the victorious composer as composer. But we must assume that the traditional rhapsodic competition continued after the model of classical festivals, with the rhapsode declaiming the traditional repertoire (Homer, Hesiod, Arkhilokhos, and others); and that festivals gave increasing recognition to the more recent composer-performer of epic (for whom, in classical times, Antimakhos of Kolophon provides a ready model), who made the rounds of local festivals with compositions in honor of the cities, rulers, heroes, or gods connected with the celebration at which he would compete (ἀγών) or offer a show of skill (ἐπίδειξις).

Pallone (1984:161), in trying to identify the earliest instance of 'poet of epics', accepts the very tentative reconstruction of *SEG* 3.368 [ἐπῶν ποιητ]ής, but inexplicably dates the inscription to the fourth century BC; the editor, however,

---

[44] One can easily find early examples of this encomiastic tradition. Thus, Diogenes Laertios 9.20 reports that Xenophanes had composed poetry about the foundation of Kolophon, his native city, and a two-thousand-line epic on the settlement of Elea. Towards the end of the fifth century BC Antimakhos of Kolophon and Nikeratos Herakleotes competed at the Lysandreia with what must have been epic poems (almost certainly hymnic encomia) in honor of Lysander, himself present for the occasion (Plutarch *Lysandros* 18.8, Test. 2 Wyss or 2 Matthews). Of course, epic hymns to various divinities are collected into the corpus of the so-called 'Homeric' hymns; no less a poet than Arkhilokhos carried the prize at a competition in Paros with a hymn to Demeter (scholia to Aristophanes *Birds* ad 1764). It is perhaps such epic compositions that (we are to imagine) formed the rhapsodic Arkhilokhean repertoire to which Plato's *Iōn* alludes (531a3). One cannot rule out the 'rhapsodizing' of other meters (in a derivative sense): after stating that Xenophanes 'wrote in hexameters, elegies, and iambs' (γέγραφε δὲ ἐν ἔπεσι καὶ ἐλεγείας καὶ ἰάμβους), Diogenes Laertios 9.18 goes on to say that 'he himself rhapsodized his own compositions' (αὐτὸς ἐρραψῴδει τὰ ἑαυτοῦ). It is clear that in later times ῥαψῳδέω, when focusing attention on the mode, rather than the substance, of performance, could be used for meters other than epic. Nevertheless, it is likely that a rhapsode schooled in epic who ventured into Arkhilokhos would sooner rhapsodize his epic hymn to Demeter than his iambs (but cf. Ford 1988:302). On Arkhilokhos' place in the repertoire of rhapsodes, see further above, pp. 350ff. Other Hellenistic instances of encomiastic epic are the infamous poets of Alexander's court and those who eulogized Antigonos Gonatas, Antigonos Soter, and others. See Hardie 1983:86–87.

dates it to the second century BC. (Cf. Steph. 2909, who himself dates it to the middle of the second century BC, specifically, to II.2/3.)[45] The scarcity in the inscriptional record of individuals that can be persuasively argued to have been both poet and rhapsode argues for a stubborn separation between the traditional and the new repertoire, a reflection perhaps of an attitude of narrow engagement best exemplified by Plato's Ion, who vehemently denied any interest in poets (even traditional ones) other than Homer.[46] The only instance I am familiar with of an individual qualified both as ῥαψῳδός and [ποιη]τής is Πόπλιος Αἴλιος Πομπηϊανὸς Παίων (Steph. 1979), from the famous inscription of the Colossus of Memnon.[47] In his case the appellative is to be taken broadly: he is called [ποιη]τοῦ πλειστονείκου, μελοποιοῦ καὶ ῥαψ[ῳδοῦ] ‖ [θε]οῦ Ἀδριανοῦ, at a time when the various Western synods of τεχνῖται of Dionysos had been consolidated into one imperial association. As his title 'rhapsode of the divine Hadrian' shows, his labor is too closely associated with the imperial cult to serve as an adequate illustration of a performer who was both a regular rhapsode and a poet.[48]

The relationship between the poet of epics and the encomiastic tradition is undeniable, and we should not be surprised to find that with increasing refinements in the competitive categories—probably responding to the rise of the prose encomium—the label 'poet of epics' would have given way to 'epic encomium'.[49] There are inscriptions, however, where 'epic encomium' and 'poet

---

[45] For the meaning of nomenclature such as 'II.2/3,' used by Stephanēs for dates and adopted here, see below, p. 492.

[46] It is helpful to refer here to Tracy 1975:60–67 no. 7h (=*FD* III 2, 48 with the supplement by Bousquet 1938:362–368), an inscription from Delphi honoring the Athenian τεχνῖται on the occasion of the fourth Pythaïs (98/97 BC). Given the number of participants named, we might reasonably have expected it to cite under both 'poets of epics' and 'rhapsodes' anyone skilled in both categories, had there been one such in the synod. But the ἐπῶν ποιητάς (line 43) are Ἀρίστων Μενελάου (Steph. 394), Διοφάνης Θεοδώρου (Steph. 782), and Λυσίας Λυσιμάχου (Steph. 1577). Whereas we do not meet again the last two in any other inscription, the first is listed as a [τραγι]κὸν ποιητάν in 17, as ᾠδός (implicitly) in line 23, and among the [π]οητὰς σατύρων in 48. The rhapsodes in this case were (line 44): Κάλλων Κάλλωνος (p. 511 item 49), Θεόδοτος Πυθίωνος (p. 510 item 47), and Ξενόφαντος Εὐμάχου (p. 513 item 53).

[47] See *SEG* 20.673–690 and Wankel 1979:134–139 no. 22. See below, p. 516 item 62.

[48] Cf. Poland 1934:2514–2519. Gangloff (2010:63) offers a suggestion by S. Follet, who construes [θε]οῦ Ἀδριανοῦ with the θεολόγου that follows. After proposing the Pythia of Ephesos or Side as possible performance venues (cf. Robert 1980:16n54), Gangloff admits: "On ne peut pas non plus préciser la nature de ses prestations rhapsodiques, surtout si celles-ci n'étaient pas agonistiques" (63).

[49] Gangloff (2010:67) notes that the 'poet of epics' disappeared at a relatively early time from the programs of the Boiotian Mouseia and the Ptoia, where the recitation of Homeric poetry was nonetheless prominent. With reference to the Mouseia during Roman imperial times, she notes that this competitive category seems to have been split into two. One concerned the emperor; the other, the Muses: "L'épreuve traditionnelle relevait probablement de l'épopée mythologique

of epics' coexist, e.g. IG VII 416.9, 13 (=*EO* 422 no. 523.9, 13): the epic encomiast is [Δ]ημοκλῆς Ἀμινίου Θηβαῖος (Steph. 645), known from Papagiannopoulos (1947–1948:75.20), not surprisingly, as an ἐπῶν ποιητής;[50] and the poet of epics is Ἀγαθοκλῆς Θεοδοσίου Νεαπολίτης (Steph. 26), not otherwise known. Another instance of this close connection is the double victory of Μήστωρ Μήστορος Φωκαιεύς (Steph. 1686) under [ἐ]πικόν and ἐπῶν ποιητής at the Ἀμφιαράϊα καὶ Ῥωμαῖα of Ὀρōπος (IG VII 418.5, 9 = *EO* 426 no. 524.6, 10).[51] It is impossible to say with certainty what the precise difference between these two competitive events must have been. Possibly, just a distinction in the subject matter: an individual vis-à-vis a deity or a city? It is clear, however, that whatever overlap these categories enjoyed did not prevent their joint appearance at the Amphiaraia of Ὀrōpos in the first century BC, as witnessed by IG VII 416, 418, 419, 420 (=*EO* nos. 523, 524, 526, and 528).[52] The contemporaneous IG VII 2727, however, from the Soteria at Akraiphia,[53] features ἐνκωμίῳ λογικῷ and ἐπῶν ποιητής, but no ἐνκωμίῳ ἐπικῷ. This confirms the intuition that the poetry of the poet of epics and the epic encomium are closely related, with the latter a peculiar instantiation of the former, perhaps openly incorporating, in epic meter, the rhetorical conventions of the prose encomium as to subject matter, arrangement, or the like.

12.3.1 Prosopography of rhapsodes

This section lists the rhapsodes extant in the inscriptional record. I include those known to us only through literary references (e.g. the writings of Plutarch or Athenaios), whose existence we have no compelling reason to doubt.[54] Abbreviations used:

---

[50] et son sujet portait sur les Muses" (68). She further suggests that the label ἐπῶν ποιηταί was abandoned perhaps because of this split or in order to open up the competition to other poetic genres and thus attract a larger number of contestants (2010:68).

[50] According to Knoepfler 2004:1264n74, Ἀ[μεινί]ου should be restored in line 8 of IG VII 2448, *contra* Dittenberger's Θ[. . . . . .]ου. If so, Steph. 646 (=Koumanoudēs 1979:53 no. 459) should be identified with Steph. 645 (=Koumanoudēs 1979:53 no. 458).

[51] A third instance, if the reconstruction [ἐπῶν ποιητὰς Δι]οφάνην Διοδώρου, Κράτερον Ἀντι[of *FD* III 2, 49.25 is accepted, is the poet Κράτερος Ἀντιπάτρου Ἀμφιπολίτης (Steph. 1488), who appears in IG VII 420.12 (=*EO* 434 no. 528.12) as winner of ἐγκώμιον ἐπικόν.

[52] In IG VII 420 and 418 ἐγκώμιον καταλογάδην should be respectively contrasted with ἐγκώμιον ἐπικόν and ἐπικόν (the elided ἐγκώμιον is readily understood from the ἐγκώμιον καταλογάδη[ν that precedes it); in 419, ἐνκωμίῳ λογικῷ with ἐνκωμίῳ ἐπικῷ (restored also in 416).

[53] For the name of this Boiotian town and its alternative spellings see Meyer 1909:125n2 and the *New Pauly* s.v. "Acraephia."

[54] I exclude Ion of Ephesus (Steph. 1305), a Platonic creation whose historical reality is hard to judge. The force of the dialog would not be diminished if Ion were wholly fictional, and nothing in the work's genre presupposes the historical reality of this figure.

EO	Β. Χ. Πετράκος *Οἱ Ἐπιγραφὲς τοῦ Ὠρωποῦ* [55]
PA	I. Kirchner *Prosopographia Attica*
PAA	J. S. Traill *Persons of Ancient Athens*
Reisch	A. Reisch *De musicis graecorum certaminibus*
Steph.	Stephanēs *Διονυσιακοὶ Τεχνῖται*

For dates, Roman numerals refer to the century (BC unless otherwise noted); an additional Arabic numeral refers to the quarter of the century in question. Thus, for example, III.3 would be the third quarter of the 3rd century BC (250–225 BC).[56] The identifications that follow Stephanēs's numbers appear in parentheses when they are inferred from the evidence; and italicized if the inference is less than certain (otherwise, straight font is used).[57] An appended question mark indicates a very high degree of uncertainty.

VI Century BC

1. Κύναιθος Χῖος (Steph. **1521**, VI/V) ῥαψῳδός

   From scholion 1c (Drachmann) to Pindar *Nemean* 2 we learn that Kynaithos was a rhapsode[58] numbered among the Homeridai,[59] whose circle of apprentices became especially famous. We are also told that Kynaithos was from Khios, where the Homeridai were based; and that, of the poetry ascribed to Homer, he 'wrote' the *Hymn to Apollo* and attributed it to him. Furthermore, Hippostratos reports that in 504–501 BC Kynaithos was the first rhapsode to perform in Syracuse the poetry of Homer.[60]

---

55 On which see *SEG* 47.487.

56 For "X/Y" read 'boundary between X and Y'; for "X–Y," 'period from X to Y.'

57 *Nota bene* that Stephanēs follows the opposite convention. I also use straight font when the inference is virtually certain, even if the professional label itself does not appear next to the name in the relevant document. An example of such 'virtual certainty' is the identification of Ἑρμόφαντος (see below, p. 499 item 17) as a κωμικὸς ὑποκριτής on the basis of IG II/III² 2325.231.

58 On Kynaithos generally see Wade-Gery 1936, Wade-Gery 1952:19–31, Burkert 1979, West 1975, and De Martino 1983 (with bibliography at 157n4).

59 For the Homeridai, see further above, pp. 334, 380 n. 169, and 383. There is some disagreement whether the scholiast counts Kynaithos himself among the Homeridai (cf. Graziosi 2002:213 and Nagy 2010a:65–66, 68, 70–72). Even if the scholion is inconclusive, the flow of its logic arguably suggests that this is so. Cf. West 1999b:371.

60 Ὁμηρίδας ἔλεγον τὸ μὲν ἀρχαῖον τοὺς ἀπὸ τοῦ Ὁμήρου γένους, οἳ καὶ τὴν ποίησιν αὐτοῦ ἐκ διαδοχῆς ᾖδον· μετὰ δὲ ταῦτα καὶ οἱ ῥαψῳδοὶ οὐκέτι τὸ γένος εἰς Ὅμηρον ἀνάγοντες. ἐπιφανεῖς δὲ ἐγένοντο οἱ περὶ Κύναιθον, οὕς φασι πολλὰ τῶν ἐπῶν ποιήσαντας ἐμβαλεῖν εἰς τὴν Ὁμήρου ποίησιν. ἦν δὲ ὁ Κύναιθος τὸ γένος Χῖος, ὃς καὶ τῶν ἐπιγραφομένων Ὁμήρου ποιημάτων τὸν εἰς Ἀπόλλωνα γεγραφὼς ὕμνον ἀνατέθεικεν αὐτῷ. οὗτος οὖν ὁ Κύναιθος πρῶτος ἐν Συρακούσαις ἐραψῴδησε τὰ Ὁμήρου ἔπη κατὰ τὴν ξθ′ Ὀλυμπιάδα, ὡς Ἱππόστρατός φησιν (scholion 1c to Pindar *Nemean* 2). For convenience I print here the English translation provided by *Brill's New*

As the earliest historically attested rhapsode (other than the likes of Theagenes or perhaps even Xenophanes),[61] Kynaithos dates to a time when the authority of the Homeric tradition was crystallizing decisively around the figure of 'Homer' as its πρῶτος εὑρετής. For this reason, since in all likelihood both he and those in his circle followed the centuries-old practice of recomposition in performance, later controversies were bound to arise about the authorship (and hence, the authority) of verses and versions attributed to them. These controversies were anachronistically framed as instances of 'interpolation' into an otherwise notionally established text. This is precisely what is reflected by scholion 1c.[62] In so far as the *Hymn to Apollo* was one of the last poems to be dissociated from the canonical *Iliad* and *Odyssey* as truly Homer's own—it was still ascribed to Homer by Thoukydides (3.104.4)—we can understand the scholiast's focus on it.[63]

Although I have no reason to deny that Kynaithos may well have reperformed this hymn—and, as one link in its line of transmission, may have had a shaping hand in the final form of the received text—scholars have been all too eager to embrace the scholion's anachronistic point of view and spin more or less plausible theories about Kynaithos' historical doings and whereabouts.[64] Perhaps the most popular is the proposal independently arrived at by Burkert and Janko that he may have "cobbled together" the Pythian and Delian sections of the hymn for (or at) the Πύθια καὶ Δήλια celebrated by Polykrates in 523/22 BC shortly before his death.[65] In particular, it has been hard to resist the notion that the

---

Jacoby: "They say that the Homeridai in ancient times were those from the family of Homer, who sang his poetry in succession. Later the name was also given to the rhapsodes, who no longer traced their descent back to Homer. Particularly prominent were Kynaithos and those associated with him, whom they say composed many epic verses and inserted them into the poetry of Homer. Kynaithos was from a Chian family, and of the poetry that bears the name of Homer, he was the one who wrote the *Hymn for Apollo* and credited it to Homer. In fact, this Kynaithos was the first who recited the epics of Homer in Syracuse, during the 69th Olympiad (504/1 BC), as Hippostratos says" (=FGH 568 F5).

[61] On Theagenes, see above, pp. 156ff.; on Xenophanes, p. 354.

[62] Scholion 1e is even more critical: Ὁμηρίδαι πρότερον μὲν οἱ Ὁμήρου παῖδες, ὕστερον δὲ οἱ περὶ Κύναιθον ῥαβδῳδοί· οὗτοι γὰρ τὴν Ὁμήρου ποίησιν σκεδασθεῖσαν ἐμνημόνευον καὶ ἀπήγγελλον· ἐλυμήναντο δὲ αὐτῇ πάνυ. Cf. Janko 1982:261–262n88.

[63] Cf. Nagy 2010a:70.

[64] Cf. West 1999b:370–371.

[65] See West 1999b:369, with reference to Burkert 1979:59–60 and Janko 1982:112–114. For the festival, see the sources in Burkert 1979:59n31. To "cobble together" is Janko's expression (1982:113), taken over by West (1999b:369) and others. Cf. Nagy 2010a:72.

sixth-century BC inscription uncovered in Gela in 1957 refers to this Kynaithos, even though there is nothing better to recommend the ascription than the alleged rarity of the name.[66]

V Century BC

2. Νικήρατος (Steph. **1817**, V.3–4) (ῥαψῳδός)

Aristotle *Rhetoric* 1413a6–9: [ἔστι] καὶ τὸν Νικήρατον φάναι Φιλοκτήτην εἶναι δεδηγμένον ὑπὸ Πράτυος, ὥσπερ εἴκασε Θρασύμαχος ἰδὼν τὸν Νικήρατον ἡττημένον ὑπὸ Πράτυος ῥαψῳδοῦντα, κομῶντα δὲ καὶ αὐχμηρὸν ἔτι. Aristotle's mention of Thrasymakhos, surely the sophist from Chalcedon made famous by Plato in the *Republic*,[67] places the *floruit* of Nikeratos during the second half of the fifth century BC. Three other instances of 'Nikeratos' have been variously related one to another and to the Aristotelian namesake. The first is the son of the Athenian general Nikias,[68] who according to Xenophon was compelled by his father to learn the poetry of Homer and could recite the entire *Iliad* and *Odyssey* by heart (*Symposion* 3.5, 4.6).[69] A second Nikeratos, called ἐποποιός by Markellinos (*Life of Thoukydidēs* 29), like Euripides, Agathon, and other Greek intellectuals, is supposed to have resided for a time at the court of the Makedonian king Arkhelaos.[70] Plutarch *Lysandros* features the third Nikeratos, this one 'of Herakleia'. He is said by

---

[66] The inscription reads: Κ]ΥΝΑΙΘΟ ΕΜΙ ΤΟ [ΑΓΑΛ]ΜΑ ΤΟ ΕΠΟΨΟ (with the characteristic red-alphabet use of the grapheme Ψ for Χ; cf. Woodard 1997a:140–141). For its publication, see Orlandini 1957:94–96 (with figs. 22–23), who dates it "nel pieno VI sec. a.C., forse anche nella prima metà di esso" (96). Cf. Dubois 1989:147–148 no. 129, who restores [σᾶ]μα on the basis of inscriptions nos. 74 and 75 in his collection. Burkert's prudence about the ascription (1979:55) has soon been discarded; so also his caution about the factuality of Kynaithos' alleged composition of the Homeric hymn (1979:57–58).

[67] Cf. Aristotle *Rhetoric* 1404a14 and 1409a2. For Thrasymakhos, see Nails 2002:288–290.

[68] Davies 1971:401 no. 10741 ("Nikias (II)," 406 no. 10808, under his father Nikias). Cf. *PA* 2.123 no. 10741 and *PAA* 13.142–143 no. 710670.

[69] See above, p. 315.

[70] συνεχρόνισε [sc. Θουκυδίδης] δ', ὥς φησι Πραξιφάνης ἐν τῷ περὶ ἱστορίας, Πλάτωνι τῷ κωμικῷ, Ἀγάθωνι τραγικῷ, Νικηράτῳ ἐποποιῷ καὶ Χοιρίλῳ καὶ Μελανιππίδῃ. καὶ ἐπεὶ μὲν ἔζη Ἀρχέλαος, ἄδοξος ἦν ὡς ἐπὶ πλεῖστον, ὡς ⟨ὁ⟩ αὐτὸς Πραξιφάνης δηλοῖ, ὕστερον δὲ δαιμονίως ἐθαυμάσθη (=Praxiphanes fr. 18 Wehrli). Wilamowitz-Moellendorff (1877:353–358) plausibly argued that Markellinos had based his synchronism on a tradition by Praxiphanes about the stay of these intellectuals at the court of Arkhelaos. Hirzel 1878 took up this suggestion and proposed that Praxiphanes' Περὶ ἱστορίας was a dialog about the value of writing history, which featured representatives of the different genres of poetry (epic, tragedy, comedy, and dithyramb). This is the point of view adopted by Wehrli (1969:112). Even if Praxiphanes' report cannot be taken as straightforwardly factual, one may safely accept the existence of Nikeratos the ἐποποιός and his chronological placement towards the end of the fifth century BC.

Douris of Samos to have bested Antimakhos of Kolophon at the festival of Hera, which in honor of Lysander the Samians had renamed Lysandreia.[71] Scholars differ in their identifications of these four figures. Diehl thinks the ἐποποιός to have been the same as Nikeratos of Herakleia (*RE* XVII, col. 313 s.v. "Nikeratos [2]"). The son of Nikias, in turn, is conventionally assumed to be the (Athenian?) Nikeratos mentioned by Aristotle in connection with Thrasymakhos (Reincke *RE* XVII, col. 313 s.v. "Nikeratos [1]"). This fits the notion that as an amateur he was defeated by the professional Pratys (so Cope 1877:3.139). Wilamowitz-Moellendorff (1924:1.103n4) apparently identified the Herakleian Nikeratos with the Aristotelian and others have followed his lead (e.g. Diehl in *RE* XVII, columns 313–314). But unless we assume that Plutarch was wrong to write Ἡρακλεώτου, Wilamowitz's equation seems impossible.[72] Plutarch, moreover, did not know who this Nikeratos was (as the τινός shows)[73] and therefore cannot have thought him to be the son of Nikias.

3. Πράτυς (Steph. **2141**, V.3–4) (ῥαψῳδός)
    Aristotle *Rhetoric* 1413a6–9. See item 2 immediately above.

IV Century BC

4. Ἄλεξις Ταραντῖνος (Steph. **127**, IV.3/4) ῥαψῳδός
    Athenaios 12.538e7–8: ... μεθ' οὓς ἐπεδείξατο ῥαψῳδὸς Ἄλεξις Ταραντῖνος (XII.54.27–28). Performed for Alexander during the wedding at Susa in 324 BC. Cf. Berve 1926:2.22 no. 44 and Heckel 2006 s.v. "Alexis." For Khares' fragment see FGH 125 F4.[74]

5. Κλεομένης (Steph. **1445**, V/IV) ῥαψῳδός
    Diogenes Laertios 8.63: αὐτοὺς δὲ τούτους τοὺς Καθαρμοὺς [ἐν] Ὀλυμπίασι ῥαψῳδῆσαι λέγεται Κλεομένη τὸν ῥαψῳδόν, ὡς καὶ Φαβωρῖνος ἐν Ἀπομνημονεύμασι. Athenaios 14.620d1–3: τοὺς δ' Ἐμπεδοκλέους Καθαρμοὺς ἐραψῴδησεν Ὀλυμπίασι Κλεομένης ὁ ῥαψῳδός, ὥς φησι Δικαίαρχος ἐν τῷ Ὀλυμπικῷ (XIV.12.20–22). For

---

71 Ἀντιμάχου δὲ τοῦ Κολοφωνίου καὶ Νικηράτου τινὸς Ἡρακλεώτου ποιήμασι Λυσάνδρεια διαγωνισαμένων ἐπ' αὐτοῦ τὸν Νικήρατον ἐστεφάνωσεν, ὁ δὲ Ἀντίμαχος ἀχθεσθεὶς ἠφάνισε τὸ ποίημα (*Lysandros* 18.4; cf. FGH 76 F71, with Jacoby's commentary in vol. 2c p. 128).

72 Cobet (1836:71) makes Nikias' son the opponent of Pratys. Näke (1817:31) in turn equates the Herakleian with the Aristotelian Nikeratos.

73 Cf. Smits 1939:183–184.

74 On Alexander's dealings with athletes and artists see Tritle 2009:122–129.

Favorinus' fragment see Mensching 1963:92–93 F18; for Dikaiarkhos', Wehrli 1944:31 fr. 87 and Mirhady 2001:86–89 fr. 85.

6. Μνασίων (Steph. **1721**, IV.4–III.2) ῥαψῳδός

According to Athenaios 14.620c, Lysanias reports that Mnasion the
rhapsode delivered the iambs of Semonides in his shows.[75] Lysanias
of Cyrene taught Eratosthenes and his *floruit* is to be dated to
III.2–3 BC.[76] Starting with Arkhilokhos perhaps as early as the
archaic period,[77] the inclusion of iambic meters and poetry in the
repertoire of rhapsodes was certainly traditional by the second half
of the fourth century. There is nothing in Athenaios' report that
requires a later date, although given Lysanias' *floruit* one cannot
preclude the first half of the third century BC.[78] Nothing further is
known about Mnasion.[79] See also item 7 immediately below.

7. Σιμωνίδης Ζακύνθιος (Steph. **2281**, IV.4–III.1) (ῥαψῳδός)

According to Athenaios 14.620c, Klearkhos told of a Simonides of
Zakynthos who sat on a stool and as a rhapsode performed Arkhilokhean poetry in the theaters (fr. 92 Wehrli).[80] Simonides must
have been a contemporary of Klearkhos. If we are to place the latter
in Athens, first under Aristotle[81] and then under Theophrastos;[82]
and if his knowledge of the rhapsode's stage manner is firsthand, as
his acquaintance with the use of the δίφρος suggests, then we may
reasonably expect Athens' own theater to be one of Simonides' performance venues. But rhapsodes cannot have delivered their poetry
in the theater of Athens much earlier than the time of Demetrios of
Phaleron,[83] and Simonides' *floruit* is perhaps to be dated as late as

---

[75] Λυσανίας δ' ἐν τῷ πρώτῳ περὶ Ἰαμβοποιῶν Μνασίωνα τὸν ῥαψῳδὸν λέγει ἐν ταῖς δείξεσι τῶν
Σιμωνίδου τινὰς ἰάμβων ὑποκρίνεσθαι (620c7–10).

[76] Lennartz 2010:51 with n. 211 and Rotstein 2010:114, 265–266.

[77] See above, pp. 350ff.

[78] Lennartz 2010: "Der Rhapsode Mnasion, der offenbar ebenfalls dem 3. Jh. angehört, habe
Aufführungen von Semonidischen ἴαμβοι veranstaltet" (295).

[79] See further above, p 482.

[80] Κλέαρχος δ' ἐν τῷ προτέρῳ περὶ Γρίφων τὰ Ἀρχιλόχου, φησίν, [ὁ] Σιμωνίδης ὁ Ζακύνθιος ἐν
τοῖς θεάτροις ἐπὶ δίφρου καθήμενος ἐραψῴδει (620c4–7). With Lennartz (2010:295n1074), I doubt
that this δίφρος has anything to do with the one in *Hymn to Demeter* 198, despite the intriguing
suggestion by Lavigne 2005:26n37.

[81] Cf. Athenaios 6.234f10–11 and 15.701c3–5, with *RE* XI, col. 580 s.v. "Klearchos [11]" and
Robert 1968:445–446.

[82] Cf. Wehrli 1983b:547.

[83] I suggested above (pp. 469f.) that Demetrios must have been the one who moved the rhapsodic
competitions from the odeion of Perikles to the theater of Dionysos. It is possible that by then
iambic rhapsodic performances had already found a home in the theater. This would explain the

the beginning decades of the third century BC.[84] Nothing further is known about this artist.[85] See also item 6 immediately above.

8. Σωσίστρατος (Steph. **2355**, IV?) (ῥαψῳδός)
   Aristotle *Poetics* 1462a6–7: ἐπεὶ ἔστι περιεργάζεσθαι τοῖς σημείοις καὶ ῥαψῳδοῦντα, ὅπερ [ἐστὶ] Σωσίστρατος.[86]

9. Τερψικλῆς (Steph. **2402**, IV.1–2?) ῥαψωιδός
   Carapanos 1878:1.40 no. 3, with pl. 23 no. 2 (=Lazzarini 1976:198 no. 142 = *SGDI* III.2.774 no. 5786). A tripod inscription from Dodona in the Ionic alphabet: Τερψικλῆς τῶι Δὶ Ναίωι ῥαψωιδὸς ἀνέθηκε. According to Kirchhoff 1887:22, "ersichtlich im ionischen Alphabet etwa der Mitte des 5. Jahrhunderts geschrieben." Carapanos too dated it to the fifth century BC. Kastelic 1995:154, on the other hand, to after 403/402 BC.[87] If Terpsikles' dedication followed his victory at a nearby festival, assuming the local manufacture of the tripod[88] and the inscription, it seems best on the basis of Lhôte 2006:15–17 §§47–49 and 329–335 §§62–69 to follow Kastelic and place it after the orthographic reform of 403/402 BC.[89]

---

reference to οὔτ' ἰάμβων οὔτε κωμῳδίας θεατάς in Aristotle *Politics* 1336b20 (cf., for example, Nagy 1996c:163–164, Lavigne 2005:22–23, and Bartol 1992:66–67). I find Lennartz's attempt to explain away Aristotle's statement forced and unpersuasive (2010:295–296). On Simonides of Zakynthos, see further Lavigne 2005:25–26 and Rotstein 2010:265.

[84] Cf. Bartol 1992:67 and Lennartz 2010:295 ("wohl spätes 4. Jh."). Wehrli 1983a:45 places Klearkhos' birth no later than the 340s BC; and his death, "tief ins 3. Jahrhundert" on account of his dialog *Arkesilaos*, which featured the participation of Arkesilaos of Pitane, head of the Academy from ca. 268 BC (frr. 11–12 Wehrli; cf. Wehrli 1983b:548). A less restrictive *terminus post quem* for his death of ca. 290 BC may be inferred from the reference to a Jew and Indian philosophy in fr. 6 (Wehrli) of his Περὶ ὕπνου (cf. Wehrli 1983a:45 and 1983b:548, and Robert 1968:447–448).

[85] See also above, p. 482 n. 20.

[86] Perhaps ὅπερ ἔτι Σωσίστρατος, which would make him a contemporary of Aristotle (Tarán prints ἐποίει). Gudeman (1934:447) thinks that Μνασίθεος ὁ Ὀπούντιος (Steph. 1715) was a rhapsode too but his reasoning is not valid. Aristotle offers two examples from spheres other than dramatic performance to show that exaggerated movement is not peculiar to tragedy. One such specialty, especially appropriate for this chapter, is rhapsody; another, the one to which διᾴδοντα refers. Stephanēs's label ᾠδός seems suitably prudent.

[87] Cf. *SEG* 46.2312.

[88] Cf. Carapanos 1878:1.84 and Cook 1902.

[89] The inscription features omega and eta; the alpha, delta, and sigma are not characteristic of the archaic alphabet of Dodona; but the rho is (Lhôte 2006:332–333). The epsilon too seems of later date. The local archaic alphabet used the psi-grapheme (in Τερψικλῆς) for the chi. For rough chronological parallels, cf., for example, Lhôte 2006:173–175 no. 80 and 227–229 no. 107 side A. Kirchhoff's dating remains possible if one supposes that Terpsikles himself inscribed the tripod or else insisted that the letter cutter use the Ionian alphabet.

10.]στρατος Σικυώνι(ος) (Steph. **2786**, IV.2–3) ῥαψ]ωιδός (αὐλ]ωιδὸς π[αῖς more likely)
    IG VII 414.4 (=*EO* 409–415 no. 520 = Manieri 2009:225–228 Oro. 5).
    Ἀμφιαράϊα] τὰ μεγάλ[α] of Ὠρōπος.
    For the date see *EO* 413 (366–338 BC, after Dittenberger), with an inventory of scholarly views; and Manieri 2009:225–228 (329/28 BC, after Knoepfler 1993:299–300, who restores [θεοί· οἵδε ἐνίκων τὰ πρῶτ]α μεγάλα [Ἀμφιάραια] in line 1 and relates this inscription to IG VII 4254 = *EO* no. 298, from 329/28 BC).[90] In IG VII 414 Dittenberger made him a κιθαρ]ωιδός, possible only on the assumption that the preceding word is abbreviated Θηβαῖ(ος) (the available space allows only for five letters). But a κιθαρῳδός appears in line 7. The restoration ῥαψ]ωιδός is marginally possible (with Θηβαῖος unabbreviated); so, for example, Frei 1900:71.II. But, as printed in *EO* 409 no. 520.3, it seems best with Preuner 1903:338–346 to supply αὐλ]ωιδὸς π[αῖς.[91]

III Century BC

11. Ἀγαθῖνος Κριτοδήμο[υ Σικ]υώνιος (Steph. **18**, III.2) ῥα[ψωι]δός
    Nachtergael 1977:420 no. 9, line 9. Ἀμφικτυονικὰ Σωτήρια of Delphi, perhaps in 258/57 or 254/53 BC.

12. Ἀρισταγό[ρας] (Steph. **306**, III.2) ῥαψωιδός
    Nachtergael 1977:408 no. 3, line 5. Ἀμφικτυονικὰ Σωτήρια of Delphi, ca. 265–258 BC.

13. Ἀριστείδης Ἀρίστωνος [. . . . .]ς (Steph. **318**, III.2) ῥα[ψωι]δός
    Nachtergael 1977:420 no. 9, line 10. Ἀμφικτυονικὰ Σωτήρια of Delphi, perhaps in 258/57 or 254/53 BC.

14. Ἀριστομένης Ἀριστομένου [. . . . .]ιος (Steph. **362**, III.2) ῥα[ψωι]δός
    Nachtergael 1977:420 no. 9, line 11. Ἀμφικτυονικὰ Σωτήρια of Delphi, perhaps in 258/57 or 254/53 BC.

15. Ἀρχέλας Θετταλός (Steph. **435**, III.1) ῥαψῳδός
    IG XI.2 105.27. In Delos in 284 BC. He is listed with the other artists under the heading οἵδε ἐπεδείξαντο τῶι θεῶι (line 16).

---

[90] Cf. *SEG* 43.208.
[91] I have not been able to find a name that ends in -στρατος whose first member is eight letters long.

16. Γλαῦκος Ἀθηναῖος (Steph. **549**, III.1) ῥαψῳδός
    IG XI.2 105.28. In Delos in 284 BC. He is listed under the heading οἵδε
    ἐπεδείξαντο τῶι θεῶι (line 16). Cf. PA 1.196 no. 2991 and PAA 4.271
    no. 276007.

17. Ἑρμόφαντος (Steph. **908**, III.3) (ῥαψῳδός), (κωμικὸς ὑποκριτής)
    According to Athenaios 14.620d, Ἰάσων δ᾽ ἐν τρίτῳ περὶ τῶν
    Ἀλεξάνδρου Ἱερῶν ἐν Ἀλεξανδρείᾳ φησὶν ἐν τῷ μεγάλῳ θεάτρῳ
    ὑποκρίνασθαι Ἡγησίαν τὸν κωμῳδὸν τὰ Ἡσιόδου,[92] Ἑρμόφαντον
    δὲ τὰ Ὁμήρου. There is no compelling reason to reject Capps's
    identification of this Hermophantos with the comic actor whose
    victory at the Lenaia ca. 240 BC is recorded by IG II/III[2] 2325.231
    (=Mette 1977:180 V.C2 col. 6.17). Capps 1900:134–135, who first pro-
    posed the restoration 'Hermophantos' in the didascalic record of the
    Lenaia when, still incomplete, it only read Ἑρμ[, also suggested that
    he was the ὑποκριτής of IG XII.6.1 176.5 (=Mette 1977:50 II.C1b.α IA.6).
    Wilhelm (1906:254; cf. 155) rejected this conjecture following
    Preuner (1903:369–370; hence O'Connor 1908:95 no. 182; cf. Ghiron-
    Bistagne 1976:324). But Preuner (1924:35–36) recanted his earlier
    judgment and the editors of IG XII.6.1 therefore date the inscription
    to "paulo post med. s. III a." The identifications are therefore possible.

18. Εὐθ]ύδημος Χάρητος Ἀθηναῖος (Steph. **948**, III.2) ῥαψῳδός
    Nachtergael 1977:423 no. 10, lines 9–10. Ἀμφικτυονικὰ Σωτήρια of
    Delphi, perhaps in 257/56 or 253/52 BC. Cf. PA 1.359 no. 5523 and
    PAA 7.241 no. 432200.

19. Εὐρύβιος Λυκίσκου Μεγαλοπολίτης (Steph. **982**, III.2) ῥαψῳδός
    Nachtergael 1977:479 no. 63, line 6; 480 no. 64, line 6.[93] Αἰτωλικὰ
    Σωτήρια of Delphi. The respective tentative dates of the festivals
    are 225/24 and 221/20 BC.

20. Ζηνόδοτος Σωπάτρου Ἀντιοχεύς ἀπὸ Πυρά[μου] (Steph. **1024**, III.4)
    ῥαψῳδός
    IG VII 1762.5 (=Jamot 1895:333–334 no. 7 = IThesp 163 = Manie-
    ri 2009:376–378 Thes. 18). The overlap of names with Ja-
    mot 1895:332–333 no. 6 (=IThesp 161 = Manieri 2009:374–376
    Thes. 17) convincingly ties no. 7 to the Μουσεῖα of Thespiai.[94]

---

[92] For the reading τὰ Ἡσιόδου see above, p. 483 n. 25.
[93] The name and specialty are fragmentary in no. 63 but wholly preserved in no. 64.
[94] All the names in no. 7 appear under the same competitive headings in no. 6 except for two:
Ζηνόδοτος the ῥαψῳδός and a Σώφιλος Σωτέ[λους] (now revised by Roesch in IThesp 163.1 to
Σώφιλος Σωπά[τρου] whom Jamot 1895:349 thinks a κῆρυξ or σαλπιστής and Steph. 2377 makes

Feyel (1942:113) persuasively argues that two celebrations of the Μουσεῖα, even if chronologically close, can hardly have had the same winners in five different categories. Yet this would be the case unless no. 6 and no. 7 refer to one and the same festival.[95] And although scholars have followed Jamot (1895:346) in thinking them to be "séparées l'une de l'autre par quelques années à peine," there is in fact no need to do so. For line 8 of no. 6 refers clearly to οἱ νικήσαντες τὸν θυμ[ε]λ[ικόν]; and hence it is only natural that it would merely list those events reclassified under the umbrella of the στεφανίτης θυμελικὸς ἀγών. Whereas no. 7 would be a fragment of the complete catalog of victors, with the addition of those events that had not been reorganized as στεφανῖται (see more on this immediately below). If we adopt this more plausible assumption, then no. 7 dates from the same time as no. 6, namely, ca. 210–203 BC.[96] The competitive events that survive on no. 7 are: ποιητὴς ἐπῷ[ν], ῥαψῳδός, αὐλητής, αὐλῳδός, κιθαριστής, κιθαρῳδός, and ἐπινίκια. Concerning the third-century BC reorganization of the Μουσεῖα by Thespiai and the Boiotian league, we learn from the decree of the Isthmian and Nemean *koinon* ratifying it[97] that recognition as

---

95 out to be a [ποιητὴς προσοδίου] (*IThesp* 163 prints [κῆρυξ?]). At any rate, his competitive event joins rhapsody and ἐπινίκια as additions vis-à-vis no. 6. For the festival, see Jamot 1895:361–366, Feyel 1942:88–132, Schachter 1981:2.163–179, Knoepfler 1996, and Manieri 2009:313–340.

95 So also Knoepfler 1996:164.

96 For the dating of no. 6 see Feyel 1942:116–117, followed by Roesch 1982:188–189 no. 32 (his dating of no. 7 is explicitly given on page 493). Cf. also Schachter 1981:2.167–168 no. II and Aneziri 2003:412 Gb1. *IThesp* dates no. 161 to 210–203; and no. 163 to 210–172, taking as the lower bound the date of IG XI.4 1061 (cf. Knoepfler 1996:155n49 and Schachter 1981:2.166n3). The modifications that Knoepfler 1996 has made to our understanding of the late third-century BC reorganization of the Mouseia do not affect the dating of IG VII 1762. The crucial piece of evidence is the year of the federal archonship of Lykinos (who appears at *IThesp* 161.7), with a *terminus ante quem* of 204 but preferentially placed by Knoepfler ca. 209 (Knoepfler 1996:158; cf. *SEG* 46.540). Knoepfler's arguments have been well received. Cf., for example, *SEG* 46.536; Aneziri 2003:412 *ad* Gb1; Le Guen 2001:1.144–145 *ad* no. 22 (a discussion of Jamot 1895:313–322 no. 1 = *SIG*³ 457); and Manieri 2009:318.

97 Fr. A was published as Jamot 1895:313–322 no. 1 (=*SIG*³ 457); fr. B, as IG VII 1735a. See, most recently, Aneziri 2003:360–361 B4, Le Guen 2001:1.141–146 no. 22, and *IThesp* 156 and 156b. Csapo and Slater 1994:244–245 no. 40 provide an English translation of fr. A. IG VII 1735 contains two resolutions side by side, often incised without a break across the width of the stone. These two texts are conventionally referred to as 1735a and 1735b. Since Feyel's analysis of them (1942:91–92 for 1735b, called by him "col. A" = *IThesp* 157; 92–93 for 1735a, Feyel's "col. B"; discussion at 93–96), 1735a has been thought connected with *SIG*³ 457 and is so presented by Aneziri 2003:360–361. This view has recently been challenged by Manieri (2009:364–366), who lists *SIG*³ 457 at 357–363 as Thes. 10 and IG VII 1735 (entire) at 363–366 as Thes. 11. The reorganization of the Μουσεῖα is discussed by Ringwood 1927:48–49, Feyel 1942:88–112, Schachter 1981:2.163–166, Rigsby 1987a:735–737, Knoepfler 1996, and Manieri 2009:318–322.

στεφανίτης ἰσοπύθιος was sought for a θυμελικὸς ἀγών of αὐλητῶν καὶ αὐλῳδῶν καὶ κιθαριστῶν καὶ κιθαρῳδῶν καὶ ἐπῶν ποιητῇ (*sic*).[98] ῥαψῳδῶν is conspicuously absent from this list, which has led some to conclude that its appearance in no. 7 was an innovation.[99] But, if Jamot's no. 6 and no. 7 are mutually related as I proposed above, this does not mean that initially rhapsodes did not take part in the reorganized festival; only that their competition remained θεματικός. There is no question, of course, that as a competitive category, if desirable, it could have been suitably subsumed under the adjective θυμελικός.[100] Both as a professional trade and a competitive category, rhapsody was more traditional than the events reorganized as στεφανῖται. Although popular with the festival public, rhapsodes perhaps fell short of the acclaim given to the artists selected for the more prestigious penteteric thymelic festival.[101] This would explain their exclusion from it. Surely rhapsodes still competed for a monetary award at the yearly Mouseia and at the more prestigious, penteteric version of the yearly festival that accompanied the penteteric thymelic ἀγών.[102]

---

[98] Here I follow Feyel 1942:112–114.

[99] E.g. Ringwood 1927:49.

[100] See, for example, Bethe 1901, Frei 1900:20, and Nachtergael 1977:321 with n. 99.

[101] See below, p. 509 item 45, for a monetary demonstration of the relative prestige enjoyed by the various specialties at Tanagra.

[102] Cf. Knoepfler 1996:161–162. It is worth noting that none of the other inscriptions (nos. 8–18) in Jamot 1895 require the absence of rhapsody. The ones that do not list rhapsodes are 8, 9, 10, 11, 14, 16, and 17. But no. 16 was reedited with additional material in *SEG* 3.334, and lines 29–30 show a [ῥαψῳδό]ς | [. . 9 . .]ίου Ὑπαταῖος (=*IThesp* 177, which prints [ῥαψῳδ]ός | [– – – –]ῃου Ὑπαταῖος, accepted by Manieri 2009:414–416 Thes. 43). No. 8 is too fragmentary: Jamot's line 12, θυμ[ελικὸς ἀγών], might have excluded mention of a rhapsode, but it has been corrected to ἐνε[ί]κων οἶδ[ε] by Roesch 1982:189 no. 33 (=*IThesp* 165 = Manieri 2009:383–385 Thes. 23). If, with Schachter (1981:2.169 no. IV), we restore ποιητ[ὴς προσοδίου] in line 13 and [σαλπιστής] in 15 (instead of ποιητ[ὴς ἐπῶν] and [αὐλητής])—a reasonable choice in light, for example, of *IThesp* 167 and 169 (other parallels in Schachter 1981:2.169n8)—there is no reason to think that it excluded a rhapsode. None of the fragmentary 9, 10, 11, and 14 (*IThesp* 166, 167, 168, and 173) preclude a possible rhapsodic event from the corresponding festival. Only no. 17, from AD 161–169 or AD 176–180 according to Roesch 1982:182 no. 5 (cf. Schachter 1981:2.179 no. XVIII), might suggest the absence of rhapsody: enough of the catalog is left for us to expect ῥαψῳδός to appear—perhaps in line 8 after the κῆρυξ or in line 17 before the κιθαριστής. But the inscription breaks after the name of the poet of new comedy and, if the list continued at that point, one cannot completely rule out the possibility that a winning rhapsode may have appeared in the text that perished. Another possible absence of traditional rhapsodic performance, though perhaps more questionable because of the fragmentary state of the text, is *IThesp* 174, dated to AD 14–29 (=Manieri 2009:407–408 Thes. 36). Here the ἐπῶν ποιητής (*sic*) is preceded by a [κ]ῆρυξ and followed by an [ἐνκωμιογρ]άφος. An examination of the tables in Manieri 2009:333–338 clearly demonstrates the regular involvement of rhapsodes in the Mouseia. (Only note

21. Ἡγησίας (Steph. **1055**, III.2/3) κωμῳδός, *(ῥαψῳδός)*
    Called ὁ κωμῳδός in Athenaios 14.620d6, it is hard to see how his performance of Hesiod could have been a *parergon* of his skill as a comic actor. (For Meineke's emendation τὰ Ἡσιόδου see above, p. 483 n. 25.) This Hēgēsias is therefore rightly classed as a rhapsode. O'Connor (1908:98 no. 209) suggests that his name should be restored in IG II/III² 2325.228 (=Mette 1977:180 V.C2 col. 6.14; cf. Steph. 1244). But the photograph in Wilhelm 1906:152–153 shows that, although the name may well start with η, the final ς must be its fifth (less likely, sixth) letter. Ἡγησίας will not fit the space. It is perhaps for this reason that Mette (1977 *ad loc.*) does not receive O'Connor's suggestion. Fanciful is O'Connor's further conjecture that this Ἡγησίας is the son of the [. . . . . . .] Ἡγησ[ίου] Ἀθηναῖος in Wörrle 1988:415 no. 7.58. See, further, Capps 1900:134 and item 17 above, p. 499.

22. Καλλίας Ἀρχετίμου Συρακ[όσιος] (Steph. **1325**, III.2) ῥαψῳδός
    Nachtergael 1977:409 no. 4, line 13. Ἀμφικτυονικὰ Σωτήρια of Delphi, ca. 265–258 BC.

23. Κλειτόριος Ἀριστείδου Ἀρκάς (Steph. **1429**, III.2) ῥαψῳδός
    Nachtergael 1977:409 no. 4, line 12; 413 no. 7, line 11; 416 no. 8, line 10; 423 no. 10, line 8–9. Ἀμφικτυονικὰ Σωτήρια of Delphi, ca. 265–252 BC.

---

that, with Schachter 1981:2.169 no. IV, the "poeta epico" at 334 under "170–150 a.C." is rather to be restored as "poeta di prosodio.") One can make the same point about Boiotian festivals generally with the help of the table in Manieri 2009:50. To return to Thespiai, little can be said with any certainty about the participation of rhapsodes in the Erotideia, a festival with only a first-century BC foundation (cf. Manieri 2009:342–343, post-Sullan for Knoepfler 1997:34–36). It seems fair to conclude that musical events were held at this festival too, even if the case is not as conclusive as Manieri claims, following Moretti 1981 and Schachter 1981:2.173–175, whatever one thinks of Roesch's proposal in *Teiresias* E.79.01 (see Manieri 2009:344–346 and 428–429). When he wrote his entry on the Erotideia, Schachter still shared the consensus at the time that this festival was solely athletic (cf. Schachter 1981:1.218–219). But it must surely be the cause of some consternation that only one epigraphic witness, *IThesp* 175 (=Manieri 2009:427–430 Thes. 53), appears to confirm the consensual reading of Pausanias 9.31.3 and Plutarch *Amatorius* 748e–749c §§1–2 (cf. Jamot 1895:367–369). *IThesp* 191 (=Manieri 2009:432–433 Thes. 57), with the lone appearance of a ποιητὴς χορῶν (line 9, in the nominative) between athletic events, *pace* Schachter and Manieri cannot adequately support their views, as Jamot (1895:368) long ago demonstrated. At any rate, even if we accept that a musical competition took place at the Erotideia and that *IThesp* 175 regards this ἀγών, we know too little about it to judge whether the absence of a rhapsode from this one inscription is significant. Its competitive events are subsumed under the label τὸν θυμελικόν (line 7).

24. Νικίας (Steph. **1820**, III.4) ῥαψωιδός
    Nachtergael 1977:481 no. 65, line 7. Αἰτωλικὰ Σωτήρια of Delphi, perhaps in 217/16 BC.

25. [Νι]κομήδ[ης (Steph. **1858**, III) [ῥα]ψωιδός
    Kontorini 1975:102, side B, line 5. [τ]ὰ μεγά[λα Ἐρεθίμια] of Rhodes.[103] Kontorini 1975:99 writes that "l'écriture ... est typique du IIIe s. av. J.-C."

26. Π[(Steph. **1971**, III.3) ῥαψωιδός
    Nachtergael 1977:476 no. 59, line 6. Αἰτωλικὰ Σωτήρια of Delphi, perhaps in 241/40 BC.

27. Πολύμνηστος Ἀλεξάνδρου Ἀρκάς (Steph. **2106**, III.2) ῥαψωιδός
    Nachtergael 1977:413 no. 7, line 10. Ἀμφικτυονικὰ Σωτήρια of Delphi, perhaps in 260/59 or 256/55 BC.

28. Πυθοκλῆς Ἀριστάρχου Ἑρμιονεύς (Steph. **2174**, III.2) ἱερεὺς τῶν τεχνιτῶν, (ἀνὴρ χορευτής), [αὐλῳ]δός, [ῥαψῳ]δός
    Nachtergael 1977:429–430 no. 15bis, lines 9–10. The restoration [ῥαψῳ]δός is uncertain (see his discussion at 321). Other occurrences of this artist in [406 no. 2bis, line 4]; 408 no. 3, lines 3–4 and 14–15; 409 no. 4, lines 7–8; [411 no. 5, line 9]; 417 no. 8, lines 30–31; 428 no. 15, line 1. Ἀμφικτυονικὰ Σωτήρια of Delphi, ca. 265–254 BC. Cf. Nachtergael 1977:317–318.

29. Σίμακ?]ος Σατύρου Ἀργεῖος (Steph. **2273**, III.3) (ῥαψωιδός)
    Nachtergael 1977:478 no. 62, line 5. Αἰτωλικὰ Σωτήρια of Delphi, perhaps in 229/28 BC. Cf. Mitsos 1952:160 s.v. [ΣΙΜΑΚ]ΟΣ(;)III.

30. Φιλοκράτης Λυσίππου Ἀργεῖος (Steph. **2530**, III.4) [ῥαψ]ωιδός
    Nachtergael 1977:482 no. 66, line 7. Αἰτωλικὰ Σωτήρια of Delphi, perhaps in 213/12 or 205/204 BC. Cf. Mitsos 1952:188 s.v. ΦΙΛΟΚΡΑΤΗΣIII.

31. [. . 4–5 . .]ν Θρασωνίδου Σινωπεύς (Steph. **2729**, III.2) ῥα[ψωι]δός
    Nachtergael 1977:416 no. 8, line 11. Ἀμφικτυονικὰ Σωτήρια of Delphi, perhaps in 259/58 or 255/54 BC.

32.]ράτης Καλλιφ[(Steph. **2762**, III.2) (ῥαψωιδός)
    Nachtergael 1977:411 no. 5, line 11. Ἀμφικτυονικὰ Σωτήρια of Delphi, perhaps in 262/61 or 258/57 BC.

---

[103] τὰ μεγάλα Ἐρεθίμι[α] on side A, line 3. Cf. Kontorini 1983:69n270. For Rhodian festivals, see Ringwood Arnold 1936.

33.]ς Ἀθηναῖος (Steph. **2886**, III.2) *(ῥαψωιδός)*
Nachtergael 1977:411 no. 5, line 12. Ἀμφικτυονικὰ Σωτήρια
of Delphi, perhaps in 262/61 or 258/57 BC.

34. ĮΑΛΛΗΣ (Steph. **2979**, III.4) ῥαψωιδός
Nachtergael 1977:483 no. 68, line 6. Αἰτωλικὰ Σωτήρια of
Delphi, perhaps in 205/204 or 209/208 BC. *Apud* Nachtergael *ad
loc.*: "ΙΑΛΛΗΣ Flacelière ('Je crois lire ΦΑΛΛΗΣ ou ΨΑΛΛΗΣ').
Βυδάλης(?) ou . . ΥΛΛΗΣ, peut-être Εὐάδης Jardé. ΑΛΛΗΣ
Nikitsky. Ḳαλλίας Klaffenbach (sur estampage)."

II Century BC

35. Ἅβρων Φιλοξένου Θηβαῖος (Steph. **12**, II.4) ῥαψῳδός
Jamot 1895:339 no. 12, line 22 (=*IThesp* 171 = Manieri 2009:399–400
Thes. 31), corrected by Roesch 1982:494.[104] Μουσεῖ[α] of Thespiai. Dated by Roesch to 110–90 BC. Knoepfler 2004:1260 prefers the upper bound, ca. 110. The order of events is: ποιητὴς
προσοδίου, σαλπιστής, [κῆ]ρυξ, ποιητὴς ἐπῶν, ῥαψωιδός, αὐλητής,
and αὐλωιδός. The epic poet is Μνάσαρχος Δάμωνος Θεσπι[εύς]
(Steph. 1712).
    Knoepfler 2004:1247.11–12 (=*SEG* 54.516 = Manieri 2009:299–301
Theb. 8), dated to ca. 120 BC (see 2004:1260).[105] At this festival, the
order of events was: σαλπικτής, κῆρυξ, ποιητὴς ἐπῶν, ῥαψῳδός,
αὐλητής, κιθαριστής, κιθαρῳδός, and ποιητὴς σατύρων. The epic
poet was Κλεώνδας Πυθέου Θηβαῖος (not in Stephanēs), on whom
see Knoepfler 2004:1261–1262.

36. Ἀείμναστος Ε[ὐφ]ραίου Θηβαῖος (Steph. **54**, II/I) κῆρυξ, ῥαψ[ῳδ]ός
IG VII 2448.3–6 (=Manieri 2009:302–303 Theb. 10). An unknown festival. Cf. Koumanoudēs 1979:4 no. 36.
    According to Roehl (1884:101), perhaps from Thespiai (as Lol-
ling had suggested), but more likely from Tanagra or Orkhomenos.
Reisch (1885:127.XI), in turn, conjectures that it may be from the
Agrionia (accepted by Pallone 1984:156n1) or from another Theban
festival. Most recently it has been assigned to the Ῥωμαῖα of Thebes

---

[104] Cf. also Roesch 1982:192 no. 38. His corrections supersede Jamot's Αμ[. . . .]λος [. . . .]ους
Θηβαῖος and A. Keramopoullos's ⟨Λ⟩ό[κ]ρ[ω]ν [Φ]ιλοσ[όφ]ου [Ἀ]θηναῖος from ΑΟ . P . N . ΙΛΟ
Σ . . ΟΥ . ΟΗΝΑΙΟΣ (in the supplement of *Ἀρχ. Ἐφ.* 1936, p. 41 no. 217).

[105] Restated at 1265 as "vers 125–20." At 1277 he admits that it may be "très peu après 118." This
allows him to explain the apparent monopoly of the catalog by Theban artists with reference to
the defection of Boiotian artists from the Isthmian *koinon* in 118/17 BC (cf. Aneziri 2003:307–316).

by Knoepfler (2004:1262–1264, photograph at 1277) and dated
at 1263 to "la fin du IIᵉ siècle, au plus tard des alentours de 100."[106]
On this occasion Ἀείμναστος won both as κῆρυξ and as ῥαψ[ῳδ]ός.
Dittenberger arrived at his date ("hunc Thebanum mecum ad
postremos alterius aut primos primi a. Chr. n. saeculi referre non
dubitabis") by comparing it IG VII 416 (inverting Reisch's reasoning
in Reisch 1885:127.XI). Note that the rhapsode precedes the ἐπῶ[ν
ποιητ]ής of lines 7–8.

37. Εἴρανος Φρυνίδου Ταναγραῖος (Steph. **822**, II.4–I.1[107]) κῆρυξ, ῥαψῳδός,
κωμῳδός, [τραγ]ῳδός

Papagiannopoulos 1947–1948:75.21–22 (=*IThesp* 170 = Manieri 2009:397
–399 Thes. 30) lists him as [Ἴραν]ος Φρυνίδου Ταναγραῖο[ς], victorious as ῥαψῳδός at the Μουσεῖα of Thespiai. Here he follows the
ποιητὴς προσοδίου, the σαλπιστής, the κῆρυξ, and the ἐπῶν ποιητής.
Nothing is preserved from the rest of the inscription to suggest a
particular relation between the poet and the rhapsode on the basis
of their relative order (it breaks with the αὐλητής immediately after
the rhapsode). The epic poet, however, is [Δημ]οκλῆς Ἀμεινίου
Θηβαῖος (Steph. 645),[108] who resurfaces in IG VII 416.9–10 (=*EO* 422
no. 523.9–10) under ἐνκωμίῳ ἐπικῷ, now preceding the rhapsode
and the epic poet (in that order). This not only underlines the close
relationship between the epic encomiast and the epic poet, but on
balance makes it likely that the rhapsode at Thespiai would have
performed not a new composition but one from the traditional
repertoire. Roesch (1982:191–192 no. 37) dates this inscription to
ca. 118–112 BC (adopted by *SEG* 32.436), although on page 494 he
restates the range as 110–90 BC. Roesch (2007:33 no. 170) reasserts
"ca. 118–112" and includes a reference to Schachter (1981:2.171n6),
where the dating is further elucidated.[109]

---

[106] Restated at 1276 as "ca. 110–100." Cf. *SEG* 54.517: "ca. 118–110 BC."
[107] For this date, which replaces Stephanēs's I.1–2, see immediately below, n. 109.
[108] The same as Steph. 646 (cf. page 491 n. 50 above).
[109] Cf. Schachter 1981:2.171n7, 2.173n2 and *SEG* 36.474. The date in the *LGPN* is ca. 80–70 BC. Its upper
boundary agrees with Gossage's ca. 80 (Gossage 1975:127, after Dittenberger in IG VII page 142
ad no. 416: "Neque vero multis annis post Sullana tempora hos catalogos incisos esse nonnulla
nomina docent"; and Bizard 1920:252–253: "postérieurs à la prise d'Athènes par Sylla"). Gossage
grounds his dating on the prosopography of IG VII 416–420, 1760 (=*IThesp* 172), 3195–3197, and
Jamot 1895:337–339 no. 12 (=*IThesp* 171). IG VII 416–420 he considers an almost continuous series
spanning twenty years, ca. 80–60 BC (Gossage 1975:120); *IThesp* 170–172, a continuous series
spanning eight, ca. 80–70 BC (1975:127). He prints a comprehensive table on page 116. To some
of these inscriptions Roesch too assigns a date during the first quarter of the first century BC

IG VII 416.25 (=*EO* 421–426 no. 523 = Manieri 2009:243–245 Oro. 16, with commentary at 252–253). Ἴρανος appears as a victorious κωμῳδός in the Ἀμφιάραα καὶ Ῥωμαῖα of Ōrōpos (the name of the festival is an editorial supplement; for the reconstruction of lines 1–2 see Petrakos 1997:423–424). The date of this inscription is discussed immediately above, n. 109. The corresponding rhapsode is Ἀρτέμων Ἰσιδότου Ἀθηναῖος, for whom see below, p. 508 item 42.

IG VII 542.1 (=Manieri 2009:277–278 Tan. 3, with commentary at 279). From a festival in Tanagra whose name is not preserved. According to Dittenberger *ad loc.*, "sine dubio hic quoque victorum recensus ad Sarapiea spectat" (accepted by Petrakos 1997:425 *ad* 523.26).[110] The name Εἴρανος Φρυνίδου Ταναγραῖος heads the list at the top of the block, followed by the competitive categories ποιητάς, αὐλητάς, κιθαριστάς, etc. Reisch (1885:129.XIII) suggests that ῥαψῳδός or κῆρυξ may have preceded his name; on the model of IG VII 540 (for which see also *SEG* 25.501), the former category is slightly more likely. The letter shapes lead Reisch to conclude that this inscription is more recent than IG VII 540,[111] which has been dated most recently to ca. 100–90/85 BC (cf. *SEG* 31.496). Thus, I.1 seems to accommodate this document (cf. Stephanēs 1988 *ad* no. 1716.)

IG VII 543.1, 3 (=Manieri 2009:278–279 Tan. 4). In line 3 he appears under [τρα]γῳδός (before ποιητάς); under what designation he is listed in line 1 is uncertain.

Bizard 1920:261 no. 11 reconstructs [Εἴ]ρανος Φρυνίδ[ου Ταναγραῖος] from IG VII 416.25–26 under κῆρυξ, apparently from the Ptoia of Akraiphia (cf. Ringwood 1927:41 and Manieri 2009:107–108 Acr. 14, who dates it to "dopo 85 a.C.").[112]

38. Μιλτιάδης Διονυσίου (Χῖος) (Steph. **1708**, II) ῥαψῳδός
   *SIG*³ 959.9, ῥαψῳδίας (=Boeckh *CIG* 2214 = McCabe *IChios* 57). For the date see Michel 1900:737 no. 898.

(e.g. "110–90" for *IThesp* 171; or "après 84" for *IThesp* 172). It seems safest, therefore, to modify Stephanēs's "I.1–2" to "II.4–I.1."

[110] For Tanagran festivals cf. Ringwood 1927:34–35.

[111] Cf. Calvet and Roesch 1966: "l'inscription fragmentaire IG, VII, 541–543, très légèrement postérieure" (315).

[112] For the festival see Holleaux 1890:59–64, 201–203; Feyel 1942:133–147; Roesch 1982:203–255; Schachter 1981:1.70–72; Rigsby 1987a; and Manieri 2009:63–77.

39.   Βοι]ώτιος (Steph. **2919**, II.1) *[ῥαψῳδ]ος*
      SEG 3.368, line 12 (=Manieri 2009:153–154 Leb. 9, with a slightly dif-
      ferent textual reconstruction). Βασίλεια of Lebadeia.[113] For the date
      see Roesch 1982:494 ("av[ant] 172" BC) with Knoepfler 1988a:274n30
      and *SEG* 38.384.

I Century BC

40.   Ἀγάθων Δαμᾶ Θεσπιεύς (Steph. **34**, I) ῥαψῳδός
      IG VII 4147.10–11 (=Manieri 2009:116–119 Acr. 18, with IG VII 4148).
      Cf. Ringwood 1927:42–43. τῶν πενταετήρων Πτωΐων.

      The name Γάιος Ἰούλιος Γαΐου Θεσπιεύς in line 15 led Hol-
      leaux, the original editor, to date it to after the dictatorship of
      Caesar, perhaps as late as the beginning of the Christian era (Hol-
      leaux 1890:190). Dittenberger disagrees, positing the end of II or
      the beginning of I BC (so Pallone 1984:156n1). Recently, however,
      Roesch (1982:226 no. 3) has approved of Holleaux's date, preferring
      the higher end of his range (i.e. the middle or second half of I BC).[114]
      The order of events is: σαλπιστής, κῆρυξ, ῥαψῳδός, ἐπῶν ποιητής,
      αὐλητής, κιθαριστής, and κιθαρῳδός. The list is preserved in full.

41.   Ἀριστόδικος Δημοκράτους Ὀπού⟨ν⟩τιος (Steph. **335**, I.1) (ῥαψῳδός)
      SEG 19.335, line 25 (=Manieri 2009:268–277 Tan. 2, which corre-
      sponds to IG VII 540 greatly improved by the addition of a much
      larger second fragment).[115] τ[ῶν] | Σαραπιείων of Tanagra, where
      he competed as rhapsode and was awarded second prize (40 Attic
      silver drachmas). To judge by the size of the award, he ranks with
      those who placed second in the categories of (epic) poet, citharist,
      (κωμῳδός),[116] and satiric poet. See below, item 45.

---

[113] For the festival, see Feyel 1942:67–87, Schachter 1981:3.109–118, Turner 1996, and Manieri 2009:137–143.

[114] Gossage 1975: "c. 50 B.C." (116). Schachter 1981: "perhaps the second half of the first century B.C." (1.66n9, with reference to Schachter 1978:96n39). Manieri 2009: "una datazione all'inizio dell'era cristiana" (118).

[115] With *SEG* 25.501, which dates it to ca. 85 BC (but cf. *SEG* 31.496, with a more cautious ca. 100–90/85 BC). For more on the dating see Schachter 1981:1.203. For the text, see further Chrēstou 1956:36–38 and Calvet and Roesch 1966:298–300.

[116] This event is listed in line 17 as τὴν κωμῳδίαν (sc. τὴν παλαιάν). Cf. Steph. 1279 and Calvet and Roesch 1966:320.

42. Ἀρτέμων Ἰσιδότου Ἀθηναῖος (Steph. **422**, I.1) ῥαψῳδός
    IG VII 416.11–12 (=*EO* 421–426 no. 523 = Manieri 2009:243–245
    Oro. 16, with commentary at 252–253). [τῶν Ἀμφιαράων καὶ
    Ῥωμαίων] of Ōrōpos.
    PA 1.155 no. 2276 (*PAA* 3.309 no. 206775), brother of Στράτων
    (Steph. 2318; in *EO* no. 523.30–33, inscribed between the columns).
    The ῥαψῳδός precedes the ἐπῶν ποιητής. Although it is possible
    that he may have performed a new composition by the epic poet,
    lines 27ff. suggest that the composer should precede the cor-
    responding performer. Thus it is more likely that the rhapsode
    performed the traditional repertoire (certainly Homer, perhaps
    Hesiod or even Arkhilokhos), while the epic poet performed his own
    composition. For the date, see above, p. 505 n. 109.

43. Ἀρχίας Σωτηρίδου Θηβαῖος (Steph. **441**, I) ῥαψῳδός
    Bizard 1920:251 no. 10, line 14 (=Manieri 2009:108–111 Acr. 15).
    Ptoia of Akraiphia. Dated by Gossage (1975:122) to ca. 70–65 BC.[117]
    Cf. Koumanoudēs 1979:35 no. 300.

44. Βίοττος [Μ]ε[ν]ελάου Χαλκιδεύ[ς] (Steph. **524**, I.1) ῥαψῳδός
    EO 415 no. 521.13–14 (=Manieri 2009:241–243 Oro. 15).[118] τὰ πρῶτα
    Ἀμφιαρᾶα καὶ Ῥωμαῖ[α]. For the use of ἱερός (as in ἐπῶν ἱερός,
    line 12) to refer to events without a winner, see Roesch 1982:228 and
    the bibliography in *EO* 419 *ad* no. 521.12. Dated to "peu après 85" BC by
    Roesch in *Teiresias* E.76.32 and to "περὶ τὸ 85 π.Χ." by Petrakos in *EO*.

45. Βουκάττης Γλαύκου Ταναγραῖος (Steph. **533**, I.1) ῥαψῳδός
    IG VII 540.5 (=Manieri 2009:268–277 Tan. 2). τ[ῶν] | Σαραπιείων of
    Tanagra. See Chrēstou 1956, Calvet and Roesch 1966, and *SEG* 19.335
    (with *SEG* 25.501).[119]
    Arguably, the ἀγωνοθέτης listed in line 1 as [Γλ]αύκου τοῦ
    Βουκάττου and the [σ]ατύρων ποιητής of line 11, an Ἀλέξανδρος
    Γλαύκου Ταναγραῖος, were his father and brother respectively.[120]

---

[117] Cf. Schachter 1981:1.66n9. For Manieri, "dopo 85 a.C." (2009:108).

[118] Cf. *SEG* 34.362 for the first seventeen lines. I infer from *Teiresias* 1976 Appendix Epigraphica p. 14 no. 32 (usually cited E.76.32) that Roesch read [Μ]ε[ν]ελ⟨ά⟩ου (printed by *SEG* and taken over by Stephanēs) from a photograph in the guide to the Amphiareion. He must have thought that the alpha marked as ⟨ά⟩ was incised as a lambda. But the letter is clearly visible as an alpha in the photograph on p. 79 of the catalog that follows (with its own pagination) the inscriptions in Petrakos 1997.

[119] Dated in *SEG* 19.335 to ca. 85 BC and in *SEG* 31.496, more cautiously, to ca. 100–90/85 BC. Gossage (1975:131) dates it to the period shortly before the Mithridatic War ("c. 90 BC" in the table on page 116; he details his reasons in 127–131). Cf. Schachter 1981:1.203.

[120] For his family tree see Calvet and Roesch 1966:331.

The rhapsode is listed after a σαλπικτής and a κῆρυξ,[121] and before a ποιητής (ἐπῶν, presumably). In lines 12–13, if the restoration of 13 is correct (which the spacing encourages), the τραγῳδιῶν ποιητής precedes his [ὑποκριτής]; this is certainly the relationship that obtains between the κωμῳδιῶν ποιητής and his ὑποκριτής in lines 14–15 (cf. Steph. 623). On balance, then, the rhapsode is not to be thought of as the poet's performer. His prize, however, is identical the actors': a crown worth 101 ¼ Attic silver drachmas.[122] At 135 drachmas for his gold crown, the (epic) poet in turn ranks with the comic and tragic poets, the citharist, and the (τραγῳδός) (for whom the inscription states his category merely as τὴν παλαιὰν τραγῳδίαν).[123]

46. Εἱέρων Ἀριστοβούλου Θηβαῖος (Steph. **820**, I.1–2) ῥαψῳδός
IG VII 419.17–18 (=*EO* 431–432 no. 526 = Manieri 2009:248–250 Oro. 19, with commentary at 252–253). τῶν Ἀμφιαράων καὶ Ῥωμαίων of Ōrōpos.

Here ῥαψῳδός follows ἐπῶν ποιητάς. Given the placement of ὑποκριτής in lines 29 and 33 after the corresponding ποιητής, one might argue that on this occasion the rhapsodes performed compositions by the epic poets. But this is unlikely given the evidence collected from other inscriptions.[124] Rather, the order here must be dictated by the close logical connection between the ἐνκωμίῳ λογικῷ 11, ἐνκωμίῳ ἐπικῷ 13, and the ἐπῶν ποιητάς 15: the distinction between a newly composed epic poem and an encomiastic hexameter poem (the poetic equivalent of the ἐγκώμιον λογικόν) was not always reflected by the nomenclature used. Where a festival featured respective competitive events for a hexameter encomium and a hexameter composition of a character other than encomiastic, it would have been natural for these two events to follow each

---

[121] I follow the text in Calvet and Roesch 1966:298–300. Their French translation follows in 303–305. For an English translation see Roller 1989:1.110–115 no. 92.

[122] For the monetary equivalences and a table of awarded amounts see Calvet and Roesch 1966:305–309. Cf. *SEG* 41.481.

[123] Cf. Steph. 2267 and Calvet and Roesch 1966:320.

[124] Of the five surviving Oropian inscriptions that feature a rhapsode and an epic poet—*EO* nos. 521, 523–524, 526, and 528—three place the rhapsode immediately before the epic poet (nos. 523–524 and 528) and two reverse the order (nos. 521 and 526). But, of the last two, only no. 526—the inscription that concerns us now—actually records an award for the epic poet; no. 521 declared the event without a winner. In all of these inscriptions, the prose and epic encomia precede (in that order) the rhapsode and the epic poet (the entry for prose encomium is conjecturally supplied for no. 523). The least that one may claim about the relative order of epic poet and rhapsode is that, if the latter had regularly performed the poetry of the former, we would expect them to be listed always in that particular order, which corresponds in fact to what we observe in the case of drama.

other in the program and in the victors' record. Regarding the date of the inscription, Gossage (1975:119–120) considers IG VII 416–420 an almost continuous series that covers a period of twenty years (the festival was penteteric). This interval he states as ca. 80–60 BC, with IG VII 419 ca. 64 BC.[125] Cf. Koumanoudēs 1979:101 no. 964.

47. Θεόδοτος Πυθίωνος Ἀθηναῖος (Steph. **1146**, I.1) (ᾠδός), ῥαψῳδός, (τραγικὸς συναγωνιστής)

Tracy 1975:62.39, 44, and 50.[126] Fourth Pythaïs of the Athenians to Delphi (98/97 BC).[127] Θεόδοτος is listed at 39 among τοὺς ᾀσομένους τούς [τε παιᾶνας] καὶ τὸν χορόν (line 21; hence the ᾠδός); again at 44 among the ῥαψῳδούς, together with Κάλλων Κάλλωνος and Ξενόφαντος Εὐμάχου (about whom see below, p. 513 item 53); and one final time at 50, also in the company of Κάλλων Κάλλωνος and Ξενόφαντος Εὐμάχου, among τοὺς τούτοις συναγωνιξαμένους (hence the τραγικὸς συναγωνιστής), where τούτοις refers to the two τραγῳδοί listed in line 49.

IG VII 1760.17 (=IThesp 172 = Manieri 2009:402–404 Thes. 33).[128] τὰ Μ[ουσεῖα] of Thespiai. The order of events is: ποιητὴς προσοδίου, σαλπιστή[ς], κῆρυξ, ἐπῶν ποιητής, ῥαψῳδός, αὐλητής, αὐλῳδός, κιθαριστής, κιθαρῳδός, σατύρων ποιητής, ὑποκριτὴς παλαιᾶς [τρ]αγῳδίας, and ὑποκριτὴς παλαιᾶς κωμ[ῳδίας].[129] The poet of epics is Μήστωρ Μήστορος Φωκαεύς (Steph. 1686), who reappears under ποειτάς at the Χαριτείσια of Orkhomenos (IG VII 3195.10 = Manieri 2009:199 Orc. 23.10) and under [ἐ]πικόν (sc. ἐγκώμιον) and ἐπῶν ποιητής at the Ἀμφιαράϊα καὶ Ῥωμαῖα of Ὠρōpos (IG VII 418.5, 9 = EO 426 no. 524.6, 10).

Cf. PA 1.440 no. 6782 with Sundwall 1910:92 and PAA 9.113 no. 505245.

48. Θεοφάνης Σωκράτου Θηβαῖος (Steph. **1186**, I.1) ῥαψῳδός

IG VII 420.14 (=EO 434–437 no. 528 = Manieri 2009:250–251 Oro. 20, with commentary at 252–253). τὰ Ἀμφι[α]ρᾷα καὶ Ῥω{ι}μαῖα of Ὠrōpos.

---

[125] See his tabulation at 122. See further above, p. 505 n. 109.

[126] The text can also be found in Aneziri 2003:354–356 A 11. It corresponds to FD III 2, 48 with the supplement by Bousquet 1938:362–368 (the relevant line numbers in the original edition are 26, 31, and 37). The unimproved text is also printed in SIG³ 711l.

[127] Some ascribe the inscription to the third Pythaïs (106/105 BC). So, for example, Pomtow in SIG³ ad loc.: "[P]ertinet nullo dubio ad Pyth. III, sc. a. 106/5." Cf. Tracy 1975:64, Nachtergael 1977:474 no. 56, and Aneziri 2003:356.

[128] Cf. Jamot 1895:339 no. 13, line 18. Roesch 1982:192–193 no. 39 and IThesp 172 date it to post 84 BC. Gossage 1975:127 to "shortly before 70 BC."

[129] These last two are equivalent to τραγῳδός and κωμῳδός respectively (see above, p. 481).

Stephanēs 1988 *ad loc.* suggests that he may be the brother of Ἡρῴδης (cf. Steph. 1121).[130] The order of competitive events at this festival was σαλπικτής, κῆρυξ, ἐγκώμιον καταλογάδην, ἐγκώμιον ἐπικόν, ῥαψῳδός, ποιητὴς ἐπῶν, etc. Lines 29–36 make the τραγῳδίας καινῆς ποιητής and κωμῳδίας καινῆς ποιητής precede their corresponding ὑποκριταί. Hence the epic poet is likely to have performed his own composition. For the inscription's date see above, p. 505 n. 109. Cf. Koumanoudēs 1979:97 no. 930.

49. Κάλλων Κάλλωνος (Ἀθηναῖος) (Steph. **1368**, I.1) (ᾠδός) ῥαψῳδός (τραγικὸς συναγωνιστής)

   Tracy 1975:61.27–28, 62.44 and 50. Fourth Pythaïs to Delphi (98/97 BC). See above, p. 510 item 47. Cf. O'Connor 1908:110 no. 284, Sifakis 1967:171, and Ghiron-Bistagne 1976:336.

50. Κράτων Κλέωνος Θηβαῖος (Steph. **1502**, I.1) ῥαψῳδός

   IG VII 418.7 (=*EO* 426–427 no. 524 = Manieri 2009:246–248 Oro. 18, with commentary at 252–253).[131] From Ōrōpos. The name of the festival is missing, since the inscription breaks off at the top, but it is probably the Ἀμφιαράϊα καὶ Ῥωμαῖα (so Gossage 1975:115). The list of competitive events appears to follow the order used in IG VII 416; among the correspondences:

EO no. 523		*EO* no. 524	
line	event	line	event
5	[κῆρυξ]	1	[κῆρυξ]
7	[ἐνκωμίωι λογικῶι]	3	ἐγκώμιον καταλογάδη[ν]
9	ἐνκωμίωι ἐπικῶι	5	[ἐ]πικόν
11	ῥαψῳδός	7	ῥαψῳδός
13	ἐπῶν ποιητής	9	ἐπῶν ποιητής
15	αὐλητής	11	αὐλητής
17	κιθαριστής	13	κιθαριστής

   IG VII 3195.11–12 (=*Del*³ 529 = Manieri 2009:199–200 Orc. 23, with commentary at 205–207).[132] τὰ Χαριτείσια of Orkhomenos. In the

---

[130] So also Gossage 1975:121–122.

[131] On this and IG VII 3195 see Gossage 1975:121. For their dates, see also above, p. 505 n. 109 and Schachter 1981:1.142 ("ca. 90–70 B.C.").

[132] Dittenberger dates IG VII 3195–3197 to the beginning of the first century BC (see IG VII p. 594 *ad* 3195). Amandry and Spyropoulos (1974:186) judge it (and 3196–3197) to be from the first

affected Boiotian dialect of the inscription (cf. Schwyzer *ad loc.* and Gossage 1975:121) the name is spelled Κράτων Κλίωνος Θειβεῖος and his category, ῥαψαϝυδός. Here ποειτάς precedes ῥαψαϝυδός, but none of the listed categories establish a preferred order for composer and performer. There is therefore no reason to infer that the rhapsode would have performed anything other than the traditional repertoire. IG VII 3196 and 3197, moreover, similarly from the Χαριτήσια of Orkhomenos and, according to Dittenberger, contemporaneous with IG VII 3195,[133] list the rhapsode *before* the poet: ῥαψῳδός 6, ποητής 8 in 3196; ῥαψῳδός 7, ποιητὴς ἐπῶν 9 in 3197. And IG VII 3197.24–34 makes πο(ι)ητής (σατύρων, τραγῳδιῶν, and κωμῳδιῶν) precede the corresponding victorious ὑποκριτής. The care taken in 3197.50 to repeat κωμῳδιῶν ποιητής for Alexandros, now victor in the category of τὰ ἐπινίκια, perhaps makes the relative order of the events worthy of special attention: it would have been more economical to list him only once, but since 'epinician' traditionally belonged after the dramatic events, Alexandros reappears at the end of the inscription, with the additional note of his triumph as comic poet.

Cf. Koumanoudēs 1979:129 no. 1215.

51. Μέντωρ Ἀπολλοδώρου Ἡρακλεώτης (Steph. **1667**, I.1) ῥαψῳδός
    IG VII 3196.6–7 (=Manieri 2009:200–202 Orc. 24, with commentary at 205–207). ἐν τοῖς Χαριτησίοις of Orkhomenos.[134] The ῥαψῳδός is followed by a ποιητής who, to judge from the contemporaneous 3197, must be a ποιητὴς ἐπῶν. The events are: σαλπιστής, κῆρυξ, ῥαψῳδός, ποιητής, αὐλητής, αὐλῳδός, κιθαριστής, κιθαρῳδός, τραγῳδός, and κωμῳδός. The relative order of ποιητής and ὑποκριτής in 3197 suggests that the rhapsode did not compete as the performer of the ποιητής.

    IG XII 9, 139.10. From a festival in the area of Amarynthos, Euboia.[135] If we accept Wilhelm's supplements (Wilhelm 1905:9),

---

[133] third of the first century BC (see 1974:224–227). Gossage (1975:121) considers 3195 the oldest of the group IG VII 3195–3197, and believes that with IG VII 1760 it bridged the gap between IG VII 416–417 and 418–420 (1975:122). This would place 3195 shortly before 70 BC (1975:127).

[133] For Gossage 1975:121, only of slightly later date.

[134] For the date, see immediately above, n. 132. For the festival, see Ringwood 1927:39–40, Schachter 1981:1.140–144, and Manieri 2009:180–183. Both this catalog and IG VII 3197 (see below) include a section with the victors at the Homolōia, on which see Manieri 2009 *ad loc.* with bibliography.

[135] Kuruniotes (1899:141) speculated that the festival was the Tamyneia. Knoepfler (1988b:388n26) thinks that it belongs to the Artemisia instead (cf. *SEG* 38.871). See Gossage 1975:123–126 for a

lines 9–10 feature [M]έντω[ρ Ἀπολλοδώρου][136] (Ziebarth prints Wilhelm's erroneous [Ἀπολλοδότου]); the diplomatic transcript by Kuruniotes 1899:140 no. 5 is ΦΛ[| ΕΝΤΩ. Wilhelm's emendation of the Φ is very plausible on internal grounds. The Λ may represent a badly preserved Α, and ΦΛ[should correspond to a competitive event. No ordinary category would fit ΦΛ; but if the Φ can be read as Ρ, ῬΑ[ΨΩΙΔΟΣ], which regularly follows or precedes the poet of epics, is the obvious choice. Wilhelm (1905:9), who dots the ῬΑ[, assumes that Kuruniotes misread the inscription: "ΦΛ wird daher vermöge eines, bei Buchstaben gerade dieser Zeit begreiflichen Versehens, statt PA verlesen und zu ergänzen sein."[137]

52. Νουμήνιος Νουμηνίου Ἀθηναῖος (Steph. **1893**, I.1) ῥαψῳδός
IG VII 3197.8 (=Manieri 2009:202–207 Orc. 25). τῶν Χαριτησίων of Orkhomenos.

A particularly fulsome catalog, which was pronounced lost by Dittenberger ("periise videtur") but resurfaced in Scotland in the 1930s, when it was studied by Tod 1934:159–162.[138] The order of events is: σαλπιστής, κῆρυξ, ῥαψῳδός, ποιητὴς ἐπῶν, αὐλητής, αὐλῳδός, κιθαριστής, κιθαρῳδός, etc. The text mentions three winning ὑποκριταί, each one *after* his respective poet, whether of satires, tragedies, or comedies.[139]

Cf. *PA* 2.151 no. 11135 and *PAA* 13.318 no. 721450.

53. Ξενόφαντος Εὐμάχου (Ἀθηναῖος) (Steph. **1913**, I.1) (ᾠδός) ῥαψῳδός (τραγικὸς συναγωνιστής)
Tracy 1975:62.38, 44, and 51. Fourth Pythaïs to Delphi (98/97 BC). See above, p. 510 item 47. Cf. Ghiron-Bistagne 1976:349.

54. [—] (I.1) ῥαψῳδός
IG VII 2727.15 (=Manieri 2009:130–132 Acr. 27). τῶν τριετήρων Σωτηρίων of Akraiphia πρῶ[τον] | ἀπὸ τοῦ πολέμου.

---

date ca. 70–65 BC, of which Knoepfler (1988b:388n26) approves.

[136] Explicit and implicit approval are expressed by Gossage 1975:123 ("the name of the rhapsode Mentor ... plausibly restored by Wilhelm") and Knoepfler 1988b:388n26 ("[l]e concours s'ouvrait alors par des épreuves de poésie épique et de rhapsodie").

[137] Although I am skeptical that Φ and Ρ might be so readily confused I see no plausible alternative to Wilhelm's restoration.

[138] For the date, see above, p. 511 n. 132.

[139] The poet of epics is the Ἀμινίας Δημοκλέους Θηβαῖος (Steph. 153) who reappears in line 25 as the victorious ποιητὴς σατύρων, and in IG VII 419.14, 16 (*EO* 431 no. 526.14, 16) as the winner at the Amphiaraia of the categories ἐνκωμίῳ ἐπικῷ and ἐπῶν ποιητάς. For one other doubtful occurrence see Roesch 1982:493.

The inscription does not preserve the name of the rhapsode. Its date is ca. 80 BC, after the Second Mithridatic War between Mithridates VI and Sulla.[140] The competitions were (by order of appearance): σαλπιστής, κῆρυξ, ἐνκωμίῳ λογικῷ, ἐπῶν ποιητής (with a Πρωτογένης Πρωτάρχου Θεσπιεύς as victor, about whom see Steph. 2156), and ῥαψῳδός. The fragment breaks at this point. A second one, included in the same entry of IG VII, may correspond to the same catalog (cf. Reisch 1885:130.XV): starting with the fragmentary name [Σ]ωσιμένης Σωσικ[—], the heading κιθαριστής follows; this probably makes [Σ]ωσιμένης an αὐλητής or an αὐλῳδός (cf. Steph. 2353).

I Century AD

55. Ἐράτων (Steph. **881**, I/II AD) *(ῥαψῳδός)*

   Plutarch *Quaestiones convivales* 645d3, 10; 736e4; and 743c11. Friend of Plutarch. Gangloff (2010:52–53) rejects Stephanēs's classification of him as a rhapsode. Plutarch never refers to him thus, but calls him Ἐράτων ὁ ἁρμονικός (645d3). He was a man of means, able to host a well-attended symposium (645d3–4). Apparently a student of *harmoniai*, we learn that he deprecated Agathon's use of chromaticism in the *Mysians* (645d10–e2). Asked at another party to sing to the lyre, he chose to perform the beginning of Hesiod's *Works and Days* (736e4–9). The host complimented him because he had adapted it (ἁρμοσάμενον) suitably to the occasion. The verb suggests Erato's selection of a fitting harmonic setting (cf. LSJ s.v. I.5). At a third appearance, all present join him in singing to the lyre Hesiod's verses about the birth of the Muses (743c10–12). Teodorsson (1989–1996:1.283) may be right to call him a "musical theorist with a practical competence," and one should therefore not consider him an ordinary rhapsode. But neither must we fail to note the evidence that Plutarch provides for epic performance to the lyre in the context of the elite symposium under Roman rule.[141]

---

[140] Cf. Gossage 1975:126–127 and Schachter 1981:3.94–95.

[141] Teodorsson (1989–1996:3.346) also calls him a "professional musician," apparently on the grounds that "[i]n Plutarch's time, singing to the lyre had become a professional competence" (he refers us to 615b). It is well known that amateur lyre-playing at the symposium was already in decline during the classical period, and one may safely assume that it was even rarer centuries later. But it is doubtful that this skill by itself would suffice to identify its possessor as a professional musician (i.e. as one who did so for a living). Gangloff's conjectural ascription of the label λυρῳδός to Erato (Gangloff 2010:53) does not add anything to our knowledge of his profession.

56. Νεικομήδη[ς] (Κῷος) (Steph. **1782**, I/II AD) ᾄδων ⟨θ⟩υμέλαισιν
Ὅμηρο⟨ν⟩
IG II/III² 9145.5–8. Epitaph from Athens. Following Kaibel (1878:34
no. 101) and Kirchner *ad loc.*, Gangloff (2010:56–57) wonders
whether Νεικομήδη[ς] might not be a *homēristēs* rather than a
rhapsode. But the mention of θυμέλαι is perfectly compatible with
the traditional rhapsody of the time, and there is no question that
the language of the epitaph is profoundly traditional. If the artist
turned out to be a *homēristēs*, this item should be added to the evidence that speaks for the continuity in the manner of performance
of both types of professionals.

57. [—] [Φι]λοκράτους Θη[βαῖος] (Steph. **2846**, I/II AD) *([ῥαψῳδό]ς)*
Bizard 1920:262 no. 12 (=Manieri 2009, 122 Arc. 20). A very small
fragment of a catalog of victors from either the Ptoia or the Soteria
of Akraiphia, for which the editor restores [σαλπιγκτής], [κῆρυ]ξ,
and [ῥαψῳδό]ς. The date is by Roesch 1982:226 no. 5.
Cf. Koumanoudēs 1979:222 no. 28.

II Century AD

58. Εὐτυχιανὸς Κορίνθιος (Steph. **993**, II.3 AD) ῥαψῳδός
IG VII 1773.18 (=Jamot 1895:340–341 no. 15 = *IThesp* 178 = Manieri 2009:412–414 Thes. 42).[142] Μουσεῖα of Thespiai. Dated to
ca. AD 150–160 by Roesch 1982:181 no. 3 (retained by *IThesp* 178 and
accepted by Manieri *ad loc.*). According to Schachter (1981:2.162n5),
this artist may be the Εὐτυχιανός mentioned in the second- to
third-century AD IG VII 1886 (=*IThesp* 1251).[143] The rhapsode is
listed after the categories of ποιητὴς προσοδίου, κῆρυξ, σαλπικτάς,
ἐνκωμιογράφος εἰς τὸν αὐτοκράτ[ο]ρα, ἐνκώμιον εἰς Μούσας,
ποιητὴς εἰς τὸν αὐτοκράτορα, and ποίημα εἰς τὰς Μούσας.

59. Κιλικᾶς (Κιτιεύς) (Steph. **1405**, II AD) *(ῥαψῳδός)*
Peek 1955:388 no. 1305, from Kition (Larnaka), Cyprus.[144] The profession must be inferred from the following statement in the epigram:

ὅς [sc. Κιλικᾶς] ποθ' ὁμηρείαισι μετέπρεπον | ἐν σελίδεσσιν
δεικνὺς ἡρώων | ἠνορέην προτέρων.

---

[142] Cf. Schachter 1981:2.176–177 no. XVI.
[143] Cf. *SEG* 36.488.
[144] Cf. Kyriazēs 1924, Seyrig 1927:147 no. 6, Sykutris 1928, Chatzēiōannou 1971–2001:4.1.220
and 4.2.157, Tsopanakēs 1984:398 no. 31, and Gangloff 2010:53–54.

Whereas δεικνύς better suits an epideictic setting (cf. Akhilleus Tatios 3.20.4), σελίδες seems more at home with a scholar. Hence the uncertainty whether Κιλικᾶς was a teacher or a performer; and, if the latter, a rhapsode or a *homēristēs*. This last I deem the least likely of the options, since written texts make an improbable choice for a *homēristēs* to designate the context of his celebrity.[145] Neither of the two remaining alternatives is satisfactory.

60. Κορ(νήλιος) Εὔκαρπος Ἀργεῖος (Steph. **956**, II/III AD) κῆρυξ, [ῥα]ψῳδός

  IG VII 4151.3–6 (=Manieri 2009:123–125 Acr. 22). Dittenberger considered 4151 from the same inscription as 4150 and 4152.[146] Discovered at the temple of Apollo Ptoios, it probably lists victors at the Ptoia of Akraiphia. The absence of instances of 'Aurelius' suggests a time *ante* AD 212. After the winner of σαλπικτῶν, we meet Κορ(νήλιος) Εὔκαρπος as victor both of κηρύκων and [ῥα]ψῳδῶν. These events are followed by [αὐλ]ητῶν and κυκ[λίων αὐλητ]ῶν. According to the editor's reconstruction, then, no poets of epics took (official) part in the festival. But cf. Roesch (1982:227 no. 7), who supplies [ποι]ητῶν ("peut-être") for Dittenberger's [αὐλ]ητῶν.
  Cf. Mitsos 1952:82 s.v.

61. Πολείταρ[χος] [– – –]α *(Ἀργεῖος)* (Steph. **2082**, II/III AD) ῥαψῳδός

  IG IV 649.4–5. Epitaph from Argos.[147] For the date see *SEG* 31.312. Cf. Feissel 1981:142 ("de l'époque impériale").
  Cf. Mitsos 1952:146 s.v.

62. Πόπλιος Αἴλιος Πομπηϊανὸς Παίων Σιδήτης καὶ Ταρσεὺς καὶ Ῥόδιος (Steph. **1979**, II.2 AD) [ποιη]τής, μελοποιός, ῥαψ[ῳδός], θεολόγος, [ἀγ]ωνοθέτης

  IEph 22 (i.e. Wankel 1979:134–139 no. 22).[148] In Bean 1965:18–19 no. 107, line 11 (=Nollé 2001:357–361 no. 70) he is described as a νέος Ὅμηρος. Cf. *SEG* 20.674–675. See my discussion above, p. 490.

63.   ]γου Ὑπαταῖος (Steph. **2859**, II.3 AD) *([ῥαψῳδ]ός)*

  SEG 3.334, line 30 = *IThesp* 177, whose text I follow (=Manieri 2009:414–416 Thes. 43, with commentary at 418–419). Μουσεῖα of Thespiai,

---

[145] Cf. Garelli-François 2000:505 on the trappings (σκευή) of the *homēristai*.
[146] Followed by Roesch 1982:227 no. 7 and Manieri 2009 *ad loc.*
[147] Fraenkel writes: "Vs. 5 vix dubium ῥαψῳδέ" (IG IV p. 112 *ad loc.*). For a text that diverges from Le Bas's, see Ross 1855–1861:2.665.d.
[148] Cf. Robert 1980:10–20, Bowie 1989:202–203 and 1990:65–66, Fein 1994:118–126, and Gangloff 2010:61–63.

ca. AD 160. Roesch (1982:181 no. 4) and *IThesp* 177
date it to "vers 150–160 ou postérieur à 169 p. C." (taken over by
Manieri 2009 *ad loc.*).

III Century AD

64. Μᾶρκος Αὐρήλιος Εὔκαιρος Ταναγραῖος (Steph. **955**, III.1 AD) κῆρυξ,
ῥαψῳδός

IG VII 1776.15–16 (=Manieri 2009:422–423 Thes. 49). See Strasser (2002:112–124), who prints a text in 112–113 and dates the
inscription to shortly after AD 212 (cf. *SEG* 52.511). The festival
appears as τῶν | μεγάλων Καισαρήων | Σεβαστήων Μουσεί|[ω]ν
(i.e. the Mouseia of Caesar Augustus). The name of the artist was
inscribed as Μ(ᾶρκος) Αὐρή(λιος) Εὔκαιρος Ταναγραῖος. The
order of events is σαλπικτής, κῆρυξ, ῥαψῳδός, πυθικὸς αὐλητής,
πυθικὸς κιθαριστής, κύκλιος αὐλητής, etc. Dated to a time in
the third century after Caracalla's citizenship edict of AD 212
(cf. Schachter 1981:2.179 no. xxi), the festival program has been
shortened vis-à-vis the one in effect towards the middle of the
second century AD (cf. IG VII 1773 and Ringwood 1927:50). Note, in
particular, that there is no competition for poets of epics or for any
sort of encomia.

IG VII 2726.1 (=Manieri 2009:128–129 Acr. 25). Roesch (1982:227–
228 no. 10) assigns the catalog to the Ptoia of Akraiphia.[149] His own
reading of the first line is [ῥαψ]ῳδῶν Αὐρ. Εὔκαιρ[ος Ταναγραῖος].[150]
Competitors followed the order [ῥαψ]ῳδῶν, [π]υθαυλῶν, χοραυλῶν,
and [κ]ιθαρῳδῶν. On the basis of Bizard 1903:297 (see immediately
below), we can assume events in trumpeteering, heraldry, and (new
epic?) poetry.[151] Both IG VII 2726 and Bizard (1903:297) must postdate Caracalla's edict (so Roesch 1982:227–228 *ad* nos. 9 and 10). The
same onomastic argument that he had applied to IG VII 1776 allows
Strasser (2002:117) to narrow the date to shortly after AD 212.

Εὔκαιρος Ταναγραῖος appears one other time in Bizard 1903:297.9–10, 12 (=Manieri 2009:125–128 Acr. 24) as victor,

---

[149] Roesch 1982:225.
[150] Manieri *ad loc.* prints [ῥα]ψῳδῶν Αὐρ. Εὔκαιρ[ος Ταναγραῖος].
[151] The similarity of the two programs becomes clear when one realizes that αὐλητὴς πυθικός and
πυθαύλης on the one hand, and αὐλητὴς κύκλιος and χοραύλης on the other, are alternative labels
for the same specialty (cf. Roesch 1982:227n112 and Strasser 2002:97–98 with *SEG* 52.1943). The
same rationale suggests that the supplement in Bizard 1903:297 line 14 should be κιθα[ρῳδῶν
rather than κιθα[ριστῶν (cf. Steph. 2937).

respectively, in heraldry (κηρύκων) and rhapsody (ῥαψῳδῶν) at the Ptoia of Akraiphia (τῶν πενταετηρικῶν Πτωΐων Καισαρείων). The events were: σαλπικτῶν, κηρύκων, ποιητῶν, ῥαψῳδῶν, πυθικ[ῶν αὐ]λητῶν, κυκλίων [αὐλητῶν], and κιθα[ριστῶν] (the inscription breaks at this point). The text details explicitly that the poet 'carried off a double prize according to the arrangements'.

PART V

ARISTOTLE ON PERFORMANCE

13

Rhapsodic *hypokrisis* and Aristotelian *lexis*

13.1 Why Aristotle on Ὑπόκρισις Matters

AS I NOTED IN THE INTRODUCTION to this book,[1] the term ὑπόκρισις is not connected solely with oratorical delivery but, more broadly, with the general notion of 'performance'. Aristotle's *Rhetoric* III.1–12 stands as a central witness to its conceptual development.[2] But before considering what the philosopher says about it, I must state my rationale for engaging in the detailed and comprehensive study that is presented in the following chapters. For, given the subject matter of this book, namely, a diachronic study of Homeric performance, one may suppose that even the sympathetic reader might question, if not the need, at least the scope and depth of the ensuing analysis. My point of entry is the reference to ῥαψῳδία at 1403b23[3] in the context of Aristotle's discussion of ὑπόκρισις:[4]

> τρίτον δὲ τούτων ὃ δύναμιν μὲν ἔχει μεγίστην, οὔπω δ' ἐπικεχείρηται, τὰ περὶ τὴν ὑπόκρισιν. καὶ γὰρ εἰς τὴν τραγικὴν καὶ ῥαψῳδίαν ὀψὲ παρῆλθεν· ὑπεκρίνοντο γὰρ αὐτοὶ τὰς τραγῳδίας οἱ ποιηταὶ τὸ πρῶτον.

> And third of these, what has the greatest power and has not yet been taken in hand, the matter of *hypokrisis*. For it has also come late to tragedy and rhapsodic delivery; for at first the poets themselves used to perform their tragedies.

'The matter of *hypokrisis*' (lit., 'what is connected with *hypokrisis*') is here said to have come 'late' to rhapsodic delivery. This observation seems to mark a

---

[1] See above, p. 1.
[2] See above, pp. 8f.
[3] Ordinarily, I will use the line numbers of Kassel's edition of the *Rhetoric* (Kassel 1976). Since these do not always agree precisely with the numbering of the more readily available *OCT* by Ross, the reader who consults the latter should know occasionally to adjust the count slightly.
[4] *Rhetoric* 1403b21–24.

development in the manner of performing Homeric poetry—for, whatever else ῥαψῳδία denotes, it must at least denote this—and hence the report has a *prima facie* claim to our attention in a study of the epic rhapsode and his craft. The coordinate mention of τραγική makes clear that what has come late to rhapsody is not the *exercise* of 'delivery': τὰ περὶ τὴν ὑπόκρισιν came late to tragic drama too, which could not exist without on-stage delivery (surely, in the context of drama, ὑπόκρισις must be what the ὑποκριτής does). The two statements that follow make clear that the philosopher is speaking about the *study* and *formal instruction* of 'delivery': 'For initially the poets themselves used to act their tragic plays'. We must remember that early plays featured only one actor.[5] Thus, if a talented poet himself acted his plays, he had no reason critically to reflect upon and write about the principles that made for successful delivery. No one needed to learn them from him. Doubtless, Aristotle assumes the poet's natural gift not only for composing but also delivering his lines effectively.[6] A second statement helps to clarify the meaning of τὰ περὶ τὴν ὑπόκρισιν: δῆλον οὖν ὅτι καὶ περὶ τὴν ῥητορικήν ἐστι τὸ τοιοῦτον ὥσπερ καὶ περὶ τὴν ποιητικήν, ὅπερ ἕτεροί τινες ἐπραγματεύθησαν καὶ Γλαύκων ὁ Τήϊος (1403b24–27). There is 'that sort of thing' in relation to rhetoric which also exists with reference to poetics;[7] which Glaukon of Teos and some others have taken in hand (in connection with poetics). Evidently, in view is studying, teaching, and writing about poetics. And οὔπω δ' ἐπικεχείρηται (1403b21–22) points in the same direction: 'not yet taken in hand' does not address the attempt to *practice* delivery, but its analysis and instruction by scholars.[8]

What could the philosopher mean when he writes that ὑπόκρισις has come to rhapsody late? Pointing to the paring of ῥαψῳδία and τραγική, someone might conclude that what Aristotle has in mind is the theatricality of rhapsodic recitation: an exaggerated stage presence, with overdone histrionic vocal intonation, gestures, attire, perhaps even too 'mimetic' an impersonation of Homeric characters when reciting their speeches. The thought of the passage would be construed thus: at length, under the influence of tragic performance, someone started to reflect upon dramatic technique—on what made for effective delivery on stage—and brought in turn such reflection, in writing and teaching, to bear on rhapsody. It is true that as early as the fourth century BC (if not before) tragic drama exerted such an influence upon rhetoric and rhapsody, with the corresponding overemphasis on histrionic delivery. But restricting Aristotle's meaning to this alone would drastically impoverish his thought, not only in

---

[5] Cf. Aristotle *Poetics* 1449a15–17.
[6] Cf. his assertion at *Rhetoric* 1404a15.
[7] ποιητική presumably includes τραγική and ῥαψῳδία.
[8] This understanding receives further support from the related ἐγκεχειρήκασι of 1404a13–15.

regard to what he says about rhetoric but also, more germanely, what he says *by implication* about rhapsody. My argument is simple to state, though it takes the following two chapters to make it convincingly: the philosopher's view of ὑπόκρισις is *not* simply the superficial one of dress, gestures, and emotive vocal delivery, which a critic of the encroachment of acting on the practice of orators and rhapsodes might decry. Vocal delivery, to be sure, is involved (for he says that ὑπόκρισις is in the voice, 1403b27); and πάθη are certainly in view, for his focus is on how to use the voice 'for each *pathos*' (πρὸς ἕκαστον πάθος 1403b27–28). But his intent is to study ὑπόκρισις as a most powerful means to the end of persuading an audience. 'Delivery', then, is an essential aspect of the orator's task, a crucial element of rhetoric, and it must be diligently considered from the point of view of the civic psychology of emotions that the *Rhetoric* undertakes to investigate.

If my reading of *Rhetoric* III.1 is correct, an examination of the first twelve chapters of the third book of Aristotle's treatise should open a window into the thought and practice of rhapsodes concerning their training and delivery of Homeric epic. For the philosopher himself states that the τὸ τοιοῦτον addressed there in connection with rhetoric came late to rhapsody too. In other words, our understanding of ὑπόκρισις in the *Rhetoric*—the only extant classical treatise that deals explicitly with delivery—will, *mutatis mutandis*, illuminate the performance of rhapsodes during the classical period. And, since at 1404a18–19 Aristotle explicitly refers to the technique of writing as an element of rhetorical practice with a role in delivery (a matter more famously treated by Alkidamas in his *On the Sophists*),[9] we are offered a glimpse of what was a cultural watershed, the adoption of writing, at a time when it was still a relatively recent phenomenon and its impact was still under searching consideration and debate.

The inquiry that follows seeks to address two principal objections. The first, that Aristotle in fact does not think of delivery in the terms just outlined: as an essential part of the oratorical task that needs to be understood, embraced, and practiced by one who desires to succeed as an orator. Rather, critics claim, Aristotle thinks delivery *inherently* an ethically objectionable matter that is best set aside and disposed of; accordingly, his goal in *Rhetoric* III.1–12 is *not* ὑπόκρισις, 'delivery', but λέξις, 'style'—and a notion of style, at that, purged from the moral stain of ties to delivery. Although this stance is variously advocated, it finds particular expression in a view of φαντασία at 1404a11 that contemptuously glosses it as 'mere appearance', 'outward show', *vel sim.* A second chief objection, built upon the first, is that the statement about writing at 1404a18–19 has nothing to do with delivery but solely, if anything, with style. By stating his

---

[9] See above, pp. 311ff.

case thus, the critic has implicitly divorced style and delivery, has made them separate in Aristotle's thought and treatment, and has mapped his views on style onto our modern own—views, in our case, that are inextricably linked to the written word and hence connote matters that can be satisfactorily captured by what is on the page, with only a derivative reference (if any) to vocal utterance or performance.

These views are so insidious—if only, because they so readily fit the mold of our own thinking and reflect a longstanding scholarly consensus—that it takes much effort to undo them. To that end, I undertake a comprehensive rereading of *Rhetoric* III.1–12 that places the philosopher's thought back in its own historical context, without distorting anachronisms, however appealing or natural to us.[10] To anticipate my results: in Aristotle's thought λέξις and ὑπόκρισις cannot be divorced, nor are they, in fact, divorced in his actual treatment. Delivery (as an element, or even the characteristic shape of, rhetorical style) is in view all throughout these twelve chapters; φαντασία is not 'outward show', but the soul's [re]presentational device that mediates between sense perception and man's critical faculties; and hence, the writing that is in view in 1404a18–19 is an element of the orator's delivery: a technique only recently introduced and used *with a view to delivery*. It is in that light that we must in particular read chapter 12 of *Rhetoric* III. Only after establishing that this is Aristotle's thought regarding oratorical delivery may one bring the investigation to bear upon the rhapsode and *his* training and practice (see above, chapter 9). For if the γραφόμενοι λόγοι of 1404a18 had really been a matter of style tied to the written word and not to delivery, one could legitimately challenge its applicability to rhapsodic performance, which, after all, is concerned not with the written word but with vocal utterance.

13.2 Relationship between Λέξις and Ὑπόκρισις

In the third book of his *Rhetoric* Aristotle turns from πίστεις,[11] his focus in Books I and II, to λέξις and τάξις ('style'[12] and 'arrangement' respectively).[13] By connecting λέξις with ὡς δεῖ εἰπεῖν and τὸ φανῆναι ποιόν τινα τὸν λόγον (1403b16–18), the philosopher explains the general meaning and scope of this term. There is, however, less terminological (if not conceptual) neatness to it than most

---

[10] For a recent commentary on this book, see now Burkett 2011. He too joins the consensus: "Unlike *lexis*, Aristotle views delivery as largely a matter of natural talent ..." (26).

[11] At *Rhetoric* 1403a36 the philosopher also refers to πίστεις with the expression τὰ περὶ τὴν διάνοιαν.

[12] Though 'style' is its usual translation, λέξις denotes broadly how thought is expressed in words. Thus, depending on the context it may be rendered as 'language', 'word choice', 'expression', *vel sim.* (Kennedy 1991:216). I will argue that *oral* expression is most often in view.

[13] *Rhetoric* 1403a36–b2 and 1403b7–8.

commentators assume, and one of the difficulties in explicating the thought of chapters 1 and 2 of the third book of the *Rhetoric* is the specific relationship between λέξις—apparently the more inclusive rubric for the subject matter of *Rhetoric* III.1–12—and ὑπόκρισις, the notion that arguably takes center stage in chapter 1.

Rhetoric 1403b18–22 marks the transition to the new subject:

τὸ μὲν οὖν πρῶτον ἐζητήθη κατὰ φύσιν, ὅπερ πέφυκε πρῶτον, αὐτὰ τὰ πράγματα ἐκ τίνων ἔχει τὸ πιθανόν· δεύτερον δὲ τὸ ταῦτα τῇ λέξει διαθέσθαι· τρίτον δὲ τούτων, ὃ δύναμιν μὲν ἔχει μεγίστην, οὔπω δ' ἐπικεχείρηται, τὰ περὶ τὴν ὑπόκρισιν.

The first thing to be examined was naturally that which comes first by nature, whence the facts themselves get their persuasiveness; second is how to compose this in language [*lexis*]; and third is something that has the greatest force, but has not yet been taken in hand, the matter of delivery [*hypokrisis*].[14]

The 'natural order' (κατὰ φύσιν) of the inquiry had led to what was 'first by nature' (ὅπερ πέφυκε πρῶτον), τὰ πράγματα, specifically, 'whence it gains τὸ πιθανόν'—this, clearly, a reference to the study of πίστεις in Books I and II. The headings that follow under δεύτερον and τρίτον are not a recapitulation of the basic outline of the *Rhetoric* (πίστεις, λέξις, and τάξις), as is the opinion of those who equate τὸ ταῦτα τῇ λέξει διαθέσθαι with πῶς χρὴ τάξαι τὰ μέρη τοῦ λόγου. For the verb διατίθεσθαι does not mean here 'to arrange' (it is therefore not a synonym of τάξαι); indeed, if *arrangement* were in view, with 'style' playing the organizing principle, we would expect κατὰ λέξιν (or similar) instead of the instrumental τῇ λέξει.[15] Rather, the *DGE* s.v. διατίθημι B.II.2 correctly cites *Rhetoric* 1403b20 under 'explicar, exponer, narrar', placing the emphasis not on the structure but on the character of the speech in view.[16] Thus, taking at face

---

14 Kennedy's 1991 translation *ad loc.* (Kennedy 1991:217–218).

15 Cf. Burkett 2011:25.

16 Though related to it, this acceptation is not the same as the (later common) 'to set forth' (LSJ s.v. B.6), a meaning illustrated by διατίθεσθαι with such objects as λόγους, ἐπαίνους, or δημηγορίαν. The *DGE* collects these instances s.v. B.II.1, a division that differs from B.II.2 in that it emphasizes the publication of the discourse. Thus, I agree with Cope (1877:3.3) when he dismisses the meaning *in publicum proponere, in medium proferre*, choices that would make τὸ ταῦτα τῇ λέξει διαθέσθαι near identical with the *third* head of Aristotle's list, ὑπόκρισις. Kennedy 1991 *ad loc.* translates, "how to compose this in language"; Dufour and Wartelle 1973, less literally, "la valeur que leur prête le style"; while Cope helpfully writes that "διαθέσθαι denotes ... the investing of the speech with a certain character, putting it in a certain state, by the use of language ... . It does not mean here distribution, ordering, arrangement, which is not the special office of the graces and properties of language or style" (1877:3.3).

value the statement of intention at 1403b15 περὶ δὲ τῆς λέξεως ἐχόμενόν ἐστιν εἰπεῖν, we should read the δεύτερον and τρίτον that follow the reference to the foregoing material (the πρῶτον) as a twofold conceptual division of λέξις—that second great head in the overall outline of the treatise as we know it today.[17]

It is clear, then, that at this stage of the argument ὑπόκρισις is seen as the second phase in the deployment of the resources of λέξις by the oratorical art: first comes the stylistic shaping of the material; then follows τὰ περὶ τὴν ὑπόκρισιν 'which', we are told 'is of the greatest moment'.[18] Aristotle does not attempt here a formal definition of ὑπόκρισις, assuming, perhaps, that its connection with the theater (τραγικῇ 1403b22–23) suffices to explain it. He soon adds that 'it [ὑπόκρισις] lies in the voice (ἐν τῇ φωνῇ), how one should use it to express each emotion' (1403b27–28).[19] The inventory that follows pertains in its entirety to the management of the voice and, generally, to oral delivery: its 'loudness', whether μεγάλη, μικρά, or μέση; its 'intonation' or 'pitch' (τόνος): ὀξύς, βαρύς, or μέσος;[20] and the 'rhythms' (ῥυθμοί) that correspond to each case. He then gathers these under the headings μέγεθος, ἁρμονία, and ῥυθμός, which must be, I think, the antecedents of the αὐτῶν at 1403b36: 'A treatise (τέχνη) about them (αὐτῶν) has not been composed yet, since the matter itself of lexis has appeared late; and, when considered aright, it seems to be vulgar'.[21]

It is at this point in the text of Rhetoric III.1 that scholars start sensing difficulties with its terminology. For some render ἐπεὶ καί 'since even' at 1403b36, as if the philosopher's treatment of ὑπόκρισις marked a detour, opening a parenthesis on 'delivery' before the matter of λέξις (properly considered) is finally taken up in section eight.[22] So, for example, Kennedy 1991 renders the

---

[17] Cope (1877:3.3) glosses τούτων in 1403b21 as "of such things as these, the divisions of Rhetoric." If he means the threefold division of rhetoric into pisteis, lexis, and taxis, this cannot be right, for then τὸ ταῦτα τῇ λέξει διαθέσθαι would have to stand for 'arrangement' (a reading refuted immediately above). It would also follow that for Aristotle τὰ περὶ τὴν ὑπόκρισιν would adequately substitute for an explicit mention of λέξις (a corollary that should discomfort those who seek to divorce these terms). The alternative is to refer τούτων to the discrete series of topics that suggest themselves in their natural order (κατὰ φύσιν 1403b18) to the scholar of rhetorical art. On this view, the philosopher might have gone on to taxis in his enumeration, but he stops at hypokrisis in order to fulfill his promise to consider lexis next (1403b15).

[18] Cf. the use of κυριώτατος at Rhetoric 1355a7, 1356a13, and 1358b17.

[19] With Cope and the anonymous commentator (Anonymi in artem rhetoricam commentarium, p. 159 ad loc., ed. Rabe), I read αὕτη at 1403b27. As Cope observes, "αὐτή seems to have no meaning here" and it is regularly translated as if it read αὕτη.

[20] The feminine gender is used throughout, which makes clear that φωνή, 'voice', is still conceptually in view under the plural τόνοι.

[21] οὔπω δὲ σύγκειται τέχνη περὶ αὐτῶν, ἐπεὶ καὶ τὸ περὶ τὴν λέξιν ὀψὲ προῆλθεν· καὶ δοκεῖ φορτικὸν εἶναι, καλῶς ὑπολαμβανόμενον (1403b35–1404a1).

[22] The logic would be a fortiori: lexis appeared late, hypokrisis the more so. Kennedy 1991:217 writes: "A third beginning is then supplied in section 3 [of Rhetoric III.1], followed by some

passage as follows: "An *Art* concerned with [the delivery of oratory] has not yet been composed, since even consideration of *lexis* was late in developing."[23] When it comes to 1404a8, however, he translates τὸ μὲν οὖν τῆς λέξεως as "the subject of expression," adding in a footnote, tellingly: "*Lexis*, here apparently including delivery." In other words, whereas he had thus far sought to separate λέξις and ὑπόκρισις, now at last he must bring them together. Kennedy is forced to make inconsistent exegetical choices—*lexis* now excluding, now including, 'delivery'—because he wishes to restrict the characterization of φορτικόν at 1404a1 to ὑπόκρισις (hence also the "since even" that suggests a detour). But now, at 1404a8–9, Aristotle speaks of the 'small necessary place' of λέξις in all teaching, a regrettable consequence (as the μὲν οὖν makes clear[24])

---

remarks on delivery, and the *actual* discussion of *lexis* does not begin until section 8" (my emphasis).

[23] Despite Kennedy's acknowledgment that "*lexis* ... refers to the 'way of *saying*' something" (1991:216, my emphasis), his perspective as a modern scholar naturally gravitates towards a reading of the *Rhetoric* that makes the *written* word its primary focus; this frame of reference in turn leads him to introduce hard distinctions—in this case, between ὑπόκρισις and λέξις—where the relation between the terms is more nuanced. Freese's translation *ad* 1403b35–36 avoids the impression of a dichotomy: "But no treatise has yet been composed on delivery, since the matter of style itself only lately came into notice" (1926:347). καί (as the "itself" hints) may well be emphatic, but if so the comparison does not intend a contrast between 'delivery' and 'style' that sets the former apart from the latter. It would signal an argument *a maiore ad minus*, one from the part to the whole: τὸ περὶ τὴν λέξιν denotes the sphere of all matters related to λέξις; if only lately did the general sphere of 'stylistic matters' itself receive scholarly attention, the correspondingly late focus on 'delivery'—a subordinate component of Aristotelian λέξις—is only to be expected. A translation like Kennedy's that renders ἐπεὶ καί 'since even' does not necessarily exclude this meaning but it tends to obscure it. Contrast this with Ross 1924, where Roberts translates *ad loc.*, "[I]ndeed, even the study of language made no progress till late in the day," but in a footnote clarifies: "From this and other indications it would seem that Aristotle regards delivery as a subordinate part of λέξις, 'expression'." And, sensitive to the 'oral' overtones of the terminology, he adds: "The classification of ὑπόκρισις under λέξις is helped by the relation of the latter to λέγειν. λέξις is 'a mode of speaking'." Cope 1877:6, in his note to §5, offers an acceptable translation, but unduly restricts the φορτικόν to ἡ ὑποκριτική (obscuring its clear, and immediately preceding, neuter referent, viz. τὸ περὶ τὴν λέξιν; see further below, p. 581 n. 6): "But no art has been as yet composed of it; for in fact it was not till late that of composition made any advance."

[24] Reviewing the uses of μὲν οὖν, Denniston (1954:470–481) divides them into three main categories: 1) retrospective and transitional οὖν with prospective μέν; 2) οὖν emphasizing a prospective μέν; 3) οὖν emphasizing an adversative or affirmative μέν. This passage falls under the first category (the repeated mention of the 'hearer' at 1404a8 and a12 makes this clear): with transitional and inferential force Aristotle retakes the immediately preceding μέγα δύναται in order to restate his point (διαφέρει γάρ τι) with an additional qualification (οὐ μέντοι τοσοῦτον), deriving from it as well a practical consequence for the study of rhetoric (ἔχει τι μικρὸν ἀναγκαῖον ἐν πάσῃ διδασκαλίᾳ). The ὅμως of a9 might seem at first to hinder my view that this section presents a restatement and an inferential summary (which would call for overall agreement with, and perhaps expansion of, the foregoing, but not for an adversative); but, just as the μὲν οὖν, this ὅμως *also* looks back, responding to the tension between the philosopher's censure of the ἡ τοῦ ἀκροατοῦ μοχθηρία that gives λέξις its force, and his implicit repudiation of any device that

of the corruption of the audience (διὰ τὴν τοῦ ἀκροατοῦ μοχθηρίαν). If φορτικόν applies only to ὑπόκρισις, and μοχθηρία in the hearer calls for λέξις (in a limited way, as a concession to weakness), then it follows that now λέξις *must* include ὑπόκρισις. But another option (defended here) opens before the interpreter: that Aristotle's view of λέξις, from the vantage point of an ideal ethics, is more radically negative than commentators usually allow, and that φορτικόν applies not only to ὑπόκρισις but to λέξις as a whole.

Those who accept the suggestion of a detour usually blame the undeniable awkwardness of the resulting thematic outline on an unfinished (or unpolished) redaction, either by Aristotle himself or by later members of the Academy who allegedly merged two originally independent works into a single treatise.[25] But the suggestion of a detour or parenthesis cannot be sustained. As argued above, following upon his clear statement of intention, Aristotle sets out to discuss λέξις, of which he reckons ὑπόκρισις a subordinate division. From our modern point of view, this choice is by no means self-evident: why should 'oral delivery' (if we accept this as a valid tentative rendering of the term) be considered part of 'style'? It is quite possible to think of 'style' as including only what can be immediately conveyed by the written word, *without* embracing matters more narrowly connected with *oral* delivery. This is the way most interpreters think about the items covered in chapters 3–11:[26] word choice suitable to prose, metaphors, similes, frigidity, grammatical correctness, conciseness, appropriateness, prose rhythm (for loud reading), periodic style, elegance, expressiveness, use of proverbs, and hyperbole. This, *we* find eminently possible to do because of the predominance in our conceptual universe of the written word (and, hence, of written discourse) over performance.[27] We think of the word, first and foremost, as reified, on the page (so to speak), and 'style', therefore, as subsuming what belongs to the literary study of written texts—with voice and its qualities logically falling under some other head, 'delivery', 'acting', or similar. My argument

---

does not strictly answer to the bare facts—this latter, an imperative of justice that only an ideal society, devoid of the corrupting allure of style, might realize. This, moreover, is not the only ὅμως in the passage: an ἀλλ' ὅμως in the previous sentence (1404a7) makes explicit the tension between the status of λέξις as περίεργα ἔξω τοῦ ἀποδεῖξαι (a6–7) and its influence (μέγα δύναται).

[25] I am not denying the possibility (which has much to commend it) that the present-day Book III of the *Rhetoric* may originally have been an independent work: this would account for the admittedly awkward double transition from *Rhetoric* II to III: ἐπεὶ δὲ δὴ τρία ἔστιν ἃ δεῖ πραγματευθῆναι περὶ τὸν λόγον at 1403a34–35 and ἐπειδὴ τρία ἐστὶν ἃ δεῖ πραγματευθῆναι περὶ τὸν λόγον at 1403b6–7. For a possible reconstruction of the historical development of the treatise, see Kennedy 1991:217 and 299–309 (his appendix II).

[26] I make clear below (see pp. 533ff.) that I disagree with this narrow construction of the contents of these chapters.

[27] Note, in this connection, the helpful distinction between *primary* and *secondary* rhetoric in Kennedy 1999:2–3.

here resists this proclivity by highlighting the *discontinuity* between Aristotle and later ancient scholars in the way they articulated the relation between λέξις and ὑπόκρισις. Although I do not fully subscribe his argument and conclusions, at least in this regard I agree with Graff 2000: "[W]hile it is true that style (λέξις, *elocutio*) would become a regular component in the major rhetorical systems after Aristotle, its status is less clear in works prior to the *Rhetoric* and also in the Aristotelian formulation of the art" (4–5). The discontinuity, however, is not simply one of content, of topics covered. It arises primarily from the emphasis the philosopher placed on the oral and aural dimensions of style and from his corresponding focus on delivery as its controlling τέλος. But as writing acquired greater pedagogical and cultural prominence, it did not take long before λέξις came to mean what we ourselves generally understand by style: the diction and composition of the written word, a set of formal qualities at times even better suited for reading than hearing. This development is already clear in Demetrios' *On Style:*[28] he shows no interest in the management of the voice, and references to ὑπόκρισις are restricted to stage acting[29] or to short, passing observations about the γραφική and ὑποκριτικὴ λέξις,[30] comments that turn on the use of σύνδεσμοι and are largely derivative of Aristotle (*Rhetoric* III.12). Typical of his attitude is *On Style* §195, where he abruptly cuts off his analysis of the scope for acting in a particular scene of Euripides' *Iōn* with the words: ἀλλ' οὐ περὶ ὑποκρίσεως ἡμῖν τὰ νῦν ὁ λόγος.[31]

---

[28] Until recently scholars dated most, if not all, of the treatise *Peri hermēneias* (or *De elocutione*; I shall refer to it by the English *On Style*) to no later than the second century BC, with a few excepting only what they thought were minor editorial touches by a later hand. During the last decade, however, several studies have advocated a later, Roman-imperial, date (Roberts 1902:64 had already advocated long ago a date in the range I BC–I AD.) See Innes 1999:312–321 and Marini 2007:1–20.

[29] *On Style* §§58, 195.

[30] *On Style* §§193–194, 226, 271.

[31] Aristotle himself planted the seeds of this development: his divergent analyses of λέξις in the *Poetics* and the *Rhetoric* implied that poetry (or, more broadly, literature) and oratory called not merely for two different styles (cf. *Rhetoric* 1404a27–28), but for entirely different ways of conceptualizing style (see below, p. 548 n. 100 and p. 588). To understand how natural it was for the study of λέξις to shift its focus from oratory to literature, we need only remember the philosopher's dismissal of ὄψις as 'least integral to poetics' because the δύναμις of tragedy did not depend on actors or on competitive performance (ἀγών) (*Poetics* 1450b16–20); and recall that he thought reading unassisted by the κίνησις of performance quite able to reveal the qualities of tragedy (*Poetics* 1462a11). *Letteraturizzazione* is the Italian term used to denote this move away from oratory—in Kennedy's words, "the tendency of rhetoric to shift focus from persuasion to narration, from civic to personal contexts, and from speech to literature, including poetry" (1999:3). It is difficult to say whether this development was already under way with Theophrastos. His writing an independent treatise on delivery (cf. Diogenes Laertios 5.48) suggests that he held to a greater autonomy of λέξις and ὑπόκρισις than Aristotle did. A passage of Athanasius (Fortenbaugh et al. 1992:558 fr. 712) shows that to voice, he added the study gestures (κίνησις τοῦ σώματος), and that he was more successful than his predecessor in integrating voice and gesture

This is not Aristotle's view: though the destabilization of the oral culture of ancient Greece was already under way in his own time (and, to go no further, chapter 12 of *Rhetoric* III may well serve as witness), ὀνόματα, 'words', are for him still primarily mimetic and a matter of the φωνή: 'The poets, as is natural, were the first to set [this] in motion; for words are instances of imitation, and the voice also, the most mimetic of all our constituent parts, was [ready at hand]'.[32] This statement, the cause of much dismay for some scholars, as one writer notes,[33] has nothing to do with the Platonic theory of words in the *Kratylos*, but is rather an admission of the degree to which, even as late as Aristotle, ποιητική and ῥητορική ('literature' and 'oratory', to use our terms), not to mention ῥαψῳδική and ὑποκριτική, were all preeminently oral professions, and scholarly study of these would not have easily dissociated their 'strictly oral' dimensions (e.g. intonation) from their (from our cultural perspective) 'more literary' qualities (say, the use of *tropoi* or grammatical correctness). A careful reading of *Rhetoric* III.3–12 will uncover many instances where the *oral* dimension of delivery is clearly in view,[34] well beyond what a study of style strictly bound to the written word would lead the scholar to expect. But Aristotle's perspective is particularly clear in chapters 1 and 12, where (as I will presently argue) ὑπόκρισις, though first apparently limited to the voice and its properties, quickly expands its purview, and soon comes to stand more generally for λέξις—while, reciprocally, λέξις stands for a style that is tailored to, and controlled by, ὑπόκρισις. This move, which has confused many a scholar, should not surprise us: though we might have wished for greater terminological clarity throughout, the philosopher's usage opens to us a window into his thought, still primarily controlled by, the oral dimensions of rhetoric, which is sooner embodied by the performance of the speaker before his audience than by the written text of his oration; this allows 'delivery' to stand for the 'stylistic shape' of the performance, including, yes, the use of metaphors, similes, elegance, conciseness, grammatical correctness, and so on.

---

with an analysis of human emotions. (Yet facial expressions are not entirely ignored by the *Rhetoric*: cf. 1386a31–33 [see below, p. 536] and 1408b5–7 [see below, p. 537].) But fragments 687 and 691 (Fortenbaugh) show an emphasis on the senses (sound and sight) that is remarkably similar to Aristotle's own (cf. *Rhetoric* 1405b6–8, b17–19). Thus, it is hard for me to tell how great a departure Theophrastos' treatment really represents. Cf. Fortenbaugh 1985.

32 ἤρξαντο μὲν οὖν κινῆσαι τὸ πρῶτον, ὥσπερ πέφυκεν, οἱ ποιηταί· τὰ γὰρ ὀνόματα μιμήματα ἐστίν, ὑπῆρξε δὲ καὶ ἡ φωνὴ πάντων μιμητικώτατον τῶν μορίων ἡμῖν· (1404a19–22).

33 Cf. Rapp 2002:2.819–820.

34 Note, for example, how at 1407b11–12, where Aristotle turns his attention explicitly to the written text (τὸ γεγραμμένον), he is chiefly concerned that it be εὐανάγνωστον, 'easy to read aloud', and εὔφραστον, which LSJ s.v. renders as 'easy to make intelligible', an acceptable gloss that has, nevertheless, an undeniable *speaking* semantic component and is therefore translated as 'easy to speak' (Kennedy), 'easy to utter' (Freese *Loeb Classical Library*), or 'leicht auszusprechen' (Rapp).

13.3 Ὑπόκρισις, Not a Detour

That Aristotle actually dealt with matters that fall strictly under the narrow definition of ὑπόκρισις (i.e. those connected with the management of the voice) should be considered *a priori* plausible. After all, at least on two different occasions he states that no one had attempted a treatise about them: at 1403b21–22 he notes that τὰ περὶ τὴν ὑπόκρισιν had not yet been taken in hand (οὔπω δ' ἐπικεχείρηται);[35] and at 1403b35–36 he adds: οὔπω δὲ σύγκειται τέχνη περὶ αὐτῶν, where, as mentioned above (p. 526), the αὐτῶν most likely points to the three qualities of the voice (1403b30–31). There is no existing manual (τέχνη), the philosopher says, 'since the [broader] field of λέξις itself has come up late' (ἐπεὶ καὶ τὸ περὶ τὴν λέξιν ὀψὲ προῆλθεν 1403b36). Here ὀψὲ προῆλθεν parallels ὀψὲ παρῆλθεν at 1403b23, this latter noting the introduction of ὑπόκρισις into the dramatic and rhapsodic arts. There is a third statement at 1404a12–15, in my opinion to be listed along with the other two; though I will consider it in detail below (see pp. 580ff.), I may now advance some of my conclusions here for the sake of clarity in my presentation. The text runs as follows:

> ἐκείνη μὲν οὖν ὅταν ἔλθῃ ταὐτὸ ποιήσει τῇ ὑποκριτικῇ, ἐγκεχειρήκασι δὲ ἐπ' ὀλίγον περὶ αὐτῆς εἰπεῖν τινες, οἷον Θρασύμαχος ἐν τοῖς Ἐλέοις.

> Now, when it [sc. *lexis*] comes [into vogue] it will have the same impact as the art of [dramatic] acting, and to a small extent some have endeavored to speak about it, for example Thrasymakhos in his *Pities*.

The ἐκείνη, as I will argue below, takes λέξις as its immediate antecedent, but does so not to the exclusion of ὑπόκρισις, which is subsumed under 'style' as the larger heading:[36] this conceptual overlap alone accounts for the grammar (which calls for λέξις) and the context (which calls for ὑπόκρισις)—a fact of great significance from which it follows that where 'style' is mentioned 'oral delivery', its primary subdivision, is preeminently in view. 'When it comes',[37] ὅταν ἔλθῃ, clearly picks up on ὀψὲ παρῆλθεν and ὀψὲ προῆλθεν; and ἐγκεχειρήκασι δὲ ἐπ' ὀλίγον answers to and qualifies οὔπω δ' ἐπικεχείρηται (1403b21–22). Should there be any need further to establish the tie between this last and the first two passages, note the statement about ἆθλα at 1404a17, with the pointed πάλιν

---

[35] By itself, this might mean that his own treatise had not yet addressed it, but the second occurrence makes the sense clear, namely, that no scholar had yet given it sustained attention. Of course, had he meant the former, this would imply that he himself would presently take it up.

[36] Thus, I agree with Cope when he glosses ἐκείνη as "that (the art which applies ὑποκριτική to Rhetoric)" (1877:3.8, his emphasis). This art, a subdivision of ῥητορική, is precisely *lexis*.

[37] For which we must doubtless supply something like 'into use' or 'into vogue.' Aristotle must have intended his own treatment in *Rhetoric* III to contribute to such bringing it into use.

that precedes it, which sends us forward to the καθάπερ clause that follows it and back to the similar comment at 1403b32–34. Aristotle's focus is on the lack of an appropriate scholarly treatment of ὑπόκρισις and, more broadly, λέξις. In light of this, is it plausible to think that he, too, would have failed to cover ὑπόκρισις in his *Rhetoric*? After pointing out the gap (twice, if not thrice), would he also have failed utterly to fill it? Scholars by and large seem to think so, and Kennedy (1991:219n8) may serve as illustration; for, translating 1404a12–13 "when delivery comes to be considered," he adds the footnote: "As it apparently was by Aristotle's student Theophrastus." If he is right, how are we to justify the philosopher's failure? One might perhaps adduce that ὑπόκρισις is not that important after all: but Aristotle calls it ὃ δύναμιν μὲν ἔχει μεγίστην (1403b21). Or one may claim that its study is undesirable, for it is only likely to corrupt the audience. But, to this view and its underlying presumptions (which I examine below and find wanting), Aristotle's own considered judgment may suffice: 'Nevertheless, the subject of *lexis* has some small necessary place in every demonstrative discipline'.[38] But, one may yet protest, what the philosopher does study is λέξις, not ὑπόκρισις, and therefore he does, after all, fill the gap. The problem with this view, however, is that it drives too wide a wedge between ὑπόκρισις and λέξις, wider than the philosopher's thought and words will allow; and that it fails to account for the two statements that are unequivocally about ὑπόκρισις in its narrow concern with φωνή: thus a glaring failure to address what Aristotle himself owns as being of the greatest moment would stand—and that, without either any explicit admission of what must then be considered by all an intentional oversight or a rationale for this *a priori* unexpected course of action.

Another option must be considered: that Aristotle *did*, in fact, treat ὑπόκρισις in chapters 3–12, though in a manner that has so failed to meet the expectations of modern scholars as to lead them to believe that he did *not* do so. A full demonstration must wait until I consider 1404a12–19 in detail below; but I can now anticipate my conviction that most scholars have read Aristotle with anachronistic expectations, tacitly presupposing that only the presence of material on delivery such as is attested in later works would justify the claim that the philosopher had indeed written, if not a whole independent treatise

---

[38] τὸ μὲν οὖν τῆς λέξεως ὅμως ἔχει τι μικρὸν ἀναγκαῖον ἐν πάσῃ διδασκαλίᾳ (1404a8–9). According to Aristotle, τὰ περὶ τὴν ὑπόκρισιν had only come to the dramatic art of late because the poets themselves had at first acted out their own tragedies. Hence there was no need to instruct others in delivery—the assumption being, perhaps, that poets were 'natural' actors (cf. 1404a15). Once some distance intervened between the poet and the performer, the conceptual space necessary for abstract study arose. But, as regards rhetoric, Aristotle lived during a time when teachers of the art were many and in great demand; so, it is only reasonable to expect that his rhetorical manual would have made sure to impart the all essential instruction in oral delivery.

on it, a least a section of his *Rhetoric* on delivery. Thus it will be helpful, at this point, to survey the chapters in question and see if there are any sections where voice and its properties—under the subheadings of loudness, harmony, and rhythm—come explicitly into play. As I do, we must remember at all times that the primary application of ὑπόκρισις is πῶς αὐτῇ [i.e. φωνῇ] δεῖ χρῆσθαι πρὸς ἕκαστον πάθος. I am not thereby conceding that only passages that explicitly discuss the voice and the emotions would qualify as a study of ὑπόκρισις, for my main contention is that, for Aristotle, all of λέξις is intimately bound with delivery; but identifying such sections would help to make the point that the philosopher, far from excluding delivery as socially noxious and unworthy of his attention, is clearly engaged with what he has already granted is of the greatest consequence for the practicing orator.[39]

13.4 Ὑπόκρισις, Not Just in *Rhetoric* III.1

I have already remarked that Aristotle considers voice to be the 'most mimetic' of man's constituent parts.[40] The corresponding connection between ὀνόματα and φωνή is grounded upon articulate sound, evident in performance but only latent on the written page. This is the starting point of λέξις, of which poets are named the pioneers (1404a19–22). Among the orators, Gorgias of Leontini provides Aristotle with a suitable illustration of the early and unsatisfactory 'poetic style'; and, lest we forget that we are dealing with rhetorical performance first, and only then with its written record, we read that 'the majority of the uneducated still think that such people [as he] *speak* (διαλέγεσθαι) best' (1404a26–27, my emphasis). A similar concern with sound surfaces at 1405b6–8, where we learn that the beauty of words (κάλλος ὀνόματος) resides in their sound (ἐν τοῖς ψόφοις) or their sense; therefore metaphors should be derived 'from things beautiful in their sound (ἐν τῇ φωνῇ), their effect, their display (τῇ ὄψει), or any other sense perception (ἄλλῃ τινὶ αἰσθήσει)'[41]—and with these words the philosopher extends the perceptual field of the audience from the immediacy of the auditory to such φαντάσματα of the other senses as might be evoked by the imagery of the metaphor.[42]

---

[39] Cf. Plutarch *Dēmosthenēs* §7.5–6.

[40] See above, p. 530.

[41] *Rhetoric* 1405b17–19.

[42] This is what is involved in 'placing the thing before the eyes' (τὸ ποιεῖν τὸ πρᾶγμα πρὸ ὀμμάτων 1405b12–13), a matter treated at greater length in *Rhetoric* III.10–11 (cf. also *Poetics* 17). For an exploration of φαντασία in connection with rhetoric, see below, pp. 561ff. One must remember that, although it takes its name from the preeminent sense, sight, φαντασία does not exclude the other senses (*De anima* 429a1–4; cf. Busche 2003:34). It is helpful to cite here Kennedy's insightful comment about Aristotle's distinctive approach to the study of metaphors:

When it comes to propriety of style, we are easily misled into thinking of it primarily (or even exclusively) in terms of word choice.[43] Such a view would not be problematic if we reckoned as part of that choice its effect on delivery, i.e. its ensuing sound shape: intonation, loudness, rhythm, the melodic line of the resulting phrase, etc. But for the average modern literate sensibility, word choice is mostly a matter of lexical semantics, and propriety connotes a register suitable to the topic and the character or social standing of the 'notional speaker' (often merely the author of the text, whose speech is usually read in silence)—without giving thought to any performative dimensions. Aristotle once again confutes such assumptions; for though he speaks of propriety as 'contracting' or 'augmenting' the tone—and illustrates his meaning *a fortiori* from poetry by censuring slaves and youth who use fine language—when it comes to a real-life example, he mentions 'the *voice* of Theodoros' (ἡ Θεοδώρου φωνή, my emphasis): 'for his [voice] seemed to belong to the one speaking, those [of the other actors] to someone else' (ἡ μὲν γὰρ τοῦ λέγοντος ἔοικεν εἶναι, αἱ δ' ἀλλότριαι 1404b23-24). A concentrated focus on the voice is all too easy to understand, considering that the actor was masked, and hence could not change his facial expression to enhance his acting.[44] He could of course gesticulate and move about the stage, but the lion's share of his dramatic art would necessarily fall to the voice. It is perhaps Aristotle's conceptual dependence upon the stage as he develops his own ideas about the orator's λέξις and ὑπόκρισις that explains why he largely failed to include in his study the use of the face, hands, and any appropriate scope for gestures.[45] But the fact remains that, in illustrating proper word choice, as he holds up the goal of a 'natural art' that hides its artifice (1404b18-19), he makes clear that his concern is with its impact on the voice, i.e. on the orator *in performance*.

"The account [of ornament] is a subtle one and seeks to penetrate to an understanding of the psychological effect of a metaphor" (1963:107). To this, he adds: "[The knowledge communicated by metaphors], like rhythm and like the sense of grammatical completion, produces a feeling of pleasure and satisfaction and is thus a characteristic of good style. Happiness is as much the object of Aristotle's theory of style as of his ethics" (112). Kennedy is acknowledging that, even when it comes to metaphor—what many would consider the most traditional of stylistic topics— the philosopher is eminently concerned with the emotions, the very target of delivery. And his concern, as we have seen by his statement at 1405b17-19, centers on the sensory qualities of metaphors.

[43] Thus, Kennedy (1991:220) titles *Rhetoric* III.2 "The *Aretē*, or Virtue, of Good Prose Style; Word Choice and Metaphors."

[44] His eyes, though visible through the mask, would have been too small for his audience to see.

[45] Stage gestures were exaggerated and, in his view, unbecomingly crude (cf. *Poetics* 26 and below, p. 553). The same attitude may underlie his vehement criticism of Kleon's manner in addressing the assembly (cf. *Athēnaiōn Politeia* 28.2).

Another place where φωνή and its properties are clearly in view is chapter 7. We must remember, as I pointed out above (see p. 533), that delivery is primarily concerned with how one should employ the voice in regard to every πάθος. Thus, when we read at 1408a10–11 that 'style will possess propriety if it is expressive of πάθος and ἦθος and proportional to its subject matter', we should immediately think of the voice in performance, how its loudness, harmony, and rhythm are to be deployed to achieve these goals.[46] Hence, to speak αὐτοκαβδάλως or σεμνῶς shall be a matter of word choice in the extended sense discussed above: not only with attention to the semantic register involved, but also to intonation, loudness, and any other quality that serves to project a persuasive persona or communicate the requisite feeling. We shall not be surprised that it is λέξις that aims to be παθητική if in Aristotle's mind, as argued above (and further, below), this term readily subsumes ὑπόκρισις; nor shall we wonder that the list at 1408a16–19 would affirm the propriety of the 'angry style' when dealing with insolence, of the 'indignant' and 'reticent' when handling impious and shameful matters, of speaking with admiration of what is worthy of praise, and humbly of pitiable things. Some readers might indeed miss here the more explicit hints offered by the *Rhetorica ad Herennium* in its section on *pronuntiatio*[47] and conclude, with its author, that *nemo de ea re diligenter scripsit*; or else judge the philosopher deficient in comparison with Cicero's *De oratore* III §§213–227. But it would be an error to let ourselves be guided by anachronistic notions of what a proper account of delivery should look like and fail to see that, in his own way (admittedly compressed by contrast), Aristotle offers guidance as to the proper voice one must use successfully to convey such πάθη as arise in the presence of insolence, impiety, shame, pity, etc. Apparently, he was satisfied to indicate the connection between a cause and its corresponding emotional response, leaving it to the student to consider how volume, melodic line, timbre, and so on should combine to express anger.[48] The outcome is that 'the one listening always

---

[46] As Rapp (2002:2.861) remarks, one should not construe that style be ἀνάλογον to its subject matter as a third requirement unrelated to its ability effectively to convey *ēthos* and *pathos*: "Natürlich liegt die Angemessenheit nicht schon dann vor, wenn die sprachliche Form 'emotional' und 'charaktervoll' ist; also wird man den letzten Teil des Definiens 'dem zugrunde liegenden Gegenstand entsprechend' auf die Merkmale 'emotional' und 'charaktervoll' zurückbeziehen müssen, so dass die Behauptung wäre: Die sprachliche Form muss dem jeweiligen Gegenstand entsprechend emotional oder charaktervoll sein."

[47] Book III, chapters 11–15 §§19–27.

[48] One might reasonably argue that, since we all have experienced (in ourselves or others) the full range of emotions under consideration, such explicit directions would have been superfluous. There is, besides, a marked tendency in the *Rhetoric* towards compression of treatment, so that material not strictly necessary is omitted or a subject already mentioned is not repeated, even when it calls for development from a new vantage point. Cf. Striker 1996:289 and 300n9 and Brinton 1988:208 on the scope of Aristotle's study of πάθη.

experiences a like feeling with the one speaking emotionally, even if he says nothing. Therefore many overwhelm their hearers by raising a clamor'.[49] Note the performative setting: the goal is a community of feeling between the hearer and the speaker.[50] Rapp (2002:2.862) calls this the "musikalisch-sympathetische Wirkung der emotionalen Rede," and he thinks that this outcome of the παθητικὴ λέξις has nothing to do with the artistic ("kunstgemäßen") emotional arousal considered in *Rhetoric* II.1–11. He is mistaken: for Aristotle makes clear that an inference takes place, an ill-founded one (παραλογίζεται 1408a20), to be sure,[51] but a mental reckoning nonetheless, which on the basis of personal experience (ἐπὶ τοῖς τοιούτοις a21) weighs the truthfulness of the claim that purports to give rise to the emotion displayed. Rapp is wrong in thinking that the mind is irrationally bewitched and thereupon does away with the qualifications set forth in *Rhetoric* II—e.g. those of chapter 8 concerning pity, where we read that "on the whole, [a person feels pity] when his state of mind is such that he remembers things like this happening to himself or his own or expects them to happen to himself or his own";[52] and that "since sufferings are pitiable when they appear near at hand ... necessarily they are more pitiable who contribute to the effect by gestures and cries and display of feelings and generally in their acting [*hypokrisis*]."[53] Nevertheless, this scholar helpfully draws

---

[49]   ... συνομοιοπαθεῖ ὁ ἀκούων ἀεὶ τῷ παθητικῶς λέγοντι, κἂν μηθὲν λέγῃ. διὸ πολλοὶ καταπλήττουσι τοὺς ἀκροατὰς θορυβοῦντες (1408a23–25). It is only natural that a section concerned with φωνή should mention causing an uproar as a strategy sometimes used to confound the audience. Just as the volume (μέγεθος) of one's voice can be modulated in accordance with the art of rhetoric without detriment to the truth, it can also serve the purposes of less principled orators. Thus, I disagree with Rapp (2002:2.863), who takes θορυβοῦντες and the concessive statements that accompany it (on which see note 50 immediately below) as paradigmatic of Aristotle's view of delivery. He thus reasserts his opinion that the philosopher has entirely excluded ὑπόκρισις from his treatment of style (as pernicious to the interests of justice), and he denies that this section develops the art of oratorical delivery.

[50]   The concessive clauses εἰ καὶ μὴ οὕτως ἔχει, ὡς ὁ λέγων (1408a22–23) and κἂν μηθὲν λέγῃ (a24) do not condone, much less enjoin, deception or encourage emotional appeals ἔξω τοῦ πράγματος. They only state the obvious: that rhetoric, as any other social endeavor, is open to the manipulation of deceit, all the more so inasmuch as its potential impact is great. On the valence of ἔξω τοῦ πράγματος, see Grimaldi 1980 *ad* 1354a15–16. On this point Halliwell (1994:212) writes: "Here the formulation (assisted by a certain latitude in the established terminology of speaking 'on/ outside the subject,' *peri/exō tou pragmatos*) somewhat elides two things that might properly be distinguished: first, an emphasis on the importance of criteria of judicial relevance; second, a general deprecation of (distortingly) emotional appeals in rhetoric (cf. 3.1.5, 1404a5–8)." I would only modify his statement to say 'a general deprecation of (potentially distorting) emotional appeals as ideally superfluous.'

[51]   See below, p. 576 n. 190.

[52]   καὶ ὅλως δὴ ὅταν ἔχῃ οὕτως ὥστ' ἀναμνησθῆναι τοιαῦτα συμβεβηκότα ἢ αὐτῷ ἢ τῶν αὐτοῦ, ἢ ἐλπίσαι γενέσθαι ἢ ἑαυτῷ ἢ τῶν αὐτοῦ (1386a1–3).

[53]   ἀνάγκη τοὺς συναπεργαζομένους σχήμασι καὶ φωναῖς καὶ αἰσθήσει καὶ ὅλως ἐν ὑποκρίσει ἐλεεινοτέρους εἶναι (1386a31–33). Both this and the quotation immediately preceding (with

attention to *Politics* VIII.5, where μέλη, 'melodies', are called μιμήματα τῶν ἠθῶν, an assertion justified by the distinct moods with which the hearers are affected in listening to the several musical modes. The passage makes clear that *pathē* are in view,[54] and it is followed by a similar statement about the effects of ῥυθμοί (*Politics* 1340b7–10). The balance is to underscore the potential inherent in the voice's ἁρμονία and ῥυθμός to communicate πάθη—precisely the stated aim of ὑπόκρισις.

The focus on delivery is unchanged in the section of *Rhetoric* III.7 that follows, where Aristotle considers λέξις as expressive of ἦθος. We may best understand his definition of ἠθικὴ λέξις, namely ἡ ἐκ τῶν σημείων δεῖξις (1408a26), if we heed Labarrière's observation that the philosopher regularly uses σημεῖα as the units of meaning of φωνή, i.e. of articulate sound, whether man's or the animals' (in contrast to σύμβολα, which he restricts to λόγος).[55] And indeed, the fitting style (ἡ ἁρμόττουσα [λέξ[ς] 1408a26) involves not only the actual words selected but also the manner of their utterance.[56] Rapp (2002:2.864) himself points out that there is no ready opportunity for deception by the speaker here (the grounds on which, he claims, Aristotle contemns delivery)—and by doing so, he undermines his own view that the doctrine of this chapter equips the orator with such artifice as will allow him to trick the audience into false inferences. The point, rather, is that only by speaking in character can the orator clothe his subject with persuasion. Rapp may be too quick, however, to assume that the listed categories cannot be blurred; for the orator who boasts of manliness, say, should not display stylistic traits that stereotype or prejudice declare typical of the female sex; nor should a defendant who pleads the naivete of youth clothe his appeal in sophisticated delivery.[57] The goal is successful μίμησις, and the voice—we well know—is the most 'mimetic' of our constituent parts. One further item proves the full involvement of voice and face in delivery: if the words uttered are harsh,

---

its supplements) are from Kennedy 1991:153–154 *ad loc.*; ἐν ὑποκρίσει should have been translated 'by their delivery'. At 1386a32 Kassel's codex F reads ἐσθῆτι for αἰσθήσει, which Spengel corrected to ἐσθῆσι.

54 The words used are ὀδυρτικωτέρως, συνεστηκότως, μαλακωτέρως, μέσως, καθεστηκότως, and ἐνθουσιαστικούς (*Politics* 1340a42–b5; cf. b10–12). For the relationship between ἦθος and πάθος in this context, see Susemihl and Hicks 1894:622–624.

55 Labarrière 1984:34–40. σημεῖον, as the unmarked term, may also apply to λόγος.

56 οὐ γὰρ ταὐτὰ οὐδ' ὡσαύτως ἂν ἀγροῖκος ἂν καὶ πεπαιδευμένος εἴπειεν (1408a31–32).

57 The material in this passage and the approach Aristotle takes is best understood if we suppose his ideas to have developed under the influence of stage acting, where the need for a successful characterization, e.g. of females by males or the old by youths, would be real and acute. Cf., for example, Plato's *Republic* 395d5–e3. Significant too is the fourth-century phenomenon of λογογραφία, which further separated composition from delivery; the professional speech writer had to place himself in his client's shoes and make him say nothing inconsistent with his origin, social status, occupation, etc. See above, p. 311 n. 76.

to avoid the appearance of artificiality and speciousness, one should not also use a harsh voice and countenance.[58]

Chapter 8 of *Rhetoric* III is yet another section where delivery is clearly in view and the canon of naturalism controls the outcome. Prose is to strike a middle course between an ἔμμετρον ('metrical') and an ἄρρυθμον σχῆμα ('arrhythmic shape'): μέτρον would make the λόγος into a ποίημα and this is to be avoided; but the lack of ἀριθμός renders the speech unformed, without boundaries, and therefore unpleasant and beyond our grasp. Aristotle has in view certain metrical shapes for cola, chosen to meet given canons of propriety detailed in this section, which avoid the sort of predictable recurrence characteristic of poetry;[59] these, he calls 'rhythm': 'Rhythm is the quantity of the pattern of *lexis*, whose sections are the meters; therefore speech must have rhythm, but not meter'.[60] But 'rhythm' is, of course, the third of the basic properties of voice (cf. 1403b30–32). This proves that we are once again dealing with ὑπόκρισις in its narrow sense of 'oral delivery'. The expressed need for σεμνότης in this context—used to disqualify the trochaic meter as 'too much like the cordax' (1408b36)—should alert us to the connection between propriety and the voice (intensity, intonation, and rhythm), a connection I have tried to highlight above (see p. 535) as I do again here. The recommendation of iambic as the λέξις of the people (οἱ πολλοί) does not focus on its abstract metrical qualities, but on its status as a performative commonplace: 'therefore, of all meters people in conversation utter (φθέγγονται λέγοντες) iambics most' (1408b34–35).

I must still consider ἁρμονία, listed as the second property of voice. There is no agreement about its meaning at 1403b31: we know it concerns τόνοι, whether the pitch is ὀξύς, βαρύς, or μέσος. Some think this refers to pitch accent at the word level,[61] but the textual evidence renders this interpretation too narrow. Cope (1877:3.5) seems to leave his options open, for he translates "accents (or

---

[58] δοκεῖ γὰρ ἀληθὲς εἶναι, ἐπεὶ οὐ λανθάνει γε ὃ ποιεῖ τὸν λέγοντα. ἔτι τοῖς ἀνάλογον μὴ πᾶσιν ἅμα χρήσασθαι· οὕτω γὰρ κλέπτεται [ὁ ἀκροατής]. λέγω δὲ οἷον ἐὰν τὰ ὀνόματα σκληρὰ ᾖ, μὴ καὶ τῇ φωνῇ καὶ τῷ προσώπῳ [καὶ τοῖς] ἁρμόττουσιν (1408b3–7). The language of 'escaping notice', 'cheating the hearer', etc. is not so much an admission of the potential for deceitfulness inherent in naturalistic art as it is a statement of the paradox essential to its success: for then *ars adeo latet arte sua*. Cf. *Rhetoric* III.2.4–5 and 8.1. Fortenbaugh (1996:161) calls to mind an interesting analogy. In *Politics* 1310a2–12, Aristotle counsels that demagogues in a democracy should *seem* to speak (δοκεῖν λέγειν) on behalf of the wealthy; whereas in an oligarchy, oligarchs should *exhibit* (ὑποκρίνεσθαι) a correspondingly favorable attitude towards the δῆμος. Fortenbaugh comments: "Those words may suggest feigned concern, and undoubtedly there are moments to be disingenuous" (161), but "[t]he verb *hypokrinesthai* ... need not imply a feigned exhibition" (161n34).

[59] ῥυθμὸν δὲ [δεῖ ἔχειν τὸν λόγον] μὴ ἀκριβῶς· τοῦτο δὲ ἔσται ἐὰν μέχρι του ᾖ (1408b31–32, supplementing from the preceding sentence).

[60] ὁ δὲ τοῦ σχήματος τῆς λέξεως ἀριθμὸς ῥυθμός ἐστιν, οὗ καὶ τὰ μέτρα τμητά. διὸ ῥυθμὸν δεῖ ἔχειν τὸν λόγον, μέτρον δὲ μή (1408b28–30).

[61] Kennedy 1991:218 and n. 5; cf. Burkett 2011:28–29.

tones of voice)" (his emphasis), and cites as *comparanda* on "the modulation of the voice in the expression of various emotions" Cicero's *De oratore* III §§215–219. In Cope 1867:380 he is nearer the rhetorical meaning when he parallels it with the Latin *apta compositio*. Of course, in its primary musical sense, it stands for "the orderly succession of certain sounds, determined by definite *intervals*, which appeals to an instinctive sense or taste in the human mind ... and constitutes 'tune' or 'melody'" (Cope 1867:380, his emphasis). The difficulty resides in transferring this concept from a musical to an oratorical context. This semantic move is attested elsewhere in Aristotle, specifically, in the *Poetics*. Indeed, at its first appearance (*Poetics* 1447a22) it refers to 'melody',[62] which explains why μέλος takes its place at a later point (1447b25).[63] But, significantly, at *Poetics* 1449a28, ἁρμονία designates a quality of prose: "For the iambic trimeter, more than any other metre, has the rhythm of speech: an indication of this is that we speak many trimeters in conversation with one another, but hexameters only rarely and when diverging from the colloquial register (ἐκβαίνοντες τῆς λεκτικῆς ἁρμονίας)."[64] Lucas (1968:86) tersely remarks *ad loc.*: "'ἁρμονίας' is said to refer to the pitch of the voice used by the Greeks in conversation (cf. R. 1403b31). We should have expected rather a reference to rhythm." Though I would take 'pitch of the voice' in the extended sense of 'melodic contour' or 'intonation' of an utterance, which was arguably the actual effect of the pitch accents at the higher level of the sentence,[65] Lucas acutely senses the intimate relationship in prose between ἁρμονία and ῥυθμός, a relationship in evidence in chapter 8 of *Rhetoric* III.[66]

The vulgate reading at *Rhetoric* 1408b32–33 is: τῶν δὲ ῥυθμῶν ὁ μὲν ἡρῷος σεμνὸς καὶ λεκτικὸς ς ἁρμονίας δεόμενος, where 'ς' is the usual abbreviation for καί. Both textual criticism and sense commend Bekker's and Spengel's text (which Cope adopts): τῶν δὲ ῥυθμῶν ὁ μὲν ἡρῷος σεμνὸς καὶ λεκτικῆς ἁρμονίας δεόμενος.[67] Kennedy (1991:238), like Kassel, follows Vettori (1548:519) instead,

---

[62] Lucas 1968 *ad loc.* writes: "I translate it by 'melody', though this does not exclude the notion of rhythm." That it entails musical tune is clear from 1447a23, which only includes instruments.

[63] The triad ῥυθμός, λόγος, and ἁρμονία at 1447a23 corresponds to ῥυθμός, μέλος, and μέτρον at 1447b25. This can be easily explained if we note that μέλος already implies words, and that μέτρον corresponds to metrical λόγος (Lucas 1968:61). 'Meters', as *Poetics* 1448b21–22 shows, are 'categories' (μόρια) of rhythms (to use Halliwell's *Loeb Classical Library* translation).

[64] Translation by Halliwell 1999. The entire passage runs thus: μάλιστα γὰρ λεκτικὸν τῶν μέτρων τὸ ἰαμβεῖόν ἐστιν· σημεῖον δὲ τούτου, πλεῖστα γὰρ ἰαμβεῖα λέγομεν ἐν τῇ διαλέκτῳ τῇ πρὸς ἀλλήλους, ἑξάμετρα δὲ ὀλιγάκις καὶ ἐκβαίνοντες τῆς λεκτικῆς ἁρμονίας (1449a24–28).

[65] Cf. Probert 2006:54–55, who in turn directs the reader to Devine and Stephens 1994:376–497.

[66] Apparently, such correlation was true even in their technical musical sense; cf. West 1992:178 and 181.

[67] See Spengel 1867:2.386–389.

who argued for the insertion of οὐ before λεκτικός,[68] and translates: "Of rhythms, the heroic [dactylic hexameter] is solemn and not conversational and needs musical intonation." To explain his translation of ἁρμονίας δεόμενος he adds the note: "That is, it is chanted. In Aristotle's time rhapsodes no longer used a lyre." The problem with this view, of course, is that one could hardly be expected to understand ἁρμονία in this unusual technical sense (i.e. 'melodic contour of non-instrumental chanting') without further explicit textual support, as its use for 'tunings' or 'attunements'[69] is by far the commonest technical one, of which the λεκτικὴ ἁρμονία is an attested extension. But by itself, ἁρμονίας δεόμενος would almost certainly be understood in its generic sense as 'lacking harmony', or, if in its technical sense, as 'lacking [instrumental] melody' or perhaps even 'needing [instrumental] melody'. 'Lacking [instrumental] melody' will not suit the contrast; 'needing [instrumental] melody' will not do either, for Kennedy's translation calls for non-instrumental chanting. As to 'lacking harmony', Cope (1877:3.86) rightly says that "[it] is absurd in itself, and contradictory to

---

[68] The *apparatus critici* in Roemer 1898 and Kassel 1976 *ad loc.* suggest that Vettori printed καὶ οὐ λεκτικός. Strictly speaking, however, although commended for its sense ("... ipse aliquando suspicatus sum desiderari particulam negandi"), neither in Vettori 1548:517–519 nor in Vettori 1579:615–617 was the emendation adopted. In either edition the Greek text reads: τῶν δὲ ῥυθμῶν, ὁ μὲν ἡρῷος, σεμνὸς καὶ λεκτικὸς καὶ ἁρμονίας δεόμενος; which he translates: "e numeris autem, herous grandis est, dignitatisque plenus et orationi aptus quique requirit harmoniam." On the assumption that the text was sound, he noted: "valet λεκτικὸς hoc in loco, sonorus ac grandiloquus. quod sane mirum videtur, cum omnis locutio λέξις a Graecis vocetur."

[69] Often called 'modes' by modern scholars, *harmoniai* represent ancient scales (i.e. distinctive series of intervals assembled as scales). In this technical sense ἁρμονία does not imply words; it might denote the music of an instrument (ψιλὴ ἁρμονία) or the voice's singing (with or without words). μέλος, on the other hand, referred primarily to the melody of singing and in this sense involved words. (Because it was the singing of poetry and it was usually accompanied by instruments, μέλος also stood for a poetic composition with musical accompaniment, especially lyric poetry.) By conceptually abstracting the music from the singing, μέλος was also at times used for ἁρμονία (West 1992:177–178). Clearly, one would be more likely to construe the statement 'the heroic meter calls for ἁρμονία' as implying that it calls for musical accompaniment than that it calls for chanting. Quite apart from the intrinsic unlikelihood of the textual reading (given the unquestionable application of ἁρμονία at 1403b31 to the voice of the orator, which rules out chanting; and the incontrovertible use of λεκτικὴ ἁρμονία in the *Poetics* 1449a28, which renders the restoration of the same expression in the present passage distinctly plausible), had this been Aristotle's meaning one would have expected τοῦ ᾄδειν δεόμενος *vel sim.* One may still argue that, for an audience familiar with the performance practice of epic (assuming *ex hypothesi* non-instrumental chanting, i.e. a reduced melody not far from speech tones; cf. West 1981:114), the meaning of ἁρμονίας δεόμενος would have been transparent: I agree. This would justify Vettori's reading and Kennedy's translation. But, even then, if ἁρμονία can be used of the melodic contour of non-instrumental chanting, given its application in the *Poetics* to the melodic contour of prose, we would still have chapter 8 of *Rhetoric* III concerned with ἁρμονία as one of the three components of φωνή that affect the orator's delivery.

the evidence of our ears, and all ancient authority." Of Vettori's emendation[70] the same writer comments that "[it] leaves ἁρμονίας δεόμενος to explain itself as it best may" (Cope 1877:3.87). But for the substitution of ἀλλά for καί, Roemer's text[71] is near identical to Spengel's and superior to Vettori's. Paradoxically, the meaning I advocate implies Kennedy's, for lacking 'the melody of common speech' suggests that 'the melody of heroic verse' (with 'melody' in its extended sense) contains non-conversational cadences such as reduced melody would produce.[72] Ross 1959 emends more heavily,[73] but his meaning is much the same in the event.[74]

Thus we have in *Rhetoric* III.8 ἁρμονία and ῥυθμός linked together as related properties of the voice in delivery: the latter denotes the measured delivery of cola for rhythmical effect, which facilitates the hearers' grasp of the orator's meaning; the former denotes the melodic contour of the speech,[75] correlated with the orator's rhythmic utterance, shaping the speech to express the necessary *ēthos* and *pathos*. This interpretation finds support in Aristoxenos, who explicitly recognized a kind of prose melody: λέγεται γὰρ δὴ καὶ λογῶδές τι μέλος, τὸ συγκείμενον ἐκ τῶν προσῳδιῶν τῶν ἐν τοῖς ὀνόμασιν· φυσικὸν γὰρ τὸ ἐπιτείνειν καὶ ἀνιέναι ἐν τῷ διαλέγεσθαι.[76] This same author also observed that 'there are three things that can be made rhythmic: utterance (λέξις),[77]

---

[70] This he quotes not as οὐ λεκτικός (as Roemer 1898 *ad loc.*) but as οὐ λογικός (Cope 1877:3.87). Cf. Demetrios *On Style* §42.

[71] τῶν δὲ ῥυθμῶν ὁ μὲν ἡρῷος σεμνὸς ἀλλὰ λεκτικῆς ἁρμονίας δεόμενος (Roemer 1898:189).

[72] Demetrios *On Style* §42 uses the term ἠχώδης. See above, pp. 343ff.

[73] τῶν δὲ ῥυθμῶν ὁ μὲν ἡρῷος σεμνῆς ἀλλ' οὐ λεκτικῆς ἁρμονίας δεόμενος.

[74] His contribution is to oppose a σεμνὴ ἁρμονία to the attested λεκτικὴ ἁρμονία, a contrast in itself plausible; and to motivate the αὐτή in the following clause: 'whereas heroic verse calls for an elevated—not a colloquial—intonation, iambic by itself [i.e. without any peculiar intonation] is the λέξις of the common people'.

[75] I do not agree with Cope (1877:3.86), who, although using 'harmony' in his translation "[to leave] open whether we are to understand by ἁρμονία 'harmony' in its ordinary musical sense," nevertheless calls this "a somewhat non-natural interpretation." The sense he favors is "an adaptation or fitting of parts into an organized whole" (i.e. 'structure' or 'style of composition'). On the impact of Greek accents upon the melodic shape of the utterance, see Allen 1973:230–234, West 1981:114–115, and p. 539 n. 65 above.

[76] *Elementa harmonica* 23.13–16 (da Rios). Barker translates: "For there is indeed said to be a kind of melody which belongs to speech, that constituted by the tone-patterns that occur in words, since tension and relaxation belong naturally to speech" (1984–1989:2.138).

[77] That Aristoxenos here means 'utterance' (the action of λέγειν) and not 'style' or any other more technical meaning is clear from its use in *Elementa rhythmica* 17.15–23 (Pighi): ὥσπερ γὰρ τὸ σῶμα πλείους ἰδέας λαμβάνει σχημάτων, ἐὰν αὐτοῦ τὰ μέρη τεθῇ διαφερόντως, ἤτοι πάντα ἢ τινα αὐτῶν, οὕτω καὶ τῶν ῥυθμιζομένων ἕκαστον πλείους λαμβάνει μορφάς, οὐ κατὰ τὴν αὐτοῦ φύσιν, ἀλλὰ κατὰ τὴν τοῦ ῥυθμοῦ. ἡ γὰρ αὐτὴ λέξις εἰς χρόνους τεθεῖσα διαφέροντας ἀλλήλων λαμβάνει τινὰς διαφορὰς τοιαύτας, αἵ εἰσιν ἴσαι αὐταῖς τῆς τοῦ ῥυθμοῦ φύσεως διαφοραῖς. ὁ αὐτὸς δὲ λόγος καὶ ἐπὶ τοῦ μέλους καὶ εἴ τι ἄλλο πέφυκε ῥυθμίζεσθαι τῷ τοιούτῳ ῥυθμῷ ὅς ἐστιν ἐκ χρόνων συνεστηκώς. Barker (1984–1989:2.185) translates the key sentence as follows: "For the same

melody (μέλος), and bodily motion; thus utterance will divide time by means of its own parts, e.g. letters, syllables, words, and all such things'.[78] A fragment of Theophrastos in Plutarch's *Quaestiones convivales* I.5.2 (623a) further reinforces the analogy between the melody and rhythm of music and the melody and rhythm of speech: [Θεόφραστος] ἀρχὰς μουσικῆς τρεῖς εἶναι λέγει, λύπην ἡδονὴν ἐνθουσιασμόν, ὡς ἑκάστου τούτων παρατρέποντος ἐκ τοῦ συνήθους καὶ ἐγκλίνοντος τὴν φωνήν (fr. 90 Wimmer).[79] In *De oratore* III §§173ff. Cicero follows Aristotle in connecting *numerus* (~ῥυθμός) and *modus* (~ἁρμονία). His usage is not uniform throughout; e.g. at §171, when he first introduces them, he apparently designates rhythm by *modus quidam* and harmonia by *forma*;[80] but once he employs the more technical *numerus*, he makes clear that *modus* stands for *harmonia*:

> Namque haec duo musici, qui erant quondam idem poetae, machinati ad voluptatem sunt, versum atque cantum, ut et verborum numero et

---

utterance [*lexis*], when disposed into durations that differ from one another, takes on differences of a sort that are equal to the differences in the nature of the rhythm themselves." Of manifest significance is the aural effect of the words in performance, a significance best captured by the gloss 'utterance', which notionally subsumes any particular rhythmic realization. We find a similar use of λέξις at Aristotle's *Sophistical Refutations* 165b23–24 and *Rhetoric* 1401a1, where παρὰ τὴν λέξιν is variously translated 'verbal', 'of diction', 'depends on language', 'beruhen auf dem sprachlichen Ausdruck', *vel sim.* Cf. Halliwell (1993:53–54), who identifies three different ways in which Aristotle uses λέξις; though I am not entirely comfortable with the manner in which he apportions the semantic range and with the illustrations adduced in support, he does to my mind correctly identify the two ends of the spectrum: "ordinary speech," roughly equivalent to my 'utterance', and "style or expressiveness," an evaluative term that, among other things, focuses on register, genre, and tone. (I would transfer to his category C some of his examples for B that, by his own admission, display a "semantic emphasis.")

78 *Elementa rhythmica* 19.15–18 (Pighi): ἔστι δὲ τὰ ῥυθμιζόμενα τρία· λέξις, μέλος, κίνησις σωματική. ὥστε διαιρήσει τὸν χρόνον ἡ μὲν λέξις τοῖς αὐτῆς μέρεσιν, οἷον γράμμασι καὶ συλλαβαῖς καὶ ῥήμασι καὶ πᾶσι τοῖς τοιούτοις. This division of λέξις is indebted to Aristotle's treatment in the *Poetics* 20. For Aristoxenos' *Elementa rhythmica* see now Marchetti 2009. The passage immediately above is found in Marchetti 2009:37 §9, with translation at 67 and commentary at 116–119. Marchetti's rendering of λέξις as 'text' is disappointingly flat and I cannot endorse it. He considers more broadly its Aristoxenian meaning at 92–99 ("a group of words chosen by the poet but which may be composed into different verses in different word order" 98). Although Barker (1984–1989:2.186) *ad loc.* prints the standard gloss 'diction', as noted in the footnote immediately above at §4 (=17.19 Pighi) he renders it more pointedly as 'utterance'.

79 The text suffers from various uncertainties which do not, however, affect the point for which I quote it. Hubert in his *Teubner* edition prints it thus: λέγει δὲ μουσικῆς ἀρχὰς τρεῖς εἶναι, λύπην, ἡδονήν, ἐνθουσιασμόν, ὡς ἑκάστου τῶν … αὐτῶν παρατρέ⟨ποντος⟩ ἐκ τοῦ συνήθους ⟨καὶ παρ-⟩ εγκλίνοντος τὴν φωνήν. Fortenbaugh et al. (1992:572–575 fr. 719A) adopt Bernardakis emendation τῶν ⟨παθῶν⟩ τούτων for τῶν … αὐτῶν and translate: "[A]nd he says that there are three sources of music, pain, pleasure and inspiration; for each of these emotions turns the voice aside and deflects it from its usual (inflection)" (575).

80 May and Wisse (2001:276) *ad loc.* translate them as 'cadence' and 'form'. At §173 Cicero repeats the terms: *modus etiam et forma verborum.*

vocum modo delectatione vincerent aurium satietatem. Haec igitur duo, vocis dico moderationem et verborum conclusionem, quoad orationis severitas pati posset, a poetica ad eloquentiam traducenda duxerunt. (§174)

The musicians—who at one time were also poets—had devised two ways of giving pleasure, verse and song; they wanted to overcome satiety of the ears by giving delight, both through the rhythm of the words and the cadence of the voice. And the ancients thought that these two things, I mean modulating the voice and rounding off a sentence rhythmically, should be transferred from poetry to eloquence, as far as the serious nature of oratory would permit.[81]

In this case, of course, the vocal melody will depend on notions of intonation and rhythm that are more familiar to us than the ancient Greek modulation, of which tonal accents were so important a component. One can speak similarly of the famous chapters 39–41 of [Longinos] *Peri hypsous*, written at a time when accentual stress had replaced pitch; and yet these sections preserve a recollection of the Aristotelian connection between ἁρμονία and ῥυθμοί in the orator's choice and arrangement of words (σύνθεσις).[82]

This survey, I trust, has shown that, far from excluding ὑπόκρισις, Aristotle has more than once explicitly made voice and its properties the focus of his study in chapters 2–11 of *Rhetoric* III. Considering the notorious thematic compression characteristic of this work, his coverage, in substance and significance, is such as to warrant the view that he does indeed endeavor to instruct the orator in proper delivery, if only we suppress anachronistic prejudices of what an adequate, comprehensive treatment of *pronuntiatio* by the philosopher should look like. My survey completed, I return to the peculiar Aristotelian relation between ὑπόκρισις and λέξις.

---

[81] May and Wisse 2001:278 *ad loc.* Wilkins 1892 *ad loc.* comments: "[H]ere [*modus*] covers variations both in duration and in pitch, i.e. what we call 'tune'." He further translates *vocis moderatio* 'the modulation of the voice', and *verborum conclusio* 'the periodic arrangement of the words'. I might also mention Hermogenes *Peri ideōn* I, where rhythm is defined thus: … καὶ τὸ ἐξ ἀμφοῖν τούτοιν [sc. συνθέσεών τε καὶ ἀναπαύσεων] συνιστάμενον ὁ ῥυθμός· ἡ γὰρ ποιὰ σύνθεσις τῶν τοῦ λόγου μερῶν καὶ τὸ ὡδί πως ἀναπεπαῦσθαι τὸν λόγον ἀλλὰ μὴ ὡδὶ ποιεῖ τὸ τοιόνδε ἀλλὰ μὴ τοιόνδε εἶναι τὸν ῥυθμόν (p. 218.22–26 Rabe).

[82] See especially §39.

13.5 Semantic Development of Ὑπόκρισις and Λέξις

In light of the foregoing considerations, regardless of the particular rendering of καί in ἐπεὶ καί at 1403b36 (cf. above, p. 526), it is important to bring out the relationship Aristotle is establishing between ὑπόκρισις and λέξις—here, that of a part to the whole, but soon to become somewhat more involved. For from 1403b18–22 and the ensuing treatment it follows that ὑπόκρισις (at least any aspect of ὑπόκρισις susceptible of 'technical' treatment, as I will clarify below, p. 583) bears such a relationship to λέξις that either term can be used to designate what might be broadly described as 'rhetorical stylistics.'[83] This intimate connection of mutual implication between ὑπόκρισις and λέξις is one that Aristotle labors to establish and explain in chapters 1 and 2 of *Rhetoric* III; and the explicit return of the term ὑπόκρισις in chapter 12, at the end of the section on λέξις (the philosopher takes up τάξις in chapter 13) should alert us to the possible presence of an intentional ring structure of sorts: ὑπόκρισις may well open and close the discussion of λέξις because, in fact, Aristotle sees successful delivery as the ultimate aim and guiding principle of his study of rhetorical style.

The term ὑπόκρισις, first employed at 1403b22 to refer to that subordinate division of λέξις that wields the greatest influence and is preeminently concerned with voice and its attendant properties, becomes at 1404a12–19, from the point of view of terminology, synonymous with λέξις itself, as I explain below.[84] This is perhaps not to be wondered at, for by exchanging the terms Aristotle merely uses the most important facet of λέξις to refer metonymically to it. The corresponding semantic development takes place in a passage prompted by the ethically equivocal status of λέξις, which becomes a necessary expedient because of rhetoric's concern with δόξα:

> ἀλλ᾿ ὅλης οὔσης πρὸς δόξαν τῆς πραγματείας τῆς περὶ τὴν ῥητορικήν, οὐκ ὀρθῶς ἔχοντος ἀλλ᾿ ὡς ἀναγκαίου τὴν ἐπιμέλειαν ποιητέον, ἐπεὶ τό γε δίκαιον μηδὲν πλείω ζητεῖ περὶ τὸν λόγον ἢ ὡς μήτε λυπεῖν μήτ᾿ εὐφραίνειν· δίκαιον γὰρ αὐτοῖς ἀγωνίζεσθαι τοῖς πράγμασιν, ὥστε τἆλλα ἔξω τοῦ ἀποδεῖξαι περίεργά ἐστιν· ἀλλ᾿ ὅμως μέγα δύναται, καθάπερ εἴρηται, διὰ τὴν τοῦ ἀκροατοῦ μοχθηρίαν. τὸ μὲν οὖν τῆς λέξεως ὅμως ἔχει τι μικρὸν ἀναγκαῖον ἐν πάσῃ διδασκαλίᾳ· διαφέρει γάρ τι πρὸς τὸ

---

[83] See below, pp. 583 and 588.
[84] See below, p. 582.

δηλῶσαι ὡδὶ ἢ ὡδὶ εἰπεῖν· οὐ μέντοι τοσοῦτον, ἀλλ' ἅπαντα φαντασία ταῦτ' ἐστί, καὶ πρὸς τὸν ἀκροατήν· διὸ οὐδεὶς οὕτω γεωμετρεῖν διδάσκει.[85]

Rhetoric 1404a1–12

But since the whole business of rhetoric is with opinion, one should pay attention to it [sc. to the matter of *lexis*],[86] not as being right but necessary, since justice, to be sure, does not at all seek more in oral argument than to cause neither pain nor pleasure; for to contend only with the facts is just, whence it follows that everything beside demonstration is incidental; this fact notwithstanding,[87] it has great power, as noted, because of the baseness of the hearer. Now then,[88] even so[89] the subject of *lexis* has some small necessary place in every demonstrative discipline, for speaking this way or that makes some difference to getting across clearly; yet not so great [a difference] but all this is

---

85   Here as elsewhere I quote Kassel 1976 *ad loc.* Ross's Greek text, despite differences in detail, ultimately bears the same meaning. He emends the vulgate οὐκ ὀρθῶς at 1404a2–3 to οὐχ ὡς ὀρθῶς; but an explicit ὡς is not required and, as Spengel (1867:2.357) notes, should be understood here from the ἀλλ' ὡς that follows. Kassel emends ζητεῖν to ζητεῖ at 1404a4; and preserves πλείω at 1404a4 and ὡς at 1404a5 over against the πλέον and ὥστε suggested by the old Latin translation (and adopted by Ross). Yet other than emphasis there is hardly a difference between 'justice is to seek nothing more (μηδὲν πλέον) than' and 'justice does not at all (μηδὲν) seek more (πλείω) than'. I prefer the transmitted infinitive ζητεῖν to Kassel's indicative ('justice is not at all to seek more than'), since ζητεῖ would call for οὐδέν. As to ἢ ὥστε vis-à-vis ἢ ὡς, the choice is semantically indifferent (cf. Smyth §2007).

86   The immediate referent in agreement with the neuters ἔχοντος and ἀναγκαίου is τὸ περὶ τὴν λέξιν at 1403b36. Alternatively, the referent might be ὑπόκρισις (from αὕτη/αὐτή at 1403b27) or τὰ περὶ τὴν ὑπόκρισιν (from 1403b22). The translation would then be: 'not as being a right, but a necessary, thing'. These more distant potential referents, however, are far less likely than the proximate τὸ περὶ τὴν λέξιν, whose case is further buttressed by its reappearance at 1404a8 in the form τὸ τῆς λέξεως. See further below, p. 581 (with n. 6). My grammatical and contextual analysis, here and below, demonstrates (*contra* Burkett 2011:36 and others) that one should not think of τὸ τῆς λέξεως as a new subject (or digression) introduced at 1404a8—a notion that, if true, would call for an earlier contrasting referent, presumably 'delivery' (ὑπόκρισις) viewed as distinct from 'style' (λέξις). The text controverts this reading: i) by unambiguously subsuming τὸ τῆς λέξεως under φαντασία 'towards the *hearer*' (πρὸς τὸν ἀκροατήν 1404a11–12, my emphasis), thus evincing that Aristotle has *aural* effects in mind (i.e. 'delivery'); and ii) by stating that its 'coming into vogue' will accomplish the same as ἡ ὑποκριτική (1404a13), plainly echoing 1403b22–26 where ὑπόκρισις is undeniably in view (and not some notion of λέξις allegedly distinct from 'delivery').

87   This ὅμως concedes that μέγα δύναται seemingly controverts τἆλλα … περίεργά ἐστιν.

88   This μὲν οὖν is transitional (see Denniston 1954:470–473), with retrospective οὖν inferentially regarding μέγα δύναται and prospective μέν anticipating the adversative οὐ μέντοι in 1404a10 (which substitutes for οὐ δέ; cf. Denniston 1954:404 §2.i).

89   This ὅμως acknowledges that the need for *lexis* in every demonstrative discipline seemingly controverts that it owes its efficacy to the baseness of the hearer.

a matter of how things will appear to the listener. Therefore, nobody teaches geometry this way.[90]

This passage contains a remarkable admission regarding the entire rhetorical enterprise, one that belies the attempt of some to restrict to ὑπόκρισις the unflattering δοκεῖ φορτικὸν εἶναι of 1403b36–1404a1, which has instead τὸ περὶ τὴν λέξιν as its proper subject.[91] On the contrary, μέγα δύναται (1404a7), as καθάπερ εἴρηται underscores, merely restates ὃ δύναμιν μὲν ἔχει μεγίστην (1403b21), and the correspondence between these two statements presupposes a clear, if qualified, equivalence between τὰ περὶ τὴν ὑπόκρισιν at 1403b22 and τὸ περὶ τὴν λέξιν as the implicit subject carried over from 1403b36 into this section. It is impossible, therefore, to divorce the philosopher's notions of λέξις and ὑπόκρισις. Accordingly, even Cope 1877 *ad loc.* must make the following admission: "[N]ot only ὑποκριτική, but the whole of Rhetoric, is directed πρὸς δόξαν. So that φορτικόν here must stand, as it often does, for the vulgarity which is shewn in unphilosophical habits of mind ... and, as applied to a study or art, may signify popular, showy, unsubstantial."

If Aristotle in this section considers λέξις an expedient, strictly speaking it is such only from the point of view of an ideal society. We are not faced here with an avoidable course of action, and therefore an unprincipled choice out of personal ease, selfish gain, or self-promotion. This is not to deny, of course, that a given speaker may harbor ethically dubious motivations; but the philosopher's point is that even an orator with the purest of intentions must have recourse to oral delivery, because no polis can boast of citizens who will embrace the bare facts of an issue without having to overcome the potential obstacles of misunderstanding and prejudice. The triumph of the ἔξω τοῦ ἀποδεῖξαι[92]—arguably necessary, but, in strict justice, superfluous[93]—is perhaps best exemplified by

---

[90] This translation draws on the discussion that follows.

[91] For my reasons to identify τὸ περὶ τὴν λέξιν as the subject, see immediately above (n. 86) and below (p. 547); see, further, p. 581 (with n. 6).

[92] On the related ἔξω τοῦ πράγματος see above, p. 536 n. 50. τὸ ἀποδεῖξαι here refers narrowly to rational demonstration (i.e. the enthymeme derived from πρᾶγμα or λόγος); for ἀπόδειξις and ἀποδεικνύναι in the *Rhetoric* see Grimaldi 1972:139–141.

[93] Too much has been made of 1404a2–7, which states that 'justice (τὸ δίκαιον) consists in not at all seeking more in connection with one's argument (or 'speech', περὶ τὸν λόγον) than that one should cause neither pain nor pleasure' (hinting at *pathos*, cf. 1378a20–22); and that 'it is just to contend (ἀγωνίζεσθαι) only with the facts' (αὐτοῖς τοῖς πράγμασιν). Accordingly, some infer that departing from this ideal would not be merely undesirable, but even *unjust*; and they think that οὐκ ὀρθῶς ἔχοντος at 1404a2–3 corroborates this view. But the comparison aims not at discriminating justice from injustice, but at evoking an ideal vision of what strict justice calls for. Although ἀγωνίζεσθαι can be used of an epideictic competition (or even a political debate), I think here Aristotle is primarily thinking of the court setting, which leads him naturally to state this ideal in terms of 'justice'. Justice, strictly speaking, must always bind defendant and plaintiff

the abuse to which it is open, e.g. by the base appeal to emotions, a practice, however, not exclusively the province of delivery (strictly considered),[94] but arguably most readily illustrated by the use of the φωνή, namely, πῶς αὐτῇ δεῖ χρῆσθαι πρὸς ἕκαστον πάθος (1403b27-28).[95] Thus, ὑπόκρισις understood strictly as 'delivery' becomes the preeminent exhibit in the trial against the potentially unethical facets of λέξις, and the connection made *exempli gratia* with the upper hand the ὑποκριταί have over ποιηταί (a parallel extended next to the political arena) follows all too naturally (1403b32-35). But even if ὑπόκρισις is 'exhibit A' (so to speak), Aristotle wishes to apply the conclusion to λέξις as a whole, as the syntactic agreement of φορτικόν with τὸ περὶ τὴν λέξιν makes clear (1403b36-1404a1), notwithstanding the efforts of many to construe the grammar otherwise.[96] From that point onward, the text is primarily engaged with λέξις (principally in its neuter form, τὸ περὶ τὴν λέξιν[97] or, at 1404a8, τὸ

---

to the facts of the case: the facts are their one and only necessary point of reference; strictly speaking, everything else must be judged superfluous. This does *not* mean, however, that the contribution of *ēthos* and *pathos* is *unjust*; simply that justice does not *require* it. This interpretation is conclusively proved by the ὥστε clause, which declares whatever else (τἄλλα) falls outside the realm of demonstration *not* unjust, but 'superfluous', περίεργα. Therefore, in 'not because it is right' (οὐκ ὀρθῶς) 'right' does not mean 'morally right' (with 'unjust' or 'morally wrong' as its opposite), but 'correct', as in 'the correct choice', the choice demanded and strictly justified by the circumstances (its opposite, then, being 'erroneous' or 'incorrect'). This is similar to its use in the expression ὀρθῶς λέγειν, 'strictly speaking' (cf. LSJ s.v. ὀρθός III.2), where accuracy and inaccuracy, correctness and error, are opposed, not justice and injustice. Jebb's translation conveys the meaning well: "... we must give our attention to this subject, considered as necessary, not as desirable in itself; for, strictly speaking, our sole aim in our language should be to give neither pain nor pleasure; our facts ought to be our sole weapons." Cf. also Dufour and Wartelle 1973 *ad loc.* On ὀρθός, Irwin (1985:391) writes: "'*Orthos*' indicates success in pursuing an end or correctness in picking it (1144a20), as opposed to error ... . It is not confined to moral rightness: nor is any special moral sense of the term required."

94 Is not striking imagery itself (to mention only one aspect of the wider field of style) quite able forcefully to affect the emotions of the hearers? Rapp (2002:2.814 §3.1) suggests that Aristotle's goal is to move the ethically objectionable ὑπόκρισις off the center of his study, in order to focus instead on those aspects of style that do not so crassly take advantage of the μοχθηρία of the hearers: "Der mündliche Vortrag wird als eine Sache der Begabung vom Zentrum der folgenden Überlegungen ausgeschlossen. Die sich tatsächlich anschließende Behandlung der sprachlichen Form konzentriert sich dagegen auf die Erleichterung des Verstehenprozesses." But here, realizing keenly that this, too, looks to affect the hearer in ways that go beyond a strict appeal to the facts themselves, he tellingly adds: "... was zwar auch *wirkungsbezogen* ist, gleichzeitig jedoch in den Dienst der Sache gestellt werden kann" (my emphasis). With this admission, the case against ὑπόκρισις contracts to whether Rapp is right in asserting—I submit that he is not—that Aristotle thinks of 'delivery' strictly as a matter of talent and not susceptible of technical treatment.

95 Cf. *De interpretatione* I 16a3-4: ἔστι μὲν οὖν τὰ ἐν τῇ φωνῇ τῶν ἐν τῇ ψυχῇ παθημάτων σύμβολα.

96 On this see immediately above, p. 545 n. 86, and further below, p. 581 n. 6.

97 As noted above, p. 545 n. 86, this must be the noun phrase implicitly in agreement at 1404a3 with the participle ἔχοντος and the adjective ἀναγκαίου.

τῆς λέξεως) and calls on ὑπόκρισις only subordinately, to make the wider point concerning λέξις by mutual implication.[98]

According to Aristotle (1404a8–10) attention to style has a small but necessary place in every διδασκαλία, for it makes a difference to clarity (πρὸς τὸ δηλῶσαι), yet not so much (τοσοῦτον)—i.e. its importance should not be overstated—but all this is φαντασία directed towards the hearer.[99] πρὸς τὸ δηλῶσαι must not be overly restricted to *intellectual* clarity[100] (as Rapp 2002:2.815 implicitly

---

[98] Here again my understanding diverges from Rapp's, much the most sensitive and careful of recent readers of the *Rhetoric*, whose translation and commentary of *Rhetoric* III is the most important extended treatment of that book to appear since Cope 1877. Rapp (2002:2.812 §1) understands the uncertainty facing the reader as to the respective boundaries of ὑπόκρισις and λέξις: "[D]ie vorigen Abschnitte [erweckten] den Eindruck ... als handle es sich beim mündlichen Vortrag und der sprachlichen Form um zwei klar voneinander getrennte Bereiche." But 1403b35–36, he adds insightfully, hints "dass das vorliegende Kapitel von einem Diskussionsstand ausgeht, auf dem sprachliche Form und mündlicher Vortrag eng miteinander verknüpft sind, bzw. letzterer einen Teilbereich der sprachlichen Form ausmacht." I find his suggestion misguided, however, that the conceptual development of the argument lies in so delimiting the purview of style that a discussion of delivery, its subordinate component, can be excluded. At 2.814 §3.1, after recalling that it is "durchaus unklar, inwieweit vom mündlichen Vortrag und inwieweit von der sprachlichen Form ... die Rede ist," he offers two possible explanations to καὶ δοκεῖ φορτικὸν εἶναι (1403b36–1404a1). The first, which I believe correct, flows readily from the text (as he himself admits): "Gemeint ist tatsächlich die sprachliche Form, denn zu Beginn des Abschnitts wird ausdrücklich das genannt, 'was die sprachliche Form betrifft'. Dann würde auch für die Behandlung der sprachlichen Form gelten, dass sie nur notwendig, aber nicht richtig ist." The second posits as aim a limited concept of style, one that has been "bereinigt," 'cleaned up' (so to say), from which delivery has been excluded, and that focuses on clarity of meaning. But the alleged goal (which I here dispute) of an unimpeachable λέξις that makes clarity its sole ambition proves elusive: for why then would Aristotle add that 'no one teaches geometry thus' (1404a12)? If in fact λέξις (in its alleged restricted sense) pursues clarity (διαφέρει γάρ τι πρὸς τὸ δηλῶσαι 1404a9–10), why would it not *also* apply to geometry and every other philosophical or scientific inquiry? But if geometry can achieve clarity without recourse to style, why should not the orator who renounces an appeal to man's baser inclinations not simply dispense with style altogether? The conclusion seems inescapable: if with a view to its effect upon the hearer ("aus Gründen der Wirkung") the orator is willing to compromise intelligibility (as Rapp claims), and, therefore, clarity becomes a stylistic trait—with style teaching us to negotiate the corresponding trade-off—how can λέξις be said to have escaped ethical indictment? Newman 2005 is another recent work that, while taking Aristotelian *lexis* seriously as more than rhetorical ornament, still views it narrowly through the lens of 'intellectual clarity' without reference to 'delivery'—as if that were all that the philosopher meant when he asserted, ὡρίσθω λέξεως ἀρετὴ σαφῆ εἶναι (*Rhetoric* 1404b1–2; cf. *Poetics* 1458a18). In rhetorical theory and practice 'expressive clarity' cannot—and for Aristotle emphatically did not—exclude full-blown consideration of ὑπόκρισις.

[99] I take καὶ πρὸς τὸν ἀκροατήν as epexegetic (cf. Smyth §2869a), i.e. as adding by way of clarification: 'I mean [φαντασία] towards the hearer'.

[100] That is, it must not be overly restricted to such clarity of thought and argument, including a perspicuous prose style, as would characterize a well-written, readily intelligible book. In the *Rhetoric* the pragmatics of oral delivery is of controlling importance for Aristotelian λέξις. Not so for his divergent conceptualization in the *Poetics*, where he defines λέξις as ἡ διὰ τῆς ὀνομασίας ἑρμηνεία (1450b13–14). This allows him at 1456b10 to sever 'poetics' from ἡ ὑποκριτική—here,

does by referring to "Gedanken" and "die gedankliche Anordnung"): Aristotle has in view such a presentation before the hearer as communicates persuasively to him in full the expressive aims of the speaker, not only conveying clearly his *logos* (in the limited sense of 1356a3–4) but also projecting a distinct *ēthos* and by its lucidity affecting the audience with the intended *pathē*.[101] Thus, at 1404b1–3, where ὁ λόγος is characterized as a kind of sign (σημεῖον γάρ τι ὁ λόγος ὤν) that fails to achieve its proper end unless it make its meaning clear (ἐὰν μὴ δηλοῖ), the philosopher implicitly calls to mind the entire communication process, with the complete circle of its constituent parts (cf. 1408a25–26).[102] It is true that here 'clarity' is ascribed to 'proper words' (τὰ κύρια ὀνόματα) and stylistic propriety to all the others mentioned in the *Poetics* 1457b1–3: loan word, metaphor, ornament, neologism, lengthening, contraction, and modification (Halliwell's terms in his *Loeb Classical Library* translation).[103] If this appears, on the surface, to restrict clarity to a mere subset of the whole range of stylistic devices (word order among them; cf. 1407b21–25 and 1410a19–22), this is but a distorted impression that fails to account for what the philosopher says or implies elsewhere. So, for example, metaphors, just classified among the τἆλλα ὀνόματα

---

understood as '[dramatic] delivery' and encompassing the knowledge of forms of utterance (τὰ σχήματα τῆς λέξεως)—as different kinds of investigation (*Poetics* 1456b8–19). On Aristotle's divergent analyses of poetic and rhetorical *lexis*, see further above, p. 529 n. 31, and below, p. 588. Cf. Morpurgo Tagliabue 1967:201–207, Halliwell 1986:344–349, and Halliwell 1993. Newman's emphasis on 'clarity' and her controlling focus on 'metaphor' prevents her from registering clearly the differences between the philosopher's respective notions of poetic and rhetorical style.

[101] Rapp (2002:2.816) uses 'Gedanken' to gloss διάνοια, which at 1403a36 seems to encompass *ēthos* and *pathos* insofar as addressed in Books I and II of the *Rhetoric*, where they are covered from the point of view of εὕρησις (cf. Grimaldi 1988:369 and *Poetics* 1456a33–b7). But his discussion suggests that with 'Gedanken' he regards *conceptual* perspicuity only. Cf. Rapp 2002:2.829 §3 and his clear statement at 2.804: "Der Gedanke ist das, was dasselbe bleibt, wenn sich die sprachliche Form allein ändert."

[102] Here I follow Ross, who adopts an emendation in Richards 1915:111 that is clearly superior to the *paradosis*: it not only accounts for the otherwise troublesome ὡς but makes for a more coherent explanation of the importance of clarity. By justifying the need for perspicuity on the grounds of the *logos* otherwise missing its target, the transmitted text offers a circular argument. Kassel's edition prints Vahlen's ὥστ' for the ὡς of cod. Parisinus 1741 (Vahlen 1867:262), a fine alternative that Kennedy 1991 and Rapp 2002 prefer. Both Ross and Kassel read τι for ὅτι. Their texts make largely the same point; either: 'for *logos*, since it is a kind of sign, will not perform its proper function unless ...' (Ross); or: 'for *logos* [is] a kind of sign, so that it will not perform its proper function unless ...'. Here *logos* is best understood as 'articulate speech' (cf. *Poetics* 1457a23–24 and *De interpretatione* 16b26–27) and as implying the speaker's oral argument.

[103] If we do not usually think of a 'metaphor' as a 'word' (ὄνομα), Aristotle does: ἅπαν δὲ ὄνομά ἐστιν ἢ κύριον ἢ γλῶττα ἢ μεταφορὰ ἢ κόσμος ἢ πεποιημένον ἢ ἐπεκτεταμένον ἢ ὑφηρημένον ἢ ἐξηλλαγμένον. Cf. Newman 2005:29; and Lucas 1968: "μεταφορά means both the transference of a word from its usual reference and the word so transferred" (204). Burkett (2011:79–80) condemns as an "error" the notion of 'metaphor' as "*one* word" (his emphasis).

that contribute to propriety of style, are nevertheless ranked at 1404b31–32 with τὰ κύρια and τὰ οἰκεῖα as alone being serviceable (χρήσιμα) to prose style, so that, if one composes (with these) well, "there will be an unfamiliar quality and [the composing may] escape notice and *will be clear* (σαφηνιεῖ 1404b36–37)."[104] In other words: we must grant a wider role to form, *including* ornamentation generally, in bringing about the requisite perspicuity;[105] and since form is connected with sense perception, this implies that φαντασία is instrumental to clarity and must be part and parcel of effective communication. The οὐ μέντοι τοσοῦτον at 1404a10–11 ('yet not so much') finds its conceptual (negative) correlative in the ἀλλά clause. The one who wishes to claim too broad a role for λέξις, Aristotle says, should consider that it works on the hearer through φαντασία: this fact will help him the better to give it its due measure, neither under- nor overestimating its import. Happily, the philosopher does not leave us to feel our way blindly to the understanding of φαντασία, but has already given us a working definition at 1370a28–30:[106] it is said to be 'a kind of weak perception' (αἴσθησις),

---

[104] Kennedy 1991:223 *ad loc.*, slightly modified (my emphasis).

[105] It may be well further to drive this point home with the aid of another passage. There, quite apart from strict conceptual clarity, we learn that, when it comes to *ēthos* (and the same might be said of the designs of *pathos* on the affections of the audience) it is essential to communicate it clearly if it is to gain its proper end: '[T]he [forensic] narrative must indicate character (ἠθικήν); and it shall be so if we know what makes for *ēthos*. One way, indeed, is to make the motivation clear (τὸ προαίρεσιν δηλοῦν); [then] the *ēthos*, of a certain kind, by the motivation being such; and the motivation, of a given sort, by its end' (1417a16–19). [In translating προαίρεσις by 'motivation' (which should be understood as *deliberate* purpose), I follow *Nicomachean Ethics* 1139a31– 33: πράξεως μὲν οὖν ἀρχὴ προαίρεσις—ὅθεν ἡ κίνησις ἀλλ᾽ οὐχ οὗ ἕνεκα—προαιρέσεως δὲ ὄρεξις καὶ λόγος ὁ ἕνεκά τινος.] Though this comment belongs to the section on τάξις and no particular stylistic devices to secure a strong ethical cast are mentioned, it is clear from the observations at 1404b18–25 that style, particularly the stylistic register selected, will further or hinder this goal insofar as it lends conviction to, or detracts from, the portrayal of the man who is (so goes the claim) motivated thus, and acts in accordance with the alleged purposes: one must seem to speak in his own voice or else he will fail to persuade his audience. This explains why τὸ πρέπον, 'propriety'—here meant as *stylistic* propriety—immediately follows clarity as the λέξεως ἀρετή. Cf. Halliwell 1993:57n12, where he makes a distinction between the "referential" and "expressive" uses of δηλοῦν in the *Rhetoric*, and lists some examples.

[106] ἐπεὶ … , ἡ δὲ φαντασία ἐστὶν αἴσθησίς τις ἀσθενής, καὶ [κἀεὶ?] ἐν τῷ μεμνημένῳ καὶ τῷ ἐλπίζοντι ἀκολουθοῖ ἂν φαντασία τις οὗ μέμνηται ἢ ἐλπίζει, … ('Since … , and [since] *phantasia* is a kind of weak perception, and in the one who recalls or hopes some sort of *phantasia* of what he is recalling or hoping for will [always?] go with [his remembering or hoping], …'). This passage is notoriously difficult and textually uncertain. Here I print Kassel's text and, with Cope, assume that the protasis εἰ δὲ τοῦτο at 1370a30 resumptively sums up the ἐπεί clauses and the optative ἀκολουθοῖ ἄν ('—if this [is so] …'). See Grimaldi 1980:251–252 and cf. *Rhetoric* 1362a29–31 on ἀκολουθέω (the optative does not so much make the attendance of *phantasia* a likely contingency as it rhetorically softens the statement the more gently to invite and elicit the assent of the reader to it). The bibliography on Aristotelian *phantasia* is massive. A partial list might include Freudenthal 1863, Cosenza 1968, Nussbaum 1978:221–269, Schofield 1992 [1978], Armisen-Marchetti 1979, Armisen-Marchetti 1980, Watson 1982, Ward 1984, Labarrière 1984,

connected not only with sense perception but also with the mental faculties of memory and hope. Nevertheless, it appears to be the universal assumption of the translators of this passage that by φαντασία Aristotle means 'external show', 'mere appearance', 'fancy'.[107] The reasons for this unanimity seem obvious: the appeals to μοχθηρία and φορτικόν (1403b35; 1404a1, a8) arguably call for a negative judgment; the concern with λέξις, Aristotle admits, far from desirable in itself, is but a necessary concession (1404a2–3); ideally, what is not strict demonstration should be superfluous (1404a6–7); the often assumed close tie between δηλῶσαι and *conceptual* clarity seems designed to render the bulk of stylistic analysis external show, superficial fancy.

13.5.1 Φαντασία, 'mere fancy'?

Nevertheless, there are good reasons to resist this interpretive consensus. Though perhaps understandable, it is but the fruit of our own prejudices against rhetoric and issues from a live suspicion of what this art portends for the pursuit of truth. Such mistrust has a distinguished ancient pedigree: the mention of μοχθηρία and the use of φορτικόν show that Aristotle is not impervious to it. All the same, I claim that the philosopher's attitude is far less negative (and, thus, more balanced) than the one that prevails among us, and that if we translate φαντασία as 'mere appearance' *vel sim.* we displace the center of gravity of his corrective and drive it to an unintended extreme. Let us revisit the reasons adduced for the consensus view. One may well regret the reality of μοχθηρία (who would not decry the weaknesses that play into the hand of oratorical abuse seeking to tread the 'facts' underfoot?), yet it is but a consequence of the ethical cast inherent in any political[108] process.[109] This is clear from the contrast

---

Rispoli 1985, Wedin 1988, Watson 1988, Fattori and Bianchi 1988, Frede 1992, Turnbull 1994, Sisko 1995, Caston 1996, Everson 1997, Labarrière 1997, Lefebvre 1997a and 1997b, Busche 1997, Manieri 1998, Lefebvre 1999, Formigari et al. 1999, Birondo 2001, Lefebvre 2001–2002, Barnouw 2002:49–147, Labarrière 2002 and 2003, Lefebvre 2003, Busche 2003, Veloso 2004, Krow 2005, O'Gorman 2005, Linguiti 2006, Stevens 2006, González 2006, Yurdin 2008, Riu 2009, and Dow 2009. For more on 1370a28–30 see below, pp. 572ff.

[107] Cope 1877 *ad loc.* renders it 'fancy', adding that φαντασία is "the mental presentation, a mere copy, without reality" (with a reference to his note on *Rhetoric* I.11.6); Kennedy 1991 and Freese 1926 prefer 'outward show'; Jebb, more cautious, retains the more traditional 'imagination' (in Sandys 1909 *ad loc.*); Roberts, too, chooses 'fanciful' (in Ross 1924); and Rapp 2002, 'reiner Anschein'.

[108] Here I employ 'political' in that basic sense most readily illustrated by Aristotle's famous dictum that ὁ ἄνθρωπος φύσει πολιτικὸν ζῷον (*Politics* 1253a2–3).

[109] I need only cite 1356a25–27, where, from the tripartite division of rhetoric into *logos*, *ēthos*, and *pathos*, Aristotle concludes: ὥστε συμβαίνει τὴν ῥητορικὴν οἷον παραφυές τι τῆς διαλεκτικῆς εἶναι καὶ τῆς περὶ τὰ ἤθη πραγματείας, ἣν δίκαιόν ἐστι προσαγορεύειν πολιτικήν ('so that it happens that rhetoric is, as it were, a kind of offshoot of dialectic and of the study of ethics which one may

drawn between rhetoric and geometry, echoed again at 1417a18–21, this time by the opposition between μαθηματικοὶ λόγοι,[110] which have no ἤθη because they lack moral purpose, and the Σωκρατικοί, which do: it is the very nature of ῥητορική—the fact that it addresses the need of the political assembly (deliberative, forensic, or epideictic) to build consensus and manage dissent—that makes not only *logos*, but also *ēthos* and *pathos* its necessary ingredients, and for this reason it holds both the promise of effective democratic governance[111] *and* the danger of the unprincipled exploitation of man's prejudice and vanity.[112]

Now, as to the phrase καὶ δοκεῖ φορτικὸν εἶναι, we are supposed to appraise it in light of the ensuing qualification, καλῶς ὑπολαμβανόμενον. Cope 1877 *ad loc.* renders it 'and rightly so considered', adding Vettori's alternative 'when considered aright', which he nevertheless rejects because the former alone "is the more *natural* interpretation of ὑπολαμβάνειν; which will not in fact bear the meaning assigned to it by Victorius 'Si vere *iudicare* volumus'" (his emphasis).

---

fairly label *politics*', my emphasis). Cf. *Nicomachean Ethics* 1094a27–b3. For the negative perspective, cf. Plato *Gorgias* 463d1–2.

[110] Aristotle considers geometry a part of mathematics, as can be gathered from many passages in his works (cf. Heath 1949:1–16). In his *Posterior Analytics* 77b26–33, for example, after stating that 'in mathematics (ἐν δὲ τοῖς μαθήμασιν) fallacy does not happen similarly', he illustrates this assertion with reference to the circle: ἆρα πᾶς κύκλος σχῆμα; ἂν δὲ γράψῃ, δῆλον. τί δέ; τὰ ἔπη κύκλος; φανερὸν ὅτι οὐκ ἔστιν ('Is every circle a figure? If one draws it, clearly yes. What then? Is the epic [cycle] a circle? Clearly not'). Another clear statement can be found in *Metaphysics* E 1026a25–27, where in a parenthetical comment the philosopher remarks: "even the mathematical sciences (ἐν ταῖς μαθηματικαῖς) differ in this respect—geometry and astronomy deal with a particular kind of entity, whereas universal mathematics applies to all kinds alike" (Tredennick's *Loeb Classical Library* translation); this shows that mathematics includes geometry as a subdivision (see Ross's note in his commentary *ad loc.*). In Proklos' *Commentary on the First Book of Euklid's Elements* 38.4–12 (Friedlein) we learn that Geminos had described geometry as a μέρος of μαθηματική, a view that goes back, in turn, to Peripatetic scholarship (specifically, to Eudemos of Rhodes), thus confirming Aristotle's own classification (cf. F. Hultsch in *RE* VII 1 s.v. "geometria," col. 1210).

[111] Hence the transmitted reading πολιτειῶν at 1403b35, which Kassel prints and Lossau 1971 justifiedly defends against the suspicions of Spengel (1867:2.357), whose conjecture was accepted by Ross in his *OCT*.

[112] One need only remember that φορτικότης had made its appearance at 1395b1–2, in the chapter on maxims, long before the matter of style was broached. There Aristotle reflected on the pleasure a hearer experiences when an orator hits upon opinions he already holds. Cope 1877 *ad loc.*: "The φορτικότης here ascribed to vulgar audiences is much the same as the μοχθηρία τῶν ἀκροατῶν III 1.5, the vices or defects, which oblige the orator to have recourse to τἆλλα ἔξω τοῦ ἀποδεῖξαι in order to convince them, because they are unable to appreciate logic alone." *Nota bene* 1395b13–14, where, as might be expected, we learn that the *ethical* character of the discourse is chiefly in view. Cf. also 1415b4–8: δεῖ δὲ μὴ λανθάνειν ὅτι πάντα ἔξω τοῦ λόγου τὰ τοιαῦτα· πρὸς φαῦλον γὰρ ἀκροατὴν καὶ τὰ ἔξω τοῦ πράγματος ἀκούοντα, ἐπεὶ ἂν μὴ τοιοῦτος ᾖ, οὐθὲν δεῖ προοιμίου, ἀλλ' ἢ ὅσον τὸ πρᾶγμα εἰπεῖν κεφαλαιωδῶς, ἵνα ἔχῃ ὥσπερ σῶμα κεφαλήν ('One must not forget that all such things fall outside the argument; they regard a hearer who is vulgar and listens to what is extrinsic to the matter, since, if he were not such, a proem is not necessary other than to headline the matter, so that it may have a head just as [it has] a body').

If Cope is right, at least he cannot claim a large following,[113] nor is it clear why his is the 'natural' translation and on what account Vettori's meaning (which glosses his translation *recte ponderatum*)[114] is not allowable: for ὑπολαμβάνειν, as LSJ s.v. III.1 states, can mean 'to take up a notion, assume, suppose', and hence 'understand a thing to be so' or 'conceive of something in a certain way'.[115] The suggestion, then, is that the label φορτικόν for τὸ περὶ τὴν λέξιν holds in a restricted, yet basic, sense; and it does not take much effort to discover that here, as before, the logic behind this dim view of style is again the interaction between the unprincipled orator and his uncultivated audience, whose weaknesses he finds all too easy to exploit for selfish ends. As noted above (p. 552 n. 112), the adjective has already made its appearance at 1395b1-2, but it is the treatment in chapter 26 of the *Poetics* that brings out most clearly its rationale. There, as the philosopher debates whether epic or tragedy is the superior μίμησις, we learn that the label 'vulgar' does not so much inhere in the subject matter or practice at hand as it is intimately dependent on the target audience and the consequent interaction between performer and public: ἡ ἧττον φορτικὴ βελτίων, τοιαύτη δ' ἡ πρὸς βελτίους θεατάς ἐστιν ἀεί (1461b27-29). In view is the practice of actors and αὐληταί who feel the need to add beyond what is proper or called for, on the assumption that the public will not otherwise notice and understand the performance. Epic, on the other hand, addresses itself πρὸς θεατὰς ἐπιεικεῖς who need not such σχήματα, tragedy πρὸς φαύλους (1462a2-4). But, he adds, the fault is not really *poiētikē*'s, but should be laid at the door of *hypokritikē* (1462a5-6).[116]

---

[113] Freese writes "and rightly considered it is thought vulgar"; Kennedy, "delivery seems a vulgar matter when rightly understood"; Jebb, "and, properly viewed, the subject is thought vulgar"; Dufour and Wartelle, "il semble d'ailleurs que ce soit là un art grossier à en juger sainement"; Rapp, "auch scheint es, richtig betrachtet, ungebührlich zu sein"; Tovar, "parece que es asunto fútil, bien considerado."

[114] Vettori 1579:544.

[115] Forming an opinion entails weighing the facts ('ponderare') and making a judgment ('iudicare'). These entailments of ὑπολαμβάνω are easily borne out by a survey of the verb elsewhere in the *Rhetoric*, where it is frequently used.

[116] One other passage may be mentioned. In *Politics* VIII.6 (1340b20ff.) Aristotle takes up the question whether the education of freeborn youth πρὸς ἀρετήν should include μουσική, specifically, learning to sing and play an instrument. The inquiry—1340b34-35 makes clear—addressing itself to those who claim that it is a menial occupation (βάναυσον εἶναι τὴν ἐπιμέλειαν), suggests that μουσική is beneficial, so long as the degree to which it is practiced is carefully regulated, and melodies, rhythms, and instruments vetted for propriety (1340b42-1341a3). Later on, at 1341b8-18, before turning his attention to 'harmonies' and 'rhythms', Aristotle again makes passing mention of the general disapproval bestowed on 'professional education' (ἡ τεχνικὴ παιδεία); he goes on, in a long parenthesis, to explain the opprobrium as follows: τεχνικὴν δὲ τίθεμεν τὴν πρὸς τοὺς ἀγῶνας· ἐν ταύτῃ γὰρ ὁ πράττων οὐ τῆς αὑτοῦ μεταχειρίζεται χάριν ἀρετῆς, ἀλλὰ τῆς τῶν ἀκουόντων ἡδονῆς, καὶ ταύτης φορτικῆς, διόπερ οὐ τῶν ἐλευθέρων κρίνομεν εἶναι τὴν ἐργασίαν, ἀλλὰ θητικωτέραν· καὶ βαναύσους δὴ συμβαίνει γίγνεσθαι· πονηρὸς γὰρ ὁ σκοπὸς πρὸς

So far, then, we have seen that μοχθηρία and φορτικόν share a common root concern, one that does not inhere so much in λέξις (and, by implication, ὑπόκρισις) as in the potentially corrupt interplay between orator and audience. On the other hand, if used in a principled way, style and delivery can play a significant role in advancing the principles of justice; for they help rhetoric fulfill its social promise, enabling truth and right to assert their natural superiority.[117] This consideration, by itself, should caution us against rendering φαντασία by so utterly dismissive a gloss as 'mere fancy'. Several additional reasons concur with this judgment. After all, the entire rhetorical enterprise is branded as πρὸς δόξαν, and interpretive consistency would demand that a φαντασία which is no more than 'outward show' tarnish with its stain the very art of oratory. Cope 1877 *ad loc.* appears to realize this when, quoting *Eudemian Ethics* I.4.2, λέγω δὲ φορτικὰς μὲν [τὰς τέχνας] τὰς πρὸς δόξαν πραγματευομένας μόνον, he adds: "This I suppose must be meant of arts that have nothing solid and substantial about them, but aim at mere outside show, ostentatious and hollow, πρὸς δόξαν contrasted with πρὸς ἀλήθειαν"; and though parenthetically he glosses πρὸς δόξαν as "directed to τὸ δοκεῖν, mere outward show, not τὸ εἶναι," he softens the outcome in translation by rendering the offending sentence: "But since the entire study and business of Rhetoric is directed to mere opinion, is unscientific." In fact, one might even question his *comparandum*, for Rackham's *Loeb Classical Library* translation of *Eudemian Ethics* 1215a29–30 is not 'ostentatious' or 'hollow', but the far more neutral "pursued only for reputation." (Reputation and truth need not be at odds.) Since the semantic range of δόξα is broad enough indeed to allow for 'show', 'ostentation' (should the context call for it), it might be inadvisable to look for guidance in the *Eudemian Ethics*, especially when the

---

ὃν ποιοῦνται τὸ τέλος· ὁ γὰρ θεατὴς φορτικὸς ὢν μεταβάλλειν εἴωθε τὴν μουσικήν, ὥστε καὶ τοὺς τεχνίτας τοὺς πρὸς αὐτὸν μελετῶντας αὐτούς τε ποιούς τινας ποιεῖ καὶ τὰ σώματα διὰ τὰς κινήσεις ('We reckon that education technical which regards contests; for in it the performer does not practice for the sake of his own virtue but for the pleasure of the audience, and a vulgar one at that. Precisely for this reason we do not deem this practice proper for free [citizens] but more typical of paid laborers. And the result is that they grow illiberal, for the target they aim at is base; for the hearer, being vulgar, is wont to change *mousikē* [for the worse], whence also it actually follows that the professionals themselves who ply their trade with him in view he makes of some such kind [i.e. illiberal], as well as their bodies on account of their motions'). Note that, once again, what qualifies a practice as φορτική (and, in this case, earns it the label θητικωτέρα) is the focus on the hearers, specifically, on their pleasure, which is compared unfavorably with personal ἀρετή, so that 'professional' practice is rendered illiberal: a θεατὴς φορτικός corrupts the τεχνῖται who ply their trade with him in view. Cf. *Politics* 1342a18–21, Plato's *Laws* II 659b–c, and especially Plato's *Gorgias* 512e5–513c2, with its insistence on the necessary conformity of the orator (as μιμητής) to his audience and their πολιτεία if he desires to wield influence in the city (μέγα δύνασθαι ἐν τῇ πόλει 513a3–4).

[117] Cf. 1355a20–24, a pivotal passage whose text is the object of much disagreement but whose implications are surprisingly tolerant of the various opinions. See further below, pp. 570f.

statement needing clarification contains a sweeping characterization of oratory as a τέχνη and the *Rhetoric* itself does not fail to provide us with parallels that, I believe, make the present one clear.

I start, then, with the passage adduced by Cope above, when he opposes πρὸς ἀλήθειαν to πρὸς δόξαν to justify his "ostentatious and hollow." This opposition does, in fact, occur at 1365b1, in the seventh chapter of *Rhetoric* I, where Aristotle considers *greater* and *smaller* in connection with the potential disagreement between opposing parties over the degree of significance of a matter that is the object of debate. The abstract notions *greater* and *smaller* are illustrated with particular oppositions, such as *often* versus *seldom*, *proper* versus *acquired*, or *ends* versus *means*. The polarity that now occupies us ('what has respect to *truth* is greater than what has respect to *doxa*') is just one of these, and the philosopher offers the following definition:

> ὅρος δὲ τοῦ πρὸς δόξαν, ὃ λανθάνειν μέλλων οὐκ ἂν ἕλοιτο. διὸ καὶ τὸ εὖ πάσχειν τοῦ εὖ ποιεῖν δόξειεν ἂν αἱρετώτερον εἶναι· τὸ μὲν γὰρ κἂν λανθάνῃ αἱρήσεται, ποιεῖν δ' εὖ λανθάνων οὐ δοκεῖ ἂν ἑλέσθαι. καὶ ὅσα εἶναι μᾶλλον ἢ δοκεῖν βούλονται· πρὸς ἀλήθειαν γὰρ μᾶλλον. διὸ καὶ τὴν δικαιοσύνην φασὶ μικρὸν εἶναι, ὅτι δοκεῖν ἢ εἶναι αἱρετώτερον· τὸ δὲ ὑγιαίνειν οὔ.

> *Rhetoric* 1365b1–8

A definition of *pros doxan* [is] what one would not choose if he is likely to escape notice. Therefore also 'faring well' would appear preferable to 'doing good'; for a man will prefer the former even if he escapes notice, but seemingly he would not choose to do good unnoticed. And everything they want to be more than to seem [would appear preferable]; for [all these things are] more *pros alētheian*. Therefore they say that even justice is a small thing, because seeming [just] is preferable to being [just]; not so with being healthy.

Aristotle could not be clearer: that has respect to *doxa* which one would not choose when likely to escape others' notice. The focus is clearly on appearances in a social context—what I might call 'social pretense' (in the spatial sense of *praetendo*) if 'pretense' did not carry such negative connotations. The concern is arguably for one's reputation in society, for affecting the views that others have of us, for creating a social standing or managing our neighbors' attitudes towards us. To use Aristotle's own word as I believe he conceives of it, this would be a matter of φαντασία, of how we appear, of being aware of and trying to control the impact that one's behavior has on the way we come across, of giving expression to a particular *ēthos* in a manner, if not so technically proficient as that of a professional orator, yet not entirely different in kind from it.[118] Such φαντασία could, of course, involve empty show and ostentation, but it need not do so; and it has a legitimate claim on our interest as social beings. The examples point this out well: doing good versus faring well, or even justice versus health. No sham is involved in the act of conferring benefits on others: the suggestion is not that it looks *as if* someone is doing good while he is not; the point is simply that the benefaction is done with an eye on the profit that accrues to one's reputation with his neighbors. As to the latter opposition (i.e. justice versus health), no one would insist on a necessary connection between doing justice and mere outward show or ostentation.[119] But, clearly, whether a person or action is just is subject to debate and opinion in ways that the physical condition of a man—healthy or diseased—is not. It is in this sense, because it is open to judgment and pretension, that justice is said to be of small value. The overriding concern, therefore, is with reputation, with social appearances (one might say *ēthos*), and this is precisely what πρὸς δόξαν is intended to convey.[120]

---

[118] Though here φαντασία and φαίνεσθαι do not themselves occur, one finds several instances of their semantic opposite in this context, viz. λανθάνω.

[119] As scholars have suggested, the choice of justice as an illustration might hint at an ongoing polemic with some of the more outrageous sophists, who may have publicly owned appearing just preferable to actually being so. (The φασί would then have specific subjects in view, which the reader in turn would be expected to identify. Thus, for example, in Plato's *Republic* II 362e4–363a5 Adeimantos notes that parents commend justice for the good repute that accrues from it and the benefits that attend on such public esteem [cf. 365b4–7, 366d7–e5, and 367b6–c1].) This would go some way towards explaining the statement, ὅτι δοκεῖν ἢ εἶναι αἱρετώτερον. It would, indeed, be surprising if this apparently sweeping and rather pessimistic judgment represented the view of the common man. Or are we to believe that most Athenians really thought the appearance of justice more desirable than its reality?

[120] Translators agree, rendering πρὸς δόξαν at 1404a2 'to influence opinion' (Freese), 'with opinion' (Kennedy), 'auf die Meinung abzielt' (Rapp), 'ne s'attache qu'à l'opinion' (Dufour and Wartelle). Jebb's 'aims at appearance' and Tovar's 'apariencia' approach Cope, but show greater restraint as neither carries the negative connotations of 'show' and 'ostentation'. Indeed, both can be argued to imply 'opinion' and hence are, in my view, acceptable equivalents. Of the other occurrences of δόξα in the *Rhetoric*, those at 1360b22, 1362b20, 1367a16, 1368b23, 1371a16, 1388a2, 1388a6, and 1404a25 clearly (1397b26 probably) carry the meaning 'reputation' (cf. also 1372b21–23); at 1381b19–20 τὰ πρὸς δόξαν (as 1381b30–31 makes clear) refers to anything that affects the opinion the public has of us (hence our 'reputation'), and is opposed to τὰ πρὸς ἀλήθειαν, 'what is actually true', for there may, of course, be a gap between one's reputation and one's true character; at 1384a23–29, too, the argument hinges on 'loss of reputation' (ἀδοξία), an opinion (δόξα) men heed only on account of those who hold it (οἱ δοξάζοντες); 'opinion' is the proper rendering too at 1369a22, 1377b18, 1378b10, 1391b24, 1395b3, 1403a32, and 1412a27 (here best translated 'expectation'), and perhaps at 1384b23 (though I rather incline, with Kennedy, to 'reputation', construing καταφρονοῦσι with τῆς δόξης and not with τοῦ ἀληθεύειν). (The well-known idiomatic παρὰ δόξαν needs no discussion.) The only other relevant section is *Rhetoric* II.1, whose principal thrust is the importance of showing oneself to be, and rendering the *krités*, of a certain type (1377b24, the former pertains to *ēthos*, the latter to *pathos*—ποιόν τινα ... κατασκευάζειν

Another reason to reject the extreme translation of φαντασία is the claim at 1404a8–9 that 'the matter of λέξις has some small [but] necessary part in every διδασκαλία'. Since arguably by this assertion Aristotle seeks to justify the place of λέξις in his study of rhetoric, interpreters have tacitly assumed that διδασκαλία, while no doubt embracing other subjects, must ultimately have ἡ ῥητορικὴ τέχνη in view. The logic of the comment would be as follows: 'style' plays a small but necessary part in *every* scientific and technical domain, for it is part and parcel of making one's meaning clear; but, if *arguendo* its status in the art of rhetoric is momentarily left open, in subjects like geometry it obviously contributes, if at all, largely dispensable ornamentation; *ergo*—one readily infers from such clearer cases—it must also lend rhetoric 'mere outward show'. Presumably, then, the statement aims to vindicate the orator's unhappy need to resort to λέξις in his practice. But this logic faces difficulties: with the words 'in every διδασκαλία' is not the philosopher claiming that style plays a small but necessary role in *teaching* any given subject (here, a τέχνη) and not, as tacitly assumed, in *practicing* it?[121] In other words, if the art of rhetoric is really in view, does not the argument then regard its teacher rather than the professional orator? In fact, it is hard to see how διδασκαλία could stand without comment for τέχνη. Perhaps we are to take 'instruction' metonymically for the knowledge imparted,[122] but this would still place a focus on the process of teaching

---

is construed *apo koinou* with αὐτόν and τὸν κριτήν, though its sense varies with either term). The point is constructing a convincing persona, articulating and sustaining a particular view of oneself, managing one's reputation with his hearers, how one comes across: hence the recurrence of φαίνεσθαι (at 1377b26, 29, 31; 1378a5, 17). Thus, there is no parallel to be found in the *Rhetoric* for Cope's translation of πρὸς δόξαν, "aim[ing] at mere outside show, ostentatious and hollow" (Cope 1877:3.7); and even his alternative, "is directed to mere opinion, is unscientific," although it contains the otherwise acceptable 'opinion', distorted as it is by 'mere' and 'unscientific', fails to offer Aristotle's meaning. The philosopher makes clear (see 1355b35–1356a4) that *ēthos* and *pathos* are ἔντεχνοι, that they are (so to speak) 'scientific'. Cf. Grimaldi 1980:38 *ad* 1355b35 on ἔντεχνοι (he uses Roemer's lineation) and 349–356.

[121] This question bears tangentially on the debate reviewed by Rapp (2002:2.92–94) *ad* 1355a1325–26, subsection 1, whether Aristotle designed his theory of demonstrative science to guide and formalize scientific research or was instead exclusively concerned with the teaching of knowledge already acquired.

[122] So the statement 'listen to my instruction,' while referring to the contents of the teaching, draws attention to the teacher's active training of his pupil. The *DGE* s.v. διδασκαλία I.3 documents its late, reified acceptation, 'doctrine', in Christian literature. But Aristotle, aligning himself squarely with the classical usage, arguably evokes the process of teaching. Thus, in *Rhetoric* 1355a25–26, with διδασκαλίας γάρ ἐστιν ὁ κατὰ τὴν ἐπιστήμην λόγος Aristotle declares that following (superlatively precise 1355a24) knowledge in one's speech is '[characteristic] of *didaskalia*' (or 'proper to' *vel sim.*). In view here is not a reified, written speech, but the orator's *speaking*: note the participle λέγοντας at 1355a25. I cannot accept Kassel's unnecessary emendation of the vulgate διδασκαλίας to the nominative case, which unduly recasts the relationship between the terms of the sentence as a straightforward identity. Neither is Rapp (2002:2.92) right to equate the (semantically broader) διδασκαλία here with the (narrower) διδασκαλικοὶ [λόγοι]

that mystifies the common interpretation. One might have expected Aristotle simply to affirm instead that 'style plays a small but necessary part in [the practice of] every *technē*.' The accompanying comment, διὸ οὐδεὶς οὕτω γεωμετρεῖν διδάσκει, fails to dissipate the puzzle; for οὕτω could be construed with διδάσκει: 'no one follows this method in teaching geometry', thus making style the province of *teaching*; or with γεωμετρεῖν:[123] 'no one teaches geometers to follow this method', a translation found nowhere, yet implied by the common interpretive framework[124] according to which style is unnecessary for the geometer.[125] Yet, arguably, something like the common interpretation seems to be required by the context, for, after all, we are dealing with style as a component of rhetorical practice, not with a meta-linguistic assessment of style's contribution to rhetorical instruction.[126]

---

in *Sophistical Refutations* 165b1–3. Not every διδασκαλία need be a λόγος guided by ἐπιστήμη; τέχνη must be allowed a place too, as one learns from the occurrence in *Rhetoric* 1355b29 of διδασκαλική in connection with τέχνη. More on this passage immediately below.

[123] Cf. *DGE* s.v. διδάσκω I.1.d and Plato *Menōn* 85e1.

[124] So, for example, although Halliwell (1993:55) glosses *didaskalia* as "systematic instruction," he also calls 'geometry' (not, *nota bene*, the *teaching* of geometry) "[Aristotle's] example of *didaskalia*"; at 56, after asserting that "[t]he *Rhetoric* defines *didaskalia* as 'discourse grounded in knowledge'," he adds that "the reference here is certainly to systematic bodies or methods ... of knowledge," thereby not necessarily implying, but certainly suggesting, speech reified as a 'body of knowledge' rather than didactic discourse and the active process of instruction (notice that he calls 'philosophy' itself '[a] knowledgeable *didaskalia*'). Admittedly, professional engagement with abstract subjects like geometry may often in practice approach teaching in manner.

[125] For example, in Plato *Theaitētos* 162e γεωμετρέω denotes the practice of geometry as discourse on, and argument about, geometry.

[126] After stating unequivocally that style has some small necessary part in *every* διδασκαλία, it would be striking if Aristotle would contradict himself by asserting that geometric instruction—arguably a διδασκαλία—does *not*, after all, call for style in any measure, however small. But, strictly speaking, this is not the nature of the claim, and the διό may simply reflect common (if inadvisable) practice: style is rarely (if ever) involved in teaching (and applying) geometry, not because the discipline has no place for it (it does, though small); but because, insofar as it offers the smallest imaginable scope for style, its neglect in this case hardly occasions any harm. In other words, established practice in connection with geometry illustrates the principle at issue by taking it to the limit. Cf. Grimaldi (1980:36) *ad* 1355b29 apropos διδασκαλικὴ καὶ πειστική: "A[ristotle] acknowledges that the use of language in all the disciplines is always something more than notional and rational. The word greatly extends the area of 'persuasive speech' and recognizes that almost all discourse with another inevitably seeks to win acceptance for itself from the other. ... A.'s examples of geometry and arithmetic and his inclusion of ἐπιστῆμαι (55b31) are even more interesting in view of the fact that no kind of persuasion is ordinarily identified with scientific discourse." Cf. Rihll 1999:12–13, 22. Aristotle *Sophistical Refutations* 165b3 (δεῖ γὰρ πιστεύειν τὸν μανθάνοντα) furnishes a rare acknowledgment of the need for persuasion in scientific discourse. Rapp (2002:2.94) reads this statement through the lens of *Topics* 159a28–30, which he interprets as stating the need for a learner to trust his teacher even before he can grasp that/why he is right ("denn niemand versucht, Falsches zu lehren" 159a29–30). But I believe that he has misunderstood the passage in the *Topics* and that he is wrong to use it to displace a learner's 'trust' away from 'commonly accepted, reputable

A solution to the puzzle, however, lies at hand in the demonstrative nature of oratorical practice.[127] Aristotle might have in mind the centrality of rhetorical 'proof' to trial and deliberative assembly (and, in smaller measure, to epideictic speeches).[128] And, in this restricted sense, the speaker can be said to 'teach' his audience the relevant facts—just as the geometer can be said to prove a particular theorem. For the former, however, the demonstration is πρὸς τὸν ἀκροατήν, whereas the latter does it, so to speak, πρὸς αὐτόν. Not that the geometrical proof cannot be directed at others; but that, by the nature of its reasoning, it is either correct or incorrect; and, if the former, it is so for one and all—the geometer as much as anyone else. Not so in the case of a rhetorical demonstration, which can be compelling to one, yet fail to convince another. This, I think, is the philosopher's point and why he speaks of διδασκαλία rather than τέχνη.[129] If so, then, φαντασία cannot be 'mere outward show' in connection

---

opinions' (τὰ δοκοῦντα in the sense of ἔνδοξα) and onto his teacher's intent not to deceive him. τῷ ... μανθάνοντι θετέον (159a29) should be rendered 'a pupil must posit' (i.e. grant) not 'a pupil must state'; τὰ δοκοῦντα (159a29) are not uniquely the *learner's*, but generally embraced, notions (cf. 100b4–6); and, as often (cf. Denniston 1954:64–65), the second γάρ clause does not qualify the first but shares its reference (the contrast drawn at 159a26–28). In fact, *Topics* 159a3–14 sets the stage by detailing explicitly the conditions under which a learner should or should not posit (i.e. grant) axioms and propositions harder to argue than the original thesis. Clearly, the analysis does not turn on the trustworthiness of the teacher but strictly on the context (learning vs. training) and the character of the claims involved (whether convincing, well-known, and so on). Note in particular the occurrence of πιστεύειν in connection with πιστά (not διδάσκαλος or ὁ διδάσκων). This is not to deny, of course, that positing or not particular claims affects the student-teacher dynamics (159a13–14). *Topics* 141a30 should suffice to settle that both teaching and learning entail demonstration.

127 *Rhetoric* 1355b26–32 owns that all τέχναι and ἐπιστῆμαι have a demonstrative facet. See Grimaldi's comment *ad loc.*, quoted in the footnote immediately above.

128 Notice the related use in *Poetics* 1456b5, which opposes φαίνεσθαι ἄνευ διδασκαλίας to ἐν τῷ λόγῳ ὑπὸ τοῦ λέγοντος παρασκευάζεσθαι καὶ παρὰ τὸν λόγον γίγνεσθαι (cf. Lucas 1968:196 *ad loc.*). Note also Aristotle *Sophistical Refutations* 165b1–3, where διδασκαλικοὶ [λόγοι] are defined as arguments that 'deduce from the principles proper to each subject and not from the opinions offered by the answerer' (διδασκαλικοὶ μὲν οἱ ἐκ τῶν οἰκείων ἀρχῶν ἑκάστου μαθήματος καὶ οὐκ ἐκ τῶν τοῦ ἀποκρινομένου δοξῶν συλλογιζόμενοι); the sentence that precedes this one makes clear that Aristotle's taxonomy concerns 'arguments used *in conversing*' (τῶν ἐν τῷ διαλέγεσθαι λόγων τέτταρα γένη, my emphasis), a perspective that brings out the discursive and demonstrative character of such arguments (cf. *Sophistical Refutations* 171a31–32, a38–b2). A few lines later (165b9) the philosopher even substitutes ἀποδεικτικῶν for διδασκαλικῶν, bringing out explicitly the tie between formal instruction and demonstration, a tie that, as just noted, given the importance of 'proof' (ἀπόδειξις) for oratory, would readily suggest the use of διδασκαλία at *Rhetoric* 1404a9. Plato too associates διδασκαλία with rhetoric. In *Gorgias* 453d7–454e2, both rhetoric and διδασκαλικαὶ τέχναι are said to work conviction (they are πειθοῦς δημιουργοί 453e4–5). For Sokrates, however, the parallel between them breaks down when it comes to truth-value: whereas πίστις can be false, μάθησις (the goal of διδάσκειν) cannot.

129 Attention to the need for persuasion in scientific discourse seems also at issue in *Rhetoric* 1355a24–29, a passage to which I have already drawn attention above. There we learn that not even fortified with the sharpest knowledge (ἐπιστήμη) would a speaker be able to convince one and all: ἔτι

with superfluous ornamentation. Rather, it concerns the demonstrative force requisite to the rhetorical project. This is also why the philosopher writes, ἀλλ' ἄπαντα φαντασία ταῦτ' ἐστὶ καὶ πρὸς τὸν ἀκροατήν, where following Kassel I do not, like others, punctuate with a comma before καί, which I take as adverbial, not conjunctive;[130] for φαντασία is present *even* in the study of geometry, but

---

δὲ πρὸς ἐνίους οὐδ' εἰ τὴν ἀκριβεστάτην ἔχοιμεν ἐπιστήμην, ῥάδιον ἀπ' ἐκείνης πεῖσαι λέγοντας· διδασκαλίας γάρ ἐστιν ὁ κατὰ τὴν ἐπιστήμην λόγος, τοῦτο δὲ ἀδύνατον, ἀλλ' ἀνάγκη διὰ τῶν κοινῶν ποιεῖσθαι τὰς πίστεις καὶ τοὺς λόγους, ὥσπερ καὶ ἐν τοῖς Τοπικοῖς ἐλέγομεν περὶ τῆς πρὸς τοὺς πολλοὺς ἐντεύξεως ('And yet, in dealing with certain people, not even if we should have the most exact knowledge would we find it easy by drawing upon it to convince them in conversation; for discourse that conforms to systematic knowledge is characteristic of *didaskalia*, and this is impossible [with such people], but rather one must fashion his proofs and [oral?] arguments utilizing what is commonly held, as we said in the *Topics* concerning conversation with the crowd'). Although in this passage the philosopher appears categorically to deprecate *didaskalia* in the context of rhetoric, in point of fact his criticism is restricted to 'instruction' (i.e. demonstrative discourse) that adheres to the canons of exacting knowledge (what we might call '*formal* instruction'). He does not intend to deny rhetoric an instructive or demonstrative force but to make room for an art of persuasion that does not regard as its own domain the collection of (demonstrative and persuasive) facts peculiar to any particular body of knowledge. Aristotle aims to preserve the distinction between a system of knowledge whose purview is bounded by its peculiar subject matter and oratory, whose search for τὸ πιθανόν embraces all others only in their common relation to λόγοι. Indeed, an argument strictly based on ἐπιστήμη would be characteristic of formal instruction, but rhetoric is a combination of 'analytical knowledge' (τῆς ἀναλυτικῆς ἐπιστήμης 1359b10) and 'that [political] science concerned with ethics' (τῆς περὶ τὰ ἤθη [πολιτικῆς] 1359b10). The philosopher affirms in 1359b8–16 that one who failed to furnish (as he ought) rhetoric or dialectic as the δυνάμεις (1359b13; cf. 55b26) that they are and instead remade them into ἐπιστῆμαι (59b13) would obscure and change the character of rhetoric from an ἐπιστήμη of speech (59b16) to one of certain underlying subjects (59b15–16, e.g. medicine, geometry, arithmetic, or some other 55b29–31). It seems, then, that Aristotle sometimes loosely applies to rhetoric the label ἐπιστήμη (it is 'an *epistēmē* of discourse' as well as a combination of analytical and ethical *epistēmai*; cf. Grimaldi 1980:93 *ad* 1359b16), sometimes disowns it (discourse based on *epistēmē* amounts to formal instruction that is impossible with the crowd). In sum, where διδασκαλία is involved the teacher brings out the clear and necessary consequences of a subject's own peculiar principles, and he secures the necessary assent of the learner. This happens characteristically in the formal instruction of an ἐπιστήμη (say, geometry), given a pupil of the requisite ability; but to adhere strictly to this manner of presentation with most members of an ordinary audience is impracticable, certainly so where considerations of *ēthos* and *pathos* play a role (cf. 1417a19): hence one must resort to commonly held notions (τὰ κοινά) for one's proofs (πίστεις) and arguments (λόγοι). Cf. Rapp 2002:2.92–96 and Grimaldi 1980:28–29.

130 My argument, of course, does not turn merely on a matter of punctuation—whether a comma should precede the καί. But understanding φαντασία as 'ostentation' has recently been helped by a tendency to weaken ever so slightly the immediacy of its connection in this sentence to the hearer: 'all this is mere show, and [all of it is directed] towards the hearer'. But if, as I claim, Aristotle has in view the orator's crafting of φαντάσματα for the hearing (and viewing) of his audience, one might expect him to say ἀλλ' ἄπαντα φαντασία ταῦτ' ἐστὶ πρὸς τὸν ἀκροατήν. And he could further emphasize the target of this φαντασία by placing an adverbial καί before πρός. This, I submit, is precisely the case; and if such is the point of the phrase, the editor should not punctuate with a pause after ἐστί. Omitting the comma by itself does not, of course, prejudice the interpretation and would be the safest editorial choice: hence neither Bekker, nor Spengel,

it is primarily πρὸς αὑτόν, not πρὸς τὸν ἀκροατήν as in the case of rhetoric or, more broadly, wherever teaching takes place and the instructive and persuasive aspects of any τέχνη are called into action.[131]

13.6 Φαντασία in the *Rhetoric*

A final reason to oppose 'mere show', 'ostentation' for φαντασία lies in the use Aristotle makes of this term.[132] The initial suggestion that in *Rhetoric* 1404a11 φαντασία meant 'pomp, ostentation' goes back to Freudenthal's "Prunk" (1863:17–18) and his attempt to explain the restriction 'if we are not speaking metaphorically' in *De anima* 428a1–4:

εἰ δή ἐστιν ἡ φαντασία καθ' ἣν λέγομεν φάντασμά τι ἡμῖν γίγνεσθαι καὶ μὴ εἴ τι κατὰ μεταφορὰν λέγομεν, ⟨ἆρα⟩ μία τις ἐστι τούτων δύναμις ἢ ἕξις καθ' ἃς κρίνομεν καὶ ἀληθεύομεν ἢ ψευδόμεθα;[133]

If then *phantasia* is that by virtue of which we say that a *phantasma* occurs to us, and if we are not speaking metaphorically, is it some one

---

Roemer, or Kassel, not even Cope and Sandys feature the comma; Ross and Dufour and Wartelle do. Yet a translation, when there is one, often makes the structure of the editor's thought clear.

[131] Once again I draw attention to *Rhetoric* 1355b29 and to Grimaldi's comment above, p. 558 n. 126.

[132] Cf. González 2006, which was based on an earlier version of this material. Less narrowly concerned with the *Rhetoric*, O'Gorman 2005 helpfully explores the psychology of *lexis*, although he places to my mind excessive emphasis on the *visual* (as opposed to the aural and cognitive) dimensions of φαντασία without comparable regard for the pragmatics of delivery. Nevertheless, his qualification of *lexis* as "phantasmatic" (26) is a step in the right direction, even if its connection to delivery remains muted (only mentioned in passing at 16, 23, 26) other than to say that style sometimes subsumes it.

[133] I have quoted Ross's text (cf. Ross 1961:286 *ad* 428a3–4), even though there is much disagreement whether the last clause is in fact a question. Note his insertion of ἆρα and his punctuation, for which he has no ms. support. Some scholars, obviously uncomfortable with φαντασία as a faculty of judgment, recast the statement as a query (to be answered later in the negative) or, like Bywater (who added ζητῶμεν εἰ), as a summary proposal for the examination that follows. (Cf. Watson 1982:106n10 and Wedin 1988:47–48 with nn. 29–30.) But contrary to the assumption of many, the list at 428a4–5 (τοιαῦται δ' εἰσὶν αἴσθησις, δόξα, ἐπιστήμη, νοῦς) need not be exhaustive (otherwise, we would expect ταῦται, not τοιαῦται, at *De anima* 428a4), and therefore φαντασία need not be, as claimed, ruled out as a faculty of judgment. [Bekker and those who depend on him (like Biehl and Hicks) print ταῦτα as the reading of LWX; but Förster (1912:108) *ad loc.*, who independently perused the witnesses and whom Ross follows, corrects Bekker and instead reports "τοιαῦται" for LW and "τοιαῦ (*sic*)" for X.] As Wedin (1988:47n30) himself acknowledges, we do not need a question here to establish that, in the event, for Aristotle φαντασία turns out to be something less than a full faculty; he might well have described it as a δύναμις that enables us to arrive at truth or falsity, while simultaneously asserting its subordinate role to the standard (truly independent) faculties. According to this view, φαντασία would then be "a system of internal [re]presentations that enables a person to have desires, beliefs, and thoughts about objects and situations in the world" (Wedin 1988:22).

faculty or disposition of those according to which we judge and [in judging] we prove true or false?

Nussbaum (1978:254), the one scholar after Cope principally responsible for popularizing Freudenthal's idea,[134] realizes that it renders Aristotle's comment in *De anima* utterly trivial: "[H]e seems to be saying, 'Assuming when we say *phantasia* we mean the faculty in virtue of which we are appeared to in such-and-such a way, and are not using the transferred sense according to which it means (mere) show, *then* it can be said that in virtue of *phantasia* we tell truth or falsehood—whereas to say, "in virtue of ostentatiousness we tell truth or falsehood" would be silly.' It will be objected that this is a trivial point. But for Aristotle it is never trivial to recognize all the senses of a word ..." (her emphasis). This last observation notwithstanding, the point *is* trivial, and it is hard to believe that Aristotle would have felt the need to preclude such a misunderstanding—not to mention that, as argued below (p. 565), this meaning was simply not commonly available until the much later time of Polybios.[135] Now, this is not the place to conduct a survey of the intricate and extensive scholarly debate on Aristotle's concept of φαντασία.[136] Some have even questioned whether he held a single, consistent view of its meaning throughout his works.[137] But if one can detect some measure of disjunction between (and at times even within) his various writings, this takes place against a background of overall conceptual coherence. It is, at any rate, clear that the meaning alleged by Cope, and widely accepted by other translators, cannot be paralleled in any other passage of Aristotle. Thus, Wedin (1988:68) notes: "Following Freudenthal, [Nussbaum] remarks that φαντασία can mean '(mere) show, pomp, ostentatiousness' and argues that this is the metaphorical sense meant in [*De anima*] 428a1–4. The remark on the point of usage is acceptable, but that 428a2 counts as a case in point is, I submit, mistaken. An initial reservation is that *only one passage* in Aristotle can be marshaled in support of the Freudenthal reading, namely *Rhetorica* 1404a11" (my emphasis).

But there are some discordant voices. Indeed, while not calling for a gloss so extreme as 'showy, ostentatious', similarly tending towards superficiality is Halliwell's proposal that the term is not used in its "psychological sense, but [taken] to mean merely 'appearance', as at *Sophistic Refutations* 4.165b25"

---

[134] Cf. Cope 1877 *ad Rhetoric* I.11.6.

[135] For a better solution to what Aristotle means by κατὰ μεταφοράν, see Wedin 1988:69–70.

[136] A debate, however, that has overlooked almost entirely *Rhetoric* III.1. For helpful overviews see Rees 1971, Schofield 1992 [1978], Watson 1988, and Wedin 1988. An expanded bibliography may be found above, p. 550 n. 106.

[137] Cf. Frede 1992:279–282.

(Halliwell 1993:59n16).[138] My problem with this comment is that his perhaps otherwise unobjectionable "merely 'appearance'"—where 'appearance' can be neutral enough simply to denote 'what appears to the thinking (or sensing) subject'—seems to connote 'mere appearance', which in turn is glossed by 'show'; thus we move quickly from 'appearance' to the objectionable 'mere ostentation or show', the very meaning that cannot be substantiated from any Aristotelian passage—unless, of course, one chooses to call 'mere show' any appearance that happens to be false (as φαντασία can certainly be). The *locus* adduced in support is a case in point: ἔστι δὲ τὰ μὲν παρὰ τὴν λέξιν ἐμποιοῦντα τὴν φαντασίαν ἓξ τὸν ἀριθμόν· ταῦτα δ᾽ ἐστὶν ὁμωνυμία, ἀμφιβολία, σύνθεσις, διαίρεσις, προσῳδία, σχῆμα λέξεως (165b24–27).[139] Doubtless here the 'appearance' in question is false: false logic is the focus of the treatise, a point its opening reiterates by referring to οἱ φαινόμενοι ἔλεγχοι (164a20–21) and by distinguishing between real syllogisms and those that seem [true] but are not.[140] There is nothing here of 'mere ostentation', for the superficiality of false reasoning is quite another from the 'sensual show' alleged at *Rhetoric* 1404a11. *Sophistical Refutations* is not, after all, an ethical treatise that looks into the motivations of deceitful sophists in order to condemn them for their ostentatiousness. Furthermore, I fail to see why this instance of φαντασία (or the one at 168b19) should not have "its psychological sense."[141] For Aristotle himself draws the parallel between the inexperienced, who reasons and refutes falsely, and 'those who view things from a distance' (164b27), a formulation strongly reminiscent of the passage in *De anima* (428b17–22) where, discussing why φαντασία can be false, Aristotle distinguishes between perception of τὰ ἴδια and perception of the αἰσθητά to which these ἴδια belong:[142] "As to the whiteness of an object, sense is never mistaken, but it may be mistaken as to whether the white object is this thing or

---

[138] Halliwell 1993:60n19 offers a mild corrective to this statement.

[139] 'The things that produce the appearance [of refutation] in consequence of language are six in number; these are: homonymy, ambiguity, combination, division, prosody, and form of expression'. An alternative (freer) translation of the first clause that better conveys the neutrality of τὴν φαντασίαν [τοῦ ἐλέγχου] as the functional equivalent of τὸν φαινόμενον ἔλεγχον (164a20–21; cf. 169b38) might be: 'The linguistic phenomena that make a fallacy look like a refutation are six in number'. φαντασία, the (psychological) movement triggered by the perception of the phenomena listed, should be carefully distinguished from φάντασμα, the attendant 'image' or 'impression'. Thus, more accurately: 'The things that cause [a refutation] to appear [to someone] ...' (or 'the appearing [of a refutation]').

[140] οἱ μὲν εἰσὶ συλλογισμοί, οἱ δ᾽ οὐκ ὄντες δοκοῦσι (164a23–24). *Contra* Poste, one should read the καί that precedes τῶν φαινομένων μὲν ἐλέγχων as epexegetic, as do Pickard-Cambridge ('i.e.'), Forster ('that is'), and Dorion ('c'est-à-dire'). See Schreiber 2003:192n1 and 173–178 (Appendix 1).

[141] LSJ s.v. 1.b places 165b25 under 'less scientifically, *appearance*', still not its fourth division 'parade, ostentation'.

[142] On ἴδια see below, p. 573.

something else."[143] This comment must in turn be read against 430b29–30: 'But just as sight perception of a proper object (τὸ ἴδιον) is [always] true, while [our perception] whether the white thing is or is not a man is not always true, so it is with immaterial objects'. Thus, when Aristotle in *Sophistical Refutations* mentions the error of 'those who view things from a distance', *De anima* leads me to believe that most likely he has in mind the misleading φάντασμα that results from viewing an object from too far a distance. I might add that the sources of false φαντασία in *Sophistical Refutations* 165b26–27, "the ambiguity of a term, the ambiguity of a proposition, the possibility of wrong disjunction, the possibility of wrong conjunction, the possibility of wrong accentuation, and similarity of termination" (Poste 1866 *ad loc.*), have their grounds on aural or visual φαντασία.[144] Such errors come from the application of νοῦς to what one hears or reads (the φαντάσματα), e.g. in syntactic or semantic parsing, where learning (and hence memory) and deductive logic are involved. This would seem to me to fall squarely under the psychological sense of φαντασία.[145]

Another discordant voice is Fortenbaugh (2002:96–100), who, opposing the analysis of human emotions as "*phantasia* apart from belief," takes an approach similar to Halliwell's: he denies any 'scientific' intent in Aristotle's account of φαντασία in the *Rhetoric* and cites in support *Sophistical Refutations* 164a20–24. Accordingly, any references to "appearance" would not pertain to the "biological faculty of *phantasia*" (96): recognizing that courts and assemblies make decisions on the grounds of probabilities, not certain knowledge, the philosopher "is careful to speak of what appears to be the case," thus "calling attention to the fact that human emotions are caused by beliefs, which may or may not be true" (97). But I fail to see why such a stance would prevent φαντασία from being the psychological faculty more fully (and precisely) discussed in *De anima*. Of course it is possible to use φαίνεσθαι without implying any particular psychological framework: the word, by itself, will not settle whether its register is technical or colloquial, nor, if technical, the degree of precision invoked. But Fortenbaugh elides the fact that not only the verb but also the noun, φαντασία, is used, for which

---

[143] Translation by Hicks 1907 *ad* 428b21–22.

[144] Concerning non-visual φαντάσματα, see Frede 1992:285.

[145] This crucial observation precludes a 'metaphorical' meaning in Simplicius' sense (*In Aristotelis De anima* 428a1–2), that is, the meaning that obtains ὅτε ἐπὶ τοῦ φαινομένου τῇ φαντασίᾳ χρώμεθα καὶ ἐπὶ αἰσθήσεως καὶ ἐπὶ δόξης 'when we use φαντασία for τὸ φαινόμενον (what appears to be the case) in both perception and belief' (Hayduck 1882:208, lines 7–8). In other words, since it involves φαντάσματα and αἴσθησις, 'appearing' in a non-psychological, transferred sense is not in view (cf. Wedin 1988:69). The verb φαίνεσθαι by itself (apart from its context) does not decide whether the 'appearing' is or is not psychological (i.e. whether it involves perception and 'images' or simply denotes 'seeming [to be the case]'); according to Simplicius, Aristotle was making clear his concern with 'psychological φαντασία.'

it is harder to argue a colloquial meaning devoid of any technical import. That Aristotle associates φαντασία and αἴσθησις at *Rhetoric* 1370a28–30, in fact, seems to militate against a strictly colloquial register for the verb and its noun, even in the context of the oratorical treatise. I would argue, moreover, that, considering the philosopher's undeniable interest in the epistemological role of φαντασία, one should assume, *ceteris paribus*, that in the rhetorical context of truth-seeking and decision-making φαίνεσθαι is more likely to bear a degree of technical precision than to be strictly colloquial, 'unscientific,' and devoid of psychological overtones. It seems to me that Fortenbaugh's rationale for a cleavage between *De anima* and the *Rhetoric* (see, for example, Fortenbaugh 2002:100) is the distinction drawn in *De anima* III.3 between φαντασία and δόξα, which allows a degree of psychological detachment to a subject who denies his φαντασία conviction (the πίστις that accompanies δόξα), resisting its implications (as when, looking at a picture, we know—however horrifying the depiction—that we need not flee from it as if from imminent danger). But it is *precisely* this effect of attachment to or detachment from a particular 'view' that opponents at law try to induce among the jury. Once rhetorical persuasion is achieved, the 'picture' carries the conviction of truth and action follows. Naturally, Aristotle need not raise in the *Rhetoric* aspects of φαντασία that follow from non-rational animals' possession of this faculty, since the purview of oratory is strictly *logos*-endowed man.[146]

Now, it is not only the case that the works of Aristotle fail to produce a single instance for which 'ostentatiousness' correctly translates φαντασία: in fact such a meaning finds no parallel in the literature before Aristotle's time. The closest approach is the use of the *verb* φαντάζειν (*not* the noun φαντασία) in Herodotos 7.10ε,[147] where, it is true, 'to show oneself' might be deemed less compelling than 'to make an arrogant display of oneself'. But we are simply not entitled to read our view of what is contextually compelling into the received lexical meaning of a term—a meaning, besides, that in this case quite adequately suits the context—unless we can support the corresponding modification of, or extension to, the lexicon by additional instances that clearly require it. Here it is not so. Artabanos' comment hinges on the contrast between ὑπερέχοντα ζῷα, 'prominent animals', and σμικρά, 'small': god strikes the former with his thunderbolts and does not suffer them to show themselves—a hyperbole allowed for its exemplary value. Some might draw the inference that 'prominent

---

[146] Cf. the helpful analysis in Rapp 2002:2.575 and 2.621 (*ad Rhetoric* 1382a21).

[147] Warning Xerxes about the peril of rash arrogance, Artabanos remarks: ὁρᾷς τὰ ὑπερέχοντα ζῷα ὡς κεραυνοῖ ὁ θεὸς οὐδὲ ἐᾷ φαντάζεσθαι, τὰ δὲ σμικρὰ οὐδέν μιν κνίζει. How and Wells 1912 *ad loc.* write: "[P]roperly show oneself (iv.124.2; vii.15.2); here *se ostentare*, 'make a show of oneself'," noting, moreover, its agreement with Polybios' usage. Powell 1938 s.v. φαντάζομαι 2 glosses it as '[to] be conceived'.

animals' are "creatures of greatness," wont "to display their pride" (to quote A. D. Godley's *Loeb Classical Library* translation): in their eyes, this may color φαντάζεσθαι, whose proper meaning is 'to appear', with a note of arrogance. But if so, such semantic coloring is strictly contextual and this instance by itself should not receive its own lemma in the lexicon (LSJ s.v. II.2). To be sure, such hypothetical contextual color would resemble the late use of φαντασία for 'outward show' and 'ostentation'—for which there are, however, no examples before Aristotle, and which, in my view, the alleged passage of the *Rhetoric* does not illustrate either. Indeed, even if *arguendo* one should grant the validity of the acceptation of the LSJ 'to make a show', one cannot argue convincingly from what would be, under those circumstances, a single, exceptional meaning of the verb φαντάζειν in Herodotos[148] that its corresponding noun, φαντασία, also in that same exceptional sense, was conceptually available to Aristotle; and, furthermore, that he actually used φαντασία with that anomalous meaning once and only once in his entire *oeuvre*, departing in so doing from other senses frequently attested elsewhere in his works. I find this unpersuasive, especially when the number of such instances of φαντασία exceed one hundred, giving more than ample scope for potential parallels—parallels that fail to materialize. Are we really to believe on the basis of a precedent so slim that, at best, only one Herodotean passage can be adduced for it that Aristotle departed from the received meaning of the noun and his own usage elsewhere, attested by many passages? Admitting such a departure would only be justified under rather stringent contextual constraints, i.e. only if the local context should categorically demand it. I have already listed several reasons that, in fact, suggest that no such necessity obtains. My case will be further strengthened if I can show that the philosopher's use of φαντασία elsewhere also suits *Rhetoric* III.1: this I shall do presently.[149] Aristotle's interest, our critics notwithstanding, is with

---

[148] I have not been able to turn up any other incontrovertible use of the verb in this peculiar sense before Aristotle. As to the noun φαντασία, the only other text cited by LSJ s.v. 4 that, in the opinion of some, might lend credence to the modern consensus on *Rhetoric* 1404a11 is [Hippokrates'] *Decorum* 7, which indeed belongs under 'ostentation' (cf. Jouanna 1999:75–111). But according to a recent detailed linguistic study by García Valdés 1992:304, "with a fair degree of certainty" the earliest possible date for this treatise is the second century AD.

[149] Quite apart from the uniqueness of Herodotos 7.10ε and the reasons just offered for a reading of φαντάζεσθαι *sensu stricto*, it is pertinent to remember that verbs and nouns do not always possess the same semantic range. In this connection, Martínez Hernández (1997:196) criticizes precisely the failure to keep lexical fields and spheres separate when verbs and nouns are mixed, forgetting "[el] carácter paradigmático del campo, que exige establecer las oposiciones sobre las que se estructura entre lexemas de una sola clase" (cf. Martínez Hernández 1997:76–77 and Coseriu and Geckeler 1981:56–59). Geckeler (1971:218) offers a clear statement of this principle: "Wenn also das Wortfeld in struktureller Hinsicht als 'ein lexikalisches Paradigma' ... charakterisiert ist, so kann es—das ist ein Wesenszug des Begriffes 'Paradigma'—notwendigerweise nur *eine* Wortart umfassen. In einem einzigen Paradigma können nicht z. B. Substantive, Verben, Adjektive und

the psychology of perception and the ways in which φαντασία subserves sense 'perception' (αἴσθησις) and 'supposition' (ὑπόληψις): 'For *phantasia* is different from both perception and thought; it does not happen without perception, nor supposition without it' (*De anima* 427b14–16).[150] If rhetoric studies the means for persuasive speech, surely its practical goal is to persuade or dissuade the audience; hence, in its polis setting and at the level of civic action, rhetoric becomes a legitimate object of interest in the study of 'animal motion', though here the ζῷον in question is one that possesses φωνή and λόγος and is eminently πολιτικόν. It is in this context that φαντασία and φαντάσματα—their role in voluntary movement—enter into the considerations of the orator and the teacher of oratory.

But before considering the *Rhetoric*'s own engagement with φαντασία, we must survey statements elsewhere that illuminate the conceptual background of this word. *De anima* 433b27–30 offers a convenient starting point: 'Thus, then, in general terms, as already stated, the animal is capable of moving itself just insofar as it is appetitive; and it cannot be appetitive without *phantasia*. Now all *phantasia* is rational [i.e. connected with reason] or perceptual [i.e. connected with perception]. Of the latter the other animals also have a share'.[151] Here Aristotle notes that motion must be traced to desire, desire that is not without φαντασία; and that φαντασία can be categorized by its connection with λόγος or perception.[152] Such λογιστικὴ φαντασία recalls a later section of the same

---

Adverbien nebeneinander funktionieren, d. h. in direkter Opposition zueinander stehen" (his emphasis). To illustrate this point, one need only consider ποιέω, ποίησις, and ποιητής, which have areas of overlap and disjunction; or, to use an English example, the word 'trip': its noun, widely used for 'short journey', now rarely (if ever) for 'nimble step' or 'stumble'; its verb in turn hardly ever for 'to make a trip or excursion'. There are also adjectives without corresponding verbs ('pregnant' is very common; 'pregnate' rare and obsolete, 'impregnate' taking its place), verbs without their nouns ('cleave', 'to part', owns 'cleft'; but 'cleave', 'to adhere', lacks a noun), etc. On such gaps, see Geckeler 1976:158–160 and Gutiérrez Ordóñez 1989:104–105. Lexical semantics is too complex to allow for unexamined extrapolations. Not even when, in their full diachronic sweep, a verb and its noun are attested with one and the same meaning should their synchrony be assumed. On this caution cf. Coseriu 1981:109–113. Cf., further, Schofield 1992:251n11.

[150] φαντασία γὰρ ἕτερον καὶ αἰσθήσεως καὶ διανοίας, αὕτη τε οὐ γίγνεται ἄνευ αἰσθήσεως, καὶ ἄνευ ταύτης οὐκ ἔστιν ὑπόληψις. Cf. *De anima* 427b27–28.

[151] Translation by Hicks 1907 *ad loc.*, modified. ὅλως μὲν οὖν, ὥσπερ εἴρηται, ᾗ ὀρεκτικὸν τὸ ζῷον, ταύτῃ αὐτοῦ κινητικόν· ὀρεκτικὸν δὲ οὐκ ἄνευ φαντασίας· φαντασία δὲ πᾶσα ἢ λογιστικὴ ἢ αἰσθητική. ταύτης μὲν οὖν καὶ τὰ ἄλλα ζῷα μετέχει.

[152] Though ἢ … ἢ are disjunctive, the alternatives need not be mutually exclusive: they may simply offer two complementary ways of viewing any φαντασία, ways that depend on the point of view chosen. That is to say, even the λογιστική may, on further consideration, turn out to be connected with αἴσθησις in a manner still to be determined. That this is in fact so becomes clear at *De anima* 432a3–10, where we learn that "apart from sensible magnitudes (παρὰ τὰ μεγέθη τὰ αἰσθητά) there is nothing, as it would seem, independently existent" (Hicks 1907 *ad loc.*);

work, which speaks of ἡ βουλευτικὴ [φαντασία] ἐν τοῖς λογιστικοῖς (434a7), 'the deliberative φαντασία in rational beings':[153] using reason a man decides whether he will do this or that (pursuing the greater good), and proves that he is not moving ἀορίστως (434a4), like the lowest animals, but measuring by a single standard; thus it follows that he is able, from many φαντάσματα, to fashion one course of action.[154] The operative word here is βουλευτική, which

---

therefore, 'it is by the perceptual forms (ἐν τοῖς εἴδεσι τοῖς αἰσθητοῖς) that the objects of thought (τὰ νοητά) exist' (my translation, taking Wedin into account). Wedin (1988:114) interprets the point of the passage as follows: "[O]ne cannot think of things that are of a kind not to have existed or, even more liberally, ... one cannot think of things whose salient parts are of a kind not to have existed." Cf. also Labarrière (1984:47n32), where "la φαντασία produite par la νόησις" should be modified to 'φαντασία involved in νόησις' vel sim. That νόησις cannot, in fact, produce φαντασία is explained below, p. 569 n. 161.

[153] ἡ μὲν οὖν αἰσθητικὴ φαντασία, ὥσπερ εἴρηται, καὶ ἐν τοῖς ἄλλοις ζῴοις ὑπάρχει, ἡ δὲ βουλευτικὴ ἐν τοῖς λογιστικοῖς (πότερον γὰρ πράξει τόδε ἢ τόδε, λογισμοῦ ἤδη ἐστὶν ἔργον· καὶ ἀνάγκη ἑνὶ μετρεῖν· τὸ μεῖζον γὰρ διώκει· ὥστε δύναται ἓν ἐκ πλειόνων φαντασμάτων ποιεῖν) (De anima 434a5–10). 'Perceptual phantasia, as noted, also exists in the other animals, but the deliberative [only] in the rational (for whether one will do this or that already is a task for reasoning; and it is necessarily the case that one measures by one [standard], for one pursues what is greater; it follows that one is actually able from more images to make one'.

[154] With Wedin (1988:82–83), I take 'deliberative phantasia' to mean 'imagination connected with deliberation', just as the λογιστική is that connected with λόγος, without prejudicing the question whether such 'imagination' always preexists reflection or else can also be forged by the deliberative process. There is no clear proof here of φαντασία as functionally complete, and Wedin's proposal (1988:45–63) may stand. This conclusion holds even if we understand the ἕν of ἓν ἐκ πλειόνων φαντασμάτων as ἓν [φάντασμα], for deliberation would still have the active role. Functional incompleteness only requires that φαντασία not be regarded as the subject of δύναται ... ποιεῖν, an interpretive point that seems entirely warranted (πράξει, διώκει, and δύναται share a common subject which must therefore be 'rational animals' vel sim.). That ἕν does not stand for ἓν [φάντασμα] but for 'one plan, thought, or course of action' plausibly follows from Wedin's observation that combining in one's head elements from different images into a single collage seems a rather odd way of conceiving the ordinary psychology of deliberation. The involvement of several images need not be "reduced to mentally pasting together images" (83, his emphasis), even if one regards this procedure as a rare possibility. Not germane to this question is De anima 434a10–11: καὶ αἴτιον τοῦτο τοῦ δόξαν μὴ δοκεῖν ἔχειν, ὅτι τὴν ἐκ συλλογισμοῦ οὐκ ἔχει, αὕτη δὲ ἐκείνην. Its correct interpretation hinges on the last clause ('but the latter [has] the former'), which Ross declared "clearly unmeaning" but in fact serves to rule out 'phantasia' and δόξα as the respective referents of αὕτη and ἐκείνην; for after 427b14–26 and 428a18–26 the mere notion that φαντασία may have δόξα is out of the question. Such a claim, moreover, seems hardly apropos in its context (hence Ross's comment and emendation). Since αὕτη cannot stand for φαντασία, neither can it be the elided noun in τὴν ἐκ συλλογισμοῦ: one must therefore read τὴν ἐκ συλλογισμοῦ [δόξαν] (with Wedin 1988:147n60 and Modrak 2001:252, contra Hicks 1907:567 and Nussbaum 1978:264n66, among many). The passage addresses the view that (at least some) animals have an attenuated form of belief (cf. Hamlyn 1968:153; Irwin 1980:127 with n. 24; Wedin 1988:147n60). If so, the question arises: does it entail phantasia? In other words, the context aims to elucidate the manner in which animals move and the role, if any, that phantasia plays in such motion. Animals that lack logos, Aristotle notes, do not have deliberative phantasia. His proof issues from the endoxical view that animals lack δόξα, at least the strong δόξα of inference (which precludes their deliberating; cf. De memoria 453a14: τὸ βουλεύεσθαι συλλογισμός

highlights the corresponding role assigned to φαντασία in deliberating a course of action.[155] There is only a small distance from this to a corresponding *symbuleutic*, i.e. social, dimension, as the orator artfully crafts φαντάσματα[156] that will prompt his hearers to 'do this or that'. This argument precludes the facile criticism that rhetoric merely addresses itself to no more than the passions of the audience, in a manipulative attempt to elicit behavior that is as irrational[157] as it is beneficial to the speaker (just as 'desire' is said at times to overpower βούλησις, *De anima* 434a12–13). No; the text tells us plainly that choosing a plan of action is the work of λογισμός, and, in so doing, promotes φαντασία (with its ethical and emotional components and the λέξις that expresses them) to a cardinal tool of the rhetorical task.

For Aristotle, then, φαντασία—the soul's [re]presentational[158] device—mediates between sense perception and the critical faculties[159] that, apprehending the object as desirable or undesirable, move one towards or away from it. But αἴσθησις is not the only cause of φαντάσματα; hope and memory too are associated with φαντασία,[160] and more generally λόγος and νόησις: τὰ μὲν γὰρ ὀργανικὰ μέρη παρασκευάζει ἐπιτηδείως τὰ πάθη, ἡ δ' ὄρεξις τὰ πάθη, τὴν δ' ὄρεξιν ἡ φαντασία· αὕτη δὲ γίνεται ἢ διὰ νοήσεως ἢ δι' αἰσθήσεως (*De motu animalium* 702a17–19).[161] The causal chain is: 'thought' or 'sense percep-

---

τίς ἐστιν); and because '[inferential] *doxa* has deliberative *phantasia*' he concludes that animals do not have deliberative *phantasia*. 'Therefore' (διό) 'the appetency [of such animals] does not have the deliberative faculty (τὸ βουλευτικόν)'. Thus interpreted, the assertions are contextually compelling and agree with Aristotle's earlier statements in the treatise. Cf. Bywater 1888:65–67.

[155] Cf. *De anima* 431b6–8: ὁτὲ δὲ τοῖς ἐν τῇ ψυχῇ φαντάσμασιν ἢ νοήμασιν, ὥσπερ ὁρῶν, λογίζεται καὶ βουλεύεται τὰ μέλλοντα πρὸς τὰ παρόντα. Clearly, these φαντάσματα are λογιστικά and βουλευτικά.

[156] *Stricto sensu*, he does not craft, but provokes, φαντάσματα: what he crafts are the visual and aural stimuli that become the object of his audience's perception and, hence, move their φαντασία (i.e. he ultimately aims at particular φαντάσματα).

[157] Or less than rational.

[158] Though my analysis does not depend for its validity on it, I am attracted to the view of φαντασία in Wedin 1988 as functionally incomplete (cf. *De anima* 429a1–2) and co-occurring with actual exercises of the functionally complete faculties (see his chapter 2 for an explication). Thus I also follow his use of brackets for '[re]presentation', which is intended, he notes, "to alert the reader to the fact that I am not foisting on Aristotle the view that we do not actually perceive objects but only make inferences to them from Hume-like images" (Wedin 1988:17n27).

[159] τῇ δὲ διανοητικῇ ψυχῇ τὰ φαντάσματα οἷον αἰσθήματα ὑπάρχει (*De anima* 431a14–15). Cf. Wedin 1988:110–113.

[160] *Rhetoric* 1370a28–30. On this passage and its context see above, p. 550 n. 106, and below, pp. 572ff.

[161] Nussbaum 1978 *ad loc.* translates: "For the affections suitably prepare the organic parts, desire the affections, and *phantasia* the desire; and *phantasia* comes about either through thought or through sense-perceptions." Since here διά governs νοήσεως, Wedin (1988:57n42) is doubtless right to insist that γίνεται διά + gen. must not be construed with "acquisitional or genetic" force. *Posterior Analytics* II.19 makes clear that νόησις cannot occasion φαντασία in the same generative sense in which perception produces it (428b10–11); hence, 'thought' cannot be said to engender

tion' → φαντασία → 'desire' → 'bodily affections' → motion.[162] As the translation indicates, in the previous passage πάθη stands for bodily changes (chillings and heatings),[163] not for the psychic affections that attend φαντασία and that are studied in *Rhetoric* II (see below, pp. 573f.). These latter πάθη would not follow, but precede, desire; in other words, they would constitute motivations for judgments or actions.[164] Perception and thought are 'critical' faculties the soul uses to judge: ἡ ψυχὴ κατὰ δύο ὥρισται δυνάμεις ἡ τῶν ζῴων, τῷ τε κριτικῷ, ὃ διανοίας ἔργον ἐστὶ καὶ αἰσθήσεως ... (*De anima* 432a15–16);[165] and if φαντασία according to Aristotle depends on perception, and thought, in turn, cannot happen without it,[166] it should not surprise us to read the following: "Now we see that the movers of the animal are reasoning and *phantasia* and choice and wish and appetite. And all of these can be reduced to thought and desire. For both *phantasia* and sense-perception hold the same place as thought, since all are concerned with making distinctions [lit., 'for all are involved in judging' (κριτικὰ γὰρ πάντα)]" (*De motu animalium* 700b17–21).[167] It can hardly be accidental that, in arguing for the usefulness of rhetoric, Aristotle should censure κρίσεις that happen μὴ κατὰ τὸ προσῆκον (*Rhetoric* 1355a22–23), implying that "the agent responsible for permitting the bad judgments is a rhetoric which

---

φαντασία (cf. Wedin 1988:42–43, 74–75). Wedin therefore translates αὕτη δὲ γίνεται ἢ διὰ νοήσεως ἢ δι' αἰσθήσεως: "imagination comes about *because of* ... thinking ... or perceiving" (57n42, my emphasis). The sense of διά + gen., then, is the very one of qualified co-occurrence expressed at *De anima* 429a2 by ὑπό + gen. (where ὑπό retains some of its locatival force; cf. Wedin 1988:52). Although both might be fairly characterized as 'causes', 'engendering' φαντασία (which for Aristotle 'thought' *cannot* do) is very different from 'arousing' φαντασία (which 'thought' arguably does). Cf. Modrak 2001:249–256.

[162] Wedin 1988:57 explains: "If, then, imagination is not a full faculty, it is surely involved in the actual use of such faculties. Perception, desire, and thought require it and so do memory and even dreams. Imagination is required because images are required not as the object toward which the faculty is directed but as a means by which a faculty accomplishes [its task]."

[163] Cf. Nussbaum 1978:154n19.

[164] On πάθη influencing judgment as opposed to action, see Striker 1996:292–293.

[165] 'The soul of animals is defined with reference to two faculties: both by its capacity to discriminate, which is the task of thought and perception ...'.

[166] διὸ οὐδέποτε νοεῖ ἄνευ φαντάσματος ἡ ψυχή (*De anima* 431a16–17).

[167] Translation by Nussbaum 1978 *ad loc.* ὁρῶμεν δὲ τὰ κινοῦντα τὸ ζῷον διάνοιαν καὶ φαντασίαν καὶ προαίρεσιν καὶ βούλησιν καὶ ἐπιθυμίαν. ταῦτα δὲ πάντα ἀνάγεται εἰς νοῦν καὶ ὄρεξιν. καὶ γὰρ ἡ φαντασία καὶ ἡ αἴσθησις τὴν αὐτὴν τῷ νῷ χώραν ἔχουσιν· κριτικὰ γὰρ πάντα. Citing a study by John Cooper, she also notes that "there is no need to interpret [κρίνειν] as implying that any kind of explicit or reflective judgment is taking place—and in particular ... it need not be associated with 'explicit verbal performance or the disposition to such—as indeed we can readily infer from [Aristotle's] ascription of κρίνειν to animals'" (Nussbaum 1978:334). The point is well taken. But a restriction necessary in the case of animals without *logos* must not disallow the otherwise legitimate implications of the philosopher's statement for the social world of the polis. Therefore, I think it is right to consider his analysis in the context of κρίσις that involves discursive thought and decision making.

does not achieve its perfection as rhetoric, and thus fails to realize its usefulness" (Grimaldi 1980:27). Though 'judgments' here are the decisions of the courts, these are but the social expression (at the civic level) of the individual's proper use of his own faculties of judgment.[168]

This line of reasoning is of a piece with Aristotle's division of the soul into two parts: one that possesses λόγος, the other ἄλογον (*Nicomachean Ethics* 1102a27–28). The former he divides further into the ἐπιστημονικόν, which studies things whose principles (ἀρχαί) cannot be otherwise, and the λογιστικόν, which makes calculating (λογίζεσθαι) and deliberating (βουλεύεσθαι) its task:[169] 'For to deliberate and to calculate are the same thing, and no one deliberates about what cannot be otherwise'.[170] Drawing our attention to the appearance of τὸ ἐπιστημονικόν at *De anima* 434a16, Labarrière (1984:30) plausibly argues that the subdivision of the soul that has λόγος is in view throughout this section of *De anima*, where the philosopher discusses the λογιστικὴ φαντασία. The effect of this terminology is to underline the involvement of λόγος—*ratio* and *oratio*—as νοῦς makes use of the corresponding φαντάσματα in forming a ὑπόληψις.[171] Like Plato before him (but with greater conceptual clarity),[172] Aristotle placed desire in the sphere of λόγος, and therefore made it, in some measure, the object of persuasion and rational appeal. We find this clearly stated at *Rhetoric* 1370a18–27:[173] ἐπιθυμία (which he defines as 'a desire for what is pleasant') can be ἄλογος or μετὰ λόγου;[174] the former kind (e.g. hunger, thirst, or sleep) does not come

---

[168] Cf. *Rhetoric* 1377b21–22, which plainly states that ἕνεκα κρίσεώς ἐστιν ἡ ῥητορική.

[169] *Nicomachean Ethics* 1139a3–8.

[170] τὸ γὰρ βουλεύεσθαι καὶ λογίζεσθαι ταὐτόν, οὐδεὶς δὲ βουλεύεται περὶ τῶν μὴ ἐνδεχομένων ἄλλως ἔχειν (*Nicomachean Ethics* 1139a12–14).

[171] Cf. Wedin 1988:145–156. One must be careful to regard 'images' (φαντάσματα) not as objects of thought but as what they really are, viz. vehicles for thought. As Wedin (1988:116) pointedly observes, "[t]o contemplate with an image is not to contemplate an image."

[172] Cf. Fortenbaugh 2002:23–44.

[173] Kassel brackets these lines as a likely Aristotelian addition (Kassel 1976:xix and *ad loc.*). However one chooses to explain the contradiction noted below (n. 174) that leads him (with Spengel 1867:1.159) to place the passage under suspicion, ultimately what matters is that we realize the underlying consistency of Aristotle's classification of causes for human action, irrespective of his terminological inconsistency.

[174] The terminology employed here contradicts 1369a1–4, where βούλησις (described as 'a desire for what is good') is assigned to λογιστικὴ ὄρεξις but ὀργή and ἐπιθυμία to the ἄλογος ὄρεξις. (My point is indifferent to the various textual uncertainties of the passage; I follow Ross's text.) The contradiction, however, is superficial, for as Grimaldi (1980:231) explains the same conceptual schema, detailed in *Nicomachean Ethics* 1102a26–1103a10, underlies both passages. Indeed, at *Nicomachean Ethics* 1102b13–14 Aristotle mentions a subdivision of the soul's ἄλογον μόριον that 'somehow shares in λόγος' ([ἄλλη τις φύσις] μετέχουσα μέντοι πῃ λόγου), for it responds differently in the continent and incontinent man. And a few lines later, at 1102b29–31, he structures the opposition as one between the φυτικόν, which 'in no wise shares in λόγος', and the ἐπιθυμητικόν (and in general the ὀρεκτικόν), which 'somehow does share [in λόγος], in that it

571

ἐκ τοῦ ὑπολαμβάνειν, 'from forming an opinion'; of the latter kind, he writes: '[I call] "attended by *logos*" all those things people desire because they have been persuaded; for often, after hearing and being persuaded (ἀκούσαντες καὶ πεισθέντες), they long to see and own'.[175] Thus, the craving in this case comes from persuasion (whence, by implication, one forms ὑπολήψεις)—in particular, from aural persuasion, 'when they have heard and have been persuaded'. I do not think that ἀκούσαντες and πεισθέντες are conceptually independent, as if the former merely referred to learning about something by word of mouth, while the latter conveys the exercise of reason that results in conviction. Rather, I believe that Aristotle has selected the common scenario of rhetorical persuasion to illustrate the division (only too apposite a choice given the subject matter of his treatise), and that the participles, conceptually subordinated, might be translated thus: 'for they often long to see and own when they are convinced by hearing [an oral argument]'. This serves well to remind us that, for Aristotle, the rhetorical endeavor is preeminently of an oral (and hence aural) nature.

Given its focus on persuasible desires, it is hardly surprising to find the first occurrence of φαντασία at this point in the *Rhetoric* (at 1370a28), where it is featured in an argument about the very desires that are open to persuasion and should therefore be of concern to the orator:

ἐπεὶ δ' ἐστὶ τὸ ἥδεσθαι ἐν τῷ αἰσθάνεσθαί τινος πάθους, ἡ δὲ φαντασία ἐστὶν αἴσθησίς τις ἀσθενής, κἀεὶ ἐν[176] τῷ μεμνημένῳ καὶ τῷ ἐλπίζοντι ἀκολουθοῖ ἂν φαντασία τις οὗ μέμνηται ἢ ἐλπίζει, εἰ δὲ τοῦτο, δῆλον ὅτι καὶ ἡδοναὶ ἅμα μεμνημένοις καὶ ἐλπίζουσιν, ἐπείπερ καὶ αἴσθησις·

Rhetoric 1370a27–32

Since the experience of pleasure inheres in perceiving a certain affection and since *phantasia* is a sort of weak perception and since some kind of *phantasia* of what a person remembers or hopes will always attend his remembering and hoping—if this is the case, it is clear that

---

hearkens to it and obeys it' (τὸ δ' ἐπιθυμητικὸν καὶ ὅλως ὀρεκτικὸν μετέχει πως, ᾗ κατήκοόν ἐστιν αὐτοῦ καὶ πειθαρχικόν).

[175] Reading πολλά adverbially, and the verbs and participles absolutely: μετὰ λόγου δὲ ὅσα ἐκ τοῦ πεισθῆναι ἐπιθυμοῦσιν· πολλὰ γὰρ καὶ θεάσασθαι καὶ κτήσασθαι ἐπιθυμοῦσιν ἀκούσαντες καὶ πεισθέντες (1370a25–27).

[176] In printing κἀεὶ ἐν I follow Roemer, who adopts Susemihl's emendation. Alternatively, the κἄν of ΘΠΓΣ (using Ross's *sigla*) or β (in Kassel's stemma) may actually be κἄν = καὶ ἐν (so Kassel, after Arnet), where the ἀεί required by the syllogism, though not explicit, is nevertheless understood. In any case, it is clear that εἰ δὲ τοῦτο summarizes the three protases, and that δέ must therefore be resumptive. Cf. Grimaldi 1980:251 and see also above, p. 550 n. 106.

pleasures accompany those who are remembering and hoping, since indeed perception [is involved here] too.

This famous passage, with its αἴσθησίς τις ἀσθενής, does not, of course, collapse the conceptual complexity of φαντασία surveyed above into a facile equation between it and perception. The enclitic τις here, as often, signals a simplification; it warns us of an approximation that, while suitable to the context and argument at hand, yet lacks the philosophical sophistication and accuracy that might be necessary and present elsewhere.[177]

The connection between φαντασία and αἴσθησις is helped by the semantic range of αἰσθάνομαι, which—Aristotle teaches in *De anima* II.6—covers not only αἰσθητά perceived in themselves, but also what might be called 'incidental objects', perceived κατὰ συμβεβηκός. The former are proper, ἴδια, to one of the ordinary senses (e.g. seeing white or tasting sweetness); or common, τὰ κοινά, to all or some (e.g. size or number). The incidental, he illustrates as follows: "An object of perception is spoken of as incidental, e.g. if the white thing were the son of Diares; for you perceive this incidentally, since this which you perceive is incidental to the white thing. Hence too you are not affected by the object of perception as such" (418a20–24).[178] It is clear that perception of incidental objects is of a higher order, in that it calls for processing and integrating with memory an array of data (proper and common).[179] And yet at one level—and certainly in popular parlance—we can still say that we 'see the son of Diares' just as we might as well say that we 'recognize' him: *seeing* considers it from the perspective of the senses, *recognizing*, from that of the mind. It is precisely this double-sidedness of perception that gives rise to the concept of an αἰσθητικὴ φαντασία, and the discourse on φαντασία seeks to understand the individual roles of soul and body and their mutual interplay when such 'perception-as-realization' takes place. Only in this sense is it right to say that we feel an emotion: not as a bare affection, as a bee may be said to be angry—for emotion is not a sensory datum impinging on the senses—but by the awareness of a relevant fact through a [re]presentational φάντασμα that is, in turn, attended by pleasure

---

[177] Cf. Watson 1982:103n6 and Wedin 1988:89. I am not hereby endorsing the widespread view of the *Rhetoric* as a treatise lacking in exactitude. For a survey of the literature for and against this view see Fortenbaugh 1974:222n4 and 223n5. Cf. also Striker 1996:286–288.

[178] Hamlyn 1968 *ad loc.* The Greek runs as follows: κατὰ συμβεβηκὸς δὲ λέγεται αἰσθητόν, οἷον εἰ τὸ λευκὸν εἴη Διάρους υἱός· κατὰ συμβεβηκὸς γὰρ τούτου αἰσθάνεται, ὅτι τῷ λευκῷ συμβέβηκε τοῦτο, οὗ αἰσθάνεται· διὸ καὶ οὐδὲν πάσχει ᾗ τοιοῦτον ὑπὸ τοῦ αἰσθητοῦ. Note how πάσχειν and αἰσθητόν are connected, just as αἰσθάνεσθαι and πάθος.

[179] Cf. Wedin 1988:94–95: "[P]erceiving Socrates qua Socrates, perhaps even qua man, involves something more than just proper perception. For one thing it involves the identity of the object, not simply feature identification. So it is likely that belief, thought, and even language may be needed as well" (95).

or pain in their various forms.[180] This explains the words ἡ δὲ φαντασία ἐστὶν αἴσθησίς τις ἀσθενής: if αἴσθησις is attended by pleasure or pain,[181] and memories and hopes—which involve φαντάσματα of the things one remembers or hopes for—are painful or pleasurable, then, on the point of analogy, φαντασία is a sort of weak αἴσθησις.[182]

The other instances of φαντασία in the *Rhetoric* follow the established norm; as Grimaldi (1980:256) notes, through "imagination, the presentative faculty," φαντάσματα affect our appetitive system. Indeed, at 1370b33 victory is said to give rise to a φαντασία of superiority (ὑπεροχή), 'which all strongly or mildly desire'; at 1371a9 honor and a good reputation are reckoned among the most pleasurable possessions, because on their account each has the φαντασία 'that he is such as a worthy man (ὁ σπουδαῖος), all the more when they say so who he thinks speak truly'; at 1371a19, elaborating on why being loved is pleasant, the reason offered is that 'there too [the one loved enjoys] a φαντασία that being good is his nature,[183] [a thing] which all who perceive it desire'; at 1378b9 the φαντασία attends 'dwelling upon the thought of revenge';[184] and at 1382a21, 1383a17, and 1384a23 the word enters into the respective definitions of fear and

---

[180] πάθος covers anything that comes about through πάσχειν (cf. *DELG* s.v. πάσχω). At *De anima* 403a7, ὀργίζεσθαι, θαρρεῖν, ἐπιθυμεῖν, ὅλως αἰσθάνεσθαι are listed as πάθη τῆς ψυχῆς (for sweetness, cold, heat, etc. as πάθη, see *Categories* 9b2–9). At 403a17–18 the list is: θυμός, πραότης, φόβος, ἔλεος, θάρσος, ἔτι χαρὰ καὶ τὸ φιλεῖν τε καὶ μισεῖν; all these happen 'with the body', the philosopher adds, 'because together with these the body feels something' (ἅμα γὰρ τούτοις πάσχει τι τὸ σῶμα 403a18–19). The concept of πάθος extends further to states of mind and body such as sleep (*De insomniis* 462a3–4: ἐὰν μὲν αἰσθάνηται ὅτι καθεύδει, καὶ τοῦ πάθους ἐν ᾧ ἡ αἴσθησις τοῦ ὑπνωτικοῦ), to μνήμη, 'memory' (*De memoria* 449b4–6), and even to φαντάσματα (*De memoria* 450a10–11: καὶ τὸ φάντασμα τῆς κοινῆς αἰσθήσεως πάθος ἐστίν [bracketed by Ross, after Freudenthal]).

[181] In ἐστὶν τὸ ἥδεσθαι ἐν τῷ αἰσθάνεσθαί τινος πάθους (1370a27–28) πάθος stands broadly for τὸ πάσχειν τι (see above, n. 180). It might thus be rendered by 'affection'—not in the narrow sense of 'emotion' (though emotions are certainly included) but the more general one of 'the state of being influenced or acted upon'. The connection of αἴσθησις with πάθη is natural, since sense organs must be *affected* by the corresponding stimuli for perception to occur (*De anima* 424b25–26). But just as every sense has its corresponding pleasure (*Nicomachean Ethics* 1174b20–21), so also the emotions (πάθη as *animi perturbationes*) are accompanied by pleasure and pain: λέγω δὲ πάθη μὲν ἐπιθυμίαν ὀργὴν φόβον θάρσος φθόνον χαρὰν φιλίαν μῖσος πόθον ζῆλον ἔλεον, ὅλως οἷς ἕπεται ἡδονὴ ἢ λύπη (*Nicomachean Ethics* 1105b21–23).

[182] Cf. Wedin 1988:89. Of course, Aristotle's reasoning does not deduce, but assumes as a premise, what I have presented as the conclusion; his goal is to argue that memory and hope are, in fact, attended by pleasure and pain: εἰ δὲ τοῦτο, δῆλον ὅτι καὶ ἡδοναὶ ἅμα μεμνημένοις καὶ ἐλπίζουσιν, ἐπείπερ καὶ αἴσθησις (*Rhetoric* 1370a30–32).

[183] I read the (notionally) underlying construction as ὑπάρχει αὐτῷ τὸ ἀγαθὸν εἶναι. Once this turns into an articular infinitive qualifying φαντασία, the τό, not strictly required, might be dropped (so cod. Parisinus 1741) to avoid the close succession of τοῦ + inf. and τὸ + inf. (Without the notionally underlying presence of τό, one would have expected ὑπάρχει αὐτῷ ἀγαθῷ εἶναι.)

[184] διότι διατρίβουσιν ἐν τῷ τιμωρεῖσθαι τῇ διανοίᾳ (1378b7–8).

courage (which involve a future expectation—the ἐλπίς noted at 1370a29—of evil or safety) and shame ('a φαντασία of loss of honor'). In none of these instances is there an emphasis on the unreality of what is '[re]presented' to the mind;[185] the focus is rather on the cognitive process that consists in entertaining a given notion or idea, a process that brings pleasure or pain to the one who engages in it. The point of view taken is δόξα,[186] often that of a third-party, and there is a keen interest in how our notions are affected by those around us. In one case we even read explicitly that the φάντασμα is what others *say* about us; and that the persuasion operative with the φαντασία is enhanced in proportion as the speakers are trustworthy—an argument that points the way to the 'scientific' (ἔντεχνον) study of reasoned emotional appeal, an appeal that, insofar as it is based on λόγος, has a legitimate place in the art of rhetoric.[187]

De anima 433a10–22 calls φαντασία a kind of thinking (νόησίς τις): like δόξα, it is a critical faculty;[188] but, significantly, in contrast to δόξα, it does not carry πίστις (*De anima* 428a20–24)—arguably the ultimate goal of rhetoric. This fundamental distinction is one that we must bear in mind as we think of the oratorical task: by affecting their φαντασία, the very [re]presentational system of the διανοητικὴ ψυχή, the speaker shapes the perception of his audience. Such molding influence works at all the available cognitive levels (including the πίστεις inherent in the αὐτὰ τὰ πράγματα, just as even the geometer must use φαντάσματα), but it pertains especially to *pathos*, as the orator endeavors to secure a desirable outcome or avoid a disagreeable one. Even a speaker's successful self-presentation, which turns on his ability to communicate proper *ēthos*, can be reinterpreted as φαντασία towards the hearers with a view to

---

[185] Concerning 1384a23, Kennedy 1991:146n56 notes: "As usual, this means a mental 'visualization' of the effects, not (as the English word may imply) a false conclusion."

[186] Labarrière 1984 argues for an understanding of λόγος that puts the accent on *oratio* rather than *ratio*. While animals do not have reason, he says, they are not entirely deprived of rationality: τὸ αἰσθητικόν—which animals obviously have—cannot be easily classified as either ἄλογον or λόγον ἔχον (*De anima* 432a30–31); besides, many (if not most) animals have φαντασία and μνήμη of particulars (*Nicomachean Ethics* 1147b5); and, as a survey readily shows (cf. Labarrière 1984:34–40), Aristotle assigns to some a kind of μάθησις and διδασκαλία, and to birds, ἑρμηνεία ἀλλήλοις and even a διάλεκτος. Moreover, following *De generatione animalium* 786b23–25 and *De anima* 420b29–33, Labarrière links φωνή—a σημεῖον of pain and pleasure (*Politics* 1253a10–11)—to αἰσθητικὴ φαντασία. The implication is that the opposition between αἰσθητική and λογιστικὴ φαντασία reflects the one between φωνή and λόγος; and hence, the λόγος in question is not so much *ratio* as *oratio*. Whether one agrees with him or not (cf. Wedin 1988:146–152), one can hardly deny that, at the very least, wherever *ratio* is involved, persuasion is active as "l'espace intersubjectif et dialogal de l'opinion et de la délibération" (32), a space that turns readily into the public sphere of δόξα where the community engages in dialog and persuasion.

[187] Cf. Brinton 1988.

[188] Even if not a *full*, i.e. independent, faculty. On its critical nature, see above, p. 570.

creating such πάθη as will move them to act to the speaker's advantage.[189] And λέξις, of course, studies which use of λόγος—including, we must always remember, φωνή and its attributes—best conveys the speaker's meaning, best achieves his goals, inducing such φαντάσματα as will support his case. Thus, he will adopt the 'style of an angry man' when there is insolence; the style of man 'disgusted' and 'cautious even to speak', with regard to impious and shameful matters; he will speak with admiration of what is worthy of praise, with lowliness of pitiable things (*Rhetoric* 1408a16–19). All these, being matters of style and delivery, will imply an appropriate register for the orator's voice—a careful choice of intonation, loudness, and prose rhythm—and a fitting countenance that does not raise the suspicion of speciousness (1408b4–7). These visual and aural stimuli translate into φαντάσματα that render style effective in expressing *ēthos* and *pathos* (1408a10–11). The resulting community of feeling between hearer and speaker creates plausibility and persuasion: 'The proper *lexis* also makes the matter credible: the mind's reasoning that one speaks truthfully is ill-founded, because when faced with such things people react in this way and consequently think that the circumstances are thus—even if[190] they are

---

[189] That such overlap between *ēthos* and *pathos* exists is generally denied by Fortenbaugh, who in a series of works (see Fortenbaugh 1996 *passim*, esp. 147, with bibliography in nn. 3 and 4) has argued that persuasion through character is not intended to arouse emotion in the audience and does not compromise the objectivity of the juror. (His only concession is that at *Rhetoric* II.1 *eunoia* is thought of as an emotion, not of the audience but *of the speaker*; but cf. *Rhetoric* 1415a35–36, where it is paired with ὀργίσαι.) By insisting on the distinction Aristotle draws between εὔνοια and φιλία in *Nicomachean Ethics* 1166b30–35, he seems to imply that should the audience, for example, see the orator manifest intense φιλία towards them (or their city), they would be inclined to mistrust him; or else that the speaker should seek to restrain such feelings for fear of warping his own or his hearers' judgment (Fortenbaugh 1996:164). Neither implication squares with intuition or actual practice. (Of course, if such protestations were overdone, they may look inauthentic and fail to convince, but this is entirely another matter.) And even if the distinction of *Nicomachean Ethics* holds, many an Athenian orator must have boasted strong affection for his city and convinced her of the honesty of his claims, or else the parody in Aristophanes *Knights* would ring hollow (cf., for example, 732, 773, and 1339–1355). Far better, then, to acknowledge with Carey (1994:35) that, "[i]n practice, *ethos* and *pathos* are closely connected, for one of the effects of *ethos*, as well as inducing a degree of trust, is also to produce a feeling of goodwill in the audience toward the speaker." (Cf. Carey 1994:39 and 43, and Russell 1990:205–206 and 212.) In other words: the orator succeeds when his εὔνοια and φιλία are reciprocated by his audience.

[190] Here εἰ καί, like κἄν at a24, must mean 'even if' (cf. Smyth §2378), for the point is not to assert the necessary disjunction between the facts and the *pathos* of the λέξις but to underline the effectiveness of the style even if such disjunction obtains. Hence, the mind's reasoning is ill-founded but not necessarily false. In Aristotelian usage, the verb παραλογίζεσθαι (1408a20) and its noun παραλογισμός—nothing suggests semantic variance between them—may be applied to inferences that, although ill-founded, hit upon the truth. Hence it need not entail, though in context it well may imply, that the conclusion drawn is not true to fact. Two considerations establish beyond question this (otherwise reasonable) semantic claim. The first is Aristotle's equating παραλογισμός and ὁ φαινόμενος ἔλεγχος/συλλογισμός in the *Sophistical Refutations* (see *Sophistical Refutations* 164a20–21 with p. 563 n. 140 above; and *Sophistical Refutations* 169b18–20,

not as the speaker [represents them]—and the hearer's feelings track those of the emoting speaker, even if he is [really] saying nothing' (1408a19-24). Thus conceived, rhetorical performance, deliberate in its λέξις and ὑπόκρισις, seeks to bring the audience under the spell of the orator: through carefully targeted sensory φαντάσματα—to which voice, gestures, and all the resources of style are instrumental—he attempts to place before his listeners a particular [re]presentation of the facts; this [re]presentation, successfully brought before his mind's eye, becomes the hearer's own λογιστικὴ φαντασία (the sensory φαντάσματα now having noetic status). The orator's design and hope is that the audience will feel the force of this φαντασία—that πίστις will attend the thinking it subserves—and that his hearers will embrace his [re]presentation with their own δόξα.[191] Thus, φαντασία not only denotes the soul's [re]presentational faculty: more loosely, it may also be used interchangeably with φαντάσματα or even stand for the oratorical technique that manipulates them for rhetorical ends. This tech-

---

170a9–10 with Schreiber 2003:174–175 and 229n3); the second, his explicit mention of a sophistic reasoning that is 'seemingly deductive' (φαινόμενος συλλογιστικός) on subjects which only dialectic is fitted for testing 'even if its conclusion is true (for it deceives about the cause)' (κἂν ἀληθὲς τὸ συμπέρασμα ᾖ (τοῦ γὰρ διὰ τί ἀπατητικός ἐστι) 171b10–11). This precise scenario is in view at *Rhetoric* 1408a19–24.

[191] At 1408b12 Aristotle refers to this embrace with the word συγγνώμη, which some erroneously think an expression of condescending toleration and translate as 'it is excusable' (e.g. Kennedy *ad loc.*: "for it is excusable that an angry person calls a wrong 'heaven-high'"). Here συγγνώμη is best taken instead etymologically as 'con-sensus', i.e. 'concurrence in view or judgment', a sort of 'critical fellow-feeling' from which the acceptations 'forbearance', 'excuse', and 'pardon' derive. In view is the audience seeing something from the speaker's vantage point once he has emotionally attuned them to his message: 'Compound words ... suit one who speaks with emotion; for there is commonality of mind with an angry speaker who calls an evil "heaven-high" ... and whenever he has already gripped his audience and has caused them to grow deeply stirred with praises, reproaches, anger, or friendship ... . For they utter such things when they are deeply stirred and also in consequence approve [of him/this], obviously because they are similarly affected' (1408b12–18: τὰ δὲ ὀνόματα τὰ διπλᾶ ... ἁρμόττει λέγοντι παθητικῶς· συγγνώμη γὰρ ὀργιζομένῳ κακὸν φάναι οὐρανόμηκες ... καὶ ὅταν ἔχῃ ἤδη τοὺς ἀκροατὰς καὶ ποιήσῃ ἐνθουσιάσαι ἢ ἐπαίνοις ἢ ψόγοις ἢ ὀργῇ ἢ φιλίᾳ ... . φθέγγονταί τε γὰρ τὰ τοιαῦτα ἐνθουσιάζοντες, ὥστε καὶ ἀποδέχονται δῆλον ὅτι ὁμοίως ἔχοντες. Note that I do not punctuate with a period before καὶ ὅταν but read καὶ [συγγνώμη] ὅταν; for the construction τε γὰρ ... ὥστε καί see Bonitz 1867:676–677 *contra* Denniston 1954:536). The relevant sense of συγγνώμη, which regards the hearers' embrace of the speaker's [re]presentation with their own δόξα, is best defined by Aristotle himself at *Nicomachean Ethics* 1143a19–24: ἡ δὲ καλουμένη γνώμη, καθ᾽ ἣν συγγνώμονας καὶ ἔχειν φαμὲν γνώμην, ἡ τοῦ ἐπιεικοῦς ἐστι κρίσις ὀρθή. σημεῖον δέ· τὸν γὰρ ἐπιεικῆ μάλιστά φαμεν εἶναι συγγνωμονικόν, καὶ ἐπιεικὲς τὸ ἔχειν περὶ ἔνια συγγνώμην. ἡ δὲ συγγνώμη γνώμη ἐστὶ κριτικὴ τοῦ ἐπιεικοῦς ὀρθή· ὀρθὴ δ᾽ ἡ τοῦ ἀληθοῦς ('The so-called "judgment" according to which we say that people "exhibit commonality of mind" and speak of "being of a mind [to]" is a right discrimination of what is reasonable. The proof: we say that the reasonable man most of all "exhibits a sympathy of judgment" and that it is reasonable to exhibit commonality of mind regarding some things. Commonality of mind is a right critical judgment of what is reasonable; and correct judgment is a judgment about the truth'). On this passage cf. Rowe and Broadie 2002:185, which renders συγγνώμονας as "having a shared sense" and τὸ ἔχειν συγγνώμην as "to be sympathetic."

nique, Aristotle tells us, works best when, drawing upon his own φαντασία, the orator turns its internal [re]presentations into sensory stimuli of adequate λέξις and σχήματα expressive of his own emotions. Then is his *pathos* best able to stir the equivalent feelings in his listeners and to excite in them a corresponding φαντασία that becomes instrumental to the art of persuasion.[192]

Aristotle's treatment, his specific guidance to the would-be orator in crafting φαντάσματα, is compressed and, by later standards, relatively undeveloped. But he is seminal in opening the way to later scholars: "Since sufferings are pitiable when they appear near at hand (ἐγγὺς φαινόμενα) ... necessarily those [people] are more pitiable who contribute to the effect by gestures and cries and display of feeling and generally by their delivery [*hypokrisis*]" (Kennedy *ad* 1386a28–33, modified).[193] By placing the evil before the mind's eye (πρὸ ὀμμάτων ποιοῦντες), speakers make it appear close (ἐγγὺς ποιοῦσι φαίνεσθαι)[194] and evoke the corresponding *pathos*. The orator's φαντάσματα are not like the ones that subserve the mind on account of the facts themselves:[195] they are rhetorically constructed by the application of λέξις to *ēthos* and *pathos*[196] and can be controverted by one's opponent. Their force is not that of logical inevitability. And this, I believe, is the note of caution Aristotle strikes when he says that λέξις, insofar as it is φαντασία towards the hearers, can only be of limited import.[197] The philosopher's comment, then, is not a dismissive aside, but offers a realistic estimate of the promise of λέξις and its corresponding limitations.

---

[192] This is elaborated in connection with the poet's art in *Poetics* 17 1455a22–32. The meaning of λέξις in τῇ λέξει συναπεργάζεσθαι (a22–23) goes beyond mere 'verbal expression' to include the rhetorical qualities of propriety (the presence of τὸ πρέπον and the absence of τὰ ὑπεναντία 1455a25–26) and vividness (ὅτι μάλιστα πρὸ ὀμμάτων τιθέμενον 1455a23). On this passage see Meijering 1987:14–17.

[193] For the Greek, see above, p. 536 n. 53. This passage of the *Rhetoric* is similar in sentiment to the beginning of *Poetics* 17, on which see immediately above, n. 192. Cf. Dupont-Roc and Lallot 1980:281–284.

[194] *Rhetoric* 1386a33–34.

[195] Even in the case of φαντάσματα strictly subservient to the 'bare facts' (such as might be employed by the geometer), one must always remember that 'forms' (universals), not φαντάσματα, are the objects of thought: τὰ μὲν οὖν εἴδη τὸ νοητικὸν ἐν τοῖς φαντάσμασι νοεῖ (*De anima* 431b2; cf. 429a27–29 and 432a2–3). Hence, Wedin (1988:91) notes: "The contemplating geometer may have an image 'before his eye,' but he does not extract information from it by inspection or any other procedure. Information is forthcoming in virtue of his *doing* something, namely, proving theorems. And although this requires images, the images merely subserve the thinking. They are not what the thinking is about" (his emphasis).

[196] For πάθη as rhetorical πίστεις see Solmsen 1938 and Conley 1982.

[197] By implication, this may be said to apply even to ῥητορική as a whole because its ultimate orientation is πρὸς δόξαν, i.e. its goal is to shape opinion.

14

The Aristotelian *tekhnē* of *hypokrisis*

14.1 Technical *hypokrisis*

WE COME AT LAST TO *RHETORIC* 1404A12–19, the section where Aristotle makes clear what approach to λέξις and ὑπόκρισις he intends to take in the rest of the treatise:

ἐκείνη μὲν οὖν ὅταν ἔλθῃ ταὐτὸ ποιήσει τῇ ὑποκριτικῇ, ἐγκεχειρήκασι δὲ ἐπ' ὀλίγον περὶ αὐτῆς εἰπεῖν τινες, οἷον Θρασύμαχος ἐν τοῖς Ἐλέοις· καὶ ἔστι φύσεως τὸ ὑποκριτικὸν εἶναι, καὶ ἀτεχνότερον, περὶ δὲ τὴν λέξιν ἔντεχνον. διὸ καὶ τοῖς τοῦτο δυναμένοις γίγνεται πάλιν ἆθλα, καθάπερ καὶ τοῖς κατὰ τὴν ὑπόκρισιν ῥήτορσιν· οἱ γὰρ γραφόμενοι λόγοι μεῖζον ἰσχύουσι διὰ τὴν λέξιν ἢ διὰ τὴν διάνοιαν.

Now, when it [sc. *lexis*] comes [into vogue] it will have the same impact as the art of [dramatic] acting, and to a small extent some have endeavored to speak about it, for example Thrasymakhos in his *Pities*; and to be good at delivery is a natural gift, and [as such] less technical, but [when brought] in connection with *lexis* [it is] technical.[1] Therefore even those who have this [technical] ability in their turn win prizes,

---

[1] Alternatively, with ἔστι as 'it is possible' governing the complementary εἶναι (Bonitz 1870:220 col. 2 lines 6–8) and τό not as the article of the infinitival clause τὸ ὑποκριτικὸν εἶναι but, more narrowly, as forming the abstract τὸ ὑποκριτικόν (cf., for example, *Poetics* 1453b1–2): 'and it is possible for the ability to perform to be a natural talent and [as such], less technical, but in connection with *lexis* [it is possible for it to be] technical'. With the grammar thus construed φύσεως is coordinated with ἀτεχνότερον (φύσεως ... καὶ ἀτεχνότερον) and one should not print a comma before the conjunction καί. I actually prefer this translation, which provides a more compelling fit for the context and more naturally accounts for the infinitive εἶναι: if Aristotle had merely intended to say that 'a capacity for acting is natural', why not simply write καὶ ἔστι φύσεως τὸ ὑποκριτικόν? At any rate, since I do not want to give the impression that the validity of my argument depends on my preferred translation, I have followed the more common 'and for someone to be *hypokritikos* is of nature'.

just as also [prizes go to] professional speakers² who are such owing to
[their natural talent for] delivery; for written speeches are more effective on account of their *lexis* than on account of their argument.³

Fortenbaugh (1985:276) has noted that the Greek of a15–16 (καὶ ἔστι φύσεως ...
ἔντεχνον) is "irritatingly compressed." The first difficulty lies in identifying
the referent of ἐκείνη: the two obvious choices are λέξις and ὑπόκρισις.⁴ Most

---

² Although not office holders *per se*, Athenian ῥήτορες were readily identified in the fourth
   century BC as a well-defined group with an important institutional role. To use a familiar label
   (with the proper adjustments; cf. Hansen 1983a), they were 'politicians' who consistently engaged
   the democratic process as public speakers. Hence one may fairly call their rhetorical *activities*
   'professional,' whether they owed their oratorical *skills* to technical training or to untrained
   talent. *Rhetoric* II.11 1388b15–18 conveniently offers Aristotle's own estimate of ῥήτορες: 'Those
   are emulated who possess these and similar things. And these things are the ones [already]
   mentioned, viz. courage, wisdom, and office (ἀρχή; cf. 1388b5); for rulers (ἄρχοντες) can do
   good to many, [I mean] generals, *rhētores*, and all those who can do such things'. For ῥήτορες as
   'politicians' and hence 'professional' public speakers, see Perlman 1963:354–355, Hansen 1981
   esp. 368–370, Hansen 1983a esp. 46–48, Hansen 1983b, Hansen 1987, Ober 1989:104–127,
   Schiappa 1999:68, and Worthington 2007. Epigraphically, ῥήτωρ is first attested in IG I³ 46a.25,
   dated by the editors to ca. 445 BC (cf. Meiggs and Lewis 1969:128–133 no. 49).
³ This translation draws on my analysis above (see in particular p. 531) and immediately below. To
   interpret this difficult passage correctly one must observe the following guidelines. Aristotle
   is primarily concerned here with exploring the technical side of the capacity for delivery (this
   follows from correctly identifying the referent of ἐκείνη). Therefore, in 'διὸ καὶ ... πάλιν ... ,
   καθάπερ ... ', structured as 'therefore also A in turn, just as B', a comparison that explains A in
   terms of a better known B—such is the logic of comparisons (cf. K-G II.2.490 §579)—one would
   expect A to regard *technical* delivery (the new consideration thitherto only to a small extent the
   subject of scholarly reflection) and B, non-technical talent (the obvious, broadly accepted fact).
   That B refers to a non-technical talent for delivery as the better known member of the comparison (and hence the one following καθάπερ) should not be controversial: whatever competitions
   (formal or informal) Aristotle has in mind when he mentions ἆθλα, it should be obvious that
   by and large *no* technical training in delivery would have assisted the majority of the competitors. Otherwise, Aristotle could not claim that delivery had only received limited and trifling
   technical attention before him. This means that the ῥήτορες who are defined as κατὰ ὑπόκρισιν
   must be professional speakers who have become such in consequence of their natural talent. This
   interpretive approach is supported by the use of τοῦτο, which more plausibly refers to the closer
   clause, περὶ δὲ τὴν λέξιν ἔντεχνον, than to the more distant, ἔστι φύσεως τὸ ὑποκριτικὸν εἶναι, καὶ
   ἀτεχνότερον. Aristotle could have made the opposite choice clear with the demonstrative ἐκεῖνο.
   A final consideration: the γάρ sentence that closes the quotation most naturally applies to the
   comparison as a whole ('therefore also A in turn, just as B') rather than to its καθάπερ clause
   alone. οἱ γραφόμενοι λόγοι, entailing as it does the technical notion of *lexis*, cannot plausibly
   apply to a natural talent for delivery; hence, if one takes the statement in its most natural sense,
   i.e. as explaining the comparison as a whole and, by implication, the *explicandum* διὸ καὶ τοῖς
   τοῦτο δυναμένοις γίγνεται πάλιν ἆθλα, the γάρ clause further supports the view that τοῦτο points
   to τὸ ἔντεχνον ὑποκριτικόν (=τὸ περὶ τὴν λέξιν ὑποκριτικὸν or ἡ περὶ τὴν λέξιν ὑπόκρισις), and not
   to the ἡ ἄτεχνος ὑπόκρισις regarded in οἱ κατὰ τὴν [ἄτεχνον] ὑπόκρισιν ῥήτορες.
⁴ See also above, p. 531. Another option, but less likely, is τέχνη, which appears at 1403b35 in the
   sense of 'treatise' (note the σύγκειται). But here it would not be acceptable in that sense, for
   ἐκείνη is picked up by περὶ αὐτῆς, and ἐγκεχειρήκασι δὲ ἐπ' ὀλίγον περὶ αὐτῆς εἰπεῖν τινες clearly

commentators assume without much discussion that the latter, i.e. 'delivery', is *exclusively* in view. Apparently, the reasons are the parallel with ὑποκριτική and the presumption that, if Thrasymakhos has dealt with 'it' in his *Eleoi*, we should look for a subject that concerns itself with πάθη; and given that these same scholars are commonly of the persuasion that only ὑπόκρισις does so (to the exclusion of λέξις), it follows *eo ipso* that not style but delivery is meant. I trust I have already succeeded in proving false the impression that Aristotle does not concern himself with ὑπόκρισις in the ensuing chapters of *Rhetoric* III, and that, therefore, the view that λέξις cannot encompass the effective expression of *ēthos* and *pathos* is a prejudice contradicted by the evidence. Such considerations, then, do not suffice to remove the ambiguity.

Pointing to ἔλθῃ one might advance that, in light of τὰ περὶ τὴν ὑπόκρισιν ... ὀψὲ παρῆλθεν of 1403b22–23, ἐκείνη must be ὑπόκρισις. The problem with this view is that the last time we have an explicit reference to this word is at 1403b27, and this, by the demonstrative αὕτη,[5] twenty-one lines before our ἐκείνη; and though 'delivery' (in its narrow sense) is still the focus of the following eight lines (b28–35), it is through its concern with φωνή and its properties (hence the περὶ αὐτῶν at 1403b35–36). Perhaps more significantly, at 1403b36 the focus is broadened to τὸ περὶ τὴν λέξιν, which henceforth remains in view as is shown by the syntactic agreement of φορτικόν and ὑπολαμβανόμενον at 1404a1 and the repetition τὸ μὲν οὖν τῆς λέξεως at 1404a8.[6] And λέξις, too, is said to have come up lately (ὀψὲ προῆλθεν 1403b36), which might just as well have triggered the ὅταν ἔλθῃ.

The parallel with acting (ἡ ὑποκριτική) at 1404a13 is more promising, for (explicit attention to) 'delivery' is said at 1403b22–23 to have come to τραγική (i.e. to tragic performance)[7] when poets stopped acting out (ὑπεκρίνοντο) their own plays. Thus, one could view ὑποκριτική as tragic ὑπόκρισις. If ἐκείνη

---

calls for a subject, not a treatise. τέχνη would be possible, however, in the sense of 'art' or 'principles that guide a professional practice', which by itself would fail to resolve whether λέξις or ὑπόκρισις or, as I argue, a combination of both is in view.

5   On αὕτη versus αὐτή see above, p. 526 n. 19.

6   The syntactic agreement by itself would not be decisive, as a superficial substitution of ὑπόκρισις by τοῦτο, without any change of the notional subject—a common occurrence—might be in view. But τὸ μὲν οὖν τῆς λέξεως is clearly intended to summarize and drive home the implications of the preceding passage, i.e. 1403b36–1404a8, and this suffices to show that the broader τὸ περὶ τὴν λέξιν, a topic neither limited to nor exclusive of ὑπόκρισις, is its subject matter.

7   τραγική, as its coordination with ῥαψῳδία shows, does not in the first instance refer to *tragica ars* but to *actio tragoediarum*. Nevertheless, 1403b24–26 assumes a natural connection between dramatic ὑπόκρισις and tragic ποιητική, and from it infers that a similar relation obtains for ἡ ῥητορική. The parallel might be closely drawn: so long as oratory remained chiefly the province of untrained, well-endowed public speakers, little explicit attention was paid to delivery; once numerous citizens of middling talent had need of it and, on this account, sought some form of training, rhetorical instruction began to focus on the rules that made for successful delivery.

referred to delivery, Aristotle would be saying that 'when delivery comes [to rhetoric], it will have the same effect [there] as acting [did in tragic drama]'; and since 'acting' would owe its origin to the application of delivery to drama, we could restate the thought thus: 'when delivery comes to rhetoric, it will have the same effect there as when delivery came to tragic drama'.[8] This comment is reasonable and apposite and has much to recommend it. But considering the capital importance Aristotle assigns to delivery and its inclusion under style, if, as I argue, the philosopher fully intends to study style on the whole from the perspective of delivery, it would be just as acceptable to refer ἐκείνη to λέξις.[9] Indeed, with the coming of rhetorical[10] λέξις would also come ὑπόκρισις. And surely, for any who hold Aristotle's perspective, the paramount significance of style coming to rhetoric would lie in the coming of *delivery* to rhetoric. When one views style and delivery in the intimate connection in which the philosopher places them, it makes no *ultimate* difference whether ἐκείνη refers to the one or to the other. Only those who have driven a wedge between them make much of the alternative selected. Strictly in terms of meaning and implications, however, I find either equally acceptable, and so perhaps does Aristotle, who apparently did not realize the profound ambiguity he would inflict on future readers by choosing the demonstrative over its referent. Such oversight would be entirely excusable (and a happy one) if in fact λέξις and ὑπόκρισις occupied roughly the same conceptual space in his mind. Nevertheless, having said this much, on contextual grounds I still prefer λέξις as the referent: for from 1403b36 on, Aristotle has addressed himself to style as the more inclusive heading, yet all the while admittedly keeping delivery in mind as its preeminent subdivision. And even though he mentions τὸ ὑποκριτικόν at 1404a15, his interest is in the 'ability to perform' insofar as it bears a connection to style, i.e. περὶ τὴν λέξιν (1404a16)—so that the controlling thought is not ὑπόκρισις in its 'natural state,' so to say, but in its 'artistic' (or 'artificial') mode. Therefore, the

---

[8] 'When delivery comes to rhetoric' would mean 'when the study of delivery comes into vogue' and orators apply their technical knowledge of it regularly and effectively.

[9] There is no difficulty, of course, in having a feminine demonstrative for what has been spoken of thus far periphrastically in the neuter as τὸ περὶ τὴν λέξιν or τὸ τῆς λέξεως, for the notional subject matter all along is the feminine λέξις. Cf. the use of feminine adjectives at 1403b29–30, notionally in agreement with φωνή, even though the preceding clause speaks of τοῖς τόνοις. Or the use of αὕτη for ὑπόκρισις at 1403b27, which until then has been referred to by a neuter plural (τὰ περὶ τὴν ὑπόκρισιν 1403b22) or the neuter singular (τὸ τοιοῦτον ... · ὅπερ 1403b25–26). One might also wonder why ἐκείνη is preferred to αὕτη. The reason is not, as one might think, to direct the reader's attention away from λέξις to the further removed ὑπόκρισις; the distance felt is rather that between the demonstrative and λέξις, which appears four lines earlier and is separated from ἐκείνη by an explanation, a qualification (with the feminine φαντασία), and an example, none of which contains or refers to 'style' at the syntactic level.

[10] On the use of 'rhetorical' to qualify 'style', see immediately below, p. 583.

subject matter does not change at 1404a12 from λέξις to ὑπόκρισις, but remains uniformly the same from 1403b36 on, namely, 'rhetorical style'.[11]

But why do I speak of *rhetorical* style? I mean to reflect the all important distinction Aristotle draws at 1404a15–16: whereas τὸ ὑποκριτικόν, 'an ability to perform', to the extent that it is a natural endowment (φύσεως) is also ἀτεχνότερον, 'less within the sphere of art (i.e. of systematic study)', yet when considered in its connection to style (περὶ δὲ τὴν λέξιν), it is ἔντεχνον, 'susceptible of artistic (i.e. systematic) treatment' (or, as Cope 1877:3.8 writes, "when applied to language (declamation) it (the practice of it) may be reduced to an art").[12] It is impossible to escape the conclusion that Aristotle differentiates between a *natural* ὑπόκρισις, strictly a matter of talent, that, undisciplined by methodical speech, remains beyond analytical purview, and a ἡ περὶ τὴν λέξιν ὑπόκρισις, where *actio* is bound with manner of speech (and manner of speech reciprocally with *actio*), and which on *that* account is of professional interest and reducible to the systematic treatment of a τέχνη.[13] Where speech is not involved (e.g. pantomime) or else is not of professional concern, the talent itself might safely do without the discipline of training. ἡ περὶ τὴν λέξιν ὑπόκρισις might as well be called, as Cope 1877:8 *ad loc.* does, "ὑποκριτικὴ [I prefer ὑπόκρισις] κατὰ λέξιν," and this is the subject matter of chapters 2–12 of the third book of the *Rhetoric*. Here, at last, it becomes clear precisely how Aristotle relates delivery—that most powerful oratorical device—to the larger field of style;[14] or, reciprocally, the philosopher spells out that a study of style that will serve the ends of the orator must be conducted with a view to delivery.[15]

---

[11] Rapp 2002:2.817–818 writes: "Tatsächlich werden im vorliegenden Abschnitt die Belange der sprachlichen Form (λέξις) mit denen des mündlichen (und vom Schauspieler verlangten) Vortrags verglichen. Daher liegt nichts näher, als unter 'ὑπόκρισις' dieselbe Kunst oder Fähigkeit zu verstehen, die schon in 1403b22 damit bezeichnet wurde, und 'jene' auf die sprachliche Form (λέξις) zu beziehen; letzteres ist schon deswegen angeraten, weil bereits im vorausgegangenen Abschnitt 1404a8–12 von der Beachtung der sprachlichen Form und nicht von der Vortragskunst die Rede war." Although I cannot agree with him that τῇ ὑποκριτικῇ in 1404a13 (which Rapp rewords as 'ὑπόκρισις') regards *oratorical* delivery, he is doubtless right to observe that the context points to *lexis* as the referent of ἐκείνη.

[12] Schloemann 2000: "Hier ist der Begriff [sc. ὑπόκρισις] eng mit dem der λέξις verbunden und hat eine viel stärkere 'technische' Konnotation: er ist auf künstlerische Gestaltung bezogen" (211).

[13] The 'coming of ἐκείνη' would then signal the arrival of 'scientific delivery,' whether we designate it by 'delivery connected with style' or 'style with a view to (or according to) delivery'. For overviews of rhetorical *actio* see Wöhrle 1990 and Steinbrink 1992.

[14] This interpretation is further supported by the lines that follow (1404a18–26), for once again style and delivery are mentioned in close succession. At 1404a18–19 written speeches are said to owe their effect more to style (λέξις) than to argument (διάνοια); after which Aristotle immediately launches into a historical survey in which the mimetic quality of φωνή plays a fundamental role and is credited with the origin of the arts of rhapsodic performance, acting (ὑποκριτική), and others—only to return immediately thereafter once more to poets as pioneers of λέξις.

[15] For a study of the intersection of rhetoric and poetics in Aristotle's treatment of λέξις, see Ricoeur 1996. There, I find much I would qualify or disagree with, but I subscribe in substance the

Also clear is what motivates the distinction between artful and artless ὑπόκρισις: after writing that 'when style-with-delivery comes, it will have the same effect as acting', the philosopher adds that 'some have endeavored *in a limited way* to talk about it' (my emphasis). Why has the scientific study of this paramount rhetorical matter been prosecuted so inadequately? Why has no one yet succeeded in drawing a full and comprehensive account of it? Aristotle replies: 'Because the ability to perform can well be a natural talent and, accordingly, less technical'. Ultimately, however, this fact cannot serve to excuse inaction, whatever the history of past failure or the theoretical challenge ahead,[16] and consequently Aristotle sets out to fill the gap and perfect the art of rhetoric with a study of 'delivery in its connection with style'.

Fortenbaugh (1985:287n27), surveying two alternative ways of reading 1404a15–16, notes: "On one interpretation, Aristotle says that the principles of style are technical ... . On another he says that when delivery is applied to style, then it (delivery) is something technical." Yet only a minority of translators (in my view, incorrectly) have followed the former reading.[17] And no wonder: for we should then expect ἡ δὲ λέξις ἔντεχνος, not περὶ δὲ τὴν λέξιν ἔντεχνον.[18]

---

central insight that the *Poetics* and the *Rhetoric* structure the field of style in ways that are distinctive and reflect their various aims. Thus, for example, observing that in the former Aristotle rejects the analysis of λέξις under "modes of speech" (i.e. illocutionary forms of speech), he writes: "Hardly has this line of analysis been alluded to when it is interrupted by the remark: 'Let us pass over this, then, as appertaining to another art ...' (1456b19). This other 'art' can only be rhetoric" (328). Ricoeur thinks that Aristotle applies himself to "clos[ing] the gap, if not fill[ing] a void" between the theory of λέξις in poetry and a "truly rhetorical theory of *lexis*" (343). I must, however, part company with him when, following the consensus view, he asserts that, as a *how*, ὑπόκρισις is further removed than λέξις from the *what* of a speech (343): perhaps so from *our* perspective, but only true of Aristotle in a limited sense, for ultimately the entire art of rhetoric is oriented towards effective and successful delivery. Valid logical distinctions cannot obscure necessary practical connections; yes, "it is through our *lexis* that we teach" (344), but in fifth- and fourth-century Greece it is preeminently in oral delivery that the act of teaching takes place. For this reason I reject his interpretation of, and rationale for, *Rhetoric* 1404a18–19: "To the degree that style is the external manifestation of discourse, it tends to separate the concern to 'please' from that of 'arguing.' It is doubtless because writing constitutes a second degree of exteriorization that the separation is particularly dangerous in this case" (344).

16 Cf. similar pronouncements regarding metaphors in *Poetics* 1459a6–7 and *Rhetoric* 1405a9–10 (with the note in Cope 1877:21–22 *ad loc.*); and yet no one would deny that much effort is expended in teaching their proper use in accordance with the principle that art improves nature. Cf. Newman 1998:76n20, Newman 2005:46n20, and Burkett 2011:91–92.

17 Namely, Roberts (in Ross 1924), Jebb (in Sandys 1909), and Rapp 2002. On the other side of the divide we find the old Latin translation (*apud* Spengel 1867), Cope 1877, Freese 1926, Tovar 1953, Dufour and Wartelle 1973, and Kennedy 1991 (cf. Arnhart 1981:165).

18 Or τὸ δὲ περὶ τὴν λέξιν ἔντεχνον, which is nowhere attested. And while one might wonder whether τό may have fallen out, the placement of δέ, between περί and τήν, rules this out (cf., for example, Aristotle *De generatione animalium* 715a14 and *Historia animalium* 491b21, 493a28, 511a27, 597a32; there are no instances of τὸ περὶ δέ). In point of fact, neither does the context recommend adding it, for the text makes good sense as is.

There is therefore no further sharpening to be found here of an alleged contrast between style and delivery, and Fortenbaugh is right in judging that "the Greek suits the latter interpretation better, which is in any case strongly supported by Aristotle's remarks in 3.12" (1985:287n27).

We must similarly understand the implication drawn at 1404a16–18, where two groups are contrasted: οἱ τοῦτο [i.e. τὸ περὶ τὴν λέξιν ὑποκριτικὸν] δυνάμενοι, namely, those who by training and profession are capable of delivering their speeches in accordance with the principles of rhetorical stylistics (in its as yet rudimentary state); and οἱ κατὰ τὴν [ἄτεχνον] ὑπόκρισιν ῥήτορες, the orators who merely have a knack for delivery, who without the sophistication and self-awareness of rhetorical instruction nevertheless show the prowess of their natural talent.[19] And just as (καθάπερ) exceptional giftedness can prove itself victorious in competition, so also (καί) the orator who is properly trained in *his* turn (πάλιν) can himself well carry off the prize.[20]

This approach contrasts significantly with the one followed in the *Poetics*, where delivery, while explicitly owned as part of style, is nevertheless declared to be of interest only to actors (ὑποκριταί) and in consequence rejected as extrinsic to

---

[19] See above, p. 580 n. 3. Interpreters have failed to grasp the distinction Aristotle is drawing here. Had he merely wanted to say "just as [prizes go] to orators on the basis of their delivery" (Kennedy's translation, which is representative of the rest), he would have written instead καθάπερ καὶ τοῖς ῥήτορσιν κατὰ τὴν ὑπόκρισιν. In the attributive position κατὰ τὴν ὑπόκρισιν *defines* these orators (it could be otherwise had Aristotle used a participle, e.g. λέγουσιν, which the prepositional clause could then modify adverbially); and if Aristotle meant to ascribe to them superior delivery, adding this qualifier was a very odd way indeed of doing so. In fact, it is hard to see how κατά by itself could bear this meaning, while the slightly modified τοῖς κατὰ τὴν ὑπόκρισιν διαφέρουσιν ῥήτορσιν would have made this plain. Once we accept the implications of the syntax and reflect on the context, it becomes clear that in this expression ὑπόκρισις must stand for τὸ ὑποκριτικόν as the natural talent that is ἄτεχνον and bears no relation to λέξις.

[20] Fortenbaugh (1985:287n29) interprets the contrast incorrectly. He is right, I think, to reject the translation in Sonkowsky (1959:261) that opposes "actors with histrionic ability" to "orators who excel in delivery" (this would invert the terms of the comparison, which should rather have had the καθάπερ go not with ῥήτορες but with οἱ τοῦτο δυνάμενοι, i.e. the alleged actors); but thinking that this chapter is an introduction to style, which he divorces from delivery, he concludes that the philosopher is only trying to show that "style, too, conveys power and produces prizes." On this reading, the γάρ sentence that follows would make the point by noting that written texts owe their power more to style than to thought (for my own notions about this, see below, section 14.2). This interpretation would be allowable if Aristotle had written ἡ δὲ λέξις ἔντεχνος at 1404a16; as it stands, the text will not permit τοῦτο to refer to style and will therefore not support an alleged literary view of style as embodied by written compositions. Fortenbaugh is otherwise correct in contrasting τὸ [φύσει] ὑποκριτικόν, 'a natural gift for delivery' ("orators gifted in delivery") with 'style'—not just any concept of style, but ἡ κατὰ λέξιν ὑπόκρισις, the choice that Cope rewords "ὑποκριτικὴ κατὰ λέξιν" and Fortenbaugh dismisses as "second best but ... at least consistent with Aristotle's focus on style." Why it is "second best" remains unexplained.

ποιητική. Indeed, at 1456b8–10 we learn that τὰ σχήματα τῆς λέξεως,[21] the 'forms of utterance' (Halliwell 1999:97 *ad loc.*), constitute one type of inquiry into matters connected with λέξις, a study which is for ἡ ὑποκριτική to know as well as for any who have such mastery (ὁ τὴν τοιαύτην ἔχων ἀρχιτεκτονικήν).[22] The ensuing list[23] makes clear that Aristotle has *performative* settings in view where a skillful employment of the voice (e.g. loudness and intonation) is essential for successful communication. Neither knowledge nor ignorance of these earns ἡ ποιητική any serious blame (ἐπιτίμημα ... ὅ τι καὶ ἄξιον σπουδῆς 1456b14–15). Protagoras' famous criticism of the opening of the *Iliad* supplies a ready illustration: for why should Homer's μῆνιν ἄειδε θεά be criticized for allegedly confusing a prayer with a command? The point is that the same form of words can be made into a prayer or a command depending on the tone of voice employed.[24] Therefore this study (θεώρημα) must belong not to poetry but to some other art, the philosopher adds. He is not thereby denying *pronuntiatio* its rightful place—surely he would have made it the part of any good rhapsode to utter the words with the solemnity and propriety that befits the invocation of a deity—but since the deficiency (if there is one) must be traced to the performer, not the poet, it is therefore possible to dissociate, as he does, the study of ποιητική from considerations of delivery. The degree to which Aristotle, for the purposes of his *Poetics*, has distanced the poetic texts of epic and tragic drama from their elocutionary performative aspects is nevertheless surprising.[25] In bringing up delivery only to dispose of it as irrel-

---

[21] The expression recalls *Rhetoric* 1408b21 and b28–29, where it is used specifically of rhythm. Though in the *Rhetoric* its semantic range is much narrower than the one we encounter in the *Poetics*, both occurrences share the performative emphasis.

[22] *Poetics* 1456b10–11. Presumably the 'architect' of acting displays a technical knowledge of his field (rationale, principles, and application), as opposed to actors who, having learned their trade by trial and error, might rely for their guidance on experience. This probably relates to the observation at *Rhetoric* 1403b22–24.

[23] οἷον τί ἐντολὴ καὶ τί εὐχὴ καὶ διήγησις καὶ ἀπειλὴ καὶ ἐρώτησις καὶ ἀπόκρισις καὶ εἴ τι ἄλλο τοιοῦτον (1456b11–13). Cf. 1457a21–22.

[24] This is not do deny Twining's obvious comment that "[of] Homer's *pronunciation* or *action* ... Protagoras knew nothing" (1812:2.251, his emphasis). All that is implied in the sophist's censure is an incorrect use of the imperative, of which there is an echo in the scholia of the Venetus A *ad loc.* (Erbse 1969–1988:1.5.41–42 §d): ὅτι κατὰ τὴν ποιητικὴν ἤτοι ἄδειαν ἢ συνήθειαν λαμβάνει τὰ προστακτικὰ ἀντὶ εὐκτικῶν. It is wrong, however, to interpret these performative settings strictly as σχήματα διανοίας (e.g. in Quintilian *Institutio oratoria* 6.3.70) and suppress in turn the 'manner of expression' (but cf. Twining 1812:2.253). Note Lucas's humane observation: "The point raised here probably arose from [Protagoras'] perception that what we call the imperative mood was associated with the tone of command ... . Those who discover new principles often try to apply them too rigidly" (Lucas 1968:198). On the notion and history of σχήματα διανοίας see Lausberg 1998:271–273 §§600–603, 335–410 §§755–910.

[25] Paradoxically, what makes such distance possible is Aristotle's belief in the inherent expressive power of διάνοια, i.e. of the argument articulated by λέξις/λόγος (1456a36–37; cf. 1462a11–13) that allows a reader to recreate the effect of performance (or at least to 'replay' the events of the

evant, the philosopher surprises the modern reader in a way that is only matched by the striking inclusion under λέξις of the principles of grammar and syntax;[26] for who could think of studying drama today without reference to staging and acting? This move parallels the dismissal of ὄψις at 1450b16–20.[27]

Note now how different the philosopher's stance is vis-à-vis rhetorical delivery: while he gives the texts of drama and epic priority over performance,[28]

---

plot, 1453b1–6) in his mind's eye. Note that the philosopher readily makes even the articulation of emotions the purview of λόγος (1456b5–8; see immediately below for an important qualification), although whatever de-emphasis on delivery this entails is partially counterbalanced by his pairing ἀνάγνωσις and τὰ ἔργα at 1462a17–18 (I adopt Madius's preferred reading over against the vulgate ἀναγνωρίσει: "ideo legendum est ἀναγνώσει, ut codices aliqui calamo exarati Venetiis habent" [Madius and Lombardus 1550:297]). To be sure, the distance between λόγος in performance and διάνοια as the verbal expression of the argument of a play abstracted from *actio* (including *pronuntiatio* and rhetorical *elocutio*) only makes sense where the text under discussion is notionally, if not actually, independent of the performer, i.e. viewed as a script that can be interpreted with a varying degree of competence. Then one may rightly question how successfully the performer has brought out the expressive potential of the text or acted out what its author intended. This argues for a significant degree of fixation already by Aristotle's time of a standard Athenian version of the *Iliad*, though it need not rule out a comparatively small degree of *mouvance*. For one, the philosopher's focus is not on epic but on drama, whose authorship and textual status are far more straightforward than those of the Homeric poems; and yet we know that even the text of Athenian tragedies experienced so-called 'textual interpolations,' which, some scholars will admit, are of histrionic origin (cf., for example, Page 1934; see also above, p. 445 n. 42). Moreover, the example selected by Aristotle, *Iliad* 1.1, is likely to have been among the earliest passages to attain fixity; the rhapsode's irrelevance (narrowly conceived) to the textual status of this line (in a poem, besides, that is notionally fixed and uniformly ascribed to the man 'Homer'), is thus, on the point of analogy, a good parallel to the corresponding 'irrelevance' of acting to drama. For the concept of 'notional fixity' and why it does not rule out a measure of *mouvance*, see pp. 173ff. above.

26 Bywater (1909:260) notes on *Poetics* 20: "This whole chapter has been condemned by Ritter and others as an interpolation; and it must be admitted that, according to our notions of the divisions of knowledge, the matter in it belongs to grammar and philology rather than to an Art of Poetry."

27 ἡ δὲ ὄψις ψυχαγωγικὸν μέν, ἀτεχνότατον δὲ καὶ ἥκιστα οἰκεῖον τῆς ποιητικῆς· ἡ γὰρ τῆς τραγῳδίας δύναμις καὶ ἄνευ ἀγῶνος καὶ ὑποκριτῶν ἔστιν, ἔτι δὲ κυριωτέρα περὶ τὴν ἀπεργασίαν τῶν ὄψεων ἡ τοῦ σκευοποιοῦ τέχνη τῆς τῶν ποιητῶν ἐστιν ('Theatrical spectacle moves the heart but it falls quite outside, and is least pertinent to, the art of poetry; for the effect of tragedy is present even without public contest and actors, and, besides, the production of visual effects belongs more to the art of the equipment and props maker than to the art of the poets'). Just as τὸ [φύσει] ὑποκριτικόν is ἄτεχνον, so also 'spectacle' is ἀτεχνότατον, not in absolute terms (for otherwise how could Aristotle *in this very passage* refer to ἡ τοῦ σκευοποιοῦ τέχνη?) but with respect to ἡ ποιητικὴ τέχνη (so, correctly, Susemihl 1874:101, 235; Gudeman 1934:190; and Halliwell 1986:340 §d). In contrast to ὑπόκρισις, however, which *can* be readily associated with λέξις—an association of φωνή with λόγος—and thus becomes the object of systematic study, the symbolic grammar of dramatic spectacle fails to benefit from a similar analytic strategy. The absence of a natural correspondence between verbal and visual language makes the crucial difference. Cf. *Poetics* 1453b1–9 and 1462a11–12.

28 Not necessarily as *written* texts (though also available thus), but as oral literature that can be actualized on demand by performance. It is doubtful that rhetorical addresses were ever similarly considered.

so secondary is the written form of an orator's speech to his public *actio* (before court or assembly) that Aristotle cannot, in his study of rhetoric, overlook delivery, and the corresponding notion of rhetorical style is quite different from the poetic stylistics that emerges in the *Poetics*.[29] And yet, even there he owns that the study of delivery is a legitimate θεώρημα of a true aspect of λέξις, however irrelevant to poetics *stricto sensu*. The difference is readily epitomized by two contrasting definitions. One is found in *Poetics* 1450b13–14: λέγω δέ ... λέξιν εἶναι τὴν διὰ τῆς ὀνομασίας ἑρμηνείαν ('By *lexis* I mean expression through wording');[30] the other, in *Rhetoric* 1403b16–18: περὶ δὲ τῆς λέξεως ἐχόμενόν ἐστιν εἰπεῖν· οὐ γὰρ ἀπόχρη τὸ ἔχειν ἃ δεῖ λέγειν, ἀλλ' ἀνάγκη καὶ ταῦτα ὡς δεῖ εἰπεῖν, καὶ συμβάλλεται πολλὰ πρὸς τὸ φανῆναι ποιόν τινα τὸν λόγον ('To speak about *lexis* is next; for it is not enough to have [in hand] what one should say, but one must also tell it as he ought to, and this contributes much to the speech coming across as being of a certain quality'; cf. 1404a35–39). This shift in emphasis is further manifest at *Poetics* 1456a38, where in remarks about the purview of λέξις and διάνοια he assigns *pathos* to the latter, with only an implicit reference to the corresponding role of *lexis* understood narrowly not as rhetorical expression but as the argument (λόγος) that falls to *inventio*.[31] It is true that here the emotions are primarily internal to the play, in and towards dramatic characters (Bywater 1909 *ad loc.*). More significantly, however, is that Aristotle seems to think of these emotions narrowly as the outworking of the μῦθος (the structure of τὰ πράγματα). Just as they are therefore unrelated to the manner of expression (to the expressive instrumentality of φωνή, gestures, and other elements of delivery), so also is ἦθος similarly divorced from *actio*: it is rather

---

[29] Addressing this distinction, Halliwell (1993:51) remarks apropos *Rhetoric* III: "[T]he subject of these chapters is rhetorical *lexis*, not *lexis* in general, a point emphasized at 3.1.10, 04a 36–9." See further above, p. 529 n. 31 and p. 548 n. 100.

[30] To this definition of λέξις, Aristotle adds the further observation, ὃ καὶ ἐπὶ τῶν ἐμμέτρων καὶ ἐπὶ τῶν λόγων ἔχει τὴν αὐτὴν δύναμιν ('which has the same potential in both verse and prose', *Poetics* 1450b14–15). In its light, his earlier statement at 1449b33–34 is but a particular application of ἡ διὰ τῆς ὀνομασίας ἑρμηνεία to metrical expression (cf. Dupont-Roc and Lallot 1980:209–210). Note the divergent point of view of *Rhetoric* 1404a28: ἑτέρα λόγου καὶ ποιήσεως λέξις ἐστίν ('The *lexis* of prose is different from that of poetry'). If the λέξις of the *Poetics* denotes 'expression' (equivalent in this sense to λόγος broadly understood as 'speech' in communication, as observed by Lucas 1968:195 *ad* 1456a37), in the *Rhetoric* the focus is more narrowly on the *form* of such expression, in particular on how it must be shaped for persuasive delivery before an audience.

[31] See *Rhetoric* 1403a36–b1 with Grimaldi 1988:369 *ad loc.* Cf. also *Poetics* 1450b4–5: τοῦτο [i.e. ἡ διάνοια] δέ ἐστιν τὸ λέγειν δύνασθαι τὰ ἐνόντα καὶ τὰ ἁρμόττοντα. Lucas (1968:195) relates τοῦ λόγου in *Poetics* 1456a37 to λέξις as 'expression'. But Aristotle not only conceptualizes rhetorical *lexis* and poetic *lexis* divergently; even the concept of λέξις that the *Poetics* explores in the following section—and tellingly fails to tie explicitly to *pathos*—diverges from the λόγος that is strictly instrumental to διάνοια. A distinction is presupposed at 1456a33–34, where λοιπόν divides into λέξις and διάνοια. And so it is that, after dismissing διάνοια and referring the interested reader to his *Rhetoric*, the philosopher then takes up λέξις at 1456b8 from the point of view of its σχήματα.

the articulation of deliberate choice, primarily through argument (the λόγος of διάνοια 1450b8–12) and secondarily through the sequence of events (πράγματα/ πράξεις 1450a20–23).[32] Once again, rhetorical style has no inherent bearing on such articulation. Yet, in the ultimate analysis, even for such ἤθη and πάθη is *lexis* as conceived in the *Rhetoric* important for plausibility and dramatic illusion vis-à-vis the spectators, all the more so if the performance is to induce in them a catharsis of 'fear and pity' (1456b1).[33]

I must address one final matter before I turn my attention to the role that writing plays in rhetorical practice, namely, the reference to Thrasymakhos at 1404a14, which might be thought to support an interpretation of ἐκείνη at 1404a12 different from the one advocated here.[34] For it is clear that αὐτῆς at 1404a14 points to the same referent as ἐκείνη, and hence it follows that, whatever its identity, Thrasymakhos is singled out as one who has taken in hand to speak a little 'about *it*' in his *Eleoi* (my emphasis). And since the title itself means 'pities', it invites translations that put the emphasis on emotional appeals *as if* entirely divorced from rhetorical considerations of a technical nature. If the substance of the *Pities* was a gross, inartistic (ἄτεχνον) appeal to emotions— without reference to λέξις, which, I have argued, constitutes for Aristotle the proper technical sphere of such appeals—mentioning Thrasymakhos can be read as correspondingly reinforcing the often alleged dichotomy between ὑπόκρισις and λέξις. This would then support the view that Aristotle's design is to characterize delivery as not only ethically obnoxious but inartistic and incapable of systematic treatment, ruling out any further consideration of it in his treatment of style—until, that is, it resurfaces somehow in chapter 12.[35]

But the little we know about the sophist from the extant sources contradicts such a tendentious reconstruction of his practice.[36] We must, of course, make

---

[32] Cf. Aristotle's comment at 1450a24–26 about ἀήθεις τραγῳδίαι ('tragedies deficient in character'; cf. Lucas 1968:103 *ad loc.*).

[33] There is, as scholars note, a parallel in the passage of the *Rhetoric* that starts at 1356a1, but with this important distinction: that, as befits an introduction, Aristotle there uses *logos* in the most general sense of 'discourse, speech' (cf. Grimaldi 1980 *ad loc.*) and makes no attempt to apportion *ēthos* or *pathos* to one or another component of the art of oratory. Therefore Kennedy's remark, "Aristotle is not thinking of style and delivery but of the thought and contents" (1991:38n41), is unnecessary and a little misleading. That the philosopher does not exclude style any more than he does thought is clear from the comment that follows, namely, that persuasion through character happens whenever the speech is spoken *in such a way as* to make the speaker worthy of trust.

[34] For the relevant *testimonia* and fragments, see DK 85 and Radermacher 1951:B.IX. For studies of his contribution to the development of prose and rhetoric, see Blass 1887:244–258, Schwartz 1892, Drerup 1901:225–251, and Kennedy 1963:68–70.

[35] See below, pp. 598ff.

[36] Quintilian's passing comment (*Institutio oratoria* 3.3.4) that Thrasymakhos had ascribed *actio* to *natura* rather than *ars* is not as definitive in its implications as might seem at first. For on the basis of *Rhetoric* 1404a15–16 the same can be said, *grosso modo*, about Aristotle himself. And yet

allowance for the more limited degree of development rhetoric as an art must have received at the hands of this pioneer when compared to Aristotle himself; for I am, after all, arguing that if, according to Aristotle, Thrasymakhos spoke about ἡ κατὰ λέξιν ὑπόκρισις only ἐπ' ὀλίγον, the philosopher—who observes and, in my opinion, regrets the lack of a τέχνη about delivery—intended to, and in actual fact did, address the gap in the scholarship of his time with his own treatment of λέξις in *Rhetoric* III.1–12. And even though he must have considered the sophist's discussion deficient enough to warrant his simultaneously holding that 'no *technē* has yet been composed' and that, all the same, Thrasymakhos and others 'have attempted to speak a little about it', tradition attests to the sophist's penning at least one τέχνη,[37] which, as Drerup (1901:227) notes, must have included not only ready-made examples but also accompanying observations of a theoretical nature. And a survey of his contributions quickly reveals that he moves largely within parameters of rhetorical stylistics not unlike those explored by Aristotle in his manual (rhythm, cola, etc.). The reality that emerges from such a survey further underscores the two facts I have endeavored to establish: first, that, far from fencing it off, delivery (in its concern with emotions) *was* indeed within the scope of Aristotle's examination of style, just as it received attention (however deficient) by Thrasymakhos; and secondly, that the subjects of rhythm, periodic structure, propriety, and so on could be conceived of and treated under the heading of delivery as a sort of rhetorical stylistics with a view to delivery (ἡ περὶ τὴν λέξιν ὑπόκρισις or ἡ κατὰ ὑπόκρισιν λέξις).

Let us, then, survey what we know about the famous sophist. The first *testimonium*, the one most emphatic and explicit about the emotional impact pursued, comes from Plato's *Phaidros* 267c: 'It seems to me that the might of the Chalcedonian has technical (τέχνη) mastery of piteously wailing speeches applied to old age and poverty, and that the man, moreover, has grown terrific both at inflaming a crowd and charming it in turn by chanting (ἐπᾴδων) to those inflamed, as he said; and he is unbeatable at both casting and wiping

---

we have seen how the philosopher, with this broad statement as a foil, introduces a technical notion of *actio* in its particular connection to *elocutio*. All the same, the logic of his thought has often escaped the modern scholar and we cannot be sure that Thrasymakhos' words, even if faithfully reported by Quintilian, were not accompanied by such instruction as would have made clear, explicitly or implicitly, that in certain respects *actio* was, after all, susceptible of systematic analysis. Quintilian may have missed this, may have depended on a source that was not sufficiently accurate or detailed, or may have chosen only to report the general statement without any further elaboration. His remark, then, may do nothing more than place the sophist all the more firmly as a forerunner of Aristotle in his approach to ὑπόκρισις.

37 The *Suidas* s.v. Θρασύμαχος states: ἔγραψε συμβουλευτικούς, τέχνην ῥητορικήν, παίγνια, ἀφορμὰς ῥητορικάς (2.726 Θ no. 462 Adler). The scholiast to Aristophanes *Birds* 880, however, mentions a μεγάλη τέχνη: is it the same as the τέχνη ῥητορική of the *Suidas*? Cf. Plato *Phaidros* 261c2 and 266c3.

off aspersions, whatever their source. Now, there seems to be general agreement on the end of speeches, which some call "recapitulation" (ἐπάνοδον), and others, by another name'.[38] After a humorous reference to his 'piteously wailing' discourses that dwelt on poverty and old age, Sokrates tells of Thrasymakhos' ability now to excite anger, now to charm the angry by his incantations (where ἐπᾴδων suggests the musical quality of his ῥυθμοί and ἁρμονία, i.e. of his voice in delivery).[39] His superior skill in fabricating and overthrowing slander seems rather to belong to his dexterity in εὕρησις (mentioned elsewhere); the term ἐπάνοδος, 'recapitulation' (cf. *Rhetoric* 1414b2), identifies the part of a speech that best lends itself to such appeals.[40]

Plutarch, in his *Quaestiones convivales* 616d mentions Thrasymakhos' Ὑπερβάλλοντες [sc. λόγοι], which, to judge from the context, must have consisted in arguments built on comparisons (συγκρίσεις). Athenaios X 416a, in turn, writes about the sophist's προοίμια: it appears, then, that he not only composed examples of closing *perorationes* but also of opening *exordia*. These two collections together may correspond to the ἀφορμαὶ ῥητορικαί of the *Suidas*. As to general qualities of style, Dionysios of Halikarnassos *Lysias* §6 (p. 14.1–2 Usener) reports that Theophrastos had credited Thrasymakhos with pioneering the middle style[41] (cf. *Dēmosthenēs* §3 p. 132.14–15 Usener), a manner of expression that 'compresses the thoughts and expresses them tersely'.[42] In *Isaios* §20 (p. 122.21–23 Usener) we also learn that Dionysios considered the sophist τῶν … τοὺς ἀκριβεῖς προαιρουμένων λόγους καὶ πρὸς τὴν ἐναγώνιον ἀσκούντων ῥητορικήν, a sentence that Usher (1974:229) *ad loc.* renders, "[of] those who preferred *factual* discourses and *practical* [*sic*][43] rhetoric designed for the law-courts" (my emphasis)—an understanding of ἀκρίβεια and ἐναγώνιος that cautions us perhaps not to jump too

---

38 τῶν γε μὴν οἰκτρογόων ἐπὶ γῆρας καὶ πενίαν ἑλκομένων λόγων κεκρατηκέναι τέχνη μοι φαίνεται τὸ τοῦ Χαλκηδονίου σθένος, ὀργίσαι τε αὖ πολλοὺς ἅμα δεινὸς ἀνὴρ γέγονεν, καὶ πάλιν ὠργισμένοις ἐπᾴδων κηλεῖν, ὡς ἔφη· διαβάλλειν τε καὶ ἀπολύσασθαι διαβολὰς ὁθενδὴ κράτιστος. τὸ δὲ δὴ τέλος τῶν λόγων κοινῇ πᾶσιν ἔοικε συνδεδογμένον εἶναι, ᾧ τινες μὲν ἐπάνοδον, ἄλλοι δ᾽ ἄλλο τίθενται ὄνομα (267c7–d4).

39 Radermacher (1951:71) comments perceptively on the rhythmic structure Plato imparts to the words τῶν γε μὴν οἰκτρογόων ἐπὶ γῆρας καὶ πενίαν ἑλκομένων λόγων (*Phaidros* 267c7–8): "Ceterum notabis puros numeros … ex quo conicias in ἐλέων exemplis admodum numerosam fuisse sophistae orationem."

40 Just as Aristotle does in *Rhetoric* III.19, though chapter 14.7 makes clear that such devices are also profitably used in *prooimia*.

41 Or *a* middle style, if Grube 1952 is right (cf. O'Sullivan 1992:114), though his insistence upon rendering λέξις narrowly as 'diction' (word choice *stricto sensu*) seems misguided, as his own comments on pp. 264–266 hint. Cf. also Innes 1985:260–262.

42 ἡ συστρέφουσα τὰ νοήματα καὶ στρογγύλως ἐκφέρουσα λέξις (§6 p. 14.9–10 Usener). Grube (1952:260) translates: "A manner of writing (or speaking) which gathers up its ideas compactly and brings them out in bold relief."

43 Presumably reading ἀσκοῦντας with F¹, although he too prints ἀσκούντων.

readily to conclusions as to the meaning of ἀκριβής in *Rhetoric* III.12,[44] where the λέξις γραφική is ἡ ἀκριβεστάτη and the ἀγωνιστική is ἡ ὑποκριτικωτάτη (1413b8–9). A little later in the same section of Dionysios' *Isaios* (p. 123.10–14 Usener) we read: Θρασύμαχος δὲ καθαρὸς μὲν καὶ λεπτὸς καὶ δεινὸς εὑρεῖν τε καὶ εἰπεῖν στρογγύλως καὶ περιττῶς, ὃ βούλεται, πᾶς δέ ἐστιν ἐν τοῖς τεχνογραφικοῖς καὶ ἐπιδεικτικοῖς, δικανικοὺς δὲ [ἢ συμβουλευτικοὺς][45] οὐκ ἀπολέλοιπε λόγους ('Thrasymakhos is pure, subtle, and terrific both at discovery and speaking at will with terseness or redundancy; but he is entirely into handbooks and epideictic, but has not left forensic [or deliberative] speeches'). Aristotle's *Rhetoric* supplies two relevant *testimonia*. At 1409a2–3 he tells us that orators have used the paean since the time of Thrasymakhos; with this, Cicero appears in broad agreement;[46] and at *Rhetoric* 1413a6–9 he recounts a brilliant instance of the sophist's use of similes.

We may quote in summary the considered judgment of Kennedy (1963:68–69): "What Thrasymachus appreciated, and perhaps he was the first to do so, was the effect of a varied rhythmic pattern ... . Furthermore, the fragment[47] shows a degree of sentence structure more developed than in any earlier writer and a tendency to avoid hiatus ... . In both these respects Thrasymachus differs from Gorgias, as he does in avoiding the artificialities of the latter's style." What emerges from this survey is not a figure narrowly concerned with inartistic emotional appeals, but one who paid broad attention to style *and* delivery, in much the same way I argue Aristotle himself does. Hence, it is understandable that the *Suidas* would say that [Θρασύμαχος] πρῶτος περίοδον καὶ κῶλον κατέδειξε καὶ τὸν νῦν τῆς ῥητορικῆς τρόπον εἰσηγήσατο (2.726 Θ no. 462 Adler).[48]

---

[44] See below, pp. 625ff.

[45] E. Schwartz *delevit*: not only is it contradicted by the testimony of the *Suidas* but, as Blass (1887:250) notes, by established facts about the sophist, including the extant fragments. It is true that as a non-Athenian he would not have had the right to address the assembly, but neither are all speeches of a symbuleutic character necessarily for oral delivery or at least for delivery by the author himself. Thus, the reported Ὑπὲρ Λαρισαίων (DK 85 B2), whose single extant line indeed reads like a political address, may have belonged to a political pamphlet or it may have been written for a Thessalian embassy (so Blass 1887:250). And the Περὶ πολιτείας (DK 85 B1) is so generic an *exemplum*, as Radermacher (1951:B.IX.10) notes, that it may well have been extracted from a rhetorical manual. (Cf. Drerup 1901:227, who thinks it must have been a political pamphlet. For Dionysios [*Dēmosthenēs* §3 p. 132.18 Usener] it is a παράδειγμα from one of his δημηγορικοὶ λόγοι.) In any case, it is surprising that one who arguably took great interest in the rhetorical impact of emotions and whose style was arguably most fitting to the oratory of the law-court should not have left any forensic speeches (as Dionysios *Isaios* §20 observes).

[46] *Orator* 175: "nam neminem in eo genere scientius versatum Isocrate confitendum est, sed princeps inveniundi fuit Thrasymachus, cuius omnia nimis etiam exstant scripta numerose."

[47] He means *Dēmosthenēs* §3, although on p. 68 he erroneously refers to "*Isaeus* 3."

[48] Cf. Grube 1952, who disputes Thrasymakhos' alleged part in the development of the periodic style. But he is countered by Innes (1985:262), who suggests that Theophrastos may have recognized the sophist as the pioneer of "the mean between the unshaped and the overperiodic sentence."

We cannot, therefore, read much into 1404a13–15, with its mention of the Ἔλεοι, for, as Fortenbaugh (1985:285n2) recognizes (his unnecessary dichotomy between λέξις and ὑπόκρισις notwithstanding): "In a work on emotional appeal remarks on style are just as appropriate as remarks on delivery."

14.2 *Hypokrisis* and the Use of Writing

Let us now return to Aristotle's statement about written speeches at *Rhetoric* 1404a18–19: οἱ γὰρ γραφόμενοι λόγοι μεῖζον ἰσχύουσι διὰ τὴν λέξιν ἢ διὰ τὴν διάνοιαν. The γάρ shows that it is an explanation of the preceding sentence, with its opposition between οἱ τοῦτο δυνάμενοι and οἱ κατὰ τὴν ὑπόκρισιν ῥήτορες. If my understanding of the identity of these two groups is correct,[49] then it follows that those skilled in that delivery which is made 'artistic' by its connection to λέξις win prizes *because* written speeches carry greater force on account of their λέξις than their διάνοια.[50] Doubtless, this need not be the *only* reason

---

[49] See above, p. 580 n. 3 and p. 585.

[50] This is an affirmation of the stylistic potential that writing holds for delivery; it does not of course assert that any and all written speeches in fact exhibited the force of their style at the expense of their argument. Some have sought to weaken the implication that οἱ γραφόμενοι λόγοι are introduced to make a point about the practice of performing orators. But, *ceteris paribus*, given its context one must surely grant not only the plausibility but even the likelihood that this implication is deliberate and true to fact. After all, it is while discussing the role of ὑπόκρισις *qua* art in its connection with λέξις that Aristotle observes that speakers who master this aspect of ῥητορική win prizes. Hence follows that the competitive success asserted of orators competent in ἡ περὶ τὴν λέξιν ὑπόκρισις must be the very fact that the ensuing γάρ clause seeks to explain when it draws attention to the 'force' of written speeches *on account of their* λέξις. Some translate οἱ γραφόμενοι λόγοι as 'speeches intended for reading', thereby dismissing any connection with performance other than perhaps an adventitious one. But no prizes were ever awarded to written speeches *qua* written, and this view effectively (and inadmissibly) severs the γάρ clause from the context it is supposed to illustrate. A sounder proposal, if in my opinion still too limiting, is that the statement chiefly regards epideictic showpieces (cf. *Rhetoric* 1414b24–25), whose authors would have hoped for a broad readership and even crafted them with reading in mind. But even under this proposal prize winning would still require their public oral performance (including perhaps reading them in public). This hypothetical scenario would only represent an extreme case of orators' dependence on scripts for their delivery. Nonetheless, I believe that a broader reference than 'epideictic' is commended both by the context, itself a general survey, and by the present participle γραφόμενοι (on which see below). Sonkowsky (1959:261) is even more definitive and asserts that "the suggestion ... that the *epideiktikon genos* is meant cannot be correct unless Aristotle is inconsistent," because "[e]pideictic in the *lexis graphikē* is the most accurately written of the three kinds of discourse and depends the least upon delivery, the counterpart of style, for its effectiveness." As a signal case of 'epideictic' (broadly understood) one might think of Isokrates. But although Aristotle knew some of his speeches and occasionally used them to illustrate his argument, these were not delivered by their author in a public setting such as would encourage the notion that they adequately illustrate the meaning, much less that they are the intended referent, of οἱ γραφόμενοι λόγοι. Isokrates famously declared himself neither well-endowed nor courageous enough to deal with the crowd and the speaker's platform (Isokrates 5.81, 12.9–10, and *Letter* 8.7); and in Isokrates 5.7

for the success of rhetorically trained speakers. But if the illustration is apposite, we must assume that some orators regularly practiced and trained for their delivery with the aid of written drafts of their own speeches.[51] Accordingly, the philosopher's argument would run thus: the acting of 'delivery' (τὸ ὑποκριτικόν) may be a matter of natural talent and, as such, less technical; but, from the point of view of style, it *can* be reduced to an art, i.e. systematized, taught, and

---

he even contrasts the (arguably private or semi-public) oral delivery of a speech with its 'publication' (διαδοθέντος τοῦ λόγου; cf. Hudson-Williams 1949). Our current knowledge of Greek rhetoric suggests that there were no formal rhetorical contests with prizes during the classical period. Isokrates explicitly says so of his own time in Isokrates 4.1–3, a passage that equates δωρεαί, τιμή, and ἆθλον. Ancient reports point to Gorgias' delivering addresses at Olympia and Delphi; the setting of Lysias 33 is Olympia (Lysias 33.2 ascribes to Herakles the convening of a twofold assembly featuring a physical ἀγών and an intellectual ἐπίδειξις [φιλοτιμίαν glosses ἀγῶνα and the Aldine δέ should be rejected]; the word choice underlines the different status of the contest and the display). Isokrates 5.12–13, 15.147, and *Letter* 1.6 confirm that ἐπιδείξεις were regularly delivered at πανηγύρεις and further suggest the absence of prizes (cf. Carey 2007:238). But if ἆθλα therefore stands not for placing first in a contest but metaphorically for success in the competitive settings of the courtroom (where plaintiff and defendant contended; cf. Plato *Euthydēmos* 305b6–9), the assembly (where competing policies were advocated), and the festival (where orators hoped that their own showpieces would receive a more enthusiastic hearing than their rivals'), then we are emphatically not dealing with 'speeches intended for reading', except perhaps in the very restricted sense of 'intended for reading aloud' where, exceptionally (cf. Alkidamas *On the Sophists* §18), delivery permitted an overt show of dependence on a script. Alkidamas' *On the Sophists* further supports connecting οἱ γραφόμενοι λόγοι with performance. It proves that written speeches were viewed by traditionalists in the rhetorical trade as unwelcome *parvenus* not to Athenian bookshops but to public delivery. It is surely significant that Aristotle follows up his comment about written speeches with further observations on the role of voice and the rise of rhapsodic and dramatic performance as τέχναι; and that he adds the opinion of the uneducated that those whose public delivery style bears heavy poetic color '*speak best*' (διαλέγεσθαι κάλλιστα). In sum, nothing suggests that οἱ γραφόμενοι λόγοι are 'speeches intended for reading', while there is much to commend the view that they are precisely what Aristotle calls them, 'written speeches'. One final point: note that the philosopher calls them neither οἱ γραπτοὶ λόγοι (cf. Alkidamas *On the Sophists* §§1, 14, 18, 25, 31–33) nor οἱ γεγραμμένοι λόγοι (cf. Plato *Phaidros* 277e5; Aristotle *Rhetoric* 1407b11–12, *Sophistical Refutations* 166b3–4, *Topics* 105b12–13, and the many mentions of γεγραμμένοι νόμοι in the *Rhetoric*), both, alternatives that would have emphasized the speeches as written products. Overlooking for a moment all the other arguments that preclude the meaning 'speeches intended for reading', if nothing else these alternatives *per se* would more plausibly hint at the circulation of written texts apart from performance. By using instead γραφόμενοι, which as a present-tense participle *cannot* in this context be particular (Smyth §§2052, 2728a), Aristotle shows that he has in view not an actually existing class of speeches but a contingency ('speeches that are [being] written' meaning 'if/whenever speeches are written') that at the very least marginally draws attention to process and practice. Such practice must in turn be regarded against the context of technical ὑπόκρισις. Cf. Alkidamas' mention of οἱ εἰς τὰ δικαστήρια τοὺς λόγους γράφοντες (*On the Sophists* §13). For Aristotelian parallels, cf. *De interpretatione* 16a3–4 (τὰ ἐν τῇ φωνῇ, 'what one speaks', versus τὰ γραφόμενα, 'what one writes'); and *Historia animalium* 515a34–35 (ὥσπερ ἐν τοῖς γραφομένοις κανάβοις) vis-à-vis *De generatione animalium* 743a2 (καθάπερ οἱ τοὺς κανάβους γράφοντες ἐν τοῖς τοίχοις).

51 And perhaps transcripts of others, not their own, whose past success commended them as models to imitate. Cf. Plutarch *Dēmosthenēs* §8.2.

learned as a discipline; and this is why they win prizes who, through training, have acquired delivery as a skill, even as they do too who have a natural knack for it; for the written speeches that orators use to prepare for and hone their delivery owe their effectiveness less to their argument than to their style—style being precisely what makes delivery susceptible of study. And so we learn that, in Aristotle's time, the technique of writing was (successfully) used by apprentices of rhetoric and by orators generally but that it remained instrumental and subordinate to delivery. We do not yet have as an ordinary occurrence speeches that are written primarily for a reading public:[52] they are first and foremost *scripts* of future performances (and only after the fact, secondarily, records of past accomplishment). The circumstances described in the *Rhetoric* represent, therefore, a midpoint in the evolution of the role of writing as a new technology in the performance culture of ancient Greece: contested in the beginning for the challenge it posed to extemporaneous speaking (and decried by Alkidamas for this reason), it gradually gained broad acceptance among professional practitioners of rhetoric and was likely common in Aristotle's time. But written speeches were still primarily scripts, ancillary and derivative, mere aids to train for the all-important moment of actual delivery.[53] As Sonkowsky (1959:273) observes, "in the Aristotelian tradition ... the techniques of delivery are not merely

---

[52] Isokrates' case is truly exceptional and resulted from his peculiar incapacitating infirmity. Compare p. 593 n. 50 immediately above with *Rhetoric* 1414a16–17. See also Harris 1989:85–86 (where "the author of the *Rhetorica ad Alexandrum*" at 86 should be corrected to 'Aristotle'). *Nota bene* that the contested (for Harris, "highly dubious") Aristotelian report preserved by Dionysios of Halikarnassos (cf. his note 99) refers to Aristotle's, not Isokrates', times.

[53] Arguably, this point of view underlies an otherwise puzzling fact: the examples Aristotle selects to illustrate his exposition in the *Rhetoric* generally fail to demonstrate first-hand, detailed acquaintance with actual forensic and deliberative speeches (Trevett 1996a). Precisely because their scripts (and transcripts) were considered ancillary and derivative they must have enjoyed, if at all, rather limited circulation (*pace* Dionysios of Halikarnassos *Isokratēs* 18; see n. 52 immediately above) and must have been hard to acquire. And ordinarily—there are exceptions—the philosopher may have considered them too ephemeral to admit of cogent and intelligible contextualization, or to suit a treatise that to escape premature obsolescence had better avoid potentially obscure historical singularities (cf. Trevett 1996a:377–378). By reason of their greater popularity, reach, and expected longevity, various poetic works were naturally (if paradoxically) a better source of stylistic *exempla* (cf. Graff 2005, esp. 322–334). The sole significant exception was epideictic rhetoric (Trevett 1996a:375–376), especially Isokrates', whose written speeches, one must assume, were considered of such polish and were so readily available to, and familiar among, those interested enough in oratory to consult Aristotle on the subject that the philosopher thought them suitable for illustration. The relatively greater difficulty of procuring oneself with actual scripts of forensic and deliberative oratory, and even an estimate of their finish and excellence that perhaps compared unfavorably with those of epideictic and poetry, do not preclude Aristotle's conviction and acknowledgment, expressed in *Rhetoric* 1404a16–19, that orators in *all* performance settings, not just where epideictic was concerned, were the better and more successful for their mastery of technical delivery, and that written scripts played a central role in reaching the desired proficiency.

something that is added in a superficial way after the process of literary composition has been completed, but something that is vitally involved in the very labors of composition anticipating the public presentation."

We are not surprised that writing should have reached this point by the second half of the fourth century BC. After all, according to the *Suidas* (s.v. Περικλῆς), roughly a century earlier even Perikles had used scripts to prepare for his public addresses: 'Public orator and popular leader; who was first to deliver a written speech in court (before him, these were improvised)'.[54] With this note, we might compare Aristotle's statement, reported by Cicero in his *Brutus*, that before Corax and Tisias 'no one was wont to speak according to method or art, but most, however, did with precision and from a written script' (§46).[55] Though some have emended 'from a written script' (*de scripto*)[56] to 'precisely ordered' (*descripte*), hence putting in doubt Aristotle's meaning,[57] it is clear, at any rate, that at first the use of scripts was contested and that to it attached a distinct onus of shame that speakers were eager to avoid; so that, if we believe Phaidros, citizens of the greatest power and dignity were ashamed to write speeches and bequeath their writings to posterity for fear

---

[54] ῥήτωρ καὶ δημαγωγός· ὅστις πρῶτος γραπτὸν λόγον ἐν δικαστηρίῳ εἶπε, τῶν πρὸ αὐτοῦ σχεδιαζόντων (4.100 Π no. 1180 Adler). On this, Blass (1887:35n5) remarks: "[D]iese letzte Notiz geht ganz entschieden auf Aristoteles oder Theophrast zurück."

[55] "Nam antea neminem solitum via nec arte, sed accurate tamen et de scripto plerosque dicere" (Cicero *Brutus* §46). Although the vulgate *descripto* has been plausibly emended to *descripte* (or even *discripte*) and *plerosque* seems arguably an overstatement, one cannot entirely rule out 'from a script' as the true reading, especially if the report of Perikles' practice preserved in the *Suidas* is accurate and goes back to peripatetic sources. Note that this assertion in the *Brutus* is immediately followed by "*scriptasque* fuisse et paratas a Protagora rerum illustrium disputationes" (my emphasis). Cf. Blass 1887:27n1, 34–39. Even if Quintilian was right to reject the attribution of certain extant writings to the famous Athenian (*Institutio oratoria* 3.1.12), and even if these same writings are the ones that Cicero (*Brutus* §27, *De oratore* II §93) apparently accepted as genuine—which of these two critics is one to prefer?—it need not follow that Cicero inferred the use of scripts from the falsely attributed texts. I am not convinced, at any rate, by the thoroughgoing skepticism of Hudson-Williams 1951 and Trevett 1996b:433–436. Plutarch's observation in *Periklēs* §8.7 (perhaps confirmed by Plato *Phaidros* 257d–e) that Perikles bequeathed no writings to posterity hardly proves that he never used scripts. In fact, that the *Suidas* should have claimed him as the first to deliver a written speech not before the assembly (as one might otherwise have expected) but in a courtroom argues for the veracity of the report; and the scrupulousness implicit in the practice agrees with the portrait of a man who was περὶ τὸν λόγον εὐλαβής (*Periklēs* §8.6). I am, however, persuaded (and Alkidamas and *Rhetoric* III.12 support the view) that *ceteris paribus* deliberative speeches were less likely to depend, and in fact less frequently depended, on a script for their delivery; and that, when they did, the scripts were probably less elaborate and detailed both as to form and content.

[56] For this acceptation of *de*, see the *OLD* s.v. 7c: "indicating personal or other source of information." E.g. *de scripto sententia dicta* (Cicero *Pro Sestio* 129); or *de tabulis publicis recitat* (Cicero *Pro Flacco* 40).

[57] See n. 55 immediately above.

that they might be numbered among the sophists.[58] To this sense of shame we might owe that all of Perikles' scripted speeches perished:[59] perhaps he disposed of them as diligently as he prepared, with their aid, to address the assembly.[60] Whatever the truth about this statesman, there is no doubt in regard to Lysias: for Phaidros introduces him as δεινότατος ὢν τῶν νῦν γράφειν (228a1–2),[61] and Sokrates assumes that his young companion not only bade Lysias repeat his speech but in the end secured possession of the script (τὸ βιβλίον 228b2). Later on, at 258a, Sokrates draws a parallel between ψηφίσματα and λογογραφία, either reckoning, in jest, decrees among the private συγγράματα of those who proposed them, or, more likely, drawing an ironic parallel between the scripts used to prepare for deliberative speeches and the actual language passed by the assembly and inscribed on stone. The picture that emerges presupposes a growing employment of λογογραφία, that is, the writing of speeches with a view to delivery, which made possible lengthy displays (ἐπιδεικνύμενος) of artistic eloquence (σοφία).[62]

Aristotle, too, mentions λογογράφοι at *Rhetoric* 1388b22, 1408a34, and 1413b13. The first two times he does so in passing, whereas the third mention occurs in chapter 12 of *Rhetoric* III, where the matter of writing resurfaces explicitly, still in the context of the philosopher's investigation of rhetorical style. Since this chapter closes his examination of the subject, it is reasonable to expect that he should take a synoptic perspective on λέξις and provide the reader with a synthetic summary of the issues involved in 'style with a view to delivery'.[63] I submit therefore that *Rhetoric* III.12 does not consider particular

---

[58] καὶ σύνοισθά που καὶ αὐτὸς ὅτι οἱ μέγιστον δυνάμενοί τε καὶ σεμνότατοι ἐν ταῖς πόλεσιν αἰσχύνονται λόγους τε γράφειν καὶ καταλείπειν συγγράμματα ἑαυτῶν, δόξαν φοβούμενοι τοῦ ἔπειτα χρόνου, μὴ σοφισταὶ καλῶνται (Plato *Phaidros* 257d4–8: 'And you yourself know, I suppose, that those of the greatest power and dignity in our cities are ashamed to write speeches and leave behind writings of their own, fearing the opinion of future times lest they be called sophists'). Cf. *Phaidros* 257c6, where λογογράφος is considered a term of opprobrium.

[59] Plutarch *Periklēs* 8.7 (156c10–11): ἔγγραφον μὲν οὖν οὐδὲν ἀπολέλοιπε πλὴν τῶν ψηφισμάτων.

[60] Cf. Blass 1887:36.

[61] To which Stallbaum 1857b *ad loc.* adds: "per totum enim librum Lysias non ut orator, sed tanquam orationum scriptor carpitur."

[62] *Phaidros* 258a6–8: ἔπειτα λέγει δὴ μετὰ τοῦτο, ἐπιδεικνύμενος τοῖς ἐπαινέταις τὴν ἑαυτοῦ σοφίαν, ἐνίοτε πάνυ μακρὸν ποιησάμενος σύγγραμμα ('Then he speaks after this, displaying his own wisdom to his fans, having composed at times a very long writing'). For λογογραφία taken broadly as 'composition of speeches' see Yunis 2011:172 *ad* 257e1–2 and Innes 2007:154 *ad Rhetoric* 1388b21–22. See also above, pp. 325ff.

[63] I agree with O'Sullivan (1996:127) *contra* Graff (2001:22 and 37) when he observes in connection with *Rheroric* III.12 that "[t]he written and the spoken, of such importance in the fifth century, continue to be the framework [for the analysis of rhetorical prose] as the world moves into an increasingly bookish Hellenistic age." Graff, on the other hand, believes that O'Sullivan over-estimates the significance of the written/spoken division and maintains that "[t]he twelfth chapter [of the *Rhetoric*] and the stylistic distinction it contains have the character of an

issues of detail but generic matters broadly applicable to the subject of delivery in its scientific connection to style. This is an important observation for, if ὑπόκρισις and writing reappear explicitly in what constitutes the capstone of Aristotle's treatment of λέξις, they must be critical elements of rhetorical style, not afterthoughts or secondary considerations. This validates the views I have propounded throughout this and the previous chapter. First, that ὑπόκρισις is not some ethically undesirable feature of the art of oratory to be fenced off and purged from style; rather, it is no more and no less than what the philosopher himself states, namely, 'that which has the greatest force', and for this reason it must remain at the heart of the oratorical practice of any successful speaker. And second, that writing in the *Rhetoric* is not primarily the instrument of speech production for a reading public but a subordinate technology at the service of delivery, and hence studied and approached as such.

---

afterthought" (22). That Aristotle should have planned and executed the composition of his treatise so haphazardly strikes me as psychologically implausible and un-Aristotelian. Such a notion is in fact belied by the deliberate manner in which the philosopher moves from one thematic head to the next. I do not mean to suggest, however, that all transitions are flawlessly executed. Aristotle was arguably comfortable with a measure of redundancy that many think awkward (e.g. at *Rhetoric* 1403a34–b8). The expectation that *Rhetoric* III.1–12 should exhibit unity of design and expository coherence seems warranted even under the assumption that it was composed as an independent work. Chapter 12 starts with a transition that is not only smooth but also of the type expected for a closing summary that ties the threads of the argument together: 'But one must not forget that a different style suits each genus [of rhetoric]'. Having surveyed λέξις without reference to, and insofar as common to all, genera, Aristotle now attempts to close with the stylistic emphases peculiar to each genus. At 1414a18–29 he notes explicitly that this has been the design of the entire section (chapters 1–12): 'To subdivide *lexis* further, [to state] that it must be pleasant and elevated, is superfluous. For why [state this] rather than [that it should be] temperate and liberal and whatever other virtue of character there is? Obviously what has been discussed will bring about that it is pleasant, if indeed the virtue of *lexis* has been rightly defined ... . So then, I am done speaking about *lexis*, from the point of view both of what is common about all [genera] and of what is peculiar to each genus'. Clearly the 'common point of view' (κοινῇ a28) regards the earlier chapters whereas the 'peculiar' (ἰδίᾳ a29), the present summation. As it is, if with Rapp (2002:2.948) one takes the presence of transitions and summations as proof that *Rhetoric* III.12 is merely an appendix, then one will be denying Aristotle the expository strategies that would precisely allow him to integrate his earlier exposition of common elements of style with his summation of the subject from the vantage point of genera. According to Rapp, the view that chapter 12 is integral to the philosopher's conception of rhetorical style remains implausible in the absence of explicit advance notice of its content earlier in the treatise. Apparently, only prior warning would adequately prepare the reader for a conclusion to 'style' that makes application to the three main social settings of rhetorical practice. Had Aristotle actually included such notice in chapter 1, I suspect that many would think it interpolated into an outline that did not include the corresponding material. On the internal coherence of *Rhetoric* III.1–12 and its integration (and, more generally, the integration of Book 3) with the rest of the treatise, cf. Grimaldi 1972, Kennedy 1991:299–305, Graff 2000:12–17, Innes 2007:151n2, and Burkett 2011:xi–xxxv.

What is it, then, that we learn from *Rhetoric* III.12? This chapter starts with what is perhaps the most commonly misinterpreted passage in the entire treatise. I quote it here, for now without a translation, for the convenience of the reader:

δεῖ δὲ μὴ λεληθέναι ὅτι ἄλλη ἑκάστῳ γένει ἁρμόττει λέξις. οὐ γὰρ ἡ αὐτὴ γραφικὴ καὶ ἀγωνιστική, οὐδὲ δημηγορικὴ καὶ δικανική. ἄμφω δὲ ἀνάγκη εἰδέναι· τὸ μὲν γάρ ἐστιν ἑλληνίζειν ἐπίστασθαι, τὸ δὲ μὴ ἀναγκάζεσθαι κατασιωπᾶν, ἄν τι βούληται μεταδοῦναι τοῖς ἄλλοις, ὅπερ πάσχουσιν οἱ μὴ ἐπιστάμενοι γράφειν.

Rhetoric 1413b3–8

Its syntax lends itself all too readily to readings that, not to put too fine a point on it, make nonsense of Aristotle's argument. Conversely, the most compelling and, I believe, correct interpretation is burdened by a choice of referents for ἄμφω and the bipartition τὸ μὲν … τὸ δέ at 1413b5–6 that is not immediately apparent and only follows from reflecting on the context and the logic of the argument. At the same time, I must emphasize that the correct identification of these referents does not call for a construal of the grammar that is in any way questionable or exceptional. Therefore, even if it does not correspond to the most immediately apparent reading, with the proper perspective Aristotle's true meaning flows with unexceptional ease. Since the context regards two pairs, the first, the 'graphic' and the 'agonistic' styles (γραφική and ἀγωνιστική), the second, the 'demegoric' and the 'dicanic' (δημηγορική and δικανική), a reasonable understanding of the immediately succeeding ἄμφω would seem 'X + Y' where 'X' is 'the one,' and 'Y' is 'the other,' element of whichever pair is in view. Yet, quite apart from the interpretive difficulties that result from any of the corresponding four possible alternatives, the neuter gender of τὸ μέν and τὸ δέ already hints that perhaps none of them is in view. Aristotle of course could have switched from the feminine-gender adjectives to a neuter bipartition ('the former [thing] … while the latter [thing]). The mismatch between the feminine λέξις and the neuter verbal predicates (ἐπίστασθαι and μὴ ἀναγκάζεσθαι) might even be enlisted to motivate the switch. But it is unarguable that, had he wanted to, he could have placed beyond doubt that he had in mind one of the four alternatives by writing ἡ μέν … ἡ δέ instead. If in fact this was his meaning, it is only too ironic that he did not take his own advice at 1407b6–9, the fourth principle of correct Greek usage (ἑλληνίζειν) ascribed to Protagoras, and failed to secure gender agreement with a view to clarity. Aristotle deserves no such criticism, however, if my interpretation below is correct. At any rate, one can infer how hard it is to make sense of the passage from how often most scholars neglect to engage or translate it. This can only be explained as a show of embarrassed silence or as proof that they are oblivious to the interpretive difficulties entailed by the commonplace rendering. On the other hand, full-length translations of the *Rhetoric*, of which I list the following samples, cannot avoid going on the record:

> One should not forget that a different *lexis* is appropriate for each genus [of rhetoric]. For the written and agonistic [style] are not the same; nor are the demegoric [deliberative] and the dicanic [judicial], and it is necessary to know both. [Debate] consists in knowing how to speak good Greek; [writing] avoids the necessity of silence if one wishes to communicate to others [who are not present], which is the condition of those who do not know how to write.
>
> Kennedy 1991:255

> Es preciso no olvidar que a cada género conviene un estilo; no es el mismo el estilo de prosa escrita que el de debate, ni el de hablar ante el pueblo que el forense. Ambos, pues, es necesario que se conozcan: es el uno saber expresarse en griego, el otro no quedar obligado a callar cuando se quiera comunicar algo a los otros, lo cual les pasa a los que no saben escribir.
>
> Tovar 1953:201

> Il ne faut pas oublier qu'à chaque genre s'approprie un style différent; car le style des compositions écrites n'est pas le même que celui des débats, et celui des assemblées n'est pas non plus celui des tribunaux. Or, il est nécessaire de connaître les deux: le style des débats suppose la connaissance du grec; grâce à l'autre, on n'est pas forcé de garder le silence si l'on veut communiquer sa pensée aux autres, inconvénient dont souffrent ceux qui ne savent pas écrire.
>
> Dufour and Wartelle 1973:73

> It must not be forgotten (lost sight of) that a different kind of language is appropriate to each different kind (of Rhetoric). For the same style is not suitable to *written* composition (that which is intended *to be read*) and that which is used in *debate* (in the *contests*, the actual struggle, of real life); nor again in (the two divisions of the latter) public and forensic speaking. The orator must be acquainted with both: for the

one (debate) implies the knowledge and power of clear expression in pure Greek, and the other freedom from the necessity (*lit.* the not being obliged to) of suppressing in silence (κατά, keeping *down*) anything that one may want to communicate to the rest of the world; which is the case with those who have no knowledge (or skill) of writing (i.e. composition).

Cope 1877:3.145 (his emphasis)

Man darf aber nicht vergessen, dass zu jeder Gattung eine andere sprachliche Form passt. Denn die schriftliche Form und die der Kontroverse sind nicht dieselbe, und auch nicht die für die politische Rede und die für die Gerichtsrede geeignete. Beides aber muss man kennen. Das eine nämlich bedeutet, dass man sich auf korrektes Griechisch versteht, das zweite, dass man nicht gezwungen wird zu schweigen, wenn man den anderen etwas mitteilen will, wie es denen ergeht, die nichts vom Schreiben verstehen.

Rapp 2002:1.150

Minime autem opus est nos fallere, aliam singulis generibus congruere locutionem. Non enim eadem est idonea scribendo, et forensibus concertationibus: neque etiam contionalis et iudicialis. Ambo autem necesse est tenere: alterum enim est scire uti Graeco sermone; alterum vero non cogi silere, siquis voluerit participem aliquem facere suar[um] cogitationum. Quo laborant, qui scribere nesciunt.

Vettori 1579:677–678

Of the two pairs of stylistic opposites that open the chapter, scholars make the latter, the δημηγορική and δικανική, an explication (by way of division) of the ἀγωνιστική, the second member of the first and more fundamental opposition around which Aristotle articulates his presentation: there is, on the one hand, a 'graphic', and on the other, an 'agonistic' style. The agonistic suits the ἀγών, i.e. a contest (in the extended sense) in which various options compete for the allegiance or support of the audience, whether in the law-court or the assembly (calling respectively for the λέξις δικανική and the λέξις δημηγορική). If the relationship commonly assumed between the first pair and the second is right, the graphic style, unlike the agonistic, does not receive a shorthand explication. Instead, after noting that 'one must know both' (ἄμφω δὲ ἀνάγκη εἰδέναι 1413b5), the philosopher appends as rationale an enigmatic statement about the possibilities closed to those who 'know not how to write': τὸ μὲν γάρ ἐστιν ἑλληνίζειν ἐπίστασθαι, τὸ δὲ μὴ ἀναγκάζεσθαι κατασιωπᾶν ἄν τι βούληται μεταδοῦναι τοῖς ἄλλοις, ὅπερ πάσχουσιν οἱ μὴ ἐπιστάμενοι γράφειν (1413b5–8). This is an observation that has baffled many. Rapp (2002:2.932) sums up the difficulty with characteristic insight: "Nicht sehr erhellend ist die Begründung, die der Abschnitt für die Nützlichkeit der schriftlichen und der kontroversen Form gibt. Wenn die Kontroverse nämlich mit der Fähigkeit in Verbindung gebracht wird, sich auf korrektes Griechisch (ἑλληνίζειν) zu verstehen, dann scheint damit nur eine minimale Bedingung genannt zu sein, und außerdem eine, die auch der schriftlichen Form zugrunde liegt ... . Ebenso wenig klar ist, warum die Eigenschaft, nicht zum Schweigen gezwungen zu sein, wenn man etwas mitteilen will, eher die schriftliche als die mündliche Form betrifft."[64]

As one readily infers from the translations quoted above, most interpreters take ἄμφω to refer to the graphic and the agonistic styles, i.e. to the *first* pair, and tie τὸ μὲν ... τὸ δέ respectively to either end of its polarity. In particular, most correlate τὸ μέν to ἡ ἀγωνιστικὴ λέξις and τὸ δέ to ἡ γραφικὴ λέξις.[65] Nothing in the grammar of the sentence hinders this approach. As noted above, the problem with it is that its rationale is specious and the resulting interpretation neither suits the context nor yields adequate sense under close examination (see below). The alert reader will not lack signs that all is not good with this consensus reading. There is no reason, for example, why ἄμφω should refer to the first pair and not the second. Only the critic's sense that the former is the more basic opposition suggests the choice. But what if in fact the second pair does not represent a subdivision of the second element of the first (ἡ ἀγωνιστικὴ λέξις)? What if instead it reprises the selfsame distinction in terms of γένη? Given that the design of *Rhetoric* III.12 is to survey style in terms of what is peculiar to each rhetorical genus, such a reprise would be eminently reasonable. On this assumption, the philosopher would have first set down the polarity that comprises the entire range of rhetorical style ('graphic::agonistic') and then he would have illustrated either end with the style of a relevant genus (demegoric and dicanic). If this is what Aristotle did, there would not be any reason to fault him for failing to give comparable due attention to the graphic

---

[64] A different attempt to construe the passage is to invert the reference of τὸ μὲν ... τὸ δέ, with the former pointing to the graphic, the latter to the agonistic, style. This is Thurot's strategy, who replaces by μόνον the μὴ of οἱ μὴ ἐπιστάμενοι γράφειν. To this, Roemer 1898 *ad loc.* writes: "sed tum verba τὸ μὲν ἑλληνίζειν ἐπίστασθαι ad λέξιν γραφικὴν referenda essent, quod fieri non potest, contra verba ἄν τι βούληται μεταδοῦναι τοῖς ἄλλοις latiore sensu intellegenda significare videntur, quod Bonitzius cum omnibus interpretibus declarat 'tradere per libros scriptos'."

[65] Greek has no set rule by which τὸ μέν consistently means 'the former' and τὸ δέ 'the latter' or vice versa. The choice must be guided by the context (LSJ s.vv. ὁ, ἡ, τό A.VI.1; cf. K-G II.2.264 §527.3a Anm. 1). As early as B 52 οἱ μέν is found to point to 'the latter' and τοὶ δ[έ] to 'the former'.

end of the polarity that engages his attention throughout the chapter. If not impossible, such an oversight at its programmatic opening is at least remarkable. Yet no neglect of either pole attaches to the alternative, which also relieves the apparent ambiguity that burdens ἄμφω, τὸ μέν, and τὸ δέ in the consensus reading: if we posit a reprise it does not matter which pair is selected, for the latter would then take up the εἴδη of the former at the level of γένη. I submit that this is in fact Aristotle's approach and that only this proposal satisfactorily explains the otherwise mystifying γάρ clause, structured as a τὸ μὲν ... τὸ δέ progression[66] that (I will show) hinges, on the one hand, on ὑπόκρισις undergirded by ἑλληνίζειν (basic but non-trivial linguistic competence, including stylistic); and, on the other, on ὑπόκρισις underpinned by the ability to write scripts that help in structuring the discourse and in training for public delivery.

The proposal that the second pair recapitulates the first seems at first precluded by the (to us) natural association of both the demegoric and the dicanic settings with rhetorical ἀγῶνες. But one must not forget that Aristotle is presenting a continuum between two poles and that for him, at least potentially if not in every actual instance, *all* three γένη—symbuleutic, forensic, and epideictic—share in delivery not only a measure of debate and competition (the ἀγών) but also a measure of written planning. Therefore, as regards their ὑπόκρισις they all fall stylistically somewhere along the continuum between the graphic and the agonistic poles. For the second pair to be able to reprise the first one only needs the dicanic and demegoric styles to be located at clearly distinct points along the continuum. This is indeed the case. In fact, the dicanic style illustrates the graphic in an even more compelling way than the epideictic because the reader could relate to it with greater immediacy: after all, resort to written scripts in the courtroom must have been commonplace by the second half of the fourth century,[67] whereas few would have had (or could be expected to have at some future time) comparable first-hand experience delivering epideictic. Any Athenian resident—every one of Aristotle's hearers and readers—might have to engage in dicanic oratory sooner or later. To that extent, Aristotle's preference for the dicanic style to illustrate in relative terms the graphic end of the stylistic range would be straightforward. And it is not as if he depended solely on the cultural context to guide the reader's interpretation. He both implied and explicitly affirmed the more markedly graphic character of the dicanic style: at 1414a17–18 we read that 'the epideictic style is the most graphic; for its effect is reading; and the dicanic, the second [most graphic]'.[68] Furthermore, in his analysis of ἀκρίβεια ('precision'), a property which the graphic style possesses

---

[66] I do not call it 'opposition' for reasons detailed on p. 606 below.

[67] Cf. Rapp 2002:2.931.

[68] ἡ μὲν οὖν ἐπιδεικτικὴ λέξις γραφικωτάτη· τὸ γὰρ ἔργον αὐτῆς ἀνάγνωσις· δευτέρα δὲ ἡ δικανική.

to a relatively greater degree,[69] he clearly contrasts the demegoric style to the dicanic: 'Now, the demegoric style seems entirely like shadow painting ... therefore, precision appears a waste and the worse ... ; the judicial plea is a more exact matter'.[70] In what may amount to a striking *Gedankenexperiment*,[71] he goes so far as to consider a trial with a single judge at which ἀγών is absent (1414a13). Having said all this, I must emphasize that my interpretation of ἄμφω at 1413b5 and of the progression τὸ μὲν ... τὸ δέ that follows it does not depend on the reader's acceptance of my proposal that the second pair at 1413b4–5 recapitulates the first. Still, this proposal makes for a more compelling reading. My argument only requires what most commentators already assume: that ἄμφω refers to the former and more basic opposition 'graphic::agonistic.'

In my reading of the passage, ἄμφω refers primarily to the 'graphic::agonistic' stylistic polarity *as a whole* and, secondarily, to Aristotle's illustration of it, i.e. to the demegoric and dicanic styles: the former as the relatively more agonistic and less graphic, the latter as the relatively less agonistic and more graphic. The statement 'it is necessary to know both' (ἄμφω δὲ ἀνάγκη εἰδέναι 1413b5) affirms the need to know the full panoply of stylistic resources and strategies, including *writing*, that make for various registers along the graphic-agonistic continuum. Thus, Aristotle makes mastery of the stylistic polarity the ideal of the well-trained orator who equipped with persuasive delivery successfully addresses audiences in any of the three chief social settings of the classical polis: the deliberative assembly, the courtroom, and the gathering of the people at festivals and other solemn occasions. There is nothing in the context of the passage or the culture of classical Greece that would lead us to expect Aristotle to proffer the ability to communicate with an absent (or distant) audience as motivation for the would-be orator's need 'to know both [styles]'. Surely, writing letters to distant relatives and friends hardly qualifies as a rhetorical accomplishment, whether it presupposes personal literacy or not. This can hardly be taken to entail or justify the need to master the graphic style, even if one takes for granted (unjustifiably, in my view) that letter writing inevitably required the interested party to know how to write. If it is to make contextual sense, the ability to write that Aristotle has in view when he mentions 'any who do not know how to write' (οἱ μὴ ἐπιστάμενοι γράφειν 1413b8) must serve *specifically* as adequate motivation for the acquisition of a particular rhetorical skill, not simply for the acquisition of basic literacy. To reduce the philosopher's meaning to the latter impoverishes his argument, effectively divesting it of rhetorical

---

[69] ἔστι δὲ λέξις γραφικὴ μὲν ἡ ἀκριβεστάτη (1413b8–9).

[70] ἡ μὲν οὖν δημηγορικὴ λέξις καὶ παντελῶς ἔοικε τῇ σκιαγραφίᾳ ... διὸ τὰ ἀκριβῆ περίεργα καὶ χείρω φαίνεται ... · ἡ δὲ δίκη ἀκριβέστερον (1414a7–11).

[71] Rapp 2002:2.937.iv.

significance and wresting it from its technical setting—a treatment of rhetorical style. The thought is recast instead as one broadly applicable to the common man without specific interest in oratory as an art. Even on these terms, the alleged meaning is remarkably flaccid, for the need that literacy is supposed to meet—writing private communications to a distant or absent audience—seems marginal and infrequent.

A more promising alternative might seem to promote the written communication from letters to rhetorical speeches. This evades the objections raised above but creates in turn its own share of difficulties. For then only in one historically exceptional case, the orator Isokrates, does the modified interpretation of the τὸ δέ clause[72] makes some sense. One may go so far as to wonder if the reading has not been formulated with him in mind and if without him anyone would have ever thought of understanding the clause thus. For without literacy Isokrates could never have communicated so widely 'to others', including distant and absent addressees, what he wished to say. But even in his case the hypothetical consequence of illiteracy, 'being forced to remain silent', seems a distinct overreach: he could always deliver his addresses orally to smaller gatherings, as he is actually known to have done on many occasions. Although ordinarily such delivery involved reading (and, therefore, also writing), I doubt that he would have been reduced to silence on the counterfactual assumption that he was illiterate. If someone answers that the consensus interprets Aristotle's comment not with regard to the bare capacity, and hence the opportunity, to communicate in writing but as regarding the skill to craft such rhetorically accomplished orations as made Isokrates famous, then he is embracing my objection: basic literacy—all that is required by assuming a distant audience—is not the philosopher's point, but writing as instrumental to rhetorical τέχνη, specifically, to the orator's scripted composition and delivery of his addresses. At any rate, the case of Isokrates is so extraordinary, and he so poorly exemplifies (or embodies the ideal of) the would-be orator that the Aristotelian treatise envisions, that he cannot possibly serve to explain the τὸ δέ limb of the progression, especially without ever so much as a contextual hint that he is in view there. We must reject as implausible any reading that reduces to so narrow and exceptional a scope what Aristotle surely intended as a general motivation, broadly applicable to his rhetorical pupils, for the need to learn the full 'graphic::agonistic' stylistic continuum. Aristotle did not intend to replicate the Isokratean model among his disciples.

---

[72] I will make clear below that, even on these terms, this consensus reading is impossible. I accept it here simply for the sake of argument.

What, then, must the reader do with τὸ μὲν … τὸ δέ? First, he should note that *stricto sensu* the subject of ἐστιν cannot be a style, e.g. ἡ γραφικὴ λέξις or (if he so choose) ἡ δημηγορικὴ λέξις: the agonistic style as a category cannot be strictly equated with any kind of 'knowing'; nor can the graphic style be equated with the absence of any given compulsion ('not being forced'). A style is a set of expressive devices and strategies (in Aristotle's case, with a view to delivery), not the *knowledge* thereof (or of any other thing). That is the reason why translators do not render ἐστιν by 'is' but by 'suppose' (Budé), 'implies' (Cope), 'bedeutet' (Rapp), 'consists in' (Kennedy), *vel sim.* Only familiarity with the consensus reading could have inured us to the inconcinnity of the statement, 'the agonistic style is to know how to speak good Greek'. To be sure, it is possible to argue oneself into accepting the conceptual sloppiness of this sentence and taking it in its only possible sense, '[*to know*] the agonistic style is to know how to speak good Greek' (my emphasis). This point may strike my reader as more than a little pedantic, but attending to it actually helps to construe the passage aright. For there is no need to impute such mental and syntactic muddle to Aristotle: the referent of τό in both τὸ μέν and τὸ δέ is the neuter infinitival clause [τὸ] ἄμφω εἰδέναι. One can hardly find fault with the positive equation of skill with skill, of 'to know' (εἰδέναι) with 'to know' (ἐπίστασθαι); or, conversely, object to the conclusion that if someone possesses a given skill he can evade a corresponding limitation. This amounts to equating 'to know' with 'not to be forced to remain silent' (μὴ ἀναγκάζεσθαι κατασιωπᾶν), an evasion predicated of 'any who know how to write' (οἱ ἐπιστάμενοι γράφειν). To construe *both* τὸ μέν and τὸ δέ as having and pointing to the *same* referent, ἄμφω εἰδέναι, entails unproblematic, ordinary syntax. Because they share a single referent I do not call the resulting balanced structure 'an opposition' but rather 'a progression [of thought]'. Another instance of τὸ μὲν … τὸ δέ with a common referent—this one, undisputed—is found in *Rhetoric* 1356b27-28:

> ἐπεὶ γὰρ τὸ πιθανὸν τινὶ πιθανόν ἐστι, καὶ τὸ μὲν εὐθὺς ὑπάρχει δι' αὑτὸ πιθανὸν καὶ πιστὸν τὸ δὲ τῷ δείκνυσθαι δοκεῖν διὰ τοιούτων, οὐδεμία δὲ τέχνη σκοπεῖ τὸ καθ' ἕκαστον, οἷον ἡ ἰατρικὴ τί Σωκράτει τὸ ὑγιεινόν ἐστιν ἢ Καλλίᾳ …
>
> *Rhetoric* 1356b26–30

For since what is persuasive is persuasive to someone, and it is persuasive and credible now immediately in and by itself, now by seeming to be proved through such things [i.e. through means persuasive and credible], and no art considers the particular, e.g. medicine what is healthful for Sokrates or Kallias ...'

It is clear that τὸ πιθανόν is picked up both by τὸ μέν and by τὸ δέ. The resulting progression of μέν ... δέ divides into inherent and derivative the reasons for the convincingness and credibility of what persuades.[73] Because in this particular case these reasons are ordinarily[74] viewed as mutually exclusive, μέν ... δέ may be taken to articulate not a constructive gradation ('first A; then, building on A, B') but an alternative ('either A or B'). Generally speaking, the relationship conveyed by μέν ... δέ depends on the particular context. This use of τὸ μέν and τὸ δέ is closely related to the adverbial one usually rendered as 'now ... now', 'partly ... partly', 'one the one hand ... on the other', 'both ... and'.[75] In the case of *Rhetoric* 1356b27–28, the only possible latitude in the construal of the grammar is whether one assumes the implicit subject τὸ πιθανόν for ὑπάρχει, with τὸ μέν ... τὸ δέ adverbial ('now ... now') or, more naturally, one grants τό in τὸ μέν and τὸ δέ deictic force as the demonstrative 'this' (τό = τὸ πιθανόν). The syntax and meaning of the particles in this case are closely paralleled at *Rhetoric* 1413b6–8.

What has hitherto led many astray is the assumption, grammatically unexceptional but of impossible meaning, that τὸ μέν pointed to one member of either pair in *Rhetoric* III.12 §1 (usually taken to be 'the agonistic style') while τὸ δέ pointed to its complement ('the graphic style'). This specious construal seemed justified by the emphasis on speaking in the first limb of the progression and the complementary emphasis on writing in the second. But this reading left out of sight the fact that up to that point in his treatise Aristotle had been exclusively concerned—and, in the cultural context even of late fourth-century Greece,

---

[73] Grimaldi's translation, "and since one thing is suasive and credible in and by itself, another by the fact that it seems to be proved by statements that are such" (1980:52 *ad* b28), although equivalent to Aristotle's meaning, is not syntactically accurate. The subject of ἐστι is τὸ πιθανόν, an abstract concept that I might somewhat inelegantly render as 'the persuasive'. This concept embraces any and every particular instance of what persuades. Since the ensuing observation is predicated of this abstract notion, *stricto sensu* it must be translated 'the persuasive is either X or Y' or, better, 'the persuasive is now X, now Y'. It may well be the case that ordinarily no instance of 'the persuasive' will be both inherently suasive at times and derivatively suasive at others (or even suasive partly in and by itself, partly derivatively), although this possibility cannot be absolutely excluded. But insofar as some instances are inherently suasive/credible and some derivatively suasive/credible, the larger notion of 'the persuasive' to which *all* belong can and must be pronounced 'now inherently persuasive, now derivatively persuasive'. Had Aristotle written instead, ἐπεὶ γὰρ τὰ πιθανὰ τινὶ πιθανά ἐστι, one could then take Grimaldi's translation as Aristotle's meaning *stricto sensu*. For another instance of the abstract τὸ πιθανόν see 1355b15–16.

[74] Nothing prevents the inherently and immediately plausible from being susceptible of inferential proof too.

[75] K-G II.2.264 §527.3a: "τὸ μέν ... τὸ δέ, τὰ μέν ... τὰ δέ und τοῦτο μέν ... τοῦτο δέ ... , teils ... teils, einerseits ... andererseits, sowohl ... als auch." See also LSJ s.vv. ὁ, ἡ, τό A.VIII.4. An adverbial construal, with the elided subject understood from the previous clause, is satisfactory too: 'For [to know both] is *both* (τὸ μέν) to know how to speak good Greek *and* (τὸ δέ) not to be forced ...'.

could only plausibly be assumed to concern himself—with the oral delivery of rhetorical prose, whether or not composed in advance with the aid of writing. For him to reduce the second limb to basic literacy would have been unthinkable and, in the context of his manual, little short of absurd.[76] Cope (1877:3.145) felt the force of this difficulty: noting that Vettori construed τὸ μὴ ἀναγκάζεσθαι ... τοῖς ἄλλοις "of actual writing, that is of *letters* to absent friends," he added that this "seems to narrow the meaning of 'writing' in such a way as to produce a somewhat ridiculous result. Surely *any* educated man, whether he be an orator and statesman or not, requires and possesses the knowledge of *writing* in that sense" (his emphasis). The specious justification for this interpretation dissolves in the light of the rhetorical stylistic continuum, which allows for precisely such apportioning of emphases as a progression that reckons ἑλληνίζειν insufficient for the perfect orator who, rising with confident proficiency to any occasion at hand, aspires for success in all of the social settings that call for public speaking. In the logic of the passage, 'knowing both' is explicated first as the linguistic competence of basic, though by no means trivial or contemptible, mastery of Greek expression, and second as the specific rhetorical skill of ὑπόκρισις that the knowledge of writing enables, when the orator prepares scripts the force of whose λέξις allows him to overcome the timidity and fear that might otherwise dissuade him from addressing the audience with the message he wants to make public. The motivation to master the entire stylistic continuum lies in the force of these two examples, a force that would be felt by any Athenian citizen (and, *a fortiori*, by any would-be orator), who could not fail to appreciate the significance of confident and effective public speaking for his social standing, legal indemnity, and political involvement.

I believe that chiefly in Aristotle's mind is the deliberative setting of the *ekklēsia* and the council, where any male citizen who wished, regardless of station,[77] so long as he had not been subject to ἀτιμία, had the right to address the people: 'The lawgiver expressly made known who should address the assembly and who should not speak before the people. And he does not drive from the platform one who is not from ancestors who have served as generals, nor indeed if he plies some trade to provide for his necessary food, but these he also heartily welcomes and for this reason again and again asks, "Who wants to

---

[76] Why introduce here this strange notion of publishing books for distant audiences? Why not simply say, 'knowing the graphic style makes possible persuasive speaking when precision is required'? If Aristotle's point was to provide a compelling example of the orator's need to master the written style, he should have chosen something that was ordinarily within the scope and interest of the citizen orator-to-be. Such would arguably be addressing the assembly and courtroom, a compelling prospect that I claim must be what Aristotle has in mind here.

[77] Plato *Prōtagoras* 319c8–d7.

address the assembly?" (τίς ἀγορεύειν βούλεται;)'.[78] It is the political resonance of this often posed question, τίς ἀγορεύειν βούλεται;—the privilege, duty, and challenge of political initiative—that motivates the philosopher's ἄν τι βούληται μεταδοῦναι τοῖς ἄλλοις.[79] Although the ideology of the Athenian state encouraged and, ideally, even presupposed the active involvement and initiative of private citizens in the political process, in practice most would have been intimidated and paralyzed by the social and legal stakes of doing so.[80] Hansen (1991:267) observes that ὁ βουλόμενος, the generic Athenian citizen who elected to take the initiative, was not "subject to *dokimasia* or *euthynai* like the magistrates; but he could always be made to answer for his initiative, even, in extreme cases, be condemned to death for it" (cf. Demosthenes 10.70). Ober 1989 adds: "The *functional* difference between the expert politician and the 'amateur' … was in part a consequence of the increased risk that political activity brought in its wake. The maze of legal difficulties in which the proposer of a controversial decree might find himself would be enough to scare most citizens away from the bema during intense debate over major issues. The general opprobrium that might follow upon a failed policy decision was also a consideration" (his emphasis). Under the circumstances, it is unsurprising that even this least graphic of all the rhetorical genera should have invited even the experienced ῥήτωρ—and, ordinarily, in the case of the ἰδιώτης probably even required him—to prepare diligently with the aid of a script before communicating his mind to others (τι [διανοίας] μεταδοῦναι τοῖς ἄλλοις).[81] The alternative would have been self-imposed silence,

---

[78] ὁ νομοθέτης διαρρήδην ἀπέδειξεν οὓς χρὴ δημηγορεῖν καὶ οὓς οὐ δεῖ λέγειν ἐν τῷ δήμῳ. καὶ οὐκ ἀπελαύνει ἀπὸ τοῦ βήματος, εἴ τις μὴ προγόνων ἐστὶν ἐστρατηγηκότων [υἱός], οὐδέ γε εἰ τέχνην τινὰ ἐργάζεται ἐπικουρῶν τῇ ἀναγκαίᾳ τροφῇ, ἀλλὰ τούτους καὶ μάλιστα ἀσπάζεται, καὶ διὰ τοῦτο πολλάκις ἐπερωτᾷ 'τίς ἀγορεύειν βούλεται;' (Aiskhines 1.27). Also reflecting this right and duty are the many references to ὁ βουλόμενος in the democratic process ([Demosthenes] 13.11 and Demosthenes 24.63; *SEG* 26.72, line 34; Aiskhines 1.23, 2.65; Andokides 1.23; *Athēnaiōn Politeia* 29.2).

[79] Cf. Demosthenes 18.170, 191; Aristophanes *Akharnians* 45, *Women at the Thesmophoria* 379, *Assemblywomen* 130; and Alkidamas *On the Sophists* §11. On political initiative in Athens see Hansen 1981, Hansen 1991:266–268, and Ober 1989:108–112.

[80] Plato *Prōtagoras* 319c1–7, although hardly an objective source, may be safely assumed to paint a realistic picture of the humiliation inflicted on a speaker by his fellow citizens. Cf. also Demosthenes 19.113 (and 19.14, one of many instances in which a speaker entreats the assembly not to interrupt with their clamoring).

[81] My suggestion assumes, of course, that the citizen in question had decided in advance to take the initiative in the debate and could therefore make a script of his planned motion; or else that the scheduled debate regarded a subject sufficiently well known and defined to allow a script readied in advance of the meeting, with minimal adjustment at the time of delivery, substantially to represent the individual's contribution to the discussion. For the view that these meetings had agendas and that one could seek to get an item added to them, see MacDowell 1975:64.B2. Obviously, Alkidamas' scornful sketch in *On the Sophists* §11 cannot be taken to preclude scripted delivery before the people; for he ridicules the thought of a ῥήτωρ hastening to his writing tablet not only upon hearing the herald asking 'Which citizen wants to speak?' but also after the water

prudent, perhaps, but one that diminished his citizenship by abridging in practice the privilege of ἰσηγορία and παρρησία.[82] A citizen who does not speak up,
who flinches from addressing an audience or delivering a speech, lacks the civic
voice in law-court or assembly enjoyed by others who need not similarly flinch
because their literacy has opened the door to scripted delivery.[83]

For Aristotle, rhetorical training must arguably start and build on
ἑλληνίζειν,[84] but it cannot stop there if it hopes to realize the full potential of citizenship in all the relevant public settings.[85] Foundational linguistic

---

clock in the courtroom is running. Yet no one, I think, will dispute the currency of scripted
forensic delivery, often facilitated by the professional λογογράφος. Cf. Mariß (2002:169–170),
especially her comment at 170 that "die Existenz eines schriftlichen λόγος δημηγορικός ... wird
suggeriert," a suggestion however that she dismisses as objectively untenable and mooted by
Alkidamas only to serve his rhetorical polemic. Be that as it may, we have the tantalizing notice
in Thoukydides 8.68 that Antiphon was the one man best able to help before court and assembly
whoever consulted with him in a matter. *Pace* Hudson-Williams (1951:69–70), the parallel
between the forensic and the deliberative settings is telling. Once again, we must beware not
to conflate the separate questions whether deliberative speeches were 'published' and whether
speakers prepared at all with the aid of writing for their addresses before council and assembly.
Such preparation could have been partial, chiefly comprising model proems, perorations,
commonplaces, topics, aphorisms and the like—all elements that could be quickly adjusted to
the need of the moment. Whatever the practice in the late fifth and early fourth centuries, all
that I need for my present purposes is that the use of scripts for demegoric addresses should
have been unexceptional enough by Aristotle's time to motivate the philosopher's recourse to
them when he makes the case for writing as needful for rhetorical proficiency and uninhibited
political engagement. I believe it is of some significance to my proposal that, starting soon after
the year 403/402 BC, in accordance with what MacDowell (1975:65) calls the "Old Legislation
Law," anyone wishing to propose a new law had to submit a written proposal in advance
(Demosthenes 20.89–99). This requirement, while eventually relaxed by the "New Legislation
Law" (Demosthenes 20.91, with MacDowell 1975:65–66), remained in force for the "Review Law"
(Demosthenes 24.20–23, with MacDowell 1975:66–68, esp. 67.D4).

82   Cf. Demosthenes 18.308 and 22.30. It is precisely the combination of voluntary speaking (ἄν
τι βούληται) and self-imposed silence (ἀναγκάζεσθαι κατασιωπᾶν) that convinces me that the
forensic setting is not primarily in view. There, one would more naturally be said 'to have to
speak' rather than 'to want to speak'; and neither plaintiff nor defendant could afford to remain
silent even if he did not enjoy the aid of a script, whether drafted in person or supplied by the
λογογράφος. On ἰσηγορία see Lewis 1971 and Hülsewiesche 2002.

83   Americans are used to a highly abstract concept of 'speech' that is deemed, at times, to include
even the way money is spent. Hence the polemic whether placing restrictions on expenditures
during political campaigns constitutes an unlawful abridgment of the constitutional right to
free speech. But surely for Aristotle 'to keep silent' must have denoted sooner one who does not
speak up than one who does not publish a written communication. On κατασιωπᾶν, see further
below.

84   Hence Rapp's remark (2002:2.932) that "[mit ἑλληνίζειν] scheint ... nur eine minimale Bedingung
genannt zu sein, und außerdem eine, die auch der schriftlichen Form zugrunde liegt ... ."

85   The consensus reading implies that ἑλληνίζειν constitutes the essence of the 'agonistic' style
and, furthermore, that both the demegoric and the dicanic are subsumed under it. This necessarily entails a corresponding reduction of the dicanic to basic oral competence, a reduction that
is hard to accept for a setting that often depended emphatically on scripted delivery.

competence is not to be despised: it involves a non-trivial mastery of the rules of Greek grammar and the conventions of Greek idiom with a view to rhetorical clarity and suasion.[86] But this necessary foundation looks ahead to the superior control over style and content that writing offers the would-be orator of average talent. The promise of stylistic precision and control over the relationship between form and content—this must be underlined—is not only to be found at the graphic end of the stylistic continuum. Whenever scripts were involved, the degree of precision that could be attained by an average speaker—one not exceptionally gifted by nature—and the control he could exert in delivery over the arrangement and stylistic expression of the material would have been considerably greater than when his address was left to his average improvisatory skills. To the extent that writing was involved at all, even if, in the nature of the case, it served to craft a naturalistically realistic debate style, 'those who knew how to write' would enjoy an immeasurable advantage. As often in life, the skills acquired by art would most dramatically improve those who were less exceptionally endowed. In retrospect, then, Aristotle's statement at 1413b7–8 does not so much concern the graphic end of the stylistic continuum as it illustrates the importance of writing to *all* styles, including the demegoric; and, to that extent, it also underlines the promise and importance of knowing the graphic style. One may safely assume that the importance of mastering the agonistic style was readily apparent to one and all. Hence, by seizing upon the demegoric genus to illustrate his argument, the philosopher renders it all the more compelling in that he shows the point at issue to be valid even where it is less obviously applicable.[87]

The view that *Rhetoric* 1413b6–8 is concerned with writing, pure and simple, irrespective of delivery, was built in disregard of the context and traded on a false parallel and several interpretive fantasies. One such fantasy is that μεταδίδωμι pointed to written communication.[88] But 'to communicate in writing' is neither its denotation nor even an ordinary connotation. The verb simply puts the accent on the impartation of one's mind, opinion, or oral argument (διάνοια,

---

[86] Cf. Kennedy 1991:231. It consists of five elements: first, the correct use of connectives; second, the use of specific names and steering clear of circumlocutions; third, the avoidance amphibolies; fourth, keeping the genders distinct; and, fifth, observing number.

[87] The fact that Aristotle is considering the necessity and importance of writing even for the demegoric style, the least precise and most agonistic of all styles, shows how misleading it is to equate 'agonistic' with 'oral' and 'graphic' with 'written.' This, which Aristotle studiously avoids, Rapp (2002:2.931) does when he writes: "Insofern der Gegenbegriff zur Form der Kontroverse der des schriftlichen Stils ist, mag man dazu neigen, die Kontroverse ganz mit dem mündlichen Stil gleichzusetzen; das entspricht der Argumentation des Kapitels auch im Großen und Ganzen, an *einer* Stelle jedoch, scheint eine mündliche Rede berücksichtigt zu sein, die nicht kontrovers ist (vgl. 1414a12–14)" (his emphasis). This last observation displays the failure of the schematism.

[88] Bonitz 1870:459 s.v. μεταδιδόναι: "tradere per libros scriptos." Cf. p. 602 n. 64 above.

δόξα, or λόγος), a nuance that is readily captured by our own 'to communicate'; or else in certain contexts it conveys the act of granting another the right to speak (lit., giving him a share in speech, λόγος). Now, as it happens, where it is used for 'to communicate', it regularly involves a speaker who addresses one or more hearers face-to-face.[89] In these contexts, the instrumentality of writing is decidedly exceptional and chronologically late. A further interpretive fantasy is that τοῖς ἄλλοις meant 'the rest of the world' (to use Cope's translation), a superset that would necessarily contain a preponderance of absent addressees (hence Kennedy's "others [who are not present]") and would therefore call for written dissemination. Besides disregarding the context, which cannot

[89] Here follows a list of such contexts: Euripides *Iphigeneia among the Taurians* 1030 'tell me what you think' (δόξης μετάδος, ὡς κἀγὼ μάθω), *Hiketides* 56–58 'share now your thought with me' (μετά νυν | δὸς ἐμοὶ σᾶς διανοίας, μετάδος δ'), *Orestēs* 153 'tell us/give us an account' (λόγου μετάδος); Plato *Phaidōn* 63c9 'or will you share [your thought] with us?' (ἢ κἂν ἡμῖν [τῆς διανοίας] μεταδοίης;), *Kratylos* 426b6–8 'these [notions], then, I will share with you if you want me to; and you, if you can find anywhere something better, try also to share it with me' (τούτων οὖν σοι μεταδώσω, ἂν βούλῃ· σὺ δ' ἄν τι ἔχῃς βέλτιόν ποθεν λαβεῖν, πειρᾶσθαι καὶ ἐμοὶ μεταδιδόναι), *Lysis* 204a2–3 'we spend our time mostly in conversation, in which we would gladly let you share' (ἡ δὲ διατριβὴ τὰ πολλὰ ἐν λόγοις, ὧν ἡδέως ἄν σοι μεταδιδοῖμεν); Aiskhines 2.52 'allow to speak' (ἀλλ' οὔτ' ἂν ὑμῖν ὁ ῥήτωρ οὗτος οὔτ' ἂν ἐμοὶ λόγου μεταδοίη); Polybios 29.27.4 'consult with his friends about the circumstances' (μεταδοῦναι τοῖς φίλοις ὑπὲρ τῶν προσπεπτωκότων), 38.8.1 'when Golosses communicated the conversation to the general' (τοῦ δὲ Γολόσσου μεταδόντος τῷ στρατηγῷ περὶ τῶν εἰρημένων); Dionysios of Halikarnassos *Roman Antiquities* 6.82.3 'for we will no longer allow you to speak' (οὐ γὰρ ἂν ἔτι μεταδοίημεν ὑμῖν λόγου), 10.9.3 'admitting no outsider either to their counsel or conversation' (μεταδιδόντες οὐθενὶ τῶν ἔξωθεν οὔτε βουλεύματος οὔτε λόγου), 10.13.7 'and not even allowing the tribunes to speak also' (καὶ οὐδὲ λόγου τοῖς δημάρχοις ἔτι μεταδόντες), 10.40.2 'but preventing those who wished to oppose the measure from speaking' (τὸ δὲ μὴ μεταδιδόναι λόγου τοῖς ἀντιλέξαι βουλομένοις; Plutarch *Quaestiones convivales* 697d7–8 'but because he participates and shares in conversation' (ἀλλ' ὅτι λόγου μεταλαμβάνει καὶ μεταδίδωσιν); [Plutarch] *Moralia* 102b3–4 'I thought it good to share with you these consolatory words to relieve your grief' (καλῶς ἔχειν ὑπέλαβον τῶν παραμυθητικῶν σοι μεταδοῦναι λόγων πρὸς ἄνεσιν τῆς λύπης); Dio Chrysostomus 37.1 'I shared my oratory with the people and your officers' (τῶν λόγων μετέδωκα τῷ δήμῳ καὶ τοῖς τέλεσι τοῖς ὑμετέροις), 38.4 'why are you giving yourself the right to speak when we have not given it to you?' (τί δὲ σεαυτῷ λόγου μεταδίδως, οὗ σοὶ μὴ μετέδομεν ἡμεῖς;), 38.5 'to have allowed a friend to speak who is willing to do so in vain' (ἀνδρὶ φίλῳ λόγου μεταδοῦναι βουλομένῳ μάτην εἰπεῖν), 56.11 'if although being a king he allowed the others to speak' (εἰ βασιλεὺς ὢν μετεδίδου λόγου τοῖς ἄλλοις); Josephus *Bellum Judaicum* 2.142 'he swears not to share their doctrines with anyone' (ὄμνυσιν μηδενὶ μὲν μεταδοῦναι τῶν δογμάτων); 1 Thessalonians 2.8 'to share with you not only the gospel' (μεταδοῦναι ὑμῖν οὐ μόνον τὸ εὐαγγέλιον); Akhilleus Tatios 4.7.8 'let her come before my eyes and converse with me' (εἰς ὀφθαλμοὺς ἡκέτω τοὺς ἐμοὺς καὶ λόγων μεταδότω); Athenaios 1.2a 'will you then agree to share with us too the fine talk you had over the cups ... ?' (ἆρ' οὖν ἐθελήσεις καὶ ἡμῖν τῶν καλῶν ἐπικυλικίων λόγων μεταδοῦναι ... ;), 14.643e–f 'all the ones I remember I will also share with you ... . But those names of flat cakes we copied we will also share with you' (ὅσων μέμνημαι τούτων σοι καὶ μεταδώσω ... . ἡμεῖς δὲ ἃ μετεγράψαμεν ὀνόματα πλακούντων τούτων σοι καὶ μεταδώσομεν); cf. Eusebios *Ecclesiastical History* 2.1.8; Cassius Dio 5.18.8; Philostratos *Vitae sophistarum* 2.18.599.9–10.

reasonably be assumed to refer to a scenario so extraneous to the rhetorical needs and practices of the classical period,[90] to regard the inability to *write* as 'the necessity to remain silent' should have been felt as decidedly odd. A natural reading of κατασιωπᾶν strongly suggests oral sound, not printed writing. In Demosthenes 41.23, *Athēnaiōn Politeia* 14.2, and Isokrates 8.38 it means, pointedly, 'not to speak up', and in the latter two *loci* the alleged cause is fear. Both the sense and the motive suit the present context very well. Even when it is applied to written communication, as happens with the late Josephus *Against Apiōn* 2.238, the verbal action it denotes, 'to speak up' (the refusal to remain silent), still occurs in the face of an opposing challenge, whether attended by fear or not. (This is also true of Demosthenes 41.23, which concerns the natural tendency to speak up and dispute false and unfair accusations.) The instances surveyed suggest that Aristotle's words about 'being forced to remain silent' were poignant and not without a sting, a sting that is largely absent from the consensus reading.

Innes (2007:154–155) is the most recent proponent of the audience of absent addressees who can only be reached in writing. Her strategy is to quote three passages from Isokrates where the orator uses οἱ ἄλλοι to deliberate rhetorical effect. In the first, Isokrates 11.44, he wants to establish a notional opposition between the addressee of his work, for whom he alleges keen pedagogical concern, and 'the rest', an interloping generality of potential hearers whose approbation sophists eagerly seek in display performances (ἐπιδείξεις) that are self-seeking and indifferent to the true well-being of their audiences. Isokrates' point is that sophistic epideictic may well have a large following and reach a numerous audience but it does not have the interest of its hearers at heart. Isokrates, in contrast, may not reach as far and may not be as popular and influential, but his goal is not thereby frustrated for it is not display and showiness: he genuinely cares for his addressee. Thus, Isokrates *Bousiris* 44 opposes ἐπίδειξιν τοῖς ἄλλοις ποιούμενος το ὑποδεῖξαί σοι βουλόμενος: the contrast is not between present and absent addressees but between a self-serving 'display' (ἐπίδειξιν) and a pedagogically informed 'indicating' (ὑποδεῖξαι).[91] The

---

[90] What fourth-century Athenian, successful in court and assembly, would have ever thought that his ability to communicate with others depended on his disseminating written documents?

[91] Livingstone (2001:185) writes: "Isocrates regularly insists that his works are not intended for ἐπίδειξις, public performance and self-display … . Isocrates' antithesis between (mere) ἐπίδειξις and practical, useful rhetoric parallels the Platonic Socrates' contrast between ἐπίδειξις and dialectic. It … reappears in places where, as here, the practical objective is to give useful advice … [I]n *Busiris* … it is all the more necessary to remind his readers that this is not ἐπίδειξις for its own sake, but for a serious purpose." On ὑποδεῖξαί σοι he adds: "[T]he verb ὑποδεικνύναι suggests a more 'restrained' presentation than ἐπιδεικνύναι … [It] means 'to illustrate', to show in brief … [and] can be used of getting a message across without stating it publicly … . In the present

orator does not imply that the interloping οἱ ἄλλοι are any more absent that the addressed σύ. Their existence is mooted only to be rhetorically excluded. Innes's second example, Isokrates 2.7, not only fails to support her point but even nicely parallels what I argue is Aristotle's meaning in *Rhetoric* 1413b7: Isokrates contrasts the composers of prose or poetry (οἱ συντιθέντες), who at the design stage hold their works in their minds (ἐν ταῖς διανοίαις), with 'the rest' (τοῖς ἄλλοις), i.e. the audiences, who acquire their knowledge of these works only in performance (ἐπιδειχθέντα). Far from establishing a contrast between the orator's speech and epideictic displays intended for an absent worldwide readership, here he calls *To Nikoklēs* a protreptic ἐπιχείρημα that serves both king and subjects (Isokrates 2.8). Finally, Isokrates 9.74 builds on the well-known *topos* of the winged word that carries an individual's name far and wide, a *topos* best known from Theognis' celebrated promise to Kyrnos: 'I have given you wings with which you will fly, soaring easily, over the boundless sea and all the land. You will be present at every dinner and feast, lying on the lips of many' (Theognis 237–240).[92] Isokrates contrasts immobile statues with λόγοι that 'can be carried out to Greece (ἐξενεχθῆναι ... εἰς τὴν Ἑλλάδα) and, once distributed among (διαδοθέντας) the leisured gatherings of enlightened men, are welcome by them'.[93] Although ἐκφέρω and διαδίδωμι may be used of publication, they neither presuppose nor require strictly written dissemination.[94] In this passage Isokrates is studiously ambiguous and does not explicitly claim that his λόγοι are *written* speeches anymore than Theognis'; on the contrary, we are explicitly told that they are mediated by performance in the leisured gatherings (ἐν ταῖς διατριβαῖς) of enlightened men. Although he acknowledges his writing soon thereafter at 9.76, such recognition is tempered by the paring of λέγειν

---

passage the idea of a concealed communication ... is reinforced by the antithesis τοῖς ἄλλοις/σοι. Compare especially *Ep.* I 6, where Isocrates uses the fact that he is writing to Dionysius personally, rather than speaking at a public festival, as evidence that his aim is serious and practical, not 'epideictic'" (185–186). There is therefore nothing here about 'the world at large' or 'absent addressees' who cannot be reached but by the medium of writing. (In fact, in *Letter* 1 Dionysios is the absent addressee, while the contrasting πλεῖστοι of §6 enjoy face-to-face delivery!) The point is narrowly rhetorical and regards grounding the orator's claim about the character of his address in the identity and scope of his alleged target audience.

[92] I take the translation from Gerber's *Loeb Classical Library* edition. σοὶ μὲν ἐγὼ πτέρ' ἔδωκα, σὺν οἷσ' ἐπ' ἀπείρονα πόντον | πωτήσηι, κατὰ γῆν πᾶσαν ἀειρόμενος ‖ ῥηϊδίως· θοίνηις δὲ καὶ εἰλαπίνηισι παρέσσηι | ἐν πάσαις πολλῶν κείμενος ἐν στόμασιν. Race (1987:149–150) explores related Pindaric precedents and echoes.

[93] τοὺς δὲ λόγους ἐξενεχθῆναί θ' οἷόν τ' ἐστιν εἰς τὴν Ἑλλάδα καὶ διαδοθέντας ἐν ταῖς τῶν εὖ φρονούντων διατριβαῖς ἀγαπᾶσθαι. I take this sentence to be the reason why Innes mentions Isokrates 9.74 even though it does not feature οἱ ἄλλοι. τοῖς ἄλλοις ἅπασιν does occur at the end of the section, but in a context that bears no relation to her argument.

[94] Hudson-Williams 1949.

καὶ γράφειν at 9.80.[95] Here, at any rate, we are far away from a public of absent, isolated readers, and Isokrates' point surely turns, at least in part, on the fact that his speech, ostensibly a gift for Nikokles (a *speculum principum*), has carried Evagoras' reputation all the way from Cyprus to Athens where (such is the conceit) it will make his intellectual temper known by embodying it 'in words that are spoken' (τὰς διανοίας τὰς ἐν τοῖς λεγομένοις ἐνούσας 9.75).[96] The public that is notionally absent from Cyprus is actually present with Isokrates, whose Athenocentric vantage point readily equates Athens with Hellas.[97]

To return to τοῖς ἄλλοις at *Rhetoric* 1413b7, the implicit contrast is clear: there is, on the one hand, the individual who wants to impart his mind; on the other, those who are apprised of it. This is the ordinary pragmatic context of the communication process. The passage gives no intimation that the receiver is distant from the emitter and hence can only be reached through writing. It is easy to demonstrate that the sense of οἱ ἄλλοι is simply 'the rest', not 'the rest [of the world]' (much less a 'rest' that is absent): in *Rhetoric* 1355a19 Aristotle uses it to contrast himself with the rest of those who have written technically about ῥητορική; at 1362a7, the opposition is between the rest of the brothers who are shameful and the one who is noble; at 1363b3, 'the rest' are all the ⟨φιλο⟩τοιοῦτοι other than the explicitly mentioned φιλόνικοι, φιλότιμοι, and φιλοχρήματοι; at 1369a16, those not already mentioned who act in accordance with their habitual characters; at 1388b7, all not included under the adjacent relative οὕς; at 1408a36, οἱ ἄλλοι are all but ὁ ἀκούων. Extending this short survey to cases other than the nominative yields the same outcome: 'the rest' is contextually defined and ordinarily does not mean 'the rest [of the world]'. There is therefore no warrant for the view advanced by the consensus other than the presupposition that writing to a distant readership is entailed by the passage. To this presupposition, a suitable meaning of τοῖς ἄλλοις is made to correspond. This sense does not flow from the statement. It is read into it.

But some believe to have found the necessary justification for this reading in Alkidamas *On the Sophists* §31. This section comes in the context of the sophist's

---

[95] Cf. Hägg 2012:33; pp. 30–41 provide a convenient introduction to the oration.

[96] Oral delivery is further suggested by ἐν εἴδόσιν ποιούμενοι τοὺς λόγους (9.5); and τοὺς δ' ἄλλους ἐθιστέον ἀκούειν περὶ ὧν καὶ λέγειν δίκαιόν ἐστιν (9.7). Isokrates inscribes his συγγράφειν (9.8) in the notional context of performance before an audience of hearers (cf. 9.4).

[97] It is well known that Evagoras was an honorary citizen of Athens (cf. IG I³ 113, Isokrates 9.54, and Demosthenes 12.10), so that Isokrates' encomium, however thin in actual biographical detail and historical accuracy, had every hope of being warmly received by his fellow citizens. Braund (1998:54) suggests that "Isocrates' oration was clearly immediately influential. Its effect can be seen in Xenophon's *Agesilaus*" (but cf. Hägg 2012:41). We also know that Athens honored Evagoras ca. 393 BC with a decree from which three small fragments have survived. In connection with it Lewis and Stroud (1979:187) remark that "the enthusiastic welcome which Konon received as a returning hero was to a large extent shared by his Cyprian patron."

justifying his paradoxical use of writing for the broadside against oratorical writing. He makes clear that he does not entirely dismiss the ability to write (τὴν γραφικὴν δύναμιν) but merely considers it inferior to performing extempore (§30). He resorts to writing, moreover, not with an attitude (οὐκ ἐπὶ τούτῳ μέγιστον φρονῶν) but only to show those who pride themselves on this skill that with little effort he succeeds in blotting out and demolishing their arguments for it. Then comes the following:

> πρὸς δὲ τούτοις καὶ τῶν ἐπιδείξεων εἴνεκα τῶν εἰς τοὺς ὄχλους ἐκφερομένων ἅπτομαι τοῦ γράφειν. τοῖς μὲν γὰρ πολλάκις ἡμῖν ἐντυγχάνουσιν ἐξ ἐκείνου τοῦ τρόπου παρακελεύομαι πεῖραν ἡμῶν λαμβάνειν, ὅταν ὑπὲρ ἅπαντος τοῦ προτεθέντος εὐκαίρως καὶ μουσικῶς εἰπεῖν οἷοί τ' ὦμεν· τοῖς δὲ διὰ χρόνου μὲν ἐπὶ τὰς ἀκροάσεις ἀφιγμένοις, μηδεπώποτε δὲ πρότερον ἡμῖν ἐντετυχηκόσιν, ἐπιχειρούμέν τι δεικνύναι τῶν γεγραμμένων· εἰθισμένοι γὰρ ἀκροᾶσθαι τῶν ἄλλων ⟨τοὺς γραπ⟩τοὺς λόγους,[98] ἴσως ἂν ἡμῶν αὐτοσχεδιαζόντων ἀκούοντες ἐλάττονα τῆς ἀξίας δόξαν καθ' ἡμῶν λάβοιεν.

On the Sophists §31

Moreover, I also apply myself to writing on account of those displays that are delivered before the multitudes.[99] For I exhort those who meet us often to make trial of us in that manner [viz. with regard to extempore delivery] since then the circumstances allow us [lit., when we are able][100] to speak elegantly and with happy appropriateness for

---

[98] Although τοὺς γραπ- before -τούς *could* have fallen out, I for one do not agree with the editors that the text must be emended. Alkidamas' complaint is precisely that the use of writing is so widespread that 'the speeches of the rest', i.e. of all others who make oratory their regular practice, are scripted and therefore do not fail to spoil their audiences. It is precisely the hyperbolic τῶν ἄλλων τοὺς λόγους that explains why Alkidamas has reluctantly given in to the practice and does not even consider that any, perhaps even a majority, of his potential new hearers may have been exposed to, much less might well appreciate, extempore speaking.

[99] For ἐκφέρω as 'oral delivery' see Hudson-Williams 1949:65–66. Cf. Mariß 2002: "[ἐκφέρειν] charakterisiert eher die mündliche Epideixis" (291).

[100] My translation seeks to capture what Mariß (2002:294) rightly observes: "Vielmehr wird die präpositionale Wendung ἐξ ἐκείνου τοῦ τρόπου durch den ὅταν-Satz erklärt und konkretisiert: 'fordern wir auf, auf jene Weise eine Probe von uns zu nehmen, wenn wir jeweils (da das Publikum das richtige ist) über jeden vorgelegten Gegenstand εὐκαίρως καὶ μουσικῶς sprechen können'." Because the temporal contingency of ὅταν hinges on the presence of the right kind of public (those who often meet Alkidamas), insofar as restricted to them this contingency turns factual and the ὅταν clause is equivalent to an explanation ('because then'). In other words, τοῖς πολλάκις ἡμῖν ἐντυγχάνουσιν notionally supplies a temporal reference point, a τότε, which ὅταν answers (Smyth §2240; cf. *On the Sophists* §13).

the occasion about every proposed subject. But for those who finally[101] come to hear us perform[102] who never yet before have met us, we endeavor to display something of what we have written; for accustomed to hear the ⟨written⟩ speeches of the others, when they hear us speak extempore they may perhaps acquire a lower regard of us than the one we deserve.

There is nothing in the passage that suggests strictly written dissemination of Alkidamas' writings. εἰς τοὺς ὄχλους ἐκφερομένων regards delivery before the crowds, with ὄχλους hinting at the sophist's contempt for the multitudes who, spoiled by their frequent hearing of speeches prepared with the aid of writing, can no longer appreciate the finer and superior skill of extempore speech-making. This negative connotation of ὄχλοι also seems present in Gorgias' *Helen* 13, which envisions crowds delighted and persuaded by speeches that are artfully written but spoken without truth; and in *Palamēdēs* 33, where a mob (ὄχλος) that can be swayed by piteous wailing, prayers, and the entreating of friends is contrasted with those who are and appear as the foremost of the Greeks and are persuaded by one who exhibits the truth with manifest justice. So it is also with Isokrates, who in *To Nikoklēs* 49–50 compares the crowds (ὄχλοι) that others seek to please, rather than admonish and counsel, with Nikokles, who receives instead his paraenetic address; and who in *Nikoklēs* 21 contrasts advisers skillful at addressing the crowds (ὄχλοι) with advisers who know how to deal with the issues.[103] Finally, Aristotle's own use of the word in *Rhetoric* 1395b28–29 also seems decidedly negative: 'For this is why the uneducated are more persuasive with the crowds than the educated, just as the poets say that the uneducated

---

[101] Mariß (2002:295) notes that here Alkidamas uses μέν ... δέ first to present, and then to expand on, a particular point of chronology: διὰ χρόνου μέν, 'after a time', is thus reprised by μηδεπώποτε δὲ πρότερον, 'never yet before'. These do not regard two different groups but one and the same set of potential hearers who finally come to hear Alkidamas perform. διὰ χρόνου draws attention to the fact that they have long had the opportunity to hear him yet have never before availed themselves of it; it also hints at Alkidamas' dissatisfied impatience with them.

[102] Mariß (2002:295) correctly renders ἀκροάσεις "Rezitation," "Lesung," and suggests recourse to τοῖς μὲν γὰρ πολλάκις ἡμῖν ἐντυγχάνουσιν for clarification. She also adds that "Schriftliches liegt jedenfalls zugrunde."

[103] Cf. Isokrates 5.81 and 15.192. An only slightly less negative assessment seems implicated by Isokrates 2.16 and 12.263. In Isokrates 4.150, in a context that does not regard public speaking, the majority of the Persians are called 'a mob without discipline' (ὄχλος ἄτακτος). The connotation of the term is neutral at 4.96, 6.64, 6.73, 6.78, 18.9, and perhaps at 11.26. But none of these regard a rhetorical context and are therefore without relevance. With a different acceptation, ὄχλος as 'mass' (i.e. 'great number') occurs at 12.192 and 15.310; at 12.211 and 15.320 it denotes 'trouble'.

are more accomplished in speaking before a crowd'.[104] Mariß (2002:291) remarks on the undertone of 'regret' in Alkidamas' acceptance of writing for delivery before crowded audiences: "[Alkidamas sagt] daß gemeinhin ἐπιδείξεις veranstaltet würden und daß er sich wegen dieses allgemeinen Trends dem Schreiben zuwende." To the hint of contempt he expresses with τοὺς ὄχλους, add the fact that in §11 ἀκρόασις refers to passive and politically inactive hearers under a tyranny (Mariß 2002:295). The entire context of §31, then, is one of oral delivery, whether the display is improvised or scripted. Hence the mention of '[vocal] recitations' (ἀκροάσεις), of an audience spoiled by 'listening' (ἀκροᾶσθαι) to the speeches of others, and of forming an opinion of Alkidamas on 'hearing' (ἀκούοντες) him speak extempore. Nothing other than the bare fact of the sophist's resort to writing and the failure of scholars to realize that, just as in the rest of the broadside, scripted delivery is in view supports the implausible reading that Alkidamas is now referring to the written dissemination of his speeches through the book market. If so, why should he refer to the alleged readership as ὄχλοι? A gathered throng was the desired ideal of the display sophist (Isokrates *Letter* 1.6): what justification does the modern scholar have to turn it into a potential multitude of individual solo readers? Hudson-Williams (1949:65) had it right: "Alcidamas, a contemporary of Isocrates, says that one reason which prompted him to compose an artistic written λόγος instead of 'improvising' was the prospect of giving recitals to crowded audiences ... . Epideictic λόγοι were intended to be read [or, better, performed] before an audience, as a play was intended to be exhibited in the theatre."[105]

---

[104] τοῦτο γὰρ αἴτιον καὶ τοῦ πιθανωτέρους εἶναι τοὺς ἀπαιδεύτους τῶν πεπαιδευμένων ἐν τοῖς ὄχλοις, ὥσπερ φασὶν οἱ ποιηταὶ τοὺς ἀπαιδεύτους παρ' ὄχλῳ μουσικωτέρους λέγειν (*Rhetoric* 1395b26–29). The other instance of ὄχλος in the *Rhetoric* is at 1414a9 (see below); it too seems to exhibit a somewhat negative color. Cf. Mariß 2002:292.

[105] An alternative way of reading the τὸ μὲν ... τὸ δέ clauses in *Rhetoric* 1413b5–6 takes ἄμφω as gathering together the graphic and the agonistic styles into a larger notion which the philosopher then considers from a different point of view. To illustrate this reading, suppose I should say: 'a student of Latin must learn both grammar and vocabulary; for one thing is to know paradigms and another to be able to read Cicero.' It would be incorrect to infer that the following two equations hold true: 'to know grammar' = 'to know paradigms' and 'to know vocabulary' = 'to be able to read Cicero'. (Knowing paradigms would be a subset of knowing grammar, while knowing vocabulary simply would not correspond to being able to read Cicero.) My point would be, rather, that merely knowing paradigms bespeaks a limited linguistic ability, while a proficient grasp of *both* grammar *and* vocabulary confers a working knowledge of the language. Note that neither grammar nor vocabulary by itself would suffice. As an alternative to the reading I have defended above, one could argue that something similar happens here: just as the knowledge of *both* styles, graphic *and* agonistic, would equip the orator successfully to address an audience, failure to master *either* would prevent him from doing so. To paraphrase Aristotle's point: 'For one thing is to know how to speak correct Greek; another to be able successfully to communicate (and, presumably, to persuade) an audience, avoiding the need to keep silent because one lacks the requisite skills.' When he uses τὸ μὲν ... τὸ δέ, the philosopher often

In my view, then, the graphic and agonistic styles are not two mutually exclusive subjects with no conceptual overlap; and so, it is not the case that knowledge of one translates into one thing (namely, speaking correct Greek), while knowledge of the other, into another (namely, not having to keep silent etc.). 'Graphic' and 'agonistic' are both connected with delivery and denote stylistic emphases that point to one or another of two ends of a continuum.[106] Ignorance of *either* emphasis would handicap the orator's delivery and compro-

---

specifies what each points to by making them follow a genitive (e.g. *Categories* 4b20, *Nicomachean Ethics* 1109a33, *Metaphysics* 1072b3, *Politics* 1334b20, or *De respiratione* 471a8) or by having ἐν + dat. indicate their sphere of reference (e.g. *On Generation and Corruption* 317a23); at least once, τὸ μὲν … τὸ δέ merely stand in apposition (*Metaphysics* 1065a21). What has misled interpreters of *Rhetoric* 1413b5–8 is the (otherwise natural) assumption that the referent of μὲν … δέ is ἄμφω; and that since ἄμφω (to put it schematically) is made of the explicitly mentioned 'X' and 'Y', τὸ μέν must equal 'X', τὸ δέ, 'Y' (or vice versa). It would then be as if the philosopher had written: ἄμφω δὲ ἀνάγκη εἰδέναι· ὧν τὸ μὲν … τὸ δέ. But no ὧν is implied and τὸ μέν may be rendered as 'one thing', while τὸ δέ, as 'another thing'. Aristotle could have written τὸ μὲν … ἄλλο δέ or τὸ μὲν … ἕτερον δέ: but perhaps he did not because this might have conveyed too sharp a contrast between speaking correct Greek and being able to speak to an audience in public address. (Note, for example, the ἓν μὲν … ἕτερον δὲ … ἄλλο δέ in *Politics* 1291b18–19, where the various categories do not overlap.) After all, we take for granted that proficient public speakers will be linguistically competent. One clear instance of τὸ μὲν … τὸ δέ which does not pick up on anything explicit that immediately precedes them is *Sophistical Refutations* 181b9–10: 'If one thing is good and another evil (εἰ τὸ μέν ἐστιν ἀγαθὸν τὸ δὲ κακόν), it is true to call them good and evil' etc. τὸ μέν and τὸ δέ do not respectively point to anything in the immediate context: they must be translated simply 'one thing' and 'another thing'. So also, according to this alternative reading, in *Rhetoric* 1413b5–8: 'One thing is to speak good Greek; another, not to be forced to keep silent' etc. The general sphere of reference, were it to be made specific, would have to be expressed somewhat along the lines of τὸν γὰρ καὶ ἐξετάζειν καὶ ὑπέχειν λόγον καὶ ἀπολογεῖσθαι καὶ κατηγορεῖν ἐγχειροῦντα with τὸ μέν … τὸ δέ (cf. *Rhetoric* 1354a5–6). A paraphrase might run thus: τὸ μὲν γάρ ἐστιν τὸν καὶ ἐξετάζειν καὶ ὑπέχειν λόγον καὶ ἀπολογεῖσθαι καὶ κατηγορεῖν ἐγχειροῦντα ἑλληνίζειν ἐπίστασθαι, τὸ δὲ πιθανῶς καὶ σαφῶς μεταδοῦναι τοῖς ἄλλοις ἐπίστασθαι (or πιθανῶς καὶ σαφῶς μεταδοῦναι τοῖς ἄλλοις οἷόν τε εἶναι). The alternative construction ἔστιν μὲν … ἔστιν δέ would have made a poorer choice; for it would only make marginal sense to write: 'it is possible, on the one hand, to know how to speak correct Greek; and possible, on the other, not to have to keep silent' etc. 'Not to have to keep silent' may well be a possible scenario, but, strictly speaking, an *inability* rather than a *possibility*. I should make clear that I consider this alternative interpretation inferior to the one I have propounded above, although effectively its meaning is much the same. I only offer it to my reader here to underline the fact that there is very little to recommend joining the consensus on this passage of the *Rhetoric*.

[106] A fact already recognized by Sonkowsky 1959: "The styles are a pair of ideal classifications; [Aristotle] recognizes a relative scale between them, along which, presumably, the two could be mixed together in varying degrees" (260–261). So also O'Sullivan 1992: "The two styles to be considered are, of course, the 'written' and the 'unwritten', but I use the quotation marks advisedly. For they are, in a sense, purely nominal designations, indicating tendency rather than method of presentation" (43). And, more recently, Schloemann 2000: "[Aristoteles] stellt Lesen … und öffentliche Rhetorik gegeneinander. Es ist dadurch nicht gesagt, daß die öffentlichen Reden auf der Ebene der Produktion mündlich sind … . Auch Reden im agonistischen Stil können schriftlich konzipiert sein" (209).

mise his ability to persuade his audience. Since *both* the graphic *and* the agonistic styles presuppose the use of written scripts in honing and rehearsing one's delivery, 'those who do not know how to write' describe individuals whose rhetorical training is wanting: laymen who approach their speech without the benefit of schooling and formal training in the discipline of oratory. At best, such people can be expected to speak good Greek but they are not up to the task of addressing the rest of their fellow citizens, whether in the law-court or the assembly. My reading, then, makes 'one must know both' equivalent to 'one must be trained in scientific delivery': this involves knowing the rules of style that make delivery an art in the first place; and these rules include suiting the style to the kind of oratory in view, that is, choosing the stylistic emphases that make the moment of truth—the performance before the audience—successful.

Thus, I translate: 'One must not overlook that a different style suits each genus of rhetoric. For the graphic and agonistic are not the same, nor the demegoric and dicanic. And one must know both: for knowing both is, on the one hand, to know how to speak correct Greek, and also, on the other, not to have to keep silent if one wishes to share something with the others—which [is what] those who do not know how to write experience'. Aristotle envisages a graded rhetorical skill: on the one hand, the foundation and ἀρχὴ τῆς λέξεως (1407a19), which was possibly shared by many an ordinary citizen[107] and reached to linguistic competence; on the other, a superior ability that was the province of the rhetorically trained,[108] who did not flinch from taking the initiative in political affairs, proposing and defending their own motions, and who were unafraid to prepare (and argue, as they must) their own cases in forensic settings. As observed above, classical Athens had many citizens who, though present in the assembly, were largely passive and easily manipulated by the naturally gifted or better trained ῥήτορες who made a career of their political activities. Though, as Ober (1989:106) notes, ὁ πολιτευόμενος vied with ῥήτωρ as a label for the professional political orator (in some ways, a label not far from our own 'politician'), the free citizen's *ideal* of civic life was to be fully and actively involved in the affairs of the polis. It is to that ideal that Aristotle addresses himself in enjoining rhetorical training—particularly, mastery of the use of written scripts as an aid to delivery—on those who wish to escape the status of mere silent spectators at their political assemblies. The degree of proficiency requisite for discharging the political responsibilities of the free citizen, in Aristotle's view, is reliably available only to the one who has mastered the skill of using written scripts to train for the moment of delivery. Ober nicely

---

[107] Cf. *Rhetoric* 1354a6–7.
[108] Cf. *Rhetoric* 1354a7–11.

captures the contrast at 1413b5–8: "Skill in public address was sine qua non for the politician. This meant not only skill at putting words together but also in putting them across" (1989:113).

The inattentive reader of the *Rhetoric* might think that the graphic style alone calls for writing, a belief that contradicts what I have advocated above. And the comment at 1414a17–18 might seem to lend credence to this view: ἡ μὲν οὖν ἐπιδεικτικὴ λέξις γραφικωτάτη· τὸ γὰρ ἔργον αὐτῆς ἀνάγνωσις. But the γάρ clause 'for its peculiar work is reading' is not primarily a statement of design, as if the philosopher thought epideictic speeches composed first and foremost for a reading public (something that may have been true of Isokrates but certainly not so of other practitioners of this genus). Rapp, who thinks that the philosopher fails to explain why the epideictic genus is the most graphic, suggests that his analysis may have been influenced by the circulation in writing of Isokrates' speeches, which Aristotle took as heuristic models. Be that as it may, this scholar is right to observe: "Allerdings scheint Aristoteles die Schriftlichkeit nicht durchgehend als ein Merkmal der vorführenden Rede angesehen zu haben, denn in Kapitel I 9 ist davon nicht die Rede, und auch in III 14, 1415b28f., spricht Aristoteles explizit von einem 'Hörer' der vorführenden Rede" (Rapp 2002:2.938). By asserting that the peculiar work of epideictic is reading, the philosopher seems to be restating the relatively lesser dependence of the epideictic style on the effective use of the voice, especially of a loud voice (1414a15–17). The employment of the common devices of style (κοινῇ 1414a28) characteristic of epideictic, e.g. how it utilizes connective particles and repetition, is contrary in tendency to the corresponding use by the more agonistic styles. This is the proper way to understand τὰ ὑποκριτικά at 1413b17: the term denotes not 'speeches suited for delivery' (as some suppose) but general stylistic devices and strategies (e.g. asyndeton),[109] viewed—in good Aristotelian fashion, as we should expect from my argument in this and the last chapter—as instrumental to delivery.[110] Thus, to connective particles as stylistic devices (subsumed, like other such resources, under τὰ ὑποκριτικά) correspond

---

[109] Cf. the use of τὰ ῥητορικά at 1375a8 and 1414a12 with Grimaldi 1980:314.

[110] In other words, it is an error to think of τὰ ὑποκριτικά as the stylistic devices and strategies of the agonistic style, as if the graphic featured analogous τὰ ἀναγνωστικά (it does not). (Graff 2001:21 goes even further and mistakenly identifies the agonistic style with τὰ ὑποκριτικά.) Since *all* genera are performed and *all* styles are conceived with a view to delivery, τὰ ὑποκριτικά denotes the entire collection of stylistic devices and strategies that an orator can choose from in order to suit the subject and setting of his address. The clarity and persuasiveness that various stylistic devices and strategies are capable of in performance are unequally devitalized when deprived of delivery. So also is the subset of them peculiar to a given style denaturalized when employed unchanged in the wrong setting (the agonistic, in the setting proper to the graphic, and the graphic, in the setting proper to the agonistic).

two delivery strategies of opposite tendency: the agonistic downplays their use and prefers relatively more frequent asyndeta, entrusting their characteristic function instead to the phrasing of the speaker's voice; the graphic, on the contrary, makes liberal use of connectives, and for this very reason depends less for its clarity and persuasiveness on a marked vocal intonation. By reason of their respective peculiar styles (ἰδίᾳ 1414a29),[111] the script of an epideictic speech survives much better the absence of vocal performance than the script of a symbuleutic or a forensic speech: the clarity and persuasiveness of the former (always inextricably tied to each other) are relatively less affected than those of the latter two. Nonetheless, there is still something logically odd about asserting that the work of the epideictic style is reading, for *stricto sensu* 'reading' cannot be the 'work' of any style (what a given style does or busies itself with) in the same way, for example, that 'to observe the cause is the work of an art' (τέχνης ἔργον 1354a11), 'to see the existing means of persuasion in each case' is the business of rhetoric (1355b10–11), or 'to know what constitution is beneficial on the basis of past history' and 'to know what constitutions the others have' is the business of the art of politics (1360a37–38). Unless style is reconceived as a 'doing', it can neither be considered 'an employment' (χρῆσις) nor can anything be said to be its product (*Eudemian Ethics* 1219a13–18).[112] One cannot even appeal to the general definition of 'the ἔργον of something' as 'its τέλος' (*Eudemian Ethics* 1219a8), for it would run counter to Aristotle's argument to think of any style (not even the most graphic of them all) as attaining its fulfillment in anything other than delivery. This is the approach adopted by Kennedy, who translates, "its objective is to be read" (1991:257). The best solution seems to me to assume that Aristotle has so deeply internalized the view of λέξις as subservient to an action—the *actio* that is ὑπόκρισις—that he allows for a conceptual overlap between the *manner* of speaking (1403b17) and the *action* of speaking before an audience. λέξις then becomes 'a manner of λέγειν', and the delivery of epideictic, as the genus most dependent on scripts because its precision calls for more extensive use of writing, naturally approaches, when it does not simply consist in, the reading of its scripts. One might even argue that the ποικιλία of style and thought characteristic of epideictic called for a more precise memorization of its script and made its commitment to memory a more critical prerequisite to delivery. To that extent, its delivery would naturally match its public reading. And, since appropriate delivery may rightly be called the *telos*

---

[111] That is, by reason of the expressive strategies characteristic of each genus, of the devices to which each of them typically resorts as well as in what manner, with what frequency, etc. it does so.

[112] Bonitz 1870:285 s.v. ἔργον: "hoc discrimen in usu voc[is] ἔργον ita est conspicuum, ut modo operae et actionis notionem complectatur, modo ipsum opus effectum significet ... ."

of any given style, ἀνάγνωσις, a delivery peculiarly suitable for epideictic, can be pronounced 'the *ergon* of the epideictic style'.[113]

Aristotle had remarked in 1413b14–19 that the speeches of the graphic poets, when subject to the *Gedankenexperiment* of delivery in an agonistic context,[114] appear thin or meager,[115] whereas those of actual orators[116] feel amateurish when read.[117] Therefore, dramatic speeches pervaded by emphases proper to

[113] Graff (2001:21) is therefore wrong to assume that "by 'reading' Aristotle here ... means a reading aloud, but presumably one lacking the dramatic vocal and gestural accompaniments of full *hupokrisis*." Unless, of course, by "full *hupokrisis*" he means the delivery peculiar to the agonistic style. If so, this would then be a trivial observation, for no one would expect Aristotle to recommend an agonistic delivery for a graphic style. He is also wrong to wedge apart the goal of delivery from those stylistic qualities that make for easy reading: "Aristotle's account here [sc. at *Rhetoric* III.8.6] emphasizes the benefits to the *reader*. That Aristotle is thinking here not of the delivery of a speech, but rather its reading (aloud but conceivably to oneself) is unambiguous. No fourth-century Greek would deliver (ὑποκρίνεσθαι) a speech from a piece of papyrus before the assembly or even in court" (Graff 2000:198–199, his emphasis). The issue whether a speaker's explicit show of dependence on a script was culturally acceptable or not in a particular social setting is a red herring. Quite apart from the undeniable benefits that a proper style would provide to the reader of lightly punctuated *scriptio continua*, it should be obvious that a script that does not make for a fluent and intelligible reading aloud, when adequately internalized for delivery, would neither make for a fluent and intelligible vocal performance. Hence Aristotle's explicit equation at 1407b11–12 between written material that is εὐανάγνωστον ('easy to read [aloud]') and εὔφραστον ('easy to give oral expression to'). Note that this last comment occurs in the section on ἑλληνίζειν, a subject that, for Aristotle, indisputably concerns the linguistic competence of oral expression. Cf. Graff 2001:28.

[114] Alternatively, one might conjecture that, at least for some of these speeches, their own dramatic context was agonistic and that, if judged accordingly, they appeared meager. If so, at any rate, fans of Khairemon's works cannot have felt this fact as a serious blemish.

[115] Without Kassel's emendation, οἱ μέν at b14 must refer to the poets (cf. οἱ ἀναγνωστικοί at b12); τῶν γραφικῶν (b15) in turn must either refer to the poets too ('and side by side, those of the graphic [class of poets] ...') or else, rather more likely, to their dramas (τῶν γραφικῶν [δραμάτων], i.e. 'those poets who compose graphic dramas'; cf. b11). With Kassel's καὶ παραβαλλόμενοι ⟨οἱ λόγοι⟩ οἱ μὲν τῶν γραφικῶν (as with Ross's similar καὶ παραβαλλόμενοι οἱ μὲν τῶν γραφέων ⟨λόγοι⟩), the comparison regards the speeches, not the poets; and τῶν γραφικῶν presumably refers to the 'graphic poets' (γραφικοί standing for ἀναγνωστικοί). I believe that ultimately none of these alternative texts differs much in meaning from any other. (I suggest a different emendation below, p. 626 n. 129.) I am not troubled by Aristotle's substituting the poets for what *stricto sensu* must be the speeches in their plays and calling them 'thin' in debate, although I can appreciate the inconcinnity between οἱ μὲν τῶν γραφικῶν and οἱ δὲ τῶν ῥητόρων and understand why the editors would wish to emend it away.

[116] If one accepts ἢ τῶν λεχθέντων at 1413b16 (see the footnote immediately below), here ῥήτορες, following its common political use, must narrowly denote assembly and forensic speakers.

[117] It is hard to know what to do with ἢ τῶν λεχθέντων at 1413b16, which Kassel brackets. I am tempted to accept it on the grounds that οἱ [λόγοι] τῶν ῥητόρων ἢ τῶν λεχθέντων nicely comprises the three rhetorical genera, which Aristotle may well be comparing *in toto* to the speeches found in those poets who are suitable for reading. The point would be that the layman who takes in hand a script devised for delivery before an audience cannot with an ordinary (non-dramatic) reading compensate for the missing ὑπόκρισις. Aristotle may have added ἢ τῶν λεχθέντων from a feeling that, by only writing οἱ δὲ τῶν ῥητόρων, he would appear to leave out

the graphic style,[118] having only marginally, if at all, been written for actual on-stage delivery, would suffer little loss of impact if they were not produced and could only be experienced by the interested reader. Note that, if my understanding of the passage is correct, to illustrate the graphic style Aristotle has selected not epideictic addresses but speeches by graphic/anagnostic poets. I believe that he owes this choice not simply to his prior resort to poets, actors, and plays to illustrate the ethical and emotional styles (although this probably contributed to it). His aim would have been not to wedge apart epideictic from the other two species of rhetoric, since, after all, he viewed all three as *inherently performative* genera whose scripts, apart from delivery, could only imperfectly represent concrete, real-life speech-making. One must remember that ordinarily epideictic speeches *were* delivered in their own characteristic settings (note the mention of a 'listener' at 1415b29).[119] One is therefore not surprised to learn that Isokrates complained about the loss of persuasiveness experienced by his written discourses, not only because popular prejudice took for granted that written speeches were composed for self-seeking display and profit but also because 'when a discourse is deprived of the prestige of the speaker, the sound of his voice, the variations that happen in rhetorical delivery, and, besides, of the critical timeliness and earnestness that attaches to the action, and … [when] someone reads it out unpersuasively and without investing it with character, but rather as one tallying up an account—in these circumstances it is natural, I think, that it should seem trivial to its hearers' (Isokrates 5.26–27).[120] If even Isokrates' epideictic writings came across as weak and ineffective when read without the requisite rhetorical vocalization, agonistic speeches would suffer comparatively greater loss and feel jejune if deprived of their intended ὑπόκρισις. It is clear, then, that Aristotle has in view the technology of writing throughout the entire chapter. This is beyond question for the graphic style, whereas with respect to the agonistic *Rhetoric* 1413b15–19 contemplates holding illustrative

---

epideictic speeches. The addition, as the superset of actually delivered speeches ('the speeches of orators or [those] from the ones spoken [that are compared]'), would not only include οἱ τῶν ῥητόρων but also incorporate epideictic. At any rate, if one follows Kassel in excising the words, it is still possible to interpret τῶν ῥητόρων as denoting all professional public speakers comprehensively. Their speeches would still comprise all three of the standard rhetorical genera.

[118] Aristotle subsumes all these emphases under the umbrella of ἀκρίβεια (see below).

[119] If my reader prefers the view that the anagnostic poets and their speeches straightforwardly represent the epideictic genus, then he need only excise ἢ τῶν λεχθέντων at 1413b16 and restrict τῶν ῥητόρων at b15–16 to symbuleutic and forensic speakers. Ultimately, the alternative preferred is of no great consequence to my overall argument.

[120] ἐπειδὰν γὰρ ὁ λόγος ἀποστερηθῇ τῆς τε δόξης τῆς τοῦ λέγοντος καὶ τῆς φωνῆς καὶ τῶν μεταβολῶν τῶν ἐν ταῖς ῥητορείαις γιγνομένων, ἔτι δὲ καὶ τῶν καιρῶν καὶ τῆς σπουδῆς τῆς περὶ τὴν πρᾶξιν, καὶ … ἀναγιγνώσκῃ δέ τις αὐτὸν ἀπιθάνως καὶ μηδὲν ἦθος ἐνσημαινόμενος ἀλλ' ὥσπερ ἀπαριθμῶν, εἰκότως, οἶμαι, φαῦλος εἶναι δοκεῖ τοῖς ἀκούουσιν.

scripts of it in one's hands and reading them aloud,[121] thus depriving the style of proper delivery (ἀφῃρημένης τῆς ὑποκρίσεως).[122] Aristotle's analysis suggests that writing had been adopted wholesale by successful rhetorical practitioners, and he correspondingly enjoins its mastery on the rhetorical apprentice.

It is now time to inquire what the philosopher means when he assigns ἀκρίβεια to the λέξις γραφική and contrasts it with ὑπόκρισις: ἀλλ᾽ ὅπου μάλιστα ὑπόκρισις, ἐνταῦθα ἥκιστα ἀκρίβεια ἔνι (1414a15–16).[123] We must notice first that the terms τὸ ἀκριβές and ὑπόκρισις are subject to degrees: this is clear enough from the superlatives at 1413b8–9 (ἔστι δὲ λέξις γραφικὴ μὲν ἡ ἀκριβεστάτη, ἀγωνιστικὴ δὲ ἡ ὑποκριτικωτάτη) and the comparative at 1414a10–11 (ἡ δὲ δίκη ἀκριβέστερον); and it is not surprising, since the inverse relation in which 1414a15–17 puts ἀκρίβεια and ὑπόκρισις[124] suggests that these are two tendencies that point to the extremes of a stylistic continuum. In other words, it is not a matter of a style being ἀκριβής, 'precise', and thus *not* ὑποκριτική, 'histrionic' (i.e. 'not bearing relation to delivery'),[125] or vice versa. What the philosopher is underlining through this contrast is that not all the elements and expressive strategies of style (τὰ ὑποκριτικά), however much they can be put at the service of delivery according to the occasion, exhibit the same intimate relationship and immediate connection to voice in its expressive use 'for each *pathos*' (1403b27–28). We readily understand, for example, that prose rhythm depends on the voice to a greater extent than the employment of metaphors; and though even instances of the latter, insofar as instrumental to delivery, are carefully designed and chosen to evoke apposite φαντάσματα,[126] when restricted to silent reading (to take an extreme, anachronistic case) metaphors retain much more of their natural effectiveness (their ἔργον; cf. 1413b18) than prose rhythm does. And however much the intonation that should attend the

[121] This observation is true regardless of how one construes the relation of the epideictic genus to the anagnostic poets and their speeches.

[122] Sonkowsky (1959:261) observes: "The technical term *lexis graphikē* must not be confused with *graphomenos logos*, which means 'a speech that is written down.' Speeches in the *lexis agōnistikē* can also be *graphomenoi*."

[123] For a concise classification of ἀκρίβεια according to its various uses, see Grant 1885:452 *ad Nicomachean Ethics* 1.7.18 1098a26–33 (cf. 1094b11–1095a13). Kurz 1970 offers a foundational study of the concept down to Aristotle's time. For 'precision' in the stylistic context, see O'Sullivan 1992 *passim* (esp. 42–62); Graff 2000:53, 101–108, 171–177, and 195–198; Graff 2001; and Innes 2007:161–164.

[124] ἀλλ᾽ ὅπου μάλιστα ὑποκρίσεως, ἐνταῦθα ἥκιστα ἀκρίβεια ἔνι. τοῦτο δέ, ὅπου φωνῆς, καὶ μάλιστα ὅπου μεγάλης.

[125] Since the analysis concerns how to suit style to the various *genera dicendi* (cf. 1413b3–5), ὑποκριτικὴ λέξις is best rendered as 'suited to the portrayal of *ēthos* and *pathos* that is the peculiar function of delivery' (note ἠθική and παθητική at 1413b10). For the sake of convenience, I will use 'histrionic' as shorthand for the fuller, more accurate translation.

[126] See above, p. 533 and n. 42.

delivery of a script may be imagined by a reader and recreated in his mind's ear, clearly this is an essentially 'histrionic' feature (to use Aristotle's terminology) that, although perhaps susceptible of '(over)precise' articulation in the context of the graphic,[127] finds a natural home in the agonistic style. The illustration supplied further clarifies what is in view: actors go after such effects in dramas, i.e. after what gives the greatest scope to their ὑπόκρισις (which is eminently concerned with giving expression to *ēthos* and *pathos*), whereas poets seek such characters.[128] Authors whose works are towards the graphic end of the stylistic continuum are the ἀναγνωστικοί, e.g. Khairemon, who is 'precise as a logographer' (1413b13).

Now follows a series of examples that are designed to show the features peculiar to either end of the stylistic continuum. Aristotle's *Gedankenexperiment* consists in taking a speech out of the context to which its style is suited, and using the resulting deficiencies to highlight the corresponding strengths when it is left in its natural rhetorical environment. Hence, compared to those crafted for competitive settings, graphic speeches seem thin;[129] whereas those delivered by professional public speakers (the implication being that they must have received high praise)[130] feel amateurish when reduced to mere scripts in the hands of the lay reader. In selecting speeches by professional public speakers, Aristotle has made his illustration as pointed as possible and rendered the ἰδιωτικοί (1413b16) sharper by contrast. As explained above, τὰ ὑποκριτικά denotes the sum total of rhetorical stylistic elements and strategies. These look to delivery and its corresponding use of the voice in whatever measure is judged appropriate. Therefore, the more critically any one of them depends for its effectiveness on delivery (on vocal articulation and the expression of character and emotion), absent ὑπόκρισις and reduced to its mark on the page the more it

---

[127] Cf. Alkidamas *On the Sophists* §16: ὅταν γάρ τις ἐθισθῇ κατὰ μικρὸν ἐξεργάζεσθαι τοὺς λόγους καὶ μετ' ἀκριβείας καὶ ῥυθμοῦ τὰ ῥήματα συντιθέναι, καὶ βραδείᾳ τῇ τῆς διανοίας κινήσει χρώμενος ἐπιτελεῖν τὴν ἑρμηνείαν ... ('For whenever one is accustomed to work out his speeches in detail and to put together the words with precision and rhythm, and to perfect his expression by using his mental process sluggishly ...').

[128] Though certainty is impossible, I think that τοὺς τοιούτους are not the actors but 'those [dramatic personae who are] such': not all the characters of a play give the same scope to histrionic displays. In any case, whatever the identity of the elided nouns, τὰ τοιαῦτα doubtless means τὰ ἠθικὰ καὶ παθητικά and οἱ τοιοῦτοι, οἱ ἠθικοὶ καὶ παθητικοί.

[129] If οἱ μέν stands for οἱ λόγοι, I believe that the text is best emended to καὶ παραβαλλόμενοι οἱ μὲν τῶν γραφικῶν ⟨τοῖς⟩ ἐν τοῖς ἀγῶσι στενοὶ φαίνονται (i.e. by construing the comparison as one between οἱ τῶν γραφικῶν and ⟨οἱ⟩ ἐν τοῖς ἀγῶσι). It is easy to see how the first τοῖς might have fallen out: 'On the one hand, those [speeches that are] of the graphic ones appear thin when compared to those [used] in *agōnes*'.

[130] Hence the glosses εὖ λεχθέντων in F (speakers are praised); and εὖ μὲν λεχθέντες (speeches are well delivered) in the anonymous commentary (*Anonymi in artem rhetoricam commentarium*, p. 221 *ad loc.*, ed. Rabe).

looks silly and lacking in persuasiveness. We are offered two examples: asyndeta and the frequent repetition of the same thing, two stylistic elements relatively more suitable for the histrionic end of the spectrum and, conversely, proportionally less suited for the graphic end.[131] Hence, rhetors put them to good use in debate contexts that call for the agonistic style. Asyndeton, in particular, requires changes in *ēthos* and *tonos* (1413b30–31). These illustrations allow us to fill in the meaning of ἀκρίβεια: the precision in avoiding asyndeta lies in making the script, by itself—without giving voice to it by way of delivery—a fuller record of the meaning and attitude of the author; the connecting particles would attempt to capture something of the missing *ēthos* and *tonos* that voice would readily impart. The more 'precise' script, when brought to life by delivery, would feature a lesser contribution of vocal phrasing to the clarity and persuasiveness of its speech. The style of the resulting communication would be comparatively less histrionic and proportionally more graphic. Concerning the effect achieved by frequent repetition in performance, a graphic style that had infrequent recourse to it would have to state more explicitly, perhaps in the form of a direct proposition adequately expressed by suitable stylistic devices, the particular *impression* effected by the repetition. Hence, if in delivery the speaker accentuates another's evil intent by piling up κλέψας, ἐξαπατήσας, and προδοῦναι ἐπιχειρήσας, the equivalent graphic statement may be reduced to the metaphoric and explicit, 'he was bent on harming you,' possibly aided, for effect, by other elements of style. The ἀκρίβεια, then, consists in a more complete propositional expression shaped by such stylistic elements as survive better a diminished role for ὑπόκρισις—the vocal expression of *ēthos* and *pathos*—all carefully targeted for the intended audience with a view to clarity and persuasiveness. When ὑπόκρισις is present and exploited to the full—i.e. when character is conveyed and emotion is elicited by the speaker's full and compelling use of the volume, *harmonia*, and rhythm of his voice—the more prolix nature of the graphic style turns, comparatively speaking, into a stylistic burden that hinders the effective expression of *ēthos* and *pathos* of which a resourceful use of voice is capable.

---

[131] Strictly speaking, it is not right to affirm that the graphic style discourages the use of frequent repetition. It would be more accurate to say that, in those social performance settings for which a relatively more graphic style is suitable, recourse to frequent repetition detracts from the effectiveness (clarity and persuasiveness) of the delivery. In such contexts a speaker would rightly disapprove of its use, and this is what is meant by 'frequent repetition of the same in the graphic style is rightly rejected as inadequate' (1413b19–20). As bundles of expressive devices and strategies with a view to clarity and persuasiveness formulated for performance in given social settings, styles are similar to genres and call for a comparable fit between cultural occasion (with its characteristic subject matter) and the manner of communication that obtains between a performer and his audience.

Now, there is a significant corollary to the Aristotelian notion of stylistic 'precision': insofar as it puts less emphasis and is less dependent on what is the essence of delivery, i.e. the use of the voice for the expression of character and the evocation of emotion, it is more appropriate to situations that may be allowed to lean for their persuasiveness more decisively on the subject matter of the orator's discourse (τὰ πράγματα). In so doing, it achieves a different balance between the possible rhetorical πίστεις. And since style/delivery often holds the potential to provoke the suspicion of the hearer, should one find himself in a situation where this suspicion is likely to arise, adopting a less histrionic style might be desirable. This, at least in part, is the situation envisaged at 1414a11–14, where a lawsuit is in the hands of one judge only.

But before I get to this, first in order of presentation is the demegoric style, which the philosopher introduces as 'altogether like *skiagraphia*'.[132] Although the nature of σκιαγραφία as a painting technique is disputed, it is clear from Aristotle's and, especially, Plato's use of it that it corresponded to a representational technique that was intelligible only from a distance.[133] Because of its illusionistic character, σκιαγραφία was used by Plato as a metaphor for illusion and deception: a case in point is *Republic* 602d2–3, where Sokrates notes that it 'falls nothing short of witchcraft'.[134] One of the central features of σκιαγραφία is a kind of mixing,[135] and for this reason Plato uses it metaphorically to criticize the fallacious commingling of what cannot (or should not) coexist as a mixture. Thus, in the *Republic* 583b, in the course of discussing the pleasures of three kinds of people—the φρόνιμος, the φιλότιμος, and the φιλοκερδής— we are told that 'excepting the man of intelligence, the pleasure of the rest is neither altogether true nor pure (καθαρά), but is a kind of shadow painting (ἐσκιαγραφημένη)' (583b3–5). The word καθαρός reappears at 586a6, where Sokrates says that those who have no experience of φρόνησις and ἀρετή have never tasted pleasure that is stable and pure (καθαρᾶς ἡδονῆς); to which he adds the question: 'Are not the pleasures they live with of necessity mixed with pains, phantoms of true pleasure and shadow painted (ἐσκιαγραφημέναις), so colored

---

[132] On σκιαγραφία, sometimes translated 'shadow painting', see Keuls 1975 [1997:107–144]; Pemberton 1976; Keuls 1978:72–87 (and the index s.v.); Rouveret 1989:24–26 and 50–59; Koch 2000:137–153; and Rouveret 2006.

[133] Insofar as it depended for its effect on viewing at a distance, we may think of it as a sort of 'classical impressionism.' Besides the passage of the *Rhetoric* that now concerns us, Aristotle refers to it in *Metaphysics* 1024b23 and *Protreptikos* fr. 104 (Düring). Some say it is also in view in *De sensu* 439b20–23 and 440a29–30. Plato makes more frequent mention of it, and a list of *loci* can be found in Keuls 1978:78–79.

[134] For a review of this and other passages where Plato touches on painting, see Demand 1975. Cf. Aristotle *Metaphysics* 1024b23, where σκιαγραφία is classed with dreams (ἐνύπνια).

[135] Disputed matters are whether it involved several colors or just hues of one and whether the mixing was by superposition or juxtaposition. Cf. Pemberton 1976.

by juxtaposition that either kind seems intense ... ?' (586b7–c1). We see that the opposition 'pure' vs. 'mixed' is central to the use to which Plato puts σκιαγραφία. So it does not come as a surprise that at *Rhetoric* 1414a13–14 Aristotle, in making his own argument, should also bring it forth while contrasting the demegoric style with a judgment that is pure (καθαρὰ ἡ κρίσις).

The demegoric style is declared to be entirely like *skiagraphia*: the greater the crowd, the more distant the view. At first one might consider taking θέα in its literal sense: on average, a large audience necessarily separates speaker from listener so that even a clear hearing of what is being said becomes difficult.[136] But this cannot have been the philosopher's point: for, in this respect, the forensic setting would have hardly provided the orator with a much better public environment, as juries sometimes numbered in the hundreds. And if this were its meaning, the comment would invert the implication of shadow painting, i.e. the growing unintelligibility of what is viewed as the spectator gets close. If the style of the assembly speaker were skiagraphic not by design but as a consequence of the limitations of his setting—the distance between him and his audience that prevents them from hearing him clearly—then, at least in principle, one could remedy the deficiency without a change in the manner of speaking simply by having them approach each other. This suggests (the possibility of) increasingly detailed intelligibility in proportion as the intervening distance is abridged. But this is precisely the opposite of what the metaphor of a stylistic σκιαγραφία implies. The literal understanding of θέα also faces the objection that, if true, the philosopher would have paralleled 'viewing' with hearing, since according to him voice, not sight, is central to delivery.[137] To this objection, one might reply that the metaphor dictates its own terms and is responsible for the lack of a precise fit. But there is a better approach: Aristotle's observation is not a veiled criticism of a style that *should*, but due to its setting cannot, be more precise. Rather, σκιαγραφία is a compelling metaphor that serves to specify the degree of precision peculiar to the demegoric style. It also helps the philosopher to explain why this style's skiagraphic lack of precision actually suits the rhetorical context for which it has been formulated. Aristotle's endorsement of this stylistic design is signaled by the use of χείρω at 1414a10 in connection with τὰ ἀκριβῆ (see below). This confirms his belief in its appropriateness for the deliberative performance setting. We must therefore take θέα in an extended sense: the statement concerns 'a distant [rhetorical] view', a notion that hints at, and is the consequence of, the various

---

[136] Cf. Johnstone 1996a.

[137] No advantage is gained by understanding θέα literally as 'point of view' (i.e. not 'opinion' but 'place from which one looks out'). One must extend its meaning into the realm of discourse (see immediately below).

and potentially divergent views of each listener in the assembly. By assimilating the delivery style, of which the speaker is the efficient cause, to a σκιαγραφία, the text commends a perspectival inversion with the hearers as viewers and the speech as the object they observe: each member of the audience has his own 'viewing', θέα, and all these θέαι are 'distant'. But distant from what? I submit that they are potentially distant from each other and from the speaker's own θέα and that they represent mutually divergent viewpoints. πορρώτερον ἡ θέα (1414a9) regards the expectation that public opinion in the deliberative assembly will grow increasingly variegated with crowd size. Divergence of views in the democratic decision-making process is the challenge that calls for rhetorical consensus building. One may equate each θέα with each citizen's δόξα, the individual opinion that the demegoric speaker is attempting to influence and draw closer to his own. The assembly setting requires his appeal to be as broad as possible, with its breadth corresponding to the size of his target. His approach should seek to circumscribe the complexity of the issue under discussion to the possibilities of a mixed deliberating body. Deliberative matters are inherently more difficult to discuss, because they must cope with uncertain outcomes and future circumstances[138] and because they cannot be treated with the intellectual precision of a philosophical argument:[139] not only are the abilities present in a mixed crowd widely variable[140] but the orator cannot possibly

---

[138] Cf. *Rhetoric* I.3, esp. 1358b2–5 and b13–17.

[139] Cf. *Rhetoric* 1369b31–32: δεῖ δὲ νομίζειν ἱκανοὺς εἶναι τοὺς ὅρους ἐὰν ὦσι περὶ ἑκάστου μήτε ἀσαφεῖς μήτε ἀκριβεῖς ('One should consider definitions to suffice when they are neither unclear nor precise about each matter'). Here, ἀκριβεῖς ('precise, exact') seems as undesirable as ἀσαφεῖς ('unclear'). This has troubled some, who have therefore tried to soften it by assuming an excess (i.e. not just 'precise' but 'excessively precise'). Kennedy even translates it as 'inexact', inverting its sense, although in an accompanying footnote he explains that by 'inexact' he really means 'overly technical'(!). But perhaps it is best understood in contrast to ἱκανούς: 'sufficiency' implies a judgment of adequacy relative to a need, while Aristotle measures 'exactness' with reference to an objective standard. If so, *eo ipso* 'a definition that suffices' cannot *stricto sensu* be objectively 'accurate'. If one wonders how precision renders a definition inadequate, the answer must be that the philosopher judges it counterproductive, exhibiting a prolixity that inhibits, rather than facilitates, discussion: 'But one must ... not look for precision in the same way in everything, but in each case in accordance with the underlying matter, and as much as belongs to the method ... . One should proceed in the same way in other cases too, so that the side issues do not overwhelm the main ones' (*Nicomachean Ethics* 1098a26–33). Thus, the two adjectives joined by repeated μήτε at *Rhetoric* 1369b32 are not like each other: obscurity is undesirable; precision, if ideally desirable, is impractical and in the real world even counterproductive. If we avoid both the undesirable and the impractical, we end up with something that is adequate, sufficient. Cf. *Nicomachean Ethics* 1094b11–14: "Now we must be satisfied (ἱκανῶς) with the statement of our science, if its distinctness be in proportion to the nature of the subject matter. For exactness (τὸ ἀκριβές) is not to be expected equally in all reasonings, any more than in all the productions of art" (translation by Grant 1885:427).

[140] Aristotle often evinces an unflattering attitude towards the promiscuous multitudes. In a crowd one is bound to find some individuals who cannot be persuaded even with the most

furnish his delivery with carefully crafted φαντάσματα that will seem persuasive to each and every one of his listeners.[141] Hence, there are limitations of precision regarding 'persuasion through the subject matter' and 'persuasion through the hearer',[142] limitations that must translate into a corresponding style that is artfully imprecise. Imprecise as to subject matter: with enough definition to capture the basic features of a particular issue, yet vague enough to do so in bold strokes that avoid philosophical niceties incomprehensible to men of average ability. Imprecise as to delivery: with such stylistic expression of *ēthos* and *pathos* as will have broad appeal to the promiscuous crowd that attends to the hearing, sidestepping private prejudice and building on common sentiment.[143] Hence, it is apparent that both in σκιαγραφία and in the demegoric style τὰ ἀκριβῆ are not only περίεργα but positively χείρω.[144] Paradoxically perhaps but with striking faithfulness to the guiding metaphor, the perspectival distance actually becomes instrumental to the clarity and persuasiveness of the demegoric style. Rhetorical style and rhetorical setting coexist in perfect symbiosis.[145]

---

exact knowledge, and on this account the speaker must resort to what is commonly held (*Rhetoric* 1355a24–29); the audience is presumed incapable of reasoning from a distant point and of arriving through many stages at a comprehensive view (1357a3–4); the judge is assumed to be a simple man (1357a11–12); maxims are of great help because hearers are vulgar (1395a32–b2); the uninstructed are more persuasive with the crowd than the educated (1395b26–28); a proem's *raison d'être* is to address remarks outside the argument to the base hearer (1415b5–9); the weakness of the audience makes lengthy interrogation inadvisable (1419a18).

[141] Cf. *Rhetoric* 1356b26–28.

[142] Cf. *Rhetoric* 1356a1–4.

[143] I think it is in that sense that Rapp (2002:2.940) writes *ad Rhetoric* 1414a8–9: "Das ist eine der wenigen Stellen, an denen Aristoteles andeutet, dass die besonderen Bedingungen der öffentlichen Rede auf Seiten der Zuhörer nicht nur aus den intellektuellen Unzulänglichkeiten der einzelnen Zuhörer ... herrühr[en], sondern auch aus den besonderen massenpsychologischen Umständen öffentlicher Reden."

[144] When the peculiar nature of the imprecision that σκιαγραφία metaphorically represents is not understood, interpreters are not able to explain why precision would be not just wasted effort but, in actual fact, *worse*.

[145] If one should ask why Aristotle does not also assimilate the dicanic style to a σκιαγραφία, the reason must be that it is susceptible of comparatively greater precision. This is so, first, because its subject matter deals with the factual past and not the uncertain future (1358b13–17; cf. 1354a26–28) and is therefore inherently more precise. And, second, because the judge's own welfare is not immediately implicated by the judicial proceedings and, for this reason, his viewpoints, convictions, and proclivities are more immediately relevant to, and more likely to be engaged by, the stylistic shape of the argument. The unprincipled orator may seek to exploit the more precise stylistic fit of the delivery to the audience by speaking off subject. Precisely this scenario is in view at 1354b31–1355a1: yet one must not take this passage as Aristotle's considered opinion about the proper working of judicial rhetoric; nor infer from it what rhetorical practice, including style, he would advocate. If his disheartening assessment of a jury's propensity for unscrupulous behavior (οὐ κρίνουσιν 1355a1) might be taken to imply that the speaker should adopt a singularly emotional delivery, this *per se* does not make the dicanic style *less* precise than the demegoric. One should also note that Aristotle himself ascribes to both the

Moving on to the forensic setting, one is struck by the fact that Aristotle does not compare ἡ δημηγορική with ἡ δικανική (the emendations of some editors notwithstanding) but with ἡ δική.[146] This proves that he is concerned with the sort of style that will suit not only the hearer peculiar to either setting (the κριτής can either be an ἐκκλησιαστής or a δικαστής)[147] but also, as I have argued above, with the corresponding subject matter: in the case of symbuleutic rhetoric, τὸ συμφέρον καὶ βλαβερόν (*Rhetoric* 1358b22). One can readily understand the philosopher's point: justice, insofar as it surveys the past and calls for a determination upon it, is less uncertain than the issues of policy that dominate deliberative assemblies. If no further considerations attended the analysis, this alone would justify the implication that the dicanic style, called to suit an inherently more precise subject matter, should reflect this precision in its own precision: with metaphors that have narrow targets, with a comparatively greater abundance of conjunctions and connectives that draw out more explicitly the logic of the argument, featuring φαντάσματα that are more acutely crafted as to their impact on *ēthos* and *pathos*, etc. Greater precision *per se*, it must be emphasized, calls for neither more nor fewer stylistic devices and strategies (although it may call for more or less frequent resort to a given device or strategy). One must eschew the notion, often presupposed by scholars, that ἀκρίβεια entails 'more of style' (it may well require restrictions, as when it calls for concision).[148] Since Aristotle's notion of λέξις is circumscribed by ὑπόκρισις, the rhetorical practice it subserves, the correct view is that a precise delivery calls for a precise style and vice versa. The inverse proportion in which the philosopher puts ἀκρίβεια and ὑπόκρισις (1414a15–16) must be understood not with regard to ὑπόκρισις as a rhetorical practice—which, as such, cannot be quantified but may be qualified (in particular, it can be more or less precise according as its stylistic means are more or less exact)—but in relation to vocal expression (loudness, *harmonia*, and rhythm) as the material cause of the homonymous technical practice. Because the degree to which character and emotion are involved as rhetorical πίστεις—I say 'the degree to which,' not 'the fact that,' because they *always* are—is in turn

---

symbuleutic and the forensic settings audiences whose judgment is obscured by love, hate, and personal interest (cf. 1354b8–11). At any rate, the converse of Aristotle's dim view of actual forensic rhetorical practice is the promise of securing a more effective hearing before an audience by a more precise stylistic fit. A final thought: the adverb παντελῶς hints perhaps that after all the metaphor of 'shadow painting' is also applicable to the dicanic style, only in a less 'absolute' sense.

[146] Cf. *Rhetoric* 1358b10–11. Rightly, Kassel *ad loc. contra* Ross, Roemer, and others.

[147] *Rhetoric* 1358b3–5.

[148] Just as a more emotional style—a style, therefore, toward the agonistic end of the stylistic spectrum (cf. 1413b9–10)—may entail more of a given device (at 1408b10–12, for example, the use of compound words, more epithets, and unfamiliar terms). On ἀκρίβεια and stylistic concision see O'Sullivan 1992:44.

proportional to the greater or lesser use of the voice, ἀκρίβεια is also inversely proportional to the stylistic prominence of *ēthos* and *pathos*.

If, as noted above, the dicanic style should match its relatively more precise subject matter with a correspondingly more precise style, this is so *a fortiori* (ἔτι δὲ μᾶλλον) when justice is in the hand of *one* judge alone.[149] Then there is no debate (ἀγών) between, nor even a gathering of, δικασταί who hold a variety of opinions;[150] then the κρίσις is 'pure' (καθαρά) because the *skiagraphic* features of deliberative settings, with their multiplicity of views (translated by the painting metaphor into distance), are absent when there is but a jury of one. 'For [then the trial] is least in rhetorical devices':[151] it is not that rhetoric *per se* and, *a fortiori*, delivery are inconsequential, but that, focused on one single individual, the scope is the narrowest possible and, for success, the orator must fine-tune every aspect of his speech (including style) to his one-member audience and to the subject matter at hand.[152] Here, Aristotle is being true to life,

---

[149] ἔτι δὲ μᾶλλον ἡ ⟨ἐν⟩ ἑνὶ κριτῇ (1414a11).

[150] Aristotle cannot mean that there is no ἀγών between opponents at law, for *that* controversy remains, whether there be one judge or many. That members of the jury did not in any formal way debate each other and that they voted immediately upon the close of the arguments is immaterial. Quite apart from the fact that individual jury members could, and probably did, speak to those seated nearby, their yelling approvingly or disapprovingly (as the case may be) as well as shouting out their reactions and engaging in other forms of disturbance—practices that speakers often complained about—should more than suffice to motivate Aristotle's view that forensic debate (the ἀγών of trial) was not to be restricted to the opposing arguments of defendant and plaintiff. Either party must have keenly felt the divergent pull of competing interests espoused, and convictions held, by diverse members of their audience. It would have been in their best interest to seek to gratify, and to avoid antagonizing, any jury member. The ensuing pull of potentially contradictory impulses must have been felt an essential element of the agonistic setting. This pull would be absent in a lawsuit before a single judge.

[151] I follow Kassel's text and understand ἡ δίκη (for ἡ κρίσις) as the implicit subject of ἐστιν with adverbial ἐλάχιστον: ἐλάχιστον γάρ ἐστιν [ἡ δίκη, i.e. ἡ κρίσις] ἐν ῥητορικοῖς. ῥητορικά are 'rhetorical devices and strategies', broadly understood (cf. 1375a8). For the superlative neuter singular ἐλάχιστον effectively used as an adverb, cf. Aristotle *Historia animalium* 494b15–16 and *Meteorologica* 343b21–22. To judge from his translation, Kennedy also understands the syntax thus. An alternative construal with ἐλάχιστον as the subject largely yields the same meaning: 'For [then] there is least [sc. scope or efficacy *vel sim.*] in rhetorical devices'.

[152] Innes (2007:162–163) suggests that the historical background to Aristotle's 'trial by one judge' is the process of arbitration (see her references *ad loc.* and Todd 1993:123–125, 128–129, also with bibliography). This is certainly possible, for although the term for 'arbitrator' was διαιτητής (not δικαστής) it not only seems reasonable to subsume him under the more general figure of a κριτής, and the arbitration procedure, under δίκη (so in *Athēnaiōn Politeia* 53.2), but Aristotle himself in *De caelo* 279b10–12 writes that 'those who intend to judge the truth adequately must be arbitrators and not legal adversaries' (καὶ γὰρ δεῖ διαιτητὰς ἀλλ᾽ οὐκ ἀντιδίκους εἶναι τοὺς μέλλοντας τἀληθὲς κρίνειν ἱκανῶς). This shows that the terminology was flexible enough to subsume under the respective labels of 'judge' and 'trial' the figure of the 'arbitrator' and the procedure of 'arbitration'. Add to this the fact that Athens featured forty magistrates (οἱ δικασταὶ οἱ κατὰ δήμους *Athēnaiōn Politeia* 48.5; cf. Demosthenes 24.112) who could render summary judgment in cases that involved small sums (*Athēnaiōn Politeia* 53.1; cf. Todd 1993:129). These too could be added

for we know from experience that a style (including, say, lavish praise) that may be acceptable in addressing a large audience may meet with suspicion if focused on one individual. When one man alone is the target of persuasion, the danger is great that he will resist the thrust of the speaker's rhetoric; for being self-conscious of, and sensitive to, the fact that the presentation is crafted *for him*, this invites him to second-guess what is said and whether the appeal to him to embrace a particular opinion is legitimate or not.[153] Consequently, the orator who would persuade one man must narrow the artifice of his delivery so as not to raise his natural suspicion; just as he ought to bear in mind his one listener as he tries to craft stylistic φαντάσματα that hold the greatest promise of persuasion. The use of εὐσύνοπτον (1414a12) is particularly apposite, picking up again on the metaphor of a σκιαγραφία: demegoric settings involve distant views that blur the precise correspondence that might otherwise obtain between the subject matter of the speech and the stylistic design of the speaker; conversely, trial by a single judge allows the orator to see more readily what in his stylistic rhetorical kit (ἐν ῥητορικοῖς) is οἰκεῖον and ἀλλότριον to the subject matter.[154] The usual reading, '[what is] proper and foreign *to the subject matter*' is acceptable (οἰκεῖον may govern the genitive or the dative). But this determines neither the sphere from which τὸ οἰκεῖον and τὸ ἀλλότριον are taken; nor the standard by which, and the point of view according to which, whatever belongs to either adjective is pronounced 'proper' or 'foreign' (as the case might be). I join the consensus in understanding the general sphere to be the presentation of the speaker, i.e. his rhetorical practice, including style. But I depart from the consensus in my choice of viewpoint and standard: it is not the opinion of the single κριτής about the closeness of the fit between the speaker's rhetorical practice and his subject matter. Instead, it is the speaker's own judgment about the appropriateness of his ῥητορικά—given the context, chiefly apprehended

---

to the historical background, if one be needed, behind the philosopher's one-judge δίκη. I do not think, however, that Innes is correct to infer the absence of ἀγών from 'arbitration'. The very fact that it was subsumed under ἡ δίκη argues otherwise. At any rate, it is also possible, with Rapp (2002:2.937), to consider the absence of ἀγών simply a *Gedankenexperiment* that allows Aristotle to demonstrate what is peculiar to the forensic setting vis-à-vis the demegoric. This ideal setting shows all the more clearly why the dicanic style is relatively more precise.

[153] Cf. in this connection Innes 2007:162–163, who draws attention to Quintilian *Institutio oratoria* 11.1.44, a passage that "ridicules the idea that the orator might speak overwhelmed by emotion 'in minor matters and minor cases ... speaking seated before an arbitrator'" (her ellipsis).

[154] Even though in my reading εὐσύνοπτον at 1414a12 regards not the judge but the speaker, the mere fact that it is used at all marks the conceptual distance traveled from *Rhetoric* 1357a3–4 and hints at the truth of Rapp's surmise that here Aristotle has in mind "ein einziger (vernünftiger; vgl. 1354a34–b1) Richter" (Rapp 2002:2.937).

under the head of style—to his one-man audience. Because for Aristotle stylistic design regards the fit in delivery between the subject matter and the audience (how to say what must be said with a view to clarity and persuasion), the speaker's judgment of pertinence and impertinence becomes one of closeness of stylistic fit between the subject matter (which 'clarity' regards) and audience (which stylistic persuasion, i.e. persuasion through *ēthos* and *pathos*, regards). This fit is what the philosopher calls ἀκρίβεια.

It is perhaps helpful to underline again that style plays an instrumental function to delivery and, as the rhetorical practice that regards 'how one must speak' (ὡς δεῖ εἰπεῖν 1403b17), it mediates the translation of subject matter (ἃ δεῖ λέγειν 1403b16) into actual vocal performance before an audience. Because style subserves delivery and the end of delivery is suasion with the use of the voice through character and emotion, proper use of style must consider the fit between the devices and strategies that shape the manner of speaking and what makes for persuasion (including the *sine qua non* of clarity) for the particular kind of audience addressed in a given setting (1356b26–34). This aspect of style, i.e. how closely it fits the target audience, most immediately regards its ψυχαγωγία. This ψυχαγωγία is circumscribed by the occasion: it not only looks to the individual hearer but also to the pragmatics of the communication. What is useful and clear for a given individual in the context of an ἐπίδειξις may be counterproductive and obfuscating to him in the more agonistic symbuleutic address. But this is not all. For style looks not only to target audience and performance occasion but also to subject matter, and with respect to the latter there is a corresponding fit between the manner of expression and the subject at hand. Stylistic 'precision', ἀκρίβεια, trades on both ends of this dual perspective, i.e. on how closely style fits both its subject matter and its target audience at a given occasion. Any failure on either end of this stylistic communicative mediation incurs a loss of persuasiveness. A speaker may owe this failure either to excessive or to defective precision: in an agonistic context, where the audience has a hard time following the logic in the heat of the moment, a style whose precision corresponds to an expansive argument compromises clarity and hence persuasiveness. One might say that argumentative fit—where the argument is detailed and expansive—compromises audience fit. In such contexts, compelling speakers adopt stylistic practices that put greater emphasis on character and emotion through the use of the voice, and the stylistic devices that subserve this greater prominence of vocal delivery are such as to commend a congruent simplification and selectivity of argumentative πράγματα. Given style's dual mediation between subject matter and situated audience, a speaker may place a comparatively greater *stylistic* emphasis on persuasion through the facts themselves or on persuasion through character and emotion.[155] The former relies less on the voice, the latter, more. The former presupposes an audience with a higher capacity to follow oral argument or a context that allows for its more reposed and effective intellection; the latter relies instead on, and seeks to exploit, the hearer's settled opinions and attitudes, his preexisting interests and commitments (emotional and intellectual), his underlying understanding and experience of the world—culture and society—in which he lives. Insofar as these constitute a more basic and reliable 'common denominator' for the audience, the agonistic style addresses itself more to these latter considerations and refers to them for guidance. On the other hand, typically (and perhaps ideally) the graphic style has a more generic audience in view, one that is more equanimous in the absence of passion and polemic. This allows this style to place a relatively greater emphasis on the closeness with which it fits the subject matter. In fact, the epideictic setting largely allowed speakers to regard, and even to construct, more uniform ideal audiences with reference to generic cultural and social stereotypes (patriotism, Panhellenism, φιλοτιμία, etc.). Because from the start they could select and shape their subject matter with regard to these generic stereotypes, epideictic made fewer and less stringent demands on the persuasive appeal through character and emotion effected by style in delivery. This afforded epideictic a potential for ἀκρίβεια greater than that enjoyed by the other two rhetorical genera. The inherently dual perspective of style as a rhetorical practice is responsible for Aristotle's shifts in emphasis between form and content, shifts which often lead modern scholars to think that he has confused two different senses of ἀκρίβεια: stylistic precision and precision of theme or argument.[156] This twofold emphasis is not the outcome of confused thinking. It is a faithful reflection of the Aristotelian conception of style and of what this conception in turn entails for stylistic precision, i.e. for the fit it effects between the 'what to say' and the 'how to say it' with a view to persuading a given situated audience in the vocal performance of delivery. But, *nota bene*, *even* in its regard for subject matter 'style' continues to look to persuasion through *ēthos* and *pathos* by the speaker's use of his voice in delivery. In other words, although 'style' as a sort of 'formal cause' takes the obligatory and inevitable account of 'τὰ πράγματα' as the rhetorical 'material cause,' it is 'persuasion' (the 'final cause') through 'vocal delivery' (the 'efficient cause') that drives Aristotle's analysis. The relation of stylistic precision to target audience is a particular manifestation of what

---

[155] I do not mean to revalidate the dichotomy between ὑπόκρισις and λέξις that I have labored to refute in this book; nor to vindicate a hard dualism of form and substance. My point is only one of relative emphasis. For Aristotle, persuasion through character and emotion can, and ideally does, regard the interests of truth and corresponds to the facts of the case.

[156] Cf. Rapp 2002:2.939 and Innes 2007:162 with n. 41.

Aristotle considered in *Posterior Analytics* 87a31–b7 in a wider context: 'A science is more precise than another ... if it depends on fewer items and the other on an additional posit' (ἀκριβεστέρα δ᾽ ἐπιστήμη ἐπιστήμης ... ἡ ἐξ ἐλαττόνων τῆς ἐκ προσθέσεως).[157] The opposite of an 'additional posit' (πρόσθεσις) is 'abstraction' (ἀφαίρεσις), and it is precisely through abstraction that epideictic constructs its public, whereas the agonistic genres circumscribe their subject matter and deliver it with rhetorical stylistic brushstrokes that will appeal to and sway a majority of their diverse audiences.[158]

The alternative understanding of dicanic stylistic precision proposed above is to be preferred to the consensus on contextual grounds. Aristotle's statements on the matter are meant to illustrate the greater precision of the dicanic style that is suitable for a trial by one judge (relative to the dicanic style employed before a numerous audience). For this reason, we expect him to explain why such a trial promotes greater precision in the speaker's stylistic design, not why a single judge is more capable of discerning when the speaker talks off subject (ἔξω τοῦ πράγματος),[159] whether he be assumed to draw on extraneous subject matter, on emotional appeals that bear no relation to, or even invert, the claims of truth, or to adopt yet some other diverting strategy. This view is to be rejected not only because there are no grounds for the claim that one judge, merely because he is one, is better able than a plurality to detect inartistic rhetorical devices that offend truth and right[160] but also because it suggests, if it does not entail, a displacement of the argument's center of gravity away from stylistic precision (ἡ ἀκρίβεια τῆς λέξεως) and towards πίστεις through αὐτὰ τὰ πράγματα (1403b19). Although one might still evade the second objection by insisting on viewing τὸ οἰκεῖον τοῦ πράγματος in relation to style (the one judge more readily sees what in the stylistic practice of the speaker properly belongs to the subject matter), the only way to make this productive of greater accuracy of style is to translate the judge's ability into the speaker's self-policing of his stylistic practice on this account. But it is implausible to assume that the judge's temperament, capacity, and whatever else makes εὐσύνοπτον predicable of him will ordinarily translate into such temperament, capacity, etc. in the speaker as will enable him, under the judge's careful watch, to modify his stylistic practice accordingly. A similar flaw does not attach to my reading, which offers the objective fact of the single-member audience and, hence, the absence of a

---

[157] Cf. Kurz 1970:128 and Barnes 1994:190.
[158] Cf. *Metaphysics* 982a25–28 and 1078a9–14.
[159] The consensus tacitly equates τὸ ἀλλότριον [τοῦ πράγματος] to τὰ ἔξω τοῦ πράγματος.
[160] To vindicate the claim one has to assume that the judge, because he is one, is *eo ipso* more proficient, perceptive, skillful, etc., an assumption for which there is no motivation other than the need to rescue the otherwise flawed reading.

multiplicity of divergent views that would otherwise blur the stylistic practice of the speaker (with a view to persuasion) as the reason for the closer fit that λέξις effects in delivery between τὰ πράγματα and the single hearer.[161] τὸ οἰκεῖον τοῦ πράγματος καὶ τὸ ἀλλότριον is not 'what in the speaker's delivery is on or off subject' but 'what pertains (οἰκεῖον) or does not pertain (ἀλλότριον) to his situated delivery of the subject matter before the single judge'.[162] This comment recalls Aristotle's observation in *Rhetoric* I.1.10: because deliberative rhetoric regards more general (i.e. public) interest, it lends itself less to speaking off subject than forensic.[163] In the assembly the κριτής judges about affairs that are pertinent to him (περὶ οἰκείων), whereas in a trial the decision is about the affairs of others (περὶ τῶν ἀλλοτρίων γὰρ ἡ κρίσις). The dicast is therefore liable to look to his own interests (πρὸς τὸ αὐτῶν) and to listen with partiality; and, after being won over by the appeal of the litigants, to give himself to them rather than render true judgment.[164] To sum up: the perspectival horizon of εὐσύνοπτον is best construed not as that of the one judge but the litigants': since he is only one, the identity and range of τὸ οἰκεῖον τοῦ πράγματος is correspondingly narrow and well defined. τὸ οἰκεῖον τοῦ πράγματος regards the manner in which the facts of the case (τὸ πράγμα) should be translated at the time of delivery with a view to clarity and persuasion into audience-directed stylistic practices. In contrast to the perspectival narrowness of the one-judge trial, before a crowd of dicasts τὸ οἰκεῖον and τὸ ἀλλότριον, translated into style for effective delivery, would be compounded and multiplied by a variegated patchwork of views, interests, and indifference. The speech, both style and subject matter in the intimacy of their mutual rhetorical connection, would be blurred into an oratorical *skiagraphia*;

---

[161] This approach meets Innes's desideratum (2007:162) that *Rhetoric* 1414a10–11 not move from stylistic precision to precision of argument. And because it does not equate τὸ ἀλλότριον [τοῦ πράγματος] with τὰ ἔξω τοῦ πράγματος it does not appear inconsistent with (or contradictory to) *Rhetoric* I.1 (1354b27–1355a1), an appearance that Rapp (2002:2.936) probes: in this passage, Aristotle regards speaking off subject less serviceable in assembly than in the law-court because members of the former have personal interest in the matter under discussion while ordinarily jurymen do not. If the exclusion of τὰ ἔξω τοῦ πράγματος is the exclusion of the ἀλλότριον [τοῦ πράγματος], and the latter exclusion makes rhetorical style more exact, then one expects the demegoric style to be more precise than the dicanic, because *ex hypothesi* it will have less frequent recourse to (the, for the setting, less serviceable) speaking off subject. This inference seems confirmed by 1355a2–3: 'There [sc. in the assembly] the judges themselves sufficiently look to this [sc. precluding the speaking off subject]'. But the facts are the inverse of this expectation. Note that the use of οἰκείων at 1354b30 and ἀλλοτρίων at 1354b33 regards a standard (of judgment) and a point of view identical to the ones I claim for the statement in 1414a12–13: they have in view what pertains or does not pertain to the κριτής—only, here the sphere is the subject matter, not the speaker's stylistic practices.

[162] I.e. εὐσύνοπτον [sc. τῷ λέγοντι *vel sim.*] Cf. *Politics* 1323b6–7.

[163] On the text of 1354b29, see Grimaldi 1980:17.

[164] This proves that the absence of *agōn* at 1414a13 cannot refer to the judge's freedom from prejudice on the grounds of his lack of personal involvement in the matter at issue.

then it would be advisable for the litigants, in crafting their speeches as to form and content, to tailor them broadly with a view to moving the entire jury towards the desirable δόξα. In such a situation, the deployment of rhetoric's full resources is all the more critical, and success depends to a larger extent on the level of the speaker's training in the oratorical art. In the opposite case, when directed to a single judge, the scope of rhetoric is the least.

Conclusion

THE STUDY OF HOMERIC POETRY, Milman Parry and A. B. Lord have taught us,[1] must necessarily consider its performance, for it was in performance that it was orally composed. And yet the times between Hellenistic Greece and our own were bridged not by sound recordings of recitations but by written artifacts like papyri and codices. How then are we to reconstruct and understand in literary-historical terms the present textual shape of the *Iliad* and the *Odyssey*? How should we variously apportion responsibility to earlier and later periods for the textual phenomena in our editions? How are we to conceive of the process that joined the early stages of relatively greater compositional freedom (though still within the parameters of the tradition)—when two performances of the 'same story' would have exhibited significant variation in their thematic construction and specific poetic diction—and stages when recitals even by different performers produced predictable lines of poetry that were largely 'the same' in sequence, content, and form?

Two avenues are open to the scholar who seeks to answer these and related questions: he may either look at the internal evidence of the extant text or consider the external evidence of its surrounding culture. It is chiefly the latter approach that I have followed here. My proposal in this book has been that, if one wishes to investigate the formation, evolution, and fixation of the Homeric poems, he can do no better than consider the figure of the epic performer and his craft. For, if it is true that the composition and performance of Homeric poetry were but two aspects of one and the same act of creative engagement with the poetic tradition, then the shape of the text must have been affected primarily by what the rhapsode, the performer of Homeric epic, did as he trained for and actually delivered his performance. Doubtless, this must have been the case until such time as the poems became primarily the province of teachers, scholars, and an educated *reading* public, and the primary agents of their transmission were no longer the rhapsodes and their festival performances.

---

[1] See especially Parry 1971 and Lord 1960; cf. also Lord 1991 and 1995.

We have seen that focusing on the rhapsode opens a window into the peculiar nature of Homeric poetics. We learned that archaic poetry cast the performer in the role of mediator between the Muse and his audience. In this capacity he could be viewed as an instrument of revelation and proclamation, and thus notionally akin, respectively, to the *mantis* and the prophet. This realization in turn gave us insight into one of the most puzzling and consequential features of Homeric poetry: its notional fixity. I demonstrated that this emic notion follows from the conviction, at the heart of Homeric poetics, that the song is but the quoted speech of the omniscient Muse to which the rhapsode has privileged access and which invests him with authority. Authority is at the root of authorship: authority to say, sing, and perform; authority to legitimize festival gatherings and religious ceremonies; authority to validate a ritual and empower their participants to achieve its ends. So long as the performance occasion was the primary determinant in the recitation of Homeric poetry, the invocation of the Muse (and, by implication, Apollo) lent authority to the rhapsode's recomposition, and the matter of individual creativity did not overtly arise. In a world of multiform oral traditions, conflicts between rival versions were bound to occur. But in these early, formative periods they were aired not by accusations that a singer had interpolated extraneous material of doubtful authorship but by branding him a liar who for the sake of his belly would readily produce whatever the audience wished to hear.

We saw that in the second half of the sixth century BC, responding to a tendency broadly attested among the Greeks to trace the origin of cultural watersheds to specific human inventors, biographical speculation about the composer of the poetry about Troy and Odysseus attracted growing interest, especially as it allowed competing states to vie for the control of so significant a cultural capital. This move, from an authorizing divinity who presides over the performance to a legitimacy based on the rhapsode's faithfulness to a human author, was helped by the notional fixity of the poetic corpus: for, just as with the quoted speech of the Muse, if a poem was the concrete end product of one man's activity, then surely it could not change with every new performance according to the individual rhapsode's recomposition and still claim faithfulness to its author—that, at any rate, was the logic regardless of what actually happened in performance. Even then, at least in the beginning, authorship was far from the totalizing notion of a unique creative source that it would eventually become. Instead, it remained closely tied to the authority, now of a *particular* performer, to produce and shape a narrative in performance.

This book also explored how the placement of the rhapsode as mediator between the audience and the source of authority naturally allowed for his twofold role as performer and *hermēneus* of his tradition. Diachronically speaking, both facets changed character with the passing of time. Originally the performer was also the composer, in fact, composer-in-performance. From the emic perspective, his hermeneutic role made reference to his explication of the divine intention (especially past, but also future), which he expressed in poetic form. From our etic stance, we would make a distinction between the relatively less fluid poetry, particularly the speeches, which the rhapsode recomposed with more predictable regularity as to form and content, and the more fluid (usually narrative) portions, which he recomposed with greater variability and by which he elaborated the μῦθος (in Aristotle's sense), stitching together the speeches into a larger whole. With the passing of time, the performance involved a decreasing measure of recomposition and the hermeneutic function gradually changed into the ἐπίδειξις of prose commentary and pedagogic lecture. It is in opposition to the rhapsode's role in classical education (as ἐπαινέτης of Homer) and his monopoly of the cultural capital of Homeric poetry that the emergent sophists defined their own practices.

The rhapsode was a privileged protagonist in the gradual transition of ancient Greece from predominantly oral to predominantly written habits of culture. This evolution, several centuries in the making, did not always proceed at the same pace. For Athens, in particular, it is clear that the late fifth and early fourth centuries were definitive and that during this time the technology of writing made great strides into the various domains of performance. I studied this transition in Parts III and V, primarily through the lens of Aristotle's *Rhetoric* and his study of oratorical delivery. I justified my increasingly Athenocentric focus with the central role that Athens' Panathenaic festival had in shaping rhapsodic practice and the transmission of Homeric poetry. We saw that Aristotle himself made the connection in his work between rhetoric, tragic drama, and rhapsody. I showed that this connection is hardly accidental: only by considering together these three preeminent domains of performance in their mutual relations and influences does one gain a proper understanding of the evolution in the training and performance practices of rhapsodes. Aristotle's own connection between rhapsody and rhetoric in the matter of ὑπόκρισις justified my applying to the rhapsode's trade, *mutatis mutandis*, the philosopher's and Alkidamas' observations about 'delivery'. In fact, I demonstrated that the treatment of ὑπόκρισις in the *Rhetoric* is broad enough to allow us to translate this concept as 'performance' and not strictly as *oratorical* performance: it is one that focuses on the voice, its expression of *ēthos* and arousal of *pathos*, and that depends for its effect on the sensory aspects of diction (especially the auditory). This was surely the case with rhapsodic performance too. Aristotle's work also offered an account of the status of writing in his own time as an aid subordinate to delivery. Insofar as the culture still prized declamation over written dissemination of speeches,

I argued that the growing role of scripts among orators illustrated the gradual introduction of writing among rhapsodes: first as transcripts, 'accidental' recordings of performances (in the philosophical sense of 'accidental'); then as scripts, aids designed for the honing of delivery, but still in tension with a measure of traditional creativity at the moment of performance; and finally, during Hellenistic and Roman imperial times, as 'scripture' largely controlling the thematic sequence and specific diction of rhapsode and *homerista*.[2]

The move from transcripts to scripts was the focus of Parts III–IV. By this time the rhapsode had evolved to where his technique was markedly histrionic. Thus, he was often compared with the actor of drama, appearing in his own right as a 'dramatic' ὑποκριτής of Homeric poetry. In adopting under the influence of drama some of the accoutrements of the acting trade, he was only bringing out the extraordinary mimetic potential already inherent in the *Iliad* and the *Odyssey*. The statement that Homer was foremost among composers of tragedy (Plato *Republic* 607a)[3]—initially a reflection that the actor, at his emergence, had taken the venerable rhapsode as his model, owing to him even the label ὑποκριτής—could now be reinterpreted to signify the mimetic potential of Homeric poetry which made its subject matter so eminently susceptible of dramatic treatment. Thus, ὑποκριτής, surely an early (if unattested) term for the rhapsode as *hermēneus* of the Homeric tradition, could now be reapplied to him by the critic who disliked his excessively histrionic delivery.

The history of the Athenian rhapsode in the late fourth century BC was marked by the state's increasing regulation of his trade. Part IV explored the central role that Lykourgos and Demetrios of Phaleron played in asserting public control by state officials over the organization of the festivals and the participation of artists. These had been matters until then left largely to the initiative of wealthy patrons. These bureaucratic regulations reinforced a tendency among performers towards specialization and doubtless gave the necessary impetus for the formation of σύνοδοι or κοινά of τεχνῖται in Athens and other cultural centers. These associations dominated the festival scene in the Hellenistic period. It was during that time that, as contemporaneous inscriptions show, the twofold office of the rhapsode, as composer and performer, explicitly unfolded into the figures of the ἐπῶν ποιητής and the continuing ῥαψῳδός. The latter kept to the traditional repertoire, whereas the former was responsible for the composition and performance of new hexametric poetry, primarily encomiastic in nature. Parallel to these was the *homerista*, who put greater emphasis on the acting out of Homeric scenes, especially fights, with appropriate dress and

---

[2]   For the sense of 'scripture' here, see Nagy 1996c:110–112.

[3]   *Republic* 607a2–3: συγχωρεῖν [χρὴ] Ὅμηρον ποιητικώτατον εἶναι καὶ πρῶτον τῶν τραγῳδοποιῶν.

props. Yet his greater emphasis on acting by no means precluded his recitation of poetry, as is often supposed.

The basic methodological leitmotif of this book has been that one cannot hope to understand the epic rhapsode and his craft except from a diachronic perspective, in the multiplicity of time-dependent, systemic relationships of reciprocal influence between the three great domains of performance in ancient Greece: oratory, tragic drama, and rhapsodic recitation. History has not been kind to the Homeric performer. It has left us with hardly any explicit reflection on his trade and practices. For this reason, my approach to him has been indirect. But against the cultural matrix explored in this work, the epic rhapsode and his craft emerge in clearer light, with more definite outlines. And with this clearer vision we also gain a deeper understanding of the cultural processes, in their full diachronic sweep, to which we owe the final textual shape and the preservation in writing of the Homeric poems.

εἴρηκα, ἀκηκόατε, ἔχετε, κρίνατε.

Appendix
The Origin of the Term *hypokritēs*

I F ONE ACCEPTS that the Panathenaia was reorganized ca. 560 BC—as seems likely not only from later reports but also from the material record of Athenian vases[1]—it is not unreasonable to assume that the rules instituted at the time for the rhapsodic competition may have sought deliberately to enhance the challenging artistry of hypoleptic performance.[2] These reforms would explain why later reconstructions of the festival's history imagined a 'Panathenaic rule' of Solonic or Peisistratean authorship.[3] As a fundamental feature of the craft of the rhapsode, hypolepsis may soon have come to dominate the average Athenian's view of rhapsodic delivery.

I have argued above (pp. 296ff.) that ὑποκριτής, like ῥαψῳδός, was an early technical label of some currency for the epic singer.[4] ἀοιδός was the most

---

[1]   The earliest Panathenaic amphoras "are dated to slightly before 560 B.C." (Tiverios 2007:1). The pride of first place, until recently given to the Burgon Amphora (see Beazley 1943:441, with the relevant bibliography conveniently assembled by Moore 1999:53n22), has now been ceded to an amphora by the potter Nikias (MMA 1978.11.13, at the Metropolitan Museum of Art; see Moore 1999). The date 560 BC matches closely the ascription of the festival (or its reorganization) to the archon Hippokleides in 566/65 BC. For this ascription and the corresponding date, see Davison 1958:26–29, Bancroft 1979:77–80, Kotsidu 1991:27–28, Neils 1992b:20–21, Kyle 1996:116– 123 (notes at 132–136), Slings 2000:69n38, and Shear 2001:507–515. On Panathenaic amphoras, see the items cited above and Tiverios 1974, Beazley 1986:81–92, Valavanis 1987, Kotsidu 1991:90– 103, Neils 1992c, Hamilton 1992, and Bentz 1998.

[2]   See above, p. 368.

[3]   A comparative study of the engagement of Greek tyrants with art and of their cultural programs would support the notion that both Peisistratos and his sons must have put their stamp on the major Athenian festivals. Cf. Shapiro 1989, Angiolillo 1997:125, Shapiro 1998, and Sancisi-Weerdenburg 2000 *passim*.

[4]   That ὑποκριτής probably existed before it was applied to the tragic actor is often acknowledged. Thus, for example, after considering the possibility that Aristophanes coined the agent noun as a "back-formation" (his term) from the surviving use of ὑποκρίνεσθαι in the sense of 'expounder, interpreter of oracles', Else (1959:101–102n93) writes: "It is simpler to suppose that ὑποκριτής already existed in the sixth century, and that its not being found in any extant text of that date is accidental. (As was pointed out above, it will not go into hexameters.)" Its prior existence as 'performer' and 'interpreter' is suggested by its occurrence during the Second Sophistic (see Zucchelli 1962:26–27), arguably, a return or reappearance of an old usage under the conservative Atticizing impulse of this cultural movement. See also Timaios *Lexicon Platonicum* o 308 (Bonelli):

traditional but, semantically, also the broadest.[5] To specify the epic singer, either ὑποκριτής or ῥαψῳδός would do. As the preeminent festival performer of his time, a strong connotation of 'on-stage delivery before an audience' attached to the archaic rhapsode. Therefore, when the need arose for Athens to select a name for the on-stage performer of drama, it was natural to extend to the actor *qua* performer a rhapsodic label that did not narrowly denote what was peculiar to rhapsodic technique. This development was all the more to be expected, insofar as the complex and integrative genre of drama grew to a significant degree in rivalry with the then queen of the festival arts, Homeric performance. The rise of Attic drama must be placed in the last thirty to forty years before the end of the sixth century BC,[6] a time when ῥαψῳδός must have carried the emphatic connotation of relay performance. Such a connotation would not do for the solo performance of the actor; neither would the centuries-old implication that ῥαψῳδεῖν involved the reworking in performance of material deeply traditional in thematic sequence and poetic diction. These considerations motivate the choice of ὑποκριτής, rather than ῥαψῳδός, for the professional performer of tragedy. With the triumphant ascendancy of drama, once 'dramatic actor' was cemented as the default acceptation of ὑποκριτής, its application to the epic singer must have grown obsolete, only to be occasionally recalled by Plato for straightforward[7] or perverse rhetorical ends.[8]

Ὁμηρίδαι: οἱ τὰ Ὁμήρου ὑποκρινόμενοι (Bonelli 2007:160; cf. 479–480); and ρ 374 (Bonelli): ῥαψῳδοί: ὑποκριταὶ ἐπῶν (Bonelli 2007:166; cf. 544); also Pollux 5.154: ἑρμηνεὺς καὶ ἑρμηνευτής, γλῶτταν συμβάλλων, γλῶτταν ὑποκρινόμενος, γλώττης ὑποκριτής; 7.188.4: τερῶν ὑποκριταί; and 7.188.8–9: ὀνειράτων ὑποκριταί. Patzer's attempt (1970:643n1) to dismiss the witness of Pollux 5.154 as an "artificial hyper-Atticism" strikes me as a feeble evasion.

5   I cannot accept as sound in the main Maslov's views of the genesis and semantic development of the term ἀοιδός (Maslov 2009). I hope to evaluate his stimulating diachronic study in a future work.

6   Even West, who discounts the traditional chronology of Thespis with radical skepticism, acquiesces "in the ancient belief that his activity began under Peisistratus" (West 1989:254). Immaterial to my argument is whether the City Dionysia goes back at least to the times of Peisistratos (so Pickard-Cambridge 1988:57–58, Shapiro 1989:86, and others) or else to the inception of Athenian democracy (so Connor 1989, with the approval of Del Rincón Sánchez 2007:103). The material point is that the definitive development of tragedy as a performance genre would have happened during the latter half of the sixth century BC. Connor himself suggests that Thespis may have performed his plays in the rural Dionysia (Connor 1989:13).

7   In the *Timaios* 71d–72b (see above, p. 220), not specifically in connection with rhapsodes, but more broadly in regard to the original respective meanings of ὑποκριτής and ὑποκρίνομαι as 'interpreter of', or 'to interpret', 'divine revelation'.

8   As I have shown above, p. 299, the Platonic juxtaposition ῥαψῳδός καὶ ὑποκριτής (*Iōn* 532d7 and 536a1) not only draws our attention to the very old connection between epic and oracular or mantic poetry, but with it Sokrates also intends to tease Ion for his overly histrionic delivery and a 'Homeric exegesis' devoid of interpretive insight. On this rhapsodic exegesis of Homeric poetry, see above, p. 299 (with pp. 275 and 289).

The foregoing account of the characteristically dramatic use of ὑποκριτής and ὑποκρίνομαι readily explains why the Attic dialect, unlike Ionic, should have rejected 'to reply' as a prevalent acceptation of ὑποκρίνομαι. The technical meaning of the *nomen agentis*, 'dramatic actor', and the acceptation of its verb, 'to act (a part)', both of doubtless currency and cultural prominence in Attica, restricted their use to the semantic sphere of dramatic performance. It also relegated the acceptation 'to answer' to the similarly constructed ἀποκρίνομαι, which received it in turn precisely under the pressure of the ascendancy of 'to act' as the characteristic acceptation of ὑποκρίνομαι.[9] I do not deny, of course, that ὑποκρίνομαι could mean 'to reply' and in actual fact acquired this sense in the dialect of Ionia. Previous scholars have already noted the semantic development that led from the judgment associated with oracular pronouncements to the notion of a formal, authoritative answer, and then, by a weakening of its meaning, to the ordinary 'to answer'.[10] Thus, Lesky (1956:473) observes that

[9] ἀποκρίνομαι, of course, was not coined *de novo*. The only innovation was to ascribe the acceptation 'to reply' to the middle voice of ἀποκρίνω, a verb long before in use for 'to separate'. Theognis 1167 instances ἀπόκρισις with the meaning 'answer', but given the nature of the *Theognidea* this could hardly serve to date the acceptation even if the authenticity of the reading went unchallenged. Otherwise, both ἀπόκρισις and ἀποκρίνομαι as 'answer' and 'to answer' appear occasionally in Herodotos, where they are often doubted. Nothing prevents the view that the historian picked up, and occasionally resorted to, Attic turns of expression. At any rate, his date is late enough not to pose any difficulties to my argument. The earliest occurrences of ἀποκρίνω in a voice other than the active are the aorist passive ἀποκρινθέντε in E 12 and ἀποκριθείς in Arkhilokhos 185.3 (those in Anaximander are all from *testimonia*). As is well known, the aorist passive was not ordinarily used in good fifth- and fourth-century Attic for 'to answer'. This later practice was condemned by Phrynikhos (*Eklogē* no. 78 Fischer s.v. ἀποκριθῆναι, on which see *TGL* 1.2.1495–1496 s.v. ἀποκρίνω and Lobeck 1820:108) and the only exceptions are Pherekrates fr. 51 K-A (*PCG* VII.129) and [Plato] *Alkibiadēs* 2.149a (Xenophon *Anabasis* 2.1.22 is dubious). Therefore, the interference of the new acceptation 'to reply' with the old 'to separate' must have been minimal. Curtius's suggestion (1866:153) that ὑπόκρισις connoted "die rasche Folge der Antwort auf die Frage," while ἀπόκρισις pointed to "die Abwechslung der redenden" may help to rationalize *a posteriori* the logic of ascribing to the latter the sense of the former, but it is unlikely to have played any part in it.

[10] That ὑποκρίνεσθαι is already used for 'to answer' in the Homeric poems has been disputed, but it is hard to deny it at H 407 and β 111, although admittedly neither passage presents a straightforward answer in reply to a specific question. But 'to answer', in Greek as much as in English, is commonly and unproblematically used to denote a verbal reaction to a given situation, even in the absence of a specific question. The pragmatics of 'to answer' cannot be tied narrowly to a corresponding question. So, the *OED* s.v. II.12: "To speak or write in reply to a question, remark, or any expression of desire or opinion; to reply, respond, rejoin; *also* To reply to an implied question, to solve a doubt" (cf. Else 1959:85, Patzer 1970:642, and Ley 1983:20–21). Proponents of the evolutionary model of textual fixation have no difficulty accepting that Homeric epic should attest to this later semantic development. At the same time, one must recognize the formal nature of the corresponding 'replies': "[T]he verb is used with emphasis and a certain formality. ... [I]t is the official or acknowledged head of the group who speaks, and he uses ὑποκρίνεσθαι to describe the decisive reaction of the group to the proposal" (Else 1959:82; cf. Patzer 1970:642 and Ley 1983:21). Hence the *LfgE* s.v. κρίνω II.3a: "give a response conveying one's decision (choice)."

"[d]er Verlauf der Entwicklung zur Bedeutung 'antworten' ist schön an *Od.*, 15, 170 abzulesen: Menelaos soll ein Zeichen deuten, aber diese Deutung ist zu gleicher Zeit der Bescheid, den er auf eine Frage gibt, die ihn gestellt wurde." The view that ἀποκρίνομαι was not simply a parallel Attic alternative to the Ionic ὑποκρίνομαι is suggested by the otherwise curious fact that the actor—if in fact he was called ὑποκριτής because he 'answered' the chorus or someone else—should not have been simply called ἀποκριτής. Drama was, after all, a genre peculiar to Attica, and ἀποκριτής never had any (potentially competing) currency as the generic noun for one who answers.[11] A helpful parallel that elucidates this point is the peculiarly narrow (technical) use of ποιητής for 'composer' vis-à-vis the much broader use of ποιέω for 'to make'. Why should Attic speakers not have concurrently employed both ἀποκρίνομαι for the ordinary meaning 'to answer' and ἀποκριτής, *ex hypothesi*, for the 'actor-as-answerer'?[12] If one should object that confusion might then arise in the corresponding (hypothetical) use of this same verb for 'to act (a part on stage)', the rejoinder is obvious: so also does ποιέω create comparable ambiguity when it is used for 'to compose' (LSJ s.v. A.1.4, the technical acceptation associated with ποιητής). Plainly, this was no object.

Thus, the facts suggest that either ὑποκριτής, as applied to the actor, did not mean 'answerer' and that the motivation for the label must be sought elsewhere, or that ἀποκρίνομαι was not available for 'to answer' at the time when ὑποκριτής was applied to the actor. But if it was not available then, the motivation for its origin remains mysterious and one is left to wonder why ὑποκρίνομαι should have been deemed insufficient or inappropriate.[13] Unless of course, as argued here, ὑποκρίνομαι (with ὑποκριτής) had already become denotative of the performance of the rhapsode, pure and simple—i.e. ordinarily it no longer

---

The unmarked Homeric verb for 'to reply' was (ἀπ)αμείβεσθαι (as Patzer 1970:642 remarks, "eigentlich nur die Wechselrede ... bezeichnend").

[11] A search of the extant literature only turns up five instances of ἀποκριτής, three of them in *etymologica* that explain ὑποκριτής as 'answerer' from the perspective of *koinē* usage: the *Lexicon* of Apollonius Sophista (p. 160, line 3 Bekker), the *Etymologicum* of Orion (column 158, lines 3–4 Sturz), and the *Etymologicum Magnum* 782.48 s.v. ὑποκριτής (col. 2190 Gaisford).

[12] Koller 1957:103 makes a similar point.

[13] Curtius (1866:150) realizes this and argues, doubtless with good reason, that old Attic shared the Ionic usage of ὑποκρίνομαι. But he cannot account for the rise of its competitor ἀποκρίνομαι and its successful displacement of ὑποκρίνομαι in the acceptation 'to answer'. It is not enough to claim that speakers of old Attic must have used ὑποκρίνομαι and that the older diction is occasionally reflected in more recent writings (he points to Thoukydides 7.44.5, which the OCT emends to ἀποκρίνοιντο without ms. warrant). This by itself neither accounts for the origin and eventual absolute dominance of ἀποκρίνομαι as 'to answer', nor does it explain why (*ex hypothesi*) the actor should have been characterized as an 'answerer'. My reconstruction, on the other hand, predicts precisely such a state of affairs. IG I³ 533 (dated to ca. 490–80? by the editors) is of little probatory value, so long as the influence of epic diction cannot be precluded (cf. Koller 1957:101n3 and Lesky 1956:473).

denotated '(exegetical) interpretation'—and upon its transference to the actor the ensuing relatively greater currency of its acceptation 'to perform (on stage)' was now felt to encroach on its non-technical one 'to reply' to a degree sufficient to provoke both a novel resort to ἀποκρίνεσθαι and its rapid embrace as an alternative to ὑποκρίνεσθαι by the linguistic community. In all likelihood, the *nomen agentis* ὑποκριτής, like ἀποκριτής, was not in use to designate the ordinary 'answerer'. Hence, it was readily deployed without interference in the theatrical context and, in turn, must have pulled into its orbit ὑποκρίνομαι, serving to root its technical acceptation 'to perform (on stage)' into common linguistic usage.[14] That, under this scenario, a similar encroachment of the technical meaning on the broader sense had not been felt before hints at the relatively rarer use of the verb ὑποκρίνομαι to designate the performance of the rhapsodic ὑποκριτής, for which verbs like ἄδειν, καταλέγειν, and (especially) ῥαψῳδεῖν were readily available and commonly used instead. The enthusiasm and vigor with which the new genre of drama was embraced by most Athenians commends the view that its basic nomenclature was broadly adopted and its impact upon the popular vocabulary for performance was swift.[15]

The numerous past attempts by scholars to explain the use of ὑποκριτής to designate the actor of Attic drama have failed to produce a consensus because the question has not been properly framed. By and large, most have assumed that a synchronic semantic approach could yield the correct answer. This presupposition led them first to establish the meaning of the verb in its several Homeric contexts, whether it should be understood as 'to interpret' or 'to answer'; then, to reduce the word to its building blocks, ὑπό + κρίνεσθαι, from which they sought the common semantic denominator that best explained *all* Homeric occurrences; they supposed that this common denominator would make clear which of the two acceptations, 'to interpret' or 'to answer', was more fundamental; and, finally, they assumed that this more fundamental meaning would satisfactorily account for the use of the verb and its agent noun in the context of Attic drama. I referred above to the semantic approach commonly adopted as 'synchronic.' In truth, it is a sort of 'synchronic diachrony': it consists in the etymological investigation of the constituent parts, verb and preverb, out

---

[14] That various derivatives of the same root—in this case the verb ὑποκρίνεσθαι, the agent noun ὑποκριτής, and the *nomen actionis* ὑπόκρισις—may be differentially attached to different semantic spheres is well illustrated by the rhetorical use of the same words: whereas ὑποκρίνεσθαι and ὑπόκρισις were adopted to refer to oratorical delivery, the agent noun was not and remained instead specific to the dramatic actor. Cf. Else 1959:80n25 (with Koller 1957:104 on ὑπόκρισις).

[15] The suggestion that it was in reaction to the use of ὑποκριτής as the label for the actor that ἀποκρίνομαι was substituted for ὑποκρίνομαι in its acceptation 'to answer' was put forward by Else (1959:101) with his accustomed sagacity (cf. Zucchelli 1962:25n50, with bibliography). Patzer (1970:647n1) calls this conjecture "ansprechend."

of which issues the disputed bifurcation into 'to interpret' and 'to answer'. Both camps assume that one of these meanings is supported both by the etymology and by all of the earliest attested uses, and that the other is an accidental synchronic concomitant, a contextual incident mistaken for the denotation. This is what I mean by the oxymoronic 'synchronic diachrony': the 'diachrony' refers to the semantic archaeology of etymological analysis; 'synchronic,' to the notion that as far as the antiquity of their origin, at least potentially, both meanings are substantially on a par. A corrective to this faulty procedure is found in a thoroughgoing diachronic perspective that combines etymological analysis and a consideration of archaic Greek performance practices, epic and dramatic. The assumption of a potential synchronic parity was bound to follow from a view of Homeric poetry that lacks the appropriate diachronic depth. If the Homeric poems were not regarded as a diachronically layered product of recomposition in performance that reached down into the late archaic and early classical periods, when ὑποκρίνεσθαι could doubtless signify 'to answer', the admission that both acceptations were present in the *Iliad* and the *Odyssey* necessarily entailed that either was synchronically derivable from the etymology.[16] Scholars who believed that, in the last analysis, only one of them was etymologically true, conceded that the notion to which the competing alternative pointed was in some measure to be found in the context, and that the definition of ὑποκρίνεσθαι ought therefore to be generously drawn to reflect this concomitance.[17]

---

[16] This view is held by the article on κρίνω in the *LfgE*, which views *both* meanings as mutually independent and equally valid: "It is not at all clear that either of the two senses below is a development of the other ... ; both senses may be independently derived from basic meaning" (s.v. II.3, column 1545).

[17] So Zucchelli 1962, whose treatment is generally accurate, but who writes in regard to the four Homeric *loci* M 228 o 170 τ 535 555 which instance ὑποκρίνεσθαι in connection with 'interpretation': "Accanto all'uso specifico testé considerato, ὑποκρίνεσθαι poté averne anche uno più ampio e generale—certamente *non secondario* rispetto al primo—poté indicare cioè il 'pronunciarsi su una questione qualsiasi'" (12, my emphasis). In this, he follows Lesky (1956:472–473), who is forced to use the word "Erklärung" to gloss the peculiar 'interpretation' that, in the interest of a uniform ('synchronic') Homeric acceptation for ὑποκρίνεσθαι, he wants to find in H 407 and β 111. I do not think that *Hymn to Apollo* 171 helps to advance the debate, because those who think that the text of the Homeric poems was already fixed in the early archaic period also date the hymn to a later time, by which ὑποκρίνεσθαι might have acquired the acceptation 'to answer' irrespective of its original meaning. All the same, because its context is explicitly one of performance, the metapoetic implications of this passage are rich: the words from the blind bard from Khios, superficially 'all of you, reply very well', may be read metapoetically as 'all of you, perform very well (the answer)'. This insight guides Nagy (2003:21–38) in his analysis of ὑποκρίνεσθαι as "responding by way of performing." (εὖ μάλα often goes untranslated or μάλα is notionally assigned to reinforce πᾶσαι; but πᾶσαι does not admit of degrees and the regular epic order when μάλα intensifies εὖ is εὖ μάλα—cf. Ψ 761 δ 96—which qualifies the verb ὑποκρίνασθαι; in Theokritos 25.19, εὖ μάλα goes with the immediately preceding φαίνεται, not

This assumption of a synchronic semantic concomitance is, in my view, a distortion of the facts. I am not denying that 'interpretation' and 'reply' may, and sometimes do, co-occur in the Homeric poems. In fact, this co-occurrence (not just in the poems, but in archaic Greek culture generally) is the key to the diachronic development that takes us from the true etymological meaning, 'to interpret', to the unmarked Ionic acceptation 'to answer'. But ὑποκρίνεσθαι originally did not *denote* 'to answer', and one muddles its meaning by reading into it the (frequent, but by no means constant) contextual concomitance of question and answer. The acceptation 'to answer' follows diachronically from the original pragmatics of the interpretation as a speech-act, i.e. as a pronouncement[18]—private interpretation is never in view—not from a semantic seed synchronically present in its original meaning that only needed time to sprout. The synchronic approach is a mirage that cannot provide resolution to the debate, and it is unnecessary once the Homeric system of poetry is granted its own diachronic depth. This realization allows for a clear diachronic ordering of acceptations—first 'to interpret' whence, in time, 'to answer'—without a forced reading of those passages which support the meaning 'to answer'.

Methodologically, there can be no objection against the etymological approach *per se*. But scholars have spent most of their efforts in determining as precisely as possible the semantic implications of the preverb ὑπό. Is it one of acting under the influence of an external agent[19] or of acting with immediacy of sequence?[20] Or perhaps, of acting in a manner that brings something out of secluded depths into open view?[21] Might it not imply a representative substitution of the inquirer by the interpreter?[22] Or refer to 'furnishing' or 'putting

---

with the following πᾶσι; cf. Theokritos 24.94 with Gow 1950–1952:2.430 *ad loc.*) We have in the *Hymn to Apollo* the overlapping occurrence of the ordinary Ionic meaning 'to answer' and the rhapsodic technical meaning 'to perform' in a context that evokes in modified fashion an old choral mode of epic performance.

[18] So Zucchelli 1962: "[D]a questi passi (ma non più che dai precedenti) risulta chiaro come poté avvenire l'ulteriore sviluppo semantico di ὑποκρίνεσθαι, il suo passaggio cioè dal significato di 'pronunciarsi' a quello di 'rispondere'" (14).

[19] Else 1959: "[O]ne important function of ὑπό in early Greek ... was to express psychological near-ness or exposure, the experience of being within immediate range of a person or object ... that was felt as having power to menace or protect. It would follow that a verb 'compounded with ὑπό' ... will tend to denote a *reaction* or *response* to such a situation" (90, his emphasis).

[20] Curtius 1866: "ὑποκρίνεσθαι wäre also gleichsam *subcertare* oder *in certamine succedere*. ... [B]ei dem dramatischen ὑποκριτής ist ... an die *Ablösung* des Chors durch den ihn aufnehmenden Schauspieler zu denken" (153, his emphasis).

[21] Schwyzer *GG* II.525: "hom. ὑπο-κρίνομαι (urspr. 'seine Meinung aus der Herzenstiefe, aus der Verborgenheit hervorgeben'; vgl. att. ἀπο-κρίνομαι!)." He is followed by Lesky 1956:472.

[22] Koller 1957: "Die Erklärung ist vielmehr in einer Gruppe von Verben zu suchen, in denen das ὑπό- 'Begleitung' und 'Vertretung' ausdrückt ..." (102).

under'?[23] Little time has been spent on κρίνεσθαι by comparison. Most proponents of 'to answer' seem to assume tacitly that, however obscure the underlying semantic rationale, the Ionic acceptation of ὑποκρίνεσθαι 'to answer' or, in its place, the identical Attic one of ἀποκρίνεσθαι, readily proves that κρίνεσθαι *can* denote 'to answer'. This justification is judged sufficient and no further effort is expended upon it.[24] Alternatively, the ancient statements relevant to the meaning of ὑποκριτής are shown to agree on relating it to 'to answer' and are marshaled as sufficient to settle the legitimacy of using κρίνεσθαι in this sense.[25] Once the verb is hastily dispatched, the investigation naturally focuses on the implications of ὑπό: whom does the actor 'answer'? Is his acting called an 'answer' because of the manner of his speaking (Curtius) or because he speaks 'in response' to another (Else)? But, with the investigation thus framed, this question is premature. One cannot reach a proper understanding of the preverb without first settling the meaning of the verb, apart from which many of the competing explanations of ὑπό seem credible and possible.

In fact, under any reasonable etymological analysis and in view of its attested use in the oldest sources, κρίνομαι cannot mean anything other than 'to separate, to pick', from which follow 'to decide', 'to judge', and the transferred sense 'to pick or judge the meaning'—in other words, 'to interpret' or 'to expound'.[26] All attempts to champion 'to answer' run aground on this shallow. The notion that a psychological process of sifting could underlie and define the essence of 'to answer' is implausible. What precisely are we to think the individual separates in his mind in order to answer a question? Would one perhaps have to imagine an array of possible answers, all fully formed and mingled together, out of which he picks the one he is to utter? Some such improbable reconstruction is unavoidable if the sense of κρίνεσθαι is to be respected.[27] On the other

---

[23] "ὑποκρίνεσθαι ... ist 'unterlegen, daruntergeben, an die Hand geben', im Sinne der Präposition bei ὑποτιθέναι und *submittere*, die auf ein 'Positives, Unterstützendes' zielt, das 'an die Hand geben' wird" (Schreckenberg 1960:119n79). Also: "Zunächst ergibt sich als Grundbedeutung des Wortes: etwas Geschautem, Gesehenem, das der deutenden Erklärung bedarf, mit Worten einen Sinn unterlegen" (112).

[24] Curtius provides a rare and telling exception. See below for the details.

[25] Curtius (1866:148) opens his article by stating forcefully the agreement of ancient sources, starting with Alexandrian scholarship down to Byzantine times, that the dramatic actor was ὁ ἀποκρινόμενος πρὸς τὸν χορόν, i.e. a "Respondent" of the chorus (149). Cf. Heimsoeth 1873, on which see Sommerbrodt 1876b.

[26] Cf. Frisk 1973–1979, Chantraine 1999, and Beekes 2010 s.v. κρίνω. Note, in particular, the Celtic cognate *go-grynu* 'to sift' < *upo-kri-nō, on which see Pedersen 1909–1913:1.124 §77.

[27] So, for example, Koller (1957:102n4) motivates the etymology of the related ἀποκρίνεσθαι as follows: "ἀποκρίνεσθαι als *Verbum dicendi*, 'antworten', muß von der Bedeutung 'für sich wählen, aussondern' ... abgeleitet werden, etwa nach einer Situation, wie sie Platon im *Staat* 337c bietet: Thrasymachos muß sich entscheiden aus den vorgelegten Möglichkeiten 2 × 6, 3 × 4, 6 × 2 oder 4 × 3 die Zahl 12 zu bestimmen ὧν ἐγὼ ἀπεῖπον, τούτων τι ἀποκρινῇ 'Du triffst daraus eine Wahl

hand, the challenge of expounding the divine will or interpreting divinely sent
σήματα (like dreams or omens), at least according to the archaic view (before
Plato's tendentious treatment of it), calls for the exegesis of a trained and intellectually engaged mantic expert who sifts through alternative interpretations
and picks out the correct one: ὧδέ χ᾽ ὑποκρίναιτο θεοπρόπος, ὃς σάφα θυμῷ |
εἰδείη τεράων καί οἱ πειθοίατο λαοί (M 228–229). This degree of psychologically
self-aware discernment is precisely what is lacking in an ordinary answer, even
when that answer is formal in nature. Individuals do not ordinarily face their
own psyche with a need to 'sift' it before they speak. Only if one colors 'answer
giving' with the interpretive judgment entailed by the verb's denotation and
pragmatics can one lend plausibility to the notion that ὑποκρίνεσθαι denotes a
qualified sense of 'to answer'. In so doing, however, one restores to it a particular variant of its true meaning, only to allege it as a concomitant factor of the
answer giving—and not, as it actually is, its true and essential meaning.

In principle, every act of the will can be reduced to a prior judgment. In this
regard, the giving of an answer is no different from any other act of speaking.
If the logic that ascribes 'replying' to the etymology of κρίνεσθαι were sound,
could we not fairly expect a derivative of κρίνω for every act of utterance? Only
one reason makes 'deciding' seem marginally more acceptable than 'separating'
as the mental process underlying the use of κρίνεσθαι in (allegedly formal)
answer giving: pragmatically, the utterance is a speech-act and, as such, it
shares its markedness with ὑποκρίνεσθαι, which involves the pronouncement of
an oracular interpretation. But once again, it is important to emphasize that one
should not confuse the pragmatics of the associated speech-act, which, however
important, is culturally contextual, with the term's own denotative meaning.
This semantic muddle is the key to Else's superficially more successful attempt
to defend the meaning 'answerer' for ὑποκριτής against the alternative 'interpreter'. But this is only the first dubious stage of his ultimately unconvincing
argument. For Else is rightly adamant that 'answering' cannot be a passing
activity of the professional who bears the title 'answerer'.[28] How does he seek
to motivate this as the defining function of the actor? His argument, in short, is
that when the poet himself performed his plays he was called τραγῳδός. Only
with the introduction of the second actor do we meet with a subordinate figure
who 'answered' the τραγῳδός. This figure would be the ὑποκριτής. After the poet

---

für dich'—diese Wahl, in Worten ausgedrückt, ist eben die 'Antwort'." Note in Koller's psychological reconstruction the fully-formed nature of the possible answers: they are laid before the
answerer, ready for his choice. Another attempt at a motivation, similarly unconvincing, is
Sommerbrodt's: "[Homer gebraucht] statt ἀποκρίνεσθαι in der Bedeutung 'antworten', die aus
ihr naturgemäß hervorgeht, (da antworten nichts anderes ist, als die Rede des Einen von der des
Andern trennen ...) das anschaulichere ἀμείβεσθαι ..." (Sommerbrodt 1867:513).

[28] See below, p. 663 n. 48, where I quote his words to this effect.

ceased acting and a professional actor took his place, all the professionals left on stage were called ὑποκριταί by an abuse of the original nomenclature. To lend plausibility to this explanation, the scholar identifies the second actor with the messenger of tragedy, whose characteristic function was to answer the question 'what happened?'[29]

Nonetheless, Else's argument lacks a foundation that might bear the weight of its conjectural reconstruction. For there is no sound basis on which to justify retrojecting to the earliest days of tragedy the late distinction between τραγῳδός as 'protagonist' and ὑποκριταί as 'supporting actors'.[30] There is, furthermore, every likelihood that the didascalic record already used ὑποκριτής in 449 BC, when the first contest for actors was held;[31] and, as Zucchelli (1962:37) remarks, if the term was already established by then, it was probably in use before poets ceased performing their own plays. Else's proposal implies that, if not immediately, at least within the compass of only a few years ὑποκριτής was also applied to the actor that replaced the poet. If, as he avers, the poet had always and exclusively been called τραγῳδός, his conjectural reconstruction would entail a striking and highly dubious departure from the traditional name for the 'protagonist' (to use our term). What about τραγῳδός would have made its transfer to the first actor so objectionable that, *ex hypothesi*, Athenians preferred instead the glaring incongruity of applying to him the very label that had hitherto designated the performer whose characteristic function was to answer the first actor? I know of no etymological analysis of τραγῳδός that ties it manifestly to the composer, nor of any other bond between this word and the poet that has the strength and specificity required to support Else's argument. The alleged renaming would have designated the first actor as his own answerer! Are we to believe that this jarring change in nomenclature happened so late after drama's adoption of ὑποκριτής that its meaning 'answerer of the poet-as-performer' had already been lost on the public? Moreover, it is hardly certain that the figure of the messenger was so fundamental to the development of tragedy that it had the definitive impact on its terminology that this theory

---

[29] Schreckenberg (1960:116–119) assigns the ἄγγελος a similar significance in the development of tragedy, although he does not, like Else, attempt to motivate the etymology of ὑποκριτής as 'one who answers the τραγῳδός' but as the original actor who "mit seiner 'Ansage' der getanzten Schau durch Worte die stoffliche Grundlage unterlegt und damit zugleich das zu Sehende 'deutet'" (114). Therefore, "ἄγγελος und ὑποκριτής sind ja ursprünglich identisch und stehen erst in einer entwickelteren Form des Dramas nebeneinander" (117). This last sentiment is at least as old as Hornung 1869:4 (cf. Fischl 1910:5, who declared it a "pervulgata ... opinio").

[30] See Pickard-Cambridge 1988:129–132.

[31] For details, see Pickard-Cambridge 1988:72–73, 102, and 126. Cf. Capps 1943:2–3.

presupposes.[32] That ancient scholars and manuscripts often refer to him explicitly by the (eminently reasonable) label ἄγγελος further undercuts Else's case.[33] For does this not make clear that generally the messenger's function was not, in fact, construed as an 'answer' to a question—whether one was posed or not—but as a 'report'?[34] Untenable too is Else's claim that, without any contextual indication to this effect, Aristotle used ὑποκριτής in two different senses: an old, narrow one that he had ascertained from his didascalic researches ('answerer' of the τραγῳδός') and the one in common use later ('actor', pure and simple).[35]

---

[32] There has been a recent resurgence of interest in the figure of the tragic messenger and his dramatic potential. See De Jong 1991, Green 1996, Green 1999, Barrett 2002, and Dickin 2009. The role is often defined functionally to embrace characters who are not explicitly cast by the manuscripts as ἄγγελοι. Although few would dispute the possibilities open to him, the significance of his contribution to the action (cf. Euboulos fr. 134 K-A and Stephanēs 1988 no. 1861 on the messenger *extraordinaire* Nikostratos), and the consummate artistry of some of the surviving messenger speeches, this is far from commending, much less requiring, that we ascribe to him the fundamental structural role and central historical import that Else argues for. For older treatments of the messenger, see Hornung 1869, Rassow 1883, Fischl 1910, Bassi 1899, Di Gregorio 1967, and Bremer 1976.

[33] ἐξάγγελος was also used, the difference turning on whether his report was from within to those outside or from outside to those within. The verb ἀπαγγέλειν denoted his reporting (cf. Bassi 1899:51n4). Some of the ancient *testimonia* about the messenger are quoted by Di Gregorio 1967:3–6.

[34] This is, of course, the primary acceptation of the tragic ἄγγελος, although the label is conventionally translated 'messenger'. Not all tragic 'reporters' are 'messengers', but all 'messengers' are 'reporters'. Else (1959:104–105) himself details instances (e.g. in Aiskhylos *Seven against Thebes*) in which the messenger "blurts out his news without waiting to be asked." The scholar excuses this on the grounds that "the situation is many times more immediate and urgent." And he adds, tellingly: "Thus the specific use of the Messenger varies strikingly—and creatively—from play to play; but his generic function ... remains constant, namely to bring into the play *a report* of significant action that has taken place off-stage" (105, my emphasis). It is still possible, if hardly compelling, to argue that no one thought of the term 'reporter', ἄγγελος, for the actor, only of ὑποκριτής in the (alleged) sense 'answerer'. And that, once the circumstances had unfolded according to Else's speculations and his label had been made common to all actors (after the poet-τραγῳδός ceased performing), nevertheless the function of the messenger was still felt to be distinct and prominent enough to call for a separate label peculiar to him. The logic of the argument is paradoxical: it first assumes that the messenger was not so markedly distinct that his denomination 'answerer' could not be shared promiscuously with all other actors (including the one whom he characteristically answered!); but that, once the label was common to all, the need for an individuating designation was felt again.

[35] See Else 1945 esp. 6, with criticism from Lesky 1956:471–472, Pickard-Cambridge 1988:130–132, and Zucchelli 1962:35–36. There is a more natural way than Else's to dispel the appearance of contradiction between Aristotle *Poetics* 1449a15–17 (καὶ τό τε τῶν ὑποκριτῶν πλῆθος ἐξ ἑνὸς εἰς δύο πρῶτος Αἰσχύλος ἤγαγε) and Themistios *Oration* 26.316d (καὶ οὐ προσέχομεν Ἀριστοτέλει ὅτι τὸ μὲν πρῶτον ὁ χορὸς εἰσιὼν ᾖδεν εἰς τοὺς θεούς, Θέσπις δὲ πρόλογόν τε καὶ ῥῆσιν ἐξεῦρεν, Αἰσχύλος δὲ τρίτον ὑποκριτὰς καὶ ὀκρίβαντας, τὰ δὲ πλείω τούτων Σοφοκλέους ἀπηλαύσαμεν καὶ Εὐριπίδου;). In quoting the latter I have adopted the reading of the codex Mediolanensis ("Ambros. gr. J 22 sup." in Schenkl's Teubner 1971 edition; cf. Schenkl 1898), τρίτον ὑποκριτάς, for what is otherwise transmitted as τρίτον ὑποκριτήν (on the choice of reading see Else 1939:141n8

Curtius's case for 'answerer' is more straightforward than Else's but also, for being more precise in its etymological analysis, the more transparently flawed. Starting from the presupposition that the almost uniformly attested ancient understanding of ὑποκρίνεσθαι must be right, he attempts to account for the application of the word to dramatic performance.[36] But he realizes that the verb κρίνεσθαι hardly allows for an ordinary sense of 'to answer': "Dass bei dem ὑποκριτής von einem Antworten im eigentlichen und gewöhnlichsten Sinne nicht die Rede sein kann, ... versteht sich im Grunde von selbst. An Fragen des Chors ist doch nur in seltenen Fällen zu denken" (Curtius 1866:151–152). Thus he selects for ὑπό the sense of 'immediate succession',[37] and for κρίνεσθαι,

---

and Lesky 1956:471). Else's approach is to harmonize by reinterpreting the passage in the *Poetics*. There, Aristotle seeks to list the μεταβολαί (1449a14) that led the number of actors to the final canonical three. It is clear that he subsumes the introduction of the first actor under his summary of the invention of drama. Perhaps because his genetic theories, which traced tragedy back to the dithyramb, for once in the intellectual history of ancient Greece benefit from drawing the focus *away* from a πρῶτος εὑρετής, he does not mention Thespis and there is no natural occasion for him to refer explicitly to Thespis' introduction of the 'first actor'. Thus silent, by default the passage hints at the ἐξάρχων as the primitive actor (even if, as to form, as Lesky 1929:12–13 observes, his 'dialog' with the chorus cannot have been like the "Sprechvers" of Thespis' actor but a variant of choral song; cf. Schreckenberg 1960:120–121 and Zucchelli 1962:34). Lesky (1929:8–9) may be right to surmise from *Poetics* 1449b4–5 (with 1449a37–38) that Aristotle admits "deutlich genug" to knowing about Thespis and his prologue, despite his earlier silence, and that Themistios must have got his information from the philosopher's Περὶ ποιητῶν. At any rate, an unforced reading of τό τε τῶν ὑποκριτῶν πλῆθος ἐξ ἑνὸς εἰς δύο πρῶτος Αἰσχύλος ἤγαγε will not support Else's contention that Aiskhylos is here said to have introduced both the first and the second ὑποκριταί and not, as it is usually understood, to have inherited one actor and added a second (Else 1945:6). Else's construal clearly contradicts the statement about Sophokles that follows (cf. Else 1957a:167–168 *ad loc.*) or else requires the impossible view that here alone Aristotle used "ὑποκριτής in its special old sense [of 'answerer' to the τραγῳδός]" (Else 1945:6n24). A better harmonizing strategy is to construe Themistios as saying that Aiskhylos introduced more than one actor—hence 'actors'. With Usener, one may then explicitly add δύο or supply it implicitly (cf. Lesky 1929:11 and Else 1945:2n8). Themistios' summary would be reporting that Thespis invented the πρόλογος and the ῥῆσις, and hence also the first actor, whereas Aiskhylos was the first to introduce a plurality of actors into his plays. If we follow Else (1959:102–103) in considering the addition of the second actor "the stroke of genius by which tragedy was really created as drama"—that is, when drama came into its own as a genre—we will not be surprised at Themistios' use of ἐξεῦρεν in this connection, rather than εἰσήνεγκε *vel sim.* This very interpretation was also originally espoused by Else: "From the point of view of true drama, then, the first actor is indispensable, to be sure, but fulfillment comes only with the second. On the other hand, the addition of a third actor ... is a detail" (Else 1939:153); to which he adds: "In other words, it need not have mattered so much to Aristotle just who added the third actor. I should interpret the remark quoted by Themistius ... in this spirit. Aeschylus brought in more than one actor, and that is what matters, not their total number" (153n51).

[36] Curtius 1866 does not look closely at the Homeric *loci* (but cf. Curtius 1868:256–257). He merely assumes that ὑποκρίνεσθαι is a synonym of the more common ἀπαμείβεσθαι and lists its occurrences (leaving out τ 535 555 and including *Hymn to Apollo* 171).

[37] I find this idea productive in the realm of rhapsodic performance and its allied terms. See above, p. 388 n. 198.

that of the Latin *certare*.[38] ὑποκρίνεσθαι, then, would amount to ἀγωνίζεσθαι, specifically, *subcertare* or *in certamine succedere* (153). By the logic of this analysis, Curtius is forced to grant that ὑποκρίνεσθαι conceives of ordinary conversation, with its questions and answers, as a sort of *concertatio*, and that ὑπόκρισις encapsulates "die rasche Folge der Antwort auf die Frage" (153). Thus, the argument moves away by degrees from his opening categorical statement that ὑποκρίνεσθαι means 'to answer' (and was so understood in antiquity) and that ὑποκριτής was the one who answered the chorus towards the inescapable conclusion that the actor-as-ὑποκριτής was so labeled because he vied with the chorus by rushing to answer their questions.[39] But if this outcome seems too strained and implausible, Curtius appears to share the feeling, for he hastens to add: "Aber bei dem dramatischen ὑποκριτής ist nicht hieran, sondern nur an die Fortsetzung der Aufführung, an die Ablösung des Chors durch den ihn aufnehmenden Schauspieler zu denken" (153). The analysis oscillates between the ancient datum Curtius seeks to uphold—the acceptation 'to answer'—and the meaning of κρίνεσθαι, which does not accommodate this goal and drives the argument away from anything that one may reasonably recognize as an ordinary reply. This accounts for Curtius's ultimate rejection of his own conclusion.[40]

Patzer 1970, in his review of Zucchelli 1962, offers yet another attempt to reconcile the etymology of ὑποκριτής and ὑποκρίνεσθαι to 'answerer' and 'to answer'. Although he rightly insists throughout that a credible answer must account for the root κρι-, like Curtius, he gradually veers away from this etymological anchor. He first proposes a definition that, at least ostensibly, seems to fall within the semantic sphere of the simple verb: "Es ergibt sich also als genaue

---

[38] Curtius 1866: "κρίνεσθαι verhält sich zum activen κρίνειν ähnlich wie *certare* zu *cernere*" (153).

[39] Sommerbrodt (1867:511) wonders, "Mit wem certirt der Schauspieler?" Obviously, not with the chorus. Nor can it be argued that a competition among actors is in view here, for his label is supposed to articulate a relationship internal to one play, and a plurality of actors for a single play was a later development. "Oder ist unter dem *certamen* das Drama selbst gemeint? Ein Drama an sich ist kein *certamen*, sondern wird erst einem andern gegenüber zu einem *certamen*" (511). Sommerbrodt also wonders why the chorus should not have been called ὑποκριτής, since it succeeds the actor as much as the actor succeeds it (512). Curtius (1868:259–260) faces these objections simply by reaffirming his views and buttressing them with an appeal to the deeply competitive character of Hellenic culture.

[40] In his reply to Sommerbrodt 1867, Curtius (1868:258) draws attention to various apparent semantic disjunctions: between ὑπηρέτης and ἐρέτης; διοικητής and οἰκητής; ἀνάβασις, ἔκβασις, πρόβασις and βάσις; and διαίρεσις, καθαίρεσις, συναίρεσις and αἵρεσις. This list is designed to ease our acceptance of his meaning 'answerer' for ὑποκριτής, a meaning that seems impossible to relate to κριτής. I for one have no difficulty relating the simple and compound nouns in the alleged *comparanda* without feeling that any violence is thereby done to the language. An obvious metaphor ties the first two; the natural meaning of οἰκέω joins the next pair; and I do not see what makes either triad respectively so far from βάσις or αἵρεσις. Nothing of the sort may be said of κριτής and ὑποκριτής or of κρίνεσθαι and ὑποκρίνεσθαι. See Sommerbrodt 1875 for a final rejoinder.

Bedeutung von ὑποκρίνομαι 'etw[as] zur (geistigen) Unterstützung einer Person auf Grund besonderer Sacherkenntnis, Überlegung oder Verantwortung entscheiden" (Patzer 1970:647). Like Else, Patzer confuses the denotative content of ὑποκρίνεσθαι ('to interpret') with its pragmatics as a speech-act, and he picks the particular sense 'to render judgment' from the broader meaning 'to utter authoritative (potentially transformative) speech'. But at least his definition explicitly includes the discriminating function of discursive thought.[41] And yet, only a few sentences later, Patzer replaces "entscheiden" by the similarly looking but, as to sense, rather different "Bescheid geben." Whereas 'entscheiden' is "ein maßgebendes Urteil fällen über, den Ausschlag geben für, endgültig bestimmen, anordnen, festlegen,"[42] 'Bescheid geben' is "Auskunft erteilen, jmdn. benachrichtigen." "Bescheid," in turn, is glossed as "Antwort, Nachricht, Auskunft," and only in an official setting ("behördlich") is it equivalent to "Entscheidung" (that is, the pragmatics makes the 'answer' authoritative and, hence, the functional equivalent of a 'judgment'). By this verbal sleight of hand, Patzer moves away from a straightforward notion of 'judgment' and offers in its stead a gloss that poses as a synonym but in fact approaches the notion of 'answer'. This allows him to add, parenthetically: "(wobei [sc. bei ὑποκρίνεσθαι] Anfrage und Bescheid sich auf Träume, Orakel, Wunderzeichen, politische Angebote ... o. ä. beziehen kann). Damit ist die Entscheidung für 'Antworter' gefallen ..." (647).

The foregoing survey makes clear that, when it comes to the original sense of ὑποκρίνεσθαι, defenders of 'to answer' are unable to adhere to a strict etymological analysis. These scholars are persuaded that the straightforward 'to interpret (a message, omen, *vel sim.*)' will not do and they labor hard to shore up what appears to them as the sole alternative. But the right etymology follows readily once the correct meaning of κρίνεσθαι is embraced. Then, the import of ὑπό is straightforward. Greek deploys this preverb in contexts that imply decoding submerged meaning or making someone aware of, and bringing to light, thoughts that are otherwise suppressed or below the subject's awareness. Such is the case, for example, with ὑπόνοια; or, to mention two Homeric examples, with ὑπομιμνήσκω (α 321 ο 3) and ὑποφήτης (Π 235).[43] Archaic liter-

---

[41] This is the case, at any rate, with "Sacherkenntnis" and "Überlegung," if not necessarily with "Verantwortung."

[42] All definitions and glosses are from the 1980 edition of the *Wahrig Deutsches Wörterbuch*, published by Mosaik Verlag.

[43] On ὑποφήτης see González 2000. Patzer (1970:645) insists that ὑπό in ὑπομιμνήσκω cannot denote "aus der Tiefe empor" because this preposition is never used in the concrete, spatial sense to indicate this manner of motion (i.e. 'from the depths upward'). Patzer trains his gun squarely at Schwyzer's definition of ὑποκρίνομαι: "urspr. 'seine Meinung aus der Herzenstiefe, aus der Verborgenheit hervorgeben'" (*GG* II.525). There is no need, however, for the motion 'up from under'. It is sufficient that ὑπό indicate the sphere in which the 'separating' or 'sifting'

ature, including Homer, clearly supports this meaning, as one can readily see from M 228 and o 170 τ 535 555. As noted above, H 407 and β 111 prove that the meaning 'to answer' was already present in Homeric diction. But while the meaning 'to interpret' for κρίνεσθαι is unproblematic, and the development from 'to interpret (an oracle)' to 'to answer (a query)' can be readily envisioned (see below), 'to answer' as the original meaning of κρίνεσθαι is impossible and there is no plausible semantic path from 'to separate or pick' to 'to answer'. Realizing this, those who champion 'to answer' as the root meaning of ὑποκρίνεσθαι in Homer focus on the fact that the corresponding interpretations are all in reply to questions (sometimes implicit), thus denying that 'interpretation' is basic to its meaning and reducing it to a concurrent secondary factor.[44]

---

takes place: 'under or below (ordinary reach or perception)'. This is surely the import of ὑπό in ὑπόνοια—an understanding or insight that is to be sought below the superficial meaning of the text, by thinking or reflecting 'under' its surface, just as παρανοέω denotes thinking that takes the subject either beyond, or else aside (and therefore away) from, what is sound, i.e. 'to think amiss'. I would also be ready to take ὑπό in the representative sense advocated by Koller (1957:102), "an Stelle eines andern entscheiden, für einen andern deuten," so long as the ὑποκριτής is understood to stand not just for the subject who benefits from his interpretation. If so construed, ὑπό would nicely encapsulate the mediating position of rhapsodic ἑρμηνεία. Koller's 'representation' is very different from the notion of 'mimetic substitution' advocated by Sommerbrodt (1867:515), for whom ὑποκριτής denotes the actor's speaking 'for another' or 'as another'. Such performative reenactment—the assumption of another's identity—cannot reasonably pose as the equivalent of 'to explain', the acceptation of κρίνεσθαι that he rightly embraces. At any rate, it should be obvious from this discussion that determining fine semantic shades of preverbs and prepositions is difficult and not always useful, precisely because their sense is often contextually underdetermined and one may justify the meaning of the overall expression in divergent, but seemingly equally valid, ways. I doubt that all, or even most, native speakers, if pressed, would have agreed on how the discrete building blocks add up semantically to the final product. So, for example, I cannot rule out Patzer's view of ὑπομιμνήσκω, which takes ὑπό as "unterstützend" and the verb as "der Erinnerung von jd. aufhelfen" (Patzer 1970:645n1). But, by the same token, neither could he legitimately dismiss 'to bring up to someone's awareness something that has grown latent'. A bare statement of his competing proposal will not do to dismiss the alternative, and I can see no justification (other than Eustathios' unperceptive comment *ad* o 3, Stallbaum 1825–1826:2.89.31–32) for his claim that ἀναμιμνήσκω provides a semantic parallel. *LfgE* s.v. μιμνήσκω II guardedly states "ὑπο-: bes[timmter] Aspekt unklar" (column 220). Moreover, *pace* Patzer, there are undeniable instances of concrete, spatial motion where ὑπό denotes, if not 'up from under', at least the comparable 'out from under'. So, for example, ὑπαΐσσω with the genitive βωμοῦ at B 310: βωμοῦ ὑπαΐξας πρός ῥα πλατάνιστον ὄρουσεν, '[the serpent] darted from under the altar and rushed toward the plane tree' (*LfgE* s.v. ἀίσσω O offers the gloss "unter etwas hervor (c. gen.) bewegen"). And ὑπόδρα < *ὑπό-δρακ < *upo-dr̥k (Beekes 2010:2.1536 s.v.) makes no reference to eyebrows (it is *not* 'looking from under one's eyebrows') but simply means 'to have a glance from below' or 'to look out from below'. Just as looking from above connotes arrogance, so here looking from below connotes disapproval and anger. Other examples may be found in Schwyzer *GG* II.524–525.

44 Thus, Else writes in regard to o 170 that, although the reply is also a prophecy that expounds a sign, "the mental labor involved in the judgment (νοήσας, said of Menelaus) is clearly distinguished from the rendering of it (ὑποκρίνασθαι)" (Else 1959:82); and concerning M 228: "The

'To interpret', the acceptation both recommended by the etymology and clearly exampled in four of the six Homeric passages, follows naturally from the revelatory nature of Homeric poetry, which, as argued above,[45] must have been in its origin closely allied to mantic and oracular speech.[46] The meaning 'to answer (solemnly *vel sim.*)' developed diachronically from the manner in which the interpretation was rendered and from the social circumstances that attended this speech-act. Therefore, one must not look for 'to answer' in the etymology of ὑποκρίνεσθαι, which can only yield 'to interpret', but in the social pragmatics of the interpretive act—in the fact that this interpretation was usually rendered 'in

'interpretation' that a diviner might give would be a statement likewise. Moreover it would be a *response*, and a responsible one (verbindlich); for if it were given it would be given in an official context, in reply to a question put to him on behalf of the people" (83–84, his emphasis). To this, Ley (1983:21) adds: "Taken together, these close analyses are sufficient to remove Lesky's principal objection to the meaning 'answer'. Even if we cannot speak of a direct question to which a reply is given, the context makes clear that in each case an answer is given in response to a demand."

45 In chapter 8, pp. 219ff.

46 This very fact effectively disposes of Patzer's objection, often repeated, to the meaning 'to interpret' on the grounds that, where it occurs, it is only in the context of dreams, oracles, and omens ("Träume, Orakel und Vorzeichen," Patzer 1970:650). Just as Patzer does not argue for an unmarked sense of 'to answer', neither am I proposing a broad and unrestricted sense of 'to explain', as if one should expect ὑποκρίνεσθαι in the context of Alexandrian philology. It is worth remarking in connection with mantic and oracular speech that Schwyzer's definition of ὑποκρίνεσθαι—'seine Meinung aus der Herzenstiefe, aus der Verborgenheit hervorgeben' (*GG* II.525)—has been unfairly pressed to imply an altered state of mind that the Swiss scholar never intended and the evidence will not support. So Else (1959:84) observes that "the problem, though it may be posed by a dream or omen and require expert judgment, is never a metaphysical or theological problem but always a perfectly concrete and practical one"; and he adds that "[n]owhere have we found a hint of trance or deep meditation, of an interpretation ('Deutung') arising out of the depths of the soul. Nowhere did the situation have this oracular or mystical character" (85). Now, I do not embrace Schwyzer's formulation, neither its focus on "Meinung"—which suggests subjective opinion rather than objective explanation—nor its reference to "the depths of the heart," because mantic interpretation does not regard something that springs solely from the heart of the seer but 'real-world' σήματα like oracles, dreams, and omens. Applied to the context of epic performance, as ὑποκριτής of the will of Zeus the rhapsode regards the real world too, reenacting before his audience the defining past, making the present intelligible to them, and establishing the framework in which they are to construe the course of future events. In other words, he is the cultural agent through whose performative authority the worldview of the audience is shaped and divinely sanctioned. The message that the rhapsode's 'interpretation' embodies is the very speech of the Muses, a message that does not spring forth from his heart as his own. It is their inspiration that occasions his mediatory *hermēneia*. To refer merely to "the depths of the heart" unhelpfully suggests the interpreter as the sole source of his ὑπόκρισις. I have, on the other hand, no problem with the formulation "to bring forth out of concealment," so long as the object of the verbal action is not envisioned simply as one's personal opinion. Drawing attention to Else's less than fair reading of Schwyzer, Zucchelli (1962:17n26) observes that a rejection of symbolic or metaphysical meaning does not preclude "che si possa parlare di penetrazione delle cose divine da parte degli interpreti (θεοπρόποι appunto!)."

answer to' (or 'as a response to') a challenge, a request, or a situation that called for a pronouncement or the expression of a viewpoint. It might seem odd at first that 'to answer', a verb that is semantically less marked, could derive from the rather more semantically dense 'to interpret'. But this development can be readily exampled. Spanish uses the verb 'contestar' for 'to answer', a verb that derives immediately from *contestor*, which in classical Latin was used narrowly and technically for 'to call to witness' or, in the legal expression *litem contestari*, for 'to join issue'.[47] It is not right, then, to reduce to 'to answer' the contexts that point to 'to interpret': not only does this strategy fail to do justice to the text, it is etymologically indefensible. Neither is it right to ignore the contexts that clearly call for the meaning 'to answer'. We must accept that the semantic development from 'to interpret' to 'to answer' was already well under way, if not completed, during the poems' long formative period of recomposition. But instead of trying to derive the two acceptations as parallel synchronic outcomes from a common pool of semantic building blocks, we should recognize that 'to answer' derives diachronically from the social pragmatics of 'to interpret'.

It is time to return to the goal of this section, that is, to accounting for ὑποκριτής as the characteristic label of the actor of Attic drama. I am persuaded that neither 'to interpret' nor 'to answer' satisfactorily explains this application of the term. One must remember what scholars on all sides agree with: that, whatever its meaning, the label ὑποκριτής must refer to the defining nature of the actor's doings on stage, at least during the beginning phases of Attic drama.[48] Views that explained it with reference to a secondary facet of his work would not be persuasive. But 'to answer' makes the actor subservient to some other dramatic agent: either to the chorus or, as Else argued, to the (implausibly sounding) 'performing poet-as-non-actor.' But the back-and-forth suggested by 'to answer' hardly seems central enough to the actor *qua* actor to make this the plausible *differentia* that called for ὑποκριτής, not to mention that ancient reports tied the historical introduction of the actor to the addition of a tragic prologue and a *rhēsis*,[49] neither of which seems to have involved the

---

[47] *OLD* s.v. Cf. the English 'to contest'. The simplex *testor* was used more often. Its acceptations were 'to invoke', 'to appeal to', 'to entreat', 'to affirm solemnly', 'to certify', 'to attest', 'to give evidence of', and 'to make a will in the presence of witnesses' (see the *OLD* s.v.). These meanings too seem far from the semantically simpler 'to answer'.

[48] Else 1959: "The crux of the matter is that ὑποκριτής, with its agent suffix, implies a *function*, not a passing activity: not simply that the bearer of that title happened on occasion to answer a question, but that it was the essence and nature of his role to answer questions: in short, that he was characteristically and consistently—vom Fach—an answerer" (102, his emphasis).

[49] This follows from the joint testimony of Themistios *Oration* 26.316d and Diogenes Laertios 3.56. Cf. Pickard-Cambridge 1988:130–131 and Lesky 1956:470 and 1983:28.

requisite dialog.[50] And there is no historical support for making the introduction of the messenger, and not just the second actor generally, the pivotal stage in the development of drama. This presupposes an inversion of dramatic priority and is too clever by half. 'To interpret', on the other hand, suggests that, when the word ὑποκριτής was first applied to the actor in the late sixth and early fifth centuries, the dramatic plot was felt to be so obscure and problematic as to call for the introduction of a figure—the actor—that would offer an 'interpretation' or 'explanation' of it. This is implausible even if the actor is thought to interpret a divinely predetermined plot,[51] and downright improbable, if one conceived by the poet.[52] To this meaning one may also object that, whereas the prologue can reasonably be thought to set the stage—and, to that extent, to aid the understanding of the audience—it is primarily through the chorus that the poet conveys reaction and reflection.[53] The chorus, not the actor, might be said to carry out a (weak) version of ὑπόκρισις understood not as 'delivery' but as 'interpretation'.

The way out of this impasse, I suggest, is to grant the rhapsode the title ὑποκριτής in its original (sacral) interpretive function, i.e. as the mediating agent of the speech of the Muses and mediating revealer of the will of Zeus (βουλὴ Διός). After centuries of the rhapsode as the preeminent solo archaic performer, ὑποκριτής came to be associated with the pragmatics of his delivery— his 'stage presence,' so to speak—and it was emulatively applied to the budding trade of dramatic acting. The thematic kinship between epic and tragedy and the mimetic character of Homeric speeches facilitated this application. In other words, by the late sixth century, the notion of 'performer' was preeminent

---

50 Zucchelli 1962: "[L]'esistenza del prologo dinanzi ai canti corali e alle *rheseis* ci vieta di vedere nell'attore un risponditore al coro, giacché una tale denominazione egli avrebbe smentito proprio al suo primo apparire davanti al pubblico" (34); "Le *rheseis* e il prologo originari dovettero dunque aver forma in sé conclusa, essere cioè principalmente dei monologhi di carattere espositivo" (35). Else (1945:4) admits, as he must, that the prologue could not have been a reply to the chorus, but he leaves open whether the ῥῆσις was. Rudberg (1947:15) wonders if the latter may have been "Stichomythie." Cf. also the attempt by Patzer 1970:651 to dispose of this difficulty.

51 Cf. Else 1959:76 and Zucchelli 1962:38.

52 Cf. Zucchelli 1962:36-37. To argue that ὑποκρίνεσθαι means 'to interpret' and yet conceive of this 'interpretation' in the sense of 'performance'—i.e. according to our modern expression 'to interpret (a play or a role)'—amounts to ignoring the etymology of κρίνω and letting the modern sense beguile our critical judgment. For, as Patzer (1970:650) rightly observes, "κρι- 'entscheiden' [bezeichnet] immer einen intellektuellen Akt." Hence, etymology cannot yield in one step the final "schauspielerisch agieren," i.e. it cannot lead "zur bloßen Ausdruckskunst des Schauspielers." Patzer therefore suggests that Zucchelli may have been inadvertently misled by the Italian sense of 'interpretare', "das sowohl auf das 'Deuten' von Träumen, wie auf das philologische 'Erklären' und auch die künstlerische 'Darstellung' gehen kann" (1970:650).

53 Else 1959: "Finally, so far as interpretation of the myths appears in Aeschylean tragedy, it is more often put in the mouth of the chorus than of the actor" (78). Cf. Zucchelli 1962:39.

in the rhapsodic use and application of ὑποκριτής, and ὑποκρίνομαι was used simply for 'to perform'. The original meanings of '(inspired) interpreter' and 'to interpret (inspired communication)' could still be activated by an appropriate context (as Plato later proves), but it would not necessarily have been an overriding association in the mind of the average festival-goer. Therefore, the meaning responsible for the reuse of ὑποκριτής to designate the dramatic actor was neither 'to interpret' nor 'to answer' but simply 'to perform'.

This view of the matter forecloses attempts, however tempting, to explore the genesis of drama through the meaning of ὑποκριτής. If this is a regrettable loss, embracing it as a fact at least allows us to shed once for all the debilitating implausibilities that burden equally both alternatives, 'answerer' and 'interpreter'. Neither carries conviction, because their indefensible assumptions and untenable implications are not true to the essential nature of drama as a performance genre. By focusing narrowly on its genesis, they presuppose early stages in the art of tragedy in which the defining generic *differentiae* of drama are missing and the resulting reconstruction cannot be recognized as a dramatic performance.[54] Aristotle's famous theories notwithstanding,[55] what is drama without the actor? How cogent is it, after all, that the essential function of the actor could be determined by a thought experiment which posits an existing strictly choral genre, to which a new figure is added as 'answerer' or 'expounder'? But even if we embrace the *Gedankenexperiment* as legitimate and useful, the difficulties that follow in its wake make clear that in either alternative we are eventually faced with a dead end. It is better, then, to admit that we have no sure hold other than the hermeneutic function of the rhapsode as the agent who reveals and expounds the will of Zeus to his audience, and who, as such, is labeled ὁ ῥαψῳδὸς καὶ ὑποκριτής. In this regard, he stands in metapoetic continuity with the epic characters who appear as subjects of interpretive ὑποκρίνεσθαι—the very characters whom he reenacts and re-presents mimetically before his audience. In the nature of the case, the transference of his designation ὑποκριτής to the actor, whose professional practice developed in direct emulation of rhapsodic performance, remains conjectural. But it commends itself to us by accounting best for all the facts while avoiding the debilitating weaknesses of the competing explanations. It builds on the close relationship between the two corresponding performance domains that this book endeavors

---

[54] Fischl 1910: "Nihilominus plane absurdum est statum quendam tragoediae ratiocinando fingere, cui dramaticum elementum prorsus defuerit. Quod quidem faciunt illi, qui Thespidem anno 534 primum actorem invenisse eumque choro dithyrambico addidisse putant ita, ut actor aliquid narraret et inter narrationes eius chorus cantaret. Talis tragoedia narrativa nusquam exstat nisi in quorundam virorum doctorum mente" (6).

[55] Curtius (1866:149) suggests that the practice of glossing the dramatic ὑποκριτής as 'one who answers the chorus' must go back to peripatetic circles, perhaps even to Aristotle himself.

to establish and fully motivates the designation by reference to what is the indisputable essence of the dramatic art: its on-stage mimetic performance.

Bibliography

Abramowicz, S. 1938. "De Homeri cum Hesiodo certamine." *Eos* 39:477–492.

Accame, S. 1963. "L'invocazione alla Musa e la 'verità' in Omero e in Esiodo." *Rivista di filologia e di istruzione classica* 91:257–281, 385–415.

Adiego, I. J. 2007. *The Carian Language.* Leiden.

Adkins, A. W. H. 1972. "Truth, ΚΟΣΜΟΣ, and ΑΡΕΤΗ in the Homeric Poems." *Classical Quarterly* 22:5–18.

Ahlberg-Cornell, G. 1992. *Myth and Epos in Early Greek Art: Representation and Interpretation.* Jonsered.

Albini, U., ed. 1954. *Platone, Ione.* I Classici della Nuova Italia 42. Florence.

Allen, T. W. 1910. "The Text of the *Odyssey.*" *Papers of the British School at Rome* 5:3–85.

———. 1924. *Homer: The Origins and the Transmission.* Oxford.

Allen, T. W., W. R. Halliday, and E. E. Sikes, eds. 1936. *The Homeric Hymns.* 2nd ed. Oxford.

Allen, T. W. and E. E. Sikes, eds. 1904. *The* Homeric Hymns. New York.

Allen, W. S. 1973. *Accent and Rhythm: Prosodic Features of Latin and Greek.* Cambridge Studies in Linguistics 12. Cambridge.

Aloni, A. 1984. "L'intelligenza di Ipparco. Osservazioni sulla politica dei Pisistratidi." *Quaderni di storia* X 19:109–148.

Aly, W. 1914. "'Ραψῳδός." Real-Encyclopädie der classischen Altertumswissenschaft, 2. Reihe, Vol. 1.1, cols. 244–249. Stuttgart.

Amadasi Guzzo, M. G. 1987. "Iscrizioni semitiche di nord-ovest in contesti greci e italici (X–VII sec. a.C.)." *Dialoghi di archeologia* serie 3, 5:13–27.

Amandry, P. 1950. *La mantique apollinienne à Delphes: essai sur le fonctionnement de l'Oracle.* Paris.

———. 1980. "À propos des oracles delphiques de l'Archilocheion de Paros." In *ΣΤΗΛΗ: τόμος εἰς μνήμην Νικολάου Κοντολέοντος,* 242–248. Athens.

Amandry, P. and T. Spyropoulos. 1974. "Monuments chorégiques d'Orchomène de Béotie." *Bulletin de correspondance hellénique* 98:171–246.

Ameis, K. F. and C. Hentze. 1877. *Anhang zu Homers* Ilias *(Schulausgabe). I. Heft. Erläuterungen zu Gesang I–III.* Zweite berichtigte und mit Einleitungen versehene Auflage. Leipzig.

———, eds. 1889. *Homers* Odysee *für den Schulgebrauch erklärt. Zweiter Band, zweites Heft, Gesang XIX–XXIV.* 7th ed. Leipzig.

———, eds. 1905. *Homers* Ilias. *Zweiter Band, erstes Heft, Gesang XIII–XV.* 4th ed. Leipzig.

———, eds. 1906. *Homers* Ilias. *Erster Band, viertes Heft, Gesang X–XII.* 5th ed. Leipzig.

———, eds. 1920. *Homers* Odysee *für den Schulgebrauch erklärt. Erster Band, erstes Heft, Gesang I–VI.* Leipzig.

———, eds. 1930. *Homers* Ilias. *Erster Band, drittes Heft, Gesang VII–IX.* 5th ed. Leipzig.

Ameis, K. F., F. S. Lehrs, F. Dübner, U. C. Bussemaker, and A. Koechly, eds. 1862. *Poetae bucolici et didactici.* Paris.

Andersen, L. 1987. *Studies in Oracular Verses: Concordance to Delphic Responses in Hexameter.* Historisk-filosofiske Meddelelser 53. Copenhagen.

Aneziri, S. 2003. *Die Vereine der dionysischen Techniten im Kontext der hellenistischen Gesellschaft.* Historia Einzelschriften 163. Stuttgart.

———. 2009. "World Travellers: The Associations of Artists of Dionysus." In *Wandering Poets in Ancient Greek Culture: Travel, Locality and Pan-Hellenism,* ed. R. Hunter and I. Rutherford, 217–236 and bibliography at 270–306. Cambridge.

Angiolillo, S. 1997. *Arte e cultura nell'Atene di Pisistrato e dei Pisistratidi: Ὁ ἐπὶ Κρόνου βίος.* Bibliotheca archaeologica 4. Bari.

Apthorp, M. J. 1980. *The Manuscript Evidence for Interpolation in Homer.* Heidelberg.

Ardizzoni, A. 1953. *ΠΟΙΗΜΑ: Ricerche sulla teoria del linguaggio poetico nell'antichità.* Bari.

———. 1962. "Intorno a due definizioni antiche di ποίημα e ποίησις." *Rivista di filologia e di istruzione classica* 90:225–237.

Arena, R. 1989. "La documentazione epigrafica antica delle colonie greche della Magna Grecia." *Annali della Scuola Normale Superiore di Pisa* 19:15–48.

———, ed. 1994. *Iscrizioni greche arcaiche di Sicilia e Magna Grecia.* Pisa.

Armisen-Marchetti, M. 1979. "La notion d'imagination chez les anciens I: Les philosophes." *Pallas* 26:11–51.

———. 1980. "La notion d'imagination chez les anciens II: La rhétorique." *Pallas* 27:3–37.

Arnhart, L. 1981. *Aristotle on Political Reasoning: A Commentary on the* Rhetoric. DeKalb.

Arnott, P. D. 1967. "The Disassociated Actor." In *Greek Drama: A Collection of Festival Papers,* ed. G. L. Beede, 2:40–51. Vermillion.

Arrighetti, G. 1992. "Esiodo e le Muse: il dono della verità e la conquista della parola." *Athenaeum* 80:45–63. French translation in Blaise et al. 1996:53–70.

———, ed. 1998. *Esiodo, Opere: Testi introdotti, tradotti e commentati.* Biblioteca della Pléiade 27. Torino.

Asheri, D., ed. 1988. *Erodoto, Le storie*, Vol. 1. Italian translation of the Greek text by V. Antelami. Rome.

Asheri, D. and S. M. Medaglia, eds. 1990. *Erodoto, Le storie*, Vol. 3. Italian translation of the Greek text by A. Fraschetti. Rome.

Asper, M., ed. 2004. *Kallimachos: Werke. Griechisch und deutsch.* Darmstadt.

Assaël, J. 2000. "Poétique des étymologies de μοῦσα, la Muse." *Noesis* 4:11–53.

Austin, J. L. 1975. *How to Do Things with Words.* 2nd ed. Cambridge.

Austin, N. 1975. *Archery at the Dark of the Moon: Poetic Problems in Homer's* Odyssey. Berkeley.

Avezzù, G., ed. 1982. *Alcidamante, Orazioni e frammenti.* Bollettino dell'Istituto di Filologia Greca, Supplemento 6. Rome.

Bachmann, L., ed. 1928. *Anecdota graeca.* Leipzig.

Bader, F. 1972. "Éphore, pylore, théore: les composés grecs en -ορος, -ουρός, -ωρός." *Revue de philologie, de littérature et d'histoire anciennes* 46:192–237.

———. 1985. "Introduction à l'étude des mythes i.e. de la vision: les Cyclopes." In *Studi indoeuropei*, ed. E. Campanile. Testi linguistici 8:9–50. Pisa.

———. 1989. *La langue des dieux, l'hermétisme des poètes indo-européens.* Testi linguistici 14. Pisa.

———. 1990. "Le liage, la peausserie et les poètes-chanteurs Homère et Hèsiode: la racine *seh₂- 'lier'." *Bulletin de la Société de linguistique de Paris* 85:1–59.

———. 1997. "Voix Divines: Réflexions Métalinguistiques Indo-Européenes." In *Studies in Honor of Jaan Puhvel II: Mythology and Religion*, ed. J. Greppin and E. C. Polomé. Journal of Indo-European Studies 21:4–53. Washington, DC.

Baechle, N. 2007. *Metrical Constraint and the Interpretation of Style in the Tragic Trimeter.* Greek Studies: Interdisciplinary Approaches. Lanham.

Bagnall, R. S. 1985. *Currency and Inflation in Fourth-Century Egypt.* Bulletin of the American Society of Papyrologists, Supplements 5. Chico.

Bagnall, R. S. and P. J. Sijpesteijn. 1977. "Currency in the Fourth Century and the Date of *CPR* V 26." *Zeitschrift für Papyrologie und Epigraphik* 24:111–124.

Bakker, E. J. 1997. *Poetry in Speech: Orality and Homeric Discourse.* Ithaca.

———. 2002a. "The Making of History: Herodotus' *Historiēs Apodexis*." In *Brill's Companion to Herodotus*, ed. E. J. Bakker, I. J. F. de Jong, and H. van Wees, 3–32. Leiden.

———. 2002b. "Remembering the God's Arrival." *Arethusa* 35:63–81.

———. 2005. *Pointing at the Past: From Formula to Performance in Homeric Poetics.* Hellenic Studies 12. Washington, DC.

Balabanēs, P. 2007. "Δραματικοί αγώνες και αρχιτεκτονική στη νότια κλιτύ της Ακροπόλεως." In *The Panathenaic Games: Proceedings of an International Conference held at the University of Athens, May 11-12, 2004,* ed. O. Palagia and A. Chōremē-Spetsierē, 127–134. Oxford.

Bancroft, S. 1979. *Problems concerning the Archaic Acropolis at Athens.* PhD diss., Princeton University.

Barber, E. J. W. 1975. "The PIE Notion of Cloth and Clothing." *Journal of Indo-European Studies* 3:294–320.

———. 1991. *Prehistoric Textiles.* Princeton.

Barker, A., ed. 1984–1989. *Greek Musical Writings.* Cambridge Readings in the Literature of Music. 2 vols. (cited as 1 and 2). Cambridge.

Barnes, J., ed. 1994. *Aristotle* Posterior Analytics. Clarendon Aristotle Series. 2nd ed. Oxford.

Barnett, H. G. 1953. *Innovation: The Basis of Cultural Change.* New York.

Barnouw, J. 2002. *Propositional Perception:* Phantasia, *Predication and Sign in Plato, Aristotle and the Stoics.* Lanham.

Barrett, J. 2002. *Staged Narrative: Poetics and the Messenger in Greek Tragedy.* The Joan Palevsky Imprint in Classical Literature. Berkeley.

Bartol, K. 1992. "Where was Iambic Poetry Performed? Some Evidence from the Fourth Century B.C." *Classical Quarterly* 42:65–71.

Bartolotta, A. 2002. *L'occhio della mente: un'eredità indoeuropea nei poemi omerici.* Studi e Ricerche 2, Circolo Glottologico Palermitano. Palermo.

———. 2003. "Towards a Reconstruction of Indo-European Culture: Semantic Functions of IE *men-.*" In *Proceedings of the Fourteenth Annual UCLA Indo-European Conference. Los Angeles, November 8-9, 2002,* Journal of Indo-European Monograph Series 47, ed. K. Jones-Bley, M. E. Huld, A. Della Volpe, and M. Robbins Dexter, 37–62. Washington, DC.

———. 2004. "Un'isoglossa indoeuropea per ΜΑΝΤΙΣ?" In *Dialetti, dialettismi, generi letterari e funzioni sociali: atti del V Colloquio internazionale di linguistica greca (Milano, 12-13 settembre 2002),* ed. G. Rocca. Hellada: Collana di storia linguistica della Grecia e del Mediterraneo orientale diretta da Mario Negri 1:97–119. Alessandria.

———. 2005. "IE *weid- as a Root with Dual Subcategorization Features in the Homeric Poems." In *Universal Grammar in the Reconstruction of Ancient Languages,* ed. K. E. Kiss. Studies in Generative Grammar 83:265–293. Berlin.

Bartoněk, A. 1966. *Development of the Long-Vowel System in Ancient Greek Dialects.* Prague.

Bartoněk, A. and G. Buchner. 1995. "Die ältesten griechischen Inschriften von Pithekoussai (2. Hälfte des VIII. bis 1. Hälfte des VII. Jhs.)." *Die Sprache* 37:129–237.

Bassi, D. 1899. "Il nunzio nella tragedia greca." *Rivista di filologia e di istruzione classica* 27:50–89.

Baumbach, M., A. Petrovic, and I. Petrovic, eds. 2010. *Archaic and Classical Greek Epigram*. Cambridge.

Baumgarten, A. I. 1981. *The* Phoenician History *of Philo of Byblos*. Leiden.

Bayer, E. 1969 [1942]. *Demetrios Phalereus der Athener*. Darmstadt. First published as *Tübinger Beiträge zur Altertumswissenschaft* 36. Stuttgart.

Bazemore, G. B. 2002. "The Display and Viewing of the Syllabic Inscriptions of Rantidi Sanctuary." In *Script and Seal Use on Cyprus in the Bronze and Iron Ages*, ed. J. S. Smith, 155–212. Boston.

Bean, G. E., ed. 1965. *Side kitabeleri. The Inscriptions of Side*. Türk Tarih Kurumu yayınlarından, V seri, sa. 20. Researches in the Region of Antalya no. 5. Ankara.

Beazley, J. D. 1927. "Some Inscriptions on Vases." *American Journal of Archaeology* 31:345–353.

———. 1943. "Panathenaica." *American Journal of Archaeology* 47:441–465.

———. 1986. *The Development of Attic Black-Figure*. Sather Classical Lectures 24. Revised ed. Berkeley.

Bechtel, F. 1963. *Die griechischen Dialekte*. 3 vols. Reprint ed. Berlin.

Beekes, R. 2010. *Etymological Dictionary of Greek*. With the assistance of L. van Beek. Leiden.

Beissinger, M., J. Tylus, and S. Wofford, eds. 1999. *Epic Traditions in the Contemporary World: The Poetics of Community*. Berkeley.

Bélis, A. 1988. "Les termes grecs et latins désignant des spécialités musicales." *Revue de philologie, de littérature et d'histoire anciennes* 62:227–250.

Bentz, M. 1998. *Panathenäische Preisamphoren: Eine athenische Vasengattung und ihre Funktion vom 6.-4. Jahrhundert v. Chr.* Antike Kunst, Beihefte 18. Basel.

Benveniste, É. 1935. *Origines de la formation des noms en indo-européen*. Paris.

———. 1954a. "Études hittites et indo-européennes." *Bulletin de la Société de linguistique de Paris* 50:29–43.

———. 1954b. "Formes et sens de μνάομαι." In *Sprachgeschichte und Wortbedeutung: Festschrift Albert Debrunner*, 13–18. Bern.

———. 1969. *Le vocabulaire des institutions indo-européenes*. 2 vols. Paris.

Bergk, T. 1872–1887. *Griechische Literaturgeschichte*. Berlin.

Bergren, A. L. T. 1975. *The Etymology and Usage of ΠΕΙΡΑΡ in Early Greek Poetry: A Study in the Interrelationship of Metrics, Linguistics and Poetics*. American Classical Studies 2. New York.

Berve, H. 1926. *Das Alexanderreich auf prosopographischer Grundlage*. 2 vols.: *Darstellung* and *Prosopographie*. Munich.

Bethe, E. 1891. *Thebanische Heldenlieder: Untersuchungen über die Epen des thebanisch-argivischen Sagenkreises*. Leipzig.

———. 1901. "Thymeliker und Skeniker." *Hermes* 36:597–601.

Bile, M. 1988. "Les verbes de paiement en crétois." *Verbum* 11:233–244.

Bird, G. D. 2010. *Multitextuality in the Homeric* Iliad: *The Witness of Ptolemaic Papyri*. Hellenic Studies 43. Washington, DC.

Birondo, N. 2001. "Aristotle on Illusory Perception: *Phantasia* without *Phantasmata*." *Ancient Philosophy* 21:57–71.

Birt, T. 1882. *Das antike Buchwesen in seinem Verhältniss zur Litteratur (mit Beiträgen zur Textgeschichte des Theokrit, Catull, Properz, und anderer Autoren)*. Berlin.

Bizard, L. 1903. "Une inscription du sanctuaire d'Apollon Ptoïos trouvée à Larymna." *Bulletin de correspondance hellénique* 27:296–299.

———. 1920. "Fouilles du Ptoïon (1903): Inscriptions." *Bulletin de correspondance hellénique* 44:227–262.

Blackburn, S. H., P. J. Claus, J. B. Flueckiger, and S. S. Wadley, eds. 1989. *Oral Epics in India*. Berkeley.

Blaise, F., P. Judet de La Combe, and P. Rousseau, eds. 1996. *Le métier du mythe: lectures d'Hésiode*. Cahiers de philologie. Série Apparat critique 16. Villeneuve d'Ascq.

Blass, F. 1887. *Die attische Beredsamkeit*, Vol. 1. 3rd ed. Leipzig. Reprint ed. 1979. Hildesheim.

Blümel, W. 1982. *Die aiolischen Dialekte: Phonologie und Morphologie der inschriftlichen Texte aus generativer Sicht*. Ergänzungshefte zur Zeitschrift für vergleichende Sprachforschung 30. Göttingen.

Boeckh, A. 1858–1874. *August Boeckh's gesammelte kleine Schriften*. Leipzig.

Boegehold, A. L. 1996. "Group and Single Competitions at the Panathenaia." In Neils 1996:95–105.

Boersma, J. S. 1970. *Athenian Building Policy from 561/0 to 405/4 B.C.* Scripta Archaeologica Groningana 4. Groningen.

Boëthius, A. 1918. *Die Pythaïs: Studien zur Geschichte der Verbindungen zwischen Athen und Delphi*. Uppsala.

Böhme, R. 1983. *Peisistratos und sein homerischer Dichter*. Bern.

Boisacq, E. 1938. *Dictionnaire étymologique de la langue grecque, étudiée dans ses rapports avec les autres langues indo-européennes*. Paris.

Bollack, J., ed. 1990. *L'Oedipe Roi de Sophocle: le texte et ses interprétations*. Cahiers de philologie. Série les Textes 11–13b. Villeneuve d'Ascq.

———. 1994. "Une action de restauration culturelle. La place accordée aux tragiques par le décret de Lycurge." In *Mélanges Pierre Lévêque 8: Religion, anthropologie et société*, ed. M.-M. Mactoux and E. Geny. Annales Littéraires de l'Université de Besançon 499:13–24. Paris.

Bolling, G. M. 1916. "The Latest Expansions Of The *Iliad.*" *American Journal of Philology* 37:1–30.

———. 1925. *The External Evidence for Interpolation in Homer*. Oxford.

Bölte, F. 1907. "Rhapsodische Vortragskunst. Ein Beitrag zur Technik des homerischen Epos." *Neue Jahrbücher für das klassische Altertum* 19:571–581.

Bonelli, M., ed. 2007. *Timée le Sophiste*. Lexique platonicien. Philosophia Antiqua 108. Leiden.

Bonfante, G. 1979. "*Mente = Manía.*" *Rendiconti della Classe di Scienze morali, storiche e filologiche dell'Accademia dei Lincei* 34:325–327.

Bonfante, G. and L. Bonfante. 2002. *The Etruscan Language*. 2nd ed. Manchester.

Bonitz, H. 1867. "Ueber den Gebrauch von τε γάρ bei Aristoteles." *Zeitschrift für die österreichischen Gymnasien* 18:672–682.

———. 1870. *Index Aristotelicus*. Berlin.

Bonneau, D. 1981. "Proposition de renouvellement de bail d'une huilerie." In *Scritti in onore di Orsolina Montevecchi*, ed. E. Bresciani, G. Geraci, S. Pernigotti, and G. Susini, 49–57. Bologna.

Bonner, R. J. 1905. *Evidence in Athenian Courts*. Chicago.

———. 1927. *Lawyers and Litigants in Ancient Athens: The Genesis of the Legal Profession*. Chicago.

Bonnet, C. 1995. "Monde égéen." In *La civilisation phénicienne et punique*, ed. V. Krings, 646–662. Leiden.

Bons, J. A. E. 1998. "Schrijven is zilver, spreken is goud: Alcidamas en schriftelijke voorbereiding van redevoeringen." *Lampas* 31:219–241.

Borchhardt, J. 1972. *Homerische Helme: Helmformen der Ägäis in ihren Beziehungen zu orientalischen und europäischen Helmen in der Bronze- und frühen Eisenzeit*. Mainz am Rhein.

Bormann, K. 1971. *Parmenides: Untersuchungen zu den Fragmenten*. Hamburg.

Bossi, F. 1986. *Studi sul* Margite. Quaderni del Giornale filologico ferrarese 6. Ferrara.

Bothe, F. H., ed. 1832–1834. *Homeri carmina*. Leipzig: Hahn.

Bottin, L., ed. 2000. *Testi greci dialettali*. Studi, testi, documenti (Università di Padova. Dipartimento di scienze dell'antichità), nuova serie 4. Padova.

Bousquet, J. 1938. "Nouvelles inscriptions de Delphes." *Bulletin de correspondance hellénique* 62:332–369.

Boutsikas, E. 2011. "Astronomical Evidence for the Timing of the Panathenaia." *American Journal of Archaeology* 115:303–309.

Bowen, J. D. and R. P. Stockwell. 1955. "The Phonemic Interpretation of Semivowels in Spanish." *Language* 31:236–240.

Bowie, E. L. 1989. "Poetry and Poets in Asia and Achaia." In *The Greek Renaissance in the Roman Empire: Papers from the Tenth British Museum Classical Colloquium*, ed. S. Walker and A. Cameron. Bulletin Supplement 55:198–205. London.

———. 1990. "Geek Poetry in the Antonine Age." In *Antonine Literature*, ed. D. A. Russell, 53–90. Oxford.

———. 1993. "Lies, Fiction and Slander in Early Greek Poetry." In Gill and Wiseman 1993:1–37.

Boyd, T. W. 1994. "Where Ion Stood, What Ion Sang." *Harvard Studies in Classical Philology* 96:109–121.

———. 1995. "Libri Confusi." *Classical Journal* 91:35–45.

Braund, S. M. 1998. "Praise and Protreptic in Early Imperial Panegyric: Cicero, Seneca, Pliny." In *The Propaganda of Power: The Role of Panegyric in Late Antiquity*, ed M. Whitby. Mnemosyne, bibliotheca classica Batava. Suplementum 183:53–76. Leiden.

Bravo, B. 1980. "*Sulān*: Représailles et justice privée contre des étrangers dans les cités grecques." *Annali della Scuola Normale Superiore di Pisa* 10:675–987.

———. 2007. "Testi iniziatici da Olbia Pontica (VI e V sec. A.C.) e osservazioni su orfismo e religione civica." *Palamedes* 7:55–92.

Bremer, J. M. 1976. "Why Messenger-speeches?" In *Miscellanea tragica in honorem J. C. Kamerbeek*, ed. J. M. Bremer, S. L. Radt, and C. J. Ruijgh, 29–48. Amsterdam.

Bremmer, J. 1988. "Oedipus and the Greek Oedipus Complex." In *Interpretations of Greek Mythology*, ed. J. Bremmer, 41–59. London.

Brinton, A. 1988. "Pathos and the 'Appeal to Emotion': An Aristotelian Analysis." *History of Philosophy Quarterly* 5:207–219.

Bronner, S. J., ed. 1992. *Creativity and Tradition in Folklore: New Directions*. Logan.

Brown, H. L. 1914. *Extemporary Speech in Antiquity*. Menasha.

Brugmann, K. 1898. "Dissimilatorische Veränderung von ē im Griechischen und Aristarchs Regel über den homerischen Wechsel von η und ει vor Vokalen." *Indogermanische Forschungen* 9:153–178.

———. 1907. *Die distributiven und die kollektiven Numeralia der indogermanischen Sprachen*. Abhandlungen der Philologisch-Historischen Klasse der Königl. Sächsischen Gesellschaft der Wissenschaften, 25. Bd., No. 5. Leipzig.

———. 1911. "Griechische und lateinische Etymologien." *Indogermanische Forschungen* 28:354–379.

Brulé, P. 1996. "La cité en ses composantes: remarques sur les sacrifices et la procession des Panathénées." *Kernos* 9:37–63.

Bryce, T. 1986. *The Lycians in Literary and Epigraphic Sources.* Copenhagen.

Buchholz, H.-G. and J. Wiesner. 1977. *Kriegswesen, Teil 1: Schutzwaffen und Wehrbauten.* Archaeologia Homerica 1, E. Göttingen.

Buchner, G. 1970–1971. "Recent Work at Pithekoussai (1965–71)." *Archaeological Reports* 17:63–67.

———. 1972. "Pithecusa: Scavi e scoperte 1966–1971." In *Le genti non greche della Magna Grecia: Atti dell'undicesimo Convegno di studi sulla Magna Grecia, Taranto, 10-15 ottobre 1971,* 361–374. Naples.

Buchner, G. and D. Ridgway. 1993. *Pithekoussai I. La necropoli: Tombe 1-723 scavate dal 1952 al 1961. Testo.* Con appendici di C. F. Russo e F. de Salvia e contributi di J. Close-Brooks, F. R. Serra Ridgway e altri. Rome.

Buck, C. D. 1902. "Note on the Form Ἀγασιλή丂ου." *Revue archéologique* ser. 3, 40:47–48.

———. 1909. "An Archaic Boeotian Inscription." *Classical Philology* 4:76–80.

———. 1998 [1955]. *The Greek Dialects.* BCP Advanced Language Series. London.

Burckhardt, J. 1963. *History of Greek Culture.* New York.

Burgess, J. S. 1999. "Gilgamesh and Odysseus in the Otherworld." *Échos du monde classique/Classical Views* 18:171–210.

———. 2000. "Review of I. M. Shear, *Tales of Heroes. The Origins of the Homeric Texts.*" *Bryn Mawr Classical Review* 02.10.18.

———. 2001. *The Tradition of the Trojan War in Homer and the Epic Cycle.* Baltimore.

Burkert, W. 1979. "Kynaithos, Polycrates, and the *Homeric Hymn to Apollo.*" In *Arktouros: Hellenic Studies Presented to Bernard M. W. Knox on the Occasion of his 65th Birthday,* ed. G. W. Bowersock, W. Burkert, and M. C. Putnam, 53–62. Berlin. Also in Burkert 2001:189–197.

———. 1985 [1977]. *Greek Religion.* Cambridge, MA. First published as *Griechische Religion der archaischen und klassischen Epoche.* Stuttgart.

———. 1987. "The Making of Homer in the Sixth Century B.C.: Rhapsodes versus Stesichoros." In *Papers on the Amasis Painter and his World,* 43–62. Malibu. Also in Burkert 2001:198–217.

———. 1992. *The Orientalizing Revolution: Near Eastern Influence on Greek Culture in the Early Archaic Age.* Cambridge, MA.

———. 1994. "Griechische *Hymnoi.*" In *Hymnen der Alten Welt im Kulturvergleich,* ed. W. Burkert and F. Stolz. Orbis Biblicus et Orientalis 131:9–17. Freiburg.

———. 2001. *Kleine Schriften I: Homerica.* Hypomnemata Suppl. 2. Göttingen.

Burkett, J. W. 2011. *Aristotle,* Rhetoric *III: A Commentary.* PhD diss., Texas Christian University.

Busche, H. 1997. "Hat Phantasie nach Aristoteles eine interpretierende Funktion in der Wahrnehmung?" *Zeitschrift für Philosophische Forschung* 51:565–589.

———. 2003. "Die Aufgaben der phantasia nach Aristoteles." In *Imagination - Fiktion - Kreation: Das kulturschaffende Vermögen der Phantasie,* ed. T. Dewender and T. Welt, 23–43. Munich.

Buttmann, P. 1869. *Lexilogus: A Critical Examination of the Meaning and Etymology of Numerous Greek Works and Passages Intended Principally for Homer and Hesiod.* 6th ed. Translated and edited by Rev. J. R. Fishlake. London.

Buxton, R., ed. 1999. *From Myth to Reason? Studies in the Development of Greek Thought.* Oxford.

Bywater, I. 1888. "Aristotelia III." *Journal of Philosophy* 17:53–74.

———. 1909. *Aristotle* On the Art of Poetry: *A Revised Text, with Critical Introduction, Translation and Commentary.* Oxford.

Cairns, F. 1983. "A Herm from Histiaia with an Agonistic Epigram of the Fifth Century B.C." *Phoenix* 37:16–37.

———. 1984. "χρέματα δόκιμα: IG XII,9,1273 and 1274 and the Early Coinage of Eretria." *Zeitschrift für Papyrologie und Epigraphik* 54:145–155.

———. 1991. "The 'Laws of Eretria' (IG XII.9 1273 and 1274): Epigraphic, Legal, Historical, and Political Aspects." *Phoenix* 45:296–313.

Calderini, A. 1911. "ΟΜΗΡΙΣΤΑΙ." *Rendiconti dell'Istituto Lombardo* 44:713–723.

Calhoun, G. M. 1919. "Oral and Written Pleading in Athens." *Transactions of the American Philological Association* 50:177–193.

Calvet, M. and P. Roesch. 1966. "Les Sarapieia de Tanagra." *Revue archéologique* 1:297–332.

Cameron, A. 1990. "Isidore of Miletus and Hypatia: On the Editing of Mathematical Texts." *Greek, Roman, and Byzantine Studies* 31:103–127.

———. 1995. *Callimachus and His Critics.* Princeton.

Camp, J. M. 2001. *The Archaeology of Athens.* New Haven.

Campbell, D. A., ed. 1993. *Greek Lyric V: The New School of Poetry and Anonymous Songs and Hymns.* The Loeb Classical Library 144. Cambridge, MA.

Cantarella, R. 1930. "L'influsso degli attori su la tradizione dei testi tragici." *Rivista indo-greco-italica di filologia* 14:39–71. Also published in R. Cantarella, *Scritti minori sul teatro greco,* 135–174. 1970. Brescia.

Capps, E. 1900. "Studies in Greek Agonistic Inscriptions." *Transactions of the American Philological Association* 31:112–137.

———. 1903. *The Introduction of Comedy into the City Dionysia: A Chronological Study in Greek Literary History.* Printed from vol. VI:261–288 of the Decennial Publications of the University of Chicago, First Series. Chicago.

———. 1943. "Greek Inscriptions: A New Fragment of the List of Victors at the City Dionysia." *Hesperia* 12:1–11.

Capuccino, C. 2005. *Filosofi e rapsodi: testo, traduzione e commento dello* Ione *platonico.* Quaderni di 'Dianoia' 3. Bologna.

Carapanos, C. 1878. *Dodone et ses ruines.* Paris.

Carey, C. 1986. "Archilochus and Lycambes." *Classical Quarterly* 36:60–67.

———. 1994. "Rhetorical Means of Persuasion." In *Persuasion: Greek Rhetoric in Action*, ed. I. Worthington, 26–45. London.

———. 2007. "Epideictic Oratory." In *A Companion to Greek Rhetoric*, ed. I. Worthington, 236–252, with bibliography at 562–593. Oxford.

Carlisle, M. 1999. "Homeric Fictions: *Pseudo-* Words in Homer." In *Nine Essays on Homer*, ed. M. Carlisle and O. Levaniouk, 55–91. Lanham.

Carpenter, R. 1933. "The Antiquity of the Greek Alphabet." *American Journal of Archaeology* 37:8–29.

Carpenter, T. H. 1991. *Art and Myth in Ancient Greece: A Handbook.* London.

Carroll, M. 1895. *Aristotle's* Poetics, *C[hap]. XXV, in the Light of the Homeric Scholia.* PhD diss., Johns Hopkins University.

Carter, J. B. and S. P. Morris, eds. 1995. *The Ages of Homer: A Tribute to Emily Townsend Vermeule.* Austin.

Casali, R. F. 1995. "Patterns of Glide Formation in Niger-Congo: An Optimality Account." Paper presented at the January 1995 LSA meeting, New Orleans, January 7, 1995. Available at http://www.eric.ed.gov/PDFS/ED383215.pdf.

———. 1996. *Resolving Hiatus.* PhD diss., University of California, Los Angeles.

———. 1997. "Vowel Elision in Hiatus Contexts: Which Vowel Goes?" *Language* 73:493–533.

Casevitz, M. 1989. "À la recherche du kosmos. Là tout n'est qu'ordre et beauté." *Le Temps de la réflexion* 10:97–119.

———. 1992. "*Mantis*: le vrai sens." *Revue des études grecques* 105:1–18.

Cassio, A. C. 1991–1993. "La più antica iscrizione greca di Cuma e τίν(ν)υμαι in Omero." *Die Sprache* 35:187–207.

———. 1994. "Κεῖνος, καλλιστέφανος e la circolazione dell'epica in area euboica." In *Apoikia. I più antichi insediamenti greci in Occidente: funzioni e modi dell'organizzazione politica e sociale. Scritti in onore di Giorgio Buchner*, ed. B. d'Agostino and D. Ridgway, AION ArchStAnt 1:55–67. Naples.

————. 1998. "La cultura euboica e lo sviluppo dell'epica greca." In *Euboica: L'Eubea e la presenza euboica in Calcidica e in Occidente. Atti del Convegno Internazionale di Napoli 13-16 novembre 1996*, ed. M. Bats and B. d'Agostino, Collana CJB 16/ AION ArchStAnt, Quaderno 12, 11–29. Naples.

————. 1999. "Epica greca e scrittura tra VIII e VII secolo a.C.: Madrepatria e colonie d'Occidente." In *Scritture Mediterranee tra il IX e il VII secolo a.C.: Atti del Seminario, Università degli studi di Milano, Istituto di storia antica, 23-24 febbraio 1998*, ed. G. Bagnasco Gianni and F. Cordano, 67–84. Milan.

————. 2002. "Early Editions of the Greek Epics and Homeric Textual Criticism in the Sixth and Fifth Centuries B.C." In *Omero tremila anni doppo*, ed. F. Montanari, 105–136. Rome.

Cassio, A. C. and G. Cerri, eds. 1991. *L'Inno tra rituale e letteratura nel mondo antico: atti di un colloquio, Napoli 21-24 ottobre 1991*. Rome.

Càssola, F., ed. 1997. *Inni omerici*. Scrittori Greci e Latini, Fondazione Lorenzo Valla. 6th ed. Milan.

Caston, V. 1996. "Why Aristotle Needs Imagination." *Phronesis* 41:20–55.

Catenacci, C. 1993. "Il finale dell'*Odissea* e la *recensio* pisistratide dei poemi omerici." *Quaderni urbinati di cultura classica* 44:7–22.

Catford, J. C. 2001. *A Practical Introduction to Phonetics*. 2nd ed. Oxford.

Catlin, H. W. 1994. "Cyprus in the 11th Century B.C.: An End of a Beginning?" In *Cyprus in the 11th Century B.C.: Proceedings of the International Symposium Organized by the Archaeological Research Unit of the University of Cyprus and the Anastasios G. Leventis Foundation, Nicosia, 30-31 October 1993*, ed V. Karageorghis, 133–141. Nicosia.

Chadwick, H. M. and N. K. Chadwick. 1932-1940. *The Growth of Literature*. Cambridge.

Chadwick, J. 1973. "The Berezan Lead Letter." *Proceedings of the Cambridge Philological Society* 199:35–37.

Chadwick, N. K. 1942. *Poetry and Prophecy*. Cambridge.

Chandler, H. W. 1881. *A Practical Introduction to Greek Accentuation*. 2nd ed. Oxford.

Chaniotis, A. 1990. "Zur Frage der Spezialisierung im griechischen Theater des Hellenismus und der Kaiserzeit auf der Grundlage der neuen Prosopographie der dionysischen Techniten." *Ktema* 15:89–108.

Chantraine, P. 1933. *La formation des noms en grec ancien*. Collection linguistique 38. Paris.

————. 1999. *Dictionnaire étymologique de la langue grecque: histoire des mots*. New ed. with a supplement. Paris.

————. 2009. *Dictionnaire étymologique de la langue grecque: histoire des mots*. New ed. with a supplement. Paris.

Chatzēiōannou, K. 1971–2001. *Ἡ Ἀρχαία Κύπρος εἰς τὰς ἑλληνικὰς πηγάς.* Leukōsia.

Cherry, J. F. 1988. "Pastoralism and the Role of Animals in the Pre- and Protohistoric Economies of the Aegean." In Whittaker 1988:6–34.

Chitoran, I. 2002. "A Perception-Production Study of Romanian Diphthongs and Glide-Vowel Sequences." *Journal of the International Phonetic Association* 32:203–222.

Chrēstou, C. 1956. "Περὶ τὰ Σαραπιεῖα τῆς Τανάγρας." *Ἀρχαιολογικὴ ἐφημερίς* 95:34–72.

Cingano, E. 1985. "Clistene di Sicione, Erodoto e i poemi del Ciclo tebano." *Quaderni urbinati di cultura classica* 20:31–40.

———. 2005. "A Catalogue within a Catalogue: Helen's Suitors in the Hesiodic *Catalogue of Women* (frr. 196–204)." In *The Hesiodic* Catalogue of Women, ed. R. Hunter, 118–152. Cambridge.

Citelli, L., M. L. Gambato, and G. Russo, eds. 2001. *Ateneo* I deipnosofisti: i dotti a banchetto. Prima traduzione italiana commentata su progetto di Luciano Canfora. Introduzione di Christian Jacob. Rome.

Citti, V. 1966. "Le edizioni omeriche 'delle città'." *Vichiana* 3:3–43.

Clay, J. S. 1988. "What the Muses Sang: *Theogony* 1–115." *Greek, Roman, and Byzantine Studies* 29:323–333.

———. 1997. "The Homeric Hymns." In Morris and Powell 1997:489–507.

———. 2003. *Hesiod's Cosmos.* Cambridge.

Clayton, B. 2004. *A Penelopean Poetics: Reweaving the Feminine in Homer's* Odyssey. Greek Studies: Interdisciplinary Approaches. Lanham.

Clédat, L. 1917. *Manuel de phonétique et de morphologie historique du français.* Paris.

Cleland, L., G. Davies, and L. Llewellyn-Jones. 2007. *Greek and Roman Dress from A to Z.* The Ancient World from A to Z. London.

Clements, G. N. 1990. "The Role of the Sonority Cycle in Core Syllabification." In *Papers in Laboratory Phonology I: Between the Grammar and Physics of Speech,* ed. J. Kingston and M. E. Beckman, 283–333. Cambridge.

Clermont-Ganneau, C. 1880. *L'imagerie phénicienne et la mythologie iconologique chez les grecs.* Paris.

Clinton, K. 1994. "The Epidauria and the Arrival of Asclepius in Athens." In *Ancient Greek Cult Practice from the Epigraphical Evidence: Proceedings of the Second International Seminar on Ancient Greek Cult, organized by the Swedish Institute at Athens, 22-24 November 1991,* ed. R. Hägg. Acta Instituti Atheniensis Regni Sueciae, series in 8° 13:17–34. Stockholm.

Cobet, C. G. 1836. *Commentatio qua continetur prosopographia Xenophontea.* Leiden.

Coldstream, J. N. 1995. "Euboean Geometric Imports from the Acropolis of Pithekoussai." *Annual of the British School at Athens* 90:251–267.

———. 2003. *Geometric Greece (900–700 BC)*. 2nd ed. London.

Cole, T. 1983. "Archaic Truth." *Quaderni urbinati di cultura classica* 13:7–28.

Colin, G. 1905. *Le culte d'Apollon Pythien à Athènes*. Bibliothèque des Écoles françaises d'Athènes et de Rome 93. Paris.

Collard, C. 1970. "On the Tragedian Chaeremon." *Journal of Hellenic Studies* 90:22–34.

Collard, C. and M. Cropp, eds. 2008. *Euripides, Fragments: Oedipus-Chrysippus, Other Fragments*. The Loeb Classical Library 506. Cambridge, MA.

Collart, P. 1944. "Réjouissances, divertissements, et artistes de province dans l'Égypte Romaine." *Revue de philologie, de littérature et d'histoire anciennes* 18:134–152.

Collins, D. 2001a. "Homer and Rhapsodic Competition in Performance." *Oral Tradition* 16:129–167.

———. 2001b. "Improvisation in Rhapsodic Performance." *Helios* 28:11–27.

———. 2004. *Master of the Game: Competition and Performance in Greek Poetry*. Hellenic Studies Series 7. Washington, DC.

Colonna, G. 1995. "Etruschi a Pitecusa nell'orientalizzante antico." In *L'incidenza dell'antico. Studi in memoria di Ettore Lepore I*, ed. A. Storchi Marino, 325–342. Naples.

———. 2002. "Gli Etruschi nel Tirreno Meridionale: Tra Mitistoria, Storia e Archeologia." *Etruscan Studies* 9:191–206.

Combellack, F. M. 1987. "The λύσις ἐκ τῆς λέξεως." *American Journal of Philology* 108:202–219.

Compton, T. 1994. "The Herodotean Mantic Session at Delphi." *Rheinisches Museum* 137:217–223.

Conley, T. 1982. "Πάθη and πίστεις: Aristotle *Rhet.* II 2–11." *Hermes* 110:300–315.

Connor, W. R. 1989. "City Dionysia and Athenian Democracy." *Classica et mediaevalia* 40:7–32.

Consani, C. 2003. *Sillabe e sillabari fra competenza fonologica e pratica scrittoria*. Quaderni della Sezione di glottologia e linguistica. Dipartimento di studi medievali e moderni, Università degli studi "G. D'Annunzio" di Chieti. Supplementi 11. Alessandria.

———. 2008. "Aspects and Problems in Mycenaean and Cypriot Syllabification." In *Colloquium Romanum: atti del XII Colloquio internazionale di micenologia (Roma, 20–25 febbraio 2006)*, Vol. 1, ed. A. Sacconi, M. del Freo, L. Godart, and M. Negri, 151–158. Pisa.

Cook, A. B. 1902. "The Gong at Dodona." *Journal of Hellenic Studies* 22:5–28.

Cook, E. F. 1995. *The* Odyssey *in Athens: Myths of Cultural Origins*. Ithaca.

Cook, R. M. 1983. "Art and Epic in Archaic Greece." *Bulletin Antieke Beschaving* 58:1–10.

Cook, R. M. and A. G. Woodhead. 1959. "The Diffusion of the Greek Alphabet." *American Journal of Archaeology* 63:175–178.

Cooke, G. A., ed. 1903. *A Text-Book of North-Semitic Inscriptions: Moabite, Hebrew, Phoenician, Aramaic, Nabataean, Palmyrene, Jewish.* Oxford.

Cope, E. M. 1867. *An Introduction to Aristotle's* Rhetoric. London.

———, ed. 1877. *The* Rhetoric *of Aristotle with a Commentary.* Revised and edited by J. E. Sandys. 3 vols. (cited as 1, 2, and 3). Cambridge.

Cosenza, P. 1968. *Sensibilità percezione esperienza secondo Aristotele.* Istituto di Storia della Filosofia dell'Università di Napoli. Quaderni di filosofia 9. Naples.

Coseriu, E. 1981. *Principios de semántica estructural.* Biblioteca románica hispánica II. Estudios y ensayos 259. 2nd ed. Madrid.

Coseriu, E. and H. Geckeler. 1981. *Trends in Structural Semantics.* Tübinger Beiträge zur Linguistik 158. Tübingen.

Cougny, E., ed. 1890. *Epigrammatum anthologia palatina cum Planudeis et appendice nova epigrammatum veterum ex libris et marmoribus ductorum,* Vol. 3. Paris.

Coxon, A. H., ed. 1986. *The Fragments of Parmenides. Phronesis* Suppl. 3. Assen.

Crahay, R. 1956. *La littérature oraculaire chez Hérodote.* Paris.

Crawford, M. H. 1975. "Finance, Coinage and Money from the Severans to Constantine." In *Aufstieg und Niedergang der römischen Welt* II.2:560–593. Berlin.

Crawford, M. H. and J. M. Reynolds. 1979. "The Aezani Copy of the Prices Edict." *Zeitschrift für Papyrologie und Epigraphik* 34:163–210.

Crespo, E. 1977. "La cronología relativa de la metátesis de cantidad en jónico-ático." *Cuadernos de filología clásica* 12:187–219.

———. 1999. "Cronología de los segundos alargamientos compensatorios en jónico-ático." In *Katà Diálekton: Atti del III Colloquio Internazionale di Dialettologia Greca,* ed. A. C. Cassio, 161–186. Naples.

Crielaard, J. P., ed. 1995. *Homeric Questions: Essays in Philology, Ancient History and Archaeology, Including the Papers of a Conference Organized by the Netherlands Institute at Athens (15 May 1993).* Publications of the Netherlands Institute at Athens 2. Amsterdam.

———. 1996. "How the West Was Won: Euboeans vs. Phoenicians." In *Die Akten des Internationalen Kolloquiums 'Interactions in the Iron Age: Phoenicians, Greeks and the Indigenous Peoples of the Western Mediterranean' in Amsterdam am 26. und 27. März 1992,* ed G. Niemeyer. Hamburger Beiträge zur Archäologie 19–20:235–260. Mainz.

Cristofani, M. 1972. "Sull'origine e la diffusione dell'alfabeto etrusco." In *Aufstieg und Niedergang der römischen Welt* I.2:466–489. Berlin.

———. 1975. "Il 'dono' nell'Etruria arcaica." *La Parola del passato* 30:132–152.

Cross, F. M. 1954. "The Evolution of the Proto-Canaanite Alphabet." *Bulletin of the American Schools of Oriental Research* 134:15–24.

Crusius, O. 1895. "Zur Kritik der antiken Ansichten über die Echtheit homerischer Dichtungen." *Philologus* 54:710–734.

———, ed. 1914. *Herondae mimiambi.* Bibliotheca Scriptorum Graecorum et Romanorum Teubneriana. Leipzig.

Csapo, E., A. W. Johnston, and D. Geagan. 2000. "The Iron Age Inscriptions." In *Kommos IV. The Greek Sanctuary*, ed. J. W. Shaw and M. C. Shaw, 101–134. Princeton.

Csapo, E. and W. J. Slater. 1994. *The Context of Ancient Drama.* Ann Arbor.

Cucchiarelli, A. 2006. "In difesa degli 'Omeristi'. Nota testuale a Petronio, *Satyr.* 59, 3." *Materiali e discussioni per l'analisi dei testi classici* 57:241–245.

Culverhouse, F. Z. 2010. *Plato's* Hippias Minor: *A Translation and Critical Commentary.* PhD diss., Claremont Graduate University.

Cunliffe, R. J. 1963. *A Lexicon of the Homeric Dialect.* Norman.

Curtius, G. 1866. "ὑποκριτής." *Berichte über die Verhandlungen der Königlich Sächsischen Gesellschaft der Wissenschaften zu Leipzig, Philologisch-historische Classe* 18:148–154. Öffentliche Sitzung am 1. Juli 1866. Herr Curtius las über zwei Kunstausdrücke der griechischen Litteraturgeschichte, pp. 141–154.

———. 1868. "Ueber die Bedeutung des Wortes ὑποκριτής." *Rheinisches Museum* 23:255–261.

Dain, A. and P. Mazon, eds. 1955–1960. *Sophocle.* Collection des universités de France. Paris.

Dale, A. M. 1963. "Stichos and Stanza." *Classical Quarterly* 13:46–50.

D'Alessio, G. B., ed. 1996. *Callimaco:* Aitia. Giambi. Frammenti elegiaci minori. Frammenti di sede incerta. Milan.

———. 2007. "῏Ην ἰδού: *Ecce satyri* (Pratina, *PMG* 708 = *TrGF* 4 F3)." In *Dalla lirica corale alla poesia drammatica: forme e funzioni del canto corale nella tragedia e nella commedia greca*, ed. F. Perusino and M. Colantonio. Testimonianze sulla cultura greca 5:95–128. Pisa.

Dana, M. 2004. "Lettre sur plomb d'Apatorios à Léanax. Un document archaïque d'Olbia du Pont." *Zeitschrift für Papyrologie und Epigraphik* 148:1–14.

Daux, G. 1936. *Delphes au IIe et au Ier siècle, depuis l'abaissement de l'Étolie jusqu'à la paix romaine, 191-31 av. J.-C.* Bibliothèque des Écoles françaises d'Athènes et de Rome 140. Paris.

Davies, J. K. 1971. *Athenian Propertied Families, 600-300 B.C.* Oxford.

Davison, J. A. 1955a. "Peisistratus and Homer." *Transactions of the American Philological Association* 86:1–21.

———. 1955b. "Quotations and Allusions in Early Greek Literature."
Eranos 53:125–140.

———. 1958. "Notes on the Panathenaia." *Journal of Hellenic Studies* 78:23–41.

———. 1968. *From Archilochus to Pindar: Papers on Greek Literature of the Archaic Period*. London.

Dawe, R. D., ed. 1993. *The* Odyssey: *Translation and Analysis*. Sussex.

De Boer, J. Z. and J. R. Hale. 2000. "The Geological Origins of the Oracle at Delphi, Greece." In *The Archaeology of Geological Catastrophes*, ed. W. J. McGuire, D. R. Griffiths, P. L. Hancock, and I. S. Stewart. Special Publications 171:399–412. London.

———. 2002. "Was She Really Stoned? The Oracle of Delphi." *Archaeology Odyssey* 5.6:47–53, 58–59.

De Boer, J. Z., J. R. Hale, and J. Chanton. 2001. "New Evidence for the Geological Origins of the Ancient Delphic Oracle (Greece)." *Geology* 29.8:707–710.

Debrunner, A. 1917. *Griechische Wortbildungslehre*. Heidelberg.

———. 1956–1957. "Δέγμενος, ἑσπόμενος, ἄρχμενος." In *Μνήμης χάριν: Gedenkschrift Paul Kretschmer*, ed. H. Kronasser, 1.77–84. Vienna.

De Gennaro, R. and A. Santoriello. 1994. "Dodona (con premessa di F. D'Andria)." *Studi di Antichità* 7:383–408.

De Jong, I. J. F. 1991. *Narrative in Drama: The Art of the Euripidean Messenger-speech*. Mnemosyne, bibliotheca classica Batava. Supplementum 116. Leiden.

Del Barrio Vega, M. L. 1987. *El dialecto de Eubea*. PhD diss., Universidad Complutense de Madrid.

———. 1991. *El dialecto euboico*. Madrid.

Della Seta, A. 1910. "Ἐξ ὑποβολῆς e ἐξ ὑπολήψεως." In *Saggi di storia antica e di archeologia*, 333–351. Rome.

Del Rincón Sánchez, F. M. 2007. *Trágicos menores del siglo V a.C. (de Tespis a Neofrón): Estudio filológico y literario*. Tesis doctorales *cum laude*, Serie L (Literatura) 45. Madrid.

Demand, N. 1975. "Plato and the Painters." *Phoenix* 29:1–20.

De Martino, F. 1983. "Cineto, Testoride e l'eredità di Omero." *Quaderni urbinati di cultura classica* 14:155–161.

Dempsey, T. 1918. *The Delphic Oracle: Its Early History, Influence and Fall*. Oxford.

Denniston, J. D. 1954. *The Greek Particles*. 2nd ed. Oxford.

Descoeudres, J. P. and R. Kearsley. 1983. "Greek Pottery at Veii: Another Look." *Annual of the British School at Athens* 78:9–53.

Des Places, E. 1969. *La Religion grecque: dieux, cultes, rites, et sentiments religieux dans la Grèce antique*. Paris.

Detienne, M. 1996 [1967]. *The Masters of Truth in Archaic Greece*. New York. First published as *Les maîtres de vérité dans la Grèce archaïque*. Paris.

Detienne, M. and J.-P. Vernant. 1989 [1979]. *The Cuisine of Sacrifice among the Greeks.* Chicago. First published as *La cuisine du sacrifice en pays grec.* Paris.

Dettori, E. 1996. "Testi 'orfici' dalla Magna Grecia al Mar Nero." *La Parola del passato* 51:292–310.

Deubner, L. 1929. "Die viersaitige Leier." *Mitteilungen des Deutschen Archäologischen Instituts (Athen. Abt.)* 54:194–200.

Devine, A. M. and L. D. Stephens. 1994. *The Prosody of Greek Speech.* New York.

Devlin, N. G. 1995. *The Hymn in Greek Literature: Studies in Form and Content.* PhD diss., Oxford University.

De Vries, S. J. 1985. *1 Kings.* Word Biblical Commentary 12. Waco.

Dickey, E. 2007. *Ancient Greek Scholarship: A Guide to Finding, Reading, and Understanding Scholia, Commentaries, Lexica, and Grammatical Treatises, from their Beginnings to the Byzantine Period.* American Philological Association Classical Resources Series 7. Oxford.

Dickin, M. 2009. *A Vehicle for Performance: Acting the Messenger in Greek Tragedy.* Lanham.

Diels, H., ed. 1897. *Parmenides' Lehrgedicht.* Berlin.

Dieterle, M. 1999. *Dodona: religionsgeschichtliche und historische Untersuchungen zu Entstehung und Entwicklung des Zeus-Heiligtums.* PhD diss., Universität Hamburg. http://www.sub.uni-hamburg.de/opus/volltexte/1999/20/.

Di Gregorio, L. 1967. *Le scene d'annuncio nella tragedia greca.* Pubblicazioni dell'Università cattolica del Sacro Cuore. Saggi e ricerche. Ser. III: Scienze filologiche e letteratura 6. Milan.

———, ed. 1975. *Scholia vetera in Hesiodi* Theogoniam. Milan.

Diller, H. 1955. "Probleme des platonischen *Ion.*" *Hermes* 83:171–187.

———. 1956. "Der vorphilosophische Gebrauch von ΚΟΣΜΟΣ und ΚΟΣΜΕΙΝ." In *Festschrift Bruno Snell zum 60. Geburtstag am 18. Juni 1956 von Freunden und Schülern überreicht,* 47–60. Munich.

Di Marco, M. 1973–1974. "Osservazioni sull'iporchema." *Helikon* 13–14:326–348.

Di Napoli, V. 2004. "Review of Θ. Παπαθανασόπουλος, *Το Τρόπαιο.*" *Annuario della Scuola Archeologica di Atene e delle Missioni Italiane in Oriente* 82, ser. III.4, II:593–600.

Dindorf, W. 1870. *Lexicon Sophocleum.* Leipzig.

———, ed. 1875–1888. *Scholia graeca in Homeri* Iliadem *ex codicibus aucta et emendata.* 4 vols. Oxford.

Dodds, E. R. 1951. *The Greeks and the Irrational.* Berkeley.

Doederlein, L., ed. 1863–1864. *Homeri* Ilias. Leipzig.

Donaldson, J. W. 1860. *The Theatre of the Greeks: A Treatise on the History and Exhibition of the Greek Drama.* 7th ed. London.

Donlan, W. 1999. *The Aristocratic Ideal and Selected Papers.* Wauconda.

Donner, H. and W. Röllig, eds. 1962–1964. *Kanaanäische und Aramäische Inschriften*. Wiesbaden.

Dorter, K. 1973. "The *Ion*: Plato's Characterization of Art." *Journal of Aesthetics and Art Criticism* 32:65–78.

Dougherty, C. 1991. "Phemius' Last Stand: The Impact of Occasion on Tradition in the *Odyssey*." *Oral Tradition* 6:93–103.

———. 2003. "The Aristonothos Krater: Competing Stories of Conflict and Collaboration." In *The Cultures within Ancient Greek Culture: Contact, Conflict, Collaboration*, ed. C. Dougherty and L. Kurke, 35–56, with bibliography at 257–282. Cambridge.

Dougherty, C. and L. Kurke, eds. 1998. *Cultural Poetics in Archaic Greece: Cult, Performance, Politics*. New York.

Dover, K. J., ed. 1968a. *Aristophanes* Clouds. Oxford.

———. 1968b. *Lysias and the* Corpus Lysiacum. Sather Classical Lectures 39. Berkeley.

———, ed. 1993. *Aristophanes* Frogs. Oxford.

Dow, J. 2009. "Feeling Fantastic? Emotions and Appearances in Aristotle." *Oxford Studies in Ancient Philosophy* 37:143–175.

Dow, S. and A. H. Travis. 1943. "Demetrios of Phaleron and His Lawgiving." *Hesperia* 12:144–165.

Drerup, E., ed. 1901. *Untersuchungen zur älteren griechischen Prosaliteratur. Wilhelm v. Christ zum 70. Geburtstag dargebracht.* Jahrbücher für classische Philologie, Suppl. Bd. XXVII.2–3. Leipzig. Reprint ed. 1974. Hildesheim.

Driessen, J. 2008. "Chronology of the Linear B Texts." In *A Companion to Linear B: Mycenaean Greek Texts and their World*, ed. Y. Duhoux and A. Morpurgo Davies, 69–79. Leuven.

Driver, G. R. 1976. *Semitic Writing: From Pictograph to Alphabet*. 2nd ed. London.

Dubois, L., ed. 1989. *Inscriptions grecques dialectales de Sicile: Contribution à l'étude du vocabulaire grec colonial*. Collection de l'École Française de Rome 119. Rome.

———, ed. 1995. *Inscriptions grecques dialectales de Grande Grèce I. Colonies eubéennes. Colonies ioniennes. Emporia*. Hautes Études du Monde Gréco-Romain 21. Geneva.

———, ed. 1996. *Inscriptions grecques dialectales d'Olbia du Pont*. Hautes Études du Monde Gréco-Romain 22. Geneva.

Dufour, M. and A. Wartelle, eds. 1973. *Aristote* Rhétorique, Vol. 3. Paris.

Dunbar, N. 1995. *Aristophanes* Birds. Oxford.

Duplouy, A. 2006. *Le prestige des élites: Recherches sur les modes de reconnaissance sociale en Grèce entre les Xe et Ve siècles avant J.-C.* Paris.

Dupont-Roc, R. and J. Lallot, eds. 1980. *Aristote, La poétique*. Paris.

Durante, M. 1968a [1958]. *"Epea pteróenta.* Die Rede als 'Weg' in griechischen und vedischen Bildern." In Schmitt 1968:242–260. First published as *"Epea pteroenta.* La parola come 'cammino' in immagini greche e vediche." *Rendiconti della Classe di Scienze morali, storiche e filologiche dell'Accademia dei Lincei* 13:3–14.

———. 1968b [1960]. "Untersuchungen zur Vorgeschichte der griechischen Dichtersprache. Die Terminologie für das dichterische Schaffen." In Schmitt 1968:261–290. First published as "Ricerche sulla preistoria della lingua poetica greca. La terminologia relativa alla creazione poetica." *Rendiconti della Classe di Scienze morali, storiche e filologiche dell'Accademia dei Lincei* 15:231–249.

———. 1976. *Sulla preistoria della tradizione poetica greca.* Incunabula graeca 64. Rome.

Durbec, Y. 2003. "Callimaque, *Aitia* fr. 26 Pfeiffer (= 30 Massimilla) et la tradition rhapsodique." *Aevum antiquum* 3:531–538.

Easterling, P. and E. Hall, eds. 2002. *Greek and Roman Actors: Aspects of an Ancient Profession.* Cambridge.

Edmunds, L. 1984. "The Sphinx in the Oedipus Legend." In *Oedipus: A Folklore Casebook,* ed. L. Edmunds and A. Dundes. Garland Folklore Casebooks 4:147–173. New York.

Edwards, A. T. 1988. "ΚΛΕΟΣ ΑΦΘΙΤΟΝ and Oral Theory." *Classical Quarterly* 38:25–30.

Edwards, G. P. 1971. *The Language of Hesiod in its Traditional Context.* Publications of the Philological Society 22. Oxford.

Edwards, M. W. 1991. *The* Iliad*: A Commentary,* Vol. 5: books 17–20. Cambridge.

Effenterre, H. van. 1985. *La cité grecque: Des origines à la défaite de Marathon.* Paris.

Effenterre, H. van. and F. Ruzé. 1994–1995. *Nomima: Recueil d'inscriptions politiques et juridiques de l'archaïsme grec.* Rome.

Egan, R. B. 2007. "Ἀναβολή, Ἀναβάλλομαι etc.: Technical Terms in Music and Poetics." *Glotta* 82:55–69.

Egetmeyer, M. 1998. "Die Silbenschriften Zyperns." In *The History of the Hellenic Language and Writing from the Second to the First Millennium B.C.: Break or Continuity?,* 233–257. Altenburg.

Eitrem, S. and L. Amundsen, eds. 1936. *Papyri Osloenses, Fasc. III.* Oslo.

Elmer, D. F. 2013. *The Poetics of Consent: Collective Decision Making and the* Iliad. Baltimore.

Else, G. F. 1939. "Aristotle and Satyr-Play. I." *Transactions of the American Philological Association* 70:139–157.

———. 1945. "The Case of the Third Actor." *Transactions of the American Philological Association* 76:1–10.

———. 1957a. *Aristotle's* Poetics: *The Argument.* Cambridge, MA.

———. 1957b. "The Origin of ΤΡΑΓΩΙΔΙΑ." *Hermes* 85:17–46.

———. 1959. "ΥΠΟΚΡΙΤΗΣ." *Wiener Studien* 72:75–107.

———. 1965. *The Origin and Early Form of Greek Tragedy.* Martin Classical Lectures 20. Cambridge, MA.

Erbse, H., ed. 1969–1988. *Scholia graeca in Homeri* Iliadem *(scholia vetera).* 7 vols. Berlin.

Ernesti, J. A., ed. 1761. *Callimachi hymni, epigrammata et fragmenta.* Leiden.

Ernout, A. and A. Meillet, eds. 1985. *Dictionnaire étymologique de la langue latine: Histoire des mots.* 4th ed. Paris.

Etiope, G., G. Papatheodorou, D. Christodoulou, M. Geraga, and P. Favali. 2006. "The Geological Links of the Ancient Delphic Oracle (Greece): A Reappraisal of Natural Gas Occurrence and Origin." *Geology* 34.10:821–824.

Eucken, C. 1983. *Isokrates: Seine Positionen in der Auseinandersetzung mit den zeitgenössischen Philosophen.* Untersuchungen zur antiken Literatur und Geschichte 19. Berlin.

Evans, A. 1928. *The Palace of Minos*, Vol. II.2. London.

Evans, J. A. S. 1982. "The Oracle of the 'Wooden Wall'." *Classical Journal* 78:24–29.

Evelyn-White, H. G., ed. 1914. *Hesiod, the* Homeric Hymns *and* Homerica. The Loeb Classical Library 57. Cambridge, MA.

Everson, S. 1997. *Aristotle on Perception.* New York.

Fachner, J. 2006. "Music and Altered States of Consciousness: An Overview." In *Music and Altered States: Consciousness, Transcendence, Therapy and Addiction*, ed. D. Aldridge and J. Fachner, 15–37. London.

Falkner, T. 2002. "Scholars versus Actors: Text and Performance in the Greek Tragic Scholia." In Easterling and Hall 2002:342–361.

Farnell, L. R. 1896–1909. *The Cults of the Greek States.* Oxford.

———, ed. 1930–1932. *The Works of Pindar Translated with Literary and Critical Commentaries.* London.

Fattori, M. and M. Bianchi, eds. 1988. Phantasia-imaginatio: *Vᵒ Colloquio Internazionale, Roma 9-11 gennaio 1986.* Rome.

Fauth, W. 1963. "Pythia." Real-Encyclopädie der classischen Altertumswissenschaft, Vol. 47, cols. 515–547. Stuttgart.

Feeney, D. C. 1991. *The Gods in Epic: Poets and Critics of the Classical Tradition.* Oxford.

Fein, S. 1994. *Die Beziehungen der Kaiser Trajan und Hadrian zu den litterati.* Beiträge zur Altertumskunde 26. Stuttgart.

Feissel, D. 1981. "Trois aspects de l'influence du latin sur le grec tardif." *Travaux et mémoires du Centre de recherche d'histoire et civilisation byzantines* 8:135–150.

Ferguson, W. S. 1974 [1911]. *Hellenistic Athens*. Reprint ed. Chicago.

Ferrara, S. 2010. "Mycenaean Texts: The Linear B Tablets." In *A Companion to the Ancient Greek Language*, ed. E. J. Bakker, 11–24. Malden.

Feyel, M. 1942. *Contribution à l'épigraphie béotienne*. Publications de la Faculté des Lettres de l'Université de Strasbourg 95. Le Puy.

Figueira, T. J. 1985. "Chronological Table: Archaic Megara, 800–500 BC." In *Theognis of Megara: Poetry and the Polis*, ed. T. J. Figueira and G. Nagy, 261–303. Baltimore.

Fileni, M. G. 1987. *Senocrito di Locri e Pindaro (Fr. 140b Sn.-Maehl.)*. Biblioteca di Quaderni Urbinati di Cultura Classica 2. Rome.

Finkelberg, M. 1986. "Is ΚΛΕΟΣ ΑΦΘΙΤΟΝ a Homeric Formula?" *Classical Quarterly* 36:1–5.

———. 1987. "Homer's View of the Epic Narrative: Some Formulaic Evidence." *Classical Philology* 82:135–138.

———. 1988. "Ajax's Entry in the Hesiodic *Catalogue of Women*." *Classical Quarterly* 38:31–41.

———. 1990. "A Creative Oral Poet and the Muse." *American Journal of Philology* 111:293–303.

———. 1998. *The Birth of Literary Fiction in Ancient Greece*. Oxford.

Finkelberg, M. and G. Stroumsa, eds. 2003. *Homer, the Bible, and Beyond: Literary and Religious Canons in the Ancient World*. Jerusalem Studies in Relgion and Culture 2. Leiden.

Finnegan, R. 1992 [1977]. *Oral Poetry: Its Nature, Significance and Social Context*. 1st Midland Book ed. Bloomington.

Fischl, J. 1910. *De nuntiis tragicis*. Dissertationes philologae Vindobonenses 10. Vienna.

Fittschen, K. 1969. *Untersuchungen zum Beginn der Sagendarstellungen bei den Griechen*. Berlin.

Flacelière, R. 1938. "Le fonctionnement de l'oracle de Delphes au temps de Plutarque." In *Études d'archéologie grecque*. Annales de l'École des Hautes Études de Gand 2:69–107, with plates I–IV. Gand.

———. 1950. "Le délire de la Pythie est-il une légende?" *Revue des études anciennes* 52:306–324.

Flashar, H. 1958. *Der Dialog* Ion *als Zeugnis platonischer Philosophie*. Deutsche Akademie der Wissenschaften zu Berlin. Schriften der Sektion für Altertumswissenschaft 14. Berlin.

Focke, F. 1943. *Die Odyssee.* Tübinger Beiträge zur Altertumswissenschaft 37. Stuttgart.

Foley, H. P., ed. 1994. *The Homeric* Hymn to Demeter: *Translation, Commentary, and Interpretive Essays.* Princeton.

Foley, J. M. 1995. *The Singer of Tales in Performance.* Bloomington.

Fontenrose, J. 1978. *The Delphic Oracle.* Berkeley.

———. 1988. *Didyma: Apollo's Oracle, Cult, and Companions.* Berkeley.

Ford, A. 1988. "The Classical Definition of ΡΑΨΩΙΔΙΑ." *Classical Philology* 83:300–307.

———. 1992. *Homer: The Poetry of the Past.* Ithaca.

———. 1997. "The Inland Ship: Problems in the Performance and Reception of Homeric Epic." In *Written Voices, Spoken Signs: Tradition, Performance, and the Epic Text,* ed. E. Bakker and A. Kahane, 83–109. Cambridge, MA.

———. 1999. "Performing Interpretation: Early Allegorical Exegesis of Homer." In Beissinger et al. 1999:33–53.

———. 2002. *The Origins of Criticism: Literary Culture and Poetic Theory in Classical Greece.* Princeton.

Forderer, M. 1960. *Zum Homerischen* Margites. Amsterdam.

Formigari, L., G. Casertano, and I. Cubeddu, eds. 1999. *Imago in phantasia depicta.* Rome.

Forsén, B. and G. Stanton, eds. 1996. *The Pnyx in the History of Athens: Proceedings of an International Colloquium Organized by the Finnish Institute at Athens, 7-9 October, 1994.* Papers and Monographs of the Finnish Institute at Athens 2. Helsinki. Bibliography at 117–129 and figures after 142.

Forssman, B. 1966. *Untersuchungen zur Sprache Pindars.* Klassisch-philologische Studien 33. Wiesbaden.

Förster, A., ed. 1912. *Aristotelis* De anima *libri iii.* Budapest.

Fortenbaugh, W. W. 1974 [1970]. "Aristotle's *Rhetoric* on Emotions." In *Aristotle: The Classical Heritage of Rhetoric,* ed. K. V. Erickson, 205–234. Metuchen. Reprinted from *Archiv für Geschichte der Philosophie* 52:40–70.

———. 1985. "Theophrastus on Delivery." In Fortenbaugh et al. 1985:269–288. Reprinted in W. W. Fortenbaugh, *Theophrastean Studies.* Philosophie der Antike 17:253–271. 2003. Stuttgart.

———. 1996. "Aristotle's Accounts of Persuasion through Character." In Johnstone 1996b:147–168.

———. 2002. *Aristotle on Emotion.* 2nd ed. London.

Fortenbaugh, W. W., P. M. Huby, and A. A. Long, eds. 1985. *Theophrastus of Eresus On His Life and Work.* Rutgers University Studies in Classical Humanities 2. New Brunswick.

Fortenbaugh, W. W., P. M. Huby, R. W. Sharples, and D. Gutas, eds. 1992. *Theophrastus of Eresus: Sources for His Life, Writings, Thought and Influence.* Philosophia Antiqua 54.2. Leiden.

Fortenbaugh, W. W. and E. Schütrumpf, eds. 2000. *Demetrius of Phalerum: Text, Translation and Discussion.* Rutgers University Studies in Classical Humanities 9. New Brunswick.

Foster, J. and D. Lehoux. 2007. "The Delphic Oracle and the Ethylene-Intoxication Hypothesis." *Clinical Toxicology* 45:85–89.

Fournier, H. 1946. *Les verbes 'dire' en grec ancien: exemple de conjugaison supplétive.* Collection Linguistique (Société de linguistique de Paris) 51. Paris.

Fowler, R. L., ed. 2000. *Early Greek Mythography: Texts.* Oxford.

Foxhall, L. 1995. "Bronze to Iron: Agricultural Systems and Political Structures in Late Bronze Age and Early Iron Age Greece." *Annual of the British School at Athens* 90:239–250.

Fraenkel, E., ed. 1950. *Aeschylus* Agamemnon. 3 vols. Oxford.

Frame, D. 2009. *Hippota Nestor.* Hellenic Studies 37. Washington, DC.

Fränkel, H. 1925. "Griechische Wörter." *Glotta* 14:1–13.

Fraser, P. M. 1972. *Ptolemaic Alexandria.* Oxford.

Frede, D. 1992. "The Cognitive Role of *Phantasia* in Aristotle." In Nussbaum and Rorty 1992:279–295.

Frederiksen, M. 1984. *Campania.* Edited with additions by N. Purcell. London.

Freese, J. H., ed. 1926. *Aristotle:* The "Art" of Rhetoric. The Loeb Classical Library 193. London.

Frei, J. 1900. *De certaminibus thymelicis.* PhD diss., Universität Basel.

Freudenthal, J. 1863. *Ueber den Begriff des Wortes φαντασία bei Aristoteles.* Göttingen.

Friedrich, J. 1921. "Καρχηδών und Carthago." *Indogermanische Forschungen* 39:102–104.

———, ed. 1932. *Kleinasiatische Sprachdenkmäler.* Berlin.

Friemann, S. 1990. "Überlegungen zu Alkidamas' Rede *Über die Sophisten.*" In Kullmann and Reichel 1990:301–315.

Friis Johansen, H. and E. W. Whittle, eds. 1980. *Aeschylus* The Suppliants. 3 vols. Copenhagen.

Friis Johansen, K. 1923. *Les vases sicyonniens: Étude archéologique.* Paris.

———. 1967. *The* Iliad *in Early Greek Art.* Copenhagen.

Frisch, P., ed. 1986. *Zehn agonistische Papyri.* Abhandlungen der Rheinisch-Westfälischen Akademie der Wissenschaften. Sonderreihe Papyrologica Coloniensia 13. Opladen.

Frisk, H. 1936. *'Wahrheit' und 'Lüge' in den indogermanischen Sprachen: einige morphologische Beobachtungen.* Göteborgs Högskolas Årsskrift 41, 3. Göteborg.

———. 1973–1979. *Griechisches etymologisches Wörterbuch.* Heidelberg.

Froehde, F. 1877. "Etymologien." *Zeitschrift für vergleichende Sprachforschung auf dem Gebiete der indogermanischen Sprachen* 23:310–312.

Furley, D. J. and A. Nehamas, eds. 1994. *Aristotle's* Rhetoric: *Philosophical Essays.* Princeton.

Furley, W. D. and J. M. Bremer. 2001. *Greek Hymns: Selected Cult Songs from the Archaic to the Hellenistic Period.* Tübingen.

Furnée, E. J. 1972. *Die wichtigsten konsonantischen Erscheinungen des Vorgriechischen. Mit einem Appendix über den Vokalismus.* Janua Linguarum, Series Practica 150. The Hague.

Gabrielsen, V. 2002. "The Impact of Armed Forces on Government and Politics in Archaic and Classical Greek Poleis: A Response to Hans van Wees." In *Army and Power in the Ancient World,* ed. A. Chaniotis and P. Ducrey. Heidelberger althistorische Beiträge und epigraphische Studien 37:83–98. Stuttgart.

Gagnepain, J. 1959. *Noms grecs en -ος et en -ā: contribution a l'étude du genre en indo-européen.* Études et Commentaires 31. Paris.

Gangloff, A. 2010. "Rhapsodes et poètes épiques à l'époque impériale." *Revue des études grecques* 123:51–70.

Gantz, T. 1993. *Early Greek Myth: A Guide to Literary and Artistic Sources.* Baltimore.

García Ramón, J. L. 1982. "La glosa de Hesiquio ζείναμεν· σβέννυμεν: una aporía fonética y morfológica." *Emerita* 50:99–119.

———. 1992a. "Homérico κόσμος, κεδνός y las pretendidas raíces IE *k̂es- 'anordnen' y *k̂ed- 'id.'" In *Homerica: estudios lingüísticos,* ed. E. Crespo, J. L. García-Ramón, H. Maquieira, and J. de la Villa. Colección de estudios 36:35–52. Madrid.

———. 1992b. "Mycénien *ke-sa-do-ro* /Kessandros/, *ke-ti-ro* /Kestilos/, *ke-to* /Kestōr/: grec alphabétique Αἰνησιμβρότα, Αἰνησίλαος, Αἰνήτωρ et le nom de Cassandra." *Mykenaïka: Actes du IXe Colloque international sur les textes mycéniens et égéens organisé par le Centre de l'antiquité grecque et romaine de la Fondation hellénique des recherches scientifiques et l'Ecole française d'Athénes (Athénes, 2-6 octobre 1990).* Bulletin de correspondance hellénique, Supplément 25:239–255. Paris.

———. 1993. "Lat. *cēnsēre*, got. *hazjan* und idg. Präsens **k̂éns-e-ti* (und **k̂n̥s-éi̯e-ti?*) 'verkündigt, schätzt', Stativ **k̂n̥s-eh₁-* 'verkündigt, geschätzt sein/werden'." In *Indogermanica et Italica: Festschrift für Helmut Rix zum 65. Geburtstag,* ed. G. Meiser. Innsbrucker Beiträge zur Sprachwissenschaft 72:106–130. Innsbruck.

———. 2007. "Mykenisch *qe-ja-me-no* und *e-ne-ka a-no-qa-si-ja,* alph.-gr. τεισάμενος und ἀνδροκτασία 'Mord' und der PN Τεισίφονος." In ΣΤΕΦΑΝΟΣ ΑΡΙΣΤΕΙΟΣ. *Archäologische Forschungen zwischen Nil und Istros: Festschrift für Stefan Hiller zum 65. Geburtstag,* ed. F. Lang, C. Reinholdt, and J. Weilhartner, 113–123. Vienna.

García Valdés, M. 1992. "Estudio lingüístico y del vocabulario de *Perì euschēmosýnēs*." In *Tratados Hipocráticos (Estudios acerca de su contenido, forma e influencia),* ed. J. A. López Férez, 287–304. Actas del VII Coloquio Internacional Hipocrático (Madrid, 24–29 de septiembre de 1990). Madrid.

Garelli-François, M.-H. 2000. "Ludions, homéristes ou pantomimes? (Sénèque, *Ep.* 117; Fronton, éd. Naber p. 158)." *Revue des études anciennes* 102:501–508.

Garner, R. S. 2011. *Traditional Elegy: The Interplay of Meter, Tradition, and Context in Early Greek Poetry.* American Classical Studies 56. New York.

Garzya, A., ed. 1958. *Euripide* Eraclidi. Traditio. Serie greca 35. Milan.

———. 1980. "Sulla questione delle interpolazioni degli attori nei testi tragici." *Vichiana* 9:3–20.

Gasparri, F. 2001. "Parchment." In *Encyclopedia of the Middle Ages,* Vol. 2, ed. A. Vauchez, 1081. Chicago.

Gastaldi, S. 1981. "La retorica del IV secolo tra oralità e scrittura: *Sugli scrittori di discorsi* di Alcidamante." *Quaderni di storia* VII 14:189–225.

Geckeler, H. 1971. *Zur Wortfelddiskussion: Untersuchungen zur Gliederung des Wortfeldes 'Alt - Jung - Neu' im heutigen Französisch.* International Library of General Linguistics 7. Munich.

———. 1976. *Semántica estructural y teoría del campo léxico.* Biblioteca románica hispánica II. Estudios y ensayos 241. Madrid.

Gehrig, U. and H. G. Niemeyer, eds. 1990. *Die Phönizier.* Mainz.

Gehrke, H.-J. 1978. "Das Verhältnis von Politik und Philosophie im Wirken des Demetrios von Phaleron." *Chiron* 8:149–193.

George, A. R., ed. 1999. *The Epic of* Gilgamesh. London.

———. 2003. *The Babylonian* Gilgamesh *Epic: Introduction, Critical Edition and Cuneiform Texts.* Oxford.

Ghiron-Bistagne, P. 1976. *Recherches sur les acteurs dans la Grèce antique.* Paris.

Giannisi, P. 2006. *Récits des voies: Chant et cheminement en Grèce archaïque.* Collection Horos. Grenoble.

Gill, C. and T. P. Wiseman, eds. 1993. *Lies and Fiction in the Ancient World.* Exeter.

Giuliani, L. 2003. *Bild und Mythos: Geschichte der Bilderzählung in der griechischen Kunst.* Munich.

Goettling, K. W., ed. 1878. *Hesiodi carmina.* 3rd ed. Leipzig.

Golden, M. 1998. *Sport and Society in Ancient Greece.* Key Themes in Ancient History. Cambridge.

———. 2008. *Greek Sport and Social Status.* Austin.

Goldhill, S. and R. Osborne, eds. 1994. *Art and Text in Ancient Greek Culture.* Cambridge.

González, J. M. 2000. "*Musai Hypophetores*: Apollonius of Rhodes on Inspiration and Interpretation." *Harvard Studies in Classical Philology* 100:269–292.

———. 2006. "The Meaning and Function of *Phantasia* in Aristotle's *Rhetoric* III.1." *Transactions of the American Philological Association* 136:99–131.

———. 2010a. "The *Catalogue of Women* and the End of the Heroic Age (Hesiod fr. 204.94–103 MW)." *Transactions of the American Philological Association* 140:375–422.

———. 2010b. "Theokritos' *Idyll* 16: The Χάριτες and Civic Poetry." *Harvard Studies in Classical Philology* 105:65–116.

———. 2015. *A Diachronic Metapoetics of Reception: Homeric* kleos (κλέος) *and Biblical* zera' (זרע). In *Diachrony: Diachronic Aspects of Ancient Greek Literature and Culture,* ed. J. M. González. MythosEikonPoiesis. New York. Forthcoming.

———. Forthcoming. "Hesiod and the Disgraceful Shepherds: Pastoral Politics in a Panhellenic Dichterweihe?" *Festschrift* for Anthony Snodgrass.

Gossage, A. G. 1975. "The Comparative Chronology of Inscriptions Relating to Boiotian Festivals in the First Half of the First Century B.C." *Annual of the British School at Athens* 70:115–134.

Gostoli, A., ed. 2007. Margite, *Omero: Introduzione, testimonianze, testo critico, traduzione e commento.* Testi e commenti 21. Pisa.

Gotō, T. 1995. "Griechisch ἐλεφαίρομαι." *Linguistica Baltica* 4:365–370. Also published as *Analecta Indoeuropaea Cracoviensia,* Vol. II: *Kuryłowicz Memorial Volume. Part One.*

Gow, A. S. F., ed. 1950–1952. *Theocritus: Edited with a Translation and Commentary.* 2 vols. Cambridge.

Graff, R. J. 2000. *Practical Oratory and the Art of Prose: Aristotle's Theory of Rhetorical Style and Its Antecedents.* PhD diss., Northwestern University.

———. 2001. "Readings and the 'Written Style' in Aristotle's *Rhetoric*." *Rhetoric Society Quarterly* 31:19–44.

———. 2005. "Prose versus Poetry in Early Greek Theories of Style." *Rhetorica* 23:303–335.

Grandolini, S. 1996. *Canti e aedi nei poemi omerici*. Testi e Commenti 12. Pisa.

Grant, A. 1885. *The Ethics of Aristotle Illustrated with Essays and Notes*, Vol. 1. 4th ed. London.

Graziosi, B. 2002. *Inventing Homer*. Cambridge.

Greaves, A. M. 2002. *Miletos: A History*. London.

Green, J. R. 1996. "Messengers from the Tragic Stage: The A. D. Trendall Memorial Lecture." *Bulletin of the Institute of Classical Studies* 41:17–30, with plates 5–13.

———. 1999. "Tragedy and the Spectacle of the Mind: Messenger Speeches, Actors, Narrative, and Audience Imagination in Fourth-century BCE Vase-painting." In *The Art of Ancient Spectacle*, ed. B. Bergmann and C. Kondoleon. Studies in the History of Art 56:37–63. Washington, DC.

Greenberg, N. A. 1961. "The Use of *Poiema* and *Poiesis*." *Harvard Studies in Classical Philology* 65:263–289.

Grethlein, J. 2004. "*Logográphos* und Thuc. 1.21.1." *Prometheus* 30:209–216.

Griffith, M. 1983. "Personality in Hesiod." *Classical Antiquity* 2:37–65.

———. 2001. "Public and Private in Early Greek Institutions of Education." In *Education in Greek and Roman Antiquity*, ed. Y. L. Too, 23–84. Leiden.

Grimaldi, W. M. A. 1972. *Studies in the Philosophy of Aristotle's* Rhetoric. Hermes Einzelschriften 25. Wiesbaden.

———. 1980. *Aristotle,* Rhetoric I: *A Commentary*. New York.

———. 1988. *Aristotle,* Rhetoric II: *A Commentary*. New York.

Grube, G. M. A. 1952. "Thrasymachus, Theophrastus, and Dionysius of Halicarnassus." *American Journal of Philology* 73:251–267.

Guarducci, M. 1926–1929. "Poeti vaganti e conferenzieri dell'età ellenistica." *Atti della Reale Accademia Nazionale dei Lincei* ser. VI 2:629–665.

———. 1967–1978. *Epigrafia greca*. 4 vols. Rome.

Gudeman, A., ed. 1934. *Aristotelis Περὶ ποιητικῆς*. Berlin.

Guillemin, M. and J. Duchesne. 1935. "Sur l'origine asiatique de la cithare grecque." *L'Antiquité classique* 4:117–124.

Guion, S. G. 1996. "Greek Syllable Structure. Evidence from Cyprian." *Diachronica* 13:63–82.

Gullick, M. 1991. "From Parchment to Scribe: Some Observations on the Manufacture and Preparation of Medieval Parchment Based upon a Review of the Literary Evidence." In *Pergament: Geschichte, Struktur, Restaurierung, Herstellung*, ed. P. Rück, 145–157. Sigmaringen.

Günther, W. 1971. *Das Orakel von Didyma in hellenistischer Zeit*. Istanbuler Mitteilungen 4. Tübingen.

Gurney, O. R. 1952. "The Sultantepe Tablets: A Preliminary Note." *Anatolian Studies* 2:25–35.

Gusmani, R. 1973. *Aspetti del prestito linguistico*. Collana di Studi Classici 15. Naples.

———. 1976. "Zum Alter des jonischen Wandels ā > η." In *Studies in Greek, Italic, and Indo-European Linguistics Offered to Leonard R. Palmer on the Occasion of His Seventieth Birthday, June 5, 1976*, ed. A. Morpurgo Davies and W. Meid, 77–82. Innsbruck.

Güterbock, H. 1957. "Narration in Anatolian, Syrian, and Assyrian Art." *American Journal of Archaeology* 61:62–71.

Gutiérrez Ordóñez, S. 1989. *Introducción a la semántica funcional*. Lingüística 20. Madrid.

Habicht, C. 1979. *Untersuchungen zur politischen Geschichte Athens im 3. Jahrhundert v. Chr*. Vestigia. Beiträge zur alten Geschichte 30. Munich.

———. 1997 [1995]. *Athens from Alexander to Antony*. Cambridge, MA. First published as *Athen. Die Geschichte der Stadt in hellenistischer Zeit*. Munich.

Hackstein, O. 1997–1998. "Sprachgeschichte und Kunstsprache: Der Perfekttyp βεβαρηότες im frühgriechischen Hexameter (und bei späteren Daktylikern)." *Glotta* 74:21–53.

———. 2002. *Die Sprachform der homerischen Epen*. Serta Graeca: Beiträge zur Erforschung griechischer Texte 15. Wiesbaden.

———. 2010. "The Greek of Epic." In *A Companion to the Ancient Greek Language*, ed. E. J. Bakker, 401–423. Malden.

Hägg, R., ed. 1983. *The Greek Renaissance of the Eighth Century B.C.: Tradition and Innovation*. Second International Symposium at the Swedish Institute in Athens, 1–5 June, 1981. Stockholm.

Hägg, T. 2012. *The Art of Biography in Antiquity*. Cambridge.

Hainsworth, B. 1993. *The* Iliad: *A Commentary*, Vol. 3: books 9–12. Cambridge.

Hajnal, I. 1995. *Der lykische Vokalismus: Methode und Erkenntnisse der vergleichenden anatolischen Sprachwissenschaft, angewandt auf das Vokalsystem einer Kleincorpussprache*. Graz.

Hall, E. 1995. "Lawcourt Dramas: The Power of Performance in Greek Forensic Oratory." *Bulletin of the Institute of Classical Studies* 40:39–58.

Hall, J. M. 2007. *A History of the Archaic Greek World ca. 1200–479 BCE*. Malden.

Halliwell, S. 1986. *Aristotle's* Poetics. Chapel Hill.

———. 1993. "Style and Sense in Aristotle's *Rhetoric* Bk. 3." *Revue internationale de philosophie* 47:50–69.

———. 1994. "Popular Morality, Philosophical Ethics, and the *Rhetoric*." In Furley and Nehamas 1994:211–230.

———, ed. 1999. *Aristotle* Poetics. The Loeb Classical Library 199. Cambridge, MA.

Hamilton, E. and H. Cairns, eds. 1961. *The Collected Dialogues of Plato Including the Letters*. Bollingen Series 71. Princeton.

Hamilton, R. 1974. "Objective Evidence for Actor's Interpolations in Greek Tragedy." *Greek, Roman, and Byzantine Studies* 15:387–402.

———. 1992. "Panathenaic Amphoras: The Other Side." In Neils 1992a:137–162.

Hamlyn, D. W., ed. 1968. *Aristotle's* De anima: *Books II and III*. Oxford.

Hammerstaedt, J. and P. Terbuyken. 1994–1996. "Improvisation." In *Reallexikon für Antike und Christentum*, Vol. 17, cols. 1212–1284. Stuttgart.

Hansen, M. H. 1981. "Initiative and Decision: The Separation of Powers in Fourth-Century Athens." *Greek, Roman, and Byzantine Studies* 22:345–370.

———. 1983a. "The Athenian 'Politicians', 403–322 B.C." *Greek, Roman, and Byzantine Studies* 24:33–55.

———. 1983b. "*Rhetores* and *Strategoi* in Fourth-Century Athens." *Greek, Roman, and Byzantine Studies* 24:151–180.

———. 1987. "*Rhetores* and *Strategoi: Addenda et Corrigenda*." *Greek, Roman, and Byzantine Studies* 28:209–211.

———. 1991. *The Athenian Democracy in the Age of Demosthenes: Structure, Principles, and Ideology*. The Ancient World. Oxford.

———. 1996. "Reflections on the Number of Citizens Accommodated in the Assembly Place on the Pnyx." In Forsén and Stanton 1996:23–33, with bibliography at 117–129 and figures after 142.

———. 2006. *Polis: An Introduction to the Ancient Greek City-State*. Oxford.

Hansen, P. A. 1976. "Pithecusan Humour: The Interpretation of 'Nestor's Cup' Reconsidered." *Glotta* 54:25–43.

Hansen, W. 1997. "Homer and the Folktale." In Morris and Powell 1997:442–462.

Hanson, V. D. 1995. *The Other Greeks: The Family Farm and the Agrarian Roots of Western Civilization*. New York.

———. 1996. "Hoplites into Democrats." In Dēmokratia: *A Conversation on Democracies, Ancient and Modern*, ed. J. Ober and C. Hedrick, 289–310, with bibliography at 401–448. Princeton.

Harder, R., ed. 1958. *Didyma II: Die Inschriften von Albert Rehm*. Berlin.

Hardie, A. 1983. *Statius and the Silvae: Poets, Patrons and Epideixis in the Graeco-Roman World*. ARCA Classical and Medieval Texts, Papers and Monographs 9. Liverpool.

Harris, J. P. 1997. *Plato's Ion: An Exegetical Commentary with Introduction*. PhD diss., University of Illinois at Urbana-Champaign.

———. 2001. "Plato's *Ion* and the End of his *Symposium*." *Illinois Classical Studies* 26:81–100.

Harris, W. V. 1989. *Ancient Literacy*. Cambridge, MA.

Harrison, A. R. W. 1968–1971. *The Law of Athens*. 2 vols. Oxford.

Harrison, E. B. 1977. "Alkamenes' Sculptures for the Hephaisteion: Part III, Iconography and Style." *American Journal of Archaeology* 81:411–426.

Harrison, J. E. 1904. "Mystica Vannus Iacchi (Continued)." *Journal of Hellenic Studies* 24:241–254.

Hartwig, P. 1893. *Die griechischen Meisterschalen der Blüthezeit des strengen rothfigurigen Stiles*. Stuttgart.

Haslam, M. W. 1979. "O Suitably-Attired-in-Leather-Boots. Interpolations in Greek Tragedy." In *Arktouros: Hellenic Studies Presented to Bernard M. W. Knox on the Occasion of his 65th Birthday*, ed. G. W. Bowersock, W. Burkert, and M. C. Putnam, 91–100. Berlin. Also in Burkert 2001:189–197.

———. 1997. "Homeric Papyri and Transmission of the Text." In Morris and Powell 1997:55–100.

Haupt, C. G., ed. 1829. *Aeschyli* Supplices. Leipzig.

Häussler, R. 1970. "Poiema und Poiesis." In *Forschungen zur römischen Literatur: Festschrift zum 60. Geburtstag von Karl Büchner*, Teil 1, ed. W. Wimmel, 125–137. Wiesbaden.

Haussoullier, B. 1898. "L'oracle d'Apollon à Claros." *Revue de philologie, de littérature et d'histoire anciennes* 22:257–273.

Hayduck, M., ed. 1882. *Simplicii in libros Aristotelis De anima commentaria; consilio et auctoritate Academiae litterarum regiae borussicae edidit*. Commentaria in Aristotelem graeca 11. Berlin.

Hayes, B. 1989. "Compensatory Lengthening in Moraic Phonology." *Linguistic Inquiry* 20:253–306.

Heath, M. 1998. "Was Homer a Roman?" *Papers of the Leeds International Latin Seminar* 10:23–56.

Heath, T. 1949. *Mathematics in Aristotle*. Oxford.

Heckel, W. 2006. *Who's Who in the Age of Alexander the Great: Prosopography of Alexander's Empire*. Oxford.

Hedreen, G. 2001. *Capturing Troy: The Narrative Functions of Landscape in Archaic and Early Classical Greek Art*. Ann Arbor.

Heger, N. 1980. "Ein *homerista* in einer Inschrift aus Noricum." In *Symmicta philologica Salisburgensia Georgio Pfligersdorffer sexagenario oblata*, ed. J. Dalfen, K. Forstner, M. Fussl, and W. Speyer. Filologia e Critica, Collana diretta da Bruno Gentili 33:235–239. Rome.

Heide, E. 2006. "Spinning *Seiðr.*" In *Old Norse Religion in Long-term Perspectives: Origins, Changes, and Interactions. An International Conference in Lund, Sweden, June 3-7, 2004,* ed. A. Andrén, K. Jennbert, and C. Raudvere, 164–170. Lund.

Heiden, B. 2007. "The Muses' Uncanny Lies: Hesiod, *Theogony* 27 and Its Translators." *American Journal of Philology* 128:153–175.

Heimsoeth, F. 1873. "De voce ὑποκριτής commentariolus." In *Index scholarum quae summis auspiciis Regis augustissimi Guilelmi Imperatoris Germaniae in Universitate Fridericia Guilelmia Rhenana per menses hibernos a. 1873-74 inde a d. 15 m. octobris publice privatimque habebuntur,* pp. iii–xiv. Bonn.

Heisserer, A. J. and R. A. Moysey. 1986. "An Athenian Decree Honoring Foreigners." *Hesperia* 55:177–182.

Heitsch, E. 1968. "Erscheinung und Meinung: Platons Kritik an Protagoras als Selbstkritik." *Philosophisches Jahrbuch* 76:23–36.

———, ed. 1993. *Platon* Phaidros. Platon: Werke III.4. Göttingen.

Heldmann, K. 1982. *Die Niederlage Homers im Dichterwettstreit mit Hesiod.* Hypomnemata 75. Göttingen.

Henderson, W. J. 1992. "Pindar fr. 140b Snell-Maehler: The Chariot and the Dolphin." *Hermes* 120:148–158.

Henrichs, A. 1994–1995. "'Why Should I Dance?': Choral Self-Referentiality in Greek Tragedy." *Arion* 3:56–111.

———. 2003. "*Hieroi Logoi* and *Hierai Bibloi*: The (Un)written Margins of the Sacred in Ancient Greece." *Harvard Studies in Classical Philology* 101:207–266.

Heraeus, W. 1930. "Drei Fragmente eines Grammatikers Ovidius Naso?" *Rheinisches Museum* 79:391–405.

Herbert, S. 1977. *The Red-Figure Pottery.* Corinth 7.4. Princeton.

Herington, C. J. 1985. *Poetry into Drama: Early Tragedy and the Greek Poetic Tradition.* Sather Classical Lectures 49. Berkeley.

Hermann, G., ed. 1806. *Homeri hymni et epigrammata.* Leipzig.

———. 1827–1877. *Opuscula.* Leipzig.

Hess, K. 1960. *Der Agon zwischen Homer und Hesiod, seine Entstehung und kulturge-schichtliche Stellung.* Winterthur.

Heubeck, A. 1972. "Nochmal zur 'innerhomerischen Chronologie'." *Glotta* 50:129–143.

———. 1979. *Schrift.* Archaeologia Homerica 3, X. Göttingen.

Heubeck, A. and A. Hoekstra. 1989. *A Commentary on Homer's* Odyssey, Vol. 2: books 9–16. Oxford.

Heubeck, A., S. West, and J. B. Hainsworth. 1988. *A Commentary on Homer's* Odyssey, Vol. 1: books 1–8. Oxford.

Heyne, C. G. 1802–1822. *Homeri carmina cum brevi annotatione, accedunt variae lectiones et observationes veterum grammaticorum cum nostrae aetatis critica.* Leipzig.

Hicks, R. D., ed. 1907. *Aristotle* De anima. Cambridge.

Higbie, C. 1997. "The Bones of a Hero, the Ashes of a Politician: Athens, Salamis, and the Usable Past." *Classical Antiquity* 16:278–307.

Hilgard, A., ed. 1965 [1901]. *Scholia in Dionysii Thracis Artem grammaticam.* Grammatici graeci 1.3. Reprint ed. Hildesheim.

Hiller, E. 1873. "Die athenischen Odeen und der προαγών." *Hermes* 7:393–406.

Hillgruber, M. 2000. "Homer im Dienste des Mimus. Zur künstlerischen Eigenart der Homeristen." *Zeitschrift für Papyrologie und Epigraphik* 132:63–72.

Hintzen-Bohlen, B. 1997. *Die Kulturpolitik des Eubulos und des Lykurg.* Antike in der Moderne. Berlin.

Hirzel, R. 1878. "Die Thukydideslegende." *Hermes* 13:46–49.

Hitzig, H. and H. Bluemner, eds. 1896–1910. *Pausaniae Graeciae descriptio.* Berlin.

Hoffmann, H. 1997. *Sotades: Symbols of Immortality on Greek Vases.* Oxford.

Hoffmann, O. 1891–1898. *Die griechischen Dialekte in ihrem historischen Zusammenhange.* Göttingen.

Holleaux, M. 1890. "Fouilles au temple d'Apollon Ptoos." *Bulletin de correspondance hellénique* 14:181–203.

Holmberg, I. 1998. "The Creation of the Ancient Greek Epic Cycle." *Oral Tradition* 13:456–478.

Holzinger, C. von, ed. 1895. *Lykophron* Alexandra. *Griechisch und deutsch mit erklärenden Anmerkungen.* Leipzig.

Hooker, J. T. 1980. *Linear B: An Introduction.* Bristol.

Hoppin, J. C. 1924. *A Handbook of Greek Black-Figured Vases with a Chapter on the Red-Figured Southern Italian Vases.* Paris.

Hornung, H. G. 1869. *De nuntiorum in tragoediis Graecis personis et narrationibus.* Brandenburg a.H.

Horrocks, G. 1987. "The Ionian Epic Tradition: Was There an Aeolic Phase in Its Development?" *Minos* 20–22:269–294.

Hose, M. 1993. "Kratinos und der Bau des Perikleischen Odeions." *Philologus* 137:3–11.

Householder, F. W. and G. Nagy. 1972. *Greek: A Survey of Recent Work.* The Hague.

How, W. W. and J. Wells, eds. 1912. *A Commentary on Herodotus.* Oxford.

Howe, T. 2008. *Pastoral Politics: Animals, Agriculture, and Society in Ancient Greece.* Publications of the Association of Ancient Historians 9. Claremont.

Hubbard, T. K. 1994. "Elemental Psychology and the Date of Semonides of Amorgos." *American Journal of Philology* 115:175–197.

———. 2001. "'New Simonides' or Old Semonides? Second Thoughts on *POxy* 3965 fr. 26." In *The New Simonides: Contexts of Praise and Desire*, ed. D. Boedeker and D. Sider, 226–231. Oxford.

Hübner, W. 1986. "Hermes als musischer Gott: Das Problem der dichterischen Wahrheit in seinem homerischen Hymnos." *Philologus* 130:153–174.

Hudson-Williams, H. Ll. 1949. "Isocrates and Recitations." *Classical Quarterly* 43:65–69.

———. 1951. "Political Speeches in Athens." *Classical Quarterly* 45:68–73.

Hülsewiesche, R. 2002. "Redefreiheit." *Archiv für Begriffsgeschichte* 44:103–143. English summary at 262.

Humphreys, S. 1985a. "Lycurgus of Butadae: An Athenian Aristocrat." In *The Craft of the Ancient Historian. Essays in Honor of Chester G. Starr*, ed. J. W. Eadie and J. Ober, 199–252. Lanham.

———. 1985b. "Social Relations on Stage: Witnesses in Classical Athens." In *The Discourse of Law*, ed. S. Humphreys. History and Anthropology 1:313–369. London.

Hunt, A. S. and C. C. Edgar, eds. 1932–1934. *Select Papyri*. London.

Hurst, A., ed. 2008. *Lycophron* Alexandra. Paris.

Hurwit, J. M. 2004. *The Acropolis in the Age of Pericles*. Cambridge.

———. 2011. "The Shipwreck of Odysseus: Strong and Weak Imagery in Late Geometric Art." *American Journal of Philology* 115:1–18.

Husson, G. 1993. "Les homéristes." *Journal of Juristic Papyrology* 23:93–99.

Iannucci, A. 2001. "ἅπαξ λέγειν: il λογογράφος tra storia e oratoria." *Seminari romani di cultura greca* 4:103–126.

Ilgen, K. D., ed. 1796. *Hymni Homerici cum reliquis carminibus minoribus Homero tribui solitis et Batrachomyomachia*. Halle.

Immerwahr, H. R. 1964. "Book Rolls on Attic Vases." In *Classical, Mediaeval, and Renaissance Studies in Honor of Berthold Louis Ullman*, ed. C. Henderson. Storia e Letteratura, Raccolta di Studi e Testi 93:17–48. Rome.

———. 1973. "More Book Rolls on Attic Vases." *Antike Kunst* 16:143–147.

———. 1990. *Attic Script: A Survey*. Oxford Monographs on Classical Archaeology. Oxford.

Ingria, R. 1980. "Compensatory Lengthening as a Metrical Phenomenon." *Linguistic Inquiry* 11:465–495.

Innes, D. C. 1985. "Theophrastus and the Theory of Style." In Fortenbaugh et al. 1985:251–267.

———, ed. 1999. *Demetrius,* On Style. The Loeb Classical Library 199. Published with Aristotle *Poetics* and [Longinos] *On the Sublime*. Cambridge, MA.

———. 2007. "Aristotle: The Written and the Performative Styles." In *Influences on Peripatetic Rhetoric: Essays in Honor of William W. Fortenbaugh*, ed. D. C. Mirhady. Philosophia Antiqua 105:151–168. Leiden.

Irwin, T. H. 1980. "Reason and Responsibility in Aristotle." In *Essays on Aristotle's Ethics*, ed. A. O. Rorty. Philosophical Traditions 2:117–155. Berkeley.

———, ed. 1985. *Aristotle Nicomachean Ethics*. Translated and annotated by the editor. Indianapolis.

Jachmann, G. 1982 [1936]. "Binneninterpolation." In *Textgeschichtliche Studien*, ed. C. Gnilka. Beiträge zur klassischen Philologie 143:528–580. Königstein. First published in *Nachrichten von der Gesellschaft der Wissenschaften zu Göttingen, Philologisch-historische Klasse*, n.F. 7:123–144 and 9:185–215.

Jackson, A. H. 1995. "An Oracle for Raiders?" *Zeitschrift für Papyrologie und Epigraphik* 108:95–99.

Jacobs, F., ed. 1821. *Achillis Tatii Alexandrini* De Leucippes et Clitophontis amoribus *libri octo*. Leipzig.

Jacoby, F. 1944. "*Patrios Nomos*: State Burial in Athens and the Public Cemetery in the Kerameikos." *Journal of Hellenic Studies* 64:37–66.

Jamot, P. 1895. "Fouilles de Thespies." *Bulletin de correspondance hellénique* 19:311–385.

Janaway, C. 1995. *Images of Excellence: Plato's Critique of the Arts*. New York.

Janko, R. 1982. *Homer, Hesiod and the Hymns: Diachronic Development in Epic Diction*. Cambridge.

———. 1990. "The *Iliad* and its Editors: Dictation and Redaction." *Classical Antiquity* 9:326–334.

———. 1992. *The* Iliad*: A Commentary*, Vol. 4: books 13–16. Cambridge.

———. 1998a. "The Homeric Poems as Oral Dictated Texts." *Classical Quarterly* 48:135–167.

———. 1998b. "Review of G. Nagy, *Poetry as Performance: Homer and Beyond*." *Journal of Hellenic Studies* 118:206–207.

Jebb, R. C., ed. 1893. *Sophocles: The Plays and Fragments with Critical Notes, Commentary, and Translation in English Prose. Part I: The* Oedipus Tyrannus. Cambridge.

Jeffery, L. H. 1962. "Writing." In *A Companion to Homer*, ed. A. J. B. Wace and F. H. Stubbings, 545–559. London.

———. 1976. *Archaic Greece: The City-States c. 700–500 B.C.* New York.

———. 1990. *The Local Scripts of Archaic Greece: A Study of the Origin of the Greek Alphabet and Its Development from the Eighth to the Fifth Centuries B.C.* Oxford Monographs on Classical Archaeology. Revised ed. with a supplement by A. W. Johnston. Oxford.

Jensen, M. S. 1980. *The Homeric Question and the Oral-Formulaic Theory.* Opuscula Graecolatina (Supplementa *Musei Tusculani*) 20. Copenhagen.

———. 2011. *Writing Homer: A Study Based on Results from Modern Fieldwork.* Scientia Danica. Series H, Humanistica, 8 vol. 4. Copenhagen.

Johnson, W. A. 2004. *Bookrolls and Scribes in Oxyrhynchus.* Toronto.

Johnston, A. W. 1983. "The Extent and Use of Literacy; the Archaeological Evidence." In Hägg 1983:63–68.

———. 1992. "A Critical View." In "Review Feature: *Homer and the Origin of the Greek Alphabet* by Barry Powell (Cambridge: Cambridge University Press 1991)." *Cambridge Archaeological Journal* 2.1:120–122.

Johnston, S. I. 2005. "Introduction: Divining Divination." In Mantikē: *Studies in Ancient Divination*, ed. S. I. Johston and P. T. Struck. Religions in the Graeco-Roman World 155:1–28. Leiden.

Johnstone, C. L. 1996a. "Greek Oratorical Settings and the Problem of the Pnyx: Rethinking the Athenian Political Process." In Johnstone 1996b.

———, ed. 1996b. *Theory, Text, Context: Issues in Greek Rhetoric and Oratory.* SUNY Series in Speech Communication. Albany.

Jones, B. N. 2008. *Relative Chronology and the Language of Epic.* PhD diss., Cornell University.

———. 2010. "Relative Chronology within (an) Oral Tradition." *Classical Journal* 105.4:289–318.

Jones, C. P. 1991. "Dinner Theater." In *Dining in a Classical Context*, ed. W. J. Slater, 185–198. Ann Arbor.

Jouanna, J. 1999 [1992]. *Hippocrates.* Medicine & Culture. Baltimore. First published as *Hippocrate.* Paris.

Judet de la Combe, P. 1993. "L'autobiographie comme mode d'universalisation. Hesiode et l'Helicon." In *La componente autobiografica nella poesia greca e latina fra realtà e artificio letterario: atti del convegno Pisa, 16–17 maggio 1991*, ed. G. Arrighetti and F. Montanari. Biblioteca di studi antichi 51:25–39. Pisa.

Kaibel, G., ed. 1878. *Epigrammata graeca ex lapidibus conlecta.* Berlin.

Kalinka, E., ed. 1901. *Tituli Lyciae lingua lycia conscripti.* Tituli Asiae Minoris 1. Vienna.

Kamptz, H. von. 1982. *Homerische Personennamen.* Göttingen.

Kannicht, R. 1982. "Poetry and Art: Homer and the Monuments Afresh." *Classical Antiquity* 1:70–86.

Karageorghis, V. 2002. *Early Cyprus: Crossroads of the Mediterranean.* Los Angeles.

Karila-Cohen, K. 2005a. "Apollon, Athènes et la Pythaïde: Mise en scène 'mythique' de la cité au IIᵉ siècle av. J.-C." *Kernos* 18:219–239.

―――. 2005b. "Les pythaïstes Athèniens et leurs familles: l'apport de la proso-pographie à la connaissance de la religion à Athénes au IIe siècle avant notre ère." In *Prosopographie et histoire religieuse: actes du colloque tenu en l'Université Paris XII-Val de Marne les 27 & 28 octobre 2000*, ed. M.-F. Baslez and F. Prévot. De l'archéologie à l'histoire, 69–83. Paris.

Kassel, R., ed. 1976. *Aristotelis* Ars rhetorica. Berlin.

Kastelic, J. 1995. "Najstarejši grški napisi v Homer." *Živa Antika* 45:135–160.

Katz, J. T. 2006. "The Riddle of the *sp(h)ij-*: The Greek Sphinx and her Indic and Indo-European Background." In *La langue poétique indo-européenne: actes du colloque de travail de la Société des études indo-européennes (Indogermanische Gesellschaft/Society for Indo-European Studies), Paris, 22–24 octobre 2003*, ed. G.-J. Pinault and D. Petit, 157–194. Leuven.

Katz, J. T. and K. Volk. 2000. "'Mere Bellies'? A New Look at *Theogony* 26–8." *Journal of Hellenic Studies* 120:122–131.

Kavitskaya, D. 2002. *Compensatory Lengthening: Phonetics, Phonology, Diachrony*. Outstanding Dissertations in Linguistics. New York.

Kawasaki, Y. 1985. "The Contest of Homer and Hesiod and Alcidamas." *Journal of Classical Studies* 33:19–28.

Kawerau, G. and A. Rehm. 1914. *Das Delphinion in Milet*. Milet: Ergebnisse der Ausgrabungen und Untersuchungen seit dem Jahre 1899, Bd. I, Heft 3. Also known as *Milet* I.3. Berlin.

Keen, A. G. 1998. *Dynastic Lycia: A Political History of the Lycians and Their Relations with Foreign Powers, c. 545-362 B.C*. Leiden.

Kelly, S. T. 1990 [1974]. *Homeric Correption and the Metrical Distinctions between Speeches and Narrative*. Originally a PhD diss., Harvard University. New York.

Kennedy, G. A. 1963. *The Art of Persuasion in Greece*. Princeton.

―――, ed. 1991. *Aristotle* On Rhetoric: A Theory of Civic Discourse. New York.

―――. 1999. *Classical Rhetoric and its Christian and Secular Tradition*. 2nd ed. Chapel Hill.

―――, ed. 2003. *Progymnasmata: Greek Textbooks of Prose Composition and Rhetoric*. Writings from the Greco-Roman World 10. Leiden.

Kerferd, G. B. 1950. "The First Greek Sophists." *Classical Review* 64:8–10.

Kerschensteiner, J. 1962. *Kosmos: quellenkritische Untersuchungen zu den Vorsokratikern*. Zetemata: Monographien zur klassischen Altertumswissenschaft 30. Munich.

Keuls, E. C. 1975. "Skiagraphia Once Again." *American Journal of Archaeology* 79:1–16.

―――. 1978. *Plato and Greek Painting*. Columbia Studies in the Classical Tradition 5. Leiden.

———. 1997. *Painter and Poet in Ancient Greece: Iconography and the Literary Arts.* Beiträge zur Altertumskunde 87. Stuttgart.

Kinkel, G., ed. 1877. *Epicorum graecorum fragmenta.* Leipzig.

Kirchberg, J. 1965. *Die Funktion der Orakel im Werke Herodots.* Hypomnemata 11. Göttingen.

Kirchhoff, A. 1887. *Studien zur Geschichte des griechischen Alphabets.* 4th ed. Gütersloh.

Kirk, G. S. 1960. "Homer and Modern Oral Poetry: Some Confusions." *Classical Quarterly* 10:271–281.

———. 1962. *The Songs of Homer.* Cambridge.

———. 1966a. "The Structure of the Homeric Hexameter." *Yale Classical Studies* 20:76–104.

———. 1966b. "Verse-structure and Sentence-structure in Homer." *Yale Classical Studies* 20:105–152.

———. 1985. *The Iliad: A Commentary,* Vol. 1: books 1–4. Cambridge.

———. 1990. *The Iliad: A Commentary,* Vol. 2: books 5–8. Cambridge.

Klawitter, U. 1998. "Improvisation." In *Historisches Wörterbuch der Rhetorik,* ed. G. Ueding. Vol. 4, cols. 307–314. Tübingen.

Klein, J. 1972. "A Greek Metalworking Quarter: Eighth Century Excavations on Ischia." *Expedition* 14:34–39.

Kleingünther, A. 1933. *ΠΡΩΤΟΣ ΕΥΡΕΤΗΣ: Untersuchungen zur Geschichte einer Fragestellung.* Philologus Supplementband 26. Leipzig.

Knecht, T. 1946. *Geschichte der griechischen Komposita vom Typ τερψίμβροτος.* Biel.

Knoepfler, D. 1988a. "L'intitulé oublié d'un compte des naopes béotiens." In *Comptes et inventaires dans la cité grecque: actes du colloque international d'épigraphie tenu à Neuchâtel du 23 au 26 septembre 1986 en l'honneur de Jacques Tréheux,* ed. D. Knoepfler. Recueil de travaux publiés par la Faculté des lettres 40:263–294. Neuchâtel.

———. 1988b. "Sur les traces de l'Artémision d'Amarynthos près d'Érétrie." *Comptes rendus de l'Académie des Inscriptions et Belles-Lettres* 132:382–421.

———. 1993. "Adolf Wilhelm et la *pentétèris* des Amphiaraia d'Oropos. Réexamen de *A.P.* LIV 7 à la lumière du catalogue IG VII 414 + SEG I 126." In *Aristote et Athènes. Fribourg (Suisse) 23-25 mai 1991,* ed. M. Piérart, 279–302. Paris.

———. 1996. "La réorganisation du concours des *Mouseia* à l'époque hellénistique: esquisse d'une solution nouvelle." In *La montagne des Muses,* ed. A. Hurst and A. Schachter. Recherches et Rencontres 7:141–167. Geneva.

————. 1997. "*Cupido ille propter quem Thespiae visuntur*: une mésaventure insoupsonnée de l'Eros de Praxitèle et l'institution du concours des *Erôtideia*." In Nomen latinum: *mélanges de langue, de littérature et de civilisation latines offerts au professeur André Schneider à l'occasion de son départ à la retraite*, ed. D. Knoepfler and A. Schneider. Recueil de travaux publiés par la Faculté des lettres 44:17–39. Neuchâtel.

————. 2004. "Les *Rōmaia* de Thèbes: un nouveau concours musical (et athlétique?) en Béotie." *Comptes rendus de l'Académie des Inscriptions et Belles-Lettres* 148:1241–1279.

Koch, N. J. 2000. *Techne und Erfindung in der klassischen Malerei*. Studien zur antiken Malerei und Farbgebung 6. Munich.

Kock, E. L. 1961. "The Sophoklean *Oidipus* and Its Antecedents." *Acta Classica* 4:7–28.

Koljević, S. 1980. *The Epic in the Making*. Oxford.

Koller, H. 1956. "Das kitharodische Prooimion." *Philologus* 100:159–206.

————. 1957. "Hypokrisis und Hypokrites." *Museum Helveticum* 14:100–107.

————. 1965. "ΘΕΣΠΙΣ ΑΟΙΔΟΣ." *Glotta* 43:277–285.

————. 1972. "Epos." *Glotta* 50:16–24.

Koning, H. H. 2010. *Hesiod: the Other Poet. Ancient Reception of a Cultural Icon*. Mnemosyne, bibliotheca classica Batava. Suplementum 325. Leiden.

Kontorini, V. N. 1975. "Les concours des grands Éréthimia à Rhodes." *Bulletin de correspondance hellénique* 99:97–117.

————, ed. 1983. *Inscriptions inédites relatives à l'histoire et aux cultes de Rhodes au IIᵉ et au Iᵉʳ s. av. J.-C.: Rhodiaka I*. Archaeologia transatlantica 6. Louvain-la-Neuve.

Köppen, J. H. J. 1804–1823. *Erklärende Anmerkungen zum Homers* Ilias. Hannover.

Kotsidu, H. 1991. *Die musischen Agone der Panathenäen in archaischer und klassischer Zeit: eine historisch-archäologische Untersuchung*. Quellen und Forschungen zur antiken Welt 8. Munich.

Koumanoudēs, S. A. 1872–1881. *Athēnaion, syngramma periodikon kata dimēnian ekdidomenon sympraxei pollōn logiōn*. Athens.

Koumanoudēs, S. N. 1979. *Θηβαϊκὴ προσωπογραφία*. Βιβλιοθήκη τῆς ἐν Ἀθήναις Ἀρχαιολογικῆς Ἑταιρείας 90. Athens.

Krajick, K. 2005. "Tracking Myth to Geological Reality." *Science* 310.5749:762–764.

Kranz, W. 1938. "Kosmos als philosophischer Begriff frühgriechischer Zeit." *Philologus* 93:430–448.

————. 1955–1957. "Kosmos." *Archiv für Begriffsgeschichte* 2:1–266.

Kretschmer, P. 1892. "Zum ionisch-attischen Wandel von ā in η." *Zeitschrift für vergleichende Sprachforschung auf dem Gebiete der indogermanischen Sprachen* 31:285–296.

———. 1894. *Griechischen Vaseninschriften.* Gütersloh.

———. 1907. "Zur Geschichte der griechischen Dialekte." *Glotta* 1:9–59.

Kreuzer, B. 1992. *Frühe Zeichner, 1500-500 vor Chr.: ägyptische, griechische und etruskische Vasenfragmente der Sammlung H. A. Cahn, Basel.* Freiburg im Breisgau.

Krings, V. 1991. "Les lettres grecques à Carthage." In Phoinikeia Grammata. *Lire et écrire en Méditerranée,* ed. C. Baurain, C. Bonnet, and V. Krings, 649–668. Namur.

———. 1995. "La Littérature phénicienne et punique." In *La civilisation phénicienne et punique,* ed. V. Krings, 31–38. Leiden.

Krischer, T. 1965. "ΕΤΥΜΟΣ und ΑΛΗΘΗΣ." *Philologus* 109:161–174.

Kroll, W. 1918. "Homeristai." Real-Encyclopädie der classischen Altertumswissenschaft, Suppl., Vol. 3, col. 1158. Stuttgart.

Krow, M. 2005. *Aristotle on Phantasia.* Master's thesis, Dalhousie University.

Kugel, J. L., ed. 1990. *Poetry and Prophecy: The Beginning of a Literary Tradition.* Myth and Poetics. Ithaca.

Kullmann, W. and M. Reichel, eds. 1990. *Der Übergang von der Mündlichkeit zur Literatur bei den Griechen.* ScriptOralia 30. Tübingen.

Kunze, E., ed. 1967. *Bericht über die Ausgrabungen in Olympia. VIII. Band: Herbst 1958 bis Sommer 1962.* Berlin.

Kurke, L. 1991. *The Traffic in Praise: Pindar and the Poetics of Social Economy.* Ithaca.

Kuruniotes, K. 1899. "Ἐπιγραφαὶ Χαλκίδος καὶ Ἐρετρίας." *Ἐφημερὶς Ἀρχαιολογική* 133–148.

Kurz, D. 1970. Akribeia: *Das Ideal der Exaktheit bei den Griechen bis Aristoteles.* Göppinger akademische Beiträge 8. Göppingen.

Kyle, D. G. 1996. "Gifts and Glory: Panathenaic and Other Greek Athletic Prizes." In Neils 1996:106–136.

———. 2007. *Sport and Spectacle in the Ancient World.* Malden.

Kyriazēs, N. G. 1924. "Ποικίλα." *Κυπριακὰ Χρονικά* 2:216–217.

La Roche, J. 1866. *Die homerische Textkritik im Alterthum.* Leipzig.

Labarrière, J.-L. 1984. "Imagination humaine et imagination animale chez Aristote." *Phronesis* 29:17–49.

———. 1997. "Désir, *phantasia* et intellect dans le De anima, III, 9–11." *Études philosophiques* 1:97–125.

———. 2002. "*Phantasia, phantasma* et *phainetai* dans le traité Des Rêves." *Revue de philosophie ancienne* 89–107.

————. 2003. "Nature et fonction de la *phantasia* chez Aristote." In Lories and Rizzerio 2003:15–30, with bibliography at 151–155.

Ladrière, C. 1951. "The Problem of Plato's *Ion*." *Journal of Aesthetics and Art Criticism* 10:26–34.

Lameere, W. 1960. *Aperçus de paléographie Homérique: à propos des papyrus de l'Iliade et de l'Odyssée des collections de Gand, de Bruxelles et de Louvain.* Publications de Scriptorium 4. Paris.

Lanata, G. 1963. *Poetica pre-platonica: testimonianze e frammenti.* Biblioteca di Studi Superiori, Filosofia antica 43. Florence.

Landi, A. 1979. *Dialetti e interazione sociale in Magna Grecia: Lineamenti di una storia linguistica attraverso la documentazione epigrafica.* Naples.

Langdon, M. K. 1987. "An Attic Decree Concerning Oropos." *Hesperia* 56:47–58.

Langerbeck, H. 1958. "*Margites*: Versuch einer Beschreibung und Rekonstruktion." *Harvard Studies in Classical Philology* 63:33–63.

Laplace, M. 1993. "A propos du P. Robinson-Coloniensis d'Achille Tatius, Leucippé et Clitophon." *Zeitschrift für Papyrologie und Epigraphik* 98:43–56.

Laroche, E. 1972. "Observations sur la chronologie de l'ionien ā > η." In *Mélanges de linguistique et de philologie grecques offerts à Pierre Chantraine*, 83–91. Paris.

Larson, J. 1995. "The Corycian Nymphs and the Bee Maidens of the Homeric *Hymn to Hermes*." *Greek, Roman, and Byzantine Studies* 36:341–357.

Laskaris, A. J. 1517. Σχόλια παλαιὰ τῶν πάνυ δοκίμων εἰς τὴν Ὁμήρου Ἰλιάδα. Rome.

Lasso de la Vega, J. S. 1956. "Sobre la historia de las vocales largas en griego." *Emérita* 24:261–293.

Latacz, J., ed. 1991. *Zweihundert Jahre Homer-Forschung.* Colloquium Rauricum 2. Stuttgart.

Latacz, J., T. Greub, P. Blome, and A. Wieczorek, eds. 2008. *Homer: Der Mythos von Troia in Dichtung und Kunst.* Munich.

Latte, K. 1940. "The Coming of the Pythia." *Harvard Theological Review* 33:9–18.

Lattke, M. 1991. *Hymnus: Materialen zu einer Geschichte der antiken Hymnologie.* Novum Testamentum et orbis antiquus 19. Freiburg.

Lauffer, S., ed. 1971. *Diokletians Preisedikt.* Texte und Kommentare. Eine altertumswissenschaftliche Reihe 5. Berlin.

Lausberg, H. 1998. *Handbook of Literary Rhetoric: A Foundation for Literary Study.* Leiden.

Lavency, M. 1964. *Aspects de la logographie judiciaire attique.* Recueil de travaux d'histoire et de philologie, 4e sér. 32. Louvain.

Lavigne, D. 2005. *Iambic Configurations: Iambos from Archilochus to Horace.* PhD diss., Stanford University.

Lazzarini, M. L. 1976. "Le formule delle dediche votive nella Grecia arcaica." *Memorie della Classe di Scienze morali e storiche dell'Accademia dei Lincei* ser. 8 19.2:47–354, with two plates.

———. 1999. "Questioni relative all'origine dell'alfabeto greco." In *Scritture Mediterranee tra il IX e il VII secolo a.C.*, 53–66. Milan.

Lazzeroni, R. 1967. "Su alcuni aspetti della lingua di Omero." *Studi e saggi linguistici* 7:49–62.

Leaf, W., ed. 1900–1902. *The* Iliad. 2nd ed. London.

Lebrun, R. 1987. "Problèmes de religion anatolienne." *Hethitica* 8:241–262.

Leclerc, M.-C. 1993. *La parole chez Hésiode: à la recherche de l'harmonie perdue.* Collection d'Études Anciennes 121. Paris.

———. 2000. "Tout ce qui est n'est pas bon à dire (Hésiode, *Théogonie*, 32, 38)." *Noesis* 4:55–72.

Lefebvre, R. 1997a. "Faut-il traduire le vocable aristotélicien de *phantasia* par 'représentation'?" *Revue philosophique de Louvain* 95:587–616.

———. 1997b. "La *phantasia* chez Aristote: subliminalité, indistinction et pathologie de la perception." *Études philosophiques* 1:41–58.

———. 1999. "L'imagination, produit d'une métaphore?: (Aristote, *De anima*, III, 3, 427b27–428a5)." *Dialogue* 38:469–489.

———. 2001–2002. "Des accidents *kata ten phantasian* à la *phantasia bouletike*: le traité *De l'âme* d'Aristote." *Kléos (revista de filosofia antiga)* 5–6:35–63.

———. 2003. "La crise de la *phantasia*: originalité des interprétations, originalité d'Aristote." In Lories and Rizzerio 2003:31–46, with bibliography at 151–155.

Le Guen, B. 2001. *Les associations de technites dionysiaques à l'époque hellénistique.* Études d'Archéologie Classique XI–XII. Paris.

Lehoux, D. 2007. "Drugs and the Delphic Oracle." *Classical World* 101:41–56.

Lehrs, K. 1964 [1882]. *De Aristarchi studiis homericis.* Hildesheim.

Lejeune, M. 1945. "En marge d'inscriptions grecques dialectales." *Revue des études anciennes* 47:97–115.

———. 1966. "Les notations de F dans l'Italie ancienne." *Revue des études latines* 44:141–181.

———. 1972. *Phonétique historique du mycénien et du grec ancien.* Paris.

Lemaire, A. 1986. "Les écrits phéniciens." In *Écrits de l'Orient ancien et sources bibliques.* Petite bibliothèque des sciences bibliques, Ancien Testament 2:213–239. Paris.

———. 2008. "The Spread of Alphabetic Scripts (c. 1500–500 BCE)." *Diogenes* 55:45–58.

Lennartz, K. 2010. Iambos: *Philologische Untersuchungen zur Geschichte einer Gattung in der Antike.* Serta Graeca: Beiträge zur Erforschung griechischer Texte 27. Wiesbaden.

Lentz, A., ed. 1867–1870. *Herodiani Technici reliquiae.* Grammatici Graeci 3. Leipzig.

Leppin, H. 1992. *Histrionen. Untersuchungen zur sozialen Stellung von Bühnenkünstlern im Westen des Römischen Reiches zur Zeit der Republik und des Principats.* Antiquitas, Abhandlungen zur alten Geschichte 41. Bonn.

Lesher, J. H. 1981. "Perceiving and Knowing in the *Iliad* and the *Odyssey*." *Phronesis* 26:2–24.

Lesky, A. 1929. "Zur Entwicklung des Sprechverses in der Tragödie." *Wiener Studien* 47:3–13.

———. 1956. "Hypokrites." In *Studi in onore di Ugo Enrico Paoli.* Pubblicazioni della Università degli studi di Firenze, Facoltà di lettere e filosofia, serie IV 1:469–476. Florence.

———. 1966 [1928]. "Das Rätsel der Sphinx." In *Gesammelte Schriften: Aufsätze und Reden zu antiker und deutscher Dichtung und Kultur,* ed. W. Kraus, 318–326. Bern.

———. 1983. *Greek Tragic Poetry.* Translated by M. Dillon. New Haven.

Leumann, M. 1942. *Die Nomina auf -ευς: ein Beitrag zur Wortbildung der griechischen Sprache.* Zürich.

———. 1950. *Homerische Wörter.* Schweizerische Beiträge zur Altertumswissenschaft 3. Basel.

Levaniouk, O. 2000. "*Aithōn*, Aithon, and Odysseus." *Harvard Studies in Classical Philology* 100:25–51.

Levet, J.-P. 1976. *Le vrai et le faux dans la pensée grecque archaïque: étude de vocabulaire,* Tome I: Présentation générale. Le vrai et le faux dans les épopées homériques. Collection d'Études Anciennes. Paris.

———. 2008. *Le vrai et le faux dans la pensée grecque archaïque: d'Hésiode à la fin du Ve siècle.* Collection d'Études Anciennes 136. Paris.

Lewis, D. M. 1959. "Law on the Lesser Panathenaia." *Hesperia* 28:239–247.

Lewis, D. M. and R. S. Stroud. 1979. "Athens Honors King Euagoras of Salamis." *Hesperia* 48:180–193.

Lewis, J. D. 1971. "Isegoria at Athens: When Did it Begin?" *Historia* 20:129–140.

Lewis, N. 1974. *Papyrus in Classical Antiquity.* Oxford.

———. 1981. "Notationes legentis." *Bulletin of the American Society of Papyrologists* 18:73–81.

Ley, G. K. H. 1983. "ΥΠΟΚΡΙΝΕΣΘΑΙ in Homer and Herodotus, and the Function of the Athenian Actor." *Philologus* 123:13–29.

Lhôte, E. 2006. *Les lamelles oraculaires de Dodone.* Hautes études du monde gréco-romain 36. Geneva.

Liebersohn, Y. Z. 1999. "Alcidamas' *On the Sophists*: A Reappraisal." *Eranos* 97:108–124.

Liep, J., ed. 2001. *Locating Cultural Creativity.* Anthropology, Culture and Society. London.

Lindgren, M. 1973. *The People of Pylos: Prosopographical and Methodological Studies in the Pylos Archives. Part II: The Use of Personal Designations and Their Interpretation.* Acta Universitatis Upsaliensis, Boreas 3. Uppsala.

Linguiti, A. 2006. "Immagine e concetto in Aristotele e Plotino." In *Incontri triestini di filologia classica IV, 2004-2005. Phantasia, il pensiero per immagini degli antichi e dei moderni: Atti del convegno internazionale, Trieste, 28-30 aprile 2005,* ed. L. Cristante. Polymnia: Studi di Filologia Classica 6:69–80. Trieste.

Lipiński, E. 1975. *Studies in Aramaic Inscriptions and Onomastics.* Leuven.

———. 1992. "Littérature." In *Dictionnaire de la civilisation phénicienne et punique,* ed. E. Lipiński, C. Baurain, C. Bonnet, J. Debergh, E. Gubel, and V. Krings, 263–264. Turnhout.

———. 2001. *Semitic Languages: Outline of a Comparative Grammar.* Orientalia Lovaniensia analecta 80. 2nd ed. Sterling.

Lippolis, E., M. Livadiotti, and G. Rocco. 2007. *Architettura greca: Storia e monumenti del mondo della* polis *dalle origini al V secolo.* Milan.

Livingstone, N. 2001. *A Commentary on Isocrates'* Busiris. Mnemosyne, bibliotheca classica Batava. Suplementum 223. Leiden.

Lledó Íñigo, E. 1961. *El concepto de* poíesis *en la filosofía griega.* Madrid.

Lloyd-Jones, H. 1963. "Review of *The Oxyrhynchus Papyri. Part 27,* by E. G. Turner, John Rae, L. Koenen, and José María Fernández Pomar." *Gnomon* 35:433–455.

———. 1978. "Ten Notes on Aeschylus." In *Dionysiaca: Nine Studies in Greek Poetry by Former Pupils Presented to Sir Denys Page on His Seventieth Birthday,* ed. R. D. Dawe, J. Diggle, and P. E. Easterling, 45–61. Cambridge.

Lobeck, C. A., ed. 1820. *Phrynichi* Eclogae nominum et verborum Atticorum *cum notis P. J. Nunnesii, D. Hoeschelii, J. Scaligeri et Cornelii de Pauw partim integris partim contractis.* Leipzig.

Lombardi, M. 1993. *Antimaco di Colofone: la poesia epica.* Filologia e critica 70. Rome.

Loney, A. 2010. *Narrative Revenge and the Poetics of Justice in the* Odyssey: *A Study on Tisis.* PhD diss., Duke University.

López Eire, A. 1970. *Innovaciones del jónico-ático (vocalismo).* Salamanca.

Lord, A. B. 1953. "Homer's Originality: Oral Dictated Texts." *Transactions of the American Philological Association* 84:124–134.

———, ed. 1954. *Serbocroatian Heroic Songs.* Collected by Milman Parry. Cambridge.

———. 1960. *The Singer of Tales.* Harvard Studies in Comparative Literature 24. Cambridge, MA.

———. 1981. "Memory, Fixity, and Genre in Oral Traditional Poetries." In *Oral Traditional Literature: A Festschrift for Albert Bates Lord*, ed. J. M. Foley, 451–461. Columbus.

———. 1985. "Memory, Meaning, and Myth in Homer and Other Oral Epic Traditions." In *Oralità: cultura, letteratura, discorso*, ed. B. Gentili and G. Paioni, 37–63. Rome.

———. 1991. *Epic Singers and Oral Tradition.* Myth and Poetics. Ithaca.

———. 1995. *The Singer Resumes the Tale.* Myth and Poetics. Ithaca.

Lories, D. and L. Rizzerio, eds. 2003. *De la* phantasia *à l'imagination.* Collection d'études classiques 17. With bibliography at 151–155. Louvain.

Lorimer, H. L. 1950. *Homer and the Monuments.* London.

Lossau, M. 1971. "μοχθηρία τῶν πολιτειῶν und ὑπόκρισις: Zu Aristot. *Rhet.* 3, 1, 1403b34f." *Rheinisches Museum* 114:146–158.

Lowenstam, S. 1992. "The Uses of Vase-Depictions in Homeric Studies." *Transactions of the American Philological Association* 122:165–198.

———. 1993. "The Arming of Achilleus on Early Greek Vases." *Classical Antiquity* 12:199–218.

———. 1997. "Talking Vases: The Relationship between the Homeric Poems and Archaic Representations of Epic Myth." *Transactions of the American Philological Association* 127:21–76.

———. 2008. *As Witnessed by Images: The Trojan War Tradition in Greek and Etruscan Art.* Baltimore.

Lucas, D. W., ed. 1968. *Aristotle Poetics.* Oxford.

Ludwich, A. 1884. *Aristarchs Homerische Textkritik nach den Fragmenten des Didymos dargestellt und beurtheilt.* 2 vols. Leipzig.

Luther, W. 1935. *'Wahrheit' und 'Lüge' im ältesten Griechentum.* Leipzig.

———. 1954. *Weltansicht und Geistesleben.* Göttingen.

———. 1958. "Der frühgriechische Wahrheitsgedanke im Lichte der Sprache." *Gymnasium* 65:75–107.

Macan, R. W., ed. 1908. *Herodotus: The Seventh, Eighth, and Ninth Books.* Vol. 1.1. London.

MacDonald, B. R. 1982. "The Authenticity of the Congress Decree." *Historia* 31:120–123.

MacDowell, D. M. 1975. "Law-Making at Athens in the Fourth Century B.C." *Journal of Hellenic Studies* 95:62–74.

Mackay, E. A. 1995. "Narrative Tradition in Early Greek Oral Poetry and Vase-Painting." *Oral Tradition* 10:282–303.

MacPhail Jr., J. A., ed. 2011. *Porphyry's Homeric Questions on the Iliad: Text, Translation, Commentary*. Texte und Kommentare. Eine altertumswissenschaftliche Reihe 36. New York.

Madius, V. and B. Lombardus, eds. 1550. *In Aristolelis librum* De poetica *communes explanationes*. Venice.

Maehler, H. 1963. *Die Auffassung des Dichterberufs im frühen Griechentum bis zur Zeit Pindars*. Hypomnemata 3. Göttingen.

———, ed. 1982–1997. *Die Lieder des Bakchylides: Text, Übersetzung, und Kommentar*. Mnemosyne, bibliotheca classica Batava. Suplementum 62 and 167. Leiden.

Malzan, W. 1908. *De scholiis Euripideis quae ad res scaenicas et ad histriones spectant*. Darmstadt.

Manieri, A. 1998. *L'immagine poetica nella teoria degli antichi:* Phantasia *ed* enargeia. Pisa.

———, ed. 2009. *Agoni poetico-musicali nella Grecia antica 1: Beozia*. Testi e commenti 25. Rome.

Marcar, A. 2005. "Reconstructing Aegean Bronze Age Fashions." In *The Clothed Body in the Ancient World*, ed. L. Cleland, M. Harlow, and L. Llewellyn-Jones, 30–43. Oxford.

Marchetti, C. C. 2009. *Aristoxenus* Elements of Rhythm: *Text, Translation, and Commentary, with a Translation and Commentary of* P.Oxy. 2687. PhD diss., Rutgers University.

Marckscheffel, J. G. W., ed. 1840. *Hesiodi, Eumeli, Cinaethonis, Asii et carminis Naupactii fragmenta*. Leipzig.

Marek, C. 1993a. "Euboia und die Entstehung der Alphabetschrift bei den Griechen." *Klio* 75:27–44.

———. 1993b. *Stadt, Ära und Territorium in Pontus-Bithynia und Nord-Galatia*. Istanbuler Forschungen 39. Tübingen.

Marini, N., ed. 2007. *Demetrio,* Lo stile: *Introduzione, traduzione e commento*. Pleiadi 4. Rome.

Mariß, R. 2002. *Alkidamas: Über diejenigen, die schriftliche Reden schreiben, oder Über die Sophisten. Eine Sophistenrede aus dem 4. Jahrhundert v. Chr. eingeleitet und kommentiert*. Orbis Antiquus 36. Münster.

Markoe, G. 1985. *Phoenician Bronze and Silver Bowls from Cyprus and the Mediterranean*. Berkeley.

Marks, J. 2008. *Zeus in the* Odyssey. Hellenic Studies 31. Washington, DC.

Marquand, A. 1887. "A Silver Patera from Kourion." *American Journal of Archaeology* 3:322–337.

Martin, R. P. 1989. *The Language of Heroes: Speech and Performance in the* Iliad. Myth and Poetics. Ithaca.

———. 2000. "Synchronic Aspects of Homeric Performance: The Evidence of the *Hymn to Apollo*." In *Una nueva visión de la cultura griega antigua hacia el fin del milenio*, ed. A. M. González de Tobia, 403–432. La Plata.

Martinet, A. 1955. *Économie des changements phonétiques: Traité de phonologie diachronique.* Berne.

Martínez Hernández, M. 1997. *Semántica del griego antiguo.* Madrid.

Marx, F. 1925. "Die Überlieferung über die Persönlichkeit Homers." *Rheinisches Museum* 74:395–431.

Maslov, B. 2009. "The Semantics of ἀοιδός and Related Compounds: Towards a Historical Poetics of Solo Performance in Archaic Greece." *Classical Antiquity* 28:1–38.

Mastronarde, D. J., ed. 1988. *Euripides* Phoenissae. Bibliotheca Scriptorum Graecorum et Romanorum Teubneriana. Leipzig.

———, ed. 1994. *Euripides* Phoenissae. Cambridge Classical Texts and Commentaries 29. Cambridge.

Matthäus, H. 2005. "ΛΑΜΠΡΟΣ ΗΛΙΟΥ ΚΥΚΛΟΣ: Phoenician Deities and Demons." In *Cyprus: Religion and Society from the Late Bronze Age to the End of the Archaic Period*, ed. V. Karageorghis, H. Mattäus, and S. Rogge, 19–39, with plates 3–4. Möhnesee.

Matthews, V. J., ed. 1996. *Antimachus of Colophon: Text and Commentary.* Mnemosyne, bibliotheca classica Batava. Suplementum 155. New York.

May, J. M. and J. Wisse, eds. 2001. *Cicero* On the Ideal Orator (De Oratore). New York.

Mayrhofer, M. 1953–1980. *Kurzgefaßtes etymologisches Wörterbuch des Altinidischen.* Heidelberg.

McCoy, M. B. 2009. "Alcidamas, Isocrates, and Plato on Speech, Writing, and Philosophical Rhetoric." *Ancient Philosophy* 29:45–66.

McDonald, W. A. 1943. *The Political Meeting Places of the Greeks.* The Johns Hopkins University Studies in Archaeology 34. Baltimore.

McLeod, W. E. 1961. "Oral Bards at Delphi." *Transactions of the American Philological Association* 92:317–325.

Meiggs, R. and D. Lewis, eds. 1969. *A Selection of Greek Historical Inscriptions to the End of the Fifth Century B.C.* Oxford.

Meijering, R. 1987. *Literary and Rhetorical Theories in Greek Scholia.* Groningen.

Meillet, A. 1897. *De indo-europaea radice men- 'mente agitare'.* Paris.

Meillet, A. and J. Vendryes. 1979. *Traité de grammaire comparée des langues classiques.* 5th ed. Paris.

Meineke, A. 1867. *Athenaei* Deipnosophistae. *Vol. IV analecta critica continens.* Leipzig.

Meister, K. 1921. *Die Homerische Kunstsprache.* Leipzig.

Meister, R. 1871. "De dialecto heracliensium italicorum." In *Studien zur griechischen und lateinischen Grammatik IV*, ed. G. Curtius, 355–469. Leipzig.

Melchert, H. C. 1992. "Relative Chronology and Anatolian: The Vowel System." In *Rekonstruktion und relative Chronologie. Akten der VIII. Fachtagung der Indogermanischen Gesellschaft, Leiden, 31. August–4. September, 1987*, ed. R. Beekes, L. A., and J. Weitenberg, 41–53. Innsbruck.

———. 2004a. *A Dictionary of the Lycian Language.* Ann Arbor.

———. 2004b. "Lycian." In *The Cambridge Encyclopedia of the World's Ancient Languages*, ed. R. D. Woodard, 591–600. Cambridge.

Méndez Dosuna, J. 1985. *Los dialectos dorios del noroeste: gramática y estudio dialectal.* Acta Salmanticensia, Filosofía y Letras 161. Salamanca.

———. 1993. "Metátesis de cantidad en jónico-ático y heracleota." *Emérita* 61:95–134.

Mensching, E., ed. 1963. *Favorin von Arelate: der erste Teil der Fragmente, Memorabilien und Omnigena historia. Texte und Kommentare. Eine altertumswissenschaftliche Reihe 3.* Berlin.

Meritt, B. D. 1961. *The Athenian Year.* Sather Classical Lectures 32. Berkeley.

———. 1977. "Athenian Archons 347/6–48/7 BC." *Historia* 26:161–191.

———. 1981. "Mid-Third-Century Athenian Archons." *Hesperia* 50:78–99.

Merkelbach, R. 1952. "Die pisistratische Redaktion der homerischen Gedichte." *Rheinisches Museum* n.F. 95:23–47.

———. 1975. "Nochmals die Bleitafel von Berezan." *Zeitschrift für Papyrologie und Epigraphik* 17:161–162.

Merkelbach, R. and M. L. West, eds. 1967. *Fragmenta Hesiodea.* Oxford.

Merle, H. 1916. *Die Geschichte der Städte Byzantion und Kalchedon: von ihrer Gründung bis zum Eingreifen der Römer in die Verhältnisse des Ostens.* Kiel.

Mette, H. J. 1961. "'Schauen' und 'Staunen'." *Glotta* 39:49–71.

———, ed. 1977. *Urkunden dramatischer Aufführungen in Griechenland.* Berlin.

Meyer, E., ed. 1909. *Theopomps Hellenika: mit einer Beilage über die Rede an die Larisaeer und die Verfassung Thessaliens.* Halle.

———. 1918. "Die Rhapsoden und die homerischen Epen." *Hermes* 53:330–336.

Michel, C., ed. 1900. *Recueil d'inscriptions grecques.* Brussels.

Michel, C. 1971. *Erläuterungen zum N der Ilias.* Heidelberg.

Mikalson, J. D. 1998. *Religion in Hellenistic Athens.* Hellenistic Culture and Society 29. Berkeley.

———. 2003. *Herodotus and Religion in the Persian Wars*. Chapel Hill.

Millard, A. R. 1970. "'Scriptio continua' in Early Hebrew: Ancient Practice or Modern Surmise?" *Journal of Semitic Studies* 15:2–15.

Millard, A. R. and P. Bordreuil. 1982. "A Statue from Syria with Assyrian and Aramaic Inscriptions." *Biblical Archaeologist* 45:135–141.

Miller, A. P. 1975. "Notes on the Berezan Lead Letter." *Zeitschrift für Papyrologie und Epigraphik* 17:157–160.

Miller, D. G. 1976. "Glide Deletion, Contraction, Attic Reversion, and Related Problems of Ancient Greek Phonology." *Die Sprache* 22:137–156.

———. 1990. "Homer and Writing: Use and Misuse of Epigraphic and Linguistic Evidence." *Classical Journal* 85:171–179.

———. 1994. *Ancient Scripts and Phonological Knowledge*. Current Issues in Linguistic Theory 116. Amsterdam.

Miller, M. C. 1997. *Athens and Persia in the Fifth Century BC*. Cambridge.

Milne, M. J. 1924. *A Study in Alcidamas and His Relation to Contemporary Sophistic*. PhD diss., Bryn Mawr College.

Mirhady, D. C. 2001. "Dicaearchus of Messana: The Sources, Text, and Translation." In *Dicaearchus of Messana: Text, Translation, and Discussion*, ed. W. W. Fortenbaugh and E. Schütrumpf. Rutgers University Studies in Classical Humanities 10:1–142. New Brunswick.

Misgav, H. 2009. "Review of B. Sass, *The Alphabet at the Turn of the Millennium. The West Semitic Alphabet ca. 1150–850 BCE. The Antiquity of the Arabian, Greek and Phrygian Alphabets*. Journal of the Institute of Archaeology of Tel Aviv University, Occasional Publications 4." *Israel Exploration Journal* 59:242–248.

Mitchel, F. W. 1973. "Lykourgan Athens: 338–322." *The University of Cincinnati Classical Studies* 2:163–214. Lectures in Memory of Louise Taft Semple delivered April 9 and 10, 1968.

Mitsos, M. T. 1952. *Argolikē prosōpographia*, Βιβλιοθήκη τῆς ἐν Ἀθήναις Ἀρχαιολογικῆς Ἑταιρείας 36. Athens.

Mitteis, L. and U. Wilcken. 1912. *Grundzüge und Chrestomathie der Papyruskunde*. Leipzig.

Modrak, D. K. W. 2001. *Aristotle's Theory of Language and Meaning*. Cambridge.

Monro, D. B., ed. 1897. *Homer:* Iliad*, Books XIII–XXIV*. 4th ed. Oxford.

———, ed. 1958 [1929]. *Homer:* Iliad*, Books I–XII*. 5th ed. Oxford.

———. 1992 [1891]. *A Grammar of the Homeric Dialect*. 2nd ed. Philadelphia.

Montanari, F. 2000. "Demetrius of Phalerum on Literature." In Fortenbaugh and Schütrumpf 2000:391–411.

Mooney, G. W., ed. 1921. *The* Alexandra *of Lycophron*. London.

Moore, M. B. 1999. "'Nikias Made Me': An Early Panathenaic Prize Amphora in the Metropolitan Museum of Art." *Metropolitan Museum Journal* 34:37–56.

Moret, J.-M. 1984. *Oedipe, la Sphinx et les Thébains: essai de mythologie iconographique*. Bibliotheca Helvetica Romana 23. Geneva.

Moretti, L. 1981. "Iscrizioni di Tespie della prima età imperiale." *Athenaeum* 59:71–77.

Morgan, C. 1990. *Athletes and Oracles: The Transformation of Olympia and Delphi in the Eighth Century B.C.* Cambridge.

Morgan, J. R. 2000. "Review of M. Finkelberg, *The Birth of Literary Fiction in Ancient Greece*." *Classical Review* 50:93–94.

Morgan, T. J. 1999. "Literate Education in Classical Athens." *Classical Quarterly* 49:46–61.

Morpurgo Davies, A. 1972. "Greek and Indo-European Semi-Consonants: Mycenaean *u* and *w*." *Minos* 12:80–121.

———. 1983. "Mycenaean and Greek Prepositions: *o-pi*, *e-pi* etc." In Res Mycenaeae: *Akten des VII. Internationalen Mykenologischen Colloquiums in Nürnberg vom 6.-10. April 1981*, ed. A. Heubeck and G. Neumann, 287–310. Göttingen.

———. 1987. "Mycenaean and Greek Syllabification." In *Tractata Mycenaea: Proceedings of the Eighth International Colloquium on Mycenaean Studies, Held in Ohrid, 15-20 September 1985*, ed. P. H. Ilievsky and L. Crepajac, 91–104. Skopje.

Morpurgo Tagliabue, G. 1967. *Linguistica e stilistica di Aristotele*. Filologia e critica 4. Rome: Edizioni dell'Ateneo.

Morris, I. 1986. "The Use and Abuse of Homer." *Classical Antiquity* 5:81–138.

———. 1991. "The Early Polis as City and State." In Rich and Wallace-Hadrill 1991:24–57.

———. 2000. *Archaeology as Cultural History*. Malden.

Morris, I. and B. Powell, eds. 1997. *A New Companion to Homer*. Mnemosyne, bibliotheca classica Batava. Suplementum 163. Leiden.

Mosconi, G. 2000. "La democrazia ateniese e la 'nuova' musica: l'odeion di Pericle." In *Synaulía: cultura musicale in Grecia e contatti mediterranei*, ed. A. C. Cassio, D. Musti, and L. E. Rossi. Annali dell'Istituto Universitario Orientale di Napoli, Dipartimento di Studi del Mondo Classico e del Mediterraneo Antico, Sezione Filologico-Letteraria. Quaderni 5:217–316. Naples.

Most, G. W. 1986. "Pindar, *O*. 2.83–90." *Classical Quarterly* 36:304–316.

———, ed. 1998. *Editing Texts*. Aporemata 2. Göttingen.

———, ed. 2007. *Hesiod: The* Shield, Catalogue of Women, *Other Fragments*. The Loeb Classical Library 503. Cambridge, MA.

Mountjoy, P. A. 1997. "The Destruction of the Palace at Pylos Reconsidered." *Annual of the British School at Athens* 92:109–137.

Mountjoy, P. A. and R. Gowland. 2005. "The End of the Bronze Age at Enkomi, Cyprus: The Problem of Level III B." *Annual of the British School at Athens* 100:125–214.

Muir, J. V., ed. 2001. *Alcidamas: The Works and Fragments.* London.

Müller, C. G., ed. 1811. Ἰσαακίου καὶ Ἰωάννου τοῦ Τζέτζου σχόλια εἰς Λυκόφρονα. Leipzig.

Müller, M. 1891. *De Seleuco Homerico dissertatio inauguralis philologica.* PhD diss., Academia Georgia Augusta, Gottingae.

Mure, W. 1854–1859. *A Critical History of the Language and Literature of Antient Greece.* 2nd ed. London.

Murray, O. 1993. *Early Greece.* 2nd ed. Cambridge, MA.

Murray, P. 1981. "Poetic Inspiration in Early Greece." *Journal of Hellenic Studies* 101:87–100.

———, ed. 1996. *Plato on Poetry:* Ion, Republic *376e–398b9,* Republic *595–608b10.* Cambridge.

Musti, D. 2002. "Tradizioni sull'*Odeion* di Atene: Ermogene e Temistocle." *Ktèma* 27:325–329.

Nachmanson, E. 1909. "Zu den neugefundenen Gedichten der Korinna." *Glotta* 2:131–146.

Nachtergael, G. 1977. *Les Galates en Grèce et les Sōtéria de Delphes.* Brussels.

Naddaf, G. 2009. "Allegory and the Origins of Philosophy." In *Logos and Muthos: Philosophical Essays in Greek Literature,* ed. W. Wians. SUNY Series in Ancient Greek Philosophy, 99–131. Albany.

Naddaff, R. A. 2002. *Exiling the Poets: The Production of Censorship in Plato's Republic.* Chicago.

Nägelsbach, C. F. 1834. *Anmerkungen zur Ilias (Buch I–II.1–483) nebst Excursen über Gegenstände der homerischen Grammatik.* Nürnberg.

Nagy, B. 1978. "The Athenian Athlothetai." *Greek, Roman, and Byzantine Studies* 19:307–313.

———. 1992. "Athenian Officials on the Parthenon Frieze." *American Journal of Archaeology* 96:55–69.

Nagy, G. 1974. *Comparative Studies in Greek and Indic Meter.* Cambridge, MA.

———. 1976. "*Iambos:* Typologies of Invective and Praise." *Arethusa* 9:191–205.

———. 1981. "An Evolutionary Model for the Text Fixation of Homeric Epos." In *Oral Traditional Literature: A Festschrift for Albert Bates Lord,* ed. J. M. Foley, 390–393. Columbus.

———. 1986. "Ancient Greek Epic and Praise Poetry: Some Typological Considerations." In *Oral Tradition in Literature: Interpretation in Context*, ed. J. M. Foley, 89–102. Columbia.

———. 1989. "Early Greek Views of Poets and Poetry." In *The Cambridge History of Literary Criticism*, Vol. I: Classical Criticism, ed. G. A. Kennedy, 1–77. Cambridge.

———. 1990a. "Ancient Greek Poetry, Prophecy, and Concepts of Theory." In Kugel 1990:56–64.

———. 1990b. *Greek Mythology and Poetics*. Mythology and Poetics. Ithaca.

———. 1990c. *Pindar's Homer: The Lyric Possession of an Epic Past*. Baltimore.

———. 1992. "Authorisation and Authorship in the Hesiodic *Theogony*." *Ramus* 21:119–130.

———. 1995. "An Evolutionary Model for the Making of Homeric Poetry: Comparative Perspectives." In Carter and Morris 1995:163–179.

———. 1996a. "Autorité et auteur dans la *Théogonie* Hésiodique." In Blaise et al. 1996:41–52.

———. 1996b. *Homeric Questions*. Austin.

———. 1996c. *Poetry as Performance*. Cambridge.

———. 1999a. *The Best of the Achaeans*. 2nd ed. Baltimore.

———. 1999b. "Epic as Genre." In Beissinger et al. 1999:21–32.

———. 2000a. "Homeric *Humnos* as a Rhapsodic Term." In *Una nueva visión de la cultura griega antigua hacia el fin del milenio*, ed. A. M. González de Tobia, 385–401. La Plata.

———. 2000b. "Reading Greek Poetry Aloud: Evidence from the Bacchylides Papyri." *Quaderni urbinati di cultura classica* 64:7–28.

———. 2001. "Homeric Poetry and Problems of Multiformity: The 'Panathenaic Bottleneck.'" *Classical Philology* 96:111–121.

———. 2002. *Plato's Rhapsody and Homer's Music: The Poetics of the Panathenaic Festival in Classical Athens*. Hellenic Studies Series 1. Washington, DC.

———. 2003. *Homeric Responses*. Austin.

———. 2004. *Homer's Text and Language*. Urbana.

———. 2009a. "Hesiod and the Ancient Biographical Traditions." In *Brill's Companion to Hesiod*, ed. F. Montanari, A. Rengakos, and C. Tsagalis, 271–311. Leiden.

———. 2009b. *Homer the Classic*. Hellenic Studies Series 36. Washington, DC.

———. 2009c. "Traces of an Ancient System of Reading: Homeric Verse in the Venetus A." In *Recapturing a Homeric Legacy: Images and Insights from the Venetus A Manuscript of the* Iliad, ed. C. Dué. Hellenic Studies Series 35, 133–167. Washington, DC.

———. 2010a. *Homer the Preclassic*. Sather Classical Lectures 67. Berkeley.

————. 2010b. "The Meaning of *homoios* (ὁμοῖος) in *Theogony* 27 and Elsewhere." In *Allusion, Authority, and Truth: Critical Perspectives on Greek Poetic and Rhetorical Praxis*, ed. P. Mitsis and C. Tsagalis. Trends in Classics. Supplementary Volumes 7:153–167. Berlin.

Nails, D. 2002. *The People of Plato: A Prosopography of Plato and Other Socratics.* Indianapolis.

Näke, A. F. 1817. *Choerili Samii quae supersunt.* Leipzig.

Neeft, C. W. 1987. *Protocorinthian Subgeometric Aryballoi.* Amsterdam.

Neils, J. 1992a. *Goddess and Polis: The Panathenaic Festival in Ancient Athens.* Princeton.

————. 1992b. "The Panathenaia: An Introduction." In Neils 1992a:13–27.

————. 1992c. "Panathenaic Amphoras: Their Meaning, Makers, and Markets." In Neils 1992a:29–51.

————, ed. 1996. *Worshipping Athena: Panathenaia and Parthenon.* Wisconsin Studies in Classics. Madison.

Neitzel, H. 1980. "Hesiod und die lügenden Musen: Zur Interpretation von *Theogonie* 27f." *Hermes* 108:387–401.

Nelson, S. A. 1998. *God and the Land: The Metaphysics of Farming in Hesiod and Vergil.* New York.

Neumann, G. 1969. "Lykisch." In *Altkleinasiatische Sprachen.* Handbuch der Orientalistik, Erste Abteilung, II. Band, 1. und 2. Abschnitt, Lieferung 2:358–396. Leiden.

————. 1995. "Altgriechisch κόσμος und seine Sippe: Grundbedeutung und Etymologie." In Verba et structurae: *Festschrift für Klaus Strunk zum 65. Geburtstag*, ed. K. Strunk and H. Hettrich. Innsbrucker Beiträge zur Sprachwissenschaft 83:203–210. Innsbruck.

Newman, S. J. 1998. *Aristotle and Metaphor: His Theory and Its Practice.* PhD diss., University of Minnesota.

————. 2005. *Aristotle and Style.* Lewiston.

Newton, C. T. 1862–1863. *A History of Discoveries at Halicarnassus, Cnidus and Branchidae.* 2 vols. London.

Nicolai, W. 1983. "Rezeptionssteuerung in der Ilias." *Philologus* 127:1–12.

Nietzsche, F. 1870. "Der Florentinische Tractat über Homer und Hesiod, ihr Geschlecht und ihren Wettkampf." *Rheinisches Museum* 25:528–540.

————. 1873. "Der Florentinische Tractat über Homer und Hesiod, ihr Geschlecht und ihren Wettkampf." *Rheinisches Museum* 28:211–249.

Nilsson, M. P. 1958. "Das delphische Orakel in der neuesten Literatur." *Historia* 7:237–250.

————. 1967. *Geschichte der griechischen Religion.* Handbuch der Altertumswissenschaft V.2.1. Munich.

Nitzsch, G. W. 1828. *Quaestio Homerica IV, sive indagandae per Homeri* Odysseam *interpolationis praeparatio.* Kiliae.

Nizzo, V. 2007. *Ritorno ad Ischia: Dalla stratigrafia della necropoli di Pithekoussai alla tipologia dei materiali.* Naples.

Nollé, J., ed. 2001. *Side im Altertum: Geschichte und Zeugnisse II.* Inschriften grieschischer Städte aus Kleinasien 44. Bonn.

Nothdurft, W. 1978. "Noch einmal Πεῖραρ/Πείρατα bei Homer." *Glotta* 56:25–40.

Notopoulos, J. A. 1964. "Studies in Early Greek Oral Poetry." *Harvard Studies in Classical Philology* 68:1–77.

———. 1966. "Archilochus, the Aoidos." *Transactions of the American Philological Association* 97:311–315.

Nünlist, R. 1998. *Poetologische Bildersprache in der frühgriechischen Dichtung.* Beiträge zur Altertumskunde 101. Stuttgart.

Nussbaum, M. C., ed. 1978. *Aristotle's* De motu animalium. Princeton.

Nussbaum, M. C. and A. O. Rorty, eds. 1992. *Essays on Aristotle's* De anima. Oxford.

Oates, J. F., R. S. Bagnall, S. J. Clackson, A. A. O'Brien, J. D. Sosin, T. G. Wilfong, and K. A. Worp. 2001. *Checklist of Editions of Greek, Latin, Demotic and Coptic Papyri, Ostraca and Tablets.* Bulletin of the American Society of Papyrologists. Supplements 9. Oakville.

Ober, J. 1989. *Mass and Elite in Democratic Athens.* Princeton.

O'Connor, J. B. 1908. *Chapters in the History of Actors and Acting in Ancient Greece.* Chicago.

O'Gorman, N. 2005. "Aristotle's *Phantasia* in the *Rhetoric: Lexis,* Appearance, and the Epideictic Function of Discourse." *Philosophy and Rhetoric* 38:16–40.

Olson, S. D. 1995. *Blood and Iron.* Leiden.

———, ed. 2012. *The* Homeric Hymn to Aphrodite *and Related Texts: Text, Translation and Commentary.* Texte und Kommentare. Eine altertumswissenschaftliche Reihe 39. Berlin.

Onians, R. B. 1951. *The Origins of European Thought about the Body, the Mind, the Soul, the World, Time, and Fate.* Cambridge.

Orlandini, P. 1957. "Noterelle epigrafiche da Gela." *Kokalos* 3:94–97, with figs. 22–24.

Osborne, M. J. 1989. "The Chronology of Athens in the Mid Third Century B.C." *Zeitschrift für Papyrologie und Epigraphik* 78:209–242.

Osborne, R. 1991. "Pride and Prejudice, Sense and Subsistence: Exchange and Society in the Greek City." In Rich and Wallace-Hadrill 1991:118–145.

———. 1996. *Greece in the Making (1200–479 BC).* London.

Ostermann, C. 1847. *Commentationis de Demetrii Phalerei vita, rebus gestis et scriptorum reliquiis pars I.* Hersfeld.

———. 1857. *Commentationis de Demetrii Phalerei vita, rebus gestis et scriptorum reliquiis pars II*. Fulda.

Osthoff, H. 1898. "Allerhand Zauber etymologisch beleuchtet." *Beiträge zur Kunde der indogermanischen Sprachen* 24:109–173, 177–213.

O'Sullivan, L. 2009. *The Regime of Demetrius of Phalerum in Athens, 317–307 BCE*. Mnemosyne, bibliotheca classica Batava. Suplementum 318. Leiden.

O'Sullivan, N. 1992. *Alcidamas, Aristophanes, and the Beginnings of Greek Stylistic Theory*. Hermes Einzelschriften 60. Stuttgart.

———. 1996. "Written and Spoken in the First Sophistic." In *Voice into Text: Orality and Literacy in Ancient Greece*, ed. I. Worthington. Mnemosyne, bibliotheca classica Batava. Suplementum 157:115–127. Leiden.

Ott, S. D. 1992. *A Commentary on Plato's Ion*. PhD diss., Brown University.

Page, D. L. 1934. *Actors' Interpolations in Greek Tragedy, Studied with Special Reference to Euripides' Iphigeneia in Aulis*. Oxford.

———. 1956. "ὑποκριτής." *Classical Review* 6:191–192.

———, ed. 1981. *Further Greek Epigrams: Epigrams before A.D. 50 from the Greek Anthology and Other Sources, not Included in* Hellenistic Epigrams *or* The Garland of Philip. Revised and prepared for publication by R. B. Dawe and J. Diggle. Cambridge.

Pagliaro, A. 1951. "La terminologia poetica di Omero e l'origine dell'epica." *Ricerche Linguistiche* 2:1–46.

Palaima, T. G. 1991. "The Advent of the Greek Alphabet on Cyprus: A Competition of Scripts." In Phoinikeia Grammata. *Lire et écrire en Méditerranée*, ed. C. Baurain, C. Bonnet, and V. Krings, 449–471. Namur.

———. 2005. *The Triple Invention of Writing in Cyprus and Written Sources for Cypriote History*. Nicosia.

Paley, F. A., ed. 1851. *Aeschylus* Supplices. Cambridge.

Pallone, M. R. 1984. "L'epica agonale in età ellenistica." *Orpheus* 5:156–166.

Pankiewicz, R. 1989. *Fluctuations de valeur des métaux monétaires dans l'Antiquité romaine*. Publications universitaires européennes. Série III, Histoire, sciences auxiliaires de l'histoire 384. Frankfurt am Main.

Papagiannopoulos, A. 1947–1948. "Ἔρευναι ἐν Θεσπιαῖς." *Πολέμων* 3:73–80.

Papathanasopoulos, T. 1999. *Τὸ Ὠδεῖο τοῦ Περικλῆ: νέα θεώρηση τοῦ μνημείου*. PhD diss., University of Crete, Rethymnon.

———. 2003. *Τὸ Τρόπαιο*. Athens.

Paquette, D. 1984. *L'instrument de musique dans la céramique de la Grèce antique: Études d'Organologie*. Paris.

Parke, H. W. 1940. "A Note on the Delphic Priesthood." *Classical Quarterly* 34:85–89.

———. 1967. *The Oracles of Zeus: Dodona, Olympia, Ammon*. Cambridge, MA.

———. 1977. *Festivals of the Athenians,* Aspects of Greek and Roman Life. London.

———. 1981. "Apollo and the Muses, or Prophecy in Greek Verse." *Hermathena* 130–131:99–112.

———. 1985. *The Oracles of Apollo in Asia Minor.* London.

Parke, H. W. and D. E. W. Wormell. 1956a. *The Delphic Oracle: The History.* Oxford.

———. 1956b. *The Delphic Oracle: The Oracular Responses.* Oxford.

Parker, R. 2004. "New 'Panhellenic' Festivals in Hellenistic Greece." In *Mobility and Travel in the Mediterranean from Antiquity to the Middle Ages,* ed. R. Schlesier and U. Zellmann. Reiseliteratur und Kulturanthropologie 1:9–22. Münster.

———. 2005. *Polytheism and Society at Athens.* Oxford.

Parry, A. M. 1989a. *The Language of Achilles and Other Papers.* Oxford.

———. 1989b. "Have we Homer's *Iliad?*" In Parry 1989a:104–140.

Parry, M. 1971. *The Making of Homeric Verse: The Collected Papers of Milman Parry.* New York.

Partee, M. H. 1971. "Inspiration in the Aesthetics of Plato." *Journal of Aesthetics and Art Criticism* 30:87–95.

Patillon, M., ed. 2008. *Corpus rhetoricum.* Paris.

Patzer, H. 1952. "ΡΑΨΩΙΔΟΣ." *Hermes* 80:314–325.

———. 1970. "Review of B. Zucchelli, Ὑποκριτής: *Origine e storia del termine.*" *Gnomon* 42:641–652.

Pavese, C. O. 1996. "La iscrizione sulla kotyle di Nestor da Pithekoussai." *Zeitschrift für Papyrologie und Epigraphik* 114:1–23.

Payne, H., A. A. A. Blakeway, and T. J. Dunbabin. 1940. *Perachora: The Sanctuaries of Hera Akraia and Limenia.* Oxford.

Pébarthe, C. 2006. *Cité, démocratie et écriture: histoire de l'alphabétisation d'Athènes à l'époque classique.* Culture et cité 3. Paris.

Pedersen, H. 1909–1913. *Vergleichende Grammatik der keltischen Sprachen.* Göttinger Sammlung indogermanischer Grammatiken. Göttingen.

Peek, W., ed. 1955. *Griechische Vers-Inschriften.* Berlin.

Pelliccia, H. N. 1995. *Mind, Body, and Speech in Homer and Pindar.* Hypomnemata 107. Göttingen.

———. 2003. "Two Points about Rhapsodes." In Finkelberg and Stroumsa 2003:97–116.

Pemberton, E. G. 1976. "A Note on Skiagraphia." *American Journal of Archaeology* 80:82–84.

Pépin, J. 1975. "L'herméneutique ancienne: les mots et les idées." *Poétique* 23:291–300.

Perceau, S. 2005. "L'un chante, l'autre pas. Retour sur la phorminx d'Achille."
   Gaia 9:65–85.

Perlman, S. 1963. "The Politicians in the Athenian Democracy of the Fourth
   Century B.C." *Athenaeum* 41:327–355.

Pernot, L. 1993. *La rhétorique de l'éloge dans le monde gréco-romain.* Collection des
   Études Augustiniennes, Série Antiquité 137. Paris.

Perpillou-Thomas, F. 1993. *Fêtes d'Égypte ptolémaïque et romaine d'après la docu-
   mentation papyrologique grecque.* Studia hellenistica 31. Louvain.

———. 1995. "Artistes et athlètes dans les papyrus grecs d'Égypte." *Zeitschrift
   für Papyrologie und Epigraphik* 108:225–251.

Peters, M. 1980. *Untersuchungen zur Vertretung der indogermanischen Laryngale
   im Griechischen.* Sitzungsberichte, Österreichische Akademie der
   Wissenschaften, Philosophisch-Historische Klasse 377. Vienna.

———. 1986. "Zur Frage einer 'achäischen' Phase des griechischen
   Epos." In O-o-pe-ro-si: *Festschrift für Ernst Risch zum 75. Geburtstag,*
   ed. A. Etter, 303–319. Berlin.

———. 1987. "Indogermanische Chronik 33, G30." *Die Sprache* 33:233–242.

———. 1998. "Homerisches und Unhomerisches bei Homer und auf dem
   Nestorbecher." In *Mír Curad: Studies in Honor of Calvert Watkins,*
   ed. J. Jasonoff, H. C. Melchert, and L. Oliver Innsbrucker Beiträge zur
   Sprachwissenschaft 92:585–602. Innsbruck.

Petrakos, B., ed. 1997. Οἱ Ἐπιγραφὲς τοῦ Ὠρωποῦ, Βιβλιοθήκη τῆς ἐν Ἀθήναις
   Ἀρχαιολογικῆς Ἑταιρείας 170. Athens.

Petrie, W. M. F. 1889. *Hawara, Biahmu, and Arsinoe.* London.

Pfeiffer, R. 1968. *History of Classical Scholarship.* 2 vols. Oxford.

Pfister, F. 1939. "Ekstasis." In *Pisciculi: Studien zur Religion und Kultur des
   Altertums, Franz Joseph Dölger zum sechzigsten Geburtstage darge-
   boten von Freunden, Verehrern und Schülern,* ed. A. Klauser, Theodor
   und Rücker, 178–191. Münster in Westfalen.

———. 1959. "Ekstase." In *Reallexikon für Antike und Christentum,* Vol. 4,
   cols. 944–987. Stuttgart.

Pfyffer, A. K., T. Theurillat, and S. Verdan. 2005. "Graffiti d'époque géométrique
   provenant du sanctuaire d'Apollon Daphnéphoros à Erétrie." *Zeitschrift
   für Papyrologie und Epigraphik* 151:51–83.

Picard, C. 1922. *Éphèse et Claros: recherches sur les sanctuaires et les cultes de l'Ionie
   du nord.* Paris.

Piccardi, L. 2000. "Active Faulting at Delphi, Greece: Seismotectonic
   Remarks and a Hypothesis for the Geologic Environment of a Myth."
   Geology 28.7:651–654.

Piccardi, L., C. Monti, O. Vaselli, F. Tassi, K. Gaki-Papanastassiou, and D. Papanastassiou. 2008. "Scent of a Myth: Tectonics, Geochemistry and Geomythology at Delphi (Greece)." *Journal of the Geological Society* 165:5–18.

Piccirilli, L., ed. 1975. *Μεγαρικά: Testimonianze e frammenti.* Pisa.

Pickard-Cambridge, A. W. 1927. *Dithyramb, Tragedy and Comedy.* Oxford.

———. 1946. *The Theatre of Dionysus in Athens.* Oxford.

———. 1988. *The Dramatic Festivals of Athens.* 2nd ed. Oxford.

Pleket, H. W. 1975. "Games, Prizes, Athletes and Ideology." *Stadion* 1:49–89. Journal also published as *Arena*.

———. 1992. "The Participants in the Ancient Olympic Games: Social Background and Mentality." In *Praktika Symposiou Olympiakōn Agōnōn, 5–9 Septemvriou 1988 (Proceedings of an International Symposium on the Olympic Games, 5–9 September 1988)*, ed. W. D. E. Coulson and H. Kyrieleis, 147–152. Athens.

———. 2001. "Zur Soziologie des antiken Sports." *Nikephoros* 14:157–212.

Pöhlmann, E. 1994. *Einführung in die Überlieferungsgeschichte und in die Textkritik der antiken Literatur,* Vol. 1: *Altertum.* Darmstadt.

Poland, F. 1934. "Technitai." Real-Encyclopädie der classischen Altertumswissenschaft, Vol. 5.2, cols. 2473–2558. Stuttgart.

Poliakoff, M. 1982. *Studies in the Terminology of the Greek Combat Sports.* Beiträge zur klassischen Philologie 146. Königstein.

Pomtow, H. R. 1881. *Quaestionum de oraculis caput selectum: de oraculis quae exstant graecis trimetro iambico compositis.* Berlin.

Popham, M. 1994. "Precolonisation: Early Greek Contact with the East." In Tsetskhladze and De Angelis 1994:11–34.

Popham, M. R., P. G. Calligas, and L. H. Sackett. 1988–1989. "Further Excavation of the Toumba Cemetery at Lefkandi, 1984 and 1986, a Preliminary Report." *Archaeological Reports* 35:117–129.

Porzig, W. 1942. *Die Namen für Satzinhalte im Griechischen und im Indogermanischen.* Untersuchungen zur indogermanischen Sprach- und Kulturwissenschaft 10. Berlin.

Porzio Gernia, M. L. 1989. "Ricostruzione linguistica e ricostruzione culturale: la funzione delle radici *men-* e *wat-* nell'antica cultura indoeuropea." *Quaderni dell'Istituto di glottologia* 1:79–91.

Poste, E., ed. 1866. *Aristotle on Fallacies.* London.

Powell, B. B. 1989. "Why Was the Greek Alphabet Invented? The Epigraphical Evidence." *Classical Antiquity* 8:321–350.

———. 1991. *Homer and the Origin of the Greek Alphabet.* Cambridge.

———. 1997. "Homer and Writing." In Morris and Powell 1997:3–32.

———. 2002. *Writing and the Origins of Greek Literature*. Cambridge.

Powell, J. E. 1938. *A Lexicon to Herodotus*. Cambridge.

Powell, J. U. 1929. "Later Epic Poetry in the Greek World." In *New Chapters in the History of Literature. Second Series*, ed. J. U. Powell and E. A. Barber, 35–46. Oxford.

Pratt, L. H. 1993. *Lying and Poetry from Homer to Pindar: Falsehood and Deception in Archaic Greek Poetics*. Michigan Monographs in Classical Antiquity. Ann Arbor.

———. 1999–2000. "Review of M. Finkelberg, *The Birth of Literary Fiction in Ancient Greece*." *CW* 93:301–302.

Prauscello, L. 2006. *Singing Alexandria: Music between Practice and Textual Transmission*. Mnemosyne, bibliotheca classica Batava. Suplementum 274. Leiden.

Preuner, E. 1903. "Griechische Siegerlisten." *Mitteilungen des Deutschen Archäologischen Instituts (Athen. Abt.)* 28:338–382.

———. 1924. "ΣΑΜΙΑΚΑ." *Mitteilungen des Deutschen Archäologischen Instituts (Athen. Abt.)* 49:26–49.

Price, S. R. F. and O. Murray, eds. 1990. *The Greek City: From Homer to Alexander*. Oxford.

Prier, R. A. 1989. Thauma idesthai: *The Phenomenology of Sight and Appearance in Archaic Greek*. Tallahassee.

Pritchard, J. B., ed. 1969. *Ancient Near Eastern Texts Relating to the Old Testament*. 3rd ed. Princeton.

Pritchett, W. K. 1986. "The *Pannychis* of the Panathenaia." In *Philia epē eis Geōrgion E. Mylōnan* II, 179–188. Athens.

Probert, P. 2003. *A New Short Guide to the Accentuation of Ancient Greek*. BCP Advanced Language Series. London.

———. 2006. *Ancient Greek Accentuation: Synchronic Patterns, Frequency Effects, and Prehistory*. Oxford Classical Monographs. Oxford.

Pucci, P. 1977. *Hesiod and the Language of Poetry*. Baltimore.

Puelma, M. 1989. "Der Dichter und die Wahrheit in der griechischen Poetik von Homer bis Aristoteles." *Museum Helveticum* 46:65–100.

Puhvel, J. 1976. "The Origins of Greek *Kosmos* and Latin *Mundus*." *American Journal of Philology* 97:154–167.

———. 1984–. *Hittite Etymological Dictionary*. Berlin.

Pulgram, E. 1981. "Attic Shortening or Metrical Lengthening?" *Glotta* 59:75–93.

Raaflaub, K. A. 1996. "Equalities and Inequalities in Athenian Democracy." In Dēmokratia: *A Conversation on Democracies, Ancient and Modern*, ed. J. Ober and C. Hedrick, 139–174, with bibliography at 401–448. Princeton.

————. 2006. "Historical Approaches to Homer." In *Ancient Greece: From the Mycenaean Palaces to the Age of Homer*, ed. S. Deger-Jalkotzy and I. S. Lemos, 449–462. Edinburgh.

Race, W. H. 1987. "Pindaric Encomium and Isocrates' *Evagoras.*" *Transactions of the American Philological Association* 117:131–155.

————. 1990. *Style and Rhetoric in Pindar's Odes.* Atlanta.

————, ed. 1997. *Pindar: Nemean Odes, Isthmian Odes, Fragments.* The Loeb Classical Library 485. Cambridge, MA.

Radermacher, L. 1931. *Der homerische Hermeshymnus.* Akademie der Wissenschaften in Wien, Philosophisch-historische Klasse, Sitzungsberichte 213.1. Vienna.

————, ed. 1951. *Artium scriptores: Reste der voraristotelischen Rhetorik.* Vienna.

Radif, L. 2004. "Il κατὰ μοῖραν 'su misura' dell'epos omerico." In *Dialetti, dialettismi, generi letterari e funzioni sociali: atti del V Colloquio internazionale di linguistica greca (Milano, 12–13 settembre 2002)*, ed. G. Rocca. Hellada: Collana di storia linguistica della Grecia e del Mediterraneo orientale diretta da Mario Negri 1:397–407. Alessandria.

Radloff, W. 1990 [1885]. "Samples of Folk Literature from the North Turkic Tribes. Preface to Volume V: *The Dialect of the Kara-Kirgiz.*" *Oral Tradition* 5:73–90. First published as *Proben der Volkslitteratur der nördlichen türkischen Stämme V: Der Dialekt der Kara-Kirgisen.* St. Petersburg.

Ramos Jurado, E. A. 1999. "Un ejemplo de exégesis alegórica, la *Teomaquía* homérica de Teágenes de Regio." In *Desde los poemas homéricos hasta la prosa griega del siglo IV d.C.: veintiséis estudios filológicos*, ed. J. A. López Férez, 45–59. Madrid.

Rapp, C. 2002. *Aristoteles* Rhetorik. Aristoteles: Werke in deutscher Übersetzung 4. In 2 parts (cited as 1 and 2). Berlin.

Rassow, J. 1883. *Quaestiones selectae de Euripideorum nuntiorum narrationibus.* Greifswald.

Real Academia Española. 1973. *Esbozo de una nueva gramática de la lengua española.* Madrid.

————. 2009–2011. *Nueva gramática de la lengua española.* In 3 vols.: *Morfología y Sintaxis I, Sintaxis II*, and *Fonética y fonología* (cited as 1, 2, and 3). Madrid.

Reece, S. 2005. "Homer's *Iliad* and *Odyssey*: From Oral Performance to Written Text." In *New Directions in Oral Theory*, ed. M. C. Amodio. Medieval and Renaissance Texts and Studies 287:43–89. Tempe.

Rees, D. A. 1971. "Aristotle's Treatment of Φαντασία." In *Essays in Ancient Greek Philosophy*, ed. J. P. Anton and G. L. Kustas, 491–504. Albany.

Reeve, M. D. 1972. "Interpolation in Greek Tragedy I." *Greek, Roman, and Byzantine Studies* 13:247–265.

———. 1973. "Interpolation in Greek Tragedy III." *Greek, Roman, and Byzantine Studies* 14:145–171.

Rehm, A., ed. 1958. *Didyma II: Die Inschriften.* Berlin.

Reich, H. 1903. *Der Mimus: Ein litterar-entwickelungsgeschichtlicher Versuch.* Berlin.

Reichel, W. 1901. *Homerische Waffen: archäologische Untersuchungen.* Vienna.

Reinhardt, K. 1996. "The Adventures in the *Odyssey.*" In *Reading the* Odyssey: *Selected Interpretive Essays,* ed. S. L. Schein, 83–87. Translated by H. I. Flower. Princeton.

Reisch, A. 1885. *De musicis graecorum certaminibus capita quattuor.* Vienna.

Reiske, J. J., ed. 1765–1766. *Theocriti reliquiae utroque sermone cum scholiis graecis et commentariis integris Henrici Stephani, Josephi Scaligeri, et Isaci Casauboni.* 2 vols. Vienna.

Renehan, R. 1976. *Studies in Greek Texts: Critical Observations to Homer, Plato, Euripides, Aristophanes and other Authors.* Hypomnemata 43. Göttingen.

Rhodes, P. J. 1993. *A Commentary on the Aristotelian* Athenaion Politeia. Oxford.

Rich, J. and A. Wallace-Hadrill, eds. 1991. *City and Country in the Ancient World.* Leicester-Nottingham Studies in Ancient Society 2. London.

Richards, H. P. 1915. *Aristotelica.* London.

Richardson, N. J. 1975. "Homeric Professors in the Age of the Sophists." *Proceedings of the Cambridge Philological Society* 201:65–81.

———. 1981. "The Contest of Homer and Hesiod and Alcidamas' *Mouseion.*" *Classical Quarterly* 31:1–10.

Ricoeur, P. 1996. "Between Rhetoric and Poetics." In Rorty 1996:324–384.

Ridgway, D. 1992. *The First Western Greeks.* Cambridge. Revised version of *L'Alba della Magna Grecia.* 1984. Milan.

———. 1997. "Nestor's Cup and the Etruscans." *Oxford Journal of Archaeology* 16:325–344.

Rigsby, K. J. 1987a. "A Decree of Haliartus on Cult." *American Journal of Philology* 108:729–740.

———. 1987b. "Megara and Tripodiscus." *Greek, Roman, and Byzantine Studies* 28:93–102.

Rihll, T. E. 1999. *Greek Science.* Greece & Rome. New Surveys in the Classics 29. Oxford.

Ringwood, I. C. 1927. *Agonistic Features of Local Greek Festivals Chiefly from Inscriptional Evidence.* PhD diss., Columbia University.

Ringwood Arnold, I. 1936. "Festivals of Rhodes." *American Journal of Archaeology* 40:432–436. Married name of I. C. Ringwood (cf. *CW* 27.21, 1934, 167 no. 42).

Risch, E. 1974. *Wortbildung der homerischen Sprache.* 2nd ed. Berlin.

———. 1987. "Zum Nestorbecher aus Ischia." *Zeitschrift für Papyrologie und Epigraphik* 70:1–9.

Rispoli, G. M. 1980. "Teagene o dell'allegoria." *Vichiana* 9:243–257.

———. 1985. *L'artista sapiente: per una storia della fantasia.* Naples.

Ritoók, Z. 1962. "Rhapsodos." *Acta Antiqua Academiae Scientiarum Hungaricae* 10:225–231.

———. 1989. "The Views of Early Greek Epic on Poetry and Art." *Mnemosyne* 42:331–348.

———. 1991. "Alkidamas *Über die Sophisten.*" *Philologus* 135:157–163.

Riu, X. 2009. "Percezione, *phantasia, mimēsis* in Aristotele." *Quaderni del Ramo d'Oro* 2:18–35.

Rix, H. 1976. *Historische Grammatik des Griechischen: Laut- und Formenlehre.* Darmstadt.

———. 1984. "La scrittura e la lingua." In *Etruschi: una nuova immagine,* ed. M. Cristofani, 199–227. Florence.

Robb, K. 1994. *Literacy and Paideia in Ancient Greece.* New York.

Robert, C. 1915. *Oidipus: Geschichte eines poetischen Stoffs im griechischen Altertum.* Berlin.

Robert, J. and L. Robert. 1983. *Fouilles d'Amyzon en Carie I.* Paris.

Robert, L. 1929. "Décrets de Delphes." *Bulletin de correspondance hellénique* 53:34–41. Reprinted in *Opera minora selecta* I:247–254. 1969. Amsterdam.

———. 1936. "Ἀρχαιολόγος." *Revue des études grecques* 49:235–254. Reprinted in *Opera minora selecta* I:671–690. 1969. Amsterdam.

———. 1968. "De Delphes à l'Oxus: Inscriptions grecques nouvelles de la Bactriane." *CRAI* 112:416–457. Reprinted in *Opera minora selecta* V:510–551. 1989. Amsterdam.

———. 1980. "Deux poètes grecs à l'époque impériale." In *ΣΤΗΛΗ: Τόμος εἰς μνήμην Νικολάου Κοντολέοντος,* 1–20. Athens.

———. 1983. "Bulletin épigraphique 475." *Revue des études grecques* 96:182–184.

———. 1989. "Discours d'ouverture du VIIIe Congrès international d'épigraphie grecque et latine à Atheènes, 1982." In *Opera minora selecta: Épigraphie et antiquités grecques* VI:709–719. Amsterdam.

Roberts, W. Rhys, ed. 1902. *Demetrius* On Style. Cambridge.

Robinson, T. L. 1981. *Theological Oracles and the Sanctuaries of Claros and Ḍidyma.* PhD diss., Harvard University.

Robkin, A. L. H. 1976. *The Odeion of Perikles: Some Observations on its History, Form, and Functions.* PhD diss., University of Washington.

———. 1979. "The Odeion of Perikles: The Date of its Construction and the Periklean Building Program." *The Ancient World* 2:3–12.

Roehl, H., ed. 1882. *Inscriptiones graecae antiquissimae praeter atticas in Attica repertas.* Berlin.

———. 1884. "Jahresbericht über die griechische Epigraphik für 1878–1882." *Jahresbericht über die Fortschritte der classischen Alterthumswissenschaft (Zehnter Jahrgang, 1882)* 32:1–154.

Roemer, A., ed. 1898. *Aristotelis* Ars rhetorica. Leipzig.

Roesch, P. 1982. *Études béotiennes.* Paris.

———, ed. 2009 [2007]. *Les inscriptions de Thespies.* Revised ed. Lyon. Electronic edition prepared by G. Argoud, A. Schachter, and G. Vottéro, available at http://www.hisoma.mom.fr/thespies.html. Cited as *IThesp.*

Rohde, E. 1925. *Psyche: The Cult of Souls and Belief in Immortality among the Greeks.* London.

Roller, D. W. 1989. *Tanagran Studies.* In 2 vols.: *Sources and Documents on Tanagra in Boiotia* and *The Prosopography of Tanagra in Boiotia.* McGill University Monographs in Classical Archaeology and History 9. Amsterdam.

Rollston, C. A. 2008. "The Phoenician Script of the Tel Zayit Abecedary and Putative Evidence for Israelite Literacy." In *Literate Culture and Tenth-Century Canaan: The Tel Zayit Abecedary in Context,* ed. R. E. Tappy and P. K. McCarter, 61–96. Winona Lake.

Romano, D. G. 1985. "The Panathenaic Stadium and Theater of Lykourgos: A Re-examination of the Facilities on the Pnyx Hill." *American Journal of Archaeology* 89:441–454.

———. 1996. "Lykourgos, the Panathenaia and the Great Altar of Athena: Further Thoughts Concerning the Pnyx Hill." In Forsén and Stanton 1996:71–85, with bibliography at 117–129 and figures after 142.

Rorty, A. O., ed. 1996. *Essays on Aristotle's Rhetoric.* Berkeley.

Rosen, R. M. 1990. "Poetry and Sailing in Hesiod's *Works and Days.*" *Classical Antiquity* 9:99–113.

Rosenthall, S. 1994. *Vowel/Glide Alternation in a Theory of Constraint Interaction.* PhD diss., University of Massachusetts, Amherst.

Rosivach, V. J. 1991. "IG 2² 334 and the Panathenaic Hekatomb." *La Parola del passato* 46:430–442.

Rösler, W. 1980. "Die Entdeckung der Fiktionalität in der Antike." *Poetica* 12:283–319.

———. 2002. "Review of M. Finkelberg, *The Birth of Literary Fiction in Ancient Greece.*" *Gnomon* 74:295–299.

Ross, L. 1855–1861. *Archäologische Aufsätze.* In 2 vols. Leipzig.

Ross, W. D., ed. 1924. *Rhetorica, De Rhetorica ad Alexandrum, De Poetica.* The Works of Aristotle 11. Translation of *Rhetorica* by W. R. Roberts. Oxford.

———, ed. 1959. *Aristotelis* Ars rhetorica. Oxford.

————, ed. 1961. *Aristotle* De anima. Oxford.

Roth, P. 1988. "The Etymology of the Term *Mantis* ('Prophet') in Ancient Greek." In *East Meets West: Homage to Edgar C. Knowlton, Jr.*, ed. R. L. Hadlich and J. D. Ellsworth, 237–245. Honolulu.

Rotroff, S. I. 1996. "Pnyx III: Pottery and Stratigraphy." In Forsén and Stanton 1996:35–40, with bibliography at 117–129 and figures after 142.

Rotroff, S. I. and J. M. Camp. 1996. "The Date of the Third Period of the Pnyx." *Hesperia* 65:263–294.

Rotstein, A. 2000. "Review of M. Finkelberg, *The Birth of Literary Fiction in Ancient Greece.*" *Scripta classica Israelica* 19:285–289.

————. 2010. *The Idea of* Iambos. Oxford.

Roueché, C. 1993. *Performers and Partisans at Aphrodisias in the Roman and Late Roman Periods.* JRS Monographs 6. London.

Rouget, G. 1985. *Music and Trance: A Theory of the Relations between Music and Possession.* Chicago.

Rousseau, P. 1996. "Instruire Persès: Notes sur l'ouverture des *Travaux* d'Hésiode." In Blaise et al. 1996:93–67.

Rouveret, A. 1989. *Histoire et imaginaire de la peinture ancienne: Ve siècle av. J.-C.- Ier siècle ap. J.-C.* Bibliothèque des Écoles françaises d'Athènes et de Rome 274. Rome.

————. 2006. "*Skiagraphia/scaenographia*: quelques remarques." *Pallas* 71:71–80.

Roux, G. 1976. *Delphes, son oracle et ses dieux.* Paris.

Rowe, C. and S. Broadie, eds. 2002. *Aristotle* Nicomachean Ethics. Translation (with historical introduction) by C. Rowe. Philosophical introduction and commentary by S. Broadie. Oxford.

Rubinstein, L. 2000. *Litigation and Cooperation: Supporting Speakers in the Courts of Classical Athens.* Historia Einzelschriften 147. Stuttgart.

Ruck, P. 1991. *Pergament: Geschichte, Struktur, Restaurierung, Herstellung.* Sigmaringen.

Rudberg, G. 1947. "Thespis und die Tragödie." *Eranos* 45:13–21.

Ruhnken, D. 1828. *Orationes, dissertationes, et epistolae.* Brunswig.

Ruijgh, C. J. 1985. "Problèmes de philologie mycénienne." *Minos* 19:105–167.

————. 1995. "D'Homére aux origines proto-mycéniennes de la tradition épique. Analyse dialectologique du langage homérique, avec un *excursus* sur la création de l'alphabet grec." In Crielaard 1995:1–96.

————. 1997. "La date de la création de l'alphabet grec et celle de l'épopée homérique." *Bibliotheca Orientalis* 54:534–604.

Ruipérez, M. S. 1989a [1956]. "Esquisse d'une histoire du vocalisme grec." In Ruipérez 1989b:63–77. First published in *Word* 12:67–81.

————. 1989b. *Opuscula selecta*. Innsbrucker Beiträge zur Sprachwissenschaft 58. Innsbruck.

————. 1991. *Estructura del sistema de aspectos y tiempos del verbo griego antiguo*. Madrid.

Rumpel, J. 1883. *Lexicon Pindaricum*. Leipzig.

Russell, D. A. 1990. "*Ēthos* in Oratory and Rhetoric." In *Characterization and Individuality in Greek Literature*, ed. C. Pelling, 197–212. Oxford.

Russell, D. A. and D. Konstan, eds. 2005. *Heraclitus:* Homeric Problems. Atlanta.

Russo, J. 1999. "Stesichorus, Homer, and the Forms of Early Greek Epic." In Euphrosyne: *Studies in Ancient Epic and its Legacy in Honor of Dimitris N. Maronitis*, ed. J. N. Kazazis and A. Rengakos, 339–348. Stuttgart.

Russo, J., M. Fernández-Galiano, and A. Heubeck. 1992. *A Commentary on Homer's Odyssey*, Vol. 3: Books 17–24. Oxford.

Rutherford, R. B. 2000. "Review of M. Finkelberg, *The Birth of Literary Fiction in Ancient Greece*." *Classical Philology* 95:482–486.

Rzach, A., ed. 1908. *Hesiodi carmina (accedit certamen quod dicitur Homeri et Hesiodi)*. 2nd ed. Bibliotheca Scriptorum Graecorum et Romanorum Teubneriana. Leipzig.

Saito, T. 1999. "The Decree of the Hephaistia in 421/0 B.C. and the Athenian Demos." *Journal of Classical Studies* 47:32–40.

Salomons, R. P., ed. 1996. *Papyri Bodleianae I*. Studia Amstelodamensia ad epigraphicam, ius antiquum et papyrologicam pertinentia 34. Amsterdam.

Samuel, A. E. 1972. *Greek and Roman Chronology: Calendars and Years in Classical Antiquity*. Handbuch der Altertumswissenschaft I.7. Munich.

Sancisi-Weerdenburg, H., ed. 2000. *Peisistratos and the Tyranny: A Reappraisal of the Evidence*. Publications of the Netherlands Institute at Athens 3. Amsterdam.

Sandin, P. 2005. *Aeschylus'* Supplices: *Introduction and Commentary on vv. 1-523*. 2nd ed. Lund.

Sandys, J. E., ed. 1909. *The* Rhetoric *of Aristotle*. Translated by R. C. Jebb. Cambridge.

Santiago Álvarez, R.-A. and M. Gardeñes Santiago. 2006. "Algunas observaciones a la 'Lettre d'Apatorios à Léanax'." *Zeitschrift für Papyrologie und Epigraphik* 157:57–69.

Sass, B. 2005. *The Alphabet at the Turn of the Millennium. The West Semitic Alphabet ca. 1150-850 BCE. The Antiquity of the Arabian, Greek and Phrygian Alphabets*. Journal of the Institute of Archaeology of Tel Aviv University, Occasional Publications 4. Tel Aviv.

Scaife, R. 1995. "The *Kypria* and its Early Reception." *Classical Antiquity* 14:164–191.

Schachter, A. 1978. "La fête des *Pamboiotia*: le dossier épigraphique." *Cahiers des études anciennes* 8:81–107.

———. 1981. *Cults of Boiotia*. 4 vols. Institute of Classical Studies, Bulletin Supplement 38. London.

Schanz, M., ed. 1881. *Platonis* Symposion. Leipzig.

Scheer, E., ed. 1881–1908. *Lycophronis* Alexandra. Berlin.

Schefold, K. 1991. "Die Bedeutung der Kunstgeschichte für die Datierung der frühgriechischen Epik." In Latacz 1991:513–526, 550–552.

———. 1992 [1978]. *Gods and Heroes in Late Archaic Greek Art*. Cambridge. First published as *Götter- und Heldensagen der Griechen in der spätarchaischen Kunst*. Munich.

———. 1993. *Götter- und Heldensagen der Griechen in der Früh- und Hocharchaischen Kunst*. Munich. Revision of *Frühgriechische Sagenbilder*. 1964. Munich.

Scheid, J. and J. Svenbro. 1996. *The Craft of Zeus: Myths of Weaving and Fabric*. Cambridge, MA.

Scheinberg, S. 1979. "The Bee Maidens of the Homeric Hymn to Hermes." *Harvard Studies in Classical Philology* 83:1–28.

Schenkl, H. 1898. "Die handschriftliche Überlieferung der Reden des Themistius." *Wiener Studien* 20:205–243.

Scherer, A. 1975. "Review of *Mélanges de linguistique et de philologie grecques offerts à Pierre Chantraine*." *Kratylos* 18:142–147.

Schiappa, E. 1999. *The Beginnings of Rhetorical Theory in Classical Greece*. New Haven.

Schironi, F. 2010. *Τὸ μέγα βιβλίον: Book-ends, End-titles, and* Coronides *in Papyri with Hexametric Poetry*. The American Studies in Papyrology 48. Durham.

Schloemann, J. 2000. "Spontaner und vorbereiteter Vortrag: *Hypokrisis* im dritten Buch der Aristotelischen *Rhetorik*." *Philologus* 144:206–216.

———. 2002. "Entertainment and Democratic Distrust: The Audience's Attitudes Towards Oral and Written Oratory in Classical Athens." In Epea *and* Grammata: *Oral and Written Communication in Ancient Greece*, ed. I. Worthington and J. M. Foley. Orality and Literacy in Ancient Greece 4:133–146, with bibliography at 191–201. Leiden.

Schmid, C. 1908. *Homerische Studien III: Die* Ilias *und die Kunst des Dramas nach den Begriffen der antiken Schulerklärung*. K. humanistischen Gymnasiums zu Weiden am Schlusse des Schuljahres 1907/08. Weiden.

Schmid, W. and O. Stählin. 1929. *Geschichte der griechischen Literatur*. Munich.

Schmidt, K. F. W. 1911. "Review of A. S. Hunt, *The Oxyrhynchus Papyri. Part 7*." *Göttingische gelehrte Anzeigen* 173:448–460.

Schmitt, R. 1967. *Dichtung und Dichtersprache in indogermanischer Zeit.* Wiesbaden.

———, ed. 1968. *Indogermanische Dichtersprache.* Wege der Forschung 165. Darmstadt: Wissenschaftliche Buchgesellschaft.

———. 1977. *Einfürung in die griechischen Dialekte.* Die Altertumswissenschaft. Darmstadt.

———. 1978. "Die theophoren Eigennamen mit altiranisch *MIΘPA-." In *Études mithriaques,* ed. J. Duchesne-Guillemin. Acta Iranica 17:395–456. Tehran.

———. 1982. "Iranische Wörter und Namen im Lykischen." In *Serta indogermanica: Festschrift für Günter Neumann zum 60. Geburtstag,* ed. J. Tischler. Innsbrucker Beiträge zur Sprachwissenschaft 40:373–388. Innsbruck.

Schnapp-Gourbeillon, A. 2002. *Aux origines de la Grèce.* Paris.

Schofield, M. 1992 [1978]. "Aristotle on the Imagination." In Nussbaum and Rorty 1992:248–277. First published in *Aristotle on Mind and the Senses,* ed. G. E. R. Lloyd and G. E. L. Owen, 99–130. Cambridge.

Schousen, M. M. 1986. *On the Rhapsode: The Position of the* Ion *in Plato's Theory of Poetry.* Master's thesis, Duquesne University.

Schrader, H., ed. 1880. *Porphyrii* Quaestionum homericarum *ad* Iliadem *pertinentium reliquiae.* Leipzig.

Schreckenberg, H. 1960. *Δρᾶμα: vom Werden der griechischen Tragödie aus dem Tanz. Eine philologische Untersuchung.* Würzburg.

Schreiber, S. G. 2003. *Aristotle on False Reasoning: Language and the World in the* Sophistical Refutations. SUNY Series in Ancient Greek Philosophy. Albany.

Schultz, W. 1909–1912. *Rätsel aus dem hellenistischen Kulturkreise.* Leipzig.

Schulze, W. 1967 [1892]. *Quaestiones epicae.* Hildesheim.

Schuman, V. B., ed. 1980. *Washington University Papyri I: Non-Literary Texts (Nos. 1-61).* American Studies in Papyrology 17. Missoula.

Schwartz, E., ed. 1887–1891. *Scholia in Euripidem.* In 2 vols. Berlin.

———. 1892. *Commentatio de Thrasymacho Chalcedonio.* Rostock. Published as *Index scholarum in Academia Rostochiensi semestri aestivo a. 1892.*

———. 1940. "Der Name Homeros." *Hermes* 75:1–9.

Schweighäuser, J. 1801–1807. *Animadversiones in Athenaei* Deipnosophistas *post Isaacum Casaubonum.* Strasbourg.

Schwenk, C. J., ed. 1985. *Athens in the Age of Alexander: The Dated Laws and Decrees of 'The Lykourgan Era' 338-322 B.C.* Chicago.

Schwyzer, E. 1914. "Zur griechischen Laut- und Wortbildungslehre." *Glotta* 5:193–197.

———, ed. 1987 [1923]. *Dialectorum graecarum exempla epigraphica potiora.* Hildesheim.

Scott, J. A. 1921. "Homer as Poet of the *Thebais.*" *Classical Philology* 16:20–26.

———. 1922. "The Callinus of Pausanias IX.9.5." *Classical Philology* 17:358–360.

Seaford, R. 1977–1978. "The 'Hyporchema' of Pratinas." *Maia* 29–30:81–94.

Sealey, R. 1957. "From Phemios to Ion." *Revue des études grecques* 70:312–355.

Setti, A. 1958. "La memoria e il canto: saggio di poetica arcaica greca." *Studi italiani di filologia classica* 30:129–171.

Seymour, T. D. 1895. *Introduction to the Language and Verse of Homer.* Boston.

Seyrig, H. 1927. "Inscriptions de Chypre." *Bulletin de correspondance hellénique* 51:138–154.

Shapiro, H. A. 1989. *Art and Cult under the Tyrants in Athens.* Mainz am Rhein.

———. 1994. *Myth into Art: Poet and Painter in Classical Greece.* London.

———. 1998. "Hipparchos and the Rhapsodes." In Dougherty and Kurke 1998:92–107.

Shear, I. M. 2000. *Tales of Heroes: The Origin of the Homeric Texts.* New York.

Shear, J. L. 2001. *Polis and Panathenaia: The History and Development of Athena's Festival.* PhD diss., University of Pennsylvania.

Shear, T. L. 1966. *Studies in the Early Projects of the Periklean Building Program.* PhD diss., Princeton University.

Shelmerdine, C. W. 1997. "Review of Aegean Prehistory VI: The Palatial Bronze Age of the Southern and Central Greek Mainland." *American Journal of Archaeology* 101:537–585.

Sherratt, S. 2003. "Visible Writing: Questions of Script and Identity in Early Iron Age Greece and Cyprus." *Oxford Journal of Archaeology* 22:225–242.

Shive, D. 1996. "Ὅμηρον ἐξ Αἰσχύλου σαφηνίζειν: *Iliad* 7.332–338 and *Agamemnon* 433–455." *Phoenix* 50:189–196.

Sicking, C. M. J. and P. Stork. 1996. *Two Studies in the Semantics of the Verb in Classical Greek.* Mnemosyne, bibliotheca classica Batava. Suplementum 160. Leiden.

Sickinger, J. P. 1999. *Public Records and Archives in Classical Athens.* Studies in the History of Greece and Rome. Chapel Hill.

———. 2004. "The Laws of Athens: Publication, Preservation, Consultation." In *The Law and the Courts in Ancient Greece*, ed. E. M. Harris and L. Rubinstein, 93–109. London.

Sider, D. 2001. "'As Is the Generation of Leaves' in Homer, Simonides, Horace, and Stobaeus." In *The New Simonides*, ed. D. Boedeker and D. Sider, 272–288. Oxford.

Sifakis, G. M. 1967. *Studies in the History of Hellenistic Drama.* University of London Classical Studies 4. London.

———. 2002. "Looking for the Actor's Art in Aristotle." In Easterling and Hall 2002:148–164.

Signes Codoñer, J. 2004. *Escritura y literatura en la Grecia arcaica*. Madrid.

Sihler, A. L. 1995. *New Comparative Grammar of Greek and Latin*. New York.

Sijpesteijn, P. J. and K. A. Worp, eds. 1983. *Griechische Texte* V. Corpus papyrorum Raineri Archeducis Austriae 8. Vienna.

Simon, E. 1981. *Das Satyrspiel* Sphinx *des Aischylos.* Sitzungsberichte der Heidelberger Akademie der Wissenschaften, Philosophisch-historische Klasse, Jahrgang 1981, Bericht 5. Heidelberg.

———. 1983. *Festivals of Attica: An Archaeological Commentary*. Madison.

Simondon, M. 1982. *La mémoire et l'oubli dans la pensée grecque jusqu'à la fin du Ve siècle avant J.-C.: psychologie archaïque, mythes et doctrines.* Collection d'Études Mythologiques. Paris.

Sisko, J. E. 1995. *Thought and Perception in Aristotle's* De anima. PhD diss., Rutgers University.

Sittl, K., ed. 1889. Ἡσιόδου τὰ ἅπαντα, Zōgrapheios Hellēnikē bibliothēkē 3. Athens.

Skeat, T. C. 1982. "The Length of the Standard Papyrus Roll and the Cost-Advantage of the Codex." *Zeitschrift für Papyrologie und Epigraphik* 45:169–175.

Slater, N. W. 1976. "Symposium at Sea." *Harvard Studies in Classical Philology* 80:161–170.

Slater, W. J., ed. 1969. *Lexicon to Pindar*. Berlin.

Slatkin, L. M. 1996. "Composition by Theme and the *Mētis* of the *Odyssey*." In *Reading the* Odyssey: *Selected Interpretive Essays*, ed. S. L. Schein, 223–237. Princeton.

Slings, S. R. 2000. "Literature in Athens, 566–510 BC." In Sancisi-Weerdenburg 2000:57–77.

Small, J. P. 2003. *The Parallel Worlds of Classical Art and Text*. Cambridge.

Smith, A. C. 2005. "'Homeric' Art in Ancient Greece: The Case of Polyphemos." *Proceedings of the Bath Royal Literary & Scientific Institution* 9. At http://www.brlsi.org/proceed05/antiquity0605.html.

Smits, J., ed. 1939. *Plutarchus'* Leven van Lysander: *inleiding, tekst, commentaar*. Amsterdam.

Smyth, H. W. 1894. *The Sounds and Inflections of the Greek Dialects: Ionic*. Oxford.

Snell, B. 1975. "ΑΛΗΘΕΙΑ." *Würzburger Jahrbücher für die Altertumswissenschaft* 1:1–18. Published also under the title *Festschrift für Ernst Siegmann zum 60. Geburtstag*.

Snell, B., R. Kannicht, and S. Radt, eds. 1971–2004. *Tragicorum graecorum fragmenta*. Göttingen.

Snodgrass, A. M. 1971. *The Dark Age of Greece: An Archaeological Survey of the Eleventh to the Eighth Centuries BC*. Edinburgh.

———. 1980. *Archaic Greece: The Age of Experiment*. London.

———. 1987. *An Archaeology of Greece: The Present State and Future Scope of a Discipline*. Berkeley.

———. 1991. "Archaeology and the Study of the Greek City." In Rich and Wallace-Hadrill 1991:1–23.

———. 1998. *Homer and the Artists: Text and Picture in Early Greek Art*. Cambridge.

———. 2006. *Archaeology and the Emergence of Greece*. Ithaca.

Solmsen, F. 1901. *Untersuchungen zur griechischen Laut- und Verslehre*. Strassburg.

———. 1938. "Aristotle and Cicero on the Orator's Playing upon the Feelings." *Classical Philology* 33:390–404. Reprinted in *Kleine Schriften* II:216–230. 1968. Hildesheim.

———. 1949. *Hesiod and Aeschylus*. Cornell Studies in Classical Philology 30. Ithaca.

Sommer, F. 1905. *Griechische Lautstudien*. Strassburg.

Sommerbrodt, J. 1867. "Ueber die Bedeutung des Wortes ὑποκριτής." *Rheinisches Museum* 22:510–516.

———. 1875. "Noch ein Wort über den ὑποκριτής des griechischen Theaters." *Rheinisches Museum* 30:456–458.

———. 1876a. *Scaenica*. Berlin.

———. 1876b. "Zu F. Heimsoeth, *De voce ὑποκριτής commentariolus*." In Sommerbrodt 1876a:288–290. Includes the note: "Bonn 1873. (Im Verzeichniss der Vorlesungen an der Universität für das Winterhalbjahr 1873 und 1874.) XIV. 4."

Sonkowsky, R. P. 1959. "An Aspect of Delivery in Ancient Rhetorical Theory." *Transactions of the American Philological Association* 90:256–274.

Spawforth, A. J. S. 1989. "Agonistic Festivals in Roman Greece." In *The Greek Renaissance in the Roman Empire: Papers from the Tenth British Museum Classical Colloquium*, ed. S. Walker and A. Cameron. Bulletin Supplement 55:193–197. London.

Spengel, L., ed. 1867. *Aristotelis* Ars rhetorica. In 2 parts (cited as 1 and 2). Leipzig.

Spiller, H. A., J. R. Hale, and J. Z. De Boer. 2002. "The Delphic Oracle: A Multidisciplinary Defense of the Gaseous Vent Theory." *Clinical Toxicology* 40.2:189–196.

Stadter, P. A. 1989. *A Commentary on Plutarch's* Pericles. Chapell Hill.

Stahl, J. M. 1907. *Kritisch-historische Syntax des griechischen Verbums der klassischen Zeit*. Heidelberg.

Stallbaum, G., ed. 1825–1826. *Eustathii archiepiscopi Thessalonicensis commentarii ad Homeri* Odysseam. In 2 vols. Leipzig.

————, ed. 1857a. Io *Platonis dialogus*. Platonis *Opera omnia* IV.2:317–378. 2nd ed. Gotha.

————, ed. 1857b. *Platonis* Phaedrus. Platonis *Opera omnia* IV.1. 2nd ed. Gotha.

Stansbury-O'Donnell, M. D. 1999. *Pictorial Narrative in Ancient Greek Art.* Cambridge Studies in Classical Art and Iconography. Cambridge.

Stanton, G. R. and P. J. Bicknell. 1987. "Voting in Tribal Groups in the Athenian Assembly." *Greek, Roman, and Byzantine Studies* 28:51–92.

Starr, R. J. 1987. "Trimalchio's *Homeristae*." *Latomus* 46:199–200.

Steinbrink, B. 1992. "Actio." In *Historisches Wörterbuch der Rhetorik*, ed. G. Ueding, Vol. 1, cols. 43–74. Tübingen.

Steinhauer, G. 1993. "Νεότερα στοιχεῖα γιὰ τὸν σαλαμίνιο θίασο τῆς Βενδῖδος." *Ἀρχαιολογικὴ Ἐφημερὶς* 132:31–47.

Stella, L. A. 1978. *Tradizione micenea e poesia dell'*Iliade. Filologia e Critica 29. Rome.

Stephanēs, I. E. 1988. *Διονυσιακοὶ Τεχνῖται. Συμβολὲς στὴν προσωπογραφία τοῦ θεάτρου καὶ τῆς μουσικῆς τῶν ἀρχαίων Ἑλλήνων.* Hērakleio.

Steriade, D. 1982. *Greek Prosodies and the Nature of Syllabification.* PhD diss., Massachusetts Institute of Technology.

Stevens, A. 2006. "Unité et vérité de la *phantasia* chez Aristote." *Philosophie antique* 6:181–199.

Stoddard, K. 2004. *The Narrative Voice in the* Theogony *of Hesiod.* Mnemosyne, bibliotheca classica Batava. Suplementum 255. Leiden.

Stoddart, S. and J. Whitley. 1988. "The Social Context of Literacy in Archaic Greece and Etruria." *Antiquity* 62:761–772.

Stone, R. M. 1988. *Dried Millet Breaking: Time, Words, and Song in the Wọi Epic of the Kpelle.* Bloomington.

Strasser, J.-Y. 2002. "Choraules et pythaules d'époque impériale. À propos d'inscriptions de Delphes." *Bulletin de correspondance hellénique* 126:97–142.

Striker, G. 1996. "Emotions in Context: Aristotle's Treatment of the Passions in the *Rhetoric* and His Moral Psychology." In Rorty 1996:286–302.

Stroh, W. 1976. "Hesiods lügende Musen." In *Studien zum antiken Epos*, ed. H. Görgemanns and E. A. Schmidt. Beiträge zur klassischen Philologie 72:85–112. Meisenheim am Glan.

Struck, P. T. 2004. *Birth of the Symbol: Ancient Readers at the Limits of Their Texts.* Princeton.

Sundwall, J. 1910. *Nachträge zur* Prosopographia Attica. Helsingfors.

Susemihl, F., ed. 1874. *Ἀριστοτέλους περὶ ποιητικῆς.* 2nd ed. Leipzig. Also titled *Aristoteles über die Dichtkunst.*

Susemihl, F. and R. D. Hicks, eds. 1894. *The* Politics *of Aristotle: Books I–V.* London.

Svenbro, J. 1976. *La parole et le marbre: aux origines de la poétique grecque.* Lund.

———. 1993. *Phrasikleia: An Anthropology of Reading in Ancient Greece.* Myth and Poetics. Ithaca.

Sykutris, J. 1928. "Epigramm aus Kition." *Hermes* 63:110–111.

Szemerényi, O. J. L. 1956. "The Genitive Singular of Masculine -ā-Stem Nouns in Greek." *Glotta* 35:195–208.

———. 1968. "The Attic 'Rückverwandlung' or Atomism and Structuralism in Action." In *Studien zur Sprachwissenschaft und Kulturkunde: Gedenkschrift für Wilhelm Brandenstein (1898-1967),* ed. M. Mayrhofer, 139–157. Innsbruck.

———. 1974. "Greek πολύς and πολλός." *Zeitschrift für vergleichende Sprachforschung auf dem Gebiete der indogermanischen Sprachen* 88:1–31.

Tanasi, M. T., G. Impagliazzo, and D. Ruggiero. 1991. "Une approche préliminaire à la caractérisation du parchemin." In *Pergament: Geschichte, Struktur, Restaurierung, Herstellung,* ed. P. Rück, 203–215. Sigmaringen.

Taplin, O. 1992. *Homeric Soundings: The Shaping of the* Iliad. Oxford.

Tarbell, F. B. 1902. "A Signed Proto-Corinthian Lecythus in the Boston Museum of Fine Arts." *Revue archéologique* ser. 3, 40:41–46.

Tarditi, G. 1968. "Sull'origine e sul significato della parola rapsodo." *Maia* 20:137–145.

Tedeschi, G. 2002. "Lo spettacolo in età ellenistica e tardo antica nella documentazione epigrafica e papiracea." *Papyrologica Lupiensia* 11:87–187.

Teodorsson, S.-T. 1989–1996. *A Commentary on Plutarch's* Table Talks. 3 vols. (cited as 1, 2, and 3). Studia Graeca et Latina Gothoburgensia 51, 53, and 62. Göteborg.

Thalmann, W. G. 1984. *Conventions of Form and Thought in Early Greek Epic Poetry.* Baltimore.

Theodoridis, C., ed. 1982-. *Photii Patriarchae Lexicon.* 3 vols.: A–Δ, E–M, and N–Φ (cited as 1, 2, and 3). Berlin.

Theurillat, T. 2007. "Early Iron Age Graffiti from the Sanctuary of Apollo at Eretria." In *Oropos and Euboea in the Early Iron Age. Acts of an International Round Table, University of Thessaly, June 18-20, 2004,* ed. A. Mazarakis Ainian, 331–344. Volos.

Thieme, P. 1968a [1954]. "Die Wurzel *vat.*" In Schmitt 1968:187–203. First published in *Asiatica. Festschrift Friedrich Weller zum 65. Geburtstag gewidmet von seinen Freunden, Kollegen, und Schülern,* 656–666. Leipzig.

———. 1968b [1957]. "Vorzarathustrisches bei den Zarathustriern und bei Zarathustra." In Schmitt 1968:204–241. First published in *Zeitschrift der Deutschen Morgenländischen Gesellschaft* 107:67–96.

Thiersch, F. 1826. *Griechische Grammatik vorzüglich des homerischen Dialektes.* Leipzig.

Thomas, C. G. and C. Conant. 1999. *Citadel to City-State: The Transformation of Greece, 1200-700 B.C.E.* Bloomington.

Thomas, R. 1992. *Literacy and Orality in Ancient Greece.* Cambridge.

Thompson, E. M. 1912. *An Introduction to Greek and Latin Paleography.* Oxford.

Thompson, H. A. and R. E. Wycherley. 1972. *The Agora of Athens: The History, Shape, and Uses of an Ancient City Center.* Athenian Agora: Results of Excavations Conducted by the American School of Classical Studies at Athens 14. Princeton.

Thompson, R. J. E. 2008. "Mycenaean Non-assibilation and Its Significance for the Prehistory of the Greek Dialects." In *Colloquium Romanum: atti del XII Colloquio internazionale di micenologia (Roma, 20-25 febbraio 2006),* ed. A. Sacconi, M. del Freo, L. Godart, and M. Negri, 2:753-765. Pisa.

Thompson, W. E. 1969. "The Inscriptions in the Hephaisteion." *Hesperia* 38:114-118.

Thompson, W. H., ed. 1868. *The* Phaedrus *of Plato. With English Notes and Dissertations.* Bibliotheca Classica. London.

Threatte, L. 1980. *The Grammar of Attic Inscriptions: Phonology,* Vol. 1. Berlin.

———. 1996. *The Grammar of Attic Inscriptions: Morphology,* Vol. 2. Berlin.

Throop, G. R. 1917. "Epic and Dramatic." In *Washington University Studies,* ed. F. W. Shipley. Humanistic Series 5.1:1-32. St. Louis.

Thumb, A. 1898. "Zur Geschichte des griechischen Digamma." *Indogermanische Forschungen* 9:294-342.

Thumb, A. and A. Scherer. 1959. *Handbuch der griechischen Dialekte,* Vol. 2. 2nd ed. Heidelberg.

Thummer, E. 1968-1969. *Pindar: die isthmischen Gedichte.* Heidelberg.

Tigay, J. H. 2002. *The Evolution of the Gilgamesh Epic.* Wauconda.

Tigerstedt, E. N. 1969. *Plato's Idea of Poetical Inspiration.* Commentationes Humanarum Litterarum 44.2. Helsinki.

———. 1970. "*Furor Poeticus*: Poetic Inspiration in Greek Literature before Democritus and Plato." *Journal of the History of Ideas* 31:163-178.

Tiverios, M. 1974. "Bemerkungen zu den panathenäischen Amphoren." Ἀρχαιολογικὸν Δελτίον 29:142-154.

———. 2007. "Panathenaic Amphoras." In *The Panathenaic Games: Proceedings of an International Conference Held at the University of Athens, May 11-12, 2004,* ed O. Palagia and A. Choremi-Spetsieri, 1-19. Oxford.

Tod, M. N. 1934. "Greek Inscriptions at Cairness House." *Journal of Hellenic Studies* 54:140-162.

Todd, O. J. 1939. "An Inelegant Verse." *Classical Quarterly* 33:163-165.

Todd, S. C. 1990a. "The Purpose of Evidence in Athenian Courts." In *Nomos: Essays in Athenian Law, Politics, and Society*, ed. P. Cartledge, P. Millett, and S. C. Todd, 19–39. Cambridge.

———. 1990b. "The Use and Abuse of the Attic Orators." *Greece & Rome* 37:159–178.

———. 1993. *The Shape of Athenian Law*. Oxford.

Tovar, A., ed. 1953. *Aristóteles Retórica*. Madrid.

Tracy, S. V. 1975. *The Lettering of an Athenian Mason*. Hesperia Supplement 15. Princeton.

———. 1995. *Athenian Democracy in Transition: Attic Letter-Cutters of 340 to 290 BC*. Hellenistic Culture and Society 20. Berkeley.

———. 2003. *Athens and Macedon: Attic Letter-Cutters of 300 to 229 BC*. Hellenistic Culture and Society 38. Berkeley.

Tracy, S. V. and C. Habicht. 1991. "New and Old Panathenaic Victor Lists." *Hesperia* 60:187–236.

Trevett, J. 1996a. "Aristotle's Knowledge of Athenian Oratory." *Classical Quarterly* 46:371–379.

———. 1996b. "Did Demosthenes Publish His Deliberative Speeches?" *Hermes* 124:425–441.

———, ed. 2011. *Demosthenes, Speeches 1–17*. The Oratory of Classical Greece 14. Austin.

Tritle, L. A. 2009. "Alexander and the Greeks: Artists and Soldiers, Friends and Enemies." In *Alexander the Great: A New History*, ed. W. Heckel and L. A. Tritle, 121–140. Malden.

Tsagalis, C. C. 2006. "Poet and Audience: From Homer to Hesiod." In *La poésie épique grecque: métamorphoses d'un genre littéraire*, ed. F. Montanari and A. Rengakos. Entretiens sur l'Antiquité classique 52:79–134. Huit exposés suivis de discussions, 22–26 August 2005. Geneva.

Tsetskhladze, G. R. and F. De Angelis, eds. 1994. *The Archaeology of Greek Colonisation: Essays Dedicated to Sir John Boardman*. Oxford.

Tsopanakēs, A. 1984. "Σύμμεικτα κυπριακά." *Hellēnika* 35:389–401.

Turfa, J. 1994. "Review of D. Ridgway, *The First Western Greeks*." *Bryn Mawr Classical Review* 94.02.19.

Turkeltaub, D. W. 2003. *The Gods' Radiance Manifest: An Examination of the Narrative Pattern Underlying the Homeric Divine Epiphany Scenes*. PhD diss., Cornell University.

Turnbull, K. 1994. "Aristotle on Imagination: *De anima* iii.3." *Ancient Philosophy* 14:319–334.

Turner, E. G. 1968. *Greek Papyri: An Introduction*. Oxford.

———. 1977. *Athenian Books in the Fifth and Fourth Centuries B.C.* 2nd ed. London.

———. 1987. *Greek Manuscripts of the Ancient World*. Bulletin Supplement 46. 2nd ed. London.

Turner, L. A. 1996. "The Basileia at Lebadeia." In *Proceedings of the 8th International Conference on Boiotian Antiquities (Loyola University of Chicago, 24-26 May 1995)*, ed. J. M. Fossey. Boeotia Antiqua 6:105–126. Amsterdam.

Twining, T., ed. 1812. *Aristotle's Treatise on Poetry*. 2nd ed. In 2 parts (cited as 1 and 2). London.

Uguzzoni, A. 1968. *Le tavole greche di Eraclea*. Pubblicazioni dell'Istituto di storia antica 7. Rome.

Untersteiner, M., ed. 1958. *Parmenide: testimonianze e frammenti*. Biblioteca di Studi Superiori, Filosofia antica 38. Florence.

Usener, H. 1896. *Götternamen: Versuch einer Lehre von der religiösen Begriffsbildung*. Bonn.

Usher, S. 1971. "Review of K. J. Dover, *Lysias and the Corpus Lysiacum*. Sather Classical Lectures 38." *Journal of Hellenic Studies* 91:147–150.

———, ed. 1974. *Dionysius of Halicarnassus: The Critical Essays*. The Loeb Classical Library 465. London.

Ustinova, Y. 2009. "Cave Experiences and Ancient Oracles." *Time and Mind* 2:265–286.

Vahlen, J. 1867. *Beiträge zu Aristoteles Poetik*. Vienna.

Valavanis, P. D. 1987. "Säulen, Hähne, Niken und Archonten auf Panathenäischen Preisamphoren." *Archäologischer Anzeiger* 467–480.

Vamvouri Ruffy, M. 2004. *La fabrique du divin: les Hymnes de Callimaque à la lumière des Hymnes homériques et des Hymnes épigraphiques*. Kernos Suppléments 14. Liège.

Vanderkam, J. C. 1992. "Ahiquar, Book of." In *The Anchor Bible Dictionary*, ed. D. N. Freedman, Vol. 1:119–120. New York.

Vanderpool, E. and W. P. Wallace. 1964. "The Sixth Century Laws from Eretria." *Hesperia* 33:381–391.

Van der Valk, M. 1949. *Textual Criticism of the* Odyssey. Leiden.

———. 1963. *Researches on the Text and Scholia of the* Iliad. In 2 vols. Leiden.

———, ed. 1971–1987. *Eustathii archiepiscopi Thessalonicensis commentarii ad Homeri* Iliadem *pertinentes ad fidem codicis Laurentiani editi*. In 4 vols. Leiden.

Vandoni, M., ed. 1964. *Feste pubbliche e private nei documenti greci*. Testi e documenti per lo studio dell'antichità 8. Milano.

Van Groningen, B. A. 1948. "Les trois Muses de l'Hélicon." *L'Antiquité classique* 16:287–296.

Van Tress, H. 2004. *Poetic Memory: Allusion in the Poetry of Callimachus and the Metamorphoses of Ovid.* Mnemosyne, bibliotheca classica Batava. Suplementum 258. Boston.

Van Wees, H. 1994. "The Homeric Way of War: The 'Iliad' and the Hoplite Phalanx (II)." *Greece & Rome* 41:131–155.

———. 1997. "Homeric Warfare." In Morris and Powell 1997:668–693.

———. 2001. "The Myth of the Middle-Class Army: Military and Social Status in Ancient Athens." In *War As a Cultural and Social Force: Essays on Warfare in Antiquity*, ed. T. Bekker-Nielsen and L. Hannestad. Historisk-filosofiske Skrifter 22:45–71. Copenhagen.

———. 2002. "Tyrants, Oligarchs and Citizen Militias." In *Army and Power in the Ancient World*, ed. A. Chaniotis and P. Ducrey. Heidelberger althistorische Beiträge und epigraphische Studien 37:61–82. Stuttgart.

Velardi, R. 1989. Enthousiasmós: *Possessione rituale e teoria della comunicazione poetica in Platone.* Filologia e Critica, Collana diretta da Bruno Gentili 62. Rome.

Veloso, C. W. 2004. "*Phantasia* et *mimesis* chez Aristote." *Revue des études anciennes* 106:455–476.

Vennemann, T. 1988. *Preference Laws for Syllable Structure and the Explanation of Sound Change (With Special Reference to German, Germanic, Italian, and Latin).* Berlin.

Verdan, S., A. K. Pfyffer, and C. Léderrey. 2008. *Céramique géométrique d'Érétrie.* Eretria XX. Lausanne.

Verdenius, W. J. 1943. "L'*Ion* de Platon." *Mnemosyne* 11:233–262.

———. 1972. "Notes on the Proem of Hesiod's *Theogony.*" *Mnemosyne* 25:225–260.

———. 1983. "The Principles of Greek Literary Criticism." *Mnemosyne* 36:14–59.

———. 1985. *A Commentary on Hesiod:* Works and Days, *vv. 1-382.* Mnemosyne, bibliotheca classica Batava. Suplementum 86. Leiden.

Vernant, J. P. 1983 [1965]. *Myth and Thought among the Greeks.* London. First published as *Mythe et pensée chez les Grecs.* Paris.

———. 1985. *Mythe et pensée chez les Grecs: études de psychologie historique.* 2nd ed. Paris.

Vettori, P. 1548. *Commentarii in tres libros Aristotelis de arte dicendi.* 1st ed. Florence.

———. 1579. *Commentarii in tres libros Aristotelis de arte dicendi.* 2nd ed. Florence.

Vine, B. 1999. "On *Cowgill's Law* in Greek." In *Compositiones indogermanicae: in memoriam Jochem Schindler*, ed. H. Eichner and H. C. Luschützky, 555–600. Prague.

Vinogradov, J. G. 1997. "Der Pontos Euxeinos als politische, ökonomische und kulturelle Einheit und die Epigraphik." In *Pontische Studien: kleine Schriften zur Geschichte und Epigraphik des Schwarzmeerraumes*, ed. J. G. Vinogradov and H. Heinen, 1–73. Mainz.

Viredaz, R. 1983. "La graphie des groupes de consonnes en mycénien et en cypriote." *Minos* 18:125–207.

Vogelzang, M. E. and H. L. J. Vanstiphout, eds. 1992. *Mesopotamian Epic Literature: Oral or Aural?* Lewiston.

Vogt, E. 1959. "Die Schrift vom Wettkampf Homers und Hesiods." *Rheinisches Museum* 102:193–221.

———. 1961. "Review of K. Hess, *Der Agon zwischen Homer und Hesiod, seine Entstehung und kulturgeschichtliche Stellung*." *Gnomon* 33:697–703.

———. 1962. "Nietzsche und der Wettkampf Homers." *Antike und Abendland* 11:103–113.

Volk, K. 2002. "ΚΛΕΟΣ ΑΦΘΙΤΟΝ Revisited." *Classical Philology* 97:61–68.

Vollkommer, R. 1991. "Zur Deutung der Löwenfrau in der frühgriechischen Kunst." *Mitteilungen des Deutschen Archäologischen Instituts (Athen. Abt.)* 106:47–64.

Vürtheim, J. 1928. *Aischylos'* Schutzflehende. Amsterdam.

Wace, A. J. B. and F. H. Stubbings, eds. 1962. *A Companion to Homer*. London.

Wachsmuth, C. 1874. *Die Stadt Athen im Alterthum*, Vol. 1. Leipzig.

Wackernagel, J. 1893. "Griech. κτεριοῦσι." *Indogermanische Forschungen* 2:151–154.

———. 1920–1924. *Vorlesungen über Syntax: mit besonderer Berücksichtigung von Griechisch, Lateinisch und Deutsch*. In 2 vols. Basel.

———. 1970 [1916]. *Sprachliche Untersuchungen zu Homer*. Reprint ed. Göttingen.

Wade-Gery, H. T. 1936. "Kynaithos." In *Greek Poetry and Life: Essays Presented to Gilbert Murray on His Seventieth Birthday, January 2, 1936*, ed. C. Bailey, E. Barber, C. Bowra, J. Denniston, and D. Page, 56–78. Oxford.

———. 1952. *The Poet of the* Iliad. The J. H. Gray Lectures for 1949. Cambridge.

Wakker, G. C. 1998. "Review of C. M. J. Sicking and P. Stork, *Two Studies in the Semantics of the Verb in Classical Greek*." *Mnemosyne* 51:357–372.

Walbank, F. W. 1967. *A Historical Commentary on Polybius*, Vol. 2. Oxford.

Walbaum, J. C. 1994. "Early Greek Contacts with the Southern Levant, ca. 1000–600 BC: The Eastern Perspective." *Bulletin of the American Schools of Oriental Research* 293:53–66.

Walberer, G. 1938. *Isokrates und Alkidamas*. PhD diss., Hansische Universität, Hamburg.

Wankel, H., ed. 1979. *Die Inschriften von Ephesos I a, Nr. 1–47 (Texte)*. Bonn.

Ward, J. K. 1984. *Aristotle's Account of* Phantasia *(Imagination, Perception).* PhD diss., University of California, San Diego.

Wathelet, P. 1966. "La coupe syllabique et les liquides voyelles dans la tradition formulaire de l'épopée grecque." In *Linguistic Research In Belgium,* ed. Y. Lebrun, 145–173. Belgium.

———. 1970. *Les traits éoliens dans la langue de l'épopée grecque.* Incunabula graeca 37. Rome.

———. 1981. "La langue homérique et le rayonnement littéraire de l'Eubée." *L'Antiquité classique* 50:819–833.

———. 2008. "Le rôle de l'eubéen et celui de l'Eubée dans lépopée homérique." *Gaia* 11:25–52.

Watkins, C. 1976. "Observations on the 'Nestor's Cup' Inscription." *Harvard Studies in Classical Philology* 80:25–40.

———. 1995a. "Greece in Italy outside Rome." *Harvard Studies in Classical Philology* 97:35–50.

———. 1995b. *How to Kill a Dragon: Aspects of Indo-European Poetics.* New York.

———, ed. 2000. *The American Heritage Dictionary of Indo-European Roots.* 2nd ed. Boston.

Watson, G. 1982. "Φαντασία in Aristotle, *De anima* 3.3." *Classical Quarterly* 32:100–113.

———. 1988. Phantasia *in Classical Thought.* Galway.

Weber, G. 1993. *Dichtung und höfische Gesellschaft: die Rezeption von Zeitgeschichte am Hof der ersten Ptolemäer.* Hermes Einzelschriften 62. Stuttgart.

Wecklein, N., ed. 1902. *Äschylos* Die Schutzflehenden. Leipzig.

Wedin, M. V. 1988. *Mind and Imagination in Aristotle.* New Haven.

Wegner, M. 1968. *Musik und Tanz.* Archaeologia Homerica 3, U. Göttingen.

Wehrli, F. 1928. *Zur Geschichte der allegorischen Deutung Homers im Altertum.* Borna, Leipzig.

———, ed. 1944. *Dikaiarchos.* Die Schule des Aristoteles, Texte und Kommentar 1. Basel.

———. 1968a. "Demetrios von Phaleron." Real-Encyclopädie der classischen Altertumswissenschaft, Suppl., Vol. 9, cols. 514–522. Stuttgart.

———, ed. 1968b. *Demetrios von Phaleron.* Die Schule des Aristoteles. Texte und Kommentar 4. 2nd ed. Basel.

———, ed. 1969. *Phainias von Eresos, Chamaileon, Praxiphanes.* Die Schule des Aristoteles. Texte und Kommentar 9. 2nd ed. Basel.

———, ed. 1983a. *Klearchos.* Die Schule des Aristoteles. Texte und Kommentar 3. 2nd ed. Basel.

———. 1983b. "Klearchos von Soloi." In *Ältere Akademie: Aristoteles - Peripatos*, ed. H. Flashar. Grundriss der Geschichte der Philosophie, *Die Philosophie der Antike* 3:547–551. Basel.

Weil, H. 1900a. *Études sur l'antiquité grecque*. Paris.

Weil, H. 1900b. "L'origine du mot 'poète'." In Weil 1900a:237–244. Paris.

Wendel, C. 1949. *Die griechisch-römische Buchbeschreibung verglichen mit der des vorderen Orients*. Halle.

West, M. L., ed. 1966. *Hesiod, Theogony*. Oxford.

———. 1967a. "The Contest of Homer and Hesiod." *Classical Quarterly* 17:433–450.

———. 1974. *Studies in Greek Elegy and Iambus*. Untersuchungen zur antiken Literatur und Geschichte 14. Berlin.

———. 1975. "Cynaethus' Hymn to Apollo." *Classical Quarterly* 25:161–170.

———, ed. 1978a. *Hesiod, Works & Days*. Oxford.

———. 1978b. "Phocylides." *Journal of Hellenic Studies* 98:164–167.

———. 1981. "The Singing of Homer and the Modes of Early Greek Music." *Journal of Hellenic Studies* 101:113–129.

———. 1982. *Greek Metre*. Oxford.

———. 1986. "The Singing of Hexameters: Evidence from Epidauros." *Zeitschrift für Papyrologie und Epigraphik* 63:39–46.

———. 1988. "The Rise of the Greek Epic." *Journal of Hellenic Studies* 108:151–172.

———. 1989. "The Early Chronology of Attic Tragedy." *Classical Quarterly* 39:251–254.

———, ed. 1989–1992. *Iambi et elegi graeci ante Alexandrum cantati*. 2nd ed. Oxford.

———. 1990. "Archaische Heldendichtung: Singen und Schreiben." In Kullmann and Reichel 1990:33–50.

———. 1992. *Ancient Greek Music*. Oxford.

———, ed. 1993. *Greek Lyric Poetry*. Oxford.

———. 1994a. "Ab ovo: Orpheus, Sanchuniathon, and the Origins of the Ionian World Model." *Classical Quarterly* 44:289–307.

———. 1995. "The Date of the *Iliad*." *Museum Helveticum* 52:203–219.

———. 1997. *The East Face of Helicon: West Asiatic Elements in Greek Poetry and Myth*. Oxford.

———, ed. 1998a. *Homeri* Ilias I. Bibliotheca Scriptorum Graecorum et Romanorum Teubneriana. Stuttgart.

———. 1998b. "The Textual Criticism of Editing Homer." In Most 1998:94–110.

———. 1999a. *Frühe Interpolationen in der* Ilias. Nachrichten der Akademie der Wissenschaften in Göttingen. I. Philologisch-historische Klasse 4. Göttingen.

———. 1999b. "The Invention of Homer." *Classical Quarterly* 49:364–382.

———. 2000. "The Gardens of Alcinous and the Oral Dictated Text Theory." *Acta antiqua Academiae Scientiarum Hungaricae* 40:479–488.

———. 2001. *Studies in the Text and Transmission of the* Iliad. Munich.

———, ed. 2003a. *Greek Epic Fragments from the Seventh to the Fifth Centuries BC.* The Loeb Classical Library 497. Cambridge, MA.

———, ed. 2003b. *Homeric Hymns, Homeric Apocrypha, Lives of Homer.* The Loeb Classical Library 496. Cambridge, MA.

———. 2007. *Indo-European Poetry and Myth.* Oxford.

———. 2011a. *The Making of the* Iliad: *Disquisition and Analytical Commentary.* Oxford.

———. 2011b. "The Homeric Question Today." The Penrose Lecture. *Proceedings of the American Philosophical Society* 155.4:383–393.

West, S., ed. 1967b. *The Ptolemaic Papyri of Homer.* Papyrologica Coloniensia 3. Cologne.

———. 1994b. "Nestor's Bewitching Cup." *Zeitschrift für Papyrologie und Epigraphik* 101:9–15.

Wetzels, L. 1986. "Phonological Timing in Ancient Greek." In *Studies in Compensatory Lengthening,* ed. L. Wetzels and E. Sezer. Publications in Language Sciences 23:297–344. Dordrecht.

Whitley, J. 1991. *Style and Society in Dark Age Greece.* Cambridge.

Whittaker, C. R., ed. 1988. *Pastoral Economies in Classical Antiquity.* Supplementary Volumes 14. Cambridge.

Wiemken, H. 1972. *Der griechische Mimus: Dokumente zur Geschichte des antiken Volkstheaters.* Bremen.

Wilamowitz-Moellendorff, U. von. 1877. "Die Thukydideslegende." *Hermes* 12:326–367.

———. 1884. *Homerische Untersuchungen.* Philologische Untersuchungen 7. Berlin.

———. 1910. *Einleitung in die griechische Tragödie.* Berlin.

———. 1911. "Ein neues Bruchstück der *Aitia* des Kallimachos." *Hermes* 46:471–473.

———. 1916. *Die Ilias und Homer.* Berlin.

———. 1920. *Platon: Beilagen und Textkritik,* Vol. 2. 2nd ed. Berlin.

———. 1922. *Pindaros.* Berlin.

———. 1924. *Hellenistische Dichtung in der Zeit des Kallimachos.* Berlin.

———. 1927. *Die Heimkehr des Odysseus: Neue Homerische Untersuchungen.* Berlin.

———, ed. 1929. *Vitae Homeri et Hesiodi in usum scholarum.* Berlin.

———. 1931–1932. *Der Glaube der Hellenen.* In 2 vols. Berlin.

Wilhelm, A. 1905. "Zwei Denkmäler des eretrischen Dialekts." *Jahreshefte des Österreichischen Archäologischen Instituts* 8:6–17.

———, ed. 1906. *Urkunden dramatischer Aufführungen in Athen*. Mit einem Beitrage von Georg Kaibel. Vienna.

Wilkins, A. S., ed. 1892. *M. Tulli Ciceronis* De oratore. Oxford.

Willcock, M. M., ed. 1995. *Pindar. Victory Odes:* Olympians *2, 7, 11;* Nemean *4;* Isthmians *3, 4, 7.* Cambridge Greek and Latin Classics. Cambridge.

Williams, J. M. 1987. "The Peripatetic School and Demetrius of Phalerum's Reforms in Athens." *The Ancient World* 15:87–98.

Willis, W. H. 1990. "The Robinson-Cologne Papyrus of Achilles Tatius." *Greek, Roman, and Byzantine Studies* 31:73–102.

Wilson, D. 1970. *The Life and Times of Vuk Stefanović Karadzić*. Oxford.

Wilson, J.-P. 2009. "Literacy." In *A Companion to Archaic Greece*, ed. R. K. A. and H. van Wees, 542–563. Malden.

Wilson, P. 2000. *The Athenian Institution of the* Khoregia: *The Chorus, the City and the Stage*. Cambridge.

Wingo, E. O. 1972. *Latin Punctuation in the Classical Age*. Janua Linguarum, Series Practica 133. The Hague.

Wismann, H. 1996. "Propositions pour une lecture d'Hésiode." In Blaise et al. 1996:15–24.

Wöhrle, G. 1990. "*Actio*: Das fünfte officium des antiken Redners." *Gymnasium* 97:31–46.

Wolf, F. A. 1876. *Prolegomena ad Homerum*. 2nd ed. Berlin.

———. 1985. *Prolegomena ad Homerum*. Translated with introduction and notes by A. Grafton, G. W. Most, and J. E. G. Zetzel. Princeton.

Wolff, H. J. 2007. "Demosthenes as Advocate: The Functions and Methods of Legal Consultants in Classical Athens." In *Oxford Readings in the Attic Orators*, ed. E. Carawan. Translated by J. Miner in consultation with G. Thür. Oxford Readings in Classical Studies, 91–115, with bibliography at 400–430. Originally presented as a lecture to the Berlin Juristic Society, 30 June 1967. Oxford.

Woodard, R. D. 1997a. *Greek Writing from Knossos to Homer: A Linguistic Interpretation of the Origin of the Greek Alphabet and the Continuity of Ancient Greek Literacy*. New York.

———. 1997b. "Linguistic Connections between Greeks and Non-Greeks." In *Greeks and Barbarians: Essays on the Interactions between Greeks and Non-Greeks in Antiquity and the Consequences for Eurocentrism*, ed. J. E. Coleman and C. A. Walz, 29–60. Bethesda.

Woodford, S. 2003. *Images of Myths in Classical Antiquity*. Cambridge.

Woodhead, A. G. 1992 [1986]. *The Study of Greek Inscriptions*. The Oklahoma Series in Classical Culture 16. 2nd ed. Norman.

Wormald, F. 1929. "A Fragment of Accounts Dealing with Religious Festivals." *Journal of Egyptian Archaeology* 15:239–242.

Wörrle, M. 1988. *Stadt und Fest im kaiserzeitlichen Kleinasien. Studien zu einer agonistischen Stiftung aus Oinoanda*. Munich.

———. 1995. "Epigraphische Forschungen zur Geschichte Lykiens V: Die griechischen Inschriften der Nekropolen von Limyra." *Chiron* 25:387–417.

Worthington, I. 1993. "Once More, the Client/*Logographos* Relationship." *Classical Quarterly* 43:67–72.

———. 2007. "Rhetoric and Politics in Classical Greece: Rise of the *Rhētores*." In *A Companion to Greek Rhetoric*, ed. I. Worthington. Blackwell Companions to the Ancient World. Literature and Culture, 255–271, with bibliography at 562–593. Oxford.

Wyller, E. A. 1958. "Platons *Ion*." *Symbolae Osloenses* 34:19–38.

Young, D. C. 1984. *The Olympic Myth of Greek Amateur Athletics*. Library of Ancient Athletics. Chicago.

Yunis, H. 1996. *Taming Democracy: Models of Political Rhetoric in Classical Athens*. Rhetoric & Society. Ithaca.

———, ed. 2011. *Plato* Phaedrus. Cambridge Greek and Latin Classics. Cambridge.

Yurdin, J. S. 2008. *Aristotle: From Sense to Science*. PhD diss., University of California, Berkeley.

Zervos, C. 1957. *L'art des Cyclades*. Paris.

Ziegler, K. 1988 [1934]. *L'epos ellenistico: un capitolo dimenticato della poesia greca*. Collana di Studi e Testi 1. 2nd ed. With an introduction by M. Fantuzzi and an appendix, *Ennio poeta epico ellenistico*, by F. de Martino. Bari. First published as *Das hellenistische Epos. Ein vergessenes Kapitel griechischer Dichtung*. Leipzig.

Ziehen, L. 1930. "Mantis." Real-Encyclopädie der classischen Altertumswissenschaft, Vol. 14.2, cols. 1345–1355. Stuttgart.

Zschätzsch, A. 2002. *Verwendung und Bedeutung griechischer Musikinstrumente in Mythos und Kult*. Internationale Archäologie 73. Rahden.

Zucchelli, B. 1962. *ΥΠΟΚΡΙΤΗΣ: Origine e storia del termine*. Brescia.

Zumbo, A. 2002. "Teagene di Reggio interprete di Omero." In *Messina e Reggio nell'antichità, storia, società, cultura: atti del Convegno della S.I.S.A.C. (Messina-Reggio Calabria 24–26 maggio 1999)*, ed. B. Gentili and A. Pinzone, 321–327. Messina.

Index of Ancient Literary Sources[†]

Aelian *Varia Historia*: 12.32, 304; 13.14, 24

Agathon *Mysians*: 514;;

Aiskhines

    Against Ktēsiphōn (Orat. 3): 166, 428; 201, 442, 442n31

    Against Timarkhos (Orat. 1): 23, 609n78; 27, 609n78

    On the Embassy (Orat. 2): 35, 443; 52, 612n89; 135, 442

Aiskhylos

    Agamemnōn: 176, 217n148; 935, 87; 977, 216; 979, 216; 981, 216; 983, 216; 989, 216; 990–993, 216; 992–993, 216; 996, 216; 1563–1564, 129

    Eumenides: 18–19, 275; 29, 275n204

    Fragments (R): fr. 161.2, 87

    Oidipous: 414;;

    Seven against Thebes: 657n34;;

    Sphinx: 413n308;;

    Suppliants: 434–436, 128, 128n80

Akhilleus Tatios: 460;; 3.20, 452; 3.20.4, 452n65, 516; 4.7.8, 612n89; 8.9, 452n66

Alkidamas *On the Sophists*: 523, 594n50;; §1, 311n78, 313n86, 594n50; §2, 312n79, 312n80, 312n82, 312n84; §§3–4, 312–313, 312n85; §3, 312n78, 313n86; §4, 313n86; §6, 311n76; §11, 312n81, 609n79, 609n81, 618; §12, 312n84; §13, 311n76, 594n50, 616n100; §14, 2, 316, 316n94, 316n96, 320n110, 380n171, 594n50; §§16–17, 316n96; §16, 626n127; §17, 316n96; §18, 594n50; §19, 319, 319n107; §25, 594n50; §26, 319n108; §§29–32, 308n64; §29, 308n64, 311n75, 329; §30, 616; §31, 308n64, 329, 594n50, 615–616, 618; §32, 594n50; §33, 319n108; §34, 317, 318n102

Anakreon (Page): *PMG* 356b, 425n349

[†]   Ordinarily, each element of an entry consists of the ancient source *locus* and a list of its occurrences in this book, separated by commas. These elements are separated in turn from each other by a single semicolon. In the rare instances when I mention a work without a *locus* I list only the occurrence: occurrences without *locus* immediately follow the title of the work, separated from each other by commas and terminated (or otherwise separated from the remainder of the entry) by two semicolons. Other than these semicolons, entries end without any punctuation. When different numbering schemes are used to cite an ancient source (e.g. Aristotle *Rhetoric* and *Vita Herodotea* under *Homerica*), I put the less precise one first.

Anakreontea: 34, 394
Andokides: 1.23, 609n78
*Anonymi in artem rhetoricam
commentarium* (Rabe): p. 159,
526n19; p. 221, 626n130
Anthologia Graeca (incl. *Anthologia
Palatina*): 4.1.17, 394; 10.67,
249n109; 14.64, 401
Anthologia Latina (Buecheler and
Riese): I.2.38 no. 487a.15–16,
453n66
Antimakhos *Thebaid*: 406;;
Aphthonios *Progymnasmata* (Patillon):
2.1, 333n7
Apollodoros *Bibliothēkē*: 1.9.25 §135.2,
450n60; 3.5.8 §§52–53, 416; 3.5.8
§52, 416; 3.10.6 §126, 64
Apollonios of Rhodes *Argonautika*:
208;; 1.5, 233; 4.150, 394; 4.1648,
396
Apollonius Sophista *Lexicon* (Bekker):
p. 160 line 3 s.v. ὑποκρίναιτο,
650n11
Apuleius *Metamorphoses*: 4.33, 288n234
Aratos *Phainomena*: 227, 408
Aristokles of Rhodes (*FHG* IV.329–
332): p. 331, 447
  On Choruses (*FHG* IV.331–332):
  448–449;;
Aristophanes
  Akharnians: 45, 609n79
  Assemblywomen: 130, 609n79
  Birds: 226, 450n60; 370, 124n57; 906,
  426n350; 1382, 450n60
  Clouds: 506, 86; 1371, 350n65
  Fragments (K-A): fr. 2, 86
  Frogs: 436n3;; 303, 446; 606, 86; 897,
  378n167
  Knights: 732, 576n189; 773, 576n189;
  1339–1355, 576n189
  Peace: 781–786, 446; 1269, 385n189

  Wasps: 53, 297n16; 1216, 371; 1222,
  371; 1225, 371; 1243–1244, 371;
  1279, 297
  Wealth: 542, 429, 429n367
  Women at the Thesmophoria: 99,
  450n60; 379, 609n79; 686, 124n57
Aristotle
  [*Athēnaiōn Politeia*]: 474n139;; 14.2,
  613; 28.2, 534n45; 29.2, 609n78;
  48.5, 633n152; 53.1, 633n152;
  53.2, 633n152; 54.2, 124n57;
  54.5, 444n37; 54.7, 475n139; 60.1,
  474–475n139
  Categories: 4b20, 619n105; 9b2–9,
  574n180
  De anima: 562, 564–565;; II.6,
  573; III.3, 565; 403a7, 574n180;
  403a17–18, 574n180; 403a18–19,
  574n180; 418a20–24, 573,
  573n178; 420b29–33, 575n186;
  424b25–26, 574n181; 427b14–26,
  568n154; 427b14–16, 567;
  427b27–28, 567n150; 428a1–4,
  561–562; 428a2, 562; 428a3–4,
  561n133; 428a4–5, 561n133;
  428a4, 561n133; 428a18–26,
  568n154; 428a20–24, 575; 428b10–
  11, 569n161; 428b17–22, 563;
  428b21–22, 564n143; 429a1–4,
  533n42; 429a1–2, 569n158; 429a2,
  570n161; 429a27–29, 578n195;
  430b29–30, 564; 431a14–15,
  569n159; 431a16–17, 570n166;
  431b2, 578n195; 431b6–8,
  569n155; 432a2–3, 578n195;
  432a3–10, 567n152; 432a15–16,
  570; 432a30–31, 575n186; 433a10–
  22, 575; 433b27–30, 567, 567n151;
  434a4, 568; 434a5–10, 568n153;
  434a7, 568; 434a10–11, 568n154;
  434a12–13, 569; 434a16, 571

De caelo: 279b10–12, 633n152
De generatione animalium: 715a14,
584n18; 743a2, 594n50; 786b23–
25, 575n186
De insomniis: 462a3–4, 574n180
De interpretatione: 16a3–4, 594n50;
16b26–27, 549n102
De memoria: 449b4–6, 574n180;
450a10–11, 574n180; 453a14,
568n154
De motu animalium: 700b17–21, 570,
570n167; 702a17–19, 569
De partibus animalium: 661b18–19,
411
De respiratione: 471a8, 619n105
De sensu: 439b20–23, 628n133;
440a29–30, 628n133
Eudemian Ethics: I.4.2, 554; 1215a29–
30, 554; 1219a8, 622; 1219a13–18,
622
Historia animalium: 491b21, 584n18;
493a28, 584n18; 494b15–16,
633n151; 501a18–19, 411; 511a27,
584n18; 515a34–35, 594n50;
597a32, 584n18
Metaphysics: 982a25–28, 637n158;
1023a32–33, 482n16; 1024b23,
628n133, 628n134; 1026a25–27,
552n110; 1065a21, 619n105;
1072b3, 619n105; 1078a9–14,
637n158; 1093a30, 482n16
Meteorologica: 343b21–22, 633n151
Nicomachean Ethics: 1094a27–b3,
552n109; 1094b11–1095a13,
625n123; 1094b11–14, 630n139;
1098a26–33, 625n123, 630n139;
1102a26–1103a10, 571n174;
1102a27–28, 571; 1102b13–14,
571n174; 1102b29–31, 571n174;
1105b21–23, 574n181; 1109a33,
619n105; 1139a3–8, 571n169;
1139a12–14, 571n170; 1139a31–
33, 550n105; 1143a19–24,

577n191; 1147b5, 575n186;
1166b30–35, 576n189; 1174b20–
21, 574n181
On Generation and Corruption: 317a23,
619n105
On Poets (Περὶ ποιητῶν): 658n35;;
Poetics: 529n31, 584n15, 586,
586n21, 588, 588n30;; chap. 17,
533n42, 578n193; chap. 20,
542n78, 587n26; chap. 26, 3,
309, 317, 446, 534n45, 553;
1447a13–16, 355n88; 1447a22,
539; 1447a23, 539n62, 539n63;
1447a28–b2, 355n88; 1447b9,
355; 1447b18, 352n72; 1447b22,
355; 1447b25, 539, 539n63;
1448a33–34, 296n10; 1448b21–22,
539n63; 1448b24ff., 353n78;
1448b31–1449a2, 296n10;
1448b35–36, 296n10; 1449a14,
658n35; 1449a15–17, 522n5,
657n35; 1449a24–28, 539n64;
1449a28, 539, 540n69; 1449a37–
38, 658n35; 1449b4–5, 658n35;
1449b25, 539; 1449b27–28, 309;
1449b33–34, 588n30; 1450a7,
308n64; 1450a20–23, 589;
1450a24–26, 589n32; 1450b4–5,
588n31; 1450b8–12, 589; 1450b11,
308n64; 1450b13–14, 548n100,
588; 1450b14–15, 588n30;
1450b16–20, 529n31, 587, 587n27;
1453b1–9, 587n27; 1453b1–6,
587n25; 1453b1–2, 579n1;
1455a17–18, 309n66; 1455a22–32,
578n192; 1455a22–23, 578n192;
1455a23, 578n192; 1455a25–26,
578n192; 1456a33–b7, 549n101;
1456a33–34, 588n31; 1456a36–37,
586n25; 1456a37, 588n30, 588n31;
1456a38, 308n64, 588; 1456b1,
589; 1456b5–8, 587n25; 1456b5,
559n128; 1456b8–19, 549n100;

(Aristotle, *Poetics, cont.*)

1456b8–10, 586; 1456b8, 588n31;
1456b10–11, 586n22; 1456b10,
548n100; 1456b11–13, 586n23;
1456b14–15, 586; 1456b19,
584n15; 1457a21–22, 586n23;
1457a23–24, 549n102; 1457b1–3,
549, 549n103; 1458a18, 548n98;
1459a6–7, 584n16; 1460a1–2,
355n90; 1461a21–23, 164;
1461a22, 164n50; 1461b27–29,
553; 1462a2–4, 553; 1462a5–6,
553; 1462a6–7, 497; 1462a11–13,
586n25; 1462a11–12, 587n27;
1462a11, 529n31; 1462a17–18,
587n25

Politics: VIII.5, 537; VIII.6, 553n116;
1253a2–3, 551n108; 1253a10–11,
575n186; 1276b4–6, 485n29;
1291b18–19, 619n105; 1305a3–7,
466n104; 1309a14–20, 466;
1310a2–12, 538n58; 1320b2–4,
466n104; 1323b6–7, 638n162;
1334b20, 619n105; 1336b13–14,
184n34; 1336b20, 497n83;
1336b27–31, 447n52; 1340a42–
b5, 537n54; 1340b7–10, 537;
1340b10–12, 537n54; 1340b20ff.,
553n116; 1340b34–35, 553n116;
1340b42–1341a3, 553n116;
1341b8–18, 553n116; 1342a18–21,
554n116

Posterior Analytics: II.19, 569n161;
77b26–33, 552n110; 87a31–b7, 637

[*Problems*]: 956b11–15, 446n47

Protreptikos (Düring): fr. 104,
628n133

Rhetoric: 529n31, 532, 548n100,
565–566, 573, 584n15, 586n21,
588n30, 588n31, 594n50, 595n53,
621;;

I, 524–525, 549n101; I.1.10, 638;
I.3, 630n138; I.7, 555; I.9, 621;
I.11.6, 551n107, 562n134; II,

524–525, 528n25, 549n101,
570; II.1–11, 536; II.1, 556n120,
576n189; II.8, 536; III, 528n25,
548n98, 581, 598n63; III.1–12,
8, 521, 523–524, 590, 598n63;
III.1–2, 544; III.1, 2, 9, 309–310,
317, 317n99, 523, 526, 530,
562n136, 566, 598n63; III.1.5,
552n112; III.2–12, 583; III.2–11,
543; III.2, 534n43; III.2.4–5,
538n58; III.3–12, 530, 532;
III.3–11, 528; III.7, 535, 537;
III.8, 538–539, 540n69, 541;
III.8.1, 538n58; III.8.6, 623n113;
III.10–11, 533n42; III.12, 310,
316, 317n99, 355n90, 524,
529–530, 544, 585, 589, 592,
596n55, 597, 597–598n63, 599,
602; III.12.1, 607; III.13, 544;
III.14, 621; III.14.7, 591n40;
III.17.10, 229; III.19, 591n40

1354a5–6, 619n105; 1354a6–7,
620n107; 1354a7–11, 620n108;
1354a11, 622; 1354a15–16,
536n50; 1354a26–28, 631n145;
1354a34–b1, 634n154; 1354b8–
11, 632n145; 1354b27–1355a1,
638n161; 1354b29,
638n163; 1354b30, 638n161;
1354b31–1355a1, 631n145;
1354b33, 638n161

1355a1, 631n145; 1355a2–3,
638n161; 1355a7, 526n18;
1355a19, 615; 1355a20–24,
554n117; 1355a22–23, 570;
1355a24–29, 559n129, 631n140;
1355a24, 557n122; 1355a25–26,
557n121, 557n122; 1355a25,
557n122; 1355b10–11,
622; 1355b15–16, 607n73;
1355b26–32, 559n127; 1355b26,
560n129; 1355b29–31, 560n129;
1355b29, 558n122, 558n126,

561n131; 1355b31, 558n126; 1355b35–1356a4, 557n120; 1355b35, 557n120

1356a1–4, 631n142; 1356a1, 589n33; 1356a3–4, 549; 1356a13, 526n18; 1356a25–27, 551n109; 1356b26–34, 635; 1356b26–30, 606; 1356b26–28, 631n141; 1356b27–28, 606–607; 1356b28, 607n73

1357a3–4, 631n140, 634n154; 1357a11–12, 631n140

1358b2–5, 630n138; 1358b3–5, 632n147; 1358b10–11, 632n146; 1358b13–17, 630n138, 631n145; 1358b17, 526n18; 1358b22, 632

1359b8–16, 560n129; 1359b10, 560n129; 1359b13, 560n129; 1359b15–16, 560n129; 1359b16, 560n129

1360a37–38, 622; 1360b22, 556n120

1362a7, 615; 1362a29–31, 550n106; 1362b20, 556n120

1363b3, 615

1365b1–8, 555; 1365b1, 555

1367a16, 556n120

1368b23, 556n120

1369a1–4, 571n174; 1369a16, 615; 1369a22, 556n120; 1369b31–32, 630n139; 1369b32, 630n139

1370a18–27, 571; 1370a25–27, 572n175; 1370a27–32, 572; 1370a27–28, 574n181; 1370a28–30, 550, 551n106, 565, 569n160; 1370a28, 572; 1370a29, 575; 1370a30–32, 574n182; 1370a30, 550n106; 1370b33, 574

1371a9, 574; 1371a16, 556n120; 1371a19, 574

1372b21–23, 556n120

1375a8, 621n109, 633n151; 1375b29–31, 150

1377b18, 556n120; 1377b21–22, 571n168; 1377b24, 556n120; 1377b26, 557n120; 1377b29, 557n120; 1377b31, 557n120

1378a5, 557n120; 1378a17, 557n120; 1378a20–22, 546n93; 1378b7–8, 574n184; 1378b9, 574; 1378b10, 556n120

1381b19–20, 556n120; 1381b30–31, 556n120

1382a21, 565n146, 574

1383a17, 574

1384a23–29, 556n120; 1384a23, 574, 575n185; 1384b23, 556n120

1386a1–3, 536n52; 1386a28–33, 578; 1386a31–33, 530n31, 536n52; 1386a32, 537n53; 1386a33–34, 578n194

1388a2, 556n120; 1388a6, 556n120; 1388b5, 580n2; 1388b7, 615; 1388b15–18, 580n2; 1388b21–22, 597n62; 1388b22, 597

1391b24, 556n120

1395a32–b2, 631n140; 1395b1–2, 552n112, 553; 1395b3, 556n120; 1395b13–14, 552n112; 1395b26–29, 618n104; 1395b26–28, 631n140; 1395b28–29, 617

1397b26, 556n120

1401a1, 542n77

1403a32, 556n120; 1403a34–b8, 598n63; 1403a34–35, 528n25; 1403a36–b2, 524n13; 1403a36–b1, 588n31; 1403a36, 524n11, 549n101; 1403b6–7, 528n25; 1403b7–8, 524n13; 1403b15, 526n17; 1403b16–18, 524, 588; 1403b16, 635; 1403b17, 622, 635; 1403b18–22, 525, 544; 1403b18, 526n17; 1403b19, 637; 1403b20, 525; 1403b21–24, 521n4; 1403b21–22, 522, 531;

(Aristotle, *Rhetoric, cont.*)

1403b21, 526n17, 532, 546;
1403b22–26, 545n86; 1403b22–
24, 446, 586n22; 1403b22–23,
526, 581; 1403b22, 544, 545n86,
546, 582n9, 583n11; 1403b23,
521, 531; 1403b24–27, 522;
1403b24–26, 581n7; 1403b25–
26, 582n9; 1403b26–31, 309n68;
1403b27–28, 523, 526, 547,
625; 1403b27, 523, 526n19,
545n86, 581, 582n9; 1403b28–
35, 581; 1403b29–30, 582n9;
1403b30–32, 538; 1403b30–31,
531; 1403b31, 538–539, 540n69;
1403b32–35, 547; 1403b32–34,
446n45, 532; 1403b35–1404a1,
526n21, 548n98; 1403b35–36,
527n23, 531, 548n98, 581;
1403b35, 551, 552n111, 580n4;
1403b36–1404a8, 581n6;
1403b36–1404a1, 546–547;
1403b36, 526, 531, 544, 545n86,
546, 581–583

1404a1–12, 545; 1404a1, 527,
551, 581; 1404a2–7, 546n93;
1404a2–3, 545n85, 546n93,
551; 1404a2, 556n120; 1404a3,
547n97; 1404a4, 545n85;
1404a5–8, 536n50; 1404a5,
545n85; 1404a6–7, 528n24,
551; 1404a7, 528n24, 546;
1404a8–12, 583n11; 1404a8–10,
548; 1404a8–9, 527, 532n38,
557; 1404a8, 527, 527n24,
545n86, 547, 551, 581; 1404a9–
10, 548n98; 1404a9, 527n24,
559n128; 1404a10–11, 550;
1404a10, 545n88; 1404a11–12,
545n86; 1404a11, 523, 561–563,
566n148; 1404a12–19, 532, 544,
579; 1404a12–15, 531; 1404a12–
13, 532; 1404a12, 527n24,
548n98, 583, 589; 1404a13–15,

522n8, 593; 1404a13, 545n86,
581, 583n11; 1404a14, 494n67,
589; 1404a15–19, 310n71;
1404a15–16, 580, 583–584,
589n36; 1404a15, 522n6,
532n38, 582; 1404a16–19,
595n53; 1404a16–18, 585;
1404a16, 582, 585n20; 1404a17,
531; 1404a18–26, 583n14;
1404a18–19, 523–524, 583n14,
584n15, 593; 1404a18, 524;
1404a19–22, 530n32, 533;
1404a24–28, 302n34; 1404a25,
556n120; 1404a26–27, 533;
1404a27–28, 529n31; 1404a28,
588n30; 1404a35–39, 588;
1404a36–39, 588n29; 1404b1–3,
549; 1404b1–2, 548n98;
1404b18–25, 550n105; 1404b18–
19, 534; 1404b23–24, 534;
1404b31–32, 550; 1404b36–37,
550

1405a9–10, 584n16; 1405a23–25,
446n46; 1405a23–24, 469;
1405b6–8, 530n31, 533;
1405b12–13, 533n42; 1405b17–
19, 530n31, 533n41, 534n42

1407a19, 620; 1407b6–9, 599;
1407b11–12, 530n34, 594n50,
623n113; 1407b11, 444n38;
1407b13–18, 444n38; 1407b21–
25, 549

1408a10–11, 535, 576; 1408a16–
19, 535, 576; 1408a19–24,
577, 577n190; 1408a20,
536, 576n190; 1408a21, 536;
1408a22–23, 536n50; 1408a23–
25, 536n49; 1408a24, 536n50,
576n190; 1408a25–26, 549;
1408a26, 537; 1408a31–32,
537n56; 1408a34, 597; 1408a36,
615; 1408b3–7, 538n58;
1408b4–7, 576; 1408b5–7,

530n31; 1408b10–12, 632n148; 1408b12–18, 577n191; 1408b12, 577n191; 1408b21, 586n21; 1408b28–30, 538n60; 1408b28–29, 586n21; 1408b31–32, 538n59; 1408b32–33, 284n223, 539, 540n68, 541n71, 541n73; 1408b32, 488; 1408b34–35, 538; 1408b36, 538

1409a2–3, 592; 1409a2, 494n67; 1409a20–21, 444n38; 1409b4, 87

1410a19–22, 549

1412a27, 556n120

1413a6–9, 315, 494–495, 592; 1413b3–8, 599–601; 1413b3–5, 625n125; 1413b4–5, 604; 1413b5–8, 310n74, 602, 619n105, 621; 1413b5–6, 599, 618n105; 1413b5, 601, 604; 1413b6–8, 607, 611; 1413b7–8, 611; 1413b7, 614–615; 1413b8–14, 356n91; 1413b8–9, 310n72, 592, 604n69, 625; 1413b8, 604, 625; 1413b9–10, 632n148; 1413b9, 356n91; 1413b10, 625n125; 1413b11, 623n115; 1413b12–13, 355; 1413b12, 623n115; 1413b13, 356n91, 597, 626; 1413b14–21, 310n73; 1413b14–19, 623; 1413b14, 623n115; 1413b15–19, 624; 1413b15–16, 624n119; 1413b15, 623n115; 1413b16, 623n116, 623n117, 624n119, 626; 1413b17, 621; 1413b19–20, 627n131; 1413b30–31, 627

1414a7–11, 604n70; 1414a9, 630; 1414a10–11, 625, 625n124, 638n161; 1414a10, 629; 1414a11–14, 628; 1414a11, 633n149; 1414a12–14, 611n87; 1414a12–13, 638n161; 1414a12, 621n109, 634, 634n154;

1414a13–14, 629; 1414a13, 604, 638; 1414a15–17, 621, 625; 1414a15–16, 625, 632; 1414a16–17, 595n52; 1414a17–18, 356n91, 603, 603n68, 621; 1414a18–29, 598n63; 1414a28, 598n63, 621; 1414a29, 598n63; 1414b2, 591, 622; 1414b24–25, 593n50

1415a35–36, 576n189; 1415b4–8, 552n112; 1415b5–9, 631n140; 1415b28–29, 621; 1415b29, 624

1417a16–19, 550n105; 1417a18–21, 552; 1417a19, 560n129

1418a23–26, 229n36

1419a18, 631n140

Sophistical Refutations: 563–564, 576n190;; 164a20–21, 563, 563n139, 576n190; 164a23–24, 563n140; 164b27, 563; 165b1–3, 558n122, 559n128; 165b3, 558n126; 165b9, 559n128; 165b23–24, 542n77; 165b24–27, 563; 165b25, 562, 563n141; 165b26–27, 564; 166b1–9, 164, 165n53; 166b3–4, 594n50; 166b15–16, 300n29; 168b19, 563; 169b18–20, 576n190; 169b38, 563n139; 170a9–10, 577n190; 171a7–11, 369n133; 171a10–11, 231n42; 171a31–32, 559n128; 171a38–b2, 559n128; 171b10–11, 577n190; 177b, 145n128; 180a20–21, 482n16; 181b9–10, 619n105

Topics: 100b4–6, 559n126; 105b12–13, 594n50; 141a30, 559n126; 159a3–14, 559n126; 159a13–14, 559n126; 159a26–28, 559n126; 159a28–30, 558n126; 159a29–30, 558n126; 159a29, 559n126

Aristoxenos

Elementa harmonica (da Rios): 23.13–16, 541n76

(Aristoxenos, *cont.*)
　Elementa rhythmica (Pighi): 542n78;;
　　17.15–23, 541n77; 17.19, 542n78;
　　19.15–18, 542n78
Arkhilokhos (West): fr. 13, 57n48;
　fr. 185.3, 649n9
Arkhimedes *Problema bovinum*: 37–38,
　386n190
Arrian *Anabasis*: 1.17.3–4, 97n83;
　3.16.5, 97n83
Artemidoros *Oneirokritika*: 4.2, 452;
　4.2.74–79, 452n64
Asklepiades *Tragōidoumena*: 414;;
Athenaios: 1.2a, 612n89; 4.148c,
　468n114; 4.148d, 468n114;
　6.234f10–11, 496n81; 7.347e,
　296n10; 9.407b, 468; 10.416a,
　591; 10.456b, 401; 12.538b–539a,
　447n50; 12.538e7–8, 495; 12.538f,
　468n114; 12.542e, 476n144;
　13.608e, 355; 14.616e, 450n61;
　14.620b–d, 448; 14.620b, 447,
　451n63, 464n97, 466; 14.620c–d,
　351n67, 482; 14.620c, 352n72,
　437n6, 496; 14.620c2, 450n60,
　483n25; 14.620c4–7, 482n19,
　496n80; 14.620c4, 450n58, 483n25;
　14.620c7–10, 482n20, 496n75;
　14.620d, 483n25, 499; 14.620d1–7,
　483n26; 14.620d1–3, 495;
　14.620d6, 502; 14.632d, 354n83;
　14.643e–f, 612n89; 15.693f–694c,
　371n139; 15.701c3–5, 496n81
Bakkhylides
　Epigrammata: 1.3, 349n57
　Epinicians: 5.9–10, 398; 8.3, 274;
　　19.6–9, 398n244
Bible
　English
　　Genesis: 1:1–2, 264n169
　　Exodus: 6:29–7:2, 221n2; 31:2–6,
　　　189
　　1 Samuel: 9:9, 221n2
　　1 Kings: 22:19–23, 164n52, 241n81

2 Kings: 6:15–17, 254
Ezekiel: 14:9, 241n81
1 Thessalonians: 2.8, 612n89
Septuagint
　Josue: 13:22, 221n2
　Regnorum I: 1:9, 221n2; 1:11,
　　221n2; 1:18, 221n2; 9:18, 221n2
　Regnorum II: 15:27, 221n2
　Paralipomenon I: 9:22, 221n2;
　　26:28, 221n2
　Paralipomenon II: 16:7, 221n2;
　　16:10, 221n2
　Isaias: 30:10, 221n2
Caesar *Bellum Gallicum*: 6.14, 293
Cassius Dio: 5.18.8, 612n89
Cicero
　Brutus: §27, 596n55; §46, 596,
　　596n55
　De legibus: 2.63–66, 466n105
　De oratore: II §93, 596n55; III §171,
　　542; III §§173ff., 542; III §173,
　　542n80; III §174, 543; III §§213–
　　227, 535; III §§215–219, 539
　Orator: 484;; 109, 484n29; 175,
　　592n46
　Pro Flacco: 40, 596n56
　Pro Sestio: 129, 596n56
Comica adespota (*PCG* VIII): fr. 599,
　445n43
Corpus Glossariorum Latinorum (Goetz):
　454;; II pp. xix–xx, 462n90; II
　p. 22 lines 40–42, 462
Demetrios *On Style*: 529, 529n28;; §42,
　541n70, 541n72; §58, 529n29;
　§§193–194, 529n30; §195, 529,
　529n29; §226, 529n30; §271,
　529n30
Demokritos (DK 68): B21, 197n85
Demosthenes
　Against Androtiōn (Orat. 22): 30,
　　610n82
　[*Against Euergos and Mnēsiboulos*]
　　(Orat. 47): 243n88;;

Against Leptinēs (Orat. 20): 89–99, 610n81; 91, 610n81
Against Meidias (Orat. 21): 205, 322n120
Against Spoudias (Orat. 41): 23, 613
Against Timokratēs (Orat. 24): 20–23, 610n81; 63, 609n78; 112, 633n152
[*Erōtikos*] (Orat. 61): 2, 382n177
First Olynthiac (Orat. 1): 8, 323
Fourth Philippic (Orat. 10): 70, 609
[*On Organization*] (Orat. 13): 11, 609n78
On the Crown (Orat. 18): 170, 609n79; 191, 609n79; 262, 446; 267, 442, 442n31; 308, 610n82
On the False Embassy (Orat. 19): second hypothesis §2, 447n49; 14, 609n80; 113, 609n80; 192, 447n50; 252, 354n86; 270, 152n12; 315, 447n49
On the Peace (Orat. 5): 6, 212n139, 447n49
Philip's Letter (Orat. 12): 10, 615n97
Derveni papyrus: 145n128
Dio Chrysostomus: 37.1, 612n89; 38.4, 612n89; 38.5, 612n89; 56.11, 612n89
Diodoros of Sicily: 2.32.4, 73n13; 16.26, 272; 17.21.7, 96; 17.64.6, 96
Diogenes Laertios: 1.48, 151; 1.57, 23n23, 383, 387, 437; 3.56, 477, 663n49; 5.48, 529n31; 5.81, 466; 6.63, 468n114; 8.63, 495; 9.18, 354, 489n44; 9.20, 489n44
Diomedes *Ars grammatica* (*Grammatici latini* 1): p. 484 (Keil), 418n318, 464n96
Dionysios of Halikarnassos
Dēmosthenēs (Usener): §3, 592n47; §3 p. 132.14–15, 591; §3 p. 132.18, 592n45

Isaios (Usener): §20, 592n45; §20 p. 122.21–23, 591; §20 p. 123.10–14, 592
Isokratēs (Usener): 18, 595n53
Lysias (Usener): §6 p. 14.1–2, 591; §6 p. 14.9–10, 591n42
Roman Antiquities: 6.82.3, 612n89; 10.9.3, 612n89; 10.13.7, 612n89; 10.40.2, 612n89
Dionysios Thrax *Tekhnē grammatikē* (*Grammatici graeci* I.1): §5 (p. 8 Uhlig), 337n23
Empedokles
Testimonies (DK 31): A33, 426n350
Fragments (DK 31): B111.2, 204n116
Purifications: 352n72, 437n6, 483n25, 484;;
Ennius *Annales*: 464n94;;
Epic Cycle
Aithiopis: 342n39;;
Kypria (Bernabé): 370n133;; fr. 1, 230, 230n39, 231n41; fr. 1.7, 231n41
Little Iliad: 370n133;;
Oidipodeia: 402–403, 402n263, 405–406n276, 412–414;;
Argumentum?, 403, 403n266, 403n267
Sack of Troy: 370n133;;
Thēbais (Bernabé): 402, 402n263;; fr. 1, 399n249
Epimenidēs (DK 3): B4, 229n37
Etymologicum Gudianum (Sturz): col. 491 line 10 s.v. ῥαψῳδία, 337n23;;
Etymologicum Magnum (Gaisford): 411.43 s.v. ζήτρειον (col. 1175), 483n25; 452.37 s.v. θνήσκω (col. 1293), 393; 574.70–73 s.v. μάντις (cols. 1630–1631), 223; 657.4–5 s.v. παιάν (col. 1858), 421n330; 782.48 s.v. ὑποκριτής (col. 2190), 650n11; 798.57–59 s.v. φορμός (col. 2233), 429n371

Euboulos (K-A): fr. 134, 657n32

Eumelos (Bernabé): *PEG* I.114 F17, 208n123

Eupolis (K-A): fr. 395, 371

Euripides

Andromakhē: 1132, 87

Bakkhai: 1100, 87

Cyclops: 455–463, 61n61

Ēlektra: 471, 400

Erekhtheus: 308, 436;;

Hēraklēs: 777–783, 474n139

Hiketides: 56–58, 612n89

Iōn: 42, 275n203; 321, 275n203; 369–372, 272n195; 413–416, 272n195; 464, 204n106; 1322, 275n203

Iphigeneia among the Taurians: 1030, 612n89

Oidipous (Kannicht): fr. 540, 402n261; fr. 540a, 402, 402n261; fr. 540a.7–10, 414n312; fr. 540a.12, 416; fr. 540b, 402n261

Orestēs: 153, 612n89

Phoinissai: 48, 400; 50, 400; 453, 87; 807, 400; 1028, 400; 1506–1507, 400; 1507, 405

Eusebios *Ecclesiastical History*: 2.1.8, 612n89

Eustathios (cited by volume, page, and line number)

Ad Iliadem (van der Valk): 1.10, 378n168; 3.851.17, 66

Ad Odysseam (Stallbaum): 2.42.30–31 to v 107, 394n226; 2.89.31–32 to o 3, 661n43

FGH: **3** F105, 233n49; **12**, 401n260; **12** F7, 401n260; **16** F10, 403n266; **70** F20, 229n33; **76** F71, 495n71; **125** F4, 447n50, 495; **485** F6n28, 151n9; **568** F5, 493n60; **785**, 37n62; **789**, 37n62

Galen

De Hippocratis et Platonis decretis: 5.244 Kühn (*CMG* 5.4.1.2, p. 132 De Lacy), 442n31

Commentaria in Hippocratis Epidemias III: 17a.607 Kühn (*CMG* 5.10.2.1, pp. 79–80 Wenkebach), 78n39, 440n22

Gellius *Noctes Atticae*: 18.5, 464n94

Gorgias

Helen: 13, 617

Palamēdēs: 33, 617

Heliodoros *Aithiopika*: 2.6.2, 378n167

Herakleitos of Ephesos (DK 22): B42, 167, 351, 399n246; B56, 167; B92, 274n198; B93, 224n18; B105, 167

Herakleitos (the Allegorist) *Allegoriae*: 52.1, 160n39; 57.2–4, 161n42

Hermogenes *Peri ideōn* (Rabe): I p. 218.22–26, 543n81

Herodas: 2.79, 118n36

Herodotos: proem, 308n64; 1.17, 349n56; 1.30.2, 378n167; 1.46–49, 178n17; 1.47, 271n191; 1.65, 271n190, 271n191; 1.65.4, 195; 1.66, 271n190; 1.73.4, 124n57; 1.85, 271n190; 1.99, 196n83; 1.99.1–4, 197n86; 1.99.1, 197; 1.146, 89; 2.44, 154; 2.53, 178n16; 2.108.1, 124n57; 2.116.6–2.117, 47n24; 2.173.1, 197n87; 3.22.2, 197, 197n88; 3.75.15, 124n57; 3.98, 429n367; 4.29, 482n16; 4.35, 426n350; 4.124.2, 565n147; 4.205.2, 124n57; 5.58, 27, 73; 5.67, 47n24, 399; 5.74, 378n167; 5.92, 271n191; 6.1, 361; 6.66, 270, 270n186, 275n205; 6.75, 270; 6.136.11, 124n57; 7.6, 155; 7.6.3, 266; 7.10ε, 565, 566n149; 7.15.2, 565n147; 7.111, 272, 275n205; 7.140–141, 178n17; 7.140.2, 179n17; 7.140.3, 179n17; 7.141,

275n205; 7.141.3, 179n17; 7.141.4, 179n17; 7.220, 482n16; 8.37, 272; 8.135, 275n205; 9.120.10, 124n57

Hesiod

Fragments (MW): fr. 25.20–33, 153n15; fr. 25.24–25, 154n15; fr. 26.13, 139n108; fr. 185.17, 139n108; fr. 195.8, 139n108; fr. 195.47, 139n108; fr. 204.44–51, 150; fr. 204.84, 362n109; fr. 205.6, 151n10; fr. 253.3, 139n108; fr. 278, 400; fr. 304, 237n69; fr. 306, 359n99; fr. 357, 339, 392, 396, 398, 410n292, 420, 424n345

Melampodia: 400;;

Shield: 8, 139n108; 47, 139n108; 202–206, 208n123; 205–206, 421; 393–396, 394n224

Theogony: 204, 234, 239, 244–245, 253, 398n242;; 1–115, 235, 264n169; 1–35, 265; 3, 285; 6, 285; 10, 256; 22–34, 219; 22–23, 213; 22, 189–190, 190n57, 227n30, 241, 241n80, 265; 25, 244n92; 26–28, 236n62, 239n75, 260; 26, 240–241, 242n83, 244, 246; 27–28, 165, 245n94, 247, 247n103, 249, 252, 254n137, 259; 27, 241, 246, 256n145, 257–260; 28, 207n120, 240–241, 241n80, 246n99, 256n145, 257, 259–260; 29, 244n92; 30, 241, 337, 348n55, 372n142; 31–32, 190, 227n29, 241; 32–33, 226; 32, 225, 227, 227n30, 264n169; 33, 227n29, 264n169; 34, 204n108, 348n55; 36, 204n108; 37–38, 235; 38, 225–227; 40–52, 212n140; 48, 357n93; 53–55, 251n120; 53–54, 204n108; 55, 235, 248–249; 56, 237n69; 65–66, 421; 71–75, 235; 78, 238; 80–103, 243; 80–92, 250; 91, 213n142; 93–95, 212n140; 94–96, 347;

94–95, 208n123, 348n55; 95, 348n55; 98–103, 235, 249n109; 100, 182n25; 102–103, 249n109; 115, 264n169; 154–210, 253n129; 176–201, 254; 202–212, 254; 226–232, 246, 250; 227, 248; 229, 236, 238n71, 259n156; 230, 236; 233–236, 250; 233, 238, 238n71, 256n145, 259n156; 236, 238n71; 252–255, 254; 326–332, 406; 330, 406, 406n279; 367–370, 228, 228n30; 369–370, 227; 442–443, 239n74; 498–500, 253n128; 507–616, 253n129; 565, 228n30; 636, 237n69; 696, 361n108; 709, 238; 722–725, 237n69; 744, 165n53; 775–806, 237; 782–783, 237n66; 783–804, 246n102; 783, 259n156; 789–790, 237n69; 789, 238; 795, 237; 797, 237; 801, 237; 803, 237; 824, 254; 886–900, 225, 253n129; 952, 154; 980, 139n108

Works and Days: 234, 244, 253n132, 514;; 1–2, 255; 3–9, 255; 3–8, 239n74; 10, 253, 255, 256n145, 263, 265n170, 265n172; 24–26, 236n63; 25–26, 182n28; 27, 265n170; 78, 259n156; 105, 255n141; 106, 265n170; 120, 243n87; 174, 265n170; 176ff., 226; 176–201, 225; 213, 265n170; 247, 151n10; 274, 265n170; 286, 265n170; 288, 393; 290, 393; 299, 265n170; 308, 243n87; 396, 265n170; 397, 265n170; 483–484, 255, 255n141; 516, 244n90; 521, 139n108; 544, 362n113, 427; 582–584, 394n224; 586, 407n283; 611, 265n170; 618–694, 227n30, 254; 633, 265n170; 641, 265n170; 648–649, 255n139; 650–657, 82; 654, 265n170; 656–658, 398n242; 657, 398n242; 658–659, 225;

(Hesiod, *Works and Days, cont.*)

658, 265n170; 659, 190, 190n55,
220, 393n216; 660–662, 227n30,
255n140; 661, 255; 662, 255; 682,
265n170; 708–709, 246n102; 709,
259n156; 752, 118n36; 765–769,
254n136; 768, 256n145; 789,
259n156; 798, 255; 814–818, 255;
818, 254n136, 255, 256n145

Hesykhios: A no. 5665 s.v. ἄοιμος,
393n213; A no. 8467
s.v. αὐτοσχεδιάζει, 440n21; Λ
no. 95 s.v. λάθει, 251; Σ no. 854
s.v. σκαπέρδα, 410n293; Τ no. 796
s.vv. τὴν ἐπιδεξιάν, 371n139; Φ
no. 781 s.v. φορμός, 429n371; Φ
no. 782 s.v. φορμο(ρ)ραφούμεθα,
428n365; Ω no. 39 s.v. ᾠδεῖον, 471

Himerios *Orations* (Colonna): 62.7
(p. 226), 208n123

[Hippokrates] *Decorum*: 7, 566n148

Homer

Iliad

Book 1 A: A 1, 181n23, 586,
587n25; A 2–5, 264n169; A 5,
230, 231n41; A 6–7, 264n169;
A 6, 181n23; A 15, 220; A 16,
194; A 28, 220; A 41, 203; A 70,
227; A 92–100, 233; A 115,
412n306; A 211, 391n206;
A 233–239, 372; A 245–246,
372; A 260–272, 200n95;
A 277–279, 40; A 279, 220;
A 286, 200n95; A 287–289,
390; A 289, 391; A 290–291,
391; A 292, 384–385, 387, 390;
A 293–296, 390; A 364, 26;
A 375, 194; A 472–474, 421;
A 487, 151n10; A 504, 203;
A 521, 421n333; A 603–604,
208n123, 288n233; A 603,
375n156; A 604, 375n156

Book 2 B: B 6, 237n65; B 11–15,
164; B 15, 164, 166n57; B 26,

166; B 32–33, 166; B 32, 165,
166n57; B 33–34, 251n120;
B 33, 166n57; B 37–38, 237n65;
B 37, 134; B 38, 237n65;
B 52, 602n65; B 58, 412n306;
B 69–70, 166; B 69, 165, 166n57;
B 70, 166n57; B 81, 237n65;
B 86, 220; B 87, 393n219; B 119,
366n124; B 121–122, 409; B 138,
207n120; B 185–186, 372n143;
B 186, 372n145; B 214, 237;
B 278–279, 372n143; B 299–300,
252; B 303–330, 233; B 308,
224n19; B 310, 661n43; B 314,
56n46; B 325, 363n115; B 349,
237n65; B 353, 224n19; B 419,
204n105; B 436, 388n195;
B 461, 104; B 476, 195n76;
B 482, 134; B 484–493, 183,
357; B 484–487, 358; B 484–486,
184, 227n30, 303; B 484, 358;
B 485–486, 199, 358; B 485,
366n125; B 486, 185n39; B 487,
358; B 488–493, 357; B 488–490,
358; B 488, 264n168, 370n136;
B 490, 264n168; B 491–493,
358; B 491–492, 358; B 493,
358; B 546–557, 150; B 557–558,
148–149, 152; B 557, 150–152,
151n11; B 558, 148–152;
B 594–600, 187n46; B 724,
56n46, 233; B 794, 373n149,
374n153; B 840, 64; B 843,
251n122; B 863, 421n334

Book 3 Γ: Γ 71, 133n89; Γ 92,
133n89; Γ 125–128, 362n110,
363; Γ 138, 133n89; Γ 151–152,
394n224; Γ 195, 56n46; Γ 208,
412n306; Γ 212, 365; Γ 214,
391n208; Γ 216–219, 372n143;
Γ 236, 194; Γ 255, 133n89;
Γ 291, 409

Book 4 Δ: Δ 47, 104; Δ 107,

372n146; Δ 124, 409; Δ 153, 26; Δ 165, 104; Δ 178, 412; Δ 192, 212n138; Δ 235, 236n65, 259n156; Δ 293, 56n46; Δ 327, 83n7; Δ 328, 83n7; Δ 381, 224n19; Δ 404, 236n65; Δ 463–471, 83n7; Δ 469, 25; Δ 504, 411n303; Δ 543, 134

Book 5 E: E 12, 649n9; E 43–47, 25; E 155, 56n46; E 176, 25; E 227, 372n145; E 384, 412; E 508, 203; E 534, 104; E 574, 56n46; E 604, 136n102; E 635, 236n65, 238n70; E 720, 347n53; E 727–728, 430; E 842, 199n95; E 866, 230

Book 6 Z: Z 27, 25; Z 159, 220; Z 163, 259n156; Z 187, 365; Z 230, 411n303; Z 286–300, 56n47; Z 321, 361n107; Z 357–358, 366–367; Z 449, 104; Z 456, 362n110

Book 7 H: 51–52, 55;; H 6, 25; H 12, 25; H 16, 25; H 77, 136n102; H 91, 363n115; H 237, 407n283; H 241, 421; H 244–272, 50; H 277, 220; H 324, 365; H 334–335, 163; H 352, 259n156; H 399–404, 392; H 407, 289, 297n11, 649n10, 652n17, 661; H 415, 374n153; H 457, 407n283

Book 8 Θ: Θ 10, 133; Θ 56, 421n334; Θ 69–72, 199n95; Θ 146, 200n95; Θ 171, 224n19; Θ 181, 185n38; Θ 185, 64; Θ 296, 372n146; Θ 334, 26; Θ 358, 56

Book 9 I: I 16, 26; I 31–51, 392; I 63, 134; I 95–99, 40; I 97, 395n228; I 168, 69; I 186–191, 373, 376; I 190, 375; I 191, 367, 372, 374n153; I 193–194, 373n150; I 236, 224n19; I 310, 204; I 344, 238; I 371, 238; I 375, 238; I 389, 139n107; I 404–405, 270n184; I 646, 134, 136n100, 137n102; I 702–703, 269n181

Book 10 K: K 19–20, 360n105; K 62, 372n146; K 169, 200n95; K 261–263, 430; K 315, 212n138; K 321, 372n144; K 328, 372n144; K 341, 56n46; K 477, 56n46; K 534, 238

Book 11 Λ: Λ 24, 393, 393n219; Λ 69, 103n110; Λ 78, 231n43; Λ 124, 372n146; Λ 240, 25; Λ 248–263, 55; Λ 257–258, 55n45; Λ 260, 25; Λ 336, 409; Λ 474, 361n108; Λ 579, 25; Λ 632–637, 129–130; Λ 653, 134, 136–137n102; Λ 699, 64

Book 12 M: M 23, 169; M 85–87, 195n76; M 164, 237n65; M 225, 200n95; M 228–229, 655; M 228, 289, 652n17, 661, 661n44; M 296–297, 362n111; M 297, 338, 369n131; M 331, 83n7; M 373, 83n7; M 377, 387n195; M 433, 252, 252n125; M 436, 409; M 453, 407n284; M 457–458, 407n284; M 458, 407; M 461–462, 407

Book 13 N: N 85, 25; N 96, 151n10; N 101, 151n10; N 195, 83n7; N 196, 83n7; N 278, 56n46; N 244, 224n19; N 358–360, 408; N 359, 408–409, 412, 424; N 360, 25, 409; N 402–423, 27n37; N 410–423, 25; N 412, 25; N 416, 26; N 420–423, 26, 26n34; N 423, 26, 27n37; N 447, 26; N 538, 26; N 599–600, 407n285; N 620, 151n10; N 684, 421n333; N 689, 83n7; N 690, 83n7; N 716, 407n285

(Homer, *Iliad, cont.*)

Book 14 Ξ: Ξ 53–54, 359n99;
Ξ 127, 230; Ξ 250, 136n102;
Ξ 389, 409; Ξ 392, 151n10;
Ξ 395, 104; Ξ 407, 407n285;
Ξ 432, 26

Book 15 O: O 11, 407n283;
O 14–17, 361n107; O 16,
361n107; O 94, 136–137n102;
O 148, 136n102; O 159, 237n65;
O 214, 104; O 291, 25; O 331,
83n7; O 337, 83n7; O 348, 133;
O 411–412, 189n53; O 413,
409; O 435, 25; O 581, 25;
O 623–629, 209n127; O 745,
372n146

Book 16 Π: Π 20, 26; Π 30, 56;
Π 79, 421n333; Π 87–90,
374n152; Π 112, 185n38;
Π 144–154, 54; Π 182,
421; Π 235, 267n176,
660; Π 269–274, 374n152;
Π 284–292, 66; Π 293,
66n85; Π 312, 25; Π 367,
200n95; Π 400, 25; Π 425, 25;
Π 431–443, 199n95; Π 465,
25; Π 466–476, 54; Π 497,
56; Π 565, 387n195; Π 610,
421n334; Π 617, 421n334;
Π 630, 409; Π 662, 409;
Π 787–804, 199n95; Π 805, 25

Book 17 P: P 1–113, 53; P 97–101,
53; P 208, 372n145; P 229,
133n89; P 288, 251n122; P 321,
199n95, 231n43; P 349, 25;
P 391, 372n145; P 400–401, 409;
P 451, 104n117; P 480, 372n145;
P 524, 25; P 612, 151n10;
P 752–754, 51

Book 18 Σ: Σ 31, 25; Σ 70, 26;
Σ 78, 26; Σ 117–119, 153; Σ 121,
154n15; Σ 188, 134, 136n100;
Σ 262, 136n102; Σ 295, 230;
Σ 323, 26; Σ 324, 134; Σ 334,

104; Σ 348, 362n108; Σ 357, 363;
Σ 362, 363; Σ 364–367, 363n118;
Σ 367, 339; Σ 400, 237n69;
Σ 503–505, 372n143; Σ 524,
374n153; Σ 603–604, 192; Σ 604,
212n138

Book 19 T: 56n47;; T 45, 391n208;
T 52–53, 55n44; T 73, 391n208;
T 74–75, 391; T 74, 387n194;
T 79, 391; T 80, 384–385,
387, 387–388n195, 391; T 81,
391n208; T 85–86, 391; T 86–88,
231n43; T 99, 138; T 107, 237;
T 230, 133; T 258, 183n30;
T 415–417, 233

Book 20 Y: 162n44;; Y 67–68,
161; Y 69, 161; Y 70–71, 161;
Y 72, 161; Y 73–74, 161;
Y 101, 409; Y 105, 138; Y 131,
230; Y 203–205, 184; Y 204,
333n7; Y 205, 184; Y 242–243,
239n74; Y 335, 387n195; Y 336,
199–200n95

Book 21 Φ: Φ 114, 25; Φ 142,
395n228; Φ 275–276, 259n156;
Φ 276, 237n65, 238; Φ 331–382,
161; Φ 391–414, 161; Φ 406, 25;
Φ 423–433, 162n44; Φ 425, 25;
Φ 426, 56n46; Φ 435–469, 161;
Φ 479–496, 161; Φ 497–501,
161; Φ 511, 138; Φ 517, 134;
Φ 578, 387n195

Book 22 X: 51;; X 30, 224n19;
X 167–181, 199n95; X 209–213,
199n95; X 213, 199n95;
X 256, 104; X 330, 25; X 335,
25; X 440, 362n110; X 470,
139n108; X 476, 385, 386n190,
387

Book 23 Ψ: 64n78;; Ψ 60,
26; Ψ 262–652, 64; Ψ 273,
372n146; Ψ 322, 133n89;
Ψ 359–361, 249n112; Ψ 576,

236; Ψ 579–580, 236; Ψ 626,
200n95; Ψ 671, 189n53; Ψ 692,
104; Ψ 712, 410n291; Ψ 726, 25;
Ψ 761, 652n17; Ψ 857, 133n89
Book 24 Ω: Ω 90, 136n102;
Ω 222–224, 237; Ω 222, 237n65;
Ω 251, 64; Ω 343, 337n25;
Ω 379, 200n95; Ω 407, 200n95;
Ω 498, 25; Ω 531, 133n89;
Ω 720–776, 375

Odyssey
Book 1 α: 193; α 1, 181n23; α 2–9,
264n169; α 2–3, 62n68; α 7, 231;
α 10, 181n23, 368, 395n228;
α 32–33, 269n182; α 34, 231;
α 121, 372n145; α 154, 269;
α 155, 234, 385; α 212, 134n94,
136n100, 137n102; α 277,
364n122; α 281–286, 366;
α 321, 660; α 325–327, 192, 365;
α 336, 212n138; α 337–341,
365; α 337–340, 193n66; α 338,
193; α 346–352, 366; α 346–349,
215, 269; α 346–347, 235; α 348,
231n43; α 351–352, 339n33, 365;
α 421–422, 192
Book 2 β: 363n115;; β 35, 230n38;
β 37–38, 372n143; β 59,
136n102; β 61, 189n52; β 80,
372n144; β 93, 362; β 97, 362;
β 98, 363, 363n115; β 111, 289,
649n10, 652n17, 661; β 120, 138;
β 124, 134n93, 136n102; β 171,
136n102; β 183, 134n93; β 186,
372n146; β 196, 364n122; β 202,
207n120; β 235–236, 361n107;
β 236, 361; β 354, 362; β 272,
136–137n102; β 340, 133n87;
β 380, 362
Book 3 γ: γ 103, 134n93; γ 113,
134n93; γ 118–119, 361; γ 118,
237n69, 339, 361–362n108, 363;
γ 153, 151n10; γ 162, 151n10;

γ 299, 151n10; γ 331, 199n95
Book 4 δ: δ 15–18, 191; δ 17–18,
421; δ 17, 212n138; δ 96,
652n17; δ 140, 238, 238n70;
δ 152, 136n102; δ 219–226,
251n120; δ 221, 251n120;
δ 225–226, 251n120; δ 411,
378n167; δ 417–418, 406n280;
δ 469–470, 199n95; δ 472–474,
199n95; δ 475, 199n95; δ 516,
26; δ 582, 151n10; δ 621,
212n138; δ 675–678, 364n121;
δ 675–676, 365; δ 676, 365;
δ 678, 365; δ 689, 136n102;
δ 691, 212n138; δ 703, 25; δ 731,
136–137n102; δ 739, 136n102,
365; δ 819, 134n93; δ 836, 370,
370n137
Book 5 ε: ε 47, 337n25; ε 61–62,
365; ε 87–90, 206; ε 87, 205;
ε 107, 237n69; ε 297, 25; ε 356,
365; ε 406, 25; ε 420, 26
Book 6 ζ: ζ 8, 366; ζ 204–205, 366;
ζ 232–234, 189n52
Book 7 η: η 215–221, 240; η 241,
370
Book 8 θ: θ 43–45, 190; θ 43,
212n138; θ 44–45, 215, 235;
θ 44, 182n28, 269n181; θ 45,
269n181; θ 47, 212n138;
θ 62–103, 182n28; θ 62–64,
184n35; θ 63, 182n28; θ 64,
184n36; θ 73–74, 181n23, 395;
θ 73, 184n36, 269; θ 74, 181,
207n121; θ 75, 395; θ 79–81,
270n184; θ 79–80, 233; θ 82,
231n43; θ 87–92, 426; θ 87,
212n138, 269, 374n153; θ 90–91,
269; θ 90, 386n190; θ 91, 191,
333n7; θ 97–107, 190; θ 134,
189n52; θ 146, 189n52; θ 159,
189n53; θ 170, 238n73; θ 173,
213n142; θ 179–181, 189n53;

(Homer, *Odyssey, cont.*)

θ 233, 25; θ 246–247, 190;
θ 254–255, 190; θ 266, 234,
385, 386n190; θ 267, 138;
θ 274–275, 412; θ 288, 138,
139n109; θ 362, 139n109; θ 429,
393, 397, 425; θ 437, 362n108;
θ 448, 189n52; θ 472, 182n28;
θ 479–481, 182n28, 213n142;
θ 479–480, 395; θ 481, 188,
189n54, 207n121, 214n146, 220;
θ 487–498, 186, 194; θ 487–491,
165, 303; θ 487–489, 213n142;
θ 487–488, 213; θ 488–489,
281; θ 488, 188, 189n54, 220,
288n233; θ 489–491, 366; θ 489,
188, 195, 195n77, 199; θ 491,
183n29, 184n33, 199; θ 492,
190, 195–196, 196n83, 198,
269, 360n100, 393n216; θ 493,
189; θ 496–498, 213n142, 230;
θ 496, 199n95; θ 499–501, 190;
θ 499–500, 181n23; θ 499,
229–230, 234, 269, 347n53;
θ 500, 269, 368, 395n228; θ 502,
196; θ 536–543, 190; θ 537,
269; θ 539, 212n138; θ 542,
269; θ 558ff., 190; θ 579–580,
231n43, 366n124
Book 9 ι: ι 14, 200n95; ι 67,
233; ι 319–328, 58; ι 319, 58;
ι 321–324, 59; ι 335, 58; ι 371,
58; ι 372, 58n52; ι 382–384, 58;
ι 384, 60; ι 534–535, 232n46;
ι 554–555, 232
Book 10 κ: κ 14–16, 365; κ 15,
151n10; κ 18, 364n122; κ 76,
26; κ 91, 151n10; κ 221, 365;
κ 227, 365; κ 237, 134n95; κ 238,
337n25; κ 254, 365; κ 277, 205;
κ 293, 337n25; κ 319, 337n25;
κ 389, 337n25; κ 397, 136n102;
κ 414, 136n102

Book 11 λ: λ 91, 220; λ 114–115,
232; λ 119–130, 233; λ 124,
151n10; λ 328–330, 370n136;
λ 363–368, 238; λ 363–366,
259n156; λ 367–368, 189n51;
λ 367, 238n73, 370; λ 368, 359,
370n135; λ 390, 136n102; λ 418,
136n102; λ 602–603, 154–155,
154n15, 155n22; λ 604, 154,
155; λ 615, 136n102; λ 616, 153;
λ 619, 154; λ 621, 154
Book 12 μ: μ 44, 192; μ 56,
370; μ 70, 170; μ 183, 192,
194, 347n53, 359n98; μ 184,
366n125; μ 187, 192; μ 189–190,
366; μ 191, 366n125; μ 192,
192; μ 197–198, 192; μ 313, 232;
μ 325–326, 232; μ 338, 232;
μ 371–373, 232; μ 387–388, 233;
μ 415–425, 57n48
Book 13 ν: ν 27–28, 421; ν 72,
372n145; ν 111, 134; ν 385,
200n95; ν 429, 337n25
Book 14 ξ: ξ 42, 136n102; ξ 69,
26n33; ξ 70, 136n102; ξ 122,
136n102; ξ 124–125, 240, 240n77;
ξ 125–127, 259n156; ξ 125,
263; ξ 126–128, 263; ξ 131–132,
360; ξ 153, 136n102; ξ 156–157,
259n156; ξ 163, 134n93; ξ 236,
25; ξ 240, 237n69; ξ 258, 151n10;
ξ 283, 136n102; ξ 352, 134n93;
ξ 296–297, 259n156; ξ 354,
26n35; ξ 365, 238; ξ 386–389,
238; ξ 387–389, 236n62;
ξ 387–388, 259n156; ξ 387, 192,
238; ξ 491, 136–137n102; ξ 501,
134; ξ 533, 104
Book 15 ο: ο 3, 660; ο 132,
372n145; ο 170, 289, 650,
652n17, 661, 661n44; ο 212,
136n102; ο 282, 372n145;
ο 324, 213n142; ο 330, 134n93;

ο 346, 136n102; ο 368, 134n93, 136n100; ο 546, 104

Book 16 π: π 40, 372n145; π 151, 136n102; π 172, 337n25; π 235, 200n95; π 335, 212n138; π 343–344, 364; π 365–370, 361; π 365, 361; π 376, 136n102; π 379, 339, 361, 363–364; π 383–384, 364; π 411, 364n119; π 421–423, 363, 364n120; π 421–422, 339; π 423, 339; π 431–432, 364; π 432, 364; π 456, 337n25

Book 17 ρ: ρ 10, 134n93; ρ 57, 362n109; ρ 110, 136–137n102; ρ 112, 134n94, 136n100, 137n102; ρ 122, 199n95; ρ 173, 213n142; ρ 243, 136n102; ρ 262, 234, 385; ρ 383–385, 182n28, 359; ρ 385, 191; ρ 427, 151n10; ρ 513, 192; ρ 514–521, 370n135; ρ 515–517, 370n136; ρ 518–521, 189, 192; ρ 518–519, 360; ρ 519, 189, 191–192, 333n7; ρ 521, 136n102; ρ 538, 136n102

Book 18 σ: σ 46, 133n89; σ 53–54, 240; σ 67, 230; σ 90–94, 26n33; σ 147, 134n93; σ 152, 194; σ 170, 200n95; σ 193, 138, 139n109; σ 212, 25; σ 238, 26; σ 239, 136n102; σ 242, 25–26; σ 304–305, 192; σ 341, 25

Book 19 τ: 363n115;; τ 29, 362n109; τ 107–307, 258; τ 137–158, 363n115; τ 143, 363n115; τ 162–163, 258; τ 203, 240n78, 258–259, 262, 262n163; τ 204–209, 258; τ 215–219, 263; τ 215–217, 259n154; τ 250, 259; τ 315, 136n102; τ 322, 134n93; τ 332, 133; τ 535–553, 233; τ 535, 289, 652n17, 658n36, 661; τ 555–556, 289; τ 555, 289,

652n17, 658n36, 661; τ 565, 204n106, 237; τ 567, 204n106; τ 577, 133n89; τ 584, 388n195; τ 592–593, 199n95

Book 20 υ: υ 11, 364n122; υ 37, 200n95; υ 72, 189n52; υ 100, 230n38; υ 105, 230n38; υ 110, 407, 407n283; υ 114, 230; υ 115, 203; υ 118, 25; υ 265, 134n94, 136n100; υ 309–310, 227; υ 310, 226; υ 351–357, 233; υ 385–386, 374n153

Book 21 φ: φ 15, 387n195; φ 75, 133n89; φ 82, 372n145; φ 94, 136n102; φ 201, 136n102; φ 212, 200n95; φ 347–348, 395; φ 386, 362n109; φ 390–391, 74n19; φ 406, 190; φ 413, 224n19

Book 22 χ: χ 31, 262n163; χ 49, 56; χ 68, 25; χ 147, 25; χ 186, 362, 431n383; χ 228, 237n69; χ 344–349, 212; χ 346, 212n140; χ 347–348, 181, 181n24, 207n121, 213n144, 359; χ 347, 207n121; χ 376, 230n38; χ 395–396, 362n109; χ 398, 362n109; χ 424, 393n216; χ 486, 200n95

Book 23 ψ: ψ 67, 232; ψ 76, 136n102; ψ 159–162, 359n99; ψ 205, 25; ψ 271, 151n10; ψ 296, 370n137; ψ 317, 26, 26n35

Book 24 ω: 363n115;; ω 2, 337n25; ω 90, 136n102; ω 128–150, 363n115; ω 133, 363n115; ω 196–198, 363n115; ω 196, 363n115; ω 197–198, 359n98; ω 197, 195; ω 199–201, 366n124; ω 227–229, 362n112; ω 288, 134n93; ω 312, 134n93; ω 313, 136n102; ω 345, 25; ω 381, 25; ω 437, 134n93

Homerica (Allen, cited by line
number)

Vita Herodotea: §15, 332n7; §16, 333;
68, 332n7; 94, 332n7; 112, 333n7,
333n9; 118, 333n7; 143, 333n7,
333n9; 145, 333n7; 193, 332n7,
333n9; 196–207, 167n60; 196,
332n7; 209, 333n7; 215–216, 333;
218, 332n7; 336, 333n7; 346–354,
167n60; 346, 332n7; 349, 333n7;
350, 333n7; 352, 333n7; 372,
332n7; 375, 332n7; 380, 333n7;
399, 333n7; 513, 333n7; 521,
333n7

Certamen: 380, 380n169;; 20, 169n63;
55–56, 332n2, 332n6; 75–101, 380;
95, 381n175, 381n176; 97–101,
381; 99, 381; 102–103, 381n175;
104, 382; 107–137, 380; 140–175,
380; 180–204, 380; 213–214,
397–398, 398n242; 337–338, 194

Vita 4: 16, 169

Vita 5: 34, 169

Vita 6: 9, 83n6

Homeric Hymns

Homeric Hymns (hymns 2–5 are
also indexed under their various
titles): 1.18 (to Dionysos), 357n93;
2.102 (to Demeter), 139n108;
2.494, 357n93; 3.20 (to Apollo),
357n93; 5.1 (to Aphrodite),
139n108; 5.9, 139n108; 5.93,
139n108; 5.293, 194n71, 393n216;
6.2 (to Aphrodite), 357n93; 7.59
(to Dionysos), 195, 360n101;
9 (to Artemis), 169; 9.3, 168;
9.9, 194n71, 393n216; 10.1 (to
Aphrodite), 138n104; 18.11 (to
Hermes), 194n71, 393n216; 19
(to Pan), 415; 19.15, 349; 19.18,
349; 19.19–21, 421; 19.21, 349;
19.27, 349; 19.28, 349n58; 20
(to Hephaistos), 359n98; 25 (to

the Muses and Apollo), 348n55;
30.18 (to Earth), 357n93; 32.2 (to
Selene), 357n93; 32.19, 357n93;
32.20, 182n25

Hymn to Aphrodite (*Homeric Hymn* 5):
1, 139n108; 9, 139n108; 93,
139n108; 109–110, 263n167; 177,
411n303; 293, 194n71, 393n216

Hymn to Apollo (*Homeric Hymn* 3):
392, 424n345, 493, 493n60,
653n17;; 1, 426n353; 20, 357n93;
157–178, 265; 165–176, 426n353;
171–173, 168; 171, 652n17,
658n36; 177–178, 426n353; 177,
265n172; 179, 426n353; 188–206,
212n140; 188–191, 235; 189,
208n123; 197–199, 421n331;
197–198, 421; 364, 406n279;
393–396, 272n195; 545–546,
426n353; 546, 264n168

Hymn to Demeter (*Homeric Hymn* 2):
138–139;; 44–45, 256; 46, 256n146;
102, 139n108; 120–121, 256n147;
121, 256; 198, 496n80; 494,
357n93; 495, 264n168, 381

Hymn to Hermes (*Homeric Hymn* 4):
287;; 3–16, 204; 3, 206; 11–12,
237n69; 25, 359n99; 32, 348n55;
40, 348n55; 52, 349; 115–137,
205; 166–173, 205n114; 173, 220,
393n216; 190–193, 249; 210,
348n55; 424, 376n160; 425–428,
203; 425–426, 348n55, 387; 426,
376, 385; 427, 203–204, 376;
428, 376; 429–433, 376; 429,
203, 203n103; 430, 204n109;
432, 203, 203n103; 433, 195;
440, 376n161; 442, 376n160,
376–377n161, 377; 443, 376n160,
376n161; 444, 376n161; 447–448,
376n160; 447, 376n161; 448,
376n161, 378n164; 450–452,
208n123; 451–452, 376n160; 451,

378n163, 393, 397; 454, 377n162;
455, 376n161; 456, 376n161;
460–462, 205n114; 464–465, 377,
393n216; 465, 376n161; 475–477,
376; 475, 376n161; 476–477, 376;
476, 421; 478, 377n161, 421;
479, 195; 480–481, 349n57; 480,
377n161; 482, 377n161; 483,
359n99; 484–485, 349; 485, 349;
486, 377n161; 490, 377n161; 496,
377n161; 499, 377n161; 516–517,
205n113; 528–532, 206n117;
529, 205, 348n55; 530, 205; 531,
206; 532, 206; 556, 288; 559, 203,
206n120; 561, 207n120; 563,
207n120; 565, 206n120; 566,
206n120; 576, 205n114; 580,
264n168
Horace *Carmina*: 1.7.6, 369n133
Hyperides *In Defense of the Children
of Lykourgos* (fr. 118 Jensen):
471n126;;
Isaios: 6, 243n88
Isokrates (also indexed under their
various titles): 2.7, 614; 2.8, 614;
2.16, 617n103; 2.43, 276n206;
4.1–3, 594n50; 4.96, 617n103;
4.120, 442n31; 4.150, 617n103;
5.7, 593n50; 5.12–13, 594n50;
5.26–27, 624, 624n120; 5.81,
593n50, 617n103; 6.64, 617n103;
6.73, 617n103; 6.78, 617n103; 8.38,
613; 9.4, 615n96; 9.5, 615n96; 9.7,
615n96; 9.8, 615n96; 9.54, 615n97;
9.74, 614, 614n93; 9.75, 615; 9.76,
614; 9.80, 615; 11.26, 617n103;
11.44, 613; 12.9–10, 593n50; 12.17,
442n31; 12.192, 617n103; 12.211,
617n103; 12.263, 617n103; 15.147,
594n50; 15.192, 617n103; 15.310,
617n103; 15.320, 617n103; 18.9,
617n103

Against Kallimakhos (Orat. 18): 9,
617n103
Against the Sophists (Orat. 13): 9,
318n102; 15, 317n101, 318n102
Antidosis (Orat. 15): 59, 444n38; 147,
594n50; 192, 317n101, 318n102,
617n103; 310, 617n103; 320,
617n103
Arkhidamos (Orat. 6): 64, 617n103;
73, 617n103; 78, 617n103
Bousiris (Orat. 11): 613;; 26, 617n103;
44, 613
Euagoras (Orat. 9): 4, 615n96; 5,
615n96; 7, 615n96; 8, 615n96; 54,
615n97; 74, 614, 614n93; 75, 615;
76, 614; 80, 615
Letters: 1.6, 594n50, 614n91, 618; 8.7,
593n50
Nikoklēs (Orat. 3): 21, 617
On the Peace (Orat. 8): 38, 613
Panathēnaikos (Orat. 12): 9–10,
593n50; 17, 442n31; 18, 318,
318n103, 318n104; 33, 318n103,
320, 320n112; 192, 617n103; 211,
617n103; 263, 617n103
Panēgyrikos (Orat. 4): 1–3, 594n50;
96, 617n103; 120, 442n31; 150,
617n103; 159, 315
Philippos (Orat. 5): 7, 593n50; 12–13,
594n50; 26–27, 624, 624n120; 81,
593n50, 617n103
To Nikoklēs (Orat. 2): 614;; 7, 614; 8,
614; 16, 617n103; 43, 276n206;
49–50, 617
Jason *On Alexander's Offerings*: 448;;
Josephus
Against Apiōn: 1.107, 37n62; 2.238,
613
Bellum Judaicum: 2.142, 612n89
Kallimakhos
Fragments (Pfeiffer): fr. 1.3, 369;
fr. 26, 349n56, 360, 367, 371
Hymn to Delos: 9, 394

(Kallimakhos, *cont.*)
  Hymn to Zeus: 78–79, 347
Kallinos (West): fr. 6, 167
Karystios *Historical Commentaries*: 448;;
Khamaileon *On Stēsikhoros*: 352n72,
  437n6, 448, 450n60;;
Klearkhos (Wehrli)
  Arkesilaos (frr. 11–12): 497n84;;
  On Riddles (frr. 84–95): 351, 448;;
  Peri hypnou (frr. 5–10): fr. 6, 497n84
Korinna (Page): *PMG* 657, 119n36
Kratinos (K-A): fr. 2, 304
Kritias (DK 88): B50, 169n63
[Longinos] *Peri hypsous*: 9 §5, 160n39;
  9 §8, 160n39; 39–41, 543; 39,
  543n82
Lucan *Pharsalia*: 5.169–174, 274n198;
  5.190–193, 274n198; 5.211–218,
  274n198
Lucian
  Adversus indoctum: §12, 450n60
  Bis accusatus: §1, 272, 275n205
  De domo: §19, 450n60
  De saltatione: §27, 450n60
  Dialogi deorum: XI §4, 450n60
  Dialogi marini: I §4, 450n60
  Hermotimos: §1.10, 378n167; §60,
    275n205
  Hēsiodos: §1, 225n25
  Iuppiter tragoedus: §6, 284n221
  Phalaris I: §13, 450n60
  Symposium: §17, 350n64
  Toxaris: §10, 425n347
[Lykophron] *Alexandra*: 10–11,
  394n226; 11, 394, 394n226; 12,
  394n226; 713, 394n226
Lykourgos
  Against Kēphisodotos (Conomis): fr. 2,
    472n126
  Against Leōkratēs: §100, 307n61;
    §101, 308; §§102–104, 307;
    §102, 23, 307–308, 308n64, 314,
    436–437, 475; §103, 307; §104,
    436n1; §110.1, 319n105; §139, 466

Lyrica adespota (Page): fr. 23
  (*PMG* 941), 208n123
Lysanias *On Iambic Poets*: 351, 448;;
Lysias: 1.29, 124n57; 33, 594n50; 33.2,
  594n50
Manetho *Apotelesmatika*: 6.5, 394;
  6.509, 394
Markellinos *Life of Thoukydidēs*: 29,
  494
Matron of Pitana (*Supplementum
  Hellenisticum*): no. 534.95–97, 149
Nonnos *Dionysiaka*: 19.102, 385n189;
  24.242, 385n189
Oppian *Halieutika*: 3.3, 394; 3.28, 394
Orion *Etymologicum* (Sturz):
  column 158 lines 3–4
  s.v. ὑποκριτής, 650n11
Ovid *Metamorphoses*: 1.4, 369n133
Parmenides (DK 28): B8.52, 196,
  196n84
Pausanias: 3.4.3, 270n186, 275n205;
  5.8.7, 167; 5.18.4, 208n123; 5.19.4,
  55n45; 7.4.10, 167; 7.7.4–5, 167;
  7.19.8, 167; 8.32.2, 208n123; 9.9.5,
  47n24; 9.29, 211; 9.30.3, 348n55,
  349n56; 9.31.3, 502n102; 9.31.4,
  234; 10.4.1, 479; 10.5–6, 275n205;
  10.7.3, 348n55; 10.13.8, 275n205;
  10.19.4, 286; 10.24.6, 253n128;
  10.29.8, 429n367
Petronius *Satyricon*: 459–460;; 59, 453;
  59.3–7, 453n67
Pherekrates (K-A): fr. 44, 86; fr. 51,
  649n9
Philo of Alexandria
  De migratione Abrahami (Wendland):
    §§71–73, 301n29; §80, 443n35;
    §111, 350n64
  De vita Mosis (Cohn): II §37, 443n35
  Quis rerum divinarum heres sit
    (Wendland): §§105–111, 301n29
Philo of Byblos *Phoenician History*:
  37–38;;

Philodemos *On Piety*: 76;;
Philostratos
  Imagines: 1.29, 385n189
  Vita Apollonii: 6.11, 296n10
  Vitae sophistarum: 1.9.493, 304;
    2.18.599.9–10, 612n89
Photios *Lexicon* (Theodoridis): 3.317
  no. 68 s.v. ῥαψῳδοί, 337n23; 3.535
  no. 195 s.v. ὑποδιδάσκαλος, 485,
  485n31
Phrynikhos the Atticist
  Praeparatio sophistica (de Borries):
    epitome p. 69 s.vv. ἐπικαττύειν
    καὶ πτερνίζειν, 445
  Eklogē (Fischer): p. 67 no. 78
    s.v. ἀποκριθῆναι, 649n9
Pindar
  Fragments (M/Sn-M): fr. 52(f).6,
    274; fr. 52(f).15–18, 421n330;
    fr. 94c, 208n123; fr. 140b, 297;
    fr. 140b.11–17, 297n13; fr. 150,
    274; fr. 179, 398n244; fr. 264,
    169n63
  Isthmian: 3/4.55–57, 337, 348;
    3/4.56–57, 360, 372n142; 3/4.57,
    348–349; 3/4.61, 350; 5.27, 422;
    8.60, 165n53
  Nemean: 1.12, 209n124; 1.60–61,
    275n202; 2, 334, 380n169; 2.1–3,
    334n11, 337; 2.2, 427; 2.3, 234;
    3.79, 422; 7.20–27, 246; 7.20–23,
    266; 7.21, 283n219; 7.77, 385n189;
    7.97, 165n53; 10.33, 386n190;
    11.18, 195
  Olympian: 5.19, 349n56, 422
  Paian: 6.6, 274; 6.15–18, 421n330
  Pythian: 1.4–5, 385n189; 3.113–114,
    207n121; 3.114, 195; 4.71–78,
    233n49; 4.178, 205; 4.226, 409;
    5.22–23, 349n57

Plato
  [*Alkibiadēs* 2]: 149a, 649n9
  Apology: 22c1, 223n7
  Euthydēmos: 305b6–9, 594n50
  Gorgias: 447c5–8, 328n136; 448d1–
    10, 328n136; 453d7–454e2,
    559n128; 453e4–5, 559n128;
    463d1–2, 552n109; 507e6–508a4,
    195n78; 512e5–513c2, 554n116;
    513a3–4, 554n116
  Greater Hippias: 285e8, 335n13
  [*Hipparkhos*]: 228b, 23n23, 80n48;
    228b5–c1, 382; 228b6–7, 308n64;
    228b8–c1, 437; 228b9–c1, 437n9
  Iōn: 235, 290, 298, 368, 368n129;;
    530a5–7, 437n5; 530b5, 299n22;
    530b6, 303n39; 530b8–9, 352n72,
    437n6; 530b10–c1, 299–300;
    530c3–4, 282, 299–300; 530c8–9,
    300n26; 530c9–d1, 300, 303,
    466n102; 530c9, 299n23; 530d2–3,
    300n25; 530d6–8, 302n36;
    530d6–7, 281, 300n27; 530d7, 194;
    531a1–2, 351n66; 531a1, 437n6;
    531a3, 489n44; 531b5–6, 300;
    531c8–d1, 169; 531d2, 283n219;
    531d6, 283n219; 532a4–6,
    351n66; 532a5, 352n72; 532b5,
    300; 532c6, 300n26; 532d6–e1,
    298n19; 532d7, 298, 299n22,
    648n8; 532d8, 300; 532e8, 308n64;
    533a4, 300, 308n64; 533b3,
    283n219; 533b5–c3, 281; 533c,
    332n2; 533c1, 334n10; 533c5–8,
    282n215; 533c5–7, 299n23;
    533c5–6, 300n26; 533c9–535a2,
    277; 533d2, 279, 299n23, 300n26;
    533d3, 280; 533e7, 279; 534a,
    278n210; 534a2, 280n212; 534a3,
    278n210; 534b3–4, 278n210;
    534b5, 280n212; 534b9, 280;
    534c1, 300n26; 534c3–4, 484;
    534c4, 279n210; 534c5–7, 280;

(Plato, *Iōn, cont.*)

534d2-4, 280; 534d5, 277n209; 534d7, 336n18; 534e4-5, 282, 299n24; 534e6-7, 283; 535a1, 283n219; 535a4-5, 279; 535a5, 282, 299n24; 535a6-10, 300n25; 535a6-7, 299n24; 535a7-9, 282; 535a7-8, 278n210; 535a9, 299n24; 535b, 282n215; 535b2-3, 309n66; 535b2, 282n215, 299-300; 535b4, 300; 535c5-8, 309; 535d2, 303n39; 535d8-e3, 282n215; 535e1-2, 471n122; 535e4-6, 309n65; 535e7-536a1, 298n20; 535e7-8, 278n210; 535e9-536a1, 278n210, 298, 298n22; 536a1-7, 278n210; 536a1, 278n210, 648n8; 536a4-7, 278n210; 536a5, 278-279n210; 536b1-2, 278n210; 536b8-c2, 305; 536b9, 278n210; 536c1-2, 282n215; 536c1, 300n26; 536d, 307n59; 536d1-3, 305n50; 536d1-2, 305; 536d3, 300n27, 305; 536d4-6, 305n51; 536d5-6, 300n27; 536d6, 305; 536d7, 300n26, 305; 537a2-4, 313n87; 538d4-5, 300; 539d3, 300; 539e7-540a3, 313n87; 541b3-5, 306n57; 541e1-3, 305n52; 541e2, 300n27; 541e3-4, 300; 542a2-3, 300; 542a5, 300n26; 542b2-3, 305n53

Kratylos: 530;; 426b6-8, 612n89

Laws: 633a, 307n59; 650a6, 87; 653d, 208n123; 655d8, 450n60; 658b, 332n2; 659b-c, 554n116; 701a3, 3; 810e11, 328; 814c6-8, 452n66; 817a-d, 446; 829c8, 335n15

Lesser Hippias: 304n45;; 363c7-d4, 305; 363d, 320n110; 365a3, 204n106; 368d6-7, 313n87; 369a4-8, 313n87

Lysis: 204a2-3, 612n89

Menōn: 85e1, 558n123

Phaidōn: 60e6-61a4, 188n49; 63c9, 612n89

Phaidros: 8, 318n102;; 228a1-2, 597; 228a2, 335n13; 228a6-b1, 335; 228b2, 597; 228d1-4, 282n217; 244b, 272; 244c, 222; 248d, 188; 252b4-6, 266; 257c4-5, 327n132; 257c5, 327n133; 257c6, 597n58; 257d-e, 596n55; 257d, 325-326; 257d4-8, 597n58; 257e-258a, 325; 257e1-2, 597n62; 257e3, 327n133; 258a, 597; 258a6-8, 597n62; 258b4, 327n133; 258c2, 327n133; 258c8, 326n129; 258d, 324; 258d1-2, 324n125; 258d4-5, 324, 324n125; 258d7, 324n125; 258d9-11, 324n125; 258d9-10, 325; 259d3-7, 188n49; 259e1-2, 326; 259e5-6, 326; 261a8-9, 325n128; 261b3-5, 326n130; 261b4, 325n128; 261c2, 590n37; 264b7-8, 327; 264b7, 327n133; 264b9-c1, 327n133; 266c3, 590n37; 267c, 590; 267c7-d4, 591n38; 267c7-8, 591n39; 271b7-8, 326n129; 271d1, 326n129; 272b1, 326n129; 272b2-3, 326n129; 275a7-b2, 328n134; 275c5-d1, 328n135; 277b6, 324, 326n129; 277d, 327n132; 277d1-4, 325; 277d1-2, 325; 277d6-e8, 324n125; 277d6, 327n132; 277d7-9, 325; 277d7, 327; 277e, 318n103, 322-323n120, 323n122; 277e5-278a1, 321; 277e5, 594n50; 277e7, 327; 277e8-9, 320n110, 322n118; 277e8, 328; 327a-28a, 474n139; 328a, 474n139

Prōtagoras: 309a6-b1, 306n54; 316d6-7, 304; 319c1-7, 609n80; 319c8-d7, 608n77; 325e1-326a1, 276n206

Republic: 337c, 654n27; 362e4–
363a5, 556n119; 365b4–7,
556n119; 366d7–e5, 556n119;
367b6–c1, 556n119; 378d5,
160n39; 383a7–8, 306n55; 383a8,
164n51; 392e–396, 3; 395a1–b1,
484n27; 395a7, 299n22; 395d5–e3,
537n57; 486c5, 87; 583b, 628;
583b3–5, 628; 586a6, 628; 586b7–
c1, 629; 595b10–c2, 296n10;
598d7–8, 296n10; 600d, 332n2;
600d5–e2, 334n10; 602d2–3, 628;
605c10–11, 296n10; 606e1–607a5,
306n56; 607a, 644; 607a2–3,
296n10, 644n3
Sophist: 230a9, 86; 261b6, 87
Statesman: 280c3–5, 431n385
Symposium: 484;; 223d1–6, 484n28
Theaitētos: 152e4–5, 296n10; 162e,
558n123; 172e4, 442n28
Timaios: 21b, 352; 21b3–4, 352; 21b7,
352n73; 23d3–4, 383n182; 24a1–2,
383n182; 71d–72b, 220, 222n6,
684n7; 71d5–72b5, 220n1; 72a6–
b5, 298n17; 72b3, 230n38
Pliny the Elder *Naturalis historia*:
18.22–23, 37
Plutarch
  Lives
    Agēsilaos: 21.4, 446n48
    Alexandros: 10, 447n50; 29,
447n50; 72.1, 447n50
    Alkibiadēs: 7.1, 276n206
    Dēmosthenēs: 7.5–6, 533n39; 8.2,
594n51; 8.4, 325n126
    Lysandros: 18.4, 494, 495n71; 18.8,
489n44
    Periklēs: 8.6, 596n55; 8.7, 596n55,
597n59; 13.9–11, 471n121;
13.11, 473n137; 17, 470n119;
17.2, 378n167
    Solōn: 8.2, 354n85; 10, 149; 10.2,
151

Moralia (also indexed under their
various titles): [102b3–4], 612n89;
389e9, 450n60; 430a7, 450n60;
623b3, 450n60; 744c5, 450n60;
1019a3, 450n60
Amatorius: 748e–749c, 502n102
[*Consolatio ad Apollonium*]:
102b3–4, 612n89
De animae procreatione in Timaeo:
1019a3, 450n60
De defectu oraculorum: 414b6–7,
275n203; 430a7, 450n60; 437c,
273n196; 438b, 272, 272n194,
273n197
De E apud Delphos: 386b, 272n194;
389e9, 450n60
De gloria Atheniensium: 349b1–6,
467
[*De Homero*]: 213, 296n10
[*De musica*]: 1132b8–c1, 352n72;
1133e7–f6, 352n72
De Pythiae oraculis: 271;; 396c–d,
284n221; 397a, 274n198; 397c,
271n189, 276n207; 397c1,
275n203; 397d1, 275n203;
402c–d, 285; 403e, 271; 404d,
224n18; 405c–e, 271n189;
405c–d, 274n199; 407b, 271
[*Lives of the Ten Orators*]: 442n30;;
841d, 438n10; 841f, 439–441;
841f8, 445n39; 842a, 445n40;
852b, 438n10; 852c, 438n10,
439n15
Praecepta gerendae reipublicae:
813e10–f5, 443n36
Quaestiones convivales: 615a–c,
371n139; 615b, 514n141; 616d,
591; 623a, 542, 542n79; 623b3,
450n60; 645d3–4, 514; 645d3,
514; 645d10–e2, 514; 645d10,
514; 697d7–8, 612n89; 736e4–9,
514; 736e4, 514; 743c10–12, 514;
743c11, 514; 743d, 209n124;

(Plutarch, *Quaestiones convivales*, *cont.*)
    744c, 286; 744c5, 450n60; 745b,
    286, 288
Pollux *Onomastikon*: 5.154, 684n4; 7.53,
    349n56; 7.188.4, 684n4; 7.188.8–9,
    684n4; 8.132.8–133.2, 472n132;
    9.116, 410n293
Polyainos *Stratēgēmata*: 1.20.1, 354n86;
    6.10.1, 446n48
Polybios: 2.12.4, 442n31; 12.13.10, 476;
    29.27.4, 612n89; 38.8.1, 612n89
Porphyry *Quaestiones Homericae*
    (Schrader): 1.96.24, 411n303
Praxiphanes (Wehrli): fr. 18, 494n70
Proklos
    Commentary on the First Book of
        Euklid's Elements (Friedlein): 38.4–
        12, 552n110
    In Platonis Rempublicam commen-
        tarii (Kroll): 1.87.12, 160n39
    Khrēstomatheia (Allen, cited by
        page and line number): 97.8–11
        (*PEG* I.6 T22 Bernabé), 369n132;
        100.5, 83n6
Protagoras (DK 80): A30, 160n39
Quintilian *Institutio oratoria*: 3.1.12,
    596n55; 3.3.4, 589n36; 6.3.70,
    586n24; 10.1.66, 445n44; 11.1.44,
    634n153
Rhetorica ad Herennium: 535;; III. chap-
    ters 11–15 §§19–27, 535n47
Rig Veda: 4.5.6, 181n24
Sappho (LP): fr. 208, 208n123
Scholia to Aiskhines *Against Ktēsiphōn*
    (Dilts): 379, 429n369
Scholia to Aristophanes
    To *Birds*: 880, 590n37; 1764, 489n44
    To *Wasps* (Koster): 1222a, 371n139
Scholia to Euripides (Schwartz)
    To *Phoinissai*: hypothesis, 401;
        26, 405; 45, 404, 416n315; 50,
        400n257, 401, 414, 416n314
Scholia to Homer
    AbT to the *Iliad* (Erbse): A 332,

296n10; A 381, 156; A 474a,
    421n330; Γ 230, 149n4; Δ 273,
    149n4; Z 466, 296n10; I 190a,
    373–374; I 190b, 374n151;
    N 359a–b, 409n288; N 359a,
    410n293; Υ 4a, 160n39; Ψ 388,
    406n279
B to the *Iliad* (Dindorf): Υ 67,
    156–157, 159, 159–160n37, 161
D to the *Iliad* (van Thiel): A 5,
    231n41; A 604, 383; K 262,
    429–430
To the *Odyssey* (Pontani or
    Dindorf): ζ 53, 394n226; τ 203,
    262n162, 263n165; χ 31, 262n162
Scholia to Lykophron (Kinkel): 7, 401
Scholia to Pindar: see *Scholia vetera* to
    Pindar
Scholia to Plato
    To *Gorgias*: 451e, 371n139
    To *Iōn*: 530a5, 337n23
Scholia to Sophokles
    To *Oidipous tyrannos*: hypothesis,
        401; 391, 337n23, 401n259
Scholia vetera to Pindar (Drachmann)
    To *Isthmian*: 4.63e, 349n59
    To *Nemean*: 2.1c, 383n181, 492–493,
        492n60; 2.1d, 337n23, 360, 367,
        378, 383; 2.1e, 493n62
Simonides
    Epigrams (Page): *FGE* no. 69,
        262n163
    Fragments (Page): fr. 72a
        (*PMG* 577a), 285, 285n224; fr. 72b
        (*PMG* 577b), 285, 285n224
    Fragments (West): fr. 20, 168
Simplicius *In Aristotelis De anima*:
    428a1–2, 564n145
Solon
    Fragments (West): fr. 1.2, 194;
        fr. 4.16, 124n57; fr. 29, 246
    Salamis: 354;;

Sophokles
  Aias: 1402, 431n381
  Antigonē: 600, 431n381
  Oidipous tyrannos: 36, 400; 130,
    400; 391, 399–400, 416; 707–725,
    284n222; 1199–1200, 400
  Philoktētēs: 857, 431n381; 1393–1394,
    422
Stobaios: 4.34.28, 168
Strabo: 1.3.7.27–28, 378n167; 3.1.3,
  369n131; 5.247, 113n13; 9.1.10,
  150–151; 9.3.5, 272; 10.3.10,
  208n123; 13.2.4, 287n230
Suidas (Adler): E no. 2898
  s.v. Ἐρατοσθένης, 351n71;
  ΕΙ no. 78 s.vv. εἰκῇ ῥαψῳδεῖ,
  320n113; Θ no. 81 s.vv. Θεαγένους
  χρήματα τά τ᾽ Αἰσχίνου, 157;
  Θ no. 462 s.v. Θρασύμαχος,
  590n37, 591–592; Κ no. 748
  s.v. καταρραψῳδήσει, 320n113;
  Π no. 1180 s.v. Περικλῆς,
  596, 596n54, 596n55; P no. 70
  s.v. ῥαψῳδός, 401n259;
  Ρ no. 71 s.v. ῥαψῳδοί, 337n23;
  Ρ no. 71.1 s.v. ῥαψῳδοί, 469n115;
  Ρ no. 71.2–3 s.v. ῥαψῳδοί,
  320n113; Φ no. 608.3 s.v. Φορμός,
  429n371
Tatian *Oratio ad Graecos* (Goodspeed):
  §31.2, 159n35
Theagenes of Rhegion (DK 8): 1,
  169n64, 321n114
Themistios *Orations*: 26.316d, 350n61,
  657n35, 663n49
Theognis (West): 412;; 237–240, 614,
  614n92; 390, 236n64; 805–810,
  225, 225n21; 1167, 649n9
Theokritos: 6.20, 385n189; 10.22, 385;
  18.58, 396; 21.13, 429n367; 23.21–
  24, 251n120; 23.24, 251; 24.94,
  653n17; 25.19, 652n17

Theon of Alexandria *Progymnasmata*
  (Spengel): 106, 308n64
Theophrastos
  Kharaktēres: 3.3.6–7, 471n121; 27.7,
    336n18
  Peri phytōn historia: 2.6.11, 429n367,
    429n371
Thoukydides: 3.104.4, 234, 493;
  4.48, 429n369; 5.16.2, 270n186,
  275n205; 7.10, 444n37; 7.44.5,
  297n11, 650n13; 8.68, 610n81
Thrasymakhos (DK 85): 589, 589n34;;
  Περὶ πολιτείας: B1, 592n45
  Ὑπερβάλλοντες: 591;;
  Ὑπὲρ Λαρισαίων: B2, 592n45
Timaios *Lexicon Platonicum* (Bonelli):
  ο 308 s.v. Ὁμηρίδαι (p. 160),
    647n4; ρ 374 s.v. ῥαψῳδοί
    (p. 166), 684n4
Timotheos *Persians*: 145n128;;
Vitruvius: V 7.2.6, 469n116; V 9.1, 472
Xenophanes (DK 21): B1.22, 246;
  B10–11, 167; B12–13, 167; B25,
  239n74
Xenophon
  Agēsilaos: 615n97;;
  Anabasis: 2.1.22, 649n9; 3.2.6.2,
    124n57
  Apomnēmoneumata: 1.1.11, 195; 4.2,
    335; 4.2.10, 301n30, 315
  Kyrou paideia: 1.6.11.9, 124n57;
    5.4.35.5–6, 124n57
  Symposion: 3.5, 276n206, 494; 3.5–6,
    301n30, 315; 3.6.7, 301n31; 4.6,
    494

Index of Documentary Sources

Bizard 1920: no. 10.14, 508; no. 11, 506; no. 12, 515

Carmina Epigraphica Graeca (*CEG*)

CEG 1: no. 70, 135n96; no. 143, 118–119n36; no. 146, 119n36; no. 268, 135n96; no. 313, 135n96; no. 334, 118–119n36; no. 355, 115n24; no. 403 (Nikandre inscription), 100, 115; no. 452.ii, 141n113; no. 454 ('Nestor's Cup'), 122, 129–146; no. 459, 128

CEG 2: no. 630, 119n36; no. 786.iv, 119n36

Corpus Inscriptionum Graecarum (*CIG*): 2214, 389, 506; 3088, 384n185, 389, 389n202; 3088.a1, 389; 3088.a4, 389

Dialectorum Graecarum exempla epigraphica potiora (*Del³* or Schwyzer 1987): 62, 118n36, 119; 529, 511; 708a3.3, 118n36; 758, 100, 115; 786, 122n49; 792a, 134n96

Διονυσιακοὶ Τεχνῖται (Steph.): **12**, 504; **18**, 498; **26**, 491; **34**, 507; **54**, 486n35, 487, 504; **127**, 495; **153**, 513n139; **306**, 498; **318**, 498; **335**, 507; **362**, 498; **394**, 490n46; **422**, 508; **435**, 498; **441**, 508; **524**, 508; **533**, 508; **549**, 499; **623**, 509; **645**, 491, 491n50, 505; **646**, 491n50,

505n108; **732**, 486–487n37; **782**, 490n46; **820**, 509; **822**, 486n35, 487, 505; **881**, 514; **908**, 483, 486n35, 487, 499; **948**, 499; **955**, 486n35, 487, 517; **956**, 486n35, 487, 516; **982**, 499; **993**, 515; **1024**, 499; **1055**, 483, 486n35, 487, 502; **1121**, 511; **1146**, 486, 486n35, 510; **1186**, 510; **1244**, 502; **1279**, 507n116; **1305**, 491n54; **1325**, 502; **1368**, 486, 486n35, 511; **1405**, 515; **1429**, 502; **1445**, 495; **1488**, 491n51; **1502**, 511; **1521**, 492; **1577**, 490n46; **1667**, 512; **1686**, 491, 510; **1708**, 506; **1712**, 504; **1715**, 497n86; **1716**, 506; **1721**, 482n20, 496; **1782**, 515; **1817**, 494; **1820**, 503; **1858**, 503; **1861**, 657n32; **1893**, 513; **1913**, 486, 486n35, 513; **1971**, 503; **1979**, 486n35, 487, 490, 516; **2082**, 516; **2106**, 503; **2141**, 495; **2156**, 514; **2174**, 486, 486n35, 503; **2267**, 509n123; **2273**, 503; **2281**, 482n20, 496; **2318**, 508; **2353**, 514; **2355**, 497; **2377**, 499n94; **2402**, 497; **2530**, 503; **2729**, 503; **2762**, 503; **2786**, 498; **2823**, 487n37; **2846**, 515; **2859**, 516; **2886**, 504; **2909**, 490; **2919**, 507; **2937**, 517n151; **2979**, 504

Ἐπιγραφὲς τοῦ Ὠρωποῦ (EO):
no. 298, 439n13, 498; no. 520,
498; no. 520.3, 498; no. 521,
509n124; no. 521.12, 508;
no. 521.13–14, 508; no. 523, 491,
506, 508, 509n124; no. 523.5, 511;
no. 523.7, 511; no. 523.9–10, 505;
no. 523.9, 491, 511; no. 523.11,
511; no. 523.13, 491, 511;
no. 523.15, 511; no. 523.17, 511;
no. 523.30–33, 508; no. 524, 491,
509n124, 511; no. 524.1, 511;
no. 524.3, 511; no. 524.5, 511;
no. 524.6, 491, 510; no. 524.7, 511;
no. 524.9, 511; no. 524.10, 491,
510; no. 524.11, 511; no. 524.13,
511; no. 526, 491, 509, 509n124;
no. 526.14, 513n139; no. 526.16,
513n139; no. 528, 491, 509n124,
510; no. 528.12, 491n51
Fouilles de Delphes (FD)
FD III 1: 497.17, 95n76
FD III 2: 11.20–22, 485; 48, 490n46,
510n126; 48.26, 510n126; 48.31,
510n126; 48.37, 510n126; 49.25,
491n51; 49.32, 487n37; 69, 468;
69.11, 468n113; 69.16–17, 468n113
Inschriften von Ephesos (*IEph*): 22, 516;
1435, 118n36
Inschriften von Olympia (*IvO*): 16.18, 114
Inscriptiones Creticae (IC)
IC 1: Lato no. 24.2, 126n66; Lebena
no. 21.2, 126n66; Olus no. 9.1,
126n66; Phaistos no. 3.1, 126n64
IC 2: Axos no. 1.3, 125n61; *Tituli
locorum incertorum* no. 1.8,
125n63, 126
Inscriptiones Graecae (IG)
IG I³: 6B.33–34, 135n96; 46a.25,
580n2; 82, 475n139; 113, 615n97;
370, 474n139; 370.67, 473n137;
375.6–7, 473n137; 472, 475n139;
509bis, 115n23; 533, 650n13;

589, 116n27; 618d, 115n23; 1231,
135n96; 1261 (Phrasikleia inscription), 115n23
IG II/III²: 334, 439n12, 473n137,
474–475n139; 334.B5–6, 474n139;
334.B18, 474n139; 334.B31–32,
474n139; 334.B32–34, 474n139;
334.B32–33, 474n139; 351, 438n10;
351.16–18, 438n10; 457, 438n10;
784, 470n117, 473, 473n134,
474n139, 476; 784.7–10, 473n136;
968.37–55, 471n124; 968.47–48,
471n124; 1060, 474n139; 1132,
467; 1132.46, 485; 1132.72, 485;
1134, 468; 1350, 468n114; 1496,
475n139; 1666.b60, 369n131;
2318, 297, 447n51; 2318.70,
297n15; 2318.202–203, 481n9;
2318.317–318, 481n9; 2325.228,
502; 2325.231, 492n57, 499; 3074,
467n110; 3076, 467n110; 3077,
467n110; 3079, 467n110; 3081,
467n110; 3083, 467n110; 3086,
467n110; 3087, 467n110; 3088,
467n110; 3157, 477; 9145.5–8, 515
IG IV: 358, 115n24; 649.4–5, 516,
516n147
IG VII: 36, 208n123; 414, 498;
414.1, 498; 414.4, 498; 414.7, 498;
416, 491, 491n52, 505, 505n109,
510–511, 512n132; 416.9–10, 505;
416.9, 491; 416.11–12, 508; 416.13,
491; 416.25–26, 506; 416.25, 506;
417, 505n109, 510, 512n132;
418, 491, 491n52, 505n109, 510,
512n132; 418.5, 491, 510; 418.7,
511; 418.9, 491, 510; 419, 491,
491n52, 505n109, 510, 512n132;
419.11, 509; 419.13, 509; 419.14,
513n139; 419.15, 509; 419.16,
513n139; 419.17–18, 509; 419.29,
509; 419.33, 509; 420, 491, 491n52,
505n109, 510, 512n132; 420.12,

491n51; 420.14, 510; 420.25, 481n10; 420.27, 481n11; 420.29–36, 511; 540, 506–507; 540.1, 508; 540.5, 508; 540.11, 508; 540.12–13, 509; 540.13, 509; 540.14–15, 509; 541, 506n111; 542, 506n111; 542.1, 506; 543, 506n111; 543.1, 506; 543.3, 506; 587, 119n36; 710, 119n36; 1735, 500n97; 1735a, 500n97; 1735b, 500n97; 1760, 505n109, 512n132; 1760.17, 510; 1760.29, 481n10; 1760.31, 481n11; 1762, 500; 1762.5, 499; 1773, 517; 1773.18, 515; 1773.20, 481n11; 1773.21, 481n10; 1776, 517; 1776.15–16, 517; 1886, 515; 2407.6, 95n76; 2448.3–6, 504; 2448.8, 491n50; 2533, 119n36; 2726, 517; 2726.1, 517; 2727, 491, 514; 2727.15, 513; 2742, 115n24; 3195, 505n109, 511n131, 511–512n132, 512; 3195.10, 510; 3195.11–12, 511; 3196, 505n109, 511–512n132, 512; 3196.6–7, 512; 3196.6, 512; 3196.8, 512; 3197, 505n109, 511–512n132, 512, 512n134; 3197.7, 512; 3197.8, 513; 3197.9, 512; 3197.24–34, 512; 3197.25, 513n139; 3197.50, 512; 4147.10–11, 507; 4148, 507; 4150, 516; 4151.3–6, 516; 4152, 516; 4254, 498

IG IX.1: 867, 114, 119n36; 869, 119n36

IG IX.1²: 1.86, 115n24

IG XI.2: 105.27, 498; 105.28, 499

IG XI.4: 1061, 500n96

IG XII.5: 893, 208n123

IG XII.6.1: 18, 118n36; 173.3, 481n10; 176.5, 499

IG XII.7: 442, 114n22

IG XII.9: 43, 114n19; 139.9–10, 513; 139.10, 512; 257, 114, 120; 1273/4, 111, 111n5, 114, 114n19, 120–121, 123

IG XIV: 645.175, 118n36; 865, 122

Inscriptions de Thespies (IThesp): 156, 500n97; 156b, 500n97; 157, 500n97; 161, 499, 500n96; 161.7, 500n96; 163, 499, 500n94; 163.1, 499n94; 165, 501n102; 166, 501n102; 167, 501n102; 168, 481n10, 501n102; 169, 501n102; 170, 505, 505n109; 171, 504, 505–506n109; 172, 481n10, 505–506n109, 510, 510n128; 173, 501n102; 174, 501n102; 175, 502n102; 177, 481n10, 501n102, 516–517; 178, 481n10, 515; 191.9, 502n102; 1251, 515

Jamot 1895: no. 1, 500n96, 500n97; no. 6, 499–501; no. 6.8, 500; no. 7, 499–501; nos. 8–18, 501n102; no. 12, 505n109; no. 12.22, 504; no. 13.18, 510n128; no. 15, 515

Milet I.3 (Kawerau and Rehm 1914): no. 31, 122n47; no. 132, 288n234; no. 132a, 121n47; no. 145, 208n123; no. 178, 289n234

Nachtergael 1977: no. 2bis.4, 503; no. 3.3–4, 503; no. 3.5, 498; no. 3.14–15, 503; no. 4.7–8, 503; no. 4.12, 502; no. 4.13, 502; no. 5.9, 503; no. 5.11, 503; no. 5.12, 504; no. 7.10, 503; no. 7.11, 502; no. 8.10, 502; no. 8.11, 503; no. 8.30–31, 503; no. 9.9, 498; no. 9.10, 498; no. 9.11, 498; no. 10.8–9, 502; no. 10.9–10, 499; no. 15.1, 503; no. 15bis.9–10, 503; no. 56, 510n127; no. 59.6, 503; no. 62.5, 503; no. 63.6, 499; no. 64.6, 499; no. 65.7, 503; no. 66.7, 503; no. 68.6, 504

Papyri: Hawara Homer, 75–76;
   MP³ 604.1, 76; MP³ 632, 76;
   MP³ 650, 76; MP³ 699, 76; MP³ 773,
   76; MP³ 778, 76n30; MP³ 819, 76;
   MP³ 821 (*olim* 822), 76; MP³ 830,
   76; MP³ 855.1 (*olim* 857), 76,
   76n29; MP³ 879, 76; MP³ 917.1
   (*olim* 919), 76; MP³ 962, 76;
   MP³ 991, 76; MP³ 998, 76–77;
   P.Berol. 16985, 76; *P.Bodl.* I 143,
   458, 461n82, 462; *P.Duk.* inv. 772,
   453n66; *P.Osl.* 189, 455, 459–462;
   P.Oxy. 0020, 76–77; *P.Oxy.* 0223,
   76–77; *P.Oxy.* 0445, 76–77;
   P.Oxy. 0519, 454, 458–460;
   P.Oxy. 0687, 76; *P.Oxy.* 1025, 457,
   460, 462, 464n95; *P.Oxy.* 1050,
   454–455, 458–459; *P.Oxy.* 1499,
   463n92; *P.Oxy.* 1815, 76;
   P.Oxy. 2075, 154n15; *P.Oxy.* 3155,
   76; *P.Oxy.* 3323, 76; *P.Oxy.* 3663,
   76–77; *P.Oxy.* 3965, 168; *P.Ryl.* 1.13
   (MP³ 203), 367; *SB* IV 7336, 456,
   459–460, 462
Peek 1955: no. 1305, 515
Sammlung griechischer Dialektinschriften
   (*SGDI*): 908, 119n36; 3188, 114n21;
   5083, 126n66; 5088, 126n66;
   5105, 126n66; 5112, 126n64;
   5270, 134n96; 5276, 120n44; 5292,
   115n25, 115n26; 5295, 120; 5351,
   114n22; 5786, 399, 497
   Eretria ⁿ3 (*SGDI* IV pp. 851–852),
   114n20
Supplementum epigraphicum Graecum
   (*SEG*): **3**.334.29–30, 501n102;
   3.334.30, 516; **3**.334.35, 481n11;
   3.334.37, 481n10; **3**.368, 489;
   3.368.12, 507; **4**.64.28–29, 120;
   19.335, 508, 508n119; **19**.335.25,
   507; **20**.673–690, 490n46;
   20.674–675, 516; **24**.303, 120n44;
   25.501, 506, 507n115, 508;

26.72.34, 609n78; **26**.845, 121;
29.337, 115n24; **29**.449, 118n36;
30.1117.7, 95n76; **30**.1118.8,
95n76; **30**.1291, 121n47; **31**.312,
516; **31**.496, 506, 507n115,
508n119; **32**.436, 505; **32**.914,
95n76; **34**.362, 508n118; **36**.473,
481n10; **36**.473.3, 481n11; **36**.474,
505n109; **36**.488, 515n143; **36**.694,
135n96; **38**.384, 507; **38**.871,
512n135; **41**.115, 477; **41**.481,
509n122; **41**.848, 116n30; **43**.208,
498n90; **45**.407, 120n44; **46**.536,
500n96; **46**.540, 500n96; **46**.2312,
497n87; **47**.487, 492n55; **52**.511,
517; **52**.536, 95n76; **52**.1943,
517n151; **54**.516, 504; **54**.517,
505n106; **54**.694, 135n96; **55**.28,
485n32
*Sylloge Inscriptionum Graecarum*³ (*SIG*³):
   450, 461n84; 457, 500n96, 500n97;
   659.5, 461n85; 696b, 485n33;
   698.15, 485; 698.28, 485; 704e,
   468; 711, 510n126, 510n127; 728k,
   487n37; 737.6, 461n85; 738a, 461;
   738a.7, 461n85; 959, 389; 959.9,
   506; 960, 389
Tracy 1975, item no. 7h (cited by page
   and line number): 490n46;; 60.17,
   490n46; 61.21, 486n37, 510; 61.23,
   490n46; 61.27–28, 511; 62.38, 513;
   62.39, 510; 62.43, 490n46; 62.44,
   490n46, 510–511, 513; 62.48,
   490n46; 62.49, 510; 62.50, 486n37,
   510–511; 62.51, 513

Index of Rhapsodes[†]

Ἄβρων Φιλοξένου Θηβαῖος
(Steph. **12**, II.4): 504 no. 35
Ἀγαθῖνος Κριτοδήμο[υ Σικ]υώνιος
(Steph. **18**, III.2): 498 no. 11
Ἀγάθων Δαμᾶ Θεσπιεύς (Steph. **34**, I):
507 no. 40
Ἀείμναστος Ε[ὐφ]ραίου Θηβαῖος
(Steph. **54**, II/I): 504–505 no. 36;
486n35, 487
Ἄλεξις Ταραντῖνος (Steph. **127**,
IV.3/4): 495 no. 4
Ἀρισταγό[ρας] (Steph. **306**, III.2): 498
no. 12
Ἀριστείδης Ἀρίστωνος [. . . . .]ς
(Steph. **318**, III.2): 498 no. 13
Ἀριστόδικος Δημοκράτους Ὀπού⟨ν⟩-
τιος (Steph. **335**, I.1): 507 no. 41
Ἀριστομένης Ἀριστομένου [. . . . .]ιος
(Steph. **362**, III.2): 498 no. 14
Ἀρτέμων Ἰσιδότου Ἀθηναῖος
(Steph. **422**, I.1): 508 no. 42; 506
Ἀρχέλας Θετταλός (Steph. **435**, III.1):
498 no. 15

Ἀρχίας Σωτηρίδου Θηβαῖος
(Steph. **441**, I): 508 no. 43
Βίοττος [Μ]ε[ν]ελάου Χαλκιδεύ[ς]
(Steph. **524**, I.1): 508 no. 44
Βουκάττης Γλαύκου Ταναγραῖος
(Steph. **533**, I.1): 508–509 no. 45
Γλαῦκος Ἀθηναῖος (Steph. **549**, III.1):
499 no. 16
Εἰέρων Ἀριστοβούλου Θηβαῖος
(Steph. **820**, I.1–2): 509–510
no. 46
Εἴρανος Φρυνίδου Ταναγραῖος
(Steph. **822**, II.4–I.1): 505–506
no. 37; 486n35, 487
Ἐράτων (Steph. **881**, I/II AD): 514
no. 55
Ἑρμόφαντος (Steph. **908**, III.3): 499
no. 17; 448–449, 483, 483n26,
486n35, 487, 492n57
Εὐθ]ύδημος Χάρητος Ἀθηναῖος
(Steph. **948**, III.2): 499 no. 18
Εὔκαιρος Ταναγραῖος, Μᾶρκος
Αὐρήλιος (Steph. **955**, III.1 AD):
517–518 no. 64; 486n35, 487

[†] Each rhapsode is identified by his name, his father's name (patronymic), and his place of origin. The list follows the Greek alphabetical order within each of these three elements. Adopted Roman names like Κορ(νήλιος) or Μᾶρκος Αὐρήλιος are placed at the end, after a comma. Elements without a beginning follow those that have one (again, in alphabetical order within each element). Thus, for example,]γου Ὑπαταῖος appears after]ράτης Καλλιφ[because]γου belongs to the patronymic while]ράτης belongs to the name. After the corresponding page and item number in the prosopography of rhapsodes follow other *loci* that mention the same individual.

Εὔκαρπος Ἀργεῖος, Κορ(νήλιος)
(Steph. **956**, II/III AD): 516 no. 60;
486n35, 487
Εὐρύβιος Λυκίσκου Μεγαλοπολίτης
(Steph. **982**, III.3/4): 499 no. 19
Εὐτυχιανὸς Κορίνθιος (Steph. **993**,
II.3 AD): 515 no. 58
Ζηνόδοτος Σωπάτρου Ἀντιοχεύς ἀπὸ
Πυρά[μου] (Steph. **1024**, III.4):
499–501 no. 20
Ἡγησίας (Steph. **1055**, III.2/3): 502
no. 21; 448–449, 483–484, 483n26,
486n35, 487, 499
Θεόδοτος Πυθίωνος Ἀθηναῖος
(Steph. **1146**, I.1): 510 no. 47; 486,
486n35
Θεοφάνης Σωκράτου Θηβαῖος
(Steph. **1186**, I.1): 510–511 no. 48
Καλλίας Ἀρχετίμου Συρακ[όσιος]
(Steph. **1325**, III.2): 502 no. 22
Κάλλων Κάλλωνος (Ἀθηναῖος)
(Steph. **1368**, I.1): 511 no. 49; 486,
486n35, 510
Κιλικᾶς (Κιτιεύς) (Steph. **1405**, II AD):
515–516 no. 59
Κλειτόριος Ἀριστείδου Ἀρκάς
(Steph. **1429**, III.2): 502 no. 23
Κλεομένης (Steph. **1445**, V/IV):
495–496 no. 5
Κράτων Κλέωνος Θηβαῖος
(Steph. **1502**, I.1): 511–512 no. 50
Κύναιθος Χῖος (Steph. **1521**, VI/V):
492–494 no. 1; 492n58, 492n59,
492–493n60, 493n62, 494n66
Μέντωρ Ἀπολλοδώρου Ἡρακλεώτης
(Steph. **1667**, I.1): 512–513 no. 51
Μιλτιάδης Διονυσίου (Χῖος)
(Steph. **1708**, II): 506 no. 38
Μνασίων (Steph. **1721**, IV.4–III.2):
496 no. 6; 351, 437n6, 448, 482,
482n20, 496n75, 496n78
Νεικομήδη[ς] (Κῷος) (Steph. **1782**,
I/II AD): 515 no. 56

Νικήρατος (Steph. **1817**, V.3–4):
494–495 no. 2; 301n30, 315–316,
316n93, 489n44, 494n70, 495n71,
495n72
Νικίας (Steph. **1820**, III.4): 503 no. 24
[Νι]κομήδ[ης (Steph. **1858**, III): 503
no. 25
Νουμήνιος Νουμηνίου Ἀθηναῖος
(Steph. **1893**, I.1): 513 no. 52
Ξενόφαντος Εὐμάχου (Ἀθηναῖος)
(Steph. **1913**, I.1): 513 no. 53; 486,
486n35, 510
Π[(Steph. **1971**, III.3): 503 no. 26
Παίων Σιδήτης καὶ Ταρσεὺς καὶ
Ῥόδιος, Πόπλιος Αἴλιος
Πομπηϊανός (Steph. **1979**, II.2 AD):
516 no. 62; 486n35, 487, 490
Πολείταρ[χος] [– – –]α *(Ἀργεῖος)*
(Steph. **2082**, II/III AD): 516
no. 61
Πολύμνηστος Ἀλεξάνδρου Ἀρκάς
(Steph. **2106**, III.2): 503 no. 27
Πράτυς (Steph. **2141**, V.3–4): 495
no. 3; 315, 494, 495n72
Πυθοκλῆς Ἀριστάρχου Ἑρμιονεύς
(Steph. **2174**, III.2): 503 no. 28;
486, 486n35
Σίμακ?]ος Σατύρου Ἀργεῖος
(Steph. **2273**, III.3): 503 no. 29
Σιμωνίδης Ζακύνθιος (Steph. **2281**,
IV.4–III.1): 496–497 no. 7; 351,
351n68, 448, 482, 482n20, 497n83
Σωσίστρατος (Steph. **2355**, IV?): 497
no. 8
Τερψικλῆς (Steph. **2402**, IV.1–2?): 497
no. 9
Φιλοκράτης Λυσίππου Ἀργεῖος
(Steph. **2530**, III.4): 503 no. 30
[. . 4–5 . .]ν Θρασωνίδου Σινωπεύς
(Steph. **2729**, III.2): 503 no. 31
]ράτης Καλλιφ[(Steph. **2762**,
III.2): 503 no. 32

]στρατος Σικυώνι(ος) (Steph. **2786**,
    IV.2–3): 498 no. 10
[——] [Φι]λοκράτους Θη[βαῖος]
    (Steph. **2846**, I/II AD): 515 no. 57
    ]νου Ὑπαταῖος (Steph. **2859**,
    II.3 AD): 516–517 no. 63
    ]ς Ἀθηναῖος (Steph. **2886**, III.2):
    504 no. 33
    Βοι]ώτιος (Steph. **2919**, II.1): 507
    no. 39
ΙΑΛΛΗΣ (Steph. **2979**, III.4): 504
    no. 34
[—] (I.1): 513–514 no. 54

Index of Greek Terms[†]

ἄγραυλοι, 219, 244, 244n91
ἀγωνίζομαι/διαγωνίζομαι, 477, 495n71
ἀγωνιστής/συναγωνιστής, 317n101,
    318n102, 378, 468n113, 481, 486,
    486–487n37, 510–511, 513
ἀγωνιστικός, 310n72, 310n73, 356n91,
    592, 599, 601–602, 625
ἀείδειν, 1, 181n23, 184n36, 186,
    188–189, 189n50, 191, 195n77,
    211n135, 212, 212n140, 213n142,
    219–220, 255n140, 277n209, 283,
    283n219, 298n19, 300, 336n18,
    337n23, 342n37, 346–347, 346n50,
    346n51, 348n55, 350n65, 352n73,
    354, 354n86, 357, 360, 365, 366,
    367, 373, 381, 383, 385, 385n189,
    386n190, 388n196, 395, 421,
    486n37, 510, 515, 540n69, 586,
    590–591, 591n38, 651
αἴσθησις, 533, 536–537n53, 550,
    550n106, 561n133, 564n145, 565,
    567, 567n150, 567n152, 569–570,
    570n161, 570n167, 572–574,
    574n180, 574n181, 574n182

ἀκρίβεια, 316n94, 591, 603, 624n118,
    625, 625n123, 625n124, 626n127,
    627, 632–633, 632n148, 635–637
ἀκριβής, 310n72, 356n91, 538n59,
    560n129, 591–592, 604n69, 604n70,
    625, 629, 630n139, 631, 637
ἀκριβόω, 301n30, 317n101
ἀκρόασις/ἀκροάματα, 312n81, 450n61,
    461n84, 616, 617n102, 618
ἀκροατής/ἀκροάομαι, 296n10,
    301n30, 315, 527n24, 528, 536n49,
    538n58, 544–545, 545n86, 548n99,
    552n112, 559–560, 560n130, 561,
    577n191, 616, 618
ἀλήθεια/λήθη, 199–200n95, 201,
    207n120, 210, 219, 220n1, 236, 238,
    238n71, 240, 241n80, 245, 247–259,
    247n106, 249n109, 249n112,
    250n113, 250n116, 251n119,
    251n120, 251n121, 251n122,
    252n125, 252n126, 253–254n133,
    255n143, 256n145, 257n150,
    257n151, 263, 263n165, 263n166,
    298n19, 301n30, 305n52, 315, 326,
    328n134, 538, 554–555, 556n120,
    561, 577n190, 577n191, 633n152

[†] Each lexical item represents any other forms of the same that are not separately listed. Thus,
    under ὑποκριτικός appear all inflected occurrences of this adjective in all genders and numbers
    other than τὸ ὑποκριτικόν and ἡ ὑποκριτική, which are separately listed (with their own inflected
    forms). The parenthetical note "and its derivatives" signals the inclusion of terms that feature the
    item in some form (thus, e.g., under γραφή are listed occurrences of παραγραφή and ὑπογραφή).

ἀλλάσσω/ἐπαλλάσσω, 406–413,
410n291, 410n292, 410n293,
410n294, 410n299, 412n304, 424
ἀμβολάδην/ἀναβάλλεσθαι, 204–204,
234, 376, 385–388, 385n189,
385–386n190, 388n196
ἀντιπαρῳδῆσαι, 150
ἀοιδός, 181n23, 182, 182n28, 184n36,
189n50, 193, 195, 201n96,
208n123, 212, 212n138, 212n140,
231n42, 235, 238, 299n24, 331,
334, 334n10, 339–340, 342,
342n40, 344–348, 347n53, 348n55,
357, 359, 365–366, 370, 370n135,
375, 395, 400, 416, 419–421, 647,
648n5
ἀοιδή, 184n36, 189–192, 190n55,
193n66, 195, 201, 203n103, 211,
214n146, 219–220, 229–230, 235,
241, 284n221, 337n23, 338–339,
342n40, 347, 347n53, 349, 349n56,
354, 359n98, 365–366, 376n160,
376n161, 378n163, 381, 393,
396–397, 397n241, 420–422,
424–425, 424n345, 426n353, 427
ἀποδείκνυμι, 308n64, 461n83, 528n24,
544, 546, 546n92, 552n112
ἀποδεικτικός, 559n128
ἀπόδειξις, 308, 308n64, 311n75, 436,
461–462, 461n83, 464, 546n92,
559n128
ἄπτερος, 362n109
αὐδή, 184n36, 190, 219–220, 241
αὐτοδίδακτος, 190n61, 207n121,
212–216, 213n142, 359
αὐτοσχεδιασμός/αὐτοσχεδιάζω,
316n94, 380, 440n21, 596n54, 616
ἀφαυρός, 406–408, 407n283, 407n284
Βύβλος, 74
γραφή (and its derivatives), 442n28,
444n38
γραφικός, 310n72, 310n73, 356,
356n91, 529, 592, 599, 602,

602n64, 603n68, 604n69, 606, 616,
621, 623n115, 625, 626n129
γράφω (and its derivatives), 151,
157n31, 157n32, 159n37, 276,
310n71, 310n74, 311n78,
312n80, 321, 321n116, 322n118,
322–323n120, 323n122, 324–326,
324n125, 325n128, 326n129,
326n130, 333n7, 354n84, 383, 440,
440n22, 489n44, 492n60, 524,
552n110, 579, 580n3, 590n37, 593,
593–594n50, 596n54, 597, 597n58,
597n59, 599, 602, 602n64, 604,
606, 612n89, 615–616, 615n96,
616n98
δέγμενος/δεδεγμένος, *see under*
δέχομαι
δέχομαι, 371–372, 371n140, 372n141,
373n149, 374n153, 377n161;
δέγμενος/δεδεγμένος, 360,
367–368, 367n126, 368n128,
371–373, 375n155, 375n156,
376–377, 376n161, 377n161
δημιουργοί, 182n28, 191, 211–212,
223n7, 313n86, 359, 559n128
διδάσκω, 187, 188–189, 214n146, 308,
326, 326n129, 545, 558
(δι)ηνεκές/διηνεκέως, 360, 362n111,
367–370, 367n127, 369n131,
369n133, 370n137
δόξα/ἔνδοξα, 196n84, 328n134,
446n48, 544, 546, 554–556,
556–557n120, 559n126, 559n128,
561n133, 564n145, 565, 568n154,
575, 575n186, 577, 577n191,
578n197, 597n58, 612, 612n89,
616, 624n120, 630, 639
ἐκεῖνος, *see* κεῖνος
ἐλεφαίρετο, 406, 406n279
ἐναντίωσις, 160–161
ἑξῆς, *see* (ἐφ)εξῆς
ἐξ ὑπολήψεως, 382–384, 388. *See also*
ὑπολαμβάνω

ἔξω τοῦ ἀποδεῖξαι, 528n24, 544, 546, 552n112
ἔξω τοῦ πράγματος, 536n50, 546n92, 552n112, 637, 637n159, 638n161
ἐπαινέτης, 186n42, 300n29, 305–307, 305n50, 305n53, 306n54, 306n56, 307n59, 597n62, 643
ἐπαινέω, 305, 305n51, 305n52, 306n55, 307, 307n59, 307n61, 436
ἔπαινος, 194n74, 300n29, 303, 353n77, 525n16, 577n191
ἐπαλλάσσω, see ἀλλάσσω
ἐπιβαίνω, 190n55, 205n114, 220, 393n216
ἐπιδείκνυμι, 300, 332–333, 332n2, 597, 597n62, 613n91, 614
ἐπιδεικτικός, 592, 603n68, 621
ἐπίδειξις, 290, 302, 307n62, 308, 308n64, 436, 461n83, 461n84, 489, 594n50, 613, 613n91, 616, 618, 635, 643
εποιεσε(ν), 112, 116
ἑρμηνεύς (ἑρμηνε-), 267, 275, 275n206, 279, 282, 290, 299, 299n24, 300–301n29, 307n62, 548n100, 575n186, 588, 588n30, 626n127, 648n4, 661n43
ἐτήτυμα/ἔτυμα, 204, 219, 238, 238n71, 245, 247, 252–254, 252n126, 253n132, 254n133, 256–261, 256n145, 256n146, 257n150, 263n168
(ἐφ)εξῆς, 282n217, 382–384, 383n182, 383–384n183, 418
ϝισϝος, 118–120
ἠθικός, 356n91, 537, 550n105, 625n125, 626n128
ἦθος/ἤθη, 535, 537, 537n54, 551n109, 552, 560n129, 588–589, 624
ἡμίθεοι, 169
ἠνεκές, see (δι)ηνεκές/διηνεκέως
θεσπέσιος, 201, 337, 360

θέσπις, 186, 190, 201, 201n96, 219, 220, 230, 241, 376n160, 376n161
θυμός and νόος, 215
καλλιστέφανος, 132, 137–141
Καρχηδών, 89, 94–97
κατὰ κόσμον, 186, 186n43, 194–195, 194n75, 194–195n76, 195n77, 197n85, 199, 204, 237, 281, 302, 360n100. See also κόσμος
καταλέγειν, 1, 186, 199–200n95, 230, 300, 485, 597n58, 651
κατὰ μοῖραν, 186, 199–200n95, 201, 230. See also μοῖρα
κεῖνος/ἐκεῖνος, 132, 134–137
κλέος/κλέα, 181n23, 183–185, 184n34, 184n36, 185n39, 185n40, 185n41, 222, 352, 353n77, 357–358, 363, 363n115, 367, 369, 373, 374n152, 395
κλέος ἄφθιτον, 185n40. See also κλέος/κλέα
κόρη, 87–88
κόσμος, 186n44, 194–198, 194n73, 194n74, 194n76, 195–196n80, 196n81, 196n83, 196n84, 197n85, 197n86, 197n88, 198n94, 239n73, 354, 354n87, 360, 360n100, 438n11, 549n103. See also κατὰ κόσμον
κραίνω (and its derivatives), 203–204, 204n106, 206, 206n117, 206–207n120, 237, 376
λέξις, 8–9, 159n37, 160, 271n189, 301n29, 309, 310n71, 310n72, 355, 356n91, 523–538, 524n12, 525n16, 526n17, 526n21, 527n23, 527–528n24, 529n31, 532n38, 538n60, 540n68, 541, 541n74, 541–542n77, 542n78, 543–544, 545n86, 546–548, 546n91, 548n98, 548–549n100, 550–551, 550n105, 553–554, 557, 563, 569, 576–590, 576n190, 578n192, 580n3, 581n4,

(λέξις, *cont.*)
    581n6, 582n9, 583n11, 583n12,
    583n14, 583–584n15, 584n18,
    585n19, 585n20, 586n25, 587n27,
    588n30, 588n31, 591n41, 592–593,
    593n50, 597–599, 598n63,
    601–602, 602n64, 603n68, 604n69,
    604n70, 606, 608, 620–622, 625,
    625n125, 632, 636n155, 637–638

λήθη, *see* ἀλήθεια

λογογραφέω, 311n76

λογογραφία, 327n133, 537n57, 597,
    597n62

λογογράφος, 311n76, 327n133,
    355n90, 356n91, 597, 597n58,
    610n81, 610n82

μάντις (-μαντ-), 182n28, 187, 205n113,
    206, 216, 220–223, 220n1, 220n2,
    223n8, 223n10, 223n11, 223n12,
    224n18, 229n36, 235, 267,
    267n176, 269, 272n196, 274–275,
    275n202, 275n205, 297, 298n17,
    299n24

μέλπω (and its derivatives), 339,
    347, 347n53, 349, 376, 420–422,
    420n329, 421n330, 421n331,
    421n332, 422n336, 424n344. *See*
    also μολπή

μεταβαίνω/μετάβηθι, 186, 194, 269,
    393n216

Μῆδος, 89–90, 93–94, 96n77

μιμνήσκω (and its derivatives),
    183–184, 220n1, 223n10, 249n109,
    249n112, 357, 381, 442n31,
    536n52, 550n106, 572, 574n182,
    612n89, 660, 660–661n43

μνήμη, 167, 167n61, 184–185n37, 211,
    378n167, 574n180, 575n186

μνημονεύω (and its derivatives),
    318n104, 319–320, 335n13,
    493n62

μνημοσύνη, 185n38, 203n103

μοῖρα, 199–200n95, 203–204, 206, 220,
    279, 282n215, 287, 305n50, 376.

    See also κατὰ μοῖραν

μολπή, 376n160, 421, 421n330. *See also*
    μέλπω

μορφή, 238, 238–239n73, 370

μοχθηρία, 527n24, 528, 544, 547n94,
    551, 552n112, 554

νεῖκος, 236–237, 237n66, 395. *See also*
    ψεῦδος

νόος, *see* θυμός

οἴμη/οἶμαι, 181, 181n23, 189–190,
    207n121, 213n142, 213n145,
    214, 214n146, 342, 347, 361n106,
    368, 375n158, 392–396, 392n212,
    394n221, 394n226, 394n227,
    396n232, 418, 427

οἶμος, 347, 376n160, 378n163,
    392–395, 393n213, 393n219,
    394n221

ὁμηριστής, 448–449, 451n63, 452,
    452n64, 454, 454n70, 456–460,
    462, 462n90, 465, 481

o-mo-pi, 393, 393n215

πάθημα/πάθος/πάθη, 309, 309n65,
    309n68, 523, 533, 535, 535n48,
    537, 537n54, 542n79, 547, 547n95,
    569–570, 570n164, 572, 573n178,
    574n180, 574n181, 576, 578n196,
    581, 589

παθητικός, 356n91, 536, 536n49,
    577n191, 625n125, 626n128

παρακαταλογή, 344n44

παραναγι(γ)νώσκω, 440, 442, 442n29,
    442n30, 442n31

παρέᾱ, 88

πίστις/πιστεύω, 524–525, 524n11,
    558–559n126, 559n128, 560n129,
    565, 575, 577, 578n196, 606, 628,
    632, 637

ποιηταὶ ἐπῶν, 481–482, 488–489,
    490n46, 491, 491n49, 491n51,
    501, 501n102, 504–505, 507–514,
    513n139, 644

προοίμιον, 201n96, 204, 205, 233,

233n51, 234–235, 239, 264n169, 265, 334, 386n190, 393n213, 395, 552n112, 591

προφήτης, 1, 206, 220–224, 220n1, 267, 267n176, 270–272, 270n186, 270n187, 272n194, 272n195, 275, 275n205, 297, 298n17, 299n24

ra-pi-ti-ra₂/ra-pte, 338, 427

ῥάπτω (and derivatives), 334, 334n10, 336–339, 336n21, 337n23, 338n27, 341, 342n40, 347, 347n53, 356–357, 360–365, 361–362n108, 362n111, 362n112, 362n113, 363n118, 364n120, 366n123, 368n130, 378n168, 396, 420–425, 420n325, 423n343, 425n347, 426n350, 427–429, 429n369, 430n377, 431, 445

ῥαφή, 338, 362, 378–379, 431n383, 431n385

ῥαψῳδέω (and its derivatives), 284n221, 318–322, 318n104, 320n112, 320n113, 328, 328n137, 332, 332n2, 332n5, 334, 340, 343, 346, 350, 354, 354n84, 378, 383, 388, 425, 425n347, 436, 437n6, 448, 449n57, 482n19, 483n26, 489n44, 492n60, 494–495, 496n80, 497, 648, 651

ῥαψῳδία, 316, 316n94, 317, 321n115, 332, 332n2, 337n23, 340, 349, 352, 355, 355n90, 389, 506, 521–522, 522n7, 581n7

ῥαψῳδική, 293, 295, 309, 312, 530

ῥαψῳδός, 1–2, 6, 278n210, 279, 282, 298–299, 298n19, 298n20, 299n22, 299n24, 301n30, 320n113, 331, 334n10, 336–338, 337n23, 340–341, 342n40, 343–347, 354, 357, 378–379, 378n168, 380n169, 382, 399–400, 399n247, 399n251, 401n259, 416–417, 448–449, 469n115, 472, 480n6, 481,

482n20, 483n25, 483n26, 484n27, 486–488, 486n37, 490, 492, 492n60, 494–518, 496n75, 499n94, 501n102, 516n147, 644, 647–648, 648n4, 648n8, 665

-ρραφέω, 428–430, 429n370; -ρραφής, 362; -ραφίη, 361n107; -ρραφίς, 428n363; -ρράφος, 431, 431n386

σκιαγραφία, 604n70, 628–631, 628n132, 628n134, 631n144, 631n145, 634

τείνυμαι, 111

Τείσων, 111, 123

τίνυμαι/τίννυμαι, 111, 123–127

ὕμνος/ὑμνέω, 219, 226, 235, 255n140, 306n56, 339, 339n33, 342n40, 347n53, 349–350, 361n106, 392–393, 393n217, 396–398, 397n239, 397n241, 398n242, 399n247, 416, 420–422, 420n329, 424–427, 424n345, 425n349, 426n350, 426n351, 426n353, 492

ὑποβάλλω, 384–385, 387–389, 387n195, 388n198, 392. *See also* ὑπολαμβάνω

ὑποβλήδην, 384–385, 385n188, 387n195, 388–391, 388n196, 388n199

ὑποβολεύς, 388, 443–444, 443n35

ὑποβολή, 384n185, 387, 387n195, 388n198, 389, 389n202; ἐξ ὑποβολῆς, 383–384, 388, 389n203

ὑποκρίνεσθαι, 1–3, 289, 289n236, 297–298, 297n16, 351, 351n69, 388n197, 388n198, 437n6, 440–443, 440n21, 433n32, 448, 452n66, 482–483, 482n20, 482n21, 483n26, 496n75, 499, 538, 623n113, 647–648n4, 648n7, 649–655, 649n10, 650n13, 651n14, 651n15, 652n17, 653n18, 653n20, 654n23, 658–662, 658n36, 659n40, 660n43, 661n44, 662n46, 664n52, 665

ὑπόκρισις, 1–2, 4–5, 8–9, 290, 297,
297n14, 302, 308–311, 309n68,
310n71, 310n73, 316–317, 316n94,
316n96, 316n97, 317n99, 321n115,
452n66, 521–535, 525n16, 526n17,
527n23, 529n31, 532n38, 536n49,
536–537n53, 537–538, 543–544,
545n86, 546–548, 547n94, 548n98,
554, 577, 579–585, 580n3, 581n4,
581n6, 581n7, 582n9, 583n11,
583n12, 584n15, 585n19, 585n20,
587n27, 589–590, 590n36, 593,
593–594n50, 598, 603, 608, 622,
623n117, 624–627, 625n124, 632,
636n155, 643, 649n9, 651n14, 659,
662n46, 664
ὑποκριτής, 1–3, 6, 9, 220n1, 221,
267, 278n210, 282n216, 289,
290, 296–299, 297n14, 297n15,
298n17, 298n19, 298n20, 299n22,
299n24, 309, 311, 351n69, 356n91,
388n198, 443, 446, 446n45,
446n48, 447n52, 465, 481, 484n27,
487, 492n57, 499, 509–513, 522,
547, 585, 587n27, 644, 647–666
passim
ὑποκριτικός, 310n72, 310n73, 356n91,
529, 592, 621, 621n110, 625–626;
τὸ ὑποκριτικόν, 310n71, 579,
579n1, 580n3, 582–583, 585,
585n19, 585n20, 587n27, 594;
ἡ ὑποκριτική, 527n23, 530, 531,
531n36, 545n86, 546, 548n100,
579, 581, 583, 583n11, 583n14,
585n20, 586, 625, 625n125
ὑπολαμβάνω, 223n8, 312n82, 383, 436,
526n21, 552–553, 553n115, 572,
581, 612. *See also* ἐξ ὑπολήψεως;
ὑποβάλλω
φαντασία, 9, 523–524, 533n42, 545,
545n86, 548, 548n99, 550–551,
550n106, 551n107, 554–557,
556n118, 559–575, 560n130,

561n132, 561n133, 563n139,
564n145, 566n148, 567n150,
567n151, 567–568n152, 568n153,
568n154, 569n156, 569n158,
569–570n161, 570n167, 574n183,
575n186, 577–578, 582n9
φάντασμα, 220, 533, 560n130, 561,
563n139, 564, 564n144, 564n145,
567–569, 568n153, 568n154,
569n155, 569n156, 569n159,
570n166, 571, 571n171, 573–578,
574n180, 578n195, 625, 631–634
φθέγγομαι (and its derivatives), 280,
284n221, 317n101, 443n35, 538,
577n191
φθόγγος/φθογγή (and its derivatives), 192, 193n65, 271n189, 286,
286n228, 391n208
φορτικός/φορτικότης, 526n21,
527–528, 527n23, 546–547,
548n98, 551–554, 552n112,
553–554n116, 581
ψεῦδος/ψεύδομαι/ἀψεύδης, 202n98,
207n120, 219, 236–238, 236n60,
236n64, 236–237n65, 237n66,
238n70, 238n71, 241, 244, 244n93,
246–247, 246n99, 249–250,
250n116, 250n118, 257–259,
257n151, 261–263, 263n165, 362,
561. *See also* νεῖκος

General Index†

accuracy (*akribeia*): 200, 259, 591, 625n123, 630n139; meaning of *akribeia* in Aristotle, 627–628, 635–636; Alkidamas on, 626n127; and clarity, 627, 635; and correption, 208, 208n122, 302n35; of court documents, 152n12, 439n14, 442, 442n29; of the demegoric style, 604, 629, 631, 631n145, 638n161; of the dicanic style, 604, 631n145, 632–633, 634n152, 637, 638n161; of the epideictic style, 622, 636; of an eyewitness report, 180, 186, 189, 195n76, 200, 209; of the fit between style and audience, 635–637; of the fit between subject matter and audience, 638; of the fit between subject matter and style, 634–637; of the graphic style, 593n50, 603–604, 611, 624n118, 625–626; and *hypokrisis*, 625, 632; of performance (singing or song), 176, 186, 189, 195n76, 202, 208, 261; of the report of an oracular answer, 224; and *skiagraphia*, 604, 604n70, 628–631, 628n132, 628n133, 628n134, 628n135, 631n144, 632n145, 633–634, 638; of style versus accuracy of subject matter and argument, 636 (*see also* accuracy: of subject matter and argument); of styles contrasted, 310, 316, 603–604, 625–626; and stylistic concision, 632, 632n148; of stylistic devices contrasted, 627; of subject matter and argument, 591, 611, 628, 630–633, 631n145, 636; verbatim, 207–208, 334–336, 341; writing offers superior stylistic, 611, 622. *See also* ἀκρίβεια; ἀκριβής; inspiration: truth/accuracy and

acting: exaggerated mimetic performance, 309, 497n86, 534n45 (*see also* acting: mimetic performance; *homēristai*: emphatically histrionic delivery of); extrinsic to poetics, 585–587; *hypokrinesthai* or *hypokrisis* denotes, 297, 536, 649; *hypokrisis* came late to *tragikē*, 521–522, 526, 581n7; mimetic performance, 4, 316, 446, 484, 529, 531, 587, 666 (*see also* acting: exaggerated mimetic performance; mimesis: of action); as 'mimetic substitution', 661n43;

(acting, *cont.*)

and rhapsody (kinship of and convergence between), 2–3, 435, 484, 487, 665 (*see also* rhapsode: actor and). *See also* rhapsodic performance: histrionic delivery

actor: as 'answerer', 655–656, 663n48 (see also *hypokrinomai*); *apokritēs* not used to label, 650, 650n11, 650n12; contest for actors, 446 (*see also* Lykourgos: contest for comic actors revived by); hermeneutic function of, 3 (see also *hypokrinomai*: in the sense of 'to interpret'); histrionic interpolations, 435, 441, 445–447, 445n42, 587n25; *hypokritēs* used to label, 9, 298–299, 309, 351n69, 388n198, 648–649, 663 (see also *hypokritēs*: passed from rhapsode to actor); *hypokritēs* versus *tragōidos* as labels for, 655–656; actors at the Panathenaia (*see* Panathenaia: actors at); the poet was also, 522, 532n38, 581; popularity of actors, 351n71, 446–447, 447n50; rhapsode as model for, 4, 296–297, 664–665 (*see also* tragedy: rhapsodic performance as model for dramatic performance). See also *hypokritēs*; performer: *hypokritēs* corresponds to; tragedy

akribeia: see accuracy

Alexandria: as Athens' heir, 441; festival calendar of, 441, 441n24; Library and Mouseion at, 441, 441n25, 480; peripatetic scholarship at, 441; Ptolemaic patronage of the arts, 441, 468, 468n114 (*see also* patronage); its rivalry with Attalid Pergamum, 441; and the text of Aiskhylos, Sophokles, and Euripides, 440–441

Alkidamas: 2, 5, 7, 9, 308n64, 311–313, 311n75, 312n84, 316–317, 316n96, 318n102, 320n110, 321n115, 329, 380–381, 380n171, 523, 594n50, 595, 596n55, 609n79, 609–610n81, 615, 616n98, 616n100, 617–618, 617n101, 626n127, 643; on accuracy (*see* accuracy: Alkidamas on); his use of *poiētēs* and *poiēma*, 312, 312n84, 317, 318n102; uses *rhapsōidikē* as a *comparandum* for the orator's use of writing (*see* rhapsodic performance: as a *comparandum* for the orator's use of writing); writes against writing, 329, 615–618. *See also* improvisation

alphabet: see writing

aorist aspect: 283n219, 321n117, 410n292, 420, 422–424, 422n338, 423n341, 423n343, 423–424n344; 'focus function' of, 423, 423n343

apodeixis: versus *agōn*, 461–462, 461n84, 489; and demonstration, 528n24, 544, 546, 546n92, 552n112, 559n128; and performance, 436, 461–462, 461n83, 464 (see also *epideixis*: *apodeixis* and). See also *epideixis*

archaic art: the blinding of Polyphemos, 57–61; Chest of Kypselos, 55–56; and the evolutionary model, 48; François Vase, 64–65; funeral games of Patroklos, 64–66; iconography of, 46–68; *Iliad* and, 49–56; the narrative shape of Homeric poetry presupposed by, 48; *Odyssey* and, 56–64; pictorial narrative derivative of poetry, 39, 61–62, 78, 404; pictorial narrative independent of poetry, 47; Sphinx in (*see* Sphinx: early iconography of);

synoptic depiction in, 58, 58n51; and the text fixation of the Homeric poems, 41–70; topical versus mythical depictions in, 65; tradition and innovation in, 40; reception, 39, 66; witnesses to epic stories independent of the Homeric poems, 67–68

Aristarkhos: atheteses and other editorial principles, 149n4, 158; on A 5, 231n41; on B 558, 148; on N 423, 26

Aristotle: his acquaintance with actual forensic and deliberative speeches, 595n53; agonistic and graphic styles as the ends of a stylistic continuum, 603–605, 608, 611, 619, 619n106, 627, 632n148 (*see also* Aristotle: agonistic and graphic styles contrasted); agonistic and graphic styles contrasted, 310, 316–317, 601–604, 607, 611n82, 621n110, 622, 626 (*see also* Aristotle: agonistic and graphic styles as the ends of a stylistic continuum; Aristotle: on the agonistic style; Aristotle: on the graphic style); on the agonistic style, 592, 599, 601, 611, 621, 625n122, 636 (*see also* Aristotle: agonistic and graphic styles contrasted); on anagnostic poets, 356, 623–624, 623n114, 624n119, 626; basic literacy, 604–605, 608, 611; his conceptual dependence on stage acting, 534, 537n57; connects rhapsodic, dramatic, and oratorical *hypokrisis*, 310; on correct Greek usage (ἑλληνίζειν), 310, 310n74, 599, 602–603, 608, 610–611, 610n84, 610n85, 618–619n105, 619n106,

620, 623n113; on the demegoric style, 599–600, 601–604, 610n85, 611, 611n87, 620, 628–631, 631n145, 634, 634n152, 638n161; on the dicanic style, 599–600, 601–604, 610n85, 620, 631n145, 632–635, 632n145, 634n152, 637, 638n161 (*see also* Aristotle: on the graphic character of the dicanic style); distant audiences, 604, 608, 608n76, 612–615; on the epideictic style, 621–623; on the graphic character of the dicanic style, 603–604 (*see also* Aristotle: on the dicanic style); on the graphic style, 317, 356, 592, 593n50, 599, 611, 621, 625n122, 627, 627n131, 636 (*see also* accuracy: of the graphic style; Aristotle: agonistic and graphic styles contrasted); *lexis* in the *Poetics* versus *lexis* in the *Rhetoric*, 529n31, 548–549n100, 583–584n15, 585–586, 588, 588n30, 588n31; *lexis*, its oral and aural dimensions emphasized by, 529–530, 530n34, 533, 548n100, 572; μεταδίδωμι, its meaning and usage in, 611–612, 612n89; *opsis* dismissed by, 587, 587n27; *Rhetoric*, the 'scientific precision' of its argument, 564–565, 573, 573n177; *Rhetoric* III, its place in the *Rhetoric*, 528n25; *Rhetoric* III.1–12, its unity and coherence, 597–598n63; on rhetorical genera (and delivery or style), 598n63, 602–603, 620, 621n110, 622, 622n111, 623–624n117, 624, 625n125, 636, 638; on stylistic accuracy (*see* accuracy; *lexis*: stylistic finish); technical delivery connected

(Aristotle, *cont.*)

    with *hypokrisis* and *lexis* by, 309–310, 317, 522–523, 536, 544, 547n94, 580n3, 582–585, 583n12, 583n13, 588, 597–598, 604, 625n125; τὸ μὲν … τὸ δέ in *Rhetoric* III.12 (1413b5–6), 599, 602–607, 602n64, 602n65, 607n73, 607n75, 618–619n105; his treatment of *hypokrisis* is relatively undeveloped, 535, 535n48, 543, 578; treats *hypokrisis* in its relation to *lexis* unlike later ancient scholars, 529, 529n31; on trial by a single judge, 604, 633–635, 637–639 (*see also* court proceedings: judgment by a single judge; rhetoric: *agōn* in); on written speeches, 310, 593, 595, 625n122 (*see also* delivery: Aristotle's technical delivery relies on writing).
    See also delivery; *hypokrisis*; *lexis*

Arkhilokhos: 57n48, 281, 343, 343n42, 346, 350–354, 351n68, 352n74, 353n77, 353n80, 353n82, 437, 437n6, 448, 450n58, 482, 483n25, 489, 489n44, 496, 508, 649n9; Panhellenic status of, 353, 353n77, 353n82; range of his *oeuvre*, 352, 352n74, 352n75, 489n44. *See also* iambic poetry

Athens: Athenian rhapsodes (*see* memorization: Athenian rhapsodes and; rhapsodes: Ionian versus Athenian rhapsodes; writing: used by Athenian [and lesser] rhapsodes); Dark-Age, 84, 84n11. See also Panathenaia; Salamis

athletes: 314–315n90

authority: *see* authorship: authorizing multiforms; 'Hesiod': authority of; 'Homer': authority of; inspiration: authority and; poetic

tradition: authority of; poetic tradition: Nereus embodies an authoritative; prophecy: authoritative proclamation of; rhapsode: cultural authority of; speech-act: authority of; truth: authority and

authorship: authorizing multiforms, 83n5; author's biography as a function of 'his' tradition, 264–265, 266n174; author's biography reflects the appropriation of 'his' poetry, 266; Hesiod's (*see* 'Hesiod': authorship of); Homer's (*see* 'Homer': authorship of); rise of the notion of, 47n24, 159, 175, 235, 266, 289, 294, 332n5, 333, 493

clarity: *see* accuracy: and clarity; delivery: and clarity; delivery: *ēthos* and *pathos* contribute to expressive clarity; *lexis*: seeks clarity; *phantasia*: instrumental to clarity (demonstrative)

compensatory lengthening (CL): 126; Attic reversion, 87, 89; Carian, 89–90, 90n44; dating the second CL, 89–97, 98; evolution of the Greek long vowels, 87; glide development (loss of syllabicity), 100–102, 104n117; Homeric futures, 104; lexical borrowing, 89, 89n38, 95–96, 96n80; Lycian, 90–94; moraic phonology, 102–103, 102n105; Naxos, 88n35, 92; -nw- clusters, 105–109; second CL, 87–88; substratum influence, 89, 94; syllabification, 86, 102, 105–109, 118–119, 118–119n36; third CL, 85–88, 89

composition in performance: *see* recomposition in performance

court proceedings: clerk, 152, 152n12, 439n14, 442; documents in, 152, 152n12, 439n14; judgment by a single judge, 633–634n152 (*see also* Aristotle: on trial by a single judge); oral versus written legal practice, 152n12. *See also* logographers

craft metaphors: see *rhaptō* and other craft metaphors

creativity: *see* delivery: as the creative center of gravity; performer: as agent of creation, transmission, and reception; performer: creative singer versus reproducing rhapsode; performer: creativity of; rhapsode: creative versus reproducing; rhapsodic performance: creative songstitching; song-culture: creative primacy of the performative setting in

Cyclops: *see* Polyphemos

deliberative speeches: 592, 592n45, 595n53; *agōn* in (*see* rhetoric: *agōn* in); deliberative setting, 2, 326, 552, 608n76, 610, 610n81, 620, 629–630, 632n145, 634n152, 635, 638, 638n161; ordinarily thought to postdate the assembly address, 325–326; published?, 610n81; script of (*see* scripts); writing used to prepare for, 325, 325n126, 596n55, 597, 603, 609, 609–610n81 (*see also* writing: as an aid to the performance of rhapsodes and orators). *See also* Aristotle: his acquaintance with actual forensic and deliberative speeches

delivery: Aristotle's notion of ('lies in the voice'), 8, 309, 523, 526, 530, 532–533, 581; Aristotle's technical delivery relies on writing, 317, 317n99, 583n14, 593–596, 594n50, 598, 603–605, 608, 611,

620, 624–625 (see also *lexis*: and writing; writing: as an aid to the performance of rhapsodes and orators); and clarity, 627 (*see also* delivery: *ēthos* and *pathos* contribute to expressive clarity); and the corruption/vulgarity of the audience, 527–528n24, 528, 544–545, 551, 552n112, 553–554, 553–554n116, 630–631n140, 632n145; as the creative center of gravity, 315; emotional, 631n145; ethically objectionable/problematic in rhetoric, 523, 527, 536n49, 536n50, 538n58, 546–547, 546–547n93, 598 (see also *lexis*: ethically equivocal); *ēthos* and *pathos* expressed through, 311, 523, 526, 535–537, 541, 625–627, 625n125, 631, 635–636; *ēthos* and *pathos* contribute to expressive clarity, 549, 550n105 (see also *lexis*: seeks clarity; rhetoric: *ēthos* and *pathos* as rhetorical *pisteis*); how *ēthos* relates to *pathos*, 537n54, 576n189; *hypokrisis* corresponds to, 1–2, 309, 547; loudness of the voice, 309, 526, 533–535, 576, 586, 632; mimetic, 309; *pathos* defined, 570, 574n180, 574n181; and the psychology of the emotions, 523, 534n42, 536, 575–576, 578; rhetorical, 4–5, 8–9, 523ff. *passim*; speaking 'outside the subject', 536n50, 631n145, 637–638, 638n161 (*see also* ἔξω τοῦ πράγματος); training in technical delivery, 620, 625, 639 (*see also* rhetoric: silence); use of voice, gestures, and appearance, 310, 315, 526, 528, 534–535, 534n44, 534n45, 538, 541, 547, 578, 586, 588, 594n50,

(delivery, *cont.*)

621, 625–627, 632–633, 635–636; writing in the service of (*see* writing: as an aid to the performance of rhapsodes and orators). *See also* Aristotle; *hypokrisis*; *homēristai*: emphatically histrionic delivery of; mimesis: voice and; rhapsode: histrionic delivery

Delphic oracle: 178, 201, 206, 270–283; cult of the Muses at, 285–286, 288, 288n234; mantic session, 270; mediation of the προφήτης, 270–272, 270n186, 270n187, 272n194, 272n195, 274–276, 284; oracular seat of Γῆ, 274, 286; *pneuma enthousiastikon*, 272, 272–273n196; prose or poetry oracles, 270–273, 270n187, 271n193, 276, 276n207 (*see also* oracular verse); Pythia, 179n17, 224n18, 268, 270–276, 270n186, 270n187, 271n193, 272–273n196, 273n197, 274n198, 284–285, 290; Pythia as προφῆτις, 275; writing at, 276n207. *See also* inspiration: ecstasy and; inspiration: *enthousiasmos*; inspiration: self-possession; inspiration: skill and; Plato: ecstasy and trance; Plato: inspiration and skill

Demetrios of Phaleron: 8, 157, 295–296, 351, 351n71, 447–448, 447n53, 447n55, 449n56, 450n57, 451, 465n100, 466–467, 466n102, 467n112, 469, 472, 476, 476n144, 496, 496n83, 644; his interest in Homeric poetry, 466; *khorēgia* abolished by, 466–467, 467n112, 469 (*see also* Lykourgos: self-serving liturgies resented by); provided the management model for the synods of *tekhnitai*, 467; reforms of, 351, 351n71,

447–449, 465n100, 466–476; and state control over performers, 465n100, 467, 476 (*see also* Lykourgos: and state control over poetic performance). See also *homēristai*: brought into the theater by Demetrios

Demodokos: 181, 182n28, 183n29, 186–187, 186n42, 186n44, 189, 193, 195–196, 195n76, 199, 201, 220, 229, 269, 269n181, 334n10, 366, 386n190, 395, 426

diachrony: cross-references in oral poetry, 209n126; diachronic analysis, 4–5, 154, 177, 277, 280, 299n22, 300n29, 331, 334, 334n10, 341–342, 346, 368n129, 380n169, 385n189, 412–413, 417, 417–418n317, 464–465n97, 648n5, 652–653; diachronic and historical analysis, 3–5, 253n132; diachronic development, 20, 24, 155n22, 239n75, 289, 332n5, 333, 335n13, 342, 348, 352, 464–465n97, 653; diachronic dynamics of diffusion and reception, 36, 239n75, 241n80; diachronic evolution, 5–6, 307n62, 347; diachronic evolution from 'song' to 'poetry', 343, 345, 352n72, 417–418n317; diachronic layering of the Homeric poems (*see* Homeric poems: diachronic layering of); diachronic perspective or understanding, 1, 1n1, 344, 396n232, 413, 652; diachronic skewing, 177, 177n14, 187, 207n121, 344, 346, 349, 349–350n60, 359; focus on, 10; Hellenistic poetry offers diachronic insight, 347–348, 347n54; historical accident versus, 16, 16n7,

18, 28n40, 29–30, 46n18, 49, 295n9; of lexical semantics and synchronic semantic outcomes, 566–567n149, 651–653, 651n14, 652–653n17, 653n18, 663; meta-poetics of reception, 186n42, 366–367; novelty (as a rhetorical narrative conceit), 193, 365–366; *prōtoi heuretai* and, 23–24, 159, 235, 277, 384, 493, 642, 658n55; synchrony versus, 144n124, 180, 276, 280n213, 331, 346, 377, 383, 392, 395, 464–465n97, 651. *See also* non-melodic recitation: diachronic melodic potential of epic; relay poetics: synchronic rhapsodic succession; sequence: diachronic rhapsodic succession

dictation: 8, 332; archaic art and, 48; as a historical accident, 22; ideological motivation for, 36, 40, 44, 44n16; R. Janko's theory, 24–29, 140n111; leisure and, 20; A. B. Lord's theory, 18–24, 44; oral-dictated text, 42, 61, 68, 85, 331; technical challenges to, 44; theories, 15–70, 16–17, 60, 67–68, 78n34; M. L. West's theory, 41, 41n3

didaskalia: 557–559, 557–558n122, 558n124, 558n126, 559n128, 560n129. *See also* rhetoric: demonstrative nature of

Dionysia: 297, 439, 446–447, 467, 469, 470n117, 476–477, 648n6; *agōnothetēs* in charge of, 467, 467n110; contest for actors (*see* actor: contest for actors; Lykourgos: contest for comic actors revived by); not the venue for rhapsodic performance under Demetrios of Phaleron, 469

Dipylon *oinokhoē*: 84, 97–98, 140n110; date of, 97; vowel contraction in, 97–99

divine will: *see* Hesiodic poems: explicate Zeus' will/mind; Homeric poems: explicate Zeus' will; notional fixity: narrative necessity and; rhapsode: his access to the divine will; truth: divine will and

drama: *see* acting; actor; tragedy

eighth-century BC 'renaissance': 212n139

emotions: *see* delivery: emotional; delivery: and the psychology of the emotions; *lexis*: and the emotions; rhetoric: and the psychology of the emotions; Thrasymakhos: emotional appeals and

Epic Cycle: 83n5, 369, 369n132; aesthetics and poetics of, 369–370n133; authorship of, 231, 231n42; comprehensiveness of, 369 (*see also* performance: comprehensiveness of); meta-phor of the κύκλος, 231, 231n42, 369n133; *neōteroi* and, 231n41; Panhellenism of, 369n133

epic poetry: Homeric epic as a 'super-genre', 202; versus non-epic poetry, 417, 417–418n317; as an oral-traditional medium of recomposition in performance, 345, 417; traditional diction, 149, 377–378, 392, 417 (*see also* Homeric poems: traditional diction); traditional referenti-ality, 379n168; 'translation' into (non-Ionic) Greek dialects, 141. *See also* non-melodic recitation: diachronic melodic potential of epic *epideixis*: 307–308, 483, 613–614, 613–614n91; versus *agōn* (see *apodeixis*: versus *agōn*); *apodeixis* and, 308, 308n64, 311, 461n83 (see also *apodeixis*: and performance); epideictic (speeches, as *genus dicendi*), 311n75, 317, 327n132, 559, 592, 593n50, 595n53, 603, 613, 618, 621–624, 624n117, 624n119, 625n121, 636–637; epideictic setting, 482n17, 483, 516, 546n93, 552, 635–636; epideictic style (*see* Aristotle: on the epideictic style); stylistic precision (*see* accuracy: of the epideictic style); writing and (*see* writing: as an aid to the performance of rhapsodes and orators). *See also* ἐπιδείκνυμι; rhapsodic performance: rhapsodic *hypokrisis* related to sophistic *epideixis*

Euboians: as audience for 'Homer', 79; *Catalogue of Ships* and, 83n7; their contact with the Levant, 29n43, 143; copies of the Homeric poems circulated by, 80, 82–83; dating of LG pottery, 112–113; Euboian dialect, 82–83, 85; Euboian formative influence on the Homeric poems, 85, 109, 130, 132–133, 135, 140–141; Homeric poems composed and written in Euboia, 81; Homeric Question and Euboia ('Euboian theory'), 81–110; Lefkandi, 82, 143; Levantine/Semitic influence at Pithekoussai, 142–143; 'Nestor's Cup' (*see* 'Nestor's Cup'); Pithekoussai, 82; Pithekoussan scribal school, 142

evolutionary model: *see* text fixation: evolutionary model of

festivals: at which rhapsodes are attested, 482n14; sacred, 464n95, 480, 480n5. *See also* Alexandria: festival calendar of; Lykourgos: and Athenian festivals; mimes: sacred festivals not open to; performance: festival performance; performance: festival calendar; reorganization of the Μουσεῖα, 500, 500n97; *tekhnitai* of Dionysos: and Hellenistic festivals

forensic speeches: 592, 592n45, 595n53; *agōn* in (*see* rhetoric: *agōn* in); forensic setting, 2, 442, 552, 608n76, 610n81, 610n82, 620, 629, 631n145, 632–635, 632n145, 634n152, 638, 638n161; script of (*see* scripts); writing and, 325–326, 326n131, 603, 610n81, 610n82 (*see also* logographers; writing: as an aid to the performance of rhapsodes and orators). *See also* accuracy: of court documents; Aristotle: his acquaintance with actual forensic and deliberative speeches; court proceedings; logographers

Gilgamesh: 29; Akkadian *Gilgamesh*, 30–31; diffusion driven by scribal training and cuneiform literacy, 31; *Gilgamesh* oral tradition, 30; and the Near-Eastern curriculum, 32; performance of, 30; writing of, a diachronic development, 29–30

Herakles: his apotheosis, 153, 153–154n15, 154n20; his *eidōlon* in the *Nekuia*, 153–154; heroic and divine, 154

hermēneuein: its meaning, whether 'to express' or 'to interpret', 301n29; as vocal expression, 300n29. *See also* recomposition in performance: in the context of rhapsodic *hermēneusis*

hermēneus: 648n4. *See also* 'Homer': as *hermēneus* of the Muse; Plato: poet as *hermēneus* of the (inspiring) gods; rhapsode: as *hermēneus* of his tradition or of the Muse; rhapsode: as *hermēneus* of 'Homer'

'Hesiod': authority of, 178, 220, 242n82, 254–255; authorship of, 165–166; construction of, 225, 225n26, 264–265, 265n170; date of, 82; dependent on the Muses, 254–255 (*see also* 'Hesiod': independent of the Muses); his *Dichterweihe*, 177n13, 182, 219–224, 225, 229, 240–242, 242n82, 258, 265, 267; his divine voice, 220, 241; his ignorance, 228; independent of the Muses, 253–254, 264, 264n169 (*see also* 'Hesiod': dependent on the Muses); individuality of, 244, 263, 263–264n168; legitimized by divine election, 265; mantic poetry (*see* mantic poetry: mantic [oracular] speech and mantic poetry); as a poet-seer, 220, 225n22, 256; as a rhapsode, 332; sang predictively, 225; his scepter (σκῆπτρον), 220, 241, 348n55; as a shepherd, 220, 241–244, 242n83, 242n84 (*see also* pastoralism); transformed into a poet of truth, 240–242, 241–242n82

Hesiodic poems: aetiological import of the *Theogony*, 253, 253n128, 253n129, 258; animal husbandry, 244n90; complementarity of the *Theogony* and the *Works and Days*, 225–226; δίκη, 254–255; episte-

mology of (*see* truth: experiential versus inspired); explicate Zeus' will/mind, 254–255; 'mere bellies' (*see* lies: 'mere bellies'); metapoetic language in, 225; *Nautilia*, 227–228n30, 254–255; overarching thematic focus of, 226, 254–255; Panhellenic claim of, 241, 252, 260, 265; Panhellenic shape of, 228–229, 258; polemic against Homeric poetry, 247n103; polis in, 244, 254; temporal scope of Hesiod's song, 226–227, 229, 253; *Theogony* as a hymn to Zeus, 234–235

Hipparkhos: 24, 43, 80, 382, 384

historical: *see* diachrony

'Homer': author of 'other' poems, 168, 333, 399; author of the 'Homeric' poems, 6, 166, 168, 175, 231, 231n42, 290, 333; authority of, 168, 178, 236, 332n5, 333; authorship of, 170, 231n42, 235, 266, 290, 333, 493, 587n25; biographical interest in, 169, 266; composing in return for livelihood, 167n60, 332–333; as culture hero, 6, 175; dialect of, 135–136; earliest attestations of the name, 167–170, 207n121; etymology of, 207n121, 231n42; as the first tragic poet, 296n10 (*see also* tragedy: roots of, in epic); as *hermēneus* of the Muse, 275, 299n24; *Hymn to Apollo* and, 265, 265n172; illiterate, 16; *ipsissima verba* of, 149; literate, 42, 68–70; as *mantis*, 235; Melesigenes, 168–169; monumental poet (*maximus poeta*), 135, 235, 331; from Oropos, 135; as prophet, 220, 225n22; references to his persona, 168; as a rhapsode, 332–334, 334n10; *Vita*

('Homer', *cont.*)

traditions, 83, 83n5, 266, 283n219, 333–334; wrote and revised his poems, 68–69, 135n97

Homeric poems: Aiolic dialect in, 85; archaisms in, 25; Argive tradition of, 53, 53–54n41; artistic unity of, 15, 379, 392; asyndeton in, 262, 411n303; Athenian *paradosis*, 150; Attic correption, 85n14; Attic dialect ('Attic coloring'), 81–82, 135; authoritative script of (*see* scripts: authoritative script of the Homeric poems); *Catalogue of Ships*, 148n3, 149, 150, 151n10, 152, 183; city editions of, 18; composed and written in Euboia (*see* Euboians); composition at verse-end and verse-opening, 137n102; criticism of, 235n58, 261, 266; cross-references in, 188, 209n126; date of, 27, 42–43, 43n10, 45, 75n21; diachronic layering of, 45n17, 297n11, 412, 652–653, 663; dialectal layers/ mixture, 81, 144n124; diffusion of, 17–18, 78; diffusion through Athens (Panathenaic 'bottleneck'), 78, 81, 84, 109–110, 135, 147, 176, 314n89; dramatic potential of, 299n21; embassy duals, 68n95, 69; enjambment in, 132–134; Epeios and the wooden horse, 189; Euboian dialect (*see* Euboians); explicate Zeus' will, 231–232; folk stories and the *Odyssey*, 56n48, 60, 60n57, 60n58, 63; formulaic extension and economy, 48n25; epichoric variants of, 53, 53n41, 83n5; Homeric tradition and, 47n24, 144n124; ideological cast of, 36, 40, 44–45n16; indirect *paradosis* of, 333; innovation and, 53n41;

interpolations in, 70, 76n29, 81, 150–154, 155n22, 163–164, 266, 358, 412, 493; *Kunstsprache*, 25, 81, 85; metapoetic language in, 177–178, 185n38, 185n41, 363n115, 385n190, 387; Meyer's law, 137n102; mimetic potential of, 3–4, 351n71, 451, 465n97, 664; mimetic pragmatics of, 375, 375n154, 389–390, 665; mistakes and inconsistencies in, 24, 27; literary echoes of, 43n11, 78n36, 168; monumentality of, 23–24, 370, 370n134 (*see also* performance: comprehensiveness of); morality of, 164, 166; multiforms of, 27, 46n24, 47, 52n35, 53, 54n41, 55–56, 60, 65–66, 151, 165–166, 166n55; narrative fluidity of, 47, 64–68, 131; *Nekuia*, 153, 153n14; non-traditional (non-formulaic) elements of, 135; notional thematic totality, 23–24, 163, 176, 209n126, 370, 379n168, 395; novelty (*see* diachrony: novelty); oracles, prophecies, dreams, and omens in, 233; orality of, 15, 48n25; oral transmission of, 35; Panathenaic rule, 23–24, 43, 78n38, 341, 371, 382–392, 382n179, 437–438, 647 (*see also* relay poetics; sequence); Panhellenism and (*see* Panhellenism); Peisistratean recension, 78, 78n37, 80n48, 147, 147n2; plus-verses, 75n23, 79n40, 333; poem versus poetic tradition, 46n24; polis in, 36, 45n16; prosody, 81, 106–107, 106n127, 208; quoted as 'text', 281; reception, 17, 18n11, 23, 27, 36; revelatory, 233, 662; ruler-shepherd in, 242n84, 243; seams, 342n39;

song-stitching not mentioned in, 344–345; structure of the *Odyssey*, 209n125; suprasegmentals, 165; thematic scope and narrative sequence of, 46, 46n24, 54n41, 163; traditional diction, 15, 17, 35, 417 (*see also* epic poetry: traditional diction); traditional themes, 15, 17, 35, 61–62, 417; Trojan-War tradition and (*see* poetic tradition: Trojan-War); ur-Homeric usage, 135; verbatim repetition in, 166n57; vulgate (received text), 26, 26n35, 46n21, 48, 50, 53, 58, 58n53, 63, 79, 130–131, 133, 137n102, 159, 165–166; written transmission of, 147, 147n2, 175–176, 295n9

Homeric Question: 15–170; Euboians and, 81–110

Homeric scholarship: 147–170; its assumptions about Homeric performance, 147; Theagenes of Rhegion (*see* Theagenes of Rhegion); Seleukos Homerikos, 156–157, 158n33

Homeridai: 7n8, 78, 80, 148, 266, 281, 302n36, 307, 334, 341, 380n169, 383, 492, 492n59, 493n60; relay performance characteristic of, 380n169; sang ἐκ διαδοχῆς, 383, 383n181, 492n60. *See also* relay poetics

homēristai (post-classical rhapsodic performance): 447–453, 449n56, 449–450n57, 451n62, 452–453n66, 453n67, 453n68, 454n69, 458–466, 461n82, 461n83, 464n94, 464n95, 464n96, 465–466n97, 469, 479–481, 480n6, 482n14, 483–484, 483n25, 515–516, 516n145, 644; brought into the theater by Demetrios of Phaleron, 448,

449n56, 451, 466; coinage of the label, 449–450n57, 465, 465n100, 481; documentary evidence for, 454–458; emphatically histrionic delivery of, 450n57, 451–453, 453n66, 459, 462, 464, 464–465n97 (*see also* rhapsodic performance: histrionic delivery); *Ennianista* and, 464n94; geographic spread of, 481–482n14; as a label for Hellenistic rhapsodes, 449–450, 480n6; mimed fights, 451–452, 451n62, 459, 462–463, 464n95, 484; old versus new, 448–449, 451, 464–465n97, 466, 469, 483; payment of, 458, 460, 463; prompter for, 459–460 (*see also* tragedy: prompter); reper- toire of, 449n57; rhapsodes at symposia, 449–450, 450n61; rhapsodes versus, 447–454; rhapsodic performance in the theater, 450–452, 453n66, 464, 465n97, 465n100, 469–470, 476 (see also *homēristai*: brought into the theater by Demetrios of Phaleron); solo performance of, 453n66, 459–461; not *tekhnitai* of Dionysos, 480–481; troupe acting, 450n57, 451, 460–461, 461n82, 464n95; vocal delivery of Homeric poetry by, 452–453, 452n66, 453n66, 453n68, 459, 461–462, 463–464. *See also* impro- visation: versus scripted perfor- mance; non-melodic recitation: Hellenistic rhapsodes sang epic 'melodically'

hymn: 396–398, 396n233, 424–425; cultic dimension of the Homeric hymns, 233–234n52; etymology of *hymnos*, 396–397; Hermes as a rhapsode performing a hymn,

(hymn, *cont.*)

204, 376–377; *hyphainō* associated with, 398; notional totality of (*see* notional fixity: notional thematic totality); as performance unit, 397–398, 397n240, 397n241, 416, 424n345, 426; poetics of proems/preludes, 233–234, 233n51, 375n158, 385, 385n189; proem and, 205, 210n131 (*see also* ἀμβολάδην; προοίμιον); rhapsodic sequencing and *hymnos*, 397. *See also* non-melodic recitation: performative implications of ἀθύρω and ἄθυρμα; rhapsodic performance: proem as the ritual framework of

hypokrinomai: in the context of 'oracular pronouncements', 649, 655, 662–663 (*see also* speech-act: pragmatics of); etymology of, 298, 652–655, 653n19, 653n20, 653n21, 653n22, 654n23, 654n25, 654n26, 654–655n27, 658–660, 660–661n43, 662–663; Homeric usage of, 651–653, 652n16, 652–653n17, 658n36, 661, 661–662n44; Ionic versus Attic usage, 297n11, 649–650, 649n9, 651n13; not a natural choice for stage acting, 297–298, 663–664; in the sense of 'to answer' (in Ionic and old Attic), 297n11, 649, 649n10, 651, 653–656, 658–660, 665n55 (see also *hypokrinomai*: its sense, whether 'to answer' or 'to interpret'); in the sense of 'to interpret', 2–3, 289, 297, 297n16, 647–648n4, 651, 653–655, 661–662, 662n46, 665 (see also *hypokrinomai*: its sense, whether 'to answer' or 'to interpret'); in the sense of 'to perform', 351, 351n69, 482–483,

482–483n21, 650–651 (*see also* performer: *hypokritēs* corresponds to); in the sense of 'to respond by way of performing', 298n18; its sense, whether 'to answer' or 'to interpret', 297n14, 651–652, 660–661 (see also *hypokrinomai*: in the sense of 'to answer'; *hypokrinomai*: in the sense of 'to interpret'). *See also* acting: *hypokrinesthai* or *hypokrisis* denotes; diachrony: of lexical semantics and synchronic semantic outcomes; performance; ὑποκρίνεσθαι; ὑποκριτικός

hypokrisis: and accuracy (*see* accuracy: and *hypokrisis*); and acting (*see* acting); Alkidamas associates scripted delivery with, 316; Aristotle and (*see* Aristotle; delivery); before Aristotle not adequately treated, 532; first attestation of, 297; *lexis* and (see *lexis*: *hypokrisis* entailed by; *lexis*: *hypokrisis* opposed to; *lexis*: *hypokrisis* with a view to); 'performance' corresponds to, 1, 521, 536, 664; in the *Poetics*, 585–586, 588; its power (according to Aristotle), 521, 525–526, 532–533, 544, 546, 582–583, 598; rhapsodic *hypokrisis* clarified by rhetorical, 523; rhapsodic performance connected with, 316, 521; *Rhetoric* III.2–11 concerned with, 528, 532–543 (see also *hypokrisis*: a thematic detour in *Rhetoric* III.1?); as the 'stylistic' shape of a performance, 530, 544; a thematic detour in *Rhetoric* III.1?, 528, 531–533, 536n49, 581, 598 (see also *hypokrisis: Rhetoric* III.2–11 concerned with); voice and (*see* delivery: Aristotle's notion of; delivery: use of voice; mimesis: voice and); writing and (*see* delivery: Aristotle's technical delivery relies on writing). *See also* Aristotle; delivery; ὑπόκρισις; ὑποκριτικός

hypokritēs: Aristotle's use of, 657, 657–658n35; in the *Fasti,* 297, 656; passed from rhapsode to actor, 299n24, 648, 651, 664–665; its sense, whether 'answerer' or 'expounder', 298n18. *See also* actor: *hypokritēs* used to label; performer: *hypokritēs* corresponds to; prophet: as interpreter (ὑποκριτής); rhapsode: as *hypokritēs;* ὑποκριτής

hypoleptic singing: *see* relay poetics

iambic poetry: and epic poetry, thematically complementary, 353; Homeric *Margites* and, 353, 353n78; as Panhellenic blame poetry, 352; *psogos* answers to *kleos,* 352; in the rhapsodic repertoire, 353–354, 450n58, 482, 483n25, 489n44; stichic meters, 352–353. *See also* Arkhilokhos; non-melodic recitation: performance mode of elegiac and iambic poetry

improvisation: Alkidamas on, 311–318, 380, 594n50, 595, 616–617; in rhetoric, 7, 380, 611 (*see also* improvisation: Alkidamas on); versus scripted performance, 312–314, 316, 316n96, 329, 335n13, 341, 380, 435, 440, 443–444, 451, 469, 476, 487, 593–594n50, 595, 596n55, 611, 616n98, 618, 622, 626 (see

also *homēristai:* prompter for; tragedy: prompter; writing: as an aid to the performance of rhapsodes and orators; writing: recomposition in performance versus). *See also* recomposition in performance

Indo-European (IE) isosyllabic meters: 137n102

inscriptions: Attic τίνεσθαι, 124, 124n57; archaic (before 650 BC), 111–146; band script, 123; dating of Euboian LG pottery, 112–113; derivative of other kinds of writing, 142; e-grade -νυμι verbs, 123; Etruscan borrowing of ϝ, 120; final iotas not written, 121–123; from Cumae, 116–129; interpunction in, 145, 444n38; Lachish ewer, 146; loss of inner -ϝ-, 112–116; Mesha inscription, 146; monophthongization in the area of Olbia, 121–122, 121–122n47; reversion of η > ā, 139n109; sanctuary of Apollo Daphnephoros in Eretria, 144; *spiritus asper,* 126; *spiritus asper* as a reflex of initial ϝ-, 118–119n36; syllabification, 118–119n36; Tataie's *lēkythos,* 127; Tell Fekherye inscription, 146; Ugaritic, 146. *See also* Index of Documentary Sources

inspiration: authority and, 168, 186, 202, 208, 211, 241, 258, 359; blindness and, 184n35; claim to, 175, 177; consistent with tradition, 179–180, 185; dancing and, 278–279n210; ecstasy and, 207n121, 221, 267–270, 274, 274n201 (*see also* Plato: ecstasy and trance); enchantment (θέλξις) and, 189–190, 192–194,

(inspiration, *cont.*)

193n69, 238 (*see also* performance: pleasure of); *enthousiasmos*, 220, 220n1, 235, 267, 272, 278n209, 443n35, 542, 542n79; inspired IE performer, 181n24; inspiring/ teaching form and content, 190–191, 207, 214n146, 241 (*see also* performance: form versus content); as a literary *topos*, 177, 177n13; lying and (*see* lies: lying inspiration); notional fixity and, 175, 181–182, 202, 208, 289–290; performative implications of, 182, 198–199, 205n113, 662n46; seeing and knowing, 184; seeing versus hearing, 183–184, 184n34; self-possession and, 267–270, 269n181, 272–273, 274n198, 290, 357, 655; 'self-taught' (*see* αὐτοδίδακτος); skill and, 187, 188, 190n57, 194, 211, 214n146, 215, 264n169, 266, 267n176, 271, 274n200, 357–359, 655 (*see also* Plato: inspiration and skill; *rhaptō*: performer's skill ascribed to the gods); Sokrates' chain of, 235, 275–281, 277n209, 278–279n210, 282n215, 298, 298n20, 304–305, 309n65, 368; teaching and, 188–189, 190n57, 214; truth/accuracy and, 165, 180, 189, 208, 211, 258 (*see also* accuracy). See also *rhaptō*: rhetoric of inspiration and

interpretation: *see* actor: hermeneutic function of; *hermēneuein*: its meaning, whether 'to express' or 'to interpret'; *hypokrinomai*: in the sense of 'to interpret'; *hypokrinomai*: its sense, whether 'to answer' or 'to interpret'; *mantis* (seer): interpreter of signs; prophecy: infallible interpretation and prediction of; prophet:

as interpreter (ὑποκριτής); rhapsodic performance: interpretation and commentary

Isokrates: 9, 79, 276n206, 311n75, 315, 317, 317n101, 318–321, 318n102, 318n103, 318n104, 320n112, 352n72, 442n31, 444n38, 593–594n50, 595n52, 595n53, 605, 613–615, 614n93, 615n97, 617–618, 617n103, 621, 624; effectiveness of written speeches lessened without delivery, 624; not an adequate illustration of Aristotle's 'being forced to remain silent' (*Rhetoric* 1413b6–7), 605, 613–615; not an adequate illustration of Aristotle's 'written speeches' (*Rhetoric* 1404a18), 593–594n50; said to have influenced Aristotle's view of the epideictic style, 621 (*see also* Aristotle: on the epideictic style). *See also* rhapsodic performance: *rhapsōideō* in Isokrates and Plato

Kalkhas: 227, 228n30, 233, 252, 253, 269, 400

Khamaileon: 157, 352n72, 437, 448, 450, 450n58, 450n60, 483n25

Klearkhos: 351, 351n71, 448, 482, 496, 497n84

kleos: 186; as affirmation of traditionality, 367; Kallimakhos and, 368–369; Penelope's, 362–363, 363n115; as song (medium of epic), 183; as sung report, 183. *See also* iambic poetry: *psogos* answers to *kleos*

Levant: *Ahiqar*, 34; Aramaic literature, 34; Carthage (*see* Phoenicia); influence from, 35–36; literacy (*see* literacy); Phoenicia (*see* Phoenicia). *See also* Euboians: their contact with the Levant; Euboians:

Levantine/Semitic influence at Pithekoussai; Near East: Levant mediated the culture of

lexis: 8–9; accuracy of (*see* accuracy; *lexis*: stylistic finish); agonistic (*see* Aristotle: on the agonistic style); Aristotelian *lexis* as the scientific study of delivery (*see* Aristotle: technical delivery connected with *hypokrisis* and *lexis* by); post-Aristotelian views of, 529; and character (*ēthos*), 535, 576, 578, 631–633, 636 (see also *lexis*: and the emotions); seeks clarity, 548–550, 548n98, 550n105, 611, 611n86, 621n110, 622, 627n131, 635; connective particles and asyndeton, 621–622, 627, 632; demegoric (*see* Aristotle: on the demegoric style); and demonstrative disciplines, 527, 532, 545, 548, 557; dicanic (*see* Aristotle: on the dicanic style); and the emotions, 309, 534n42, 535, 547, 547n94, 569, 576–578, 576n190, 581, 631–633, 636 (*see also* delivery: *ēthos* and *pathos* expressed through; πάθημα); epideictic (*see* Aristotle: on the epideictic style); ethically equivocal, 544–547, 546–547n93, 552–553 (*see also* delivery: ethically objectionable/problematic in rhetoric); graphic (*see* Aristotle: on the graphic style); *harmonia*, 538–539, 627, 632 (see also *lexis*: 'prose melody'); how *hypokrisis* relates to, 524–530, 546, 548n98, 587n27; *hypokrisis* opposed to, 523–524, 526–527, 527n23, 532, 547n94, 548n98, 581, 584n15, 585, 585n20, 598; *hypokrisis* entailed by, 527–528,

527n23, 531, 535, 544, 546, 582–583, 583n12 (see also *lexis*: τὰ ὑποκριτικά; *lexis*: *hypokrisis* with a view to); *hypokrisis* with a view to, 524, 529–530, 534, 544, 582, 584n15, 597, 606, 619, 621, 621n110, 622, 624, 626, 627n131, 632, 635, 638 (see also *lexis*: τὰ ὑποκριτικά; *lexis*: *hypokrisis* entailed by); *hypokritikē* (histrionic), 625n125 (*see also* Aristotle: technical delivery connected with *hypokrisis* and *lexis* by); mediates the vocal expression of subject matter, 635–636; metaphor, 533, 533–534n42, 549–550, 549n103, 625, 632; in the *Poetics* (*see* Aristotle: *lexis* in the *Poetics* versus *lexis* in the *Rhetoric*); precision of (*see* accuracy; *lexis*: stylistic finish); propriety of style, 534, 537–538, 549–550, 550n105, 578n192, 634–635, 638, 638n161; 'prose melody' (rhythm and *harmonia* of speech), 539–543, 625 (see also *lexis*: *harmonia*); repetition, 621, 627, 627n131; *Rhetoric* III.12 offers a synoptic perspective on, 597–598; rhetorical genera and (*see* Aristotle: on rhetorical genera); 'rhetorical style' (*see* Aristotle: technical delivery connected with *hypokrisis* and *lexis* by); 'rhetorical stylistics' (see *lexis*: *hypokrisis* with a view to); rhythm, 538, 625, 627, 632; semantic range of, 541–542n77, 542n78; and sensory *phantasmata* beyond the auditory, 533, 533–534n42, 547n94, 576; social setting and, 627n131, 629, 631; stylistic finish, 314, 316, 329, 611, 627 (*see also* accuracy); τὰ

(lexis, cont.)

ὑποκριτικά, 310n73, 621, 621n110, 626–627 (see also lexis: hypokrisis entailed by; lexis: hypokrisis with a view to; rhetoric: rhētorika); translated 'style', 524n12; and writing, 310, 523–524, 593n50, 604, 608, 611, 620–621. See also accuracy; Aristotle; delivery; hypokrisis; λέξις; non-melodic recitation: melos versus harmonia; rhetoric: stylistic emphasis on various pisteis

lies: blurring the distinction between truth-telling and lying, 236n62, 240, 246n99, 246n100, 259; challenge to judge the veracity, 236–237, 236n62, 237n65; competition/strife and lying, 236–237, 239, 252; concept of, 236n60, 238; as fiction, 239n75, 244–245 (see also truth: fiction and); ineffectiveness of, 237–238; lying inspiration, 239, 241, 241n81, 258–261; 'mere bellies', 240, 240n77, 241n82; Odysseus' lies, 236n62, 258–259, 263; Panhellenism and, 239–240; pseudos used regardless of culpability, 238, 238n70; singer contrasted with liar, 238–239; truth and, 206–207n120, 235–266. See also truth

literacy: 5, 16, 166; in archaic Greece, 45n16; Cypriot, 143; ethnogenesis and, 144n124; Mesopotamian, 29; northwest Semitic, 34–35, 144. See also Aristotle: basic literacy; Gilgamesh: diffusion driven by scribal training and cuneiform literacy

logographers: 7, 325, 327, 327n133, 537n57, 597, 610n81, 610n82; distinction between clients and, 311n76; involvement in Athenian

lawsuits considered ordinary, 325–326; 'logographer' as a term of opprobrium, 597n58; logographia as 'composition of speeches', 327n133, 597n62; stylistic precision exemplified by, 626. See also λογογραφέω; λογογραφία; λογογράφος

Lykourgos (the Athenian statesman): 8, 23, 295–296, 307, 307n60, 314, 319n105, 435–441, 438n10, 444–446, 444n38, 466, 470, 471–472n126, 472, 472n132, 475–476, 644; and Athenian festivals, 439; authoritative texts of the canonical tragedians established by, 437, 439–441; building program of, 436 (see also Lykourgos: theater of Dionysos finished by; Panathenaia: Panathenaic stadium and theatron); contest for comic actors revived by, 439; and the finances of the lesser Panathenaia, 438–439; reforms of, 435–447; self-serving liturgies resented by, 466 (see also Demetrios of Phaleron: khorēgia abolished by); and state control over poetic performance, 444–445, 467 (see also Demetrios of Phaleron: and state control over performers); theater of Dionysos finished by, 438n10, 439

lyre: number of strings in the archaic, 286–287, 287n230

Lysanias: 351, 351n71, 448, 482, 496

mantic poetry: 3, 6, 219–235; ecstatic inspiration (see inspiration: ecstasy and); etymology of φαίνω and φημί, 229–230, 230n38; inner vision, 224 (see also inspiration: seeing and knowing; inspiration:

seeing versus hearing); μανία as a marked mental state, 221–223; μανία as punitive, 222; mantic (oracular) speech and mantic poetry, 182, 201, 220, 223–224, 225n23, 229–230, 662; reveals, 224, 254, 488; root *men-, 216, 221, 223, 223n14, 267. *See also* oracular verse; prophecy

mantis (seer): 221n2; Epimenidēs, 222n5, 229, 253n131; etymology of, 223, 223n10, 223n11, 223n12, 223n13; the future not his sole concern, 222, 229, 253, 253n131; interpreter of signs, 222, 297, 655, 662n46; Muse as, 274 (*see also* prophet: poet as); poet-seer, 224 (*see also* 'Hesiod': as a poet-seer); 'prophet' was once interchangeable with, 223–224. *See also* Kalkhas; prophet

mediation: notion of, 3; Pindar as mediator, 275. *See also* Delphic oracle: mediation of the προφήτης; *lexis*: mediates the vocal expression of subject matter; Muses: rhapsode as mediator of; Near East: Levant mediated the culture of; Plato: rhapsode mediates the epic poet according to; rhapsode: as *hermēneus* of his tradition or of the Muse; rhapsode: as *hermēneus* of 'Homer'; rhapsode: mediates the epic poet

memorization: Athenian rhapsodes and, 8, 315, 329; memorizing and remembering, 7, 19, 48n25, 49, 79–80, 155, 163, 207, 221, 257, 279n210, 282, 294–295, 303, 303n41, 305–306, 313–316, 313n87, 319, 319n105, 331–332, 335, 339, 341, 435, 451, 536, 550n106, 572–574,

622. *See also* memory; Muses

memory: memorializing, 19, 69n97, 250; as a mental faculty (or the exercise thereof), 551, 564, 569, 570n162, 573–574, 574n180, 574n182; as *pharmakon* of forgetfulness, 251n120; social memory (*see* rhapsode: activates social memory in performance). *See also* memorization; Muses

mimes: 453n66, 458–459, 462, 462n86, 464n95, 479–480; *homēristēs* and *biologos* (mime), 460, 462, 462n89, 464n94, 480; not *tekhnitai* of Dionysos, 464n95, 479; pantomimes versus, 452n66, 459, 459n78, 583; sacred festivals not open to, 464n95

mimesis: 188, 355–356, 366, 484; of action, 355n90, 356; by actors (*see* acting: exaggerated mimetic performance; acting: mimetic performance); educational value of poetic, 308, 436; mimetic arts/ artists, 188, 355n88; mimetic delivery (*see* delivery: mimetic); mimetic impulse of rhapsodes (*see* rhapsodic performance: histrionic delivery); mimetic potential of the Homeric poems (*see* Homeric poems: mimetic potential of); Plato and (*see* Plato: on mimetic poetry); and pragmatics (*see* Homeric poems: mimetic pragmatics of; rhapsodic performance: self-referential mimetic pragmatics of); same actor cannot be good at both tragic and comic mimesis, 484; voice and, 530, 533, 537, 583n14; words and, 530. *See also* acting: as 'mimetic substitution'

morality: divine, 164–166, 241n81, 246n99; double determina-

(morality, *cont.*)

tion, 164n52, 241n81; theodicy, 164n52. *See also* Homeric poems: morality of

multiforms: 190n58, 415. *See also* authorship: authorizing multiforms; Homeric poems: Argive tradition of; Homeric poems: multiforms of; Salamis: Megarian multiform about; Sphinx: multiforms of the riddle of; truth: multiforms and

Muses: 197n85; Apollo and the, 182, 182n26, 187, 189, 201, 208n123, 285–286, 286n226; called Μνεῖαι, 209; divine song-masters, 187, 194, 213; divine speech (of Muses, Apollo, or Zeus), 3, 180, 186, 201–202, 206, 274, 662n46, 664; divine speech of, quoted, 208, 265–266, 285; etymology of μοῦσα, 223, 285n225; as eyewitnesses, 180, 183–184, 186, 211, 246, 303; guarantee the truthfulness of the telling, 179, 208 (*see also* inspiration: truth/accuracy and); IE background, 181n24; invocation of, 180, 210n131, 233, 381; local poetry delegitimized by, 260–261; and lying (*see* lies: lying inspiration); as *manteis* (see *mantis*: Muse as); memory (total recall), 184–185, 184–185n37; Mnēmosynē and, 204, 204n110, 208–209, 248–250, 249n109, 376; and oblivion (poetic/performative forgetfulness), 210, 236, 249–250; Olympian, 244n92; rhapsode as mediator of, 4, 6, 179n17, 202, 208–217, 224, 301n29; singer loved by, 182n28; three in number at Askra (Μελέτη, Μνήμη, Ἀοιδή), 211; three in number at Delphi, 286–287. *See*

also Delphic oracle: cult of the Muses at; 'Hesiod': dependent on the Muses; 'Hesiod': independent of the Muses; 'Homer': as *hermēneus* of the Muse; memory; performer: as attendant of the Muses; rhapsode: as *hermēneus* of his tradition or of the Muse

Near East: *Gilgamesh* (see *Gilgamesh*); Greek acquaintance with the literature of, 33, 35; influence from, 35–36; Levant mediated the culture of, 29; libraries in, 31–32; Mesopotamian popular literature, 32; oral traditions of poetry in, 30, 32–33; scribal trade in, 32; written epics from, 29–33

neoanalysis: 53–54n41; performance traditions and, 54n41; *Quellenkritik* and, 54n41

'Nestor's Cup': 78, 82, 84, 122–123; band script in, 123; defamiliarizing (high-register) diction, 135–136; *de novo* composition, 130–131; Homeric diction and, 130, 132–133, 134–135n96, 137; 'I am' inscriptions, 131; irony in, 131; and textual fluidity (*see* text fixation: textual fluidity); Pylian saga and, 130–131; its relationship to the Homeric tradition of the eighth century, 129–132, 136, 140n110, 141. *See also* Index of Documentary Sources: *CEG* 1 no. 454

non-melodic recitation (solo performance without musical accompaniment): 343–356; ἀείδω used for, 346; characteristic of stichic and elegiac verse, 343; diachronic melodic potential of epic, 450, 450n60; from melodic performance to ordinary speech, 343–344n44; from 'song' to 'poetry' (*see* diachrony: diachronic evolution from 'song' to 'poetry'); Hellenistic rhapsodes sang epic 'melodically', 450, 450n58, 450n60 (*see also* non-melodic recitation: singing versus reciting); instrumental accompaniment (*see* rhapsodic performance: instruments used during); Khairemon's *Centaur*, 355–356, 355n88, 355n89, 355n90, 356n91; *melos* versus *harmonia*, 540n69 (see also *lexis*: *harmonia*; *lexis*: 'prose melody'); performance mode of elegiac and iambic poetry, 343n42 (*see also* iambic poetry); performative implications of ἀθύρω and ἄθυρμα, 348–349; recitative (*see* non-melodic recitation: from melodic performance to ordinary speech); ῥαψῳδέω applied to solo, non-melodic recitation of stichic and elegiac verse, 343, 346, 350, 354, 449n57; ῥαψῳδία used etymologically, 355, 355n90; sewing/stitching and, 343; singing versus reciting, 341, 341n36, 345–347, 346n49, 346n50, 346n51, 350n65, 352n73, 354–355, 419 (*see also* non-melodic recitation: Hellenistic rhapsodes sang epic 'melodically'); solo performance and, 341, 343, 400, 416–417, 426, 483; Xenophanes rhapsodized his own poetry, 354, 354n83, 354n84. *See also* performance; rhapsodic performance; tragedy: prologue and ῥῆσις of

notional fixity: 6, 165, 173–182, 175, 175n8, 180, 182; artistic freedom and (*see* performer: artistic freedom of); divine will and (*see* truth: divine will and); emic versus etic perspective, 174–175, 179–180, 294n4; of form and content, 175, 179, 202; insists on exact identity, 174n5, 179; inspiration and (*see* inspiration: notional fixity and); narrative necessity and, 199–200n95, 232, 289 (*see also* truth: divine will and; truth: κατὰ μοῖραν); notional thematic totality, 176n11, 397, 397n240 (*see also* Homeric poems: notional thematic totality); prophecy and, 178–179, 178–179n17, 224; recomposition in performance compatible with, 177, 294n4; text fixation and, 175–176, 294n4, 435, 587n25; variants polemically opposed, 165, 176n11, 248, 266. *See also* text fixation; truth

odeion of Perikles: 470, 470n117; built by Perikles or Themistokles, 470n119, 472, 472n126; designed not as a music hall, 470–471, 470n119, 471n123; Panathenaic *mousikoi agōnes* held at, 470n119; transfer of the rhapsodic performances from, to the theater of Dionysos, 470–472, 470n117, 471n124 (*see also* Panathenaia: relocation of the Panathenaic rhapsodic contests)

Onomakritos: 154–155, 266

oracular poetry: *see* mantic poetry

oracular verse: 284–288; hexameter used for divine speech, 284–286, 288; oral-traditional, 284; quoting divine speech as (*see* Muses: divine speech of, quoted); verse used at oracular seats other than Delphi, 288–289n234. *See also* mantic poetry

oral culture: *see* song culture
oral poetry: composed not in perfor-
     mance, 48n25, 420, 424, 587n28;
     genre of, as performance occa-
     sion, 342n38; indifference
     towards writing, 69n97; notion
     of 'word' in, 174; poetics of,
     175n7; primacy of the story in,
     207; truth in, 210n131 (*see also*
     truth); worldview of, 178. *See
     also* diachrony: cross-references
     in oral poetry; epic poetry: as
     an oral-traditional medium of
     recomposition in performance;
     Gilgamesh: *Gilgamesh* oral tradi-
     tion; Homeric poetry: orality of;
     Homeric poetry: oral transmis-
     sion of; Near East: oral traditions
     of poetry in; oracular verse;
     performance: oral technique;
     recomposition in performance
oratory: *see* rhetoric
Panathenaia: 17, 23, 371n138; actors
     at, 476–478; athletic events,
     64; audience at, 24, 164, 176;
     competitive rules at, 176,
     314, 329, 352, 368, 369n133,
     389, 389n202, 417, 435, 439,
     647; Homeric poems alone
     performed at the penteteric,
     23, 369n133, 436–437, 439,
     475–476; managed by *athlothetai*
     and/or *hieropoioi*, 467, 467n109,
     473, 473n137, 474–475n139;
     Panathenaic amphoras, 647n1;
     Panathenaic 'bottleneck', 81,
     176 (*see also* Homeric poems:
     diffusion through Athens);
     Panathenaic rhapsodes, 314,
     314n90; Panathenaic rule (*see*
     Homeric poems: Panathenaic
     rule); Panathenaic stadium
     and *theatron*, 438, 438n10;

program at the lesser (whether
     it featured *mousikoi agōnes*),
     437, 471n124, 472–476; reloca-
     tion of the Panathenaic rhap-
     sodic contests, 438n10 (*see also*
     odeion of Perikles: transfer of
     the rhapsodic performances
     from, to the theater of Dionysos);
     rhapsodic performance at, 78,
     83, 147n2, 315n90, 368, 380, 417,
     439; rhapsodic performance
     judged against an authoritative
     script (*see* scripts: authoritative
     script of the Homeric poems);
     rhapsodic performance venue at
     (see *homēristai*: rhapsodic perfor-
     mance in the theater; odeion of
     Perikles; Panathenaia: relocation
     of the Panathenaic rhapsodic
     contests); sixth-century reor-
     ganization of (*see* Panathenaia:
     Solonic or Peisistratean
     reforms of the); Solonic or
     Peisistratean reforms of the, 24,
     45, 352, 382n179, 384, 647. *See also*
     Lykourgos: and the finances of
     the lesser Panathenaia
Panathenaic rule: *see* Homeric poems:
     Panathenaic rule
Panhellenism: 18, 45n16, 180;
     aesthetics of reception and, 23;
     Apollo and Panhellenic *mousikē*,
     205n113; of the Epic Cycle
     (*see* Epic Cycle: Panhellenism
     of); epichoric (local) versus
     Panhellenic, 18, 53–54n41, 83n5,
     165, 211, 240, 240n77, 260; forma-
     tive Panhellenic period of the
     Homeric tradition, 144n124, 166,
     176; itinerancy and, 144n124,
     182n28, 212, 212n139, 236 (*see also*
     rhapsode: itinerancy of); local
     praise poetry versus Panhellenic

epic, 144n124, 353n77; lying
and (*see* lies: Panhellenism and);
Panhellenic linguistic consciousness, 144n124; Panhellenic
praise poetry, 353 (*see also* iambic
poetry: as Panhellenic blame
poetry); Panhellenic scope
('expansion aesthetics') (*see*
performance: comprehensiveness of); Panhellenic status of
Κυθέρεια, 139n109; polis and,
45n16, 176; trade, travel, and,
62, 244, 244n89, 271n184. *See
also* Arkhilokhos: Panhellenic
status of; Hesiodic poems:
Panhellenic claim of; Hesiodic
poems: Panhellenic shape of;
Homeric poems: city editions of;
iambic poetry: as Panhellenic
blame poetry; Muses: Olympian;
Polyphemos: Cyclops episode and
Panhellenism
pastoralism: 243–244, 243n86,
243–244n88, 244n89; farming
versus, 243n88; polis and,
243–244n88; and settlement
patterns, 244n91
patronage: *see* Alexandria: Ptolemaic
patronage of the arts; performance: patronage of; *tekhnitai*
of Dionysos: patronage of, by
Hellenistic rulers
performance: accuracy of (*see* accuracy: of performance); *aoidē* as
(activity/faculty of) 'singing'
versus 'song', 190, 191n63, 214,
214n146, 426n353; aural shape
of the verse, 136n100, 418–419;
comprehensiveness (monu-
mentality) of, 176, 180, 195n76,
228n30, 241, 370, 379n168,
395, 395–396n230 (*see also* Epic
Cycle: comprehensiveness of;

Homeric poems: monumen-
tality of; sequence: expansion
aesthetics signaled by διηνεκές/
διηνεκέως; recomposition in
performance: thematic contraction and expansion); epistemology of epic performance,
184; festival calendar, 35, 237n69,
369 (*see also* performance:
festival performance); festival
performance, 2–3, 8, 17–18,
17n10, 49, 84, 163, 188, 212, 236,
276, 315, 345, 350n60, 375n158,
379n168 (*see also* performance:
festival calendar); form versus
content in, 191–192, 207 (*see
also* inspiration: of form and
content); *hypokrinesthai* denotes
'to perform' (see *hypokrinomai*:
in the sense of 'to perform');
hypokrisis corresponds to (see
hypokrisis: 'performance' corresponds to); 'I am' inscriptions,
131; linear chronology of epic,
194–195n76, 199n95, 209n125,
209n126; occasion, 174, 211, 417;
oral technique, 42; patronage of,
206, 240–241, 244n89, 440 (*see
also* patronage); performance
culture (*see* song culture); pleasure of, 190–192, 191n63, 194,
235 (*see also* inspiration: enchantment); poetry as medium of, 177;
political legitimacy and, 40; pragmatics of, 177, 180, 185n39, 375;
recurrent (repeated), 209, 336,
416; of self-standing episodes,
60–62, 418; sequential (*see*
sequence); skill in, 174, 176, 418
(*see also* inspiration: skill and);
social, notion of, 2; song as well
ordered speech, 194–195, 195n77,
198; time (present, past, and

(performance, *cont.*)

future) and, 203, 209, 225, 253; truth of (*see* truth); verse line as a unit of performance, 145–146, 418–419; 'word' as unit of utterance, 174, 207n121, 208; writing and (*see* writing: as an aid to the performance of rhapsodes and orators). *See also* acting; *epideixis*; *hypokrinomai*; *hypokrisis*; recomposition in performance; rhapsodic performance

performer: as agent of creation, transmission, and reception, 27, 248, 277, 277–278n209, 341; artistic freedom of, 174–175; as attendant of the Muses (Μυσάων θεράπων), 182, 187n46, 208n123; and audience, 180, 313 (*see also* delivery: and the corruption/vulgarity of the audience); creative singer versus reproducing rhapsode, 299n24, 329, 331–332, 334, 339–340 (*see also* rhapsode: creative versus reproducing); creativity of, 173n1, 174, 180, 213n144, 295–296, 335n13; *hypokritēs* corresponds to, 1, 647–648n4, 648, 650–651, 664–665; poet versus, 277–281, 277n209; professional identity of (see *tekhnitai* of Dionysos: professional identity of performer); professionalization of, 17, 446, 449n57, 465, 465n100 (see also *tekhnitai* of Dionysos: professionalization of performance and); rhetorical pose of, 180, 183, 185–186, 185n39, 193, 213, 213n143, 213n144; role of, 177; same performer cannot be both a good rhapsode and a good actor, 299n22; truth of (*see* truth); 'voice' of, 178. *See also* actor; *homēristai*; rhapsode; *tekhnitai* of Dionysos

phantasia: as 'appearance', 562–564, 564n145; pre-Aristotelian meaning of, 565–566, 565n147, 566n148; Aristotle's definition of, 550–551, 550n106; essential to thought, 567, 570, 578n195; as a faculty of judgment, 561n133, 562–565, 568n154, 569n158, 569–570n161, 570, 570n162, 575, 575n188, 578n195; in its full psychological sense (see *phantasia*: as a faculty of judgment); glossed as 'mere appearance, outward show', 523, 551, 551n107, 554–556, 557n120, 559, 561–562; includes senses other than sight, 533n42, 561n132, 564n144, 625; instrumental to clarity (demonstrative), 550, 560; memory and hope connected with, 551, 561n133, 569, 574; and perception (*aisthētikē phantasia*), 550–551, 555, 567, 568n153, 569–570n161, 570, 572–574; and the psychology of perception (see *phantasia*: as the soul's [re]presentational device); and reason/thought (*logistikē phantasia*), 567–568, 567–568n152, 571, 575n186, 577 (see also *phantasia*: as a faculty of judgment); in the *Rhetoric*, 572–578; rhetorical (deliberative), 565, 568–569, 568–569n154, 569n156, 571–572, 575–578, 625, 631–632, 634; as the soul's [re]presentational device, 524, 563–564, 567, 569, 573–575, 573n179; towards the hearer, 548, 548n99, 550, 559, 575, 578. *See also* φαντασία

Phemios: 181, 188, 190n61, 192–193, 193n66, 193n69, 207n121, 212–213, 213n142, 213n144, 216, 269, 269n182, 281, 332n2, 334n10, 339n33, 359, 365–366, 395; as a rhapsode, 332n2

Phoenicia: alphabet, 36; Carthaginian literature, 36–37; Phoenician literature, 29n43, 36–37, 45–46; written literature, 33–40

Plato: *anakrisis* in, 321, 322n; associates rhapsodic performance with scripted delivery, 322, 323n122; conflates literary criticism and inspiration/poetic composition, 281–282, 282n215, 303–304 (*see also* rhapsodic performance: unity of declamation and commentary in); on crossing generic boundaries in performance, 484; on ecstasy and trance, 268–269, 272–273 (*see also* inspiration: ecstasy and); on inspiration and skill, 188, 222, 222n6, 223n7, 277, 283; Ion called ὁ ῥαψῳδὸς καὶ ὑποκριτής by, 298–299, 648, 648n8, 665; mantic art according to, 222; on mimetic poetry, 188, 309, 446; and *mousikē*, 188; poet as *hermēneus* of the (inspiring) gods, 282–283, 299n24; rhapsode mediates the epic poet according to, 275n206, 276, 282–283, 283n218, 289, 304 (*see also* rhapsode: as *hermēneus* of 'Homer'); tendentiousness of, 267, 368n129, 648, 655; his view of inspiration (*see* inspiration: Sokrates' chain of); on writing, 321–324, 322n118, 327. *See also* rhapsodic performance: *rhapsōideō* in Isokrates and Plato

poetic tradition: 47n24, 176n11; archaic Greek epic, 175, 179; Argonautic, 170; authority of, 367; continental, 239n75; Iliadic, 65, 418; interaction between poetic traditions, 231n41; of the *Kypria*, 230; Nereus embodies an authoritative, 250; Odyssean, 61, 63–64, 153n14, 418; Odyssean *nostos*, 60; poem versus, 46–47n24; Pylian, 130–131; rivalry between poetic traditions, 148, 151, 236; Southslavic, 165, 173–175, 179, 210n131; Theban-War (Theban cycle), 168, 399, 402, 405n276, 412, 414–415; Trojan-War (Trojan cycle), 47n24, 230, 369n132, 370n133; Wǫi epic, 210n131. *See also* authority; authorship

poet of epics: 488n39; composition versus performance (of epic), 489; encomiastic traditions and, 488–491, 489n44; new epic poetry composed and performed by, 488; popularity of, 482n17, 490n49; rhapsode versus (see *tekhnitai* of Dionysos: rhapsode versus poet of epics)

poiēsis: as *carminum factio*, 332–333n7

Polyphemos: 57–63; Cyclops episode and Panhellenism, 62

precision: *see* accuracy

prophecy: about the past, 179n17; affects the future, 179n17, 206n120; authoritative proclamation of, 221n2; 'bee-maidens' and, 205n113, 206n120, 287–288; infallible interpretation and prediction, 201; notional fixity and (*see* notional fixity: prophecy and); poetry and, 177, 201, 201n96, 205n113, 488; reveals, 179n17;

(prophecy, *cont.*)
truth and, 178–179n17. *See also* Delphic oracle; divine will; mantic poetry
prophet: 3, 221n2; Apollo as *mantis* and, 274–275; as interpreter (ὑποκριτής), 3, 6, 221, 276, 289, 297–299, 647n4, 648n7, 655 (see also *hypokrinomai*; *hypokritēs*); *mantis* versus, 206, 220–221, 274–275; poet as, 274; Teiresias as *mantis* and, 274–275. *See also* Delphic oracle: Pythia; Delphic oracle: Pythia as προφῆτις; *mantis*
quantitative metathesis (QM): 99–105; synizesis and, 99–105
reception: of traditional poetry, 242, 245. *See also* archaic art: reception; diachrony: diachronic dynamics of diffusion and reception; diachrony: metapoetics of reception; Homeric poems: reception; Panhellenism: aesthetics of reception and; performer: as agent of creation, transmission, and reception
recomposition in performance (of diction, themes, and sequence): 7, 16n3, 19–20, 22–23, 26, 35–36, 41n3, 63, 66–67, 79, 155, 164–166, 174–175, 177–178, 211, 290, 290n238, 295, 313, 342, 381, 412–413, 416–418, 493, 652, 663; acceptable range for, 6, 45n17, 47n24, 165, 180, 290n238, 295, 313, 332–333, 412, 435 (*see also* performer: artistic freedom of; performer: creativity of); centrifugal (divergent), 44, 176; centripetal (convergent), 49, 68, 176, 209n126; in the context of rhapsodic *hermēneusis*, 302–304, 303n43, 328 (*see also* rhapsodic performance: unity of declamation and commentary in); as a defining characteristic of rhapsodic performance, 348, 416–417, 648; entailed by formulaic extension and economy, 48n25; layering of themes in, 155n22 (*see also* Homeric poems: diachronic layering of); mistakes and inconsistencies due to, 24; *mouvance*, 335–336, 335n14, 587n25; neoanalysis and, 54n41; notional fixity and (*see* notional fixity: recomposition in performance compatible with); 're-compose' what is scattered, 379, 384; suddenly arrested, 44, 295n9, 331; thematic contraction and expansion, 24, 210n131, 226–227, 264n169, 290, 314, 369n133, 379n168 (*see also* performance: comprehensiveness of). *See also* improvisation; oral poetry: composed not in performance; poet of epics: composition versus performance; rhapsodic performance; writing: recomposition in performance versus
relay poetics (of hypoleptic singing): 367–397, 371n138, 380n169, 417, 647–648; of Akhilleus and Patroklos, 372–375, 374n152; Akhilleus and Patroklos' narrative hypolepsis, 369n131; δέγμενος/δεδεγμένος and, 367–368, 371; (δι)ηνεκές and, 367–369; founded on the poetics of solo seam-stitching, 417 (*see also* sequence: poetics of seam-stitching); of Hermes and Apollo, 376–377; Kallimakhos and, 367–370; synchronically reenacts the *paradosis*, 368; synchronic rhapsodic succes-

sion, 277–281, 313–314, 314n88, 320, 342, 352, 360n103, 368, 377, 381, 383, 392, 400–401, 401n258, 416, 424, 424n345, 426n351. *See also* Homeric poems: Panathenaic rule; Homeridai: relay performance characteristic of; sequence

revelation: *see* Homeric poems: revelatory; mantic poetry: reveals; prophecy: reveals; rhapsodic performance: revelatory

rhapsode: his access to the divine will, 224, 230, 301n29, 662n46, 664–665; activates social/cultural memory in performance, 185n38, 208–209, 246, 248–249, 256, 303, 303n42; actor and, 309, 435, 476, 484, 487 (*see also* actor: rhapsode as model for; *hypokritēs*: passed from rhapsode to actor); as apprentice, 187, 194, 213, 216, 276; as artisan, 195; coinage of the term, 339, 341, 346, 348, 399, 417–418; creative versus reproducing, 5, 281, 329, 331, 338–341, 339n33, 348, 417 (*see also* performer: creative singer versus reproducing rhapsode); cultural authority of, 301, 304, 335n13 (*see also* rhapsode: as educator); earliest attestations of ῥαψῳδός, 399–416; as educator, 278n209, 300n29, 301, 304, 306, 319n108, 335n13, 643; as ἐπαινέτης of Homer, 186n42, 194n74, 300n29, 302–303, 305–308; etymology of, 336–338, 419; as *hermēneus* of his tradition or of the Muse, 2–4, 275n206, 290, 299, 299n24, 302, 661n43, 662n46, 664–665 (*see also* rhapsodic performance: interpretation and commen-

tary); as *hermēneus* of 'Homer', 282, 290, 299, 309 (*see also* Plato: rhapsode mediates the epic poet according to); 'Hesiod' as (*see* 'Hesiod': as a rhapsode); 'Homer' as (*see* 'Homer': as a rhapsode); versus *homēristēs* (see *homēristai*: rhapsodes versus); as *hypokritēs*, 282n216, 289–290, 296–305, 647, 647–648n4, 650–651, 662n46, 664 (*see also* prophet: as interpreter); Ion, 6, 8n8, 276, 279–282, 282n215, 290, 298–300, 299n22, 303–305, 309, 309n65, 321, 334, 351, 368n129, 437n5, 466n102, 490, 491n54, 648n8; Ionian versus Athenian rhapsodes, 7–8, 314–316, 314–315n90; itinerancy of, 70, 83, 248, 295n9, 319, 354n84, 400n253, 416 (*see also* Panhellenism: itinerancy and); Kallimakhos and the rhapsodes (*see* relay poetics: Kallimakhos and); as *mantis*, 3, 256; mediates the epic poet (*see* Plato: rhapsode mediates the epic poet according to); as mediator of the Muse (*see* Muses: rhapsode as mediator of); Nikeratos, 301n30, 315–316, 316n93, 494–495; Phemios as (*see* Phemios: as a rhapsode); poet of epics versus (see *tekhnitai* of Dionysos: rhapsode versus poet of epics); as prophet, 3, 6, 224; repertoire of, 63, 193, 248, 343, 351, 351n71, 482–483, 488–490 (*see also* iambic poetry: in the rhapsodic repertoire; rhapsodic performance: of poetry other than epic); *rhapsōidos*, marked term vis-à-vis unmarked *aoidos*, 334, 334n10, 344–345, 368n129, 416, 647–648, 648n5;

(rhapsode, *cont.*)

sacred (sacrosanct) status of, 212, 213n142; self-conscious (or not), 207n121, 248; Sphinx as (*see* Sphinx: as a rhapsode); staff (ῥάβδος) of, 205–206, 337, 348n55, 360, 360n102, 367, 372, 372n142, 399n246; among the *tekhnitai* of Dionysos (see *tekhnitai* of Dionysos: rhapsodes among); as a term of derision, 334, 341–342, 342n37, 399 (*see also* rhapsode: *topos* of the rhapsodes' stupidity); *topos* of the rhapsodes' stupidity, 301, 316n93, 320, 648n8 (*see also* rhapsode: as a term of derision); Xenophanes (*see* non-melodic recitation: Xenophanes rhapsodized his own poetry). *See also* Athens: Athenian rhapsodes; Demodokos; festivals: at which rhapsodes are attested; Homeridai; *homēristai*; Index of Rhapsodes; Theagenes of Rhegion: was a rhapsode

rhapsodic performance: addresses the god, 234n52; adorning 'Homer', 281, 290, 300, 302, 302n36, 370n134 (*see also* κατὰ κόσμον, κόσμος); at the Asklepieia, 437n5; authority of (*see* speech-act: authority of); combined with another performance specialty (see *tekhnitai* of Dionysos: rhapsodic performance combined with another specialty); as a *comparandum* for the orator's use of writing, 312, 317, 380; competitive (agonistic), 176, 371, 374, 379, 380–382; competitive and cooperative dynamics of: 68, 352, 374, 375n158, 377–382; cooperative, 342, 378–380, 392; creative song-stitching, 338–342,

418; defined not by the degree of originality or the use of dactylic hexameter, 343; *differentia* of, 416–419; expansion aesthetics of (*see* performance: comprehensiveness of); god presiding over, 234; histrionic delivery, 3, 7, 296, 302, 302n38, 308–311, 316, 351, 351n69, 351n71, 469, 476, 522, 648n8 (*see also* acting: and rhapsody; delivery; *homēristai*); Homeric poetry associated with, 399; *hypokrisis* and (*see* *hypokrisis*); instruments used during, 343–346, 348n55; interpretation and commentary (rhapsodic exegesis), 282, 290, 299–300, 299n24, 300n29, 302, 304, 307n62, 316, 318n103, 319–320, 328–329; melic roots of, 344, 348–350; oriented towards the past, 225; at the Panathenaia (*see* Panathenaia: rhapsodic performance at); of poetry other than epic, 343, 346, 350–354 (*see also* iambic poetry: in the rhapsodic repertoire); proem as the ritual framework of, 205, 210n131, 230, 233–235, 233n50, 334, 375n158, 385; quoting the speeches of the characters in the poems, 298n18; 'reactive' performance (*see* sequence: 'reactive' [hypoboletic] performance); recomposition in performance as a defining characteristic of (*see* recomposition in performance: defining characteristic of rhapsodic performance); revelatory, 187, 214n146, 224, 229–230, 256, 275, 275n206, 488, 662, 664–665; rhapsodic elaborations of Homeric passages, 81; rhapsodic *hypokrisis* related to sophistic *epideixis*, 290, 302, 304–305, 319, 464 (see also *epideixis*); rhapsodic sequencing (*see* sequence); rhapsodic succession (*see* sequence: diachronic rhapsodic succession); *rhapsōideō* in Isokrates and Plato, 318–329; *rhaptō* and (see *rhaptō*); self-referential mimetic pragmatics of, 376, 415, 665; sewing and the poetics of sewing, 338–341, 343, 359–360, 393, 396–398, 398–399n245, 420, 427 (*see also* rhapsodic performance: creative song-stitching; sequence); sewing/stitching versus plaiting and/or weaving, 342n40, 368n130, 419–420, 427–431; singing versus reciting (*see* non-melodic recitation: singing versus reciting); solo performance (*see* non-melodic recitation: solo performance and); stitching (*see* rhapsodic performance: sewing and the poetics of sewing); technical terms of (with metapoetic echoes), 194, 198, 213n142, 248, 249n112, 250, 349, 360n100, 362–363, 373, 385, 385–386n190, 387–390, 392–394; by *tekhnitai* of Dionysos (see *tekhnitai* of Dionysos: epic performance by); in the theater (see *homēristai*: rhapsodic performance in the theater); unity of declamation and commentary in, 320–321 (*see also* Plato: conflates literary criticism and inspiration/poetic composition; recomposition in performance: in the context of rhapsodic *hermēneusis*; rhapsodic performance: interpretation and commentary); weaving and, 348n56, 368n130, 393, 427–428. *See also* delivery; *hypokrisis*; non-melodic recitation; performance; Plato: associates rhapsodic performance with scripted delivery; recomposition in performance; sequence

rhaptō and other craft metaphors: artistry of performing gods, 359; craft metaphors not applied to mortal singers, 359; craft metaphors used for self-interested telling, 360; etymology of ῥάπτω, 338, 338n27, 338n28, 338n29, 338n30; etymology of κασσύω, 428n361; *hyphainō* and *rhaptō*, 357, 361–365, 363n116; IE metaphor for composition, 356–357, 364; metapoetic reading of *rhaptō*, 357, 361; non-IE origin of *rhaptō*, 428; performer's skill ascribed to the gods, 357–359, 361 (*see also* inspiration: skill and); *rhapsōidos* draws attention to compositional technique and performance practice, 357, 648; *rhaptō* used for composition *and* performance ('planning' *and* 'execution'), 356–357, 360–367; *rhaptō* used for fabrication of plots, 357, 360; rhetoric of inspiration and *rhaptō*, 357, 359, 360–361, 364; rhetoric of novelty (*see* diachrony: novelty); syntax of *rhaptō*, 420, 420n325, 424–425, 427

rhetoric: *agōn* in, 601, 603–604, 633n150, 634n152, 638n164 (*see also* Aristotle: on trial by a single judge); and animal motion, 567, 567n151, 569–570 (see also *phantasia*: rhetorical);

(rhetoric, *cont.*)

civic importance of, 608–610, 609n78, 609n79, 609n80, 610n82, 620–621; concerned with *doxa*, 544–546, 554–555, 556n120, 575, 577, 577n191, 578n197, 630, 639; concerned with τὰ ἔξω τοῦ ἀποδεῖξαι, 546–547, 552n112 (*see also* ἔξω τοῦ ἀποδεῖξαι); delivery (*see* delivery; *hypokrisis*); demonstrative nature of, 559–560 (see also *didaskalia*); *epideixis* (see *epideixis*); ethical status of, 552, 631n145; *ēthos* and *pathos* as rhetorical *pisteis*, 547n93, 549, 551n109, 552, 557n120, 569, 575–576, 578, 578n196, 632, 635–636, 636n155 (*see also* delivery: *ēthos* and *pathos* contribute to expressive clarity); improvisation in (*see* improvisation: in rhetoric); natural talent versus acquired skill in, 579–580, 579n1, 580n3, 583–585, 594–595, 611 (*see also* delivery: training in technical delivery); *pisteis* in, 628, 631, 635–636 (*see also* rhetoric: *ēthos* and *pathos* as rhetorical *pisteis*); its promise fulfilled with the help of *lexis* and *hypokrisis*, 554, 569, 576–577, 632n145, 636n155; and the psychology of the emotions, 523, 574–575; rhapsody and, 7, 523–524; *rhētores*, 580n2, 609, 620, 623n116, 623–624n117, 624n119; rhetorical contests during the classical period, 594n50; rhetorical view (θέα), 629–631, 629n137, 634, 638; *rhētorika*, 633–634, 633n151 (see also *lexis*: τὰ ὑποκριτικά); and scientific discourse, 558n126, 559–560n129; silence, 609–610, 610n83, 613 (*see also* delivery: training in technical delivery); style (see *lexis*); stylistic emphasis on various *pisteis*, 635–637; truth in, 326, 551, 636n155, 637; writing and (*see* writing: use by orators). *See also* Aristotle

Salamis: Athens and, 83n7; court proceedings and the quarrel about, 152, 152n12 (*see also* court proceedings); Matron of Pitana knew B 558, 149–150; Megarian multiform about, 151; quarrel between Athens and Megara about, 147–153

Sankhouniathon: 37–38

scripts: 9, 19, 79, 130, 163, 163n48, 282, 294, 311, 313, 335–336, 380, 587n25, 595, 603, 609, 609–610n81, 620, 622, 626; authoritative script of the Homeric poems, 435, 439; Lysias' use of, 597; *paranagignōskein*, 440, 440n20, 442–443, 442n29, 442n30, 442–443n31 (*see also* παραναγι-(γ)νώσκω); Perikles first to use, 596, 596n55; propriety of scripts, 335, 335n13, 594n50, 623n113; script of the Homeric poems archived, 439, 439n14; from transcripts to, 295–296, 314, 332n7. See also *hypokrisis*: Alkidamas associates scripted delivery with; improvisation: versus scripted performance; Plato: associates rhapsodic performance with scripted delivery; transcripts

self-referential chorality: 216, 653n17

sequence (rhapsodic sequencing): 200n95, 395–396, 417, 649n9, 653, 653n20, 658–659; ἄλλη ἀοιδή as 'the rest of the song', 381–382, 382n177; audience awareness of, 418–419, 418n318; 'capping' challenges, 380–382; diachronic rhapsodic succession (*paradosis*), 368–369, 371, 377, 383, 383n181, 392, 396; enjambment, 371, 380–382, 419 (*see also* sequence: poetics of seam-stitching); expansion aesthetics signaled by διηνεκές/διηνεκέως, 370, 370n137 (*see also* performance: comprehensiveness of); *hymnos* and (*see* hymn: rhapsodic sequencing and *hymnos*); 'mending' in performance, 378–379, 379n168; notional, 181n23, 379n168; οἴμη (narrative thread) and, 181, 207n121, 342, 368, 371, 375n158, 392–396 (*see also* sequence: οἶμος and); οἶμος and, 347–348, 378, 378n163, 393–396 (*see also* sequence: οἴμη and); poetics of repetition, 369, 418–419; poetics of seam-stitching (interlocking of successive phrases, verses, and themes), 340, 371, 379–381, 379n168, 380n169, 388–389, 392, 395–396, 416–419; (poetics of) synchronic rhapsodic succession (*see* relay poetics); 'reactive' (hypoboletic) performance, 383–384, 388–389, 389n203, 391; relationship between syntactical and metrical periods, 208, 418–419; shifting the performance backward/forward, 190, 194, 395, 396n230, 397n240, 426, 426n353 (*see also* μεταβαίνω); *skolia* and, 371, 371n139, 377, 377n162; starting point of, 181n23, 379n168, 385n190; stichic (additive) style of epic, 208, 342, 371, 418; stitching together self-standing performance units, 342, 418, 426–427; thematic sequence

(continuity), 23, 313–314, 369, 378–380, 383–384, 392, 395–396, 418; three modes of, 368. *See also* ἐξ ὑποβολῆς; ἐξ ὑπολήψεως; ἐφεξῆς; Homeric poems: Panathenaic rule; relay poetics

skiagraphia: *see* accuracy: and *skiagraphia*

Solon: 24, 124n57, 194, 196, 246, 327n133, 354n83; his poetry at the Apatouria, 352, 352n73; his recitation of the *Salamis*, 354–355, 354n85, 354n86, 354n87; on Ajax and Salamis, 148–152, 149n7, 152n13. *See also* Panathenaia: Solonic or Peisistratean reforms of

song culture: 5–6, 9, 15, 19, 33, 35, 46, 166, 175, 177, 209n126, 245, 385n190, 413; *aoidos* as the unmarked term for singer (*see* rhapsode: *rhapsōidos*, marked term vis-à-vis unmarked *aoidos*); creative primacy of the performative setting in, 314; definition of 'poetry', 343, 343–344n44; definition of 'song', 343; destabilized, 530; folk transmission of epic stories in, 66; increasing dependence of, on writing, 294, 595, 597n63; Kirgiz singers, 21; primacy of aurality in, 335 (*see also* writing: presupposes oral expression)

sophists: their interaction with the audience, 328n136; lectures or showpieces (ἐπιδείξεις) of, 290; rhapsodes emulated by, 4, 318–321, 319n108

speech-act: ἄπτερος applied to ineffectual speech, 362n109 (*see also* lies: ineffectiveness of); authority of, 202, 204, 206, 220,

(speech-act, *cont.*)

237, 245, 304, 366, 662n46; ineffectual speech (*see* speech-act: ἄπτερος applied to ineffectual speech; lies: ineffectiveness of); κραίνω and, 203–204; notion of, 3, 201–202n97; paradigmatic (archetypal), 210–211; performative (efficacious) speech, 3, 198–199, 198n94, 201–206, 236, 250, 252, 275, 376n159, 662n46; performative Homeric subgenres, 202–203; pragmatics of, 653, 655, 660, 662–663 (see also *hypokrinomai*: in the context of 'oracular pronouncements'); scepter as emblem of authoritative speech, 372 (*see also* 'Hesiod': his scepter; rhapsode: staff of); singing epic as a (sacral) speech-act, 185, 201, 203–204, 233, 266, 284; and utterance, 174n3

Sphinx: audience of, 403–404; character of, 403–404, 405n274, 405n276; and contests of riddles, 400, 400n256, 400n257; diction of the riddle's 'vulgate' text, 402, 406–413; early iconography of, 403–404n271, 404–405, 404n272, 406n276, 413–414; folklore study of, 403n265; multiforms of the riddle of, 401, 415; Oidipous' manner of defeating, 405, 405n275; oral-traditional character of the riddle of, 412, 414–415; proto-IE background of, 406; as a rhapsode, 400–401, 401n259, 415–416; as a songstress, 400; source of the riddle's 'vulgate' text, 402, 412–415; text of the riddle attested on vases, 413–414, 413n308, 414n310

style: see *lexis*

succession: *see* sequence

syllabification: *see* compensatory lengthening: syllabification; inscriptions: syllabification

technology of writing: 70–80, 144, 304n46; length and surface of scrolls, 75–77

tekhnitai of Dionysos: 446, 479n2; Athenian synod, date of its founding, 467–468; Athenian synod, its preeminence, 468; Athenian synod, reasons for its founding 467; Διονυσοκόλακες, 446; epic performance by, 480 (see also *tekhnitai* of Dionysos: rhapsodes among); and Hellenistic festivals, 479, 479n4; *homēristai* and (see *homēristai*: not *tekhnitai* of Dionysos); honorary decrees for, 461, 480; mimes and (*see* mimes: not *tekhnitai* of Dionysos); patronage of, by Hellenistic rulers, 468, 468n114 (*see also* patronage); performing more than one genre, 484; professional ethos of the synods of, 486; professional identity of performer, 468–469; professionalization of performance and, 446, 465, 468 (*see also* performer: professionalization of); professions attested among, 481; rhapsodes among, 480n6 (see also *tekhnitai* of Dionysos: epic performance by); rhapsode versus poet of epics, 482, 488–490 (*see also* poet of epics); rhapsodic performance combined with another specialty, 486–487; social standing of, 446, 480; and specialization, 449n57, 465, 484–488, 486n34; *termini ante quos* for non-Athenian synods, 468n114. *See also* Demetrios of Phaleron:

provided the management model for the synods of *tekhnitai*

text fixation (of the Homeric poems): ninth-century BC, 71, 109; eighth-century BC, 24, 27, 73, 109; early archaic, 55, 295n9; seventh-century BC, 109; sixth-century BC, 147; by Theagenes' time, 156, 161; by Aristotle's time, 587n25; alleged references to specific lines (in our text), 152, 157; archaic art and (*see* archaic art: and the text fixation of the Homeric poems); dictation and (*see* dictation); differential crystallization of different parts, 48n26, 60, 151n11, 155, 158, 587n25; and editorial redaction, 41n3; entailed by the scholia B to Υ 67, 162; evolutionary model of, 5, 16n3, 17, 23, 25, 27n38, 42, 45n17, 46–48, 60, 68–69, 109–110, 133, 140n111, 144n124, 147, 159, 294–295, 649n10; gradual, 68, 176, 294n4, 392; only possible with writing, 41, 43, 69; oral-dictated text (*see* dictation); performance driven, 176; quoting 'Homer' as text (*see* Homeric poems: quoted as 'text'; text fixation: alleged references to specific lines); in sixth-century BC Athens, 44; textual fluidity, 131–132, 140, 159, 164 (*see also* Homeric poems: narrative fluidity of); of theme, form, and sequence, 294n4, 392; of theme versus diction, 155, 159; truth and (*see* truth: fixity and); written textual artifact, 18, 40, 43, 45, 47, 62, 64, 77–79, 130, 147–148, 162–163, 295n9, 439, 441n26. *See also* notional fixity

Theagenes of Rhegion: 140n111, 147, 156–167, 301n31, 321n114; and allegoresis, 156, 156n23, 160; Anaximander and, 162n42; and the Homeric gods, 156; Homeric text of, 158; his study of 'Homer', 159, 169n64; theomachy (*Iliad* 20) and, 160, 160n39; was a rhapsode, 157, 162, 162n42, 493; against Xenophanes, 158

Theognidea: 412–413, 649n9

Theophrastos: 336n18, 429, 429n367, 429n371, 471n121, 496, 529–530n31, 542, 591, 592n48

Thespis: 346, 350, 350n63, 648n6, 658n35. *See also* tragedy: rise of Attic drama

Thrasymakhos: ancient *testimonia* about, 590–592; concerned with style and delivery, 592–593; and the dichotomy between *hypokrisis* and *lexis*, 589; and emotional appeals, 589; *hypokrisis*, a natural talent according to, 589–590n36; rhetorical stylistics of, 590; subject matter of his *Eleoi*, 589; wrote a *tekhnē*, 590, 590n37

thymelikoi agōnes: 469, 469n116, 470n117, 500–501, 502n102

tradition: *see* archaic art: tradition and innovation; authorship: author's biography as a function of 'his' tradition; epic poetry; *Gilgamesh*: *Gilgamesh* oral tradition; 'Homer': *Vita* traditions; Homeric poems: Argive tradition of; Homeric poems: Homeric tradition and; Homeric poems: poem versus poetic tradition; Homeric poems: traditional diction; Homeric poems: traditional themes; inspiration: consistent with tradition;

(tradition, *cont.*)

kleos: as affirmation of traditionality; Near East: oral traditions of poetry in; neoanalysis: performance traditions and; 'Nestor's Cup': its relationship to the Homeric tradition of the eighth century; oracular verse: oral-traditional; Panhellenism: formative Panhellenic period of the Homeric tradition; poetic tradition; poet of epics: encomiastic traditions and; reception: of traditional poetry; rhapsode: as *hermēneus* of his tradition or of the Muse; Sphinx: oral-traditional character of the riddle of

tragedy: messenger of, 656–657, 656n29, 657n32, 657n33, 657n34, 664; prologue and ῥῆσις of, 346, 350, 350n63, 350n65, 663–664, 664n50; prompter, 388, 443–444 (see also *homēristai*: prompter for); rhapsodic performance as model for dramatic performance, 350, 445, 648 (*see also* actor: rhapsode as model for); rise of Attic drama, 648, 648n6, 663, 665 (*see also* Thespis); roots of, in epic, 296, 296n10, 664. *See also* nonmelodic recitation: Khairemon's *Centaur*

transcripts: 8–9, 19–20, 20n17, 44n16, 55, 57, 78–79, 147, 163, 163n48, 175–176, 294, 311, 313–314, 435; Euboian, 82. *See also* scripts; writing: as an aid to the performance of rhapsodes and orators

truth: ἀληθέα versus ἔτυμα, 238n71, 245, 247, 252–259; ἀλήθεια characteristically verbal, 247–248, 252, 256, 257n151; authority and, 165, 236, 245, 248; characteristic use of ἀληθέα, 252, 256; claims

to, 165; coinage of ἀληθείη, 247–248, 252; divine will and, 199n95, 201, 230; etymology of ἀληθείη, 247n106, 248–249, 249n112, 251–252; etymology of κόσμος, 198n94; excellence and, 179, 179n18; experiential versus inspired, 247, 252–258, 253n127, 253n132, 253–254n133, 257n150; fiction and, 178, 240, 246n99, 259–261, 263 (*see also* lies: as fiction); fixity and, 175; inspiration and (*see* inspiration: truth); κατὰ κόσμον (order and truth), 186n43, 194, 194–195n76, 198n94, 201; κατὰ μοῖραν, 199–200n95; meaning of ὁμοῖος, 259–263; multiforms and, 176n11, 236, 248; ornamentation versus truthful telling, 174–175; reality and, 194n76, 195, 201, 210n131, 211, 252; rhetoric and (*see* rhetoric: truth in); skepticism and, 211; of song, 174, 199; standards of plausibility in judging, 257–258, 260–263. *See also* ἀλήθεια/λήθη; ἐτήτυμα; inspiration; lies; Muses

Venetus A: 231n41, 586n24

Venetus B: 161, 161n41

writing: as an aid to the performance of rhapsodes and orators, 7–9, 145–146, 145n127, 310–318, 322, 324, 324n125, 327, 435, 524, 530n34, 593n50, 595–598, 596n55, 603, 605, 608–609, 617–618, 620 (*see also* delivery: Aristotle's technical delivery relies on writing; writing: presupposes oral expression); alphabet, 27–28, 28n41, 34, 36, 71, 76, 82, 92n51; alphabet and commerce, 143–144n124; alphabet and Homer: 143n124, 295n9; Aristotle on (*see* Aristotle:

on the graphic style; Aristotle: on written speeches; delivery: Aristotle's technical delivery relies on writing; *lexis*: and writing); Athenian book trade, 78, 276n206, 294, 435, 444n38; borrowing the alien practice of, 36, 144; Byblos and, 74; Carpenter's *argumentum ex silentio*, 71; combined with oral composition, 69n97, 313–314; continuity of the practice of, during the Dark Age, 71–73, 213n4, 213n5; Cypriot syllabary, 72; Delphic oracle and (*see* Delphic oracle: writing at); derivation of the Greek alphabet, 71, 71n3, 142; eighth-century bookhand, 141–146; epichoric alphabets, 79n41, 144n124; ideology of, 36; of the *Iliad*, 68–69; leather and parchment, 43, 73–74, 74n14, 76–77; Linear-B, 72–73, 107–108, 145n128; materials for, 35, 43, 71–72, 74–75, 79, 143, 295n9; Metroon archive, 437n7, 439n14, 440, 441n26; mistakes and inconsistencies and, 25; old-Athenian alphabet, 147; from orality to writing (*see* song culture: increasing dependence of, on writing); papyri and, 29, 43, 70, 73–76, 75n21; Plato and (*see* Plato: on writing); polemical introduction of the technology of writing, 295, 311–312, 594n50, 595–597; presupposes oral expression, 327–328, 335, 593–594n50, 595, 607–608, 612–613, 616–618, 621 (*see also* song culture: primacy of aurality in); recomposition in performance versus, 19, 293, 311

(*see also* improvisation: versus scripted performance; song culture: increasing dependence of, on writing); role of, in the preservation and transmission of knowledge, 335; scribal culture, 35; *scriptio continua*, 145n128; technical challenges, 27, 35, 69–70, 75, 295n9; technology of (*see* technology of writing); used by Athenian (and lesser) rhapsodes, 8, 313, 315, 329 (*see also* memorization: Athenian rhapsodes and). *See also* deliberative speeches: writing used to prepare for; rhapsodic performance: as a *comparandum* for the orator's use of writing; text fixation: only possible with writing; text fixation: written textual artifact

CPSIA information can be obtained
at www.ICGtesting.com
Printed in the USA
JSHW032118150822
29286JS00002B/5